Written, updated and revised by the Editors at FL Memo with assistance from Sue Ashtiany and Michal Stein, Nabarro Nathanson

FL Memo Limited

Important Disclaimer

This publication is sold on the understanding that the information provided within it is for guidance only, and that the publisher is not in business to provide legal or accounting advice or other professional services. Readers entering into transactions on the basis of, or otherwise relying on, such information should seek the services of a competent professional adviser.

Whilst every care has been taken to ensure the accuracy of the contents, the editors and the publishers cannot accept responsibility for any loss occasioned to any person acting or refraining to act as a result of any statement in it.

ISBN : 0-9548452-1-8

FL MEMO LTD
185 Park Street
Bankside
London SE1 9DY

Telephone (020) 7803 4666, Fax (020) 7803 4699
Email: flm@flmemo.co.uk
Website: www.flmemo.co.uk

British Library Cataloguing in Publication Data.
A catalogue record for this book is available from the British Library.

FL MEMO

Employment

2006

Law and Practice

Human Resources

Abbreviations

The following are the main abbreviations used in this book:

ACAS	Advisory Conciliation and Arbitration Service
CA	Court of Appeal
CC	County court
ChD	Chancery Division, High Court
cl(s)	Clause(s)
CS	Court of Session
DDA 1995	Disability Discrimination Act 1995
DDA 2005	Disability Discrimination Act 2005
DPA 1998	Data Protection Act 1998
EA 2002	Employment Act 2002
EAT	Employment Appeal Tribunal
EEA	European Economic Area
EC	European Community
ECJ	European Court of Justice
EPA 1970	Equal Pay Act 1970
ERA 1996	Employment Rights Act 1996
ERelA 1999	Employment Relations Act 1999
ERelA 2004	Employment Relations Act 2004
ET	Employment tribunal (formerly Industrial tribunal (IT))
EU	European Union
EWCA Civ	England and Wales Court of Appeal (Civil Division) Decision
HC	High Court
HL	House of Lords
HSWA 1974	Health and Safety at Work etc. Act 1974
ICR	Industrial Cases Reports
ITEPA 2003	Income Tax (Earnings and Pensions) Act 2003
IRLR	Industrial Relations Law Reports
NIC	National Insurance Contributions
NMWA 1998	National Minimum Wage Act 1998
PAYE	Pay as you earn
para(s)	Paragraph(s)
PILON	Pay in lieu of notice
QBD	Queen's Bench Division, High Court
reg(s)	Regulation(s)
RRA 1976	Race Relations Act 1976
s(s)	Section(s)
SAP	Statutory adoption pay
Sch	Schedule
SDA 1975	Sex Discrimination Act 1975
SI	Statutory Instrument
SMP	Statutory maternity pay
SPP	Statutory paternity pay
SRP	Statutory redundancy pay
SSCBA 1992	Social Security Contributions and Benefits Act 1992
SSP	Statutory sick pay
TULRCA 1992	Trade Union and Labour Relations (Consolidation) Act 1992
TUPE	Transfer of Undertakings (Protection of Employment) Regulations
UCTA 1977	Unfair Contract Terms Act 1977
VAT	Value Added Tax

Contents

All references in this handbook are to paragraphs.

Preface

Employment Memo 2006 is a well-established handbook providing **practical guidance** and **dynamic and fast moving commentary** on employment law and practice. It is accessible and easy to navigate, whilst retaining depth of coverage on a wide range of employment issues.

Employment Memo 2006 has been significantly revised so that readers are to **up to date with all the recent developments** that have occurred over the last year and includes new commentary and practical advice on:

- the forthcoming legislation on age discrimination;
- the recent recognition of civil partnership status;
- new domestic information and consultation requirements;
- the proposed new TUPE regulations; and
- numerous case law developments, for example, on work-related stress, compromise agreements, annual leave and statutory maternity pay.

Irrespective of experience and background, Employment Memo 2006 is an **invaluable resource** for readers ranging from legal advisers/practitioners and HR specialists to business professionals and company directors.

Employment Memo 2006 primarily **covers** the law applying to England and Wales. Whilst reference is made in this edition to the legal systems in Scotland and Northern Ireland, specialist advice should be sought where applicable. Public sector employment and those working at sea are also largely outside the scope of this handbook.

This handbook is intended to reflect law and practice as at 5 December 2005. In order to provide readers with a reliable source of information throughout the year, an **online updating facility** is available via our website (www.flmemo.co.uk), where changes in law and practice that have arisen since publication are detailed.

FL Memo Ltd
December 2005

CHAPTER 1

Types of employment relationship

OUTLINE ¶¶

This chapter sets out the distinction between employees and self-employed workers and the distinction between the latter and those that are in business for their own account who can be termed self-employed persons. The "classic" working relationship is that of employer-employee where an employee works for his employer under a contract of employment. Further, the most common employment arrangement is that of **full-time permanent employment** and this is the standard relationship used in this book unless otherwise stated. 1

With the increase of a **flexible work** ethos and the importance of a work-life balance, there is an increasing number of staff who have flexible work arrangements, including **part-time** and **agency** workers. The legal, contractual and practical issues involved are discussed in Chapter 6.

Directors are office-holders and may also be employees. The subject is discussed in Chapter 7. 2

There are also special rules relating to **apprentices**, **trainees** and **young persons** and these are discussed outside this chapter in the specific topics as follows: 3

Type of worker	Para.
Apprentices	
National minimum wage	¶2865
Trainees	¶6350
Working time	¶3615
Young persons	
Working time	¶3720
Right to time off to study	¶6330
Government backed training initiatives	¶6370
Health and safety	¶4880

SECTION 1

Employees and workers

10 Traditionally, UK law focused on the relationship between employer and employee. As a result, the main employment rights **apply to employees** only (i.e. those who work under a contract of employment) and those who are employed under other contracts are excluded. However, as a result largely of the implementation of EC Directives into UK law, there is a range of newer employment rights that **apply to** a larger group called **workers**. Generally, the term workers includes employees and other persons employed under other contracts for personal service but excludes those who are in business for their own account and are providing these services to a client or customer.

Employees

11 The main Act on employment rights gives a **standard definition** as follows (s 230(1) ERA 1996): 'an "employee" means an individual who has entered into or works under (or, where the employment has ceased, worked under) a contract of employment.'

A **contract of employment** is defined as a contract of service or apprenticeship, whether express (orally or in writing) or implied (s 230(2) ERA 1996).

Slightly different definitions can be found in other Acts and regulations such as health and safety legislation, business transfer regulations, trade union law and statutory maternity, adoption, paternity and sick pay regulations. How each of these definitions differs from the standard definition is discussed in the relevant topics.

12 The **main employee statutory rights** are shown in the table below. In addition, employees are **also entitled** to the rights of workers (see below). Most are only activated when the employee has been continuously employed for the requisite **qualifying periods** (¶1080).

Employee's right to:	Para.
Written statement of main terms	¶1405
Not to be discriminated against on grounds of sex, racial group, disability, religion or belief, or sexual orientation	¶5200
Equal pay	¶5600
Not to suffer unlawful deductions	¶3050
Itemised pay statements	¶2985
Guarantee payments	¶7860
Sick pay	¶4110
Maternity, adoption and paternity rights	¶4420
Parental rights	¶4620
Safe place of work	¶4810
Minimum period of notice	¶8131
Written statement of reasons for dismissal	¶8310
Continuity of employment on transfer of undertaking	¶7980
Redundancy rights	¶8730
Unfair dismissal rights	¶8380
Pay during medical suspension	¶4862
Equality for fixed-term employees	¶1950
Request flexible work	¶1813
Access to statutory dispute resolution procedures	¶6500

Workers

A person is a worker when he is either: 13
- an **employee** working under a contract of employment; or
- working under a contract (other than a contract of employment) and is offering his personal service in return for remuneration to the employer who is not his client or customer. Such a contract is often called a "contract for personal services." Such workers can be referred to as **non-employee workers**.

Worker or business undertaking? Those who are self-employed and are in business to provide a client or customer with professional or other services are not workers. These are considered to be sufficiently at arm's-length and in an independent position to look after themselves. For example, a consultant running a consultancy practice or a freelancer who is working for many companies. Such persons can be labelled "**self-employed persons**" and are outside the scope of this book. 14

However, self-employed contractors/freelancers, subcontractors, home and casual workers who are in a subordinate and dependent position and are not providing their services in a client or professional relationship will be **workers** albeit self-employed. For example, the Court of Appeal and the EAT have held that self-employed, labour-only subcontractors were good examples of those who would be unlikely to be carrying on a business undertaking and therefore likely to be within the classification of workers (*Byrne Brothers (Formwork) Ltd v Baird* [2002] IRLR 96, EAT; *Wright and Redrow Homes (Yorkshire) Ltd* [2004] ICR 1126, CA). 15

EXAMPLE In *Byrne Brothers (Formwork) Ltd v Baird*, B, a sub-contractor, was not contractually entitled to holiday pay under his subcontractor's agreement with his contractor BB. However, as B was offering his personal service in return for remuneration (delegation was only allowable where the subcontractor was unable to provide the services and required the express prior approval of BB) and was not in an independent position to be said to be in business for his own account, B was held to be a worker and entitled to holiday pay.

This is based on the **definition** given by legislation as follows (s 230(3) ERA 1996): 16
'a worker (except in the phrases "shop worker" and "betting worker") means an individual who has entered into or works under (or, where the employment has ceased, worked under):
a. a contract of employment, or
b. any other contract, whether express or implied and (if it is express) whether oral or in writing, whereby the individual undertakes to do or perform personally any work or services for another party to the contract whose status is not by virtue of the contract that of a **client or customer** of any profession or business undertaking carried on by the individual;
and any reference to a worker's contract shall be construed accordingly.'
There are similar legislative provisions for other worker rights, for example worker rights under the trade union law, national minimum wage and working time regulations.

The **main worker statutory rights** are shown in the table below. There are **no qualifying periods** that need to be achieved before the worker can benefit from these newer employment rights. 17

Worker's right to:	Para.
Breaks and rest periods	¶3710
Paid annual leave	¶4000
Equality for part-time workers	¶1870
National minimum wage	¶2865
Trade union activities	¶7100
Whistleblowing rights	¶2700
Right to be accompanied at discipline and grievance hearings	¶6780
Health and safety rights	¶4860

SECTION 2

Employee or self-employed?

30 The distinction between those in employment and those who are self-employed is significant for employment and tax law purposes.

Those that are self-employed have less stringent **tax** rules on the deductibility of expenses, benefit from cash flow advantages, and pay less in **social security contributions** (NIC). However, employees have more statutory **rights** than the self-employed and their contracts of employment often give contractual benefits (e.g. contractual sick pay) which are not normally applicable to those who are self-employed. Those who are self-employed workers do have the benefit of some more recent statutory rights (see above) which in turn do not apply to self-employed persons (i.e. those who are genuinely in business for their own account).

Employers may also be **vicariously liable** for employee misdeeds.

Companies are increasingly using contractors or agency workers to provide certain services, to respond to work fluctuations or to provide cover when employees are absent. The reason for this shift is outside the scope of this book and is due not only because of the emergence of a more flexible work ethos but also due to company economics and the increased responsibilities with regard to worker rights. Persons may also prefer the significant control over how much tax they pay if they are self-employed regardless of the loss of employment rights that would result.

MEMO POINTS 1. Contractors who **supply their services through** an intermediary service company, often called a **personal service company** are taxed as if they are employees of that company.

2. **Agency workers** have a general employment relationship with their agencies. Further, in certain circumstances, it may be possible for an agency worker to be an employee of either the agency or the client (end-user). The Court of Appeal has given guidance on the relationship between the agency and its worker and between the worker and the client (*Brook Street Bureau (UK) Ltd v Dacas* [2004] IRLR 358, CA). See ¶¶2048, 2050 for further details.

31 It is, though, usually **clear** whether a person is employed or self-employed. However, there are circumstances where it is **not clear** or it is in dispute. Such disputes usually occur when one party is trying to enforce his legal rights, for example he claims he has been unfairly dismissed and the employer asserts that he is self-employed and therefore not entitled to make a claim. Typically, disagreement as to status arises where there is no written contract between the parties or where there is a written contract but the parties disagree as to its interpretation and/or effect.

Disputes may also occur where Revenue and Customs disagrees with the type of tax and NIC contributions that are being paid.

Further, the **consequences** of treating an individual as self-employed when he is actually employed are likely to fall on the employer, who may be **liable to account for** the **PAYE** (¶6810) and **NIC** (¶6925) that should have been deducted over the course of the employment. Alternatively, Revenue and Customs may not impose a retrospective charge and in such cases will only require the employer to commence deduction of PAYE/NIC.

In situations where there is doubt over whether an individual is employed or self-employed, it is therefore in the employer's interests to ensure that the individual is making the appropriate tax/NIC payments under the self-employment regime.

32 Case law gives guidance on how to distinguish between those in employment and those who are self-employed and the following **two tests** have to be satisfied for there to be an employment relationship:
- there must be mutuality of obligation and the work must be personally performed; and
- the worker must not be in business for his own account.

Mutuality and personal performance

In an employment relationship, both parties must be under an irreducible minimum of obligation. This must amount to one party providing work usually for remuneration and exercising sufficient control over the other party who must personally perform the work required (*Montgomery v Johnson Underwood Ltd* [2001] IRLR 269, CA). 35

MEMO POINTS The Court of Appeal in *Montgomery v Johnson Underwood Ltd* has noted that as the nature and manner of carrying out employment develops, so will the courts' view as to the nature and extent of mutual obligation and control. Therefore, what will amount to mutuality of obligation and sufficient control may change in the future.

Mutuality of obligation With regard to **permanent employees**, it is usually clear that there is an obligation on the employer to provide work and on the employee to work. 37

This may be less clear with regard to non-permanent staff who are **casual or seasonal**. To ascertain the status of a casual staff member, it must be determined if he is employed for the **specific periods** he works. If he has separate contracts of employment for each of these periods, he will be an employee from the start to end of each period worked.

When a casual staff member has a series of **specific contracts** of employment, he is continuously employed for the duration of each contract and will be able to rely on the main statutory rights once the necessary qualifying periods of employment have been achieved. However, periods of non-employment will usually break his continuity of employment unless the statutory continuity rules are satisfied (¶1010). It may, therefore, be difficult for casual staff to obtain the necessary qualifying periods with regard to rights for which long periods are required (principally the right not to be unfairly dismissed and redundancy payments).

In certain circumstances, the courts have held that there may be a **general contract** of employment if the casual worker has a long-standing relationship with the employer which is so regular and constant that it creates an irreducible minimum of obligation on each party (*Nethermere (St Neots) Ltd v Gardiner and Taverna* [1984] IRLR 240, CA). Such a contract is often called an "**umbrella**" or "**global**" contract of employment and whether such a contract is created will depend on all the circumstances. If there is an umbrella contract, subject to the statutory continuity rules, continuity is presumed to run from the beginning of the first assignment and there will be no gaps in the employment relationship or breaks in continuity when the employee is not working between assignments. 38

Court decisions in recent years, though, have appeared to move away from identifying such umbrella contracts, especially if a casual staff member is only paid when work is available, is not obliged to accept work and does not work when there is none (*Carmichael v National Power plc* [2000] IRLR 43, HL; *Clark v Oxfordshire Health Authority* [1998] IRLR 125, CA; *Bunce v Postworth Limited t/a Skyblue* [2005] IRLR 557, CA).

EXAMPLE In *Clark v Oxfordshire Health Authority*, the Court held there was **no umbrella contract** where C, a staff nurse who worked for the Authority, was only offered employment at one of the Authority's hospitals when it was available. Although C worked regularly for over three years, there were gaps when she did not work. When C worked she was paid hourly and was subject to PAYE and NIC deductions. However, she was not entitled to guaranteed or continuous work, she received no payment during periods she was not working and was not entitled to holiday or sick leave.

The principle of mutuality of obligation is also relevant to establishing the status of **volunteers**. A volunteer will not be an employee if he receives no pay other than the reimbursement of expenses and is not obliged to attend work or be provided with work. The existence of required standards and guidelines if the volunteer did attend work does not create mutuality of obligation (*Melhuish v Redbridge Citizens Advice Bureau* [2005] IRLR 419, EAT). 39

Sufficient control of employer The employer must have sufficient control over an employee for there to be an irreducible minimum of obligation (*Ready-Mixed Concrete (South East) Ltd v Minister of Pensions and National Insurance* [1968] 2 QB 497, as supported by recent decisions). In general, an employer can tell an employee what to do, and also how and when to do it, and in such circumstances it is clear that the employer has sufficient control. 40

The courts have noted that in many kinds of employment, direct supervision and control by an employer is absent, for example highly-skilled employees may have little day-to-day control exercised on them, and in such circumstances the courts will look to see if there is a "sufficient **framework of control**" i.e. overall control (*Montgomery v Johnson*, above).

41 Control can be exercised indirectly as long as there is a sufficient degree of **actual** control (*Motorola Ltd v (1) Davidson and (2) Melville Craig Group Ltd* [2001] IRLR 4, EAT). Further, if there is a sufficient degree of control, it is irrelevant that another party may have similar or greater powers of control.

This has been the case with **agency workers** where a company (the client/end-user) which has been supplied with an agency worker exercises actual control over the worker (see ¶2046).

42 However, if there is **no contract of any kind** between the worker and the client it is irrelevant whether there is sufficient control as there cannot be an employment relationship (*Hewlett Packard Ltd v O'Murphy* [2002] IRLR 4, EAT; *Esso Petroleum v (1) Jarvis and (2) Brentivine* [2002] All ER 112, EAT).

EXAMPLE In *Hewlett Packard Ltd v O'Murphy*, a computer specialist (O'Murphy) who as an employee of a company he had set up (Circle Technology (CT)) provided services to Hewlett Packard (HP) continuously for a number of years as part of a team and was integrated into the workforce. His work was provided through CT (who paid his remuneration) under a contract with an employment agency, which had a separate agreement with HP to provide computer services. HP terminated this agreement when HP considered that O'Murphy was incapable of efficiently performing the work expected of him. EAT held that as there was no contract of any kind between O'Murphy and HP (except for a confidentiality agreement that had been agreed between O'Murphy and HP), there was no employment relationship between them.

43 It is generally considered problematic for a **controlling shareholder** to be an employee of the company to which his shares relate, as he may be able, by virtue of his shareholding, to control whether or not he is dismissed. His dual role may also give rise to a conflict of interests. If, however, it can be shown that there is no such conflict and that the controlling shareholder cannot decide issues relating to his employment, it is possible for him to be an employee.

Although the service agreement is a significant factor, it is not determinative and all the relevant factors must be considered in determining whether or not he is an employee. The courts will look at the reality of the situation, as they did in *Bunting v Hertel (UK) Ltd*, EAT case 1453/99, where the EAT held that there was no actual employment relationship despite what, on the surface, may have seemed as one. In particular, the **following factors**, posed here as questions, should be considered, and answers which show that a controlling shareholder has no effective control with regard to his employment go towards indicating that he may be an employee. However, these factors do not create rigid guidelines and each case must be determined on its **particular circumstances** (*Secretary for Trade and Industry v Bottrill* [1999] IRLR 326, CA as affirmed by *Sellars Arenascene Ltd v Connolly* [2001] IRLR 222, CA):

1. Was there a genuine contract of employment or was it a sham?
2. What degree of control was exercisable over the controlling shareholder? To determine this, the relevant considerations include:
– was the company controlled by the board of directors?
– was the controlling shareholder a member of the board and, if so, how many other directors were there (i.e. to what extent was his influence diluted)? and
– was there any provision to stop the controlling shareholder voting on matters he had a personal interest in?
3. What was the actual conduct of the parties?

EXAMPLE **Controlling shareholder is an employee**
In *Sellars Arenascene Ltd v Connolly*, C was a majority shareholder of Arenascene (through his majority holding of its parent company). He was the managing director and chairman though did not have sole control of the board. He had a written contract of employment with express provisions for his duties, hours of work, holidays. In looking at all the relevant factors, the Court confirmed that C was an employee.

Controlling shareholder is not an employee
In *Bunting v Hertel (UK) Ltd*, the two shares in a company, PMS, were held by B and another on trust for B's family. Neither trustee had a casting vote. B was also the sole director and so had effective control. PB, his wife, was the company secretary. Neither B nor PB had a written contract of employment though they both received a salary from which tax and NIC was deducted. The EAT held that B and PB were not employees.

Personal performance A person must perform his contract personally (*Ready-Mixed Concrete (South East) Ltd v Minister of Pensions and National Insurance* [1968] 2 QB 497). 45

Where a person can **choose to perform** his contract by sending someone else in his place, he will not satisfy this requirement. In such circumstances, the person need never perform the contract personally and therefore cannot be employed (*Express and Echo Publications Ltd v Tanton* [1999] IRLR 367, CA). This is the case even if the power of substitution is **fettered** (*Staffordshire Sentinel Newspapers Limited v Potter*, EAT case 0022/04).

EXAMPLE In *Express and Echo Publications Ltd v Tanton*, a driver was made redundant and re-hired. A clause in the new contract provided that 'in the event that the contractor is unable or unwilling to perform services personally, he shall arrange at his own expense entirely for another suitable person to perform the services.' From time to time the driver did in fact provide a substitute driver. Consequently, the Court accepted that the driver had been re-hired as a self-employed contractor.

However, **substitution** is acceptable in a limited capacity, if agreed, where a person is **unable to perform** (as opposed to choosing not to perform) (*Macfarlane v Glasgow City Council* [2001] IRLR 7, EAT). 46

EXAMPLE In *Macfarlane v Glasgow City Council*, M, a gymnastics instructor, could arrange for a replacement from a register of coaches maintained by the Council if she was unable to take a class. The replacements were paid directly by the council. The EAT held that M was an employee and such agreed substitution was not contrary to personal performance.

Not in business for own account

For a person to be employed he must show that he is not in business for his own account (*Market Investigations Ltd v Minister of Social Security* [1969] 2 QB 173; affirmed by *Lee v Chung* [1990] IRLR 236, PC). 50

All the circumstances should be considered. Further, *Lee v Chung* held that: 51
– there is **no exhaustive list** of the factors that are relevant and that considering factors cannot be done by way of a mechanical exercise of running through items on a checklist to see whether they are present or not;
– there are **no strict rules** as to the relative weight of the various factors and the weight should be determined in relation to each individual case.

The object of the test is to **paint a picture from the accumulation of detail** and it is a matter of evaluation of the overall effect, which is not necessarily the same as the sum of the individual factors (*Hall Inspector of Taxes v Lorimer* [1994] IRLR 171, CA).

Though there is no exhaustive list, the courts have identified a number of **important factors** that are helpful (*Stevenson Jordan and Harrison Ltd v MacDonald and Evans* [1952] 1 TLR 101, CA; *Lee v Chung* [1990] IRLR 236, PC). 52

These are posed as questions:

Affirmative answers **indicate employment**:
1. Is it the parties' intention that there should be an employment relationship?
2. Do the terms of any contract or agreement (including the "label" applied by the parties themselves) indicate an employment relationship?
3. Is the person an integral part of the employer's business?
4. Is he receiving any benefits and does he get paid annual leave?
5. Is he subject to the employer's disciplinary rules and procedures?
6. Does the employer pay him using the PAYE scheme with tax and NIC deducted?

Affirmative answers **indicate self-employment**:
1. Is he using his own equipment or tools?
2. Is he responsible for hiring his own helpers if needed?
3. Does he take any degree of financial risk and has he opportunity to profit from his work?
4. Is he effectively selling his services and expertise over and above having the required expertise and skill to perform his work?

If there is **no documentation** regarding the working relationship between the parties, then it is essential that all evidence which is relevant to the possible formation of an oral or implied contract of service is considered (*Franks v Reuters Ltd and another* [2003] IRLR 423, CA).

53 **Intention of the parties** As can be seen above, the parties' intention as to their status is a **factor** in determining whether there is an employment relationship. To this end, the general rules of construction will apply with regard to construing the agreement between the parties (¶1118). These have been specifically applied as follows:

If the relationship between the parties is ambiguous, any **clearly stated intention** as to what they consider their relationship to be is a factor that will go towards indicating their position (*Massey v Crown Life Insurance Co Ltd* [1978] IRLR 31, CA). However, **all the circumstances** will be considered, and the courts will look behind the parties' intention and labels to determine the true relationship (*Young & Woods Ltd v West* [1980] IRLR 201, CA). Therefore, where factors indicate that there is an employment relationship, or they are neutral with regard to this, a label to the contrary attributed by the parties, although important, cannot necessarily be treated as being a determinative or decisive factor (*Dacas v Brook Street Bureau (UK) Ltd* [2003] IRLR 190, EAT, confirmed by the Court of Appeal ([2004] IRLR 358, CA)). Likewise, even where an agreement contains an "entire agreement" clause, the tribunal is entitled to look at both the written agreement and at the parties' conduct and how they operated their agreement in practice (*Royal National Lifeboat Institution v Bushaway* [2005] IRLR 674, EAT).

Where the intention of the parties has **not been clearly stated**, the other terms of the contract may give an indication of intent. The courts will look at the written contractual documents to see if the terms as a whole truly reflect the parties' intention at the time these documents were entered into and then whether this position has changed and, if so, how and when (*Secretary of State for Education and Employment v Bearman* [1998] IRLR 431, EAT). If there are any other circumstances relating to the parties' intention and the terms of the contract, such as any oral agreements/exchanges and conduct as well as any other supporting documentation, the courts will consider all these factors in determining the position between the parties.

54 The Court of Appeal has emphasised that a contract of employment can be **implied** as a **necessary inference** from the conduct of the parties and from the circumstances surrounding the parties and the work done. This case has been applied where a worker who was providing his services (via his own company which had been set up specifically for this purpose), through an agency, solely to an end-user, was deemed to be an employee of the end-user under an implied contract of employment (*Cable & Wireless v Muscat*, EAT case 0661/04). In this case, the end-user had control over the worker, supplied him with all his equipment and the worker's holidays were arranged to suit the end-user.

It may also be possible for a contract to be implied in between an agency worker on a long-term assignment and the end-user (¶2051).

CHAPTER 2

Pre-employment

OUTLINE

¶¶

500 The **recruitment and selection** of the right candidates is of vital importance to employers. Legal issues also impinge on this process, namely that the employer must ensure he is not discriminatory and that the data protection rules are complied with. Once a successful applicant has been identified, the employer can make him an **offer** of employment which may be subject to certain conditions, for example, receipt of references, passing a medical or evidence that the individual can work legally in the UK.

501 Employers can also only employ an individual who has an automatic right or permission to live and work in the UK and an employer will commit a criminal offence if he does not do so. However, if an individual does not fall within one of these groups, the employer maybe able to apply for a work permit.

SECTION 1

Recruitment and selection

510 Getting the right size and composition of workforce is a crucial **employment planning** decision. Getting it wrong may mean bearing the costs of overstaffing or redundancies, or having insufficient employees to meet demand, which may result in lost sales opportunities and revenue. There may be fluctuating staffing requirements throughout the year, or even on a weekly or daily basis.

The recruitment process is important in **selecting** the right applicant for the job. If an unsuitable applicant is appointed the employer will have to invest management time (including extra training and more supervision) to deal with the situation, which may involve a higher absence rate and staff turnover, and low morale. The employer may also need to invoke disciplinary procedures for poor performance. If the employee is dismissed, the employer may face an unfair dismissal claim.

MEMO POINTS ACAS has published a useful guide on recruitment and induction, which can be obtained on its website: www.acas.org.uk

511 The recruitment and selection **process** involves identifying the qualifications and experience required for the particular vacancy, formulating a job description, deciding whether and where to advertise, implementing appropriate selection and interviewing processes and keeping records of each stage.

The employer should take steps to ensure that the process is **non-discriminatory** or he may face a discrimination claim, which could lead to a substantial award of damages being made against him. The process should also be **monitored** on a regular basis to ensure that it is up to date and that it complies with relevant legislation, in particular, in relation to equal opportunities. The information generated during the process must be handled in accordance with **data protection** obligations.

Recruitment checklist

512 **The vacancy**

• determine how the vacancy should be filled
– redistribute duties among existing employees?
– recruit/promote internally?
– recruit external candidate?
– redeploy potentially redundant staff?
• determine if it requires a full-time or part-time employee on a temporary, fixed-term or permanent basis

The job details

• compile a job description (including pay details) and person specification or review and update existing ones as required, in all cases avoiding discrimination

Recruitment method

- consider the most appropriate recruitment method
- where necessary, compile a job advert, taking care to:
– comply with the company image/house style
– use clear, unambiguous language
– avoid discriminatory contents
– ensure that any description of salary/benefits corresponds to the terms and conditions which will apply

The application form

- ensure the form covers all the information required from the applicant, based on the skills and abilities required to do the job
- if necessary, consider other formats as a reasonable adjustment
- standard of completion/English should only be a factor if essential to the job
- a health questionnaire could be included as a distinct part
- consider a question on disability – if completed form reveals disability, duty to make reasonable adjustments applies
- consider asking applicant to disclose criminal convictions – in most cases, "spent" convictions need not be disclosed
- check whether applicant needs a work permit

Short-listing

- ensure that selection is free of bias by involving more than one person
- process personal details separately
- train selectors

Selection

- decide on the most appropriate method of selection (interview, tests, assessment centre)
- review selection criteria and plan for interview
- make reasonable adjustments as appropriate for disabled applicants

The interview

- be prepared to give applicant information on the job and the company
- ask job-related questions
- avoid discrimination
- do not make promises which conflict with the terms and conditions
- assess candidate according to selection criteria and relevant weighting
- take notes and retain them

The decision

- compare the interview/test scores and agree on the most suitable candidate
- notify all applicants as soon as possible

Data protection

- ensure compliance with data protection obligations throughout the recruitment and selection process

Conditions to the employment

- confirm qualifications
- check references
- consider whether a medical is required
- has candidate provided proof of right to live and work in the UK?
- is a work permit required?
- is the candidate subject to restrictive covenants?

Appointment

- consider whether to make a conditional or unconditional offer
- consider enclosing a written contract of employment with the offer letter
- ask the candidate to sign and return the offer letter/contract to signify his acceptance
- if an unconditional offer is accepted (or a conditional offer is accepted and the conditions have been satisfied), it cannot be withdrawn

I. Recruitment policies and planning

A. Company recruitment policy

520 Company size rather than company sector tends to determine company policy on recruitment. A company may need to recruit a new employee because it is **expanding**, or in order to **replace** an employee who has left.

If there is a **vacancy**, the employer should consider whether it requires a full-time or part-time employee, on a temporary, fixed-term or permanent basis. The job duties and the terms and conditions (including the level of remuneration) should be reviewed and updated where necessary.

The employer should consider whether **existing staff** could be **redeployed** as part of their career development, or in order to avoid or minimise possible redundancies elsewhere in the company.

The company's recruitment policy may be affected by the process of human resource planning, discussed below.

B. Human resource planning

525 An organisation's staff (i.e. its human resources) is one of the resources necessary to meet its business objectives. Human Resource Management is, therefore, important to the success of a business, with Human Resource Planning (HRP) being an essential element of good management.

HRP varies considerably from one organisation to another. Many organisations do not plan ahead or have regard to future needs, but recruit as the need arises to fill current vacancies, whilst others rely on complex statistical analysis to forecast business requirements. HRP is often equated with **Manpower Planning**, which, in essence, is concerned with simply forecasting the quantity (and to some extent quality) of the workforce with a view to matching supply to demand. HRP certainly includes Manpower Planning but, in some organisations, HRP goes further and embraces organisational culture, attitudes, employee development, employee behaviour and commitment, organisational development, motivation, training and development and establishing best work methods.

HRP may be less important in relatively stable organisations with little technological innovation, fairly constant demand, low labour turnover and a ready supply of suitable labour. However, the following factors may result in a **need for HRP**:
- demography (i.e. the fact that labour supply changes on a national and regional basis);
- market change, whether growth or decline;
- organisational culture change;
- company development such as site relocation, business acquisitions;
- statutory change (for example, new employment laws);
- Government initiatives such as "New Deal", and plans for education and training; and
- new technology.

HRP may have the following **benefits**:
- anticipating and responding to changes in demand for labour;
- attracting and retaining the required number of employees with appropriate skills;
- achieving the best possible utilisation of staff;

– tailoring training and development to ensure effective performance in current roles and staff development for future roles at the same or higher levels;
– reducing reliance on external recruitment;
– promoting equal opportunities and diversity within the workforce; and
– assisting the process of monitoring, influencing and controlling labour costs.

Objectives

HRP is essentially **concerned with** delivering: 526
– the **right quantity and quality of people** (i.e. the correct numbers of staff offering the desired mix of skills and the levels of outlook, attitude and motivation necessary for the organisation to achieve its objectives);
– at the **right place** (so that the right mix of people and skills is available at each different location, including, for example, planning for opening of a new facility, partial or total closure of a location or transferring key tasks between locations);
– at the **right cost** (to fit in with overall organisational strategy in terms of funds available, relativities, competitiveness, reward strategy and, especially in a production environment, unit labour cost); and
– at the **right time** (taking into account the hours and patterns of work, including responding to the various peaks and troughs in demand for the organisation's products or services, across shifts, weeks, months, seasons or even years).

The HRP process

HRP requires the collection, collation and analysis of information in order to identify and anticipate the organisation's staffing requirements. The process can be **computerised** (both off the shelf and tailored software packages are available) and spreadsheet packages can assist statistical analysis. Where subjective judgements are required, data may need to be analysed **manually**. 527

Forecasting demand for and supply of labour The first step is to forecast the organisation's **demand for labour** (at one or more points in time, usually from 1 to 5 years ahead) as follows: 528
– gather information such as details of business plans, management expectations, forecasts, productivity and current technology;
– assess current labour requirements including skills, numbers, and location; and
– forecast labour requirements by assessing future needs taking into account as many relevant factors as possible, including market changes (both product-related and customer-led change, different delivery patterns, changes to product shelf life and product life cycles), the need for new skills, increased or reduced numbers of current skills, reflecting increased or reduced capacities, changes in productivity and technological developments.

The next stage is to forecast the **supply of labour** as follows:
– gather information relating to the organisation including existing staff numbers, skills, likely turnover, age profile;
– to consider how many staff may be due for retirement, retention factors, stability, reward strategy, recruitment strategy, and training plans;
– gather information external to the organisation including, where relevant, data on the local labour market, other external environmental factors which may impact upon the business, possible changes and trends in labour supply; and
– forecast likely availability of labour, taking into account, where relevant, the skills mix and any locational factors.

Gap between supply and demand A **comparison** of forecast demand with forecast supply establishes whether there is a potential gap (i.e. over-supply, under-supply or a combination of both across different skills, levels or locations). The employer should then seek to establish the cause(s) of the gap. 529

Possible **causes of a shortage of labour** include:
– high staff turnover;
– recruitment difficulties arising from, for example, the perceived negative aspects of the job, the image of the organisation or the industry in which it operates, location, lack of reward, poor advertising campaigns, or inefficient recruitment processes;
– lack of suitable skills;
– lack of internal or external mobility (i.e. reluctance to relocate);
– restricting policies;
– financial constraints preventing improvements to attraction, retention, training and development or reward;
– high absence levels; and
– seasonal fluctuations in demand.

Possible **causes of a surplus of labour** include:
– falling demand for labour (following less demand for the organisation's products or services, a shift in demand for specific skills, or the introduction of new technology/productivity improvements);
– organisational structure (resulting in limited promotional opportunities);
– restricting policies (for example, a union agreement to avoid compulsory redundancy);
– financial constraints; and
– seasonal fluctuations in demand.

530 **Reducing the impact** Once he has established the cause of the gap, the employer can take appropriate action to reduce the impact. Sometimes the reasons for a gap may be outside his control (for example, national skills shortages). However, a **review of the following areas** (and implementation of appropriate action) may, individually or in combination, close specific gaps:
– recruitment practices (for example, the methods of recruitment, the media used to advertise, the style and content of the advert with specific regard to the actual target audience, the response time to applications etc.). A **proactive recruitment strategy** will assist effective HRP, in that it responds to and attempts to reconcile both the short and longer term staffing needs. This may result in the recruitment of staff with potential for training and development, or recruiting on a short-term basis in the knowledge that labour reductions will be required within a period of time;
– reward structures;
– organisational image;
– induction process;
– management of absence;
– job redesign;
– policies and agreements;
– productivity;
– working practices/reallocation of duties;
– flexible working patterns (for example, introducing or extending shift working);
– alternatives to full time permanent staff (for example, part-time staff, temporary/agency staff, job share, short-term contracts, interim placements, outsourcing and home working);
– organisational culture (including management style, communication, policies and procedures, recognition of contribution and performance, employee participation/involvement, training and development, and reward strategy);
– training and development (to improve current and future job performance, productivity, the ability to fill skills shortages, career progression, staff turnover and recruitment);
– job security and redundancy; and
– planning to avoid redundancy.

C. Government assistance

New Deal

As part of the Government's Welfare to Work agenda, it has introduced several New Deal schemes aimed at assisting those who would otherwise have difficulty getting a job. As part of the schemes, the employer commonly receives **funding** and **training** subsidies to minimise the costs of recruiting these employees. In return, employers are expected to keep the employee on after the scheme is completed. More details on these schemes are provided at Chapter 18. 535

II. Equal opportunities

The company should aim to promote equality of opportunity during the recruitment and selection process. As a result of this, many employers have an **equal opportunities policy** (¶5850), which, like all good practice policies, they should take care to observe. 540

Several **codes of practice** offer guidance for employers to help them to avoid discriminating, including those published by the Equal Opportunities Commission, the Commission for Racial Equality, and the Disability Rights Commission. The codes emphasise the close link between equal opportunities and good employment practice, and that promoting equal opportunities should lead to better work relationships and better use of human resources. The codes deal in general terms and employers will need to adapt the guidelines in a way appropriate to the size and structure of their organisation. Small businesses, for example, may not be able to carry out all of the detailed recommendations and will require simpler procedures than those in larger organisations. The codes' recommendations are incorporated where appropriate below. 541

In certain limited circumstances, it is lawful to discriminate in a job for which the sex, sexual orientation, racial group or religion or belief of the worker is a **genuine occupational qualification or requirement** (¶580; see also Chapter 16 for further details). 542

Discrimination on grounds of sex, race, disability, religion or belief, or sexual orientation

For a full discussion of discrimination, see Chapter 16. 543

It is unlawful for an employer to discriminate against prospective employees on the grounds of sex, race, disability, religion or belief, or sexual orientation (s 6 SDA 1975; s 4 RRA 1976; s 4 DDA 1995; reg 6 SI 2003/1660; reg 6 SI 2003/1661):

a. in the **arrangements made** for the purpose of determining who should be offered employment. For example:
- the job description;
- the person specification;
- the job advert;
- the application form;
- not being short-listed for an interview (*V Saunders v Richmond upon Thames Borough Council* [1977] IRLR 362, EAT);
- the selection process, including the location and timing of interviews, assessment techniques, interviewing (for example, the appointment of a biased interviewer (*Brennan v J H Dewhurst Ltd* [1983] IRLR 357, EAT)) and selection criteria; or
- the final selection;

b. by **refusing or deliberately omitting to offer** employment. For example:
– refusing to consider an application (*Owen & Briggs v James* [1982] IRLR 502, CA) or to interview (*Panesar v The Nestle Co Ltd* [1980] IRLR 64, CA); or
– telling an applicant that the vacancy has been filled when it has not (*Johnson v Timber Tailors (Midlands) Ltd* [1978] IRLR 146, IT); or
c. in the **terms** on which employment is offered (see section 2). For example, part-time work, domestic leave, company cars and benefits for dependants should be available to both male and female employees in the same or not materially different circumstances.

MEMO POINTS Selection arrangements are **one-off acts** (not continuing acts) for the purpose of compliance with time limits for discrimination claims (¶9460).

544 If an employee or applicant has suffered discriminatory treatment, he will be entitled to a **remedy** (¶5700).

545 Discrimination may be direct or indirect. It may also take the form of victimisation (a form of direct discrimination) or harassment. **Sex** discrimination includes discrimination on the ground of **marital status** (i.e. on the basis that the applicant is married, as opposed to unmarried), **civil partnership status** and on the ground of **gender reassignment**.

EXAMPLE Direct discrimination
1. Refusal to consider a woman for a lorry driver's job because of her sex.

Indirect discrimination
2. Requiring all job applicants to have previously been employed by the Armed Forces (fewer women than men would be eligible to apply).
3. Imposing a mobility requirement (it may be more difficult for women to comply).

546 In the case of a **disabled person**, unlawful discrimination occurs when the employer:
– for a reason which relates to his disability, treats that disabled person less favourably than he would treat other people to whom that reason does not apply (¶5505), although in certain circumstances, such discrimination will not be unlawful (¶5510);
– on the ground of his disability, treats that disabled person less favourably that he would treat a person not having that particular disability, whose relevant circumstances, including his abilities, are the same as, or not materially different from, those of the disabled person (¶5550) (this treatment cannot be justified); or
– fails to comply with the duty to make reasonable adjustments in relation to the disabled person (it is no longer possible for an employer to justify such a failure) (¶5515).

EXAMPLE An employer rejects a suitable disabled applicant, A, because he thinks her wheelchair will get in the way in the office. He appoints applicant B, who is no more suitable for the job but who does not use a wheelchair. A has therefore been treated less favourably than B for a reason related to her disability (i.e. the fact that she uses a wheelchair), which did not apply to B. Unless the employer can demonstrate that this treatment falls within the scope of the lawful treatment permitted by the Disability Discrimination Act 1995, he will have unlawfully discriminated against A.

547 There is no requirement to treat a disabled person more favourably than other applicants, but employers are obliged to make **reasonable adjustments** to working conditions or the workplace so that the disabled person is not at a substantial disadvantage. The disabled person may be able to offer suggestions as to what adjustments may assist. Less favourable treatment is justified if the disabled person cannot do the job concerned, and no adjustment which would enable the person to do the job is practicable.

EXAMPLE An applicant for a typing job, C, has arthritis in her hands and is, on the face of it, not the best person for the job as her typing speed is too slow. However, if a reasonable adjustment could be made, such as an adapted keyboard, to overcome C's speed problems, the employer would be obliged to make the adjustment and reconsider her application in the light of that adjustment.

548 **Discrimination questionnaires** In order to decide if he has sufficient **grounds to bring a discrimination claim**, a job applicant can serve a questionnaire on the employer asking for **information about** the successful applicant (for example, details of their sex, skills, qualifica-

tions and experience) and the recruitment process (for example, how many men and how many women applied, the sex or race of all those interviewed, their qualifications and experience, etc) (s 74 SDA 1975; s 65 RRA 1976; s 56 DDA 1995; reg 36 SI 2003/1660; reg 33 SI 2003/1661). For further discussion on discrimination questionnaires, see ¶5711.

Positive action It is permissible to adopt positive measures **to encourage applications** from potential employees who are members of particular racial groups, religions or beliefs, or a particular sex which have been under-represented in particular work (see Chapter 16). Applications from other racial groups, religions or beliefs, or members of the opposite sex should also be sought, as withholding information from one group or sex in an attempt to encourage applications from other groups or from the opposite sex would be unlawful. 549

Discrimination in selection to achieve a "racial balance" or, for example, an equal number of male and female employees is not allowed. Selection must ultimately be based on merit. Discrimination against able-bodied people is not prohibited by the disability discrimination legislation, and so a **disabled applicant** could be selected over an able-bodied applicant in order to increase the number of disabled employees in the workplace.

Age discrimination

Age discrimination is currently **not specifically prohibited**. However, it is proposed that direct and indirect age discrimination will **become unlawful from** 1 October 2006. At the time of writing, the Government has published **draft** Employment Equality (Age) Regulations 2006, together with the final consultation document on age discrimination (Equality and Diversity: Coming of Age). See ¶5254 for a summary of the draft regulations and current proposals. For general advice, see ACAS's advice leaflet "Employing older workers". 550

MEMO POINTS Until age discrimination legislation comes into force, such discrimination may be held to be **unlawful on other grounds**. For example, an employer who discriminates on grounds of age may find that he has indirectly discriminated on grounds of sex where an employer imposes an upper age limit for applicants with which fewer women than men can comply due to their being out of the labour market while bringing up children (*Price v Civil Service Commission* [1977] IRLR 291, EAT). See memo points to ¶5254 for further examples.

Discrimination on trade union grounds

It is unlawful to refuse employment on the grounds of membership or non-membership of a trade union (s 137 TULRCA 1992) (¶7563). 551

III. Recruitment procedure

It is advisable for both a member of human resources and the line manager/supervisor to be involved in the entire recruitment and selection process, including the short-listing for interview, the interview itself and the final selection. In small companies, there may not be a separate human resources function and it will therefore fall to the line manager/supervisor to carry out the recruitment process. 570

A. Profiling

1. Job descriptions

575 The first step in the recruitment process is to give careful consideration to the vacant position, identifying the main purpose of the job, the key tasks involved and the responsibilities of the jobholder. A member of human resources should work closely with the line manager/supervisor for the job to ensure proper identification and accuracy.

This information will form the basis of a job description, which should be **broadly drafted** (especially in the case of senior employees), as it will define the scope of the employee's contractual duties. If the scope is sufficiently broad, the employer should be able to move the employee to other duties without the need to obtain his consent to a variation of contract.

The job description usually **deals with** the following:
– job title;
– main purpose of job;
– main duties and responsibilities;
– to whom the jobholder will report; and
– for whom he will be responsible.

In order to avoid an inference of discrimination, the job title must be neutral in terms of gender, race, religion or belief and sexual orientation, unless a genuine occupational qualification or requirement applies (see Chapter 16).

2. Person specification

577 The next step is to consider the qualifications, skills and experience required by the job holder, with the line-manager again taking a major role.

There should be a direct and precise connection between the person specification and the job description to ensure that the focus is on the applicant's ability to do the job rather than unrelated personal characteristics.

The **criteria** of this person specification may include:
– relevant qualifications, knowledge and attainments;
– the length and type of experience required;
– special skills or aptitudes (e.g. oral or written skills, manual dexterity); and
– physical abilities (e.g. normal or corrected vision), disposition (e.g. reliability), and circumstances (e.g. has a current driving licence, owns a car), where these are a justifiable requirement for the job.

The specification should make clear those criteria which are "essential", and those which would be merely "desirable", and more weight should clearly be given to the essential elements.

578 Employers in the **finance sector** must comply with regulations on staff recruitment and development (Financial Services and Markets Act 2000), which apply to all employees. In the context of recruitment, the employer must ensure that the applicant is competent, in particular, by relating the applicant's skills and knowledge to that required for the particular job, taking reasonable steps to obtain information about the applicant's previous activities and training, and identifying whether further training is required. The employer must also ensure that references are taken from suitable sources.

Qualifications and requirements

The employer should consider whether any requirements specified in the person specification might be indirectly discriminatory. Even a quality described as "desirable" as opposed to "essential" may constitute a discriminatory requirement if it is clear that it was a deciding factor in the selection process (*Falkirk Council v Whyte* [1997] IRLR 560, EAT). 579

In order to avoid discrimination claims, the employer should take the following action:

Liability	Employer action
Sex discrimination	– avoid prescribing requirements that effectively inhibit applications from one sex or from married people or from civil partners
Racial discrimination	– avoid prescribing requirements such as length of residence or experience in the UK – where a particular qualification is required, make it clear that a fully comparable qualification obtained overseas is as acceptable as a UK qualification – avoid requiring a standard of English higher than that needed safely and effectively to perform the job
Disability discrimination	– be able to justify imposing essential health requirements – avoid unnecessary or marginal requirements in job specifications (for example, that the employee be "energetic", when in fact the job in question is largely sedentary) – be able to show that any qualifications required are relevant and significant in terms of the particular job and the particular applicant, and that there is no reasonable adjustment (for example, the reassignment of the duties to which the qualification relates) which would change this
Religion or belief discrimination	– avoid unnecessary requirements that the applicant needs to follow a particular faith
Sexual orientation discrimination	– avoid offering benefits packages which are available to married employees only
Age discrimination (expected from October 2006)	– avoid using upper age limits or age ranges in job adverts, or phrases which imply age restrictions, such as "young graduate" or "mature person" – ensure that the levels of experience and qualifications required are necessary to the position – do not make assumptions based on age, for example, that young people lack supervisory experience, or that older people do not have IT skills

Genuine occupational qualification/requirement

It is permissible, in relation to certain jobs, to impose a requirement that applicants be of a particular sex, racial group or sexual orientation, or to belong to a particular religion or belief where there is a genuine occupational qualification (GOQ) or requirement (GOR) for that job (s 7 SDA 1975; ss 4A, 5 RRA 1976; reg 7(2) SI 2003/1661; reg 7(2) SI 2003/1660). If a GOQ/GOR has been identified for a particular job, the position should be reviewed from time to time to see whether it is still applicable. For further details on GOQs and GORs, see ¶5290 and ¶5402. 580

B. Recruitment methods

A vacancy can be publicised in a range of ways, and more than one method is often used (see table). 585

To avoid discrimination, employers need to give some thought as to which method(s) to use. Not advertising or advertising in certain publications with a narrow readership or using particular recruitment methods may restrict the groups of applicants who can apply. In order to avoid claims of **indirect discrimination**, the employer should place adverts in publications that will reach both sexes and a wide age-range, and will not unjustifiably exclude or disproportionately reduce the numbers of applicants from a particular racial group, religion or belief. People of different age groups, for example, may use different methods of looking for a job: younger people are more likely to use careers services, Jobcentres, newspapers or the internet, while many older people prefer to rely on community and business networks.

In cases of **positive action**, it is permissible for job adverts to be placed specifically to reach members of under-represented groups (for example, through the use of ethnic minority press, as well as other newspapers), and for employment agencies and careers offices in areas where these groups are concentrated to be used.

In general, recruitment by **word of mouth** or on **personal recommendation** is not recommended, as it may give rise to a claim of discrimination (for example, sex or race). However, the courts have recognised that recruitment to **highly specific posts** such as personal confidential advisers might be limited to individuals well-known to the person they are serving (*Coker v Lord Chancellor* [2002] IRLR 80, CA).

Method	Description	Comment
Word of mouth	Informal and cost-effective, relying on introduction of applicants through existing employees or an employers' network.	If used by itself, will usually give smaller selection of suitable applicants. Should be avoided where workforce is wholly or predominantly white or black (and labour market is multi-racial), or where workforce is predominantly of one sex.
Internal recruitment	More formal than word of mouth. Relies on internal promotion (may use company intranet).	Exploits and develops existing employees' skills and training, benefiting both company and individual employees. Likely to boost motivation within workforce if employees can progress their careers within the company.
National newspapers	Expensive. Appropriate if large response is desirable or for more senior vacancies.	Likely to reach a wide and ethnically diverse readership.
Local newspapers and radio	Suitable for less specialised jobs. Can be used to target groups in a particular local area.	
Trade and specialist journals	Less expensive than national press. Targets applicants for specialist and professional vacancies.	
Employment/ recruitment agencies	Often specialise in particular type of work or industry (e.g. secretarial, IT), with job seekers registered with them. "Executive search" companies or "head-hunters" exist for higher management or specialist applicants, who are often approached directly.	See memo points. Can deal with all or part of recruitment process. Employer should check agency's equal opportunities policy to ensure recruitment methods conform to legal requirements and employer's own practice. Both agency and employer have responsibility to ensure that recruitment process operates fairly. Agency has specific responsibilities as suppliers of job applicants to prospective employers, in addition to own responsibilities as employers of agency staff.

Method	Description	Comment
The internet	Increasingly used as means of recruitment, particularly for graduate-level and technical jobs. Some companies include job vacancies on own internet web site. Employment agencies increasingly use internet. In some cases, applications may be made directly via e-mail.	Many unskilled workers do not have access and so unlikely to be suitable means of recruitment of such staff.
Jobcentres	Provide free nationwide recruitment and advisory service, displaying employers' vacancies and referring potential applicants. Administer some Government training programmes. Disability Employment Advisers (DEAs), supported by local Disability Service Teams, can assist in recruitment of disabled applicants, and advise on practical and financial help available (particularly where employer obliged to make reasonable adjustments).	See memo points. Jobcentres, schools, colleges and careers offices may have a specific, narrow source of applicants (e.g. single sex schools).
Local schools, colleges, career services	Regular contact with local schools and colleges will ensure that employer's needs with respect to particular skills and abilities are known, and work experience or "shadowing" schemes can be useful to both students and employer. Careers services can give employers information on suitable school leavers under 18.	
Trade unions	May supply applicants to employer.	Should not be used if results in members of a particular racial group or of one sex only (or a disproportionately large number of them) applying.
Training and Enterprise Councils (Local Enterprise Councils in Scotland)	Provide general information on local labour market and skills balance available. Operate recruitment service and may put forward trained workers, and tailor further training to employer's needs.	

MEMO POINTS When recruiting through employment agencies, Jobcentres, career offices, schools and other third parties, it is unlawful for employers to give **instructions to discriminate**, for example by indicating that certain groups will or will not be preferred, and/or to bring **pressure** on them **to discriminate** against members of a particular sex, racial group, disability, religion or belief, or sexual orientation (ss 39, 40 SDA 1975; ss 30, 31 RRA 1976; s 16C DDA 1995; reg 3(1)(a) SI 2003/1660; reg 3(1)(a) SI 2003/1661). It is also unlawful for a person knowingly to **help another to discriminate** on the grounds of disability (s 57 DDA 1995). If an employment agency, for example, refused to consider an application from a disabled person on the instructions of the employer, the agency could be liable for aiding the company.

C. Job adverts

590 Adverts should be designed and **presented** so as to attract the right sort of applicant for the job. They should therefore be tailored to the level of the target audience, and consistent with the **company image**, using the company logo (if there is one) as appropriate. It may be advisable to require that all job adverts are authorised by human resources or a senior line manager before they are issued.

If the employer becomes aware that a particular applicant's **disability** places him at a substantial disadvantage, the employer will be required, as part of his obligation to disabled applicants to make reasonable adjustments, to provide information about jobs in **alternative formats** (for example, large print, in Braille, on tape or computer disk). What is reasonable will depend on the circumstances (including the time available before the new employee is needed and the ease with which the applicant's request can be met) (¶5515).

The advert should be based on the **objective analysis** that was carried out to devise the job description and person specification. It should be concise and easily understood, clear as to what the job is, specific with respect to the qualifications, experience, skills and abilities needed, and should avoid generalisations such as "attractive salary" or "appropriate qualifications".

Adverts for **internal recruitment** should contain the same information as those used externally, and vice versa.

Equal treatment

591 **Pay rates** must comply with legislation on equal pay (¶5600).

592 The employer must avoid **discriminatory wording**, and should ensure that he advertises in such a way that encourages applications from both able-bodied and disabled applicants of any sex, racial group, religion or belief, sexual orientation and, ideally, a wide age-range. The employer may also be liable for discrimination if, in the advert, he has set **requirements or criteria** for the job that are indirectly discriminatory. For further details, see ¶5807.

MEMO POINTS It is proposed that from 1 October 2006, discriminatory wording in relation to age will also be unlawful (¶550).

593 In addition to the availability of individual remedies, if an advert indicates an intention to discriminate, the Equal Opportunities Commission, the Commission for Racial Equality and the Disability Rights Commission can **enforce** the provisions relating to discriminatory wording by issuing a non-discrimination notice and seeking a restraining injunction from the civil courts. See ¶5790 for further information.

595 The advert can include a **statement of commitment to equal opportunities**. Some organisations are accredited with the "double tick" symbol by the Employment Service, which they can use in their adverts as a sign of public commitment to good practice in the employment and retention of people with disabilities.

Contractual status

596 Employers should ensure that any **description of benefits and salary** included in the advert corresponds to the terms and conditions of employment set out in the offer letter and/or contract of employment for the successful applicant. Any **discrepancy** could give rise to legal action, although adverts are normally not part of the employment contract. The wording of the advert is usually taken to be no more than an indication of the terms that would apply if the applicant were engaged. If, therefore, an employee accepts a written job offer that contains terms different to those of the advert, he cannot normally rely on the advert as evidence of contractual terms.

However, where the terms are in writing but are ambiguous, giving rise to a **dispute as to the interpretation** of the contract, the tribunal can consider the wording of the advert in order to ascertain the intentions of the employer at that time (*Pedersen v The Mayor and Burgesses of the London Borough of Camden* [1981] IRLR 173, CA).

If the applicant is engaged but the job offer is not put in writing (and there are no written terms and conditions of employment), the employee may be able to rely on the advert as proof of his terms.

D. Applications

A job advert usually asks applicants to send in their **CV** (curriculum vitae) (with a covering letter), or to write in for an **application form**. Each has its advantages, as the following table shows: 600

Application form	CV
Uniform format makes it easier to compare one application with another.	Although reviewing CVs may be more time-consuming for the employer, using a CV is likely to make the recruitment process shorter and less complicated.
Employers can ensure that all the required information is provided.	CVs may not provide the information required.
Applicants may be put off applying because forms are time-consuming to complete and may be intimidating.	CVs are less time-consuming for employees as, once they are compiled, they can be used for multiple applications.
Applicants may find the form inadequate as they are unable to control the information given.	Applicants can control the information provided, focusing on their strengths.
Applicants have less scope to lie, as the form sets out the information to be provided, can state that references and qualifications will be checked, and that information must be current and accurate (and warn that inaccuracy will be serious misconduct possibly leading to dismissal).	Some applicants may leave gaps on their CV, distort facts or even tell lies (e.g. stating they have worked for a particular employer when they have not).

If possible, applications should be **acknowledged** promptly, and the timetable for short-listing, interviewing and appointment given. Some organisations may state that, if nothing further is heard by a particular date, the applicant can conclude that he has been unsuccessful. Other organisations will send out a formal notification that the applicant has not been short-listed for interview. 601

To reduce the risk of an appointment based on **inaccurate information**, either in the CV or in the application form, the employer may want to: 602

a. ask applicants to produce original examination certificates (making this a pre-condition of employment, where necessary), take copies, and contact the institutions for further confirmation if in doubt;

b. in the interview

– ask searching questions about their qualifications;

– investigate gaps evident from the CV and go through the applicant's employment history; and

– observe the applicant's body language for signs of lying (e.g. lack of eye contact, shifting in their seat, blushing, pausing before speaking and repetition);

c. review any psychological tests (¶650) used for signs of lying; and

d. take up references.

603 Some statements are unlikely to give rise to **legal liability** because they are "sales talk", for example, broad statements such as "team player". However, fraudulent or negligent misrepresentations or mis-statements made by an applicant that are relied on by the employer, causing him to suffer loss as a result, may entitle the employer to damages. The **employer's loss** in these circumstances may include costs associated with having to start the recruitment process again, for example, advertising or employment agency fees. However, in practice, it is not likely to be cost-effective to bring an action for damages against an employee.

604 If the employee has not been truthful, the employer will only be justified in **dismissing** the employee if the deception is relevant to the particular employment and/or any terms of the contract. The employer's verification of information provided by the applicant is dealt with in ¶680 below.

1. Application forms

607 Companies may have a standard application form, or a series of application forms for different departments or different types of employee. As for the job advert, the application form should **focus** on the skills and abilities required to do the job, as identified in the job description and the person specification.

The employer should consider allowing applicants to apply in ways other than completing an application form (for example, typewritten, by telephone or on tape), as the **format** of the form might place a disabled applicant (for example blind or partially sighted applicants, or those with dyslexia) at a disadvantage.

The **standard of completion** can be a guide to the applicant's suitability, if writing and presentation skills are essential to the job. Reliance on this factor may, however, lead to a disability discrimination claim. Application forms should not require a higher standard of English than is required to do the job, as this may discriminate against those whose first language is not English.

608 The application form can include a question as to whether the applicant will need a **work permit** to work in the UK. The employer will need to check at some stage during the recruitment process whether the applicant can lawfully work in the UK (¶750). In order to avoid racial discrimination, the question must be asked of all applicants and not just those whom the employer suspects (for example, because they have a foreign name) may need a work permit.

609 The application form should state whether **references** will be required. References are discussed further at ¶704.

2. Disability issues

611 The application form can include a question asking whether the applicant is disabled and if so, whether the individual will require any adjustments (both during the selection process and in order to do the job in question), and what these might be. If the employer obtains information as a result of questions asked in the application form, he will be under a statutory duty to make reasonable adjustments (s 4A DDA 1995, as amended by reg 4 SI 2003/1673).

Employers should take all reasonable steps to find out whether or not a person has a disability that is likely to place him at a substantial disadvantage (Code of Practice on employment and occupation (DD Code)). If an employer's agent or employee (for example, a member of human resources, a line manager, or company doctor) knows of the applicant's disability and its disadvantageous effect, the employer will have "constructive" knowledge of it, and the duty to make reasonable adjustments will apply.

3. Criminal convictions

An employer may need to know about his employee's criminal convictions where, for example, there is an obligation to disclose such information on registration forms for regulatory authorities. For some posts this information may be relevant as it may reflect on the individual's character and suitability for the job. If this information is required by the employer a question as to whether the applicant has any criminal convictions should be included on the application form. 615

Unless the employer has **expressly asked** for information on past convictions, no action can be taken against an employee for failure to disclose convictions which are not spent.

Spent convictions

If questions about past convictions are raised on an application form or at a job interview, prospective employees are not generally obliged to reveal convictions that are "spent" (Rehabilitation of Offenders Act 1974, as amended). Convictions become spent after a certain period of time has elapsed from the date of conviction (the "rehabilitation period"), depending on the nature of the sentence imposed. 616

Sentence	Rehabilitation period
Imprisonment, custody or detention for life or detention at Her Majesty's pleasure	Never rehabilitated
Imprisonment, youth custody, detention in a young offender institution, or corrective training for a term exceeding 30 months	Never rehabilitated
Imprisonment, youth custody, detention in a young offender institution, or corrective training for between 6 and 30 months	10 years/5 years (if offender under 18 when convicted)
Imprisonment or youth custody for 6 months or less	7 years/3 years (if offender under 18 when convicted)
Probation (for convictions on/after 3 February 1995), fines	5 years/2 years (if offender under 18 when convicted)
Probation (for convictions before 3 February 1995), conditional discharge, binding over, care or supervision order	1 year or the duration of the order/bond, if longer
Absolute discharge	6 months
Disqualification from driving	Period of disqualification

MEMO POINTS A **suspended sentence** is treated as one that has taken effect (the rehabilitation period is the same as for the full sentence). If an offender is sentenced for several offences, the rehabilitation period will depend on the time actually served. For example, if two prison terms of 6 months are served **concurrently**, the rehabilitation period is 7 years. If they are served **consecutively**, the rehabilitation period is 10 years.

Exceptions Employees in **certain occupations and professions** are obliged to disclose any spent convictions (Rehabilitation of Offenders Act 1974 (Exceptions) Order SI 1975/1023, as amended). The application form should clearly state whether the job is being treated as an exception. 617

Most of the exceptions relate to the administration of justice, national security, social and health services with patient contact (in particular, those with access to vulnerable groups such as the infirm, elderly, mentally ill and young people under the age of 18), specific areas of the financial sector, certain professions (doctors, lawyers, accountants, pharmacists), and taxi drivers.

There is a further exception for any office or employment concerned with the provision of accommodation, care, leisure and recreational facilities, schooling, social services, supervision or training to **persons under 18**, where the holder of the office or employment would have access in the course of his normal duties to such persons, or where the normal duties are carried out wholly or partly on the premises where such provision takes place.

An applicant to whom an exception applies must disclose spent convictions if the question asked relates either to the applicant himself or, where relevant, to a **person who lives in the same household**, and the provision of the services mentioned would normally take place in that household.

618 **Implications** A "rehabilitated person" must be treated as a person who has not committed or been charged with or convicted of the offence in question, and must not be prejudiced in any way by virtue of that conviction or its non-disclosure (s 4 Rehabilitation of Offenders Act 1974). The implications are as follows:

Rejecting applicant	**Spent** conviction (or failure to disclose) not grounds for rejecting applicant or employee from any office, profession, occupation or employment. Convictions that are **not spent** (or where an **exception** applies) can be good reason for rejection.
Dismissal	**Spent** conviction (or failure to disclose) not grounds for dismissal, even if occupation/employment is sensitive (it is generally accepted that a dismissal on these grounds will be **automatically unfair** (¶8390)) (*Property Guards Ltd v Taylor and Kershaw* [1982] IRLR 175, EAT). Concealing convictions that are **not spent** when applying for a job (or where an **exception** applies and full disclosure not given as required) can provide fair reason for dismissal (*Torr v British Railways Board* [1977] IRLR 184, EAT).
Providing reference	If employer/ex-employer refers to **spent** conviction in reference, employee may be sue for defamation. Defence of justification may be available, unless revelation made with malice.

Criminal record and other checks

619 The employer may need to find out whether the applicant has **current or spent convictions**, such as where the position involves a specified position of trust. In certain circumstances an application may be made to the Criminal Records Bureau (CRB) which is set up to provide three levels of checks on the criminal records of individuals (Police Act 1997):
- enhanced;
- standard; and
- basic (not yet implemented).

CRB also acts as a central access point not only to criminal records information, but also to the Department for Education and Skills (DfES) **List 99** and the Department of Health **POCA list** (Protect Of Children Act List Service), which lists people considered unsuitable to work with children. The latter two lists will be included in the checks regarding enhanced or standard disclosure to work with children or vulnerable adults, and the disclosure will record whether the applicant is included on any of those lists.

MEMO POINTS 1. For **more information**, see the CRB's website: www.crb.gov.uk
2. In **Scotland**, applications are made to Disclosure Scotland.

620 Applications for enhanced and standard disclosures must be **signed by** the individual about whom the check is being made and countersigned by an organisation registered with the CRB. This may be the organisation that is recruiting, but if an employer does not want to register he can use another registered organisation to sign on his behalf (known as an umbrella body).

621 Checks are carried out by the CRB for a prescribed fee, depending on which type of check is required and will result in the issue of one of the following certificates:
1. **Enhanced Criminal Record Certificate (ECRC) (enhanced disclosure)**. This check is **appropriate for** sensitive jobs that come within the exceptions of the Rehabilitation of Offenders Act 1974 (Exceptions) Order SI 1975/1023, as amended (¶617), which include the regular caring for, training, supervising or being in sole charge of those aged under 18, or of vulnerable

adults. It is also used when certain licences are applied for (e.g. gaming and lottery licences) and for judicial appointments. The Certificate will record all convictions (including spent convictions), cautions, reprimands and warnings or state that there are none, and may also include information provided by the local police.

The original disclosure will then be **issued to** the individual and a copy sent to the registered entity. Local police forces can also disclose further information directly to the registered entity where such information cannot be included in the certificate itself because its disclosure may hamper detection or prevention of crime.

2. **Criminal Record Certificate (CRC) (standard disclosure)**. This check is **appropriate for** jobs that come within the exceptions of the Rehabilitation of Offenders Act 1974 (Exceptions) Order SI 1975/1023, as amended (¶617), where there is a position of trust. Such positions of trust include professional posts (e.g. accountants) or jobs which involve regular contact with those aged under 18 or with vulnerable adults. The Certificate records details of all convictions (including spent convictions), cautions, reprimands and warnings, or will state that there are none. It will also show if the individual is barred from working with children and other vulnerable groups. Local police forces will not be involved in the checking procedure.

The original disclosure will then be **issued to** the individual and a copy sent to the registered entity.

3. **Criminal Conviction Certificate (CCC) (basic disclosure)** (not yet implemented). Although basic disclosure checks were due to be introduced in the summer of 2002, their implementation has been delayed. It is anticipated that when it is introduced this check will be appropriate for most employers. It will disclose details of recorded offences (other than spent convictions) over the previous 6-year period or will state that there are none.

Unlike enhanced and standard disclosures an individual will be able to apply directly to the CRB and a basic disclosure will only be **issued to** the individual.

CRB registration Only organisations which are registered with the CRB are entitled to counter-sign an application for a **standard or an enhanced check**. 622

Those registering must sign up to the **CRB's Code of practice** which requires that all disclosure material is kept confidential and used fairly. The Code requires the registered entity to have a written policy on the **handling and storage of disclosure material** to ensure that information obtained is kept securely and only for as long as is necessary, usually not more than 6 months, before being disposed of. Organisations must also have a written policy on the **recruitment of ex-offenders** with a view to avoiding unfair discrimination and **must also**:

a. ensure that application forms for positions where a standard or enhanced disclosure will be requested:

– inform applicants that such a request will be made for successful applicants; and

– state that a criminal record will not necessarily be a bar to obtaining the position (or include this statement in accompanying material);

b. discuss any matters revealed with the applicant before withdrawing an offer of employment;

c. make applicants who are subject to disclosure aware of the CRB Code and make a copy available on request; and

d. give guidance on the recruitment of ex-offenders to those involved in the selection process.

The CRB can **refuse to issue** standard and enhanced disclosures if it suspects that the CRB Code is not being adhered to.

It is a **criminal offence** for employees of registered bodies/recipients of standard and enhanced disclosures to disclose information contained in the certificates other than in the course of their duties.

The requirements for registration do not apply where **basic checks** are made. However, as basic disclosure will involve sensitive personal data the data protection principles will apply (¶5951). 623

624 **Fees** There is a one-off fee of £300 when an organisation **registers** with the CRB to enable it to receive enhanced or standard disclosures. This includes the cost of the lead countersignatory. There is also a a one-off fee of £5 for each additional countersignatories.

The fee payable by a registered body for **each disclosure** is as follows: £34 for an enhanced criminal record certificate (enhanced disclosure) and £29 for a criminal record certificate (standard disclosure), although this fee is waived in the case of volunteers. Organisations can to ask the applicants to pay them for the disclosure.

4. Health questionnaires

625 The applicant could be asked to complete a health questionnaire as a **supplement to the application form**. This is common where the job involves driving work and in industries where there is an exposure to certain chemicals. The degree of detail requested on a health questionnaire will depend on the **nature of the job** and the sort of medical conditions that may affect the applicant's ability to carry out that job. Advice can be obtained from the local Employment Medical Advisory Service, which is part of the Health and Safety Executive. Sometimes a health questionnaire is required for **pension or insurance purposes**.

A health questionnaire could also form the basis of the health assessment required under the working time regulations for **night workers** (¶3701).

MEMO POINTS It may be appropriate with manual based jobs in **certain industries** such as oil or construction to require an employee to remain in **excellent health** throughout his employment and in such cases the employer should state this as an express term of the contract. If an employer subsequently dismisses an employee on this term he will need to show that the requirement was reasonable and that he was justified and acted reasonably in relying on it.

626 Only information that really needs to be known should be obtained and employers requiring health questionnaires to be completed must ensure that they comply with the data protection **sensitive data condition** (¶5951). This means that, in general, employers should only use health questionnaires where it is necessary for the protection of health and safety, to prevent discrimination on the grounds of disability, to satisfy other legal obligations or if the applicant has freely given his explicit consent. Medical information should be **obtained separately** and kept separate from the application form. Information about an applicant's health which has been collected for occupational or insurance purposes should not be made available to the employer unless this is necessary to administer the scheme.

The health questionnaire should be treated as **confidential**, and it is advisable that steps are taken to ensure that only the employer's medical adviser sees the completed form.

The employer should **rely on** his medical adviser's professional opinion as to whether the applicant is fit to do the job, or whether a medical examination is required (¶706).

627 If the answers reveal that the applicant is **disabled**, the employer will be under a statutory duty to make reasonable adjustments (¶5515).

628 If a prospective employee has **deliberately concealed** a condition (for example a history of mental illness) the employer may be able to void the contract, especially if the condition recurs. The employer must ensure that in such circumstances he voids the contract and dismisses the employee due to this deception (using his disciplinary procedure) and not due to his illness. It is useful to state on any medical questionnaire that any deliberate concealment or deception will be treated as a matter of gross misconduct which could lead to the dismissal of the employee. The employer will then be on firm ground if he finds out the employee has made a serious concealment or deception and he dismisses the employee, after following his disciplinary procedure, on the grounds of gross misconduct. However, if the concealment has no impact on the employee's work and is a condition that will not re-occur, the employer must act carefully and reasonably and ascertain the reason why the employee concealed his condition before disciplining him.

References are another good way of ascertaining a prospective employee's attendance record and many employees specifically ask appropriate referees what kind of attendance and sickness record a prospective employee has. 629

IV. Selection

A. Short-listing for interview

In some companies, **human resources staff** will be involved in the sifting of application forms and the short-listing of applicants to be invited to the next stage of the selection process, commonly an interview. To avoid any possibility of bias, it is preferable for two or more selectors (including a member of human resources and the direct line manager/supervisor of the vacant post) to be involved in this process. 630

Selectors should be **trained** to ensure that they are aware of their legal obligations (in particular, to avoid discrimination) and that they should base their decisions on objective **selection criteria**, which are founded on the key skills and experience identified in the job description and person specification (and not on prejudices and stereotypes (*Horsey v Dyfed County Council* [1982] IRLR 395, EAT)). 631

It is good practice for the selectors who do an initial review for interview selection not to see unnecessary **personal details**, as this reduces the risk of discrimination on irrelevant, unlawful grounds. In smaller organisations it may not be possible for the sifting and selection processes to be separated. 632

Where certain **qualifications** have been validly stipulated, the selectors should shortlist those applicants who have the appropriate qualifications (or overseas equivalents). If an applicant has alternative evidence of the necessary level of competence, the employer may be able to waive the requirement for the particular qualification stipulated. 633

If, having selected on the basis of qualifications, there are too many applicants to interview, the selectors should consider the relevance and length of the applicants' **work experience**, keeping a note of the criteria applied.

If the employer knows that an applicant has a disability and is likely to be at a substantial disadvantage because of the employer's arrangements or premises, he should consider whether a **reasonable adjustment** may bring the disabled person within the number of applicants to be considered for the position even though he would not otherwise be selected because of that disadvantage. If the selectors **need more information** to be able to make that judgement, they should put the disabled person on the shortlist for interview if that is the normal method of seeking additional information on applicants. 634

All applications should be processed in exactly the same way, and there should not be separate lists of male and female or married and single applicants. Decisions about short-listing should not be made until the closing date for applications. 635

B. Selection methods

640 The selection process can involve a number of **different approaches** including:
- interviews;
- practical tests;
- psychometric tests;
- role plays;
- team exercises; and
- assessment centres.

Which approach is adopted will depend on the needs and seniority of the job, the skills of the recruiter and the resources and objectives of the company. More senior or specialised jobs may require more detailed and sophisticated techniques to test the applicant's skills and personal characteristics. In any case, the employer should ensure that the process does not discriminate on grounds of sex, marital status, sexual orientation, racial group, religion or belief, disability or age, but is specifically related to the job requirements.

1. Interviews

643 The interview is the most common method of selection. It has two main purposes, to assess the applicant's suitability, and to give him information about the job and the company.

644 **Assessing the applicant's suitability** The interview should be organised in such a way as to promote **fair treatment** of all applicants. It may be helpful to have a written interview procedure specifying the manner in which interviews should be conducted. For example, this could specify the number of interviewers (such as a human resources specialist, together with the line manager), and the types of questions that can and cannot be asked. This will help to ensure that there is a consistent form to the interviews, and that the required information is obtained from each applicant.

In addition to receiving training in their legal obligations, interviewers should be trained in interviewing techniques.

Interviews can vary in the **degree of formality**, depending on the nature of the job and the type of company. The interview may be conducted one-to-one, by a series of one-to-one interviews, or by panels of two or more people.

Panel interviews tend to be more formal but may be helpful in bringing a range of ages, racial backgrounds and both male/female presence so as to reduce the risk of unlawful discrimination. The number of panel members should ideally be kept to a maximum of three or four, unless there is a pressing reason for exceeding these numbers. Members of the panel may have particular areas of expertise, which they can concentrate on with the applicant. However, the applicant may feel outnumbered and less relaxed, and it may be difficult to achieve a rapport with large numbers present. The environment can be made less intimidating by avoiding formal surroundings, such as a boardroom, and formal layouts (e.g. sitting the applicant opposite a long line of panel members behind a formal table). Panel interviews need to be chaired by one member so that it is well structured and not subject to random interruptions from the various panel members.

Sometimes a member of human resources will conduct an **initial screening interview** in order to pre-select applicants for general suitability and competence. The disadvantage of this approach is that the applicant may be inconvenienced by being asked to attend on more than one occasion, and there is a danger of repetition in sequential interviews. Following a screening interview, there may be a **first interview** (either panel or one-to-one) involving the line manager/supervisor for the vacant position. This stage may identify a few suitable applicants, who may be invited to return for a **second interview**. A second interview may be used to undertake a more detailed analysis of the strengths and weaknesses of the remaining applicants. At this stage, more senior members of the company may be involved in the interview in order to make a final selection. The various stages of the interview process described above may be condensed in smaller organisations.

Providing information to the applicant Employers should recognise that interviews also give applicants the opportunity to find out about the company, the job, how much it pays and other employment terms. The interviewer should be equipped to answer these questions. A badly prepared interviewer can create an unfavourable impression of the company and may deter suitable applicants. 645

2. Selection tests

Selection tests can be used as an aid to measure an applicant's **practical ability**, or **personality traits** and **intelligence**. The employer should give careful thought as to whether or not to use tests, and they should not be used (particularly in the case of personality tests) in isolation, but rather in conjunction with other selection techniques. 647

If tests are used, they should be specifically related to job and/or career requirements, should measure an applicant's actual or inherent ability to do or train for the work or career against objective criteria, and the employer should have a policy about using tests, storing results and giving feedback to applicants. They should be administered by people who are trained and competent to do so, and applicants should be given an explanation of the nature and purpose of the tests before they are taken. The results should be confidential to the selectors and the applicant.

Tests should be gender **neutral**. Tests should also not contain irrelevant questions or exercises on matters which may be unfamiliar to racial minority applicants.

Routine testing of all applicants may discriminate against particular individuals or place them at a substantial disadvantage. If it does, the tests themselves or the way the results are assessed may need to be revised to take account of **specific disabled applicants** unless the nature and form of the test are necessary to assess a matter relevant to the job. If an applicant's disability inhibits his performance, it may be a reasonable adjustment to accept a lower "pass rate". Whether this is acceptable will depend on how closely the test is related to the requirements of the job, and what adjustments the employer would have to make if the disabled applicant was appointed.

EXAMPLE 1. A man with dyslexia, E, applies for a job that involves writing letters within fairly long deadlines. He can generally write letters very well but has difficulty doing so in stressful situations. At the interview, applicants must do a test of their letter-writing ability immediately on arrival and within a short time, putting E at a substantial disadvantage compared to other applicants. A reasonable adjustment would be for the employer to allow E more time to settle in and longer to write the test.

2. A disabled applicant, F, takes the numeracy test set by the employer for prospective employees and does not achieve the stipulated level. If the job requires a high level of numeracy, it may be reasonable to reject F. If, however, little numerical work is required and F is otherwise suitable, it is likely to be a reasonable adjustment for the employer to waive the requirement.

Tests should be subject to regular **review** to ensure that they remain relevant and free from any unjustifiable bias, either in content or in the scoring mechanism. 648

Practical tests If the job involves practical skills (e.g. typing, shorthand, or manual or dexterity skills), tests can be used before or at the time of the interview to measure an applicant's ability. The test must not be discriminatory and must strictly relate to the actual requirements of the job. 649

Psychometric and psychological tests These tests set out to measure personality traits and intelligence, in particular reasoning, problem solving, decision-making, interpersonal skills, and confidence. 650

The use of such tests is not widespread and is sometimes considered controversial, for example, those tests measuring personality. Guides on their use are available (for example, from the Institute of Personnel and Development).

The data protection implications of using **automated processes** in the selection process are discussed below.

3. Role plays, exercises and assessment centres

653 Larger companies may use assessment centres to put applicants (often senior management or fast-track graduates) through interviews, tests, and individual and group exercises. These may take place in a residential setting over a few days. The exercises may include presentations, role-plays and team events. This method is the most time consuming, but can give an accurate indication of likely job performance. The identification of the skills required to do the job and the choice of exercises to test those skills will be critical to the effectiveness of this method.

C. Arranging and preparing for interviews

660 **Travel expenses** The letter inviting an applicant for interview should indicate whether the company will pay his reasonable travel expenses, making it clear whether it will reimburse first or second class travel and/or what mileage rate will be applied to car travel. It may be appropriate to offer a subsistence payment (either actual expenditure incurred based on receipts submitted, or a notional allowance).

661 **Evidence of qualifications** The letter should also indicate what the applicant should bring with him to the interview, such as evidence of his qualifications.

662 **Disabled applicants** The statutory duty to make **reasonable adjustments** in relation to disabled applicants applies where the **employer knows**, and could reasonably be expected to know, that the disabled person in question is or may be an applicant for the post, or that a particular applicant has a disability which is likely to place him at a disadvantage, for example, where the application form has revealed that an applicant has a disability (s 4A DDA 1995, as amended by reg 4 SI 2003/1673).

If the employer is **not aware** in advance of an applicant's disability and the need to make reasonable adjustments to the arrangements, he should nevertheless seek to do so as soon as he learns of the disability and the disadvantage. What may reasonably be required in these circumstances may be less extensive than if advance notice had been given.

Reasonable adjustments might include the following:

– rearranging the time of the interview;

– accommodating a hearing impaired applicant by ensuring that the interviewer faces the applicant, is well lit, speaks clearly and is prepared to repeat questions, or providing a hearing loop or signer;

– paying additional expenses to meet any special requirements, for example travelling expenses for a support worker or reasonable cost of travel by taxi, rather than by bus or train, if this will eliminate any substantial disadvantage to which the arrangements would otherwise put the disabled applicant;

– holding the interview in an alternative room if an applicant turns up unexpectedly in a wheelchair which cannot access the designated interview room; and

– allowing the applicant with a learning disability to bring a friend or relative to assist when answering questions that are not part of tests.

For further details, see ¶5515.

Interviewer preparation The interviewer should re-read the application form, job and person specifications, and identify areas to develop further in the interview. The interviewer should plan questions, considering whether to ask only a few questions in order to encourage the applicant to talk at length on certain areas, and/or to structure a series of short questions covering several different topics. If there is to be a panel interview or a series of interviews, the topics to be covered by each member of the panel or each separate interviewer should be agreed. 663

The interviewer should consider, in advance, what information the applicant might ask for, and be ready to answer questions about the company and the job.

D. Conducting interviews

It may be useful for the applicant to be given a **tour of the company**/the relevant department and to meet employees with whom he would be working. This will be of particular interest to applicants who are new to the job market (e.g. school-leavers), but will also give the employer an opportunity to assess the applicant's interaction with other employees. 665

If possible, there should be no interruptions (for example, in-coming telephone calls). The interviewer should begin the interview by introducing himself and any other interviewers. He should give some background information about the company and the job. The applicant could be made to feel at ease by beginning with straightforward questions. As the interview progresses, it is more productive to avoid questions that merely call for a "yes" or "no" answer. The interviewer should ensure that all the relevant areas are covered. As the applicant speaks, the interviewer should listen, making notes on important points.

The interview should be **scheduled** to last a certain time, and the interviewer should try to keep within the time allowed, leaving enough time for the applicant to raise any questions he may have. Applicants should be told when they are likely to know the **outcome** of the interview.

Interview questions Unless they have been specifically asked, applicants are not obliged to offer information to prospective employers. It is up to the interviewer to elicit the information required by the employer. 666

The interviewer does not have to ask all applicants the same questions, particularly if there are certain areas, for example, gaps in an applicant's employment. However, interviewers should be aware of the need to ask **job-related questions**, focusing mainly on the job requirements, and should not ask questions that might indicate an intention to discriminate on the grounds of sex, marital status, race, disability, religion or belief, sexual orientation or age. For example, women should not be singled out and asked about their childcare arrangements. If questions are to be asked about matters that could be regarded as discriminatory (for example, **domestic circumstances**), it would be advisable to ask the same questions of all applicants. Questions about marriage plans or family intentions should not be asked, as they could be construed as showing bias against women.

Questions about an applicant's **background, character and private life** may infringe his right to privacy under human rights legislation (Human Rights Act 1998).

It is also advisable for the interviewer to ascertain when the applicant would be able to start the new job. If the applicant is currently employed, he will have to give **notice of termination** to his current employer. This may affect whether the employer decides to offer employment to a particular applicant. It is a commercial decision for the employer whether he is prepared to wait for the applicant to be free to start the new job. It may be possible for the applicant to negotiate a shorter period of notice with his current employer.

The interviewer could ask about a disabled applicant's **disability** if it is, or may be, relevant to the person's ability to do the job, after a reasonable adjustment if necessary. Indeed, this information may be required to assess what adjustments should be made. It should not, however, be used to discriminate against him and discriminatory questions should be avoided.

EXAMPLE A disabled applicant, G, is asked in an interview whether he may require extra leave because of his disability. The need for extra time off work may be a substantial factor relevant to the person's ability to do the job and so the question is unlikely to be discriminatory.

667 **Promises** Interviewers should take care not to make any promises during the interview that conflict with the employer's standard terms and conditions of employment unless these have been approved in advance. Oral promises have been enforced where the interviewer had authority to make them, even where these conflict with signed contract terms.

If any unusual agreement is reached during the interview, it is advisable to record it in writing and amend the offer letter and/or contract of employment as appropriate.

E. The decision

670 Interviewers should record their assessment of each applicant against the agreed selection criteria. In reaching a final decision, the interviewers should compare their results, taking into account the relative weighting of the criteria. Ideally, assessments of an applicant should be written up as soon as possible after the interview to assist in the decision making process and also to monitor the fairness of the process.

The decision should be made as soon as possible after the interview, test or assessment. A scoring system or assessment based on the selection criteria should allow a speedy comparison of results.

Notes of the scores and reasons for decisions should be kept.

671 If an applicant meets the required standard, the appointment process can begin. All applicants should be **informed of the outcome** as soon as possible, or informed of any delay. Rejection letters should be short and to the point. Employers are not obliged to give **reasons** why a particular applicant was unsuccessful. If reasons are given, the employer must ensure that they are accurate, because if the recruitment or selection process is subject to legal challenge, the rejection letter may have to be disclosed. If there is any discrepancy between the rejection letter and the evidence before the tribunal as to the real reason for rejection, the employer's defence to any claim will be weakened.

V. Monitoring and data protection

Monitoring and review

675 Monitoring applications can help to ascertain how people found out about the vacancy, and therefore how **advertising** can be used to best effect in the future.

Application forms should be reviewed periodically to ensure that they comply with legal requirements, and that they cover all the information needed to decide which applicants to short-list for interview.

The recruitment process should also be monitored as part of the company's **equal opportunities programme** so that the profile of applicants can be identified in order to ascertain whether there are any barriers to the recruitment of particular groups. For these purposes, **personal details** such as sex, marital status, ethnic origin or date of birth should be requested in a distinct part of the form that can be separated and re-introduced at the end of the recruitment process. It should be clear that this information is for monitoring purposes only and need only be provided on a voluntary basis.

Data protection

Data protection principles are discussed in Chapter 17. The application of these principles to recruitment and selection is discussed below and is based on the Recruitment and Selection Part of the Information Commissioner's Employment Practices Code (part 1 DP Code). 676

Employers are also advised to follow the DP Code's general recommendations with regard to data management (¶6000).

An applicant can ask for **access** to interview notes (and other personal data) if these form part of a set of information about him, for example, if they are filed together with the application form and references or, in the case of an existing employee, in his personnel file (¶5980).

Managing data protection Those involved in the recruitment and selection process should be **trained** so that they understand their own responsibility for data protection compliance, and serious data protection breaches should be a **disciplinary offence**. 677

Employers should also only request data about an applicant that is **relevant** to the recruitment and selection process.

Advertising Applicants should be informed of the name of the organisation to which their information will be provided and how it will be used, unless this is self-evident (normally the case with adverts for specific jobs, where the employer's name is on the advert). If the link between the requested information and its potential use is unclear, an explanation must be given. 678

If a **recruitment agency** is used, it must identify itself when placing an advert on behalf of an employer and explain how an applicant's personal data will be used and disclosed (unless this is self-evident). If the information may be used in connection with future vacancies, this should be clearly stated in the advert. The advert need not identify the employer.

The agency can pass the information to the employer provided the applicant understands that it will do so. If the employer is to receive the information about the applicant, the applicant must informed of the employer's identity and how the information will be used, unless this is self-evident.

If the employer wishes to remain anonymous at the early stages of the recruitment process, the agency may send information on an anonymous basis about an applicant to him. Once the employer wishes to receive personally identifiable information about the applicant so that the application can be pursued further, he must then be identified to that applicant.

Applications Again, the application form should state to whom the information is being provided and how it will be used, unless this is self-evident (normally the case with applications for specific jobs). If the employer receives an **unsolicited application**, he need only provide the above explanation if the application is to be retained and the use of the information or period of retention would not be self-evident to the applicant. 679

Any information requested should be **relevant** to the recruitment decision to be made (or to a related purpose, such as equal opportunities monitoring), and should be proportionate (in terms of its **extent and nature**) to the position. Certain questions will be relevant to some positions and not others, and the application form should be tailored accordingly. There should be a clear statement on the application or surrounding documents which explains what information might be required about applicant in addition to the information directly supplied by him. This should also state from whom this information will be sought.

Information about **criminal convictions** should only be requested if the role justifies such a request, in which case the form should clearly state that spent convictions do not have to be declared, unless an exemption applies (¶616).

The form should explain what checks may be made to **verify** the information provided (see below), including details of any further sources of information about the applicant.

If **sensitive data** are requested, special conditions must be satisfied (¶5951). Only sensitive data questions that have to be asked at the initial application stage should be requested.

The employer should provide a **secure method for sending** applications. If applications are to be sent by post or by fax, access to them once received should be limited. If applications are made on-line, the employer should ensure a secure method of transmission (for example, by using encryption-based software). Once received, the application must be **securely stored**.

MEMO POINTS In the context of recruitment and selection, **sensitive data** may include:
– relevant criminal convictions to assess suitability for certain types of employment;
– disabilities to ensure reasonable adjustments are made during the recruitment and selection process; and
– racial or ethnic origin and/or sexual orientation to ensure that the processes are non-discriminatory.

680 **Verification** An employer may need to **check the information provided** to him by a job applicant. In most cases this can be done on the production by the applicant of documentary evidence, such as original certificates of educational qualifications. In some cases, however, the employer may need to obtain third party verification, such as following up references from previous employers or checking financial references. In such cases employers should:
– fully **explain to the applicant** how the checks will be carried out. This should be done as soon as is reasonably practicable in the recruitment process. If external sources are to be used to check information, this should be explained to the applicant; and
– **obtain a signed consent** from the applicant if he needs to get documents or information from a third party (for example, confirmation of qualifications) unless consent has been indicated in some other way, for example the applicant has already written to the third party confirming that the information can be sent to the employer. Employers should not force applicants to use their subject access rights to obtain **records from another organisation** (i.e. making it a condition of getting the job) unless they are under an obligation to require the collection and verification of any criminal records (¶615) and this is sought from the Criminal Records Bureau (CRB). Generally, where CRB disclosure is requested this should be confined, as far as practicable, to the applicant that the employer intends to appoint.

If the checks produce **discrepancies**, the applicant should be given the **opportunity to explain**.

Verification should be limited to the checking of information specifically requested in the application form or during the recruitment process and should be proportionate to the requirements of the positions being applied for.

682 **Short-listing** Personal data should be **used consistently** and all short-list methods should be checked with sources of good practice such as the Equal Opportunities Commission or Commission for Racial Equality.

If an **automated short-listing system** is used as the sole basis for making a decision about an applicant's work performance or reliability (for example, short-listing purely on the basis of answers provided through a touch-tone telephone in response to psychometric questions posed by a computer), the applicant should be informed and permitted to make representations, which should be taken into account before a final decision is reached.

Tests based on the **interpretation of scientific evidence** (for example, psychological tests) should only be used and interpreted by individuals who have been properly trained.

683 **Interviews** The collection of personal data at interview, their recording, storage and use are subject to data protection principles (for example all notes should be destroyed after a reasonable time taking into account the employer's need to protect himself from any potential discrimination claim). These should, therefore, be relevant to, and necessary for, the recruitment process (or defending any challenge to that process). Interviewers should be made aware that interviewees may have a right to request access to their interview notes, and they (or those in contact with the applicants) should be taught how to deal with such requests.

684 **Pre-employment vetting** Enquiries to third parties about the applicant's background and circumstances should be confined to situations where there are particular and significant risks to the employer, clients, customers or others (for example, government workers with access to classified information, employees who work with children or certain vulnerable adults) and where there is no less intrusive and reasonably practicable alternative.

The **extent and nature** of information sought must be justified by the position and proportionate to the risks faced (the aim should be to obtain **specific information**, as opposed to a general intelligence gathering exercise). If sensitive data are collected, special conditions must be satisfied (¶5951). Wherever practicable the relevant information should be obtained directly from the applicant and, if necessary, then verified.

The applicant should be **informed** early in the process that vetting is to take place and how it will be done. The vetting itself should be **carried out** at an appropriate point in the recruitment process and comprehensive vetting should only be conducted on a successful applicant.

An approach should only be made to **sources** likely to provide the required information. If it is necessary to obtain **documents or information from a third party**, the applicant's consent should be obtained. The applicant's family and close associates should only be approached in exceptional cases.

Information from **unreliable sources** should be discounted. The applicant should be permitted to make representations in relation to **adverse information** that will affect the decision to appoint.

If **information** is obtained **about a third party**, that party should (so far as practicable) be made aware of that fact.

Retention of recruitment records All personal data obtained during the recruitment process should be **securely stored or destroyed**. The employer must carefully consider which information from the application form should be **transferred to the on-going employment record** (irrelevant information should be deleted). For example, information about the applicant's former salary should not be kept. 685

There must be a clear business **need for keeping** any recruitment **records**. No recruitment record should be held beyond the statutory limitation period for bringing a claim which may have arisen out of the recruitment process unless, again, there is a clear business reason for exceeding this period and in such cases, anonymising the recruitment information should be considered. **Information obtained by vetting** should be destroyed as soon as possible, or in any case within 6 months. A record of the result of the vetting or verification may be retained. With regard to criminal convictions disclosure from the Criminal Records Bureau, such information should be deleted after verification unless the information is relevant to the on-going relationship.

If information about **unsuccessful applicants** is to be kept on file for future vacancies, they should be informed and given the opportunity to have such information removed (the application form itself can allow the applicant to indicate his wishes).

SECTION 2

Offer and appointment

Once a successful applicant has been identified, the employer can make him an **offer** of employment. Consideration should be given to whether this offer should be subject to any **conditions**, for example, receipt of references, passing a medical or evidence that the individual can work legally in the UK. It may be necessary to apply for a work permit for some applicants from overseas. 700

It is advisable that the **appointment** of the successful applicant is documented. The essential terms should be communicated in an **offer letter**, which may be accompanied by a more detailed written contract of employment. In either case, the applicant should signify his acceptance of the offer in writing. Once an unconditional offer of employment is accepted or any conditions have been satisfied, a binding contract of employment will come into existence. 701

A. Pre-conditions to employment

702 It is a criminal offence for an employer to employ a person aged 16 or over who does not have the **right to live and work in the UK**. The employer should, therefore, obtain **documentary proof** of such a right from successful applicants. If this has not been established, the employment should be made conditional on proof being produced to the employer's satisfaction.

If an applicant does not have the right to work in the UK, the employer could consider **applying for a work permit**. If a work permit is required, the employment should be made conditional on a permit being granted. If an employer suspects in advance that he may need to do so he should ensure that any advert meets the requirements of Work Permits (UK) (the organisation which deals with work permit applications), seeking specific advice if necessary.

These issues are discussed in section 3 below.

Other pre-conditions are discussed immediately below.

Confirmation of qualifications

703 The job may require the holder to have particular qualifications, registrations, training or licences, and the applicant should be asked to provide proof that he has the necessary qualifications etc, perhaps by bringing the appropriate documentation to the interview. If the employer is to make the check himself, the applicant should be informed, and copies of the relevant checks and responses should be kept on file (subject to the data protection obligations discussed in ¶676).

References

704 It is common to specify that one of the referees should be the applicant's current employer, which may cause problems if the latter is not aware that his employee is looking for a new job. It may, therefore, be helpful for the application form to state whether references will be taken up and at what stage of the recruitment process (for example, prior to the interview or after an offer has been made). It is advisable for the company to require references "**satisfactory to the employer**", i.e. a subjective test. If the employer asks for "satisfactory references", there may be scope for dispute as to whether the references provided are in fact satisfactory.

When **taking up references** the employer should:
– consider why he needs a reference and what he wants to find out (for example, dates of previous employment, position held, attendance and conduct);
– specify his needs carefully, perhaps using a list of structured questions, relevant to an assessment of the applicant's abilities (a copy of the job description could be sent to the referee);
– decide who in the organisation would be best placed to provide a reference and how best to approach the referee; and
– recognise that roles may be reversed and that he may be asked to provide a reference in the future.

The employer should obtain the **applicant's permission** to contact his referee, either in the application form itself or at a later stage in the selection process. References can be obtained over the telephone, but a **written reference** gives the referee time to think and compose a structured response.

The prospective employer should use the reference provided to **supplement his own view** of the applicant, as formed from the application form and the performance at interview. It is unwise to rely solely on references, as they may be biased.

When checking references, the employer should take care not to disclose to prospective employees any **confidential information** received from the referee.

To **avoid any allegation of discrimination**, the process of checking references should be consistent.

An applicant can request access to references received by the prospective employer (¶5980). Where a worker has requested to see a reference received by the employer which enables a third party to be identified, the employer must make a judgement as to what information is reasonable to withhold (part 2.9.3 DP Code).

When **giving a reference**, an employer owes a **duty of care** to the subject of that reference (the employee), and the latter will be able to sue the employer for damages if he suffers loss as a result of the employer's negligent preparation of the reference (¶8324). As a result, many employers limit references to factual matters such as the employee's dates of employment and job title, which may be of limited value to prospective employers. 705

The employer should (part 2.9.1-2 DP Code):

– set out a company policy which states who can give references, in what circumstances, and the policy that applies to the granting of access to them. Anyone who is likely to become a referee should be aware of the policy;

– not provide confidential references about a worker unless sure that this is the worker's wish; and

– establish at the time the worker's employment ends whether or not he wants references to be provided to future employers or others.

Medicals

Where relevant, the recruitment process should make it clear that any job offer is subject to passing a medical. However, a medical should only be required where it is necessary for the prospective job. Particular reference should be made to the guidance in the Information about Workers' Health Part of the Information Commissioner's Employment Practices Code (part 4 DP Code). Employers must ensure that the testing is a **necessary and justified measure** to: 706

– determine whether the applicant is fit or likely to remain fit to carry out the job in question;

– meet any legal requirements for testing; or

– ascertain eligibility for a pension or insurance scheme.

Medical examination or testing should be carried out at an **appropriate point** in the recruitment process, i.e. where there is a likelihood of appointing them.

The employer must obtain the applicant's **informed and freely given consent** to a medical examination or testing (unless another sensitive data condition has been complied with (¶5951)), particularly if it involves invasive checks such as blood tests. To be informed, the applicant must fully understand the nature of the tests and how the information obtained through testing will be used.

If a **medical report** is sought (whether from an applicant's doctor or specialist direct to an employer, or to the employer's medical adviser), the applicant's **consent** must be obtained, and the applicant has a **right to see** the report (Access to Medical Reports Act 1988). However, if the medical is conducted by the company doctor, the employer will not be bound by these requirements.

An employer should avoid requiring a medical check for **disabled applicants** and not others, as this is likely to constitute unlawful discrimination unless the employer has objective justification, which may be the case where the disability is relevant to the job (for example, a job requiring lifting or carrying where the applicant's condition affects these abilities) or due to the environment in which the job is done. Where there is a **specific condition**, the employer must ensure that he obtains the medical report from the most appropriate authority (for example, in *Paul v National Probation Service* [2004] IRLR 190, EAT, the employer erred in obtaining and relying on information given by the applicant's GP instead of the applicant's consultant who had specialist knowledge of his condition). The employer can take account of medical evidence that shows that the disability affects the person's ability to do the work when deciding whether to appoint a particular applicant. However, where a report highlights potential problems that might affect whether the employer employs the applicant, the 707 employer must **discuss** things further with the applicant and he is under a duty to take reasonable steps **to adjust** the job on offer (*Paul v National Probation Service*).

Similarly, **older applicants** should not be singled out simply because of their age, and employers should not make assumptions about the capability or medical fitness of applicants based purely on age.

Restraints on taking up employment

709 The employer should ascertain the applicant's **current notice period**. If the applicant leaves his current employment to take up the new post without giving the proper notice, the new employer may be liable for inducing a breach of contract.

The employer should also establish whether the applicant is restricted in taking up new employment by **restrictive covenants** in his current contract of employment. If so, the employer should review the contract and decide whether the restrictions affect his decision to make an offer.

If it is not possible to clarify this before making an offer, the offer could be conditional on the contract being produced and the employer being satisfied that the applicant's ability to perform the duties of the job offered is not restricted. Alternatively, the employer could seek a warranty in the contract of employment to the effect that the applicant will not be in breach of his existing or former terms of employment or of any other obligation binding on him by reason of his entering into the employment contract.

B. Appointment

710 The legal requirements for a valid contract are discussed in detail at ¶1111. Care needs to be taken to ensure that a **binding contract** is not formed between the employer and a successful applicant before it is intended to be.

In some cases, the offer of employment will be **conditional** on certain requirements being satisfied (see above). It is advisable for the employee not to resign his current employment until he is satisfied that all such conditions will be met. Once all conditions are satisfied, the employer could write again to the successful applicant to confirm that the offer of employment is now unconditional. If this is accepted, there will be a binding contract of employment.

If there are no conditions to be met (or all conditions have already been satisfied), the employer may send an **unconditional offer** letter to the employee. If this is **accepted**, there will be a binding contract of employment. The employer may wish to require acceptance within a certain time, so there is a definite time within which he must leave the offer open before turning to another applicant.

711 **Offer letter** Although an offer can be oral, it is advisable for it to be made in writing. The offer letter will contain a formal offer of the job, and will set out the essential terms and conditions of employment. These should be consistent with the details of the job that were given in the job advert, and should cover the following:
– job title;
– any pre-conditions to the offer;
– whether the employment is subject to a probationary period;
– main terms, namely salary, hours, benefits, pension arrangements, holiday entitlement, place of employment; and
– start date and arrangements for the first day.

The offer letter could form the **statutory statement of written particulars**, in which case it must contain all the necessary information (¶1420). To avoid any confusion over the terms offered and accepted, the employer may wish to set out the terms in a **written contract of employment**, a copy of which the new employee is asked to sign and return. The contract could be enclosed with the offer letter, and should contain and, where necessary, expand on the essential terms contained in the offer letter.

It is advisable for the offer to require **acceptance** in writing. Note that acceptance is effective as soon as a letter of acceptance is posted. 712

Terms The employer should take care not to discriminate in the terms on which employment is offered. In the case of **disabled employees**, the employer must consider whether any reasonable adjustments need to be made to the terms and conditions which would otherwise apply, for example, changing working hours so that a disabled employee who has difficulty using public transport during rush hours can avoid those times. 713

Increasingly employers are giving "**golden hellos**" to new employees, which can involve substantial bonuses being paid on joining the company. 714

Relocation assistance and cultural acclimatisation is particularly beneficial when dealing with international transfers and people relocating their home in order to start employment. For employees relocating from overseas, the initial months of employment might also include language tuition and assistance on finding accommodation and appropriate schooling for children. 715

Pre-contractual negotiations In some cases, the successful applicant may not be willing to accept the terms offered. The employer may be prepared to negotiate, in particular, where there are no other suitable applicants and the employer does not wish to start the recruitment process again. The employer should avoid negotiating different terms where these would create discrepancies between that applicant and existing employees, in terms of existing reward structures and terms and conditions of employment. This may leave the employer vulnerable to **discrimination or equal pay** claims. 716

If negotiations do take place, the **outcome** should be recorded in writing, for example as an amendment to the written contract of employment, or as part of a revised offer letter. The latter may be more appropriate where the arrangement agreed is temporary.

If the employer is **not prepared to amend** the terms of his offer, either from the outset or at the conclusion of negotiations, he should write to the applicant stating this fact and either repeating the original offer (perhaps giving the applicant a certain period in which to respond before the offer lapses), or withdrawing that offer altogether.

Withdrawing an offer If a **pre-condition** to employment is **not satisfied** (for example, satisfactory references are not received), the employer may wish to withdraw the offer of employment. He should do so formally by letter, taking care that he has reasonable grounds to do so (for example, a reasonable belief that the unsatisfactory reference received is valid). Legally, a withdrawal is not effective until it is communicated to (i.e. received by) the applicant. 717

Once an **unconditional offer** is **accepted** (or a conditional offer is accepted and the conditions have been satisfied), it cannot be withdrawn as a valid contract exists. This is so even though the date when the employee is due to start work may be delayed. The **employer** should therefore not make an offer until he is sure that he wants to go ahead. If the employer attempts to withdraw the offer after it has been accepted, he could face a claim for breach of contract, and possibly also unfair dismissal and/or discrimination. If the **employee** changes his mind after accepting the offer, this will also amount to a breach of contract, entitling the employer to compensation. In practice, it is unusual for the employer to sue the employee for his losses (for example, the additional recruitment costs in finding a replacement).

SECTION 3

Right to work

750 An employer can only employ an individual who has permission to live and work in the UK. Individuals fall into different categories for immigration purposes, depending on their citizenship or nationality. Certain individuals can **automatically live and work** in the UK, whilst others may be given **permission to work**, for example, as a result of their ancestry or due to their high level of skills. If an individual does not fall within one of these groups, the employer could consider applying for a **work permit**.

MEMO POINTS 1. The **Home Office** (HO), which incorporates the **Immigration and Nationality Directorate** (IND) and **Work Permits (UK)** (WPUK), is responsible for immigration control and the work permit scheme through caseworkers in the UK and immigration officers at ports of entry.
2. The **Foreign and Commonwealth Office** (FCO) is responsible for most entry clearance officers in British embassies, consulates and High Commissions around the world. They handle applications for entry clearance (¶774) and are occasionally joined by immigration officers. The HO and FCO set up the **joint entry clearance unit** to facilitate liaison between the two departments.
3. "The statement of changes to the immigration rules" (as amended from time to time and referred to in this section as "the **Rules**") contain the outline rules for most immigration categories of entry to the UK. The IND publishes sections of its **interpretation** of the Rules (used by its caseworkers and immigration officers) on the internet. It also creates **concessions**, which either arise out of accumulated experience or, more recently, are specially devised to cover new policies. These concessions may, in due course, be incorporated into the Rules.

A. Who has the right to work?

British citizens

760 British citizens are exempt from immigration control (i.e. they can **automatically settle and work** in the UK). British citizenship may be conferred by **birth** (depending on the place of the birth and the immigration status of the individual's parents or their citizenship) or by **descent** (if the individual was born outside the UK and his father or (if born after 1 January 1983) his mother, was a British citizen other than by descent). Citizenship may be acquired by **naturalisation** by meeting certain requirements (including a residence requirement of 5 years or 3 years if married to a British citizen) or **registration** (principally for children, for example, children born or living in the UK whose parents were not British citizens or settled in the UK when they were born).

Commonwealth citizens

762 A Commonwealth citizen, like any other national, may be a British citizen by descent (see above). Some Commonwealth citizens have a "**right of abode**" in the UK and if so they have the right to the same treatment as a British citizen in the UK, although they cannot hold a British passport and have no free movement rights in the EU. These are:
– Commonwealth citizens born or legally adopted outside the UK before 1 January 1983 whose mother was born in the UK; or
– female Commonwealth citizens who married a male with the right of abode in the UK before 1 January 1983.

MEMO POINTS **Commonwealth countries** are Antigua and Barbuda, Australia, the Bahamas, Bangladesh, Barbados, Belize, Botswana, Brunei, Canada, Cameroon, Cyprus, Dominica, Fiji, the Gambia, Ghana, Great Britain, Grenada, Guyana, India, Jamaica, Kenya, Kiribati, Lesotho, Malawi, Malaysia, Maldives, Malta, Mauritius, Mozambique, Namibia, Nauru, New Zealand, Nigeria, Pakistan, Papua New Guinea, Saint Christopher and Nevis, Saint Lucia, Saint Vincent and the Grenadines, Seychelles, Sierra Leone, Singapore, Solomon Islands, South Africa, Sri Lanka, Swaziland, Tanzania, Tonga, Trinidad and Tobago, Tuvalu, Uganda, Vanuatu, Western Samoa, Zambia, and Zimbabwe.

Commonwealth citizens with a UK born grandparent will be required to obtain **leave to enter** (¶771), which will be granted if they satisfy certain requirements. This leave will allow them to work. 763

Some Commonwealth citizens must obtain a **residence permit** if they wish to stay in the UK for more than 6 months (¶774).

EEA nationals

The following countries are part of the EEA: Austria, Belgium, Cyprus, Czech Republic, Denmark, Estonia, Finland, France, Germany, Gibraltar, Greece, Hungary, Iceland, the Republic of Ireland, Italy, Latvia, Liechtenstein, Lithuania, Luxembourg, Malta, the Netherlands, Norway, Poland, Portugal, Slovakia, Slovenia, Spain, Sweden and the United Kingdom. 765

EEA nationals have an **automatic right to work** or look for work, study, or establish themselves in business in any of the EEA countries (Immigration (European Economic Area) Regulations SI 2000/2326). These rights are called the **rights of free movement** under EC law.

MEMO POINTS 1. **Irish nationals** are EEA nationals but in practice they are treated as having settled status in the UK.
2. Switzerland is not in the EEA but **Swiss nationals** have the same right of free movement as EEA nationals under an agreement with the EU.

After 4 years' continuous residence in the UK, the EEA national (except if studying in the UK) can apply for **settlement** provided he has lived here in accordance with EC law (for example, he has not claimed public funds (for an extended period)). He must do so if he (or his family) wishes to obtain British citizenship. 766

Other nationals

If the individual does not fall within one of the groups discussed above, he will require leave (permission) to enter or remain in the UK (i.e. there is **no automatic right** to enter and work). 768

Indefinite leave An individual with indefinite leave (commonly called **permanent residence** and also known as "**settlement**") can live and **work** in the UK **without restriction** on the length of his stay or the type of work he can do. 770

Settlement is usually acquired after a certain period of limited leave.

Limited leave In most cases, leave to enter the UK is initially granted for a **limited period** and may also be subject to additional **restrictions** (for example, relating to the type or amount of work that can be done). Limited leave usually needs to be **extended** at least once before indefinite leave is granted, in which case **leave to remain** (granted by the Home Office in the UK) will be required. 771

Categories of limited leave include Commonwealth citizens with UK ancestry, highly skilled migrants, working holidaymakers, students, businessmen, investors, sole representatives, investors, innovators, and retired people of independent means.

If the individual does not have settled status and does not fall within one of the categories of limited leave above (or if that category does not allow him to take the particular employment), the employer must apply for a **work permit** for him. A work permit is another type of limited leave which may lead to settlement. It is subject to **restrictions** in that it is granted for a limited period, for a particular job with a particular employer. 772

Leave to enter Leave to enter is granted by immigration officers at the port of entry, unless prior entry clearance is required, in which case it is granted overseas as part of that application (see below) except for visitors. 773

774 **Entry clearance and residence permits** In addition to leave to enter, entry clearance (called **visas or entry certificates**) or residence permits may be required. This depends on the individual's **nationality** (visa nationals always require entry clearance – a list is available from the Home Office or the Foreign and Commonwealth Office) and the **purpose of entry**.

Entry clearance is initially granted by the British High Commission, consulate or embassy nearest to where the applicant lives. Other than for visitors (see below), entry clearance is now also treated as a **grant of leave to enter**, and all entry clearances now state the length of the permission to enter and other conditions applicable to the individual.

Residence permits are now required for non-visa nationals who are citizens of non-EU countries who wish to stay or are granted leave to stay for more than 6 months in the UK. The permits are issued by the IND and will not be necessary if entry clearance has been granted unless an individual needs to extend their stay. The relevant countries are: United States, Canada, South Africa, Singapore, Malaysia, South Korea, Hong Kong (other than British Nationals (Overseas)), Japan, Australia and New Zealand.

775 **Refusal of entry** Entry clearance, leave to enter/remain are all subject to a number of **general criteria** (for example, an application may be refused if the person's presence is considered "not conducive to the public good"). In addition, entry will be refused if the individual does not satisfy the criteria **specific to the relevant category** of entry.

776 **Visitors** Visitors are **not allowed** to establish a business, produce goods, provide services or **take employment** and visits are not allowed for more than 6 months at a time.

However, a **business visit** may be permitted and the following principles are applied in practice:
– the visit should **not normally last** more than a few days/weeks (repeated business visits look suspicious);
– the visitor **cannot be paid** a salary in the UK;
– certain **types of services** may be provided, for example the visitor may come from an overseas sister company to advise, consult or liaise with UK colleagues (but not to manage a UK team); and
– the visitor can **observe** UK work practices.

The IND provides further guidance in relation to **specific categories** of visitor, available on their website.

A person will be **refused entry** as a visitor if he is coming to wait for a work permit to be granted (even if he does not start work during that time) or to settle on the basis of a forthcoming marriage.

777 **Asylum seekers and refugees** Asylum seekers may be granted **permission to work** (commonly after a 6-month period while their asylum application is considered).

Once refugee status or exceptional leave to remain is granted, the individual will have a right to work as part of the conditions of his status.

B. Proof of right to work

780 It is a **criminal offence** for an employer to employ a person aged 16 or over who does not have permission to live and work in the UK (s 8 Asylum and Immigration Act 1996). The penalty is a fine of up to £5,000 in respect of each employee, depending on the seriousness of the offence and the employer's financial circumstances. Any director, manager, secretary or similar officer of the company will be jointly liable with the company if the offence was committed with their consent or as a result of their negligence.

MEMO POINTS The Government has published a new Immigration, Nationality and Asylum Bill, which proposes tougher criminal penalties (up to a 2 year custodial sentence and unlimited fines) and a new civil penalties scheme for employers (with fines of up to £2,000 per illegal employee) against employers who employ illegal workers.

To avoid committing a criminal offence, the employer should obtain from successful candidates **suitable documentation**, check they meet the legal requirements and that they apply to the applicant, and keep a **copy** of the documentation on file (Immigration (Restrictions on Employment) Order SI 2004/755). In the case of a passport or other travel document, the front page and any page containing specified information (including the holder's personal details, the holder's photograph and/or signature and the date of expiry) must be scanned. All other documents must be photocopied or scanned in their entirety. It should be emphasised that employers must now satisfy themselves that the documentation **relates to** the employee. 781

This evidence when **obtained before** the applicant has started employment will provide the employer with a defence in cases of unintentional breach. However, if the employer knows the employee cannot take the job offered because of his immigration status, the defence will not be available. 782

Satisfactory **documentary proof** falls into **two groups**. The first group consists of "secure" documents that represent sufficient evidence in their own right; the second consists of those which, in combination, amount to satisfactory proof. 783

First group (sufficient evidence in their own right) consists of:
- a UK passport describing the holder as a British citizen or as a citizen of the UK and Colonies with the right to live in the UK;
- a passport containing a certificate of entitlement issued by or on behalf of the UK Government which certifies that the holder has a right to live in the UK;
- a passport or national identity card, issued by a State which is party to the EEA Agreement or any other agreement forming part of the Communities Treaties which confers rights of entry to or residence in the UK, which describes the holder as a national of that State;
- a UK residence permit issued to a national of a State which is party to the EEA Agreement or any other agreement forming part of the Communities Treaties which confers rights of entry to or residence in the UK;
- a passport or other travel document or a residence document issued by the Home Office which is endorsed to show that the holder has a current right of residence in the UK as the family member of a named national of a State which is a party to the EEA Agreement or any other agreement forming part of the Communities Treaties which confers rights of entry to or residence in the UK, and who is resident in the UK;
- a passport or other travel document endorsed to show that the holder is exempt from immigration control, has indefinite leave to enter, or remain in, the UK or has no time limit on his stay;
- a passport or other travel document endorsed to show that the holder has a current leave to enter, or remain in, the UK and is permitted to take the employment in question, provided that it does not require the issue of a work permit; and
- a registration card which indicates that the holder is entitled to take employment in the UK.

The second group (two verifying documents required for satisfactory evidence) consists of: 784

a. a document issued by a previous employer, Revenue and Customs, the Department for Work and Pensions' Jobcentre Plus, the Employment Service, the Training and Employment Agency (Northern Ireland) or the Northern Ireland Social Security Agency, which contains the NI number of the person named in the document and either:
- a birth certificate issued in the UK, which specifies the names of the holder's parents;
- a birth certificate issued in the Channel Islands, the Isle of Man or Ireland;
- a letter issued by the Home Office, to the holder, which indicates that the person named in it has been granted indefinite leave to enter, or remain in, the UK;
- an Immigration Status Document issued by the Home Office, to the holder endorsed with a UK Residence Permit, which indicates that the holder has been granted indefinite leave to enter, or remain in, the UK;

– a letter issued by the Home Office, to the holder, which indicates that the person named in it has subsisting leave to enter, or remain in, the UK and is entitled to take the employment in question in the UK; or
– an Immigration Status Document issued by the Home Office, to the holder, endorsed with a UK Residence Permit, which indicates that the holder has been granted limited leave to enter, or remain in, the UK and is entitled to take the employment in question in the UK; or
b. a work permit or other approval to take employment issued by Work Permits UK; and either
– a passport or other travel document endorsed to show that the holder has current leave to enter, or remain in, the UK and is permitted to take the work permit employment in question, or
– a letter issued by the Home Office to the holder, confirming the same.

Further **guidance** is available from the Home Office as to whether a particular document will provide the employer with a defence. The IND website also gives guidance on UK **passport stamps** issued by immigration officers and whether these signify that the holder has the right to work. Employers are advised to look at this site (or contact the Home Office) if in any doubt.

785 In order to avoid **racial discrimination** claims, the employer should treat all applicants in the **same way**, in particular by:
– treating the documents that constitute documentary proof in accordance with the rules as of equal value, unless the employer knows the person is not allowed to take the job because of his immigration status;
– not making assumptions about an applicant's immigration status on the basis of his colour, race, nationality or ethnic or national origins. An employer who rejects a job applicant simply because he assumes that the person has no right to work in the UK may well be committing unlawful racial discrimination. For example, an employer who rejected the application of a person he (incorrectly) assumed did not have the right to work in the UK was found guilty of indirect racial discrimination (*Grampian Health Board v Cole*, EAT case 470/85).
– not enquiring about an applicant's immigration status, apart from asking him to produce proof as required by the rules;
– treating all applicants in the same way at each stage, either by requesting proof from all applicants or by informing all applicants that the successful applicant will be asked to produce such a document. For example, an employer who offered a job applicant a lecturing post, subject to verification of her right to work in the UK without a permit, was found to have discriminated against the applicant on racial grounds because he had only asked her (and no other applicant) to produce evidence of her right to work in the UK (*Karimjee v University of Newcastle-upon-Tyne*, EAT case 545/84); and
– not assuming that an applicant is an illegal worker if he cannot produce proof of his right to work (the employer should refer the applicant to a Citizens Advice Bureau or other agency for advice and keep the position open for as long as possible).

786 Although it is advisable that all applicants are treated the same way, a recent EAT decision has allowed an employer to apply a **different policy** in respect of evidence of leave to enter or remain in the UK to job applicants from outside the EU as against those from inside the EU. The EAT held that although this was discriminatory on the grounds of race as it was permitted by the Asylum and Immigration Act 1996 it was protected from a discriminatory claim (under s 41 RRA 1976 (i.e. that an act of discrimination will not be unlawful if done under statutory authority)) (*Olatokun v Ikon Office Solutions*, EAT case 0074/04).

CHAPTER 3

Starting employment

OUTLINE ¶¶

Most employers have an **induction programme** so that new employees can settle into their new jobs easily and effectively. In particular, certain groups, for example school/college leavers and employees with disabilities, may require extra help and guidance. To ensure that an induction programme is working well, it may be useful to have a **review** of it with employees after they have been in their jobs for a certain period in order to ensure that the process was successful or identify any problems. 900

In these initial stages, most employers will also make the employment conditional on the satisfactory completion of a **probationary period** to ensure that new employees are able to perform their duties.

SECTION 1

Induction

Induction is important from a **human resource management** perspective. The focus of induction is good practice, rather than legal compliance. Induction programmes aim to ensure that **new recruits** settle into the company quickly and easily so that they can become effective employees as soon as possible. An effective induction process can encourage closer identification with and knowledge of the company and thus can also help to reduce staff turnover. 910

Employees moving from one part of the company to another also need induction training, but this will be more limited than for a new recruit, focusing on the new aspects of their changed role. 911

1. Form and duration

Form

Induction can take the following forms, which may be used on their own or in combination: 915
- one-to-one briefings from the line-manager or a member of human resources;
- group briefings with other new staff; and/or
- receipt of a copy of the staff handbook.

Which forms are appropriate will **depend on** the nature of the job, the size of the company, its business sector, strategy, business values and beliefs. If there are trade union or other employee representatives, it may be useful to consult with them when planning an induction programme.

The **degree of formality** may vary, as may the amount of specific training involved. In many companies, the induction programme is carried out informally by the new recruit's line-manager on a day-to-day basis. If a number of recruits join at the same time, group induction sessions could be used to cover issues of general application.

In some companies, a **"mentor" or "buddy" system** may be used, so that the new recruit has a more experienced employee to approach with day-to-day queries or problems.

916 Whichever form of induction is used, it is advisable to follow a structured approach. A **written checklist** can be provided to the employee of the topics to be covered in the induction, who will deal with them, and when. This checklist is usually compiled by the human resources department in consultation with other people involved in the programme, including the appropriate line-manager/supervisor, trade union and/or employee representatives, safety representatives, and training officers.

The induction programme may include a large amount of information, and it is important that the programme is carefully structured to avoid "information overload".

Timing and duration

920 It is useful for the induction programme to take place at the beginning of the new recruit's employment, as it can be more difficult to schedule induction sessions once the employee is established in his new job. The induction process can extend over several days or even weeks.

Special plans may need to be made for **shift and night workers**.

2. Key points of induction programme

Reception

925 In order to make a good first impression, the new recruit should be made to feel welcome, and the employer should make **arrangements for his arrival**, including:
- designating someone to meet him on arrival;
- carrying out necessary personnel checks (for example, copy of P45, NI number); and
- putting in place any necessary security arrangements (for example, providing the new recruit with a security pass).

Information

926 The employee should be informed/reminded of the following:
- **company information**, i.e. an overview of the company's organisation, its history, products, services, markets, clients, and future plans and aspirations. A member of human resources may be charged with this task, and reference could be made to the staff handbook, which commonly contains such information;
- **the job**, i.e. what it entails, how the department/work area fits into the company structure, what standards are expected, how performance is assessed, who he will be working with, and who he reports to. His line-manager, supervisor or department head may be best placed to provide this information, and introduce him to immediate work colleagues and others with whom he will come into contact;
- **the terms and conditions of employment**, including hours, holiday entitlement, and notice provisions. Details will be found in the statement of particulars (¶1400) or written contract of employment (¶1127), and also the staff handbook (¶1480). The human resources officer is likely to be responsible for supplying this information;

– **pay details**, including the pay date and method. This should be set out in the statement of particulars or the written contract, and the human resources officer should be able to answer any further queries;
– **company rules and codes of conduct**, such as dress codes. These are often set out in the staff handbook, to which the employee could be referred;
– **security arrangements**, in respect of access to the workplace, document control, use and storage of equipment, and personal items at work;
– **health and safety**, including applicable health and safety rules, emergency procedures, and any special hazards or requirements (see Chapter 15). Any health and safety training needs (which may be required to give employees the necessary physical and mental abilities to do their jobs) should be identified during the recruitment process and addressed again during the induction programme. If necessary, the employer should carry out a risk assessment (¶4910). The company's health and safety adviser may be involved in this part of the induction programme, and the employee should also be introduced to the workplace safety representative;
– **data protection rights**, including the nature and source of any information kept about the employee (see Chapter 17);
– **company policies** (e.g. equal opportunities, bullying and harassment) and **procedures** (e.g. those relating to discipline, grievance, and absence). These are often set out in the staff handbook (see ¶1480 for further information);
– **training (formal and informal) and employee development**, including an explanation of any formal appraisal/performance management systems (see Chapter 18). The induction stage may be an appropriate time to assess the employee's training requirements and formulate a personal training plan. This stage may be led by the company's training officer, if it has one;
– **benefits and facilities**, including explanation and further information, where necessary. For example, information on any private medical insurance cover should be provided, as should information on any employee incentive schemes;
– **employee representation**, including information on trade union membership, and consultation procedures (see Chapter 21). The employee should be introduced to any trade union or employee representatives, who should be given the opportunity to explain their role; and
– **layout of the office/department**, including a tour of the offices so that the new recruit can see where he is working, and where he can find the toilets, first aid, cafeteria etc.

3. Special cases

The employer should be sensitive to the fact that starting work may be more difficult for school-leavers, people returning to work after a career break, those changing career direction or arriving from overseas, employees with disabilities, and members of ethnic or religious minority groups. 930

School and college leavers **Health and safety training** is particularly important in the case of young new recruits who may have little or no experience of workplace environments, thus making them more vulnerable to accidents. Employers must take these factors into consideration and take extra steps to make such recruits aware of potential risks. 931

Employers have specific duties to young workers under health and safety legislation to assess risks to workers under 18 before they start work, and to address specific factors in the **risk assessment** (¶4920).

Employees returning from a career break or changing direction New recruits may have been out of the workplace for some time in order to care for children, change direction in their careers, or spend some time working abroad. The employer needs to be sensitive to the fact that such employees may feel apprehensive about their return, and may feel out of touch with recent developments in their area of work. He must therefore ensure that such employees obtain the necessary **training and experience** to enable them to feel confident in their new jobs. 932

933 **Employees with disabilities** Employees with disabilities may face problems of access, equipment, or dealing with colleagues. Advice for employers on how to provide for such employees is available from Disability Employment Advisers, supported by Disability Service Teams via local Jobcentres. Financial assistance may be available to the employer to assist him in adapting his premises or investing in equipment in order to comply with his duty to make **reasonable adjustments**.

934 **Minority groups** In general, new recruits who are members of an ethnic or religious minority group should follow the same induction programme as other new recruits. However, the employer should be sensitive to any **cultural or religious issues or customs** that may impact on the programme.

SECTION 2

Probation

940 The employer may wish to engage a new employee **subject to the satisfactory completion** of a probationary period. If so, the employer should make this clear, and should also state (preferably in the offer letter and/or contract of employment):
- the **duration** and whether the employer reserves the right to extend where there are doubts as to the probationer's performance;
- whether any particular **terms** will **not apply** during the probationary period; and
- whether any **terms** are **varied** (for example, termination on shorter notice than after the employment is confirmed, or a requirement that all accrued holiday entitlement be taken prior to the end of the probationary period).

The employee's statutory rights cannot be disapplied (¶9203).

941 Set out below is a **sample probation clause**, taken from the model short form contract of employment for general staff (¶9910).

EXAMPLE 3. Your employment is subject to a probationary period of [*number*] months, during which your performance and conduct will be appraised and monitored. [Employer] reserves the right to extend your probationary period should this be considered necessary by [your manager].
During the probationary period, your employment may be terminated by [employer] or by you giving [*notice period during probation, if different from general position*]. On successful completion of the probationary period, the provisions of clause [16 *general termination provisions*] will apply in respect of the termination of your employment.

1. Rights and obligations during probation

945 **Probationer's rights** Apart from any express statements of non-application or variation of contractual terms, a probationer has the **same rights and obligations** as other employees. He will start to accrue continuous employment at the beginning of the probationary period. He has the same right to a statement of particulars, and may, for example, in common with any other employee in a similar situation, bring a claim of race, sex, disability, sexual orientation, or, religion or belief discrimination.

946 **Employer obligations** During the probationary period, the employer is obliged, by an implied term, to take reasonable steps to **appraise** the employee, giving guidance by advice or warning where necessary in order to ensure that the required level of competence is achieved (*White v London Transport Executive* [1981] IRLR 261, EAT).

While there is no implied term to train probationers, or to support, assist, or offer guidance to them specifically during the probationary period, any **contractual training terms** (i.e.

relating to the provision of adequate training and/or agreements on training) highlighted in the recruitment or induction stage will usually be most appropriate during the probationary period.

2. Completion

At the end of the probationary period, the probationer's performance should be reviewed. The outcome of the review will depend on whether the employer is satisfied with the probationer's performance, still has doubts about him, or has decided that he is not suitable. The employer's assessment should take into account any appraisals of performance during the course of the probation and any other relevant factors. **950**

Confirmation If the **employer is satisfied** that the probationer is suitable, the employment should be confirmed, and the probationary period will come to an end. **951**

Extension If there are **doubts** as to the probationer's suitability, the probationary period can be extended if the employer has expressly reserved the right to do so. If he has not, the probation can be extended by agreement at the review stage. The probationary period should not be extended unnecessarily, and should only be done where the employer has genuinely been unable to come to a decision in the initial probationary period. **952**

Dismissal If the employer concludes that the probationer has **not met the required standard**, the employer can dismiss him. Nevertheless, if the employer is contemplating dismissing the probationer at the end of his probationary period, the statutory dismissal and disciplinary procedure will apply and, consequently, the employer must ensure that he meets the minimum statutory requirements of the applicable procedure (¶6500). **953**

The probationer may be qualified to bring an **unfair dismissal** claim if he has been **continuously employed for** 1 year, or earlier if he is dismissed for an inadmissible reason, such as trade union activities or membership. **954**

To **defend** a claim, the employer must have a statutory fair reason for the dismissal (for example, capability or conduct), and must also act fairly in dismissing the employee. It is not automatically fair to dismiss a probationer, rather this will be one factor that the tribunal would take into account in reaching its decision on the fairness of the dismissal. Moreover, if the employer fails to follow an applicable statutory dismissal and disciplinary procedure, this may impact on the fairness or otherwise of the dismissal and any compensation which may be awarded to the employee (¶¶6510, 8436).

In reaching its decision, the employment tribunal will apply the **statutory test** applicable to all employees, i.e. whether the employer acted reasonably in all the circumstances (including the size and administrative resources of his undertaking) in treating the reason for the dismissal as a fair reason for dismissal (*Anandarajah v Lord Chancellor's Department* [1984] IRLR 131, EAT). Consequently, the following **considerations** should be taken into account:

– whether the employer observed the implied term to maintain appraisal of the probationer throughout the period of probation, giving guidance by advice or warning when such is likely to be useful or fair; and

– whether an appropriate officer/manager made an honest effort to determine whether the probationer came up to the required standard, having informed himself of the appraisals made by supervising officers/managers and any other facts recorded about the probationer (*The Post Office v P A Mughal* [1977] IRLR 178, EAT).

CHAPTER 4

Continuity of employment

OUTLINE ¶¶

1000 Some employment rights are **only activated** after certain periods of continuous employment (called qualifying periods), for example the right to bring a claim of unfair dismissal or the right to a redundancy payment. The length of continuous employment is also used to **calculate** the amount of a statutory award, such as a redundancy payment.

The **basic rule** is that there is continuity of employment from the start of employment until that particular employment ends. Breaks in the contract of employment with the same employer or changing employment will break continuity except in certain circumstances.

1001 With regard to **statutory rights**, a period of continuous employment cannot be modified by contractual agreement (*Collison v British Broadcasting Corporation* [1998] IRLR 238, EAT; *Morris v Walsh Western UK Ltd* [1997] IRLR 562, EAT).

However, if an employee is entitled to **contractual rights** based on his length of employment, although the parties may choose to rely on the continuity rules to calculate this period, they are free to alter them if they agree to do so (*Secretary of State for Employment v Globe Elastic Thread Co Ltd* [1979] IRLR 327, EAT). For example, with regard to calculating a contractual redundancy payment, an employer may agree to count a period that would not be continuous under the continuity rules or to add an extra period.

SECTION 1

Employment with same employer

General rule

1010 Where an employee is employed under a contract of employment and at least part of his time satisfies the requirements for continuity, there is a **presumption of continuity** (s 210(5) ERA 1996). This presumption can be rebutted by evidence from either party. Where an employee has asserted continuity based on this presumption, the burden of proof will be on his employer to prove that continuity had actually been broken (*Nicoll v Nocorrode Ltd* [1981] IRLR 163, EAT).

This presumption does not apply if the contract becomes **illegal** (*Hyland v J H Barker (North-West) Ltd* [1985] IRLR 403, EAT).

Continuity will be preserved even if the employee is **not required to perform** any work. 1011

Special cases

The following rules apply to **successive contracts of employment** with the same employer: 1013

Gap between two contracts – less than one week Any week during the **whole or part** of which the employee is under a contract of employment counts in computing continuity (s 212(1) ERA 1996). 1014

If the employee's contract is terminated and is re-started or a different contract is commenced with the same employer at a later date, the gap between the two contracts will not break continuity, regardless of what the employee did during it, as long as **at least 1 day in each week** is under a contract of employment with that employer (*Sweeney v J & S Henderson (Concessions) Ltd* [1999] IRLR 306, EAT (Scotland)).

EXAMPLE In *Sweeney v J & S Henderson (Concessions) Ltd*, S resigned on Saturday, 15 February 1997, and immediately took up another employment. He regretted that decision and was re-employed by his original employer on Friday, 21 February. The EAT held that continuity was not broken during this break in employment with regard to his original employer, as he was employed by him during the week ending 15 February and for part of the following week (21 February).

Such gaps can also occur where: 1015
- the employee moves from one type of work to another;
- the employee moves from one site or department to another; or
- the terms of the contract of employment change.

EXAMPLE Different type of work

In *Tipper v Roofdec Ltd* [1989] IRLR 419, EAT, T, a lorry driver, was dismissed on Friday, 22 May 1987, as a consequence of a 12-month driving ban. His employer found him alternative employment clearing a site, which he began on the following Monday. The EAT held that continuity was preserved and the fact that the first employment was frustrated (i.e. no longer possible because of the driving ban) was irrelevant.

Different department

In *Wood v York City Council* [1978] IRLR 228, CA, W changed jobs within the Council who employed him by resigning from one job to take up another position in a different department. The CA held that continuity was preserved.

Gap between two contracts – greater than one week Gaps between two contracts which are greater than a whole week will break continuity unless they fall under one of the following special circumstances where the employee was (s 212(3), (4) ERA 1996): 1017
1. absent from work on account of a temporary cessation of work;
2. absent from work in circumstances such that, by arrangement or custom, he is regarded as continuing in the employment; or
3. incapable of work as a result of illness or injury (limited to 26 weeks).

As long as **each week** where there is no contract of employment satisfies one of these special circumstances it is irrelevant why the previous contract came to an end.

1. There will be a **temporary cessation** or suspension of normal working when the employer is unable to provide work and the employee is laid off, for example, when there is a shortage of supplies or orders. The courts have held that temporary means a relatively short time and in determining this, all the relevant circumstances, particularly the length of the period of non-employment in relation to the period of employment as a whole, will be taken into consideration (*Flack and others v Kodak Ltd* [1986] IRLR 255, CA). In *Flack and others v Kodak Ltd*, the Court of Appeal held that employees in a photo-finishing department, who had been employed intermittently over a number of years, depending on work requirements, did have 1018

their continuity of employment preserved in their non-employment periods. In *Ford v Warwickshire County Council* [1983] IRLR 126, HL, the House of Lords held that the weeks between the summer and autumn school terms where there was no contract of employment was a temporary cessation of work and continuity was preserved.

The **intention** of an employer to re-employ the employee at a later date does not in itself indicate that the cessation of work was temporary, though it is a factor that will be taken into consideration (*Sillars v Charringtons Fuels Ltd* [1989] IRLR 152, CA).

1019 2. If, by **arrangement or custom**, the employee is regarded by the employer as continuing in employment, even though there is no contract of employment for those weeks (because the employee is between fixed term contracts or has a break between contracts of employment), continuity is preserved.

An "arrangement or custom" requires that, in advance of the break, there was agreement between the parties that they regarded the relationship as continuing despite the termination of the contract of employment (*Booth v United States of America* [1999] IRLR 16, EAT). A guarantee of re-engagement is not, in itself, sufficient for there to be an arrangement for continuity of employment between the parties (*Curr v Marks & Spencer plc* [2003] IRLR 74, CA). For there to be no break in continuity, both parties must **mutually acknowledge** that their employment relationship continues despite the employee's break from work, **before** the period itself takes place. This cannot be retrospectively done on re-employment.

Continuity will also be preserved between when an employee was dismissed and when his internal appeal (using his employer's contractual internal appeal procedures) was upheld and reinstatement ordered (*London Probation Board v Kirkpatrick* [2005] IRLR 443, EAT). The EAT held that in these circumstances it was not necessary for this to have been specifically agreed at the time the employee was dismissed. The EAT went on to comment that even if agreement was required in such circumstances, this could be implied as reinstatement was one of the possible outcomes of a successful appeal. Readers should note that this decision has been largely overtaken by application of the statutory dispute resolution procedures, as a decision to re-engage or reinstate an employee arising out of the use of these procedures will now automatically preserve continuity (¶1027).

1020 This need not be relied on where the employer allows the employee to take unpaid leave and the contract of employment subsists, as continuity will not be broken in any event. If though, the contract has been **terminated**, this exception has to be complied with for continuity of employment to be preserved.

MEMO POINTS This exception does not apply with regard to **contractual entitlements** as the parties can retrospectively agree to treat such period as continuous.

1021 3. In exceptional circumstances, the weeks where there is no contract of employment and the **employee is ill** or injured will not break continuity when the employee is re-employed. This is limited to a non-contractual period of 26 weeks.

Continuity will be preserved for the period between termination or suspension and re-employment if during this period the employee was **not able to work** due to his illness or injury. For example, continuity will not be broken if an employee leaves his employment due to ill health but is re-hired when he recovers if this happens within 26 weeks.

The employee can **temporarily work** for another employer during this period as long as he remains unable to do the work that he would have done for his employer if he still had a contract (*Donnelly v Kelvin International Services* [1992] IRLR 496, EAT).

1024 **Redundancy and re-employment within four weeks** If an employee has been made redundant and starts **suitable alternative employment** within 4 weeks of termination of the original contract, his continuity will be preserved (s 138 ERA 1996). However, a gap of more than 4 weeks will break continuity.

1025 Further, the receipt of a **genuine redundancy payment** will break continuity for the **purposes of redundancy payments only** if the employee is later reinstated or re-engaged unless he is re-employed on the condition that the redundancy payment is repaid (s 214 ERA 1996; Employment Protection (Continuity of Employment) Regulations SI 1996/3147; and *Secretary of State for Trade and Industry v Lassman* [2000] IRLR 411, CA). This prevents the employee being entitled to another statutory redundancy payment for this first period if he is made redundant again.

Where such, or part of, such a payment, is purely contractual or ex gratia, then this requirement to repay to retain continuity does not apply to the non-statutory part (*Rowan v Machinery Installations (South Wales) Ltd* [1981] IRLR 122, EAT).

Reinstatement and re-engagement Reinstatement and re-engagement orders by the court as a result of a successful unfair dismissal claim, require the employer to take the employee back in either the same or a similar role and in such cases continuity will be preserved (¶8681). The position is the same in respect of a decision to re-engage or reinstate an employee taken arising out of the use of a statutory dispute resolution procedure where such a procedure applies (¶6510). 1027

SECTION 2

Change of employer

1035 Although periods of continuous employment normally relate to employment by the same employer, there are **special circumstances** where a change of employer does not break continuity (s 218 ERA 1996). The **most common** of these is where there has been a transfer of a business or undertaking.

Type of change	Reference (ERA 1996)
Whole or part of trade, business, or undertaking is **transferred** from one person to another [1]	s 218(2)
Employer dies and employee is taken into employment of personal representatives or trustees [2]	s 218(4)
Change in partners, personal representatives or trustees [3]	s 218(5)
Employee moves to another employer who, at that time, is an **associated employer** [4]	s 218(6), s 231
Act (local or public) changes a contract of employment resulting in the original **body corporate employer** being replaced by some other body corporate [5]	s 218(3)
Health service employee is employed by another health service employer [6]	s 218(8)-(9)

1. If a part is transferred it does not need to be self-contained, though the transfer must make some sense as a **transfer of business** and it must not solely be a transfer of assets (*Melon v Hector Powe Ltd* [1980] IRLR 477, HL). The sale must put the new owner in possession of a **going concern** (or one that has the potential of being a going concern if it is not one at the time of transfer, for example where the transfer relates to an insolvent company (*Teeside Times Ltd v Drury* [1980] IRLR 72, CA)).
The burden of proof is on the employee to show that the transfer satisfied these conditions and this will be a question of fact. However, a tribunal will not put an over-strict burden of proof on the employee who may have little knowledge of the company's financial dealings (though a tribunal may nevertheless require more than the employee stating that it was business as usual under the new owner).
The courts have held that the **time of transfer** is not limited to a precise date but can be spread over a longer period during which the process of transfer takes place, any part of which is sufficient for the employee to be in the transferor's employment (*Clark & Tokeley Ltd v Oakes* [1998] IRLR 577, CA). If the question of the time of transfer is disputed, it will be a question of fact that the tribunal will determine on looking at the evidence.
It should be noted that such transfers are also **commonly governed** by the specific rules regarding transfers of undertakings (**TUPE** rules), which provide for the transfer of employee contracts to the transferee and the preservation of continuity (¶7980). However, where TUPE does not apply, continuity may nevertheless be preserved under these rules as the right to continuity under ERA 1996 is a distinct and separate right.

2. Where an **employee is a personal representative**, he can contract with himself in his different capacities (*Rowley Holmes & Co v Barber* [1977] ICR 387, EAT).

3. Continuity of employment can be preserved where the **number of partners** in the partnership is reduced to one (*Stevens and anor v Bower* [2004] IRLR 957, CA). The Court of Appeal commented in this case that continuity could also be preserved under the exception relating to transfer of undertaking (see note 1, above) though it considered the change in partners, personal representative or trustees exception preferable in such circumstances.

4. Any two employers are associated if one is a company in which the other has **direct or indirect control**, or both are directly or indirectly controlled by a third person who need not necessarily be a company.
The **definition of company** in this context encompasses partnerships of companies (*Pinkney v Sandpiper Drilling Ltd* [1989] IRLR 425, EAT) and foreign companies (*Hancill v Marcon Engineering Ltd* [1990] IRLR 51, EAT). Whether there is control depends on who has **effective control** (i.e. usually those who have the majority shareholding or board control). Effective control can extend to a company owned equally between two brothers which was held to be associated with the brothers' partnership (*Tice v Cartwright* [1999] ICR 769, EAT).

5. For continuity to be preserved, the employee must have been **transferred** from one body corporate to another as part of the statutory scheme to which the Act relates. This may include privatisations of public companies (*Gale v Northern General Hospital NHS Trust* [1994] IRLR 292, CA).

6. This only occurs where there is **relevant** employment. This is defined as employment in which persons are engaged while undergoing professional training that involves their being employed successively by a number of different health service employers.

SECTION 3

Calculating period of continuous employment

The period of continuous employment is assessed on how many successive weeks are continuous, and is, therefore, determined on a **week-by-week basis** running from Sunday to Saturday. 1040

Consequently, there is continuous employment if each **consecutive week** after the first week of continuity satisfies the requirements for continuity (see sections 1 and 2 above) (s 210(4) ERA 1996). If not, the week(s) in question will **break the continuity** and a new period of continuous employment will start at the beginning of the first week that does again satisfy the requirements. For example, if the employee changes employment, continuity will usually be broken and a new period will start when he begins his new employment.

In relation to a specific statutory right, award or payment, the **relevant period of employment** is calculated by identifying the start date and the end date (i.e. the date when the employment ends or the date necessary for the entitlement of the right). Depending on the right, this is determined in complete calendar months or years of service.

EXAMPLE Employee A has worked for the same employer since 1 January 1997. On 31 December 2004 he is made redundant but is re-employed on 1 March 2005. This breaks continuity and his new period of continuous employment is calculated from when he restarted his employment. If he is made redundant again, he will only be entitled to a redundancy payment based on this new start date. However, if A had been re-hired within 4 weeks of being made redundant, continuity would have been preserved, see above.

1. Start date

Continuous employment starts on the first day of employment (s 211(1) ERA 1996). This is the start date as stated in the employee's contract of employment and may be different from the actual start date (*The General of The Salvation Army v Dewsbury* [1984] IRLR 222, EAT). 1045

EXAMPLE In *The General of The Salvation Army v Dewsbury*, D's contract of employment commenced on 1 May 1982 though the first date she actually worked was 4 May as 1-3 May was a bank holiday weekend. However, her period of continuous employment was held to have started on 1 May.

MEMO POINTS For the purposes of redundancy only, an employee's period of continuous employment cannot begin until he is **18 years old**. In such circumstances, an employee has two start dates: one that applies to all rights other than redundancy and begins on the start date of the contract of employment; and a later date for the right to redundancy payments that begins on the date of his 18th birthday.

It is **proposed** that periods of service before the age of 18 will no longer be discounted under the draft regulations on age discrimination, which are expected to come into force from 1 October 2006 (¶8991).

In special circumstances, the start date may be **moved back** (so increasing the period of continuous employment) if a change of contract does not break continuity. In such cases, it will be calculated as starting from the **beginning of the original employment**. 1046

Conversely, the start date will be subsequently **brought forward** (so reducing the period of continuous employment) if the employee **takes part** in a **strike/lockout** (ss 211(3), 216 ERA 1996). If an employee does not take part, there will be no deduction to his period of continuity. 1047

In such cases, the number of days between the last working day before the strike/lockout and the date when work was resumed (including non-working days) will be deducted from his start date. These days are calculated in relation to the workforce, or part of workforce, that is striking/taking part in a lockout. Therefore, if an employee has a rest day at the beginning of the strike, that day is still deductible. Likewise, if he restarts work before the end of the strike any such days are still deducted. On the other hand, if an employer requires the employee to recommence work at a date after the strike has ended, any such days of non-work are not deducted.

EXAMPLE Employees B, C and D work a 5-day week from Monday to Friday.
Employee B has a rest day on Monday, the day a strike by the workforce starts. The strike ends on that Thursday, and work is resumed by the workforce on Friday. However, Employee C is told by his employer not to come back to work until the following Monday. Finally, Employee D returned to work on Wednesday, a day before the strike ended.
All the employees will have 6 days deducted (Saturday before the strike through to the Thursday the strike ended) even though they all worked a different number of days for different reasons.

MEMO POINTS It is possible to read the legislation as giving a double jeopardy by way of a double deduction which would occur by 1) discounting any weeks that do not count (i.e. where during each week or part of each week, the employee takes part in a strike) and 2) bringing forward the start date as shown above. However, it is unlikely that this was the intention of the legislation.

1048 Further, for the purpose of continuity with regard to **redundancy payments** only, employees **working overseas** who are not paying NIC will have their start date brought forward by 7 days for every week so worked (ss 211(3), 215 ERA 1996).

2. Relevant end date

1055 The end date is determined to ascertain whether an employee has the sufficient length of continuous employment (i.e. qualifying period) necessary to activate a statutory right or to calculate a statutory payment. The relevant end date is, therefore, either the end date of the qualifying period or the termination date of the contract.

1056 As the different periods needed for each right to be activated are expressed in either a set number of **calendar months or years**, so are the relevant lengths of continuity (s 210 ERA 1996).

EXAMPLE Employee E was employed on 1 January and Employee G was employed on 1 February. The right to minimum notice is activated after 1 month of continuous employment. E will have the right to minimum notice after 1 calendar month which will be from 1 February and G will have the right from 1 March. As January always has more days than February it can be seen that G has actually obtained the right after having been employed for a fewer number of days.
Rights based on a calendar year follow the same pattern. Therefore, in a leap year a new employee will have to be employed for an extra day to obtain the rights that his colleagues who did not start in a leap year obtain after a calendar year.

1057 If the employee has been dismissed, the relevant end date is the date on which the termination takes effect called the **effective date of termination** (EDT) (¶8340) (s 97(1) ERA 1996). This is the date on which:
– the notice expires (if the contract is terminated by notice); or
– where termination is given without notice, the date that should have been given for expiry of the statutory notice to which the employee is entitled. This can result in a gap between when the employee stopped working and when the termination takes effect. The fact that an employee stopped working prior to the effective date of termination is irrelevant in calculating the period of employment.

1058 However, if there is a **continuation order** the contract remains in force from the EDT or settlement of the case to determine for any purpose (for example, the amount of a basic award or statutory redundancy payment) the employee's period of continuous employment (¶8704).

SECTION 4

Qualifying periods

As already noted, many of the main statutory rights will depend on whether or not the necessary qualifying periods of continuous employment have been achieved. 1080

The following table is a summary of those that have qualifying periods and the lengths needed. Other statutory rights do not require a qualifying period and can be brought on the first day of service, and in some cases, even before the employment has begun (for example, where sex discrimination in relation to recruitment is claimed).

Right/complaint	Length of qualifying period from start of employment unless otherwise indicated	Reference (ERA 1996 unless otherwise indicated)
Additional maternity leave Adoption leave Paternity leave	26 weeks, see ¶4405 for start date	s 73; reg 5 SI 1999/3312; regs 4, 15 SI 2002/2788
Guarantee payments during lay off	1 month	s 29
Minimum period of notice	1 month	s 86
Parental leave	1 year, see ¶4405 for more details	s 76; reg 13 SI 1999/3312
Pay during medical suspension	1 month	s 65
Pay during ordinary maternity leave Pay during ordinary adoption leave Pay during paternity leave	26 weeks, see ¶4405 for start date	ss 164; 171ZA-B, 171ZL SSCBA 1992
Redundancy payments	2 years	s 155
Right to request flexible working (parents of young children)	26 weeks	reg 3 SI 2002/3236
Time off to look for work when under notice of redundancy	2 years	s 52
Unfair dismissal	1 year unless automatically unfair, see ¶¶8393-4 for more details	s 108
Written reasons for dismissal	1 year	s 92

EXAMPLE Employee I starts his job on 1 January 2000 and works continuously until 31 July 2005 when he is made redundant.
Redundancy payments are payable after 2 years' continuous employment and are calculated on the number of whole years of continuous employment. I has the 2 years' continuous employment necessary to entitle him to a redundancy payment and his length of employment with regard to the calculation of the redundancy payment itself is 5 whole years.

MEMO POINTS In general, **fixed term workers** are no longer subject to any special rules on qualifying periods since the implementation of the Fixed-term Employees (Prevention of Less Favourable Treatment) Regulations SI 2002/2034. However, it appears that there is still a bar to equal treatment under the collective redundancy provisions in s 282 TULRCA 1992 which provides that the provisions relating to the **procedure for handling redundancies** (notably the consultation requirements) do not apply to employment under a fixed term contract for a term of 3 months or less, or for a specific task that is expected to last for more than 3 months. This provision has not been repealed by the recent regulations and, it seems, results in an apparent anomaly following the introduction of the new regulations which prohibit the less favourable treatment of fixed-term workers by an employer with regard to comparable permanent employees.

CHAPTER 5

Employment contract, variation and breach

OUTLINE ¶¶

Once a successful candidate has accepted a job offer and any pre-conditions are satisfied, the employment can be confirmed. This chapter focuses on the formation and terms of contracts of employment, as opposed to contracts for services (where a person does work for or provides services to another as part of his own business). The distinction between employment and self-employment is discussed at ¶30. **1100**

A contract of employment is a type of contract. It must, therefore, meet the **formal requirements** that apply to all legally binding contracts, including offer and acceptance, consideration and an intention to enter into a legally binding agreement (¶1110). **1101**

A contract of employment is usually a written document. However, its **form** may vary significantly, ranging from a short oral agreement to a detailed written contract and can be a combination of written and oral agreements (¶1125). **1102**

The contract may be made up of both express and implied terms (¶1150). **Express terms** may be contained in a document called the contract of employment (see the model contract of employment for general staff at ¶9910) or may be incorporated by reference to other documents, for example collective agreements between the employer and a recognised, independent trade union. Not all terms will be enforceable – those which are illegal (e.g. those which defraud Revenue and Customs) will be void. **1103**

Some terms are **implied** into all contracts as characteristic of the employment relationship, such as the employee's duty to give personal service, and the employer's duty to pay for work done. When the contract is silent, the courts may imply specific terms on the basis that the parties can be taken to have intended those terms to apply. Statute may also intervene to impose further obligations on the parties and further protections for the employee, such as the statutory minimum notice periods.

There is no statutory requirement to have a written contract, but the employer is obliged to provide **certain information** about the terms of employment to the employee **in writing** (¶1400). **1104**

Contractual terms may also be set out in a **staff handbook**, which can also contain non-contractual **policies and procedures** (¶1480; see also the policies checklists at ¶9940). **1105**

1106 During the course of the employment, the employer or the employee may wish to change the contractual terms (or a change may be imposed, for example, by a change in the law) (¶1600).

1107 The **breach** of a contractual term, by either party, will entitle the innocent party to a remedy for breach of contract. If the breach is sufficiently serious, it may entitle the innocent party to terminate the contract, i.e. permit the employer to summarily dismiss the employee, or the employee to treat himself as constructively dismissed (¶1700).

SECTION 1

Formation

1110 It is compulsory for details of certain terms to be provided to the employee in writing (¶1405). However, in order to avoid ambiguity and prevent disputes, it is advisable for all of the terms of the contract of employment to be in writing, preferably in a document that is signed by both the employer and the employee (see model contract of employment at ¶9910). If terms are agreed orally, it is advisable that these should be confirmed in writing.

It is **common practice** for the terms and conditions specific to each employee to be set out in a written contract of employment, with further terms of general application to the workforce to be set out in a staff handbook, which may also include policies and procedures that, although relevant to the employment relationship, do not form part of the contract of employment between employer and employee (¶1480).

A. Legal requirements

1. Legal capacity

1111 Parties to a contract must have legal capacity to enter into it. There are legal restrictions on the ability of minors, the mentally impaired and drunk people to enter into binding contracts.

An ordinary contract of employment with a **minor** is usually valid at common law. However, there are statutory restrictions which may apply to make the contract totally illegal (¶1305). Local authorities are empowered to regulate the employment of minors in their jurisdiction and so restrictions may vary from area to area.

2. Binding contracts

1112 As for all legally binding contracts, an employment contract must comprise four elements: an offer (i.e. of employment); acceptance of that offer; consideration (i.e. something provided by one party in return for the other party's contribution to the contract); and intention to enter into a legally binding agreement.

Offer and acceptance

1113 An offer of employment is commonly made to a successful candidate by way of an offer letter (¶711), which may give outline terms and conditions of the employment offered and also details of any conditions which must be satisfied for the employment to be confirmed (for example, providing acceptable references, obtaining a work permit or passing a medical). Once a potential employee has accepted an offer of employment and any conditions have been satisfied, a binding contract of employment comes into existence.

Any **change** to the agreed terms will be a variation (¶1600). 1114

If either party wishes to **terminate** the contract, it will have to do so in accordance with the terms of the contract (i.e. by giving the other party the applicable period of notice and complying with any other terms relating to termination), even if the employee has not yet started work. If it does not, this will amount to a breach of contract (¶1650) entitling the innocent party to compensation for the breach, although in practice, it is unusual for the employer to recover his losses (for example, additional recruitment costs in finding a replacement) from the employee in these circumstances. 1115

Consideration

The consideration is normally salary or wages in return for work, but it can take other **forms**, for example share options, provision of accommodation or other benefits. 1116

Where there is no consideration for the work done, as is usually the case for **volunteer workers**, there is unlikely to be a binding employment agreement. Where a volunteer receives an expenses payment, which is limited to reimbursement for actual costs incurred (for example, travel expenses for the actual cost of getting to/from the place of work), the volunteer will not be working in a manner consistent with a binding employment contract (*Melhuish v Redbridge Citizens Advice Bureau* [2005] IRLR 419, EAT). If there is no such limitation on expenses, this may provide sufficient consideration for employment.

If an agreement is **executed as a deed**, there is no need for consideration.

Where the employer wants to **vary the employment contract** (¶1600) by asking the employee to agree to a change, that agreement should be supported by consideration. Sometimes the offer of continued employment on the new terms will be sufficient consideration to support an agreed change.

Intention to enter into a legally binding agreement

For the parties to enter into a legally binding agreement, they must intend to do so. 1117

General principles of construction If there is a dispute as to the parties' intentions, the court or tribunal will construe the contract applying the general principles set out below (*Davies v Hotpoint Ltd* [1994] IRLR 538, EAT). 1118

The original written agreement should be read as a whole and objectively in the context of its factual matrix, genesis and aim (*Prenn v Simmonds* [1971] 1 WLR 1381, HL), together with any documents containing or confirming the particulars of the contract, to ascertain the parties' intention in relation to the terms of the contract **at the time the agreement was reached**.

The tribunal should adopt a construction which gives effect to all the words of the contract and, if possible, **avoid** a construction which makes contractual words otiose or produces absurd consequences.

An employee will be deemed to have actual knowledge of the terms of a contract he has **signed** and, consequently, has no recourse if he later discovers that one of the terms is more onerous than he expected (*Peninsula Business Services Ltd v Sweeney* [2004] IRLR 49, EAT). However, the parties cannot be presumed to have taken on a "one-sided bargain" unless there are clear words which makes this plain (*Brand v Compro Computer Services Ltd* [2005] IRLR 196, CA). Moreover, it should be noted that if a clause is **unreasonable** it may fall foul of the Unfair Contract Terms Act 1977 (¶1340).

The parties' **subsequent conduct** is not generally admissible in construing the original agreement, but it will, however, be relevant to show that the original contract has been varied, whether by the addition of a new term or the variation of an existing one (*Wickman Machine Tool Sales Ltd v L Schuler AG* [1974] AC 55, HL; *Hooper v British Railways Board* [1988] IRLR 517, CA). However, a **practice in place before and after** an agreement is entered into may assist in resolving a contractual ambiguity in that agreement, as it is part of the factual matrix against which the agreement should be construed (*Dunlop Tyres Ltd v Blows* [2001] IRLR 629, CA).

EXAMPLE 1. In *Pedersen v The Mayor and Burgesses of the London Borough of Camden* [1981] IRLR 173, CA, P responded to a **job advertisement** that indicated that the primary duties of the post were as a bar steward, with catering assistant duties as a subsidiary matter. The offer letter indicated that P would be assigned catering duties when not required at the bar. The Court held that the offer letter contained the terms of P's contract, but that it could also look at the advertisement (even though it was not part of the contract) to ascertain Camden's exact intentions in relation to the scope of the job duties. In the light of the advert and the letter, the Court agreed that the parties had intended P's duties to be primarily as a bar steward and that a move entirely to catering duties was a breach of contract.
2. In *Hooper v British Railways Board*, H's contract (which incorporated a BRB Council minute) stated that, if declared unfit by BRB's medical officer, he would be paid his basic salary until he resumed work. The Court held that a **subsequent BRB Council minute** (which stated that any such payment would only be made on a short-term basis) could not be relied on by BRB as evidence of its intention as to the original terms. Further, BRB had not shown that H had accepted the subsequent minute as a variation to the original agreement.
3. In *Dunlop Tyres Ltd v Blows*, the contractual terms of a collective agreement were ambiguous as to payments for public holidays. However, a **30-year-old practice** of paying employees triple time for working such holidays which existed before and continued after the agreement was acceptable to resolve the ambiguity.
4. In *Judge v Crown Leisure Ltd*, EAT case 0443/04, a conversation at CLL's Christmas party at which a manager **expressed a general intention** of raising an employee's salary "in due course" did not amount to a legally enforceable variation of the employee's contract since the EAT found there was no intention to create legal relations at the Christmas party and the manager's remarks were merely words of comfort. A different result might have ensued had the comments not been general or aspirational in nature.

3. Certainty

1120 In addition, the terms of a contract must be sufficiently certain for the courts and tribunals to be able to interpret them. Therefore, an agreement to agree terms at a later date is likely to be unenforceable.

B. Form

1125 If the formal legal requirements are met, there will be a binding contract, the form of which can be **oral, written** or a **combination of both**.

1126 **Oral contracts** A short conversation during which the employer offers a job on certain outline terms (for example, a salary of X amount with X days' paid holiday per year) that is accepted by the employee will, subject to the parties' intention (see above), be a binding contract. There is clearly more scope for dispute as to the terms of the contract in the case of oral agreements.

1127 **Written contracts** The employment terms may be found in a single document or, more commonly, in a range of written documents, including documents specific to the employee and those common to all staff, the most important of which are set out in the table:

Offer letter accepted by employee	¶711
Signed contract	¶¶1110, 9900
Staff handbook	¶1480
Codes (e.g. of conduct)/Rules (e.g. dealing rules)	¶1480
Applicable collective agreements	¶1270

A written contract can be entered into or varied by email.

Save where the parties have intended that all the employment terms and conditions are to be only found in one document, the identification of, for example, policies and procedures as part of the contract is a matter of fact. In *O'Flynn v Airlinks the Airport Coach Co Ltd*, EAT case 0269/01, there was no evidence that only one document was to contain the contract terms. Therefore, whether the employer's drugs and alcohol policy formed part of the employee's contract of employment was a finding of fact, taking into account the immediacy of the implementation of the policy, the employee's knowledge of the policy and its consequences and the fact that she had not objected to it.

Combination of both The contract may be partly oral, partly in writing. For example, if the employer tells the employee at the time he is selected that he will be entitled to a company car and the parties then sign a written contract that does not deal with this entitlement, the contract between the parties may (depending on the authority of the promisor and the wording of the written document) comprise the oral promise of the company car in addition to the terms contained in the written document. 1128

SECTION 2

Terms

As a contract of employment can be formed by a variety of methods, including a brief oral exchange, it often falls to the courts and tribunals to attempt to identify what the terms and conditions are. 1150

Terms may be **express**, for example, by oral or written agreement between the parties. Such terms can be incorporated into the contract from another source, for example, those that are agreed through collective bargaining with trade unions or those contained in the staff handbook. If there is an express term, that term will normally prevail. Some express terms will be void as being illegal or contrary to public policy (e.g. those which defraud Revenue and Customs or are for an immoral purpose).

Where the contract is silent, the courts will look to see whether a specific term should be **implied**, for example, by virtue of custom and practice or whether the term is one that has been identified by the courts over time as characteristic of the employment relationship.

In some cases, statute will impose certain obligations or minimum standards which will override an express term (e.g. the right to statutory minimum notice).

I. Express terms

Terms can be expressly agreed by the parties, either orally or in writing. Written terms may be found in a range of documents (¶1127). If the employer has complied with the obligation to provide written particulars, these will provide evidence of the employment terms and, if signed and accepted by both parties as such, will be contractual terms (¶1405). 1155

An express term will normally prevail over a **conflicting implied term**, and courts are unwilling to imply terms that would contradict express terms (*Stevedoring & Haulage Services Ltd v Fuller* [2001] IRLR 627, CA). Further, where a written employment contract states that it sets out the "whole agreement" between the parties, the courts are unwilling to imply any other terms. However, an express term will be **overridden by the law** in certain circumstances (¶1185), for example, the equality clause implied by the equal pay legislation. 1156

EXAMPLE In *Stevedoring & Haulage Services Ltd v Fuller*, F's contract stated that the company was not obliged to provide work for him, and that he was not obliged to accept any work offered. The Court declined to imply obligations to offer and accept a reasonable amount of work (¶1200 and ¶1233) as this would clearly contradict the express terms.

1157 See Appendix at ¶9910 for a model contract.

II. Specific terms implied by the courts

1170 In the absence of an express term, the courts may have to decide if it is possible to imply a particular term, on the basis that the parties can be **taken to have agreed** it. The court's role is not to determine what the parties should have agreed but what the **parties' intention** when entering the agreement must have been (¶1117). A court will not invent terms where they are neither expressly nor impliedly agreed and will not imply a term just because it is reasonable.

Where the parties' intentions can be ascertained entirely from documents, the meaning and effect of the contract is a question of law. However, where the parties' intentions have to be determined not only from documents but also from oral communications and conduct, the terms of the contract are a question of fact for the tribunal. The court will examine the facts, and whether or not a term may be implied from those facts is a question of law, rather than a question of fact (*Carmichael v National Power plc* [2000] IRLR 43, HL). This distinction is relevant as only a question of law may be appealed to a higher court.

1. Obvious terms

1172 A term may be implied if it is so obvious that the parties must have intended it and that both their responses to the suggestion of "an officious bystander" that a particular provision be included in their contract would have been "Oh, of course" (*Shirlaw v Southern Foundries (1926) Ltd* [1939] 2 All ER 113, HC (affirmed by the Court of Appeal); *Deeley v British Rail Engineering Ltd* [1980] IRLR 147, CA).

EXAMPLE In *Ali v Christian Salvesen Food Services Ltd* [1997] IRLR 17, CA, the Court declined to imply a term that the employees' annualised hours contract should be pro-rated in relation to overtime payments stated to be payable once the annual target was reached. The contracts had been carefully negotiated by union representatives, which led the Court to conclude that the question of pro-rating had deliberately not been dealt with. It was therefore not obvious that a pro-rating term had been agreed.

2. Business efficacy

1174 A term may be implied if it is necessary to give the contract business efficacy, i.e. to make the contract work (*Liverpool City Council v Irwin* [1977] AC 239, HL). An implied term of this kind should be **no wider than is necessary** to give the contract business effect and must be **sufficiently precise** (*Marshall v Alexander Sloan & Co Ltd* [1981] IRLR 264, EAT; *Lake v Essex County Council* [1979] IRLR 241, CA).

EXAMPLE 1. If the contract is silent on the need for flexibility in relation to the place of work, the courts may imply a mobility clause on the grounds that it is essential to make the contract work, as was decided in *Courtaulds Northern Spinning Ltd v Sibson and TGWU* [1988] IRLR 305, CA, in relation to a heavy goods vehicle driver. However, where mobility is not essential to the contract, the court will not imply such a clause, as was decided in *Aparau v Iceland Frozen Foods plc* [1996] IRLR 119, EAT, in relation to a cashier working for a supermarket chain.
2. In *Morley v Heritage* [1993] IRLR 400, CA, the Court refused to imply a term into M's contract entitling him to a payment in lieu of accrued but untaken holiday on the termination of his employment

on the grounds that it was not needed to give business efficacy to the contract. Note that legislation on working time now provides for such a payment to be made (¶4000).

3. In *Aspden v Webbs Poultry and Meat Group (Holdings) Ltd* [1996] IRLR 521, QBD and in *Villella v MFI Furniture Centres Ltd* [1999] IRLR 468, QBD, the High Court implied a term that the employer would not terminate the employment in circumstances which would deprive the employee of his **contractual permanent health insurance benefit** (¶4200). If the employer was able to terminate in those circumstances, the contractual terms relating to company sick pay and permanent health insurance benefit would not work.

4. The Court will imply a term to the effect that an employer must take reasonable steps to bring to the employee's notice the existence of a particular term (for example, **enhanced pension entitlement**), where the employee must take some action in order to take advantage of that term and where the employee cannot otherwise be expected to be aware of the term unless it is drawn to his attention (*Scally v Southern Health and Social Services Board* [1991] IRLR 522, HL). Note, though, that having taken such reasonable steps, there will be no implied duty on the employer to ensure that the information is actually communicated to the employee (*Ibekwe v London General Transport Services Ltd* [2003] IRLR 697, CA).

3. Conduct of the parties

A court may imply a term based on the conduct of the parties **at the time of the agreement**, provided that, although nothing was said, it is clear the parties intended that term to apply. **Subsequent conduct** is less reliable as evidence of the original agreement, as it may in fact evidence a variation to that agreement (¶1600). 1176

4. Custom in that trade, industry or area

A term may be implied if it is customary in that trade, industry or area, on the basis that the parties must be taken to have agreed such a term. The custom must be "reasonable, notorious and certain", i.e. fair, well known (although not necessarily to every single employee working in that trade, industry or area) and precise (*Sagar v H Ridehalgh & Son Ltd* [1931] 1 Ch 310, CA; *Bond v CAV Ltd* [1983] IRLR 360, QBD). 1178

EXAMPLE In *Sagar v H Ridehalgh & Son Ltd*, the Court accepted that the practice in the Lancashire weaving industry of **deducting wages** for poor workmanship was an implied term of employment. The practice had been in operation for over 30 years, was generally well known and followed in at least 85% of other mills in the area.

5. Employer custom and practice

A term may be implied by virtue of the custom and practice of the particular employer (*Duke v Reliance Systems* [1982] IRLR 347, EAT). Factors determining whether this is possible include whether the relevant policy has been drawn to the attention of the employees and whether the practice has been followed without exception for a substantial period of time. However, with regard to **discretionary benefits**, it does not necessarily follow that the fact that a benefit has been granted for a number of years will always be deemed to be an implied term (*Campbell v Union Carbide Ltd*, EAT case 0341/01). 1180

EXAMPLE 1. In *Quinn v Calder Industrial Materials Ltd* [1996] IRLR 126, EAT (applied in *Albion Automotive Ltd v Walker* [2002] EWCA Civ 946, CA) and *Pellowe v Pendragon plc*, EAT case 804/98, the employers provided management with guidelines on **enhanced redundancy payments**. In *Quinn v Calder Industrial Materials Ltd*, these were followed on the four occasions between 1987 and 1994 that redundancies were made, and in *Pellowe v Pendragon plc* the formula had been followed for over 20 years. In both cases, despite their awareness of past payments, the management manual had **not** been **communicated directly to employees**. In *Quinn v Calder Industrial Materials Ltd*, the EAT noted that payment of the enhanced terms was not automatic but required a **management decision on each occasion**. The EAT in each case could not, therefore, infer that the parties intended the enhanced redundancy terms to be contractual.

2. In *Campbell v Union Carbide Ltd*, above, the EAT emphasised that the fact that the employer had made **discretionary ill-health payments** for a number of years did not in itself demonstrate the employer's intention that such payments were contractual, rather that he made such payments for the sake of good industrial relations.
3. In *Cook v Diageo*, EAT case 0070/04, a reference in a collective agreement and employees' terms and conditions to **"occasional" holidays** did not oblige the employer to fix such holidays by reference to local public holidays, although this had usually been the case in the past. There was nothing to demonstrate that the intention of the parties to the collective agreement was to create a contractual obligation that the occasional days would always be on local public holidays. The employer's actions had therefore not undergone the passage from policy to contractual obligation.

III. Terms implied by statute

1185 Parties are generally free to agree terms and conditions, and any expressly agreed terms will normally prevail unless the law intervenes to **override** and/or **vary** any contradictory or inconsistent express terms. For example, the **equality clause** overrides any terms which are less advantageous than those applying to a member of the opposite sex doing the same or like work, or work of equal value (¶5605), and the **statutory minimum notice period** will prevail where the contract is silent or is less favourable (¶8131).

1186 Statute also intervenes to **imply certain rights** and minimum standards in favour of the employee, some of which are subject to qualifying periods of service (¶1080).

Any dismissal of an employee who is seeking to assert his statutory rights is automatically unfair (¶8395).

The most important implied statutory rights are:

Right	Para
Written statement of main terms	¶1405
Not to be discriminated against on grounds of sex, race, disability, religion or belief, or sexual orientation	Chapter 16
Equal pay	¶5600
National minimum wage	¶2865
Not to suffer unlawful deductions from wages	¶3050
Guarantee payments	¶7860
Itemised pay statement	¶2985
Sick pay	¶4110
Family friendly rights including maternity, paternity, adoption and parental leave and the right to request flexible working	Chapter 14
Payments during medical suspension	¶4862
Safe place of work	¶4810
Breaks and rest periods	¶3710
Paid annual leave	¶4000
Time off in certain circumstances	¶3910
Trade union membership and activities	¶7560
Right to be accompanied at disciplinary and grievance hearings	¶6780
Continuity of employment on transfer of undertaking	¶7980
Minimum period of notice	¶8131
Redundancy rights	¶8730
Unfair dismissal rights	¶8380
Written statement of reasons for dismissal	¶8310

IV. Terms implied by common law as characteristic of the employment relationship

The courts have identified certain terms which they regard as characteristic of the employment relationship and which they will therefore imply into all contracts of employment. These "common law" terms deal with the parties' respective **rights and duties**. 1195

MEMO POINTS As such terms are characteristic of employment relationships, the presence or absence of these implied rights and duties may serve to indicate the status of the worker, i.e. whether he is an employee or is self-employed (¶30).

In practice, many of these implied rights and duties are **made express**. For example, the employer may wish to extend the protection of his confidential information by express agreement, or may wish to bring certain duties to the employee's attention so that he is clearly made aware of them. 1196

The most important implied duties are: 1197

Employee duties [1]	
Service	¶1200
Competence	¶1202
Due diligence and care	¶1205
Obedience	¶1208
Fidelity – not to compete against employer or solicit employer's customers – behave honestly – account for profits – notify employer of misdeeds of other staff – disclose information received from third parties – inventions and copyright to belong to employer – work according to reasonable interpretation of contract	¶1213 ¶1215 ¶1216 ¶1217 ¶1218 ¶1219 ¶1220 ¶1221
Confidentiality	¶1223
Notice	¶1226

1. Directors are subject to additional duties, including their fiduciary duties to the company (¶2133).

Employer duties	
Payment of agreed wages	¶1230
Payment of contractual sick pay for reasonable period where contract silent as to duration	¶1231
Provision of work in certain circumstances	¶1233
Care for employee's health and safety	¶1237
Provision of grievance procedure	¶1239
Reasonableness and mutual trust and confidence	¶1241
Indemnity for costs	¶1255
References (if provided, must be accurate and compiled with reasonable care)	¶1257
Notice	¶1260

A. Employee duties

1. Service

1200 The employee must give **personal service** (i.e. he must not delegate or assign his duties) (*Ready-Mixed Concrete (South East) Ltd v Minister of Pensions and National Insurance* [1968] 1 All ER 433). This means that he must be **ready and willing to work** (*Henthorn and Taylor v Central Electricity Generating Board* [1980] IRLR 361, CA). Sickness absence will not breach this duty (*O'Grady v M Saper Ltd* [1940] 2 KB 469), but participating in a strike may do so, as the employee cannot be said to be ready and willing to work (*W Simmons v Hoover Ltd* [1976] IRLR 266, EAT).

See ¶3007 on the employer's right to deduct some or all of the employee's wages if he refuses to work.

2. Competence

1202 It is also an implied term that the employee will be **reasonably competent** to do the job.

There is an implied term that an employer will take reasonable steps to maintain an appraisal of an employee during a **probationary period** (¶946).

1203 **Incompetence** will be a breach of contract (¶1700). Depending on the seriousness of the breach, the employer may be entitled summarily to dismiss the employee. Less serious cases will require careful management by the employer and, if necessary, implementation of disciplinary procedures.

MEMO POINTS **Incapacity** (which includes incompetence) is a statutory fair reason for dismissal, which will enable the employer to defend a claim of unfair dismissal as long as he has acted reasonably in treating the incapacity as a sufficient reason for dismissal (¶8450).

3. Due diligence and care

1205 An employee is obliged to **take reasonable care** in the performance of his duties generally, and in particular, to take care of the employer's property (*Lister v Romford Ice and Cold Storage Co Ltd* [1957] 1 All ER 125, HL).

If the employee is negligent and, for example, injures a fellow employee, the employer may be **vicariously liable** for his actions. This means that legal responsibility is imposed on the employer, even though he is free from blame. For the employer to be liable, the employee's negligent act must be committed in the course of his employment. Where it is unclear whether this is the case, the **test** will be whether the act is so closely connected with the employment that it would be fair and just to hold the employer liable (*Lister v Hesley* [2001] IRLR 472, HL). The employer may also be vicariously liable for **acts of discrimination** committed by employees in the course of their employment, and the test currently applied for negligence is similar to the statutory test in health and safety cases (¶4850).

EXAMPLE In *Lister v Hesley*, a warden of a children's residential school sexually abused boys in his care. Given that the employer undertook to care for the boys through the services of the warden, and that the acts were committed in his working time and on the employer's premises, there was a sufficiently close connection between his acts and his employment to make the employer liable.

1206 **Negligence** will be a breach of contract, entitling the employer to sue the employee for damages and, in very serious cases, to dismiss the employee without notice.

MEMO POINTS Failure to exercise reasonable skill may provide a defence to an unfair dismissal claim if it constitutes one of the statutory fair reasons for dismissal (for example, incapacity or misconduct) (¶8450).

4. Obedience

An employee must carry out the **reasonable and lawful instructions** given by or on behalf of the employer, even where the employer is in breach of the duty of trust and confidence (see below) by issuing an instruction in bad faith. 1208

Whether an instruction is reasonable will depend on the circumstances (in particular, the nature and scope of the employee's duties) and whether the employee is contractually obliged to comply with it (*Macmillan Inc v Bishopsgate Investment Trust plc* [1993] IRLR 393, ChD). For example, if an employee's contract states that he can be required to take part of his annual leave during the employer's Christmas/New Year shut down period, it will be reasonable for the employer to require the employee to do so.

An employee is obliged to comply with orders that provide for a **new method of doing his job** (as opposed to doing a different job) (¶1616).

Disobedience can amount to a sufficiently serious breach of contract such as to justify summary dismissal. 1209

MEMO POINTS **Misconduct** (which includes disobedience) may constitute a statutory fair reason for dismissal (¶8490).

An employee is not obliged to obey **unreasonable or unlawful instructions**. For example, it is usually reasonable for an employee not to obey an instruction that would put him in danger. However, employees in the fire or police services, for example, may be expected to accept a higher degree of risk as part of their duties. 1210

EXAMPLE In *L G Morrish v Henlys (Folkestone) Ltd* [1973] IRLR 61 NIRC, M was held to have been unfairly dismissed for refusing to participate in the falsification of the employer's records.

If the employer insists on the employee carrying out an instruction that falls **outside the scope of his duties**, the employer will be in breach of contract and the employee may, if the breach is fundamental, be entitled to resign and claim that he has been constructively dismissed (*O'Brien v Associated Fire Alarms Ltd* [1969] 1 All ER 93, CA). 1211

5. Fidelity

The relationship between employer and employee is founded on a continuing bond of trust and confidence (¶1241). This tends, in the case of employees, to manifest itself in the more specific common law duty of fidelity (i.e. "to serve the employer faithfully within the requirements of the contract" (*Ticehurst and Thompson v British Telecommunications plc* [1992] IRLR 219, CA)), which encompasses the duty of confidentiality discussed below. The duty of fidelity is implied into every contract of employment (*Robb v Green* [1895] 2 QB 315). It ends with the termination of the employment, apart from the obligation not to use or disclose the employer's trade secrets. The principal aspects of the duty of fidelity are discussed below. 1213

Breach of the duty of fidelity can amount to gross misconduct. 1214

MEMO POINTS A dismissal for breach of the duty of fidelity could amount to a statutory fair reason for dismissal.

a. No competition

1215 The scope of this duty obliges an employee, during his employment, not to compete **with his employer's business**, either by working for competitors of the employer or setting up a competing business, and further not to solicit the employer's customers. After the employment ends there is no implied term that an ex-employee will not compete with his former employer. Express terms in restraint of trade may be used, but may be unenforceable (¶2500).

b. Honesty

1216 The employee must behave honestly. To determine the extent of the duty and the seriousness of any breach, the nature of the employer, the role of the employee, and the degree of trust required of the employee will be relevant factors. **Financial wrongdoing** amounting to gross misconduct, for example, does not necessarily require deliberate dishonesty or deceit (*Neary and Neary v Dean of Westminster* [1999] IRLR 288, Special Commissioner). **Unauthorised access to a computer** (¶6223) is comparable to dishonesty and may also amount to gross misconduct.

c. Account for profits

1217 The employee is obliged to account to the employer for "**secret profits**" (*Boston Deep Sea Fishing and Ice Co v Ansell* [1888] 39 ChD 399). This means that the employee "must not make a profit out of his trust; he must not place himself in a position where his duty and his interest may conflict; he may not act for his own benefit or the benefit of a third party without the informed consent of his employer" (*Attorney General v Blake* [2001] IRLR 36, HL). This **includes** taking bribes or "backhanders" but could also include benefits such as free "air miles" or gifts for private use, if the benefit to the employee is more than minimal.

Where the employee's **outside activities do not conflict** with his duty to the employer (as determined by his contractual obligations), he will not be obliged to account for any financial gain unless there is an express provision to that effect (*Nottingham University v Fishel* [2000] IRLR 471, QBD).

MEMO POINTS However, although the employment relationship is not a fiduciary one, equity may impose **fiduciary duties** (including a duty to act in the interests of another) as a result of the specific contractual obligations undertaken. These additional duties may oblige an employee to account for profits where he has benefited from his position (¶2665).

d. Other duties

1218 **Notify misdeeds** There is no general duty either to notify the employer of his own misconduct (*Bell v Lever Bros Ltd* (1932) AC 161, HL, although it has since been observed that *Bell v Lever Bros Ltd* does not provide any authority for the assertion that an employee can never be under a duty to notify his employer of his own misconduct (*Item Software (UK) Ltd v Fassihi* [2004] IRLR 928, CA)), or to notify misdeeds of other staff.

However, depending on the contract and the circumstances (in particular, whether the employee is so placed in the hierarchy of the workplace as to have a duty to report on the misconduct of superiors and/or subordinates (*Swain v West (Butchers) Ltd* [1936] 3 All ER 261, CA), an employee may **specifically be obliged** to notify the employer of serious misdeeds by other staff (*Sybron Corporation v Rochem Ltd* [1983] IRLR 253, CA). Directors and senior employees also have a positive duty to disclose breaches of their own fiduciary duty (¶2138) (*Tesco Stores Ltd v Pook and others* [2004] IRLR 618, ChD).

If the duty to disclose does apply, it is no defence that the employee was not specifically asked to volunteer the information (*Sybron Corporation v Rochem Ltd*), or that he would thereby incriminate himself.

Disclose information received from third parties An employee is under a duty to disclose information received from third parties which relates to the employer's business if received in the course of employment. An employee is not, however, generally obliged to disclose information received outside the course of his employment, even if it is of value to the employer (*Macmillan Inc v Bishopsgate Investment Trust plc* [1993] IRLR 393, ChD). 1219

Inventions and copyright When made in the course of the employment, inventions and copyright normally belong to the employer unless there is agreement to the contrary. Legislation also regulates ownership of intellectual property rights (¶2310). 1220

Work according to his contract An employee must work according to a reasonable interpretation of his contract. For example, a **work-to-rule** was held to be a breach of contract even though the employees were, strictly speaking, carrying out the express terms of the contract properly and fully (*Secretary of State for Employment v ASLEF (No 2)* [1972] ICR 19, CA). 1221

Withholding goodwill can also breach the implied term of fidelity and justify withholding pay (¶3009).

6. Confidentiality

During his employment an employee is bound by the common law duty of confidence which prevents him from using or disclosing the employer's confidential information and trade secrets. After the employment ends the implied duty only applies to trade secrets, so express provisions are needed to protect confidential information (¶2500). 1223

An employer may seek damages or an injunction if the employee has **breached** the implied duty of confidence or an express post-termination restriction (¶2640). 1224

MEMO POINTS The dismissal of an employee in order to preserve confidentiality may be fair for statutory purposes, relying on the statutory defence of "some other substantial reason" to defend an unfair dismissal claim (¶8530).

7. Notice

Legislation provides for a minimum notice period (¶8131). An express term may provide for a period of notice equivalent to or greater than the statutory minimum period. 1226

Where the contract is silent as to the amount of notice required to terminate the employment, it is an implied term that "**reasonable notice**" of termination will be given. This is discussed further at ¶8129.

B. Employer duties

1. Payment of agreed wages

It is an implied term that the employer will pay for the **work done** (¶2817). 1230

Where the employment contract provides for **sick pay** but is silent on the duration of the obligation to pay, a term may be implied to give effect to the presumed intention of the parties (¶1117). The presumption is that the employer will pay for a **reasonable period** only, which will depend on the term normally applicable in the particular industry as determined, for example, by reference to the relevant national agreement (*Howman & Son v Blyth* [1983] IRLR 139, EAT). 1231

2. Provision of work

1233 The employer does not have an implied obligation to provide work, as long as the employee is paid (*Turner v Sawdon & Co* [1901] 2 KB 653). However, the employer may be obliged to provide work if the consideration provided by him is more than merely to pay the agreed wages, extending to an obligation to permit the employee to do the work (*Langston v AUEW (No 2)* [1974] IRLR 182, NIRC). Whether there is a right to work is a **question of construction** of the particular contract in the light of its surrounding circumstances (*William Hill Organisation Ltd v Tucker* [1998] IRLR 313, CA, approving *Langston v AUEW (Nos 1 and 2)* [1974] IRLR 15, CA and 182, NIRC).

An **obligation to provide work** has been identified in the **following circumstances**:
– where earning capacity depends on working, such as pieceworkers, workers on commission and those who regularly work overtime or nights (*Langston v AUEW (Nos 1 and 2)*);
– workers dependent on publicity, such as actors (*Herbert Clayton and Jack Waller Ltd v Oliver* [1930] AC 209, HL); or
– workers needing regular exercise of their skills (*Langston v AUEW (Nos 1 and 2)*; *William Hill Organisation Ltd v Tucker*).

EXAMPLE In *William Hill Organisation Ltd v Tucker*, the employee was a senior dealer in the specialised business of spread betting. His contract expressly imposed an obligation on him to work those hours necessary to carry out his duties in a full and professional manner and emphasised that T would have every opportunity to develop his skills. When T resigned without giving the required period of notice, WH wanted to put him on garden leave, although it had no express right to do so. The Court held that T's special skills required frequent exercise, and that the express contractual terms were inconsistent with an implied term allowing him to collect wages without doing any available work. There was, therefore, an obligation to provide work during the employment, including the notice period.

1234 It is advisable for the employer to reserve an express contractual **right to suspend** the employee during the employment, and to put him on "**garden leave**" during the notice period, in order to defeat any argument that there is an implied obligation to provide work. Garden leave is discussed further at ¶2529.

Where the employer has expressly reserved the right to make a **payment in lieu of notice** (¶8145), the employee has no right to work out his notice period (*Marshall (Cambridge) Ltd v Hamblin* [1994] IRLR 260, EAT).

3. Health and safety

1237 There is an implied term that employers must take **reasonable care** of their employees' health and safety. The health and safety obligations of the employer both in statute and common law are discussed at ¶4800.

4. Grievance

1239 There is an implied term that an employee's grievances will be **promptly and properly** dealt with. Employee grievances are discussed further in Chapter 19.

MEMO POINTS **Compulsory statutory dispute resolution procedures**, including a statutory grievance procedure, may also need to be followed (see ¶6500 for further details).

5. Reasonableness and mutual trust and confidence

There is no general obligation on the employer to act fairly and reasonably (*Western Excavating (ECC) Ltd v Sharp* [1978] IRLR 27, CA), as to imply such a term would be too wide and uncertain (*Post Office v Roberts* [1980] IRLR 347, EAT). Therefore, an employer's unreasonable conduct alone is insufficient to found a claim for constructive dismissal, as a fundamental breach of contract is required in such cases (*Western Excavating (ECC) Ltd v Sharp*). 1241

There is, however, an implied term that an employer will **not exercise** his power under a **contractual provision on unreasonable grounds**. This means that the employer must exercise: 1242
- an express right to suspend, for example, on reasonable grounds for no longer than is reasonably necessary (*McClory v Post Office* [1993] IRLR 159, ChD);
- an express mobility clause on reasonable grounds i.e. not "capriciously" (*White v Reflecting Road Studs Ltd* [1991] IRLR 331, EAT), but for business reasons (*HSBC Bank plc v Drage*, EAT case 369/02 & 1036/03); and
- discretion in relation to contractual bonuses in a rational manner and in good faith (¶2833).

The courts may also be willing to imply a term to the effect that the employer will take **reasonable care in making statements** in the context of a proposed **business transfer** where (*Hagen and others v ICI Chemicals & Polymers Ltd* [2002] IRLR 31, QBD): 1243
- the transfer will impact on the future economic interests of his employees;
- the transfer will be unlikely to take place if a significant number of the employees object; and
- the employer has access to information unavailable to the employees, which he knows will carry considerable weight with them.

An obligation to treat the employee in a reasonable manner may, however, be implied if it can be identified under another head, such as **business efficacy** (*Aspden v Webbs Poultry and Meat Group (Holdings) Ltd* and *Scally v Southern Health and Social Services Board*; ¶1174). 1244

Trust and confidence The courts have also upheld an obligation to treat the employee in a reasonable manner as part of the duty to preserve the relationship of **mutual trust and confidence** (*Imperial Group Pension Trust Ltd v Imperial Tobacco Ltd* [1991] IRLR 66, ChD). This means that the employer will not, without reasonable and proper cause, **conduct** himself in a manner calculated or **likely to destroy or seriously damage the relationship** of trust and confidence which should exist between him and the employee (*Woods v WM Car Services (Peterborough) Ltd* [1981] IRLR 347, EAT (affirmed [1982] IRLR 413, CA)). It is not necessary for the employer's conduct to be targeted in some way at the employee, nor is it necessary for the employee to know of that conduct while still employed (*Malik v Bank of Credit and Commerce International SA* [1997] IRLR 462, HL). 1245

This obligation is **not diminished** by factors such as the overall working environment (for example, one in which abusive language is acceptable) or the seniority and remuneration of the employee (*Horkulak v Cantor Fitzgerald International* [2003] IRLR 756, HC, confirmed on appeal [2004] IRLR 942, CA). In this case, the Court rejected the argument that high levels of remuneration entitled an employer to apply different standards of treatment to a city broker compared with other less well-paid employees.

The obligation is confined to matters arising during the subsistence of the employment relationship, and it does not apply in relation to the **manner of a dismissal** (i.e. the acts immediately surrounding the dismissal) (*Johnson v Unisys Ltd* [2001] IRLR 279, HL). However, if an employer breaches either the implied term of mutual trust and confidence or the duty of care in taking steps in relation to an employee **prior to and leading up to** dismissing the employee such that the employee would be entitled to a contractual or tortious remedy (which existed **independently** of any action in respect of the fairness of the dismissal) and the employee had suffered direct financial loss as a result of the employer's conduct, then *Johnson v Unisys Ltd* will not bar such an action (*Eastwood and Williams v Magnox Electric plc* heard jointly 1246 with *McCabe v Cornwall County Council and anor* [2004] IRLR 733, HL). In *Eastwood and Williams v Magnox Electric plc* and *McCabe v Cornwall County Council and anor*, the employees brought court proceedings (after bringing successful claims for unfair dismissal in the tribunal) claiming that they had suffered financial loss as a direct result of psychiatric illnesses brought on by their employers' unfair treatment of them in the events prior, and leading up, to their dismissals. The House of Lords considered that, ordinarily (with the exception of suspension), an employer's unfair treatment of an employee in the events leading up to dismissal would not cause financial loss. However, **exceptionally**, financial loss might be suffered and in such cases, the cause of action preceded and was independent of the subsequent dismissal. Note, however, that any such claim will be subject to the principle of double recovery.

In *King v University Court of the University of St Andrews* [2002] IRLR 252, CS, the implied term of trust and confidence arising from a provision in the contract of employment entitling the employer to terminate the contract with notice for "good cause shown" was held to only cease **once a decision to dismiss has been made** and consequently subsisted during the employer's investigation and evaluation of disciplinary charges.

1248 The implied term of trust and confidence has been **applied** in a wide variety of circumstances, including the following:

EXAMPLE 1. In *Malik v Bank of Credit and Commerce International SA*, the bank went into liquidation after having operated for some time in a corrupt and dishonest manner. This conduct amounted to a breach of the implied contractual obligation of mutual trust and confidence as the employee's **employment prospects** were tainted by the employer's reputation.

2. The term may be breached if the employer exercises an express contractual right, such as a **mobility clause**, in a way that has a particularly onerous impact on the employee. When exercising such a clause, the employer is subject to an implied duty to give reasonable notice, to co-operate with and not frustrate the employee's attempt to perform the contract (*United Bank Ltd v Akhtar* [1989] IRLR 507, EAT), and to communicate fully with the employee (*White v Reflecting Road Studs Ltd* [1991] IRLR 331, EAT).

3. In *French v Barclays Bank plc* [1998] IRLR 646, CA, the Court found that the employer had breached the implied term by **changing the terms of a bridging loan** made to F when he relocated, as required by the bank, from one branch to another. The housing market had collapsed and F was unable to sell his house at the agreed price. The bank demanded that he accept a lower sum or pay interest on the bridging loan.

4. **Providing** an employee's prospective employer with **a reference** that reveals complaints made about the employee, of which he is unaware, amounts to a breach of the implied term (*TSB Bank plc v Harris* [2000] IRLR 157, EAT).

5. **Sexual harassment** can amount to a breach of the implied term (*(1) Reed and (2) Bull Information Systems Ltd v Stedman* [1999] IRLR 299, EAT).

6. Dismissing the employee in circumstances which would deprive him of his **contractual health benefits**, such as permanent health insurance benefit, may amount to a breach of the implied term (¶1716) (*Aspden v Webbs Poultry and Meat Group (Holdings) Ltd* [1996] IRLR 521, QBD; *Villella v MFI Furniture Centres Ltd* [1999] IRLR 468, QBD).

7. **Suspending** an employee pending the outcome of an investigation into an allegation of child sexual abuse amounted to a breach of the term (*Gogay v Hertfordshire County Council* [2000] IRLR 703, CA).

8. **Offering a particular benefit** (a new contract) to an entire class of employees except for one amounted to a breach of the term (*Transco plc (formerly BG plc) v O'Brien* [2002] IRLR 444, CA).

9. Seeking to **impose new terms and conditions of employment** in an aggressive manner, giving only perfunctory and misleading explanations as to the effect of the new terms, amounted to a breach of the implied term of trust and confidence (*Cantor Fitzgerald International v Bird and others* [2002] IRLR 867, QBD).

10. **Inviting an employee to resign** after the employee failed to improve following a warning for poor performance with the suggestion that the employee would be treated favourably in respect of her compromise/severance package should she tender her resignation (*Billington v Michael Hunter and Sons Ltd*, EAT case 578/03).

11. **Failing to notify** an employee of a **vacancy** that had **arisen during her maternity leave** if the vacancy is one for which the employee believed she would have been suitable (*Visa International Service Association v Paul* [2004] IRLR 42, EAT). In this case, it was irrelevant that had the employee applied, she would not have been short-listed for the position in any event.

1249 The duty of trust and confidence does not alter the premise that **neither party** to the contract is **obliged to disclose his breach** of the contract to the other (*Bell v Lever Bros Ltd* [1932] AC 161, HL, although see ¶1218). For example, when entering into compromise agreements (¶9315) with an employee, the employer is not obliged by the duty of trust and confidence to make any disclosure that it has previously acted in breach of that implied term (e.g. by carrying on a dishonest and corrupt business) (*Bank of Credit and Commerce International SA v Ali* [1999] IRLR 226, ChD).

The employer's conduct must be serious to breach the duty of trust and confidence, and there will be no breach if the employer had **reasonable and proper cause** for his actions (*Gogay v Hertfordshire County Council*, above; *Hilton v Shiner Ltd – Builders Merchants* [2001] IRLR 727, EAT). It is not necessary to show that the employer **intended** such a breach, and an employer who breaches the term on the basis of a mistake may still be liable (*Transco plc (formerly BG plc) v O'Brien*). 1250

The **test** as to whether an employer had reasonable and proper cause for his actions is an objective one and, consequently, it is not necessary for the employee to actually lose confidence for there to be a breach (*Meikle v Nottinghamshire County Council*, EAT case 0033/03 confirmed on appeal ([2004] IRLR 703, CA)).

If there is such a breach, it will always be a **repudiatory breach** for the purposes of a claim of constructive dismissal (*Morrow v Safeway Stores plc* [2002] IRLR 9, EAT).

The employee will be entitled to **damages** in respect of his financial loss (¶1725). 1251

The **rules of construction** of a contract are unchanged and there is no positive obligation on the courts to construe contracts of employment in a way which furthers mutual trust (*Hill v General Accident Fire & Life Assurance Corporation plc* [1998] IRLR 641, CS). 1252

6. Indemnity for costs

The employer is generally expected to pay for or reimburse costs/expenses incurred by the employee in the course of his employment. 1255

7. References

There is no implied term entitling an employee to a reference. 1257

If, however, one is provided, the employer owes the employee a duty of care to ensure that it is **accurate** (¶8324). In such circumstances, there is an implied term that the reference will be compiled (and the information on which it is based will be verified) with **reasonable care**. If it is not, the employee may have a remedy for negligent misstatement (*Spring v Guardian Assurance plc* [1994] IRLR 460, HL). The employer must also take care not to breach the implied term of **trust and confidence** when providing a reference (¶1241).

8. Notice

Where the contract is silent as to the amount of notice required to terminate the employment, it is an implied term that **reasonable notice** of termination will be given (¶8129). This may be greater than the statutory minimum in some cases. 1260

Where the employer has reserved the right to make a **payment in lieu of notice**, the employment will terminate immediately if the employer exercises it. 1261

V. Incorporated terms

A. Collective agreements

1270 These are agreements **made between** the employer (or employers' association) and a recognised, independent trade union. Such agreements may **deal with**, for example, wages and salaries, benefits, holidays, working hours, and disciplinary matters.

MEMO POINTS Note that it is possible for a shop steward (or, presumably, another individual union official with apparent or ostensible authority) **acting as agent**, to bind union members into collectively agreed terms he agrees with the employer, even though he has not consulted with the workforce over such terms and is not considered by the union to be a proper signatory to such an agreement (*Harris v Richard Lawson Autologistics Ltd* [2002] ICR 765, CA).

1271 To be **enforceable** as **between the employer and the employee**, the collective agreement must be incorporated into the individual employee's contract. If it is, it does not matter that the terms are not legally enforceable between the union and the employer, nor that the employee does not approve of them (*Tocher v General Motors Scotland Ltd* [1981] IRLR 55, EAT), or is not a member of the union (*Young v Canadian Northern Railway Company* [1931] AC 83, PC).

EXAMPLE In *Marley v Forward Trust Group Ltd* [1986] IRLR 369, CA, the provisions of a collective agreement relating to enhanced redundancy payments were incorporated into M's contract. The collective agreement itself stated that the provisions were **binding in honour only** as between the employer and the union. However, the Court held that M could rely on the redundancy provisions as being a **legally binding** term of his contract.

1272 There may be **more than one** applicable collective agreement (for example, a national and a local agreement). If there is a conflict between those agreements, the question as to which terms are incorporated into the individual contract will depend on the intention of the employer and employee.

1273 If the **terms** are **not expressly incorporated**, they will not be enforceable as between the employer and the employee merely because the employer joins the employers' association that negotiated the agreement (*Hamilton v Futura Floors Ltd* [1990] IRLR 478, CS), nor merely because the employee is a member of the union that negotiated the agreement. Nor can union members generally argue that the union negotiates collective agreements with the employer as their agent, such that they could automatically take advantage of terms agreed on their behalf.

Method of incorporation

1275 The provisions of a collective agreement may be incorporated into an employee's contract by agreement with the employee (for example, where the written contract of employment expressly provides for incorporation) or by implication by virtue of the custom and practice within the industry.

1276 **Incorporation by individual agreement** To incorporate the collectively agreed terms, the wording of the individual employee's contract must make it clear that agreements reached with the recognised union (or particular terms of those agreements) will be binding on the employer and the employee. The contract may incorporate the agreements generally or by reference to specific provisions.

1277 **Incorporation by custom and practice** The provisions of a collective agreement may be incorporated by virtue of the custom and practice within the industry if it is clear that the employer and employees have **assumed an obligation to observe** those provisions. In *Henry v London General Transport Services Ltd* [2002] IRLR 474, CA, the court stated that **clear evidence** was required to establish custom and practice but that once custom and practice had been established, it would cover all contractual terms. It is not enough that the parties have habitually observed the provisions. If such an inference would be inconsistent with an express term of the contract, no such inference will be drawn (*Gascol Conversions Ltd v J W Mercer* [1974] IRLR, CA).

Which terms will be incorporated?

Whether part of a collective agreement is incorporated into individual contracts depends on the contractual **intention** of the employer and the employee (¶1117). If there is **no express incorporation**, incorporation may only be inferred if the particular provision is apt to be a term of the contract. If a collective agreement is **expressly incorporated by general words**, it will be for the courts and tribunals to consider, together with the words of incorporation, whether any particular part of the agreement is apt to be a term of the individual's contract. If it is not apt, the inference will be that that part is not incorporated. To **avoid ambiguity**, the employer may therefore wish to specify in the contract which parts are incorporated. **1279**

Provisions considered to be **inappropriate** to be enforceable by individual employees are commonly concerned with general industrial relations and policy issues rather than individual rights and obligations, and include: **1280**
- joint consultation and procedural issues, including redundancy provisions (a "last in first out" selection procedure) (*Alexander v Standard Telephones & Cables Ltd (No 2)* [1991] IRLR 286, QBD; *LTI Ltd v Radford*, EAT case 16/00);
- broad policy issues (e.g. long-term plans on business continuity, retraining and redundancy) (*British Leyland (UK) Ltd v McQuilken* [1978] IRLR 245, EAT);
- collective issues (e.g. collective bargaining and dispute resolution procedures) (*Tadd v Eastwood and Daily Telegraph Ltd* [1983] IRLR 320, QBD; *National Coal Board v National Union of Mineworkers* [1986] IRLR 439, ChD);
- union recognition; and
- "no strike" clauses. Note that incorporation of a provision of a collective agreement restricting an employee's right to take industrial action is prohibited, unless certain conditions are met (¶7428).

In deciding whether a particular provision of a collective agreement is suitable for incorporation into individual employees' contracts, a tribunal must bear in mind that certain terms are not intended to give rise to any contractual obligation on the employer's part and, therefore, the **content and character** of the relevant provisions must be considered in determining whether it is appropriate that they should be incorporated into an employee's contract (*Kaur v MG Rover Group Ltd* [2005] IRLR 40, CA overturning the High Court's decision).

EXAMPLE In *Kaur v MG Rover Group Ltd*, the Court held that the statement "There will be no compulsory redundancy" in a collective agreement which covered other manpower and industrial relations issues was merely aspirational, vague and only related to a commitment at a collective level. It was, therefore, not a provision which could be incorporated into the employee's individual contract.

Variation

The **employer cannot change** a term incorporated into an individual contract by a unilateral variation, abrogation or withdrawal from the collective agreement but must agree with the recognised union to vary the collective agreement. If the collective agreement is not varied by agreement, the individual contracts will remain unaffected (*Robertson and Jackson v British Gas Corporation* [1983] IRLR 302, CA; *Lee v GEC Plessey Telecommunications* [1993] IRLR 383, QBD). **1282**

Therefore, where an employee's written contract states that his pay will "normally be in accordance with" rates which had been collectively agreed, a term will be implied into the contract that the employer will **notify** the employee if and when he intends to depart from the normal position (*Glendale Managed Services v Graham and others* [2003] IRLR 465, CA).

1283 Similarly, an **employee cannot unilaterally withdraw** his agreement once he has agreed that the provisions of a collective agreement are incorporated into his contract (*Tocher v General Motors Scotland Ltd* [1981] IRLR 55, EAT). If the provisions of a collective agreement are incorporated, the employee cannot withdraw from those provisions by resigning as a union member.

1284

EXAMPLE In *Airlie v City of Edinburgh District Council* [1996] IRLR 516, EAT, the EAT construed the pay provisions of a collective agreement which had been incorporated into A's contract and concluded that it gave the employer the right to alter the bonus scheme after a period of consultation.

1285 **Incorporation of the changes** If a collective agreement (or particular provisions of it) is varied by agreement between the employer and the union, it will be incorporated into the individual employment contract if the employer and the employee **expressly agree** to incorporate such provisions as renegotiated from time to time or "for the time being in force."

In the absence of express agreement, it is usually possible to **interpret** the agreement that incorporates the collective agreement/provisions into the employee's contract as being an agreement to incorporate it/them as renegotiated from time to time.

MEMO POINTS In *Singh v British Steel Corporation* [1974] IRLR 131, IT, the tribunal held that the employer could not unilaterally vary the contract by means of an agreed variation to the collective agreement incorporated into S's contract. S had been told that his terms of employment were in accordance with the collective agreement, but no reference was made to any revision of the agreement.

The *Singh v British Steel Corporation* case has been criticised (despite the fact that the EAT took a similar approach in *Land and Wilson v West Yorkshire Metropolitan County Council* [1979] IRLR 174, EAT) because it was founded on the premise that the union had no authority to vary S's terms because he had resigned as a union member. However, in light of the principle that union membership is irrelevant if the provisions are incorporated (as seen above), the better view is that he was bound by the collective agreement despite his resignation because he had impliedly agreed to incorporate the collective terms as renegotiated from time to time.

1286 If there is an express or implied agreement to incorporate provisions of collective agreements as renegotiated from time to time, then any variations to those provisions will **automatically vary** the individual contract.

EXAMPLE In *Higgins v Cables Montague Contracts Ltd*, EAT case 564/93, H's statement of particulars stated that his terms of employment were in accordance with, and subject to, collective agreements currently in force between the company and the union. The EAT held that an agreement between the company and the union to reduce wages by 20 per cent as a result of the company's financial difficulties was binding on H.

1287 If there is **no agreement to incorporate** collectively agreed terms as renegotiated from time to time, variations to the collective agreements must be incorporated into the individual contract, either by individual agreement or by virtue of custom and practice (as seen above). For example, it may be possible to infer an agreement to vary the contract by the parties' conduct, i.e. the application by the employer of the revised terms and the acceptance of those terms by the employee.

Termination of the collective agreement

1289 If the terms of the collective agreement have been **incorporated into the individual employee's contract**, the termination of the collective agreement will not automatically remove those terms from the individual contract, and the parties can continue to enforce them (*Robertson and Jackson v British Gas Corporation* [1983] IRLR 302, CA).

Sale of the business

1292 If the business transfers to a new employer **under the transfer (TUPE) regulations** (¶7900), any collective agreement made between the original employer and a trade union recognised by him in respect of the transferring employees (and incorporated into their contracts of employment) will have effect after the transfer as if made between the transferee employer and that trade union. The new employer will have to take account of any terms that have been incorporated into the employees' contracts, and a variation of those terms may, if in connection with the transfer of the business, be ineffective (¶8010).

B. Work rules

There is a distinction between collective agreements (which result from negotiations and agreement between the employer and the trade union) and work rules (which are unilateral, made only by the employer) (*Cadoux v Central Regional Council* [1986] IRLR 131, CS). The employer is entitled to introduce work rules for the conduct of his employees within the scope of the contract. A set of **rules, a policy or a code of practice** circulated by the employer (and often included in the staff handbook (¶1480)) may be incorporated into an individual's contract of employment if it can reasonably be inferred from the circumstances that the parties must have intended the rules to become contractual terms. To avoid any uncertainty, it is good practice for introductory wording expressly to state whether the provisions are binding or not. **1295**

In the absence of express wording, a provision will be contractually binding if it should properly be regarded as **conferring a right**. If, on the other hand, it should properly be regarded as merely setting out **guidelines on good practice** (*Wandsworth London Borough Council v D'Silva and another* [1998] IRLR 193, CA), it will not be binding. **1296**

EXAMPLE Contractually binding

1. In *Dal v Orr* [1980] IRLR 413, EAT, the EAT found that rules in the employees' handbook gave the employer a contractual right to alter shift systems and hours of work. The employer was therefore not in breach of contract when he did so.
2. In contrast to *Grant v South-West Trains Ltd* (see below), in *Taylor v Secretary of State for Scotland* [2000] IRLR 502, HL, the Court accepted the tribunal's earlier finding that an equal opportunities policy (which included an undertaking not to discriminate on the grounds of age) was contractual as it had been notified by a circular in the same way as changes and additions to contractual terms were notified.

Mere guidelines

1. In *Grant v South-West Trains Ltd* [1998] IRLR 188, QBD, SWT adopted an equal opportunities policy which referred to its "commitment" not to discriminate on grounds of sexual preference and its "aim" to eliminate unfair discrimination. G's contract provided for an opposite sex spouse to receive travel concessions. G's partner was of the same sex and SWT refused to provide travel concessions for her. The Court held that the equal opportunities policy had not been incorporated, but was a statement of policy in "general, idealistic terms, and not of contractual obligations". There was no evidence of an intention to be bound, and the policy imposed no obligations on SWT. The Court also said that the policy could not, in any case, be imported into the contract to override a clear, express provision.
2. In *Wandsworth London Borough Council v D'Silva and another* (see above), the council revised its code of practice on staff sickness to introduce tighter absence monitoring procedures and more frequent reviews of long-term absence. The Court held that the language of the code did not provide an appropriate foundation on which to base contractual rights but rather aimed to provide guidance. The sickness procedure was designed to be flexible, and this flexibility was inconsistent with the creation of contractual rights. The employers were therefore entitled unilaterally to amend the code.
3. In *Secretary of State for Employment v Association Society of Locomotive Engineers and Firemen (No 2)* [1972] 2 All ER 949, CA, the Court held that if the staff handbook, for example, contains numerous sets of rules, the courts might conclude that the rules are instructions as to how the employee should carry out his contractual obligations, rather than being contractual obligations in themselves.

VI. Unenforceable terms

A. Illegal terms and terms contrary to public policy

1305 A contract may be **unenforceable** by the parties if its terms are:
- directly **prohibited by statute** (e.g. the contract may be illegal because the employee is a child (¶4881), or because the employee does not have a legal right to work in the UK (¶750));
- **unlawful** (e.g. to do an unlawful act, most often to defraud Revenue and Customs);
- **contrary to public policy** (e.g. for an immoral purpose, such as the procurement of prostitutes); or
- lawful, but the contract is **performed illegally** (e.g. where the employer in practice makes additional undisclosed cash payments to make up for the amount of tax and national insurance deducted).

Relevant factors when assessing enforceability

1306 Whether a party can enforce a contract is likely to depend on the factors set out below.

1307 **Parties' intentions and awareness** If the parties intend an otherwise lawful contract to be used for unlawful means (most commonly, defrauding Revenue and Customs), it will be illegal and void (*Tomlinson v Dick Evans U Drive Ltd* [1978] IRLR 77, EAT). However, a scheme whose only purpose is to reduce the amount of deductions that ought to be paid will be lawful if it is entered into in **good faith**, constitutes a proper method of reducing tax and is/will be disclosed to Revenue and Customs (*Lightfoot v D & J Sporting Ltd* [1996] IRLR 64, EAT).

It is irrelevant that the parties did not realise that their actions were illegal (*Salvesen v Simons* [1994] IRLR 52, EAT). As the Court found in *Miller v Karlinski* [1945] 62 TLR 85, CA, "ignorance of the law cannot excuse them". In *Salvesen v Simons*, the parties claimed that income was taxable under Schedule D when it should have been taxed under Schedule E (as it was then) but neither party to the arrangement knew or suspected that the arrangement was illegal. Since the **incorrect classification** had been **deliberate**, even this relatively minor tax evasion was sufficient to render the contract unenforceable, thereby preventing the employee from bringing an unfair dismissal claim. Similarly, an employee who **lies** to the Contributions Agency regarding the nature of his work in order to maintain the benefits of self-employed status (even though he is an employee) will taint his contract with illegality and prevent him from claiming unfair dismissal (*Soteriou v Ultrachem*, EAT case 0250/01).

On the other hand, in *Young & Woods Ltd v West* [1980] IRLR 201, CA, it was held that the label applied by the parties as to the classification of the contract was wrong. The contract was, however, not void for illegality as the parties had made an **honest mistake**. The Inland Revenue (now called Revenue and Customs) had a duty to reclaim tax deductions that were granted to Mr West as self-employed, but he was nevertheless entitled to claim unfair dismissal.

1309 **Participation in the illegality** The employee may be unable to enforce the contract if he was a party to or knew of the employer's illegality (*Newland v Simons and Willer (Hairdressers) Ltd* [1981] IRLR 359, EAT).

Whether the contract is unenforceable will depend on the following factors:
- whether, looked at subjectively, the employee in fact **knew or came to know** of the illegal act (and not whether the employee ought to have known of that illegal act), although in cases of statutory illegality the knowledge of the parties is irrelevant;

– the extent to which the employee **colluded** with the employer in allowing the illegality to take place (the contract will be unenforceable only if the employee has **actively participated** in the illegality);
– whether the **employee benefits** from the illegality; and
– the **relative conduct** of the parties.

EXAMPLE Unenforceable
In *Tomlinson v Dick Evans U Drive Ltd* [1978] IRLR 77, EAT, T knew that no tax was being deducted from the weekly cash payment and she **did nothing to complain**. She lost her right to a redundancy payment and her protection from unfair dismissal.

Enforceable
1. In *Hall v Woolston Hall Leisure Ltd* [2000] IRLR 578, CA, the Court found that H had acquiesced in the illegality only because she was **powerless to change** the situation. Mere knowledge and acquiescence without more were insufficient to bar her from enforcing the contract.
In *Hewcastle Catering Ltd v Ahmed and Elkamah* [1991] IRLR 473, CA, the employer involved the employees in his scheme to evade VAT. The employees subsequently gave evidence to Customs and Excise, and were dismissed by the employer as a result. Despite their involvement in the illegality, the Court allowed their unfair dismissal claim, in part because they had **not benefited** from the fraud themselves, and further because their **conduct was minor and insignificant** compared to the employer's.
2. In *Cannon t/a Barkway Park Golf Club v Sadler*, EAT case 385/01, S received a taxable benefit in the form of a car which she did not declare to the Inland Revenue (now called Revenue and Customs). However, she had **not participated** in any fraud or dishonesty and there was **no scheme intended to defraud** the Revenue and so could bring an unfair dismissal claim.
3. In *Wheeler v Quality Deep Ltd (trading as Thai Royale Restaurant)* [2004] EWCA Civ 1085, a Thai national waitress working in the UK whose **English was poor** was **deemed not to have knowledge** of the fact that her employer had not deducted tax and NIC from her pay and so could bring an unfair dismissal claim.

Infrequent or incidental illegality The **duration or frequency** of the illegality may be relevant. The issue will depend on the particular circumstances, including the amount and frequency of the payments and why they are made. A court will also consider whether the illegality is **merely collateral or incidental** to the employment contract. 1311

EXAMPLE 1. In *Annandale Engineering v Samson* [1994] IRLR 59, EAT, the EAT held that an **occasional, irregular payment** made when the employer's greyhound won a race, and which did not form part of S's regular remuneration (as defined in the contract or implicit in its performance) did not render the whole contract illegal/unenforceable where tax was not deducted.
2. In *McConnell v Bolik* [1979] IRLR 422, EAT, B, without the knowledge of the employer, failed to disclose on his **tax return** to the Inland Revenue (now called Revenue and Customs) details of a particular benefit he had received from the employer. B's failure was a matter for him and the Revenue, and did not make the contract of service illegal.
3. In *Coral Leisure Group Ltd v Barnett* [1981] IRLR 204, EAT, B, in the course of his employment, procured and **paid for prostitutes** for his employer's customers. The EAT held that this immoral purpose was collateral to the contract as B did not enter into the employment with the purpose of doing that unlawful act. B was therefore able to bring a complaint of unfair dismissal.
4. In *Cannon t/a Barkway Park Golf Club v Sadler*, EAT case 385/01, the **provision of the car** was not central to S's unfair dismissal claim but amounted to a collateral illegality which did not taint the whole contract.

Consequences of illegality

If **part of a contract is illegal**, the whole arrangement will be affected. The courts will not readily sever an offending term so that the remainder of the contract can be enforced (*Miller v Karlinski* [1945] 62 TLR 85, CA). 1313

A contract can be illegal **throughout** or for **part of its duration** only. Statutory continuity of employment (¶1080) is not preserved during the period of illegality. While a contract is illegal, rights cannot normally be claimed or enforced. For example, the rights to bring an unfair dismissal claim or a claim for a redundancy payment depend on the applicant being an employee working under a valid contract of service (*Tomlinson v Dick Evans U Drive Ltd*). 1314

1315 Case law indicates that, if a contract is "tainted with illegality", an employee can bring a **sex discrimination claim** (as such a claim is based in tort, not in contract, and only relies on the contract to establish an employment relationship) (*Leighton v (1) Michael and (2) Charalambous* [1996] IRLR 67, EAT), unless the claim is inextricably bound up with the illegal conduct (*Hall v Woolston Hall Leisure Ltd*, see example at ¶1309). It seems likely that the same reasoning would apply to **race, disability, religion or belief and sexual orientation discrimination claims** (as they are, like sex discrimination, statutory torts).

EXAMPLE In *Leighton v (1) Michael and (2) Charalambous* [1996] IRLR 67, EAT, L was permitted to bring a claim of sexual harassment and victimisation despite the fact that her employers were not deducting income tax or national insurance contributions from her wages, which made her contract illegal.

B. Other unenforceable terms

Discriminatory terms

1330 Terms that are discriminatory will be void and unenforceable against the victim of discrimination (s 77 SDA 1975; s 72 RRA 1976; s 9 DDA 1995; reg 35 SI 2003/1660; reg 35 SI 2003/1661).

No contracting out

1335 An employee or employer cannot usually contract out of any applicable employment legislation. However, where a conciliation officer is involved in **settling** certain claims or a valid **compromise** agreement has been signed (¶9330), contracting out will be permitted in those circumstances (¶¶9220-1).

EXAMPLE The Public Interest Disclosure Act 1998 (the "whistleblowing" legislation which amended the ERA 1996) states that any provision in an agreement, including a contract of employment, will be void so far as it purports to preclude the worker from making a protected disclosure. Therefore, in order to ensure that a confidentiality provision can be enforced, it should expressly state that it does not restrict or limit the worker's right to make such a disclosure.

Unfair Contract Terms Act 1977 (UCTA)

1340 Recent case law shows that UCTA can apply to contracts of employment. The effect of UCTA is to make certain terms always unenforceable, and certain others subject to a test of reasonableness (memo point 1).

1341 Terms which exclude or restrict liability for **death or personal injury** resulting from negligence are always unenforceable (s 2(1) UCTA 1977).

1342 Terms which exclude or restrict liability for negligence in the case of loss or damage **other than for death or personal injury** are subject to the test of reasonableness (s 2(2) UCTA 1977).

1343 Where the employee either deals as a consumer (memo point 2) or on the employer's written standard terms of business (memo point 3), terms excluding or restricting liability for **contractual breaches** (memo point 4) or entitling the employer to perform his contractual obligations in a substantially different way than that reasonably expected of him (or to give no contractual performance at all) are subject to the test of reasonableness (s 3 UCTA 1977). Special rules apply to share option schemes (memo point 5).

MEMO POINTS 1. To satisfy the **test of reasonableness**, a term must be a fair and reasonable one to be included having regard to the circumstances which were, or ought reasonably to have been, known to or in the contemplation of the parties when the contract was made (s 11 UCTA 1977).
2. To **deal as a consumer**, the employee must not make the contract in the course of a business (including a profession) or hold himself out as doing so, whilst the employer must make the contract in the course of a business (s 12 UCTA 1977). In *Brigden v American Express Bank Ltd* [2000] IRLR 94,

QBD, the Court held that, as an employee, B did deal as a consumer. Note, however, that the Unfair Terms in Consumer Contracts Regulations SI 1994/3159, based on the corresponding European Directive, do not apply to contracts of employment.
3. It could be argued that an employee deals with the employer on the latter's **written standard terms of business** if he is employed under a standard form contract of employment.
4. To be covered by UCTA, the clause must attempt to exclude or limit liability, or permit substantially different performance, for example, a term restricting liability for wrongful dismissal. This should be contrasted with a clause that merely **sets out the parties' rights and liabilities** (not covered by UCTA), for example the disapplication of the employer's disciplinary procedure during the first 2 years of employment (*Brigden v American Express Bank Ltd*). A genuine liquidated damages clause (¶1703) is unlikely to be an exclusion clause.
5. UCTA does not apply to "any contract so far as it relates to the creation or transfer of securities or of any right or interest in securities" (Sch 1 para 1(e) UCTA 1977). Therefore, in *Micklefield v SAC Technology* [1990] IRLR 218, ChD, the Court held that a term in a **share option scheme** purporting to exclude the employee's right to compensation for the loss of rights on dismissal was not void under UCTA. The Scottish UCTA provisions did not include an equivalent securities exception, and so such an exclusion was held to be void there (*Chapman v Aberdeen Construction Group plc* [1991] IRLR 505, CS).

Terms in restraint of trade

Terms that impose restrictions on an employee's activities after the termination of his employment will be unenforceable if their main purpose is to prevent competition. The term may be enforceable if it goes no further than is strictly necessary to protect the employer's legitimate business interests, such as confidential information or trade secrets, and goodwill. These issues are discussed in detail at ¶2500. 1355

Terms restricting right to take industrial action

Such terms cannot form part of an individual employee's contract of employment unless certain conditions are satisfied (¶7428). 1360

SECTION 3

Information to be provided in writing

There is **no statutory requirement** to have a written contract but the employer is obliged to provide certain written particulars of the contract terms to the employee, so that he is aware of the main terms of his employment. 1400

It is **common practice** to have a written contract of employment, which includes all the information that the employer is obliged to provide in writing, as well as other, non-obligatory terms. A model short form contract of employment for general staff is provided at ¶9910, and a model service agreement, which is suitable for senior executives and directors is provided at ¶9920. 1401

There may be **other provisions** relating to the employment, such as codes of practice, or policies and procedures, which may be contained in a staff handbook. These may be contractual terms or may be mere instructions or guidelines as to how the employee should carry out his job (¶1480). 1402

1. Obligation to provide written particulars

There is no requirement for a contract of employment to be in writing, but the employer must provide written details of the main terms and conditions of employment to all employees whose employment lasts for at least 1 month (ss 1, 198 ERA 1996; Implementing Proof of Employment Relationship EC Directive 1991/533). This obligation is commonly referred to as the requirement to provide a "statutory statement" or "written particulars" of terms and conditions of employment. 1405

A model statement of particulars is provided at ¶9900.

If, after 1 month's employment, the **employment ends** before the statement is provided, the employee is still entitled to receive one (s 2(6) ERA 1996).

2. Status of statement of particulars

1410 The statement of particulars does not constitute the contract of employment (*Robertson and Jackson v British Gas Corporation* [1983] IRLR 302, CA). It does, however, provide strong (but not conclusive) evidence of the terms of that contract (*System Floors (UK) Ltd v Daniel* [1981] IRLR 475, EAT). Given that it is the employer who issues the statement, it is harder for him to prove that the statement does not reflect the contractual terms. If, on the other hand, the employee has good evidence of the terms of the contract, the statement is considered to be "persuasive" only, and refutable by the employee's evidence.

1411 It is common practice for employers to include the obligatory particulars in a written contract, which is signed by both the employer and the employee. From 1 October 2004, this is now expressly permitted by the legislation (s 7A ERA 1996 as inserted by s 37 EA 2002). The particulars may form the **foundation of the contract**, with non-obligatory terms being added as required by the employer or the nature of the job. A model contract is provided at ¶9910.

Some employers, however, find that the statement of particulars is sufficient in which case it will become a written contract of employment if **both parties agree** that the **stated terms are correct** (for example, by signing the statement to that effect) (*Gascol Conversions Ltd v J W Mercer* [1974] IRLR 155, CA).

The statement does not become a contract by virtue only of the employee's **acknowledgement of receipt** (*System Floors (UK) Ltd v Daniel*) or **mere acquiescence** (*Aparau v Iceland Frozen Foods plc* [1996] IRLR 119, EAT). In *Aparau v Iceland Frozen Foods plc*, A did not sign the statement. She did, however, continue to work according to its terms for more than 12 months without objection. This was not enough for the EAT to find that she had impliedly accepted those terms. The statement did not, therefore, constitute the contract.

3. Contents

1420 The statutory statement must contain the following particulars:

Particulars	ERA 1996
Identity of the parties	s 1(3)(a)
Start date	s 1(3)(b)
Date continuous employment began (¶1045)	s 1(3)(c)
Job title or brief description of main characteristics of work*	s 1(4)(f)
Applicable notice period (¶8127)*	s 1(4)(e)
Expected duration (temporary employees) or expiry date (fixed term contracts)	s 1(4)(g)
Place of work or indication that employee may work at various places, a list of those places (where known) and employer's address*	s 1(4)(h)
Hours of work, including terms relating to normal working hours (and overtime)*	s 1(4)(c)
Scale/rate of remuneration and intervals of pay*	s 1(4)(a)(b)
Holiday entitlement, including public holidays, holiday pay and sufficient information to allow precise calculation of entitlement (including on termination)*	s 1(4)(d)(i)
Sickness provisions, including terms relating to incapacity due to sickness or injury, and details of any sick pay provisions*	s 1(4)(d)(ii)
Pension provisions*	s 1(4)(d)(iii)

Particulars	ERA 1996
Contracting out certificate	s 3(5)
Disciplinary rules [1]	s 3(1)(a)
Dismissal, disciplinary and grievance procedures [2]	s 3(1)(aa), (b)
Collective agreements directly affecting terms, and details of parties where employer is not a party	s 1(4)(j)
Work outside UK for more than 1 month, including duration, currency of remuneration, other pay and benefits, and terms relating to return to UK	s 1(4)(k)

* Must be correct as at specified date, which must be no later than 7 days before the date they are provided.
1. These requirements [i.e. the disciplinary rules and the procedures] do not apply to rules, disciplinary decisions, decisions to dismiss, grievances or procedures relating to health or safety at work (s 3(2) ERA 1996, as amended by s 35 EA 2002).
2. With regard to the disciplinary and grievance procedures, the statutory statement must, in all cases, identify to whom and how a grievance or complaint about a disciplinary decision or any decision to dismiss an employee should be made (including details of appeal stages).
Note that the exemption for small employers who employ less than 20 employees on the date the employment began has been removed.

The above list of information to be provided is not exhaustive – the statement must contain particulars of all of the **essential elements** of the contract (*Lange v Georg Schünemann GmbH* [2001] IRLR 244, ECJ). **1421**

4. Statement of no terms

The parties are not obliged to agree terms in relation to the statutory particulars (*Morley v Heritage plc* [1993] IRLR 400, CA). If, in fact, there are **no terms relating to a required particular** (for example, if the employer does not offer any contractual sick pay above the employee's statutory entitlement), the statement should state this (s 2(1) ERA 1996). Applicable disciplinary rules and disciplinary or grievance procedures must nevertheless be stated. **1425**

EXAMPLE In *Morley v Heritage plc*, M was claiming a payment for untaken holiday accrued at the time of the termination of his employment on the basis that the employer was legally required to provide sufficient detail of any terms relating to **holiday pay** so that any such entitlement could be precisely calculated. The Court held that no such provision need be implied into contracts of employment merely because the legislation recognises that employment contracts can include such a provision. Note that the regulations on working time now provide for such a payment to be made (¶4000).

5. Form of statement

Subject to the time limit for provision of the particulars (¶1440), employers can give the statement in **instalments** (ss 1(2), 2(4) ERA 1996). **1430**

However, certain particulars must be **included in a single document**. These are:
- the identity of the parties;
- the start date and date of continuous employment;
- job title;
- place of work;
- hours of work;
- pay details; and
- holiday entitlement.

Reference to other reasonably accessible documents For the following particulars, the statement may refer the employee to another document, as long as this is reasonably accessible, i.e. one which he has reasonable opportunities of reading in the course of his employment, or which is made reasonably accessible to him in some other way, such as the staff handbook or the employer's notice/bulletin board, if this is accessible to all employees (s 6 ERA 1996): **1431**
- the applicable notice period (for this particular, the employer can refer the employee to the relevant statutory provisions or collective agreement if these are reasonably accessible to him);

– sickness;
– pension;
– disciplinary rules; and
– dismissal and disciplinary procedures (although the written particulars must at least identify (i) the person (by description or otherwise) to whom the employee can apply if he is dissatisfied with any disciplinary decision or decision to dismiss him or if he has a grievance, and (ii) how that application should be made, including details of any further appeal stages).

6. Timing

1440 The statement (whether provided in a single document or in instalments) must be provided **within** 2 calendar months of the beginning of the employment (s 1(2) ERA 1996). A contract of employment or letter of engagement given to an employee **before** the beginning of his employment is acceptable (s 7B ERA 1996, as inserted by s 37 EA 2002).

The particulars marked with an asterisk in the table above should be correct as at a specified date not more than 7 days before they are given to the employee (to ensure they are as up-to-date as possible) (s 1(4) ERA 1996).

1441 **Overseas employees** If, before the end of the 2-month period, the employee is due to go overseas to work for more than 1 month, the statement must be provided before he leaves the UK (s 2(5) ERA 1996). Similarly, if he is posted abroad for more than 1 month during the course of his employment, details of the posting must be provided within 1 month or prior to the departure, if earlier.

7. Changes to statement

1450 If there are **any changes** to the statement (for example, a salary increase), the employer must, within 1 month of the change, give the employee a written statement containing details of the change (s 4 ERA 1996). For those terms where there have been no changes, the new statement may refer back to the previous one, indicating that there has been no change.

The change must be notified in a single document (not in instalments) but reference can be made to another reasonably accessible document for the details of the change, as for the original statement (¶1402).

If the change relates to the **name** or **identity of the employer** (where the employee's continuity of employment (¶1010) is preserved), the employer does not need to provide a new statement but must notify the employee in writing of that change and, in the case of a change in the employer's identity, give the date the employee's period of continuous employment began (s 4(6) ERA 1996).

MEMO POINTS If the change involves a change to any **contractual term**, the employer should obtain the employee's consent (¶1601).

8. Enforcement

1460 If the employer fails to provide the statement or to notify a change, or if the statement provided is incorrect, the employee can apply to the employment tribunal for a remedy (s 11 ERA 1996).

Remedies

1461 If, during the course of certain tribunal proceedings (including unfair dismissal and discrimination claims) in which the employment tribunal finds in favour of the employee, it becomes evident that the employer had **failed to provide**:
– a written statement;

– a complete or accurate statement; or
– notification of a change to the written statement

at the date the proceedings were begun, the tribunal must award **minimum compensation** of 2 weeks' pay to the employee and may, if it considers it just and equitable to do so, increase the award to 4 weeks' pay (s 38 EA 2002). This award will be in addition to any damages in respect of the employee's claim which was the subject of the proceedings.

A week's pay is subject to a **statutory cap**. For details of how a week's pay is calculated, see ¶2920.

In addition, an employee can bring a **stand-alone action** in respect of his employer's failure to comply with his duty to provide a statutory statement of written particulars. The remedy will depend on whether the statement was not provided at all, was incomplete or inaccurate, or whether a change was not notified.

No statement, incomplete statement, or failure to notify change If the employer fails to provide a statement, provides an incomplete one, or fails to notify a change, the employee can apply for a determination as to what particulars should have been provided (s 11(1) ERA 1996). Those particulars are then deemed to have been given by the employer (s 12 ERA 1996). 1462

Incorrect statement If the statement provided is incorrect, either the employer or the employee can apply to the tribunal, which can affirm, amend or replace the existing particulars (s 11(2) ERA 1996). If it does, the employer is deemed to have provided the corrected version (s 12 ERA 1996). Again, there is no right of damages for an employee under such an action. 1463

Determining or amending particulars When determining what particulars are missing or how existing particulars ought to be amended, the tribunal must decide whether the term had been agreed orally or by necessary implication (*Mears v Safecar Security Ltd* [1982] IRLR 183, CA). If so, it should be included in the statement. If not, the tribunal is entitled to take account of all the facts and circumstances, in particular the subsequent statements or conduct of the parties and from that, infer the term necessarily agreed by them. 1464

The **tribunal's role** is limited to identifying and declaring the particulars that ought to have been included, and does not extend to interpreting any ambiguous ones (*Construction Industry Training Board v Leighton* [1978] IRLR 60, EAT). In the absence of both express and implied agreement, the tribunal should not invent a term for the parties (*Eagland v British Telecommunications plc* [1992] IRLR 323, CA).

SECTION 4

Staff handbook

The staff handbook (also known as "employee handbook", "company handbook", or "company manual") is a source of **non-contractual rules** of conduct, employee behaviour, rights and miscellaneous information about the company. In addition to non-contractual provisions, the handbook may also contain **statutory particulars** (¶1400) and **contractual terms** of employment (for example, terms relating to holiday entitlement or a policy which the employer wishes his employees to be legally bound by, such as equal opportunities). 1480

The company's rules, policies and procedures make clear what conduct is acceptable/unacceptable, and ensure that employees' conduct and performance meet minimum standards. Policies can also help the employer to comply with his statutory duties, such as his health and safety obligations, and an effective implementation of these policies may provide a defence to employee claims, such as harassment and discrimination. Breach of these provisions may therefore be treated as a disciplinary/capability issue, with disciplinary action being taken as appropriate (¶6538), unless the provision is contractual (either expressly or through custom and practice, see below) in which case any breach (by either the employer or the employee) will give rise to a claim for breach of contract (¶1700).

1482 Employers must make clear (by an express statement where appropriate) which parts of the handbook are contractually binding (¶1155), as an employer should obtain employees' consent to vary contractual terms (¶1601), and breach of such terms will entitle the innocent party to a remedy for breach of contract (¶1700). It is important to note that even if a particular provision or policy is labelled by the parties as "non-contractual", it is possible for such a provision or policy to be deemed contractual (through "**custom and practice**") if it has been followed without exception for a substantial period of time (¶1180).

1485 An example of a staff handbook is given in outline below. The handbook can be used as a source of reference to provide **information on the organisation**, and is an important communication tool, allowing the company to impart a sense of its culture, ethos and goals. As such, the handbook can play an important role in the induction of new employees (¶910), helping them to learn about the company and settle in to their new role. The handbook also serves a practical purpose, informing staff of the benefits, amenities and services available to them.

1486 Some of the **statutory written particulars** (for example, sickness provisions and information on pensions (¶1431)) can be provided in a reasonably accessible document such as the staff handbook. Further, it may be practical to include **provisions of general application** (such as dismissal, discipline and grievance procedures, sick pay and pensions) in the handbook, with variations (if any) applicable to particular employees or groups of employees set out in their individual contracts or issued as a supplement. However, where terms are particular to one individual (such as salary or individually agreed bonus arrangements), they should be included in the individual's contract of employment.

1487 The handbook may contain **rules, policies and procedures** or these may be issued separately. These should be easily accessible to employees, as it is important that they are known and understood by all members of staff. These rules will vary from organisation to organisation, depending on the particular circumstances. It is advisable for them to be in writing, as there is then less scope for misunderstanding.

1490 When **compiling** a new staff handbook, the following **four steps** could be followed:
- consultation;
- design and format;
- issue; and
- updating.

Checklists which set out the usual issues an employer must consider when formulating his rules, policies and procedures are found at ¶9940.

1491 It may be useful to **consult** with:
- trade union and/or employee representatives;
- employees/managers with responsibility for particular areas covered in the handbook; and
- solicitors/the in-house legal department to ensure compliance with the law.

1492 The **language** used should be simple and easy to read. The handbook should be clear and concise, avoiding too much detail. The **presentation** of information should be user-friendly and engaging, with use of diagrams, charts and pictures where appropriate. An index should be included for ease of use. Consideration should be given as to whether it may be necessary to provide **translations** for non-native English speakers.

It is good practice for the staff handbook to be accessible to all staff. As technology advances, it is becoming more common for the handbook to be issued on the company intranet. If the handbook contains statutory particulars (¶1400), it must be **reasonably accessible** to all staff, which may require a hard copy to be distributed.

It may be useful to provide space in the back cover for supplements or amendments to be added. Loose-leaf formats may prove cost effective in that they can be easily updated. The handbook could include space for employees to make their own notes, either in the margin or at the back of the book.

Before issuing the handbook, the employer should ask a number of employees to give **feedback** on content, style and format.

To ensure that all employees can access the handbook, the safest course may be to **issue** a 1493
copy to all employees when they join the company. It is advisable for employees to be asked to return a written acknowledgement of receipt.

The handbook will need to be **updated** from time to time to take account of organisational, 1494
practical and legal changes. If there are any changes to the statutory particulars, in addition to issuing a new statement detailing the change, the handbook may also need to be revised. If the provision to be varied is contractual, the employee's consent should be obtained, unless the employer has already reserved the right to make such changes (¶1615).

Example staff handbook outline 1495

Introduction
- about the company (history, structure, activities, location, mission statement)
- introduction to handbook
- contractual status of contents
- reserve right to change

Terms and conditions
- hours, overtime, time off in lieu
- flexible working
- holiday provisions
- sickness absence/sick pay
- notice periods, lay off arrangements

Remuneration and benefits
- salary/job and salary banding
- expenses
- pensions
- private medical cover
- permanent health insurance
- life assurance
- accident and travel insurance
- company car policy
- season ticket loans
- eye tests
- sports and social
- staff canteen
- parking
- childcare

Core policies and procedures
- family-friendly rights
- equal opportunities
- sex/race/religion or belief/sexual orientation harassment
- disability harassment
- harassment complaints procedure
- disciplinary rules
- disciplinary procedure
- grievance procedure
- whistleblowing
- sickness absence procedure
- data protection

Other policies and guidelines
- change in personal circumstances
- references
- time off for trade union activities and duties
- time off for public duties (e.g. jury service)
- compassionate leave/family emergencies
- relationships at work
- private telephone calls/correspondence
- recording of telephone calls
- right of search
- timekeeping
- dress and appearance
- health and safety, fire, security
- smoking
- drugs/alcohol misuse
- personal property
- public statements
- conflicts of interest/outside employment
- gifts
- protection of intellectual property
- internet and e-mail
- software and computer usage
- company property
- client confidentiality
- disclosure
- trade union policy (membership and representation, recognition and collective bargaining)

Regulations
- dealing rules
- insider dealing
- personal transactions
- money laundering

Career development
- induction
- training
- appraisals/performance reviews
- transfers/secondments

For further discussion on the main policies and procedures, please refer to the specific 1498
chapters which deal with each topic in detail, in particular:
- equality at work (¶5200);
- discipline and grievance (¶6500);

- dress and appearance (¶5826);
- drugs and alcohol (¶4960);
- internet and email (¶6215);
- smoking (¶4980);
- family-friendly rights (¶4400);
- data protection and monitoring (¶5900); and
- company information and confidentiality (¶2300).

Policy checklists are set out at ¶9940.

SECTION 5

Varying terms and conditions

1600 A contract of employment is a legally binding agreement (¶1112), which means that the parties are bound by its terms. However, it is likely that over the course of the employment relationship, the terms of the contract may need to change.

1601 **Employees** may seek to vary the contract, for example by requesting a reduction in working hours or a change from full-time to part-time working to accommodate new domestic responsibilities, or asking for a pay rise. In many cases, the employee's only recourse is to seek the employer's agreement. If the employer does not agree, the employee may decide to accept the situation, resign or, where practical, implement the change, in which case he will be in breach of contract, and (depending on the seriousness of the breach) the employer may be justified in dismissing him.

More commonly, **employers** may want to vary the terms of a contract for various reasons, including the need to react to economic circumstances, to respond to changes in the market place and/or technological advances, or to reorganise the business to make it more efficient or profitable. In particular, an employer may seek to change terms relating to pay or benefits, working hours or shift patterns, duties or place of work. If the change is one which is favourable to the employee he is unlikely to resist it. If, however, the change is unfavourable, there may be scope for dispute. In such circumstances, the change will be a breach of contract unless the employer has a contractual right to vary the contract, obtains the employee's consent, or terminates the existing contract in accordance with its terms and offers a new one containing the variation. These are discussed below.

1602 Changes may also be triggered by sources outside the employer/employee relationship. **Legislation** can impose changes to contract terms. Certain statutory rights, such as the right to maternity pay and to redundancy payments, are automatically implied in employment contracts. If the statute itself changes, the contract will be automatically changed to give the employee an automatic entitlement to the current right. For example, the employee's entitlement to statutory redundancy pay is automatically increased with statutory changes which increase in line with price movements.

The commercial factors involved in a **transfer of undertakings** may give rise to a desire to harmonise terms and conditions, and special considerations will apply in these circumstances. Variation in the context of a business transfer is discussed in detail at ¶8010.

Changes may be negotiated between the employer and a trade union, resulting in amendments to applicable **collective agreements**. The incorporation of collective agreements is discussed at ¶1275, and, given that amendments to collective agreements must also be incorporated into the individual contract of employment, variations involving collective agreements are also discussed in that section.

1603 The variation may have several **legal implications**. For example, it may infringe legislation on discrimination or equal pay, constitute an unlawful deduction from wages, or give rise to a claim of unfair dismissal. The employer must take care to observe the working time regulations, restrictions on Sunday working, and take into account any health and safety considerations when varying any terms.

The **means of variation** will depend on whether the change relates to a non-contractual provision or a contractual term. 1604

Non-contractual provisions can be varied by the employer at any time, without the need for employee consent (¶1482). In addition to variations following changes in the law or an applicable collective agreement, **contractual terms** can be varied by any of the following means:
- by virtue of a contractual right;
- by agreement (either express or implied); or
- by the employer unilaterally imposing a change.

If contractual terms have effectively been varied and the variation relates to any of the **written particulars** that the employer is obliged to provide (¶1420), the employer must, within 1 month of the change, issue a new statement of particulars giving details of the change. A failure to do so will not affect the variation, but will entitle the employee to a remedy for failure to provide the statutory particulars. 1605

The employer cannot vary contractual terms merely by amending the statement of written particulars, as it is usually only evidence of the terms of the contract, rather than the contract itself. However, if the employee continues to work without protest after receiving the amended statement, this may provide evidence that he has impliedly agreed to the new terms (¶1640).

A. Contractual right to vary

The employer may have a contractual right to vary the contract either because it is sufficiently broadly drafted so that the proposed variation falls within its scope, or because there is an express or implied right in the contract to make that variation. 1615

If the employer has a contractual right to vary, the employee will be in breach of contract if he refuses to comply with the new terms.

1. Scope of existing terms

The terms of the contract can be express, implied (by the courts or by statute), or incorporated (by reference to other documents, such as collective agreements). A proposed change may in fact be within the scope of the existing contract terms, in which case the employer does not need to seek the employee's consent. Whether the change is within the scope will **depend on** the construction of the contract. Case law has shown that the ambit of an employee's contractual obligations, especially in **small companies**, may be wider than the ambit of the duties that he actually performs (*Glitz v Watford Electric Co Ltd* [1979] IRLR 89, EAT). 1616

EXAMPLE 1. In *Cresswell v Board of Inland Revenue* [1984] IRLR 190, ChD, the employees were instructed to transfer from a manual accounting system onto a computerised one. They resisted this **new method of work**, but the Court held that their contracts required them to adapt to new techniques and methods of carrying out work within the scope of their duties.

2. In *Glitz v Watford Electric Co Ltd*, G's **job description** in her contract referred to her position as a copy typist/general clerical duties clerk. The employer moved her to operate a duplicator machine and the Court held that such a task fell within the ambit of general clerical duties, given the small number of clerical staff in a small office and the resulting need for flexibility.

2. Express right

Flexibility clauses

1618 The contract of employment may contain an express flexibility clause, i.e. one that gives the employer the right to make unilateral changes to a specific contract term (for example, the employee's job duties or location), or to the terms in general.

If the clause gives the employer a **general right** to vary terms, the extent of that right will be limited to changes of a minor and non-fundamental nature (*United Associated for the Protection of Trade v Kilburn*, EAT case 787/84). If the employer makes significant changes, the employee may still be able to claim constructive dismissal (¶8230).

A common example of a specific flexibility clause is a **mobility clause** that gives the employer the right to move the employee to another location without seeking the employee's consent at the time of the transfer (*Rank Xerox v Churchill* [1988] IRLR 280, EAT). However, an employer should consider whether such a clause could amount to a discriminatory work condition before requiring such a provision in a contract of employment (¶5200).

1619 If the employer has a contractual right to change terms (for example, where the employer reserves the right in contractual work rules to make changes to them without employee consent), an employee will have no redress if the employer exercises that right, even where benefits are withdrawn as part of that change (*Cadoux v Central Regional Council* [1986] IRLR 131, CS).

1621 **Interpretation** The courts will take a strict approach to the interpretation of flexibility clauses. Careful drafting (in particular, clear language) is crucial for various reasons, including the fact that, due to a legal rule of construction, any **ambiguity** is resolved against the person seeking to rely on it. If, therefore, a flexibility clause is unclear, it will be construed against the employer (*Bainbridge v Circuit Foil UK Ltd* [1997] IRLR 305, CA).

Further, the courts will construe the flexibility clause to see if its **scope** extends to cover the circumstances of the particular variation, and they will not readily interpret the contract so as to enable a party to vary contractual provisions with which he is required to comply (*Wandsworth London Borough Council v D'Silva and another* [1998] IRLR 193, CA). Therefore, it is advisable that care is taken when drafting the clause to ensure that contemplated changes fall within its scope. For example, if the employer wishes to be able to change the number of hours worked by the employees as part of a right to alter shift patterns, it is advisable to reserve a specific right to do so.

EXAMPLE 1. In *National Semiconductor (UK) Ltd v Church*, EAT case 252/97 and *SmithKline Beecham plc v Johnson*, EAT case 559/96, the EAT held that clauses which gave the employers the right to vary existing **shift patterns** did not extend to giving them the right to increase or reduce the **number of hours worked**.
2. In *Baynham v Philips Electronics* (UK) Ltd, 7 July 1995 (unreported), QBD, the employer was contractually obliged to provide healthcare cover to a number of former employees. An express term permitting the employer to vary the contract was held by the Court to be intended to apply to matters such as changes to duties and job title, and did not permit the employer to withdraw the healthcare **after the employment had terminated**.
3. In *Land Securities Trillium Ltd v Thorney* [2005] IRLR 765, EAT, the EAT held that a clause which stated that the employee would "perform to the best of your abilities...**any other duties which may reasonably be required** of you and will at all times obey all reasonable instructions given to you" did **not give** the employer **carte blanche** to require the employee to undertake any duties they wished her to but expressly imposed a requirement of reasonableness on the employer's request.

1623 **Implied limitations** The employer is obliged by an implied term to exercise a flexibility clause on reasonable grounds (¶1242) and, although there is no implied term requiring him to operate the clause in a reasonable manner, he may also be restricted by the implied term of mutual trust and confidence (¶1245), for example, where a transfer to other work involves a drop in pay. Business efficacy (¶1174) may also require the employer to give reasonable notice of the exercise of the clause.

EXAMPLE **Transfer involving a drop in pay**

In *White v Reflecting Roadstuds* [1991] IRLR 331, EAT, *BPCC Purnell Ltd v Webb* EAT case 129/90, and *Hussman Manufacturing Ltd v Weir* [1998] IRLR 288, EAT, White, Webb and Weir were transferred to **alternative work**, from **one department to another**, and from the **night-shift to the day-shift** respectively. In White's case, the EAT held that the resulting drop in pay did not breach the duty of trust and confidence, whilst in Webb's case it did because Webb's wages dropped from £305 to £225. In Weir's case, the EAT held that a drop in wages would only breach the implied term in exceptional cases, and Weir's decrease of £17 per week was not such a case.

Relocation

In *United Bank Ltd v Akhtar* [1989] IRLR 507, EAT, A was given very little notice of his **transfer from Leeds to Birmingham** and was not given any relocation allowance, which was at the discretion of the employer. As a matter of business efficacy, the employer's right to exercise the mobility clause was subject to a duty:
- to give reasonable notice;
- not to exercise his discretion to provide relocation expenses in such a way as to prevent the employee from performing his contractual duties; and
- not to act in such a way as to undermine the relationship of mutual trust and confidence.

Sex discrimination A mobility clause may be challenged on the grounds that it constitutes sex discrimination, in that it has a disproportionately adverse effect on workers of one of the sexes (often women) compared with workers of the opposite sex. If so, the clause will be indirectly discriminatory and will not be valid unless it can be objectively justified by the employer (¶5310). The Court of Appeal has ruled that a mobility clause was indirectly discriminatory against women since women were more likely than men to be "second earners" and, consequently, would find it harder than men to relocate (*Mende-Hill and the National Union of Civil and Public Servants v British Council* [1995] IRLR 478, CA). 1625

Redundancy A mobility or flexibility clause that allows the employer to transfer the employee to other locations or other duties may have an impact in redundancy situations. For example, if work is no longer available at the employee's place of work, the employee may be taken to be redundant and the legal rules regarding redundancy would apply. If the employee can be required to work at other locations, he may attempt to argue that he is not technically redundant if work is available at such locations. However, the courts currently give more weight to where the employee actually worked (as opposed to where he may be required to work), so that if an express mobility clause has not been exercised in practice, it will not affect the redundancy situation. 1627

3. Implied right

The employer may be taken to have an implied right to change contract terms if the change is needed to give the contract **business efficacy** (¶1174), i.e. to make the contract work and, by extension, to ensure that the business (to which the employment relates) continues. The term must be both "necessary" and "obvious". It could involve changes in work practices to take account of changed market conditions, but is unlikely to be able to be used to reduce pay rates. 1630

Implied mobility clause A term is often implied that the employee is expected to work **within reasonable daily travelling distance of his home** (*Jones v Associated Tunnelling Co Ltd* [1981] IRLR 477, EAT). Therefore, if the employer moves the employee from one place of work to another (which is, for example, no further from his home than the first), the employer may not need an express right to do so and may not be, therefore, in breach of contract. However, other factors will also be relevant, including whether the move from one location to another may entail a loss of status (for example, the EAT identified a distinction between a central London legal secretary and a suburban one (*Blatchfords Solicitors v Berger*, EAT case 207/00)). However, where a mobility clause is not needed to make the contract work, the courts will decline to imply any term as to mobility at all (*Aparau v Iceland Frozen Foods plc* [1996] IRLR 119, EAT). 1631

As the scope of implied mobility clauses is uncertain, it is preferable for express mobility clauses to be used if employees may be required to move workplace.

B. Mutual agreement

1635 If there is no right in the contract to vary terms and conditions, the contract, in common with other legal agreements, can be varied by the mutual agreement of the parties to it. This agreement can be **express or implied**.

1636 **Consideration** As with any type of contract, a variation will not be binding if there is no consideration for it. For example, the employer may offer to give the employee an **extra day's holiday** in return for the employee agreeing to work longer hours. If the employer wants to promote the employee to a position with more responsibility, the consideration is usually an **increase in salary**.

In the context of **pay negotiations**, the consideration for the pay rise is the settlement of the pay claim and the continuation of the same employee in the same employment (*Lee v GEC Plessey Telecommunications* [1993] IRLR 383, QBD).

It may be possible to rely on the offer of **continued employment** as the consideration for the agreement to vary the existing terms.

1. Express agreement

1638 The parties can agree **orally or in writing** to a variation to the original contract (note that an agreement by e-mail is likely to amount to an agreement in writing (¶6222)). For example, if an employer wishes to change work practices, he could seek the employee's agreement, possibly in return for a pay increase. If the employee agrees, the contract is amended to take account of the change. Pay rises and promotions are common agreed variations to the original contract. However, both parties must intend to enter into a legally binding agreement for any variation to be enforceable (*Judge v Crown Leisure Ltd*, EAT case 0443/04) (¶1117).

It is preferable for such an agreement to be in writing, as there is more scope for dispute with oral agreements, in which case it would be a question of evidence as to whether a variation had been agreed (*Simmonds v Dowty Seals Ltd* [1978] IRLR 211, EAT).

Of course, there will be no agreement if the employee was forced to accept the change, for example by threat of dismissal.

2. Implied agreement

1640 Over the course of the employment relationship, certain terms may change without any formal agreement having been reached. For example, new methods of work may be introduced, including the introduction of new machines, or the employee may take on a new task. Where a change is introduced or imposed by the employer and the **employee continues to work without protest** for a significant period of time whilst being aware of that change, the employee may be taken impliedly to have agreed to the change, and there will be no breach of contract by the employer.

1641 Whether implied agreement can be identified will depend on various factors, including the employee's conduct and the nature of the change. There may be uncertainty as to whether the worker's subsequent conduct is evidence of an affirmation of the new terms. In *Henry v London General Transport Services Ltd* [2002] IRLR 474, CA, the Court affirmed the principle that when an employee **makes clear his objection** to work that is being done under new terms of employment imposed by the employer, he will not be taken as having affirmed the contract by continuing to work and to draw pay for a limited period of time. However, if the employee does **not make his objection known** and complies with the new terms such compliance will normally show that he has accepted them. Similarly, if an employee indicates that he accepts the new terms and conditions only "**under duress**", this will not be sufficient to constitute working under protest (unless there is sufficient duress in the legal sense to negate the employee's consent) and will not be sufficient to invalidate the variation (*Hepworth Heating Ltd v Akers*, EAT case 846/02).

However, the fact that an employee has continued to work without protest after the introduction of a varied term does not necessarily mean he has consented to the change. In such circumstances, **great caution** should be exercised before finding an implied acceptance of the new term, especially if the new term does not have **immediate effect** (*Jones v Associated Tunnelling Co Ltd* [1981] IRLR 477, EAT). 1642

EXAMPLE In *Aparau v Iceland Frozen Foods plc* [1996] IRLR 119, EAT, A's employer issued her with new terms and conditions of employment that contained a mobility clause. A did not sign and return the copy, but continued to work under the new conditions for **more than 12 months**. The EAT held that it could not be accepted that A had impliedly accepted the new terms as the clause had **no immediate practical effect**. The effect would only be felt if and when the employer attempted to exercise the mobility clause.

If it can be implied from the employee's conduct that he has **agreed to the variation**, there will be no breach of contract by the employer, so the employee will have no claim for damages, and will not be able to resign and claim constructive dismissal. 1643

MEMO POINTS It should be noted that the fact that employees have **previously expressly agreed to a variation** of their terms and conditions (for example, the imposition of short-time working) does not mean that there is an ongoing implied agreement to work on varied terms and conditions in the future (*International Packaging Corporation (UK) Ltd v Balfour* [2003] IRLR 11, EAT). An employer cannot therefore make unilateral variations (see below) on this basis.

C. Unilateral variation by the employer

If the employer has no contractual right to vary and the employee is unwilling to agree to a variation, the employer can either abandon his proposed changes or insist on implementing them. 1645

If the employer insists on implementing the changes, he will be in **breach of contract** and this method of introducing a change therefore carries the highest risk of legal liability. The new terms are not legally binding on an employee unless he **accepts** them (either expressly or impliedly, i.e. by not protesting), in which case the change will be agreed and the employer will not be liable for breach of contract. 1646

Where the variation involves a reduction in wages or other change to remuneration, the employee may also be able to bring a claim of **unlawful deductions from wages** (¶3050). 1647

1. Breach of contract

Any unilateral change amounts to a breach of contract, which gives the employee the right to a remedy, which may include damages or an injunction, or (in certain circumstances) compensation for unlawful deduction from wages (¶3080). If the variation affects a **large number of employees**, the unions may be involved in seeking redress on their behalf. 1650

It is no defence for the employer to show that he had sound business reasons for imposing the change or that he acted reasonably in the circumstances (although these may be a defence in cases of unfair dismissal (¶1665)).

Repudiatory or fundamental breach

Where the breach is fundamental (¶1701), the employee who rejects the change has **several options**: 1651

– he can continue to work under the new terms (whilst making his rejection of them clear to the employer), and seek a remedy for breach of contract (¶1700). Further, if the change involves radically different terms, the courts may consider the employee to have been unfairly dismissed from his old contract (¶1652);

– where practical, he can continue to work under the old terms and refuse to work under the new ones (for example, those relating to hours of work or job duties). If he is dismissed in these circumstances, the employee could bring claims of unfair and wrongful dismissal; or

– he can resign and claim that he has been constructively dismissed (¶8230), in which case the employer may be liable for both wrongful and unfair dismissal and will not usually be able to rely on any post-termination obligations or restrictive covenants.

2. Imposition of new contract

1652 The unilateral imposition of **radically different terms** may be interpreted as a dismissal of the employee from the old contract and the immediate entry into a new contract on different terms. For example, where the variation involves a complete change in the employee's job content and the employee continues to work, he will be treated as having accepted the termination of the old contract and entered into a new contract. This may allow the employee to claim that he has been **unfairly dismissed** from the old contract (*Hogg v Dover College* [1990] ICR 39, EAT). Whether the imposition of a new contract can be identified depends on a careful assessment of the surrounding circumstances, and will be a matter of fact and degree in each case (*London Borough of Southwark v Mungul*, EAT case 1359/99). If the changes are found not to amount to a withdrawal of the old contract, the court may find that the imposition of new terms amounts to a repudiatory breach which the employee has waived by continuing to work without complaint.

EXAMPLE 1. In *Hogg v Dover College*, the employer introduced new terms giving H lower status, shorter working hours and less pay. The EAT held that he could claim that he had been unfairly dismissed from his old contract.

2. In *Alcan Extrusions v Yates and others* [1996] IRLR 327, EAT, Y worked under a shift system that operated from Monday to Saturday morning, and was paid overtime for working at weekends and on bank holidays. The employers fundamentally changed the system by introducing a continuous rolling shift pattern, changing hours of work and including weekends and bank holidays, thereby affecting Y's overtime. Holiday provisions, shift premiums and start-up payments were also changed to Y's detriment. The EAT held that the new terms were so radically different from the old that Y could be said to have been dismissed from the old contract.

1653 The **terms of the new contract** will be a matter of construction (*S W Strange Ltd v Mann* [1965] 1 All ER 1069, ChD). The courts will, therefore, attempt to identify the intention of the parties (¶1118).

3. Dismissal and re-engagement

1655 If the employee refuses to agree to a change that the employer is determined to introduce, rather than vary contracts unilaterally the employer could terminate the existing contract and offer a new one that includes the variation. If he gives the appropriate **notice of termination** (¶8120) (and complies with any other contractual obligations relating to the termination of employment), there will be no breach of contract as a result of taking such action, thus avoiding liability for **wrongful dismissal** and constructive dismissal claims. If no notice is given and the employee refuses a reasonable offer of employment on new terms, an award of compensation for wrongful dismissal may be reduced by reason of his **failure to mitigate** his loss (*Marenghi v Western Baths Club*, EAT case 1508/00) (¶8171).

The notice of termination must be clear and unambiguous. A notice from the employer that he is only willing to continue to employ the employee after a period of notice on revised terms is unlikely to be construed as notice of dismissal and re-engagement (*Burdett-Coutts v Hertfordshire County Council* [1984] IRLR 91, QBD).

If the employee accepts the new contract and starts working under it immediately following the termination of the old contract, **statutory continuity** is preserved. 1656

Termination of the existing contract will be a dismissal for unfair dismissal purposes, and qualifying employees will therefore be able to bring an **unfair dismissal** claim (*Banerjee v City and East London Area Health Authority* [1979] IRLR 147, EAT; *St John of God (Care Services) Ltd v Brooks* [1992] IRLR 546, EAT). However, an employee who is offered a new contract on reasonable terms without substantial changes is unlikely to be awarded much (if anything) by way of compensatory award if he succeeds in claiming unfair dismissal. The employee will, however, normally receive the basic award in full (¶8575). 1657

The employee may also be eligible for a **redundancy payment** (¶8990). If twenty or more employees are dismissed, there may be collective redundancy **consultation obligations** (¶8916). 1658

Negotiated settlements If the employer dismisses and re-engages an employee on reasonable terms, the employer could consider offering a **financial inducement**, calculated by reference to the unfair dismissal basic award, to persuade the employee to accept changes in terms of employment. In such circumstances, it is advisable for the employer to **seek a waiver** (in a compromise agreement) of the employee's right to bring an unfair dismissal claim in connection with the variation of his employment terms (¶9322). 1659

4. Liability for unfair dismissal

If the employer dismisses an employee who refuses to agree to a variation, or if the employer imposes a change in fundamental breach of contract causing the employee to resign and claim constructive dismissal, the employee may be able to claim that he has been unfairly dismissed. 1665

Fair reason In order to avoid liability for unfair dismissal, the employer must show that he has one of the five statutory fair reasons for dismissal. In some cases, **redundancy** may be pleaded, but the most common statutory reason put forward is the catch-all "**some other substantial reason**" (SOSR). This is discussed in detail at ¶8530. 1666

Where the employee claims **constructive dismissal**, the employer must be able to justify the variation that caused the employee to resign and treat himself as dismissed.

Fair procedure In addition to having a statutory fair reason, the employer must also be able to show that he acted fairly in all the circumstances in dismissing for the statutory fair reason. See ¶8550 for further discussion. 1667

Automatic unfair dismissal It is automatically unfair to dismiss an employee because he brought proceedings against the employer or alleged that the employer had infringed a relevant statutory right. In the context of a variation of employment terms, the employee may have asserted his right not to have unlawful deductions from wages (¶8395). 1668

5. Redundancy issues

The implementation of changes to employees' terms and conditions may give rise to a redundancy situation (¶8745). Redundancy is a **statutory fair reason for dismissal**, and may therefore be a defence to an unfair dismissal claim. 1675

Individual redundancy If the employer wishes to **dismiss and re-engage** the employee (¶1655), his offer of employment on revised terms may constitute an offer of suitable alternative employment, in which case an employee who unreasonably refuses the offer would not be entitled to a redundancy payment in respect of the termination of the "old" job. If an employee accepts the new terms, his redundancy entitlement is rolled-over into the new 1676 contract as his **continuity of employment** is preserved if he commences the new contract within 4 weeks following the termination of the old contract. The employee is allowed a 4-week "**trial period**" in redundancy cases where there is re-engagement on revised terms.

1677 **Collective redundancy** If the employer proposes to impose measures involving the termination of existing contracts in respect of a group of **twenty or more employees** at one establishment within a period of 90 days or less, the dismissals will give rise to a redundancy situation for **collective consultation** purposes (¶8916) where the reason(s) for the dismissal do not relate to the individuals concerned (*GMB Man Truck & Bus UK* [2000] IRLR 636, EAT). This often occurs where employees are dismissed and re-engaged in order to harmonise terms following the sale of a business subject to the transfer regulations (¶7900). The employer will be obliged to consult trade union representatives or employee representatives, in addition to consulting individually with employees.

SECTION 6

Breach of contract

1700 It is important to distinguish between non-binding provisions and binding contractual terms (¶1112) as the innocent party can only bring a claim for breach of a contract in respect of a **binding contractual term**, whether this is express or implied.

The circumstances giving rise to a breach of contract may also support **other claims** (such as unfair dismissal). Conversely, a dismissal in accordance with the terms of the contract may still be unfair for statutory purposes. Certain **disclosures** of a breach of contract will also bring the employee within the protection of the whistleblowing legislation (¶2700).

1701 The remedies available will depend on whether the breach is fundamental or not. A **fundamental breach** is one that is serious enough to be considered to be a repudiation of the contract. This will depend on the circumstances of the case, but to be fundamental the breach must go to the root of the contract and be incompatible with the continuance of the employment relationship (i.e. the party committing it clearly no longer intends to be bound by the terms of the contract). The **innocent party** may choose to treat himself as discharged from the duty to perform the contract any further, thus terminating it (although he must do so within a reasonable time of the breach). Alternatively, he can waive the breach (in which case the contract is "affirmed", i.e. it continues), and seek another remedy. In either case, he can claim damages.

1702 The most common remedy for a breach of contract is an action for **damages**. Other remedies include the equitable remedies of **injunction** and **declaration** of the parties' rights.

1703 The parties can **pre-agree** the amount of compensation payable in the event of a breach of contract (most commonly, premature termination) by way of an agreed or liquidated damages clause, thus avoiding the need for legal action. Such a clause will be **enforceable** if it is a genuine pre-estimate of the loss likely to result from the early termination (*Dunlop Pneumatic Tyre Co Ltd v New Garage and Motor Co Ltd* [1915] AC 79, HL). If it is not, it may (depending on its construction in the light of the contract as a whole and the surrounding circumstances as at the time the contract was made) be held **unenforceable** for being a penalty clause. The pre-agreed amount should, therefore, not be "extravagant and unconscionable" in comparison with the greatest conceivable loss, nor should the same fixed sum be payable for a range of breaches regardless of the amount of loss suffered.

EXAMPLE In *Giraud UK Ltd v Smith* [2000] IRLR 763, EAT, S's contract allowed the employer to deduct a sum from his final payment in the event that he failed to give notice and work out his notice period. This was held to be a penalty clause as it was not a genuine pre-estimate of loss as the employer was not restrained from recovering his actual loss if this was greater than the pre-agreed sum.

To obtain a remedy, the innocent party should **apply to** the courts or, in some circumstances (depending on the monetary value of the claim, the remedy sought, and whether the breach arises, or is outstanding, on termination (¶9425)), the employment tribunals. 1704

I. Employee remedies

If the employer's breach is **fundamental** (see below for examples), the employee is entitled to resign and claim that he has been constructively dismissed. If he chooses not to (i.e. he waives the breach), or if the breach is **not fundamental**, he can bring an action for damages, arrears of salary or other payment, or bring a statutory claim in respect of wages unlawfully deducted, as appropriate. 1710

Where **damages are not an appropriate remedy** (for example, where working hours are changed with no resulting financial loss), the court may grant a declaration (setting out the employer's obligations) and/or an injunction (requiring him to fulfil those obligations) (*MacRuary v Washington Irvine Ltd*, EAT case 857/93).

EXAMPLE In *Rigby v Ferodo Ltd* [1987] IRLR 516, HL, the employer's unilateral reduction of the employee's contractual wages was a fundamental breach of contract. R did not accept the breach as repudiation of the contract, but rather **continued working**, indicating nevertheless that the variation was unacceptable to him. He successfully sued for damages for sums due under the contract, i.e. by reference to the level of his wages prior to the employer's unilateral reduction.

Timing of claims Where the employee can present his claim to an **employment tribunal**, he must do so **within** 3 months of the effective date of termination (¶8345) (or, where there is no such date, within 3 months of the last day on which the employee worked). The time limits can be **extended** for such period as the tribunal considers reasonable if it is satisfied that it was not reasonably practicable to present the claim in time. If the claim is brought in the **High Court or county courts**, it must be presented within 6 years of the date of the breach. 1711

Pre-employment breaches The employee need not have commenced employment in order to bring a breach of contract claim, as if he has **accepted an unconditional offer** of employment there is a valid contract. Therefore, if the employer terminates the contract before the start date, the employee can bring a wrongful dismissal claim (¶8155) (*Sarker v South Tees Acute Hospitals NHS Trust* [1997] IRLR 328, EAT), and possibly a discrimination or unfair dismissal claim (where no period of qualifying service is required, e.g. for reasons relating to pregnancy or trade union membership). 1712

A. Constructive dismissal

If the employer commits a fundamental breach of contract, the employee is entitled to **treat himself as discharged**, i.e. he may resign and claim that he has been constructively dismissed (¶8230). 1715

A breach often arises in the context of a **variation** of terms and conditions. Whether a variation amounts to a fundamental breach is a question for the courts. If an employee is to claim that he has been constructively dismissed, he must choose within a **reasonable time** to treat the varied contract as at an end, otherwise he will normally be taken to have affirmed the variation to his terms and conditions (*Western Excavating (ECC) Ltd v Sharp* [1978] IRLR 27, CA; see also ¶8242). If there has been a **delay** before the employee resigns (for example, whilst pursuing a formal grievance), the entire period of delay should be taken into account in deciding whether the claim can be upheld and not just the period between the end of the formal grievance period and the employee's subsequent resignation (*Cow v Surrey and Berkshire Newspapers Ltd*, EAT case 716/02).

There is **no affirmation** of an employee's contract where, even if he does not indicate that he is working under protest, his behaviour demonstrates that he has no intention of returning to work under the circumstances that resulted in a material breach (*Forbes v Salamis (Marine & Industrial) Ltd*, EAT case 0085/03). Furthermore, simply by drawing sick pay during this period does not indicate that he has affirmed the contract and this is neutral as to that effect.

EXAMPLE Variation amounting to fundamental breach
- a deliberate reduction of an employee's **pay**, whatever the amount of the reduction (*Cantor Fitzgerald International v Callaghan* [1999] IRLR 234, CA);
- a decision to reduce **wage levels** following the termination of a local collective agreement, despite the fact that the previous collectively agreed rate had been incorporated into the individual's contract (*Gibbons v Associated British Ports* [1985] IRLR 376, QBD);
- a change of **job duties** (*Genower v Ealing Hammersmith and Hounslow Area Health Authority* [1980] IRLR 297, EAT) or an instruction (not contemplated by the contract) to employees to cease their normal work and carry out other work (*Hughes v London Borough of Southwark* [1988] IRLR 55, QBD);
- a decision to put a salaried employee on **short-time working** where his contract did not include a right to do so, and neither he nor his union had given their agreement (*Miller v Hamworthy Engineering Ltd* [1986] IRLR 461, CA);
- a proposal (i.e. an anticipatory breach) unilaterally to vary **working hours** and to serve notice of dismissal if the employee refused to agree (*Greenaway Harrison Ltd v Wiles* [1994] IRLR 380, EAT);
- replacement of full-time work by **part-time and temporary work** (*Hogg v Dover College* [1990] ICR 39, EAT);
- seeking to impose new terms and conditions in an **aggressive manner**, giving only perfunctory and misleading explanations as to the effect of the new terms (*Cantor Fitzgerald International v Bird and others* [2002] IRLR 867, QBD);
- failure to take **reasonable care for the health and safety** of the employee (*Marshall Specialist Vehicles Limited v Osborne* [2003] IRLR 672, EAT); and
- a unilateral decision to stop an employee **working at home** if the employee can establish that he is contractually entitled to work at home and if it impacts significantly on the employee's working practices (*France v Westminster City Council*, EAT case 0214/02).

1716 The implied term of **trust and confidence** introduces a grey area, in that the application of the term can be wide-ranging. Examples of breaches of that term might include changing non-contractual conditions of employment such that the employee feels less secure about his position, removing support systems (e.g. other employees who assist the employee) so that the employee cannot do his job, changing reporting lines so that it appears that management has lost confidence in the employee or, as in *Blackburn with Darwen Borough Council v Stanley*, EAT case 0429/04, an ongoing failure to address an employee's complaints of bullying and harassment (either through a company procedure or otherwise). A breach of this implied term will always be fundamental (*Morrow v Safeway Stores plc* [2002] IRLR 9, EAT).

1717 In some cases, breaches by the employer may have a **cumulative effect**, such that, taken together, they amount to repudiatory conduct breaching the implied obligation of trust and confidence (¶8234).

1718 The employee may be justified in resigning if the employer indicates that he intends to commit a fundamental breach (an "**anticipatory breach**"). This is discussed further at ¶8233.

1719 An employee who has been constructively dismissed may seek compensation for wrongful dismissal and/or unfair dismissal. In either case, the calculation of damages will be based on the same approach as would be taken where the employer has actually terminated the employment.

B. Damages

The **aim of any award** of damages is to put the employee into the position he would have been in had the employer performed his obligations in accordance with its terms. Employment tribunal awards are subject to a statutory cap (¶9428) (the High Court and the county court are not subject to these limits). 1725

An employer can be held liable in damages for breach of **any express or implied term** of the contract of employment. For example, damages may be awarded for breach of the following duties:
- to give the required period of **notice** to terminate the employment;
- to **pay** for work done; and
- to observe the duty of **mutual trust and confidence**.

A termination of employment in breach of contract (most commonly for failure to give the required period of notice) is known as **wrongful dismissal**. See ¶8156 and following for details on calculating damages in these circumstances.

Damages awarded will be linked to any **financial loss** suffered, with no award for injured feelings or distress (*Johnson v Unisys Ltd* [2001] IRLR 279, HL, see also *Dunnachie v Kingston upon Hull City Council* [2004] UKHL 36, HL), as such damages are only recoverable where the object of the breached contract was specifically to provide pleasure, relaxation, or entertainment (*Bliss v South East Thames Regional Health Authority* [1985] IRLR 308, CA). 1726

Damages may also be recovered for the financial losses associated with **psychiatric illness** suffered as a result of a contractual breach (¶4945). 1727

C. Other remedies

Action for arrears of salary/other payments

As long as he can prove that he worked or was ready and willing to carry out his contractual duties, the employee may have a debt action for arrears of salary if the **employer has withheld payment** of salary (or other sums or benefits) due under the contract (*Miles v Wakefield Metropolitan District Council* [1987] IRLR 193, HL). 1730

MEMO POINTS 1. The employee may not be entitled to bring an action for arrears if he only gives **partial performance** (¶3007), or the employer **terminates without notice** (the employee's remedy will be damages for wrongful dismissal (see above)) (*Gunton v Richmond-upon-Thames London Borough Council* [1980] IRLR 321, CA).
2. If the breach involves a reduction in wages or other change to remuneration, the employee may alternatively be able to bring a claim of **unlawful deductions from wages** (¶3050).

Injunctions

The High Court and county courts (but not the employment tribunal) have the power to grant injunctions (orders requiring a party to do or not do a particular thing), which is an equitable remedy. As time may be a crucial issue (for example, where the employee is about to be dismissed), the courts can order an **interlocutory** (i.e. temporary) injunction. The circumstances in which injunctions will be granted are discussed in detail below. They will not normally be granted where **other procedures** are more appropriate (for example, in the case of unpaid wages the employee could make an application for summary judgment in an action for arrears of salary (see above) (*Jakeman v South West Thames Regional Health Authority and London Ambulance Service* [1990] IRLR 62, QBD)). 1732

1733 The court can impose **conditions** when granting an injunction, for example, that the employee will work in accordance with the employer's instructions (*Wadcock v London Borough of Brent* [1990] IRLR 223, ChD).

1734 The granting of an injunction is subject to the **general rule** that there cannot be specific performance of a contract of employment, i.e. the courts will not order the performance of a contract of employment where this would involve requiring an employee to work for an employer (or force an employer to allow the employee to work for him), when the employer has sought to terminate that employment.

1735 The courts will only grant an injunction in **exceptional circumstances** to enforce a contractual term where there is still mutual trust and confidence between employer and employee. It will only do so if it is clear on the evidence (taking into account the nature of the work, the people with whom the work must be done and the likely effect on the employer and his operations) that the employer still has sufficient confidence in the employee's ability and other necessary attributes for it to be reasonable to make the order, and that it is just in all the circumstances to do so (*Powell v Brent London Borough Council* [1987] IRLR 466, CA). In particular, an injunction may be granted where the parties agree that the employment contract subsists, and should subsist, in some form, such that the provisions to be enforced can be put into effect without requiring any greater degree of contact and mutual co-operation than the parties themselves are prepared to accept (such as the implementation of contractual disciplinary procedures when an employee is on suspension (*Peace v City of Edinburgh Council* [1999] IRLR 417, CS)).

EXAMPLE 1. In *Irani v Southampton and South-West Hampshire Health Authority* [1985] IRLR 203, ChD, an injunction was granted restraining the employer from dismissing the employee before completing a **contractual disputes procedure**.

2. In *Barros D'Sa v University Hospital Coventry and Warwickshire NHS Trust* [2001] IRLR 691, CA, an injunction was granted to restrain the employer from dismissing the employee where he had acted outside the **contractual disciplinary procedure**.

3. In *Peace v City of Edinburgh Council*, P was on disciplinary suspension. The Court granted an injunction restraining an anticipated breach of contract on the basis that it did not compel the resumption of duties, but rather prohibited the employer choosing to implement **alternative disciplinary procedures** in place of older contractual ones.

4. In *Hughes v London Borough of Southwark* [1988] IRLR 55, QBD, an injunction was granted restraining the employer from **implementing an instruction** (that the employees should cease their normal work and carry out other work) that the employer was **not entitled to give**.

5. In *Anderson v Pringle of Scotland* [1998] IRLR 64, CS, the employer was restrained from dismissing the employee in breach of a **contractual redundancy selection procedure**. In contrast, in *Alexander v Standard Telephones & Cables Ltd* [1990] IRLR 55, ChD and *(No. 2)* [1991] IRLR 286, QBD, the High Court refused to grant an injunction to enforce contractual redundancy procedures based on seniority as the selection had been made on the basis of capability, which indicated that the employer had less confidence in A than in the retained employees. A's remedy was in damages only.

6. In *Wishart v National Association of Citizens Advice Bureaux Ltd* [1990] IRLR 393, CA, W accepted an **offer of employment** which was conditional on receipt of satisfactory references. The Association was not satisfied with the references received and the Court refused to grant an injunction to require it to allow W to start work as W had been rejected on grounds of suitability, thus indicating that the Association would have no confidence in him to do the job.

7. In *Hill v C A Parsons & Co Ltd* [1971] 3 All ER 1345, CA, an injunction was granted restraining wrongful dismissal in order to enable the employer to **resist external pressure** from trade unions.

Declarations

1740 An employee can apply to the courts for a declaration of his rights (*Gunton v Richmond-upon-Thames London Borough Council* [1980] IRLR 321, CA). However, a declaration cannot require the employer to act in accordance with the contract (an injunction would be required) but merely states the parties' rights, thus bringing moral pressure on the employer to respect those rights. Many of the cases in which a declaration has been granted involve public sector employers, where the pressure to comply may be greater than for private employers.

II. Employer remedies

In cases of **fundamental** breach, the employer can treat the contract as discharged and dismiss the employee without notice or payment in lieu of notice (known as "summary dismissal"), and can also sue for damages. If the breach is **not fundamental**, the employer will not be justified in dismissing (he will be liable for wrongful dismissal if he does so (*Wilson v Racher* [1974] IRLR 114, CA)). In such cases (or where the employer waives the breach such that the employment continues), his remedy will be in damages or withholding the employee's wages. In very rare cases, he may be entitled to an account of profits. 1750

Again, where **damages are not an appropriate remedy**, the court may grant an injunction (for example, to enforce a restrictive covenant).

Timing of claims If the employer is bringing a counterclaim (¶9426) in an **employment tribunal**, he must do so **within** 6 weeks from receipt of the employee's claim, although the time limit can be **extended** for such period as the tribunal considers reasonable if it is satisfied that it was not reasonably practicable to present the counterclaim in time. If the claim is brought in the **High Court or county courts**, it must be presented within 6 years of the date of the breach. 1751

A. Dismissal without notice

In cases of fundamental breach, the employer can dismiss the employee without notice (known as **summary dismissal**). Whether a breach is sufficiently serious to be considered repudiatory will depend on **various factors**, including the nature of the employment and the employee's past conduct. **Examples** of fundamental breach include gross misconduct (such as disobedience or dishonesty), serious negligence/incompetence, a serious breach of duty, and going on strike (*W Simmons v Hoover Ltd* [1976] IRLR 266, EAT) (¶1701). 1755

However, a dismissal in the above circumstances may nevertheless be unfair for statutory purposes, for example for failing to follow a fair procedure. In cases of strike where industrial action is protected, dismissal will be automatically unfair in certain circumstances (¶7521).

A further factor is whether the **contract expressly states** that certain conduct will result in summary dismissal. For example, the contract may state that gross misconduct includes acts of discrimination or harassment, theft or dishonesty, fighting or other disorderly behaviour, being under the influence of drugs or alcohol at work, and serious incidents of general misconduct, such as poor time keeping or sub-standard work (¶6538). 1756

MEMO POINTS If the contract defines the circumstances in which the employer can summarily dismiss the employee, whether or not he was justified in doing so is a question of construction of the contract rather than the application of the common law doctrine of fundamental breach.

B. Damages

An employee can be held liable in damages for breach of **any express or implied term** of the contract of employment. For example, damages may be awarded for breach of the following duties: 1760
- to give the required period of **notice** to terminate the employment;
- **fidelity** (*Sanders v Parry* [1967] 2 All ER 803);
- to give **personal service** (i.e. failure or refusal to perform contractual obligations); and
- to work with **due diligence and care** (*Janata Bank v Ahmed* [1981] IRLR 457, CA).

EXAMPLE In *Janata Bank v Ahmed*, A was Assistant General Manager in the bank's London branch. The Court confirmed an award of damages of approximately £35,000 in respect of the bank's losses caused by A's negligence, which included authorising an overdraft for £5,000 without making any credit checks.

1761 Actions for damages against employees are rare due to the cost to the employer in terms of personnel time and legal fees, the fact that employees often lack the financial resources to meet any claim, and the detrimental effect such actions may have on industrial relations. Also, it may be more practical for the employer, in the case of an employee refusing to work normally, to withhold wages or salary instead (¶1770).

Calculation

1763 Damages should put the innocent party into the position he would have been in had both parties to the contract performed their obligations in accordance with the contract. If, for example, the employee **fails or refuses to perform his obligations** under the contract, the employer could claim damages on the basis of the cost to him of finding a **replacement employee** less any sum that he would have paid to the employee in breach. It may be more expensive to find a replacement at short notice, or on a temporary basis and the employee in breach will be liable for this extra cost (*Richards v Hayward* [1841] 2 Man & G 574).

The employer may also be able to claim for any **consequential loss** (e.g. the value of work lost as a result of the employee's non-performance) where the consequences of the breach might reasonably be expected to have been in the contemplation of the parties when they entered into the contract of employment.

Alternatively, the employer may wish to recover the **wasted expenditure** incurred as a result of the employee's breach.

EXAMPLE In *Anglia Television Ltd v Reed* [1972] 1 QB 60, CA, Anglia had engaged R, an actor, to play the lead role in a film. R subsequently backed out and **refused to perform**. Anglia could not find a substitute and abandoned the production. As it was unable to establish what profit the film might have made, Anglia sued to recover its **wasted expenditure**, including the cost of employing other staff involved in the production of the film. The Court held that both pre- and post-contractual expenditure was in the reasonable contemplation of the parties at the time the contract was made as being likely to be wasted if R decided to pull out.

1764 If the employee breaches his duty of care, he will be liable not only for loss incurred by the employer in relation to the employer's property, but also for any loss suffered by the employer as a result of **vicarious liability** (i.e. where the employer is obliged to compensate third parties in respect of the actions of his employees) (*Lister v Romford Ice and Cold Storage Co Ltd* [1957] AC 555, HL).

C. Other remedies

1770 An employer is entitled to **withhold the wages** of an employee who is not performing his contractual duties, and may deduct an amount in respect of any **consequential financial loss** incurred as a result of the employee's breach of contract, where this can be identified (¶3006). In any event, the employer must be careful not to make an **unlawful deduction** from wages (¶3050).

Injunctions

1771 As in the case of employee remedies, the equitable remedy of injunction may be available in appropriate circumstances. Again, **interlocutory** injunctions are often sought.

A court will **not grant** an injunction or order specific performance of an obligation in order to compel an employee to work (s 236 TULRCA 1992). 1772

An injunction may, however, be **granted** in the following circumstances:
- to enforce post-termination confidentiality provisions or restrictive covenants, to the extent that enforcement of these provisions is strictly necessary to protect the employer's legitimate business interests; and
- to restrain the employee from working for another employer during the notice period, either by enforcing an express clause prohibiting the employee from working for other employers or the implied duty of fidelity.

Further information on the enforcement of confidentiality obligations and restraints by way of injunction is provided at ¶2645.

Account for profits

In exceptional circumstances, the employee may be compelled to account to the employer for any profit he has made as a result of a breach of contract (regardless of whether the employer has suffered any loss). For further details see ¶2665. 1775

CHAPTER 6

Flexible working

OUTLINE ¶¶

1800 With the **increase of a flexible work ethos**, atypical, flexible work arrangements have become increasingly prevalent in the workplace. Section 1 details the growing number of options available while sections 2-4 focus on the particular issues of home-working, part-time working and fixed-term working. **Agency work** is also a way to work flexibly and is discussed in section 5.

1801 The **status** of the part-time, fixed-term, agency or home-worker must be established as some rights only apply to employees. With regard to agency workers, a distinct body of case law has arisen as to their status.

SECTION 1

Types of flexible working

Flexible working arrangements can be any working pattern other than the worker's normal working pattern. A certain amount of flexible working has always occurred, for example, shift-working, fixed-term working and agency working, usually as a result of the employer's particular business demands and requirements. However, the increase of women at work, single parents, instances of both parents working and the growing acknowledgement of the necessity for a "work-life" balance has given rise to an increasing number of flexible working options. These, when tailor-made to fit the business of the employer, can be of benefit to both the employer and worker. 1810

Many workers find that flexible working helps with home commitments, the "work-life" balance, as well as reducing the time, cost and stress that commuting brings. Employers also find that flexible working gives them better staff retention and lower workplace overheads and the **DTI encourages companies** to consider flexible working where appropriate.

The following are **examples** of the wide range of working arrangements now being used: 1811
- **annualised hours**: organising the worker's working time based on the number of hours worked over the year rather than a week. This is usually used to accommodate high and low demands for work;
- **career breaks**: allowing the worker an extended period of unpaid leave. Schemes may limit taking a career break for a particular purpose (for example, for childcare though this is less pertinent given the increased maternity rights and the introduction of adoption leave). Usually, most schemes require the employee to resign with the employer giving a commitment to the employee to re-employ him at the same level or grade when he returns to work. It is important both parties are clear before the break begins as to whether the employment relationship continues during the break or not (see ¶1019);
- **compressed hours**: allowing the worker to work his total number of agreed hours over a shorter period, for example, working his weekly hours over four rather than five days;
- **flexitime**: allowing the worker choice about his working hours, usually outside certain agreed core times;
- **home working**: as well as the more traditional full-time working at home for, for example, manual workers and telesales, this is being increasing used by office workers by dividing their time between the workplace and home;
- **jobsharing**: typically, two workers working on a part-time basis so that together they can cover a full-time job;
- **matching hours/days to school hours and term times**: allowing workers to be available for their children when they are out of school either by adjusting their daily hours of work and/or by allowing workers to take unpaid leave during school holidays;
- **shift working**: working in shifts which is also particularly useful for employers with longer than the standard working day production or service demands;
- **staggered hours**: allowing workers to start and finish their days at work at different times;
- **sabbaticals**: usually given by some large companies in the form of a career break or extended leave with pay as a reward for long service. Sabbaticals are usually allowed to be taken for any reason and are often seen as a way for workers to "recharge their batteries";
- **term-time working**: allowing workers to take unpaid leave during school holidays;
- **voluntary reduced hours**: allowing workers to choose to work less hours or become part-time; and
- **zero hour contracts**: workers agreeing to be available for work as and when required though with no particular number of hours or times of work being specified.

Request for flexible work

Workers who have young children aged up to 6 (or 18 if disabled) have the right to request flexible working (¶4690). 1813

1815 However, there is **no actual legal right** for such a worker or any worker **to change his hours of work**. Whether it is possible depends on the contract, and it will be a matter of negotiation between the worker and the employer (¶1601). If a change of terms is **agreed**, either the contract is varied or a new contract is issued.

1816 Although an employer is not generally obliged to offer flexible work arrangements, a refusal to consider forms of flexible working, at the request of a **female worker with childcare responsibility**, may amount to indirect sex discrimination if it cannot be justified on objective grounds, e.g. on business or administrative grounds (*Robinson v Oddbins Ltd*, EAT case 188/96). Further, a number of cases have established that an employer insisting on inflexible work practices which make life difficult for working mothers, e.g. an inflexible shift system, may be committing unlawful indirect sex discrimination (*Chief Constable of Avon & Somerset Constabulary v Chew*, EAT case 503/00; *London Underground Ltd v Edwards (No. 2)* [1998] IRLR 364, CA).

EXAMPLE On her return from maternity leave, a worker requests to change her work arrangements from full-time to jobshare. The employer refuses:
- citing a clause in the worker's contract of employment which requires her to work at least 9: 00-5: 00 and to do additional hours as the job may require;
- stating that it is too expensive to have the job shared; and
- stating that the job in question cannot be shared effectively (even though this was not tried before).

A tribunal faced with a sex discrimination claim by the worker will have to decide whether the employer had properly considered the request (e.g. did his objections apply to the particular circumstances of case?) It is likely to disregard the contractual provisions and will need to decide, on the facts, whether it was commercially and organisationally viable to perform the post on a jobshare basis. Even if the post could not be shared, a tribunal will consider whether other flexible work arrangements would have been possible.

SECTION 2

Working at home

1820 Home-working is an increasingly popular form of flexible working and there are a substantial and increasing number of employees who work fully or partly from home as part of a shift to more flexible working. This is often referred to as "**teleworking**" where IT is used to facilitate splitting work between the home and workplace or where primarily mobile workers use their home as an administrative base. Workers can range from those who are working completely from home processing information and/or taking calls to senior employees who work part of the week at home instead of the office. There are now estimated to be over two million people in the UK who use IT to help them work away from the traditional office environment.

Employers and home-workers should **address the following contractual and practical issues**, principally concerning the organisation of work, the equipment and set-up including health and safety, and confidentiality and company information.

1821 It is advisable that a **move to home-working** (be it for all or part of the employee's working time) should be done on a trial basis to assess its viability and success. Such a period will be usually for 2-3 months with a review at the mid-point to resolve any issues that may have arisen. During the trial period, it is usual for the employee to have stricter reporting obligations and duties than after a successful completion so that the volume of work being produced at home can be assessed.

Employee considerations

1823 A home-worker should consider the following as there may be:
- differences to his home insurance policies which should be checked;
- tax implications in using his home for business purposes, for example he may become liable for capital gains tax if he moves home;

– planning permission considerations if he wishes to extend his home for business purposes; and
– lease implications in using his home for business purposes and any lease should be checked to ensure it can be used for business purposes and if such use affects the rateable value.

1. Organisation of work

Place of work

The **contract of employment** should state the place of work. If it does not, this must be evidenced in a written statement (¶1405). Therefore, it must be stated (either in the original document or by variation) if the employee is required or permitted to work at home for all or part of his time at work. 1825

Working practices

Employers can introduce more comprehensive and stricter **contractual obligations** on the working practices of home-workers, for example requiring a home-worker to: 1827
– regularly report and communicate with his line manager;
– be contactable at certain periods;
– inform in an agreed time scale when he is on holiday or sick;
– work certain hours;
– attend the workplace at certain times;
– be more formally supervised; and
– keep a record of his time-keeping.

It is necessary to ensure that workers have their regulatory daily and weekly **rest periods**, and in-work rest breaks; and that they do not exceed the average weekly working time limit unless by written agreement (¶3688). To this extent, requiring the home-worker to fill out time sheets will provide the employer with the necessary records to ensure compliance.

To prevent feelings of isolation and a lack of motivation as much **contact with work colleagues** as possible should be encouraged and the home-worker should be regularly informed of any developments or problems in the company. For example, established and regular interaction through electronic networking facilities (email, intranet and on-line discussions) and by telephone and post are important. Good access to the home-worker's line manager is also important and the home-worker should be encouraged or required to attend the workplace to facilitate face-to-face discussions and to attend certain team/company meetings. Finally, when at the workplace, innovative organisational practices such as establishing "social club facilities", "soft seating areas" for informal conversations and "hot desking" can further facilitate additional patterns of communication. 1828

How the employer can organise cover, if necessary, when the home-worker is **absent** due to sickness or on holiday should be addressed. 1829

2. Equipment and set-up

Equipment

Employers may **supply** home-workers with equipment necessary to perform their duties. For example, a lap-top, PC, fax machine, answerphone, separate telephone line or other equipment. What the home-worker needs, how equipment is maintained and how any problems with it are solved should be addressed (for example, who will be available to help the home-worker with hardware or software problems at home). The employee should also be given training, if necessary, to ensure he is using the equipment properly. 1835

1836 The employer should ensure that any equipment is sufficiently **insured** as the employee's home insurance may not cover it. In such circumstances, the **policy** should be checked to see if:
– it needs to be extended; and
– if any security measures need to be complied with, for example the need to secure equipment when not in use.

1837 Employers can introduce tighter contractual terms on **expenditure and care** of company property for home-workers. If a home telephone or fax machine is being used, there should be a written agreement as to how the business use is paid for, for example itemised bills may be required before payment and/or the employer may agree to pay a certain percentage of non-itemised bills. It is also useful to state contractually who will bear the **cost of moving** and setting-up equipment if a home-worker moves home.

1838 The employer should make sure that the home-worker is aware of any **email or internet policies** in relation to using the workstation equipment and he should clarify whether the home-worker can use equipment provided by the employer for personal purposes outside working hours.

Health and safety

1840 Employers have health and safety obligations (both common law and statutory) (¶4810) with regard to their **employees** even when they are working from home (Workplace (Health, Safety and Welfare) Regulations SI 1992/3004 extend employer liability to a home or part of home that is converted into a workplace).

It is, therefore, necessary to ensure that home-workers use any company equipment safely and that adequate materials are provided. To this end it may be appropriate to **inspect** the home workstation and how the home-worker uses it. At the very least, an **ergonomic questionnaire** should be filled out and signed by home-workers to ensure that the rules relating to workstations and VDUs are complied with. Like with assessments at the workplace, these should be repeated as appropriate (see in particular the requirements as set out by the Health and Safety (Display Screen Equipment) Regulations SI 1992/2792 as amended). Employers should also ensure that there are adequate first-aid provisions and that any reportable injuries are reported.

1841 The general statutory duty also applies to anyone who is affected by the home-worker's work and consequently extends to **members of the employee's household** and any **visitors** to the home. Therefore, if there are others in the home-worker's household that may have access to the equipment (especially if it is in a general living area of the home), it is necessary to ensure that this is not a safety risk, for example cables should be out of the way and equipment which could cause electrical shocks should be out of reach of young children.

1842 To ensure health and safety compliance, it is useful to have a contractual term that allows for **access to the home** for this purpose either by the employer or a health and safety inspector.

3. Confidentiality and company information

1845 Employees have an implied duty of fidelity and good faith (¶1213) towards their employer (though this does not apply to those that are self-employed). Both, though, are subject to the general duty of confidentiality (¶1223). It is useful to include **contractual terms** to augment, clarify and highlight the employer's right to confidentiality and good faith and it may be appropriate to introduce stricter terms on the confidentiality and non-competition/solicitation covenants. At the very least, employers should emphasise to home-workers that the same obligations exist as for whose working at the workplace. Employers can reserve a contractual **right of entry** to obtain company information if the home-worker breaches these clauses or it is reasonable to expect him to do so.

Security issues

Employers may wish to make it clear contractually that the home-worker is responsible for the security of confidential information. Where necessary, the employer should supply the home-worker with a lockable filing cabinet for such purposes. 1847

Potential breaches of security can also occur with the use of a laptop or PC in three main ways:
– laptops may be lost or stolen, or the display on the laptop may be seen by other people, for example while travelling on trains;
– unauthorised access to corporate systems due to careless use of passwords and/or phone numbers; and
– information in transit over the internet may be read by a third party unless it is sufficiently encrypted.

Care with the use of laptops and PC should be emphasised and employers should make employees aware of the risks supported with clear policies.

4. Discrimination

Employers must ensure that if they offer different terms and conditions to home-workers they do not discriminate against them especially if such workers are **predominately female**. In such cases, a home-worker may have a claim under the equal pay and/or sex discrimination legislation. Further, if home-workers are **predominately part-time**, they may have a claim for equal treatment (under the Part-time Workers Regulations (see ¶1890)). 1850

Potential discrimination can occur with regard to **pay and career development** and employers should ensure that home-workers are paid appropriately and that they have an equal opportunity to participate in **training courses**.

SECTION 3

Part-time workers

Employers must ensure that part-time **workers** are **not treated less favourably** than full-time staff (Part-time Workers (Prevention of Less Favourable Treatment) Regulations SI 2000/1551 (referred to in this section as the regulations) as amended by Part-time Workers (Prevention of Less Favourable Treatment) Regulations 2000 (Amendment) Regulations SI 2002/2035). Employers and workers cannot contract out of the regulations and any term (express or implied) in the contract of employment or in any other contract, will be void in so far as it seeks to exclude or limit the operation of any of the regulations or stop workers from bringing proceedings under them (reg 9 SI 2002/2035). 1870

MEMO POINTS The regulations implement the EC Part-time Work Directive 1997/81 and in particular, clauses 1-4 of the framework agreement on ensuring equal treatment. As a result, the courts and tribunals can look at the Directive for guidance when interpreting the regulations.
The Directive also promotes the development of part-time work on a voluntary basis and the flexible organisation of working time to take into account the needs of both employers and workers. The **DTI guidance notes** on part-time workers (The Law and Practice – a detailed guide for employers and part-time workers (referred to in this section as the guidance notes)) reflect this aspiration as well as giving guidance on regulatory compliance. The guidance notes recommend that more types of job and levels of management should be opened to part-time workers and they give best practice recommendations on how this can be achieved. Although the guidance notes do not have any legal status, a court or tribunal may infer that an employer has breached the regulations if he has not followed the relevant best practice recommendations.

As most part-time work arrangements are undertaken by women who, statistically, often have the prime responsibility for child-care arrangements, if employees suffer less favourable treatment as a result, this may also constitute **indirect sex discrimination** (see ¶5323). 1871

Less favourable treatment with regards to pay between part-time and full-time workers may also give rise to an **equal pay claim** (see ¶5600). Where national legislation provides that both part-time and full-time workers will be remunerated for overtime worked only when at least 3 additional hours per month have been completed, such a condition will be contrary to Article 141 of the EC Treaty of Rome and the EEC Equal Treatment Directive 1976/207 if considerably more women than men are affected by it and the condition cannot be objectively justified (*Elsner-Lakeberg v Land Nordrhein-Westfalen* [2005] IRLR 209, ECJ). The European Court of Justice ruled in this case that the condition to have worked 3 additional hours per month was a greater burden on part-time workers than their full-time counterparts and offended the principle of equal pay.

Part-time employees also have a separate right to equal treatment with regard to **pensions** and some may also be entitled to past benefits if they were deprived of them (see ¶3435).

MEMO POINTS The former need for an employee to work a minimum number of hours a week to be continuously employed has been removed (Employment Protection (Part-time Employees) Regulations SI 1995/31).

A. Scope

1880 The protection under the regulations is given to all **workers** who are not full-time and are therefore considered to be part-time (regs 1(2), 2(2) SI 2000/1551). A full-time worker is defined as one who is paid wholly or in part by reference to the time he works and is identifiable as a full-time worker having regard to the custom and practice of the employer in relation to his other workers under the **same type of contract**. A part-time worker is only entitled to the protection given under the regulations if he can **compare** himself to an identified comparable full-time worker (i.e. a comparator) **unless** he is entitled to compare his part-time terms and treatment to his old full-time terms and treatment.

MEMO POINTS The ECJ has held that a casual worker who worked on demand (i.e. there was no guarantee of particular hours of work) was a worker within the meaning of the EEC Equal Treatment Directive 1976/207 and the EC Part-Time Work Directive 1997/81. However, working under such a contract could not in itself amount to indirect sex discrimination or discrimination against part-timers as there is no full-time comparator (i.e. a full-time worker working on demand) (*Wippel v Peek & Cloppenburg GmbH & Co KG, Case C313/02* [2005] IRLR 211, ECJ).

1881 To determine whether a **comparator** has the same type of contract as a part-time worker, the **different types of contract** are divided into the following four groups. The comparator and part-time worker must belong to the same group (reg 2(3) SI 2000/1551):

1. employees under a contract that is not a contract of apprenticeship;
2. apprentices;
3. workers who are not employees; and
4. any other type of employment relationship (any other description of worker that it is reasonable for the employer to treat differently from other workers on the ground that workers of that description have a different type of contract). Note that this is a miscellaneous group.

The Court of Appeal has recently held (overturning the EAT on this point) that the four groups are mutually exclusive, and that group 4. is purely a residual group for "other" descriptions of workers who do not fall into one of the other groups. Consequently, only the actual type of contract (i.e. employee, apprentice, worker who is not an employee, any other type of worker) should be considered and not secondary factors such as other contractual terms and conditions. The Court emphasised that to do otherwise would severely limit the application of the statutory protection given to part-time workers and that applying the test of reasonableness to differences in contractual terms and conditions should be only considered when deciding whether the employer was justified in treating the worker less favourably on objective grounds (¶1890) (*Matthews and others v Kent and Medway Towns Fire Authority and others* [2004] IRLR 697, CA).

MEMO POINTS Previously, before 1 October 2002, fixed term contracts were distinguished from open ended employment contracts. This change was brought in by the Part-time Workers (Prevention of Less Favourable Treatment) Regulations 2000 (Amendment) Regulations SI 2002/2035 to bring the UK in line with the EC Fixed-term Work Directive 1999/70.

Comparison to comparator

A comparator is **defined** in relation to a part-time worker. He is a full-time worker who, at the time of the alleged unequal treatment (reg 2(4) SI 2000/1551): 1882

– is employed by the **same employer** under the same type of contract and engaged in the **same or broadly similar work** having regard, where relevant, to whether he has a similar level of qualification, skills and experience; and

– works or is based at the **same establishment**. Where there is no full-time worker at that establishment who could be a comparator, he can work or be based at a **different establishment**.

The Court of Appeal has recently confirmed the EAT's decision to allow factual differences to be taken into consideration (*Matthews and others v Kent and Medway Towns Fire Authority and others*, above). Consequently, tribunals are entitled to take into consideration not only the core obligations, but also other factors such as additional functional duties and other additional matters. In *Matthews and others v Kent and Medway Towns Fire Authority and others*, the tribunal could consider not only the accepted core activity of fire-fighting and dealing with other emergencies which was common to both groups, but also the additional educational, preventive and administrative tasks of full-time fire-fighters and the differences in relation to entry standards, probationary standards and training, and subsequent training. The Court of Appeal made no comment as to the desirability of the tribunal's decision (which was that because of these factual differences part-time fire-fighters could not be compared to full-time fire-fighters) as the tribunal had correctly approached the question and the way it applied the facts was not perverse i.e. a decision which no reasonable tribunal would have reached.

Comparison to previous treatment

In two situations, a part-time worker who used to work full-time can be his own comparator regardless of whether he has a new contract or a variation of his existing contract, as long as the terms are for a decreased number of weekly hours (regs 3(1), 4 SI 2000/1551). This applies to a full-time worker who is either: 1884

– **transferring to part-time work**; or

– **returning part-time after absence** if he was a full-time worker immediately before it, continues to work for the same employer within a period of less than 12 months from the first day of absence and does the same job or a job at the same level. Where the contract continues, any contractual variation made during this absence will be taken as included.

If a **new contract** has been agreed, it need not be the same type contract. For example, a full-time secretary with a permanent contract could transfer or return as a part-time secretary, with protection under the regulations, on a fixed term contract if the above conditions are satisfied. 1885

B. Equal treatment

A part-time worker has the right **not be treated less favourably** due to his part-time status than a comparable full-time worker with regard to his contractual terms unless the treatment can be justified on objective grounds (regs 5-6 SI 2000/1551). A part-time worker also has the right **not to be subjected to any other detriment** by any act, or deliberate failure to act, of his employer (reg 5(1)-(2) SI 2000/1551). 1890

In determining whether a part-time worker has been treated less favourably, the **pro rata** principle is applied unless inappropriate (reg 5(3) SI 2000/1551).

A part-time worker is not subject to less favourable treatment where the **real reason for the difference** in treatment between himself and a full-time comparator is not by reason of his status (*Gibson v Scottish Ambulance Service*, EAT case 0052/04). The EAT in a majority decision held that the appropriate test in such circumstances was the subjective "by reason that" test (as set out by the House of Lords in *Chief Constable of West Yorkshire Police v Khan* (a case on racial discrimination) and reinforced recently by the Court of Appeal in *The Law Society v Bahl* (a case on sex and race discrimination). The question that must be determined is "why did the alleged discriminator act as he did? What, consciously or unconsciously, was his reason?" Consequently, the reason or motivation for the difference in treatment must be determined to ascertain where the part-time worker has been treated unequally. In this case the real reason for the difference in the number of stand-by hours the part-time worker had to do compared to his full time comparator was held to be an issue of demand in the local area and consequently not was because he was a part-time worker.

MEMO POINTS The EAT in *Gibson v Scottish Ambulance Service* also gave tacit support to the tribunal's analysis that the "sole" reason for the less favourable treatment must be because of the worker's part-time status for a claim to succeed. If this is followed, it provides a further restriction to the protection offered by the regulations.

Request for written statement

1891 If a part-time worker believes that he is being treated less favourably than a comparable full-time worker he has the right to ask his employer **to give reasons for his less favourable treatment**. He should make his request to his employer in writing, and is entitled to receive a written statement from his employer within 21 days of that request (reg 6 SI 2000/1551).

A written statement is **admissible** as evidence in any proceedings concerning a part-time working claim (¶1920) and if it appears to the tribunal that the employer deliberately, and without reasonable excuse, omitted to provide a written statement, or that the written statement is evasive or equivocal, the tribunal may draw any inference which it considers just and equitable to draw, including an inference that the employer has infringed the right in question.

1892 The right to request a written statement does not apply where the treatment in question consists of the **dismissal of an employee** as in such cases the employee is entitled to a written statement of reasons for his dismissal (¶8310).

Remuneration and benefits

1893 Part-time workers must receive the same basic **rate of pay** as comparable full-time workers unless a lower hourly rate can be justified on objective grounds (for example, where the pay scheme is performance-related and they can be shown to have a different level of performance (measured in a fair and consistent appraisal system)). In general, the same principle applies to **enhanced or special rates** of pay such as bonus pay, shift allowances, night work or weekend work. However, part-time workers do not have an automatic right to **overtime payment** once they work beyond their normal hours until they have reached the normal hours of their comparable full-time workers (reg 5(4) SI 2000/1551).

When comparing wages of part-time workers to full-time workers, the **wages as a whole** should be compared (*James and ors v Great North Eastern Railways*, EAT case 0496/04). In this case, full-time workers were paid at a higher rate for some of their contractual hours, which meant that overall their rate was higher than their part-time colleagues. Consequently, unless the employer could justify this on objective grounds, this amounted to less favourable treatment.

1894 Part-time workers are entitled to receive a pro rata level of **benefits** in line with the number of hours they work, unless exclusion can be objectively justified. For example, **share option schemes** may be excluded if the value of the share options is so small for a part-time worker that the potential benefit to him would be less than the likely cost of realising them.

It may be inappropriate to pro rata certain benefits, for example health insurance or company cars, and employers can exclude such benefits from part-time workers if it can be justified on objective grounds. For example, providing a car to a part-time worker might be at a disproportionate cost to the company or may not meet any real need.

The guidance notes state that in such situations, employers might, by way of **best practice**, calculate the financial value of the benefit to a full-time worker and apply that value pro rata to a part-time worker. Alternatively, if the benefit or allowance was given to a full-time worker, for example every year, then a part-time worker working half the full-time hours might be given the benefit or allowance every 2 years. Likewise, other benefits such as **clothing or travel allowance** or **staff discounts** might also be extended to part-time workers in line with these principles.

Detrimental pay differentials between a part-time worker and his full time comparator may give rise to a claim under the regulations and/or the equal pay legislation (¶5600). 1895

EXAMPLE An employer pays a different rate of pay to part-time and full-time workers doing a similar job. He tries to justify the pay differential on the basis that his full-time workers gained experience and developed their skills more quickly than his part-time workers. The employer's argument was rejected by the ECJ on the basis that it was generalised. According to the ECJ, pay practices should depend on the particular circumstances of each case and, in particular, on the relationship between the nature of the duties performed and the experience the employee gained from performing those duties after a certain number of working hours (*Nimz v Freie und Hansestadt Hamburg* [1991] IRLR 222, ECJ).

Leave Part-time workers are entitled to statutory annual leave (¶4000). Part-time employees are also entitled to maternity, adoption, paternity and parental leave (¶4400). 1897

If these entitlements have been extended or enhanced by contract (or, in certain circumstances, practice), for example increased annual leave or a career break scheme, part-timers are entitled to the same entitlements on a pro rata basis.

Public and bank holidays The guidance notes recommend the adoption of **best practice** to avoid any practical difficulties in ascertaining whether a part-time worker is entitled to leave on public and bank holidays. 1899

If a company gives the day off to all staff who ordinarily work on the day of the public/bank holiday but no time off in lieu to any other members of staff, it will probably not be unlawful. For example, a part-time worker who works Monday-Wednesday inclusive would be entitled to bank holiday Mondays off, but a part-time worker who works Wednesday-Friday inclusive would not. The guidance notes suggest that, as a matter of **good practice**, employers should compensate for the disadvantage suffered by those workers who do not receive particular days off as a result of their working pattern by allowing a pro rata entitlement of days off in lieu.

Recruitment

Although the regulations do not cover external recruitment, the guidance notes recommend as **best practice** that employers periodically review whether the posts they are offering could be performed by part-time workers. Likewise, if approached by an applicant for a full-time post who wishes to work part-time, employers should give consideration as to whether part-time work arrangements could fulfil the requirements of the post. 1901

The guidance notes recommend that employers make a **wider range of jobs** available for part-time and as **best practice**, that at all levels of the company, including skilled and managerial positions, employers should seek to maximise the range of posts designated as suitable for part-time working or job-sharing. Companies should recognise that just because a worker works part-time does not mean that he does not want to continue to develop a career and that reducing or blocking his chances to move around the company may demoralise or cause him to look for job opportunities elsewhere. Conversely, allowing part-time workers to apply for other posts ensures that the employers will be able to pick the best person for the job.

Part-time workers should be given equal opportunity to seek **promotion**, indeed part-time staff may be willing to work full-time on promotion if, for example, the extra pay will allow them to afford childcare.

1902 Giving part-time workers less **information on job vacancies** will amount to less favourable treatment and the guidance notes recommend that employers should examine their advertising practices to see if there is anything that might disadvantage part-time workers. For example, part-time workers may not hear about vacancies that are filled by informal management practices such as word of mouth.

As **best practice**, the guidance notes recommend that employers should periodically review how individuals are provided with information on the availability of part-time and full-time positions. Companies should consider how to make it easier for workers to vary their hours, including transferring between part-time and full-time work, to the benefit of both workers and employers.

1903 The guidance notes recognise that **staff representatives** of formal or informal bodies representing the workforce may find it useful to be kept informed of some or all of the following:
– overall human resource policy with regard to part-time work and any plans to change it;
– number and location of part-time workers;
– whether any requests to change hours have been refused, and if so, why;
– training opportunities for part-time workers and take up; and
– the steps taken to ensure equal access to promotion.

Training

1905 Employers should be aware that training may be inconvenient to part-time workers, for example a part-time worker with personal commitments may find it difficult to attend. As **best practice**, the guidance notes recommend that the provision of training should be arranged to ensure that it is as conveniently located and timed for part-time workers. Where this is not possible, a range of **other measures** might be considered to support their career development:
– paying part-time workers (at their normal rate of pay) for the hours they attend outside their normal working hours; or
– offering
· an equivalent course from an alternative provider at a more convenient time and place;
· the comparable level and quality of training in another area; or
· other training methods, for example open or distance learning (by correspondence, phone or internet/email) courses.

MEMO POINTS In certain circumstances, part-time work can be a form of **training in its own right**, for example workers who are on a career-break can find periods of part-time work a useful way to keep in touch with developments in their companies and their area of work. Further, employers may find that this not only keeps the services of the worker during a career break but when the worker returns he is immediately able to play a full role in the company.

Jobsharing

1907 Jobsharing arrangements consist of dividing a full-time job between two part-time workers. This division can be in a number of ways to suit the circumstances, for example, one worker may work mornings, the other afternoons, or each may work two and a half days each. Sometimes, depending of the type of work involved it may be appropriate to have a handover period when both are working.

Employers often benefit from having two people working on a project, with their combined energy, skills and experience and depending on the agreement, jobsharers may provide cover when one is on holiday or sick. As a result, the guidance notes recommend that as **good practice** employers should seriously consider requests for jobsharing. The drawback is that it may be difficult to organise a jobshare arrangement due to the need to find two workers who can do the job, are capable of working together and who want to work complementary hours. Therefore, the guidance notes recommend that as best practice **larger companies** should keep a database of those interested in entering jobsharing arrangements.

Indirect sex discrimination

Moreover, a **provision or policy, recruitment criterion or practice** which requires all persons to work full-time is likely to constitute indirect sex discrimination (¶5323), since more women than men need to work part-time to balance their work requirements with childcare responsibilities. This is an important aspect to the discrimination legislation since the regulations do not protect persons who want to move into or out of part-time work. Staff in this position, who believe that their employer's policies make it difficult for them to do so, may only complain if they can demonstrate that the provision, criterion or practice has an adverse impact on them as women (or, possibly, men). Cases increasingly recognise that problems associated with part-time working (e.g. lack of career progression, reduced benefits) are predominantly female problems. Therefore, tribunals and courts will often not require much by way of statistical evidence to be persuaded that an issue of indirect discrimination has arisen (*Greater Manchester Police Authority v Lea* [1990] IRLR 372, EAT). **1909**

If an employer's provision, criterion or practice is found to have a detrimental effect on part-time workers, the employer's only **line of defence** is to show that he had an objective reason, not connected with sex, for applying the particular provision, etc. For example, there might be good business, commercial or administrative reasons for the difference in treatment. Rarely will it be open to an employer to argue that part-timers are less productive or experienced than their full-time counterparts. However, each case will be considered on its facts. **1910**

EXAMPLE An employer has the following promotion criteria: workers must have completed at least 5 years' full-time service before they may be promoted to a managerial post. A female part-time worker has applied for the post, but was not promoted because, although she has worked for the employer for 5 years, she has only worked 3 days a week. To try to justify this criterion on the basis that 5 years' full-time work is necessary for workers to gain the necessary experience for a managerial post, is likely to be regarded as a generalisation. Instead, the employer should examine the nature of the duties performed by the worker and the experience she gained in practice during the time she has actually worked.

C. Change of terms

See ¶1813 for a general discussion on the right to **request flexible working**. **1915**

As **best practice**, the guidance notes currently recommend that employers should look seriously at requests to work part-time and where possible, explore with their workers how this change could be accommodated. Further, employers should also consider establishing a procedure for discussing with workers whether they wish to change from full-time to part-time for any reason.

The guidance notes suggest that it is helpful if employers have a **procedure for handling requests** for part-time work together with discussions focusing on any particular worker's tasks and responsibilities and how a change in hours could fit in. **1916**

Questions that may be useful in forming the **basis of a policy** for handling such requests are as follows:
- does a worker need to be present in the post during all working hours? If so, can the post be filled as a job share and is there a suitable candidate?
- can all the necessary work be done in the hours requested?
- can the job be redefined to make it easier to do part-time?
- is there another job of similar level that the worker could do part-time?
- is the change for a known period?
- how much would it cost to recruit and train a replacement if the worker left?

– what benefits would the company get, for example staff retention, lower wage bill and assurance of staff coverage for peak periods? and
– what would be the effect on the morale and commitment of other staff?

1917 On the other hand, if there is a **request for increasing hours**, questions that may be useful in forming the **basis of a policy** for handling such a request are as follows:
– is there sufficient work for an increase in hours?
– could the extra hours be used to reorganise a number of jobs more efficiently?
– can the company afford the increase in pay? and
– will the increase save money on recruitment?

If it is the **employer** who wishes to change the hours worked to correspond with operational needs, he must nevertheless be careful that he has a good business reason to do so and that he has not indirectly discriminated against the worker.

D. Remedies

Right not to be treated less favourably or suffer detriment

1920 A part-time worker can bring a claim to an employment tribunal if his employer has infringed his right to not be treated less favourably or if he has suffered a detriment (regs 7-8 SI 2000/1551).

A part-time worker has the right not to be subjected to any detriment by any act, or any deliberate failure to act, by his employer if the reason(s) or ground(s) is that he has:
– alleged that the employer has infringed his rights;
– refused (or proposed to refuse) to waive a right;
– brought proceedings against the employer in pursuance of his rights;
– requested a written statement of the reasons for less favourable treatment;
– given evidence or information in connection with proceedings brought by another worker; or
– otherwise done anything further to his rights to the employer or any other person.

The worker has the same right if the detriment or act was because the employer believes or **suspects** that he has done or intends to do any of the above.

If the **allegation**(s) that the employer infringed a worker's rights (or acted or did not act because of his belief or suspicion) is false and not made in good faith, the worker will have no right to claim.

1921 As seen, an employer has a **defence** if he can show that the treatment was justifiable on objective grounds (reg 5(2) SI 2000/1551).

1922 Complaints must be made **within** 3 months beginning with the date of the act or failure to act or if it is part of a series of similar acts or failures, the last of them. However, a tribunal may **extend** this period if it considers it just and equitable to do so (¶9475).

1923 If the **claim is successful**, the tribunal can:
– make a declaration;
– order the employer to pay compensation; and
– recommend that the employer take, within a specified period, whatever action it considers reasonable to obviate or reduce the adverse effect on the worker.

If the employer fails, without reasonable justification to comply, it can make an order for compensation (or increase the amount of compensation if one has already been made).

MEMO POINTS Previously, before 1 October 2002, there was a requirement that complaints of less favourable treatment in relation to an occupational pension scheme be limited to a backdating period of 2 years before the date on which the complaint was presented. This is no longer the case (Part-time Workers (Prevention of Less Favourable Treatment) Regulations 2000 (Amendment) Regulations SI 2002/2035 which was brought into force to comply with the terms of the judgment of the House of Lords in *Preston v Wolverhampton Healthcare NHS Trust* [2001] IRLR 237, HL).

Right not to be unfairly dismissed

Any dismissal of an employee will be **automatically unfair** (¶8390) if the reason (or, if more than one, the principal reason) for the dismissal is one of those covered by the right not to suffer a detriment (reg 7 SI 2000/1551). 1925

MEMO POINTS Non-employee workers who are so dismissed should rely on the right not to suffer a detriment (see above) though compensation is awarded on the same basis as for unfair dismissal.

SECTION 4

Fixed-term contracts

Workers may be contracted to work for a **fixed period only** or to **perform a particular task** 1950
with the contract terminating at the end of this period or on the completion of the task. Such contracts are called fixed-term contracts.

MEMO POINTS Prior to 1 October 2002, there was a distinction between fixed-term contracts for a specified period and contracts for a specific task or performance. However, this distinction is no longer relevant and contracts for a specific task or performance are now regarded as fixed-term contracts.

Fixed-term employees have the **right not to be treated less favourably** than comparable 1951
permanent employees (i.e. employees with employment contracts for an indefinite or indeterminate term) of the same employer doing similar work, unless the treatment is objectively justified. Further, all fixed-term employees are now entitled to the main statutory employment rights, for example the right not to be unfairly dismissed, the right to a written statement of the reason for dismissal and the right to statutory redundancy payments. It is also automatically unfair to dismiss those employees who seek to rely on the regulations.

A fixed-term employee may also become a permanent employee if he has served under **successive fixed-term contracts**.

MEMO POINTS 1. The previous imbalance between the employment rights of fixed-term and permanent employees was addressed by the Fixed-term Employees (Prevention of Less Favourable Treatment) Regulations SI 2002/2034 which came into force on 1 October 2002 (referred to in this section as **the regulations**).
The regulations derive from the EC Fixed-Term Work Directive 1999/70 which, like the EC Part-Time Work Directive 1997/81, extends to protect those with 'an employment contract or employment relationship as defined by law, collective agreement or practice in each member state.' Under the Part-time Workers (Prevention of Less Favourable Treatment) Regulations SI 2000/1551 (which derive from EC Part-Time Work Directive 1997/81) protection is extended to "workers" whilst under the (fixed-term) regulations protection is only granted to the narrower category of "employees."
2. The **DTI guidance notes**, "Fixed-Term Work, A guide to the regulations", are a useful guide to regulatory compliance.

As a result of the new right to comparable treatment, employers may have to change existing 1952
contract terms to ensure that fixed-term employees are not treated less favourably than permanent employees.

It should be noted that **permanent employees do not have a comparable right** to equal treatment and consequently fixed-term employees may have more favourable terms without permanent employees having a right for recourse under the regulations.

If an employer employs a number of staff on fixed-term contracts, the majority of whom are 1953
women, he must ensure that those fixed-term employees are treated no less favourably than their permanent counterparts, as such less favourable treatment may constitute **indirect sex discrimination**.

EXAMPLE In *Whiffen v Milham Ford Girls' School* [2001] IRLR 468, CA, it was the school's redundancy policy to dismiss all fixed-term staff before applying objective selection criteria to the remainder of the school's permanent employees. The Court of Appeal found that such a policy was indirectly discriminatory on the ground of sex since W was able to demonstrate that a considerably smaller proportion of female staff could comply with the redundancy selection policy criterion that an employee had to be employed on a permanent contract to avoid being dismissed at an early stage in the redundancy process than the proportion of men who could comply with it.

1954 For further discussion on indirect sex discrimination, see ¶5300.

A. General

1. Scope

1960 A **fixed-term employee** is defined as a person with a contract of employment which is due to end when (reg 1(2) SI 2002/2034):
– a specified date is reached;
– a specified event does or does not happen; or
– a specified task has been completed.

Such contracts of employment are referred to as fixed-term contracts.

Examples are those who are employed specifically to cover for maternity, parental or paternity leave; employees who do "seasonal" or "casual" work, such as agricultural workers and shop assistants employed during busy periods such as Christmas; employees hired to cover unusual peaks in demand, as in the tourist industry; and employees whose contracts will end on the completion of a specified task, such as painting a house or installing a computer system.

An employee with a fixed-term contract as defined above will still come under the protection of the regulations even if the contract allows for **termination before the expiry date** by notice to either party (*Allen v National Australia Group Europe Ltd* [2004] IRLR 847, EAT).

1961 The regulations do not cover **non-employee workers** (i.e. workers with a contract for services) (¶13).

Workers are excluded from the protection afforded by the regulations, as are **apprentices**.

Likewise, **students on work experience placements** of 1 year or less that are being undertaken in connection with an undergraduate, post-graduate or teacher training course are also excluded. However, students who take on fixed-term employment during their holidays or gap year are covered by the regulations as long as the job is **not part of their course**.

Comparable permanent employee

1963 In order to ascertain whether a fixed-term employee is being treated less favourably than other employees of the same employer it is necessary to compare his employment terms with that of a comparable permanent employee.

The **definition** of a comparable permanent employee is (reg 2(1) SI 2002/2034):
– a permanent employee employed by the same employer as the fixed-term employee;
– to do the same or broadly similar work of the fixed-term employee having regard, where relevant, to whether they have similar levels of qualifications and skills; and
– who works or is based at the same establishment as the fixed-term employee he is being compared with. Where there is no comparable permanent employee at that establishment the comparison can be made with a permanent employee working or based at another establishment of the employer.

2. Equal terms

A fixed-term employee has the right **not to be treated less favourably** than comparable permanent employees on the grounds that he is a fixed-term employee, either with respect to his contract terms or by subjecting him to any other detriment unless it can be objectively justified (regs 3-4 SI 2002/2034). However, the fact that an employee has a fixed-term contract as opposed to a permanent contract cannot, in itself, amount to less favourable treatment (*Department for Work and Pensions v Webley* [2005] IRLR 288, CA overturning *Webley v Department for Work and Pensions*, EAT case 0033/04). 1965

Some areas where a fixed-term employee may be disadvantaged include qualifying periods of work, or in the conditions for accrual of entitlements or benefits, training opportunities or being considered for permanent employment. The fixed-term employee may also be disadvantaged in other areas, such as pay or annual leave. Less favourable treatment, for example, can occur when a fixed-term employee does not get an employment benefit that a comparable permanent employee gets. The benefit may be offered to the comparable permanent employee under his contract of employment or it could be a benefit that is generally available to permanent employees but not to fixed-term employees. The permanent employee may also get non-contractual benefits, such as bonus payments, or he may be given training opportunities which are not offered to fixed-term employees even though all other contract terms are identical. In each case the employer may be treating the fixed-term employee less favourably than the permanent comparable employee.

To ensure that the employer is not treating his fixed-term employees less favourably, he should **offer** them the **same terms** as for comparable permanent employees. These may be **pro-rated** as appropriate so that the fixed-term employee can receive or be entitled to such proportion of the pay or benefit as is reasonable in the circumstances having regard to the length of his employment and the terms on which the benefit is offered (reg 1(2) SI 2002/2034). Therefore if benefits, such as annual season tickets, are offered to permanent employees but the duration of the fixed-term contract is for only 6 months, the fixed-term employee could be offered a 6 monthly season ticket under the pro-rating principle. Likewise, if a contract is for 6 months, the employee should receive half of an annual benefit; if the contract is for 4 months, he should receive one third. 1966

The employer must also provide fixed-term employees with the same opportunities for **internal recruitment** as their permanent counterparts and must give them the same information on permanent vacancies within the organisation as they provide to permanent employees. The posting of vacancy notices on a notice board, accessible to all employees, will usually be sufficient to show that this obligation has been met. However, if the employer limits the availability of vacancies to permanent employees this will amount to less favourable treatment. 1967

Fixed-term employees must be offered access to an **occupational pension scheme** on the same basis as permanent employees. Vesting periods (i.e. the qualifying period of work that must be met before an employee becomes a member of the pension scheme) are **not required to be pro-rated** to accommodate fixed-term employees and the same period should apply to both fixed-term and permanent employees. 1968

The fixed-term employee is **not obliged to accept** entry into the scheme, even when offered. Where the length of employment is not sufficient to provide any, or provides little, benefit under the scheme, the employee may decide not to join. If this happens the employer is **not required to offer** alternative pension benefits such as contributing to a private pension scheme unless similar arrangements are offered to comparable permanent employees. Where membership of a pension scheme offers little or no benefits to the fixed-term employee the employer may wish to point this out to him at the time of recruitment.

Given that access to an occupational pension scheme may be of little value to a fixed-term employee, the employer and the fixed-term employee can agree that alternative compensation is provided to the employee instead.

1970 **Objective justification** Less favourable treatment may be objectively justified by the employer. If this is the case then there will be **no breach** of the regulations. What amounts to objective justification will **depend on the circumstances** but employers should ensure that they have **good reason** for treating a fixed-term employee less favourably. Each case should be decided on its own circumstances with the employer weighing up the costs against the benefits obtained.

1971 Objective justification may exist if the less favourable treatment is a **necessary and appropriate means** of achieving a **legitimate business objective**. Equally, the **cost to the employer** in offering a particular benefit may be disproportionate to the benefit actually received by the fixed-term employee and, as a result, the employer may be objectively justified in withholding the benefit. There may, for example, be objective justification for an employer not to offer a fixed-term employee access to the occupational pension scheme where the scheme has a vesting period which exceeds the length of the fixed-term contract, or if the employer makes instead a reasonable level of payment into a stakeholder or private pension scheme of the fixed-term employee.

A further example is given in the DTI guidance notes where there is a fixed-term employee on a contract of 3 months and a comparable permanent employee with a company car. The employer may decide not to offer the car to the fixed-term employee if the cost of doing so is high and the need of the business for the employee to travel can be met in some other way.

Comparison

1973 In order to ensure that fixed-term employees are treated comparably with permanent employees or to ensure that different terms and conditions can be objectively justified, the employer should make a comparison, which can be done either on a term-by-term basis or on a package basis.

1974 The **term-by-term approach** involves taking each individual term and condition and showing that they are identical, or, if appropriate, pro-rated for the fixed-term employee.

1975 The **package approach** involves showing that the overall package of terms and conditions afforded to the fixed-term employee taken as a whole, is no less favourable than the comparable permanent employee's overall package (reg 4 SI 2002/2034). The employer will be able to balance a less favourable term against a more favourable one, the only limitation being that the overall value of the fixed-term employee's employment package should be at least equal to that of the permanent comparable employee. In using the package approach the employer may be able to objectively justify the absence of a particular benefit from the fixed-term employee's package.

The DTI guidance notes suggest that when assessing the **value of benefits** for the purposes of the comparison their objective monetary worth should be used. For example, if a fixed-term employee has fewer paid holidays per year than comparable permanent employees, his salary could be increased by the value of the days' holiday to which he is not entitled.

Request for written statement

1977 If a fixed-term employee believes that he is being treated less favourably than a permanent comparable employee he has the right to ask his employer **to give reasons for his less favourable treatment**. He should make his request to his employer in writing, and is entitled to receive a written statement from his employer within 21 days of that request (reg 5 SI 2002/2034).

A written statement is **admissible** as evidence in any proceedings concerning a fixed-term working claim (¶2010) and if it appears to the tribunal that the employer deliberately, and without reasonable excuse, omitted to provide a written statement, or that the written statement is evasive or equivocal, the tribunal may draw any inference which it considers just and equitable to draw, including an inference that the employer has infringed the right in question.

The right to request a written statement does not apply where the treatment in question consists of the dismissal of an employee as in such cases the employee is entitled to a written statement of reasons for his dismissal (¶8310). 1978

3. Successive fixed-term contracts

Where a fixed-term employee's contract is renewed or re-engaged after at least **4 years of continuous employment**, the renewal or re-engagement will take effect as if the contract was permanent unless the employer can justify the fixed-term status on objective grounds (reg 8 SI 2002/2034). 1980

Whether successive periods of fixed-term contracts count towards this period or not will depend on continuity of employment rules and whether there is continuity of employment as a result (see ¶1010 for information on continuity). However, any period of continuous employment before 10 July 2002 will not count towards the 4-year period and the **start date** for the purposes of **counting continuous employment** will be 10 July 2002. As a result, the earliest date that a worker with successive fixed-term contracts can be considered as a permanent employee will be 10 July 2006.

The **permanent contract** that arises will be regarded as one of indefinite duration and any clause in the fixed-term contract (that has been converted into the permanent contract) which purports to limit its duration will be void. Consequently, once a fixed-term contract takes effect as a permanent contract the statutory minimum notice period (¶8131) will apply unless a longer period has been agreed. 1981

Objective justification The employer may be able to show objective justification for not recognising the renewal or re-engagement as permanent employment where a further fixed-term contract (DTI guidance notes): 1983
- is required to achieve a legitimate objective, such as a genuine business objective;
- is necessary to achieve that objective; and
- is an appropriate way to achieve that objective.

If there is objective justification, the employer is not required to accept that the fixed-term employee has become a permanent employee and the contract that is renewed will continue as a fixed-term contract.

Extension beyond four years Employers and employees may also, by the **use of collective agreements** (¶1270) **or workforce agreements** (¶4652), extend the validity of fixed-term contracts beyond the 4-year period. Such agreements are recognised on the basis that they prevent the abuse of successive fixed-term contracts (reg 8 SI 2002/2034). They may be used where there is a specific recognition or need for successive fixed-term contracts, such as where sports professionals or actors are to be employed over successive seasons. Collective or workforce agreements may vary the limit on successive contracts, upwards or downwards, or limit the use of such contracts by adopting one or more of the following: 1985
- a limit on the total duration of successive fixed-term contracts;
- a limit on the number of successive fixed-term contracts; or
- a list of permissible objective reasons justifying renewals of fixed-term contracts.

Request for written statement

If the **employee believes** that he has **met the condition of successive fixed-term** contracts amounting to 4 years of continuous employment he may make a written request to his employer asking that he confirm, in writing, that his employment be considered as permanent. The employer is **required to respond** within 21 days of the request being made either confirming that the employment is now permanent or giving reasons why the employee remains on a fixed-term contract (reg 9 SI 2002/2034). 1987

Such a written statement is **admissible** as evidence in any proceedings before a court, an employment tribunal and the Commissioners for Revenue and Customs and if it appears to a court/tribunal in any proceedings that the employer deliberately, and without reasonable excuse, omitted to provide a written statement, or, that the written statement is evasive or equivocal, it may draw any inference which it considers just and equitable to draw.

B. Termination

1990 The termination of a fixed-term contract is **recognised as a dismissal** for the purposes of the fixed-term employee's statutory rights, even if mutually agreed at the start of the contract. **Non-renewal by mutual consent** will not, however, amount to a dismissal.

Dismissal before end of contract

1992 In guaranteeing work for a fixed period, the employer is liable to pay for the whole of that period if the employee is willing and able to perform the work. Therefore, where the fixed-term contract is prematurely terminated by the employer, the employee can claim that he has been **wrongly dismissed** and the employer has a liability to pay him for the remainder of the period. However, if there is a **notice clause** in the fixed-term contract which provides that the contract may be terminated on notice, the employer's liability will only be for pay during that notice period.

1993 If the fixed-term contract is for 3 months or less and does not contain a contractual notice period, the employee is entitled to **one week's notice** period if the contract is terminated after he has completed 1 month or more of continuous service.

1994 If the employee continues to **work after expiry** (without an express extension or renewal), then, in the absence of a specific notice period, the employment can be terminated by either party giving reasonable notice to the other.

Dismissal at end of contract

1996 A fixed-term contract will be expected to **automatically terminate** at the end of the fixed period and therefore if the contract has run its full term, the fixed-term employee cannot claim that he has been wrongly dismissed. However, as the expiry of a fixed-term employment contract without renewal is deemed to be a dismissal for the purposes of the employee's statutory rights, he may bring a **claim for unfair dismissal** if the non-renewal is unfair, for example, if the employer has not followed the correct procedures by failing to consult with an employee before his fixed-term contract ends (¶8380). In order to bring a claim for unfair dismissal the employee must have been employed for at least 1 year.

1997 Fixed-term employees also have an **automatic right not to be unfairly dismissed** (¶8390) if the reason for dismissal or, if more than one, the principal reason for the dismissal is that the employee (reg 6 SI 2002/2034):
– brought proceedings against his employer under the regulations;
– requested a written statement from the employer (i.e. asking for written justification of less favourable treatment or for a written statement of variation);
– gave evidence or information in connection with such proceedings brought by any employee;
– otherwise did anything under the regulations in relation to the employer or any other person;
– alleged that the employer had infringed the regulations. Any such allegation must be made in good faith;
– refused (or proposed to refuse) to forgo a right conferred by the regulations;
– declined to sign a workforce agreement for the purposes of the regulations; or
– being an employee representative or prospective representative performed any functions or activities as such.

This also applies if the employer dismisses the employee because he believes or **suspects** the employee will or has done any of the above.

Further, the employee has the right not to be **subjected to any detriment** (i.e. any detrimental act short of dismissal) by any act, or failure of his employer to act, on one of the above grounds. 1998

The EAT has given **guidance** as to how the right not to suffer a detriment will apply to fixed-term employees and has done so by applying discrimination cases to this area of law (*Coutts and Co plc and another v Cure and another* [2005] ICR 1098, EAT). Firstly, claims must be for both less favourable treatment and a detriment (applying the House of Lords' decision in *Chief Constable of West Yorkshire v Khan* (a racial discrimination case)). A detriment will occur when a reasonable employee would or might take the view that he had been disadvantaged in the circumstances in which he had to work (applying the House of Lords' decision in *Shamoon v Chief Constable of the Royal Ulster Constabulary* (a sex discrimination case)). The EAT also pointed out that where it can be shown that a detriment was due to the employee's fixed-term status it is irrelevant whether or not the employer also discriminated against other groups not covered by the fixed-term regulations (for instance, other non-permanent employees). 1999

Secondly, the **3-month limitation period** begins on the date the detriment occurred (applying the Court of Appeal's ruling in *Cast v Croydon College* (a sex discrimination case)). In this case, the detrimental act was held to have occurred when the details of the bonuses to be paid were finalised (which included a statement that fixed-term employees would be excluded) and not when the promise of the non-contractual bonus was first made.

Redundancy

Fixed-term employees should not be selected for redundancy merely because they are not permanent employees. If, however, they have been employed for specific tasks or periods, the employer may have objective justification in selecting them for redundancy at the end of their contracts when these specific tasks or periods have been completed. 2000

Where the employer has a **redundancy policy** that specifies the criteria to be applied in the redundancy selection process, such as last in first out, the same criteria should be applied to both fixed-term and permanent employees, unless different criteria can be objectively justified by the employer.

Fixed-term employees have a **right to statutory redundancy payments** once they have been continuously employed for 2 years or more and they are made redundant at the end of their contracts. Consequently an employer **cannot exclude** fixed-term employees from the statutory redundancy payments scheme. Fixed-term employees may, however, be excluded from any contractual redundancy payment scheme if the exclusion is objectively justified. 2001

Sometimes the employer will provide **extra compensation** to his employees in redundancy situations to compensate them for the unexpected loss of employment, or the employer may provide certain services, such as **outplacement services**, to his employees as part of the redundancy policy. As the fixed-term employee will, generally, have **no expectation of employment** beyond the term of the fixed-term contract the employer may be objectively justified in excluding him from such benefits. 2002

Waiver of redundancy rights Any waiver of redundancy rights contained in a fixed-term employment contract is invalid. 2003

MEMO POINTS Prior to 1 October 2002, a fixed-term employee could waive his right to a redundancy payment (though not with regard to redundancy payments for lay-offs or short-time working). Where the waiver is contained in an employment contract **entered into before 1 October 2002** it will be valid until such time as the employment contract is renewed or extended, at which point it will no longer be valid.

C. Remedies

2010 A fixed-term employee can bring a claim to an employment tribunal if his employer has infringed his right to **not be treated less favourably** (regs 7 SI 2002/2034).

The regulations also give him the **right not to be unfairly dismissed** or to **suffer a detriment** on specific grounds (¶¶1997, 1998).

If the **allegation**(s) that the employer infringed an employee's rights (or acted or did not act because of his belief or suspicion) is false and not made in good faith, the employee will have no right to claim.

2011 As seen, an employer has a **defence** if he can show that the treatment was justifiable on objective grounds (reg 3(3) SI 2002/2034).

2013 Where the fixed-term employee believes that he is entitled to permanent status as a result of **successive fixed-term contracts** the following requirements must be met before an application is made in the employment tribunal (reg 9 SI 2002/2034):
– the employee must have written to the employer requesting confirmation of the status of employment (i.e. whether permanent or not);
– the employer must have failed to respond or given a statement giving reasons why the contract remains fixed-term; and
– the employee must be employed by the employer at the time the application is made.

2014 Complaints must be made **within** 3 months beginning with the date of the act or failure to act or if it is part of a series of similar acts or failures, the last of them. However, a tribunal may **extend** this period if it considers it just and equitable to do so (¶9475).

Where the employee's claim is in respect of the employer's failure to provide him with the opportunity to secure permanent employment (reg 3(2) SI 2002/2034), the time limit is 3 months from the date that other individuals were informed of the vacancy.

2015 If the **claim is successful**, the tribunal can:
– make a declaration;
– order the employer to pay compensation; and
– recommend that the employer take, within a specified period, whatever action it considers reasonable to obviate or reduce the adverse effect on the employee or order the employer to re-employ the employee if it is practicable and just to do so.

If the employer fails, without reasonable justification, to comply, the tribunal can make an order for compensation (or increase the amount of compensation if one has already been made).

SECTION 5

Agency workers

2040 Agency workers are **often used** by employers (referred to here as end-users) to help on a short-term basis, either due to an increased workload, or to act as a cover for absent staff. These will be hired from **employment businesses** (referred to as agencies for the remainder of this section) who supply them "on assignments" where they will work under the end-user's instructions and control. Such workers are often temporary or casual workers of the agency, often referred to as "temps", and they will often sign on with one or more agencies to increase their chances of getting a regular supply of work.

There is no obligation on the part of an agency worker to accept an assignment, though once he does he is bound by various obligations according to that agency's written statement of terms and conditions. Likewise, in return the agency will be obliged to pay the worker for work done in accordance with the assignment. Usually, the end-user pays the agency for the services of the worker and the agency pays the worker directly according to its agreement with him.

MEMO POINTS 1. Employers may also use "**employment agencies**" which, broadly speaking, introduce work-seekers to clients for direct employment by them. With this arrangement, the work-seeker's contract (either as a worker or employee) will be with the client and not with the agency. This is usually known as "permanent recruitment" even though the employment may only be for a fixed time.
2. **Proposals for a new EU Directive** on the rights of agency workers (temps engaged via an intermediary employment business) are to be reconsidered and rewritten before they come back on the EU legislative agenda, which will create further delay. The aim of the proposals is to create parity of working conditions and benefits between temporary and permanent workers in all member states.

Agencies must ensure that (Conduct of Employment Agencies and Employment Businesses Regulations SI 2003/3319): 2042
- confidentiality is kept;
- agreement about its terms is obtained from the agency worker and that this is put in writing;
- information about the end-user is given to the agency worker on assignment;
- the agency worker's right to take direct employment with the client is protected; and
- the use of agency workers is restricted for the purposes of strike-breaking.

Note that the rules regulating the conduct of agencies (SI 2003/3319) which replace the previous regulations contain many **new provisions**, the main ones being as follows:
- limitations on any terms in the agreement between an agency and the end-user that prevent the agency worker from taking up a permanent job with the end-user unless a fee is paid;
- the requirement for an agency to confirm the identity of the agency worker and that he has the experience, training and qualifications that the end-user expects for that position;
- an on-going obligation on an agency to inform the end-user when it receives information about an agency worker which indicates that the worker might be unsuitable for the position;
- the requirement for an agency to obtain information on any health and safety risks known to the end-user and the steps taken to prevent or control those risks; and
- the requirement for an agency to obtain references on agency workers who are to work with vulnerable persons.

MEMO POINTS For further details, see the DTI's Guidance on the Conduct of Employment Agencies and Employment Businesses Regulations 2003.

Discrimination

Agencies are prohibited from committing unlawful discrimination on the grounds of sex, race, sexual orientation, or religion or belief (i) in the terms on which they offer to provide any of their services; (ii) by refusing or deliberately omitting to provide their services; or (iii) in the way they provide their services (s 15 SDA 1975; s 14 RRA 1976; reg 18 SI 2003/1661; reg 18 SI 2003/1660). Where, however, it is lawful for an employer to refuse to offer a job on grounds of sex, race, sexual orientation, or religion or belief (for example, because there is a genuine occupational qualification), an agency will be allowed to discriminate in relation to that job on the grounds of sex, race, sexual orientation, or religion or belief. In addition, an agency may not be liable if it can prove that (i) it had acted in reliance on a statement made to it by the employer to the effect that it could lawfully refuse to offer employment on grounds of sex, race, sexual orientation, or religion or belief; and (ii) it was reasonable for it to rely on the employer's statement. 2043

For the purposes of the **disability discrimination** legislation, a **principal** (who, for the purposes of the Disability Discrimination Act 1995 (DDA 1995), is the **end-user**) is prohibited from discriminating against a disabled agency worker (i) in the terms on which he is able to work; (ii) by not allowing him to work or continue to work; (iii) in the way he affords the worker access to any benefits or by refusing or deliberately omitting to afford him access to them; or (iv) by subjecting him to any other detriment (s 4B(1) DDA 1995). In addition, it is unlawful for an end-user to subject a disabled worker to harassment (s 4B(2) DDA 1995).

Moreover, if, by virtue of a **provision, criterion or practice** applied by or on behalf of all or most of the end-users to whom a disabled worker is or might be supplied, or a **physical feature of the premises** occupied by an end-user, a disabled person is likely, on each occasion when he is so supplied, to be placed at a substantial disadvantage in comparison with persons who are not disabled, the **agency worker's employer** (who, under the principles of common law, could be the employment agency or, more exceptionally, the end-user (¶¶2048, 2050)) is under a duty to make any reasonable adjustments to prevent such disadvantage from being suffered as he would have to make as if the provision, criterion, or practice were applied by him or on his behalf or (as the case may be) if the premises were occupied by him (s 4B(4), (5) DDA 1995). Note that end-users are under the same duty to make reasonable adjustments as if they were the actual employer of the agency worker. However, if a step is required to be taken under the duty to make reasonable adjustments in relation to a disabled agency worker by that worker's employer (i.e. the employment agency), the end-user is under no obligation to take that step (s 4B(7) DDA 1995).

These provisions **aim** to ensure that where a person, for the purposes of the DDA 1995, is the principal of an agency worker, he will be treated as having the same obligations as if he were the agency worker's actual employer (para 9.6 DD Code).

Main statutory rights

2044 The main **agency worker statutory rights** are shown in the table below. Some of these rights are dependent upon various qualifying criteria being satisfied (see relevant paragraph numbers). Those rights that do not have a qualifying period of continuous employment are commonly referred to as "Day One" rights and are, therefore, of particular importance to agency workers. These include the right to a national minimum wage, restrictions on working time and annual leave.

Agency worker's right to:	Para.
National minimum wage	¶2868
Paid annual leave	¶4000
Working time rules	¶3615
Statutory sick pay (Revenue and Customs has advised that if a worker is treated as an employee for NIC purposes, they will also be treated as an employee for statutory sick pay purposes)	¶4123
Statutory maternity pay, statutory adoption pay, and statutory paternity pay (again where agency worker is an employee. Pregnant workers who are not employees may be entitled to maternity allowance)	¶4420
Right to be accompanied to disciplinary and grievance hearings	¶6780
Right not to be discriminated against on the grounds of sex, race, sexual orientation, or religion or belief	¶5200

Status

2046 Agency workers will have a general employment relationship with their agency and this will usually be as a worker. However, in certain circumstances where the agency worker is on a long-term assignment (i.e. a number of years, though it has recently been suggested that this may be any period over a year), it may be possible for an agency worker to be an employee of either the agency or the end-user.

2048 **Agency/agency worker relationship** Agencies will usually hire agency workers under **general terms of engagement** (i.e. the basis on which the person is "on the books" of the agency) which amounts to a contract for services (employer-worker relationship). These general terms usually fall short of being a contract of employment (an employee-employer relationship) as there is usually a lack of mutuality of obligation (i.e. no obligation on a worker to accept a particular job offer or on the agency to make an offer) which is fundamental for there to be a contract of employment (¶35).

However, even if there is only a contract for services with regard to the general relationship between the agency, there may be a contract of service (i.e. of employment) between the agency worker and the agency in relation to a **specific assignment**, which will last for the duration of the assignment (*McMeechan v Secretary of State for Employment* [1997] IRLR 353, CA). If there is just one agreement between the agency worker and the agency, this agreement can be interpreted in different perspectives according to whether it is being considered in the context of the general engagement or in the context of a single assignment. When considering the agreement in the context of a particular assignment, if the two tests of employment are satisfied (¶32), the agency worker will be an employee of the agency for the purposes of that assignment. Such a contract of employment may be oral or implied (*Franks v Reuters Ltd and another* [2003] IRLR 423, CA). 2049

However, recent Court of Appeal decisions have indicated that with regard to **long-term assignments** where an end-user has exclusive day-to-day control of the agency worker and where it is the end-user who tells the agency when it no longer requires the worker, there will not be an implied contract of employment between the agency and the agency worker as the two tests for employment will not have been satisfied (i.e. sufficient control and mutuality of obligation) (*Brook Street Bureau (UK) Ltd v Dacas* [2004] IRLR 358, CA; *Bunce v Postworth Limited t/a Skyblue* [2005] IRLR 557, CA). In particular, in such cases the Court has emphasised that it will look at the reality of the situation with regard to who actually exercises control over the worker.

The EAT has also applied the guidance given by the Court of Appeal in *Brook Street Bureau (UK) Ltd v Dacas* [2004] IRLR 358, CA and in doing so has found that a worker who was providing his services (via his own company which had been set up specifically to provide his services), through an agency, **solely to the end-user**, was an employee of the end-user under an implied contract of employment. This was because the end-user had control over the worker, it supplied the worker with all his equipment and holidays were arranged to fit in with it. Further, although substitution of the worker's services was contractually allowable under the agency agreement, it was never done and (although the agency agreement expressly stated that the worker was not an employee of the end-user) the end-user referred to the worker as its employee in its departmental structure.

EXAMPLE **Employee of agency**

In *McMeechan v Secretary of State for Employment*, M had no general agreement with his agency though for each assignment, he had a job sheet that included a standard written statement of terms and conditions. However, although the terms stated that M was a self-employed worker, the Court held that M was an employee of the agency when he was on a specific assignment.

Not employee of agency

In *Brook Street Bureau (UK) Ltd v Dacas*, the agency had a written temporary worker agreement with D and was responsible for her discipline and pay, whereas the end-user, Wandsworth Council (WC), had exclusive day-to-day control and could decide when it no longer wanted D. D had been assigned to WC for 6 years until WC asked for her to be withdrawn. The Court held that the agency was not D's employer as it was not obliged to provide D with work and it did not have sufficient control over D.

End-user/agency worker relationship There is usually no employer-employee relationship between the end-user and the agency worker even though there may be sufficient control for an employer-employee relationship (*Motorola Ltd v (1) Davidson and (2) Melville Craig Group Ltd* [2001] IRLR, EAT). This is because whether there is a relationship will depend on both tests of employment being satisfied (i.e. sufficient control and mutuality of obligation, ¶32) and there being a contract of some sort between the end-user and the agency worker (*Esso Petroleum v (1) Jarvis and (2) Brentivine* [2002] All ER 112, EAT). 2050

There will be, though, at a minimum, a legal relationship between end-users and agency workers, which will mean that, depending on the contractual relationship between them and the agency, end-users may be vicariously liable for any wrong these workers do while working for them. An end-user may also be liable for a personal injury claim if an agency worker is injured.

EXAMPLE In *Motorola Ltd v (1) Davidson and (2) Melville Craig Group Ltd*, an agency worker, D, was recruited by MCG (on behalf of Motorola) to work for Motorola. D did not have a contract of employment with Motorola and filled out time sheets as supplied by MCG which contained its terms and conditions. According to this agreement, MCG controlled when and where D worked. Motorola did, though, exercise day-to-day control over D while he was at work.
The agreement between MCG and Motorola stated that if Motorola found a worker unsuitable, MCG had to remove him. As this sanction was so akin to an employer's power to dismiss (if Motorola did not want D to continue, he would be dismissed albeit through MCG), the EAT held that this indirect control amounted to a **sufficient degree of control**.

2051 However, with regard to **long-term assignments** over a period of years, as distinct from weeks or months typical of temporary or casual work, a contract of employment may be implied (*Franks v Reuters Ltd and another* [2003] IRLR 423, CA; *Brook Street Bureau (UK) Ltd v Dacas*, above). In *Brook Street (UK) Ltd v Dacas*, the Court of Appeal indicated that in the future, tribunals should consider this possibility and make findings of fact relevant to this issue. As to the likelihood of whether a tribunal would find the end-user is the employer, Sedley LJ suggested that any such arrangement for a year or more inexorably inferred such employment, although Munby J raised serious misgivings over such an inference. This has recently been borne out in a recent EAT decision in which the EAT, in applying this case law, confirmed that the tribunal had correctly assessed all the relevant factors and was entitled to hold that the agency worker was an employee of the end user from the start of her assignment regardless of the fact that her terms as an agency worker were different to the terms she was given once she was taken on permanently (*Royal National Lifeboat Institution v Bushaway* [2005] IRLR 674, EAT). The EAT went on to comment that an employee's terms of employment may well be very different at different times in his employment and what mattered was whether at any one time they indicate employment or self-employment.

It is advisable that end-users re-address the position of any agency workers who are used for long periods as it is now more likely that tribunals will judge them to be their employees. It should be noted that the same considerations are likely to apply to any temporary workers on long-term assignments.

CHAPTER 7

Directors

OUTLINE ¶¶

Directors are **office-holders** and are, therefore, officers of the company. They serve on the board of directors, in accordance with the company's memorandum and articles of association. 2100

There are **different categories** of director. These categories include: 2101
- **executive** directors, who are usually actively involved in the management of a company. They will often be employed by the company and are likely to have service agreements which set out the terms relating to their status as both a director and employee of the company (see ¶9920).
- **non-executive** directors, who are not usually actively involved in the management of the company and who may work on a part-time basis. Their function is often to monitor the management activities of the executive directors and to provide an independent balance on the board.
- **nominee** directors, who are appointed by a particular shareholder or group of shareholders. They are often found in group companies, where the parent company will nominate one of its own directors to sit on the board of a subsidiary to monitor its activities.
- **alternate** directors, who, if it is permitted in the company's articles, can be appointed by a director to take his place on the board.
- **de facto** directors, who claim or purport to act as directors, but have either not been validly appointed or continue to act as directors after they has been removed from office. A tribunal or court, for example, may decide that an individual is a de facto director, even though he is not formally a director, because of his responsibilities and duties.
- **shadow** directors, who are individuals in accordance with whose directions or instructions the directors of the company are accustomed to act (but not merely someone whose advice, given in a professional capacity, is acted upon by the directors, for example, a solicitor) (s 741(2) Companies Act 1985).

The above categories are not necessarily mutually exclusive (for example, an alternate director could be appointed to stand in for a managing director, who is usually an executive director).

However, all directors, irrespective of their title, are subject to the **same duties and liabilities** arising from their directorships.

A director's tenure of office does not automatically confer employee status on him. However, it is usual for directors who work full time in managing the company to be **employees** of the company. 2102

MEMO POINTS Whilst it is often the case that an executive director will be an employee, and a non-executive director will not be an employee, this is not always the case. For example, an individual could be an employee of a company but also sit on the board as a non-executive director.

A distinction should also be drawn between a director who is an office-holder and a senior employee whose job title includes the word "director." The latter is not a statutory board director.

2103 Where directors are employees, they are **bound by** the implied duties of all employees and any express terms in their employment contracts. They also remain subject to additional obligations as directors. This Chapter focuses on issues relating to directors as employees of the company. These issues also affect directors of public companies and these are discussed further in section 6 below.

MEMO POINTS The rules and legislation governing directors (relating to, for example, their appointment, conduct, remuneration, removal and termination) are summarised in this chapter as a more detailed review of the legislative provisions is outside the scope of this book.

1. Appointment and employment

2110 It is possible for a director to become an employee of the company and, similarly, an existing employee may become a director. Alternatively, an individual may be appointed as a director and engaged as an employee at the same time. If a director is required to work full-time in return for remuneration, the courts are likely to regard him as an employee, although the decision will be based on the circumstances of each particular case.

It is common, particularly in small companies, for a director to have a **controlling interest in the company's shares**. He may also be an employee, in which case certain issues arise (¶43).

2111 Some people **may not be directors** because they are the subject of a disqualification order preventing them from being a director of a company, or from being concerned or taking part in any way in the promotion, formation or management of a company for a certain period (Company Directors Disqualification Act 1986).

2112 Directors are **appointed** either by an ordinary resolution of the shareholders in general meeting or by a resolution of the board (subject to re-appointment by shareholders at the next AGM) (Table A, regs 76-79 SI 1985/805). Any procedural requirements will be set out in the articles of association.

Service agreements

2115 A director who is an employee of his company has a **contract of employment**, which is often called a service agreement to reflect his higher status than general staff. This agreement may be express or implied and need not be in writing (although as an employee, certain statutory written particulars of employment must be provided (¶1405)).

A **model service agreement** is provided at ¶9920. As for general staff, employers should carefully consider the contractual terms appropriate for their particular organisation. The model service agreement is intended to serve as guidance only and **should be tailored** to meet the specific requirements of the employer, and in relation to the particular role. The agreement may also be subject to **detailed negotiation**, in which case specialist legal advice should be sought. Reference should also be made to the company's articles of association, which will override any inconsistent term in the service agreement.

2116 The service agreement may deal with the director's **outside interests**, and may seek to limit his holding of securities in competing companies. The company may also wish to **protect its information** and other business interests by including express clauses on intellectual property, confidentiality, garden leave, and post-termination restrictive covenants (¶¶2310, 2400, 2529, 2550).

2117 The terms of the service agreement must be **approved by the board**, unless the managing director, for example, has been given authority by the board to set the terms of employment of the executive directors (Table A, regs 72 and 84 SI 1985/805). When setting the terms, the board (or managing director) must act in the best interests of the company. As the board cannot override the articles of association, any conflicting provisions in the service agreement will be ineffective.

The company can only enter into a service agreement with its directors that it can terminate by notice (or in specified circumstances) for a **period up to** five years (s 319 Companies Act 1985). For **longer periods**, shareholder approval in general meeting must be obtained. Without approval, any express term referring to a longer period will be void, and the contract will be deemed to be terminable on reasonable notice (¶8129). 2118

Remuneration The **fees** of directors, as office-holders, are governed by the articles of association and any shareholders' resolutions passed pursuant to them (Table A, reg 82 SI 1985/805). In practice, this sum is usually incorporated into their salaries as employees. 2119

As an employee, an executive director will receive a **salary** according to the terms of his service agreement. He may also be entitled to a bonus and other benefits, including pension, private health insurance, share options, company car etc. The company may also provide directors' liability insurance cover (¶2147). The total value of the director's salary and benefits may be set by a remuneration committee of the board.

The company's annual accounts must **disclose** details of all of the directors' emoluments (including any fees paid, salary, bonuses and benefits), pensions, share options/gains, money/assets paid or received under any long term incentive schemes, and any compensation that has been paid to directors for loss of office (s 232 Companies Act 1985, as amended and Sch 6 Pt I Companies Act 1985). 2120

Directors' remuneration must not be paid free of **income tax**, or calculated by reference to, or varying with, their income tax liabilities (s 311 Companies Act 1985). Special charging provisions apply to the taxation of benefits payable to directors and higher-paid employees. 2121

Inspection of agreements Unless the contract will expire or can be terminated by the company without compensation within the following 12 months, the company must make a copy of a director's service agreement (or a written memorandum of its terms) available for inspection without charge to all shareholders during business hours at an appropriate place (usually the company's registered office or principal place of business) (s 318 Companies Act 1985). 2122

Removal and termination

If a director's **employment** is terminated, he will not automatically lose his directorship, as the correct procedures for removal must be followed. When dismissing an executive director, the company should therefore ensure that the director either resigns, or is removed from, his office as a director. The **grounds for dismissal** should be drafted in broad terms, reflecting the grounds stated in the articles of association for the director to lose his office. 2125

Service agreements often contain a clause dealing with the **reconstruction or amalgamation** of the company (see **sample clause** below, taken from the model service agreement (¶9920)). The object of this clause is to prevent the director from claiming damages for breach of contract where he is offered employment on no less favourable terms with the company's successor following its liquidation or reorganisation. 2126

EXAMPLE If the Employment is terminated by reason of the liquidation of the Company in order to effect its reconstruction or amalgamation, the Executive will have no claim against the Company provided that he is offered employment with the company or undertaking resulting from the reconstruction or amalgamation on terms and conditions that are no less favourable to him than the terms of this Agreement.

The articles of association will provide for the removal of a director as an **office-holder**. Regardless of any provisions to the contrary in the articles or in the service agreement, a director can be removed by ordinary resolution of the shareholders in general meeting following a special procedure (s 303, 304, 379 Companies Act 1985). 2127

MEMO POINTS A director who is also a shareholder may be able to block such a shareholder resolution if the articles provide for enhanced voting rights in these circumstances (*Bushell v Faith* [1970] 1 All ER 53). Such a provision is usually only found in small companies.

If a director is removed from office, he will remain an ordinary employee (but not an office-holder) of the company unless it is an express or implied term of the employment contract that he must be a director, in which case the employment will also terminate. Alternatively, a director's service contract may specifically provide that on removal from the board, the director's employment will automatically terminate. In such cases, the Court of Appeal has held that such dismissal may be legitimate on the grounds of 'some other substantial reason' (¶8530), and therefore, potentially fair.

Often the directorship and the employment are **inter-dependent** (for example, the managing director must be a director). If this is the case, removal from the board may result in the individual being entitled to damages for wrongful dismissal, if he is not given the required notice of termination of his employment, and possibly for unfair dismissal or redundancy. Contractual provisions allowing the company to call for the director's resignation from office should therefore be exercised with caution. The inclusion of an express agreement in the service agreement that the termination of any directorship will not amount to constructive dismissal may assist the company's defence to any such claim.

2128 In some cases, the articles of association will provide for a director to cease to hold office on the occurrence of **certain specified events** (for example, if he becomes bankrupt, is mentally ill, or is absent from board meetings for more than 6 months) (Table A, reg 81 SI 1985/805). The employment may be made subject to similar provisions, in which case there would be no breach of the employment contract (and therefore no claim for damages) if it were terminated in those circumstances (*Shindler v Northern Raincoat Co Ltd* [1960] 1 WLR 1038).

2129 Executive directors (including the managing director) are exempt from the requirement of standard form articles of association that a third of the total number of directors **retire by rotation** at each AGM (Table A, regs 73, 84 SI 1985/805). The articles can be amended to exclude the requirement for all types of directors. If the requirement does apply, the retiring directors are subject to re-election at the AGM, giving the shareholders the opportunity to review the composition of the board.

2130 Although the service agreement commonly provides that the director must not **resign his directorship** without the company's consent, he cannot be restrained from doing so. The company's remedy would be for breach of contract.

2131 **Termination payments** Any payments for compensation for the loss of office or on retirement, including transfers of the company's property or business, that do not represent damages for breach of contract or pension for past services (often referred to as a "**golden handshake**") will require the prior approval of the shareholders by ordinary resolution (ss 312-313, 316 Companies Act 1985).

MEMO POINTS The DTI has consulted on its **proposed reforms** to directors' severance pay (Rewards for failure: Directors' remuneration – contracts, performance and severance), but has put on hold its plans to introduce any legislation on this matter for the time being. Instead the Government has decided to monitor how effectively the Directors' Remuneration Report Regulations SI 2002/1986 (¶2171) are working in practice, although it has not ruled out the possibility of future legislation in this area.

2. Duties

2133 As an **employee**, a director will be subject to common law implied duties (¶1195) and any **express duties** set out in his service agreement. These should be described in broad terms, reflecting the wide obligations owed by the director to the company. It may be useful for the service agreement to provide that the board can specify his duties from time to time, giving it the flexibility to **vary the duties** as required by changing circumstances. Express provisions relating to the director's duties may be subject to negotiation, particularly if he has other interests (which should not conflict with his duties to the company (¶2116)).

If it is envisaged that another person may be appointed to **act jointly** with the director, an express right should be reserved in the service agreement to prevent the director from claiming that he has been constructively dismissed by virtue of a loss of status.

MEMO POINTS The Government has consulted on its proposed company law reform, which includes a new statutory statement of directors' duties. More information and a copy of the Company Law Reform Bill can be obtained from the DTI website at http://www.dti.gov.uk/cld/review.htm.

As an **office-holder**, he will be subject to additional duties, which include acting within the powers delegated to him, observing his fiduciary duties, and exercising proper care and skill. The positions of director and employee are often inter-dependent, such that it is important to consider the duties to which a director is subject as a whole. 2134

Duties under the articles of association As the company's representatives, directors must act within the powers delegated to them. The company's articles of association determine the powers delegated to the board and how they should be exercised, which in turn are usually delegated to the individual director. 2135

Duty to obey instructions Directors must obey the company's instructions without departing from them, unless the company allows them the discretion to do so. A director must, therefore, **act within his authority**. It is often the case that directors do not have any specific instructions from either the shareholders or the board. If the instructions are vague or unclear, the director will discharge this duty by following a reasonable course of action in what he believes to be the company's best interests. Directors are usually granted a wide discretion to act within the company's articles. In exercising his discretion, a director must always work within the boundaries of his powers set out in the memorandum, articles, shareholder resolutions and agreements. As long as a director remains within these powers when acting on vague or unclear instructions, he will not be in breach of this duty. 2136

Duty of personal performance A director's **appointment** is personal and cannot be delegated. However, delegation of a director's **functions** is usually permitted by the articles. If the articles are silent on the matter, delegation may be authorised by the shareholders by a special resolution. Delegation of a director's **office** may also be permitted and it is common for articles to permit directors to appoint alternates. 2137

Fiduciary duties Given the position of trust which directors have within the company, all directors (non-executive and executive) owe certain fiduciary duties to the company. These duties are distinct from and go further than the duty of fidelity applicable to all employees (¶1213). A director's duties include the following: 2138

– **acting in good faith** in what he considers to be the best interests of the company, i.e. of the shareholders (current and future). This includes the director's duty to **disclose** his **own misconduct** (*Item Software (UK) Ltd v Fassihi* [2004] IRLR 928, CA);
– not putting himself in a situation where his **personal interest conflicts** with that of the company, although it may be possible for him (after full disclosure of his position) to obtain consent from the company to act in such circumstances; and
– **exercising his delegated powers** only for the purposes for which they are granted, and within the scope of such powers.

Where a director uses his powers for a purpose other than in pursuance of his office, he is **personally liable** for any loss caused as a result.

EXAMPLE 1. In *Bishopsgate Investment Trust Ltd v Maxwell (No 2)* [1994] 1 All ER 262, M, a director, signed documents transferring some of the company's assets to a bank for no consideration and for the sole benefit of a third party. M was held liable to the company for the loss of these assets.
2. In *Item Software (UK) Ltd v Fassihi and ors* [2003] IRLR 769, HC (confirmed on appeal ([2004] IRLR 928, CA)), F, an executive director, sought to divert the business flowing from a major contract from IS Ltd to a rival company with which he had close connections and had placed himself in a position where his personal interests conflicted with those of IS Ltd. No losses were suffered by IS Ltd as a result of these breaches alone, but there was an additional fiduciary duty on F to disclose his misconduct

at the time he committed it and, consequently, he was liable for losses suffered by IS Ltd resulting from the loss of the contract.

2139 Consequently, in relation to **confidentiality and restraints**, a director must not place himself in a position where his personal interests and those of the company conflict, or attempt to make a secret profit. For example, a director will be in breach if he takes for himself the benefit of a contract which he had been ostensibly negotiating on behalf of the company (*Cook v Deeks* [1916] AC 554).

A director's fiduciary duties will not prevent him from taking **preparatory steps** to the extent that employees may do so (¶2512).

In contrast to the duty of fidelity, fiduciary duties **may continue** after the fiduciary relationship (i.e. the directorship) ends. In particular, former directors must not take for themselves or another, a maturing business opportunity which the company is actively pursuing, where they resigned at least in part in order personally to take advantage of that opportunity or where the opportunity only arose as a result of their position as director (*Island Export Finance Ltd v Umunna* [1986] BCLC 460, HC). However, like employees (¶2415), former directors may use their **own skill and knowledge** (including, for example, market information learned during the directorship) for their own benefit and in competition with the company.

2140 A director must also **account for any profit** he has made as a direct result of his position. For example, as a director, he may have information about business opportunities, such as business contracts soon to be available. He must not use this information to his own advantage by entering into any such contract in his own name. If he did so, he would be obliged to account to the company for any profit made, unless the shareholders approved of his action by ordinary resolution in general meeting after he had made full disclosure of the relevant facts.

2141 **Duty of proper care and skill** Directors must exercise their responsibilities with proper care and skill (*Dorchester Finance Co Ltd v Stebbing* [1989] BCLC 498). An employed director may also have express duties of skill and care under his service agreement.

2142 Generally, a director must attend diligently to the affairs of the company, exercising the **degree of care** that a reasonable person would exercise on his own behalf. A higher degree of diligence is required of executive directors than of non-executive directors.

2143 The office of director does not require the holder to possess any particular skills. The **level of skill** required of a director is generally subjective, i.e. measured according to the knowledge and experience of the individual. However, a **director of an insolvent company** must exhibit the general knowledge, skill and experience that he actually has and which might reasonably be expected of someone carrying out his function within the company. Otherwise, he may incur personal liability for wrongful trading (¶2165). Increasingly, this dual subjective and objective test is being applied by the courts to assess a director's skill in ordinary breach of duty cases, and it is anticipated that the reformed company legislation will stipulate that this test should be used (*Norman and another v Theodore Goddard (a firm)* and others [1991] BLLC 1028).

2144 It is acceptable for a director to rely on other board directors and other office-holders. Where it is reasonable for him to do so, a director may **delegate** his powers (including appointing an alternate director) and there is no right of action against him for the actions or defaults of properly appointed delegates.

Indemnity and insurance

2147 When civil or criminal proceedings are brought against a director by a third party in connection with the performance of his duties, the company may **indemnify** the director against any liability incurred by him where judgment is given in his favour, he is acquitted or the court grants relief because he acted honestly and reasonably and ought fairly to be excused (see below) (s 310 Companies Act 1985; Table A, reg 118 SI 1985/805). A company **cannot** otherwise **indemnify** directors for negligence, default or breach of duty.

Where the company obtains or maintains directors' **liability insurance cover** on behalf of its directors in any financial year, this must be disclosed in the directors' report. This insurance covers liabilities incurred in the performance of the director's duties. The amount of any premium paid on a director's behalf is a benefit in kind, which is taxable as such under special provisions. Consequently, if an insurance policy is a qualifying policy, the taxable amount of the premium is cancelled out by the cost to the director of obtaining cover i.e. it is a taxable benefit but the value of the benefit is nil.

Breach of duties

If a director breaches his agency or fiduciary duties or fails to exercise proper care and skill, the company can take action against him in order to recover its loss. In some cases, the company may choose to ratify the director's actions by ordinary resolution (special resolution is required if the breach exceeds the limits of the company's memorandum), for example, where his personal interests have been in conflict with the company's, or where he has made a profit from his position as a director. **2150**

In cases of **serious breach**, the company may be entitled to remove the director from office and possibly to terminate his employment (¶8155).

A director may **escape liability** for negligence, default, breach of duty or breach of trust at the court's discretion if he can show that he acted honestly and reasonably and ought fairly to be excused (s 727 Companies Act 1985). **2151**

3. Statutory obligations

The following table gives a **summary** of a director's statutory obligations. **2155**

Obligation	Reference (Companies Act 1985)
Act within **powers of memorandum**	s 35
Disclose interest in **contract/proposed contract** with company (including, for example, own service agreement) [1]	s 317
Disclose interest (and those of spouse/civil partner and minor children) in **company's shares/debentures**	ss 324, 328
Have regard to **employee interests** [2]	s 309
Make disclosures and obtain shareholder approval for **compensation for loss of office**	s 313, 314
Obtain shareholder approval (by an ordinary resolution) of **substantial property transaction** with company [3]	s 320
Observe **restrictions** on company making loan, acting as creditor or giving security to directors or persons connected with them	ss 330-346
Comply with statutory **accounting requirements**, including production of directors' report [4]	Part VII; s 234, Sch 7, paras 9, 11
Maintain up-to-date **records** and file returns with Registrar of Companies	ss 221, 363

1. Obligation arises at the **first board meeting** at which a contract is to be discussed. **Non-compliance** usually results in a fine but if the director has also failed to comply with general duties of disclosure, any resulting transactions will be voidable, i.e. can be made void at the option of the innocent party (*Guinness plc v Saunders* [1990] 2 AC 663).

2. Duty is **owed to company** and not directly to employees, so latter cannot complain if directors give priority to shareholders' interests.

3. Substantial property transaction means **buying** a non-cash asset exceeding a certain value from, or **selling** such an asset to, the company.

4. **Directors' report of companies** with an average of 250 employees must include:
a. information on the employment of disabled persons; and
b. a statement on steps taken to develop arrangements to:
– provide employees with relevant information,
– consult employees or their representatives on matters affecting them,
– encourage performance through share or other incentive schemes, and
– achieve employee awareness of financial/economic factors affecting company performance.
See further memo points to ¶2172.

4. Personal liability

2160 A limited company is treated as a separate legal entity having its own rights and duties. As such, directors are generally not held responsible for the company's debts or defaults. In **certain circumstances**, however, the director may be personally liable if he has:
– given a personal guarantee;
– acted outside his actual authority, such that the company seeks an indemnity for loss suffered as a result of an action brought by a third party who had assumed he had authority;
– acted entirely outside his authority (actual and "apparent") whilst purporting to act on the company's behalf, with the result that a third party has a direct right of action against him;
– acted illegally as a director (i.e. while under a disqualification order);
– failed to maintain proper up-to-date records and/or make the appropriate returns to Companies House or breached other statutory duties under the Companies Act 1985; and
– committed an offence under certain health and safety legislation.

2161 A company may be liable for **involuntary manslaughter** (i.e. death caused by gross negligence) if a specific employee who is sufficiently senior to embody the company can be identified as individually guilty of the same crime. At present, the company's directors are not personally liable for the crime (unless, of course, they are individually guilty), although they may be liable for a health and safety offence (see above) in respect of the death.

MEMO POINTS A draft bill for **reforming corporate manslaughter** is progressing through Parliament (see memo points to ¶5073 for more details).

5. Insolvency of the company

2165 If a company is insolvent or is likely to become insolvent, various offences may be committed by a director, the most important of which are (Insolvency Act 1986):
– **misfeasance**, i.e misapplying, retaining or becoming otherwise accountable for any money or other property of the company or being guilty of any misfeasance or breach of any fiduciary or other duty in relation to the company (s 212 Insolvency Act 1986);
– **fraudulent trading**, i.e. knowingly carrying on the company's business with the intention of defrauding creditors of the company or of any other person, or for any other fraudulent purpose (s 213 Insolvency Act 1986); and
– **wrongful trading**, i.e. failing to take every reasonable step to minimise the potential loss to the company's creditors when he knew, or ought to have concluded, that there was no reasonable prospect that the company would avoid going into insolvent liquidation (s 214 Insolvency Act 1986).

In all cases, the court can require the director to **contribute to** the company's assets. Fraudulent trading is also a **criminal offence** punishable by imprisonment and/or a fine. A director can also be disqualified if his conduct whilst the company is insolvent renders him unfit (s 6 Company Directors Disqualification Act 1986).

2166 If a director is involved in entering into a **transaction at an undervalue**, or the granting of a **preference**, when the company was insolvent (or which caused the company to become insolvent), the transaction or preference can be set aside and the director may be liable to make up any loss to the company (ss 238-241 Insolvency Act 1986).

6. Directors of public companies

2170 In addition **more onerous conditions** apply to public company directors who:
– must leave office by the first annual general meeting following their 70th birthday, unless there is a resolution to the contrary (s 293 Companies Act 1985);
– must not deal in options to sell or buy quoted shares or debentures of their company or of certain associated companies (s 323 Companies Act 1985);
– face more stringent restrictions in relation to company loans;

– are bound by "insider dealing" provisions, as they are likely to have "inside information", i.e. specific or precise unpublished information relating to an issuer or securities which, if made public, would have a significant effect on the price of any securities (Criminal Justice Act 1993).

A company is a **public company** if its memorandum of association so states and it has registered or re-registered as such (for which it must meet certain requirements, including having a minimum share capital of a certain amount) (ss 11, 118 Companies Act 1985).

A **listed public company** must also comply with its continuing obligations under the Listing Rules of the London Stock Exchange (the so-called "Yellow Book"). These contain a number of obligations with regard to the display of directors' contracts and particularisation of directors, their emoluments, etc., in the context of takeover bids, offers and circulars. Directors must comply with its "Model Code" in relation to their **dealings in the company's securities**. It may be useful for the service agreement expressly to refer to the director's obligation to comply with the Model Code and the insider dealing provisions (see **sample clause** below, taken from the model service agreement (¶9920)). 2171

EXAMPLE The Executive will comply (and will procure that his wife and minor children comply) with all applicable rules of law (including, in particular, Part V of the Criminal Justice Act 1993), Stock Exchange codes, rules and regulations, and all rules, policies and codes of conduct of the Company as issued from time to time in relation to the holding of and dealing in shares, debentures or other securities.

MEMO POINTS In respect of financial years ending on or after 31 December 2002, certain quoted companies are required to publish a **Directors' Remuneration Report** within their annual report, in addition to the disclosure requirements discussed above (Directors' Remuneration Report Regulations SI 2002/1986). This report is subject to shareholder approval. Information to be provided includes details on individual directors' remuneration packages (including emoluments, share options, long term incentive plans, pensions, compensation and excess retirement benefits); a statement of the company's directors' remuneration policy for the following financial year; the circumstances surrounding the consideration by the directors of directors' remuneration issues (including the role of the board and remuneration committee); and certain information to be set out concerning each director's contract of service or contract for services.

The directors are responsible for the good **corporate governance** of their company, initiated by the Cadbury and Greenbury Reports, and clarified and consolidated by the Hampel Report, which includes detailed provisions in relation to duties, remuneration and training of directors. This resulted in the Principles of Good Governance and Code of Best Practice published by the London Stock Exchange, together with consequent amendments to the Listing Rules. 2172

The Financial Reporting Council (FRC) has produced a **revised Combined Code of Corporate Governance**, published in July 2003, which is to apply to reporting years commencing on or after 1 November 2003. This includes the Code itself and related guidance (the Turnball guidance on Internal Control, the Smith guidance on Audit Committees and various items of good practice from the Higgs report). The revised Code makes specific recommendations with regard to board structures, re-election of non-executive directors, rules relating to the appointment of chief executives to the role of chairman, the role of chairmen and senior independent directors, the constitution of the nomination committee, and roles of the audit and remuneration committees.

MEMO POINTS The DTI has published draft guidance to the accounts and audit provisions in the Companies (Audit, Investigations and Community Enterprise) Act 2004 and associated secondary legislation. It provides details of a new statement in the directors' report about the disclosure of information by directors to auditors and guidance on the Act's requirements regarding employees providing information and explanation to auditors. It will be finalised when all the secondary legislation described in the guidance has been laid before Parliament.

The **takeover of a company** may be subject to the City Code on Takeovers and Mergers, which may restrict the company's ability to amend or enter service contracts during the course of a takeover offer if this would involve an abnormal increase in the director's remuneration or a significant improvement in his terms of service. 2173

CHAPTER 8

Assignments

OUTLINE ¶¶

2200 An employer may want an employee to work for the **benefit of another undertaking** during the course of his employment, for example, if the employee's job is such that it needs to be performed in a different office, or when the employer wants the employee to gain additional experience. This is referred to as an assignment or secondment of the employee. This chapter outlines the issues involved, including the special rules and considerations that apply to assignments abroad.

2201 The terms assignment and secondment are often used interchangeably. However, the term **secondment** can be used where there is a specific contract between the employer and a third party undertaking and the employee is specifically seconded to support that contract, for example, where an employee is provided to another company to act as consultant to a specific project.

The term **assignment** may be used both for secondment situations and those where an employee works for an affiliate (i.e. an entity within the same group of companies as the employer and under the same direction and control of the employer), or at a branch office of the employer. This might also be referred to as an intra-group assignment.

Where the assignment is to another country the term **posting** is commonly used, although the term detachment is being used more and more frequently. Notwithstanding the use of all these different terms the concept behind them is identical, i.e. the employee continues to be employed by his employer but the work that he carries out is for the benefit of another undertaking.

2202 This chapter does **not cover** situations that involve the legal assignment of the employee's contract of employment to another entity which results in a **change in the identity of the employer**. Such legal assignments would arise, for example, where all or part of the employer's business is transferred to a third party and, as a consequence, the third party takes over the employment of those employees who support that business. Such transfers are dealt with in Chapter 24 on TUPE.

SECTION 1

Prerequisites for assignment

The **period of assignment** may be for a **short term**, for example when the employee is asked to carry out a specific task in a branch office of the employer which only takes a few days, or it may be for a **longer term**, for example when an employee is seconded to the office of a third party to provide technical support to a project. In each instance, the employment contract remains in place and the employee **remains employed** by the employer throughout the period of assignment, with the period counting for continuity of service. Furthermore, the expectation is that the employee will return to his original job at the end of the period of assignment. 2210

Employee consent

Before an employer assigns his employee he needs to find out whether he has the employee's consent to the proposed assignment. Although many employees consider assignment as a positive step in their career progression, there may be instances when the employee does not wish to move from his current position. 2211

Consent will **already exist** if the contract of employment specifically provides for the assignment of an employee as part of his job, for example, where a management accountant is employed to assist affiliated companies in setting up their accounting systems. Alternatively, the contract of employment may contain a **mobility clause** under which the employer is entitled to relocate his employee (¶1618). Where there is no express mobility clause, one may be **implied** under the principle of business efficacy if the employee is expected to carry out his work at different locations (¶1631). It is **good practice** for the employer to consult with the employee prior to deciding on any assignment. 2212

When there is **no mobility clause** (either express or implied), the employer must obtain the employee's express consent prior to any assignment and this will amount to a variation of the employment contract.

An employer owes an implied **duty of trust and confidence** to his employees (¶1242). The failure of the employer to act reasonably in matters relating to an assignment could result in a breach of that duty with the possible outcome that the employee could claim against him for breach of contract (*United Bank Ltd v Akhtar* [1989] IRLR 507, EAT). 2213

Effect on the terms of employment

When **variations** to the employment contract are necessary as a result of the assignment, they must be **agreed** and the employer cannot unilaterally make variations to the terms without the employee's consent (¶1600). Variations to some terms are required by law to be **evidenced in writing** (¶1400) but it is **good practice** for all changes arising from an assignment to be agreed by way of written amendment or variation of the employment contract. 2215

Issues such as the **control and direction** of the employee during the period of assignment will need to be addressed, and the employee will need to know who he is to report to. The employer's **grievance and disciplinary procedures** and **health and safety procedures** may need amendment to accommodate the circumstances of the assignment. The assignment may also affect any employee performance evaluation, if carried out during the period of the assignment, and input from the other undertaking in this should be considered. The employer retains ultimate responsibility for these procedures and should also ensure that an adequate **health and safety policy** applies to any workplace to which the employee is assigned (¶4901). Any working practices of the other undertaking, including those that affect the **hours of work** of the employee, should be taken into account. 2216

The employment contract may need to incorporate **new terms** that are agreed in connection with the assignment and depending on the particular circumstances. They will usually 2217 include details on the identity of the other undertaking, and the place of work. Terms covering the financial arrangements, the duration of the assignment, and the termination of the assignment and the employee's return at the end of the assignment will need to be considered.

2218 The employee may be given **additional benefits or reimbursement of costs** such as:
- paid **home leave**: if the assignment is to a place far from the employee's home the employer may agree to pay for the employee and his family to return home at regular intervals;
- payment of **housing costs**: if the employee is asked to relocate to a different area from his original workplace location he may incur additional housing costs which the employer may agree to meet in full or subsidise; and
- payment of **school fees**: the relocation may affect an employee's family and the employer may agree to pay for the school fees of the employee's children either in the original workplace location or in the new location.

The employer usually agrees to cover the employee's **costs of travel** to the new place of employment and, if appropriate, the **relocation costs** to the new workplace and his return to the original workplace.

2219 As an assignment is not intended to be permanent the parties must agree the **duration of the assignment** and, if for a fixed-term, the date on which it is to end. The parties should also agree on the terms and condition of the **return** to the original place of employment, covering issues such as the employee's seniority and the availability of his original job on his return.

2220 Both the employer and the employee should agree in advance their respective rights and responsibilities arising on **early termination** of the assignment because of the following events:
- the employee's acts or omissions;
- the employer's recall of the employee to his original workplace;
- the other undertaking no longer requiring the employee; or
- external circumstances e.g. when there is an event of force majeure (i.e. acts of God, war, earthquake or similar events beyond the control of the parties which prevent the continuation of the contract).

Agreement between the employer and the other undertaking

2222 It is good practice to evidence in writing any agreement concerning a secondment, especially where the other undertaking is a **third party** but also if it is an intra-group assignment. The agreement should reflect the issues discussed above and, depending on the circumstances of the secondment, the extent of the other undertaking's involvement.

2223 The employer may require the other undertaking to cover the **remuneration and costs** of the employee including those relating to the additional benefits and costs which are incurred in connection with the secondment. Reimbursement may be either to the employer or directly to the employee.

The parties should also agree in advance which **other costs** are recoverable from the other undertaking and in which circumstances, for example, where the secondment is terminated early. If there are associated employer costs that arise on early termination the employer may want to obtain an indemnity to cover them. The cost of arranging and placing of **insurance cover** for the benefit of the employer may also be met by the other undertaking.

Finally, the employer may want to include a "hold harmless" and **indemnity clause** in the agreement, whereby the other undertaking will cover him with respect to claims, damages and actions arising from the employee's acts or omissions during the period of secondment.

SECTION 2

Assignment abroad (posting)

There are various situations where an employer may want to assign his employee to work abroad. The employer may be part of a multi-national group with offices throughout the world, or he may provide consultancy services to clients who have offices abroad. 2230

The employer will need to consider the **immigration requirements** of the country of posting and ensure that work visas and similar requirements are met. He will also need to check its **employment laws** to ensure that the posting does not breach them and it may be advisable to obtain the advice of a local lawyer for this purpose. 2231

The same issues of employee consent and how the assignment will have an effect on the employee's contract of employment will apply to a posting (¶¶2210, 2215). Issues that specifically apply to postings may be covered in the employer's expatriation handbook whilst further issues may need to be discussed and agreed between the employer and the employee. 2232

A. Contractual issues

Where the employer frequently posts his employees abroad, some terms and conditions relating to postings may be contained in an **expatriation handbook** or similar document. Therefore, although the employment contract itself may not specifically contain the terms and conditions of posting, the terms in the handbook will apply if specifically incorporated into the employment contract by reference. 2235

Other **terms, personal** to the individual postings, will not be contained in the handbook but will need to be agreed on a case-by-case basis. Agreements regarding some terms are required by law to be evidenced in writing (¶1400) but it is good practice for terms arising from an assignment to be agreed by way of written amendment or variation of the employment contract.

It is usual for the following issues to be discussed and agreed prior to a posting.

Remuneration

Remuneration will cover: 2236
- any incentive payments to encourage the employee to accept the posting;
- additional benefits relating to relocation costs, home leave, housing costs and school fees. These are more likely to be offered and expected in postings abroad and usually form part of the incentive package offered to employees; and
- currency of remuneration, rate of exchange, how and when paid, the place of payment and whether there is an allocation of remuneration between UK sterling and foreign currency.

Tax position

The length of the posting may affect the employee's residence status in the UK (¶3102) or he may have to pay tax in the country of posting as well as in the UK. The employer may agree to augment the employee's salary to make up any loss that he suffers as a result of his paying higher taxes as a result of his posting. 2237

NIC and benefits

Payment of UK NICs establish an employee's entitlement to certain contribution-based UK state benefits as well as counting towards his state pension accrual (¶6931). Generally, if an employee is temporarily posted abroad, Class 1 NIC may still be paid for the first 52 weeks 2238 (in certain circumstances this may be extended for a further 52 weeks). Continuing payment of UK NICs may also be recognised by the country of posting, exempting the assignee from making social security contributions in the country of posting and entitling him to the state benefits, for example health care, of that country (see below for a summary and ¶7000 for a more detailed discussion).

2240 When the posting is to an **EEA state** the employee is expected to contribute towards the social security system of the state in which he is working (EC Regulation 1971/1408; ¶7026).

However, **special circumstances** will **exempt** a UK employee who continues to have Class 1 UK NICs paid on his behalf whilst he is posted abroad (¶7028). These circumstances exist when the posting is:
- to another EEA state;
- in continuation of his employment;
- for a period expected to be less than 12 months; and
- not taking the place of someone else who works for the employer and who has come to the end of the time they have to spend here.

Consequently, the employee will **not be required** to make social security contributions in the EEA state of posting but may still obtain **certain state benefits**, the most relevant for employees being healthcare cover.

Where the special circumstances exist the employer should apply for a certificate of continuing liability from the National Insurance Contributions Office (NICO) before the employee is posted. This certificate, also called a **Form E101**, when shown in the country of posting, will evidence the employee's exemption from social security contributions in the country of posting.

If the **posting is extended** beyond the initial period the exemption may be extended for up to a further 12 months with the consent of the state of posting (¶7029). Application must be made by the employer to NICO and, if successful, will be evidenced by the issue of a **Form 102**.

MEMO POINTS For the purposes of this section the term 'EEA state' covers the EU Member States and the EEA countries (i.e. Austria, Belgium, Cyprus, Czech Republic, Denmark, Estonia, Finland, France, Germany, Gibraltar, Greece, Hungary, Iceland, the Republic of Ireland, Italy, Latvia, Liechtenstein, Lithuania, Luxembourg, Malta, the Netherlands, Norway, Poland, Portugal, Slovakia, Slovenia, Spain, Sweden and the United Kingdom) and Switzerland.

2241 The same **recognition of continuing liability for UK NICs** applies where the special circumstances set out above exist and the employee is posted to a country which has an appropriate **reciprocal agreement** with the UK (¶7036). The employer must apply for a certificate of continuing liability from NICO before the employee is posted abroad and this will be recognised in the country of posting, exempting him from making contributions towards that country's social security system and, in some cases, allowing him to obtain state benefits within that country. The benefits provided in the country of posting will depend on the scope of the relevant reciprocal agreement.

2242 Where the temporary posting of less than 12 months is **to another country**, and Class 1 NICs continue to be paid in the UK the employee will, as seen above, retain his right to UK state benefits on his return to the UK. However, in the absence of a reciprocal agreement between the UK and the country of posting it is unlikely that the employee will be able to claim any state benefits in the country of posting save those that are paid through his UK employer, such as statutory maternity pay or statutory sick pay. However, contributions may also be due in the country of posting (this may lead to a **double charge**), which may entitle the employee to certain state benefits in the country of posting (¶7044).

Healthcare

2245 In the UK, the provision of state healthcare cover under the National Health Service (NHS) is not dependent on a person having made NICs but on his residence in the UK. When an employee is posted abroad his entitlement to state healthcare cover will depend on the country to which he is posted.

If a UK national is **posted to an EEA state**, the employee and the members of his family will be entitled to the full state healthcare cover of that state. Entitlement is evidenced by **Form E128** which should be obtained in the UK from NICO before the employee is posted abroad. As the level of healthcare provided by each EU member state differs, **some services**, such as the ambulance service, that are provided by the NHS without charge to the patient, may not be included in the state healthcare cover of the state of posting and **must be paid for by the patient**. Additional healthcare cover may need to be taken out privately to cover such extra expenses, and the employer may agree to provide and pay for this. Alternatively the employer might agree to directly reimburse the employee as and when such expenses are incurred. 2246

Entitlement to state healthcare cover under Form E128 will not extend to an EEA state other than the one in which the employee works, although urgent treatment will be covered for him and his family. The employee should apply for Form E111 to cover himself and his family when visiting other EEA states.

MEMO POINTS Gibraltar is not included in the definition of EEA (see memo point above) for the specific purpose of healthcare cover. Before commencing a posting there the UK employee should get in touch with the Gibraltar Health Authority to establish whether healthcare cover will be provided or if he will have to pay into the Gibraltar Group Practice Medical Scheme.

If a UK employee is **posted** to a country **outside the EEA**, the extent of healthcare cover provided to him will depend on whether there is an agreement between that country and the UK to provide healthcare cover. This can be checked with the Department for Work and Pensions before the employee is posted. 2247

EXAMPLE The United States of America does not extend its state healthcare cover to UK residents who are there, even though it has a reciprocal agreement with the UK covering social security contributions and benefits.

If the state healthcare cover or the medical facilities of the country of posting is inadequate the employer should consider funding private healthcare cover for the employee and his family during the posting. 2248

Emergency repatriation If the posting is to a country of political instability or if there are inadequate medical facilities the employer may consider obtaining additional insurance protection and emergency return cover. 2249

Pension

The employee's **UK state pension accrual** will not be affected as long as Class 1 NICs are made in the UK for him whilst he is posted abroad. Should the posting exceed 52 weeks and the employer is unsuccessful in extending the certificate for continuing liability (Form E102 or equivalent) contributions can continue to be made in the UK, thereby protecting the employee's pension accrual. Unfortunately, this could result in Class 1 NICs being made in the UK as well as contributions being made in the country of posting. In order to protect his UK state pension accrual the employee has the choice of continuing to make UK NICs as voluntary Class 2 payments. 2250

Employer contributions to a **UK occupational** pension scheme should continue whilst the employee is posted abroad and the employee can continue to make voluntary contributions to such schemes whilst posted abroad subject to Revenue and Customs limits.

B. Applicable law

2255 The rights conferred on the parties under the employment contract will be decided and applied by reference to the proper or applicable **law of the contract**, whilst the right to bring an action before a specific court will depend on whether that court has valid **jurisdiction** over the issue. The law of the contract and jurisdiction are two separate concepts, and, as a result, the court of jurisdiction may be required to apply the law of another country to the dispute before it.

The principles which identify which law will apply are set out in the Contracts (Applicable Law) Act 1990 which incorporates into UK law the EU uniform rules adopted under the 1980 Rome Convention on the law applicable to contractual obligations. The **specific principles** relating to contracts of employment set out below apply to any contract which has a foreign element.

2256 The parties to a contract **may choose** which law will determine their respective rights and obligations under the contract. However, even if the parties agree that the law of a country outside the UK is to govern the contract, a UK employee **cannot be deprived of applicable UK statutory employment rights** (¶2280).

2257 If the parties have **not chosen any law**, the law of the contract will be:
– the law of the state in which the employee habitually carries out his work under the contract, even if he is temporarily employed in another state; or
– if it is not possible to ascertain where he habitually carries out his work, the law of the state in which the place of business through which he was engaged is situated.

The place where the employee **habitually carries out his work** is where he has established the effective centre of his working activities or where he in fact performs the essential part of his duties vis-à-vis his employer. This is ascertained by considering where he has an office, spends most of his working time, organises his work and where he returns after each business trip abroad.

The above also applies where the employee carries out his duties in **more than one state** (*Rutton v Cross Medical Ltd* [1997] IRLR 249, ECJ). Where the employee works in more than one EEA state but the above factors fail to conclusively establish the habitual place of employment, the habitual place of work may be decided by the length of time that an employee spends in each state and where he has worked the longest (*Weber v Universal Services Ltd* [2002] IRLR 365, ECJ).

EXAMPLE 1. The parties have not chosen any law but the UK employee habitually carries out his work in France. French law will apply to the contract.
2. If the same employee is only seconded to France for a short period of time, he will habitually carry out his work in the UK, and UK law will apply to the contract.
3. The employee does the same job for 6 months in France, 11 months in Germany and 5 months in the UK. In the absence of the factors in ¶2257 conclusively showing otherwise, the habitual place of work is Germany.

C. Applicable jurisdiction

2260 A court or tribunal in the UK would have jurisdiction over an employment dispute between a UK employee working in the UK and his UK employer. However, where an international element is involved, specific rules apply as to where the claim should be brought, and will depend on where the **employer and the employee are domiciled**.

MEMO POINTS Within the **EU**, the rules of jurisdiction for contracts, including employment contracts, are defined within EC Regulation 2001/44 (the Rules). This replaces and updates the Brussels Convention on Jurisdiction and the Enforcement of Judgments in Civil and Commercial Matters 1968 as amended by the

San Sebastian Convention. For Denmark only, the Brussels Convention remains in place. The Rules are adopted into UK legislation under the Civil Jurisdiction and Judgments Order SI 2001/3929 which also amends the Civil Jurisdiction and Judgments Act 1982.

Similar rules are also recognised in the **EFTA states** (Switzerland, Liechtenstein, Norway and Iceland) and are contained in the Lugano Convention 1988, signed by the EFTA states and also by the EU member states. Consequently, the principles which decide where an employment claim can validly be brought, by either the employer or the employee, are the same within the EU member states and EFTA, and the judgment of a competent court in any of these states will be recognised in the other states.

Claims within EU

When the employer and the employee are both domiciled in an EU member state, the following will apply, depending on whether it is the employer or the employee who is bringing the claim. 2261

If the **employer makes a claim** against his employee he may only do so in the courts of the member state where the employee is domiciled (s 5 Art 20 EC Regulation 2001/44; Sch 4 s10(3) Civil Jurisdiction and Judgments Act 1982 as amended by SI 2001/3929).

An **employee can choose** where to bring a claim against his employer. He can do so (Art 19 EC Regulation 2001/44; Sch 4 s 10(2) Civil Jurisdiction and Judgments Act 1982 as amended by SI 2001/3929):
- either in the member state where he is domiciled; or
- in the member state where he habitually carries out his work (or where he last worked).

If he does not or has not habitually carried out his work in any one country, then he can claim in the state where the business he works for is situated.

EXAMPLE A habitually carries out his work in the UK but is domiciled in France. He is employed by a French company. He can choose to bring a claim against his employer either in the UK (the place where he habitually works) or in France (his country of domicile).
If he did not habitually work in any one country, then he could bring his claim in France, as his employer is situated there.

Domicile What constitutes domicile depends on how the **law of the relevant state** defines the term and this will differ between each EU state. When determining whether a party is domiciled in an EU state or not, the court where the claim is brought will apply its internal law to ascertain domicile. If it decides that the party is not domiciled in the state where the claim is placed, the court will apply the law of the state where he might be domiciled to establish whether he is domiciled there or not (Art 59 EC Regulation 2001/44). 2262

In the UK, an employee will be domiciled in the UK when he is resident in the UK and the circumstances of his residence indicate that he has a substantial connection with the UK i.e. if he has been resident in the UK for the last 3 months or more. A company will be domiciled in the UK if it is incorporated in the UK or has its central management or control in the UK (Sch 1 para 9 SI 2001/3929).

EXAMPLE B, a UK national, has been seconded for 3 years to Germany by his UK employer. B has acted in breach of contract and the UK employer wants to claim against him. B is now living in Germany. His UK employer, in deciding where to bring his claim, needs to know whether B is domiciled in the UK or in Germany.
The courts in the UK cannot hear the claim as B has been living in Germany for more than 3 months and therefore is not considered as domiciled under UK law. Whether B is considered as domiciled in Germany will depend on German law.

Agreed jurisdiction In limited circumstances, an employer and employee may **agree** that a specific court of a member state will have jurisdiction. However, this will only be valid if the agreement is arrived at **after the dispute** has arisen or if it allows the employee to bring proceedings in courts other than those identified above (Art 21 EC Regulation 2001/44; Sch 4 s 10(5) Civil Jurisdiction and Judgments Act 1982 as amended by SI 2001/3929). 2264

EXAMPLE C, a German national, is employed by an American company with an office in the UK, under a contract of employment that contains a jurisdiction clause that allows any dispute to be heard in the courts of England and Wales. C is seconded to France and habitually carries out work there. In the event of an employment dispute the employer will not be able to rely on the jurisdiction clause to bring the dispute before the courts of England and Wales, as it was entered into before the dispute arose.

MEMO POINTS Different rules apply to other types of contract.

2265 **Recognition of judgment** **Judgments made** by a competent **court in one EU member state** will be automatically recognised by other EU member states without the need for any special procedure, save for purely formal checks on the documents (EC Regulation 2001/44; Sch 1 s 8(1) SI 2001/3929). This ensures the EC objective of the free movement of judgments in civil and commercial matters between EU member states. **In the UK**, the judgment of a competent court of another EU member state must be registered for enforcement in the part of the UK (i.e. England and Wales, Scotland or Northern Ireland) where it is to be enforced. The procedure of recognition in other EU member states is to have the judgment declared as enforceable in that state.

EXAMPLE 1. A UK employer successfully sues his employee in Germany, on the basis that this is the country of domicile. He can have that judgment recognised in any other EU member state where the employee may reside.
2. The UK employee sues his German employer in Germany. During the proceedings the employer relocates to Italy. On obtaining a judgment in his favour, the employee will be able to serve the judgment on the employer in Italy with minimal involvement of the Italian courts.

Claims made in EFTA states

2266 **Similar rules** are applied where the employer or the employee are domiciled in EFTA member states, namely Switzerland, Liechtenstein, Norway and Iceland, and, under the Lugano Convention 1988, judgments made in those states will be recognised in the EU member states.

Claims made in other states

2268 **In the UK**, jurisdiction is based on the domicile of the defendant (Sch 4 s 1 SI 2001/3929). Where either the employer or the employee is domiciled outside the EU or EFTA, the claimant must find the court where the claim will be properly heard.

If an **employer** in the UK has a claim against an employee now domiciled outside the EU or EFTA, he must find out if the courts of the country in which the employee is domiciled admit the claim and what legal redress he can obtain if he is successful. In many cases, it is impractical to pursue a claim against an employee if he has left the EU/EFTA jurisdiction.

If it is the **employee** who has a claim against an employer who is domiciled outside the EU or EFTA, he may bring his claim before a UK employment tribunal. However, any award made against the employer by the tribunal will be unenforceable if there are no assets or presence within the UK.

2270 **Exceptions** In some circumstances an employment claim may be brought in an appropriate court in the UK even if the defendant is not domiciled in the UK. Such proceedings may be issued **with the permission of the court** in England and Wales if:
- the employment contract was made in England;
- it was breached in England;
- it is subject to English law; and
- it specified that the courts of England and Wales had jurisdiction.

In order to obtain the permission of the court to proceed against a defendant who is not domiciled in the jurisdiction, the claimant has to show that he has a **good arguable case** and that the court is the appropriate forum for the action. If the court agrees to serve the defendant out of the jurisdiction and he fails to make an appearance, the case may be heard against him in his absence.

MEMO POINTS Similar rules, allowing proceedings against an absent defendant, apply in the courts of Scotland and Northern Ireland.

Courts in the UK can also decide not to hear a claim if they consider that it can be **dealt with more conveniently** by a court of another country (this is also known as the doctrine of forum non conveniens). 2271

EXAMPLE D, who lives in New York, is employed by Company X, which is incorporated in New York with its offices there. D is seconded to Company Y to carry courier packages to London. D delivers the packages and then returns to New York with packages from Company Y's branch office. If D brought a claim against Company X for breach of contract in an English and Welsh court, the court would be entitled to invoke the doctrine of forum non conveniens and require that the case be heard in New York as all the relevant parties are resident there.

MEMO POINTS This doctrine may not be used to deprive an employment tribunal of jurisdiction. It is based on the common law whilst the tribunal's jurisdiction to hear cases is derived under the statutory law and regulations.

Recognition of judgment Even if the claimant is successful and judgment is awarded in his favour by a court in the UK, he will have to translate that judgment into one that can be applied in the country where the defendant is located. As seen above, this is not a difficult process where EFTA and EU member states are concerned, but the enforcement of judgments outside those states can prove to be a complicated process and its success will depend on whether there is a **reciprocal agreement** between the UK and the other country. 2273

MEMO POINTS Recognition will be by specific statutory instrument, for example, under the Reciprocal Enforcement of Foreign Judgments (Canada) Order SI 1987/468, the UK recognises civil and commercial judgments of the Federal Court of certain Canadian provinces as the Canadian courts recognise similar judgments made by courts in the UK.
It should be noted that there is **no bilateral treaty** or international convention between the **United States and any other country** on reciprocal recognition and enforcement of judgments.

D. Statutory employment rights

UK employment law gives employees and workers in the UK certain statutory employment rights (¶12 and ¶17). **Within the EU**, a worker will continue to benefit from the protection of these rights even when posted abroad by his UK employer, as long as he habitually carries out his work in the UK or if his employer has a place of business there (Sch 1 Art 6 Contracts (Applicable Law) Act 1990). **Outside the EU**, it is necessary to establish the territorial jurisdiction of each of the relevant pieces of legislation from which the statutory employment rights are derived. The Employment Rights Act 1996 (which provides, amongst others, the statutory right not to be unfairly dismissed) is silent as to its territorial jurisdiction but the Court of Appeal has recently held that the right not to be unfairly dismissed covers "employment in Great Britain". It also gave guidance as to how such employment can be determined, particularly in the context of temporary postings abroad, in respect of which the Court stated that an assessment of all the circumstances of the case should be made (*Serco Ltd v Lawson* [2004] IRLR 206, CA). Although the principles in this case have been applied in *Crofts and others v Cathay Pacific Airways Limited and others* [2005] ICR 1436 CA, at the time of writing, the decision in *Serco Ltd v Lawson* is on appeal to the House of Lords. It is hoped that the appeal hearing will produce clear guidance going forward. 2280

Whilst the employer and the worker are free to agree to enhance these rights, they may **not reduce or exclude** them, so even if they agree to choose a law other than the laws of England and Wales, Scotland or Northern Ireland, these UK statutory employment rights will still protect the employee. Therefore, the right of a worker not to be unfairly dismissed under UK statutory employment law cannot be avoided by the parties agreeing, for example, that Japanese law will govern the employment contract.

Posting within EU

2282 All EU member states must ensure that certain **minimum rights** apply to workers of that state and to workers temporarily posted to that state (Posted Workers EC Directive 1996/71). Therefore, where a UK worker is posted to another EU member state the minimum employment rights provided by that state should be available to him during his posting. Similarly, where a worker domiciled in another EU member state is posted to the UK, he is entitled in this country to the same protection as that given to a UK employee.

MEMO POINTS All EU member states have state legislation or mandatory collective agreements that conform to EC Directive 1996/71, save Belgium and Luxembourg. In the UK, most of the Directive requirements already applied to workers, whether working permanently or temporarily in the UK, by the implementation date of 16 December 1999. Where employment legislation did not conform to the Directive, changes were made to legislation to accommodate its requirements e.g. the Employment Relations Act 1999 removed the territorial limits from the ERA 1996 thereby extending the rights to all employees in the UK including those temporarily posted there.

2283 The minimum employment rights afforded to posted workers **are**:
- maximum work periods and minimum rest periods;
- minimum paid annual holidays;
- minimum rates of pay, including overtime rates;
- conditions of hiring out workers, in particular the supply of workers by temporary employment undertakings;
- health, safety and hygiene at work;
- protection for pregnant women, or those who have recently given birth;
- protection of children and of young people; and
- non-discrimination.

2284 Member states may **exclude or derogate** from the minimum rates of pay and minimum paid annual leave provisions with respect to certain work or where the posting is for a period of less than 1 month. They also have the power to **extend local collective agreements** to posted workers and this can affect the level of rights afforded to workers seconded to an EU member state.

EXAMPLE An employer who wants to second his UK employee to work in France will find that not only will the French minimum terms and conditions apply but also the requirements of a local (i.e. French) collective agreement requiring that there must be an employment contract written in French.

2285 A **UK worker posted to another EU member state** is entitled to the benefit of both UK statutory employment rights and the minimum employment rights of the country of posting. Whilst he may enforce the latter against his employer in the country of posting, this will not prejudice or prevent him **from bringing proceedings** in the UK. As a result, a UK employer may find himself defending a claim in the UK and in the member state where his employee was posted (with respect to the minimum rights protection of that state).

CHAPTER 9

Company information and confidentiality

OUTLINE ¶¶

2300 The ownership of **intellectual property rights** (IPR) can be an important issue for businesses and individuals who may wish to ensure that they are entitled to such rights, either legislatively or contractually.

2301 IPR may amount to a trade secret or confidential information, and how and when an employer can protect against disclosure to a third party is often vital to his business. **Confidential information** and **trade secrets** although not defined by legislation have been held to include many types of sensitive company information, for example a recipe may be a trade secret and a client list may amount to confidential information. Confidential information and trade secrets obtained during the employment (and as a result of it) are **protected against disclosure** to a third party by the implied duty of fidelity during employment and is often supplemented, clarified and highlighted by express contractual terms. This duty also **prevents** an employee **competing** with his employer's business or soliciting its customers during employment.

However, this duty does not apply **post employment** (with the exception of disclosures of trade secrets). Therefore, employers who wish to restrict ex-employees' activities (particularly in the case of senior employees) must do so by way of express contractual terms, known as **restrictive covenants**.

2302 Finally, the protection afforded to an employer (by the implied duty of confidentiality and any express contractual terms) is subject to **whistleblowing** legislation, which protects workers who due to a sense of public duty reveal **serious employer misconduct**.

SECTION 1

Intellectual property rights

2310 Intellectual property is created by the intellectual effort of individuals. Businesses and individuals need to consider their intellectual property rights (IPR) to ensure that they identify and protect these rights and that they have ownership where appropriate. Where employees may be creating original work or invention, it is also advisable for their contracts of employment to have express terms on IPR.

IPR are split into registered and unregistered rights. Unregistered rights, i.e. copyright, design rights and database rights exist automatically, and no formalities are required to create these rights (Copyright Designs and Patents Act 1988 as amended by the Copyright and Rights in Database Regulations SI 1997/3032). Consequently, employees are likely to be creating such rights on an everyday basis. On the other hand, registered rights, i.e. patents (Patents Act 1977, as amended), registered designs (Registered Design Act 1949) and trademarks only exist on completion of various procedural steps. Companies should have procedures in place to enable them to recognise when work is or will be created that is capable of registration and to ensure that any such rights are registered.

MEMO POINTS Trademarks are signs that are capable of being represented graphically and which distinguish goods/services/undertakings from others. Issues of ownership rarely arise in connection with the employer/employee relationship, so are not discussed in this chapter.

Unregistered rights

2311 **Copyright** is a right that automatically **exists** in (ss 1(1), 3, 3A Copyright, Designs and Patents Act 1988):
– original literary, dramatic, musical (including a computer program, database and table or compilation), or artistic works. The general requirement of originality requires that the work must not be copied but produced using the author's own independent skill. Consequently, this is not a high hurdle to clear as long as the work is not a copy;
– sound recordings, films, broadcasts or cable programmes; and
– typographical arrangements of published editions.

Copyright in literary, dramatic or musical works does not exist until the **work is recorded** (whether this is in writing or otherwise). 2312

EXAMPLE 1. A person may deliver a speech without notes and copyright will not exist in that speech unless the speech is recorded at the time of delivery (whether by television or sound recording). However, if he prepares for the speech by writing notes prior to delivery, copyright will exist in the notes as a literary work.
2. A musician may have composed a "tune" in his head, but copyright in it as a musical work will not exist unless he records it (for example on a score).

The same piece of work may **create different copyrights**. 2313

EXAMPLE A marketing director gives an informal presentation to the board as to the future marketing direction of the company. No record/recording is made of the presentation. He did not make notes prior to the presentation and therefore no copyright exists. Later, he prepares a formal report in writing and copyright will exist in the written report (as a literary document). There may also be a publisher's copyright in any published version of the report. He then gives a verbal presentation of the report, which is recorded by means of video equipment for training purposes. He uses the copyright work (the written report) and a further copyright work is created in the film recording.

Design rights protect designs of functional items. A design right automatically **exists** in (s 213(1)-(2) Copyright Designs and Patents Act 1988): 2314
– an original design. A design is not original if it is commonplace in the relevant design field at the time of its creation. Whilst there is no fixed assistance on what will amount to the relevant design field, this is likely to be the area in which those designing that type of design would have been involved; or
– the design of any aspect of the shape or configuration of an article.

Excluded are (s 213(3) Copyright Designs and Patents Act 1988):
– methods or principles of construction. It is the design itself and not the method by which it is made that is protected; or
– features of shape or configuration which:
· enable the article to be connected to or placed around another article so that either article can perform its function. This is the so called 'must fit' exception and includes any feature which enables it to be connected to or placed in/around another article to enable either to perform its function;
· are dependent on the appearance of another article, which is intended by the designer to form an integral part. This is the 'must match' exception; or
· are surface decoration. Therefore, the surface pattern of an article cannot amount to a design right.

Databases are also protected by specific database rights. A database right automatically **exists** in an original database and this is satisfied if, by reason of selection or arrangement of the contents of the database, the database constitutes the author's own intellectual creation. 2315

Registered rights

A **patent** may be **granted** to an invention, if it is (s 1(1), (3) Patents Act 1977): 2316
– new;
– involves an inventive step; and
– is capable of industrial application.

However, this does **not include** anything that:
– would encourage offensive, immoral or anti-social behaviour; or
– is for any variety of animal, plant or biological processes for the production of animals or plants. This does not include micro-biological processes or its products.

A **design** in respect of an article or set of articles may be **registered** if it is new (s 1(2) Registered Designs Act 1949). It is important to note that there must be a design and an article to which the design is applied for the design to be protected by registration. A design is defined as any features of shape, configuration, pattern or ornament applied to an article by an industrial process where the finished article appeals to and is judged by the eye. 2317

Excluded are:
– methods or principles of construction; and
– features of shape or configuration of an article which are:
· dependent solely on function (that is if the feature of the shape or configuration can be attributed to or caused by the article's function and there has been no embellishment to those features); or
· dependent upon the appearance of another article which is intended to be an integral part of the article in question (i.e. the two articles must be an integral part of each other and this must have been the intention of the author/designer).

A. Ownership

2330 Individuals or groups of individuals use their intellectual ability to create IPR and this is, therefore, not limited to individuals who are specifically employed to invent. For example, an employee may be employed to invent or produce literary/musical works; a salesman may write his company's next advertising campaign; and a director may design new packaging for a company product.

It is important to ascertain who is the owner of the right or to whom the right has first been granted. Generally, this will be the **employer** where the employee has created the IPR as part of his employment. It is also possible, in most cases, to **transfer** ownership where required by contractual agreement between the parties, although there are certain formalities that have to be met.

1. Unregistered rights

2335 Where the employee in the **course of his employment** makes the work or right, **the employer** is deemed to be the first owner of the work (subject to an agreement to the contrary) (ss 11(2), 215(3) Copyright Designs and Patents Act 1988; reg 14(2) Copyright and Rights in Databases Regulations SI 1997/3032).

2. Registered rights

Patents

2340 A patent is granted to the **inventor** who is defined as (s 7 Patents Act 1977):
– the actual deviser of the invention;
– any person who is entitled to the invention by law, i.e. deemed to be the inventor (for example, the employer, if his employee makes the invention in the circumstances set out below); or
– any person who has an enforceable agreement with the inventor (for example, the employer, who has a contract of employment with the employee that transfers ownership, though this cannot apply to patents that have not been already created).

There is an assumption that unless proved to the contrary, anyone applying for a patent is assumed to be the inventor or somebody entitled to the invention (s 7 Patents Act 1977).

2341 The employer will be **deemed to be the inventor** where the employee makes the invention (s 39 Patents Act 1977):
– in the circumstances an invention might reasonably be **expected to result**:
· in the course of **normal duties** of the employee, for example if designing or inventing formed part of his duties. It is also considered to be in the course of normal duties if he is required to overcome problems (by way of inventions) as they arise; or
· in the course of **duties specifically assigned** to him if outside his normal duties; or

– in the course of his duties when because of the nature of his duties and responsibilities he had a **special obligation** to further his employer's business as may be the case with a more senior employee. However, the decision as to whether the invention belongs to the employer will depend not only on the employee's position and status but also his attendant duties.

EXAMPLE A director with specific responsibility for manufacturing within a company invents a new machine for packing the products. As his responsibilities include the packaging of the products and he has an overall responsibility to the company as a director, the right to the invention is more likely to belong to the company. However, if the finance director came up with the same invention, it is less likely that the company would be able to claim the invention.

The invention must put into effect the objectives of the employee's duties. Consequently, any invention that is in reality **coincidental to** his **duties** will not belong to the employer (*Harris' Patent* [1985] RPC 19). 2342

EXAMPLE An employee is employed to devise and develop new chemicals as solvents. Any patents for solvents will belong to his employer. If, by accident, he created a chemical that is an industrial lubricant, then the invention would not automatically belong to the employer. However, if the same employee was requested to widen his research to consider the best way to lubricate certain machinery within the factory and then came up with the lubricant, the employer would automatically gain the right to the invention.

Employee compensation If the employer is deemed to be the inventor, the employee may be entitled to statutory compensation to be paid by his employer where, having regard to the size and nature of the employer's undertaking, an invention or the patent (or a combination of both) is granted to an employer that is of outstanding benefit to him (s 40 Patents Act 1977 as amended by s 10 Patents Act 2004). The invention must, however, be the subject of the patent and a claim for compensation cannot relate to aspects of an invention which are not covered by a patent. 2343

The **amount** of the award should be a fair share of the benefit that the employer has or might reasonably be expected to derive from the invention or the patent (or from the grant or assignment of any right in the invention, or any right under an application for the patent, to a person connected to the employer) (s 41 Patents Act 1977 as amended by s 10 Patents Act 2004). Employers should therefore ensure that their arrangements for rewarding employee compensation in respect of such benefits reflect these provisions.

Registered designs

The employer will be treated as the first owner of the design where it is created by an employee in the **course of his employment**, or it has been **commissioned** by him (s 2 Registered Design Act 1949). Otherwise, registered designs are granted to the **designer**. 2344

B. Express terms

Where employees may be creating original work or invention, it is advisable for their contracts of employment to have express terms on IPR, principally to ensure that their employer has ownership. Although the employer will be deemed to be the owner in most cases (as seen above), it is often useful to have an express term to highlight, clarify and augment these rules. This can be seen as a 'belt and braces' approach. Employers should seek **legal advice** with regard to any express terms they may wish to introduce into employees' contracts, as the exact wording will depend on the requirements of the business. 2350

The following wording is taken from the model Service Agreement (see ¶9920) (which is designed for directors and senior employees), and therefore refers to the 'Executive'. It is a relatively standard clause, intended to be used as a starting point, and should be tailored according to the circumstances of the employer.

EXAMPLE **Definition and Interpretation**

In this Agreement:

'Intellectual Property Rights' means all rights in and to intellectual property in the UK and internationally including without limitation patents, trade marks, copyright, design rights and rights in databases whether or not any of the above are registered and including applications for registration of any of them.

'Inventions' means all inventions, works and information including, without limitation, discoveries, designs, databases, ideas, methods, programs, diagrams and reports (and any drafts thereof) made or discovered by the Executive (alone or with others) in connection with the Employment or relating to or capable of being used in those parts of the businesses of the Company or any Group Company in which the Executive is involved.

18. Intellectual Property

18.1. The Executive will promptly communicate full details of any Inventions to the Company. All Intellectual Property Rights in the Inventions will belong to the Company or the appropriate Group Company, as the case may be.

18.2. The Executive will not disclose or exploit any Invention unless authorised by the Company or in the proper performance of his duties.

18.3. The Executive hereby assigns to the Company or any other Group Company as appropriate to the extent allowed by law all his existing and future rights (including Intellectual Property Rights), title and interests in all Inventions.

18.4. To the extent that any right in such Inventions may not be assigned to the Company or other Group Company, the Executive will hold all such rights on trust for the Company.

18.5. In any event, at the request and expense of the Company, the Executive will give it all information and assistance as may be necessary to enable the Company effectively to exploit the Intellectual Property Rights, and will execute all documents and do all things which may be necessary to vest all such rights in the Company (or as it may direct) as legal and beneficial owner and to secure appropriate protection for all such rights anywhere in the world.

18.6. The Executive hereby irrevocably appoints the Company to take any action in his name and execute any document on his behalf for the purpose of giving to the Company (or its nominee) the full benefit of the provisions of this clause. If there is any doubt as to whether such a document or action has been executed or carried out within the authority conferred by this clause, a certificate in writing signed by any director or the secretary of the Company will be conclusive evidence that such is the case.

18.7. The Executive waives all of his moral rights (as defined in the Copyright, Designs and Patents Act 1988) and any corresponding foreign rights in respect of all Inventions where the Intellectual Property Rights belong to the Company or appropriate Group Company by virtue of this clause, to the extent that such waiver is permitted by law.

18.8. The Executive will promptly notify the Company in writing if he becomes aware of any infringement or suspected infringement of any Intellectual Property Right in any Invention.

18.9. Rights and obligations under this clause will survive the termination of the Employment in respect of Inventions made during the Employment and will be binding on the Executive's personal representatives.

2352 **In connection with employment** An invention is contractually defined in this model clause as all things made in connection with the employment. The question is, what is the executive required to do under his employment contract? Obviously, with a more senior employee such as this, the duties in the contract are often quite vague (by necessity) if he is required to carry out such duties as the Board may from time to time direct. As a result, work or invention made in "connection with the Employment" may be open to dispute.

2353 **Involvement with business** The model clause definition of invention continues '... or relating to or capable of being used in those parts of the businesses of the Company... in which the Executive is involved.' This passage broadens the definition further. By just how far will depend on the circumstances. There is always going to be room for dispute as to what 'being involved' means. It is likely that the size of the company or group of companies will be a practical factor in the implementation of this clause. If there are several businesses within the company and the executive's only real involvement on a day-to-day basis is in one of them, it is likely that only those inventions relating to, or capable of being used, in that business will be covered by this definition.

An alternative may be to widen the definition further, perhaps stating that all inventions made in connection with the employment, or relating to or capable of being used by any part of the company or group of companies, belong to the company. The need for this type of clause will be heightened if the employer is part of a large group and/or the duties and responsibilities of the employee are vague.

Ownership

Having established what inventions are covered under the terms of the contract, what provisions are made for their ownership? 2354

Clause 18.1 This requires that the executive communicates details of inventions to the company. When considering the definition of invention this may seem a considerable task and indeed if the executive was required to list every invention (as defined) then it would be a considerable task. However, no specific method of notification is required and this makes the clause workable. The company would require and need notification of inventions, to ensure that they are protected (by registration if appropriate), valued and exploited if possible. The need for this clause is clear; an invention that may be valuable to the company is less likely to be so if only one person knows about it. 2355

Clause 18.2 Certain registered rights are not capable of protection unless they have the required degree of novelty. This clause simply requires that the executive does not disclose inventions unless authorised or in the proper performance of his duties. Whilst this clause will not prevent unwitting disclosure that may destroy that novelty, it may prevent some types of disclosure and will give the company a remedy for breach of contract in some circumstances. 2356

Clause 18.3 This clause assigns or transfers the rights in inventions to the company. With regard to copyright, design and database rights, the rights will be owned by the employer immediately upon the right coming into existence (ss 223, 91 Copyright Designs and Patents Act 1988; Copyright and Rights in Databases Regulations SI 1997/3032). Also, where the right to apply for a registered design is assigned to the employer, then the employer is considered to be the owner of that design (s 2(2) Registered Designs Act 1949). The position with regard to patents is different. Contracts with employees (or parts of contracts) are unenforceable if it diminishes the employees' rights in the invention. Therefore, the attempted assignment of future inventions capable of patent protection is not enforceable (s 42 Patents Act 1977). 2357

Clause 18.4 This covers any invention that is not assigned in clause 18.3, so that the executive holds those inventions on trust for the company. This can be considered a fall-back provision. 2358

Clauses 18.5 & 18.6 These clauses are self-explanatory and require the executive to provide necessary assistance to allow exploitation and protection of the rights. The second clause allows the company to take whatever steps are required to obtain the full benefits of the clause. 2359

Clause 18.7 This refers to moral rights. These are rights that are laid down in the Copyright Designs and Patents Act 1988: 2360
- to be identified as author;
- to object to derogatory treatment of work;
- not to have false attribution of work; and
- of privacy of certain photographs.

The executive waives those rights under this clause.

Clause 18.8 This requires the executive to notify the company of any suspected infringement of any intellectual property rights. 2361

Clause 18.9 This ensures that clause 18 survives the termination of the contract. 2362

SECTION 2

Confidential information and confidentiality

2400 Confidential information and trade secrets obtained during the employment (and as a result of it) may be protected against disclosure to a third party by the **implied duty** of fidelity or the express terms of the contract of employment. The **degree of protection** provided by the express term will depend on the type of information, and the timing of the disclosure. Employees are free to impart or use trivial information in any way they please, at any time. Unauthorised disclosure of trade secrets is prohibited both during and after employment, whilst confidential information is only protected against disclosure during employment. **Express contractual terms** can restrict the disclosure of both confidential information and trade secrets during and after employment.

There is no definitive legal **definition** of confidential information or trade secrets, although there is court guidance. Where confidentiality is important to an employer, it is advisable to have a **policy**, which helps identify and categorise the different types of information employees may be given or use.

2401 The duty of confidentiality is subject to **whistleblowing** legislation, which protects workers who disclose information to another party in certain circumstances (¶2700). Any express terms which restrict the employee's right to make a protected disclosure are void.

A. Protection against disclosure

2405 In summary, there are three types of information which are protected as follows:

	Protected during employment	Protected post employment
Trivial information	X	X
Confidential information	✔	X (unless express contractual term)
Trade secrets	✔	✔

1. During employment

Confidential information and trade secrets

2410 During employment, an employee is bound by the **implied duty** of fidelity (see also ¶1213), and he can only use confidential information and trade secrets for the benefit of his employer. An employee will be in breach if he uses or discloses such information for his own benefit (or that of another employer), for example by making, copying or deliberately memorising lists of the employer's customers to use as a 'springboard' to launch himself into business after his employment ends.

The duty applies during and outside working hours (*Hivac Ltd v Park Royal Scientific Instruments Ltd* [1946] 1 All ER 350, CA).

This duty also **applies to employers**, for example with regard to information held as part of personnel records, if the information has the necessary quality of confidence (*Dalgleish v Lothian and Borders Police Board* [1991] IRLR 422, CS). Employers are also bound by their obligations under data protection legislation with regard to personal data (¶5900).

Many employers include **express terms** of confidentiality which can clarify, highlight and supplement this implied duty. 2411

2. Post employment

Confidential information

When an employee has left employment, he is **entitled to use** confidential information for his benefit (or that of another employer) to the extent that such information has become part of his own **general skill and knowledge** (*Robb v Green* [1895] 2 QB 315). Confidential information will become part of an employee's skill and knowledge if it is inevitable that such information will be carried away in his head (*Roger Bullivant Ltd v Ellis* [1987] IRLR 491, CA). 2415

This does not include confidential information that has been **deliberately memorised**.

EXAMPLE In *Roger Bullivant Ltd v Ellis*, E took certain documents from RB Ltd, including a card index listing RB's trade contacts which amounted to confidential information, and set up in competition with his former employer. The Court upheld an injunction preventing E from contracting with those people on the list and, as it was unable to distinguish between those people whom E could have lawfully contacted (because they had become part of his general knowledge) and those he could not, the injunction applied to all of them.

If an employer wishes to protect against disclosure of confidential information after the employment has ended, he will need an **express term** in the contract of employment. 2416

MEMO POINTS It is arguable, however, whether such an express term can survive termination where the person seeking to rely on the term has committed a **repudiatory breach of contract** (*Campbell v Frisbee* [2002] IRLR 728, CA). Note, however, that this case involved a contract for services rather than an employment contract and that no final determination on the issue was required from the Court of Appeal.

Trade secrets

An employer is protected by the **implied duty** of fidelity against an ex-employee using a trade secret for his own benefit (or that of another employer), even if it has become part of his general knowledge (*Johnson & Bloy (Holdings) Ltd and Johnson & Bloy Ltd v Wolstenholme Rink plc and Fallon* [1987] IRLR 499, CA). 2417

However, as the distinction between trade secrets and confidential information is sometimes not clear (see below), it is often advisable for an employer who wishes to protect against disclosure of a trade secret to have an **express term** to clarify, supplement and augment the implied duty.

B. Categorisation of information

In summary, the **three different types** of information are as follows: 2425

Trivial Information	Information of a trivial nature which is easily accessible from public sources, which would not be considered by any reasonable person to be confidential at all (for example, details of registered intellectual property rights published by the Patent Office)
Confidential Information	Information which the employee must treat as confidential, either because he is expressly told that it is confidential (unless it is actually trivial) or because of its very nature or character it is obviously confidential
Trade Secrets	Specific trade secrets

2426 Just because information can once be classed as confidential information or a trade secret, it does not necessarily always remain so. The information may lose its confidential nature due to the **passage of time** or because the information becomes **available to the public** by some other means. Whether information has become available to the public will depend on if it has been made available to a substantial number of people (*Stephens v Avery* [1988] FSR 510).

1. Confidential or trivial?

2430 It is usually clear what is confidential information and what is trivial information. The **basic requirements** for information to be confidential are that it must:
- have the necessary quality of confidence; and
- be communicated in circumstances importing an obligation of confidence.

2431 **Quality of confidence** **Public knowledge** of the information may be relevant when assessing whether the information has the necessary quality of confidence. It is not clear whether **unauthorised and wrongful publication** by the employee or a third party will destroy confidentiality. It has been held that the employee should not escape his duty of confidentiality if he has wrongfully disclosed the information (*Speed Seal Products Ltd v Paddington* [1986] 1 All ER 91, CA), although the information has arguably lost the required quality of confidence.

Information will not be regarded as confidential if it is in the **public interest** for it to be disclosed (i.e. the public's interest in discovering wrongdoing outweighs the individual's right to confidentiality) (the so-called 'just cause' defence). This may include disclosure of the commission of a crime or a fraud. The disclosure must be made to the most appropriate person or body, and the employee must have reasonable grounds to support his allegations. The whistleblowing legislation may also apply to disclosures made in such circumstances (¶2700).

2432 **Circumstances of communication** Information is more likely to be confidential if the importance placed by the employer on it (and the need to keep it confidential) is made clear by him. Thus the express terms that the employer seeks to apply, and the degree to which he restricts access to the information, will be relevant. However, confidential information is by its very nature confidential regardless of whether it is **labelled confidential** or not. Therefore, an employee cannot disclose confidential information simply because it is not labelled as such, nor can an employer prevent the use or disclosure of information merely by labelling it as confidential if it is actually trivial.

2. Confidential or trade secret?

2435 It is often more difficult to ascertain whether confidential information is so highly confidential that it is a trade secret. Unfortunately, in practice, the terms have been used interchangeably and the courts have recognised that the distinction is not an easy one (*Thomas Marshall (Exports) Ltd v Guinle* [1978] IRLR 174, ChD). There is **no definitive legal definition of trade secrets**, although the courts do give **guidance** as to how to make the distinction.

Some trade secrets are **readily identifiable** as such, for example, secret processes of manufacture such as chemical formulae (*Amber Size and Chemical Co Ltd v Menzel* [1913] 2 Ch 239), or designs or special methods of construction (*Reid and Sigrist Ltd v Moss Mechanism Ltd* [1932] 49 RPC 461). Trade secrets are not confined to technical information but can include highly confidential information of a non-technical or non-scientific nature (*Lansing Linde Ltd v Kerr* [1991] IRLR 80, CA).

2436 Whether or not information amounts to a trade secret is a **question of degree**. For example, a document that lists the ingredients for a specific food product is clearly more confidential (and may amount to a trade secret) than a list of suppliers for certain raw materials. However, if they are of a sufficiently high degree of confidentiality, customer or supplier lists/requirements and pricing information (such as pricing in tender documents) will also be trade secrets.

Four specific factors (set out below) must be considered when determining whether information is of a sufficiently high degree of confidentiality to amount to a trade secret (*Faccenda Chicken Ltd v Fowler* [1986] IRLR 69, CA; confirmed in *A T Poeton (Gloucester Plating) Ltd v Horton* [2000] ICR 1208, CA). They must all be taken into account, and none is conclusive on its own.

Nature of the employment

A higher duty may be imposed on employees who **habitually handle** confidential information and trade secrets than those who only receive such information **occasionally or incidentally**. 2437

Nature of the information

Information that is highly confidential in nature and of paramount importance (for example, the Coca-Cola formula) is likely to be a trade secret (but the list of suppliers of its raw ingredients may not be). The employer must make a realistic assessment of the information in question, and the courts are unwilling to overestimate the degree of confidentiality of a document. The **employer's categorisation** of the information cannot determine the issue, and his description of confidential information as a trade secret will not make it one if the nature of the information is such that it does not actually have a sufficiently high degree of confidentiality. 2438

EXAMPLE 1. In *Lock International plc v Beswick* [1989] IRLR 481, ChD, documents which were described as confidential information or trade secrets were not, as they were extremely general.
2. In *Brooks v Olyslager OMS (UK) Ltd* [1998] IRLR 590, CA, detrimental information about the employer's solvency, ability to carry on business for a period of time and relationship with its holding company was not capable of amounting to a trade secret.

Communication of confidentiality

If the **employer made it clear** that the information was highly confidential, then it is more likely that the information will amount to a trade secret. Consideration will also be given to the number and types of employees who have **access** to such information. Information is more likely to be a trade secret if it has a limited and restricted distribution. 2439

However, where the **employee is fully aware** of the confidential nature of a particular process or piece of information, the employer's failure to impress the confidentiality on him will not prevent it from being highly confidential, and the matter is often one of common sense (*Lancashire Fires Ltd v SA Lyons & Co Ltd* [1997] IRLR 113, CA).

EXAMPLE 1. In *Lancashire Fires Ltd v SA Lyons & Co Ltd*, the employer was a manufacturer of decorative gas fires. The employee was a products manager, involved in the development of new products and the refinement of the manufacturing process. Although the employer had **not precisely specified** what he considered to be confidential, the mould technology used still amounted to a trade secret as it was highly confidential, and the employer was not required to point out the precise limits of this confidentiality.
2. In *Faccenda Chicken Ltd v Fowler*, F was the company's sales manager, with access to sales information which included names, addresses and requirements of customers, delivery routes, dates and times, and prices paid. F left and set up a competing business, making use of the sales information. In the absence of express terms, he was free to use this information as it did not amount to a trade secret, in part because the information was **generally known** to junior employees and not restricted to senior management, and no **express instruction** had been given to treat it as confidential.

Isolation from other information

If the information forms part of a wider base of information that is widely known or readily available, it is less likely to possess the necessary high quality of confidentiality to constitute a trade secret. For example, if the information in question is part of other information which is trivial or merely confidential and it cannot be easily isolated, then it is less likely to be a trade secret. 2440

EXAMPLE In *Faccenda Chicken Ltd v Fowler* (see previous example), the pricing information could have amounted to a trade secret, but was not isolated from the rest of the sales information, so F was free to use all that information.

C. Express terms

2450 Contracts of employment can contain express terms which prevent disclosures of both confidential information and trade secrets.

The following wording is taken from the model Service Agreement (¶9920) (which is designed for directors and senior employees), and therefore refers to the 'Executive'. Similar wording can be found in the model Contract (¶9910). The example clauses are intended to be used as a starting point and, given the complexity of the issues involved, employers would be advised to seek legal advice with regard to any express terms they may wish to introduce into employees' contracts to reflect their business needs and environment.

EXAMPLE Definition and Interpretation

In this Agreement:

'Confidential Information' includes but is not limited to client or trade secrets and confidential or commercial information relating to the organisation, business, finances, clients, customers, dealings and affairs of the Company and other Group Companies [*define confidential information further, if possible*]

17. Confidentiality

17.1. The Executive acknowledges that during the course of the Employment, he will have access to and is likely to obtain Confidential Information.

17.2. Without prejudice to any common law duties owed to the Company, the Executive agrees that he will not, during or after the Employment, except as authorised by the Company or as required by law or his duties, use, divulge or disclose to any person, firm or organisation, any Confidential Information which may come to his knowledge during the Employment. The Executive further agrees to use his best endeavours to prevent the unauthorised use or disclosure of such information.

17.3. This restriction will not apply to information which becomes public (other than through unauthorised disclosure by the Executive), and is not intended to exclude or restrict his right to make a protected disclosure under the Public Interest Disclosure Act 1998.

17.4. The Executive is likely to obtain Confidential Information belonging to or relating to other Group Companies. The Executive will treat such information as falling within the terms of clauses [17.2 and 17.3] above, and those clauses will apply with any necessary amendment to such information. The Executive will, at the Company's request, enter into an agreement or undertaking with other Group Companies in the same terms as clauses [17.2 and 17.3] above.

17.5. Unless it is [a formal/an agreed] part of the Executive's duties, the Executive will not, without the prior written consent of the Board, communicate with any press, radio or television representative on any issue relating to the business or affairs of the Company or any Group Company or to any officers, employees, customers or clients of any such company.

2451 The employer can use the contract of employment (or a separate confidentiality policy) to **define** confidential information. Although this label will not make trivial information confidential (or confidential information a trade secret), it serves to emphasise the importance placed by the employer on the information (¶2432), and may make the employee aware of its confidential nature (¶2438). It may be appropriate to have a more detailed analysis of what kinds of information would be confidential in a **supporting policy**.

2452 A provision in an agreement (including a contract of employment) that purports to preclude an employee from making a protected disclosure under the **whistleblowing** legislation is void (¶2700). It is therefore advisable to exclude protected disclosures from the scope of any confidentiality clause.

2453 If the employee will obtain confidential information of other **Group Companies** (as defined in the Service Agreement – ¶9920), the contract could require him to enter into direct confidentiality undertakings with those companies.

The company may wish to limit the employee's freedom to **speak to the press**. The sample wording requires the Executive to obtain the Board's consent and if he failed to do so he would commit a breach of the agreement, which, if sufficiently serious, could entitle the company summarily to terminate the employment. 2454

After the employment has ended, the employer may also seek to protect his trade secrets and confidential information by way of a **restrictive covenant** (¶2500). There is some uncertainty as to what class of information can be protected in this way. It has been held that the information need not amount to a trade secret (*Lansing Linde Ltd v Kerr* [1991] IRLR 80, CA, approved in *FSS Travel and Leisure Systems Ltd v Johnson* [1998] IRLR 382, CA), but would extend to such information as warranted legitimate protection (*SBJ Stephenson Ltd v Mandy* [2000] IRLR 233, QBD). This would include information which (i) its owner used in a trade or business; (ii) dissemination of which he limited or at least did not encourage or permit on a widespread basis; and (iii) which, if disclosed to a competitor, would be liable to cause real or significant harm to the owner (for example, marketing strategies/other business plans, if these are sufficiently concrete) (*Lansing Linde Ltd v Kerr*; *Scully UK Ltd v Lee* [1998] IRLR 259, CA). It is therefore possible that some types of confidential information may not be protected. 2455

SECTION 3

Restraints and restrictive covenants

An employee has an **implied duty** not to compete with his employer's business or solicit his customers **during employment**. This is the duty of fidelity, which also prevents employees from disclosing trade secrets and confidential information (¶2400). Employers may also wish to impose **express contractual provisions** to highlight, supplement and extend this implied right. 2500

The implied duty does not apply **post employment** (with the exception of disclosures of trade secrets). Therefore, employers may wish to restrict an ex-employee's activities (particularly in the case of a senior employee) by way of express contractual terms, known as **restrictive covenants**. These terms must be **agreed with the employee**. This is usually done by including them in the contract of employment. However, if, at the time of termination, there are no existing restrictive covenants, the employee could be asked to agree to enter into such covenants, perhaps as part of a negotiated termination settlement (¶9276). 2501

There are **different types** of restrictive covenant, including a restriction against competing with the employer's business ('non-compete' covenants), from soliciting or dealing with his customers or clients ('non-solicitation' and 'non-dealing' covenants), and from soliciting his employees ('anti-poaching' covenants). Other post-termination provisions may indirectly restrict the employee's activities, for example where outstanding commission will not be paid if he joins a competitor.

As an alternative or supplement to restrictive covenants, employers may seek to put an employee on so-called '**garden leave**' during his notice period, which means the employee does not attend work, and must not take up other employment during the garden leave period. 2502

Both restraints during employment (including garden leave provisions) and restrictive covenants are subject to the public policy **doctrine of restraint of trade** that ensures that employees retain the ability to earn a living and use their skill and knowledge. 2503

Where appropriate, **sample wording** is provided in this chapter, which is intended to be used as a starting point. Given the complexity of the issues involved, employers would be advised to seek **legal advice** with regard to any express terms they may wish to introduce into employees' contracts to reflect their business needs and environment. 2504

I. Restraints during employment

A. Implied duty

2510 The implied duty of fidelity (¶1213) includes the duty **not to compete** with the employer's business, either by working for competitors or by setting up a competing business, and encompasses a duty **not to solicit his customers or suppliers** (*Wessex Dairies Ltd v Smith* [1935] 2 KB 80, CA). This duty applies during the period of employment (even outside working hours (*Hivac Ltd v Park Royal Scientific Instruments Ltd* [1946] 1 All ER 350, CA)) unless the employer gives the employee express permission to compete.

In addition to the implied duty of fidelity which they may owe as employees, **directors** are bound by their fiduciary and other duties, which are independent of any contract of employment (see ¶2138).

Working for a competitor

2511 The implied duty can prevent an employee working for a competitor during his employment if it causes or may cause **significant harm** to his employer's interests, which will depend on the circumstances of the case. Rather than rely on this concept, employers who wish to restrict the activities of employees during their spare time should consider using an express term (see below).

EXAMPLE No breach

1. In *Nova Plastics Ltd v Froggatt* [1982] IRLR 146, EAT, an odd-job man who did some work for a competitor during his employment was not in breach, as the nature of the work done would not significantly contribute to any competition.

Breach

2. In *Hivac Ltd v Park Royal Scientific Instruments Ltd*, skilled manual employees of H Ltd worked for H Ltd's sole competitor on Sundays. They could be said to be causing H Ltd significant harm as they were advancing the interests of its only competitor.

Intention to compete

2512 An employee will not breach the implied term of fidelity by merely indicating an intention to set up in competition with his employer at some time in the future. An employee is free to make **preparations** to compete with his employer outside working hours, subject to any express provision. For example, he may set up a company, arrange finance and order equipment and material (*Balston Ltd v Headline Filters Ltd* [1990] FSR 385, ChD), as long as these do not go further than taking **preliminary steps** (which will be a question of degree in each case) (*Lancashire Fires Ltd v SA Lyons & Co Ltd* [1997] IRLR 113, CA – see example below).

However, if an employee goes **beyond the intention to compete** and there are grounds for considering that he is or intends to abuse his confidential position or that he is in actual competition with his employer, he will be in breach of his implied duty. For example, an employee will be in breach if he competes with his employer for the future business of one of his employer's customers.

EXAMPLE No breach

1. In *Laughton and Hawley v Bapp Industrial Supplies Ltd* [1986] IRLR 245, EAT, L and H **wrote to their employer's suppliers** requesting product lists, price lists and details of terms, with a view to starting up a competing business several weeks later. Merely indicating an intention to compete in the future was not a breach.

Breach

2. In *Adamson v B & L Cleaning Services Ltd* [1995] IRLR 193, EAT, A was a foreman in a firm of contract cleaners. One particular contract was up for renewal and A put his name forward for the tender list and refused to undertake not to submit a **competitive tender while employed** by B & L. This amounted to a breach.

3. In *Marshall v Industrial Systems & Control Ltd* [1992] IRLR 294, EAT, M, the managing director, had formed a plan with another key employee to **deprive the employer of his best client** and to persuade another senior employee to join them. This amounted to actual competition and therefore a breach.

4. In *Lancashire Fires Ltd v SA Lyons & Co Ltd*, above, the employee planned to set up a business in competition with his employer. He entered into an agreement giving him **financial backing, bought equipment and rented premises**, which he renovated in his spare time, installing equipment in readiness for production, going further than mere preliminary steps and thus breaching the implied term.

5. In *Wessex Dairies Ltd v Smith* (¶2510), a milkman was held to be in breach of his implied duty when he **solicited customers** on his last day by informing them that he had set up his own business and would be able to supply them with milk after he left his employment.

An employee will not be in breach of the implied term by **seeking employment with a competitor**, unless he intends to abuse the employer's confidential information or his position with the employer. A dismissal in these circumstances will only be justified if there are solid grounds for believing that the employee intends to commit such a breach (*Harris & Russell Ltd v Slingsby* [1973] IRLR 221, NIRC; approved in *Laughton and Hawley v Bapp Industrial Supplies Ltd*). 2513

B. Express terms

Express terms may be advisable to clarify, highlight and supplement an employee's implied duty, and much will depend on the employer's specific needs. However, such clauses are subject to the doctrine of restraint of trade (¶2551). 2520

Working for a competitor

Set out below is sample wording from the model contract of employment (¶9910). This may be suitable for **general staff**. 2521

EXAMPLE 12. Outside interests

For the duration of this contract (including without limitation any period of garden leave), you will not undertake any other employment without the prior written permission of [*job title*], or engage in any outside activity, paid or unpaid, which might interfere with the effective discharge of your duties or adversely affect [employer] in any way. If such permission is given, you must advise [employer] of your additional working hours and [employer] reserves the right to withdraw its consent at its absolute discretion.

Employers can have an express term which **specifically prohibits** employees working for a **competitor** during their employment (*William Robinson & Co Ltd v Heuer* [1898] 2 Ch 451, CA). However, the courts have held that preventing an employee from working for **anyone else** (i.e. a blanket restriction) is an unreasonable restraint of trade (*William Robinson & Co Ltd v Heuer*; *Symbian Ltd v Christensen* [2001] IRLR 77, CA). 2522

An employer can include a term that the employee must obtain his **consent** before undertaking outside work. Failure to obtain consent would be a breach of contract entitling the employer to damages if he has suffered any loss (¶2660). Note that there is no general principle obliging an employee to inform the employer if/when he is doing outside work, even if he is doing so in breach of contract. 2523

In order for the employer to be able to comply with his obligations under the **working time regulations** (¶3605), it is advisable for the contract to oblige the employee to notify him of any hours worked for other employers. 2524

2525 As the implied term does not cover **preparatory activities**, the contract could also include an express term restricting such activities during the employment. For example, an express term prohibiting employees from holding a material interest in a company which might impair their ability to act at all times in the best interests of the employer may prevent an employee from **setting up an off-the-shelf company** for future competition purposes, even where that company remains dormant during the employment (*Ward Evans Financial Services Ltd v Fox* [2002] IRLR 120, CA).

2526 Set out below is sample wording from the model Service Agreement (¶9920). This may be suitable for **directors and other senior employees**. This is intended to be used as a starting point and should be tailored according to the requirements of the employer.

EXAMPLE 15. Outside Interests
15.1 The Executive will disclose in writing to the Board all his interests in any business (apart for any interest in a Group Company) throughout the Employment.
15.2 Subject to clause [15.3] below, during the Employment (including without limitation any period of garden leave), the Executive will not, without the prior written consent of the Board or except as a representative of the Company, be engaged, concerned, or interested, directly or indirectly, in the conduct of any other business of a similar nature to or which competes with that of the Company (or any Group Company) [or which is a supplier or customer of the Company (or any Group Company)].
15.3 The Executive may hold or be interested in shares or other securities of any company [which are listed or quoted on any recognised stock exchange or dealt on the Alternative Investments Market] provided that the interest of the Executive in such shares or other securities does not extend to more than [5%] of the total amount of such shares or securities.

2527 The employer may wish to ascertain what outside interests the employee has, in particular where these interests may compete with those of the company or prevent him devoting sufficient time to his duties. The agreement should therefore oblige the executive to **disclose** his outside interests to the board.

2528 The company could seek to limit the executive's competing outside interests by **limiting his holding of securities** in any competing company to a certain percentage. It may wish to include a different percentage for quoted and unquoted securities. For quoted companies, an appropriate figure would be between 5 and 10%.

Garden leave

2529 When the employer or, more commonly, the employee gives notice to terminate the employment (or where the employee intends to leave without giving proper notice), the employer may wish to distance him from confidential information, customer connection and staff, and to stop him going straight to a competitor (or setting up in competition) with such information and knowledge. He could achieve this by putting the employee on 'garden leave', which means that he remains employed (and is paid and receives his full contractual benefits) **during the notice period**, but does not attend work or carry out his job duties.

Garden leave may be a useful option where the employer wishes to remove the employee from the business immediately, without incurring the risk of restrictive covenants being held to be unenforceable if the employee is wrongfully dismissed (¶8155), or where there are no restrictive covenants.

2530 It is advisable to have an **express contractual right** to put the employee on garden leave, as otherwise a skilled employee may be able to argue that the employer has an implied duty to provide him with work and the opportunity to exercise his skills (¶1233; *William Hill Organisation Ltd v Tucker* [1998] IRLR 313, CA), in which case the employer's breach of contract in putting the employee on garden leave may entitle him to resign and claim constructive dismissal (¶8230).

Note that there may be an obligation to inform any relevant **regulatory body** that the employee is on garden leave and not performing normal duties.

Set out below is sample wording from the model Service Agreement (¶9920). This may be suitable for **directors and other senior employees**, but could also be used for general staff if required in the circumstances. It is intended to be used as a starting point and should be tailored according to the requirements of the employer.

EXAMPLE 21. Garden Leave

[Once notice to terminate the Employment has been given by either party in accordance with clause [2.3] of this Agreement,] OR [During the last [*number*] months of the [initial fixed-term/fixed-term,] or if the Executive resigns without giving the required period of notice and the Company does not accept that resignation, the following provisions will apply for [such period as the Company in its absolute discretion may decide/a maximum period of [*period*]]:

21.1. the Company will not be obliged to provide the Executive with any work or require him to perform any duties or may require him to perform such specific duties as are expressly assigned to him by the Company for such period as the Company in its absolute discretion may decide;

21.2. the Company may exclude the Executive from its premises or the premises of any other Group Company and may require him not to be involved in the business of such companies;

21.3. the Executive's salary and all contractual benefits [excluding any bonus] will continue to be paid or provided;

21.4. the Executive will remain bound by his obligations under this Agreement and, in particular, by clause [15] [*outside interests*];

21.5. the Executive will return all of the Company's property including without limitation all Confidential Information;

21.6. the Company may require the Executive not to have any contact or communication with any of its [employees, customers, clients, or professional contacts] in relation to the business of the Company or any Group Company;

21.7. the Company may make such announcements or statements to any of the [employees, customers, clients, or professional contacts] of the Company or any Group Company or any other third parties concerning the Executive as it in its sole and absolute discretion may decide;

21.8. the Company may require the Executive immediately to resign without claim for compensation from any office which he holds in the Company or any Group Company. If he fails to do so, the Executive hereby irrevocably appoints the Company to be his attorney to execute any document or do anything in his name necessary to effect his resignation.

[The Company reserves the right to require the Executive to take holiday which is accrued up to the commencement of garden leave and which will accrue to the date the Employment terminates during the period of garden leave on such day or days as the Company may specify. No contractual holiday entitlement shall accrue during such period, save that the Executive's entitlement to annual leave pursuant to the Regulations shall continue to accrue during such period.]

[At the end of any period of garden leave imposed, the Company may make a payment in lieu of the balance of [any required period of notice (whether given by the Executive or the Company)] OR [the initial fixed-term/fixed-term], less any deductions the Company is required to make by law.]

Garden leave provisions used to be treated by the courts with greater flexibility than post-termination restrictive covenants. However, case law, as it currently stands, suggests that they may also be subject to the doctrine of restraint of trade (see below) (*William Hill Organisation Ltd v Tucker*, above; *Symbian Ltd v Christensen* [2001] IRLR 77, CA). This may affect the **length and scope** of any garden leave injunction granted against an ex-employee (¶2651). 2531

If the employment is for a **fixed term** (without provision for termination by notice prior to expiry), the facility to impose garden leave for any unexpired part of the fixed term should be limited to a reasonable period of time. In any case, the **garden leave period** should not be excessive taking into account the nature of the employee's work and his need regularly to exercise his skills in order to maintain them or to preserve his reputation in the market. The garden leave period may, therefore, be shorter than the notice period.

Whether or not there is an express garden leave clause, the courts may grant an injunction to enforce the **duty not to compete** (whether express or implied) during the employment, which arguably continues to bind him during the notice period as he remains employed. Blanket restrictions (¶2522) may be limited by the courts to a specific competitor (*Symbian Ltd v Christensen*, above). 2532

MEMO POINTS It has been suggested that an express garden leave clause operates to terminate the duty of fidelity (and the implied duty not to compete) because it ends the relationship of employer and employee even though the contractual relationship continues. The contract would therefore have to contain an express term (see sample clauses at ¶2521 and ¶2526 above) preventing the employee from working for a competitor for the duration of the contract of employment (*Symbian Ltd v Christensen*).

2533 If the employee has been on garden leave during all or part of his notice period, it is still possible, depending on the circumstances, to impose **restrictive covenants** as well (see below). The period of such covenants need not necessarily be reduced by the period spent on garden leave (*Crédit Suisse Asset Management v Armstrong* [1996] IRLR 450, CA). However, a court may take into account the existence of a garden leave clause in determining the validity of a restrictive covenant. An express set-off will, therefore, probably assist the enforceability of the covenants, and will be appropriate unless the employer is confident that the minimum length of necessary protection is the period of garden leave plus the restricted period of the covenant.

EXAMPLE In *Crédit Suisse First Boston (Europe) Ltd v Padiachy* [1998] IRLR 504, QBD, P was an equities research analyst. His contract with CSFB contained a non-solicitation covenant (with respect to clients and employees) for 12 months after the termination of his employment and a non-compete covenant for 3 months. After giving notice, P was put on 3 months garden leave. The court refused to enforce the non-compete covenant taking into account the speed with which the market changes and the 3 months of exclusion from the market during the garden leave period, and also the existence of the non-solicitation covenant.

II. Post-employment restrictive covenants

2550 The implied duty (with the exception of disclosures of trade secrets) does not apply after the employment has ended and in the absence of any express contractual obligation, employees are free to compete with their employers after the termination of their employment. **Fiduciary duties** may extend beyond the end of the fiduciary relationship (¶2510).

Any express contractual terms that restrict an ex-employee's activities after termination are called restrictive covenants and are subject to the restraint of trade doctrine.

Restraint of trade

2551 The doctrine of restraint of trade holds that any contractual term which seeks to restrict an individual's freedom to earn a living and use his skill and knowledge is, in principle, void and unenforceable.

However, such terms may be enforced if it is both reasonable in the interests of the parties, and reasonable in the interests of the public.

2552 To be reasonable in the **interests of the parties**, the **employer** must have a legitimate business interest to protect (see below), and the restraint must be no wider than is necessary to protect that interest (for example, the duration, geographical area and restricted activities of a covenant must be limited to that necessary to achieve the protection required in each particular case). If these tests are satisfied, the courts will then consider the restraint from the **employee's** point of view to assess whether it is fair in the light of the general principle of restraint of trade. The severity of the restraint on the employee will be balanced against the employer's need for protection and is judged on the facts of each case.

The three-stage **process of assessing** the **reasonableness** of such restrictive covenants has recently been reiterated by the High Court (*TFS Derivatives Ltd v Morgan* [2005] IRLR 246, QBD). It is first necessary for the court to decide what the covenant means when properly construed. Having done this, if the court concludes that there is an element of ambiguity and that there are two possible ways in which the covenant can be construed, one of which would make the clause unlawful in restraint of trade, but the other of which would be lawful, the court should adopt the latter on the basis that the parties are deemed to have intended to negotiate a lawful contract which is not contrary to public policy. The second stage is to find evidence that the employer has legitimate business interests which are worthy of protection in respect of the employee's employment. The third stage is for the employer to demonstrate that the covenant is no wider than reasonably necessary to protect those legitimate business interests.

The courts will balance the parties' private interests with the **interests of the public** in maintaining a business environment of healthy competition. For example, an agreement between two employers not to employ each other's staff is likely to be void as an unlawful restraint of trade (*Kores Manufacturing Co Ltd v Kolok Manufacturing Co Ltd* [1958] 2 All ER 65, CA; *Esso Petroleum Ltd v Harper's Garage (Stourport) Ltd* [1967] 1 All ER 699, HL). 2553

This section will focus on the interests of the parties and, in particular, the tests that the employer must satisfy to achieve a potentially enforceable restraint. 2554

A. Legitimate business interests

The courts will closely examine the **subject of a restraint** in order to decide whether the employer has a real legitimate business interest to protect. Whether he does will depend on the nature of the employer's business, and the employee's position within that business. The **types of interest** that the employer can seek to protect are: 2560
- trade secrets or other confidential information (¶2425 and section 2 above);
- customer/client connection (i.e. goodwill); and
- a stable workforce.

EXAMPLE Interest

1. In *Dawnay, Day & Co Ltd v de Braconier d'Alphen* [1997] IRLR 442, CA, the Court held that the employer, D, had a legitimate interest in protecting the **customer connection** established by ex-employees as inter-dealer brokers, as D had incurred considerable expense in establishing and fostering that connection.

No interest

2. However, in *Cantor Fitzgerald (UK) Ltd v Wallace* [1992] IRLR 215, QBD, the employer sought to enforce a non-compete covenant (to protect goodwill) in respect of W and other former inter-dealer brokers. The Court held that, where the true skills and art of a job lie in the **personal qualities** of the person performing it (as was the case with W and the other brokers, whose success depended on their personality and ability to get on with the traders), there is no proprietary right which the employer can claim to protect for himself as part of his business.

The connection of an **employment agency** with the pool of workers available for temporary employment is also capable of being a protectable business interest (*Office Angels Ltd v Rainer-Thomas and O'Connor* [1991] IRLR 214, CA). 2561

B. Scope of covenant

To have a better chance of being enforced, the covenants should be **carefully drafted** to suit the specific circumstances of the employer and each particular employee. The employer should not include every conceivable type of covenant to try and ensure blanket protection. If he did so, a court may conclude that he has not given careful consideration to what protection he really requires. 2565

The **type of restriction** considered reasonable for a particular employee will depend on the nature of his work, in particular, whether he has access to confidential information, and/or has contact with the employer's customers such that they tend to identify him with the business. For example, it would not be appropriate to include a covenant protecting customer connections in the contract of an employee who has no contact with customers. 2566

Different covenants may be suitable in different industries, geographical areas, and in relation to different positions within the same company.

2567 The **reasonableness of a particular covenant** will depend on various factors, including the duration, the geographical area, the scope of the restricted activities, the definition of prohibited customer, and the link between the interest and the restraint. A long restricted period (for example, 2 years) is less likely to be enforced than a shorter period, and it may be necessary to have different restricted periods for different covenants. The various factors do not apply in isolation, but all interrelate. For example, the longer the time, the smaller the geographical area must be, and the narrower the scope of the activities.

2568 Set out below is sample wording from the model Service Agreement (¶9920). This may be suitable for **directors and other senior employees**, but could also be used for general staff if required in the circumstances. It is intended to be used as a starting point and should be tailored according to the requirements of the employer.

EXAMPLE 24. **Post-termination restrictive covenants**

24.1 During the Employment, the Executive is likely to obtain trade secrets and confidential information and personal knowledge of and influence over the Group's clients, customers and employees. As a result, the Executive agrees to observe the following restrictive covenants after the Termination Date:

24.1.1. The Executive covenants that he will not, for a period of [*period*] from the Termination Date [(less any period of garden leave imposed by the Company)] and within [*insert geographical area of restriction*], on his own account or for or with any other person, directly or indirectly carry on or be engaged in any activity or business which is or is intended to be in competition with the business of the Company or any Group Company which was carried on by such company at the Termination Date and with which the Executive was concerned or connected at any time during the [*number*] months prior to the Termination Date.

24.1.2. The Executive covenants that he will not, for a period of [*period*] from the Termination Date [(less any period of garden leave imposed by the Company)], in competition with the Company or any other Group Company, on his own behalf or for or with any other person, directly or indirectly seek orders from or solicit the custom of Company Clients.

24.1.3. The Executive covenants that he will not, for a period of [*period*] from the Termination Date [(less any period of garden leave imposed by the Company)], in competition with the Company or any other Group Company, on his own behalf or for or with any other person, directly or indirectly deal or otherwise do business with Company Clients.

24.1.4. The Executive covenants that he will not, for a period of [*period*] from the Termination Date [(less any period of garden leave imposed by the Company)], in competition with the Company or any other Group Company, on his own behalf or for or with any other person, directly or indirectly entice or try to entice away from the Company or any other Group Company any person who was at the Termination Date and/or any time during the [*number*] months prior to the Termination Date [a senior or key employee, director, *list class of employee*] of such a company and with whom the Executive had worked closely at any time during that period.

24.1.5. The Executive shall at the request of the Company enter into a direct agreement or undertaking with any other Group Company by which he will accept restrictive covenants corresponding to the restrictive covenants contained in this clause [24]. The Executive acknowledges that the provisions of this clause [24] constitute severable undertakings given for the benefit of the Company and all other Group Companies and may be enforced by the Company on its own behalf or on behalf of any other Group Company.

24.1.6. Before accepting any employment, appointment or engagement with any third party either during the Employment or at any time during the period of [*period*] after the Termination Date, the Executive shall draw the provisions of this clause [24] to the attention of such third party.

24.1.7. [Each of the covenants set out above is entirely separate and independent of the others and is considered and accepted by the parties [each of whom has taken legal advice] to be reasonable and necessary for the protection of the legitimate interests of the Company and the Group Companies. If any covenant or part thereof shall be found void, invalid or unenforceable by any court of competent jurisdiction, but would be valid if some words were deleted, or the period reduced, such covenant shall apply with such modification as may be necessary to make it valid and effective.]

24.1.8. [In the event of any covenant or part thereof being declared void, invalid or unenforceable by any court of competent jurisdiction, all other covenants or parts thereof shall remain in full force and effect and shall not be affected.]

24.1.9. After the Termination Date, the Executive will not without the consent of the Company represent himself still to be connected in any way with the Company or any Group Company.

1. Non-compete covenants

See clause 24.1.1. of the model Service Agreement, reproduced above. **2570**

Protectable interests

Non-compete covenants prohibit the ex-employee from engaging in a competitive activity. They are, however, viewed very cautiously by the courts and will be unenforceable and will not be upheld if their effect is limited to restricting competition. **2571**

They will only be upheld in order to give **adequate protection** to the employer's legitimate interests, and will only be enforced where a non-solicitation or non-dealing covenant would provide inadequate protection (*Office Angels Ltd v Rainer-Thomas and O'Connor* [1991] IRLR 214, CA), for example where the employer's customers, although regular, are not readily identifiable (for example, hairdressing businesses), or where their solicitation by the ex-employer would be difficult to detect. **2572**

The courts have upheld non-compete covenants on two grounds: to protect the employer's confidential information and customer connection.

Confidential information A covenant will only be enforced where: **2573**
- it is not possible to protect the confidential information in any other way (for example, because it is difficult to monitor the observance of a confidentiality undertaking or to distinguish between information which is confidential and information which is not (*Lawrence David Ltd v Ashton* [1989] IRLR 22, NICA)); and
- the information is capable of causing real damage in the hands of a competitor (¶2455).

Customer connection The employer must show that the ex-employee had acquired influence over his customers. However, in order to be a protectable interest, the customer connection must be a proprietary interest of the employer, rather than a result of the personal qualities of the employee (*Dawnay, Day & Co Ltd v de Braconier d'Alphen*; *Cantor Fitzgerald (UK) Ltd v Wallace* – see example at ¶2560). **2574**

Prohibited area

Non-compete covenants are usually drafted as area covenants (i.e. by reference to a 'prohibited area'), which can be **defined by reference** to a: **2575**
- radius taken from the employer's place of business; or
- territory or region which reflects the scope of the employee's duties or the employer's operations.

In any case, non-compete covenants should only operate in respect of an area where the employer has **legitimate business interests** (*Greer v Sketchley Ltd* [1979] IRLR 445, CA), and there must be a 'functional correspondence' with the interest that the employee is seeking to protect (*Office Angels Ltd v Rainer-Thomas and O'Connor* [1991] IRLR 214, CA). This means that there must be a **close link** between the prohibited area and the actual operations of the employer's business, reflecting, for example, the likely distribution of the employer's customers.

EXAMPLE In *Office Angels Ltd v Rainer-Thomas and O'Connor*, R-T and O'C were a branch manager and a consultant of the employer, an employment agency. The non-compete covenants were limited to a radius of 1,000 metres from the branch at which they worked. Nevertheless, the location of that branch meant that the prohibited area covered most of the City of London. As such, it was too wide, and therefore unenforceable.

The reasonableness of the **geographical extent** of the restriction will depend on the circumstances of each case. In *Lansing Linde Ltd v Kerr* [1991] IRLR 80, CA, the employers failed to justify the extension of their covenant to all countries in which the group operated. However, in some circumstances a national or even **worldwide** covenant may be justifiable (*Scully UK Ltd v Lee* [1998] IRLR 259, CA). **2576**

If **no area is stated**, the covenant will be deemed to be worldwide, and therefore harder to uphold.

2577 If the employer's real concern is to prevent the ex-employee dealing with his customers, a non-solicitation/non-dealing covenant may be sufficient to protect his interests, particularly where customer contact is not confined to a particular area (for example, where dealings are over the telephone). An area covenant is more likely to be reasonable where the employer's business involves **clients visiting his premises** to receive the service or use the business (e.g. hairdressers, estate agents).

An area covenant will be unenforceable if it is not an effective means of **protecting customer connection** (for example, because the number of customers within that area would be too high, including those with whom the employee had no previous dealings). In such cases, it may be necessary specifically to limit the covenant to customers with whom the employee had dealings during the latter stages of his employment for there to be a valid covenant.

Specific competitors

2578 An alternative to the prohibited area non-compete covenant is to identify specific rival businesses, with which the ex-employee must not be involved (*Littlewoods Organisation Ltd v Harris* [1977] 1 WLR 1472, CA).

Restricted activities

2579 Non-compete covenants are often criticised on the grounds that they would prohibit the ex-employee from taking part in activities that would not be harmful to the employer (for example, where he joins a competitor but in a business area that does not compete with the employer, or in a role where his knowledge of the employer's confidential information or customer connection is of no use).

It is advisable, therefore, to limit the scope of the activities to the **particular sector** of the industry in which the employee is involved (*Scully UK Ltd v Lee*), and within that sector, to specify the **exact nature of the occupation(s)** in which the employee is prohibited from working.

EXAMPLE Unreasonably wide scope

1. In *Wincanton Ltd v (1) Cranny (2) SDM European Transport Ltd* [2000] IRLR 716, CA, the covenant, contained in a booklet containing standard terms and conditions, prohibited C from working in competition with 'any business carried on by the company'. This was too wide because it was of a **standard form** and was plainly intended to apply to a wide range of situations.

2. In *J A Mont (UK) Ltd v Mills* [1993] IRLR 172, CA, the restriction was unreasonable because it restrained M from working 'in **any capacity** whatsoever' and 'in **any sector** of the tissue industry'.

3. In *Marley Tile Co Ltd v Johnson* [1982] IRLR 75, CA, J was restricted from supplying, selling or fixing products similar to the employer's. The covenant was too wide because it was not limited to the roofing business and could therefore extend to **purposes other than roofing**.

Duration

2580 The duration of the covenant will also be critical to its enforceability. However, there are no hard and fast rules for determining whether a particular period is reasonable. Restrictions of more than 1 year would, in most cases, be unreasonable.

EXAMPLE In *Barry Allsuch & Co v Harris*, 4 May 2001, HC, a non-compete covenant prohibiting a former employee from working as an estate agent within a specified area for 2 years was unreasonable. Covenants imposed by other estate agencies in the area were for a maximum of 6 months and there was no evidence to suggest that the longer period was justified.

2581 In the case of restraints protecting **confidential information**, it will depend on the "shelf life" of the information (i.e. how quickly the industry changes), and the length of time for which it will be valuable to the ex-employee. In the case of restraints protecting **customer connection**, it will depend on the length of time the employer will need to rebuild the relationship with clients following the ex-employee's departure.

2. Non-solicitation covenants (customers)

See clause 24.1.2. of the model Service Agreement, reproduced at ¶2568. 2585

These covenants seek to protect the **employer's customer connection** by preventing the ex-employee from soliciting the custom of the employer's clients and customers. The Service Agreement **defines** Company Clients as 'any person, firm or company who was at the Termination Date and/or any time during the [*number*] months prior to the Termination Date a customer or client of, or in the habit of doing business with, the Company or any other Group Company and in respect of which the Executive had dealings, whether directly or indirectly'.

Prohibited customers

It may be appropriate to use a **prohibited area** definition in order to clarify the identity of customers who cannot be solicited. However, the covenant may be unenforceable where the class of prohibited customers is very large in number (*Marley Tile Co Ltd v Johnson* – see example at ¶2579). 2586

It is therefore advisable for the pool of prohibited customers to be restricted to those who were customers, and with whom the employee had dealings, within a **specified period** (which should be as short as possible in the circumstances) **prior to the termination date**. The length of this period may depend on the regularity of contact between the ex-employee and customers. For example, if the ex-employee would deal with most customers every 6 months, then a period of 6 months might be appropriate. 2587

The courts have, however, upheld non-solicitation covenants where there is **no time limit** on the past period when such dealings took place (*Dentmaster (UK) Ltd v Kent* [1997] IRLR 636, CA), and even where there was **no link** between the ex-employee and clients (*G W Plowman & Son Ltd v Ash* [1964] 2 All ER 10, CA). Although this may be justified in the case of very senior employees (for example, the managing director), there is a high risk of the covenant being found to be unreasonable. It is therefore advisable to restrict the scope of the covenant to those clients with whom the ex-employee had dealt.

It may be appropriate to restrict the covenant to those customers who were still **customers on the termination date**. However, if it is not immediately apparent whether or not a particular individual or company was a customer of the employer on any specified date (for example, because customer contact is typically irregular), such a restriction will not be appropriate. 2588

The covenant should not usually extend to **prospective clients**, i.e. those who became customers after the termination date, as the ex-employee could have no influence over such customers (*Konski v Peet* [1915] 1 Ch 530). However, where sufficient influence exists, a covenant may be upheld (*International Consulting Services (UK) Ltd v Hart* [2000] IRLR 227, QBD).

EXAMPLE In *International Consulting Services (UK) Ltd v Hart*, the Court upheld a covenant restraining the ex-employee from soliciting anyone who, during the 12 months immediately prior to the date of termination, was negotiating with the employer for the supply of services and with whom the employee or one of his subordinates had dealt. 'Negotiations' was interpreted as meaning a discussion between the parties about the terms of a contract which both parties have in view and which is a real possibility. The Court found that the ex-employee had an influential position such that any previous contact might have given him a rapport with the customer, and that he might have had some input into the preparation of a proposal for negotiations.

Duration

The reasonableness of the period chosen will depend on the length of time the employer will need to rebuild the relationship with clients following the ex-employee's departure. 2589

3. Non-dealing covenants

2595 See clause 24.1.3. of the model Service Agreement, reproduced at ¶2568. See ¶2585 above for definition of Company Clients.

A covenant prohibiting an employee from dealing with customers also seeks to protect the employer's **customer connection**, but is more onerous than a non-solicitation covenant. A non-dealing covenant may be enforceable where it is unlikely to be possible to prove that the ex-employee has solicited or will solicit customers (*PR Consultants Scotland Ltd v Mann* [1996] IRLR 188, CS), or if he may be able to take advantage of the employer's customer connection without actively doing so (for example, where they approach him independently).

A non-dealing covenant should be used in conjunction with a non-solicitation covenant in order to prohibit the ex-employee from dealing with the employer's customers **regardless of who initiated the approach**.

The comments made above in respect of the enforcement of non-solicitation of customers apply equally to non-dealing covenants.

4. Non-solicitation covenants (employees)

2600 The employer may be concerned that the employee may seek to take other members of staff with him when he leaves the company. There is no implied term that will prevent an ex-employee enticing other staff to leave the employer (although there may be liability for inducing a breach of contract). An express non-solicitation or 'anti-poaching' covenant can be used to try to prevent this situation and to protect the employer's interest in a **stable workforce**.

The employer's need for protection arises because the ex-employee may seek to exploit the knowledge that he has gained of employees' qualifications, rates of pay and other terms. Although there has been much debate as to whether the employer has a legitimate interest to protect, the courts are increasingly willing to recognise an interest in maintaining a stable, trained workforce where the employer can show an **investment in a complement of skilled staff** (*Dawnay, Day & Co Ltd v de Braconier d'Alphen* [1997] IRLR 442, CA).

Prohibited employees

2601 The definition of prohibited employees needs careful consideration. The clause is most likely to be enforceable if it is limited to current employees with a particular level of seniority or expertise. It should not normally cover clerical or secretarial staff, or any staff who are unskilled and could readily be replaced. The employer must therefore consider in each case the **category of employees** the covenant should seek to protect.

The tighter the definition, the greater the prospect of enforceability. For example, a covenant restraining the ex-employee from soliciting anyone who was, during his employment, "a **director or senior employee**" was upheld (*Dawnay, Day & Co Ltd v de Braconier d'Alphen*), as was a covenant restraining the ex-employee from soliciting anyone working "in a **senior capacity**" (*Alliance Paper Group plc v Prestwich* [1996] IRLR 25, ChD).

Conversely, a covenant restraining the ex-employee from soliciting "**any employees** of the company" was held to be unenforceable as being unreasonably wide (*Hanover Insurance Brokers Ltd v Shapiro* [1994] IRLR 82, CA). However, a covenant restraining the ex-employee from soliciting "any individual who was an **employee or director**" was held to be enforceable where the company had invested a great deal in the training of both its broking and support staff, and therefore had a legitimate interest in protecting the stability of the workforce as a whole in the circumstances (*SBJ Stephenson Ltd v Mandy* [2000] IRLR 233, QBD).

2602 It may assist the test of reasonableness if the covenant is linked with the ex-employee's **exercise of personal influence**, i.e. by defining the prohibited employee as someone with whom the departing employee worked closely. As the departing employee's knowledge or personal influence will decrease with time, this link could be limited to staff with whom the ex-employee worked closely **during the latter stages** (for example, 6 months) of his employment.

The covenant will be invalid if it includes **new employees** who join the employer after the departing employee has left (*Hanover Insurance Brokers Ltd v Shapiro*). 2603
The covenant could expressly state that it does not include employees who approach the ex-employee in response to a **properly advertised vacancy**.

Duration

The reasonableness of the period chosen will depend on the period over which the influence or knowledge of the departing employee is likely to diminish. 2604

5. Indirect restrictions

An indirect restraint is a clause which penalises the ex-employee after the termination, for example, by providing that **outstanding commission** will not be paid if the employee joins a competitor (*Sadler v Imperial Life Assurance Co of Canada Ltd* [1988] IRLR 388, QBD; *Marshall v N M Financial Management Ltd* [1996] IRLR 20, ChD, on appeal [1997] IRLR 449, CA). Such restraints must also go no further than is necessary to protect the employer's legitimate business interests (¶2560). 2610

C. Other factors affecting enforceability

Context of agreement

Restrictive covenants entered into as part of a **business or share sale** (where the person accepting the restriction is the vendor) will be easier to enforce, even if the vendor is also an employee of the business (*Allied Dunbar (Frank Weisinger) Ltd v Weisinger* [1988] IRLR 60, ChD; *Systems Reliability Holdings plc v Smith* [1990] IRLR 377, ChD). The purchaser has an interest in protecting the newly acquired business from any **competing activities of the vendor**, particularly where the sale price included an element for goodwill. 2615

EXAMPLE In *Allied Dunbar (Frank Weisinger) Ltd v Weisinger*, W was a self-employed sales associate of AD. He had built up a highly successful practice, which was dependent on his personal connections and customer recommendations. W sold his practice to AD, including its goodwill and connection, and agreed to stay on as a consultant for 2 years and to be bound by non-compete and non-solicit covenants for a further 2 years after his consultancy ended. The Court indicated that it would adopt the less stringent approach applying to the protection of the goodwill of a business sold by the covenantor to the covenantee and that the covenants were therefore enforceable even though W had been engaged as an employee during the intervening 2-year period.

Employer's fundamental breach of contract

It is a general legal principle that a party **may not take advantage of its own breach** of contract. If, therefore, the employer terminates the employment in breach of contract (for example, by not giving the required period of notice), or the employee resigns following the employer's repudiatory breach, the employer will not be entitled to enforce any of the employee's obligations that are stated to continue or take effect after the termination (*General Billposting Co Ltd v Atkinson* [1909] AC 118, HL). A breach of the implied term of trust and confidence (¶1241) will also lead to restrictive covenants being unenforceable. 2616

The employer **cannot circumvent** this principle by **expressly stating** that the restrictive covenants will be enforceable however the employment is terminated, or even where the employer terminates in breach. Restrictions stated to apply after the termination of employment "how- 2617 ever that comes about and whether lawful or not" are unenforceable because they are "manifestly wholly unreasonable" (*Living Design (Home Improvements) Ltd v Davidson* [1994] IRLR 69, CS).

Wording such as "terminated for any reason whatsoever" and "irrespective of the cause or manner", which may indicate that the covenant will apply even where the employee is dismissed in breach of contract, has been held to render the entire covenant clause unenforceable (*D v M* [1996] IRLR 192, QBD). It is not likely to be possible to sever the offending wording by applying the blue pencil test (¶2633) so as to leave the rest of the clause to be enforced (*Living Design (Home Improvements) Ltd v Davidson*).

However, it has since been held that the **mere existence of a provision** stating that the covenants will apply following the termination of the employment "howsoever occasioned" or "howsoever arising" will not necessarily make the covenant unreasonable and unenforceable, although if the employer actually terminated in breach, they would be (*Rock Refrigeration Limited v Jones* [1996] IRLR 675, CA).

2618 Where the employer has a contractual right to terminate the employment by making a **payment in lieu of notice**, he will not be in breach of contract if he does so, and can therefore rely on any post-termination restrictions (*Rex Stewart Jeffries Parker Ginsberg Ltd v Parker* [1988] IRLR 483, CA). If the employer makes a payment in lieu of notice where he has no contractual right to do so, this may still amount to a wrongful dismissal unless the employee consents to it. The safest course would therefore be to repeat any post-termination restrictions in settlement documentation (¶9300).

MEMO POINTS It is suggested that if the employee is asked to **reaffirm his post-termination restrictions in the settlement documentation**, then the employer should consider allocating some additional consideration to the obligations to ensure that he will be able to enforce the restrictions at a later date.

Garden leave

2619 A court may take into account the existence of a garden leave clause in determining the validity of a restrictive covenant (see ¶2529).

Payment in respect of restricted period

2620 The concern underlying the doctrine of restraint is not only to ensure that employees can earn their living, but also to uphold the public interest in competition and the proper use of the employee's skills. **In general** therefore, it makes no difference to the enforcement of restrictive covenants that the ex-employee is remunerated during the period of restraint (*JA Mont (UK) Ltd v Mills* [1993] IRLR 172, CA).

However, in **certain circumstances** (for example, where a senior employee receives an additional payment as part of a termination agreement), a payment may be taken into consideration in assessing the reasonableness of a covenant (*Turner v Commonwealth & British Minerals* [2000] IRLR 114, CA).

2621 Payment for goodwill will be relevant to restrictive covenants entered into as part of a **business or share sale**.

Transfer of undertakings

2622 Under the transfer regulations, the rights and obligations of the transferor employer will pass automatically to the transferee employer, and restrictive covenants may, therefore, be enforced by the transferee employer against employees who have transferred to it in certain circumstances (see ¶7980).

The transferee employer may wish to impose **new covenants** on the transferred employees. However, at the time of writing, any variation of terms in connection with the transfer will be legally ineffective, even where the employees were better off overall after the change (¶8010).

MEMO POINTS It is expected that the new TUPE regulations, due to become effective on 6 April 2006, will expressly permit contractual variations made in connection with the transfer to be agreed (¶8015).

D. Courts' approach

Interpretation

As with any binding contractual term, covenants must be **sufficiently certain**. If they are not, they will be void for uncertainty, although the courts are slow to come to that conclusion (*Dawnay, Day & Co Ltd v de Braconier d'Alphen* [1997] IRLR 442, CA). 2630

An employer should avoid drafting '**multiple choice**' restrictions (for example, including a prohibited area by reference to 'London, Manchester, Birmingham, England and Wales, the UK'), in the hope that the courts will enforce one of the choices. The risk in this approach is that the clause may be held to be void for uncertainty.

If a contract includes a covenant which is unreasonably wide in its scope, it will normally be held void and of no effect. However, it may be possible to **construe the covenant** as having a more limited application, in which case it may meet the reasonableness requirement. The courts will apply the normal rules of construction, construing the covenant realistically to give effect to the **intention of the parties** (¶1117). They will reject a literal interpretation of the words used if that would contradict the obvious intention of the parties, will limit general wording, where necessary, to reflect the assumed purpose of the restraint, and will discount remote possibilities in which the covenant could operate unreasonably. 2631

EXAMPLE 1. In *Hanover Insurance Brokers Ltd v Shapiro* (¶2601), S was prohibited from soliciting the insurance broking business of clients of the employer, the parent company and that company's subsidiaries. S argued that the extension to other companies made the clause unreasonably wide. The Court took a flexible approach and decided that, as the parent and other subsidiaries were not involved in insurance broking, the clause could be construed as referring only to the employer.
2. In *G W Plowman & Son Ltd* (¶2587), the employer sought to enforce a covenant restraining A from canvassing customers. Although the covenant did not mention the kind of goods to which it applied, the Court held that it should be construed in the light of the contract as a whole. As the contract did make reference to the employer's products (corn and agricultural merchandise, and animal feed), the clause was limited to those products and was therefore not too wide.
3. In *Home Counties Dairies Ltd v Skilton* [1970] 1 All ER 1227, CA, S, a milkman, was restrained from serving or selling milk or dairy produce to, or soliciting orders from, those who had been customers of the employer during the last 6 months of the employment and who had been served by him. The Court discounted the argument that the covenant could cover the situation where both the milkman and the customer moved to another area, in which case the application of the covenant would be unreasonable. Further, the Court rejected a literal reading of the covenant which might have led to the conclusion that S was restrained from becoming a grocer, as this also involved the sale of dairy produce. The covenant had to be considered in the context, concerning the employer's trade as a dairyman and the employee's trade as a milkman.

The reasonableness of the covenant is assessed in the light of the facts and circumstances as they were at the time **when the contract was entered into**, although the parties' reasonable expectations are also to be taken into account (*TSC Europe (UK) Ltd v Massey* [1999] IRLR 22, ChD). 2632

When the employer seeks to enforce a covenant by way of an injunction, the courts will also assess whether the covenant is reasonable at that time.

Unreasonable covenants

If, having construed a post-termination restriction, a court finds it to be unreasonable, the restriction will be unenforceable in its **entirety**. A court will not rewrite a covenant so as to make it reasonable and, therefore, enforceable, nor will it enforce a restriction in **more limited terms** than those imposed by the restrictive covenant (*J A Mont (UK) Ltd v Mills* [1993] IRLR 172, CA). 2633

If a single clause contains several restrictions (for example, a non-compete and a non-solicit covenant), the court may decide the enforceability of **each restriction** separately. If one restriction is unreasonable, the courts may be able to sever the unreasonable part without

affecting the enforceability of the remaining restriction. **Individual words or phrases** may also be severed in this way, providing that (*Sadler v Imperial Life Assurance Co of Canada Ltd* [1988] IRLR 388, QBD):
- what is left makes independent sense without the need for further changes;
- the remaining terms continue to be supported by adequate consideration; and
- the sense of the agreement is not changed.

This is known as the "**blue pencil test**". This test will be used 'where the part so enforceable is clearly severable, and even so only in cases where the excess is of trivial importance, or merely technical, and not a part of the main purport and substance of the clause' (*Mason v Provident Clothing and Supply Co Ltd* [1913] AC 724, HL). For example, a covenant might be drafted to stop an ex-employee soliciting customers of the employer and other group companies for 3 years after termination. A court might be prepared to sever the reference to other group companies, but it will not change the 3-year period to 1 year in order to make it enforceable. To facilitate the application of the blue pencil test where necessary, it is advisable to deal with each type of restriction in a separate and distinct clause.

EXAMPLE In *Rex Stewart Jeffries Parker Ginsberg Ltd* (¶2618), P's contract restrained him from soliciting anyone who to his knowledge 'is or has been' during his employment a customer of the company or any associated companies. The Court agreed that there were four distinct restrictions which prohibit the soliciting of:
- those who had been customers to the date of termination;
- those who might have become customers after the date of termination;
- customers of the company; and
- customers of associated companies.

The second and the last prohibition were unreasonable, and so the judge deleted the reference to 'is or' and the part of the clause relating to associated companies, thus limiting the restriction to customers of the company up to the date of termination, making it reasonable and enforceable.

2634 Some agreements contain **express wording** stating that, if any restriction is found to be void but would be valid if some part of it were deleted, those restrictions will apply with such modifications as may be necessary to make them valid or effective (see wording of clause 24 of the model Service Agreement, reproduced at ¶2568). The court accepted such wording in *Hinton & Higgs (UK) Ltd v Murphy and Valentine* [1989] IRLR 519, CS, but in *Living Design (Home Improvements) Ltd*, above, it considered that such wording did not enable it to do anything more than the blue pencil test, and that it did not extend the courts' powers to enable them to rewrite the contract.

III. Enforcement and remedies

2640 An **employee/ex-employee** can apply to the court for a declaration that an express term/covenant is invalid and unenforceable, or for summary judgment against the employer on the grounds that the employer's claim has no real prospect of success.

2641 An **employer** may be justified in **dismissing** an employee for breach of his implied duty of fidelity/express term and the dismissal could amount to a fair dismissal (¶8422). However, it is likely that at this stage, the damage will have been done so as an enforcement measure it will not be effective other than to serve as a deterrent to other employees.

An employer must also be careful before he takes such action, if he merely believes that an employee is going to breach an implied or express term. In such cases, to justify dismissal, the employer would need strong evidence to show that he knew that the employee was going to disclose confidential information, compete or solicit.

2642 If the ex-employee has taken **confidential documents** belonging to the employer, the employer can ask the court to order the employee to preserve these documents or to **deliver them up** (*Roger Bullivant Ltd v Ellis* [1987] IRLR 491, CA). In extreme cases, the court may grant a search order, which would permit the employer to enter particular premises in order to **search** for them. Such orders will only be granted sparingly, and there is a heavy evidential burden on the employer to show that there is a grave danger or real possibility that evidence might be destroyed if the order is not granted (*Lock International plc v Beswick* [1989] IRLR 481, ChD).

1. Injunction

In practice, the usual remedy for a threatened or actual breach of an implied or express term/restrictive covenant is an injunction (granted by the High Court and county courts, but not employment tribunals), which prevents the employee/ex-employee (most usually the ex-employee) from breaching or further breaching the term/covenant. In many cases the employer requires immediate relief and will apply straight away for an '**interlocutory**' or '**interim**' (i.e. temporary) injunction pending the trial of the action. Where the matter is extremely urgent, the employer can apply to the court without notifying the ex-employee (an '**ex parte**' application), although notice should usually be given where the employer's interests will not be prejudiced by doing so. 2645

If, unusually, the period of the restrictive covenant enforced by an interlocutory injunction has not expired before the matter comes to trial, the court may grant a **permanent** injunction.

For an injunction to be **granted**, the requirements of the civil court rules and related practice direction must be satisfied (reg 25 Civil Procedure Rules SI 1998/3121). Previous guidance given by the House of Lords will probably continue to be relevant (*American Cyanamid Co v Ethicon Ltd* [1975] 1 All ER 504, HL). This requires the employer to show that there are serious issues of law and fact to be tried (i.e. that he has an arguable claim), and if so, that, on the balance of convenience, the injunction should be granted. If the court is in doubt as to the balance of convenience, it will favour maintenance of the status quo. 2646

In making its decision, the **court will consider** whether:
- damages would be an adequate remedy; and
- more harm will be done by granting or refusing to grant an injunction (taking into account the employer's cross-undertaking in damages, see ¶2649).

It will also take account of the right to **freedom of expression** guaranteed by the Human Rights Act 1998.

Damages will probably not be considered an adequate remedy:
- if the ex-employee does not have the financial means to meet an award;
- if damages are difficult to quantify;
- to restrain the misuse of confidential information; or
- to enforce non-solicitation or non-compete covenants.

EXAMPLE In *Wincanton Ltd v (1) Cranny (2) SDM European Transport Ltd* [2000] IRLR, 716, CA, C was restricted by a customer non-solicitation covenant. However, the Court of Appeal refused to grant an injunction because (i) there were only 3 months of the 12 months' restriction left to run, such that the balance of convenience lay in C's favour, and (ii) Wincanton, who had been able to quantify their loss by reference to the loss of specific customer contracts, could be **adequately compensated** by way of damages. Wincanton should therefore have concentrated their efforts in securing a speedy trial.

Normally, the **court will not consider** the merits of the parties' case (*American Cyanamid*, followed in *Lawrence David Ltd v Ashton* [1989] IRLR 22, NICA). However, if the grant or refusal of an injunction at the interlocutory stage would in effect **dispose of the action** (for example, because a speedy main hearing is not possible and the action cannot be tried before a restraint has expired or nearly expired), the court may also consider the employer's prospect of success at the main hearing (*NWL Ltd v Woods* [1979] IRLR 478, HL, followed in *D v M* [1996] IRLR 192, QBD). This will result in a more onerous burden on the employer than merely establishing an arguable claim. 2647

An employer seeking an injunction to enforce **confidentiality obligations** must specify in detail the information they claim to be confidential (*Lock International plc v Beswick*). The duration or shelf life of the confidential information will be relevant to the court's decision on whether to grant an injunction and for how long. For example, in the case of an employee who has 2648 copied client lists for use as a 'springboard' to launch into business after his employment ends, the court may grant an injunction so as to neutralise the unfair advantage gained for as long as the information is likely to be commercially sensitive.

2649 Seeking an injunction is **costly**, both financially and in terms of management time. The employer must therefore weigh up the damage to his business against the costs of seeking this remedy. He must be prepared for the following:
– to give a cross-undertaking in damages (i.e. an undertaking to pay damages to the ex-employee in respect of any loss suffered by him if the court decides at the main hearing that the interlocutory injunction should not have been granted);
– to demonstrate that he could afford such damages;
– to meet his own legal costs, which are likely to be substantial given the amount of work and the speed with which an application must be made; and
– to pay the ex-employee's legal costs if the employer loses.

If the matter proceeds to a main hearing and the employer is successful, he may be able to recover part of his legal costs from the ex-employee.

However, one advantage is that a successful application for an interlocutory injunction may actually be, in effect, a final injunction as the ex-employee may be financially unable to continue fighting the action. Many cases involving negotiations are resolved at this stage.

2650 Given the uncertainties surrounding the enforcement of post-termination restrictions and the cost of seeking an injunction, employers may consider their use and enforcement as a **tactical deterrent**, rather than a weapon of legal protection. If an ex-employee has breached or is about to breach a covenant, the **threat of legal proceedings** alone (for example, a letter from his former employer's legal representative) may be sufficient to stop him.

Garden leave injunction

2651 If the employee works for a competitor during his notice period while on garden leave, the employer can apply to the court for a garden leave injunction. The court **may grant** an injunction if:
– the employer is not in breach of contract;
– the period is not excessive;
– the employer continues to pay the employee's salary and benefits;
– the employer undertakes not to claim damages from the employee if he chooses not to work for him during the notice period; and
– the employer can show that he will suffer serious and unquantifiable damage if the injunction is not granted, in terms of the fostering of the rival business or the confidential information that the employee knows (if the employee has confidential information but this is not relevant to the rival's business, an injunction would not be granted) (*Evening Standard Co Ltd v Henderson* [1987] IRLR 64, CA; *Provident Financial Group plc and Whitegates Estate Agency Ltd v Hayward* [1989] IRLR 84, CA).

2652 The **scope and period** of any injunction granted will be limited to that which is absolutely necessary to protect the employer's legitimate interests (*GFI Group Inc v Eaglestone* [1994] IRLR 119, QBD). In contrast to the enforcement of restrictive covenants, a court may, if necessary, **narrow the scope** of the restriction, for example, by preventing the employee from working for specified competitors or competitors generally, such that he could take up **non-competitive work** during garden leave (*Provident Financial Group plc and Whitegates Estate Agency Ltd v Hayward*; *Symbian Ltd v Christensen* [2001] IRLR 77, CA). The courts will carefully examine the length of the notice period, and will **limit the duration** of the garden leave period where the notice period is excessively long.

EXAMPLE Period reduced

1. In *GFI Group Inc v Eaglestone*, above, the court refused to grant an injunction restraining E, a foreign exchange options broker, from joining a competitor firm for his entire notice period of 20 weeks, as two other brokers (whose contracts provided for only 4 weeks' notice) had already joined the competitor firm. This meant that, to a certain extent, the damage to GFI's customer connection

had already been done, and it was not necessary for the protection of GFI's interests to hold E to the full period of 20 weeks. A shorter period of 13 weeks was held to be sufficient.

Period not reduced

2. In *Eurobrokers Ltd v Rabey* [1995] IRLR 206, ChD, the court granted an injunction restraining R, a money broker, from joining a rival firm for his notice period, up to a maximum of 6 months. In this case, a lavish and expensive customer connection had been furthered at the employer's expense, and this goodwill was something that the employer was entitled to protect. The injunction for the full 6 months was necessary given that the potential damage of being deprived of the opportunity to put new traders in place to deal with R's customers was not quantifiable in monetary terms.

Injunction against second employer

Injunctions may also be brought against a second employer who is **inducing a breach**, as happened in *Hivac Ltd v Park Royal Scientific Instruments Ltd* [1946] 1 All ER 350, CA, where the Court ordered an injunction against the second employer, who was a competitor, on the basis that the employees of the first employer were in breach of their implied duty of fidelity by working for this second employer on Sundays. 2653

2. Damages

Where the employer has reacted slowly to the ex-employee's activities, or where financial compensation is a sufficient remedy (such that no injunction is granted), the employer may proceed to a trial of the matter seeking damages for breach of contract or an account of profit (see below). This will be **assessed** on the loss suffered by the employer as a result of the breach and is **calculated** by reference to the profits on contracts or opportunities lost as a result of the ex-employee's activities. While it is relatively easy to describe that loss, problems often arise in proving that the loss directly resulted from that breach. An employer may also have difficulty quantifying his lost profits. 2660

EXAMPLE No actual loss

1. In *Nottingham University v Fishel* [2000] IRLR 471, QBD, F was in breach of an express term which required him to obtain consent before undertaking paid work abroad. However, as the University suffered no actual loss, it was not entitled to damages.

Difficult to quantify loss

2. A company is experiencing severe competition from a number of small start up companies in the same geographic area. One of its sales managers left his employment taking with him confidential product information that was protected by an express contractual provision in his contract of employment. He established a further company in competition. His ex-employer suffers severe financial hardship. However, it may prove difficult to show what loss was a result of that breach and what was due to other non-related causes i.e. the other start up companies.

Damages against second employer

If the ex-employee has gone to work for a competitor, it may be more financially viable to issue proceedings against the second employer for unlawfully interfering with contractual relations, and **inducing** (or aiding and abetting) a **breach** of contract (i.e. by inducing/attempting to induce the employee to breach a restrictive covenant or confidentiality undertaking). 2661

MEMO POINTS A second employer may also be liable for breach of the **equitable duty of confidence**, which is independent of the employment contract, if he receives information from a new employee which he knows has been obtained in breach of that employee's previous obligations or duties (*Attorney General v Guardian Newspapers Ltd* [1988] 3 All ER 545 (known as the Spycatcher case)). In this case, the newspaper was held to be in breach of confidence when it published material which it knew was in breach of the writer's (the ex-secret service agent, Peter Wright) contract with a third party (the Crown).

3. Account for profits

2665 This remedy is available for a breach of **equitable fiduciary** duties, which may nevertheless be imposed in the context of a contract of employment as a result of specific contractual obligations undertaken by the employee which place him in a position where he must act solely in the interests of the employer. It is **assessed** on the profit made by the employee and not the loss suffered by the employer.

EXAMPLE In *Nottingham University v Fishel* [2000] IRLR 471, QBD (see example above), F, the scientific director of an infertility clinic set up by the university also carried out private clinic work in the UK and abroad. Junior embryologists from the university worked for him privately. As F directly benefited from his position, he was obliged to account for the profits he made as a result of their work, even though the university had suffered no loss.

MEMO POINTS In exceptional circumstances, this remedy may be available for a **breach of contract** if the employer has a legitimate interest in preventing the employee's profit-making activity (*Attorney General v Blake* [2001] IRLR 36, HL). In this case, B published an autobiography in breach of his contract with the Crown not to disclose information about his work as an ex-secret service employee.

SECTION 4

Whistleblowing

2700 Legislation protects workers who, out of a sense of public duty, reveal **serious employer misconduct** (ERA 1996 as amended by the Public Interest Disclosure Act 1998). Such workers are often termed whistleblowers. In these circumstances, whistleblowing takes precedence over and above a worker's private contractual and common law duties of confidentiality to his employer (¶2400). Further, any **contractual term** or any other agreement that **purports to prevent** a worker from making a protected disclosure will be void and, to avoid this, confidentiality clauses should state that such disclosures are allowable (¶2450) (s 43J ERA 1996).

2701 To be protected, a worker must usually make the disclosure to his employer or to an appropriate public authority and only in certain circumstances or if exceptionally serious will a worker be justified in disclosing the information to the general public or another body. This gives employers, in most cases, an opportunity to resolve the issues internally and to facilitate this it is advisable that employers have a **whistleblowing policy**. For a checklist to assist in formulating such a policy, see ¶9940.

2702 In reality, workers may still find themselves with a stark choice, for although they may have legal protection not to be victimised or be dismissed, they may feel unable to continue with their employment after making a protected disclosure. However, if they are **victimised or dismissed**, they will be entitled to bring a claim against their employer. Given the highly explosive nature of certain disclosures and the damage they may have on public confidence in a company or organisation, companies/organisations will often want to **settle** any such claims rather than have their 'dirty laundry' washed out in a tribunal or have sensitive information revealed.

2703 If there is a threat of a public disclosure, an employer may wish to seek an **injunction** though this will only be given if it is in the public interest. Naturally, once there has been a public disclosure, there is little a company can do other than clean up its act and try to restore public confidence, though many companies/organisations will try to down play any such disclosures as much as possible.

A. Scope of protection

Whistleblowing protection applies to all **workers** and is specifically extended to include four groups of working individuals as follows (s 43K ERA 1996): 2710
- agency workers;
- home-workers (where working in a place other than a workplace and includes those who perform the work personally or otherwise);
- trainees (other than those provided by an educational establishment); and
- certain NHS doctors, dentists, ophthalmologists and pharmacists.

Qualifying disclosures

To qualify for protection, the disclosure must, in the **reasonable belief** of the **worker making the disclosure** (judged on the facts as understood by the worker at the time of the disclosure (*Darnton v University of Surrey* [2003] IRLR 133, EAT)), show that one or more of the **following events** has happened, is happening or is likely to happen (s 43B ERA 1996): 2711
- criminal offence;
- failure to comply with any legal obligation;
- miscarriage of justice;
- danger to health and safety of any individual;
- danger to the environment; or
- deliberate concealment of any of the above.

Failure to comply with a **legal obligation** includes a breach of contract (of employment or for services) where there is a breach of a legal obligation of the contract and the disclosure has resulted in the dismissal of the worker (*Parkins v Sodexho Ltd* [2002] IRLR 109, EAT as applied in *Wilson Odong v Chubb Security Personnel*, EAT case 819/02). However, if the worker mistakenly believes that a legal obligation exists, when in fact it does not, he will not be protected under the legislation by claiming he reasonably believed that a legal obligation existed (*Kraus v Penna plc and another* [2004] IRLR 260, EAT). Rather, his reasonable belief relates to what he perceives to be the facts and the basis on which he considers it reasonable to rely on them.

The event is called a **relevant failure**. It is immaterial whether the relevant failure occurred, occurs or will occur in the **UK or elsewhere**, and whether the law applying to it is UK law or the law of another country or territory (s 43(2) ERA 1996).

MEMO POINTS Excluded are disclosures where it is a **criminal offence to disclose** the information, for example civil servants to the extent that they are bound by the Official Secrets Act. Further, information protected by **legal professional privilege** (or, in Scotland, confidentiality between a client and professional adviser) is also excluded.

A disclosure will still qualify even if the **person who receives the information** on the relevant failure is **already aware** of the information contained in the disclosure and in such cases the worker will be deemed to have brought the information to his attention (s 43L(3) ERA 1996). 2713

However, the right does not extend to a worker **threatening to make a disclosure**. Consequently, if an employer threatens or pressurises a worker not to reveal a relevant failure, the worker will not be protected until he actually makes a protected disclosure. 2714

Protected disclosures

Protection is only given to qualifying disclosures that have been **disclosed in an acceptable manner**. These ensure that except in certain or exceptional circumstances, the worker does try to resolve the matter internally, or through any other appropriate channel, before going public with any qualifying disclosure. Qualifying disclosures that are disclosed in the correct manner are called protected disclosures. 2715

2716 **Standard** protected disclosures are made to the following (s 43A ERA 1996):
- employer or appropriate person;
- appropriate public authority; or
- legal adviser.

Only in special cases, can there be **wider disclosure** to other bodies or persons, most often in the form of publicity.

2717 Regardless of how the disclosure is made it must be made in **good faith**. Consequently, a disclosure which is predominantly motivated by the worker's personal antagonism towards his employer, that is, to "advance a grudge" will not be made in good faith (*Street v Derbyshire Unemployed Workers' Centre* [2004] IRLR 687, CA). Where there is an allegation that an employee has not made a disclosure in good faith, there must be cogent evidence provided to support such an allegation and the more serious the allegation, the more cogent the evidence required (*Lucas v Chichester Diocesan Housing Association Ltd*, EAT case 0713/04). Moreover, the allegation must be brought explicitly to the employee's attention in advance of any hearing, for example, in the employer's response to the tribunal claim (formerly referred to as a notice of appearance) and not just in written submissions made at the tribunal. In considering such an allegation, importance should be placed by the tribunal on the chronology of events leading up to the disclosure, together with the impression given by witnesses.

B. Acceptable methods of disclosure

2725 Disclosures should be made to the employer especially if there is an appropriate internal procedure to facilitate this. Barring this, disclosure can be made to an appropriate public authority, or in certain circumstances or if exceptionally serious, to the public.

If a worker is concerned about the implications of a relevant failure he knows about or suspects he can seek **legal advice and guidance**. Qualifying disclosures made in such a manner are protected (s 43D ERA 1996). Therefore, if a worker is uncertain as to his rights, whether the information he has is a qualifying disclosure or which if any of the following disclosures to make, he can seek legal advice without recourse from his employer. For example, if an employer finds out that a worker has gone to a legal adviser and fears that as a result of the advice the worker will make a public disclosure, he may dismiss the worker before he has time to act. In such cases, any qualifying disclosure the worker makes to the adviser is protected and the worker will be protected from such employer action.

1. Internal disclosure

2730 A qualifying disclosure is protected if it is disclosed to the **employer** (s 43C ERA 1996).

Disclosures **should be made** to the employer especially if there is an appropriate **whistleblowing policy and procedure** unless another method of disclosure can be justified. Indeed, if there is an adequate policy, it will be difficult for a worker to show that he could have reasonably believed that he would have been victimised for making a disclosure to his employer.

A whistleblowing policy **should cover** how different types of worker can disclose internally or externally to an appropriate person. For example, a different procedure may be appropriate for agency or self-employed workers compared to employees. Further, it may be necessary to vary the person to whom a disclosure should be made, depending on the status of the worker and the type or seriousness of the allegation. For example, a senior manager may require disclosure to a non-executive director if the allegations relate to an alleged malpractice by senior management. If the policy requires disclosure to a person other than the employer, the worker will be treated as if he made the disclosure to his employer. The policy should also make it clear that malpractice in the workplace is a matter that will be taken seriously by the employer and it should seek to encourage employees to discuss any genuine suspicions they have. A **checklist** which sets out what provisions should be covered in a whistleblowing policy can be found at ¶9940.

Employers must ensure that such policies are **communicated** to their workers so that they are aware of the relevant procedures if they need to make a qualifying disclosure.

Disclosures not relating to employer

Where the worker reasonably believes that the relevant failure relates solely or mainly to: **2731**
- the conduct of a person other than his employer; or
- any other matter for which a person other than his employer has legal responsibility;

it should be made to that **other person**.

EXAMPLE If a supplier is regularly supplying less than the agreed amount to the employer, the worker may make disclosure to the supplier and gain protection. However, if the worker discovers that the supplier and his employer are defrauding Revenue and Customs over supplies then his disclosure will only be protected if it is made to his employer and disclosure to the supplier alone will not give the worker protection.

2. Disclosure to a public authority

A qualifying disclosure is protected if it is made to an **appropriate** public authority (s 43F ERA 1996). There are a number of regulators, commissioners and watchdogs which have been specified as an appropriate public authority for disclosures within their remits (SI 1999/1548). For example, the Secretary of State for Trade and Industry (for disclosures regarding fraud, and other misconduct, in relation to companies, investment businesses, insurance businesses or multi-level marketing schemes (and similar trading schemes); insider dealing; and consumer safety) and the Director of the Serious Fraud Office (for disclosures regarding serious or complex fraud). A full list of these appropriate public authorities for disclosures by private employees can be found at ¶9980. **2735**

To be protected, the worker must also **reasonably believe** that the information falls within the remit of that public authority and that the information disclosed, and any allegations contained in it, are substantially true.

3. Public disclosure

In the **following circumstances**, a qualifying disclosure to the public or any other body is protected if, at the time the worker makes the disclosure, (s 43G ERA 1996): **2740**
- he reasonably believes that he will be subject to a detriment (i.e. victimised) if he discloses to his employer;
- there is no appropriate public authority and he reasonably believes that it is likely that evidence relating to the relevant failure will be concealed or destroyed if he makes a disclosure to his employer; or
- he has previously made a disclosure of substantially the same information to his employer.

However, the following **conditions** must be satisfied: **2741**

1. the worker must reasonably believe that the information disclosed and any allegations contained in it are substantially true;
2. it must be reasonable in all the circumstances for the worker to disclose in this manner.

In determining reasonableness, particular regard is given to:
- the identity of the person to whom the disclosure is made;
- the seriousness of the relevant failure;
- whether the relevant failure is continuing or is likely to occur in the future;
- whether the disclosure is made in breach of a duty of confidentiality owed by the employer to any other person. For example, where a doctor's receptionist believes she has discovered a malpractice and disclosure would breach patients' rights to privacy;

– any action by the employer or appropriate person that has been taken or should have reasonably been taken where there has been a previous disclosure of substantially the same information. In assessing the reasonableness of the employer's response to the previous disclosure, a tribunal will look at whether the worker complied with any employer policy and procedures on whistleblowing; and

3. the disclosure must not be for purposes of personal gain. Therefore, the main motive for selling a story about a relevant failure must not be to make money. This does not preclude the worker receiving money for his information if he can show that his main motivation was that he was acting in the public interest rather than out of self-interest. Naturally, this will be a question of degree and a worker may find it harder to convince a court or tribunal that his motivation was a public duty to see justice done if he sells his story for a large sum of money (for instance to a tabloid newspaper) where there were other ways which would have been just as, or more, effective in disclosing the information.

Disclosure of an exceptionally serious nature

2742 If the relevant failure is of an exceptionally serious nature, wider public disclosure can occur at any time (s 43H ERA 1996). What is exceptionally serious is a matter of judgement and the worker will most likely need to show the matter was so serious that it was in the public interest to disclose the information in this manner. Nevertheless the conditions for public disclosure have to be satisfied, though the requirement of reasonableness will be easier to satisfy on the consideration of all the circumstances. In such situations, particular regard is only given to the identity of the person to whom the disclosure is made.

C. Protection and remedies

2760 A protected disclosure must not result in the worker being disciplined and/or dismissed. A worker **cannot be** held in **breach of contract** if he makes a protected disclosure, as it is not a breach of his implied duty of fidelity and any express term that purports to make such a disclosure an express breach is void.

2761 Further, a worker has legal protection from any **detrimental acts or omissions** (i.e. victimisation) which have occurred as a result of a protected disclosure and any dismissal for a reason connected with a protected disclosure, in relation to an employee will be **automatically unfair**.

The **disclosures** may occur **before the whistleblowing rules came into force** as long as the detrimental act/omission or dismissal occurred when the rules were in force (i.e. after 2 July 1999) (*Miklaszewicz v Stolt Offshore Ltd* [2002] IRLR 344, CS; *Meteorological Office v Edgar* [2002] ICR 149, EAT). This is because although the disclosure was not protected at the time it was made, it is a protected disclosure, and the employer should know it was protected, when he acts as a result of it and causes the employee to suffer a detriment or dismissal.

This is most likely to occur when there is a long train of events/conduct stretching over a number of years. Naturally, though, as a matter of proof, the longer ago the disclosure is, the harder it may be for the employee to prove that a future act of detriment or dismissal is in relation to it.

EXAMPLE 1. In *Miklaszewicz v Stolt Offshore Ltd*, M was dismissed by SO in 1993 as a result of a disclosure he made of malpractice to the Inland Revenue (now called Revenue and Customs). He continued to work in the same industry and found himself by reason of various transfers of undertakings to be employed again by SO in 1999. In 2000, SO dismissed M on the grounds of redundancy though M held it was due to his previous disclosure. The EAT held that M did have a claim for unfair dismissal as the disclosure was now protected at the time of dismissal.
2. In *Meteorological Office v Edgar*, E, a television weather reporter, made an internal complaint against his manager, G, in March 1999, which was subsequently protected by the time the detrimental acts were alleged to have occurred the following year.

Right not to suffer a detriment

A worker has the right not to be subject to any detriment by any act, or a deliberate failure to, act on the ground that he **made a protected disclosure**, for example he has been passed over for promotion (s 47B ERA 1996). Such legal protection only applies **during employment** (*Fadipe v Reed Nursing Personnel* [2001] EWCA Civ 1885, CA). 2763

Tribunals will apply a **strict causation test** to establish whether a worker has suffered a detriment. As a consequence, it is not sufficient for the detriment to be merely 'related to' the protected disclosure but rather there must be an analysis of the employer's mental thought process which caused him to subject the worker to a detriment (*London Borough of Harrow v Knight* [2003] IRLR 140, EAT). 2765

If the worker has suffered a detriment he can bring a **claim** to the employment tribunal. The complaint must be **made before** the end of 3 months beginning with the date of the detrimental act/failure to act, or date of the last of such acts/omissions. If it is not reasonably practicable for the complaint to be brought within 3 months, the tribunal can extend this period as it considers reasonable (s 48(3) ERA 1996). 2766

If the tribunal finds the complaint well-founded, it can make (ss 48(1A), 49 ERA 1996): 2767
- a **declaration** to that effect; and
- if appropriate an award of **compensation** to be paid by the employer.

The **amount** of compensation is the amount the tribunal considers just and equitable in all the circumstances, having regard to (s 49(2)(5) ERA 1996):
- the victimisation suffered; and
- any loss which resulted from the victimisation. Loss includes any expenses reasonably incurred or the loss of any benefit because of the victimisation, though the worker has a duty to mitigate his loss as far as possible.

Detriment under the whistleblowing legislation is a form of discrimination and, consequently, the guidelines laid down in *Vento v Chief Constable of West Yorkshire Police (No 2)* (¶5751) will apply with regard to the level of compensation for injury to feelings (*Virgo Fidelis Senior School v Boyle* [2004] IRLR 268, EAT).

If the detrimental act **results in dismissal**, workers who do not have a contract of employment will be entitled to the same level of compensation as if they were an employee who has been unfairly dismissed (see below) (s 49(6) ERA 1996).

The tribunal will take into consideration the extent to which the worker caused or **contributed** to the detriment claimed and it will reduce the amount of compensation if it feels it is just and equitable to do so.

Right not to be unfairly dismissed

Any **dismissal** of an employee due to the making of a protected disclosure will be automatically unfair (s 103A ERA 1996) (see ¶8390). As a result, no qualifying period of continuous employment is necessary and there are no age limits (s 108(3)(ff) ERA 1996). An employee will also be unfairly dismissed, if the reason or principal reason for selecting him for **redundancy** is that he made a protected disclosure (s 105(6A) ERA 1996). 2769

MEMO POINTS Non-employee workers who are so dismissed or so selected for redundancy should rely on the right not to suffer a detriment (see above) though the compensation is awarded on the same basis as for unfair dismissal.

The employee can also claim **interim relief** and this will be given if the tribunal considers it likely that he will succeed at the full hearing (ss 128-129 ERA 1996) (¶8700). If so, the tribunal will order the employer to continue his contract by reinstating him or re-engaging him on similar terms and conditions. 2770

The amount of **compensation** that can be awarded, if the complaint is successful, is uncapped (s 124(1A) ERA1996 as amended by Public Interest Disclosure (Compensation) Regulations SI 1999/1548). 2771

CHAPTER 10

Remuneration

OUTLINE ¶¶

Remuneration can be made up of the following: basic pay, overtime, bonuses, incentive payments and commissions, benefits, employee share schemes and a pension scheme. Employees may also be entitled to sick pay (see Chapter 13) and maternity, adoption or paternity pay (see Chapter 14). Further, an employee may be entitled to guarantee payments for workless days (see Chapter 23) and medical suspension payments if prohibited to attend work for health reasons (see Chapter 15). **2800**

This chapter details the remuneration package, the minimum level of pay, the forms and rate of pay, deductions from pay and taxation. A checklist as to what a policy on remuneration could contain can be found at ¶9940.

MEMO POINTS The Inland Revenue is now called Revenue and Customs.
This chapter refers to Revenue and Customs' material and with regard to this the following abbreviations are used: SP (Statement of Practice) and ESC (Extra Statutory Concession).

SECTION 1

Pay

Employers and workers are **free to negotiate** and agree terms on remuneration, subject to certain employment rights such as the right to equal pay and the right to be paid at least the national minimum wage (ERA 1996; National Minimum Wage Act 1998; Part-time Workers (Prevention of Less Favourable Treatment) Regulations SI 2000/1551; Working Time Regulations SI 1998/1833; and Equal Pay Act 1970). **2805**

The employee has an implied **right to be paid** in accordance with his express contractual terms as long as he is ready and willing to work or he is absent due to illness/other unavoidable circumstances. Any **failure to pay** will give rise to a breach of contract. Further, employees have **special protection** against their employer making unauthorised deductions which includes unlawful deductions and deductions made in an incorrect manner. Only in specific circumstances can employers make (for example, a contractual term allowing for deduction of wages due to unauthorised absences), or be required to make (for example due to an attachment of earnings order), **lawful deductions** from their employees' remuneration. **2806**

Employees and directors must pay **income tax** on their earnings (i.e. what tax legislation defines as employment income and includes certain lump sum payments made on commencement, termination or variation) and on the value of most benefits. Lump sum payments on **2808**

termination or variation that are not earnings (for example compensation for breach of contract on termination) will be taxable under a special provision which allows for certain exceptions including the exemption of the first £30,000 from tax. The payment of expenses by the employer is also subject to tax but employees/directors will be able to claim a deduction for business expenses that are incurred wholly, exclusively and necessarily in the performance of their duties. Special rules apply to certain expenses, for example travel expenses.
For payroll and NIC issues, see Chapter 20.

MEMO POINTS Pay is used here to refer to wages or salary. Remuneration is used to denote all employment income (i.e. pay, overtime, bonuses and benefits) and pension rights. For tax purposes, the term earnings is used to denote all chargeable employment income, which can include additional elements such as certain lump sum payments on commencement, variation or termination of employment.

I. Elements of remuneration

A. Remuneration package

2810 Depending on the type and seniority of the employee and the size and type of his employer's business, his remuneration will **include** one or more of the following:
- basic pay;
- overtime;
- performance-related additional payments, for example bonuses, incentive payments and commissions;
- allowances, for example a daily allowance, London weighting allowance or a stand-by allowance;
- benefits, for example health cover;
- permanent health insurance (¶4200);
- employee share schemes; and
- a pension scheme (¶3400).

1. Basic pay

2815 The employee has an implied right to be paid in accordance with his **express contractual terms** as long as he is **ready and willing to work** or he is absent due to illness or other unavoidable circumstances (*Miles v Wakefield Metropolitan District Council* [1987] IRLR 193, HL). As a result, pay can only be validly withheld or deducted if there is a specific term of the contract that allows for the deduction and the burden of proof will be on the employer to show he can do so.

EXAMPLE 1. In *Beveridge v KLM UK Ltd* [2000] IRLR 765, EAT, B, after a long period of sickness absence, wanted to return to work and produced a doctor's certificate to show she was fit for work. However, KLM refused to take her back until their own doctor was satisfied that she was fit for work. The EAT held that she had an implied right to be paid from when she was willing to work and had been certified as fit to do so.
2. In *Miller v Hamworthy Engineering Ltd* [1986] IRLR 461, EAT, M's employer, H, introduced a system of 'work sharing' as an alternative to immediate redundancies. This had to be agreed by M's union each time H wanted to decrease the hours of work, in which case M's normal contractual terms on remuneration were waived. The EAT held that M's contractual terms were not waived when the reductions to his working hours were not accepted by his union and he was ready and willing to work under his existing terms.

If, on the other hand, the employee is **not ready and willing to work** or declines to perform part of his job, his employer is entitled to withhold wages for the period in question without terminating his contract of employment and without relying on any right to damages for breach of contract. 2816

If the amount of pay is **not expressly stated**, there is an implied term which gives the employee the right to be reasonably remunerated for work done if it can be shown that there was an **intention to pay** (*Way v Latilla* [1937] 3 All ER 759). This is called the "quantum meruit" principle. 2817

This principle has also been used to quantify a contractual right to a **bonus** (*Powell v Braun* [1954] 1 WLR 401).

Employers can include express contractual terms to **increase or decrease pay**. Pay can be validly increased or decreased by **collective bargaining** where the relevant collective agreement is incorporated into the workers' contracts. If the worker wishes to contest that the terms have not been incorporated into his contract he must make a **clear, prompt and continuing objection** (*Henry v London General Transport Services Ltd* [2001] IRLR 132, EAT). 2818

Pay increases

It is useful to expressly state whether **pay reviews** and increases are contractual or discretionary. 2821

Where the **contract is silent**, the courts are reluctant to imply a contractual right to a pay increase and past annual increases do not give rise to such a right (*Murco Petroleum Ltd v Forge* [1978] IRLR 50, EAT).

Most employers **provide salary reviews** on an annual basis with a right to an increase subject to their **discretion**. In such cases, the employee does not have a right to an increase. However, if the employer decides not to exercise his discretion, he must nevertheless ensure that he did not act arbitrarily, capriciously or unfairly in not increasing pay (*FC Gardner Ltd v Beresford Ltd* [1978] IRLR 63, EAT). 2822

Some employers give **contractual automatic increases** depending on length of service, qualifications, age, and banding/grade of the employee. More rarely (and most often with regard to senior employees), employers may provide a contractual right to an annual increase which is linked to inflation and calculated by reference to an appropriate index (such as the retail prices index). 2823

2. Overtime

In the absence of an express or implied contractual term that allows for overtime (paid or unpaid) there is no obligation to work overtime. On the other hand if an employee voluntarily works longer hours in the absence of an express contractual term, he has no general implied right to be paid for the extra hours worked (*Ali v Christian Salvesen Food Services Ltd* [1997] IRLR 17, CA). 2825

EXAMPLE In *Ali v Christian Salvesen Food Services Ltd*, A was contractually entitled to be paid overtime once he had worked a set number of hours in his pay year. The Court held he was not entitled to paid overtime when he was dismissed during a pay year as he had not yet reached this number and the agreement was silent as to what should happen in such circumstances.

It is, therefore, necessary to have an **express contractual term** covering when overtime is allowable and the terms of entitlement. Contractual overtime is usually paid for extra hours or for unsociable working hours and is often expressed as a multiple of the employee's hourly rate, for example one and a half times the hourly rate. However, sometimes **time off in lieu** is given as an alternative and any contractual terms should set this out. 2826

Such terms must at least be evidenced in writing (¶1400).

3. Bonuses, incentive payments and commissions

2828 **Commission payments** are regular contractual payments which depend on the employee's performance. These may be based on a percentage, for example on a percentage of sales received, or on set amounts, for example a fixed amount per sale. Usually, commission payments are additional to a basic salary and may form a substantial part of the employee's remuneration. Occasionally, the employee's salary may be based solely on commission payments.

2829 **Bonuses** and **incentive payments** are usually offered as a reward for performance and/or loyalty, and will be usually in the form of additional payments or awards such as share options.

Bonuses are usually calculated on an individual basis based on the **employee's performance** in the required period (for example, on a yearly basis as a result of an appraisal of his year's work). Alternatively, bonuses can be based on the **company's performance** or the employee's group/department's performance.

In contrast, **incentive schemes** will usually set individual, group or company targets which will need to be achieved in the required period before any payments can be made.

MEMO POINTS **Profit-related pay**, a special Government scheme which enabled the employer to provide a tax-free payment by linking a part of his employees' remuneration to the profits of the business, has been phased out and there is no longer any relief for any profits periods beginning on or after 1 January 2000.

2830 Employers may wish to state the **terms** as to when any payments will be made, for example that the employee must still be in employment, without notice of termination having been given on either side, at the date of payment (which can be later than the period to which it relates (usually the company's financial year)).

However, such terms must not be **discriminatory** (*Gus Home Shopping Ltd v Green and McLaughlin* [2001] IRLR 75, EAT; *Caisse Nationale d'Assurance Vieillesse des Travailleurs Salaries v Thibault* [1998] IRLR 399, ECJ).

EXAMPLE Discriminatory

In *Gus Home Shopping Ltd v Green and McLaughlin*, GHS introduced a discretionary **loyalty bonus** largely contingent on the effective transfer of the department (in which G and M worked) over the preceding 6 months. The EAT held that GHS discriminated against G and M when it disqualified M from receiving a bonus and reduced G's bonus because they were absent on maternity leave/due to a pregnancy-related sickness during this period.

Not discriminatory

However, in *Lewen v Denda* [2000] IRLR 67, ECJ, a bonus that was calculated by reference to actual performance or contributions was not held to be discriminatory in relation to a worker on maternity leave.

2831 Schemes can be **contractual** i.e. the employee will have a right to the payment/share options as long as he has satisfied any express conditions. In some circumstances employees may wish to negotiate contractual bonuses, sometimes with a guaranteed element, for example a **retention bonus** in a takeover situation.

2832 However, most employers will normally wish to avoid any obligation to make payments, etc and will include an express contractual term indicating that the terms of the bonus/incentive payments may be varied. Such schemes are called **discretionary**. If an employer wishes to have the option to withdraw a bonus scheme, he should make this clear in express contractual terms otherwise, as well as incurring potential liability for a breach of contract claim, he may be liable for an unauthorised deduction if he does not make a payment (*Kent Management Services Ltd v Butterfield* [1992] IRLR 394, EAT). Where the employer wishes a scheme to remain discretionary, he must be careful not to create a contractual entitlement by **custom and practice**, for example, he should state that he is exercising his discretion on each occasion a bonus is awarded.

Once a discretionary bonus is **declared on certain terms**, this creates an obligation to pay it on these terms and withholding some or all of the bonus will be an unlawful deduction of wages (¶3050). This applies equally to discretionary bonuses granted under contract and those given by custom or by an ad hoc decision (*Farrell Matthews & Weir v Hansen* [2005] IRLR 160, EAT).

However, the exercise of any discretion is not absolute and the employer must not exercise it irrationally or perversely (*Mallone v BPB Industries plc* [2002] IRLR 452, CA; *Clark v Nomura International plc* [2000] IRLR 766, QBD). Indeed, the employee is entitled to expect his employer to exercise his discretion **rationally and in good faith** (*Horkulak v Cantor Fitzgerald International* [2004] IRLR 942, CA). This applies to anticipatory as well as actual payments/awards and is part of the implied term of trust and confidence. 2833

If the employer does act irrationally or perversely, the employee will be able to bring a breach of contract claim. Further, the employee may have the right to claim that he has been constructively dismissed and claim wrongful dismissal (compensation may include an element for the "lost bonus"). The employee may also have a claim under sex, race, religion or belief, sexual orientation, or disability discrimination provisions if he has been treated less favourably as a result.

EXAMPLE 1. In *Mallone v BPB Industries*, under the rules of a share option bonus scheme, executives who ceased employment could at certain times still exercise options which had been awarded to them subject to BPB's discretion to allow only a fraction of the options to be so exercised. The fraction consisted of a denominator of 36 and a numerator which was chosen by BPB. On the day of M's dismissal, BPB determined that this numerator should be zero resulting in the cancellation of his share options.

This was held to be an irrational exercise of BPB's discretion as the options had been awarded because of good service and there was nothing in the circumstances of M's dismissal that warranted the total removal of his options.

2. In *Horkulak v Cantor Fitzgerald International*, H, who held a senior managerial position in a firm of brokers, resigned due to bullying and abusive behaviour which had amounted to a breach of his implied contractual term of trust and confidence. He successfully claimed damages for wrongful dismissal on the basis that had he remained in employment, he would have received his discretionary annual bonus given that in the context of his employment in a high-earning and competitive activity his bonus clause was properly viewed as part of his remuneration structure. Further, he was entitled to expect that his employer would have exercised this discretion rationally and in good faith.

Where a **bonus should have been awarded**, the court will determine what the employee would have received had his employer acted rationally and in good faith taking into account the employee's expectations as to what a reasonable employer would have awarded in the circumstances (*Horkulak v Cantor Fitzgerald International* [2004] IRLR 942, CA). Where necessary, it will apply the quantum meruit principle (i.e. the right to be reasonably remunerated for work done) to determine the amount of the award if it is not quantified (*Powell v Braun* [1954] 1 WLR 401). 2834

In **practical terms**, to ensure that a bonus scheme is fair and transparent, employers should ensure that: 2835
- the terms of the scheme are clear and unambiguous and set out the factors that will be taken into account in determining awards;
- the same criteria and methods of calculation are used for all employees (or specified groups of employees, for example employees, managers and directors) covered by the scheme;
- discretionary bonuses are awarded rationally and in good faith and not irrationally or perversely i.e. in a manner that no reasonable employer would have done; and
- the terms are non-discriminatory.

4. Benefits and employee share schemes

Employers often provide employees with benefits (called benefits in kind) as well as a basic salary and other cash payments. These may be offered as part of an offer package to entice prospective employees to work for them and to assist in the retention of staff. Certain benefits, such as private health care and gym membership may also aid their employees' health and well-being. 2837

Flexible benefit packages have increased in popularity and are typically **made up of** a set of "core benefits" provided to all staff (e.g. pension, private medical cover), with a menu of add-ons funded from the employee's total package value, for example by sacrificing other benefits (e.g. giving up a day's holiday or accepting a lower grade company car) or from deductions from salary. A points system can be used, whereby the employee is given a certain number of points that he can use to "buy" a range of benefits, according to his personal requirements. A flexible benefit package scheme should be **set out** in a policy which deals with the operation and administration of the scheme (e.g. limiting the number of times employees can make changes to their options).

For a comprehensive list of the main types of benefits, see ¶3155 (for non-taxable benefits) and ¶3190 (for taxable benefits).

2838 Such benefits are generally taxable as being a **payment made other than in cash** to an employee or director (or a member of his family or household) as a result of his employment. If and how a benefit is **taxable** will depend on whether he is classed as a relevant or lower paid employee (¶3146).

2839 Employers may also provide employees with **share schemes** which give their employees discounted or free shares in their company or an option to buy the shares at a reduced rate at a later date. The **taxation** of such schemes depends on the structure of the package and whether it has Revenue and Customs approval (¶3340).

B. Other types of payments

Lump sum payments

2845 Employees may also receive lump sum payments on the **commencement, variation or termination** of their contract. Such payments are often made as compensation for the loss or surrender of rights, or instead of notice of termination. Alternatively, a lump sum payment may simply be made to reward an employee for past or future services. For tax issues, see ¶3115.

Gratuities

2846 Employees may receive gratuities **from a third party**, for example waiters and waitresses are usually given tips by their customers. The employer may have in place a system whereby these gratuities are pooled in a "tronc" and then distributed amongst the employees.

Gratuities that have been added to a cheque or credit-card will need to be administered through payroll and will form part of the employee's earnings.

Expenses

2847 Employees may also **incur** expenses which will be:
– reimbursed by their employer either for specific expenses incurred or by way of an expense allowance;
– paid by them without reimbursement; or
– paid by their employer directly.

The payment of expenses by the employer is subject to tax (¶3265) but the employee will be able to make a claim for business expenses.

Loans

2848 Employers may give their employees an advancement on their wages or loans for specific purposes, for example to go on a course or to buy a season ticket.

It is useful to have a **separate written agreement** for each loan agreement setting out the terms as these are likely to vary depending on the type of loan. Such agreements should include **terms** on:
– the amount of the loan;

– the circumstances in which it becomes repayable; and
– when the deductions are to be made, for example a percentage of the loan in each pay period until the loan is paid off with the authority to deduct an outstanding amount if the employee leaves before the loan is completely paid off.

The employer may require repayment of all or some of the **cost of a training course** if the employee leaves the company within a set period after completing the course or fails to successfully complete it. However, such costs will only be enforceable in a breach of contract claim if they are a genuine pre-estimate of loss suffered by the employer (in not having a trained employee) and not a penalty clause against the employee (*Neil v Strathclyde Regional Council* [1984] IRLR 14, CS). Whether or not there is a genuine pre-estimate of loss is a question of construction that depends on the terms and circumstances of the contract at the time the contract was made. 2849

In any event, an express clause in the contract or in a separate agreement is necessary for the employer to make a lawful deduction. Further, all loan repayments (other than for the repayment of an advancement of wages) must comply with the statutory protection against unauthorised deductions. 2850

II. Level

Employers and workers are **free to negotiate** and agree terms on pay **subject to the following rights**: 2860
– of workers to be paid a minimum wage (¶2865) and to be paid for statutory annual holiday entitlement (¶4000); and
– of part-time workers not to be treated less favourably than full-time workers (¶1870).
Further, those who are employees have the following **additional rights** to:
– equal pay (¶5600; ¶1950)
– pay for time off in certain circumstances (¶3930);
– statutory sick pay (¶4170);
– statutory maternity pay, statutory adoption pay and statutory paternity pay (¶4700);
– guarantee payments with regard to workless day (¶7860); and
– medical suspension payments if there is a risk of a health hazard (¶4862; ¶4876 on maternity grounds).

A. Right to a minimum wage

A worker's average hourly rate **must not be less** than the national minimum wage (NMW) (National Minimum Wage Act 1998 (NMWA 1998); National Minimum Wage Regulations SI 1999/584 (as amended) and referred to in this section as the regulations). 2865

MEMO POINTS Where the employee is paid less than the national minimum wage, any basic and compensatory unfair dismissal awards will be based on the national minimum wage (*Paggetti v Cobb* [2002] IRLR 861, EAT).

Any **provision** in any agreement (whether a worker's contract or not) is void in so far as it purports to **exclude or limit** the operation of the statutory rules or to preclude a person from bringing proceedings under them (s 49 NMWA 1998). However, agreements prohibiting the bringing or continuance of proceedings are permissible if it is part of a conciliation or valid compromise agreement. 2866

Entitlement

2867 To be entitled, the worker must (s 1 NMWA 1998; reg 12 SI 1999/584):
- be above compulsory school leaving age; and
- work, or ordinarily work, in the UK.

2868 A **worker** is **defined widely** (s 54(3) NMWA 1998). All workers other than those who are genuinely self-employed are covered and there are specific provisions to ensure that agency workers and home workers are included (ss 34-35 NMWA 1998). An agency worker will be deemed to be a worker of either the agency or the client and this will depend on who pays the worker.

Excluded are students on sandwich courses, and teacher trainees on work experience. Family members working in the family business are also excluded (reg 2(4) SI 1999/584).

Minimum wage rates

2869 The rates from 1 October 2005 are as follows (National Minimum Wage Regulations 1999 (Amendment) SI 2005/2019 which amends SI 1999/584)):

Worker	Hourly rate	Reference (SI 1999/584)
16 to 17 years (does not apply to apprentices)	£3.00	reg 13(1A)
18 to 21 years	£4.25	reg 13(1)
22 and over	£5.05	reg 11
22 and over taking part in accredited training for at least 26 days	£4.25 for first 6 months of employment then £5.05	reg 13(2)
18 to 25 years on a contract of apprenticeship	No entitlement for first 12 months then according to age	reg 13(2)

MEMO POINTS Many **agricultural workers** may be entitled to a higher rate under agricultural wages regulations.

1. Calculation of average hourly rate

2870 In order to determine whether a worker has been paid the NMW, it is necessary to calculate his average hourly rate of pay. This is calculated in **three steps** by (reg 14 SI 1999/584):
- taking the worker's gross pay in a pay reference period;
- deducting any amounts in that period that do not count towards NMW; and
- dividing this by the total number of hours which the worker has done in that period.

If a worker's average hourly rate is below the NMW, his wages must be increased to at least the NMW for that period.

a. Gross pay in pay reference period

Gross pay

2875 Gross pay is the **gross amount of included payments** the worker receives.

Included payments (reg 30 SI 1999/584)	Excluded payments (regs 8, 31, 36 SI 1999/584)
Pay including overtime payments	Advances of wages/salary or a loan
Bonuses and incentive payments or commissions	
Tips and gratuities paid through payroll system [1]	Tips and gratuities not paid through payroll system
Allowances attributable to worker's productivity	Allowances not attributable to worker's productivity [2]

Included payments (reg 30 SI 1999/584)	Excluded payments (regs 8, 31, 36 SI 1999/584)
Accommodation benefit provided by employer can be off set to a maximum of £26.25 per week. The daily rate is £3.75	Benefits in kind other than accommodation
Payments by worker for goods and services provided by employer where he is free to choose whether to buy	Payments by worker for goods and services provided by employer where he is required to buy (for example a bank requiring its workers to bank with it)
	Reimbursement of expenses
	Pension payments
	Payments by way of award under a suggestions scheme
	Redundancy payments
	Court/tribunal awards or similar settlements

1. *Nerva v RL & G Ltd* [1996] IRLR 461, CA, confirmed by the European Court of Human Rights (*Nerva v UK* [2002] IRLR 815, ECHR)
2. *Aviation & Airport Services Ltd v Bellfield and others*, EAT case 194/00; *Laird v AK Stoddart Ltd* [2001] IRLR 591, EAT

Pay reference period

The relevant pay reference period is 1 month (reg 10(2) SI 1999/584). Where a worker is paid by reference to a shorter period (for example, weekly or hourly), it is to that period. Therefore, workers who are paid monthly, weekly or hourly, will have a pay reference period of 1 month, 1 week and 1 hour respectively. 2876

Employers who pay their workers at intervals of more than a month apart, for example quarterly, have to make sure that the workers receive the NMW at least on a monthly basis.

EXAMPLE A 21-year old shop worker, A, is paid solely by commission. He works 40 hours a week and is paid weekly. He should be paid a minimum of £170 per week (£4.25 x 40).

	Pay reference period			
	1	2	3	4
Commission earnings	£180	£200	£175	£140
Average hourly rate of pay	£180/ 40	£200/ 40	£175/ 40	£140/ 40
	= £4.50	= £5.00	= £4.38	= £3.50

A is paid over the NMW in his first three pay reference periods. However, his employer must increase A's pay in pay reference period 4 by £30 (£170 – £140).

Calculating gross pay in reference period

The gross pay in a pay reference period is the gross pay **in that period** plus any payments earned in that period which are not paid until the **next period** (for example, where payment for overtime or a commission is not calculated or paid until the next pay period) (reg 30 SI 1999/584). 2877

However, if a payment has been earned but is not paid in the period it is earned or in the next period and is paid in a later **subsequent period**, it must be included in the calculation of gross pay in that subsequent period. Note though, there is a special rule relating to annual bonuses and a proportion of an **annual bonus** can count toward pay allocated to a previous pay period (DTI guide to NMW). For example, if an annual bonus is paid in December and the pay reference period is 1 month, a twelfth of the bonus can be allocated to the November pay period for NMW purposes. The rest of the bonus will count towards the NMW in December and does not affect the NMW calculations for January-October. 2878

MEMO POINTS Payments made in a later pay reference period are taken into account where the worker has to complete a record of the amount of work done before any entitlement to payment arises and he has failed to submit the relevant record before the fourth working day before the end of that following pay reference period.

EXAMPLE B, a 22-year old shop worker is paid £3.00 per hour plus commissions. He works 35 hours a week and is paid weekly. The commissions earned are paid in the next pay reference period. He should be paid a minimum of £176.75 per week (£5.05 x 35).

	Pay reference period			
	1	2	3	4
Earnings	£105	£105	£105	£105
Commission	none	£25	£75	£100
Average hourly rate of pay	(£105 + 25)/ 35	(£105 + 75)/ 35	(£105 + 100)/ 35	(£105 +?)/ 35
	= £3.71	= £5.14	= £5.86	= £?

B's employer must increase B's pay in his first pay reference period by £46.75 (£176.75 – (£105 + 25)).
B is paid over the NMW in his second and third pay reference periods.
It is not possible to calculate B's average hourly rate in pay reference period 4 until his commission has been calculated and paid in period 5.

b. Deductions to gross pay

2880 For the purposes of NMW, the **following amounts** must be deducted from the gross pay (reg 31 SI 1999/584):
– payments that have been included in an **earlier pay reference period**;
– overtime and shift **premium payments** in so far as they are additional to the normal rate of pay; and
– payments made in respect of periods in which the worker is **absent from work** or is taking part in **industrial action**.

To **calculate the premium element** of an overtime payment, the lowest basic rate that is paid to the worker must be subtracted from the overtime payment.

EXAMPLE Worker C is paid weekly based on a basic 25-hour week at £5.05 per hour. He works an additional 5 hours at night and is paid a premium rate of £6.05 per hour and he also works 5 hours overtime on Saturday for which he is paid at a premium rate of £6.50 per hour.
His gross pay for the week will be £189.00 (£5.05 x 25) + (£6.05 x 5) + (£6.50 x 5).
However, the premium element of £12.25 (((6.05 – 5.05) x 5) + ((6.50 – 5.05) x 5)) must be deducted giving £176.75.
His average hourly rate for the week is, therefore, £176.75/ 35 = £5.05.

2881 On the other hand, the following actual deductions made by the employer are **ignored** (reg 33 SI 1999/584):
a. tax and NIC; and
b. any deductions in respect of:
– the worker's conduct for which he is contractually liable;
– the repayment of a loan or recovery of an accidental overpayment; and
– the purchase of shares, options or other securities, or the interest in a partnership.

c. Total number of hours worked

2885 This is calculated by reference to the type of work the worker performed in the relevant pay period. The rules and calculation of hours differ for each type of work, for example certain periods of time may be excluded. Where a period of time is excluded from the calculation of the total hours, any pay that the worker may receive for excluded time is also ignored in calculating the average hourly rate.

There are four different **types of worker** identified for this purpose:
- salaried hours workers;
- time workers;
- output workers; and
- unmeasured time workers who work unspecified hours or who do not fall into the other categories above.

Salaried-hours and time workers

A worker is a **salaried-hours** worker if he is (reg 4 SI 1999/584): 2886
- paid an annual salary for a set basic number of minimum hours per year; and
- paid in equal instalments, for example 12 monthly or 52 weekly instalments.

A worker is a **time** worker if he (regs 3, 15 SI 1999/584):
- has set hours or times at which he is expected to work but is not paid an annual salary; or
- does piece work or commission work in set hours.

Time that is to be counted for salaried-hours workers and time worked workers is as follows: 2887

Period of time to be counted	Salaried-hours worker	Time worker
time required to be at work	Y	Y
rest breaks	Y	N
time on standby or on-call at or near the place of work [1]	Y	Y
absences paid at normal rate of pay	Y	N
absences not paid at normal rate of pay and any absences due to industrial action	N	N
time spent travelling in connection with work during normal working hours/normal range of hours	Y	Y
commuting between home and work	N	N
time spent on training at or away from the place of work during normal working hours	Y	Y
Y = yes N = no		

1. For example, in *Scottbridge Construction Ltd v Wright* [2003] IRLR 21, CS, W, a nightwatchman, who was paid by reference to the time he worked and was permitted to sleep at the workplace while at work, was entitled to NMW for all the hours he was required to be on the premises. Workers on standby at home are also entitled to NMW for all the hours they are available to for work (for example, answering telephones calls from customers) even if they are free to undertake other activities, such as watching TV or reading when not answering calls (*British Nursing Association v Inland Revenue (National Minimum Wage Compliance Team)* [2003] ICR 19, CA).

Output worker

A worker is an "output worker" if he is paid not for the time that he works, but for the number of pieces he produces or the number of tasks (for example sales or deals) he performs (reg 25(1) SI 1999/584). Consequently, his **hours of work are not fixed** by his employer. This is commonly known as "piece work" or "commission work." 2889

The system **to calculate** the total number of hours worked in such cases provides for the determination by the employer of the "**mean hourly output rate**" on an actual or estimated basis (National Minimum Wage Regulations 1999 (Amendment) Regulations SI 2004/1161 amending National Minimum Wage Regulations SI 1999/584).

Since 6 April 2005, the number of hours taken by a worker in producing pieces or performing tasks during the pay reference period will be treated as being 120% of the number of hours that a worker working at the mean hourly output rate would have taken to produce or perform the same number of pieces or tasks.

MEMO POINTS This new system, introduced on 1 October 2004, replaced the previous system of "fair estimate agreements."

2890 To determine the mean hourly output rate, the employer must conduct a **satisfactory test or estimate** of the speed at which the workers produce the subject piece or perform the subject task (reg 26A SI 1999/584).

To conduct a **test**, the employer can choose a sample of these workers that, in respect of the speed at which the workers work, is representative of all them. To be performed satisfactorily, the chosen group must be tested in working conditions similar to those in which the workers work. The hourly output rate is then calculated by dividing the total number of subject pieces or subject tasks (or the fraction of a piece or task) produced or performed by the tested workers per hour during the period of the test by the number of workers in the group tested.

2891 If necessary, employers can make an **estimate** of the average speed, in terms of pieces or tasks per hour, at which the workers are likely to work. For an estimate to be satisfactory, the employer must test the average speed, in terms of pieces or tasks per hour, at which a sample of workers of the employer work either:
- in similar conditions to produce a piece or perform a task that is reasonably similar to the subject piece or subject task; or
- in different working circumstances but on the same subject piece or subject task.

In both circumstances, the employer must fairly adjust the average speed to take into account any differences that would affect the speed of production or performance.

2892 Having conducted a satisfactory test or made a satisfactory estimate, **subsequent changes** to the workforce will not require a new test or estimate unless the employer has reason to believe that the changes materially affect the mean hourly output rate.

2893 A **written notice** must be given to the worker at any time before the beginning of the pay reference period and must contain (reg 25(2) SI 1999/584):
- statements conveying that it is being given to inform the worker that, to secure compliance with NMW legislation, he will be treated with regard to his production of the subject piece or performance of subject task during the pay reference period as working for a certain period of time and for the purposes of determining this, the employer has conducted a test or made an estimate to ascertain what the mean hourly output rate is;
- the mean hourly output rate and the rate the worker is to be paid for the production of a single subject piece or performance of a single subject task; and
- the telephone number of the NMW helpline, which is identified as such.

Unmeasured time worker

2895 This covers those who work **unspecified hours** and all other workers who do not fall into the other three categories above (reg 6 SI 1999/584). It includes, in particular, work where there are certain tasks to be done but no specified hours or time when they must be done. They are most often domestic staff with no set hours, output or annual salary. This group includes live-in care workers (*Walton v Independent Living Organisation Ltd* [2003] ICR 688, CA).

2896 To calculate the total number of hours worked in such cases, the employer and worker can have a "**daily average**" **agreement**. This must be in writing and agreed between them before the start of the pay reference period it covers, setting out the daily average number of hours which the worker is to work in this period (the employer must be able to show that this figure is realistic).

If there is no agreement, the employer must nevertheless ensure that he pays at least the NMW for every hour worked with regard to each pay period.

2. Compliance

Records

Employers are required to keep records for 3 years (s 9 NMWA 1998; reg 38 SI 1999/584). These must be sufficient to establish that the worker has been paid at least the NMW. The records required must be in a form which enables them to be produced in a single document. 2900

If the **worker** has reasonable grounds to believe that he is being/has been remunerated for any pay reference period at a rate which is less than the NMW, he can give **notice** to his employer **requesting the production of the relevant records** relating to periods listed in the notice (s 10 NMWA 1998). The worker has a **right to be accompanied** by another person chosen by him if stated in the notice. 2901

The employer must give the worker reasonable notice of the time and **place** at which the relevant records will be produced, which must be:
– the worker's place of work;
– any other place at which it is reasonable, in all the circumstances, for the worker to attend to inspect the relevant records; or
– such other place as may be agreed between the worker and the employer.

The records must be **produced**: 2902
– **before** the end of the period of 14 days following the date of receipt of the production notice; or
– **at such later** time as may be agreed during that period between the worker and the employer.

The worker is entitled to make a **copy** of the records.

Enforcement

Revenue and Customs' NMW enforcement officers can **require employers** to (s 14 NMWA 1998): 2903
– produce records;
– allow access to premises; and
– provide information in order to determine whether there has been compliance.

Information so obtained must only be used for the purposes of the NMW rules or for criminal or civil proceedings (s 15 NMWA 1998).

MEMO POINTS 1. It should be noted that **Revenue and Customs** can **disclose information** which comes into its possession in the course of its duties such as during an employer tax compliance visit (s 39 NMWA 1998). Disclosure in such circumstances is to the Secretary of State who will pass the information on to NMW enforcement officers.
Officers can disclose information obtained from the employer to the worker and vice versa (s 16A NMWA 1998 as inserted by s 44 ERelA 2004).
2. In the **agricultural sector**, the relevant officers are called agricultural wages inspectors.

Where it appears that the employer is paying, or has in the past paid, below the NMW, the enforcement officer can issue **enforcement notices** requiring him to comply with the NMW and to make up the loss suffered by his workers within a specified period (s 19 NMWA 1998). Enforcement notices can be served with regard to non-compliance even after the workers to whom they relate have left their employment, but cannot relate to pay reference periods which ended more than 6 years before the enforcement notice is served (s19(2A), (2B) NMWA 1998) (as amended by the National Minimum Wage (Enforcement Notices) Act 2003 which closed the loophole created by *Inland Revenue Commissioners v Bebb Travel plc* [2003] ICR 1271, CA). 2904

Failure to comply may result in (s 20-21 NMWA 1998):
– the issue of a penalty notice for non-compliance which imposes a financial penalty on the employer, related to the period of his failure to comply with the enforcement notice, in addition to any arrears of the NMW; and/or

– the enforcement officer bringing employment tribunal or civil court proceedings against the employer on behalf of that employer's workers.

If the employer does not agree with the enforcement notice or any penalty notice, he can **appeal** to an employment tribunal within 4 weeks of its issue. If the tribunal finds that the amount specified is wrong, it will rectify the notice and state what the correct amount should be. Where there is unsatisfactory evidence, the tribunal will do its best to estimate the accurate figure (*Commissioners of Inland Revenue v St Hermans Estate Co Ltd* [2002] IRLR 788, EAT).

MEMO POINTS While enforcement notices relating to arrears due must cover all pay periods up to 3 months before the date of the notice, they need not cover more recent periods. Further, a single enforcement notice may relate to more than one worker irrespective of whether the employer's failure to pay the NMW is a previous or ongoing failure (s 19 NMWA 1998 as amended by s 45 ERelA 2004).
The Act will also give new rights to enforcement officers enabling them to withdraw and replace an enforcement notice or a penalty notice (s 46 ERelA 2004 which will insert new s 22A to 22F NMWA 1998). No date has yet been given for commencement but it is expected to be by April 2005.

2906 **Criminal offences** If none of the above enforcement measures has an effect, the employer will commit a criminal offence if he:
– refuses or wilfully neglects to pay NMW;
– fails to keep records or falsifies records; or
– obstructs an enforcement officer or knowingly provides false information.

The maximum penalty is a fine up to £5,000 (level 5 on the standard scale).

3. Remedies

2910 A worker has two general remedies and two specific remedies under the NMW rules if he is not paid the NMW.

General remedies

2911 A worker can bring a claim for an **unauthorised deduction** from wages (¶3050) if he is not paid the NMW or if his employer reduces the number of his hours of work in order to offset the extra cost of implementing the NMW (as happened in *Burr v Buckle & Bowen-Jones t/a Industrial Cleaning Services*, ET case 1502147/99). The employer will also be liable to a claim if he changes the payment arrangements without consent to fund the payment of the NMW (*Laird v AK Stoddart Ltd* [2001] IRLR 591, EAT). A worker can also bring a claim for **breach of contract** if there is an unlawful deduction (¶1710).

In both cases, the **burden of proof** is on the employer to establish that the worker has been paid at least the NMW (s 28 NMWA 1998).

EXAMPLE In *Laird v AK Stoddart Ltd*, above, L's employer increased L's hourly rate to comply with the NMW by consolidating part of L's attendance allowance into the basic hourly rate. If L had not consented to this change, this would have amounted to an unauthorised and/or unlawful deduction. However, as L had agreed to this variation in his payment arrangements there was no unauthorised and/or unlawful deduction.

Specific remedies

2912 Workers also have the right **not to suffer detriment** as a result of their request to be paid the NMW (s 23 NMWA 1998). Any **dismissal** of an employee in such circumstances will also be **automatically unfair** (s 104A ERA 1996).

MEMO POINTS Non-employee workers who are so dismissed should rely on the right not to suffer a detriment though compensation is awarded on the same basis as for unfair dismissal.

2913 The worker can also make a complaint to the employment tribunal if his employer **fails to comply** with a **request for information** in respect of a pay period (s 11 NMWA 1998). If the tribunal finds the complaint well-founded, it will:

– make a declaration to that effect; and
– order the employer to pay the worker an award of 80 times the relevant NMW.

The complaint must be made **within** 3 months from the date by which the records should have been produced.

B. A week's pay

The **following entitlements and rights** are calculated by reference to a week's pay: 2920
a. statutory redundancy pay;
b. special redundancy pay for lay-offs or short-time working;
c. guarantee payments;
d. guarantee debts on the employer's insolvency;
e. medical suspension payments;
f. paid annual leave;
g. paid time off:
– to perform duties as an employee representative/candidate or as a member/candidate of an SNB, EWC, or information or consultation body;
– to look for new employment under notice of redundancy;
– for a young person to study; and
– for antenatal care; and
h. the following awards:
– unfair dismissal awards (basic, compensatory and additional);
– award due to infringement of the right to written particulars;
– award due to infringement of the right to minimum statutory notice;
– award for employer's failure to allow worker to be accompanied to disciplinary/grievance hearing or hearing regarding flexible working;
– award for employer's failure to consider/correctly consider employee's request for flexible working;
– protective award for employer's failure to consult on redundancy; and
– award for employer's failure to consult on training (statutory recognised unions).

The broad aim of the rules relating to a week's pay is to **ascertain the minimum amount** to which the employee would be entitled under his contract if he worked a normal week.

The rules give **four different formulae** for calculating a normal week's pay and which formula to use will depend on the type of employee. Once the correct formula is identified, it is applied to the calculation date which is the date used for calculating a week's pay. This date will vary depending on the entitlement.

Where the employee is paid **less than the national minimum wage**, the calculation of a week's pay should be based on the NMW he should have received and not what he was actually paid (*Paggetti v Cobb* [2002] IRLR 861, EAT). 2921

Maximum limits

There is a **statutory cap** on the amount of a week's pay with regard to certain entitlements and rights, the most important of these relating to (s 227 ERA 1996): 2923
– **statutory redundancy payments**; and
– basic awards and additional **awards in unfair dismissal cases**.

The **current maximum** is set at £280 for cases in which the calculation date (¶2955) falls on or after 1 February 2005.

MEMO POINTS This is likely to be increased in February 2006 and will be covered in updates to this edition.

The following table sets out when the statutory cap applies and maximum limits to the amount of any award:

Entitlement or right subject to the statutory cap for a week's pay: £280	Maximum limit	Reference	Para.
Employer's insolvency: guaranteed debts	£2,240 (arrears of pay) £1,680 (holiday pay)	s 186 ERA 1996	¶9054
Flexible working: failure to consider/correctly consider employee's request	£2,240	s 227 ERA1996; reg 7 SI 2002/3236	¶2923
Redundancy pay: statutory (SRP)	£8,400	ss 162, 227 ERA 1996	¶9005
Right to be accompanied: disciplinary/grievance hearing	£560	s 11(5) ERelA 1999	¶6790
Right to be accompanied: flexible working hearing	£560	reg15 SI 2002/3207	¶4720
Trade unions (statutorily recognised): employer's failure to consult on training	£560	s 70C TULRCA 1992	¶9005
Unfair dismissal: basic award	£8,400 (minimum in certain cases: £3,800)	ss 117-122, 227 ERA 1996	¶¶8575+, 8999
Unfair dismissal: compensatory award	£56,800 (no limit where dismissed unfairly or selected for redundancy for reasons connected with health and safety)		¶8587
Unfair dismissal: additional award (employer's failure to follow statutory disciplinary/grievance procedures)	£1,120	ss 117-122, 227 ERA 1996	¶8577
Unfair dismissal: additional award (failure to re-employ or reinstate employee)	between £7,280 and £14,560		¶8688
Written particulars: employer's failure to provide statement/incomplete or inaccurate statement	£560 or £1,120	s 38 EA 2002	¶1461

2924 **Guarantee payments** have a daily limit of £18.40 for a workless day and are only payable for a maximum of 5 workless days in any 3 month period (i.e. £92).

MEMO POINTS 1. This is likely to be increased in February 2006 and will be covered in updates to this edition.
2. The right to remuneration for **redundancy time off** is subject to a maximum of 40% of the employee's week's pay although a week's pay in such circumstances is not subject to the statutory cap (¶8885).

1. Type of calculation

2930 Each of the four formulae relate to a different type of employee. These **types are as follows**:
– employees with normal working hours (i.e. the hours are constant from week to week);
– regular employees with a flat (i.e. paid by the number of hours they work) or variable rate (i.e. paid by piece, product or commission);
– shift or rota workers; and
– employees with no normal working hours.

Whichever of the four formulae is used, a week's pay is calculated by reference to the employee's pay. 2931

The courts have held that, for these purposes, **pay includes** the employee's wages or salary including any regular bonuses or like payments if the employee is entitled to them (*Mole Mining Ltd v Jenkins* [1972] ICR 282, NIRC; *S and U Stores Ltd v Wilkes* [1974] IRLR 283, NIRC). Ex gratia payments are, therefore, not included.

Pay does **not include** benefits in kind, cash payments by a third party and payment for expenses where they represent a true reimbursement. Additional expense payments may be included, therefore, if it can be shown that the payment represented a profit which exceeded the employee's real expense.

MEMO POINTS Agricultural workers can include benefits in kind where such benefits are included in the minimum wage set by agricultural wages regulations (*W A Armstong & Sons Ltd v Borrill* [2000] ICR 367, EAT).

---

a. Employees with normal working hours

No variation

If an employee's pay for work done in normal working hours does not vary, a week's pay is the pay due for the **basic hours** the employee is contracted to work. This can include **premium rates** if the normal hours he works attract this higher rate, for example because he is a night-worker. **Regular contractual bonuses or allowances** (except expense allowances) which do not vary with the amount of work done are also included (s 221(2) ERA 1996). 2935

However, it does not include any **commission payments** which are paid over and above basic salary (*Evans v Malley Organisation Ltd t/a First Business Support* [2003] IRLR 156, CA). Likewise, **overtime** pay can only be included if it is obligatory and guaranteed by the contract of employment. Voluntary overtime must be excluded (*Bamsey and others v Albon Engineering and Manufacturing plc* [2004] IRLR 457, CA).

MEMO POINTS With regard to **statutory annual leave pay** which is based on a week's pay, this inability to include commissions or overtime payments could suggest that the Working Time Regulations do not correctly implement the EC Working Time Directive and it may, therefore, be open for workers employed by public authorities to try and rely on the Directive directly.

This must be the amount payable under the contract of employment in force on the calculation date (see below). 2936

Variation

If there is a variable element with regard to the employee's pay, the following special rules apply. 2937

Flat or variable rates If an employee has normal working hours but his pay varies with the amount of work done (for example, under piece rates) or where pay is partly made up of variable productivity bonuses or commissions, then a **week's pay is** his average hourly rate over a 12-calendar week period times the number of normal weekly working hours (s 221(2) ERA 1996). 2938

The **formula** to calculate the average hourly rate is as follows: 2939

$$\text{average hourly rate} = \frac{\text{pay over the 12-calendar week period}}{\text{total number of hours during this period}}$$

This **12-week calendar period** is **ascertained by** reference to the calculation date (see below). If the calculation date is on the weekly payday, the period will end on this date. If not, it will end on the payday of the previous pay week to ensure that 12 complete calendar weeks are taken into consideration. If the employee's pay period is more than a week, the payday is deemed to be a Saturday (s 335(1) ERA 1996). 2940

2941 Hours worked as **voluntary overtime** are included as part of the total number of hours worked over the 12-week period. However, where pay for such work is higher than pay for the same work done in normal working hours, the pay must be adjusted (i.e. the premium element must be ignored and it is brought down to the level it would have been if the same work had been done in normal working hours) (*British Coal Corporation v Cheesbrough* [1990] ICR 317, HL).

As with the general rule, full pay for overtime hours can be included if it is **obligatory and guaranteed**.

2942 12/13 of any quarterly **bonus**, or 12/52 of any annual bonus, can be included provided the bonuses are not paid specifically for some time outside the 12-week period (DTI guide on a week's pay).

2943 **Any hours** in which the employee was **not working** are not included and consequently any pay for hours not worked, for example under a guaranteed week agreement, are ignored.

Further, **any week** in which no work was done should be replaced by the last previous week when the employee did work, to bring the total number of weeks up to 12.

2944 If the employee has **less than 12 weeks' service**, the parties can look to other factors that might be relevant in ascertaining the average hourly rate, for example the working hours of other employees of the employer and/or the expected pattern of working based on the terms on which the job was offered.

2945 **Shift or rota workers** Where an employee is contracted to work normal hours but on days or at times which differ from week to week or over a longer period, a **week's pay is** the average weekly working hours times the average hourly rate (see above) (s 222 ERA 1996).

2946 The **formula** to calculate the average weekly working hours is:

$$\text{average weekly working hours} = \frac{\text{total number of normal working hours during 12-week calendar period (see above)}}{12}$$

b. Employees with no normal working hours

2950 For an employee with no normal working hours (for example, an employee paid wholly by commission), the amount of a **week's pay is** the average weekly pay over the 12-week calendar period (s 224 ERA 1996).

2951 The **formula** to calculate the average weekly pay is:

$$\text{average weekly pay} = \frac{\text{total pay during 12-week calendar period (see above)}}{12}$$

2. Calculation date

The calculation dates for awards and payments under the following entitlements are as follows (ss 225-226 ERA 1996; TULRCA 1992; ERelA 1999; EA 2002; SI 1981/1794; SI 1998/1833; SI 2002/3207). 2955

Entitlement or right	Calculation date used for calculating a week's pay
Annual leave	Date on which time off was taken or on which it should have been permitted.
Time off to perform duties as an employee representative/candidate or as a member/candidate of a SNB, EWC, or information or consultation body	
Time off for young person for study or training	
Flexible working: employer's failure to consider/correctly consider employee's request	Day on which flexible working application was made.
Guarantee payment	Day in respect of which guarantee payment is due unless contract has been varied or new one entered into to provide for short-time working, in which case it is the last day on which original contract was in force.
Medical suspension payments	Day before that on which suspension began. Where suspension for maternity reasons falls during maternity leave, day before leave began.
Minimum statutory notice	Day before first day of notice period.
Redundancy: employer's failure to consult appropriate representatives/comply with election requirement	Date protective award made.
Redundancy pay: statutory (SRP)	Date on which statutory minimum notice was given. Where notice is longer than statutory minimum, date on which minimum notice would have to have been given to end employment on same day as it actually ends. Where less than statutory minimum is given, date on which employment ends.
Right to be accompanied: disciplinary/grievance hearing	Where claim made in unfair dismissal claim: date on which employer's notice was given, or, if no notice, the EDT. Otherwise: date on which hearing took place or was to have taken place.
Right to be accompanied: flexible working hearing	Date on which hearing took place or was to have taken place.
Special redundancy payments for lay-offs or short-time working	Day before lay-off or short-time working began.
Time off for antenatal care	Day of appointment.
Time off to look for work or to arrange training for redundant employees	Day on which employer's notice was given.
Trade unions (statutory recognised): consult on training	Date of employer's failure to consult.
Unfair dismissal: basic award	Same as for redundancy payments.
Unfair dismissal: additional award (failure to reinstate or re-engage employee order)	Date on which employer's notice was given or, if notice was not given, the EDT.
Written statement of reasons for dismissal	Date on which employer's notice was given or, if notice was not given, the EDT.

EXAMPLE **Redundancy payments**
A is entitled to 4 weeks' statutory notice when he is given notice on 1 January 2005.

Scenario 1: He is given his statutory notice. His calculation date will be the same date as the date he is given notice, i.e. 1 January 2005.

Scenario 2: He is given 3 months' notice. His employment will, therefore, end on 31 March. However, his calculation date will be 4 weeks before that date (i.e. the date on which minimum notice would have had to be given for the employment to end on the same day as it actually ends) and will be 3 March.

Scenario 3: He is given 2 weeks' notice. His calculation date will be the date his employment ends, i.e. 14 January.

The **maximum week's pay** applicable will be the rate in force on the calculation date. Therefore the maximum will be £270 (as it was until 1 February 2005) in scenarios 1 and 3 and £280 in scenario 2.
Note that the calculation date is different to the **relevant date** (used for the purposes of calculating A's length of service and the amount of his redundancy payment) which is the date his statutory notice period ends, i.e. 28 January (¶8340).

III. Payment

A. Forms and rate of pay

2980 Levels and intervals of pay will normally be fixed by **express contractual terms**. Where there is no written contract of employment or where it does not cover these provisions, the employer must provide his employee with a **written statement of particulars** (¶1400).

2981 The **rate of pay** is commonly expressed as:
– a yearly sum for a fixed number of hours per week payable in monthly instalments;
– a sum for a lesser period, for example weekly or daily for a fixed number of hours payable on a monthly, weekly or daily basis; or
– an hourly rate payable on a weekly, daily or hourly basis.

2982 If there is a **collective agreement** between the employer and a recognised trade union for the purpose of pay bargaining, the contract of employment should provide that the amount to be paid is incorporated into the contract (*Airlie v City of Edinburgh District Council* [1996] IRLR 516, EAT).

2983 Earnings (i.e. basically the tax term for remuneration) are subject to income tax and NIC.

B. Itemised pay statements

2985 An employee is entitled to be given by his employer, at or before the time at which any payment of wages is made to him, a **written** itemised pay statement **containing** (s 8 ERA 1996):
– the gross amount of the wages;
– the amounts of any variable or fixed deductions from that amount;
– the net amount of wages payable; and
– where different parts of the net amount are paid in different ways, the amount and method of payment of each part payment.

With regard to **fixed deductions**, the employer need only state the aggregate amount of fixed deductions including that deduction, if he has given the employee, at or before the time at which the pay statement is given, a **standing statement of fixed deductions** (s 9 ERA 1996). 2986

The standing statement must be in **writing**, effective at the **date on which the pay statement is given** and must **contain** in relation to each deduction comprised in the aggregate amount of deductions:
- the amount of the deduction;
- the intervals at which the deduction is to be made; and
- the purpose for which it is made.

A standing statement will be effective at the date on which it is given to the employee and can remain effective for 12 months after which it will be necessary to re-issue the statement. A **re-issued statement** should be consolidated and must incorporate the particulars of any notices of amendment (see below). The first re-issue must be **made within** 12 months of when the first standing statement was given and thereafter should be re-issued at intervals of not more than 12 months.

A standing statement can be amended if necessary to add a new deduction, to change the existing deduction or to cancel it. The **notice of amendment** must be given to the employee in writing and must contain the particulars of the amendment. 2987

Remedies

The employee can bring an application to an employment tribunal if the employer **fails to provide** an itemised pay statement (s 11 ERA 1996). 2988

Both the employee and the employer can also bring an application where a question arises over the **particulars of the information** given in a pay or standing statement. Questions cannot relate solely to the accuracy of the amount stated in such particulars nor can they relate to whether the employment has been, or will be, contracted out of the Second State Pension (formerly referred to as SERPS).

Any application must be **brought** while the employee is employed or within 3 months of the date on which employment ended (s 11(4) ERA 1996). This time limit can be extended as the tribunal considers reasonable where it accepts that it was not reasonably practicable for the application to have been made in time.

In both cases, the tribunal will **determine** what the itemised pay statement should contain. 2989

The tribunal will also make a **declaration** if the employer has failed to give a pay statement or if a pay or standing statement does not, in relation to a deduction, contain adequate particulars (s 12(3) ERA 1996). In such cases, if the tribunal further finds that any unnotified deductions have been made during the period of 13 weeks beginning with the date of the application (whether or not the deductions were made in breach of the contract of employment), the tribunal may order the employer to **pay** the employee a sum **up to** the aggregate of the unnotified deductions (s 12 (4) ERA 1996).

This has been used by the tribunals to penalise employers for not complying with these legal requirements and it is, therefore, irrelevant whether or not the employee was aware of the deduction and whether the employer was contractually entitled to make the deduction (*Miller v Leicestershire County Council* [1978] IRLR 433, IT). Alternatively, a tribunal may decide it is only appropriate in the circumstances to award any shortfall between what the employee should have received and what he did in fact receive (as it did in *Scott v Creager* [1979] IRLR 162, EAT).

IV. Deductions

3000 The employer may be able **lawfully** to make a deduction if:
- he has an express contractual right to do so;
- he is obliged to do so by a statutory order; or
- the employee has refused to perform all his duties.

Otherwise, it is **unlawful** and the employee will be able to bring a breach of contract claim. For example, if the employer tries to make a deduction by varying the contractual terms unilaterally by imposing a pay cut. Deductions made with regard to overpayments must also be **valid**. In certain circumstances, the employer may be also estopped from recovering the overpayment.

3001 Further, employees have **special statutory protection** with regard to certain deductions and, within this group, unlawful deductions are unauthorised as are any deductions made in an incorrect manner. In such cases, an employee can bring a claim in an employment tribunal for the repayment of the unauthorised deduction.

MEMO POINTS All deductions must be adequately set out in itemised pay statements.

A. Lawful deductions

1. Contractual deductions

3005 The employer has **no implied right** to withhold pay or make deductions and an **express clause** will be needed. **Specific** clauses providing for deductions in specific circumstances, for example for poor performance, stock deficiencies, unauthorised absences, season ticket loans, training costs etc. are usually considered reasonable.

However, a **general** clause allowing the employer to vary pay will not allow him to reduce pay as this is likely to be held unreasonable.

MEMO POINTS Whether or not an employer has an express clause allowing him to deduct wages for **poor or incomplete performance**, he may alternatively be able to claim damages for breach of contract in respect of that performance. If the breach is sufficiently serious (i.e. it is fundamental), the employer will be entitled to dismiss and consequently stop paying wages. Poor performance should first be dealt with under an appraisal system to find out the causes for it and whether training, support or increased supervision will solve the problem. If not, it may be a disciplinary matter.

3006 **Common specific clauses** giving the employer the right to deduct from wages are as follows for:
- overpayments of wages or expenses;
- unauthorised absences;
- loans;
- any losses caused by the employee's breach of his duties or by his negligence (for example, damage to company property); and
- any other amount which the employee owes (for example, season ticket loans) from the final salary payment, including any overpaid holiday.

There may also be a **right to suspend** without pay in certain circumstances (for example, until a serious matter has been dealt with by a disciplinary hearing).

Refusal to work

3007 If the employee refuses to **perform all** of his contractual duties, he is not entitled to his full contractual wage and his employer can deduct a sum **equal to the proportion of time** the employee deliberately refuses or fails to fulfil his contractual duties (*Miles v Wakefield Metropolitan District Council* [1987] IRLR 193, HL). This is based on the quantum meruit principle (¶2817).

The same principle will apply to **go-slows**.

MEMO POINTS An alternative way of reducing the employee's wages for **part-performance** is by **setting-off** the loss due to the employee's breach of contract against his wages (*Sim v Rotherham Metropolitan Borough Council* [1986] IRLR 391, HC). However, the end result is the same.

The employer is entitled to **withhold the whole of** the employee's **pay** if he makes it clear that part-performance is not acceptable (*Wiluszynski v London Borough of Tower Hamlets* [1989] IRLR 259, CA). 3008

EXAMPLE In *Wiluszynski v London Borough of Tower Hamlets*, the Court held that the Council was entitled to withhold the whole of W's wages as it had made it clear to him that his refusal to perform part of his duties (answering councillor's enquiries) was unacceptable. This was so even though this was a very small part of his duties and he had performed the substantial part of his contract.

MEMO POINTS A refusal to work part of the day is underperformance and will allow the employer to discipline accordingly. A sufficiently serious breach may be fundamental allowing the employer to summarily dismiss the employee.

Withholding of goodwill

A withholding of goodwill can breach the implied term of fidelity and justify a withholding of pay (*Ticehurst and Thompson v British Telecommunications plc* [1992] IRLR 219, CA). 3009

EXAMPLE In *Ticehurst and Thompson v British Telecommunications plc*, T, who had withdrawn her goodwill as part of a concerted action by union members, was not permitted to return to work and was not paid after taking industrial action until the dispute was settled because she refused to sign an undertaking to work normally in accordance with the terms of her contract of employment. The Court held that she had not proved that she was ready and willing to perform in full her obligations under her contract of employment and that the withholding of pay was not unlawful.

Overpayments

Recovery will only be possible if the employer can show that the overpayment was due to a mistake in fact (for example, an error in computation). If it is, the deduction will be **valid**. However, if the overpayment was due to a mistake of law (for example, the employer did not realise that he did not legally have to pay the employee for a particular absence) then the deduction will be **invalid**. In such cases, the employee can bring a claim to prevent the deduction or for reimbursement in the civil courts. 3010

Further, an employer may also be prevented (**estopped**) from claiming repayment (called "restitution") if the following conditions are satisfied: 3011
- he has made a representation of fact which led the employee to believe that he was entitled to treat the money as his own;
- the employee must have, in good faith and without notice of the employer's claim, consequently changed his position for the worse where it would be inequitable in all the circumstances to require him to repay some or all of the amount (*Home Office v Ayres* [1992] IRLR 59, EAT; *Lipkin Gorman v Karpnale Ltd* [1991] 3 WLR 10, HL); and
- the payment must not have been primarily caused by the fault of the employee.

2. Statutory deductions

An employer may be legally required to make the following deductions which he must pass on to a third party: 3015
- attachment of earnings;
- student loans; and
- trade union subscriptions.

a. Attachment of earnings

3017 The employer may be statutorily bound to make a deduction from his employee's earnings if the courts have made an attachment of earnings order (Attachment of Earnings Act 1971). In such cases, the employer will pass the money deducted onto the relevant court office.

Scope

3018 An attachment of earnings order can be made by a court against the employee's earnings in relation to the following if the employee has **failed**, or is likely to fail, **to pay** the sums due in a satisfactory manner (s 1 Attachment of Earnings Act 1971):
- judgment debts made in the county court or the balance of it if it has been part-paid;
- maintenance orders made in the High Court, county court or magistrates' court;
- fines or compensation order made in the magistrates' court on the conviction of an offence;
- payments under a legal aid contribution order; or
- payments under a county court administration order.

There are specific regulations in relation to attachment of earnings for failure to pay council tax (¶3028) and for failure to pay child support maintenance by an absent parent (¶3029).

Procedure

3019 When an employer **receives** an attachment of earnings order, he must make the deductions that are set out in it (s 6 Attachment of Earnings Act 1971). The order will state:
- what the employee's **attachable earnings** are;
- what sum is to be deducted from the earnings on each pay day (called **normal deductions**); and
- the earnings below which no deduction can be made (called **protected earnings**).

MEMO POINTS **Earnings** include (s 24 Attachment of Earnings Act 1971):
- basic pay;
- overtime payments;
- any other fee, bonus, commission or other emolument referable to his employment;
- statutory sick pay;
- compensation for loss of office; and
- company occupational pensions and annuities over the guaranteed minimum pension.

Excluded are:
- any social security payments, for example statutory maternity pay, pensions or allowances; and
- pensions or allowances payable due to disability.

3020 The employer must make the stated deductions **on the relevant pay days** subject to the protected earnings limit.

If all or part of the normal deductions **cannot be made on a pay day** because the amount is greater than the difference between the employee's attachable earnings and his protected earnings, the outstanding arrears created on that pay day can be carried forward to the next pay day. This carrying forward of arrears does not apply to orders relating to debt judgments or payments under an administration order.

3021 Where the employer receives **more than one attachment of earnings order** in relation to an employee, he must comply with the orders in date order except that orders relating to judgment debts or payments under administration orders must always be complied with last.

This can only occur when there is an **excess** between the attachable earnings and the protected earnings after the normal deduction is made in accordance with the first order. This excess is then applied to the other attachment orders in the required order.

3022 The deductions must be shown on the employee's itemised pay statement.

The employer must also give the employee a **written statement** stating the total amount of the deduction, the intervals at which the deductions are to be made, and the purpose for which it is made (ss 8, 9 ERA 1996). Such statements will be **valid for** 12 months.

If there is a **change to the statement**, for example if there is a deduction or an alteration or cancellation of an existing order, the employer must give written notice to the employee. In such circumstances, the employer should also issue an updated statement.

Administrative cost The employer is entitled to make a deduction up to £1 to cover any administrative costs involved in making the deduction (s 7 Attachment of Earnings Act 1971; Attachment of Earnings (Employer's Deduction) Order SI 1991/356). The employer must inform the employee of the deduction in the written statement. 3023

Compliance

The employer must comply **within** 7 days to: 3024
- an attachment of earnings order;
- a variation to it; and
- a notice stopping or discharging the order.

The court may also require the employer to **supply the court** with a signed statement of the employee's earnings and anticipated earnings within a specified period (s 14 Attachment of Earnings Act 1971).

The employer must also **notify the court** (that made the order): 3025
- if the employee is no longer employed by him or within 10 days of termination of his employment (s 7 Attachment of Earnings Act 1971); or
- within 7 days of becoming his employer or finding out that the new employee has an attachment of earnings order against him. In such circumstances, the employer must also inform the court in writing and include a statement of the employee's earnings and anticipated earnings (s 15 Attachment of Earnings Act 1971).

Penalties If the employer fails to comply with any of the above provisions, he can be subject to **criminal proceedings** in a magistrates' court (s 23 Attachment of Earnings Act 1971). If found guilty, he may be liable to a maximum fine of £500 (level 2 on the standard scale). Alternatively, he may be fined up to £250 in the **High Court or county court**. 3026

Further, if the employer deliberately makes a **false statement**, he may also be liable to imprisonment for up to 14 days.

The employer has a **defence** if he can prove that (s 23(5) Attachment of Earnings Act 1971):
- he took all reasonable steps to comply with the order; or
- he did not know and could not reasonably be expected to have known that the debtor was not employed by him, or had stopped working for him, and that he gave notice of this fact as soon as was reasonably practicable when he knew.

Specific rules

The relevant bill authority (i.e. the district or borough council) can make an attachment of earnings order for the payment of any outstanding **council tax** once it has obtained a liability order from the magistrates' court (reg 37 Council Tax (Administration and Enforcement) Regulations SI 1992/613 as amended). The employer must comply with this order if it relates to one of his employees and non-compliance is a criminal offence with a maximum fine of £1,000 (level 3 on the standard scale). These rules are very similar to the general rules above. 3028

The amount to be deducted is specified for any given level of net earnings.

MEMO POINTS **Earnings** have the same meaning as with general attachment of earnings order. Net earnings are gross earnings after the deduction of income tax, NIC and pensions contributions.

The relevant rules relating to the attachment of earnings order in relation to the payment of **child support maintenance** by an absent parent are also very similar to the general rules (Child Support (Collection and Enforcement) Regulations SI 1992/1989). 3029

b. Student loan deductions

3030 Student loans are available to help students meet their expenses whilst they are studying and are known as "income-contingent" loans because repayment is related to the borrower's level of income. Revenue and Customs are now responsible for collecting repayments, although the loans continue to be administered by the Student Loans Company. In most cases, the employer **collects** student loan repayments by making deductions from the borrower's pay and **passes the amount on** to Revenue and Customs.

For when and how much to deduct, see ¶6911.

c. Union subscriptions

3035 There is no legal obligation on an employer to have (or keep) any arrangement for direct deduction of dues and whether the employer does so will depend on the agreement between the employer and the union.

The employer must have **written permission** from the worker (which must not have been withdrawn) before he can make any deduction from wages for trade union subscriptions. The worker retains the ability to withdraw authorisation at any time. **Notice of withdrawal** must be given in writing and must be received in time for it to be reasonably practicable for the employer to ensure that no deduction is made. There is no time limit on the length of the worker's authorisation (Deregulation (Deduction from Pay of Union Subscriptions) Order SI 1998/1529).

3036 If the worker contracts out of paying into the **political levy**, the employer must make sure that he only deducts the flat subscription fee. In such cases, the worker must give notification in writing that he is exempt from making payments to the political fund, and this amounts to withdrawal of any authorisation to deduct (s 86 TULRCA 1992). The employer cannot refuse to deduct the flat subscription fee, if contributions are deducted in respect of other workers.

3037 A union member claiming that the employer has **not complied** with his duties can apply to the county court for a declaration. The complaint must be made within a period of 3 months. The court can order the employer to take steps to comply within a specified time.

B. Unauthorised deductions

3050 Certain deductions that are **not made in compliance** with these rules are unauthorised and consequently are reimbursable. The employer also loses his right to the deductions and will not be able to recover them even in the proper manner.

The same rules apply to the right not to have to make **payments to the employer** (s 15 ERA 1996).

3052 The employer cannot include a provision in the worker's contract or have an agreement with him which excludes or limits the right of the worker to **contract out** of his right not to suffer an unauthorised deduction, unless certain exceptions apply (¶9333).

1. General rule

First limb

3055 No deduction from a worker's wages **may be made unless** (s 13 ERA 1996):
- it is required or **permitted** by the contract or by statute; or
- the worker has given his **prior written consent**.

Consequently, where an employer unilaterally imposes a variation to employees' contracts (for example, by introducing short-time working), unless he is entitled, either expressly or impliedly, to reduce the wages paid to employees, any reduction of wages as a result will constitute an unlawful deduction of wages (*International Packaging Corporation (UK) Ltd v Balfour* [2003] IRLR 11, EAT).

Where any deductions are to be made pursuant to a contractual provision, a copy of these provisions must be **shown to the worker** or, if not in writing, its effect notified in writing to the worker, prior to any deduction.

Wages include (s 27 ERA 1996): 3056
- basic pay;
- any fee, bonus, commission, holiday pay or other emolument referable to his employment, whether payable under his contract or otherwise. Therefore, non-contractual bonuses are included if they can be shown to be normally expected and are treated as wages payable on the day on which payment is made (*Kent Management Services Ltd v Butterfield* [1992] IRLR 394, EAT);
- the following benefits in kind: vouchers, stamps or similar documents which have a fixed value expressed in monetary terms and are capable of being exchanged for money, goods or services (for example, luncheon vouchers);
- statutory sick pay, statutory maternity/adoption/paternity pay, guarantee payments, suspension on medical grounds and suspension on maternity grounds payments;
- payments for paid time off when payment is required by statute;
- pay under a protective award; and
- sums payable due to an order for reinstatement, re-engagement or the continuation of the contract.

Discretionary and **ex gratia payments** are wages if they are for service and are made (or the intention to make them existed) before termination of employment. This includes discretionary bonuses that have been declared on certain terms but not yet paid (be it under contract, by custom or by an ad hoc decision) (*Farrell Matthews & Weir v Hansen* [2005] IRLR 160, EAT). **Commission payments** that become payable after termination are wages as they are made in connection with the employee's employment (*Robertson v Blackstone Franks Investment Management Ltd* [1998] IRLR 376, CA). Likewise **garden leave payments** are wages as the contract subsists during the time the payments are made. **Payments in lieu of notice** are not as they relate to a period after the termination of the employment (*Delaney v Staples* [1992] IRLR 191, HL). In any event, payments in lieu of notice are also expressly excluded (see below) when they are compensation for loss of office (*Foster Wheeler (London) Ltd v Jackson* [1990] IRLR 412, EAT).

The following payments are **excluded** from the definition of wages and therefore are not protected by these rules: 3057
- all other benefits in kind;
- payments made in respect of expenses;
- pension, allowance or gratuity payments in connection with the worker's retirement or as compensation for loss of office;
- any payments relating to the worker's redundancy; and
- any payments made/received otherwise than in his capacity as a worker.

MEMO POINTS **Advances** under a loan agreement or advances of wages are also excluded from the definition of wages but this does not apply in relation to unauthorised deductions of wages and the employer must not make an unauthorised deduction in respect of such advances.

Second limb

A **deduction** will occur where the total amount of any wages that are paid on a pay day by the employer are **less than the total amount** of wages that are properly payable by him to the worker on that pay day (*Murray v Strathclyde Regional Council* [1992] IRLR 396, EAT). For example, if the worker is paid monthly, a reduction with regard to the first month's payment will be a deduction if it is made against another month's payment. If an employee is **not paid any of his salary** on time, this also constitutes a breach of the employee's statutory right not to 3058 have deductions made from his wages (*Elizabeth Claire Care Management Limited v Francis*, EAT case 147/05).

If the amount properly payable is **not certain**, then any reduction to a pay packet is not classified as a deduction (*New Century Cleaning Co Ltd v Church* [2000] IRLR 27, CA).

> EXAMPLE Employee A is paid on the last day of each month. A's February pay packet is reduced to take into account a contractual entitlement to deduct pay for certain types of absence which occurred in January and February.
> The reduction in relation to absent days in February is part of the calculation as to what is the total amount of wages properly payable in February and is, therefore, not classified as a deduction. However, the reduction in relation to absent days in January is not part of this calculation and is a deduction.

3059 The protection will not apply to reductions that are made as a result of an **error in the employer's computation** (i.e. the process of counting and calculating) (s 13(4) ERA 1996; *Morgan v West Glamorgan County Council* [1995] IRLR 68, EAT).

An error in computation will not include the employer's conscious decision to withhold a payment because he **wrongly believes he has the right** to do so under the contract (*Yemm v British Steel plc* [1994] IRLR 117, EAT; *Morgan v West Glamorgan County Council*, above).

> EXAMPLE In *Morgan v West Glamorgan County Council*, above, the Council demoted M because it believed it could do so. However, the Council did not have a contractual right to do so and the resultant reduction in M's wages was held not to be an error of computation and was an unauthorised deduction.

2. Deductions not protected

3065 The **following deductions** are not protected if they are (ss 14, 16 ERA 1996):
- to reimburse the employer for an overpayment of wages or expenses;
- made as a result of disciplinary proceedings held due to a statutory provision;
- due to a statutory payment required to be made to a public authority;
- for taking part in a strike or other industrial action;
- to satisfy a tribunal or court order for payment to the employer with the worker's written prior agreement/consent; or
- payments to third persons with the worker's written prior agreement/consent.

3066 If a deduction is made under one of the above exceptions, it is irrelevant whether the deduction is lawful or not for the purposes of the protection given by the rules (*SIP (Industrial Products) Ltd v Swinn* [1994] IRLR 323, EAT).

3. Special protection for retail employment

3070 Special protection covers workers who carry out **retail transactions** directly with the public or are involved with the collection of such amounts and applies with regard to cash shortages and stock deficiencies (s 17 ERA 1996). **Cash shortages** are defined as a deficit arising in relation to amounts received in connection with retail transactions (i.e. the sale or supply of goods or the supply of services (including financial services)). **Stock deficiencies** are defined as such deficiencies in relation to retail transactions.

3071 There are **limits** on the amount of any deductions due to cash shortages and stock deficiencies that can be made and on when such deductions can be made (s 18 ERA 1996):
- the employer cannot deduct **more than** one-tenth of the gross amount of wages payable to the worker on each pay day; and
- he must make such a deduction **within** 12 months beginning with the date when the employer discovered or ought reasonably to have discovered the shortage or deficiency.

There are also limits on **payments to the employer** with regard to cash shortages and stock deficiencies as follows (ss 20-21 ERA 1996): 3072
- the employer must notify the worker in writing of his total liability in respect of the shortage or deficiency;
- he cannot require payment of more than one-tenth of the gross amount of wages payable to the worker on each pay day or the balance of that amount after any of the above deductions; and
- his demand for payment must be in writing and on the pay day. This must not be made earlier than the first pay day on or after notification and must be made within 12 months beginning with the date when the employer discovered or ought reasonably to have discovered the shortage or deficiency.

The **restriction to one-tenth** of the gross amount of wages does not apply to the final instalment of wages nor to a payment after this as long as it is made within the 12 months set out above (s 22 ERA 1996). After this period the employer cannot receive payments or recover them by bringing proceedings.

If proceedings are brought against a retail worker to recover such sums, any sums to which he is found to be liable to pay must not be recovered at a rate that exceeds these special provisions. 3073

4. Remedies

The worker can **bring a claim** to an employment tribunal that an unauthorised deduction or payment has been made or received (s 23(1) ERA 1996). Retail workers can also bring a claim that a deduction or payment made was over the limit allowed. In deciding whether it has **jurisdiction to hear** a deduction from wages claim, a tribunal must make findings of fact if necessary (*Gill and others v Ford Motor Co Ltd; Wong and others v BAE Systems Operations Ltd* [2004] IRLR 840, EAT). In this case, the tribunal should not have refused to hear such a claim because the employer stated that due to industrial action the wages in question were not protected, as whether the applicant had actually taken part was in dispute. Instead, the tribunal should have considered the evidence to make a finding on the disputed facts to ascertain whether it had jurisdiction to hear the claim. 3080

The **time limit** for bringing a claim is 3 months beginning with the date of payment from which the deduction was made or the date the payment was received by the employer, whichever is relevant (s 23(2) ERA 1996). If there is a series of deductions or payments, the time limit runs from the date of the last deduction or payment. The tribunal can **extend** this period if it is satisfied that it was not reasonably practicable to have presented the claim in time. In such cases the tribunal will indicate what extension is reasonable (s 23(4) ERA 1996).

Where the tribunal finds that the complaint is well-founded it will (s 24 ERA 1996): 3081
- make a **declaration** to that effect; and
- will **order** the employer to pay the worker as appropriate.

If the amount deducted is greater than that which has been held to be lawfully deducted, the tribunal will order the employer to **pay the difference** between the actual amount deducted and the amount which was lawfully deducted (s 25 ERA 1996).

Any sums paid or repaid to the worker as a result of a tribunal claim **cannot be subsequently lawfully deducted** and consequently the employer loses his right to make the deduction for that sum or part of it (*Potter v Hunt Contracts Ltd* [1992] IRLR 108, EAT). This is a sanction against making unauthorised deductions and in such cases the employer's only course of action would be to bring a common law action against the worker in the county courts. 3082

SECTION 2

Tax

I. Earnings

A. Regular earnings

3100 When an individual who is resident or ordinarily resident in the UK performs the duties of his office or employment wholly in the UK for a UK employer, the individual will be **taxed** on the earnings arising from that office or employment (s 62(2) ITEPA 2003). The amount of earnings subject to tax will be **reduced** to take account of travel and subsistence expenses incurred necessarily, and other expenses incurred wholly, exclusively and necessarily, in the performance of the duties of the employment (¶3270).

MEMO POINTS For tax purposes, the term "emoluments" has been superseded by the more user-friendly term "earnings" and, consequently, will be referred to as such. Employment income used to be **taxable under Schedule E** and the term "taxable under Schedule E" is still often used as a convenient reference.

Liability

3102 Tax payable on earnings arising from the individual's office or employment is divided into **three cases**, based on the **residence status** of the employee, **where the duties are performed** and the **location of the employer**.

General rule (s 15 ITEPA 2003): Earnings will fall under the general rule if the employee is:
– domiciled, resident and ordinarily resident in the UK; or
– not domiciled but resident and ordinarily resident in the UK and his duties are performed (either wholly or partly in the UK) for a UK employer.

Not resident or not ordinarily resident (s 25 ITEPA 2003): This applies to earnings received in the UK by employees who are either not resident or not ordinarily resident in the UK. Where duties are performed partly in the UK and partly overseas, earnings must be apportioned between the two.

Remittance basis (ss 22, 26 ITEPA 2003): This applies to earnings from work done abroad:
– by employees who are resident but not ordinarily resident in the UK, regardless of whether the work was done wholly or partly abroad; and
– income received by non-domiciled employees of an overseas employer.

Residence

3103 In the majority of cases the residence of an individual will be a question of fact which will have a simple answer (for example someone has lived in the UK all his life). Residence is more difficult to determine when an individual arrives in, or leaves, the UK. The tests use the number of days spent in the UK to determine residence. However, these cannot be applied in advance, and so provisional criteria are applied for individuals arriving in, or leaving, the UK.

Although an individual will generally be resident for tax purposes in **one country**, it may be possible to be resident in **more than one country**, in which case the relevant double taxation agreement will decide in which country the individual is resident. It is also possible for an individual not to be resident in any country.

MEMO POINTS The UK has concluded **double taxation agreements** with most countries, which contain a tie breaker clause for situations where an individual would otherwise be resident in both territories. Where tax is actually suffered in both countries, double taxation relief may be available.

183 day test An individual who is physically present in the UK for 183 days in any tax year is resident for that tax year. This rule applies whether the stay is for one continuous period or a succession of visits. 3104

MEMO POINTS 1. As an **exception**, an individual who is a Commonwealth or Irish citizen, who is ordinarily resident in the UK, will remain UK resident, even where he is temporarily absent from the UK in excess of 183 days.
2. It is common practice to ignore **days of arrival and departure** when counting the number of days for each test. However, parts of a day can be taken into account where relevant.
3. Even in a **leap year**, the test is still 183 days.

91 day test Where an individual makes **regular visits** to the UK, he will be UK resident, although he will never be considered resident in a year in which he does not set foot in the UK. 3105

If an individual is present in the UK for an average of 91 days per annum in a 4 year period, the individual will become resident in the UK on the first day of the 5th tax year.

For these purposes, the average is taken to be:

$$\frac{\text{Total visits to the UK (in days)}}{\text{Relevant tax years (cumulative days)}} \times 365 = \text{Average annual visits}$$

Ordinary residence

An individual may be ordinarily resident for a year despite not setting foot in the UK during that year. 3106

Ordinary residence is a more general concept and denotes **greater permanence** than residence. An individual may be resident for a tax year, for example where he is temporarily working in the UK, without becoming ordinarily resident. In contrast, an individual may be ordinarily resident, by virtue of living in the UK throughout his life, but not resident for a number of years because of employment abroad.

If either of the following two **criteria** are satisfied, an individual will be treated as ordinarily resident:

a. he visits the UK and has available accommodation which implies a stay in the country of 3 years of more (i.e. excluding a lease for a period shorter than 3 years); or

b. his visits average 91 days or more per tax year (the same test as for residence).

Domicile

Domicile is a general concept which is a question of law. An individual must have a domicile, but cannot have more than one at the same time. Domicile is not **necessarily the same** as place of residence or nationality. 3107

MEMO POINTS An individual acquires a **domicile of origin** at birth. This is normally the domicile of the father at the time of birth unless the child is born of unmarried parents, in which case the domicile of the mother is taken. Whilst the domicile of origin may be abandoned in later life, it may be revived if a domicile of choice is no longer upheld. Once the individual reaches the age of 16, he may acquire a **domicile of choice**. In order to do so, the individual must physically reside in a new country, with the intention to remain there indefinitely, and must sever all ties with his former domicile. A domicile of choice can be lost by ceasing to live in the country, and having no intention of ever living there permanently. If a domicile of choice is abandoned, the individual reverts to his domicile of origin until such time, if ever, that another domicile of choice is acquired.

For earnings

3110 Earnings can essentially be summarised as a payment in return for acting, or being, an employee. Earnings are **defined as** (s 62 ITEPA 2003):
- any salary, wages or fee;
- any gratuity or other profit or incidental benefit of any kind obtained by the employee if it is money's worth; or
- anything else that constitutes an emolument of employment.

The factors **which must be taken into account are**:
- whether there is a direct link to the employment;
- its monetary value; and
- the time when the remuneration is assessed.

Providing the earnings arise from the office or employment, they are assessable for tax whether or not they are received from the employer (*Hochstrasser v Mayes* [1960] AC 376, HL).

MEMO POINTS 1. **Money's worth** is defined as something that is:
- of direct monetary value to the employee; or
- capable of being converted into money or something of direct monetary value to the employee.

2. Employees are taxable on **commission** received in respect of goods, investments and services sold to third parties during the course of their employment: Revenue and Customs' SP 4/97. Where the employee is obliged to pass on the commission to another party, wholly, exclusively and necessarily to perform his employment duties, he will be able to claim a deduction for the amount paid.

Payment derived from employment

3111 Not all payments made by employers to employees constitute earnings. Conversely some payments made by persons other than the employer will constitute earnings. The crucial test is whether the payment is derived from the employment, which essentially includes the situation of a reward for services, rendered either in the past, currently, or in the future, or to encourage the employee generally.

Each case will be addressed on its merits, but as with employment status, a body of case law exists from which the **following tests** have evolved:

Type of payment	Details
Gifts	Recognition of the person, such as gifts on marriage, does not constitute earnings. However gift vouchers given to employees at Christmas were held to be earnings because the primary reason for the gift was the position of the individuals as employees, with a secondary reason of encouraging future productivity. (The fact that the employees were not contractually entitled to the payment was ignored).
Prizes	A payment relating to exceptional examination performance was held not to be earnings, as it was paid for personal reasons. However employees earning more than £8,500 per annum are still assessed (¶3194).
Compensation	May not be earnings. In the case of a payment made to an employee on the withdrawal of a savings-related share option scheme (¶3380), it was held that the payment was a recognition of the loss of the right to benefit from the scheme, and not made as a result of employment.
	However a payment to an employee in return for giving up a benefit was held to be taxable as earnings.
	Where an employer reimburses an employee in respect of bank charges, which have arisen due to a failing on the part of the employer, this will not be earnings.
Inducement	May be earnings if it can be shown that there is link between the payment and future services. A payment may be taxable even where the old employer, or an unrelated third party, makes a payment to induce an individual to take up employment with another employer.
Reasonable expenses	Paid to a teacher attending a course voluntarily has been held not to be earnings.

Type of payment	Details
Payments from someone other than the employer	Generally earnings, including tips to waiters or taxi drivers.
Payments to a third party	By the employer on behalf of the employee are earnings taxable on the employee. So payment of the employee's health club bill is taxable as earnings.
Payments made in exceptional circumstances	May not be taxable.
Payment anticipated by employee	It is likely that such a payment will be earnings.

Value of remuneration

Monetary payments made in the form of cash, cheque or bank transfer are the most common forms of earnings, and are easy to value. By their very nature, **non-monetary** remuneration, such as benefits in kind (¶3150) or shares (¶3340), does not have an immediate cash value, so special valuation rules exist. 3112

Time of assessment

Monetary earnings are assessed on a receipts basis, irrespective of when the services which relate to the earnings were actually performed (s 15 ITEPA 2003). There are special rules for non-monetary earnings such as benefits in kind, including vouchers. 3113

In most cases it is straightforward to ascertain when earnings are assessable, however, the following rules apply if earnings are paid:
– in a tax year **before commencement** of the employment, when the earnings will be assessed as occurring in the tax year when the employment commences;
– **after cessation** of the employment, such as the case of continuing medical benefit, when the earnings are assessed on a receipts basis; or
– **after death**, when it is likely that the employee's death estate will be assessed to income tax on a receipts basis.

Earnings for **employees** other than directors are treated as received on the earlier of the following dates (s 18(1) ITEPA 2003): 3114
– when the payment of earnings is made; or
– when the employee becomes entitled to the payment.

For directors, the rules are extended so that earnings (whether arising from the directorship or a different role) are treated as received on the earliest of the following dates (s 18(1) ITEPA 2003):
– when the payment of earnings is made;
– when the director becomes entitled to the payment;
– when sums on account of earnings are credited in the company accounts or records (regardless of whether the director has the right to draw the money);
– where the amount of earnings for a period has already been determined, the date on which the period of account ends; or
– where the period of account has already ended, the date when the amount of earnings for a period is determined.

MEMO POINTS It is common for a **general accrual** to be made for directors' bonuses in the draft accounts, which is then approved at the AGM. In this case the date of AGM will be the key date, unless the directors are also shareholders, when the date of the decision regarding the amount of bonuses will be the operative date.

B. Lump sum payments

3115 In addition to earnings paid in the normal course of employment, payments may also be made in the form of a lump sum on the commencement, termination or variation of employment. Such payments are often made as compensation for the loss or surrender of rights, or for failure to give notice of the termination of employment. Alternatively, a lump sum payment may simply be made to reward an employee for past or future services.

The nature of a lump sum payment will determine whether and how it is taxed.

1. Payments on commencement of employment

3120 The crucial question with respect to payments made on the commencement of employment, is whether the payment is a **reward** or an **inducement** for becoming an employee, in anticipation of future services. If this is the case, the payment will be taxed as earnings. In contrast, payments that are shown to be **compensation** for giving up an advantage relating to a previous employment will be free from income tax.

2. Payments on termination or variation of duties

Taxable as earnings

3123 The general rule is that termination payments are taxable in full as earnings if they arise out of a **contractual liability** or constitute a **reward for past services**.

The same criteria apply to lump sum payments paid on the variation of employment in connection with a change of duties.

MEMO POINTS Where a P45 is issued before the taxable termination payment is made, basic rate tax must be deducted from the taxable amount (reg 37 SI 2003/2683). Otherwise, the usual payroll procedures should be observed, and the taxable amount should be included on the P45.

Taxable under section 401

3124 Any other payments validly made on termination or variation in connection with a change of duties, will not be taxable as earnings. Instead, they are taxable under section 401 (s 401 ITEPA 2003).

There are four exemptions to the general charge under this regime which are **free from tax**:
- the £30,000 tax free amount;
- payments on death or disability;
- payments to an approved pension scheme; and
- certain payments relating to foreign service.

In addition the following **costs incurred by the employer** on behalf of the employee may be exempt from tax:
- outplacement counselling;
- retraining; and
- legal costs.

3125 **Tax free amount** This is the most common exemption, and the **maximum** exemption for each employment is £30,000 (s 401(1) ITEPA 2003). The exemption is applied first to cash payments and then benefits.

For these purposes **two or more payments** will be treated as deriving from the same employment and therefore eligible for only one £30,000 exemption where the payment is from:
- the same employer; or
- different employments with the same or associated employers (i.e. employers under common control).

If the threshold is **not used up in one tax year**, it can be carried forward and set against payments made in respect of the same employment in future tax years.

EXAMPLE A's employment with B Ltd was terminated on 31 December 2005. As compensation for the loss of employment, A was given a cash sum of £25,000 (payable in two equal instalments, on 31 December 2005 and 31 December 2006), and the use of his company car until 31 December 2006. The cash equivalent of the car for the termination payment was £3,000 for the period 1 January 2006 to 5 April 2006, and £8,000 for the period from 6 April 2006 to 31 December 2006.

The £30,000 exemption will be applied as follows:

	£
2005/06	
Termination payment	12,500
Cash equivalent of car	3,000
	15,500
Less: exemption (restricted)	(15,500)
	NIL
2006/07	
Termination payment	12,500
Cash equivalent of car	8,000
	20,500
Less: balance of exemption (30,000 – 15,500)	(14,500)
Taxable car benefit	6,000

Payments on death or disability Tax will not be **charged** on any payment or other benefit provided by an employer (s 406 ITEPA 2003): 3126
- in connection with the termination of employment on the death of an employee; or
- on account of injury to, or disability of, an employee.

To qualify under the latter exemption it must be established that either an injury or disability exists, and it was for this reason only that the employer made the payment.

This exemption must be considered at the time of the termination, as a **subsequent medical condition** cannot be cited as the reason for any payment.

MEMO POINTS For these tax purposes, the term **disability** covers not only a condition resulting from a sudden affliction but also continuing incapacity to perform the employment duties, arising from deterioration of physical or mental health caused by chronic illness. There must be medical evidence confirming the nature of the disability.

Payments to an approved pension scheme Where a lump sum is paid under the provisions of an approved occupational pension scheme, it will be exempt from tax and NIC if the payment is (s 407 ITEPA 2003): 3127
- compensation for either loss of employment or a decrease in earnings due to ill-health; or
- has been earned by past service.

MEMO POINTS Special **employer contributions** to an approved pension scheme (personal or occupational) will be exempt from tax and NIC, if the related benefits are within the scheme rules (s 408 ITEPA 2003). Similarly, tax will not be charged where the employer purchases an **approved annuity** from a life office for an employee.

Periods of foreign service A payment may be fully or partially exempt where an employee has undertaken foreign service **during** his employment (s 413 ITEPA 2003). A period of foreign service is essentially **defined** as a period when earnings are not liable to UK income tax. 3128

The following table sets out the **criteria** to be satisfied for the payment to be fully exempt:

Period of service up to termination	Period of foreign service
Any duration	At least 75% of the whole period of service
More than 10 years	The last 10 years of service
More than 20 years	At least 50% of the whole period of service, including any 10 of the last 20 years

3129 Where the employee's foreign service **does not meet the criteria** above, the termination payment will be taxed as follows (s 414 ITEPA 2003):
a. deduct the tax free sum of £30,000; and
b. apply the following fraction to the remaining amount to calculate the taxable payment.

$$\frac{\text{Foreign service}}{\text{Total service}} \times \text{Amount otherwise chargeable to tax}$$

3130 **Outplacement counselling** Where this is provided by the employer, the costs incurred (including related travel expenses) are not taxable on the employee, if all of the following conditions are met (s 310 ITEPA 2003):
a. the employee must have been employed for a 2-year period ending either when the counselling begins, or when the employment ends;
b. the only or main purpose of the counselling is to enable the employee to adjust to losing his job or find some other method of earning income (including self-employment);
c. the counselling is generally available to employees or a particular class of employee; and
d. the counselling consists of the giving of advice, imparting skills, or providing normal office facilities or equipment.

MEMO POINTS 1. In relation to **a**. above, **before 6 April 2005**, the employee must have been full-time during the 2 year period. For 2005/06 onwards, part-time employees are afforded the same relief.
2. Any amount attributable to outplacement counselling does not use up the £30,000 **tax free amount**.
3. There is tax relief for the costs of **re-training** provided by the employer in the event of redundancy (¶3210).

Legal costs

By concession, where an **employer agrees to pay** the employee's legal costs in relation to the termination of his employment, this would normally be a taxable benefit for the employee: Revenue and Customs' ESC A81.

However the employee will be **exempt from tax**, where either of the following conditions are met.
a. The dispute is **settled outside Court** and;
– the employer pays the solicitor direct;
– the fees paid only relate to the termination of employee; and
– the fees are paid under a specific term in the settlement agreement.
b. The dispute is settled under by a **Court Order** and payment is made under such an order (even if the payment is made direct to an employee).

Reporting requirements

3131 Employers must provide Revenue and Customs with a report including **details of** any payments or benefits in excess of £30,000 paid to employees on the termination or variation of employment, unless the payment is purely in cash and form P45 has not already been issued (reg 91 SI 2003/2682). The report must be submitted by 6 July following the end of the tax year. There is **no requirement** to report a termination package **worth less** than £30,000.

The report should **state** the following (reg 92 SI 2003/2682):
– the total package (including estimates where necessary);
– the payments and benefits paid in the year of termination;
– any future payments and benefits to be paid; and
– the total number of years in which the package will be paid with details of any event which would reduce this period.

Employees must be **provided with** the same information as contained within the report (reg 96 SI 2003/2682). The employee should include the termination payment on his tax return, to ensure the correct amount of tax is paid.

MEMO POINTS If an event occurs which causes the **reported payments to change**, a further report should be made by 6 July following the tax year in which the event occurs.

3. Specific provisions

Redundancy payments

Statutory redundancy payments are exempt from income tax. Such payments will however reduce the £30,000 tax free limit available for some termination payments (¶3124). 3132

EXAMPLE B was made redundant and received £15,000 of statutory redundancy pay. He was also given his company car (cash equivalent £17,000) as compensation. Although the redundancy pay will not be subject to tax, it will reduce the amount of the exemption available with respect to the car to £15,000 (30,000 – 15,000).
The taxable amount will therefore be £2,000 (17,000 – 15,000).

As with the general rule, **contractual** redundancy payments made under a company scheme which are genuine payments solely to compensate for loss of employment through redundancy will be taxed as a termination payment. However, payments which are really a terminal bonus as a reward for past services are taxable as earnings. 3133

Payments in lieu of notice

A payment in lieu of notice (PILON) includes the following: 3134
- a contractual payment made instead of giving adequate notice;
- a discretionary payment made by the employer instead of giving notice; and
- a payment agreed between the employer and employee at the time of termination with no prior contractual commitment or understanding.

The tax treatment will depend on whether the PILON has been made in breach of contract. If the contract of employment **provides for a PILON** to be made by the employer and the employer pays the employee according to this clause, there is no breach of contract and the payment is taxed as earnings. If, however, the contract of employment does **not provide for a PILON** and the employer fails to give the employee notice, any payment made to the employee for his notice period will be in breach of contract. The payment is deemed to constitute compensation for this breach and will not be treated as earnings.

Where an employer has established a practice of making non-contractual payments in lieu of notice, this may create an **implied term** in the employment contract, and subsequent payments to other employees in the same situation may be deemed to be taxable.

If a contractual PILON is subject to the **employer's discretion**, the payment will still constitute earnings as there is no breach of contract (*EMI Group Electronics Limited v Coldicott (HM Inspector of Taxes)* [1999] IRLR 630, CA). It may be argued that the employer did **not exercise his discretion** but instead breached the contract and paid compensation (*Cerberus Software Limited v Rowley* [2001] IRLR 160, CA). In such circumstances, all the factors need to be considered to ascertain whether the employer has exercised his discretion or not and to assess whether this is the case, Revenue and Customs have stated that it will consider the following factors to be relevant: Revenue and Customs' Tax Bulletin issue 63: 3135
- the settlement is substantially the same in value as the exercise of the discretion would have produced. If so, it goes towards indicating that the employer did exercise his discretion;
- the payment has characteristics normally associated with compensation or damages for breach of contract rather than those associated with a contractual payment (for example, where the payment has been reduced to reflect the fact that the employee has secured alternative employment before the end of the notice period). If so, it goes towards indicating that the employer did not exercise his discretion; and
- the decision not to exercise discretion is evidenced in writing. If so, it goes towards indicating that the employer chose not to exercise his discretion.

From *Richardson (HM Inspector of Taxes) v Delaney* [2001] IRLR 663, ChD, it can be seen that for any payment to be treated as compensation in breach of contract, it is advisable that **termination occurs before** any payment is agreed.

Garden leave

3137 If the employee is on garden leave, any payments made during the period will be taxable as earnings, because the employee is still employed until the end of the notice period, even though he is not attending his place of work.

Ex gratia payments on retirement or death

3138 Ex gratia payments of **lump sums or gratuities** made on the retirement or death of an employee (or in anticipation of retirement) by virtue of any arrangement will be **deemed to be** a retirement benefits scheme: Revenue and Customs' SP 13/91 (¶3127).

This does **not apply** to payments on redundancy or loss of office, or because of death or disability due to accident or ill health.

MEMO POINTS Revenue and Customs consider that an **arrangement exists where** the payment flows from any prior formal or informal understanding with the employee, or as a result of any system, plan, pattern or policy. Revenue and Customs provide the following examples of an arrangement:
- a decision at a meeting to make an ex gratia payment on the retirement of an employee;
- where a personnel manager makes an ex gratia payment under a delegated authority; or
- where it is common practice for an employer to make an ex gratia payment to a particular class of employee.

3139 Such retirement benefit payments will be subject to tax in full unless the employer obtains Revenue and Customs **approval** for the scheme, in which case the payments can be made without a charge to tax. However, an ex gratia **pension** paid to an employee (or his spouse or dependants) will always be chargeable to tax whether or not the scheme is approved.

An employer may **apply** for approval of an arrangement to pay an ex gratia lump sum where the payment:
- satisfies the normal requirements for tax approval of a retirement benefits scheme (including the limits on benefits); and
- is the only lump sum relevant benefit potentially payable in respect of the employment (unless the payment is made on retirement and there is a scheme providing death in service benefits). This means that the employee should not be a member of another retirement benefits scheme that is either approved or being considered for approval, or of a relevant statutory scheme.

Restrictive covenants

3140 Where an employer makes a payment in respect of a covenant (whether legally valid or not) given by an employee the intention of which is to restrict his activities or his ability to compete with his employer, the payment will generally be taxable as earnings (s 225 ITEPA 2003).

In practice, where restrictive covenants are part of a termination settlement, it is usual for a nominal amount to be allocated to such restrictive covenants in compromise agreements on the basis that such sums will be taxed as earnings (¶9278).

Unfair dismissal

3143 Where damages for unfair dismissal are awarded by an employment tribunal, the tax treatment will depend on whether the employee is reinstated.

Where reinstatement or re-engagement occurs, a compensation payment for arrears of pay from the date of dismissal to the date of reinstatement or re-engagement is assessable as earnings. However, this was recently held not to apply to a negotiated settlement following an order to reinstate/re-engage (*Wilson (Inspector of Taxes) v Clayton* [2004] IRLR 611, ChD). Otherwise any compensatory awards are a valid termination payment.

II. Benefits and expenses

Most benefits in kind are assessable on most employees. Usually an employee will also be assessed on expenses incurred by the employer, subject to making a claim for a business expense deduction against earnings. Benefits and expenses should include VAT where relevant, and are not subject to deduction of income tax through the payroll. Instead, the employer reports any relevant items to Revenue and Customs on forms P11D or P9D, and the employee pays tax through his PAYE code for the next year, or through his self-assessment return. 3145

Classification of employees

The rules for benefits in kind and expenses depend on the type of employee, defined as follows (s 216 ITEPA 2003): 3146

Term	Definition	Directors (¶3148)
Relevant employee	An individual who either earns £8,500 or more per annum	✔
Lower paid	An individual earning less than £8,500 per annum	X (with a limited exception)

Summaries of the different tax treatment for benefits and expenses depending on the type of employee can be found at ¶3194 and ¶3270 respectively.

To determine whether the **threshold** of £8,500 has been met or exceeded, the following items should be taken into account, on the basis of amounts earned in the tax year (s 218 ITEPA 2003): 3147
- salary;
- all benefits received whether taxable on all employees or under the provisions relating to relevant employees (including share schemes etc), excluding exempt income;
- any deemed earnings arising from the personal service company provisions; and
- expenses incurred by the employee and reimbursed by the employer (other than when a dispensation (¶6900) is in force).

Deductions may be made for approved pension contributions and contributions under payroll giving schemes. No deduction is made for expenses of employment.

MEMO POINTS 1. If an employee is employed for only **part of the year**, the threshold is compared to the annualised earnings.

2. Where a person has **two or more employments** with the same employer, the total income from all employments is aggregated. If the threshold is exceeded, the employee is treated as a relevant employee for all of the employments (s 220 ITEPA 2003).

Directors

As directors are in a position of control, they may be able to influence the level of benefits which they receive and are therefore identified separately (s 67 ITEPA 2003). 3148

A director (including a shadow director, whose instructions the directors usually follow) is **treated as** a relevant employee **unless** he earns less than £8,500 per annum, does not have a material interest (essentially more than 5% of the ordinary share capital of a company) and either:
- he is a full-time working director (devoting substantially the whole of his time to the service of the company in a managerial or technical capacity); or
- he is a director of a non-profit making company or charitable organisation.

A. Benefits

3150 A benefit in kind (referred to in this section as a benefit) **is usually** a payment made other than in cash to an employee or director (or a member of his family or household) by reason of his employment. Certain minor benefits which are available to all employees of an employer may be specifically exempted.

The **general test** is whether such a payment is one made in return for acting as, or being, an employee. This means that payments or provisions made by an employer (other than a company) in the normal course of his **social relationships** will not constitute benefits. It is not necessary for the benefit to be from the employer for it to be taxable, although it must be provided by **virtue of the employment**. For example, a car provided to a professional footballer by a car dealer would be an assessable benefit.

Goods and services provided to an employee as a result of his employment will not be assessable if they are **for business purposes only**. Where there is an **element of private use** or where an **asset is transferred** to the employee an assessable benefit may arise.

3151 A benefit may also arise where a payment is made to a member of an employee's **family or household** as a result of the employment (s 721(5) ITEPA 2003). Family is generally defined as the employee's spouse, parents and children (and their spouses) and dependants. Household has the same definition but also includes servants and guests.

3152 This section identifies various benefits and explains the valuation rules applicable to each type. Exempt benefits are discussed before taxable benefits, and reference should be made first to the table at ¶3155, before consulting the table at ¶3190.

1. Non-taxable benefits

Summary

3155 The following table provides a summary of the benefits which are not taxable on any employee.

General area	Specific benefit	Basic conditions	Legislation reference (ITEPA 2003)	¶¶
Subsistence	Meals and drinks	Provided to all employees on similar terms.	s 317	¶3157
	Luncheon vouchers	Up to 15p per day.	s 89	
	Homeworking allowance	Up to £104 per annum. Further amount if appropriate evidence retained.	s 316A	¶3326
Travel	Workplace parking space	For cars, motorbikes and bicycles (also vans from 6 April 2005).	s 237	
	Mileage allowances	If within certain limits dependent on mileage.	s 229	¶3303
	Free transport	Travel, accommodation and subsistence provided during a public transport strike.	s 245	
		Employer subsidised public bus services.	s 243	
		Work bus provided for journey between home and workplace, including minibuses with at least 9 seats.	s 242	
		Travel between workplace and home for occasional late night working (9pm or later), less than 60 nights a year.	s 248	
		Provision of alternative transport when expected car sharing arrangements are not available.	s 248	
		Travel from home to workplace for disabled employees.	s 246	
	Cycling	Cycles and related safety equipment made available to all employees, and used mainly for commuting.	s 244	
		Provision of breakfast to cyclists on an unlimited number of designated cycle to work days.	SI 2002/205 reg 3	
	Use of a heavy goods vehicle	Exceeding 3,500kg fully laden and mainly used for business purposes.	s 238	
Training and counselling	Work related training	Includes retraining programs on redundancy.	ss 250, 251, 311, 312	¶3159
	Scholarships	Not received by reason of employment.	s 211	¶3162
	Welfare counselling	Made available to all employees on similar terms. Not relating to finance (other than debt), tax, legal issues, or leisure.	SI 2000/2080	
	Pensions advice	From 6 April 2005, external advice paid for by the employer up to £150 per annum.	SI 2004/3087	

General area	Specific benefit	Basic conditions	Legislation reference (ITEPA 2003)	¶¶
Provision of equipment	Computer equipment	Where value of equipment is less than £2,500, and made available on similar terms to all employees (not just directors).	s 320	¶3165
	Mobile phones (including car phones)	All private use exempt except if paid for by voucher, or employer pays bill in employee's name.	s 319	¶3167
Medical costs	Medical check ups	Routine health checks and medical screening for employees and their families.	Tax Bulletin 7	
	Overseas medical costs	Medical insurance and treatment during foreign visits where performing employment duties.	s 325	
Miscellaneous	Childcare	Workplace facilities exempt.	s 318	¶3171
		First £50 per employee per week of direct nursery payment exempt.	s 318A	¶3173
	Parties and functions	Cost up to £150 per head. Event must be available to employees generally.	s 264	¶3175
	Removal expenses	Up to £8,000 exempt.	s 271	¶3177
	Job related accommodation	Where necessary or for better performance of duties, or for security reasons.	ss 99, 100	¶3201
	Long service awards	For at least 20 years of service; Not cash; and Maximum £50 per year for each year of service up to 20 years.	s 323	¶3180
	Sports facilities	Available to all employees but not to general public. From 6 April 2005, facilities also made available by an employer, who is not the employee's own employer, is also exempt.	s 261 SI 2004/3087	
	Staff suggestion schemes	Open to all employees on equal terms.	s 321	¶3182
	Entertaining and gifts from third parties	Cost of gift to donor is £250 or less.	s 324	¶3184
	Personal equipment for disabled individuals	Provision of equipment and services to enable duties of employment to be performed.	SI 2002/1596	

Provisions of meals and canteen facilities

3157 A benefit does not arise where employees are provided with canteen facilities, even if the canteen is not in the employer's premises, or under his control (s 317 ITEPA 2003). The **basic premise** of the exemption is that all staff of the employer, or at least all at a particular location, are provided with a meal, however the exemption also applies where:
- meals are provided on a reasonable scale; and
- the employer gives free or subsidised meal vouchers to staff for whom meals are not provided.

MEMO POINTS 1. The exemption also extends to **light refreshments** such as tea and coffee.
2. From 6 April 2005, no benefit arises where free or subsidised canteen facilities are made available at the **premises of another employer** (SI 2004/3087).

Work related training

Where an employee attends training **courses** paid for by his employer, no benefit arises provided the training is related to his current employment or to a position with the employer to which he is likely to be appointed (ss 250, 251 ITEPA 2003). In addition to the actual training course, this exemption covers any **associated costs** (for example, accommodation, examination fees and registration fees which become payable as a result of achieving a qualification) and **assets provided** for use by the employee during the period of training, or in his employment. 3159

The exemption does **not apply** to entertainment and recreation costs or courses provided as an inducement or reward for services.

Certain benefits provided for employees at a **time of redundancy** are not taxable (s 311 ITEPA 2003). These include training courses (including related travel costs) of up to 2 years' duration, allowing the employee to retrain for a new career. The exemption will apply where the employee's job has already been terminated, or he ceases to be employed within 2 years of the beginning of the course. Counselling services in connection with redundancy are also excluded from the charge to tax (¶3130). 3160

MEMO POINTS **Before 6 April 2005**, the course had to be wholly or substantially full-time, and its duration was limited to 12 months.

Scholarships

Generally income from a scholarship is exempt from tax for the recipient (ss 211-213 ITEPA 2003). However, where an employee, or a member of his family or household, receives a scholarship by reason of employment, it will be taxable on the employee (unless the employer is an individual, and the scholarship is made as a result of a social relationship). 3162

By **exception**, where the employer makes a scholarship available to a member of the employee's family or household, but only as a result of fortuitous circumstances (such as the employee's child wins the scholarship through a public exam), the income will be exempt, if all of the following conditions are met:
– the scholarship is not provided by reason of employment;
– the funds are provided by a trust fund or a scheme;
– the scholarship is to be held by an individual in full-time education, such as a school or university student; and
– less than 25% of the payments made by the trust are scholarship payments provided by reason of employment.

An employee who receives a scholarship from his employer for undertaking a **full-time educational course** for the 2005/06 academic year, will by concession, be exempt from tax up to a maximum of £15,000 per annum (a rate of £1,250 per month): Revenue and Customs' SP 4/86. If this limit is exceeded the whole amount will become taxable. 3163

MEMO POINTS 1. **To qualify** for the exemption, the employee must be enrolled in the educational establishment for at least one academic year with an average attendance of not less than 20 weeks per year. The exemption does not apply to payments for periods spent at work (whether during college vacations or otherwise).
2. For **earlier academic years** (including 2004/05) the limit was £7,000 per annum, and the payments were only NIC free if paid under a training contract.

Computer equipment

The provision of computer equipment (including peripheral items, such as printers and software) for an employee to use at home is **wholly exempt if** (s 320 ITEPA 2003): 3165
– the ownership of the equipment is not transferred to the employee;
– the equipment is available on terms which do not favour directors; and

– the market value of the equipment (including ongoing maintenance costs) does not exceed £2,500.

Where the **cash equivalent** (taking 20% of the market value) of such a benefit exceeds £500, only the excess will be taxable.

Mobile phones

3167 The provision of a mobile phone (including a car phone or blackberry) is not an assessable benefit (s 319 ITEPA 2003). However there are two potential situations where an income tax charge **may still arise, if** the employer:
– pays amounts relating to a contract in the name of the employee, income tax will be due on any rental element; or
– provides the employee with a pay as you go phone, any vouchers purchased will be taxable.

Childcare

3169 The tax relief afforded to employees with **parental responsibilities** has been improved from 6 April 2005, and the following now potentially qualify:
– employer provided childcare facilities; and
– direct payment for childcare by the employer.

From 6 April 2005, where an employer offers either scheme, it must be open to all employees or to all those working at a specific site where the scheme is offered.

MEMO POINTS Employers can include childcare as **part of an overall package** which offers the benefit:
a. as an addition to the existing salary;
b. as part of a flexible benefits scheme; or
c. in return for a sacrifice of salary.
In respect of **b**. and **c**. above, the employer should ensure any salary reduction is carefully structured, and recorded in the employee's terms and conditions of employment. Otherwise the reduction will not be effective for tax or NIC purposes.

3171 **Facilities** To be excluded from taxation (and also NIC), childcare facilities must be housed in non-domestic premises that are **provided** either **by** the employer, or by a group of people including the employer (s 318 ITEPA 2003). The employer must be wholly or partly responsible for managing and financing the provision of childcare facilities. Any registration requirements for either the staff or the premises must be met.

Childcare may be provided **to** any child under 18 years of age (including a stepchild) of the employee, who either lives with the employee or is maintained fully by the employee, or for whom he has a parental responsibility.

MEMO POINTS 1. There are many **commercially marketed schemes** which involve an employee entering into a salary sacrifice arrangement, whereby he gives up an amount of pay equal to the cost of the nursery place that is provided. The employer pays for the nursery place for the employee's child, but also pays an additional annual fee per place. The employer appoints a scheme promoter to act as agent at meetings with the nursery management committee.
Revenue and Customs may attack these arrangements as follows:
– the salary sacrifice is not effective, so the full salary is taxable;
– the nursery place is in reality a contract between the employee and nursery, so the amount paid by the employer is taxable as earnings; or
– the financing and management criteria are not met because the arrangements are a sham.
2. **Before 6 April 2005**, there was no requirement for facilities to be made available to all employees or individuals working at the location where the scheme was offered.

3173 **Direct payment** From 6 April 2005, the first £50 per week per employee of any direct childcare payment has become exempt from tax (and NIC), regardless of the number of children involved (ss 318A, 270A ITEPA 2003). The contract must be between the employer and the childcare provider. Alternatively the employer can provide vouchers with a face value of up to £50 per week which will also be exempt (the administration costs incurred by the employer are not an assessable benefit for the employee).

For this exemption, a **qualifying child** is a child aged 15 or less, up to 1st September following the child's 15th birthday; and either:
– a child or stepchild of the employee who is maintained (wholly or partly) at the employee's expense; or
– is resident with the employee, for whom he has parental responsibility.

Two employees can receive exempt benefit for the same child.

The **type** of childcare which qualifies for the exemption includes registered or approved care provided by:
– a registered childminder;
– a school or educational establishment;
– a school or local authority, for children who are at least 8 years old, in relation to pre- and after-school care; and
– a registered nanny in the child's own home.

However, care provided by the employee's partner (married or unmarried) will not qualify. Care provided in the child's house by a relative is also precluded.

MEMO POINTS 1. **Nannies** should be registered as childminders for their costs to qualify for this exemption.
2. The definition of **relative** includes parents, grandparents, siblings, aunts and uncles.
3. For **disabled children**, the age requirement is extended by a year to 16.
4. The provision of childcare facilities which are tax exempt may affect a claim for **tax credits**, in which case Revenue and Customs should be notified.

Parties and functions

There is an exemption which applies to an **annual party** (e.g. a Christmas party), or similar annual event (e.g. a summer barbecue), provided for employees where the cost per head does not exceed £150, and the party is either available to (s 264(3) ITEPA 2003): 3175
– all employees generally; or
– all those working at a specific location, where the employer has more than one location.

If the employer provides **two or more annual functions**, no charge arises in respect of the events for which the costs per head do not exceed £150 in aggregate. If the aggregate cost per head exceeds £150 per head, then the events within the limit are exempt (choosing the best combination), and the others are taxable.

The **cost of the function** is calculated by adding together all costs, including VAT and transport, and dividing by the number of all attendees (including non-employees).

Removal expenses

When an individual relocates due to his employment, removal expenses **up to a maximum** of £8,000 may be paid by the employer without being treated as a benefit, where they consist of (ss 271-289 ITEPA 2003): 3177
– reimbursements from his employer in respect of removal costs; or
– costs directly incurred by the employer.

For these purposes, **relocation includes** the situation where an employee moves:
– in order to take up a new employment;
– as a result of being given a new job within the organisation; or
– where the location of the current employment changes.

The relocation must be **necessitated by** the old residence not being within a reasonable daily travelling distance of the workplace. The new home obviously must be within commutable distance.

MEMO POINTS 1. Where **payments exceed £8,000**, the excess will be taxed, although **lower** paid employees (¶3192) are only assessable on payments made to them in respect of their costs, not on expenses directly incurred by the employer (s 287 ITEPA 2003).

2. Revenue and Customs take a common sense approach to **reasonable daily travelling distance** taking into account both travelling time and distance.

3178 The removal **costs** may include the following (s 272 ITEPA 2003):
– fees in connection with selling the previous residence and acquiring the new one (including stamp taxes and legal costs);
– fees in connection with an abortive acquisition, where the intended new residence is not acquired due to circumstances outside the employee's control, or other reasonable circumstances;
– costs of transporting belongings including insurance, reconnection fees etc;
– costs of replacing equipment which is not suitable for use at the new residence (e.g. replacing a gas cooker with an electric one where the new residence is not connected to the gas supply);
– travel and subsistence costs (e.g. costs incurred in going to view possible properties); and
– bridging loan expenses to the extent that the loan is used to purchase the new residence and does not exceed the proceeds from the sale of the old residence (including loans by the employer).

Generally, qualifying removal costs must be **incurred by** the end of the tax year following the tax year in which the employee relocated, although Revenue and Customs have discretion to extend this time limit.

Long service awards

3180 For service in excess of 20 years, awards **consisting of** assets or shares in the employing company valued at up to a maximum of £50 for each year of service (up to 20 years) can be made to staff without a tax charge (s 323(2) ITEPA 2003). Where the maximum has been exceeded and the award was made in cash, an assessable benefit will arise for all employees. Relevant employees (¶3146) will also be assessable where an award in excess of the maximum is made in the form of an asset.

Staff suggestion schemes

3182 Awards may be made to employees under qualifying staff suggestion schemes (ss 321, 322 ITEPA 2003). **To qualify**, a staff suggestion scheme must be open to all employees on equal terms and the suggestion concerned must be outside an employee's normal duties.

Awards are usually only made when a suggestion is **implemented** and should not exceed:
– 50% of the expected net benefit of implementation in the first year; or
– 10% of the expected net benefit over 5 years subject to an overriding maximum of £5,000.

Where a cash award is non-qualifying it will be assessable on all employees. Relevant employees (¶3146) will also be assessable where a non-qualifying award is made in the form of an asset.

MEMO POINTS 1. Suggestions made during **meetings** are considered part of the employee's normal duties.
2. Where the award **exceeds** £5,000, the excess is taxable.
3. Where a suggestion is **not implemented**, but the employer wants to encourage future suggestions, the maximum award is £25.

Third party gifts and entertaining

3184 **Goodwill gifts** (such as a bottle of wine from the employer's client) can be received by an employee without an income tax charge where all of the following conditions are met (s 324 ITEPA 2003):
– the cost to the donor is less than £250 (including the cumulative cost of all gifts within the same tax year);
– the gift is a voucher to acquire goods, or an actual good;
– the donor is not connected to the employer, or anyone connected with him; and
– the gift is unsolicited and not given in return for the employee's service.

Where someone other than the employer entertains an employee, including hospitality of any kind, there will be no taxable benefit if all of the following conditions are met (s 265 ITEPA 2003): 3185
- the entertaining was not procured by the employer, or anyone connected with him;
- the person providing the entertainment is not connected with the employer; and
- the hospitality is not provided in return for any services of the employee.

If these **conditions are not met**, the third party must provide the employee with information about the amount of the benefit, which the employee should then include as assessable income on his tax return.

2. Taxable benefits

Summary of common benefits 3190

Benefit	Taxed on		Legislative reference (ITEPA 2003)	¶¶
	Lower paid	Relevant (£8,500+)		
Accommodation	✔	✔	s 102	¶3200
Ancillary expenses and services for accommodation	×	✔	s 315	¶3218
Vouchers and credit cards	✔	✔	ss 73, 266	¶3208
Permanent health benefits	✔	✔	s 660	¶3211
Medical insurance	×	✔	s 325	¶3194
Use of assets [1]	×	✔	s 205	¶3215
Transfer of assets	✔ [2]	✔	s 206	¶3216
Company cars	×	✔	s 114	¶3221
Car fuel	×	✔	s 149	¶3229
Company vans	×	✔	s 154	¶3233
Cheap loans	×	✔	s 173	¶3238
Payment of director's PAYE	×	✔	s 223	¶3247

1. Excluding cars, phones and accommodation.
2. See ¶3192.

Lower paid employees

With the exception of living accommodation and vouchers (which have specific valuation rules), lower paid employees are **principally assessable** only on items that can readily be converted into cash. 3192

This means that, in the absence of specific legislation, lower paid employees are only assessable on items which can be sold. For example, the right to use a car cannot be sold and therefore a lower paid employee would not be assessable. However, a gift of a car would be assessable as the employee could sell the car for cash. The cash equivalent of **an asset transferred** is the second-hand value, i.e. the amount the benefit can be sold for. No comparison is made with the market value of the asset.

Relevant employees

Relevant employees are taxed on every benefit received by reason of employment, such as private medical insurance, prizes, or gym membership, unless a specific exemption exists (s 201 ITEPA 2003). Generally, the time at which the benefit becomes taxable is when it can be enjoyed by the employee, which may be later than the time when the expenditure is incurred by the employer. Where an assessable benefit arises, the cash equivalent of the benefit is included as income of the employee and taxed accordingly. 3194

3195 The **cash equivalent** is generally calculated as follows.

Full cost to provider of benefit	£
Full cost to provider of benefit	X
Less: employee contribution	(X)
Cash equivalent	X

However, where a **cash alternative** is offered in lieu of the benefit, the value of the benefit will be the amount of cash offered. The exception to this is living accommodation, where the benefit will be valued under the rules in ¶3200 if this provides a higher figure than the amount of cash offered.

MEMO POINTS Where the benefit consists of the provision of **in-house benefits** arising out of **surplus capacity**, the cash equivalent is usually the marginal cost incurred by the provider the benefit. For example, in the case of a school educating the sons of teachers for reduced fees, the cost of providing education was not the fees that other parents paid, but the marginal cost to the school in having one extra pupil attend (*Pepper v Hart* [1993] AC 593).

a. Benefits chargeable on all employees

Living accommodation

3200 Living accommodation is not specifically **defined** but it is taken to mean all kinds of residential accommodation with the exception of overnight accommodation, a stay in a hotel room or board and lodging.

The provision of living accommodation, other than job related accommodation, by reason of employment will constitute a **benefit for** all employees whether provided to the employee himself, or a member of his family or household (s 102 ITEPA 2003). Ancillary services provided with the accommodation are only taxable on relevant employees (¶3146).

3201 The provision of living accommodation **in connection with the employment** will not be taxable where it falls within one of the **following exceptions** (ss 99-100 ITEPA 2003):

a. where it is necessary for the proper performance of the employee's duties that he should occupy the accommodation e.g. a caretaker;

b. where the accommodation is provided for the better performance of the duties of his employment, and his is one of the kinds of employment where it is customary for employers to provide living accommodation for employees e.g. farm workers; or

c. where, because of a special threat to the employee's security, special security arrangements are in force and he resides in the accommodation as part of those arrangements e.g. the chairman of a company providing politically sensitive and therefore high risk services.

The exemptions outlined in **a.** and **b.** above will not be available to a **director** unless he is a full-time working director with either:
- no material interest in the company; or
- he is a director of a non-profit making or charitable company.

MEMO POINTS 1. Providing accommodation for the **employee's convenience** is not job related accommodation, and the exemption does not apply.
2. A further exemption is available where a **local authority provides** accommodation for an employee on terms which are not more favourable than those made available to non-employees.

3202 **Valuation of the benefit** Where taxable living accommodation is provided to an employee, the way in which the benefit is valued depends on the cost of the property. All accommodation is subject to the same cash equivalent calculation, but property with a cost to the employer in excess of £75,000 is also subject to an additional charge. Where the ownership period of the person providing the accommodation exceeds the 6 years before it is first occupied by the employee, cost is substituted by the market value at the date the property is first occupied (including any improvements made between acquisition and first occupation), provided the original costs of purchase and subsequent improvements were in excess of £75,000.

MEMO POINTS 1. If a **cash alternative** is offered instead of the accommodation, this may affect the value of the taxable benefit.
2. **Shared accommodation** is taxed by apportioning the benefit fairly between the employee occupants.

Vouchers and credit cards

When any employee (or a family member) receives **vouchers or credit tokens**, an assessable benefit arises (s 75 ITEPA 2003). A voucher is defined for this purpose as any voucher, stamp or similar document, or token capable of being exchanged for money, goods or services and includes transport vouchers and cheques. A credit token is something which allows the holder to obtain goods or services on presentation, without actually being surrendered at that time. 3208

The following are specifically **excluded** from the benefit rules:
- luncheon vouchers of up to 15p per day;
- childcare vouchers with a face value of up to £50 per week per employee;
- non-cash vouchers or credit tokens provided to enable an employee to obtain the use of a parking space at or near his place of work; and
- non-cash vouchers or credit tokens provided to an employee by someone other than the employer to obtain entertainment or hospitality that is not in recognition of the employment.

Vouchers give rise to a tax liability as if the employee had received a **sum equal** to the cost of providing the voucher. Where a **credit token** is used, the **cash equivalent** is the expense incurred for the provision of the credit token. Where the token can be used on multiple occasions, the value of the benefit at each use is the additional cost to the employer. Initial or annual subscriptions are ignored, as is interest.

For both vouchers and credit tokens, a **deduction** will be made against the taxable benefit for any sum made good by the employee.

MEMO POINTS 1. **Pay as you go** mobile phone vouchers are taxable.
2. Concessions are available which allow some **employees of passenger transport undertakings**, such as railway companies, to receive non-taxable travel vouchers.

Strictly, where a **credit card** is made available to any employee by reason of his employment, the employee will be taxed on any cost incurred on the card, including any subscription cost, but not any interest for late payment (s 94 ITEPA 2003). 3209

The following **exceptions** exist, however, when:
- the employer receives Revenue and Customs' approval that no tax liability will result from purely business use of the credit card; or
- the credit card is used to pay for exempt benefits, such as workplace parking, third party entertainment, incidental overnight costs or other exempt travel expenses.

If the credit card is used to purchase **readily convertible assets**, PAYE should be applied by the employer.

Permanent health benefits

Where the employer pays into a permanent health insurance policy, and the employee receives benefits whilst suffering from ill-health, the employee will be taxed on those benefits as if they were earnings. 3211

If the policy is not funded by the employer, any benefits will be exempt.

---

b. Benefits charged on relevant employees only

Assets made available

Where assets are made available (other than cars or vans) for a relevant employee's private use, the **cash equivalent** of the benefit is based on the annual value of the asset (s 205 ITEPA 2003). The annual value is calculated as 20% of the market value of the asset when first 3215 made available to the employee. Any expenses incurred in connection with the provision of the asset are added to the benefit. Where the employer pays rent or a hire charge for the asset and this is greater than the annual value calculated above, the amount paid is substituted for the annual value.

The **exceptions** are (s 207 ITEPA 2003):
– land which is valued on the basis of the rent which might reasonably be expected to be obtained on letting; and
– computer equipment which may be exempt (¶3165).

3216 Where assets are **transferred** to a **lower paid employee**, the amount of benefit is the second-hand value of the asset (s 206 ITEPA 2003).

Where assets (other than bicycles and computers) are transferred to a **relevant employee**, a benefit arises which is equal to the higher of the market value at the following times:
– at the time of transfer; or
– when first made available to an employee, if the asset has already used by the employee, less amounts already taxed (both on the employee in question and other employees (¶3215)).

This amount is then **reduced by** any price paid by the employee.

MEMO POINTS In certain circumstances, the provision of computers and bicycles is exempt from tax (¶3155). From 6 April 2005, the benefit, chargeable on the transfer of a previously loaned computer or bicycle (which qualified for exemption whilst loaned) into an employee's ownership, is based on the asset's current market value only. So where the employee buys the asset from the employer at this value, no benefit will arise.

Ancillary services for living accommodation

3218 Ancillary services provided in connection with living accommodation may give rise to an assessable benefit for relevant employees, and **include**:
– heating, lighting or cleaning;
– repairs, maintenance or decoration (excluding structural alterations);
– council tax; and
– furniture or other effects normal for domestic occupation.

The **cash equivalent** of the benefit is generally the cost to the employer (e.g. if the employer provides a cleaner, the cash equivalent of the benefit will be the cleaner's wages and the cost of items such as cleaning materials) (ss 203 – 205 ITEPA 2003). The **exception** to this rule is where the ancillary service is in the form of an asset (for example a television) which is made available to the employee. In this case the cash equivalent will be valued in accordance with the rules for assets made available for the private use of employees (¶3215).

3219 Where the provision of living accommodation is not taxable because the employee satisfies one of the **exceptions** in ¶3201, the amount assessable in respect of ancillary services is restricted to 10% of the taxable earnings (excluding this benefit) from the employment, and then reduced by any amounts paid by the employee (s 315 ITEPA 2003).

In addition, **council tax** paid by the employer in relation to job-related accommodation is not assessable (s 314 ITEPA 2003).

MEMO POINTS **Taxable earnings** are defined as remuneration after deducting pension contributions, and deductible expenses, including capital allowances.

Company cars

3221 A benefit occurs when a car (often referred to as a company car) is provided, by reason of the employment, and is **available** for private **use** by a relevant employee (including a member of the employee's family or household) (s 114 ITEPA 2003). A car is **defined** as any mechanically propelled road vehicle, with the exception of vehicles that are unsuitable for private use, or used to convey goods or burden (other than passengers). Invalid carriages are also excluded from the definition.

The employer should **report** the provision of a car to an employee within 28 days of the end of the quarter in which the car is first made available.

A car is treated as being available for **private use** unless such use is both prohibited by the employer, and none actually occurs (s 118 ITEPA 2003). 3222

Pool cars (including vans) are treated as not being available for private use, and where an employee has use of a genuine pool car an assessable benefit will not arise (s 167 ITEPA 2003). A car is treated as a pool car if all of the **following conditions** are satisfied:
– it is made available to, and actually used by, a number of employees and is not usually used by one of them to the exclusion of the others;
– it is not normally kept overnight at or near the home of any of the employees who use it; and
– any private use is incidental to its business use.

A car (including the provision of fuel and other related expenses) made available to a **disabled employee** by an employer, will not constitute a benefit where all of the following conditions are satisfied (s 247 ITEPA 2003): 3223
– the car has been specially adapted for the employee's needs (or is an automatic car where required);
– the car is only available for business travel, home to work travel and travel to training, and any other private use is prohibited; and
– no private use actually occurs.

Where accessories are added to **convert a car** for a disabled person, the price of such accessories is not a benefit (s 125 ITEPA 2003). If the vehicle is an **automatic car** provided to a disabled employee, the carbon dioxide emissions figure for an equivalent manual car should be used (s 138 ITEPA 2003).

Accessories provided for use in the performance of the **duties of the employment** are not assessed as a benefit. A mobile phone is not treated as an accessory (ss 172, 126, 127 ITEPA 2003). The price of **other** accessories (not supplied as standard) which are added when a car is first made available, will increase its price. If accessories are added later, the price of such accessories is added to the price of the car for the year in which the accessories are added and in all subsequent years. 3224

In both cases the **price** of an accessory is usually taken to be the list price. Individual accessories with a price of less than £100 are ignored.

MEMO POINTS **Replacement accessories** are normally ignored unless the replacement is superior to the original. In such a case the price of the car is increased by the difference between the price of the new accessory and the price of the original.

Valuation of the benefit The **cash equivalent** of the benefit of a car made available for private use by an employee is a percentage of the list price of the car (which cannot exceed 35%), **determined by** the level of the car's carbon dioxide (CO_2) emissions and the date it was first registered. There are no reductions for high business mileage. Cars **registered before 1 January 1998** will not have a CO_2 emissions figure and therefore the benefit continues to be based on the engine capacity (whether petrol or diesel). Additional discounts of the standard charge apply to **dual fuel cars** and there is no assessable benefit on the cost of conversion. 3225

Once the cash equivalent is calculated there is no separate charge on any **other costs** associated with the provision of the car (such as insurance and servicing). The exceptions to this rule are the cost relating to the provision of a chauffeur which is assessed as a separate benefit under the normal rules (¶3194), and the provision of fuel for private motoring (¶3229).

MEMO POINTS 1. The **price of the car** is the list price, if it has one or, if not, the notional price, reduced by any capital contributions made by the employee (s 121(1) ITEPA 2003). The price actually paid for the car is irrelevant. The **maximum price** of a car is restricted to £80,000.
The **notional price** is the price which might reasonably be expected to be the list price if its manufacturer, importer or distributor had published one, for an equivalent car sold in the UK in a single open market sale on the day before its first registration.

2. Where an employee makes one or more **capital contributions** to the cost of a car, the price of the car is reduced by the amount of the total contributions in that and earlier years, subject to a maximum of £5,000. No such deduction is made if the car's price exceeds £80,000.

3227 The cash equivalent by also be **reduced** to take account of any periods of unavailability or any employee contributions, in that order (s 143 ITEPA 2003).

A **period of unavailability** will arise when the car:
– is made available or withdrawn part way through the year; or
– is off the road for a period of at least 30 days (which may run into a new tax year).

Any amount **paid by the employee** as a condition of using the car during the tax year, reduces the cash equivalent (s 144 ITEPA 2003).

Car fuel

3229 If private fuel is provided for a car by reason of employment, a further benefit arises, unless the car is a pool car (¶3222) (s 150 ITEPA 2003).

Where fuel is provided for a **non-company** car, the value of the benefit is the cost of providing the benefit. Where private fuel is provided for a **company car** (¶3221), the **cash equivalent** of the benefit is calculated by multiplying a fixed sum (£14,400 from 6 April 2003) by the appropriate percentage determined by the level of the car's carbon dioxide (CO_2). Often an employee will be better off paying for private fuel himself, rather than being charged a fuel benefit.

To avoid any benefit but ensure the employee and employer are not out of pocket, either the employee can **fully reimburse** the employer for private fuel, or the employer can reimburse the employee for business fuel. **Partial reimbursement** by the employee will not reduce the fuel benefit.

3231 The cash equivalent of the fuel will be **reduced** where (s 152 ITEPA 2003):
– the cash equivalent of the car benefit is reduced because it is unavailable for use throughout the tax year; and
– free fuel ceases to be available to an employee from any date to the end of the tax year (although if free fuel is provided later in the same tax year, no reduction is due).

Company vans

3233 Where an employer makes a van (s any mechanically propelled road vehicle (not exceeding 3500 kg fully laden) which is primarily suited to the conveyance of goods of any description) available for the **private use** of a relevant employee (or a member of his family or household), an assessable benefit arises. Until 6 April 2007, no additional benefit arises where fuel is provided for private use.

From 6 April 2005, an employee who uses a van for mainly business purposes and who takes it **home overnight** is not taxed on a benefit where (s 168 ITEPA 2003, Sch 14 Finance Act 2004):
– he only uses the van for commuting; and
– any other private use is insignificant.

MEMO POINTS Revenue and Customs has published guidance on the interpretation of **insignificant**, which is deemed to take its dictionary meaning of "too small or unimportant to be worth consideration."

3235 The **cash equivalent** of the benefit is a standard charge, which is set at (s 154 ITEPA 2003, Sch 14 Finance Act 2004):
– £500 for a van which is less than 4 years old at the end of the tax year; and
– £350 for an older van.

The amount of the cash equivalent is **reduced** proportionately for each day where the van is either unavailable (¶3227) or is a shared van. Any payments made by the employee for private use may also be deducted from the cash equivalent.

MEMO POINTS **From 6 April 2007**, the following changes will apply:
– the standard charge will increase to £3,000;

- there will be no discount for older vans; and
- a fuel benefit of £500 will apply for any private fuel provided.

Shared vans A van is a shared van for any period throughout which it is available (but not necessarily used) **simultaneously** to more than one employee of the same employer (s 156 ITEPA 2003). 3236

There are two ways in which the **cash equivalent** can be calculated, although it is important to note that the total benefit for any individual employee can never exceed £500 (or £350 for older vans), irrespective of the number of vans made available to him. The employee may choose, on a tax year by tax year basis, which method to use.

Cheap loans

A relevant employee (including his relatives) who receives a cheap loan or credit by reason of his employment will be **liable to tax** on (s 175 ITEPA 2003): 3238
- the cash equivalent of the cheap interest rate (if this is lower than the official rate of interest); and
- any waiver of the loan (¶3245).

MEMO POINTS 1. An employee will also be taxable on **loans obtained** in the following circumstances:
- the employer guarantees or facilitates a loan;
- a loan is provided by a shareholder in a close company as a result of the employment; or
- the employer takes over a loan from another person.

2. **Relative** includes the following for the purposes of these rules:
- the employee's spouse;
- the parents, children and more remote ancestors or descendants of both spouses;
- the siblings of both spouses; and
- the spouses of all those mentioned above.

The following types of loan are **exempt** from these rules, and so no benefit arises if the loan: 3239
a. is an advance made by an employer to pay for necessary expenses and/or incidental overnight expenses where the amount outstanding does not exceed £1,000 and the advance is spent within 6 months of it being made;
b. is made on a commercial basis by an employer whose business includes the making of loans provided a substantial proportion of loans are made to the public, and the terms received by the employee are comparable to those received by the public at arm's length;
c. is a fixed term loan with a fixed rate of interest, which, at the time the loan was made, was not less than the official rate of interest;
d. is made as a result of a personal or family relationship;
e. would wholly qualify for tax relief if interest was charged; and
f. balance is below £5,000 throughout the tax year (aggregating all loans from the employer, but ignoring any such loans qualifying for tax relief).

Valuation of the benefit There are two ways in which the **cash equivalent** can be calculated which are based on calculating the difference between the interest paid by the employee and what would have been paid at the official rate of interest. Each year the employee should check both methods to see which is the more beneficial. This will be dependent on a number of factors such as whether the loan balance varies. Revenue and Customs may insist that the strict method is applied. 3240

Loan waivers

Where a loan provided by reason of employment is written off, it is **usually** taxable as regular earnings (¶3100)(s 188 ITEPA 2003). **Otherwise** an assessable benefit will arise for relevant employees, and the **cash equivalent** is the amount of the loan written off. 3245

A loan written off after the **death of the employee** does not lead to an assessable benefit (s 190 ITEPA 2003).

PAYE paid for directors

3247 Where the employer **does not deduct PAYE** from the earnings of an individual in the following circumstances, then the PAYE itself becomes earnings if (s 223 ITEPA 2003):
– the individual has been a director at anytime during the tax year;
– the employer pays the PAYE to Revenue and Customs; and
– there is no reimbursement to the employer by the director.

For these purposes a director is defined as for a relevant employee (¶3146).

B. Expenses

1. General principles

3265 As a general rule, where an **employer settles an expense**, the employee will be treated as having received earnings upon which he will be taxed, subject to a claim for expenses incurred in relation to the duties of employment, or to a dispensation arranged by the employer (s 72 ITEPA 2003).

Less common is the situation where the employee incurs **expenses which are not reimbursed by the employer**, in which case the employee will be at a disadvantage, having incurred expenses out of taxed income. Again a claim should be made, in order to deduct business expenses against taxable income.

EXAMPLE A receives an annual salary of £30,000 from B Ltd and incurs £1,500 of employment expenses in the tax year.
1. If B Ltd does not reimburse A, he will have a net salary of £28,500 but in the absence of a claim he will still be taxed on income of £30,000.
2. If B Ltd reimburses A, he will (in the absence of a claim) be treated as if he had received earnings of £31,500.
In both cases A will effectively pay tax on £1,500 which he has in fact used to pay expenses.

If the conditions are satisfied, A can submit a claim which will reduce earnings by the amount of the expense:
2. No reimbursement

	£
Salary	30,000
Less: claim	(1,500)
Taxable	28,500

3. Expenses reimbursed

	£
Salary	30,000
Reimbursed expenses	1,500
	31,500
Less: claim	(1,500)
Taxable	30,000

3270 There are **three ways** in which employment expenses are incurred:
– the employee pays the expenses and is reimbursed by the employer either for specific expenses incurred or by way of an expense allowance;
– the employee pays the expenses without reimbursement; or
– the employer pays the expenses directly.

The **tax treatment** is different for each type of payment, depending on the type of employee, as follows:

Payment method	Lower paid employee	Relevant employee	¶¶
Reimbursement	Not taxable unless excessive	Taxable but may claim deduction	¶3274
No reimbursement	May claim deduction	May claim deduction	¶3276
Employer pays directly	Not taxable	Taxable but may claim deduction	¶3277

Timing

Expenses are **deemed to be incurred** in the same tax year as the earnings they relate to, even if that is a different tax year to when they were paid (s 328 ITEPA 2003). 3273

EXAMPLE B incurred employment expenses on 15 March 2006 (i.e. 2005/06) which were reimbursed to him on 12 April 2006 (i.e. 2006/07).
The reimbursed expenses will be assessable in 2006/07 and B will therefore be deemed to have incurred the expenses in 2006/07.

Expenses paid by employee and reimbursed by employer

Relevant employees (¶3194) are assessed on any cash payment made to them arising from the employment. The result of this provision is that any expenses paid to an employee (whether as an expense allowance or as reimbursement of expenses incurred) are considered to be earnings (ss 70, 216 ITEPA 2003). For example an employee who is reimbursed for a train fare incurred on a business trip would be liable to tax and NIC on that amount. Employers are obliged to declare to Revenue and Customs all expenses payments made to employees, unless a dispensation is in place. 3274

Where the relevant conditions are satisfied (¶3278) a claim may be submitted which will allow the taxpayer to **deduct** a corresponding amount from his taxable income. The net effect is therefore that an employee will not be taxed on genuine business expenses.

In practice, where it can be shown that specific expenses payments will always be covered by such a claim, a **dispensation** (¶6900) can be obtained which will avoid the necessity of completing a P11D and having to make an expense claim.

MEMO POINTS Expenses reimbursed to **lower paid employees** are not taxable where the reimbursement is an:
- exact repayment of expenses incurred in performing the duties of employment;
- allowance to cover expenses whilst away from home; or
- Revenue and Customs agreed scale allowance.

Any excessive payments, however, may be taxable.

Expenses incurred by employee with no reimbursement

Where the appropriate conditions are satisfied, **any employee** who incurs expenses without reimbursement may claim a deduction against his taxable earnings. Revenue and Customs will however often query the validity of expenses where there has been no reimbursement by the employer. 3276

Expenses incurred directly by the employer

For **relevant employees**, expenditure incurred directly by the employer will be assessable as earnings although a corresponding claim for a deduction can be submitted providing the conditions (¶3278) are satisfied. 3277

For **lower paid employees** the direct payment of bills on behalf of an employee will not be taxable unless it is the payment of a monetary liability. For example the direct payment of a telephone bill (i.e. where the bill is addressed to the employer) is not subject to tax whereas a mobile phone top up voucher will be subject to tax.

2. Claiming a deduction for expenses

3278 For an expense to **be allowable as a deduction** from employment income an appropriate claim (known as a section 336 claim) must be submitted to Revenue and Customs (s 337 ITEPA 2003).

The **conditions** for making a claim depend on the nature of the expense:
– qualifying **travel** expenses must have been incurred necessarily in the performance of the duties of the employment;
– **capital allowances** claimed in respect of assets must relate to expenses incurred necessarily in the performance of the duties of the employment (ss 15, 36 CAA 2001); and
– all **other expenses** must have been incurred wholly, exclusively and necessarily in the performance of the duties of the employment (s 336(1) ITEPA 2003).

A stand-alone claim can either be made at the same time as the P11D (¶6897) is submitted, or a claim can be entered on an employee's tax return.

3279 The phrase **wholly, exclusively and necessarily** is derived from the legislation but each element has been the subject of a great deal of interpretative case law. The general conclusion has been that where all of the elements apply, the expenses must relate specifically to the office or employment rather than to the individual who holds the office or employment. This means that the duties of the office or employment must require the outlay of the expense, any personal benefit being incidental.

Wholly and exclusively

3280 An expense may be incurred for the **purposes** of the employment but may not wholly and exclusively relate to that employment. For example if a company decided to install a telephone in the home of an employee so that he could make business calls, the cost of the business calls would be deductible but the line rental would not. This is because the line can be used to make personal calls and is not therefore wholly and exclusively used for the employment.

Necessarily

3281 The requirement for an expense to have been incurred necessarily in the performance of duties **means** that it would not be possible to perform the duties without the expense being incurred. There is no corresponding requirement for self-employed individuals which is the main reason that it is easier for them to claim a deduction for expenses.

In the performance of duties

3282 The issue of whether an expense is incurred in the performance of duties is primarily a **question of fact**. Further, a distinction must be drawn between expenditure incurred to put the employee in a position to perform his duties efficiently, and expenditure incurred as part of those duties.

Limit on deduction

3283 The amount of a deductible expense is limited to the amount of the earnings from which it is to be deducted. It is not possible for an allowable loss to be created, and surplus expenses cannot be set against other income, including income from other employments.

3. Expenses subject to special rules

Summary

3284 Some expenses in employment do not fall within the general principles outlined above because the conditions for claiming a deduction are different or because special rules are required for calculating the amount of the expense. These expenses are covered in greater detail as follows:

Expense	Para.
Travel and subsistence	¶3285
Business entertaining	¶3322
Subscriptions	¶3324
Working at home	¶3326
Payroll giving	¶3328
Capital allowances	¶3329
Employee's liability and indemnity insurance	¶3330

a. Travel and subsistence

Employees are taxed on travel and subsistence expenses incurred by reason of the employment and paid for or provided by the employer (or a third party) either directly or by way of reimbursement (s 337 ITEPA 2003; Booklet 490). 3285

Where the expenses are incurred necessarily in the performance of the duties, the employee will be able to claim a deduction from his earnings.

Qualifying situations

Whether travel and subsistence expenses (referred to for the remainder of this section as travel expenses) are incurred in the **performance of the duties** of the office or employment will depend in part on the nature of the journey. Broadly, a deduction will not be available if the journey represents ordinary commuting or private travel. 3286

A journey directly from the office to a client site for a meeting will be an allowable deduction but the following scenarios are not as clear cut:
– travel between home and workplace;
– travel between home and workplace where home is also a place of work;
– travelling between two employments; and
– travelling between two centres of the same employment.

Each of these scenarios is considered in the following paragraphs.

Qualifying travel expenses Qualifying travelling expenses are defined as those incurred in the performance of the duties of the employment which are: 3287
– necessarily incurred in travelling in the performance of those duties; or
– other travelling expenses attributable to the necessary attendance of the employee at any place of work (other than expenses connected with ordinary commuting or private travel).

Ordinary commuting is deemed to be travel between the employee's home and the permanent workplace, where the employee regularly attends to perform his duties of employment (s 338 ITEPA 2003).

Private travel is deemed to be travel from the employee's home to somewhere other than a workplace. The primary purpose of the trip is the key issue. For example, if an employee undertakes a journey in order to carry out employment duties, but he also visits a relative in the same town after work, the journey will not be private travel.

Travel between home and workplace As a **general rule** the cost of travel between an employee's home and his normal place of work will not be a deductible expense. However, an **exception** allows employees to claim a deduction for qualifying travelling expenses between home and a temporary workplace. 3288

A **temporary workplace** is a place that the employee attends in the performance of the duties of the employment for the purpose of performing a task of limited duration (s 339 ITEPA 2003). If there is no substantial effect on the journey time or expense normally incurred, travel to such a temporary workplace would still constitute ordinary commuting. 3289

3290 A workplace will **become permanent** if it is attended (or is likely to be so) for a period of continuous work of more than 24 months during which time 40% or more of the employee's working time is spent there. It is therefore possible for an employee to have more than one permanent workplace at the same time.

Where the workplace is **expected to be temporary**, but then it is decided that the employee will actually be spending more than 24 months there, the following rules apply:
– travel expenses incurred up to the date when the decision is made are deductible;
– travel expenses after that date relate to ordinary commuting, and no deduction can be claimed.

MEMO POINTS 1. Where the period of continuous work is 24 months or less but is likely to represent all of the employee's **remaining period of employment** the workplace cannot be treated as temporary.
2. If the employee travels **direct from home to a temporary workplace**, he can claim the full cost as a deduction.
3. Where the employee **passes the permanent workplace** on the way to a temporary workplace, but does not stop there, he can claim a deduction for the whole journey from home to the temporary workplace.

3291 An **exception** to the rules on travelling expenses applies to area-based employees (such as salesmen or estate workers) who will be treated as if their permanent workplace is a specific area (s 339(8) ITEPA 2003). An **area-based employee** is one:
– whose duties are defined by reference to an area (although they may require attendance outside that area);
– who attends various places in that area in the performance of his duties; and
– where none of those places represents a permanent workplace.
Travel from home to the boundaries of the area will not be allowable as a deduction but expenses within the area will be allowable. Where the area-based employee lives within the area all travel within the area will be allowable.

3292 **Home is also a workplace** Expenses incurred in travelling between home and a place of work may be deductible if the employee is genuinely using his home as a base of operations, and there is an objective requirement for him to perform his employment duties at home. Where an employee works at home for reasons of convenience only, his home does not become a workplace.

3293 **Travelling between two employments** The cost of travelling between two different employments or between two different employers will not be a deductible expense (s 340 ITEPA 2003).

By exception, expenses incurred by a director or employee when travelling between two companies within a group will be deductible. For this purposes, group means a company and its 51% subsidiaries.

3294 **Travelling between two centres of employment** An employee who is required to attend more than one place of work in the performance of his duties may claim a deduction for the expenses of travelling between two places of work (provided they are both part of the same employment).

Amount of deduction

3300 Where travel expenses qualify for relief, the amount of the deduction is the full cost with no adjustment for the saving that the employee made by not having to travel to his normal workplace.

For these purposes travelling expenses will include:
– fares on train, bus, plane etc.;
– vehicle hire charges;
– costs associated with an employee's use of his private car;
– toll fees and car parking; and
– subsistence expenses where an overnight stay is required.

Where expenditure is **not attributable to the business travel** (for example the cost of private telephone calls, laundry and newspapers) it will not qualify as a deduction under these provisions. Instead a fixed sum is allowed for incidental expenses based on the number of nights spent away from home (¶3306).

MEMO POINTS **Subsistence** is not defined by the legislation but is taken to be the additional costs of living away from home. If the employee has continuing commitments at home and is obliged to live away from home in order to carry out the duties of his employment, the additional costs will normally be allowed in full. Where the employee does not have a permanent residence (where he normally lives in a hotel or club for example) then a subsistence deduction will not be available.

In most cases the **full cost** will be the actual amount paid such as the cost of a ticket or of a hotel room. Special rules apply to determine the expense incurred by an employee who uses his own car for business journeys. 3301

A deduction is **only available** for the expenditure actually incurred, so an employee who chooses to take a coach rather than a plane will only receive a deduction for the cost of the coach, even if the employer reimburses the cost of a plane fare. The employee will therefore be taxed on the difference. 3302

Similarly, the fact that travel costs were not the cheapest available will not prevent a claim being allowed for the full amount of the expenditure incurred. For example, the cost of a first class ticket will be allowable even if a standard class ticket was available. However, where the cost of travel and subsistence is **unusually lavish**, Revenue and Customs may seek to tax an element of the cost, on the basis that it was provided by way of a reward. For example, if an employee who usually travels standard class and stays in two star hotels flies first class to New York and stays in a five star hotel, an element of the cost of the trip may be deemed to be a reward for past performance.

Use of employee's own vehicle or bicycle There is a statutory **exemption** from tax for the following approved mileage allowance payments which are made to an employee in respect of a qualifying vehicle (s 230 ITEPA 2003). The payments must be made by the employer and are not available if the employee is a passenger in the vehicle, or if the vehicle is a company vehicle. 3303

Vehicle	Mileage in tax year	Rate per mile
Cars and vans	Up to 10,000 miles	40p
	Excess over 10,000 miles	25p
Motorcycles	No restriction	24p
Bicycles	No restriction	20p

If an employee is entitled to, but **does not receive**, mileage allowance payments as described above, he may be able to claim a deduction from earnings, being: 3304
- the amount of mileage allowance payments to which the employee would have been entitled; less
- any payments which he actually received.

If the employee receives **excess mileage payments**, he will be taxable on the excess, and only this amount should be entered on the employee's tax return.

A driver who takes **passengers** with him in a car or van will not be taxable on any related payment of up to 5p per passenger per mile, paid by his employer. The passenger must also be engaged on business travel for the employer. If no passenger allowance is payable by the employer, the employee cannot claim a deduction. 3305

Incidental overnight expenses The expenses which fall under this provision are those considered incidental to the individual's stay away from his usual abode during a qualifying absence from home (ss 240, 241 ITEPA 2003). For example, this might include telephone calls home, laundry or newspapers. 3306

A **qualifying absence** from home is any continuous period during which the individual is obliged to stay away from home for at least one night.

Personal incidental expenses are not earnings providing they are below the de minimis **limit** of £5 per night in the UK and £10 per night outside the UK. Where the de minimis limit is exceeded, the whole amount (not just the excess) will become taxable.

3307 Where the employee spends **more than one consecutive night** away, the total expense for the period is compared to the total of the de minimis amounts for the nights spent away. There is no requirement for each night to be looked at in isolation. Where the employer pays the expenses directly and the expenses for a number of employees are aggregated so that separate identification would be difficult, Revenue and Customs will accept a reasonable apportionment of the expenses.

Where the expenses of travelling to a particular place would not be deductible, this prohibits any claim for related accommodation expenses. For example, where a salesman makes a visit to relatives on the way to a client, the cost of travel from the office to the relatives' house will not be deductible, and neither will the cost of hotel accommodation nearby.

Foreign elements

3310 Where an employee, who is resident and ordinarily resident in the UK (¶3102), performs the **duties** of his office or employment **wholly overseas** then a deduction will be allowed for the cost of travelling to and from any place in the UK at the beginning and end of the employment (s 341 ITEPA 2003).

Such an employee who performs the duties of his employment **partly overseas** can claim a deduction for an unlimited number of visits to the UK provided each journey (s 370 ITEPA 2003):

– to the UK is made after carrying out duties that can only be performed outside the UK; and

– the journey outwards is undertaken in order to commence or resume such duties.

The deduction is made from taxable earnings but is restricted to the amount borne or reimbursed by the employer.

If the employer is foreign, the employee must be UK domiciled to claim a deduction.

3311 Where the employee holds **two or more offices or employments**, and the duties of at least one are performed wholly or partly outside the UK then the cost of travelling from one to another will be deductible from the earnings of the destination employment (s 342 ITEPA 2003).

3312 Where, for the purpose of enabling the employee to perform the duties of the overseas employment, expenses are incurred on **board and lodging** outside the UK a deduction will be allowed (s 376 ITEPA 2003). Where the board and lodging is only partly provided to enable the employee to perform his duties the allowable deduction will be apportioned.

A deduction will be available if the employer incurs the expense of certain journeys by the employee's **spouse or any child** of his, where he is absent from the UK for a continuous period of 60 days or more for the purpose of performing the duties of employment (s 371 ITEPA 2003). The journeys must be made to accompany him at the beginning of the period of absence or to visit him during that period, and there is a limit of two return trips by the same person in any year of assessment.

2. Other expenses

Business entertaining

3322 Expenses incurred in entertaining customers are **strictly** not wholly, exclusively and necessarily incurred in the performance of the duties of an employment because of the dual function of feeding the employee as well. Often an employer will provide an employee with an allowance to be used for business entertaining purposes (ss 356, 357 ITEPA 2003). **In practice** Revenue and Customs do not seek to tax reimbursed entertaining expenses, gifts or entertaining allowances on the principle that the employer will not be able to claim a deduction for the expenditure, and to tax the employee would create a double charge.

Staff entertaining is a deductible expense, unless the entertaining of non-employees is the main purpose of the expenditure (s 358 ITEPA 2003).

Subscriptions

Two types of subscriptions are **allowable as a deduction** from earnings (ss 343, 344 ITEPA 2003): 3324
- where the performance of the employment duties requires membership of a certain organisation, and it is a condition of employment; or
- where the performance of the duties of the employment is directly affected by the knowledge concerned or involves the exercise of the profession concerned.

The latter type of subscription is only eligible as a deduction if it is approved by Revenue and Customs, and a list of approved bodies can be obtained from www.hmrc.gov.uk/list3/index.htm

Working at home

No liability to income tax arises where an **employer makes a payment** to an employee in respect of reasonable additional household expenses which the employee incurs whilst working from home (s 316A ITEPA 2003). The annual limit for such payments since 6 April 2003 is £104 (£2 per week). Amounts over this figure can also be paid free of tax, provided the employer can provide supporting evidence that the payment is wholly in respect of additional household expenses incurred by the employee in carrying out his duties at home. 3326

MEMO POINTS With regards to homeworking payments, it is possible to seek an arrangement with the local Revenue and Customs office so that **payments in excess** of £104 per annum can be made without the need to retain documentary evidence.

If the **employer does not pay** any homeworking allowance, Revenue and Customs will allow an expense deduction where the employee does not have a permanent office base, and where communication between the employee and his employer or customers takes place at the employee's home. It should be noted however that to make such a claim the employee should strictly be able to show that a part of his home is used exclusively in the performance of the duties of his employment. If this is the case, any subsequent reliance on the capital gains tax exemption for private residences may be restricted. 3327

Payroll giving scheme

Employees may be able to make **charitable donations** direct from their salary, where the employer operates an approved payroll giving scheme (s 713 ITEPA 2003). Under the scheme, an employee arranges for a regular amount (with no maximum limit) to be withheld from his salary by his employer, which is allowed as a tax deductible expense against his earnings. 3328

The amounts withheld are then passed by the employer to an approved agent (or charity) for onward distribution to nominated charities.

MEMO POINTS 1. The employer must deduct the amount from earnings when calculating the **PAYE** (but not NIC) deductions. Therefore the employee obtains tax relief at source, so a donation of £100 will only cost a basic rate taxpayer £78, and a higher rate tax payer £60.
2. The following **employer grants**, based on the size of the payroll, are available to businesses with less than 500 employees, who set up a new scheme in the period from April 2004 to December 2006: Revenue and Customs' Employer's Bulletin 19:
- under 200 employees – grant of £300;
- 200 to 249 employees – grant of £400; and
- 250 to 499 employees – grant of £500.

Capital allowances on assets other than cars

3329 Where expenditure is incurred necessarily on **plant and machinery** (other than a car) for use in the performance of the duties of the employment, capital allowances may be claimed.

Employee's liability and indemnity insurance

3330 Where an employee has incurred a liability (to the employer or a third party) as a result of negligence in his capacity as an employee, he will be able to obtain a deduction for the following **types of expense** (s 346 ITEPA 2003):

a. insurance premiums paid to indemnify the employee against liability for his acts or omissions whilst undertaking his employment duties;

b. payments to settle an uninsured liability for the same acts and omissions as in **a.**; and

c. payments of costs incurred which relate to the liability, such as court fees.

An employee may also claim relief for payments under this provision made in relation to a **previous employment** (s 555 ITEPA 2003). The payments must be made within the 6 years following the year of assessment in which the employment ceases. Relief is given in the year in which the payment is made, and unused relief cannot be carried forward.

III. Share schemes

3340 In line with the general income from employment principles, an employee or director will be chargeable to income tax when, by reason of employment, he acquires **shares** (including securities) in the employer company for **free or for a reduced price**. Broadly, the tax charge is levied on the value received by the employee, which will be calculated under the rules for unapproved schemes, unless the shares are made available within a Revenue and Customs' approved scheme. The most common type of charge in relation to an unapproved scheme is where the employee receives shares for less than market value, when he will be treated as if he had received a loan from the employer. There are many other situations in which a tax charge can arise however, and readers are referred to the *Tax Memo* for further details.

An **approved scheme** allows the employer to make shares or options available to the employees without a charge to income tax or with a reduced tax charge, providing all prescribed conditions are met in relation to the following criteria:
- eligible employees;
- type of company;
- restrictions on shares; and
- scheme specific approval requirements.

The main types of approved schemes are summarised below, with a focus on the main objectives and uses of each type of scheme, the types of employees who are eligible and the tax relief available. Further details can again be found in the *Tax Memo*.

Reporting requirements

3342 Revenue and Customs require **annual reports** to be submitted so that they can monitor both approved and unapproved schemes. The annual report must include all reportable events and must be submitted by 7 July following the tax year, whether or not a return (form 42) has been issued. If there are no reportable events, and a return has been received, a nil return should be submitted. The obligation to report is imposed on:
- the employer;
- the person from whom the shares were acquired;
- the person who issued the shares; and
- any host employer (where the actual employer is abroad).

Where more than one person has responsibility to report, the duty to report is not met until one of them has met the disclosure requirements. There are penalties for failure to report.

1. Approved company share option plans

Approved company share option plans (ACSOPs) are discretionary share option schemes which means that the options may be granted to employees on a selective basis rather than to the workforce as a whole. 3350

Where an employee holds share options under an ACSOP, there will generally be no income tax charge on the grant or exercise of the options, nor on the subsequent increase in value of the shares. Capital gains tax on the eventual disposal of the shares will therefore normally be the only charge to tax in respect of an ACSOP.

The costs incurred by a company in setting up an ACSOP are allowable for corporation tax purposes.

An individual will only be **eligible** to join an ACSOP if, in relation to the company which established the scheme, (or in the case of a group scheme, a participating company) he is (Sch 4 para 8 ITEPA 2003): 3351

- a full-time director; or
- an employee who is not a director of the company.

Extent of tax relief

The general rule is that, providing the conditions outlined below are met, no income tax charge will arise on either the grant or exercise of an option under an ACSOP. 3355

Where an ACSOP has been approved by Revenue and Customs the **grant of an option** will not give rise to an income tax charge (s 518 ITEPA 2003). 3356

A tax charge may arise however where, exceptionally, the subscription price proves to be less than the market value of the shares on the date of the grant (s 526 ITEPA 2003). For example, a rise in a company's share value at the time of its flotation would give rise to such a charge. Schemes can specify market value by reference to published prices on recognised investment exchanges.

The **exercise of an option** under an ACSOP will be free from income tax provided the option is exercised at least 3 but no more than 10 years after it was granted to the director or employee (s 524 ITEPA 2003). 3357

Where share options obtained by a person under an ACSOP are exercised after his death, tax relief will still be available provided the exercise takes place within 10 years of the grant.

Individuals ceasing to be a full-time director or qualifying employee because of: 3358

- injury;
- disability;
- redundancy; or
- retirement.

and who exercise the option within 6 months from the day on which they cease to be a director or employee will still receive the tax advantages. This applies even where the option is exercised less than 3 or more than 10 years after it was granted to the director or employee. Such employees and directors are referred to as "good leavers".

2. Enterprise management incentives

The enterprise management incentive scheme (EMI) enables small higher risk trading companies to grant qualifying share options with a value up to £100,000 to eligible employees without income tax consequences. 3360

An employee must be an employee of that company or, if that company is a parent company, of that company or a qualifying subsidiary of that company. He must not have a material interest in the company or if that company is a parent company, any group company. 3362

There are also strict criteria as to the type of company which can be involved in EMIs.

To be **eligible**, the employee's committed time must amount to (Sch 5 para 29 ITEPA 2003):
– at least 25 hours a week; or
– if less, 75% of his working time.

For these purposes, committed time means the time that the employee is required to spend on the business of the company or, if the relevant company is a parent company, on the business of the group. Committed time also includes any time that the employee would have been required to spend in this way but for:
– injury, ill-health or disability;
– pregnancy, childbirth, maternity or paternity leave or parental leave;
– reasonable holiday entitlement; or
– not being required to work during a period of notice of termination of his employment.

The employee must also not have a material interest in the company (i.e. basically, he must not own more than 30% of the ordinary share capital).

Extent of tax relief

3365 The **grant of an option** will not give rise to an income tax charge (s 529 ITEPA 2003).

3366 Special rules apply to the **exercise of an option** where it occurs **within 10 years** of the date of the grant and those rules are dependent on whether the option is to acquire the shares at or less than the market value.

Exercise price	Income tax implication	Reference
Equal or above market value at grant	No charge	s 530 ITEPA 2003
Less than market value at grant	Charge on the difference between: – market value (at the lower of grant and exercise); and – amounts paid by the employee for both the option and shares	s 531 ITEPA 2003

MEMO POINTS Where the option is exercised more than 10 years after the date of the grant, it will fall outside the EMI scheme and it will be subject to the normal rules for unapproved share option schemes, and a tax charge will arise on exercise.

3367 Where a **disqualifying event** occurs **before the exercise of a qualifying option** and that option is not exercised within 40 days of the event, the tax benefits of EMI status are lost (s 532 ITEPA 2003).

The amount chargeable on the **subsequent exercise** of the option is (or is increased by) the amount by which the market value of the shares on the exercise of the option exceeds the market value of the shares immediately before the qualifying event.

The following table summarises disqualifying events for EMI purposes (ss 534-539 ITEPA 2003).

Disqualifying event	Notes
The relevant company becomes a 51 per cent subsidiary of, or becomes under the control of another company	A disqualifying event will not occur where, within the permitted period, a replacement option is granted in respect of shares of the company which has taken control
The relevant company ceases to meet the qualifying trading activities requirement	
The employee ceases to be an eligible employee by breaching the employment or working time conditions	
The shares no longer meet the EMI criteria as a result of variation in the terms of the option to increase the market value of the shares under option	

Disqualifying event	Notes
Alterations which affect the value of the shares under option or which alter the rights attaching to any shares in the company (not necessarily the shares under option) are made without prior Revenue and Customs approval	Revenue and Customs are required to give approval to the alteration unless it appears that the effect of any changes is to increase the value of the shares under option or to breach the requirements of the EMI provisions. An appeal against a refusal by Revenue and Customs to approve an alteration must be lodged within 30 days of the notice of Revenue and Customs' decision
A conversion is made in the class of shares to which the option relates	Where the whole of one class of shares is converted into one new class of shares the conversion is not a disqualifying event if, before the conversion, the majority of the class of shares in question were not held by: – employees and directors of the company (or of an associated company); or – by an associated company
The grant of certain company share option plan options (i.e. an approved share option other than a SAYE option) if the result is that the employee holds unexercised options with a value of more than £100,000	This applies where the ACSOP option is granted by reason of a person's employment in the company which issued the EMI option or the group
A company qualified on the basis that it was preparing to carrying on a trade but the trade is never carried on or, alternatively the trade does not commence within 2 years of the grant of the option	

A disqualifying event will also be treated as occurring if, in a tax year, the employee's **actual working time** is less than 25 hours per week, or (if less) 75 per cent of his working time (s 535(6) ITEPA 2003). Actual working time is the time the individual spends as an employee in a relevant employment on the business of the relevant company or group. 3368

The test is carried out on a monthly **cumulative basis** from the beginning of the tax year. If the working time requirement is not met, qualifying status is lost at the end of the month preceding the month in which the test is failed. Where the employee **commences employment** during the tax year, the test is done cumulatively for the period in which he is in employment.

If the test is failed before an option is granted, then that grant is treated as it had never been a qualifying option.

3. Share incentive plans

Share incentive plans (**SIPs**) allow shares to be appropriated to employees without giving rise to an income tax charge. A trust is set up in order to hold the shares until they are appropriated. Employee-elected trustees to SIPs to bolster the use of employee ownership in private companies are also encouraged (Employee Share Schemes Act 2002). 3370

An employee who is awarded shares under a SIP is known as a participant.

The **purpose** of a SIP must be to give employees a continuing stake in the company (Sch 2 para 5 ITEPA 2003). A scheme with the purpose of making advantageous salary payments to employees is unlikely to be approved. 3371

Broadly, the scheme allows for **four different types of shares**:
a. free shares – appropriated to the employee by the employer;
b. partnership shares – purchased by the employee through deductions from his salary;
c. matching shares – offered by the company in a ratio relating to the number of partnership shares purchased; and
d. dividend shares – purchased with dividends reinvested on behalf of the employee.

Revenue and Customs' **conditions for approval** of an SIP are different for each type of share. The scheme must **provide for** the participation of every employee:
– who is eligible; and
– who is resident and ordinarily resident in the UK.

3372 An individual will be **eligible** if he is an employee of the company that established the plan or of a company participating in a group scheme. A qualifying period may be specified within the terms of the scheme which must not exceed:
– 18 months ending with the date of the award in the case of free shares;
– 18 months ending with the date of the salary deduction in the case of partnership or matching shares; or
– 6 months ending with the start of the accumulation period where relevant to partnership shares.

A qualifying period must apply to all employees but different periods may be specified for different awards.

3373 Every employee who is eligible to participate must be **invited** to do so. The scheme must not contain features that would discourage employees (or a particular group of employees) from joining (Sch 2 para 8 ITEPA 2003). For example, a scheme that requires employees to sacrifice other benefits in order to be eligible would be unlikely to receive approval.

Participation must be on the **same terms** for all employees but free shares may be allocated by reference to criteria such as length of service, remuneration levels or hours worked. Performance measures may also be used to determine the allocation of free shares but these must be calculated in accordance with specified criteria.

Extent of tax relief

3375 Subject to the certain conditions, shares that cease to be subject to the plan will attract income and capital gains tax relief.

Shares **cease to be subject to the plan** when:
– they are withdrawn from the plan;
– the participant ceases to be employed by the company (or any associated companies); or
– the trustees dispose of the shares to meet PAYE obligations.

Specific rules apply to free or matching shares, partnership shares, dividend shares and capital receipts.

3376 With regard to income tax, each tax year employers can give employees up to £3,000 worth of free shares, and employees can buy up to £1,500 of partnership shares free of tax as long as the shares **are left in the plan for** at least **5 years**.

However, an income tax charge will arise if the shares cease to be subject to the plan **less than 5 years** from the date of the award, but the amount of the charge will depend on the type of share and the timing of the withdrawal. Capital receipts may also give rise to an income tax charge.

3377 Further, employers also get a **corporation tax deduction** for the costs in setting up a SIP.

4. Savings-related share option schemes

3380 A savings-related share option scheme (SRSOS) allows directors and employees to acquire shares using the funds from a savings scheme. Providing the scheme is approved and all of the conditions are met, the grant of the share options will be tax free and so will the increase in value of the shares between the grant of the option and its exercise. Interest and bonuses paid on the funds in the scheme are exempt from tax.

The costs incurred by a company in setting up a SRSOS are allowable for corporation tax purposes.

The persons **eligible** to participate in the scheme must include every person who (Sch 3 paras 6-8 ITEPA 2003): 3381
– is an employee or full-time director of the company which has established the scheme (or in the case of a group scheme, a participating company);
– has been employed by the company throughout the qualifying period; and
– is resident and ordinarily resident in the UK.

For these purposes, a director is deemed to be full-time if he normally devotes at least 25 hours per week (excluding meal breaks) to the duties of his office. A director may aggregate all of the hours that he works for the participating companies in a group scheme.

MEMO POINTS The company may specify a **qualifying period** (of up to 5 years) throughout which the employee or director must have been employed by the company. This allows the company to exclude employees and directors who have been employed for a shorter period.

The company has **discretion to permit** the following to participate under the scheme: 3382
– part-time directors;
– employees or directors who have been employed for less than the qualifying period; and
– employees who do not satisfy the residency condition.

Those employees or directors who do participate in the scheme must do so on similar terms but there may be variation in the rights issued to participants based on their remuneration, length of service or other similar factors.

The **shares** under a SRSOS must be **acquired out of savings** (and interest) with a certified contractual savings scheme (SAYE) which is approved for this purpose by Revenue and Customs. The contribution that each participant makes under the SAYE contract must secure, as near as possible, a repayment equal to the amount required for the purchase of the shares under the option concerned. The scheme must not permit a participant's contributions under all SAYEs to exceed £250 per month and may impose a minimum contribution limit, although this may not exceed £10 per month. Monthly contributions as low as £5 per month are permitted. 3383

The price at which shares may be acquired (the **subscription price**) must be specified at the time when the rights are obtained by the participant. The price must not be manifestly less than 80% of the market value of the shares at the time when the rights are acquired (or at an earlier time that has been agreed in writing with Revenue and Customs). Provision may be made in the scheme to allow for adjustments to the following to take count of any variation in the share capital of which the scheme shares form part: 3384
– the subscription price; and
– the number of shares subject to the option.

Extent of tax relief

Providing all of the conditions outlined above have been satisfied, **income tax** will not be chargeable on the **grant of an option** under a Revenue and Customs' approved SRSOS. 3385

Similarly, where a SRSOS **option is exercised** within the terms of the scheme, the charge to income tax that would normally apply under the general rules will be exempted (s 519 ITEPA 2003). The general rule with regard to the **exercise of the option** under a SRSOS is that it must not be capable of being exercised before, or more than 6 months after, the date on which the repayments under the SAYE scheme are due (known as the bonus date). The bonus date will be 3, 5 or 7 years after the commencement of the SAYE scheme and this period must be determined at the time when the option is granted. By exception, an earlier exercise may be permitted:
– on the death of the participant;
– on the cessation of employment for approved reasons; and
– following a takeover.

MEMO POINTS Where the shares acquired under a SRSOS are eventually sold, the resulting gain or loss will be subject to capital gains tax. For these purposes, the acquisition cost of the shares will be taken to be the actual price (as opposed to the market value) paid for the shares by the participant.

SECTION 3

Pensions

3400 Many employers offer **occupational pension schemes** (OPS) (also known as retirement benefit schemes) by which they can make tax efficient retirement provision for their employees. An employer who offers such a scheme has certain legal obligations to his employees generally, the members of the scheme and its trustees. Alternatively, some employers will offer to pay into their employees' **personal pension schemes**.

3401 Further, unless employers offer suitable pension schemes to their employees, those who have more than five employees and have at least one relevant employee (see below) must provide their relevant employees with access to a **designated stakeholder pension**.

MEMO POINTS Detailed information on the tax charges and their various calculations with regard to the different schemes and benefits is beyond the scope of this book and readers should refer to the *Tax Memo* and contact Revenue and Customs with regard to specific issues.

3402 Individuals are also entitled to receive a **state retirement pension** once they have reached the state pension age (currently 60 for women, 65 for men). This is made up of two elements:
– a basic flat rate; and
– the second state pension (previously called the state earnings related pension scheme (SERPS)).

Employees and directors with an appropriate personal or stakeholder pension can **opt out** of the earnings related element of the state pension scheme (the second state pension (S2P)). In such cases, the employee will pay the full rate of national insurance on their earnings and Revenue and Customs' National Insurance Contributions Office (NICO) will pay an amount known as the minimum contribution into his appropriate pension scheme.

MEMO POINTS The **state pension age** is to be equalised at age 65, to be phased in over 10 years from 6 April 2010 (Pensions Act 1995).

3403 A **new pensions regime** will replace all of the existing tax provisions in relation to pensions from 6 April 2006 resulting in the tax treatment for all types of approved schemes, including occupational schemes, being amalgamated into the rules for registered schemes. In addition, the tax treatment of unapproved schemes will also change. Further details can be obtained from Revenue and Customs and can also be found in the *Tax Memo*.

I. Occupational pension schemes (OPS)

3405 An OPS can be set up for any number of employees and can include all or some of the employer's workforce. It is usually in a form of a trust with legally appointed trustees and is separate from the employer's business. The trustees can delegate the day-to-day management of the scheme to an administrator who will be named in the scheme documentation and can be the employer or a named trustee(s). There is a legal requirement for at least one third of the trustees to be nominated by scheme members.

The **tax treatment** of the contributions made by the employer, and of the benefits received out of the scheme, will depend on whether the scheme is **approved** by Revenue and Customs.

A. General principles

There are **two main types** of OPS and the level of benefits under each is calculated differently. The first is a **final salary scheme** (also known as a defined benefits scheme) where the employer guarantees a pension which is a fraction of the employee's salary based on the number of years of service. This type of pension is now being phased out by many companies or is being limited to existing employees. 3410

The other main type of scheme is a **money purchase scheme** (also known as a defined contribution scheme) where the benefits under the scheme ultimately depend on the amount that the fund has built up and the level of contributions made by the employee and the employer. Consequently, there is no set promise or guarantee about the level of benefits that the employee will receive on retirement.

Both types usually offer a **pension** or a pension and a **lump sum** on retirement. Some may also allow for part of the pension to be given up in **exchange** for a lump sum on retirement. The rate of exchange will depend on the scheme's rules and current legislation, and may apply to all members or a certain group/member. It is usually expressed as a ratio and is referred to as the "commutation factor." 3411

Schemes can also give **benefits on death**, for example the payment of a lump sum and/or a pension to the surviving spouse and/or dependants. Indeed, some may be **limited to such payments**. Such benefits will be "death in service" if the employee dies before reaching the normal retirement date (NRD) and/or "death on retirement" payable when the employee dies during retirement. The tax rules will vary depending on the type of benefit.

Normal retirement date

Each scheme should set out the age at which the employee is expected to start to receive his pension, called the normal retirement date (NRD). It is **distinct and independent** from the state pension age, contractual retirement age (CRA) and normal retiring age (NRA) (¶8211), though it may be the same date. 3412

The NRD must be the same for **men and women** as pension is "pay" for the purposes of EU equal pay provisions (*Barber v Guardian Royal Exchange Assurance Group* [1990] IRLR 240, ECJ). However, an employer may have different retirement ages for **different jobs**, provided the disparity is not gender-based.

Early retirement Early retirement occurs if the employee leaves his job and takes his retirement benefits before his NRD. This may be offered as an **alternative to redundancy** and the scheme may provide for one or more of the following if there is early retirement: 3413
- immediate payment of the employee's full pension (with no reduction for early payment);
- payment of part of the pension as a lump sum;
- additional years' service for the purpose of calculating pension entitlement; and
- payment of the whole or part of any termination payment into the scheme to increase the pension entitlement.

In general, the statutory tax rules allow an employee to retire early from the age of 50 years although with regard to approved schemes not before this age (unless due to ill health or in a specialised occupation such as a sportsman).

Most schemes will provide for early retirement due to **ill health**, commonly granting immediate payment of full pension, perhaps with additional pensionable service added on in order to calculate an enhanced ill health pension. Some schemes apply a tiered system, such that full prospective pensionable service is used for complete incapacity and actual pensionable service is used when the employee can do some work (but not his normal duties). 3414

Some schemes will also allow for commutation on the grounds of **serious ill health**. If so, and the employee's life expectancy is severely shortened, the scheme will commute the whole of his retirement benefit into a lump sum.

Medical evidence is normally required to prove that the employee's ill health prevents him from carrying out his normal employment. Often, the incapacity must be expected or likely to be permanent, with provisions for suspension of pension payments if the employee is able to resume work before reaching pensionable age.

The employer is bound by his duty to act in **good faith** when deciding whether the employee meets any definition of incapacity (*Mihlenstedt v Barclays Bank International Ltd and Barclays Bank plc* [1989] IRLR 522, CA) and the scheme **rules must be construed** in a purposive and practical way (*Derby Daily Telegraph Ltd v The Pensions Ombudsman and Thompson* [1999] IRLR 476, ChD).

MEMO POINTS **Personal pensions** can also come into payment early, at a reduced rate, and the employee should check his policy, if necessary.

1. Approved schemes

3420 Revenue and Customs-approved OPSs attract the following **tax reliefs**:
- relief from income tax and NIC on employee contributions;
- relief from corporation tax on employer contributions;
- relief from income tax on the benefit of any employer contributions (i.e. such payments are not treated as a benefit in kind);
- exemption from income tax and capital gains tax on the income and growth of the scheme's investments; and
- tax-free cash lump sum payments on retirement or death if entitled.

In a recent case the House of Lords held that a director who retired as an executive director, but continued as a non-executive director, had retired for the purposes of a Revenue and Customs' approved scheme, and, therefore, the pension payments paid to him were not taxable. The fact that the taxpayer remained in his non-pensionable position as a non-executive director did not affect his right to receive a pension when he retired from his only pensionable occupation (*Venables and others v Hornby* [2004] STC 84, HL).

3421 Essentially, Revenue and Customs will give **tax approval** if:
- employer contributions are paid into the scheme; and
- the money held by the scheme and the benefits paid out of the scheme are in the form of pension benefits and do not exceed set maximum limits.

Limits on contributions

3422 The amount of contributions which an **employee** can make to an OPS is limited to a maximum of 15% of his remuneration in any one tax year. Remuneration for these purposes is salary, commission, bonuses, and taxable benefits in kind. Income from share incentive schemes and termination payments is excluded. Many schemes may impose a lower maximum, or simply use salary to calculate maximum payments.

However, unlike personal pension schemes, there is no limit to the level of contributions that the **employer** can make. Instead, statutory limits are applied to the amount of benefit that can be derived from a scheme.

Employer and employee contributions are not aggregated for these purposes and an employer may make unlimited contributions without affecting the employee maximum. Where there is a shortfall between the contributions that the employee can make and the maximum contributions allowed, some schemes will allow the employee to make **additional voluntary contributions** (AVCs).

MEMO POINTS The employee is also entitled to make free-standing additional voluntary contributions (FSAVCs) into a personal pension scheme to utilise any balance of tax relief available.

2. Unapproved schemes

There are **two types** of unapproved retirement benefit schemes: funded and unfunded. A **funded scheme** is one where the employer makes arrangements for future benefits by paying into an insurance policy or by setting up a separate trust fund. An **unfunded scheme** is one where the employer simply gives an undertaking that, at some date in the future, he will pay pensions or other retirement benefits. 3425

Unapproved schemes are not as tax efficient as approved schemes but are commonly used to "top-up" pension provision for executives whose earnings are above the earnings cap (currently for earnings over £102,000 (for 2004/2005 tax year), and who are therefore restricted on the amount that can be paid into an approved scheme.

B. Employer obligations

Duty to members

Any powers an employer may have under the rules of an OPS must be exercised in **good faith** and he must treat his employees in a reasonable manner as part of the duty to preserve the relationship of mutual **trust and confidence** (*Imperial Group Pension Trust Ltd v Imperial Tobacco Ltd* [1991] IRLR 66, ChD). 3430

Consequently, such powers must be exercised with a view to the efficient running of the scheme and to preserve his employees' rights and the pension fund. In particular, this creates a contractual obligation to take reasonable steps to bring to the employees' attention the existence of new or varied beneficial terms (*Scally and others v Southern Health and Social Services and others* [1991] IRLR 522, HL).

EXAMPLE In *Scally*, a collective agreement amended the employees' individual contracts introducing a beneficial OPS right contingent on the employees taking appropriate action. The employer was held to be under an implied duty to draw this to his employees' attention.

However, there is no implied duty on an employer to make employees aware of their **pension rights** generally although there is a corresponding duty in tort to take reasonable care in any information he does give (*Hagen and others v ICI Chemicals & Polymers Ltd* [2002] IRLR 31, QBD). Therefore, if the employer negligently misrepresents information to his employees, he will be in breach of his duty of care. 3431

Further, the implied duty also does not stretch to requiring the employer to give financial advice, for example that the employee is not choosing the most financially advantageous option when exercising his rights under the scheme (*University of Nottingham v Eyett* [1999] IRLR 87, ChD; *Outram v Academy Plastics* [2000] IRLR 499, CA). If, on the other hand, the employer does give advice, he is under an implied duty to ensure that the **information** is not misleading, inaccurate or negligent.

Duty to trustees

Trustees of the scheme who are also employees have the right to take reasonable **paid time off** for training and for the performance of their duties (ss 58-60 ERA 1996). This does not apply to election candidates. Trustees have the right to be remunerated for the work they would have done had they not had the time off (¶3910). 3432

Trustees also have the **right not to suffer a detriment or be dismissed** because of their duties or the performance (or proposed performance) of their duties as trustees (ss 46, 102 ERA 1996). 3433

Discrimination

3435 A detailed discussion of pension-related discrimination is beyond the scope of this book. However, the main principles are discussed below.

3436 **Sex discrimination** The current inequality between men and women relating to their **state retirement ages** (65 and 60 respectively) is due to be removed starting in 2010 with the result that the state pension age will be equalised at 65 for both sexes by 2020. Note, however, that it has been unlawful for employers to discriminate between men and women in respect of **contractual retiring ages** since 1987 (s 2(1) SDA 1986) (¶8207).

3437 It is also unlawful to discriminate in respect of access to, and benefits payable under, **occupational pension schemes**. The law relating to this matter has developed in a piecemeal manner.

3438 Article 141 of the EC Treaty of Rome requires that men and women must receive equal pay for equal work. 'Pay' is now deemed to include any benefits paid under an occupational pension scheme (*Barber v Guardian Royal Exchange Assurance Group* [1990] IRLR, 240, ECJ). However, any claim relating to **treatment under** (as opposed to access to) an occupational pension scheme which is based on the principle of equal treatment enshrined in *Barber*, is restricted to **pensionable service on or after 17 May 1990** (the date of the *Barber* decision).

Following *Barber*, domestic legislation was implemented to provide that all occupational pension schemes would incorporate the **"equal treatment rule"**, including any provisions which provide for the benefit of scheme members' dependants (ss 62(1)-(2), 63(1) Pensions Act 1995). Later ECJ cases further clarified that the principle of equality extends to the trustees of an occupational pension scheme (*Coloroll Pension Trustees Ltd v Russell* [1995] ICR 179, ECJ) and that survivors' benefits are also covered (*Ten Oever v Stichting Befrijfspensioenfonds voor het Glazenwassers en Schoonmaakbedrijf* [1995] ICR 74, ECJ).

MEMO POINTS The Treaty of Rome has direct effect in the UK and does not require further domestic implementing legislation.

3439 However, in contrast, ECJ case law has held that the **right to join** an occupational pension scheme is within the scope of Art 141 but is not subject to the same time limitation as in *Barber* (*Vroege v NCIV Instituut voor Volkshuisvestuing BV* [1994] IRLR 651, ECJ), although employee contributions would need to be backdated in respect of any period of retrospective membership claimed (*Fisscher v Voorhuis Hengelo BV* [1994] IRLR, 662, ECJ).

A long-standing issue of access to occupational pension schemes has involved **part-time workers**, many of whom were previously excluded from access to their employers' occupational pension schemes. It has been held that the exclusion of part-time workers (many of whom were women) from their employers' occupational pension schemes constituted indirect sex discrimination, on the basis that the exclusion adversely affected more women than men. Despite the ECJ decisions in *Vroege* and *Fisscher*, UK domestic legislation did not previously allow claims regarding access to be backdated in respect of pensionable service more than 2 years before the date on which the complaint was presented.

However, following a referral to the ECJ from the House of Lords, this is no longer the case (*Preston v Wolverhampton Healthcare NHS Trust* [2001] IRLR 237, HL) and domestic legislation has now been introduced to implement the *Preston* decision (Part-time Workers (Prevention of Less Favourable Treatment) Regulations 2000 (Amendment) Regulations SI 2002/2035).

However, a **distinction should be drawn** between claims relating to benefits payable under, as opposed to access to, an occupational pension scheme, where the time limitation in *Barber* continues to apply (*Quirk v Burton Hospital NHS* [2002] IRLR 353, CA).

EXAMPLE In *Quirk v Burton Hospital NHS*, a male nurse, who would be financially worse off than his female counterparts if he decided to retire early was held not to have suffered discrimination contrary to the equal pay rights under art 141 and could not claim equality of treatment in respect of pensionable service prior to 17 May 1990.

The Court of Appeal has dealt with a number of issues in the on-going equal pay case of *Preston*, and has recently held that (*Powerhouse Retail Ltd and others v Burroughs and others* [2004] IRLR 979, CA): 3440
– an employer will breach the EPA 1970 if he makes membership of a pension scheme compulsory for full-time employees, but does not permit part-time employees to join. However, he will not breach the Act if he permits (but does not compel) part-time workers to become scheme members, even if membership for full-time employees is compulsory (note: this is now unlawful);
– any breach ceases when the barrier for part-time workers is removed, even if the employer does not inform his workers, provided that his failure to inform was not, in itself, on discriminatory grounds (note: employees may be able to bring a separate contractual claim against the employer, for failing to inform them of the availability of advantageous contractual benefits); and
– where TUPE applies, liability under the EPA 1970 and Article 141 EC Treaty for failure to provide equal access to pension benefits remains with the transferor. The time limit for bringing a claim runs from the date of the transfer.

In addition, the Pensions Act 1995 has amended the SDA 1975 to provide that **discrimination** against a woman in respect of her access to membership of, or rights to benefits payable under, an occupational pension scheme is unlawful in relation to terms of employment, opportunities for or access to benefits, or subjecting an employee to any detriment (s 6 SDA 1975). The SDA 1975 does not cover any other pension-related discrimination except in respect of transsexuals (s 6(8) SDA 1975). 3441

The principle of equality is also now incorporated in the **equal pay** legislation (s 6(1B) EPA 1970, as amended by the Pensions Act 1995). This extends the principle of equal treatment to cover any term in the contract relating to a person's membership of or rights under an occupational pension scheme, unless the term is one in relation to which the equal treatment rule would be excluded. 3442

Disability discrimination Every occupational pension scheme is taken to include a non-discriminatory rule in relation to access to, and benefits under, the scheme. From 1 October 2004, both the trustees and managers of an occupational pension scheme are prohibited from discriminating against or harassing a disabled person in carrying out their functions as trustees and managers (s 4G DDA 1995). In addition, trustees and managers are under a duty to make reasonable adjustments where a provision, criterion or practice (including a scheme rule) is applied by or on behalf of the trustees and managers, or any physical features of premises occupied by the trustees and managers, places a disabled person at a substantial disadvantage compared with a non-disabled person. In such circumstances, the trustees and managers are under a duty to make any reasonable adjustments which would prevent the provision, criterion, practice or physical feature from having that effect (s 4H DDA 1995). This might include altering the pension scheme rules or the trustees'/managers' premises. There is no defence of justification for failure to make such reasonable adjustments. 3443
See ¶5450 for further details on disability discrimination.

Other discrimination Moreover, all occupational pension schemes are now subject to the principle of non-discrimination against any person in relation to access to such schemes and entitlement to benefits under them on the grounds of **sexual orientation** or **religion or belief** (reg 9A SI 2003/1660 as inserted by reg 3 SI 2003/2828; reg 9A SI 2003/1661 as inserted by reg 3 SI 2003/2827). Trustees and pension scheme managers must also implement this rule. 3444
See ¶¶5260, 5375 for further details on sexual orientation and religion or belief discrimination.

MEMO POINTS It is expected that direct and indirect **age discrimination** will become **unlawful from** October 2006 and, at the time of writing, the Government has published draft Employment Equality (Age) Regulations 2006 (see ¶5254 + for a summary of the draft regulations).
It is proposed that certain **age-related rules or practices** in occupational pension schemes will be **exempted** from the draft regulations, such as using minimum and maximum ages for admission to schemes or entitlement to benefits. A Schedule to the draft regulations contains a full list of the rules or practices which will be exempted.

It will, however, be **unlawful** for trustees or managers of an occupational pension scheme, when carrying out their functions, **to harass or discriminate** against a member or prospective member of the scheme on the grounds of age. Every occupational pension scheme will be treated as including a **non-discrimination rule** and trustees and managers will be given power to alter schemes to comply with the rule.

Data protection compliance

3445 The **administrator of the OPS** has the general responsibility for the administration of the scheme, including keeping membership records, corresponding with members, reporting changes to the scheme to the relevant authorities and providing the scheme's actuary with information. If the employer takes on this responsibility it will usually be through a director or a senior member of his staff, most likely in the human resources department. The **function of the scheme administrator** will extend to the processing of personal and sensitive data of both workers and non-workers if scheme members include past employees, and, in some cases, spouses and dependants.

3446 Where employers have administrative obligations in relation to such schemes or are, in fact, party to a scheme, they must ensure that they comply with the data protection rules (¶5945) (for example, where the data is personal and sensitive (¶5925), explicit consent should be obtained).

Further, as **good practice**, employers should (part 2.4 DP Code):

– remember that they do not have a right of access to personal information required for the administration of an OPS. The information should not be used for general employment purposes. For example, if a worker gives his medical records to the scheme administrator for the purposes of the OPS these records should not be used by the employer for non-OPS purposes, such as in deciding whether the worker is eligible for sick pay or not. If information is collected on behalf of the insurer, the employer must ensure there is a secure method of collection;

– limit the exchange of information with a scheme provider to the minimum necessary for operation of the scheme; and

– ensure that when a worker joins a scheme it is made clear what, if any, information is passed between the insurer and the employer and how it will be used. Unless told otherwise, workers are entitled to assume that information they give to a doctor, nurse or other health professional will be treated in confidence and not passed to others.

Employers are also advised to follow the DP Code's general **recommendations** with regard to data management (¶6000)

MEMO POINTS The Data Protection (Processing of Sensitive Personal Data) Order SI 2000/417 sets out more detailed provisions for processing information in establishing and administering an occupational pension scheme and information that is required to determine eligibility for, and benefits payable under, such a scheme.

3447 The employer who acts as scheme administrator should also be conscious of data protection compliance when **providing information to others** in connection with the administration of the scheme. Therefore, if the scheme actuary requires information on the age profile of scheme members in order to carry out a valuation of the scheme, any information that could identify individual scheme members should be anonymised before being sent out. The scheme administrators must ensure that they comply with the data protection rules (¶5945) (for example, where the data is sensitive (¶5925), explicit consent should be obtained).

C. Compliance

The Pensions Regulator is the **new regulatory body** for work-based pension schemes in the UK, having taken over from OPRA (the Occupational Pensions Regulatory Authority) on 6 April 2005 (Pensions Act 2004). A work-based pension scheme is defined as any scheme that an employer makes available to employees and includes all occupational schemes and any stakeholder and personal pension schemes where employees have direct payment arrangements. 3460

The Pensions Regulator has the **following objectives**:
- to protect the benefits of members of work-based pension schemes;
- to promote good administration of work-based pension schemes; and
- to reduce the risk of situations arising that may lead to claims for compensation from the Pension Protection Fund.

To meet these objectives, the Pensions Regulator has a **wide range of statutory powers** (wider than those previously available to OPRA), including:
- the power to issue improvement notices requiring schemes to take specific action;
- the ability to gather information to identify schemes most likely to present a risk to scheme members' benefits;
- increased powers to suspend, prohibit and remove trustees; and
- powers to require those involved with schemes to report suspected breaches of pensions legislation to the Pensions Regulator.

Remedies

An employee will have several options if his employer or trustees do not comply with: 3461
- the statutory pension rules or any other appropriate statutory rules, for example the right to equal pay;
- the rules of the scheme; or
- the implied duty of good faith or mutual trust and confidence.

Claims **against** the **employer** can be brought in the civil courts as a contractual claim (*Harris v Lord Shuttleworth* [1994] ICR 991, CA) whereas claims regarding **trustees** should be brought as a tortious action. Alternatively, the employee can bring a claim in the employment tribunal if it arises on, or is outstanding at, the termination of his employment, although this will be limited to the statutory maximum (currently £25,000) (Employment Tribunals Extension of Jurisdiction (England and Wales) Order SI 1994/1623). 3462

The employee can also complain to the **Pension Ombudsman** who can determine claims of maladministration against employers, trustees, or the scheme's managers or administrators. However, the Ombudsman cannot act if the employee has already brought an action in the civil courts or employment tribunal. There is a time limit of 3 years to make a claim though this can be extended at the Ombudsman's discretion (Personal and Occupational Pension Schemes (Pension Ombudsman) Regulations SI 1996/2475). Decisions can be appealed to the High Court. 3463

II. Stakeholder pensions

General rule

3470 If an employer has **more than five employees** and has **at least one relevant employee**, he must provide all his relevant employees with access to a designated stakeholder scheme **unless** he is exempt from doing so because (Welfare Reform and Pensions Act 1999; reg 22 Stakeholder Pension Schemes Regulations SI 2001/1403):
– he offers access to a **qualifying OPS** to all employees within 12 months of starting employment; or
– there is a term in his relevant employees' contracts which states that he will make contributions to a **qualifying personal pension scheme**.

The employer can offer access to an OPS to some employees and offer to contribute to a personal pension scheme for the rest of his employees as long as all relevant employees can benefit from one of the schemes.

3471 **Relevant employees** **All employees** and **office holders** are relevant employees.
However, the following employees and office holders are **excluded** if (reg 23 SI 2001/1403):
– they have worked for the employer for less than 3 calendar months;
– their earnings are below the National Insurance lower earnings limit for one or more weeks within the last 3 months;
– they are a member of their employer's OPS;
– they are excluded from their employer's OPS because they did not join when first invited to do so, or have opted out of the scheme;
– they cannot join the OPS because its rules do not admit members under 18 years old or because they are within 5 years of the scheme's NRD; or
– they cannot join a stakeholder pension scheme because of Revenue and Customs restrictions (e.g. they do not live in the UK).

3472 **Qualifying OPS** To qualify, all employees must be allowed to join within 12 months of starting employment. Membership does not have to be extended to those that are under 18 years old or are within 5 years of NRD. No particular level of benefits is required and a "death benefits only" scheme will be adequate. Further, the benefits do not have to be the same for each member and different benefit categories can be offered (though the employer must be careful he is not discriminatory).

If an employer plans to make any amendments to his OPS to enable it to qualify, he must remember that any amendments to approved schemes must be agreed by Revenue and Customs.

3473 **Qualifying personal pension scheme** To qualify, the employer must contribute an amount equal to at least 3% of the employee's basic pay to all relevant employees who are at least 18 years old. This can be conditional on matching employee contributions (but not more than 3% for new employees joining an existing scheme after 7 October 2001). Any new schemes set up after 7 October 2001 are limited to matched contributions of 3% or less. Further, the scheme must have no "exit charges" or penalties (i.e. for stopping contributions or for transferring the pension). The employer must deduct employee contributions if asked to do so and pay them to the trustees or manager/administrator of the scheme.

A. Procedure

Before the employer can designate a stakeholder scheme (which must be one that is **registered** with Revenue and Customs and the Pensions Regulator), he must **consult** with his relevant employees and any organisations that represent them (for example, trade unions and staff associations). The regulations do not give assistance as to what will amount to satisfactory consultation and the Department of Work and Pensions' stakeholder guide for employers states that it is up to the employer how this is done. However, the guide does suggest that an employer might: 3475
- already have a discussion process in place;
- give details about possible stakeholder pension schemes to employees at a meeting; or
- give employees written details and ask for their views.

Employers should not give **financial advice** in relation to the scheme

After consultation, it is the employer who must make the **final decision** about which scheme to designate. The employer does **not have to consider** the performance of the scheme as long as he is satisfied that: 3476
- the scheme is registered with Revenue and Customs and the Pensions Regulator;
- it offers membership to all his relevant employees; and
- he has given his employees information on the designated scheme.

Once a **scheme has been designated**, the employer must give adequate **information** to his employees so that they can decide whether to join the scheme. As well as the name and address of the scheme, the DWP guide suggests that employers should also give other appropriate contact details such as a named representative, phone and fax numbers and an e-mail address. The scheme provider may provide its own literature or leaflets that can be passed on the employees. 3477

Employers must allow reasonable access for **representatives** of the scheme to **visit the workplace** and to talk to employees about the benefits of joining the scheme.

Employees that **decide to join** the scheme must be told within 2 weeks, in writing, of how the employer plans to run the payroll deduction system including (reg 25 SI 2000/1403): 3478
- how the employee can ask for a change in contribution (for example, whether it should be in writing or by phone to a particular person);
- how often the employer will accept changes;
- how the employee can ask for his contributions to stop; and
- that any change in contributions will be made no later than the pay period after the request.

The employer can **refuse a request** to vary or make deductions if the employee has already made a change in the last 6 months. In such cases, he must write to the employee to explain why the request has been refused and when another request can be made.

Requests to stop contributions can be made at any time, though the employer must explain that no subsequent request need be acted on for 6 months. However, in such cases employee contributions can be made directly to the scheme.

The scheme must accept **employee contributions** of £20 or over and may accept payments of less (reg 17 SI 2000/1403). 3479

B. Compliance

3485 The employer must make sure that a **record** of the direct payment payroll arrangements is maintained showing the rates and dates of contributions (s 111A Pension Schemes Act 1993; reg 2 SI 2000/2692). These must include separate entries for the contributions payable by the employer and the employee and must be kept for a minimum of 6 tax years.

3486 **Penalties** The Pensions Regulator may impose a **civil penalty** of up to £50,000 for a company and £5,000 for an individual employer if the employer has failed to (s 10 Pensions Act 1995; s 111A (12) Pension Schemes Act 1993):
- designate and provide access to a stakeholder scheme;
- offer payroll deduction facilities; and
- keep or provide records.

3487 Further, an employer will be guilty of a **criminal offence** if he is knowingly involved in the fraudulent evasion of direct payment arrangements. This is subject to a maximum fine in the magistrates' court, and to an unlimited fine and up to 7 years in prison in the criminal courts.

CHAPTER 11

Time on

OUTLINE ¶¶

Time at work is regulated by legislation and generally concerns all workers (Working Time Regulations SI 1998/1833 as amended). Employers must ensure that the limits on the hours worked and breaks given comply with these regulations. Further, there are stricter obligations with regard to night workers and young workers. 3600

Workers also have the right to paid annual leave and this is discussed in Chapter 12.

Further, **shop and betting employees** have special rules relating to them if they work or may be required to work on Sundays (ss 36-43 ERA 1996; Sunday Trading Act 1994). 3601

SECTION 1

Working time

3605 The **minimum regulatory standards** that employers must comply with concern (Working Time Regulations SI 1998/1833 as amended, referred to as the regulations):
- the average weekly working time and night work;
- daily and weekly rest periods, and in-work rest breaks; and
- annual leave (¶4000).

While employers must ensure compliance with the regulations, workers are not obliged to make use of their entitlements and an employer cannot force a worker to take an entitlement that is made available to him (subject to health and safety considerations).

3606 Subject to the ability of workers to opt-out of the average weekly working time, neither employers nor workers can **contract out** of any of the regulations (regs 4, 5, 35 SI 1998/1833; *Witley & District Men's Club v Mackey* [2001] IRLR 595, EAT). Any term in the contract of employment or in any other contract, express or implied, will be **void** in so far as it seeks to exclude or limit the operation of any of the regulations or where it seeks to stop workers from bringing proceedings under them.

However, a **relevant agreement** can affect the application of the regulations. This is **defined** as any workforce agreement (¶4652) that applies to the worker, any provision of a collective agreement (¶7123) which forms part of a contract between him and his employer, or any other agreement in writing which is legally enforceable as between the worker and his employer (for example, the contract of employment). A written statement giving the statutory particulars relating to the terms and conditions of employment is unlikely to amount to a relevant agreement, as it is usually only evidence of the employment contract (¶1410).

3607 If employers **breach** certain provisions of the regulations they will commit a criminal offence. The courts have imposed a contractual obligation on employers with regard to the average weekly working time which workers will be able to enforce. Workers also have the right to bring a claim against employers in an employment tribunal to protect their working time rights.

MEMO POINTS The regulations are the implementation of the EC Organisation of Working Time Directive 1993/104 and aspects of the EC Protection of Young People at Work Directive 1994/33.

Summary of the application of the rules

3608 The following tables (for young workers, see ¶3720 and for workers in certain sectors, see ¶3640) show when the different regulatory standards apply.

	48 hour weekly limit	Night time limit	Daily and weekly rest	In-work breaks	Compensatory rest	Annual leave
Hours worked:						
Set and determined time under the control of the employer	✔	✔	✔	✔	n/a	✔
Unmeasured time	X	X	X	X	X	✔
Additional hours – as working time	✔	✔	✔	✔	n/a	✔
Additional hours – as unmeasured hours	X	X	✔	✔	n/a	✔
Due to distant commuting	✔	X	X	X	✔	✔
Due to foreseeable surge of activity in agriculture, tourism and postal services	✔	X	X	X	✔	✔

	48 hour weekly limit	Night time limit	Daily and weekly rest	In-work breaks	Compen-satory rest	Annual leave
Due to unusual and unforeseeable circumstances beyond control of employer	✔	X	X	X	✔	✔
Due to exceptional events which could not reasonably have been avoided by the employer	✔	X	X	X	✔	✔
Due to an accident or the imminent risk of an accident	✔	X	X	X	✔	✔
Due to shift work	✔	✔	X	✔	✔	✔
Due to collective or workforce agreement	✔	X	X	X	✔	✔
✔ = entitlement to right; X = no entitlement to right; n/a = not applicable						

I. Scope of regulations

The legal requirements on working time apply to all workers (reg 2(1) SI 1998/1833) and also apply to: 3615

a. **agency workers** (reg 36 SI 1998/1833). This is regardless of whether the agency worker comes under the general definition of worker or not. In the latter case, the regulations will apply as if there is a contract between the agency worker and whoever pays or is responsible for paying the agency worker in respect of the work (whether the agent or the principal); and

b. persons who are **receiving relevant training**, other than under a contract of employment (regs 42, 2(1) SI 1998/1833). Relevant training is **defined** as work experience provided in relation to a training course or programme, training for employment, or both, other than work experience or training where:

– the immediate provider is an educational institution/person whose main business is the provision of training; and

– which is provided on a course run by that institution/person.

Workers may be **totally or partially excluded** from certain rights **if they**:

– have unmeasured or partially unmeasured working time;

– work in shifts; or

– work in air, rail, road, sea, inland waterway and lake transport and sea fishing.

Further, workers can be partially excluded from certain rights **where**:

– it is needed for flexibility, continuity or other special reasons; or

– there is an agreement to do so in a collective or workforce agreement.

These are covered in detail as follows. It should be noted though, that even if such workers are excluded in whole or in part, an employer cannot require them to work such hours that would result in a breach of the employer's implied duty to take reasonable care for the health of his employees (¶4815) (*Johnstone v Bloomsbury Health Authority* [1991] IRLR 118, CA).

1. Unmeasured and partially unmeasured working time

Unmeasured

3625 Workers are excluded from all the regulations save those regarding annual leave (¶4000) if they have unmeasured working time (reg 20(1) SI 1998/1833). This occurs in the following three circumstances where:

a. the workers have **complete control** over the hours they work. For example, this will include managing executives who need to control their own work time, directors and those in similar positions who have autonomous decision-making powers. It will also include those who decide how and when they work, what is and what is not done, and who determine the time and effort that are devoted to their various tasks and objectives. Any additional hours worked will also be unmeasured working time;

b. the workers' time is not monitored or pre-determined by their employers because of **specific characteristics of the activity** in which the workers are engaged. For example, sales representatives who need to visit customers, often over a wide area, will determine themselves the hours worked. Workers who are engaged to complete a particular project or task, for example, home piece-workers (i.e. workers who are paid per piece or item produced), may fall within this exception, as their work is not measured by the number of hours; or

c. the workers are **family workers**.

Partially unmeasured

3627 For workers who are not excluded or do not have unmeasured working time, **any additional hours** worked over and above their normal contractual hours of work will qualify as (reg 20(2) SI 1998/1833):

– working time; or

– partially unmeasured working time.

The distinction is important because, if the additional hours worked are classified as partially unmeasured working time, they will not be subject to the rules concerning the average weekly working time (¶3680) and night time work (¶3695). Such hours will, therefore, not be included in calculating whether workers are within these limits.

3628 The **definition** of partially unmeasured working time is any time worked **without being required** to do so. Consequently, time worked that is set by the employer or is not controlled by the worker will amount to working time. The test is whether the worker had any choice if these hours could be worked or not. If the latter, then the hours worked are working time, but if it was a choice that the worker made without being required or asked to by his employer, then it is unmeasured.

It is often difficult to determine whether the hours a worker does outside any predetermined or requested hours constitute working time. To help with this distinction, the **DTI guide on working time** gives examples as to when additional hours worked would be working time. These illustrate the fine line between the employer's and the worker's subjective opinion as to the purpose and the control of the additional hours worked, and are as follows:

EXAMPLE 1. Worker A is paid by the hour. He occasionally works overtime, for which payment is made. The working time does not fall within the scope of this exception because it is measured.

2. Worker B's work is closely supervised. B is told what to do and when. B's working time does not fall within the scope of this exception, as it is not determined by B.

3. Worker C's contract specifies that she is to work 42 hours a week, but she regularly works longer because the volume of work is greater than could be done in the time. The nature of her job means that C works to deadlines and has to complete her work. She cannot control the volume of the work. The extra hours do not fall within the scope of this exception because she is required to do the work.

4. Worker D's contract also requires a working week of 42 hours, but the volume of work coming to him is greater than someone could reasonably be expected to do in that time. However, he has discretion and a clear choice over how much work is done, how his work is done and how to meet his objectives, for example he can prioritise his tasks and so, if he chose to, he could limit his

working week. Therefore, to the extent that he can limit them, the time worked beyond that required by his contract falls within the scope of this exception.
5. Worker E, whose contract requires a working week of 40 hours, works in an environment where colleagues habitually do a 12-hour day even though the work does not always necessitate such hours. Worker E works the long hours because she is led to believe that her employer considers it unacceptable to work shorter hours. Therefore, the time does not fall within the scope of this exception because she is required by her employer to work the extra time.
6. Worker F has a managerial or professional role which allows him to decide how and when he works, chooses what is done, establishes priorities and determines the time and effort that are devoted to tasks. Time worked above F's contracted hours will fall within the scope of this exception because he can determine the volume of his work.
7. Worker G for reasons of personal interest or self-motivation, chooses to go beyond the work that is expected of her, for example spending additional hours studying, thinking and reading about her work in addition to any formal employer-required training. Such time will fall within the scope of this exception because G determines the duration of the additional hours of work.
8. Worker H is a well paid sales representative who chooses to work beyond the hours necessary to meet her targets for reasons of personal motivation, for example additional commission. These additional hours will fall within the scope of the exception because H determines the volume of her work.

2. Shift workers

In certain circumstances, shift workers' right to **daily and weekly rest periods** may not apply (reg 22 SI 1998/1833). Any worker whose work schedule is part of shift work is a shift worker. Shift work is defined as any method of organising work in shifts so that workers succeed each other at the same workstations according to a certain pattern. This pattern includes a rotating pattern and may be continuous or discontinuous, with the need for workers to work at different times over a given period of days or weeks. 3635

If a **shift worker changes shift**, or where the work is split up over the day as may be the case for cleaning staff who have a morning and evening shift, it may not be possible for him to take his full rest entitlements before starting a new shift. If this happens, the entitlement to daily and weekly rest will not apply.

Shift workers who have had their rest entitlements affected will be entitled to **compensatory rest** (¶3717).

3. Workers in certain sectors

This sub-section refers to the special series of rules that apply to workers in **air, rail, road, sea, inland waterway and lake transport, sea fishing**, and **other work at sea (for example, offshore work in the oil and gas industry)**. In most of these sectors, different rules apply to non-mobile and mobile workers. 3640

MEMO POINTS These sectors were excluded from the original directive (EC Working Time Directive 1993/104 which was implemented in the UK by the Working Time Regulations SI 1998/1833) as it was agreed that these sectors required their own special rules. As a result, there are four specific Directives which concern specific groups (EC Aviation Directive 2000/79, EC Seafarers' Directive 1999/63, EC Seafarers' Enforcement Directive 1999/95 and EC Road Transport Directive 2002/15). How these have been implemented or when they are due to be implemented are detailed below. It should be noted that where there has not been implementation to date, these Directives can only be directly relied upon by workers of public bodies and authorities.

Outside the ambit of these specific Directives are non-mobile workers and certain groups of mobile workers working within these sectors. The EC Horizontal Amending Directive 2000/34 has expanded the original Directive to either fully or partially include such workers. This Directive has been implemented in the UK by the Working Time (Amendment) Regulations SI 2003/1684 which amend the original working time regulations.

MEMO POINTS **Doctors in training** are subject to an average weekly working limit of 58 hours (reg 7 Working Time (Amendment) Regulations SI 2003/1684 which adds a new reg 25A SI 1998/1833). On 1 August 2007 this will be reduced to 56 hours and on 1 August 2009 it will be further reduced to 48 hours.

Non-mobile workers

3642 Non-mobile workers (for example, administrative/clerical workers) are protected by the regulations in (Working Time (Amendment) Regulations SI 2003/1684):
- road, rail, air, sea, and inland waterway and lake transport;
- sea fishing; and
- other work at sea (for example, offshore work in the oil and gas industry).

Mobile workers

3644 The minimum regulatory standards (¶3605) generally apply to mobile workers although special exemptions and derogations will apply depending on the type of mobile worker. Some mobile workers are covered not by the regulations but by other legislation. For more information, readers are referred to the relevant regulatory/legislative source as set out below.

Mobile workers **protected by the regulations** are as follows:
1. those not covered by the EC Road Transport Directive 2002/15 (including all drivers not covered by EEC Community Drivers' Hours Regulation 3820/1985 (tachograph rules)) (for example, people carriers, couriers, taxis, white vans);
2. rail transport workers. Special exemptions apply to workers whose activities are intermittent, spent on trains and whose activities are linked to railway transport timetables and ensuring the continuity and regularity of railway traffic;
3. workers in aviation who are not covered by the EC Aviation Directive 2000/79 including those who work in corporate and general aviation as opposed to commercial air transport; and
4. offshore workers. Special derogation to allow for the weekly working time limit of 48 hours to be averaged over 52 weeks.

Mobile workers **protected/to be protected by other legislation** are as follows:
1. those covered by the EC Road Transport Directive 2002/15 (i.e. commercial drivers and crews of heavy good vehicles and public service vehicles) (or, in some cases, the AETR (the European agreement concerning the work of crews of vehicles engaged in international road transport) are now covered by new working time regulations) (Road Transport (Working Time) Regulations SI 2005/639) which have implemented this Directive. Special provisions allow for a maximum of 60 hours work in any single week (subject to compliance with the average weekly working time limit) and night workers are restricted to 10 hours working time in any 24-hour period;
2. those in civil aviation covered by the EC Aviation Directive 2000/79, including all mobile workers in commercial air transport (both flight crew and cabin crew), which has been implemented through the Civil Aviation (Working Time) Regulations SI 2004/756. Special provisions concern the maximum annual working time of crew members, adequate health and safety protection services and facilities at work along with adequate rest breaks to be given to crew members where work is organised in a certain pattern. Crew members are also entitled to a minimum number of rest days, free from all duties, in every calendar month and year;
3. seafarers on sea-going ships covered by the EC Seafarers' Directive 1999/63 which has been implemented through the Merchant Shipping (Hours of Work) Regulations SI 2002/2125. Special provisions require employers to ensure seafarers have at least the specified minimum hours of rest;
4. those in inland waterway and lake transport covered by the EC Horizontal Amendment Directive 2000/34 implemented through the Merchant Shipping (Working Time: Inland Waterways) Regulations SI 2003/3049 (which amends the Merchant Shipping Act 1995); and
5. sea fishermen covered by the EC Horizontal Amendment Directive 2000/34, still to be implemented.

4. Flexibility, continuity or other special reasons

In certain circumstances, workers will be excluded from the entitlements regarding (regs 21, 4(5) SI 1998/1833): 3650
- length of night work;
- daily and weekly rest periods; and
- in-work rest breaks.

Workers still keep their entitlement to annual leave. Employers will also have to make sure workers do not exceed the average weekly working time. In calculating this, the relevant reference period (¶3681) will be **any 26-week period**.

Workers will only be subject to these limited entitlements while they fall under one of the **following three categories** and they will be entitled to **compensatory rest** (¶3717):

1. Distant commuting Where a worker's place of work and home (or different places of 3652
work) are distant from one another, it may be beneficial to let him work more flexible hours (reg 21(a) SI 1998/1833). Flexibility may be desirable to allow him to work longer hours for a short period to complete a task more quickly, or because continual changes in the location of work make it impractical to set a pattern of work. Such working practices must be by agreement with the employer and will be acceptable as long as the average weekly working time is adhered to.

EXAMPLE Worker A's employer has agreed that A can work flexible hours because he lives far from work. This results in some days being worked without a break so that A can leave before the rush hour.
Worker B is a site worker and he needs flexible hours as he regularly visits different sites.

2. Continuity of service or production Employers may require the need for continuity of 3654
service or production as may be the case in (reg 21(b), (c) SI 1998/1833):
- services relating to the reception, treatment or care provided by:
  · hospitals or similar establishments,
  · residential institutions, or
  · prisons;
- work at docks or airports;
- press, radio, television or cinematographic production;
- postal and telecommunications services;
- gas, water and electricity production, transmission and distribution, household refuse collection and incineration;
- industries in which work cannot be interrupted on technical grounds (as may be the case where there is a need to keep machinery running);
- research and development activities;
- agriculture; or
- security and surveillance activities by security guards or caretakers (including any worker who is providing a permanent presence in order to protect property and persons).

3. Special events or circumstances Employers may require greater flexibility with regard 3656
to their workers' working hours in the following circumstances:
- a foreseeable surge of activity (as can happen in relation to agriculture, tourism, and postal services);
- an occurrence due to unusual and unforeseeable circumstances beyond the control of the employer;
- exceptional events, the consequences of which could not have been avoided despite the exercise of all due care by the employer; or
- an accident or the imminent risk of an accident.

When considering whether a derogation from the entitlement to an in-work rest break can be invoked, the need for continuity of service or production must relate to the activities of the workers concerned as opposed to those of the employer (*Gallagher and others v Alpha Catering*

Services Ltd t/a Alpha Flight Services [2005] IRLR 102, CA). Without such interpretation, the protection given by the regulations would be vulnerable to abuse by employers who deliberately understaff their workplaces to ensure a need for continuity of service or production is maintained. Moreover, when considering the meaning of "foreseeable surge of activity", this must refer to something more acute than mere fluctuations in activity which takes place as a matter of course.

5. Collective or workforce agreement

3660 A collective agreement or workforce agreement may **modify or exclude** the following regulations with regard to particular workers or groups of workers (reg 23 SI 1998/1833):
- length of night work limit;
- daily and weekly rest periods; and
- in-work rest breaks.

Workers who are affected will be entitled to **compensatory rest** (¶3717).

Such workers are still entitled to annual leave. Employers will also have to make sure that workers do not work over the average weekly working time limit. The **relevant reference period** (¶3681) in calculating the average weekly working time can be up to 52 weeks if it is necessary for objective or technical reasons or for reasons concerning the organisation of work.

II. Minimum standards

3670 Limitations are set as to how long a worker can work during a set period of time (the average weekly working time) though workers can opt out by agreement. Workers are also entitled to weekly, daily and in-work rest periods.

3671 **Working time** is **defined** as when a worker is working at his employer's disposal and is carrying out his employer's activities or duties (reg 2(1) SI 1998/1833). Both these elements must be satisfied for time worked to be regarded as working time. Additional periods can be counted as working time if allowed under a collective or workforce agreement.

For example, time worked that is **paid hourly**, **prescribed hours** of work, work done under **close supervision**, or **expressly or implicitly requested periods** of work will be working time. Implicitly requested periods of work include longer hours worked either because:
- of the requirements of the work, for example, to finish a delivery or meet a deadline; or
- the worker may suffer a detriment, for example be passed over for promotion, if he does not work longer hours.

Working extra hours **without being required** to do so will be partially unmeasured working time (¶3628) and will not be subject to the following regulations concerning the average weekly working time and night time work.

3672 Where the worker is obliged to be **present and available** at his workplace with a view to providing his professional services, it is regarded as working time.

This includes time spent resting or sleeping at the workplace where such facilities are provided (for example, providing on-call hospital doctors with beds for use when they are not attending to patients) (*Landeshauptstadt Kiel v Norbert Jaeger* [2003] IRLR 804, ECJ). However, where the worker is not present at his place of work but is **on call**, his time is not regarded as working time if he is free to pursue leisure activities although if a worker is called to his place of work while on call, his time at his place of work in response is, naturally, working time (*Sindicato de Médicos de Asistencia Publica (SIMAP) v Conselleria Sanidad Y Consumo de la Generalidad Valenciana* [2000] IRLR 845, ECJ).

The following table sets out specific activities as examples of what counts towards working time: 3673

Periods included as working time	Periods excluded as working time
Working/business lunch or corporate entertaining	Lunch break
Working at home with prior consent of employer	Taking work home without prior consent
Time spent travelling if it is an essential part of work (for example, a sales representative)	Time spent travelling to and from a place of work
Time on call where the worker is at his place of work or is restricted as to what he can do and cannot pursue leisure activities	Time on call where the worker is otherwise free to pursue leisure activities
Time spent on relevant training (for example, training a machine operator)	Time spent on other training or activities (for example, training and playing football in a company team)

A. General system of average weekly working time

A worker's working time, including overtime, **must not exceed** an average of 48 hours a week (7 days) in any reference period (reg 4(1) SI 1998/1833) unless he has **opted out**, see ¶3688. 3680

MEMO POINTS A **day** is taken as a period of 24 hours beginning at midnight (reg 2(1) SI 1998/1833).

Reference period

This average is calculated over a reference period. For each worker, this is **any 17-week period** of work, unless a relevant agreement has pre-defined specific **consecutive periods of 17 weeks**. Employers, therefore, can require workers to work more than 48 hours a week for some of the weeks within a reference period as long as some of the other weeks are less than 48 hours to compensate and to ensure that the average remains 48 hours or less. 3681

If the worker has worked less than 17 weeks then the working time is calculated for the period he has worked up to the date of calculation. If he is a **night worker** he will also be subject to the night work limit (see below).

Where there is the need for **flexibility, continuity or other special reasons** (¶3650), the average weekly limit will still apply but it should be noted that the reference period will be any 26-week period.

An **extended reference period** is allowed up to 52 weeks under a workforce or collective agreement (reg 23 SI 1998/1833).

MEMO POINTS The European Commission has published its proposals for amendments to the EC Organisation of Working Time Directive 1993/104 and has proposed that the reference period should be allowed to be up to 52 weeks. It has also proposed that no worker should work more than 65 hours in any individual week. Whether these proposals will be approved is uncertain.

Calculating average weekly working time

Average weekly working time is calculated by dividing the number of hours worked by the number of weeks in the reference period. 3684

EXAMPLE A worker has a standard working week of 40 hours and does overtime of 10 hours a week for the first 10 weeks of the 17-week reference period.
The total hours worked is:
17 weeks of 40 hours and 10 weeks of 10 hours of overtime
(17 × 40) + (10 × 10) = 780
Average weekly working time:
780/17 = 45.9 hours a week.

3685 The number of working days taken into account must be days worked and **days of absence** due to sickness, annual leave or maternity, paternity, adoption or parental leave are excluded from the reference period. Actual days worked (equal to the number of days of absence) must, therefore, be added to the reference period by including the appropriate number of worked days immediately after the reference period has ended.

If the reference period is set to start at a specific date by a relevant agreement, the inclusion of extra days immediately after one reference period has ended will not affect the date on which the subsequent reference period starts. Such extra days are counted twice, both in the reference period in which there was absence and in the subsequent reference period.

3686 The **average weekly hours** can be calculated by using the formula:

$$\frac{(A + B)}{C}$$

A is the total number of hours worked **during** the reference period;
B is the total number of hours worked **immediately after** the reference period equal to the number of days missed during that period due to absence;
A + B are the total hours worked; and
C is the number of weeks in the reference period.

Opting out

3688 Individual workers can voluntarily agree to work **more than the average weekly limit**. This must be **agreed in writing** and it must allow the worker to terminate it (regs 4, 5 SI 1998/1833). Any such agreement can be for a specified or an indefinite period, and can have a notice period of up to 3 months. If no notice period is specified, only 7 days' written notice will be required to end the agreement. If it is obvious from the outset that the worker may exceed the average weekly limit, the opt-out can be included in the contract of employment.

The ECJ has recently emphasised that a worker's consent to opting out of the average weekly working time limit "must be given not only individually but also **expressly and freely**" (*Pfeiffer and others v Deutsches Rotes Kreuz, Kreisverband Waldshut eV, Case C397-403/01* [2005] ICR 1307, ECJ). Consequently, employers must ensure that not only do they have a written agreement with each worker who is opting out (which can be included in the worker's contract of employment) but that it is made clear to them that they have the freedom to choose whether or not to opt-out.

Where an opt-out agreement **covers only part** of a reference period, this must be excluded from the average weekly hours formula (above) and an equivalent period must be added to the end of the reference period. This may occur if the opt-out is for a specified period or if it has been terminated.

MEMO POINTS The European Commission has published its **proposed amendments** to the Working Time Directive 1993/104. Its main proposals are that Member States should only be allowed to apply the opt-out if it is expressly allowed under a collective bargaining arrangement. However, if there is no collective arrangement or workers' representation, individual consent would be allowed to be obtained, though it is proposed that this must be writing and limited to a maximum of 1 year although this can be renewed. Further, it is proposed that consent should not be given at the same time as the worker's contract is signed or during any probationary period.

These proposals attracted much criticism, particularly in the UK (which is the only Member State which allows workers to opt-out as a general rule) and were opposed by the Council of Ministers in June 2005 (in a blocking action led by the UK), which has prevented voting. The Council will need to vote before the issue returns to the European Parliament (which has voted to phase out the right to opt out by 2010) though this is now unlikely to happen until sometime during 2006.

B. Night time working

Night time is defined as a period of at least 7 hours (which must include the period from midnight to 5 am) which is determined by a relevant agreement. If there is no agreement night time will be from 11 pm to 6 am (reg 2(1) SI 1998/1833). 3695

A **night worker** is defined as any worker 'who, as a normal course, works at least 3 hours of his daily working time during night time, or who is likely, during night time, to work at least such proportion of his annual working time in a collective agreement or a workforce agreement.' The term night worker is therefore intended to apply to workers who work at night as part of a regular shift pattern rather than on an occasional or infrequent basis.

Stricter controls operate on **young workers** (¶3720).

Normal hours of night work

A night worker should not exceed an average of 8 hours work for each 24 hours over the reference period (reg 6 SI 1998/1833). The **reference period** and **extended reference period** are the same as for the average weekly working time. 3696

The night working limit is a **separate limit** to the average weekly working time. Employers must ensure that night workers also comply with the weekly average.

Calculating normal hours of night work The hours of night work are calculated by dividing the number of a worker's **normal hours** of working time in the reference period by the total number of days in the period, less the number of rest days to which the worker was entitled. This calculation is **based on** normal hours worked (which can include overtime where it is part of the worker's normal hours) and not actual hours worked. 3697

Average night hours can be calculated using the formula:

$$\frac{A}{(B-C)}$$

A is the number of normal working hours during the reference period;
B is the number of days during the reference period; and
C is the number of hours of weekly rest to which a worker is entitled (i.e. 24 hours for each 7 days (¶3712)) divided by 24. Note that this is not the total amount of hours that the worker is at rest in each week but only the hours making up the weekly rest period to which he is entitled.

EXAMPLE A night worker normally works 4 12-hour shifts each week.
Therefore, A is for a 17-week reference period:
17 weeks of 4 shifts of 12 hours
17 × (4 × 12) = 816
B is the number of days during the reference period:
17 × 7 = 119 days
There are 17 weekly rest periods of 24 hours to which the worker is entitled during the reference period.
Therefore, C is:
17 × (24/24) = 17
The calculation of the total of hours divided by the number of days a worker could be required to work:
816/(119 – 17) = 8, giving an average of 8 hours in each 24-hour period.

Work involving special hazards or strain

Where a night worker's work involves special hazards or heavy physical or mental strain, there is a limit of 8 hours on the worker's actual daily working time. The **8-hour limit** must be observed in any period of 24 hours during which the night worker performs such work. 3699

A night worker is regarded as being involved in special hazards or heavy physical or mental strain if either:
- the collective or workforce agreement identifies the work as such; or
- it is recognised as such in a risk assessment made by the employer under the Management of Health and Safety at Work Regulations SI 1999/3242.

Health of night workers

3701 An employer must offer a worker a free health assessment **before assigning him** work that makes him a night worker (reg 7 SI 1998/1833). If the worker has already had a health assessment due to a previous assignment and the employer has no reason to believe that the assessment is no longer valid (because it was a recent assessment and there are no indications of any health problems), the employer will have satisfied this requirement.

3702 Free health assessments must be offered at **regular intervals** as appropriate (reg 7(6) SI 1998/1833). If a night worker is doing hazardous work or has a medical condition that might be affected by the work then free health assessments should be offered at **shorter intervals** than with regard to other night workers.

Where a registered medical practitioner advises that a worker is **suffering from health problems** which are considered to be connected with the worker working at night and it is possible for the employer to transfer the worker (to work which the worker is suitable for and which allows him to stop being a night worker) then the employer must do so.

C. Rest periods

3710 Workers are **entitled** to weekly, daily and in-work rest periods. Stricter controls operate on employers of young workers. Employers must ensure that workers can take their rest, but are not required to ensure that they do so.

Periods of inactivity or sleep during working time while workers are on-call do not count towards their rest periods, particularly if they are not guaranteed a minimum number of hours of continuous rest (*Landeshauptstadt Kiel v Norbert Jaeger* [2003] IRLR 804, ECJ).

Daily and weekly rest periods

3711 These are **separate entitlements**. Weekly rest is additional to any paid annual leave to which workers may be entitled.

3712 A worker is entitled to **daily rest** of 11 consecutive hours during a 24-hour period (reg 10 SI 1998/1833).

A worker is entitled to **weekly rest** of an uninterrupted rest period of not less than 24 hours in each 7-day period (reg 11 SI 1998/1833). This may be averaged over a 2-week period so that the worker is entitled to either two uninterrupted rest periods of not less than 24 hours each or one uninterrupted rest period of not less than 48 hours.

In-work rest breaks

3715 A worker is entitled to an uninterrupted break of 20 minutes when his daily working time is more than 6 hours (reg 12 SI 1998/1833). It should be a break in working time and should not be taken either at the start or at the end of a working day. It should not overlap with a worker's daily rest period.

Where the **pattern of work** is such as to put the health and safety of the worker at risk, employers must make sure that workers are given adequate rest breaks to negate this risk which may exceed those specifically required by the regulations (reg 8 SI 1998/1833). Such circumstances include monotonous work or uninterruptible work, for example, repetitive work on a factory line, or work involving special hazards or heavy physical or mental strain.

Compensatory rest

3717 Where the rest periods or in-work rest breaks do not apply or have been modified (in relation to shift workers (¶3635), those working in conditions that require flexibility, continuity etc (¶3650), those working under a collective or workforce agreement which has modified or excluded certain rights (¶3660) and young workers (¶3720)), workers must be permitted to take equivalent periods of compensatory rest wherever possible (reg 24 SI 1998/1833). In exceptional cases, where it is not possible for objective reasons to give compensatory rest, the employer must give the worker such protection as may be appropriate in order to safeguard his health and safety.

The daily rest entitlement may be incorporated into the weekly rest entitlement if this is justified by objective or technical reasons or reasons concerning the organisation of work.

Compensatory rest should be provided **within** a reasonable time from when the entitlement to rest was not applied or modified.

D. Young workers

Employers with young workers have stricter controls with regard to the night time limit. Young workers are also entitled to longer rest periods and there are restrictions on whether these can be altered or modified. 3720

The **definition** of a young worker is a worker who is 15 to 17 years old and is over compulsory school age (reg 2(1) SI 1998/1833). Children of compulsory school age are not workers within the meaning of the regulations (*Addison & another (trading as Brayton News) v Ashby* [2003] ICR, 667, EAT). Such children are covered by other regulations (Children (Protection at Work) Regulations SI 1998/276) (¶4880). 3721

Further, there are **additional health and safety requirements** which limit the type of work a child or young person can do (¶4880).

Day time limit

Young workers must **not work for more than** 8 hours a day or 40 hours a week **unless** (regs 5A, 27A(1) SI 1998/1833): 3722

– it is necessary to maintain continuity of service/production or as a response to a surge in demand for a service/product;
– there is no adult available to perform the task; and
– the employer ensures that the training needs of the young worker are not adversely affected.

This cannot be averaged out over a period of time nor can young workers opt out. Employers must also take all reasonable steps to ensure that this limit is complied with (reg 5A(4) SI 1998/1833).

Night time limit

Young workers must **not work at night between** 10 pm and 6 am, or between 11 pm and 7 am if the contract of employment provides for work after 10 pm (regs 2, 6A SI 1998/1833). 3724

However, as **exceptions**, young workers are (reg 27A SI 1998/1883): 3725

a. permitted to work at night if they work in a hospital or similar establishment or are employed in connection with cultural, artistic, sporting or advertising activities; and

b. permitted to work between 10 pm and midnight and between 4 am and 7 am if they are employed in agriculture, retail trading, postal or newspaper deliveries, a catering or bakery business, or a hotel, public house, restaurant, bar or similar establishment;

if it is necessary to maintain continuity of service/production or as a response to a surge in demand for a service/product, there is no adult available to perform the task, and the employer ensures that the training needs of the young worker are not adversely affected. In such cases, the employer must ensure that the young worker has the opportunity of a **free assessment of his health and capacities** before working such hours.

Further, where in such circumstances young workers are required to work during a period which would otherwise be a rest period or in-work break, they must be **supervised** by an adult worker where such supervision is necessary for their protection and they must be allowed an equivalent period of **compensatory rest** (¶3717).

Daily and weekly rest periods

3727 A young worker is entitled to daily rest of 12 consecutive hours in each 24-hour period during which he works (reg 10(2) SI 1998/1833).

A young worker is also entitled to weekly rest of 2 days each week which cannot be averaged over a 2-week period (reg 11 SI 1998/1833). This weekly rest may be reduced to 36 hours, where justified by technical or organisational reasons, for example, where such reasons are inherent in the nature of the work or its desired purpose.

The minimum daily and weekly rest periods can be interrupted in the case of activities involving periods of work that are split up over the day or do not last long.

In-work rest breaks

3729 A young worker is entitled to an in-work rest break of 30 minutes when daily working time is more than 4.5 hours (reg 12(4) SI 1998/1833).

Alterations or modifications to rest periods and in-work breaks

3731 A young worker's entitlement to daily rest periods and in-work rest breaks may be modified or excluded where he has to undertake tasks because there is no adult worker available. In addition, these tasks must (reg 27 SI 1998/1833):

a. need to be performed immediately;
b. be of a temporary nature; and
c. be due to:
– unusual and unforeseeable circumstances, beyond the employer's control; or
– exceptional events, the consequences of which could not have been avoided by the employer regardless of whether due care has been taken.

If a young worker is required to work in these conditions, the employer must allow him to take an equivalent period of **compensatory rest** (¶3717) within the following 3 weeks.

III. Records

3740 Employers must keep records, which **adequately show** that the average weekly working time and night work limits for workers and the maximum working time and night work provisions for young workers have been complied with in regard to each worker, and all records must be **retained for** 2 years (reg 9 SI 1998/1833). An up-to-date record of any workers who have opted out of the average weekly working time limit will need to be kept by employers but there is no need to record how many hours they actually work (reg 4(2) SI 1998/1883).

Employers will not be expected to keep a running total of how much time workers work on average each week, and will only be expected to make occasional checks on workers who do standard hours and who are unlikely to reach the average weekly working time limit. However, employers should monitor the hours of workers who appear close to the working time limits to ensure that such workers do not exceed these limits.

Records can be based on time sheets produced by workers or information produced on requiring workers to clock in and out of their places of work. If there are no time sheets or clocking in and out procedures, the normal contractual hours can be used as a guide with the employer adding any working time done above this, for example, from overtime sheets. Employers might be able to use existing records maintained for other purposes, for example pay, or they may have to make new records.

Employers should require workers to inform them of any hours they work for other employers (as these will count towards the limit on working time) so that they can ensure that the working time limits are complied with.

There is no requirement to keep records to show that the entitlements to **daily** and **weekly rest periods** and **in-work rest breaks** have been complied with. However, as an employee can make a complaint to an employment tribunal if the employer breaches the regulations with regard to these entitlements, it is advisable for both parties to keep adequate records. 3741

Should any disputes arise as to the number of hours worked, it will be a factual and evidential issue which the tribunal or court will decide.

Records of **health assessments** must also be **kept for** 2 years and they must not be disclosed to any person other than to the worker to whom the assessment relates, unless (regs 9, 7(5) SI 1998/1833): 3742
- the worker has given his consent in writing to the disclosure; or
- disclosure is confined to a statement that the assessment shows the worker to be fit for night work.

IV. Enforcement and remedies

Employers will commit a criminal offence and will be subject to penalties if they do not comply with certain of the rules. 3750

Workers can also ensure that employers comply with certain of their entitlements and have two enforcement options available to them. The first is from a contractual obligation on employers which will be enforceable in the civil courts. The second is from a regulatory obligation on employers which can be enforced through the employment tribunals.

Workers may also have a specific action in an employment tribunal for unfair dismissal and have the right not to suffer detriment.

Summary of enforcement provisions 3751

Working time provision	Offence/Complaint	Where enforced	Penalty/Remedy
Average weekly working time	Criminal offence	Magistrates' court Crown Court	Fine Fine
	Breach of contract	Civil courts	Declaration of rights Injunction
Night time limit and provisions	Criminal offence	Magistrates' court Crown Court	Fine Fine
Adequate rest breaks during monotonous work			
Records			
Daily and weekly rest periods	Breach of regulations	Employment tribunal	Declaration Compensation
In-work rest breaks			
Compensatory rest			
Annual leave (¶4000)			
Specific protection from unfair dismissal in relation to working time and annual leave (¶4000)	Unfair dismissal	Employment tribunal	Reinstatement Re-engagement Compensation
Right not to suffer detriment for insisting on working time and annual leave (¶4000) rights	Breach of right	Employment tribunal	Declaration Compensation

A. Criminal offences and penalties

3755 The authority **responsible for enforcing** the regulations is the Health and Safety Executive except where the relevant requirements apply in relation to workers employed in premises for which the local authority has control in which case responsibility lies with that local authority (reg 28 SI 1998/1833).

An employer will commit an offence on failing to comply with (reg 29 SI 1998/1833):
– average weekly working time and the maximum working time for young workers, both of which he must take all reasonable steps to observe;
– the night time limit and the provisions regarding night work for young workers, both of which he must take all reasonable steps to observe;
– giving compensatory rest where necessary with regard to night time workers and young night time workers;
– the requirement to provide free health assignments for night time workers and young night time workers;
– providing young night time workers with supervision by an adult worker where necessary for their protection;
– his duty to transfer a night time worker to day work on advice from a doctor where it is possible to do so;
– giving adequate rest breaks for workers with monotonous or repetitive work; or
– keeping records.

The penalties are:
– in the **magistrates' court**, a fine not exceeding the statutory maximum; and
– in the **Crown Court**, a fine as decided appropriate by the judge.

B. Remedies

Breach of contract

3760 The regulations impose an implied contractual obligation on employers not to require workers to do more than the **average weekly working time** (*Barber v RJB Mining (UK) Limited* [1999] IRLR 308, QBD). This creates a freestanding legal right under the contract of employment or any other relevant contract and a worker can bring an action against his employer in the **civil courts** for a declaration of his rights.

In *Barber v RJB Mining (UK) Limited*, the High Court made a declaration of the workers' rights and enforced these rights using injunctions. This declaration meant that the workers were entitled to refuse to continue working until their average working hours came within the specified limit.

Breach of regulations

3761 Workers can bring a complaint against their employers in an **employment tribunal** for breach of the following entitlements (reg 30 SI 1998/1833):
– daily and weekly rest periods;
– in-work breaks;
– compensatory rest (including compensatory rest with regard to young workers); and
– annual leave.

The worker must **bring** his **complaint within** 3 months starting on the date when: 3762
– it is alleged that the exercise of the right should have been allowed (where the alleged rest period or leave extended over a day, the date on which it should have been permitted to start); or
– a payment should have been made as compensation in relation to an annual leave entitlement.

This period may be extended if considered reasonable by the tribunal, and if the tribunal is satisfied that it was not reasonably practicable for the complaint to be presented before the end of the 3-month period.

Where a **tribunal finds** a **complaint well founded**, it will make a declaration to that effect, 3763
and may make an award of compensation (s 18(1) ERA 1996). A tribunal will award whatever it considers to be just and equitable in all the circumstances having regard to:
– the employer's default in refusing to permit the worker to exercise his right; and
– any loss sustained by the worker that is attributable to the matters complained of.

Right not to suffer detriment

A **worker** can make a complaint for detrimental effect, or deliberate failure to act by his 3765
employer, which has occurred as a result of him (s 45A ERA 1996):
– having refused (or proposing to refuse) to comply with a requirement which his employer imposed (or proposed) in contravention of the regulations;
– refusing (or proposing to refuse) to forgo a working time or annual leave right;
– failing to:
· sign a workforce agreement for the purposes of the regulations, or
· enter into, or agree to vary or extend, any other agreement with his employer; or
– being a representative of members of the workforce for the purposes of workforce agreements, or being a candidate in an election in which any worker elected will become such a representative, and performing (or proposing to perform) any function or activities in his role.

Workers can also suffer a detriment for **alleging an infringement** for any of the above acts or for bringing proceedings against their employers.

It is irrelevant and immaterial whether or not a worker did have the right or whether a right has been infringed. However, all claims must be made in **good faith**.

Contractual **changes to accommodate opting back in** are not detrimental if they are necess- 3766
ary to facilitate the reduction of working hours and are not, on weighing up their advantages and disadvantages, substantial or material (*Clamp v Aerial Systems*, EAT case 0266/04).

EXAMPLE In *Clamp v Aerial Systems*, an engineer, C, who drove to appointments had an opted-out working week of 60 hours which was unregulated. When he opted back in his employer calculated C's hours from the start of his first job to the end of his last job. When he had no first job, his working time now started from a designated spot on the motorway. The EAT held that discounting C's time spent travelling to and from work was not detrimental as it is common ground that time spent travelling to and from a place of work is not working time and in any event his salary was the same as before. Further, requiring him to wait at a designated spot rather than at home had more advantages than disadvantages and meant that he started his working day earlier. Consequently, despite the fact that C could no longer wait at home, this was not a detriment.

MEMO POINTS The EAT also commented in this case that reducing a worker's pay, if his hours are reduced on opting back in, would not be a detriment as long as the worker's hourly rate of pay remains the same.

Right not to be unfairly dismissed

Any dismissal of an employee will be **automatically unfair** (¶8390) if the reason (or, if more 3769
than one, the principal reason) for the dismissal is one of those covered by the right not to suffer a detriment (s 101A ERA 1996).

MEMO POINTS Non-employee workers who are so dismissed should rely on the right not to suffer a detriment (see above) though compensation is awarded on the same basis as for unfair dismissal.

SECTION 2

Sunday trading

3800 Although Sunday is normally regarded as an ordinary working day, shop and betting employees have **special rules** relating to them if they work or may be required to work on Sundays (ss 36-43 ERA 1996; Sunday Trading Act 1994).

Unless a shop or betting employee is employed solely to work on Sundays, he has the **right to opt-out** of Sunday working and, if he was such an employee when the various rules came into force, he is automatically protected and cannot be required to work on Sundays. In this section, opted-out employees and those who are automatically protected will be referred to as **protected employees**. If protected, employees can nevertheless opt-in and expressly agree to work on Sundays, or on a particular Sunday.

3801 Within 2 months of becoming a shop or betting employee, the employer must give the employee an **explanatory statement** setting out the employee's rights with regard to Sunday working.

3802 Any contractual term, made either before or after the employee was protected that purports to override his protection is unenforceable (s 37 ERA 1996). If a protected employee has opted-in to Sunday working, his contractual terms are varied only to the extent necessary to give effect to any subsequent express agreement to work on Sundays or on a particular Sunday.

3803 There is no statutory right for an employee working on Sundays to receive an enhanced hourly **rate of pay** (s 45 ERA 1996). However, most employers do offer special overtime rates or premiums to encourage employees to work on Sundays and this is legally acceptable. Therefore, a protected shop or betting employee has no remedy if his wage is reduced because, although he does the same hours, he no longer works on Sundays. Likewise, a protected employee has no remedy if the employer does not provide him with any other benefit that is related to Sunday working.

MEMO POINTS Small shops whose floor area for the display, sales and serving of goods are not more than 280 metres can open freely on Sunday and larger shops can open for up to 6 continuous hours between 10 am and 6 pm (there are exemptions for certain types of large shop).

I. Shop employees

Definitions

3810 A shop employee is an employee who, under his contract of employment, is or may be required to do shop work (s 232 ERA 1996). Shop work is work in or about a shop that is open for serving customers. This includes sales assistants, check-out operators, shop managers and supervisors, and those working around the shop such as shelf-fillers and security staff. As the rules relate to shops opening on Sundays, those employed, for example shelf-fillers or stock-takers, while the shop is closed are excluded.

EXAMPLE A, a shelf-filler, works when the shop is closed and is required to work Sunday mornings, 6.00 am until 10.00 am prior to the shop opening at 12.00 noon. A is not a shop employee.
His colleague, B, is a cashier and works behind the till when the shop is open including Sundays from noon until 5.00 pm. B is a shop employee.

3811 A **shop** is defined as any premises where a retail trade or business is carried on and includes barbers, hairdressers, hiring of goods (other than for use in the course of a trade or business) and retail auctions. It does not include restaurants or other catering businesses that sell meals, refreshments or alcoholic drinks for consumption, either on the premises or immediately off the premises, or the sale of programmes, catalogues and similar items at a theatre or place of amusement.

Where premises are mainly used for other purposes, only the **part of the premises**, which is used wholly or mainly for the purposes of retail trade, or which is used together with a wholesale trade (i.e. the sale, resale or hire of goods for use in the course of a business) is within the definition of a shop.

A. Protected employees

What, if any, protection a shop employee has will depend on when he became a shop employee and his contractual terms (s 36 ERA 1996). 3815

Excluded employees

Where a shop employee's contractual terms state that he is to work solely on Sundays, he obviously has no protective rights with regard to Sunday working and is termed an excluded employee regardless of when he became a shop employee. 3816

1. Shop employees on 25 August 1994

Regardless of whether there are contractual terms, where a shop employee was employed as a shop worker (but not to work only on Sundays) he will be automatically protected (s 36(2) ERA 1996). It is irrelevant whether or not the employee performed regular or occasional Sunday work before this date. 3820

Where there are contractual terms, an automatically protected employee, as with opted-out employees, has no right to work extra hours if he chooses not work on Sundays and his pay or any other benefits can be reduced accordingly (¶3803). 3821

2. Shop employees employed after 25 August 1994 with no contractual terms

Where there are no contractual terms requiring, or allowing for Sunday working, the shop employee is automatically protected (s 36(3) ERA 1996). He can surrender his protection (i.e. opt-in) (¶3845). 3825

3. Shop employees employed after 25 August 1994 with contractual terms

Where there are contractual terms requiring or allowing for Sunday working, the shop employee has the right to be protected (ss 40-41 ERA 1996). If the employee exercises this right, he will have opted-out. This right is obtained when the employee gives the employer a written notice called an opting-out notice. The employer must inform the employee of his right to opt-out. Even if he opts-out, the employee can always opt-in again. 3830

Opting-out

The opting-out notice must be signed and dated by the employee, stating that he objects to Sunday working. The employee does not need to give any reason as to why he does not wish to work on Sundays. 3831

3832 **Notice can be given** at any time while he is a shop employee and is effective 3 months from the date of the notice. If the **employer does not issue** the required **explanatory statement** (see below) within 2 months of the employee becoming a shop employee, the opting-out notice period is reduced to 1 month.

During this opting-out notice period, the employee can be required to work on Sundays or on a particular Sunday in accordance with his contractual terms.

3833 **Employers' duty to inform of opt-out rights** Before the end of 2 months from when the employee became a shop employee, the employer should give the employee an **explanatory statement** (s 42 ERA 1996). This statement is **legally prescribed as follows**:

"*You have become employed as a shop worker and are or can be required under your contract of employment to do the Sunday work your contract provides for.*

However, if you wish, you can give notice, as described in the next paragraph, to your employer and you will then have the right not to work in or about a shop on any Sunday on which the shop is open once 3 months have passed from the date on which you gave notice.

Your notice must:
– *be in writing;*
– *be signed and dated by you; and*
– *say that you object to Sunday working.*

For 3 months after you give the notice, your employer can still require you to do all the Sunday work your contract provides for. After the 3 month period has ended, you have the right to complain to an employment tribunal if, because of your refusal to work on Sundays on which the shop is open, your employer:
– *dismisses you; or*
– *does something else detrimental to you, for example, failing to promote you.*

Once you have the rights described, you can surrender them only by giving your employer a further notice, signed and dated by you, saying that you wish to work on Sunday or that you do not object to Sunday working and then agreeing with your employer to work on Sundays or on a particular Sunday."

3834 **In summary**, the statement sets out the employee's statutory rights, in particular:
– the right not to work on Sundays after serving an opting-out notice on the employer;
– when the notice takes effect; and
– after the opting-out notice period:
· the employee has the right to complain to an employment tribunal if the employer dismisses him or subjects him to a detriment or causes him to suffer a detriment (for example, fails to promote him) because he does not agree to work on Sundays or on a particular Sunday; and
· the employee must give an opting-in notice (¶3845) to surrender his protective rights, if the employee subsequently does not object to Sunday work or wants to work on Sundays.

EXAMPLE On 1 January 2005, in accordance with his contractual terms, A starts work as a shop employee as he is moved from stocking shelves when the shop is closed to working behind the till as a cashier. A is required to work every Sunday in accordance with these terms. His employer must inform A of his legal rights in the prescribed statement by 29 February 2005.

1. A's employer **serves the prescribed form** in early February and in response A gives his employer an opting-out notice on 12 February, which is effective 3 months later. Consequently from Sunday, 16 May, A cannot be required to work (or any Sunday thereafter as long as he remains a shop employee), unless A opts-in to Sunday working. During the 3 months notice period though, A will be obliged to work in accordance with his contractual terms and can therefore be required to work on Sunday.

2. A's employer does **not serve the prescribed form** by 29 February. A is aware of his rights from talking to other employees, and so gives notice to his employer on 1 March that he does not want to work on Sundays. As a result, his protection starts on 1 April, 1 month after he gives notice.

Implication for employees on opting-out

If a shop employee chooses to exercise his right to not work on Sundays, he cannot insist on working extra hours (i.e. any hours in excess of hours normally worked before he stopped Sunday working) on the other days of the week to make up for not working on Sundays (s 38 ERA 1996). This applies even if the contractual terms state a specified number of working hours per week. In such cases, the shop employee's number of specified hours can be reduced if he stops working on Sundays. 3837

Where it is not apparent from the contractual terms what part of the remuneration payable, or other benefit due, was attributable to working on Sundays, the employer can **reduce the amount of remuneration paid**, or the extent of any other benefit proportionately (s 39 ERA 1996). 3838

B. Opting-in

A protected employee can surrender his protection and **opt-in** to work on Sundays by (ss 36, 41 ERA 1996): 3845
- giving his employer a written opting-in notice, signed and dated by him, that expressly states that he wishes to work on Sundays or that he does not object to Sunday working; and
- after giving notice, expressly agreeing with his employer to work on Sundays or on a particular Sunday.

A protected employee can, therefore, **modify** his protection, by expressly agreeing to work particular Sundays, for example Sundays in December, or enter into a rotational pattern, for example every fourth Sunday. If the employee limits the Sunday work that he is prepared to do, he will remain protected with regard to general Sunday working.

After opting-in, an employee retains his right to **opt-out again** on giving an opting-out notice. 3846

EXAMPLE A, who has opted-out of Sunday working, decides that he would like to take advantage of the special rates that his employer has chosen to give for those working on Sundays.
1. A sees his employer and agrees to work on Sundays. A signs and dates a form (to ensure proper compliance, the form has been prepared by the employer for use by employees), which expressly states that he now wishes to work on Sundays and agrees to work on Sundays in general. A is now required to work on Sundays as long as he is a shop employee unless he subsequently opts-out.
2. A sees his employer about working on the four Sundays leading up to Christmas. A signs and dates a form (to ensure proper compliance, the form has been prepared by the employer for use by employees), which expressly states that he now does not object to Sunday work and in which he agrees to work the four Sundays leading up to Christmas. A is now required to work these specified Sundays (but no other Sunday) as long as he is a shop employee unless he subsequently opts-out. However, A can further agree in writing to modify his protection and work on Sundays in general or another particular Sunday(s).

C. Remedies

A protected employee must be continuously employed as a shop employee to the appropriate date necessary to apply the relevant protective remedy. For example, where a protected employee is dismissed for not working on Sundays, the appropriate date is the effective date of termination. 3860

If there is a **break** in his continuity of employment **as a shop employee**, the employee will lose his protection. In such situations, the employee has to give an opting-out notice to regain these rights if he is **subsequently required to work** as a shop employee.

Not to suffer a detriment

3861 If a protected employee suffers any detriment, as a result of the employer's act or deliberate failure to act for any of the same reasons as outlined above in the case of dismissal, he can make a complaint to an employment tribunal (s 45 ERA 1996). Any detriment **includes** situations where an employee has been refused promotion, overtime or training due to these reasons. It **does not include** failure to pay remuneration, or provide any other benefit, in respect of Sunday work that the employee has not done. Nor does it include any failure to provide the employee with any work, remuneration or other benefit that the employer is not obliged to provide.

Not to be unfairly dismissed

3862 Any dismissal will be **automatically unfair** (¶8390) if a protected employee is dismissed and the reason or the principal reason for the dismissal is that (s 101 ERA 1996):
– he refused (or proposed to refuse) to do shop work on Sundays or on a particular Sunday (this does not apply to employees who refuse to perform any such contractual duties during their opting-out notice period); or
– he gave (or proposed to give) an opting-out notice to his employer.

II. Betting employees

3880 Identical rules apply to betting employees though the date these rules came into force is different (s 36 ERA 1996). Therefore, the level of protection will depend on whether the employee was a betting employee **on or after 2 January 1995** instead of on or after 24 August 1994.

3881 A **betting employee** is an employee who, under his contract of employment, is or may be required to do betting work (s 233 ERA 1996). **Betting work** is work:
– at a track for a bookmaker when the bookmaker is doing work, which consists of or includes dealing with betting transactions; and
– in a licensed betting office when open for use for betting transactions.

A betting transaction includes the collection or payment of winnings on a bet and any transaction in which one or more of the parties are acting as a bookmaker. A bookmaker is a person who whether on his own account or as an employee or agent, carries on, regularly or occasionally, the business of receiving or negotiating bets or conducting pool betting operations, or holds himself out, or permits himself to be held out, as such a person.

CHAPTER 12

Time off

OUTLINE ¶¶

The law imposes **minimum requirements** on employers entitling employees to: **3900**
– paid or unpaid time off during working hours in certain circumstances, for example for some trade union duties;
– annual leave; and
– family-friendly leave: maternity, paternity, adoption and parental.

Employers can provide **more generous contractual terms** to employees, providing them with enhanced annual leave and paid time off during working hours to attend to non-work duties and obligations.

Employers may also give additional time off for certain personal reasons, which is often called **compassionate leave**. The extent and amount of any compassionate leave will be usually within the employer's discretion, though employers will often provide guidelines as to when they may grant such leave. Employees do have a statutory right to time off to care for dependants although this is unpaid and only applies to employees taking time off to deal with unforeseen events with regard to their dependants.

SECTION 1

Time off during working hours

I. Right to time off

3910 The minimum requirements entitling employees to paid or unpaid time off **during working hours** are outlined in the table below. Working hours are defined as any time when, in accordance with the employee's contract of employment, he is required to be at work. These rights are effective from the start of employment except for the right to time off under notice of redundancy and parental leave.

The extent of time off is subject to various tests, depending on the type of right, all based on the necessity of the employer acting reasonably. This is discussed in the relevant subject chapters with the exception of the right to take time off for public duties. For the right to take the following types of leave, see Chapter 14:
– maternity;
– adoption;
– paternity; and
– parental.

Employee	Purpose of time off		paid
Companion	accompany worker to discipline/ grievance hearing, flexible working hearing	¶¶6784, 4722	B
EWC, SNB or information or consultation body member or candidate	perform duties	¶¶7767, 7830	A
Negotiating representative	perform duties	¶7706	A
Information and consultation representative	perform duties	¶7740	A
Pregnant	antenatal care	¶4410	A
Public official	certain public duties	¶3920	X
Redundancy: employee representative and candidate in election	perform duties	¶8931	A
Safety representative and representative of employee safety	certain health and safety duties	¶5030	B
Trade union member	certain trade union activities, consulting ULR	¶7601	X
Trade union official	certain trade union duties	¶7603	B
Trustee of occupational pension scheme	perform duties	¶3432	B
Union learning representative (ULR)	training and perform duties	¶7607	B
Under notice of redundancy	look for new employment or training	¶8885	A
With dependants	care of dependants	¶4740	X
Young person	study or training	¶6330	A
A = at appropriate hourly rate	B = for work would have done	X = no right to paid time off	

Public officials

An employee who is a justice of the peace has the right to take time off to perform any duties of his office (s 50 ERA 1996). 3920

Further, an employee who is a member of any of the following has the right to time off to attend a meeting of the body or any of its committees or sub-committees, and to perform duties as approved by the body for the purpose of discharging the functions of the body or of any of its committees or sub-committees (s 50(1), (2) ERA 1996): 3921

Type of body	England and Wales	Scotland (where different)
Local authority	a local authority; the Common Council of the City of London; a National Park authority; or the Broads Authority	a council (instead of a local authority)
Statutory tribunal	magistrates and employment tribunals	
Police authority	a police authority; the Service Authority for the National Criminal Intelligence Service or the Service Authority for the National Crime Squad	
Board of prison visitors	a board of prison visitors	a prison visiting committee
Health body	a National Health Service trust; a Health Authority	a Health Board
Education body	a managing or governing body of an educational establishment maintained by the local education authority; or a governing body of a grant-maintained school, further education corporation or higher education authority	a school council or board; a board of management of a self-governing school or college of further education; a governing body of a central institution; a governing body of a designated institution
Environmental body	Environment Agency	Environment Protection Agency

The employer must allow the employee a **reasonable amount** of time off taking into account all the circumstances, in particular (s 50(4) ERA 1996; *C Riley-Williams v Argos Ltd*, EAT case 811/02): 3922

– how much time off is required for the performance of the duties of the office or as a member of the body, and how much time off is required for the performance of the particular duty;

– how much time the employee already takes off further to any trade union duties and activities; and

– the circumstances of the employer's business and the effect of the employee's absence on the running of it.

It may be considered reasonable to expect an employee who has **extensive duties** to devote part of his annual leave to the performance of them but this will depend on all the circumstances (*Borders Regional Council v Maule* [1993] IRLR 199, EAT).

If the employee holds **several public offices** he may be expected to organise them so that the time taken off is reasonable.

II. Right to remuneration

3930 Where there is the right to statutory pay, such statutory remuneration is calculated on one of two systems depending on the right. A right to statutory pay does not affect any right of an employee to contractual remuneration under his contract of employment.

A. Statutory remuneration

At appropriate hourly rate

3935 Where indicated in the table at ¶3910, an employee who is entitled to take paid time off is remunerated for the period of absence at the appropriate hourly rate.

With regard to the right to take time off when **under notice of redundancy**, this is subject to a maximum limit of 40% of a week's pay (s 53(5) ERA 1999).

3936 **Regular working pattern** The appropriate hourly rate, in relation to an employee, is the amount of a week's pay (¶2920) divided by the number of his normal working hours in the week in which time off has been taken. For time off taken under a notice of redundancy, this is the week in which the notice of dismissal is given.

> EXAMPLE E has taken time off.
> E has a regular working pattern and his normal working hours were 40 hours at the time E took time off. E's 1 week's pay is £300.
> E's appropriate hourly rate is 300 divided by 40 = £7.50

3937 **Irregular working pattern** Where the number of normal working hours differs from week to week or over a longer period, the appropriate hourly rate is ascertained by dividing the employee's week's pay by his average normal working hours calculated over the period of 12 weeks ending with the last complete week before the day on which the time off is taken (or the notice of dismissal is given).

> EXAMPLE Like E, employee F has also taken time off.
> F, though, has an irregular working pattern. In the 12 weeks before the day on which F started to take time off, he worked a variety of hours: 35, 4 × 40, 32, 3 × 38, 34, 2 × 36 = 447. F's 1 week's pay is also £300.
> The average number of normal working hours is 447 divided by 12 = 37.25
> F's appropriate hourly rate is 300 divided by 37.25 = £8.05

3938 Where the employee has been employed for less than 12 weeks, the appropriate hourly rate is calculated by dividing 1 week's pay by a number, which fairly represents the number of normal working hours in a week. The following must be taken into consideration as appropriate:
- the average number of working hours in a week that the employee could expect to work according to his contract; and
- the average number of normal working hours of other employees engaged in relevant comparable employment with the same employer.

Remuneration for work that would have been done

3940 Where the employee's **remuneration does not vary** with the amount of work done, he is entitled to be paid as if he had worked for the whole of the time off.

If it **does vary**, he must be paid an amount calculated by reference to his average hourly earnings. The average hourly earnings are:
- those of the employee concerned; or

– if no fair estimate can be made of those earnings, the average hourly earnings for work of that description of persons in comparable employment with the same employer or, if there are no such persons, a figure of average hourly earnings which is reasonable in the circumstances.

The employer is required to remunerate the employee for his time off work, which may not be the whole time of the duty or training if it is outside working hours. If part of the activity is **outside working hours** and the employee is given time off in lieu, he will not be entitled to be paid for it (*Hairsine v Hull City Council* [1992] IRLR 211, EAT). 3941

EXAMPLE H, a shop steward, is given permission by his employers to attend a union course.
On the day of the first session, which ran from 9 am to 4 pm, H was rostered to work the late shift between 3 pm and 11 pm. H went to work after the session ended until 7 pm. H will be paid for the 1 hour of the session that he was rostered to work, and for the time he actually worked. H, though, will not be paid for the time he took off (between 7 pm and 11 pm) because he had attended the course.
If H had attended a course from 3 pm to 11pm, he would have been entitled to be paid for the entire shift. If H's shift had been from 9 am to 4 pm, he would have been entitled to be paid for the entire shift.

Similarly, part-time workers, who are remunerated for work that would have been done, are only entitled to be paid for the **part-time hours** not worked, even if the duty or training is a full-time event. However, this may be contrary to the right to equal pay under Article 141 of the EC Treaty, as part-time workers affected are predominantly female compared to a male full-time workforce (*Arbeiterwohlfahrt der Stadt Berlin eV v Bötel C-360/90* [1992] IRLR 423, ECJ; *Kuratorium für Dialyse und Nierentransplantation eV v Lewar C-457/93* [1996] IRLR 637, ECJ). The EAT has required payment for the whole period in these circumstances (*Davies v Neath Port Talbot County Borough Council* [1999] IRLR 769, EAT). 3942

EXAMPLE In *Davies v Neath Port Talbot County Borough Council*, the EAT held that a part-time worker was entitled under Article 141 to be paid by her employers as if she was a full-time worker, when she was given time off to attend on a full-time trade union training course on her duties as a health and safety representative. The EAT held the employer must remunerate the employee for the whole of the training. In doing so, the EAT disapproved of another EAT decision (*Manor Bakeries Ltd v Nazir* [1996] IRLR 604, EAT) which had held that attending a union conference was not work under Article 141.

MEMO POINTS As *Davies v Neath Port Talbot County Borough Council* is a later EAT decision and is in line with decisions of the ECJ, it is suggested that this is the course UK law will follow.

B. Set off against remuneration

Any contractual remuneration paid to an employee in respect of a period of time off goes towards discharging any statutory liability of the employer to pay in respect of that period (either at the appropriate hourly rate or by remuneration for work that would have been done). Similarly, any payment of remuneration that is due under statute in respect of that period goes towards discharging any liability of the employer to pay contractual remuneration for that period. 3945

III. Remedies

An employee can **bring an action** in an employment tribunal that his employer has failed to allow him to take time off to which he is entitled. Where an employee had the right to paid time off, he can also claim for the whole or part of any amount to which he is entitled. In all cases, where a tribunal finds a complaint well-founded, the tribunal will make a **declaration** to that effect. 3960

3961 If the claim is successful, the tribunal can order **compensation** and, where relevant, an **award for payment**.

The following table sets out:
– the type of compensation available on a successful complaint to a tribunal when time off has been refused; and
– the type of award for payment, where relevant, on a successful complaint to a tribunal that the employer has failed to pay the amount of remuneration due.

Right to time off	Complaint Time off refused	Basis of compensation	Complaint Failure to pay amount due	Basis of award	Reference
Antenatal care	✔	2	✔	3	s 57 ERA 1996
Care of dependants	✔	1	n/a	n/a	s 57B ERA 1996
EWC, SNB or information and consultation body members or candidates	✔	2	✔	3	reg 27 SI 1999/3323
Information and consultation representative	✔	2	✔	3	reg 29 SI 2004/3426
Negotiating representative	✔	2	✔	3	reg 29 SI 2004/3426
Notice of redundancy	✔	4	✔	4	s 54 ERA 1996
Public official	✔	1	n/a	n/a	s 51 ERA 1996
Redundancy: employee representative and candidate in election	✔	2	✔	3	s 63 ERA 1996
Representative of employee safety	✔	1	✔	3	Sch 2 para 2 SI 1996/1513
Safety representative	✔	1	✔	3	reg 11 SI 1977/500
Training for young persons	✔	2	✔	3	s 63C ERA 1996
Trade union member	✔	1	n/a	n/a	s 170 TULRCA 1992
Trade union official	✔	1	✔	3	ss168-169 TULRCA 1992
Trustee of occupational pension scheme	✔	1	✔	3	s 60 ERA 1996
Union learning representatives (ULR)	✔	1	✔	3	ss 168A, 169 TULRCA 1992

1. Compensation is awarded according to what tribunal considers just and equitable in all circumstances, having regard to:
– employer's default in refusing time off, and
– any loss sustained by the employee attributable to employer's refusal.
With regard to an employer's refusal to allow an employee to take time off for trade union duties, compensation for this failure under TULRCA 1992 is wide enough to encompass cash reparation for the individual for the wrong done to him, independent of any specific loss he may have suffered (*Skiggs v South West Trains Limited* [2005] IRLR 459, EAT).
2. Compensation is equal to remuneration to which employee would have been entitled.
3. Where the employer has failed to pay amount due, in whole or in part, he will be ordered to pay the employee this amount.
4. The employer will be ordered to pay:
– remuneration for the time taken off;
– the amount that the employee should have received, or would have received if he had been allowed to take the time off; or
– both.
This is subject, in respect of the period of notice, to a limit of 40% of the employee's week's pay. Any award for payment for time off refused is not set against any contractual remuneration received.

The **time limit** for presenting such claims is 3 months beginning with the date on which it is alleged that the time off should have been permitted or paid. This period can be extended by the tribunal, as it considers reasonable, if it is satisfied that it was not reasonably practicable for the complaint to be presented before this date. 3962

SECTION 2

Annual leave

Workers are entitled to **paid statutory annual leave** from when they start work (Working Time Regulations SI 1998/1833 as amended, which will be referred to in this section as the regulations). Any term in the contract of employment or in any other agreement, express or implied, will be void so far as it seeks to exclude/limit this entitlement or the right to bring a claim under the regulations (reg 35 SI 1998/1833). 4000

A **relevant agreement** can alter or exclude some of the procedural requirements. This is **defined** as any workforce agreement (¶4652) that applies to the worker, any provision of a collective agreement which forms part of a contract between him and his employer, or any other agreement in writing which is legally enforceable as between the worker and his employer (for example, the contract of employment).

MEMO POINTS An **agency worker** will be treated as being employed by either the agent or the end-user, whichever is responsible for paying him or, if that cannot be established, by whichever party in fact pays the worker (reg 36 SI 1998/1833).

Contractual terms, express or implied by the custom and practice of the industry/employer, can also **enhance** the minimum statutory entitlement by increasing the number of days of paid annual leave and/or allowing for unpaid annual leave. See ¶9910 for a model clause. 4001

MEMO POINTS There is no longer a 13-week qualifying period before entitlement (Working Time (Amendment) Regulations SI 2001/3256). Before 25 October 2001, workers could not claim the right to paid annual leave unless they had been employed for 13 continuous weeks (*Voteforce Associates Ltd v Quinn*, EAT case 1186/00).

A. Entitlement

A worker is **entitled to** 4 weeks' paid leave in each leave year (ss 221-224 ERA 1996, reg 13(1) SI 1998/1833). This is not additional to any contractual entitlement and taking **contractual paid leave** in a particular leave year will count against the worker's statutory entitlement. 4005

A **week's leave** is equivalent to the time a worker works in a week. For example, for a worker working 5 days a week, the entitlement corresponds to 20 days' annual leave, whereas a part-time worker, working 2 days a week, is entitled to 8 days' paid annual leave. If a part-time worker's working time is set in terms of hours, then his annual leave can also be expressed in terms of hours.

The Court of Appeal has held that a worker on **long-term sick leave** is not entitled to statutory annual leave if they are **absent from work throughout that leave year** (*Commissioners of Inland Revenue v Ainsworth and others* [2005] IRLR 465, CA overruling *Kigass Aero Components Ltd v Brown & other cases* [2002] IRLR 312, EAT and *Bold Transmission Parts Ltd v Taree* [2002] IRLR 312, EAT). However, this decision did not address the resultant issue of whether statutory annual leave continues to accrue during sick leave (to be taken after the worker **returns** to work at some time **during** the remainder of the leave year). With regard to absences which do not cover the whole leave year, employees should be allowed to take their full entitlement (though any accrued 4006 annual leave running into another leave year will be lost unless preferential contractual terms apply (¶4018)).

MEMO POINTS *Commissioners of Inland Revenue v Ainsworth and others* is being appealed to the House of Lords.

4007 If a worker is **sick while on holiday**, such days may be treated as sick days and not part of his annual leave if the worker has complied with any notification and evidence requirement which are required by SSP rules or by the employer's sick pay scheme.

Public and bank holidays

4009 Christmas Day and Good Friday are English and Welsh public holidays at common law whereas bank holidays are set by legislation in the banking industry, which provides for financial dealings to be suspended on these designated days. A bank holiday may also be appointed by Royal Proclamation (for example, the Golden Jubilee bank holiday on 3 June 2002).

There is no statutory entitlement or general implied right to bank or public holidays with, or indeed without, pay. Therefore, whether these days are leave days will depend on the contract between the employer and the worker, and there will need to be either an **express term** giving a right to some or all designated public and bank holidays (for example, 20 days' holiday plus bank and public holidays) or an implied term due to the custom and practice of the industry/employer. If there is **no contractual right** to a particular public holiday, the worker is not entitled to an additional day's paid leave (*Campbell & Smith Construction Group Ltd v Greenwood* [2001] IRLR 588, EAT).

EXAMPLE 1. In *Campbell & Smith Construction Group Ltd v Greenwood*, G was contractually entitled to a winter holiday of 7 working days in addition to Christmas Day, Boxing Day and New Year's Day. His employer always set 31 December as one of these days. In 1999, the Government appointed 31 December 1999 as an extra bank holiday to mark the Millennium. The EAT held that G was not entitled to an additional day's leave as the date was already part of the 7-day paid leave.

2. In *Cook v Diageo* [2005] EAT case 0070/04, the reference in a collective agreement and employees' terms and conditions to "occasional" holidays did not mean that the employer was required to fix such holidays by reference to local public holidays (although this had usually been the case). Further, there was nothing to demonstrate that the intention of the parties to the collective agreement was to create a contractual obligation that the occasional days would always be on local public holidays.

4010 Paid leave on bank or public holidays will **count toward** the annual statutory entitlement.

EXAMPLE On the standard basis of 6 bank holidays and 2 public holidays per annum and on the basis that the following workers are employed full-time for 5 days a week (therefore, entitling them to 20 days' statutory annual leave).

– Worker A has a contract giving him 4 weeks of annual leave plus bank and public holidays. He will not be entitled to any further leave. Worker B has a contract giving him 4 weeks of annual leave without bank and public holidays. He will not be entitled to any further leave.

– Worker C has a contract giving him 3 weeks of annual leave plus bank and public holidays. He will not be entitled to any further leave. Worker D has a contract giving him 3 weeks of annual leave without bank and public holidays. He will be entitled to 5 further days leave per annum.

– Worker E has a contract giving him 2 weeks of annual leave plus bank and public holidays. He will be entitled to 2 further days leave per annum. Worker F has a contract giving him 2 weeks of annual leave without bank and public holidays. He will be entitled to 10 further days leave per annum.

Payment in respect of leave

4013 A worker is entitled to be paid, in respect of any period of annual leave to which he is entitled, at a **rate** of 1 week's pay for each week's leave (reg 16 SI 1998/1833). For the calculation of 1 week's pay see ¶2920.

Any contractual pay to a worker in respect of a period of leave will go towards **discharging the employer's liability** to paid leave (reg 16(5) SI 1998/1833). This does not include vague contractual provisions on remuneration which purport to include holiday pay as a 'rolled-up' element (*Caulfield and others v Marshalls Clay Products Ltd*; *Clarke v Frank Staddon Ltd* [2004] IRLR 564, CA; *McCarthy and others v Blue Sword Construction Ltd*, EAT case 0223/03; *Smith v AJ Morrisroes & Sons Ltd, JJ Cafferkey & Co Ltd v Byrne, Wiggins v Borth Yorkshire County Council* [2005] ICR 596, EAT). However, a **rolled-up element** can go towards discharging liability if:

– there is a mutual agreement for genuine payments for holidays; and

– the rolled-up element represents a true addition to the contractual rate of pay for time worked.

The courts have given **guidance** as to the best way that this could be evidenced as follows:

– the provision for rolled-up holiday pay must be clearly incorporated into the contract of employment. This can be done by an express agreement, by incorporation from a collective agreement or by custom and practice;

– the percentage or amount allocated to holiday pay (or sufficient information for this to be calculated) should be identified in the contract, and preferably also in the payslip;

– records should be kept of the holidays taken (or of absences from work when holidays can be taken); and

– reasonable practical steps should be taken to ensure that workers take their holiday before the end of the relevant holiday year.

EXAMPLE **No mutually agreed addition**

1. In *Smith v AJ Morrisroes & Sons Ltd*, the employer purportedly varied S's contract during his employment so that it included holiday pay which was funded by deducting an amount from S's daily pay which was paid back as holiday pay. The EAT held that the purported rolled-up element did not represent a true addition to S's pay and, therefore, did not discharge his employer's liability to give paid leave.

2. In *JJ Cafferkey & Co Ltd v Byrne*, the contract that B was asked to sign at the beginning of his employment expressly provided for a rolled-up element to B's daily rate. However, the total for the daily rate including the holiday pay element was the same as the "going rate" for the job. The EAT held that the purported rolled-up element did not represent a true addition to S's pay and, therefore, did not discharge his employer's liability to give paid leave.

Incorporated term

In *Wiggins v Borth Yorkshire County Council*, W was a freelance teacher paid on an hourly basis. The EAT found that W's terms and conditions were set out in national documents on teachers' pay and conditions which gave his leave entitlement and sufficient information as to how the pay element for this entitlement was calculated by reference to full time teachers. Consequently, W's employer had discharged his obligations and was paying W for leave as required.

The Court of Appeal in *Caulfield and others v Marshalls Clay Products Ltd* firmly held that neither it nor the EAT were, as a matter of law, bound to follow decisions of the Scottish Court of Session and consequently it ignored an earlier contrary decision from the Scottish Court of Session which had indicated that such rolled-up elements were never acceptable (*MPB Structures Ltd v Munro* [2003] IRLR 350, CS). However, for the avoidance of further doubt and because the Court of Appeal acknowledged that it was unsatisfactory for there to be contradictory decisions between the Court of Appeal and the Court of Session, it referred the question of rolled-up elements to the European Court of Justice (ECJ). **4014**

The Advocate General gave his opinion on 27 October 2005 on this matter and has indicated that, in line with the English courts, rolled-up holiday pay is acceptable as long as the precise proportion of holiday pay is shown in a transparent fashion (*Robinson-Steele v R. D. Retail Services Ltd*; *Clarke v Frank Staddon Ltd*; *Caulfield and others v Marshall Clay Products Ltd*, Joined Cases C-131/04 and C-257/04). The Advocate General went on to note that if rolled-up holiday pay is used employers should ensure that they have contractual arrangements in place to make sure that their workers take their statutory annual leave entitlement.

The ECJ decision is expected shortly and usually follows the Advocate General's opinion; the online updating service will report this decision as soon as it is known.

Requesting leave

4015 It is **standard practice** to allow workers to choose when they take their leave. Many employers, though, do set **certain conditions**, for example that only a certain number of workers may take leave at the same time or that workers may not take more than a certain number of consecutive working days off in one go.

4016 There are **procedural notification** requirements that need to be followed when either the employer or the worker requests leave though a relevant agreement can exclude these provisions. If excluded, the employer and worker can agree their **own provisions**.

An **employer requesting** a worker to take leave at specified times, must give notice to his worker of at least twice the period of the leave to be taken (reg 15 SI 1998/1833). Similarly, a **worker requesting** to take leave at specified times, must give the same prior notice to his employer. However, the employer's permission is required and employers can refuse their workers the permission to take any leave requested, but if they do so they must notify the workers within a period equivalent to the period of leave.

Untaken annual leave

4018 Untaken annual leave is "lost" at the end of the leave year. The **statutory entitlement** cannot be replaced in the leave year by a payment in lieu except where the employment relationship is terminated (¶4023) (reg 13(9) SI 1998/1833). In such cases, payment in lieu can be given for untaken leave in the leave year that termination occurs. However, **under the working time rules**, no payments can be made for untaken leave with regard to previous leave years.

4019 With regard to any **contractual entitlement**, whether any such days unused can be carried over to the next leave year will depend on the terms of the contract and will often be a matter of employer discretion.

B. Calculation of leave

4020 Entitlement to paid leave relates to the **leave year** and this **starts** on the date provided for in any relevant agreement (reg 13(2) SI 1998/1833). If there are no such provisions and where the worker started work on or before 1 October 1998, the leave year will start on this date and on each subsequent anniversary. Where the worker starts work after 1 October 1998, the leave year starts on the date on which the worker started his employment and on each subsequent anniversary. Where a worker starts work **part way through** his **leave year**, his entitlement is proportionate to the amount of the leave year that he works (reg 13(5) SI 1998/1833).

First year of employment

4021 Workers whose employment began after 25 October 2001, will be able to take their entitlement on a **pro rata arrangement** during their first year of employment (reg 15A SI 1998/1833). This is calculated in relation to the proportion of the employment year worked. Therefore, the 4 weeks' annual entitlement will accrue over the course of his first year of employment at a rate of 1/12 of this entitlement starting on the first day of each month.

Where this calculation does not result in an exact number of days, the figure will be rounded up to the nearest half day. Therefore, where a particular case includes a fraction of a day other than a half-day, the fraction is treated as a half-day if it is less than a half-day and as a whole day if it is more than a half-day. This does not apply for the purposes of calculating a payment in lieu on the termination of employment (see below).

EXAMPLE Worker G starts full-time work on 1 January 2006 resulting in a 20-day annual entitlement (4 weeks x 5 days). He will accrue his year's entitlement leave at a rate of 2 days per month for the next 10 months, i.e. 20 divided by 12 = 1.67 rounded up to 2.

Termination of employment

If a worker's employment is terminated, his leave entitlement is proportionate to the part of the leave year that has been worked (reg 14 SI 1998/1833). As a result, a worker is **entitled to** be paid in lieu for any leave accrued of this period that has not been taken. 4023

The **calculation** of this payment in lieu can be provided for in a **relevant agreement**. This is usually given as the same rate as remuneration but there may be circumstances where, due to the behaviour of the worker, it might be appropriate to allow for this sum to be reduced. However in such circumstances, the sum payable must be at least something and cannot be nothing otherwise it would breach the regulations, as a contract of employment cannot deny such payment on termination to which the worker was entitled (*Witley & District Men's Club v Mackey* [2001] IRLR 595, EAT).

EXAMPLE In *Witley & District Men's Club v Mackey*, W was dismissed for dishonesty and under his contract such a dismissal rendered that outstanding holiday pay would not be payable on termination. However, the EAT held that was contrary to provision preventing contracting out of any of the working time regulations.

If the method of calculation is **not set out** in a relevant agreement, the following formula must be used: 4024

$$(A \times B) - C$$

A is the worker's leave entitlement.
B is the proportion of the worker's leave year that had been worked before his effective date of termination.
C is the period of leave taken by the worker between the start of the leave year and the effective date of termination.

EXAMPLE Worker H works 5 days a week (therefore, his leave entitlement is 20 days (4 x 5 days' leave during the leave year). His employment is terminated 6 months into the leave year (i.e. half the leave year has been worked) during which he has taken 3 days' leave.
Therefore the employer must pay H the equivalent of 7 days ((20 x 0.5) – 3) payment in lieu.

The regulations do not provide a formula for **calculating a day's leave or a day's pay**. Consequently, there are diverging views as to how a worker's payment in lieu of unused holiday entitlement should be calculated. In the absence of an express contrary provision, the Apportionment Act 1870 will apply so that the rate is calculated on the basis of daily accrual using calendar days. On this basis, a day's pay is calculated by dividing annual salary by 365 (*Thames Water Utilities v Reynolds* [1996] IRLR 186, EAT). Whilst this method was confirmed as correct in *Taylor v East Midlands Offender Employment* [2000] IRLR 760, EAT, in this case the EAT also held that a worker who was entitled to 10 days' accrued holiday pay on the termination of his employment was in fact entitled to 14 calendar days' pay since the entitlement was based on 2 working weeks and that this would include 2 working weekends. The EAT has since held (*Leisure Leagues UK Ltd v Maconnachie* [2002] IRLR 600, EAT) that the daily rate of pay is calculated by dividing the worker's annual salary by the number of working days in the leave year, as opposed to the number of calendar days in the year. This decision is surely right. 4025

However, there is a further view that payment in lieu of unused holiday entitlement should focus on the weekly rather than the daily rate of pay. The regulations in fact refer to an entitlement of 4 weeks' annual leave rather than 20 days' annual leave. Following **DTI guidance**, it appears that a week for this purpose is the same amount of time as a normal working week (therefore if a worker works 5 days a week, he will be entitled to 20 days' annual leave). The regulations provide that in respect of each week of leave, a worker is entitled to receive a week's pay. In respect of a worker who works (say) 35 hours per week and receives an annual salary, a week's pay will be his annual salary divided by 52. Therefore, to calculate payment in respect of unused holiday entitlement on termination of employment, the worker's total annual holiday entitlement should be multiplied by the proportion of the leave year 4026 that has expired. From this figure, the period of leave that the worker has taken (expressed in weeks) should be subtracted.

EXAMPLE Worker J works 5 days a week (therefore his leave entitlement is 4 weeks). His employment is terminated 6 months into the leave year (i.e. half the leave year has been worked) during which he has taken 8 days' leave.
J will have accrued holiday entitlement of 2 weeks and will have taken 1.6 weeks' paid holiday. Therefore the employer must pay J the equivalent of 0.4 weeks, that is, 40% of a week's pay.

4027 Where a worker has taken holidays in **excess of his entitlement**, and if provided for by a **relevant agreement**, his employer can recover the sum equal to the gross salary paid in respect of such holidays from his final payment of wages. However, if there is **no relevant agreement**, then his employer cannot recoup any 'overpayment' made in respect of annual holiday pay (*Hill v Chapell* [2003] IRLR 19, EAT)

C. Records

4030 There is no requirement to keep records to show that the entitlements to paid annual leave have been complied with. However, as a worker can make a complaint to an employment tribunal if the employer breaches the regulations with regard to these entitlements, it is advisable to keep adequate records. Should any disputes arise as to the number of hours/days worked, it will be a factual and evidential issue for the tribunal or court to decide.

D. Remedies

4040 Workers can bring a **complaint** against their employers in an employment tribunal for **breach of their entitlement** to annual leave.

Workers also can make a complaint for **any detrimental effect**, or any deliberate failure to act by their employer, which has occurred in connection with this entitlement.

Employees can also bring a claim for **automatic unfair dismissal** (¶8390), if they are dismissed in connection with their entitlement to annual leave. Non-employee workers who are so dismissed should rely on the right not to suffer a detriment though compensation is awarded on the same basis as for unfair dismissal.

See ¶¶3761 – 3766 for further details.

4041 The Court of Appeal has held (overruling the EAT on this point) that applications to recover unpaid annual leave or pay in lieu can **only be made under the working time regulations**. Consequently, employees cannot bring claims for unlawful deduction of wages and are, therefore, limited to presenting claims within 3 months of the date the payment was due (*Commissioners of Inland Revenue v Ainsworth and others* [2005] IRLR 465, CA overruling *List Design Group Ltd v Douglas and others, List Design Group Ltd v Catley* [2003] IRLR 14, EAT and *Canada Life Ltd v Gray and another*, EAT case 0657/03).

MEMO POINTS *Commissioners of Inland Revenue v Ainsworth and others* is being appealed to the House of Lords.

CHAPTER 13

Sickness, injury and absence

OUTLINE ¶¶

Certain prudent steps can be taken at the **recruitment stage** to ensure that prospective employees will be fit and able to perform their duties though care must be taken that employers do not discriminate in doing so (¶706). **4100**

See also Chapter 15 for the **duties** the employer has with regard to the health and safety of his employees including stress-related/psychiatric illnesses.

When an employee is unable to work due to sickness/illness or injury (referred to in this chapter as sickness or illness), he is generally entitled to **statutory sick pay (SSP)** paid by his employer. Alternatively, his employer may provide a company scheme giving **occupational sick pay (OSP)** instead of paying SSP. In addition, he may provide **permanent health insurance (PHI)** if the employee continues to be sick or has a serious illness. In managing OSP and in providing information to the insurers of PHI, the employer may require information from the employee as to his health which has data protection implications. **Private healthcare** is a popular and common benefit (see ¶9920 for model wording for such a clause) and cover may be extended to include the employer's spouse and dependant children, commonly at an additional cost to the employee. **4101**

MEMO POINTS 1. The provisions relating to SSP are **contained and regulated** by the Social Security Contributions and Benefits Act 1992 (SSCBA 1992) and Statutory Sick Pay (General) Regulations SI 1982/894 (as amended and referred to in this chapter as the regulations).
2. Revenue and Customs also publish **help books** on SSP for employers (E14 and E14 (Supplement)). Though these have no legal status they are useful as an indication of the position Revenue and Customs take on certain procedural issues as well as outlining the scope and breadth of the regulations.

4102 The Court of Appeal has held that a worker on **long-term sick leave** is not entitled to statutory annual leave if they are **absent from work throughout that leave year** (*Commissioners of Inland Revenue v Ainsworth and others* [2005] IRLR 504, CA overruling *Kigass Aero Components Ltd v Brown & other cases* [2002] IRLR 312, EAT and *Bold Transmission Parts Ltd v Taree* [2002] IRLR 312, EAT). However, this decision did not address the resultant issue of whether statutory annual leave continues to accrue during sick leave (to be taken after the worker **returns** to work at some time **during** the remainder of the leave year). With regard to absences which do not cover the whole leave year, employees should be allowed to take their full entitlement (though any accrued annual leave running into another leave year will be lost unless preferential contractual terms apply (¶4018)).

MEMO POINTS The same principles are likely to apply to other types of absences, for example maternity/adoption leave and sabbaticals.

4103 If a worker is **sick while on holiday**, such days may be treated as sick days and not part of his annual leave if the worker has complied with any notification and evidence requirement which are required by SSP rules or by the employer's OSP scheme.

4104 Where the employee has a **long-term illness** or is **persistently sick**, his employer may be able to **dismiss** him fairly if he has a genuine business reason for doing so. However, employers must be careful not to discriminate against disabled employees.

Alternatively, the employer may choose to offer the employee early retirement on the grounds of ill health. Occupational pension schemes usually provide for this and see ¶3414 for the typical requirements that need to be satisfied before such payments are made. These may grant extra pensionable service to calculate enhanced ill health provisions or tiered benefit (i.e. full prospective pensionable service where the employee is unable to perform any work and actual pensionable service where he is able to do some work though not his usual/previous job).

Any dismissal **without good cause** which would deprive the employee of the benefit of an early retirement occupational pension or a PHI scheme may be a breach of the implied term of trust and confidence (see section 3).

In relatively rare situations, an employee's ill health may **frustrate** his employment contract bringing it to an end and in such cases there is no dismissal.

4105 **Pregnant employees** have special protection during their pregnancy and maternity leave and any dismissals due to a pregnancy-related illness will amount to direct discrimination (¶5320).

4106 The absence record of employees can be part of valid **redundancy selection criteria** where it is used as a factor measuring reliability of future attendance (¶8830). The weighting of this factor depends on all the circumstances, taking into account any special circumstances and disabilities.

SECTION 1

Statutory sick pay (SSP)

Employers **must pay** statutory sick pay (SSP) or at least the equivalent occupational sick pay (OSP) (see section 2) usually **from** the fourth qualifying day to employees who are employed earners and who are absent due to their incapacity i.e. sickness (s 151 SSCBA 1992). 4110

Employers are free to choose **whether or not to operate** the following rules of the SSP scheme if they give OSP at or above the SSP rate for each day of SSP entitlement. Employers must **not** make their employees **contribute** directly or indirectly towards SSP (or the equivalent amount of SSP in an OSP scheme).

SSP is **funded by** the employer. However, if the SSP paid in any tax month **exceeds** 13% of the gross Class 1 primary and secondary contributions payable for that month, the excess may be recovered by reducing the amount of PAYE, NIC and student loan deductions payable to Revenue and Customs. 4112

Any **dispute** as to whether SSP is due to an employee will be determined by Revenue and Customs and not by an employment tribunal (*Taylor Gordon & Co Ltd (t/a Plan Personnel) v Timmons*, EAT case 159/03). 4113

Records

Employers are required to maintain **full records** of the employee's absence from work in order that entitlement to SSP may be checked by Revenue and Customs. To aid employers, Revenue and Customs have produced an optional form **SC2** "self-certification form" which can be used for employees to certify themselves as sick for the first 7 days of sickness. Also optional, is Revenue and Customs' form **SSP2** "record sheet" which has been produced to particularly help small businesses operate the SSP scheme. 4115

Employers must complete and give to their employees Revenue and Customs' form **SSP1** (or their own computerised version) if they are off sick for 4 or more days and are not entitled to SSP, or, if their entitlement has stopped during their time off sick. This form will set out why the employee is not entitled to SSP and will enable him to claim appropriate social security benefits. Employers must also provide employees, if requested, with a completed leaver's certificate (form **SSP1(L)**) if they leave employment within 8 weeks of receiving SSP.

Payments of SSP are **subject to PAYE and NIC deductions** and must also be recorded on the deductions working sheet (P11) and on the annual return (P35) (¶6877). 4116

Penalties

Employers who **fail** to **produce** any document or record required under the SSP scheme face an initial penalty of £300 with further penalties of £60 per day for continuing failure. Employers who fail or repeatedly refuse to **make payments** of SAP or SPP will be liable to a penalty of up to £3,000 (s 11 EA 2002). 4118

Further, employers who **fraudulently or negligently** (s 12 EA 2002):
– make any incorrect payments of SSP;
– produce any incorrect document or record, provide any incorrect information, or make any incorrect return; or
– receive incorrect payments in connection with the recovery of SSP;
will be liable to a fine of up to £3,000.

MEMO POINTS Note that **employees** will face similar penalties if they fraudulently or negligently:
– make any incorrect statement or declaration in connection with claim; or
– provide any incorrect document or information which has been required to be produced to an HMRC officer.

A. Employed earner

4120 Employed earners i.e. **employees who pay Class 1 NIC** qualify for SSP from their **employers who contribute** to their NIC payments if they have **average weekly earnings** (or the equivalent period if paid monthly) for the 8 weeks prior to the PIW (¶4142) of at least the lower earnings limit for NIC.

All employees, regardless of their length of contract, are treated exactly the same for SSP purposes. Consequently, all employees, including those with **contracts of 3 months or less**, will be entitled to SSP provided they satisfy the remaining qualifying conditions.

Agency workers

4123 Agency workers who are employed by their agency on a series of contracts cannot claim SSP from their agency when they are **not employed** to work for a client. When employed, the same rules as above will apply in determining qualification.

If a worker qualifies, his entitlement continues for the duration of the contract or until he is fit for work, regardless of whether the agency is required to provide a **replacement** for the client. Therefore, if the contract is **terminated** purely for the purpose of avoiding SSP, the worker will remain entitled to SSP (reg 4 SI 1982/894).

Employees with more than one job

4125 Whether an employee, who has more than one job with the same or with different employer(s), qualifies for SSP with regard to one or all jobs will depend on whether he is an employed earner for each job.

Where there are two or more concurrent contracts with the same employer (or employers trading in association) and his earnings are in both cases **aggregated for NIC**, the employee must be incapable of work under all his contracts before he is entitled to SSP (regs 20-21 SI 1982/894). For example, an accountant working for associated companies must be unable to perform all his duties under his contracts to qualify, if his earnings are aggregated for NIC.

However, if the contracts are separate and the employee's earnings are **not aggregated for NIC** (usually because he is working for different employers), he will qualify for SSP with regard to the job he is incapable of performing even if he remains capable of performing the other(s). For example, a man could be a manual labourer during the day and work for another employer as a bingo caller in the evening. In such circumstances, he will be able to claim SSP from his daytime employer if he breaks his arm and is unable to perform his duties even though he can still perform his evening job of calling numbers.

Pregnant employees

4127 A pregnant employee does not qualify for SSP during a 26-week period called a **disqualifying period** unless she has suffered a miscarriage or an abortion (s 153(2), (11), (12) SSCBA 1992; reg 3(4)-(5) SI 1982/894).

4128 If she is **entitled** to statutory maternity pay (**SMP**) or maternity allowance (**MA**), this period will start at the beginning of the week when she is first entitled to either of these payments and will last for the duration of entitlement (which is 26 weeks).

If she is **not entitled** to SMP or MA and is **receiving SSP**, her disqualifying period will start with the earliest of the following dates:
– the day after the date of birth; or
– the first day she is sick with a pregnancy-related illness on or after the start of the fourth week before the baby is due.

If she is not entitled to SMP or MA and is **not receiving SSP**, her disqualifying period will start with the earliest of the following dates:
– the beginning of the week in which the birth occurred; or

– the beginning of the week in which she is first off sick with a pregnancy-related illness if this is on or after the start of the fourth week before the baby is due.

SSP will only be payable **after the disqualifying period** has ended. If a PIW (¶4142) is formed before or during the disqualification period, a new PIW after the disqualifying period must be at least 57 days (i.e. more than 8 weeks) later for SSP to be payable. Otherwise, under the PIW rules it would be treated as a linked PIW (¶4155). 4129

Employees absent due to a trade dispute

An employee does not qualify for SSP if at the **beginning of his incapacity** (or the start of his employment contract if later) he is absent because of a trade dispute unless he can show that he had no direct interest in it either on or before the start of his sickness (Sch 11 SSCBA 1992; reg 3 SI 1982/894). He is deemed to be **directly interested** if the outcome of the dispute will be applied across the workforce automatically by the employer due to a collective agreement or because of established custom and practice (*Presho v Insurance Officer* [1984] IRLR 74, HL). 4132

A trade dispute is **defined** as any dispute between employers and employees, or between employees, which is connected with the employment or non-employment or the terms and conditions of employment of any persons, whether or not they are employed by the employer (s 27 SSCBA 1992).

B. Incapacity to work

To qualify for SSP, an employee must be off sick with a disease or disability that renders him **incapable of performing** any work which he can reasonably be expected to do under his contract (s 151(4) SSCBA 1992). Therefore, if an employee is able to perform contractual work other than his usual duties, he will not qualify. 4135

If an employee is suffering a **bereavement**, his employer should decide whether to accept the time taken off due to bereavement as sickness, for example due to shock or depression. Naturally, if there is an extended period of absence and an employee produces a medical certificate stating he is suffering from shock or depression, his employer should treat the time taken off as sickness unless he has good reason not to (¶4230).

The **exception** to the rule of incapacity is when an employee is **deemed incapable** of work even though he is actually capable of it. This happens where (reg 2(1) SI 1982/894): 4136
– he is excluded from work on a certificate of a Medical Officer for Environmental Health and is under medical observation because he is a **carrier** of, or has been in contact with, an infectious disease; or
– a doctor states that the employee should not work for **precautionary or convalescent reasons**. For example, a doctor may deem a pregnant woman incapable of work if there is an outbreak of rubella (German measles) at her place of work, to prevent the risk of serious harm to her unborn child.

Extent of incapacity

An employee must be incapable or deemed to be incapable for the **whole** of each of the **working days** he is absent. Therefore, if an employee has done even a short period of work in a working day it will not be treated as a day of incapacity for SSP purposes. If, on the other hand, an employee turned up to work but was unable to start due to incapacity, the day will be treated as a day of incapacity. 4138

Night shift workers

Work done in any shift which **extends over midnight** is treated as having been done entirely on the first of the two days (reg 2(2) SI 1982/894). Therefore, if an employee becomes incapable 4139 of work after the end of such a shift, the second day is deemed to be a day of incapacity even though he did some work during that day.

> EXAMPLE Employee B works from 11pm to 7am on Mondays to Fridays. B works his Monday shift to Tuesday morning but becomes ill on Tuesday and is off sick until his next Monday shift. His days of incapacity are Tuesday to Sunday (or Saturday or Friday depending whether he remained sick for all or part of the weekend).

Period of incapacity to work (PIW)

4142 The employee will only qualify if the days of incapacity create a period of incapacity to work (PIW). A PIW is formed when he is **incapable** of work for at least **4 or more consecutive calendar days**. As PIW is measured in consecutive calendar days, all days of incapacity count towards determining its length including weekends, holidays and any other days in which the employee is not expected to work. The PIW ends when the employee's incapacity ends.

Odd days of incapacity of **up to 3 consecutive calendar days** do not count and cannot create PIWs.

> EXAMPLE Employee C is off sick on Monday and Tuesday. His employer must ascertain whether he was sick over the weekend from Saturday (i.e. if he had been required to work he would have been unable to do so) before SSP is due. If so, a PIW will have been formed, if not and the employee was only sick on Sunday or Monday, a PIW will not have been formed.

C. Period of entitlement

Start of entitlement

4145 The entitlement starts from the **4th qualifying day of a PIW** and is payable on all qualifying days after that for up to a **maximum** of 28 weeks (i.e. 196 days) (s 151 SSCBA 1992).

SSP is only payable on qualifying days. Consequently, the rate for qualifying days is the weekly rate for SSP divided by the number of qualifying days in that week. For example, if the qualifying days are Monday-Friday, the daily rate on these qualifying days will be the weekly rate divided by 5 (¶4165). If there is only 1 qualifying day in the week then the rate for that day will be the full weekly rate.

> MEMO POINTS The employee must have normal or average **weekly earnings** (or the equivalent period if paid monthly) for the 8 weeks prior to the PIW of at least the lower earnings limit for NIC to be entitled. This needs to be calculated afresh with regard to each PIW if necessary.

4146 There are slightly different rules when a PIW is **linked** with one or more PIWs i.e. when they are less than 57 days apart from each other (¶4155). Where a new PIW occurs which is **not linked** to previous PIWs, the employee's entitlement will start afresh.

The **first 3 qualifying days** are called **waiting days**.

4147 **Qualifying days** The employer and employees or their representatives can **choose** which days of the week are qualifying days (s 151(2) SSCBA 1992). These will **normally be** the days of the week on which the employee is contracted to work.

Choosing qualifying days must be by agreement, with at least 1 qualifying day a week (s 151(3) SSCBA 1992). These must not be determined by the actual days an employee is off sick.

If qualifying days **cannot be agreed**, the following rules determine the qualifying day(s) to be:

– the day(s) on which the employee is required to work and Wednesdays if the contract does not specify a day(s). For example, if the employee is contracted to work Monday to

Wednesday every other week, his qualifying days would be Monday to Wednesdays on the weeks he is required to work and Wednesdays on the weeks he is not; or

– every day of the week except those on which there is agreement that the employee does not work if there is no agreement on which days he is required to work. For example, if there is no agreement, but the employer and employee agree that Saturday and Sunday are days on which none of the workforce are required to work, the qualifying days will be deemed to be Monday-Friday.

EXAMPLE Employee D is contracted to work Monday to Friday and these are his qualifying days. D is off sick Wednesday to the following Tuesday. As it is over 3 consecutive calendar days long, he has formed a PIW (¶4142) which runs from that Wednesday to the following Tuesday.
He has 5 qualifying days within that period: Wednesday, Thursday, Friday and the following Monday and Tuesday. He will be entitled to SSP from the fourth qualifying day and therefore will be entitled to SSP on the Monday and Tuesday he is off sick.
Employee E is a part-time employee working Monday to Wednesday, which are his qualifying days. E is off sick during the same period and therefore has the same PIW as D.
However, he only has 3 qualifying days within that period: Wednesday and the following Monday and Tuesday. He will not be entitled to SSP as the first 3 qualifying days are waiting days.
Employee F who works from 6pm on Sunday to 9am on Monday, has agreed with his employer that Sunday is his 1 qualifying day in the week.
He works his shift but is sick on Monday which is his first day of PIW. He returns to work four Sundays later. The PIW lasts for 27 calendar days.
However, there are only 3 qualifying days in this PIW (the three Sundays he did not work) and as these are waiting days, F does not qualify for SSP.

Where staff work on a **rota system** or have an **unusual working pattern**, the Revenue and Customs manual suggests that for simplicity employers should agree with their employees or their employee's representatives that the same day(s) in every week is a qualifying day(s). **4148**

End of entitlement

An employee's entitlement will end on the last qualifying day of his PIW. This will occur **at the earliest** of the following events where (s 153(2), (11), (12) SSCBA 1992): **4150**
– he recovers and is able to return to work;
– he reaches the maximum entitlement of 28 weeks of SSP;
– he travels outside the EEA (unless he is a mariner, airman or an employee working on the continental shelf);
– the contract ends (unless it was terminated by the employer in avoidance of SSP); or
– she is a pregnant employee and has reached her disqualifying period.

In all but the first situation when the employee returns to work, he may be entitled to other state benefits when his SSP ends, for example incapacity benefit or severe disablement allowance. Pregnant employees may be able to claim statutory maternity pay (SMP) or maternity allowance (MA) and/or other state benefits.

1. Linked PIWs

If **two or more** PIWs occur **within 8 weeks** (i.e. 56 calendar days or less), they are treated as linked and are regarded as a **single period of entitlement**. A PIW with a **former employer** does not count. **4155**

EXAMPLE Employee G is off sick 27 October to 4 November 2005 and 31 December 2005 to 3 January 2006. G's PIWs are separated by exactly 56 days and are therefore linked.
Employee H is off sick 27 October to 4 November 2005 and 29 December 2005 to 3 January 2006. H's PIWs are separated by less than 56 days and are therefore linked.
Employee I is off sick 27 October to 4 November 2005 and 5 January to 12 January 2006. I's PIWs are separated by more than 56 days and are therefore not linked (and see below).

4156 As linked PIWs are regarded as a single period of entitlement, the following rules occur:
1) **Waiting days** are carried forward by a previous linked PIW.

EXAMPLE Employees J's, K's and L's qualifying days are Monday to Friday. All are sick from Sunday to Friday. Their PIWs run from Sunday to Friday within which there are 5 qualifying days, Monday to Friday.
J's last PIW was more than 56 days ago and is therefore not linked. Therefore, J's waiting days are Monday to Wednesday and he is entitled to SSP for Thursday and Friday.
K's PIW is linked to a previous PIW which had occurred 4 weeks previously. This previous PIW was from Tuesday to Friday, K's waiting days were Tuesday to Thursday of that week and he was paid SSP for that Friday. All his waiting days have been served and he is entitled to SSP for Monday to Friday in his new linked PIW.
L's PIW is linked to a previous PIW which had also occurred 4 weeks previously. This previous PIW was from Friday to Monday and therefore L's waiting days were Friday and Monday. L has 1 waiting day to serve to be entitled to SSP and, therefore, Monday of the new linked PIW will be his final waiting day and he will be entitled to SSP for Tuesday to Friday of that week.

4157 2) The SSP **maximum entitlement** of 28 weeks is spread over the linked period.

EXAMPLE Employee O has used up 4 weeks of entitlement in a previous PIW. This PIW is linked with a newly formed PIW which is 56 or less days apart from it. O has 24 weeks of entitlement left which can be paid in this new PIW.

4158 3) If a series of linked **PIWs lasts longer than 3 years**, entitlement to SSP ends after the third year. This will apply regardless of whether the maximum entitlement of 28 weeks has reached.

EXAMPLE Employee P has a number of linked PIWs from 6 May 2002 to 5 May 2005. Therefore, his PIWs have lasted 3 years.
If P is off sick creating a new PIW on or before 1 July 2005, the PIWs will be separated by 56 days or less and P's employer is not liable to pay SSP as the entitlement ends after 3 years of linked PIWs.

2. Non-linked PIWs

4160 Where a PIW occurs **over 8 weeks** after the end of the last PIW, it will not be linked to the previous PIW. In such cases, each PIW will be treated as a **separate period of entitlement**. This means that the first 3 qualifying days are waiting days and SSP will not be payable on these days. The maximum entitlement of 28 weeks will start afresh. Note again, a **PIW with a former employer** will not count.

EXAMPLE Employee Q started work on 2 January 2006. Q is off sick from 14 January to 18 January 2006 and 17 March to 26 March 2006.
Q's first PIW (14 January to 18 January) cannot be linked to the last PIW from his previous employer so his employer does not need to check if the last PIW from the previous employer was separated by more than 56 days or not.
Further, Q's second PIW with his employer is separated by more than 56 days from his first PIW and is therefore not linked. Therefore, his first 3 qualifying days do not count and his 28 week maximum entitlement starts again.

D. Rate

4165 SSP is **payable at** a fixed weekly rate of £68.20 from April 2005 (s 157(1) SSCBA 1992; Statutory Paternity Pay and Statutory Adoption Pay (Weekly Rates) Regulations SI 2002/2818 as amended by Social Security Benefits Up-rating Order SI 2005/522). The daily amount payable depends on the number of qualifying days during the week (¶4147). For example, if the qualifying days are Monday to Friday, the daily rate for being off sick on a qualifying day will be a fifth of the weekly rate.

Revenue and Customs provide a table (in E14 and E12) setting out the daily rate for all the available combinations of qualifying days.

MEMO POINTS The fixed weekly rate is likely to increase in **April 2006**. See the online updates and the newsletters to this edition.

SECTION 2

Occupational sick pay

Employers can **opt out** of the SSP scheme if they have a company scheme, namely an OSP scheme that matches or exceeds the amount payable under SSP. 4170

Where an employer has contractual terms on incapacity to work due to sickness and/or an OSP scheme, it is advisable that he **sets out** these terms in the **contract of employment**. Where there is no written contract of employment or where it does not cover these provisions, employers must provide employees with a **written statement of particulars** relating to them (¶1400). 4171

The following wording is taken from the model Contract (¶9910).

EXAMPLE 10. Sickness absence

10.1. [[Employer's] sick pay arrangements are explained in [*reasonably accessible document*].]
OR
[If you are absent from work due to sickness or injury, you (or someone on your behalf) must inform [your manager] of the reason for and likely duration of your absence no later than [*time*] on the first day of absence [*note: For SSP purposes, the employer cannot specify notification before a specific time on the first qualifying day*]. If your sickness absence lasts 7 calendar days or less, you must complete a self-certification form on your return to work [*note: For SSP purposes, the employer cannot insist on evidence of incapacity in the first 7 days of sickness*]. For absences lasting more than 7 calendar days, you must produce a medical certificate from your doctor stating the reason for your absence. You must keep [your manager] regularly informed of your absence and likely duration of your absence. Further medical certificates are required for each further [week] of sickness absence.] [Failure to notify [employer] of your absence may render you subject to disciplinary action and may also bar you from receiving sick pay.]

10.2. [Employer] may require you to undergo a medical examination at its expense by a medical practitioner appointed or approved by [employer] and you authorise that medical practitioner to disclose to [employer [and its advisors]] the result of the examination and discuss with it [or them] any matters arising from the examination which might impair the proper performance of your duties.

10.3. [[Employer] does not operate a sick pay scheme. Your entitlement is to Statutory Sick Pay (SSP) only.] OR [Subject to any right [employer] may have to terminate your employment, you will be paid your normal basic remuneration (inclusive of any Statutory Sick Pay (SSP)) [and provided all contractual benefits] for [*number*] working days of absence due to sickness or injury in any calendar year. Thereafter, you will be paid half your normal basic remuneration (inclusive of any Statutory Sick Pay (SSP)) [and provided all contractual benefits] for a further [*number*] working days of absence due to sickness or injury in that calendar year. Any payments to which you are entitled under any social security scheme (whether or not claimed by you) may be deducted from any sick pay paid to you by [employer]. Entitlement to payment is subject to notification of your compliance with this clause [10].]

Where there is an OSP scheme, the provisions should state how much will be paid, how it will be paid and for how long. An employer can also choose to cover some employees and not others in a scheme though he must ensure that he does not discriminate against his employees on grounds of sex, sexual orientation, race, religion or belief, or disability in doing so. 4172

A **typical scheme** will give full pay on sickness for a certain period reducing to a percentage of full pay for a following set period with no further sick pay thereafter. Sometimes no OSP will be payable in a probation period and/or the level of entitlement may increase with length of service. If **no duration** is stated, a term may be implied to give effect to the presumed intention of the parties (¶1170). The presumption is that the employer will pay for a reasonable period only, which will depend on the term normally applicable in the particular industry as determined, for example, by reference to the relevant national agreement (*Howman & Son v Blyth* [1983] IRLR 139, EAT).

The scheme should also set out any **conditions** to which it is subject (commonly self-certification for periods of absence up to 7 days, and the production of a medical certificate for long periods).

4175 **Data protection** Employers must ensure that they comply with the data protection rules (¶5945) (for example, where the data is sensitive (¶5925), explicit consent should be obtained).

Further, as **good practice**, employers should (part 4.2 DP Code):
– make workers aware how information relating to their health will be used and who will have access to it. Unless told otherwise, workers are entitled to assume that information they give will be treated in confidence and not passed on to the employer or another third party;
– not compromise the confidentiality of communications between workers and their occupational health professionals, for example if emails can be used as a form of confidential information, this should not be monitored; and
– act in a way that is consistent with the Guidance on Ethics for Occupational Physicians from the Faculty of Occupational Medicine.

Employers are also advised to follow the DP Code's general **recommendations** with regard to data management (¶6000) and its good practice recommendations with regard to information about their workers' health (see ¶5040).

No OSP scheme

4190 If there is no OSP scheme, the employer must ensure that this is stated either in the contract or written particulars. A failure to do so may result in an **implied right** to any existing scheme (*Mears v Safecar Security Ltd* [1982] IRLR 183, CA). In deciding whether there is such a right, a tribunal will consider all the facts and circumstances to see whether a term can be implied. Relevant circumstances are the knowledge of the parties at the time the contract is made, the nature of the contract and how the parties have behaved since the employee started work. Such a term may be also implied from the custom or practice in the industry.

SECTION 3

Permanent health insurance

4200 Many employers also provide permanent health insurance (PHI), otherwise known as long-term disability cover or even more generally as sickness and accident benefit. PHI usually gives employees the equivalent or a proportion of a salary if they have a long-term illness and cannot return to work, and is nearly always provided by an insurer who will have an agreement with the employer to provide cover to his employees in the event of such illness. Such payments are normally triggered after the employee has been sick for a set period of time and will continue until the employee either recovers from his illness and returns to work or reaches retirement age.

PHI **premiums** are not taxable as a benefit for employees. However, the payment of PHI benefits during an employee's illness will be treated as earnings and consequently will be taxable as employment income.

Note that PHI premiums are deductible for the employer if the policy enables him to continue paying his employees' salaries during illness or if it covers revenue loss.

The following wording is taken from the model contract of employment for general staff (¶9910).

EXAMPLE 7.3 [Permanent health insurance]
Subject to [employer's] right to terminate your employment, if you comply with any eligibility or other conditions imposed by [employer] or by the relevant insurance provider, you may be eligible to receive payments under [employer's] permanent health insurance arrangements. The terms and level of such cover will be in accordance with the [employer's] policy from time to time in force.

To **ensure an employer has no contractual liability** to provide payments if the **insurer refuses or cannot pay** an employee's claim, it should be expressly stated that the benefit is provided in accordance with the terms of the insurer's policy from time to time in force (which may be changed by the insurer without notice to the employee). The employer should also ensure that he has an express clause which gives him the right to change insurers, vary the entitlement or discontinue the scheme. Further, if there are major exemptions to the payment of the benefit (for example the ending of payments if an employee leaves employment), the employer must ensure that the employee is aware of these exemptions, for example, the employee should be shown the policy or told to read it, otherwise the employer may be liable for these exemptions (*Villella v MFI Furniture Centres Ltd* [1999] IRLR 468, QBD). It should be noted that the terms of PHI policies will be interpreted in a realistic and practical way (*Walton v Airtours plc and Sunlife Assurance Company of Canada* [2003] IRLR 161, CA). 4201

If the above is not expressly stated, the employer may have a **contractual liability** to the employee. This will depend on what is outlined in any other documents provided to the employee and any other representations made to him. In such circumstances, if there is a contractual liability and the insurer refuses to pay a claim, the employer may have an obligation (as part of his general duty of trust and confidence) to challenge an insurer's assessment of the employee's fitness if the employee has no other means of redress. The duty to challenge will depend on whether the claim is genuine and the employer's view as to whether the claim would be successful (*Marlow v East Thames Housing Group Ltd* [2002] IRLR 798, QBD). In certain circumstances, the employer may even be liable for continuing payments if the insurer stops making them (*Jowitt v Pioneer Technology (UK) Ltd* [2002] IRLR 790, EAT, which has been overturned on appeal, but this point remains unaffected). 4202

Dismissal of an employee **without good cause** in circumstances which will deprive him of the benefit of a PHI scheme may be a breach of the implied term of trust and confidence (*Aspden v Webbs Poultry and Meat Group (Holdings) Ltd* [1996] IRLR 521, QBD; *Adin v Sedco Forex International Resources Ltd* [1997] IRLR 280, CS) (¶1241). This includes dismissing the employee for specious or arbitrary reasons, for no reason at all or solely with the view of preventing, or bringing to an end, any such payments (*Hill v General Accident Fire & Life Assurance Corporation plc* [1998] IRLR 641, CS). 4203

However, there is no implied term to prevent dismissal if otherwise **justified**, for example if the employee was summarily dismissed for a fundamental breach of contract due to his gross misconduct or if he is made redundant, even if one of the results is that entitlement under a PHI scheme ends.

EXAMPLE In *Briscoe v Lubrizol Ltd* [2002] IRLR 607, CA, B's misconduct in failing to attend meetings to discuss his long-term absence and failing to respond to requests for contact amounted to a fundamental breach entitling his employers to dismiss B even though there was a PHI scheme.

If an employee has successfully brought a personal injury claim against his employer as a result of an injury sustained at work, any insurance payments will be regarded as a contractual benefit and will not be taken into account in the **assessment of damages** (*Lewicki v Brown & Root Wimpey Highland Fabricators Ltd* [1996] IRLR 565, CS). 4204

Data protection If an employee becomes unfit for work and makes a claim, the insurer might justifiably approach the employer for a report as to his fitness and to determine whether suitable alternative work is available. This could involve the disclosure of some health information and employers must ensure that they comply with the data protection rules (¶5945) (for example, where the data is sensitive (¶5925), explicit consent should be obtained). 4206

Further, as **good practice**, employers should (part 2.4 DP Code):
– remember that they do not have a right of access to personal information needed by a third party for the administration of employment-related benefits. The information should not be used for general employment purposes. If information is collected on behalf of insurer, the employer must ensure there is a secure method of collection;
– limit the exchange of information with a scheme provider to the minimum necessary for operation of the scheme; and
– ensure that when a worker joins a scheme it is made clear what, if any, information is passed between the insurer and the employer and how it will be used. Unless told otherwise workers are entitled to assume that information they give to a doctor, nurse or other health professional will be treated in confidence and not passed to others.

Employers are also advised to follow the DP Code's general **recommendations** with regard to data management (¶6000) and its general good practice recommendations with regard to information about their workers' health (see ¶5040).

Alternative to PHI cover

4208 Some employers who do wish to give the benefit of PHI prefer to give their employees a sum of money to purchase their own PHI cover. Such payments are a taxable benefit.

SECTION 4

Management of sickness

4210 Employers are free to choose the procedure for **monitoring and control** of sickness absence though they must make employees aware of any company policy and procedural rules.

4211 Employers are entitled to ask for **reasonable evidence** of incapacity, for example self-certification or a sick note from the employee's doctor. A sick note is strong evidence of incapacity and should usually be accepted as conclusive unless there is **evidence to the contrary**, for example a sick note states the employee is unable to work due to an ankle injury but he is seen playing football (*Bailey v BP Oil Kent Refinery Ltd* [1980] IRLR 287, CA). At the very least, this example may indicate that the employee was reckless as to trying to make a full and speedy recovery if the sick note indicated that he should rest his ankle as a recuperative measure.

Generally, if an employee is doing anything **away from work** while he is off sick which suggests that he is not genuinely sick, this is a matter which properly concerns the employer (*Hutchinson v Enfield Rolling Mills Ltd* [1981] IRLR 318, EAT). In *Hutchinson v Enfield Rolling Mills Ltd*, the employer acted reasonably when he dismissed H who took part in a union demonstration when he was off sick regardless of the fact that H had a sick note from his doctor stating he was suffering from sciatica.

Information about workers' health

4213 **Contractual or procedural terms** on the right to ask employees to attend an occupational medical practitioner (i.e. company doctor) for check-ups or when a medical issue affects their work may prove useful in the management of employee sickness and may highlight a potential problem early on.

Further, if necessary, it may provide an employer with a medical assessment as to the capability of an employee. An occupational health doctor/professional often has a better understanding of the employer's business and the employee's work than the employee's own GP which may aid this assessment. Tribunals also often put more weight behind a occupational health report for this reason.

4215 Employers must ensure that they comply with the **data protection rules** (in particular the requirements relating to sensitive data (¶5925)) when obtaining, using, handling and retaining information about workers' health. Further, the Data Protection Code sets out core principles and good practice recommendations for employers to follow. See ¶5040 for details.

Policy and procedure

Provisions on sickness and sick pay should be supported by a policy and procedure which will usually be found in supporting documentation or the staff handbook. It is advisable that any policies and procedures are not contractual. A policy and procedure concerning sickness should help ensure that absence is minimised and that the employer deals with his employees fairly and consistently. The latter is especially important if an employer reaches the stage where he wishes to dismiss an employee who has a long-term illness or is persistently ill (¶4245 and ¶4280). **4220**

It is advisable that the procedure is **separate** from the employer's disciplinary procedure for all cases of ill health as opposed to misconduct. For example, if the employer wishes to put the employee on guard that his attendance record due to sickness is unacceptable, a caution would be more appropriate than a disciplinary warning. This helps maintain good employment relations as a warning often carries a suggestion that the employee is required to change or improve his conduct and this may be inappropriate where absence is due to ill health.

The procedure should include **informal and formal discussions/consultations**, though if the employee is **unable to attend** such meetings, the employer should write to see if he would be prepared to deal with the process by correspondence. **4221**

See the Appendix at ¶9940 for a checklist as to what such a policy could contain.

Sickness records

Sickness records are almost certain to include sensitive data (¶5925) and employers must make sure that they comply with the data protection rules (¶5945). **4223**

Further, as **good practice**, employers should (part 2.3 DP Code):

- keep sickness and accident records separate from absence records. Sickness or accident records should not be used for a particular purpose when records of absence can be used instead;
- ensure that the holding and use of sickness and accident records is either with explicit consent or required by health and safety legislation;
- only disclose information from sickness or accident records about an employee's illness, medical condition or injury where there is a legal obligation to do so, where it is necessary for legal proceedings or where the worker has given explicit consent to the disclosure; and
- not make sickness, accident or absence records of individual workers available to other workers, other than to provide managers with information in so far as this is necessary for them to carry out their managerial roles.

As good practice, the employer should **only disclose** information from sickness or injury records about an identifiable worker's illness, medical condition or injury where there is a legal obligation to do so, where it is necessary for legal proceedings or where the worker has given his explicit consent to the disclosure (part 2.3 DP Code).

Employers are also advised to follow the DP Code's general **recommendations** with regard to data management (¶6000) and its general good practice recommendations with regard to information about their workers' health (see ¶5040). **4224**

A. Disciplinary matters

4230 If a prospective employee has **deliberately concealed** a condition, for example a history of mental illness, the contract may be held to be void, especially if the condition recurs. The employer must ensure that in such circumstances he dismisses the employee due to the deception and not his illness.

4231 If the employee has **deliberately deceived** his employer about his health, be it a deliberate concealment or lie, the employer should use his disciplinary procedure. For example, if an employee rings in sick but was at Wimbledon watching tennis, this may well amount to gross misconduct justifying immediate dismissal under his employer's disciplinary rules. Likewise, if an employee **abuses** his employer's policy on **self-certification** of short-term sickness absence procedure by stating that he was sick when in fact he had been on holiday (as happened in *Bailey v BP Oil Kent Refinery Ltd* [1980] IRLR 287, CA).

4232 Dismissals on the grounds of conduct may be justified if there has been gross misconduct as a result of **unauthorised absences, malingering** or **persistent, significant and consistent failures** in following the employer's reporting procedures. However, in such circumstances, the employer must ascertain the state of the employee's health to determine if it had any bearing on his actions.

4233 Any failure by the **employer to follow his procedure** will be taken into account, but it should be weighed against all the other circumstances. In *Bailey v BP Oil Kent Refinery Ltd*, the employer had failed to comply with the agreed company disciplinary procedure by failing to make contact with the appropriate union official who should have been informed when the dismissal was being contemplated. The Court of Appeal held that though this failure should be taken into account, it should be weighed against all the other circumstances and in these circumstances the dismissal was not unfair. Here, the requirement was not a condition precedent to dismissal but merely that the employer should keep the union official informed of what he was considering so that the official could take such action as he thought fit.

MEMO POINTS Employers must also ensure that they have followed a **statutory disciplinary procedure**. See ¶6500 for further details.

B. Long-term illness

4240 Where an employer is considering the status of an employee who has a long-term illness, he must **investigate** the situation as far as is possible and obtain a medical opinion as to the employee's current and future capability. The employer should discuss the employee's capability with him (once medical evidence has been obtained or after such a request has been refused), so that he is in a better position to make a decision as to whether the employee is likely to return to work, and what the business consequences are for a continued absence.

1. Dismissal

4245 An employer may wish to dismiss an employee who has a long-term illness with **no reasonable expectation of recovery** in an acceptable and reasonable period. Dismissal on the grounds of incapacity is a statutory fair reason for dismissal (¶8450).

In order to avoid liability for unfair dismissal, the employer should ensure that he has undertaken an appropriate medical investigation, consulted with the employee, and considered whether the employee could be employed in some **alternative capacity**. In doing so, he must act reasonably in **all the circumstances**. This includes considering the type of illness, the likely length of continuing absence, and whether recovery is possible within a period that is reasonable and acceptable. This should be balanced against the genuine **business needs of the employer** (*K Spencer v Paragon Wallpapers Ltd* [1976] IRLR 373, EAT). Therefore, it is a balance between the needs of the employer to get the work done and whether he should be expected to wait any longer, and if he should, for how long. As with all unfair dismissal claims, the tribunal will look at whether the employer's response was within the range of reasonable responses a fair and reasonable employer would make (*Rolls-Royce Ltd v Walpole* [1980] IRLR 343, EAT).

In assessing the fairness of a dismissal, the tribunal can take into account any medical reports obtained by the employer during the notice period (*White v South London Transport Ltd* [1988] ICR 293, EAT).

The fact that an employee has not exhausted his sick pay entitlement will not automatically make his dismissal unfair as the existence of a contractual sick pay procedure does not indicate that there is a guaranteed period of sickness absence before dismissal will be considered. However, if sick pay is contractual, dismissal before the right to it has ended may be unfair unless the employer has strong evidence that dismissal at that time was necessary. Further, automatic dismissal when sick pay entitlement has run out will not necessarily be fair. Note, that if dismissal stops or prevents payment under a PHI scheme, this might be in breach of an implied duty (¶1241). 4246

Disabled employees

A person is **defined** as disabled if he has a physical or mental impairment which has a substantial and long-term adverse effect on his ability to carry out his **normal day-to-day activities** (s 1 DDA 1995). This definition is wide and many employees suffering long-term illnesses will be termed disabled (¶5455). 4248

If an employee is disabled, his employer must make all **reasonable adjustments** to facilitate his return from long-term sick leave (s 4A DDA 1995). These can include:
- modifying the way the job is structured;
- changing particular duties within his role;
- providing retraining or redeployment to another post; and
- allowing time off for rehabilitation.

Further, if necessary, he must also consider whether there is **suitable alternative employment**. Only then, can the employer consider dismissing the disabled employee on grounds of incapacity.

Therefore, before an employer dismisses an employee due to his incapacity, he must consider if the reason for dismissal **relates to a disability**, as if it does, he must ensure that he does not discriminate against his employee (*H J Heinz Co Ltd v Kenrick* [2000] IRLR 144, EAT). In addition, an employer must not discriminate against a disabled employee by treating him less favourably on the ground of disability than he would treat a person not having that particular disability whose relevant circumstances (including his abilities) are the same, or not materially different from, those of the disabled person (s 3A(5) DDA 1995). (Note that there is **no qualifying period** that needs to be satisfied before an employee can bring a disability discrimination claim and there is **no limit** to the amount of award that can be given in such cases.) 4249

EXAMPLE In *H J Heinz Co Ltd v Kenrick*, K was frequently off sick. Although, his condition was never satisfactorily identified, he told the company's medical adviser that he thought he had chronic fatigue syndrome (CFS). During the last period of absence, K was warned that he was at risk of being dismissed if there was no indication of a likely date for his return. K's doctor could not give a return date. After nearly a year's absence, K was still certified unfit for work and Heinz dismissed him despite the fact that K had asked Heinz to wait until he had seen an immunologist before acting. A diagnosis of CFS was later confirmed.

Heinz was found liable for disability discrimination, as it should have ascertained whether K was disabled by waiting until he had seen the immunologist. It should then have considered making any reasonable adjustments such as lighter duties or changes to his working hours.

4250 Long-term sickness absence is a common reason for **less favourable treatment** for a disability-related reason (for example, a dismissal) of a disabled worker. However, if an employer can demonstrate that the reason for the less favourable treatment was both 'material to the circumstances of the particular case' and 'substantial' then the treatment will be justified (s 3A(3) DDA 1995). An employer will only be able to **justify** less favourable treatment of a disabled employee for a reason related to his disability if he can show that the less favourable treatment would have been justified even if the required reasonable adjustments had been made (s 3A(6) DDA 1995). Moreover, such less favourable treatment **cannot be justified** where it constitutes less favourable treatment on the ground of that person's disability which falls within the scope of the new definition of 'direct' disability discrimination (s 3A(4) DDA 1995).

Examples of where an employer's action in dismissing a worker on long-term sick leave were justified include where a worker was physically incapable of performing the functions of his job due to his disability (*Allen v H Hargrave & Co*, case 150/99, EAT); where the employee was a key worker in a small team whose duties needed to be carried out on a full-time basis and was not suitable for job-sharing or temporary cover (*Sillifant v North & East Devon Health Authority*, case 14001241/97, ET); where temporary cover was not considered suitable, reasonable or realistic (*O'Rourke v Harrogate District Hospice Care Limited*, case 1807515/99, ET); and where an employee was deemed unfit for any duties, even light work and there was no indication as to when the employee might next be able to work again (here the employer was unable to consider any reasonable adjustments to the employee's working arrangements) (*Joy v Connex South Central*, EAT case 975/01). However, case law in this area is constantly changing and each case will be determined on its own particular facts. It is therefore important to keep informed of recent developments. See ¶5500 for further details and for a detailed discussion of disability discrimination.

The Code of Practice on employment and occupation (DD Code) (¶5500) recognises that there are circumstances in which an employer may be justified in **terminating** the employment (¶5510). In the same way, where an employer's other statutory obligations (for example, health and safety) conflict with the provisions of the DDA 1995, they will take precedence provided there are no reasonable adjustments which the employer can make (¶5503).

Medical evidence and investigation

4251 Employers must, as far as they are able, inform themselves of the **true medical position** so they can make a rational and informed decision as to whether to dismiss. However, they cannot be expected to be medical experts and the decision to dismiss is not a medical question but one that is answered in the light of the available medical evidence (*East Lindsey District Council v Daubney* [1977] IRLR 181, EAT; *A Links & Co Ltd v Rose* [1991] IRLR 353, CS).

4252 To **obtain medical evidence**, the employer may ask the employee to attend a medical examination by an **occupational health doctor** or adviser. If he does not have a contractual right to do so, the employer will need the employee's consent before requesting him to attend an examination. In such cases, the employer is not bound by the medical access rules. Alternatively if this is not possible or where specialist advise is needed which cannot be provided by any occupational health service, the employer should try to obtain a report from the **employee's own GP**. In such cases, the following **medical access rules** must be complied with (ss 3-5 Access to Medical Reports Act 1988):
- the employee must consent; and
- the employer must inform the employee of his right to withhold his consent, his right to have a copy of the report before his consent is given and his right to amend or correct errors.

Where an employee **refuses to provide unequivocal consent** to his occupational health report/GP/specialist, the employer is entitled to make his decision on the basis of the limited material available to him.

EXAMPLE In *Elmbridge Housing Trust v O'Donoghue* [2004] EWCA Civ 939, CA, O **refused** to provide unequivocal consent to her occupational health report being passed to her employer, EHT, after a **prolonged attempt** by EHT to persuade her otherwise and was deemed to have been fairly dismissed on the grounds of capability after three and a half months on sickness absence. The Court held that the dismissal was within EHT's band of reasonable responses given that, without access to the occupational health report, EHT was entitled to conclude that O was incapable on the basis of the limited material available to it.

MEMO POINTS Employers can apply to the county court if a **doctor refuses** to comply (s 8 Access to Medical Reports Act 1988).

It may also be appropriate and necessary to obtain a report from a **specialist** in the relevant field, rather than rely solely on the company doctor and/or the employee's GP (*Crampton v Dacorum Motors Ltd* [1975] IRLR 168, IT). This is especially so when a GP gives an unconfirmed diagnosis or it is one that is required to be made (or is better made) by a specialist. 4253

The employee may also be prepared to apply for his actual **health records** made by his doctor in addition to any medical report. These may give a useful insight as to what was being said or reported at the doctor's surgery and ascertaining what drugs the employee is taking (Access to Health Records Act 1990). The doctor can refuse this request if such access would cause harm to the patient (s 4 Access to Health Records Act 1990). 4254

Conflicting reports Where there are conflicting medical reports, the employer may act reasonably if he accepts the less favourable report of an occupational health doctor who knew the nature and importance of the employee's job particularly with regard to the risks it entailed (*Singh-Deu v Chloride Metals* [1976] IRLR 56, IT, where a paranoid schizophrenic who worked with hazardous materials was fairly dismissed on the medical report of the occupational health doctor despite the fact that a specialist had thought he was capable of resuming work). 4256

Prior consultation

The employer **must consult** with the employee before dismissal unless there are wholly exceptional circumstances, for example to prevent the employee discovering a pessimistic prognosis (*East Lindsey District Council v Daubney* (¶4251); *Eclipse Blinds Ltd v Wright* [1992] IRLR 133, CS). A discussion will enable the situation to be weighed up, bearing in mind the employer's need for work to be done and the employee's need for time to recover his health. Further, discussions and consultations may show facts and circumstances that the employer was unaware of and which may throw new light onto the situation. Alternatively, the employee may wish to seek medical advice on his own account which, when brought to the notice of the employer's medical doctors or advisers, may cause them to change their opinion. 4258

EXAMPLE In *Eclipse Blinds Ltd v Wright*, W's health had deteriorated and she was often ill and off work. The employer obtained a report from W's doctor which stated that he could not see any possibility of her returning to work in the near future and that her ultimate prognosis was not good.
As W had told her employer that she thought she was improving and clearly did not know the seriousness of her illness, the director, who took the decision to dismiss her, decided to write to her instead of discussing the situation where it might be difficult to avoid disclosing information about her health. These particular facts led the Court to hold that this was an **exceptional case** where consultation was not required.

In certain cases where the employee has mobility problems, or where it has been difficult to keep in contact with him, a **home visit** may be appropriate. However, the employer should first check with the employee's doctor that he is fit to undergo an investigatory process or a welfare visit. 4259

2. Frustration

In relatively rare circumstances, a contract may be brought to an end due to an employee's illness frustrating the contract. In such cases, the contract is **nullified** and the parties cannot choose to keep it alive though they can, naturally, agree to enter into a new contract. If a contract is frustrated, there is no dismissal and, therefore, no possibility of an unfair dismissal claim. Further, the EAT has indicated that a contract may be frustrated even if it contains an 4270 ill health termination procedure which has not yet been concluded, as whether the employee has been expressly dismissed is not determinative of whether the contract is frustrated (*Hogan v Cambridgeshire County Council* [2001] IRLB 677, EAT).

Frustration only **occurs** when it is no longer practical to regard the contract as continuing and only happens if the employee has been ill for a lengthy period and has no likelihood of return (*Notcutt v Universal Equipment Co (London) Ltd* [1986] IRLR 218, EAT). In particular, a contract cannot be frustrated during the period in which any contractual sick pay is payable if the employee returns to work or is likely to do so (*Harland & Wolff Ltd* [1972] IRLR 90, NIRC).

4271 The **relevant factors** that a tribunal will take into account are (*Egg Stores (Stamford Hill) Ltd v Leibovici* [1976] IRLR 376, EAT):

– the length of past employment;
– how long it had been expected that the employment would continue;
– the nature of the job;
– the nature of the illness;
– the employer's need for a replacement;
– the risk to the employer of acquiring obligations in respect of redundancy payments or compensation for unfair dismissal to any replacement employee if the employee returns;
– whether wages have continued to be paid;
– the acts and statements of the employer; and
– whether in all the circumstances a reasonable employer could have been expected to wait any longer.

The tribunal will also look at the intention of the parties as their **conduct** may be relevant as evidence to whether the changed circumstances were so fundamental that they went to the root of the contract (*Hogan v Cambridgeshire County Council*).

EXAMPLE In *Collins v Secretary of State for Trade and Industry*, EAT case 1460/99, C, who had worked for many years with a transport company, was off work from February 1996 due to a severe injury to his right hand. He received SSP and later incapacity benefit and disability living allowance. He remained "on the books" of his employer receiving a Christmas voucher and P60s at the end of each tax year showing zero pay. In late 1998/1999 he was offered to stay on their books or take a redundancy payment. He chose the former. However, soon after the company went into receivership. The EAT held that the contract was frustrated due to his injury and that the Secretary of State therefore was not obliged to pay C's application for a state redundancy payment.

4272 However, as frustration could prevent an employee claiming unfair dismissal and/or disability discrimination, and may prevent any permanent health insurance payments, tribunals are reluctant to find a contract has been frustrated (*Williams v Watsons Luxury Coaches Ltd* [1990] IRLR 164, EAT). This is particularly true if the employee was disabled and a reasonable adjustment could have facilitated a return to work or where the contract needs to continue for permanent health insurance payments to be made.

C. Persistent short-term absences

4280 The same considerations as for long-term illnesses apply when dealing with an employee who is persistently off sick with short-term absences except that a formal medical investigation may not be necessary (see below).

All such situations **should be treated** with sympathy, understanding and compassion (*Lynock v Cereal Packaging Ltd* [1988] IRLR 510, EAT). However, if the employee has an unacceptable attendance record and has, despite **cautions**, failed to improve, dismissal may be appropriate and this is capable of constituting a fair reason ("some other substantial reason") for unfair dismissal purposes (¶8530). Cautions should be given using the employer's sickness procedure rather than giving a disciplinary warning unless the absences are not due to genuine sickness. The employer should firstly give a **fair review** of the poor attendance record and the reasons for it and allow the employee an opportunity to make representations before issuing any cautions.

The employee should also be cautioned when he has reached a stage when it has become impossible to continue with his employment i.e. when a reasonable employer is entitled to say "**enough is enough**." If there is **no adequate improvement**, the employer may be justified in dismissing him (*International Sports Co Ltd v Thomson* [1980] IRLR 340, EAT). In such cases, the employee does not have to be incapacitated at the time of the dismissal (*Lynock v Cereal Packaging Ltd*, above).

MEMO POINTS Employers must make sure that they also follow the **statutory disciplinary procedures**. See ¶6500 for further details.

As with long-term dismissals, the employer must have sufficient grounds to fairly dismiss the employee and must act reasonably in **all the circumstances**. As with all unfair dismissal claims, the tribunal will look at whether the employer's response was within the range of reasonable responses a fair and reasonable employer would make (*Rolls-Royce Ltd v Walpole* [1980] IRLR 343, EAT). The employer should be clear as to the reason for dismissal because procedural requirements vary according to whether the reason is poor attendance (conduct) or sickness (capacity). The courts have held that in relation to persistent short-term absences this includes the nature of the illnesses, the likelihood of recurrence, the existence of any underlying sickness that has resulted in the persistent absences, the length of the absences, and the periods of good health in between such absences. These factors should be balanced against the genuine business needs of the employer. 4281

Medical investigation

Where there are unconnected intermittent periods of absence, the employer is not obliged to make medical enquiries as such investigations are rarely fruitful because of the transient nature of the employee's symptoms and complaints (*Lynock v Cereal Packaging Ltd*, above). However, any indication that there may be an underlying cause should be investigated. 4283

EXAMPLE In *International Sports Co Ltd v Thomson* [1980] IRLR 340, EAT, T was off sick for about 25% of the time in the last 18 months of her employment due to a series of minor ailments mostly supported by sick notes. The acceptable level of absence as agreed with her union was 8%. T was issued with four separate warnings (persistent absence was dealt with under the employer's disciplinary procedure) over nearly a year, with the final warning stating that if there was no improvement she would be dismissed. T did not improve and was dismissed. The company had consulted its occupational doctor prior to dismissal who had advised that there was no useful purpose in examining T because she had no illnesses that could be subsequently verified. Further, on examining the sick notes, the occupational doctor could not see any common link between the illnesses. The EAT held that this was reasonable behaviour by the company and that it could not be expected to investigate the illnesses further.

CHAPTER 14

Family-friendly rights

OUTLINE

¶¶

There have been significant additions and enhancements to the rights of employees who are prospective/new parents and parents of young/disabled children in recent years. The complete package of family-friendly rights (subject to any qualifying requirements) is as follows: **4400**

a. pregnant employees have:
- the right to take paid time off to attend antenatal classes;
- the right to take enhanced maternity leave starting before or on the birth of their child;
- special protection when they are off sick due to a pregnancy/post-birth-related illness (¶5321) or their job is made redundant during maternity leave; and
- the right not be exposed to health and safety risks (¶4873);

b. adoptive parents have the right to take adoption leave starting just before or on the placement of their child and also have special protection if their job is made redundant during their leave;

c. expectant fathers (and the adoptive parent not taking adoption leave) have the right to take paternity leave on the birth/adoption of their child;

d. employees of young/disabled children have the right to:
- take unpaid parental leave; and
- request flexible working; and

e. workers have the right to take unpaid time off to **care for dependants**.

Employers can choose to give **more favourable contractual or non-contractual terms**, for example longer leave and contractual paid leave. With regard to maternity, adoption and paternity leave, **composite rights** will be formed of the most favourable elements of any enhanced right and the statutory minimum requirements (ML: reg 21 SI 1999/3312; AL/PAL: reg 30 SI 2002/2788). This includes statutory procedural requirements and, consequently, if an enhanced term is silent with regard to any procedural matter or has a more onerous requirement, the statutory procedural rules will apply. Slightly different rules apply to parental leave (¶4645).

MEMO POINTS 1. These rights are largely **contained** in the ERA 1996 and SSCBA 1992 (both as amended by the EA 2002) and, also, with regard to:
- maternity and parental leave – Maternity and Parental Leave etc Regulations SI 1999/3312 (as amended); Statutory Maternity Pay (General) Regulations SI 1986/1960 (as amended);
- paternity and adoption leave – Paternity and Adoption Leave Regulations SI 2002/2788 (as amended); Statutory Paternity Pay and Statutory Adoption Pay (General) Regulations SI 2002/2822 (as amended); and
- flexible working – Flexible Working (Procedural Requirements) Regulations SI 2002/3207; Flexible Working (Eligibility, Complaints and Remedies) Regulations SI 2002/3236 and ACAS (Flexible Working) Arbitration Scheme (England and Wales) SI 2003/694).

2. The **DTI** publishes the following **guides** for employers and employees on:
- maternity rights (PL 958 Rev 9 and PL 507 (basic summary));
- adoptive parents (PL 518 and PL 515 (basic summary));
- working fathers (PL 517);
- parental leave (PL 509 and PL 510 (short guide)); and
- flexible working (PL 520 and PL 516 (basic summary)).

Revenue and Customs also publishes **help books** for employers on:
- statutory maternity pay and leave and statutory paternity pay and leave (E15 and E15 (Supplement) (further guidance)); and
- statutory adoption pay and adoption leave and statutory paternity pay and paternity leave (E16 and E16 (Supplement) (further guidance)).

These have no legal status though are useful to indicate the scope and breadth of the regulations. The DTI guides also contain good practice guidance and the Revenue and Customs help books can also indicate the position Revenue and Customs will take on certain procedural issues.

3. The Government proposes to **enhance the existing family-friendly rights** and, further to its response to the DTI's consultation paper – Consultation on Work and Families: Choice and Flexibility, has published a draft Work and Families Bill. New measures in the bill and pursuant regulations include:
- extending statutory maternity pay;
- a power to extend paternity leave rights;
- extending the right to request flexible working to carers;
- introducing "keeping in touch days" so that, where employees and employers agree, an employee on maternity leave can work for a few days without losing her right to maternity leave or a week's statutory pay; and

– extending the period of notice for return from maternity leave.
See the online updates and newsletters for the progress of this bill.
4. Where the rights refer solely to a pregnant employee or new mother, the **references will be to 'she'** and not to 'he'. Also where gender is of particular relevance, **'he/she'** will be used instead of 'he'.

4402 For ease of reference, and where appropriate, the following codes will be used:
– CML: compulsory maternity leave;
– ML: maternity leave; AL: adoption leave; PAL; paternity leave; PL: parental leave;
– OML: ordinary maternity leave; OAL: ordinary adoption leave;
– SMP: statutory maternity pay; SAP: statutory adoption pay; SPP: statutory paternity pay; and
– AML: additional maternity leave; AAL: additional adoption leave.

Summary of paid and unpaid leave 4405

		PAID LEAVE			UNPAID LEAVE		
		ORDINARY MATERNITY LEAVE (OML)	ORDINARY ADOPTION LEAVE (OAL)	PATERNITY LEAVE (PAL)	ADDITIONAL MATERNITY LEAVE (AML)	ADDITIONAL ADOPTION LEAVE (AAL)	PARENTAL LEAVE (PL)
1	QUALIFICATION FOR LEAVE	pregnant employees	– employees who are adopting; and – notified and agreed to placement by approved agency	employees who are: – biological father or mother's husband, civil partner or partner/spouse, civil partner or partner of adoptive parent; and – take leave to care for newborn or support mother/adoptive child or support adoptive parent	no additional requirements		employees who have parental responsibility/ registered as father: – for child under 5/5 years after adoption (where child born/adopted on or after 15/12/99); or – until 31/03/05/ adopted child's 18th birthday if sooner (where child born/adopted between 15/12/94 and 14/12/99)
	QUALIFICATION FOR PAY	employed earner: pay Class 1 NIC and earning at least the lower earnings limit for Class 1 NIC for 8 weeks up to and including the 15th week before EWC or ending with week notified of match			n/a		
2	QUALIFYING PERIOD FOR LEAVE	none	26 weeks' continuous employment ending with week in which they are notified of match by approved agency	26 weeks' continuous employment by end of 15th week before EWC or ending with week adoptive partner notified of match	26 weeks' continuous employment by end of 15th week before EWC	no additional requirements	– for child born/adopted on or after 15/12/99: 1 year's continuous employment with current employer; and – for child born/adopted between 15/12/94 and 14/12/99: 1 year's continuous employment with an employer between 15/12/98 and 9/01/02
	QUALIFYING PERIOD FOR PAY	26 weeks' continuous employment by end of 15th week before EWC			n/a		

		PAID LEAVE			UNPAID LEAVE		
		ORDINARY MATERNITY LEAVE (OML)	ORDINARY ADOPTION LEAVE (OAL)	PATERNITY LEAVE (PAL)	ADDITIONAL MATERNITY LEAVE (AML)	ADDITIONAL ADOPTION LEAVE (AAL)	PARENTAL LEAVE (PL)
3	DURATION	up to 26 weeks		1 or 2 whole weeks	up to 26 weeks from end of OML/OAL		13 weeks (18 weeks for disabled child) for each child Fallback scheme: taken as whole week(s), maximum of 4 weeks per child per year
4	PAY	first 6 weeks, earnings-related rate then standard rate	standard rate		n/a		
5	START DATE	from 11th week before EWC. Automatic on birth/absence due to pregnancy-related illness during 4 weeks before EWC	from 14 days before expected placement	within 56 days of birth	at end of OML/AML		fallback scheme: from when entitled subject to correct notification (and any employer postponement)
6	NOTICE TO TAKE LEAVE	before end of 15th week of EWC employer must respond within 28 days setting out when due back if full entitlement (OML or OML and AML) is taken	within 7 days of notification of adoption employer must respond within 28 days setting out when due back if full entitlement (OAL and AAL) is taken	before end of 15th week of EWC/within 7 days of notification of adoption	no additional requirements		fallback scheme: at least 21 days before leave
	NOTICE FOR PAY ENTITLEMENT	28 days before start date. Usually satisfied by giving notice to take leave			n/a		

		PAID LEAVE			UNPAID LEAVE		
		ORDINARY MATERNITY LEAVE (OML)	ORDINARY ADOPTION LEAVE (OAL)	PATERNITY LEAVE (PAL)	ADDITIONAL MATERNITY LEAVE (AML)	ADDITIONAL ADOPTION LEAVE (AAL)	PARENTAL LEAVE (PL)
7	EVIDENCE FOR LEAVE ENTITLEMENT	on request. Usually satisfied by giving evidence for pay entitlement			n/a		fallback scheme: on request
	EVIDENCE FOR PAY ENTITLEMENT	maternity certificate	matching certificate	self-certificate and declaration	n/a		
8	TERMS AND CONDITIONS DURING LEAVE	all terms except remuneration			most terms suspended		
9	NOTICE TO RETURN	28 days before intention to return: – before end of OML; or – immediately after OML if entitled to AML no notice if return at end of maternity leave (ML) entitlement	28 days before intention to return before end of OAL and AAL no notice if return at end of AL entitlement	none	see OML/OAL		none
10	JOB ON RETURN	same job (unless after a period of AML, AAL or PL of more than 4 weeks in which case same as AML/AOL)			same job unless not reasonably practical, in which case suitable alternative employment		– less than 4 weeks (other than after AML or AAL): same job; or – more than 4 weeks and any leave after AML or AAL: same as AML/AAL
11	ENFORCEMENT AND REMEDIES	right not to suffer detriment and right not to be unfairly dismissed in relation to above rights					

SECTION 1

Rights of prospective/new parents

I. Time off for antenatal care

4410 Pregnant employees have the right to time off to **attend antenatal classes** (s 55 ERA 1996). These must be made by appointment and on the advice of a GP/midwife/health visitor. Antenatal classes are not defined though the DTI guide on maternity rights suggests that antenatal care is not restricted to medical examinations and could, for example, include relaxation or parentcraft classes if it is medically advised.

The employee must **inform her employer** that she is pregnant and that she has an antenatal class for which she needs time off to attend. For the **second and subsequent appointments** (for which she needs time off) the employer can also ask her to produce:

- a certificate from a GP/midwife/health visitor stating that the employee is pregnant; and
- an appointment card or some other document showing that the appointment has been made.

4411 Employers must **not unreasonably refuse** to permit employees to take such time off (s 57 ERA 1996). There may be circumstances where the employer could reasonably refuse time off, for example if the employee could have reasonably made her appointment outside working hours (*Gregory v Tudsbury Ltd* [1982] IRLR 267, IT). However, each case will be decided on its merits and it is unlikely that an employer could reasonably expect an employee to make an appointment outside working hours given that she will probably have little or no control as to the appointment times. If she does have some choice, it may be considered reasonable for her to organise them, if she can, at the beginning or end of her working day.

There may also be circumstances where it may be reasonable for the employer to re-arrange the employee's working schedule to make up the time, especially if she is working part-time. However, as this may give rise to a claim for discrimination, unless the employee wants to make up time, it is advisable that the employer does not require it.

Right to remuneration

4413 Employees have the right to be remunerated for time off at the appropriate hourly rate (s 56 ERA 1996) and see ¶3935.

II. Maternity, adoption and paternity leave

4420 Pregnant employees and adoptive parents have, subject to certain qualifying conditions, the right to take paid ordinary leave and unpaid additional leave. Further, new fathers and adoptive parents (who have chosen not to take adoption leave) have the right to take paid paternity leave.

A. Ordinary leave and paternity leave

1. Ordinary maternity leave

Employees (including apprentices) (reg 2(1) SI 1999/3312) who are pregnant are entitled to take **up to** 26 weeks' leave. 4425

The **earliest** this can **begin** is the 11th week before the expected week of confinement (EWC) (s 71 ERA 1996; reg 4 SI 1999/3312) and the **latest** on the day after birth (¶4436).

The EWC is defined as the week beginning with midnight between Saturday and Sunday in which it is expected that childbirth will occur. Childbirth includes premature living or stillborn babies born after 24 weeks of pregnancy.

EXAMPLE If Employee A's baby is due on Wednesday 30 August 2006, the EWC will start on Sunday 27 August and the earliest A can start her OML is Sunday 11 June.

Prohibition against work for two weeks after birth Employers must not permit employees who are entitled to OML to work in the 2 weeks after the date of the birth (s 72 ERA 1996; reg 8 SI 1999/3312). This is called **compulsory maternity leave (CML)**. This applies to any type of work and not just attending work at the workplace. For example, an employee must not be permitted to work at home or from the hospital during this period. Any breaches will result in the employer being liable for a criminal offence unless he can show that he did not require the employee to work and had no intention that she should do so. 4427

CML counts as part of the OML and the same entitlements and conditions apply. Indeed, as OML commences automatically on birth in any event (see below), this does not have an impact on maternity leave except for the criminal prohibition on doing any work during this period. This prohibition does not apply during the rest of maternity leave (though, on a separate point, it should be noted that working during any week of leave will disallow the employee from claiming SMP for that week).

MEMO POINTS 1. OML may be extended to the end of CML if CML does not fall within this period (reg 7(1) SI 1999/3312). However, this is unlikely to happen as even if OML was started at the beginning of 11th week before EWC, the birth would have to be over 15 weeks late before OML would need to be extended.
2. Factory workers must not be permitted to work for 4 weeks after the date of birth (s 205 Public Health Act 1936).

Notice requirements

The employee can choose when to start OML as long as she gives adequate notice, although there are two circumstances in which her OML will automatically commence (see below). In return for notifying her employer, her employer must reply setting out when her maternity leave will end if she takes her total entitlement (¶4585). 4429

The employee must notify her employer, **before** the end of 15th week before EWC (reg 4 SI 1999/3312): 4430
- that she is pregnant;
- her EWC; and
- her proposed start date for OML.

These requirements can be **given separately**.

EXAMPLE Example from ¶4425 continued:
Employee A must notify her employer by Saturday 20 May 2005.

4431 The **employer can request** that:
a. the proposed date is given in writing; and
b. the employee provides evidence of her entitlement. This will take the form of a certificate from a GP or midwife that states the EWC. The most usual certificate to be produced is the MAT B1 certificate. The earliest this certificate will be given is 20 weeks before EWC. This is the form that is also usually used as evidence for SMP and, consequently, satisfying the requirements for SMP will also satisfy this request.

4432 **Failure to give adequate notice** must be disregarded if it was **not reasonably practicable** for the employee to notify her employer correctly and in time. For example, because she does not realise she is pregnant or she only starts to work for her employer after notification was due. In such cases, she should notify her employer as soon as reasonably practicable, i.e. when she finds out she is pregnant or starts employment.

MEMO POINTS If it should have been **reasonably practicable**, the employer may be able to insist that the employee postpones her start date to ensure that she gives at least 3 weeks' notice (that is the shortest notification period possible i.e. the period from the end of the 15th week (latest date to give notice) to the beginning of the 11th week of EWC (earliest date to start leave)).

4434 **Changing start date** The employee can change her start date (reg 4(1A) SI 1999/3312). Consequently, if she wants to:
– bring her original **start date forward**, she must give at least 28 days' notice before her new start date; and
– take her original **start date back**, she must give at least 28 days' notice before the original start date.
She can choose to further vary the start date using the same procedure. Each change must be notified in writing if requested.

Automatic commencement

4436 Regardless of whether the employee has specified a start date in accordance with the notice requirements above, her OML will automatically commence the **day after** either of the following two situations (reg 6 SI 1999/3312):
1. the employee is **absent** wholly or partly **because of her pregnancy at any time from** the beginning of the 4th week before EWC. Technically, as the employee need only be absent because of the pregnancy, she need only be a few minutes late for work due to, for example pregnancy-related fatigue, for this to automatically start OML. However, the DTI guide suggests that short periods including odd days of absence can be disregarded at the employer's discretion if the employee wishes to defer the start of her OML to her chosen date.
Leave due to illness that is **unrelated to pregnancy** (for example, flu) must be treated as sick leave and does not automatically commence OML.
2. the employee has **given birth**.

EXAMPLE Example from ¶4425 continued:
Employee A has given notice that she would like to start her OML on 16 August 2006.
1. A is off sick because of pregnancy-related back problems in the 4th week before EWC on 2 August. Her OML should automatically start on 3 August unless the employer disregards this day's absence because A wishes to delay the start of her OML.
2. A gives birth on 16 August. Her OML will automatically start on 17 August.

MEMO POINTS Before 6 April 2003, OML could automatically commence in 1. at any time from the start of the 6th week before EWC. This was considered to give unnecessary uncertainty and so was reduced. Also note that automatic commencement now starts the day after either of the two situations above occurs instead of on the day itself.

4437 In both circumstances, the employee must **notify** her employer that she is absent from work wholly or partly because of pregnancy/giving birth as soon as it is reasonably practicable. The employer must in return, give her notice as to when her maternity leave will end (¶4585).

2. Ordinary adoption leave

All employees (including apprentices) (reg 2(1) SI 2002/2788), i.e. both male and female, who are **notified by an approved adoption agency** of a match with a child/children are entitled to take leave **up to** a maximum of 26 weeks (reg 18 SI 2002/2788). Such employees are called adopters. The right is the same irrespective of whether **more than one child is matched**. If a couple is **adopting jointly**, they can choose who takes adoption leave. In such cases, the other one can take paternity leave. 4440

OAL can **begin** from the actual date of the child's placement or from a fixed date which can be up to 14 days before the expected date of placement (regs 16, 18 SI 2002/2788).

Eligibility

To be eligible, the adoptive parent must have (reg 15 SI 2002/2788): 4442
- been **continuously employed** with the employer for at least 26 weeks ending with the week in which he/she is notified of being matched with a child; and
- **notified his/her agency** that he/she agrees to the child being placed with him/her on the expected date of placement.

MEMO POINTS With regard to taking paternity leave to support a spouse/civil partner/partner who is **adopting from overseas**, this is covered by s 80B ERA 1996; ERA 1996 (Application of Section 80B to Adoptions from Overseas) Regulations SI 2003/920; Paternity and Adoption Leave (Adoption from Overseas) Regulations SI 2003/921; Social Security Contributions and Benefits Act 1992 (Application of Parts 12ZA and 12ZB to Adoptions from Overseas) Regulations SI 2003/499; Statutory Paternity Pay (Adoption) and Statutory Adoption Pay (Adoptions from Overseas) Regulations SI 2003/500; Statutory Paternity Pay (Adoption) and Statutory Adoption Pay (Adoptions from Overseas) (Administration) Regulations SI 2003/1192 and Statutory Paternity Pay (Adoption) and Statutory Adoption Pay (Adoptions from Overseas) (No. 2) Regulations SI 2003/1194.
In such cases, the employee must receive an official notification. For further details, see the legislation listed above and latest version of the DTI guide on parents adopting a child from overseas. Assistance can also be obtained from the Department of Health Intercountry Adoption Team.

Notice requirements

Employees must notify their employer as to when the child is expected to be placed for adoption and the date on which they want AL to begin (reg 17 SI 2002/2788 as amended by reg 3 SI 2004/923). This must be given no later than 7 days after being notified of having been matched with the child. If this is not reasonably practicable, it should be done as soon as it is. 4444

The **employer can request** that: 4445
a. the notice is given in writing; and
b. the employee provides evidence of his/her entitlement. This takes the form of one or more documents from the adoption agency that states:
- the name and address of the agency;
- the date on which the employee was notified that he/she had been matched with the child; and
- the expected date of placement.

The "**matching certificate**: statutory adoption leave and pay" (¶4489) can be used and will provide all the information required.

MEMO POINTS Employers can no longer request the name and date of birth of a child in respect of whom leave is taken.

Failure to give adequate notice must be disregarded if it was **not reasonably practicable** for the employee to notify his/her employer correctly and in time. In such cases, it should be done as soon as it is reasonably practicable. 4446

Changing start date The employee can change his/her start date (reg 17(4) SI 2002/2788). Consequently, if he/she wants to vary the date: 4448
- to the date on which the child is **actually placed** for adoption, he/she must give at least 28 days' notice before the expected date of placement; and
- to **another set date**, he/she must give at least 28 days' notice before that date.

He/she can choose to further vary the start date using the same procedure. Each change must be notified in writing if requested.

3. Paternity leave

4455 Eligible employees are entitled to either 1 or 2 whole weeks paid paternity leave where they wish to take leave (regs 4, 8 SI 2002/2788):
- to **care** for a newborn or newly adoptive child; or
- to **support** the child's mother or adoptive parent.

4456 Paternity leave must also **be taken**:
- as either 1 or 2 whole weeks; and
- within 56 days of the date of birth or placement.

The **earliest start date** is on the date of birth or placement.

Eligibility

4458 To be eligible for paternity leave, the employee must (regs 4, 8 SI 2002/2788):
a. have been **continuously employed** for 26 weeks:
– before the end of the 15th week before the EWC and be either the biological father of the child or the mother's husband, civil partner or partner; or
– ending with the week in which the adoptive parent is notified of being matched for adoption and be either married to, the civil partner or the partner of the adoptive parent; and
b. have or be expected to have **responsibility for the upbringing** of the child where he is the child's father. Where the spouse, civil partner or partner of the adoptive parent is not the child's father, he/she must have or be expected to have the main responsibility along with the mother or adoptive parent.

With regard to adoption leave, where a **couple** is **adopting jointly**, they can choose which one takes adoption leave leaving the other to take paternity leave if desired.

MEMO POINTS 1. A **partner** is a person (whether of a different sex or the same sex) who lives with the mother or adoptive parent and the child in an enduring family relationship but is not a relative of the mother or adoptive parent. A relative in this context is a mother's or adoptive parent's parent, grandparent, sister, brother, aunt or uncle. The regulations have also been amended to include **civil partners** (SI 2005/2114 which gives same-sex couples the right to form a civil partnership and gain legal recognition).
2. With regard to taking paternity leave to support a spouse/civil partner/partner who is **adopting from overseas**, this is covered by s 80B ERA 1996; ERA 1996 (Application of Section 80B to Adoptions from Overseas) Regulations SI 2003/920; Paternity and Adoption Leave (Adoption from Overseas) Regulations SI 2003/921; Social Security Contributions and Benefits Act 1992 (Application of Parts 12ZA and 12ZB to Adoptions from Overseas) Regulations SI 2003/499; Statutory Paternity Pay (Adoption) and Statutory Adoption Pay (Adoptions from Overseas) Regulations SI 2003/500; Statutory Paternity Pay (Adoption) and Statutory Adoption Pay (Adoptions from Overseas) (Administration) Regulations SI 2003/1192 and Statutory Paternity Pay (Adoption) and Statutory Adoption Pay (Adoptions from Overseas) (No. 2) Regulations SI 2003/1194.
In such cases, the employee must receive an official notification. For further details, see the legislation listed above and the latest version of the DTI guide on parents adopting a child from overseas. Assistance can also be obtained from the Department of Health Intercountry Adoption Team.

Notice requirements

4460 Employees must notify their employer **no later than** the end of the 15th week before EWC or no later than 7 days after being notified of having been matched with the child (regs 6, 10 SI 2002/2788):
- of the EWC or the date which the adoptive parent was notified and the expected date of placement;
- whether 1 or 2 weeks of leave is to be taken; and
- the chosen start date.

The employee must give **further notice**, as soon as reasonably practicable, of the actual date of birth or placement. 4461

The **employer can request** that: 4462
a. the notices are given in writing; and
b. the employee provides a signed declaration as evidence of his/her entitlement. This must state:
– that he/she is taking the leave to care for a newborn or newly adoptive child or to support the child's mother or adoptive parent;
– that he/she is the biological father of the child/the mother's husband/civil partner/partner or married to/civil partner/the partner of the adoptive parent; and
– that he/she has or is expected to have responsibility (or main responsibility if required) for the child's upbringing.

Revenue and Customs provides **model self-certificates and declarations** (form SC3 (Becoming a parent) and form SC4 (Becoming an adoptive parent)) which can be used.

Failure to give adequate notice must be disregarded if it was **not reasonably practicable** for the employee to notify his/her employer correctly and in time. In such cases, it must be done as soon as it is. 4463

Changing start date The employee can change the start date (regs 6(4), 10(4) SI 2002/2788). Consequently, if he/she wants to vary the date to: 4465
– the **date of birth or placement**, he/she must give at least 28 days' notice before the first day of the EWC or the expected date of placement;
– a date that is a **set number of days** after the date of birth or placement, he/she must give at least 28 days' notice before that set number of days taken after the first day of the EWC or the expected date of placement; or
– **another set date**, he/she must give at least 28 days' notice before that date.

He/she can choose to further vary the start date using the same procedure. Each change must be notified in writing if requested.

B. Statutory pay

Although statutory pay **runs in parallel** with ordinary leave/paternity leave, there are additional qualifying conditions for statutory pay and, therefore, an employee may find that he/she has the right to take leave but not to be paid. An employee is still entitled to statutory pay, even if he/she **decides not to return to work** after the leave has ended. However, the employee will not be entitled to statutory pay for any week in which he/she **works during the pay period**. 4470

Statutory pay is paid by employers who can recover most, and in certain circumstances, all of the amount. Any agreement will be void in so far as it purports to exclude, limit or modify any provision of the SMP scheme or require an employee to contribute to any costs incurred by the employer (SMP: s 164 SSCBA 1992; SAP: s 171ZO SSCBA 1992; SPP: s 171ZF SSCBA 1992).

Other forms of support: social benefits If an employee is **not entitled to statutory maternity pay**, the employer should complete the HMRC form SMP1 and give it to the employee. This form sets out why the employee is not eligible and enables the employee to claim social security benefits. The main benefit, subject to certain qualifying conditions, is a **maternity allowance** which is paid by the DWP through the Benefits Agency. Pregnant employees may also be eligible for a **Sure Start Maternity Grant**. 4472

Those who do not qualify for statutory pay (or maternity allowance), or whose income during their leave falls short of their needs, may also be able to claim **income support** and/or **housing and council tax benefits**. These are income-related benefits with maximum levels set yearly. Further, they may be entitled to the **working tax credit** (for working households on low incomes) and the **child tax credit** (for those who are responsible for a child/ children).

MEMO POINTS A guide to maternity benefits (NI17A) gives further information on these benefits and is available from Jobcentre Plus/Social Security offices and at the Department of Work and Pensions (DWP) website: www.dwp.gov.uk

1. Entitlement

4475 As well as satisfying the requirements to take ordinary leave/paternity leave, to qualify for statutory pay (SMP: s 164 SSCBA 1992; SAP: s 171ZL SSCBA 1992; SPP: s 171ZA-B SSCBA 1992):
1. the individual must be an **employed earner**. That means that he/she must be an employee or office holder (for example, a director) aged over 16 years and pay Class 1 NIC, and have average weekly earnings of at least the lower earnings limit for Class 1 NIC.
The **average weekly earnings** are determined by reference to the 8 weeks up to and including the qualifying week (the **relevant period**).
The **qualifying week** is:
– SMP: the 15th week before EWC;
– SAP: the week in which he/she is notified of a match for adoption; and
– SPP: the 15th week before EWC/the week in which the adoptive parent has been notified of a match for adoption.
2. he/she must have **26 weeks' continuous employment** up to and including the qualifying week. Continuity will be preserved in any 1 week as long as the employee is employed for at least part of that week (see memo points below for further details of this and other exceptions as to when continuity will be preserved in periods of non-employment).

4476 MEMO POINTS 1. Slightly modified rules of continuity apply and continuity will be **preserved** during a period of **non-employment** (SMP: reg 11 SI 1986/1960; SAP/SPP: reg 33 SI 2002/2822):
a. as long as the employee is employed for at least part of each week; or
b. with regard to a whole or part of a week of non-employment (i.e. no contract of employment) if the employee:
– was incapable of working due to sickness or injury (limited to 26 weeks); or
– absent:
• due to a temporary cessation of work;
• by arrangement or custom; or
• with regard to SMP: due to pregnancy or birth (which is limited to 26 weeks unless the employee returns to work after AML or returns as a result of an offer of suitable alternative work) or due to taking paternity leave.
See ¶1010 for the ambit of such absences. Further, a **change of employer** will break continuity unless it falls under one of the continuity rule exceptions (¶1035).
The employee must be **re-employed after his/her absence**.
2. Further, if an employee is **reinstated or re-engaged** as a result of:
– an unfair dismissal claim;
– action by an ACAS conciliation officer (before the employee had presented an unfair dismissal claim);
– a designated dismissals procedure agreement; or
– the statutory dispute resolution procedure.
the interval between dismissal and re-employment will be counted as continuous (SMP: reg 12 SI 1986/1960 as amended by SI 2005/358; SAP/SPP: reg 34 SI 2002/2822 as amended by SI 2005/358).
Where there has been a **stoppage due to a trade dispute**, an employee's continuity will not be broken, but the weeks in which the trade dispute occurred will not count toward calculating his/her period of continuous employment unless he/she can prove that he/she did not have a direct interest in the trade dispute (SMP: reg 13 SI 1986/1960; SAP/SPP: reg 35 SI 2002/2822).

4478 **SMP: Dismissal or resignation after qualifying week** As long as these conditions are satisfied, a pregnant employee will continue to be entitled to SMP even if the employee is dismissed or resigns after the qualifying week before commencing OML.

MEMO POINTS Before 6 April 2003, this only applied to dismissals.

Informing employee if not entitled

If an employee is not entitled to SMP/SAP/SPP, the employer should give his employee the relevant **form SMP1** "Why I cannot pay you SMP"/form **SAP1** "Why I cannot pay you SAP"/-form **SSP1** "Why I cannot pay you SSP" as appropriate. If there is a dispute, the matter can be referred to Revenue and Customs for a formal decision. 4480

MEMO POINTS 1. The forms are **available from** Revenue and Customs. Form SMP1 is also available from Jobcentre plus/social security offices and the Department of Work and Pensions.
2. The employer can **produce** his own computerised or paper versions although he must make sure that he includes the employee's name, address and NI number and the reason why he cannot pay SMP/SAP/SMP or, if some payments have been made, the reason why he is now stopping the payments, the date these payments will stop and, with regard to SMP, how many weeks have/are to be paid. It is helpful if the employer also includes information on what the employee should do if he/she disagrees with his decision and who to contact or what to do to find out about other government help and assistance.

Disputes

Any dispute as to whether SMP, SAP or SPP is due to an employee will be determined by Revenue and Customs and not by an employment tribunal (*Taylor Gordon & Co Ltd (t/a Plan Personnel) v Timmons* [2004] IRLR 180, EAT). 4482

2. Notice and medical evidence

Notice Employees must give notice, in writing if required, 28 days **before** they wish their statutory pay to start (SMP: s 164(4); SAP: s 171ZL; SPP: s 171ZC SSCBA 1992). The notice requirements for leave will suffice (except if, with regard to maternity leave, the employee gives notice in the 15th week of EWC that she wishes to start OML in the 11th week before EWC). If it is **not reasonably practicable** to give notice in time, he/she should do so as soon as it is. 4485

Where statutory pay is to start on the date of birth or placement for adoption, or on a set number of days after either of these dates, the employee must give further notice of the actual date as soon as is reasonably practicable.

MEMO POINTS Before 6 April 2003, notice for SMP was 21 days.

Medical evidence: SMP An employee must provide her employer with medical evidence of the EWC and the week of actual birth where relevant (reg 22(1) SI 1986/1960). This must be **submitted no later than** the end of the 3rd week of the statutory pay period unless the employer accepts that there was a good reason not to do so. The very latest, though, the evidence can be given is the end of the 13th week. 4487

This evidence is usually in the form of a **maternity certificate** (MAT B1) (though the employer can accept other medical evidence) from her GP or midwife. It must **contain** (Statutory Maternity Pay (Medical Evidence) Regulations SI 1987/235):
- the employee's name;
- the EWC, and if the certificate is issued after the birth, the actual date of birth. A birth certificate will also be sufficient evidence of the date and week of actual birth;
- the date of the examination on which the certificate is based;
- the date on which the certificate is signed. This must not be earlier than the 20th week before EWC; and
- the address of the GP or midwife, his registered number and the expiry date of his registration.

Evidence: SAP/SPP An employee must provide his/her employer with (reg 24 SI 2002/2822): 4489

a. for SAP: evidence of the adoption and a declaration that he/she has elected to receive SAP and not SPP. Revenue and Customs' **form SC4** "Becoming an adoptive parent" provides a declaration form that can be used. Evidence of adoption must be from the adoption

agency who will provide a letter or a "**matching certificate**: statutory adoption leave and pay". The evidence must **include**:
– the name and address of the agency;
– the name and address of the employee;
– the date on which the employee was notified that he/she had been matched with the child; and
– the expected date of placement (or actual date if it has already occurred); and
b. for SPP: a declaration of his/her family commitment. Revenue and Customs' **forms SC3** "Becoming a parent" and **SC4** "Becoming an adoptive parent" provide a declaration that can be used.

These must be **submitted at least** 28 days before the start of the statutory pay period. If this is not reasonably practicable, it must be given as soon as it is, for example Revenue and Customs' Help Book on pay and time off for adoptive parents notes that sometimes there is very little time between the date the adoption agency informs the employee of a match and the date the child is placed with him/her and in such circumstances late notice must be accepted.

Failure to give notice/evidence

4491 If an employee does not give adequate notice/evidence, his/her employer can refuse to pay statutory pay and if he does so the employee will lose his/her right to it. In such cases, the employer should give the employee the appropriate form setting out why his/her request for statutory pay has been refused (¶4480).

3. Rate

4495 Statutory pay should be treated as earnings. Consequently, they are **subject to** PAYE and NIC deductions and any lawful contractual deductions, for example pension contributions and trade union subscriptions. However, deductions in relation to attachment of earnings must not be made.

Contractual payments to which the employee is entitled during this period can be **offset**.

During first six weeks of OML

4497 The first 6 weeks of OML is paid at 90% of the employee's normal weekly earnings (the **earnings-related rate**).

In relation to **pay rises**, an employee on maternity leave is entitled to be treated the same as other employees who remain at work. From 6 April 2005, where an employee is awarded a pay increase (or would have been awarded such an increase had she not been absent on statutory maternity leave and the pay increase applies to the whole or any part of the period between the beginning of the relevant period and the end of her statutory maternity leave (both her OML and AML), then her normal weekly earnings must be calculated as if such an increase applied in each week of her relevant period (¶4475) (reg 21(7) SI 1986/1960 as amended by Statutory Maternity Pay (General) (Amendment) Regulations SI 2005/729, following *Alabaster v (1) Woolwich plc, (2) Secretary of State for Social Security (C-147/02)* [2005] ICR 695, ECJ).

As a result, employers must be careful not to delay any pay reviews of employees on maternity leave and must ensure that they review such employees' pay in tandem with other employees. Where staff are offered formal appraisals, employers must remember to include those on maternity leave as to do otherwise may give rise to claims of sex discrimination. Pay increases must then be included when calculating the employee's normal weekly earnings.

Revenue and Customs have given guidance in their October 2005 Employer's Bulletin on the **time limits** that will apply to a claim for the re-calculation of SMP paid for past periods where there may have been a pay increase that was not included at the time. They advise that employers should consider all claims within 6 years of when the SMP was paid. If the employee has left the employer's employment any claim must also be within 6 months of leaving. As employers are only required to keep records for 3 years (¶4510), Revenue and Customs consider it reasonable for the employer to request the employee to provide sufficient evidence to substantiate her claim if he no longer has the necessary records. Any such arrears properly and reasonably calculated are recoverable (¶4504).

MEMO POINTS 1. If the pay increase has occurred after the first 6 weeks of OML (and consequently, the earnings-related rate has been already calculated and paid), it can only be presumed that the employer must make an additional payment equal to the difference between the revised rate (which takes account of the increased normal weekly earnings) and the rate paid at the time.
2. The Court of Appeal has held that employees can bring a claim for unpaid back-dated pay increases under the equal pay regime despite the fact that there is no male comparator (*Alabaster v (1) Barclays Bank PLC and (2) The Secretary of State for Social Security* [2005] ICR 1246, CA).

During all other statutory pay periods

Statutory pay is payable for the rest of OML and throughout OAL and PAL at the **standard set rate** of £106 (or 90% of the employee's normal weekly earnings (¶4475) if this is less than £106). 4499

MEMO POINTS This set rate is likely to be increased in April 2006.

4. Recovery

The employer can recover 92% of the statutory pay by reducing the amount of PAYE, NIC and student loan deductions paid to Revenue and Customs (SMP: regs 5-6 Statutory Maternity Pay (Compensation of Employer) Amendment Regulations SI 1994/1882 as amended; SAP/SPP: regs 3-4 SI 2002/2820). 4505

However, **small employers** are entitled to recover 100% plus an additional amount (4.5% of the total SMP/SAP/SPP paid for the tax year) to compensate for the secondary Class 1 NIC payable on SMP/SAP/SPP. A small employer is one where the total Class 1 NICs for the previous tax year were £45,000 or less (Statutory Maternity Pay (Compensation of Employers) Amendment Regulations SI 2004/698).

5. Records

The employer must **keep** records **for** 3 years after the end of the tax year in which the employee's statutory pay ends that show (SMP: reg 26 SI 1986/1960; SAP/SPP: reg 9 SI 2002/2820): 4510
- the day statutory pay started;
- the number of weeks in that tax year for which statutory pay was paid and the weekly amount; and
- any week of statutory pay in that tax year where no statutory pay was paid together with the reasons why.

Forms SMP2 (for SMP), **SAP2** (for SAP) and **SPP2** (for SPP) can be used as appropriate. The employer must also keep the employee's evidence of entitlement for the same period.

MEMO POINTS 1. The forms are **available from** Revenue and Customs.
2. The employer can **produce** his own computerised or paper versions although he must make sure that he includes the employee's name, address and NI number, a record of the payment dates and the amount paid, the date the pay period began and a record of any weeks when the statutory pay was not paid together with the reasons why.
With regard to SMP, it may also be helpful to record:
- the EWC and qualifying week;
- the date of birth;
- the date the employee told the employer she planned to start her leave;
- the date she planned to start her leave; and
- if the employee has changed her start date, when the employer was told of the new date and the new date.

With regard to SAP, it may also be helpful to record:
– the date the employee was told by the adoption agency that he/she had been matched with a child;
– the date the child was expected to be placed;
– the date the child was placed;
– the date the employee told the employer he/she planned to start his/her leave;
– the date he/she planned to start his/her leave; and
– if the employee has changed his/her start date, when the employer was told of the new date and the new date.
With regard to SPP, it may also be helpful to record:
– the EWC and qualifying week/or the date the adoptive parent was told by the adoption agency that he/she had been matched with a child and the date the child was expected to be placed;
– the date of birth/the date the child was placed;
– the date the employee told the employer he/she planned to start his/her leave;
– the date he/she planned to start his/her leave; and
– if the employee has changed his/her start date, when the employer was told of the new date and the new date.

4516 Employers must also be able to show the **correct accounting** of such payments, as appropriate, on the following records:
– deductions working sheet (P11);
– end of year returns (P14); and
– annual return (P35).

Further, the employer should be able to produce for **inspection** by the Revenue and Customs if required all appropriate wage sheets and all other documents and records which concern the calculation or payment of such statutory payments within 30 days of a notice being issued to that effect (SMP: 26A SI 1986/1960 as amended by SI 2005/989; SAP/SPP: reg 10 SI 2002/2820).

6. Penalties

4520 Employers who **fail** to **produce** any document or record required under any of the statutory payment schemes will face an initial penalty of £300 with further penalties of £60 per day for continuing failure. Employers who fail to or repeatedly refuse to **make payments** will be liable to a penalty of up to £3,000 (s 11 EA 2002).

Further, employers who **fraudulently or negligently** (s 12 EA 2002; ss 113A-B Social Security Administration Act 1992):
– make any incorrect payments;
– produce any incorrect document or record, provide any incorrect information, or make any incorrect return; or
– receive incorrect payments in connection with the recovery of such payments

will be liable to a fine of up to £3,000 with regard to SMP/SAP and £300 with regard to SPP.

MEMO POINTS Note the **employees** will face similar penalties if they fraudulently or negligently:
– make any incorrect statement or declaration in connection with claim; or
– provide any incorrect document or information which has been required to be produced to a Revenue and Customs' officer.

C. Additional leave

1. Additional maternity leave

An employee who has qualified for OML will be **entitled** to 26 weeks of **unpaid** AML if she has also been continuously employed for at least 26 weeks by the end of the 15th week before EWC (s 73 ERA 1996; reg 5 SI 1999/3312). This is the same qualifying period as for SMP. 4530

AML is added to the end of OML and **starts** the day after it ends.

EXAMPLE Employee B's EWC starts on Sunday 26 March 2006. Consequently, B must have been continuously employed from at least the Saturday of the 40th week before EWC, 25 June 2005, to at least the Sunday of the 15th week, 11 December 2005, to be entitled to AML.

MEMO POINTS Before 6th April 2003, the qualifying period was 1 year's continuous employment by the beginning of the 11th week before the EWC and AML was limited to a maximum of 29 weeks after birth.

If an employee does not qualify for AML she may be entitled to take a shorter period of leave in the form of unpaid parental leave. 4531

2. Additional adoption leave

An employee who has qualified for OAL will be **entitled** to 26 weeks of **unpaid** AAL (s 75B ERA 1996; reg 20 SI 2002/2822). 4535

AAL is added to the end of OAL and **starts** the day after it ends.

D. Terms and conditions during leave

Ordinary leave and paternity leave The following are the **statutory minimum requirements** (OML: s 71 ERA 1996, reg 9 SI 1999/3312; OAL: s 75A ERA 1996, reg 19 SI 2002/2788; PAL: s 80C ERA 1996, reg 12 SI 2002/2788). As with every aspect of family-friendly rights, the employer can provide for more favourable contractual or non-contractual terms. 4540

The employee's **contract of employment continues** during ordinary leave and he/she is: 4541
- entitled to the benefit of the express and implied terms and conditions of employment which would have applied if he/she had not been on leave; and
- bound by any obligations arising under these terms and conditions except for those that require him/her to work and attend his/her place of work.

Terms and conditions are defined as including all matters connected with the employee's employment whether or not they arise under his/her contract of employment **except** for those concerning remuneration. For example, failing to notify an employee of a vacancy that had arisen during her maternity leave will breach the implied term of trust and confidence if the vacancy was one that the employee would have believed she was suitable for (it is irrelevant that had she applied, she would not have been short-listed in any event) (*Visa International Service Association v Paul* [2004] IRLR 42, EAT). 4542

Remuneration is defined as wages or salary and includes any **payment related to the employee's performance**, for example bonuses, commissions or profit-related pay (OML: reg 9(3) SI 1999/3312; OAL: reg 19(3) SI 2002/2788; PAL: reg 12(3) SI 2002/2788). In such circumstances, the employee will only be entitled to whatever part relates to the time he/she was at work 4543 before he/she took leave. They must be paid this pro rata amount even if it is paid while he/she is absent. Consequently, any bonus that is given equally to all staff (or a distinct group of staff of which the employee is a member), and is not related to individual performance should not be treated as remuneration and must be paid in full.

4544 ML: Where a **bonus** is not work-related (i.e. not related to the work the employee does during the period in question), non-payment or reduced payment may also be discriminatory (*Gus Home Shopping Ltd v Green and McLaughlin* [2001] IRLR 75, EAT; *Caisse Nationale d'Assurance Vieillesse des Travailleurs Salaries v Thibault* [1998] IRLR 399, ECJ).

EXAMPLE **Not work-related**

In *Gus Home Shopping Ltd v Green and McLaughlin*, GHS introduced a discretionary **loyalty bonus** largely contingent on the effective transfer of the department (in which G and M worked) over the preceding 6 months. The EAT held that GHS discriminated against G and M when it disqualified M from receiving a bonus and reduced G's bonus because they were absent on maternity leave or pregnancy-related sickness during this period.

Work-related

In *Hoyland v Asda Stores Ltd* [2005] ICR 1235, EAT, a pro rata reduction of an annual bonus for the period of absence on maternity leave was made with regard to a scheme which allowed for reductions on absence for any reason for more than a specified period during the year in question. The EAT held that this was not discriminatory as the scheme was work-related, for although the bonuses were unrelated to individual productivity, they were paid in recognition of the work undertaken by employees as a whole (with attendance being rewarded as this contributed to the overall performance of the business).

4545 Remuneration does not include all other benefits such as contractual annual leave, an **occupational pension scheme** or **benefits in kind**, for example a company car, private health cover and luncheon vouchers. Nor does it cover payments made in lieu of a benefit, for example a car allowance. Consequently, ordinary leave will count towards pensionable service and an employee on ordinary leave will be entitled to employer contributions.

4546 As the contract continues, any period of ordinary leave will count towards his/her statutory **continuity of employment**. The same applies to any contractual rights that are based on continuity, for example occupational pension scheme or seniority.

4548 **Additional leave** Unless there are more favourable/preferential contractual terms, although an employee's contract continues during additional leave, most of its terms and conditions are **suspended** and he/she only **remains entitled** to (AML: s 73 ERA 1996, reg 17 SI 1999/3312; AAL: s 75B ERA 1996, reg 21 SI 2002/2788):

a. any contractual terms and conditions relating to:
- notice of termination;
- compensation in the event of redundancy;
- disciplinary or grievance procedures; and

b. the benefit of his/her employer's implied obligation of trust and confidence.

In return, an employee is **bound** by:

a. any contractual terms and conditions relating to:
- notice of termination;
- disclosure of confidential information;
- acceptance of gifts or other benefits;
- participation in any other business; and

b. his/her implied obligation of good faith.

4549 As the contract continues, any period of additional leave will count towards his/her statutory **continuity of employment**. This does not apply with regard to contractual rights that are based on continuity, for example pension contributions or seniority, as these terms are suspended (unless otherwise agreed).

4551 **Accrual of annual leave** During ordinary leave (OML/OAL) and PAL, the employee will be entitled to any enhanced contractual annual leave that accrues. However, even if there are no enhanced terms, the statutory entitlement to annual leave still accrues. On the other hand, during additional leave (AML/AAL) he/she will not be entitled to any contractual annual leave provision (unless otherwise agreed), though he/she will be entitled to accrue statutory annual leave. Statutory accrual can be set off against any contractual allowance and vice versa.

EXAMPLE Example using ML:
Employee C's leave year is agreed by the parties to run from 1 January each year. C has 24 days contractual leave. If there had been no preferential terms, she would have been entitled to the statutory minimum of 4 weeks (i.e. 20 days in this case as she works 5 days a week) for every leave year.
1. C's OML runs from 1 January 2005 to 30 June 2005. During this time she accrues enhanced contractual leave. On the basis that her holiday entitlement accrues at a rate of 2 days per complete month worked, C will accrue 12 days during her OML. (If she had only been entitled to statutory annual leave, she would have accrued 10 days).
2. C's AML runs from 1 July 2005 to 31 December 2005. There are preferential terms entitling her to contractual leave during AML and she accrues a further 12 days. If there are no preferential terms entitling her to contractual leave during AML, she will accrue 8 days of statutory annual leave during this period (i.e. 10 – 2 contractual days that are set off).

Annual leave cannot be taken during maternity, adoption or paternity leave (DTI guides). **4552**
The ECJ has confirmed that a worker is entitled to take her annual leave at a time other than during her **maternity leave** and has held that this principle should not be adjusted where the woman's maternity leave period coincides with a period of annual leave specified in a collective agreement (e.g. when there is a general shutdown of the workplace) (*Merino Gomez v Continental Industrias del Caucho SA, C-342/01* [2004] IRLR 407, ECJ). This may cause practical problems where an employee takes maternity leave that stretches over 2 leave years as untaken leave cannot be carried over to the next leave year (¶4018). Consequently, to ensure compliance with the working time rules an employee may need to take leave before she goes on OML to ensure that it is not "lost" when she returns to work in the following leave year (this may be problematic if the employee is in her first year of employment as a pro rata arrangement exists and she may not yet have accrued all the leave to which she will be entitled before she starts her OML).

E. Right to return

As long as an employee **returns immediately** after the leave period or has given the requisite notice to return earlier, he/she has exercised their right to return. Therefore, if he/she **fails to return** without good reason on the specified date it is a disciplinary matter. **4560**
ML: If the employee has a good reason (for example, illness) for not returning on the specified date, any dismissal will be a breach of contract and is also likely to constitute discrimination (*Halfpenny v IGE Medical Systems Ltd* [1999] IRLR 177, CA).

If the employer does **not allow him/her** to **return** or to return to a job to which he/she is entitled, the employee is deemed to have been **unfairly dismissed** unless the employer can justify his actions. Further, if the employer proposes a material change in the employee's job as a condition of return, this may also give rise to a claim for **constructive dismissal**. This can happen before the employee is due to return if the employer has made it plain that there is to be a material change (*Nelson v Kingston Cables Distributors Ltd*, EAT case 662/99). **4561**

Parents with young children also have the right to request flexible working (¶4690). **4562**

Redundancy situations during maternity or adoption leave

Special rules apply where, during leave, it is not practicable by reason of redundancy for the employer to continue to employ the employee under his/her existing contract of employment (ML: reg 10 SI 1999/3312; AL: reg 23 SI 2002/2788). In such circumstances, the employer must offer the employee any **suitable and appropriate vacancies** that are available. In such cir- **4564** cumstances, the employee is entitled to be offered such an alternative before the end of his/her employment under his/her existing contract and, if accepted, the new job will take effect immediately on its termination. This takes precedence over offering suitable vacancies to any other employees who have been selected for redundancy. Further, whether it is economically undesirable for the employer is also irrelevant (*Community Task Force v Rimmer* [1986] IRLR 203, EAT).

4565 The **new contract** of employment must be:
– for work that is of a kind which is suitable and appropriate for the employee. Consequently, the employer will have to take into account any added domestic responsibilities the employee may have and an increase in travelling time and additional childcare costs may mean that an alternative job is not suitable; and
– on terms that are not substantially less favourable to the employee as to his/her capacity, place of work and other terms and conditions.

Alternative employment can be with his/her employer, his successor, or an associated employer.

4566 If there is a suitable vacancy and the **employer does not offer** it to the employee, the dismissal will be automatically unfair.

1. Job entitlement

4570 Employees after ordinary leave and additional leave have the right to return to the same or in certain circumstances a similar job. A job is **defined** as meaning (s 235(1) ERA 1996):
– the nature of the work in accordance with the contract of employment;
– the capacity (for example, seniority); and
– the place of work.

4571 Employees may wish to return on **different terms**, for example part-time or a different working pattern. Although an employee has no legal right to require such a change, he/she has a right to request flexible working.

ML: It should also be noted that an employer's refusal to permit an employee to return part-time or job share may result in indirect discrimination if there was no justification for full time work (*Colman Coyle v Georgiou*, EAT case 535/00; *British Telecommunications plc v Roberts and Longstaffe* [1996] IRLR 601, EAT).

Ordinary leave and paternity leave

4573 An employee on ordinary leave is **entitled** to return to the same job in which he/she was employed before his/her absence **unless** he/she returns after a period of AML, AAL or paternity leave of more than 4 weeks in which case the situation is the same as for additional leave (see below) (OML: reg 18(2) SI 1999/3312; OAL: reg 26(1) SI 2002/2788; PAL: reg 13(1) SI 2002/2788).

4574 This must be with the seniority, pension and similar rights that he/she would have been entitled to if he/she had not been absent, and on no less favourable terms and conditions (s 71(4), (7) ERA 1996). Therefore, an employee is entitled to any pay increases or other enhanced terms that he/she would have got had he/she not been absent.

EXAMPLE Same seniority

In *Edgell v Lloyd's Register of Shipping* [1977] IRLR 463, IT, before taking maternity leave, E was employed as a bookkeeper with authority to sign cheques and reported to the manager (although these aspects were not part of her contractual job description). On her return, E was offered a post as bookkeeper on the same grade but with no authority to sign cheques and reporting to a supervisor. The changes were held to be administrative resulting from a reorganisation while she was on leave and, therefore, not contractual. As a result, she had been offered the same job with the same seniority.

Not same seniority

In *McFadden v Greater Glasgow Passenger Transport Executive* [1977] IRLR 327, IT, before taking maternity leave, M was employed as an established grade CG3 clerk. When she returned to work, M was told her position had been filled and she was placed in another department as a supernumerary i.e. an un-established grade CG3 clerk. The tribunal held that M had not been allowed to return to the same job.

Likewise, if a contractual term has been validly **changed to his/her detriment** during his/her leave, he/she will be bound by it (for example, if a collective agreement has changed his/her contract and reduced the time that can be taken during a lunch break). **4575**

If the contract allows for a **range of work** the employee can perform, for example that the employee should perform duties as required by the employer to meet his business needs, or the **job description** is in general terms only, he/she can be required to change the nature of his/her work. The employer may wish to invoke these provisions if there has been a reorganisation in the employee's absence. **4576**

Likewise, if the employee's work is only described in the contract by a **job title**, an employer will be able to offer a different range of work to perform that job title function. For example if an employee's job title is canteen manageress (with no further description), he/she will be given the same job on return even if he/she finds that due to economy cuts he/she is now only responsible for providing snacks instead of a full meal service.

Where the contract allows for **mobility**, the employer may be able to require him/her to change his/her place of work. However, the employer must take into account any domestic responsibility due to the child that may make offering a job at a different place be unreasonable. **4577**

ML: An employer must also be careful that he does not discriminate against her in requiring her to attend a different place of work.

Additional leave

An employee on additional leave has the same right to return to the **same job** on the **same rate of pay** that he/she had before leave began **except** if it is no longer reasonably practicable to do so (other than due to redundancy). In such circumstances, he/she must be given another **suitable and appropriate job** (AML: reg 18(2) SI 1999/3312; AAL: reg 26(3) SI 2002/2788). **4579**

The onus will be on the employer to show that it was not reasonably practicable to give the employee the same job back. For example, he would have difficulty showing this if he filled the employee's position in his/her absence because the **temporary replacement** was better at the job. However, if the employer considered all alternative options before making a replacement employee permanent, he may be able to support a claim that it was not reasonably practicable to give the employee his/her job back.

The same or a suitable and appropriate job must be on: **4580**
– remuneration no less favourable than what would have been applicable from the commencement of the ordinary leave i.e. the same rate of pay including any pay increases in the period of absence; and
– other terms and conditions no less favourable than those that would have been applicable at the end of ordinary leave. This is because nearly all terms are suspended during AML/AAL so the parties have to look at what the employee would have had as his/her terms and conditions at the end of the ordinary leave.

2. Notice requirements for maternity and adoption leave

Employer: end date

As a result of an employee's notice of his/her proposed or varied start date (or of a reason which results in automatic commencement of OML), his/her **employer must give him/her notice** of when his/her leave will end (i.e. ML: the end of OML or the end of AML if she is entitled to it; AL: the end of AAL) (ML: reg 7(6) SI 1999/3312; AL: reg 17(7) SI 2002/2788). **4585**

This must be **within** 28 days of notification unless the employee has notified his/her employer of a change to his/her start date in which case the employer must notify him/her of the new end date within 28 days of the varied start date.

Model letters that employers can use are provided at Annex A of the DTI guide to maternity rights and Appendix 3 of the DTI guide for adoptive parents.

4586 If the employer **fails to notify** in time, he cannot complain or reprimand his employee for coming back:
– too early (i.e. without giving at least 28 days' notice that he/she wishes to come back before the end of his/her leave (see below)); or
– too late (i.e. after the leave has ended) where the employee reasonably believed that his/her leave had not ended, or, where the employer has given less than 28 days' notice it was not reasonably practicable for the employee to return on that date.

Employee: early return

4588 An employee does not have to give notice of his/her return immediately after his/her full leave entitlement ends (i.e. ML: the end of OML or the end of AML if she is entitled to it; AL: the end of AAL). However, if he/she wishes to return earlier, he/she must **give at least** 28 days' notice to that effect (ML: reg 11 SI 1999/3312; AL: reg 25 SI 2002/2788). Failure to do so will entitle his/her employer to postpone his/her return until the notice requirement has been satisfied or he/she comes to the end of his/her leave entitlement, whichever is earlier.

Consequently, with regard to adoption leave and maternity leave (if an employee is entitled to additional maternity leave), he/she will have to give 28 days' notice if he/she does not wish to take it and plans to return immediately after ordinary leave.

4589 The notice requirement does **not apply** where the employer has failed to properly notify the employee as to when his/her leave will end (see above).

MEMO POINTS 1. Before 6 April 2003, the notice period for ML was 21 days.
2. Employers no longer have the right to request notification of when employees expect to return from maternity leave if they are entitled to AML. The employer can still ask but must make it very clear that the employee is under no obligation to respond and that she will not be discriminated against or lose her right not to suffer a detriment/be automatically unfairly dismissed if she chooses not to.

3. Effect of termination of placement during adoption leave

4595 If a child's placement is terminated during adoption leave, **special rules** in relation to when adoption leave will end apply if (reg 22 SI 2002/2822):
– the employee has started adoption leave before the placement and the adoption agency has notified the employee that the child will no longer will be placed with him/her; or
– the child dies/is returned to the adoption agency during adoption leave.

In such circumstances, unless adoption leave is due to end earlier, it will end 8 weeks after the end of the week during which:
– the employee is notified the adoption will not take place; or
– the child dies/is returned.

SECTION 2

Rights of parents with young/disabled children

Parents with young/disabled children can take unpaid parental leave (PL). Employees on maternity, adoption or paternity leave can also take PL immediately after such leave. If an employee does not qualify for parental leave, he/she may be entitled to take unpaid time off in the form of care for dependants although this is only designed for short periods to aid resolution with any problems arising from the care of the employee's dependants. 4620

Parents with young/disabled children also have the right to request flexible working.

I. Parental leave

A. Minimum standards

All employees (including apprentices) have the right to take unpaid parental leave for the **purpose of caring for the child** for whom they are responsible. The employee's rights to **take the leave last until** the child's 5th birthday, or in case of adoption until 5 years have elapsed following placement (reg 15 SI 1999/3312). 4625

To be entitled, parents must have completed 1 year's **continuous employment** with their current employer.

Employers can offer more favourable **contractual terms** than the following minimum standards, for example, longer leave, contractual paid leave, no qualifying period, or making it available to a larger group of staff.

MEMO POINTS Employees with children born or adopted between 15 December 1994 and 14 December 1999 had the right to take leave until 31 March 2005, or in the case of adoption until the child's 18th birthday if that had been sooner (reg 15 SI 1999/3312). To have been entitled, parents must have had completed 1 year's continuous employment with an employer between 15 December 1998 and 9 January 2002.

Responsibility for child

An employee has responsibility for a child if he/she has (reg 13(2) SI 1999/3312): 4632

- "parental responsibility." This covers mothers, and also fathers who are married to the mother at the time of birth. It also includes those who have acquired responsibility as a result of a court order or a formal agreement with the mother, for example, adoptive parents who take responsibility when the adoption order is made (Children Act 1989); or
- been registered as the father on the birth certificate. This covers fathers who are unmarried to the mothers at the time of birth.

MEMO POINTS The Government is planning to allow unmarried fathers who register the birth jointly with the mother, parental responsibility and when they do so unmarried fathers will not have to rely on the second limb above.

As long as parents have parental responsibility they do not have to live with the child to be entitled to take leave. On the other hand, step-parents or foster parents who have not formally obtained parental responsibility will not be entitled to take parental leave. 4633

As a **good practice example**, the DTI guide on parental leave indicates that employers who wish to improve on this right can do so by extending it to employees who have informal responsibility for looking after a child, for example step-parents, foster parents and even grandparents.

4635 **Purpose of caring for child** Leave must be taken for the purpose of caring for that child (reg 13 SI 1999/3312). The regulations are silent as to what amounts to leave for the purpose of caring for a child but it is likely to include (DTI guide on parental leave):
- spending more time with young children;
- accompanying a child during a hospital stay;
- checking out new schools;
- settling a child into new childcare arrangements; and
- enabling the family to spend more time together, for example by taking the child to see his grandparents.

If an employee takes leave without a **valid reason**, it is a disciplinary matter.

Duration

4637 An employee is **entitled** to 13 weeks' leave in respect of **each child** (reg 14 SI 1999/3312). This is extended to 18 weeks in respect of a **disabled child** (reg 14A SI 1999/3312).

This entitlement applies as a total, therefore, if an employee has had 4 weeks' leave with a previous employer, he/she will be entitled to 9 weeks' leave with his/her present employer. The DTI guide on parental leave gives as a **good practice example** that employers can disregard leave taken in a previous job.

4638 A **week's leave** is taken to be the period for which the employee is **normally required** under his/her contract of employment to work in the course of a week. For example, if an employee works 3 days a week, a week's leave would amount to 3 days' leave.

Where the period for which an employee **works varies** from week to week or over a longer period, or where he/she is normally required to work in some weeks but not in others, a week's leave will be calculated by dividing the total of the periods for which he/she is normally required to week in a year by 52 (i.e. the number of weeks in a year).

EXAMPLE Employee A is contracted to work 5 days a week on alternative weeks.
A week's leave would be 5 x 25 divided by 52 = 2.5 days

4639 Where **leave is taken** in blocks of **less than 1 week** (except where the fallback scheme applies), a week is only deducted from an employee's overall entitlement of 13 weeks when these short periods of leave add up to what would be a normal or average working week.

B. Procedure

4645 To give employers as much flexibility in the implementation of parental leave so that it can suit the needs of their business and the workforce, employers may make their own **arrangements** as to how and when parental leave can be taken. If there is **no** such **arrangement** then the fallback scheme will apply.

Arrangements must result in provisions on parental leave (including a specific entitlement to it) to be **incorporated** into the employee's contract or operate by reference to a:
- **collective agreement** i.e. union agreement; or
- **workforce agreement** i.e. non-union group agreement.

4646 Where terms on parental leave have been **incorporated individually** into the employee's contract of employment (i.e. been formed by a non-union individual agreement), the fallback scheme applies. Therefore, if the contract is **silent or less favourable** with regard to some or all of the procedural requirements, the fallback scheme applies.

Where there is a collective or workforce arrangement, the fallback scheme does not apply and therefore the terms can be **more or less favourable** though they cannot be less favourable than the minimum standards. As the fallback scheme does not apply, if the arrangement is silent about some or all of the procedural requirements, the only procedural requirement will be that of the common law requirement of reasonableness. 4647

There is no requirement to keep **records** though it is advisable to keep a track of how much leave has been taken. 4648

1. Collective and workforce agreements

Collective

A collective agreement is defined as any agreement or arrangement made by or on behalf of one or more independent trade unions and one or more employers or employers' associations and see ¶1270. 4650

Workforce

This is a non-union agreement formed with **relevant members** of the workforce (Sch 1 SI 1999/3312). These are **defined** as all the employees except those whose terms and conditions are provided for to any extent in a collective agreement. The agreement must apply to all of the relevant members or to all of the relevant members who belong to a particular group. A particular group could be a group of relevant members who undertake a particular function, work at a particular workplace or belong to a particular department or unit within their employer's business. 4652

The **agreement must be** (Sch 1 para 1 SI 1999/3312): 4653
- in writing and signed by the representatives of the workforce or of the particular group except those who are not a relevant member on the date on which the agreement is first made available for signature or if the employer has 20 or fewer employees on this date, the agreement can be signed by a majority of members; and
- in effect for a specified period of not more than 5 years.

Representatives are employees elected to represent the relevant members of the workforce or particular group. Elections must follow the following rules (Sch 1 para 3 SI 1999/3312):
- the employer determines the number of representatives;
- the candidates are relevant members of the workforce or particular group and no eligible member can be unreasonably excluded;
- all relevant members of the workforce or particular group are entitled to vote and may vote for as many candidates as there are representatives to be elected;
- the election is, so far as is reasonably practicable, in secret; and
- the votes are fairly and accurately counted.

Before the agreement is available for signature, the employer must **provide** all relevant members with copies of the text of the agreement and such guidance as will enable the agreement to be reasonably understood by them. 4654

2. Fallback scheme

Evidence of entitlement

Employees must comply with any **request by their employer** to produce for inspection evidence of their entitlement (Sch 2 paras 1-2 SI 1999/3312). Such evidence amounts to that which may reasonably be required to show: 4660
- the employee's responsibility or expected responsibility for the child for whom the employee proposes to take leave;

– the child's date of birth or the date of adoption placement; and/or
– the child's entitlement to a disability living allowance, if relevant.

Notice

4662 Employees must give notice (orally or in writing) of their intention to take leave **at least** 21 days before the leave is due to begin (Sch 2 SI 1999/3312).

The notice must **specify** the date on which the period of leave is to begin and end.

4663 Where the employee is an expectant father/adoptive parent and the **leave is to begin on the date of birth/placement**, notice must be given at least 21 days before the beginning of the EWC/beginning of the week of the expected placement and must specify the EWC/expected placement and duration of leave. If it is not reasonably practicable to give 21 days' notice then notice must be given as soon as it is reasonably practicable, this may particularly be the case with regard to adoptive parents as placements can often be given on short notice.

Periods of leave

4665 An employee must take parental leave **in blocks of** 1 or more weeks unless the child is entitled to a disability allowance. Therefore, the period of leave will be rounded up to the nearest complete week in calculating how much of the employee's entitlement has been used. However, this has recently been rejected by the Court of Appeal which held that under the fallback scheme, parental leave must be taken in complete blocks of 1 or more weeks and an employee is not entitled to take less than this (*New Southern Railway Ltd (formerly South Central Trains Ltd) v Rodway* [2005] ICR 1162, CA).

MEMO POINTS This only concerns the fallback scheme and does not apply if preferential contractual terms allow for leave to be taken in shorter periods. Further, where the need to provide child care arises unexpectedly, an employee will be able to take time off to deal with this situation under the right to time off to care for dependants.

4666 An employee may **not take more than** 4 weeks of leave in respect of each child during a particular year. A year is calculated as starting on the date on which the employee **first becomes** entitled to leave with regard to each child or where his/her entitlement has been interrupted at the end of a period of continuous employment (for example, when he/she has changed jobs and is working for another employer), on the date on which the employee **most recently became** entitled to take parental leave. Subsequent years will start on the 12 month anniversary of that date.

This deters an employee from using parental leave to work part-time after, say maternity leave. If the employee works for 3 out of her five-day week and takes off 2 days a week as parental leave, she can only do this for 4 weeks in any year, and the time off will reduce her remaining entitlement in respect to that child to 9 weeks.

4668 **Postponement** An employer may postpone a period of parental leave **unless** it relates to an employee taking leave from the date of birth or date of placement (Sch 2 para 6 SI 1999/3312).

The employer can postpone leave for **up to 6 months** if he considers that the operation of his business would be unduly disrupted if the leave is taken. This may be the case if, for example, the work is at a seasonal peak, a significant proportion of the workforce will be on parental leave at the same time or the employee's role is such that his/her absence at that particular time would unduly harm the business.

If, because of postponement, the period of leave falls **after the child's 5th birthday**, then the employee is allowed to take it after this date.

4669 The employer must give the employee **notice** in writing of the postponement, the reasons for it, and the new dates, not more than 7 days after the employee's notice was given to him.

C. Terms and conditions

The employee's terms and conditions during parental leave are the same as those on additional leave (¶4548). 4675

D. Right to return

An employee is entitled to return as follows, where parental leave is: 4680
– less than 4 weeks (other than after additional maternity leave/additional adoption leave): same job entitlement as for ordinary leave and paternity leave (¶4573); and
– more than 4 weeks and any leave after additional maternity leave/additional adoption leave: same job entitlement as for additional leave (¶4579).

II. Right to request flexible working

Employees with children under 6 years (or under 18 if disabled), subject to certain qualifying conditions, have the right to request a flexible working pattern which will have to be given serious consideration by their employer (ss 80F-I ERA 1996; Flexible Working (Eligibility, Complaints and Remedies) Regulations SI 2002/3236). 4690

However, this does not give employees the right to work flexibly in itself and if the employer refuses an application, the tribunals cannot force the employer to accept flexible working practices. Rather the right focuses on providing a **set vehicle** which employees can use to facilitate the discussion and hopefully mutual agreement of flexible working practices (Flexible Working (Procedural Requirements) Regulations SI 2002/3207). Consequently, the **initial onus** is on the employee to present a carefully thought-out application well in advance of when he/she would like the change in working pattern to take effect. As a result of this application, the employer must follow a set procedure the aim of which is to help **facilitate discussion** and enable each party to gain a clear understanding of each other's thinking with the employer only refusing a request where there is a clear business reason for doing so.

The following **changes can be requested** (s 80F(1)(a) ERA 1996): 4691
– a change to the hours the employee is required to work;
– a change to the times the employee is required to work; and/or
– working from home.

See ¶1810 for a range of flexible working arrangements.

If the request is accepted this will result in a **permanent change** to the employee's contract (unless otherwise agreed, for example a trial period may be initially appropriate to assess viability or to last for a set period). Consequently, any changes do not have to be limited to the child's 6th birthday (18th if disabled) and will depend upon what is agreed between the parties. It should be noted that where any changes are permanent there is no right to revert back the former working pattern and any subsequent reversion or change must be agreed. 4692

Qualification

The right only applies to employees with children under 6 years (or disabled children under 18) who (s 80F ERA 1996; reg 3 SI 2002/3236): 4694
a. have been **continuously employed** for at least 26 weeks;

b. are either the mother, father, adoptive parent, foster parent or guardian, **or**, their spouse, civil partner or partner (including partners of the same sex);
c. have/are expected to have **responsibility for the child's upbringing**; and
d. make the request to enable them to **care for the child**. This can cover a range of circumstances, for example to enable the employee to spend more time with his/her children or to enable him/her to drop his/her children off at school.

MEMO POINTS 1. A **partner** is a person (whether of a different sex or the same sex) who lives with child and the mother, father, adoptive parent, foster parent or guardian in an enduring family relationship but is not a relative of the mother, father, adoptive parent, foster parent or guardian. A relative in this context is a mother's, father's, adoptive parent's, foster parent's or guardian's parent, grandparent, sister, brother, aunt or uncle. The regulations have also been amended to include **civil partners** (SI 2005/2114 which gives same-sex couples the right to form a civil partnership and gain legal recognition).

1. Making a request

4700 The request must be made by **formal application** and to be able to make a valid request the **date of the application** (s 80F(3)-(4) ERA 1996):
– must be at least 2 weeks before the child's 6th birthday (or 18th if disabled); and
– at least 12 months after the date of any previous application.

4702 **Form and content of application** The application must be **dated and in writing** and can be by letter, on a form provided by the employer or by email (reg 4 SI 2002/3236). The DTI has also produced a **Form FW(A)**: Flexible Working Application Form which can be used.

4703 The application **must state** (s 80F ERA 1996; reg 4 SI 2002/3236):
– that the application is being made under the statutory right to request flexible working;
– that he/she is responsible for the upbringing for the child and that he/she is the mother/father etc (see qualification, above). Such self-certification will suffice;
– the flexible working pattern applied for and the date which he/she would like it to start. This date should allow time for the application to be considered and implemented. There is no set time, but the DTI guide on flexible working suggests that employees should expect it to take around 14 weeks or longer if a problem arises;
– what effect, if any, the employee thinks the proposed change would have on the employer and explain how, in his/her opinion, it can be dealt with. Employees are not expected to know every factor that might influence their employer's decision but they should show that they have considered the factors that they are aware of; and
– whether a previous application has been made to that employer and, if so, when.

EXAMPLE Examples of possible requests:
A claims processor requests on his application to **compress his hours** from 9 am – 5 pm Monday to Friday to 8 am – 6 pm Monday to Thursday. He states that he will still be working the same number of hours a week and will be able to continue to manage his existing caseload. He also states that most claims are received earlier in the week and that Friday is normally the quietest day.
A tyre fitter requests on his application that he would like to **start work an hour later** each day. He accepts that this would mean a reduction in his pay and states that he has asked the other fitters working in the branch whether they would be able to manage, and they have no problems with this. Mornings are usually less busy than afternoons, and they believe they would be able to handle any eventualities that may occur.
An shop assistant requests on her application to **change her hours** from 8 am – 1 pm to 10 am – 3 pm. She states that early mornings tend to be the quietest time and that the other two assistants agree that they will cover this period. She also states that as the lunch period is the busiest time, her new working pattern would result in an increase in the number of customers that could be served.
A manager requests on his application that he would like to **work from home** one day a week in order, by avoid commuting, to care for his young child in the early evening. He states that he has asked other colleagues for their opinions and they have no objection. He also states that as he has a computer with broadband Internet access at home, he can readily stay in contact with the office.

The DTI guide on flexible working recommends that as best practice employers should acknowledge the application. An **acknowledge slip** is included in **Form FW(A)**. 4704

Alternatively, if the employee has **failed to provide all of the required information**, the employer should inform the employee of what they have omitted and ask him/her to re-submit the application. The employer is under no legal obligation to consider the application if it is incomplete.

2. Procedure for considering request

Meeting to hear request The employer must **arrange a meeting** with the employee to discuss the request and how it can be best accommodated **within** 28 days of receipt of the application, unless the employer has already agreed to it in writing setting out the contract variation agreed to and the date it will take effect (reg 3 SI 2002/3207). 4710

Where the **manager** who would ordinarily consider the application is **absent** due to annual leave or sickness, this **period only starts** to run from the earlier of the manager's return or 28 days after the receipt of the application (reg 13 SI 2002/3207).

Notification of decision **Within** 14 days of the meeting, the employer informs his employee in a **written dated form** that he either (regs 4-5 SI 2002/3207): 4712

- **agrees** the request, specifying the variation of contract terms agreed to and the date on which they are to take effect; or
- **rejects** the request, providing **clear business grounds** why the application cannot be accepted including sufficient explanation as to why these reasons apply as well as setting out an appeal procedure.

DTI **Forms: FW(B)** "Application acceptance form" and **FW(C)** "Application rejection form" can be used as appropriate.

The business grounds must relate to one or more of the following grounds (s 80G ERA 1996): 4713

- burden of additional costs;
- detrimental effect on ability to meet customer demand;
- inability to re-organise work among existing staff;
- inability to recruit additional staff;
- detrimental impact on quality;
- detrimental impact on performance;
- insufficiency of work during the periods the employee proposes to work; and
- planned structural changes.

The DTI guide on flexible working suggests that an explanation of around two paragraphs will usually be sufficient, although the actual length will depend on the particular circumstances. In particular, it should:

- say why the business ground is relevant and why it cannot be accepted;
- avoid unfamiliar jargon;
- include all relevant and accurate facts; and
- not be overly complex or unnecessarily long.

For example, an appropriate explanation (given as an example by the DTI guide on flexible working) for rejecting a request not to work on a Thursday in a small manufacturing factory might be:

"I am sorry that I cannot grant your request to change the days that you work, but to allow you to not work on a Thursday would have a detrimental effect on the performance of the business.

Thursday is our busiest day of the week, when all staff are required to ensure that the machinists can continue making curtains while stock is received, and finished curtains are packaged ready to be despatched the following morning. You are aware that on a Thursday morning we receive our weekly delivery of fabric. This requires the involvement of all staff to help move the material from the delivery bay into the storeroom, before the newly made curtains can be prepared for despatch the following morning.

As I indicated when we met to discuss the application, if you decide to change the day you would prefer not to work to one earlier in the week, then I would be happy to reconsider your application."

4715 **Appealing a refusal** The employee can appeal against any refusal by giving **written dated notice** within 14 days of the notification of the decision (reg 6 SI 2002/3207). This must set out the grounds of appeal, for example that the employee challenges a fact given by the employer to explain why a business reason applies, that a new fact has come to light (like another employee now being prepared to cover time the employee does not want to work) or propose an adapted working pattern that accommodates the business grounds as set out in the refusal.

4716 The employer should arrange a **meeting to discuss the appeal within** 14 days of receiving the employee's written notification. The employee has the same right to be accompanied as for the meeting to discuss the application.

Within 14 days of this meeting, the employer must inform his employee in a **written dated form** that he either:

– **upholds** the appeal, specifying the variation of contract terms agreed to and the date on which they are to take effect; or

– **dismisses** the appeal, stating the grounds for the dismissal including sufficient explanation as to why these grounds apply.

DTI **Form FW(E)** "Appeal Reply Form" can be used.

Extension of procedural time limits

4718 Any of the following time limits can be extended **by agreement** (reg 12 SI 2002/3207):

a. with regard to employers:

– time to arrange meeting or appeal; and

– time to give decision after meeting or appeal; and

b. with regard to employees: time to choose whether to appeal.

In all circumstances, the employer must send a **dated written record** of the agreed extension to the employee stating the period the extension relates to and the date on which the extension ends.

The **DTI Form (FW)F**: "Extension of Time Limit" can be used.

3. Right to be accompanied to meeting

4720 The employee has the **right to be accompanied** to either the meeting to discuss the request or appeal by a colleague or trade union representative as long as he also works for the employer (reg 14 SI 2002/3207). The employee can ask if a companion from outside the employer's organisation can attend, for example a trade union representative who is not employed by the employer, though the employer is under no obligation to accept any such request. The **role of the companion** is to support the employee and to this end he can address the meeting on behalf of the employee and confer with the employee during it, but cannot answer questions on behalf of the employee.

MEMO POINTS There is no general right for the companion to be a trade union representative as with the right to be accompanied to discipline or grievance hearings (¶6782).

4721 The employee should contact his/her companion as soon as he/she is given the date of the meeting. If the companion is unable to make this, the employer must accept an alternative time as proposed by the employee that is convenient time for all parties and which takes place within 7 days of the date of the original meeting. If this cannot be achieved, the employee should consider an alternative companion who can attend the meeting.

4722 Companions are entitled to **paid time off** to act as a companion (reg 14(6) SI 2002/3207).

4. Withdrawal of request

The **employee can withdraw** his/her application at any time by notifying his/her employer orally or in writing, though if he/she does so he/she cannot make a new application under this right within 12 months of the date on which the application was made (reg 17 SI 2002/3207). 4725

The **employer can also deem** that the application has been withdrawn if:

a. the employee **misses two meetings** to discuss the request/the appeal without reasonable cause; or

b. the employee unreasonably **refuses to provide** the employer with **information necessary** for the employer to be able to consider the application. For example, an office worker may request to work 3 days a week at home but refuses to comply with any checks to ensure that their working space at home satisfies health and safety standards.

The employer must confirm the withdrawal of the application in writing (unless already so provided by the employee). 4726

The DTI's **Form FW(G)**: "Notice of Withdrawal" can be used.

SECTION 3

Time off to care for dependants

This right was created to help employees to take time off to **deal with unforeseen events** with regard to their dependants. As a result, an employee can take **unpaid time off** to take whatever action is necessary (s 57A(1) ERA 1996): 4740

a. to provide assistance when a dependant falls ill (including mentally ill), gives birth or is injured or assaulted;

b. to make arrangements for the care of a dependant who is ill or injured;

c. when a dependant dies;

d. because of the unexpected disruption or termination of arrangements for the care of a dependant; or

e. to deal with an incident involving the employee's child that occurs unexpectedly during school.

A dependant is defined as a spouse, child, parent or person living in the same household as the employee other than those who are employed by the employee and tenants, lodgers or boarders (s 57A(3)-(5) ERA 1996). With regard to the responsibilities of the employee under **a.**, **b.** and **d.**, a dependant can be any person who reasonably relies on the employee for assistance or to make arrangements when such events occur. This is the widest of all the family-friendly rights in that it relates to all dependants as detailed above and not just employees' children.

The employer must allow the employee a reasonable amount of time off so that he/she can take whatever actions are necessary. What is **necessary** will depend on the particular circumstances of each case, and factors include the nature of the incident that has occurred, the relationship between the employee and the dependant and the extent to which anyone else can provide assistance. For example, where a dependant has died, this includes taking time off to make funeral arrangements, attend the funeral, register the death, apply for probate etc. However, it does not include time off to deal with the emotional effects of bereavement (*Forster v Cartwright Black Solicitors*, EAT case 0179/04). What is **reasonable** will depend again on the circumstances of the employee and any disruption, inconvenience and cost to the employer must be ignored (*Qua v John Ford Morrison Solicitors* [2003] ICR 482, EAT). 4741

EXAMPLE Examples of what may be necessary:
Employee A taking time off when one of his parents dies to take action that is necessary as a consequence of the death.
Employee B attending a problem arising at her child's school.
Employee C assisting and making arrangements for an elderly neighbour, who relies on C, after he falls and injures himself.

Employee D sorting out alternative care arrangements for his friend, who requires care and relies on D, after his friend's carer does not turn up.

4742 The employee must **inform his/her employer** of the reason for his/her absence as soon as reasonably practicable (s 57A(2) ERA 1996). Unless this cannot be complied with until the employee has returned to work, he/she must also tell his/her employer how long he/she expects to be absent. If the employee does not properly notify his/her employer, he/she loses his/her right to take time off under this right (*Qua v John Ford Morrison Solicitors* [2003] IRLR 184, EAT) and any unauthorised absences will be a disciplinary matter.

However, given that the right to take time off to care for dependants concerns taking time off to deal with **unexpected, urgent and often difficult situations**, all that needs to be communicated is sufficient information for the employer to understand that something has occurred to cause a care arrangement to break down making it necessary for the employee to be urgently absent from work (*Truelove v Safeway Stores plc* [2005] ICR 589, EAT). Employers should not require a formal procedure to be used nor should they expect employees to make their application with any formality.

4743 If there is a **significant change in the circumstances** which results in the employee needing to extend the leave to more than what would be reasonable and necessary under the original circumstances, then he/she should re-notify his/her employer as soon as is reasonably practicable (*MacCulloch and Wallis Ltd v Moore*, EAT case 51/02).

SECTION 4

Remedies

4760 Employees have a right not to suffer a detriment, be unfairly dismissed or be discriminated against as a consequence of exercising their rights to time off, leave and statutory pay. They also have additional specific remedies that will apply to each of these rights.

4761 It is recommended that an employee who believes that he/she is entitled to make a complaint to a tribunal should **first seek to resolve** it by mutual agreement with the employer, for example through a grievance or internal appeals procedure where one exists. Any compensation awarded by a tribunal may be reduced if the employee has not tried to resolve the matter in this way.

Further, **external dispute resolution** by third party mediation or conciliation, for example by using the services of an ACAS conciliation officer, may be more desirable than pursuing an application through the tribunals. In particular, there is a **dispute resolution scheme** for employees to use with regard to complaints regarding the right to request flexible working (ACAS (Flexible Working) Arbitration Scheme (England and Wales) Order SI 2003/694).

A. General

4765 As well as the following rights, it should be noted that an employee may, in certain circumstances, also have a claim for **sex discrimination or equal pay** (¶¶4544, 4560, 4577, 5261, 5320 and 5600). This now applies directly with regard to a women suffering a detriment or being dismissed due to exercising her rights to time off to take antenatal care, maternity leave and pay (¶5320), and possibly indirectly in relation to time off to care for dependants and adoption leave.

Pregnant employees and those on maternity leave also have special protection, and any dismissals or detrimental treatment during this period due to a pregnancy/post-birth-related illness will amount to direct discrimination.

Not to suffer a detriment

An employee has the right not to be subjected to any detriment (other than dismissal) by an act or deliberate failure to act because of (ss 47C, 47D ERA 1996; reg 19 SI 1999/3312; reg 28 SI 2002/2788; reg 16 SI 2002/3207): 4767
- a reason connected with pregnancy or childbirth;
- taking maternity/adoption/paternity/parental leave;
- time off to care for dependants;
- exercising his/her right to request flexible working; or
- being a companion for a colleague at his/her meeting to request flexible working.

Complaints must be made **within** 3 months beginning with the date of the act or failure to act (or if it is part of a series of similar acts or failures, the last of them) (s 48 ERA 1996). However, a tribunal can **extend** this period if it is satisfied that it was not reasonably practicable for the employee to make the complaint in time. 4768

If the claim is successful, the **tribunal can** (s 49 ERA 1996): 4769
- make a declaration; and/or
- order the employer to pay compensation.

Compensation will be the amount the tribunal considers just and equitable in all the circumstances having regard to the infringement and any loss which is attributable to the act, or failure to act. It will include any expenses reasonably incurred as a consequence and any loss of benefit(s) which the employee might reasonably be expected to have had but for the act or failure to act. If the tribunal finds that the employee caused or contributed to the action, it will reduce the amount of compensation by such proportion as it considers just and equitable in the circumstances.

Automatic unfair dismissal

An employee has the right not to be automatically unfairly dismissed (¶8390) on the **same reason(s)/ground(s)** as above (ss 99, 104C ERA 1996; reg 20 SI 1999/3312; reg 29 SI 2002/2788). Further, an employee will be held to be automatically unfairly dismissed where the dismissal is on the **grounds of**: 4771
- a health and safety provision that could require a maternity suspension; or
- redundancy during maternity or adoption leave if the employer fails to offer any available suitable alternative employment.

For a dismissal to be automatically unfair because of a reason connected with the pregnancy of the employee, the employer must have **knowledge of the pregnancy** or must have believed the employee to be pregnant. It is not enough that the employer should have deduced from the employee's symptoms that she was pregnant (*Ramdoolar v Bycity Ltd* [2005] ICR 368, EAT). However, the EAT in this case did comment that it may be possible for a dismissal to be automatically unfair where the employer dismissed the employee because he had a suspicion that she might be pregnant.

There is a **small employer exception** in cases of employees returning after AML or AAL where the number of employees (employed by the employer or any associated employer) is five or fewer immediately before the end of the leave (or immediately before the dismissal if before). In such cases, the employee must bring an claim for unfair dismissal under the general scheme and show that the dismissal was unfair and/or the correct procedure was not followed, see ¶8410. 4772

B. Specific

4780 **Time off for antenatal/to care for dependants** Employees have the right to complain to an employment tribunal if the employer has failed to allow the employee time off (ss 57, 57A ERA 1996):
– to attend antenatal classes or pay her for such time; or
– to care for dependants.

4782 **Parental leave** Employees have the right to complain to an employment tribunal that his/her employer (s 80(1) ERA 1996):
– unreasonably postponed a period of requested leave; or
– prevented/attempted to prevent him/her from taking leave.

4784 **Right to request flexible working** Employees have the right to complain to an employment tribunal if their employer has not followed the correct procedure or has rejected the application on a ground that is not a valid business reason or is based on incorrect facts (s 80H ERA 1996). The employee must first exhaust all internal procedures before making a claim.

Employees also have the right to complain to an employment tribunal if their employer has refused them the right to be accompanied at the flexible working meeting (reg 15 SI 2002/3207).

Procedure

4786 Complaints must be made **within** 3 months beginning with the date of the act or failure to act or if it is part of a series of similar acts or failures, the last of them. With regard to flexible working claims, this must be within 3 months of either the date when the employee was notified of the final internal appeal decision or the date on which the alleged breach of duty was committed. However, a tribunal may **extend** this period if it is satisfied that it was not reasonably practicable for the employee to make the complaint in time (¶9465).

Remedies

4788 **Time off for antenatal care:** If the claim is well-founded, the tribunal must make a **declaration** to that effect.

With regard to unreasonable refusal to allow time off for antenatal care, the tribunal will order the employer to **pay** the employee what she should have received for the period requested (s 57(4) ERA 1996). Likewise, if the employer allowed the time off but refused to pay either the whole or part of it, the tribunal will order the employer to pay the amount outstanding (s 57(5) ERA 1996).

Time off to care for dependants: The tribunal may also order the employer to pay **compensation** (s 57B(3)-(4) ERA 1996). The amount of compensation will be such as the tribunal considers just and equitable in all the circumstances having regard to the employer's behaviour and any loss sustained by the employee, which is attributable to the matters complained of.

Parental leave: The tribunal may also order the employer to pay **compensation** (s 80(3)-(4) ERA 1996). The amount of compensation will be such as the tribunal considers just and equitable in all the circumstances having regard to the employer's behaviour and any loss sustained by the employee, which is attributable to the matters complained of.

Flexible working (right to request): The tribunal can make an order for the **reconsideration** of the application (s 80I ERA 1996). The tribunal may also order the employer to pay **compensation** (s 80I ERA 1996). The amount of compensation will be such as the tribunal considers just and equitable in all the circumstances though this is **limited** to 8 weeks' pay (which is subject to the statutory cap) (¶2923) (reg 7 SI 2002/3236). It should be noted that the tribunal has no power to order the employer to comply with the request for flexible working.

(right to be accompanied): The tribunal can make an order for **compensation** for **up to** 2 weeks' pay (which is subject to the statutory cap) (¶2920) (reg 15 SI 2002/3207).

CHAPTER 15

Health and safety

OUTLINE ¶¶

Employers have a **general statutory duty** to ensure the health and safety of their workers whilst at work (Health and Safety at Work etc Act 1974 (HSWA 1974) as amended; Management of Health and Safety at Work Regulations SI 1999/3242 as amended). In addition, there are many **specific acts and regulations** which cover working conditions and safety at work. For the rules relating to working time, see Chapter 11. 4800

Breaches of these duties can, depending on the circumstances, lead to criminal proceedings and fines. Further, individual directors and managers can be personally prosecuted and fined, or, in extreme cases, imprisoned as a result of offences committed by their company or organisation. A worker may also bring a civil claim for damages where he has suffered injury as a result of a breach.

MEMO POINTS 1. SI 1999/3242 is based on the EEC General Health and Safety Directive 1989/39. There are also numerous other EU directives on specific health and safety topics, for example protective equipment, and these have been generally implemented by corresponding regulations.
The European Commission has the responsibility of taking enforcement proceedings against any Member State, in the European Court of Justice, in respect of any failures to implement directives. There are also two bodies established by Council Directives: the **Advisory Committee** on Safety Hygiene and Health Protection at Work which the EC consults on draft directives, and the **European Agency** for Safety and Health at Work which has functional links with the Committee and EU. The Agency's objectives include encouraging improvements in the working environment and providing technical, scientific and economic information on health and safety at work to EU bodies and Member States.
2. Practical guidance on the regulations is given by **Approved Codes of Practice** (referred to as HS Codes) issued by the Health and Safety Commission. Where an employer fails to comply with a code, this does not in itself give rise to a liability in criminal or civil law. However, failure to comply may be accepted by the courts as evidence of a breach of the relevant legislation unless the employer can prove that the requirement was met in some equally, or more, effective way.

4801 Employers also have a common law **tortious duty** to take reasonable care of the health and safety of employees. Claims under this head are frequently used by employees bringing personal injury claims against their employers and in the last few years there have been a growing number of cases of psychiatric injury caused by stress at work.

Employers also have an **implied contractual duty** to take reasonable care of their employees' health and safety and also an implied contractual duty of trust and confidence.

Breach of either of these duties will entitle the employee to bring a claim for damages. It should be noted that the courts and tribunals often do not distinguish between claims for damages brought under tort or contract and, in practice, the result will be the same.

MEMO POINTS An **employer's liability** towards his employee, when arising in connection with the employment contract, will be **capable of transfer** under TUPE. Consequently, the employee will be able to sue his current employer for a breach of the employer's duty of care that occurred under his original employment (¶7980).

4803 Finally, there may also be the possibility of **other claims for damages**:
- constructive dismissal;
- unfair dismissal and the right not to suffer a detriment; and
- disability discrimination.

There are also a number of **other related claims**, namely, claims relating to time off for safety representatives/representatives of employee safety, pay on medical suspension, maternity-related rights and whistleblowing.

4805 **Workers** also have a statutory duty to take reasonable care. They may also be bound under express contractual terms relating to health and safety. **Employees** also have a tortious and implied contractual duty to take reasonable care. Disciplinary action may be taken against those who are in breach of these duties and in certain circumstances may justify dismissal (see ¶6540). Further, such behaviour may also reduce the amount of damages that they might be able to obtain as a result of a successful court or tribunal claim.

Insurance requirement

4807 **Employers** carrying on a business in the UK are obliged to maintain **insurance against liability** for bodily injury or disease sustained by employees in the course of their employment in the UK (Employers' Liability (Compulsory Insurance) Regulations SI 1998/2573).

MEMO POINTS However, where employees are **working abroad**, the failure by the employer to provide **personal accident insurance** will not be a breach of his common law or implied duties (*Reid v Rush & Tomkins Group plc* [1989] IRLR 265, CA).

SECTION 1

Scope of protection

The health and safety obligations of the employer are to be found under the law of tort, contract and statute. 4810

A. Tortious duty

Employers have a common law duty under tort to take **reasonable care** of their employees' safety. What is considered reasonable will depend on the circumstances and what steps the employer took or should have taken to prevent the harm from arising. This is not, therefore, an absolute duty. For example, working in a war zone involves risks that cannot be guarded against even by the exercise of reasonable skill and care for the safety of the employee (*Tarrant v Stuart Ramage* [1995] IRLR 35, QBD). Consequently, where the terms of the employment contract require an employee to perform a task where there is an obvious health risk, the scope of the employer's duty will be narrower than if that term did not exist (*Johnstone v Bloomsbury Health Authority* [1991] IRLR 118, CA). 4815

However, where an employee runs the risk of physical danger to himself (other than when this is a necessary, reasonable and acceptable part of his job) if he continues in employment, the employer is under a duty to dismiss him (*Coxall v Goodyear Great Britain Ltd* [2003] 1 WLR 536, CA).

The courts have recognised that an employer **will have shown reasonable care** by providing his employees with a safe place of work, safe tools and equipment and a safe system of working (*Wilsons and Clyde Coal Co Ltd v English* [1938] AC 57, HL). 4817

Generally, an employer will only breach his duty of care if he fails to take **reasonable steps** to prevent the harm, bearing in mind the magnitude of the risk, the gravity of any harm, the costs and practicability of preventing it and any justifications for running the risk.

The employer's duty is owed to **each individual employee** (*Paris v Stepney Borough Council* [1951] AC 367, HL). With regard to this, an employer will not be expected to put extra precautions in place to protect an employee with an **unusual susceptibility** unless the employer is aware or ought to have been aware of that employee's vulnerability (*Barber v Somerset County Council* [2004] IRLR 475, HL; *Paris v Stepney Borough Council*, above). Similarly an employer is entitled to take into account an employee's **particular skill or experience**. 4818

EXAMPLE In *Pickford v ICI plc* [1998] IRLR 435, HL, the House of Lords found that the employer did not have a legal duty specifically to warn a qualified and experienced senior secretary (who had responsibility to organise and plan her own work) that she should intersperse other work with her typing to avoid risk of Repetitive Strain Injury (RSI). RSI was not reasonably foreseeable in her case. The Court contrasted P's position with that of typists in the accounts department, to whom the employer was obliged to give instructions, warning and advice about the need to take breaks.

The employer's practice must be objectively measured against the **standard of the reasonable employer**, and if damage is not **reasonably foreseeable**, the employer will not be liable. For example, the possibility that there will be an explosion when using welding equipment in tanks containing combustible material would be reasonably foreseeable. 4819

Where the damage is **not foreseeable**, for example if the employee's job involves the use of a chemical which is not known to have long term effects, the employer will not be liable for the employee's ill health which occurs as a result of the exposure, if the chemical was used correctly in the light of the then current knowledge.

4820 The **damage suffered** by the employee, which can be physical injury or financial loss, must be shown to have been **caused by** the employer's negligence and the onus is on the employee to show that the injury was caused by his employer's breach of duty.

EXAMPLE In *Volex Group plc v Jane Wilson Evans* [2002] EWCA Civ 225, CA, E's claim failed because she had not proved that her illness was caused by the fumes from her employer's machinery.

4821 However, where the employee has **worked for two employers** and the damage suffered might have been caused by either employment, both employers may be liable (*Fairchild v Glenhaven Funeral Services Ltd* [2002] IRLR 533, HL). In *Fairchild v Glenhaven Funeral Services Ltd*, the House of Lords held that where an employee had been negligently exposed to asbestos during the course of employment with more than one employer and his asbestos-induced illness could only have been caused by the employment, it was sufficient to prove that each of the employers had materially increased the risk of injury. Consequently, the employee was entitled to recover from both the employers, even though it was not clear which particular employment had been the actual cause of the illness.

With regard to **whether** liability for the injury **should be apportioned** between the **different employers** to reflect the amount of exposure suffered during each period of employment, the Court of Appeal has held that in applying the principle in *Fairchild v Glenhaven Funeral Services Ltd* any employer who had contributed to the injury should be liable for the whole loss. Consequently, there should be no apportionment between employers, although this could be subject to a reduction in damages based on the contributory negligence of the employee (*Barker v Saint Gobain Pipelines plc* [2004] EWCA Civ 545, CA). Further, with regard to the question of whether the employee's injury might have resulted from exposure during a period of self-employment meant that he was no longer an "innocent victim", the Court of Appeal felt that the employee's widow should not be deprived of redress for the injury caused by the employee's employment simply because his exposure to the harmful substance during a **period of self-employment** might have contributed to his injury. The Court of Appeal acknowledged that this was based on the policy decision of seeking the fairest solution on the whole.

4822 Employers who **occupy premises** must also take such care as is reasonable in all the circumstances to ensure the premises are safe. This duty is owed not only to employees but also to **visitors** and in some cases, trespassers.

B. Contractual duties

4840 There is an implied contractual term that the **employer** has a duty to take reasonable care which mirrors the duty under tort (*Marshall Specialist Vehicles Limited v Osborne* [2003] IRLR 672, EAT).

The employer's duty of care is also covered by the implied term of **trust and confidence**. This obligation is confined to matters arising during the subsistence of the employment relationship, and does not apply in relation to the manner of a dismissal (¶1241).

4842 **Damages** are assessed on the basis of whether the injury was within the reasonable contemplation of the parties at the time the contract was made (the test of "remoteness").

4843 Where the **breach of duty is fundamental**, an employee is entitled to resign and claim constructive dismissal (¶8230). The requirements for establishing liability also mirror the duty under tort (*Marshall Specialist Vehicles Limited v Osborne*, above).

4844 **Employees** will also have an **implied contractual duty** to follow employer instructions and take reasonable care as well as express terms relating to health and safety.

C. Vicarious liability

An employer may be vicariously liable for his employee's acts or omissions and he may be held responsible if his **employee injures someone** in the course of employment, even when the employer did not specifically authorise the act that caused the injury. 4850

Whether the action is taken in the **course of employment** will be determined by looking at the job being done in general terms and not whether the employer authorised each step of the task carried out by the employee (*Fennelly v Connex South Eastern Ltd* [2001] IRLR 390, CA). The correct **approach** is to concentrate on the relative closeness of the connection between the nature of the employment and the employee's wrongdoing and not whether the acts could be viewed as authorised (or a wrongful and unauthorised mode of doing an authorised act) (*Lister v Helsey Hall Ltd* [2001] IRLR 472, HL; *Dubai Aluminium Co Ltd v Salaam* [2003] WLR 1913, HL followed in *Mattis v Pollock (t/a Flamingo's Nightclub)* [2003] EWCA Civ 887). This should be taken broadly: what is important is whether the employee's wrongdoings can be closely connected with the employment so that when "looking at the matter in the round" it is just and reasonable to hold the employer vicariously liable (*Bernard v Attorney-General of Jamaica* [2005] IRLR 398, PC).

An employer may also be in breach of his duty if he fails to protect an employee against **harassment, bullying or victimisation by fellow employees**, particularly when he knows that acts carried out by his employees during their employment may cause physical or mental harm to a fellow employee and does nothing to prevent it when it is in his power to do so (*Waters v Commissioner of Police of the Metropolis* [2000] IRLR 720, HL). 4851

An employer may also be vicariously liable for the **acts of its contractor's employees** where the employer has control over the way in which they work (*Hawley v Luminar Leisure plc and others* [2005] EWHC 5, QB). In such circumstances, the contractor's employees will be "temporary deemed employees" for the purposes of vicarious liability. In this case, the employer who was the owner of a nightclub was held to be vicariously liable for an assault carried out by a doorman employed by a security company but over whom the employer had control. 4852

MEMO POINTS 1. As a **practical measure**, if employers want to limit their exposure to such liability, they must ensure that any contractors they hire retain the responsibility for controlling and supervising their employees. Where control and supervision cannot be left to the contractor, employers should ensure that the contractor's employees are properly trained and supervised at all times.
2. **Dual vicarious liability** is possible (i.e. more than one "employer" is liable) if, on the facts of a particular case, the core question is who was entitled, and in theory obliged, to control the employee's relevant negligent act so as to prevent it, the sensible answer would be each of two "employers" (*Viasystems (Tyneside) Ltd v Thermal Transfer (Northern) Ltd and others* [2005] EWCA Civ 1151).

Finally, the Court of Appeal has recently held that employers can be vicariously liable for a **breach of a statutory duty imposed only on its employees**; in this case under the Protection from Harassment Act 1997 (legislation originally introduced to give protection from stalkers) (*Majrowski v Guy's and St Thomas's NHS Trust* [2005] ICR 977, CA). Like with all claims under vicarious liability, the employer will only be liable if the acts or omissions are done in the course of employment (i.e. there is sufficient closeness between the wrongdoing and the employee's duties to make it fair and just to hold the employer vicariously liable). 4853

MEMO POINTS A claimant can bring a claim under the **Protection from Harassment Act 1997** where the wrongdoer has engaged in a course of conduct (i.e. conduct or speech on at least two occasions) which was intentional and which, by any objective standard, he knew or ought to have known amounted to harassment (*Banks v Ablex Limited* [2005] EWCA Civ 173). As well as giving another potential cause of action for employees who have been harassed or bullied at work, it should be noted that there are certain aspects of bringing a claim under this Act which may appeal to potential claimants. For example, claims do not have to be type specific (like harassment claims under the protection from sex and sexual orientation discrimination, racial and religion or belief discrimination, and disability discrimination), nor do victims need to show they have suffered a recognised psychiatric illness (general anxiety or distress will suffice) or that their injury was foreseeable as is required for personal injury claims.

D. Statutory duties

1. Employer's duties

a. General duty

4860 Employers have a general statutory duty to ensure the health and safety of their workers whilst at work **as far as is reasonably practicable** (s 2 HSWA 1974). The duty extends to risks arising from:
– the work;
– the manner of conducting the employer's undertaking;
– the plant and substances used; and
– the condition of the premises.

4861 The employer's duty is to take steps to **eliminate identified risks** if it is reasonably practicable to do so. What is reasonably practicable will depend on the circumstances and the degree of risk in a particular job or workplace balanced against the time, trouble, cost and physical difficulty of taking measures to avoid or reduce that risk. In the event of a claim being made, the **burden of proof** will be on the employer to prove that it was not reasonably practicable to have taken steps which would have avoided or reduced the risk. In certain circumstances, this duty is one of strict liability.

EXAMPLE In *R v Gateway Foodmarkets Ltd* [1997] IRLR 189, CA, the practice at a local depot was to frequently leave a trap door open. R, a worker, fell through the trapdoor and died. The offence (under s 2 HSWA 1974) was held to be one of strict liability and it was, therefore, irrelevant that the practice was not known or sanctioned by head office.

MEMO POINTS The HS Codes provide **further guidance** on what is reasonably practicable.

4862 **Pay during medical suspension** In certain circumstances, an employer may be required by law to suspend an employee on medical grounds, or he might be recommended by a Code of Practice to suspend an employee. If so, provided that the statutory requirement or recommendation is specified in one of the prescribed regulations (s 64(3) ERA 1996), an employee who has to be **suspended** from his normal work on medical grounds may be entitled to payment during his period of suspension (s 64(2) ERA 1996). Suspension simply means that the employee, although still employed by the employer, is not provided with work or does not perform the work he normally performed before the suspension (s 64(5) ERA 1996). However, this does not mean that the employee is not suspended if he performs a task other than his normal work.

In order to **qualify** for the right to payment during suspension, the employee must have been continuously employed for 1 month (¶1080) and must not be physically or mentally incapable of undertaking work (s 65(3) ERA 1996). Certain categories of employment are excluded from the right. Moreover, an employee may **lose his right** to payment during suspension if his employer has offered to provide him with suitable alternative work during the suspension and the employee has unreasonably refused the work, or if the employee has not complied with reasonable requirements imposed by his employer to ensure his services are available (s 65(4) ERA 1996).

An employee may receive **payment** during a period of medical suspension at the statutory rate for up to 26 weeks. The amount of payment is based on a week's pay for every week of suspension (pro-rated, if necessary) (¶2920).

4863 Employers have additional specific duties with regard to the medical suspension of women of childbearing age and new or expectant mothers (¶4874).

Premises The employer, as an occupier of premises, has a duty for the safety of employees, visitors and, in some cases trespassers (Occupiers Liability Acts 1957 and 1984). Further, where an employer has, to any extent, control of non-domestic premises used as a **workplace**, or a place where others may use plant and substances provided for their use, statutory health and safety duties also arise with respect to those premises (s 4 HSWA 1974; Workplace (Health, Safety and Welfare) Regulations SI 1992/3004). 4864

A person or organisation is in **control of premises** if they have obligations under a tenancy or contract for the maintenance or repair of premises, or the health and safety of plant or substances to the extent of the contractual duties imposed upon them. These obligations extend to employers who **use premises** as a place of work, or use the machinery or materials there. The obligation on the employer is not absolute but he is expected to take such steps as it is reasonable for a person in his position to take to ensure that, as far as is reasonably practicable, the premises, the plant and machinery are safe (s 4 HSWA 1974).

Where the workers of one employer **work on the premises of another**, the employer in charge of the premises should provide the employer of the visiting staff with comprehensible information on any risks that the host employer's activities may cause to the visiting workers and the relevant precautions that are required. Further, there is a duty on the host employer to provide both the employer of the visiting workers, and the workers themselves, with details of the staff nominated by the host employer to implement emergency procedures on the premises (reg 11 SI 1999/3242). 4865

Non-workers Employers also have a statutory duty to take reasonable steps to protect non-workers from risks to their health and safety as a result of the employer's activities, so far as is reasonably practicable (s 3(1) HSWA 1974). Non-workers include visitors to an employer's workplace, members of the public affected by the work undertaken or contractors and their workers undertaking work for the employer. The duty extends to the provision of information, instruction or training where this is needed to avoid putting non-workers at risk. 4867

Where an employer engages a **contractor** to undertake work on his behalf, or on his premises, the employer has responsibilities in relation to the competence of the contractor to undertake the work safely, and the information provided to the contractor in relation to risks on the employer's premises, or in relation to the work involved. Employers must, therefore, assess the competence of the contractors to be engaged and ensure that they are provided, so far as is reasonably practicable, with sufficient information and, if necessary, instruction and training to reduce the risks (ss 2-3 HSWA 1974; regs 11-12 SI 1999/3242). 4868

There are additional requirements where **large construction contracts** are undertaken, or in the case of any **demolition work**. 4869

b. Specific duties

Specific health and safety duties that employers are required to comply with are **as follows**: 4870
- the management of health and safety issues including general risk assessments and appropriate information and training (SI 1999/3242);
- safe workplace (SI 1992/3004) including electricity (Electricity at Work Regulations SI 1989/635) and fire precautions (The Regulatory Reform (Fire Safety) Order SI 2005/1541);
- provision and maintenance of safe plant and equipment (Provision and Use of Work Equipment Regulations SI 1998/2306), the reduction of risk where manual handling operations involve a risk of injury (Manual Handling Operations Regulations SI 1992/2793) and the reduction of risk with regard to working at heights (Work at Height Regulations SI 2005/735);
- physical working conditions, including ventilation, heating, lighting and welfare issues (SI 1992/3004), noise (Control of Noise at Work Regulations SI 1989/1790), vibrations (Control of Vibrations at Work Regulations SI 2005/1093) and display screen equipment (Health and Safety (Display Screen Equipment) Regulations SI 1992/2792);

– provision of protective clothing, personal protective equipment (PPE) and safety signs (Personal Protective Equipment at Work Regulations SI 1992/2966); and
– provision for first aid (Health and Safety (First Aid) Regulations SI 1981/917).

There are also **detailed requirements** relating to specific problems, for example dangerous substances, asbestos, lead and the transportation of hazardous materials.

MEMO POINTS **Using hand-held mobile telephones** while driving is a criminal offence (there is an exemption for emergency calls where it is not possible for the driver to stop). Note that employers may be liable if they require their employees to use hand-held phones whilst driving on business or if they fail to expressly ban such use.

4871 Compliance will be usually satisfied by taking **all reasonable steps**. However, with regard to certain risks the employer's liability will be **absolute** and the employer has to take action not just when it is reasonably practicable for him to do so. For example, there is an absolute obligation on the employer to ensure that work equipment is maintained in an efficient state, in efficient working order and in good repair (*Stark v The Post Office* [2000] EWCA Civ 64; SI 1998/2306).

Further, where a risk assessment has identified certain risks, **specific action** must be taken by the employer.

4873 **Women** Whilst an employer's statutory duties extend to all of his workers regardless of gender, he has **additional obligations** to protect women of childbearing age and new or expectant mothers from certain specified risks (SI 1999/3242). He is required to carry out a specific assessment of health and safety risks for workers in this group and must identify the measures needed to avoid any risks (¶4910).

MEMO POINTS The health and safety responsibilities covering pregnant workers and those who have recently given birth or are breastfeeding (i.e. new and expectant mothers) are a result of the implementation of EEC Pregnant Workers Directive 1992/85.

4874 Employers are obliged to take **preventive and protective measures**. These include all reasonable and practical measures to:
– avoid risks, for example removing the hazard or preventing exposure to the risk;
– reduce or remove the effect of risks that cannot be avoided, for example by providing aids to help with manual handling duties;
– adapt the design of the workplace and any equipment to suit the worker; and
– develop an overall prevention policy covering technology, organisation of work, work conditions, social relationships and the influence of factors relating to the work environment.

MEMO POINTS These are in line with the general principles as set out in the Introducing Measures to Encourage Improvement of Health and Safety EEC Directive 1989/391.

4875 The employer also has a **specific duty to remove** a **new or expectant mother from a risk** after she has **notified** him in writing that she is pregnant, has given birth within the previous 6 months or is breastfeeding (reg 16 SI 1999/3242). It is, therefore, essential for a pregnant or breastfeeding worker to **inform** her employer in writing as soon as she is aware that she is pregnant, or has given birth or is breastfeeding. The employer has no obligation under this specific duty to protect her or her child if she does not do so.

Where relevant, the employer can require that she produces, within a reasonable period, a written certificate from a registered medical practitioner or midwife confirming that she is pregnant (reg 18 SI 1999/3242). This specific duty will not apply if the employer knows that she is no longer a new or expectant mother or if he cannot establish whether she remains so.

EXAMPLE In *Day v T Pickles Farms Ltd* [1999] IRLR 217, EAT, the worker told her employer that she was pregnant and gave him a medical certificate to say that she was suffering from "hyperemesis gravidarum" which is severe vomiting associated with pregnancy. The EAT held that as there had been written notification, it was for the employer to prove that it was not adequate and did not indicate pregnancy.

The **following progressive steps** must be taken until a risk is removed: 4876

1. **Alter** the new or expectant worker's **working conditions** or **hours of work** if it is reasonable to do so.

2. **Offer** her **suitable alternative work** (¶8867) if available. A worker can refuse the alternative work and the employer will have to go to step three and suspend her for as long as is necessary to protect her or her child. However, if a worker unreasonably refuses suitable alternative work, she will lose her right to be paid remuneration during the period of suspension from her normal duties.

EXAMPLE In *British Airways (European Operation at Gatwick) Ltd v Moore and Botterill* [2000] IRLR 296, EAT, B's removal from flying duties to ground crew did not amount to suitable alternative work as the loss of her cabin crew member's flying allowance meant that the ground crew terms were substantially less favourable than her normal terms.

3. **Suspend** her **from work** as long as is necessary to protect her safety or health or that of her child. A new or expectant mother must also be suspended from work if working at night is affecting her health and safety and there is no suitable daytime work. 4877

A worker on maternity suspension is **entitled** to be paid remuneration at her full normal rate for as long as the suspension continues. This is calculated by reference to a week's pay (¶2920) in respect of each week of suspension (or proportionately for part of a week). The right to paid suspension does not affect any contractual right to remuneration, though any contractual remuneration will be offset.

A worker's **employment will continue** during maternity suspension and therefore the period will count towards continuity for both statutory and contractual rights.

A worker on maternity suspension will start her **maternity leave** on her chosen date or date of childbirth, if earlier. If the period of suspension is likely to apply up to the birth she must give notice when she wishes to start her leave otherwise it may start automatically at the beginning of the fourth week before the expected week of confinement (EWC) (¶4436).

Where a new or expectant mother is engaged in **night work** and the employee provides a medical certificate from a registered medical practitioner or registered midwife stating that for health and safety reasons the employee must not work at certain times as specified in the certificate, the employer must either change her hours of work or suspend the employee for as long as is necessary (reg 17 SI 1999/3242). 4878

Young persons and children Special restrictions apply to the employment and working conditions of children and young persons. A **child** is, unless otherwise specified, a person who is not over the compulsory school age (s 58 Education Act 1944) and a **young person** is a person over compulsory school age but under 18 (s 114(1) Education Act 1944). 4880

MEMO POINTS The basis for rules and restrictions applying to young persons and children is the EC Young Workers Directive 1994/33. This has been implemented by:
- Children (Protection at Work) Regulations SI 1998/276;
- Health and Safety (Young Persons) Regulations SI 1997/135 (which amended the then Management of Health and Safety at Work Regulations (now SI 1999/3242)); and
- Working Time Regulations SI 1998/1833.

Employers are prohibited from employing **children** in a factory or industrial undertaking, but children above the age of 13 may be employed in non-industrial undertakings, subject to local authority bylaws. These bylaws restrict the number of hours which children may work and generally require that an application be made to the local authority for the issue of an employment card before the child starts work. 4881

Further, all work must be **light**. This is not defined by the appropriate regulations, however, EC Directive 1994/33 defines light work as any work that is not likely to be harmful to a child's safety, health, development, attendance at school or participation in work experience.

Employers can employ **young persons** in a factory or industrial undertaking as well as a non-industrial undertaking. However, they must ensure that young persons are protected at work from any risks to their health or safety which are a consequence of their lack of 4882 experience, their absence of awareness of existing or potential risks or the fact that they have not fully matured (reg 13D SI 1999/3242).

4883 It is **prohibited** for an employer to employ a young person in work which:
– is beyond the young person's physical or psychological capacity;
– involves harmful exposure to agents which are toxic or carcinogenic, cause heritable genetic damage, or harm the unborn child, or which in any other way chronically affect human health;
– involves harmful exposure to radiation;
– involves a risk of accidents which it may reasonably be assumed, cannot be recognised or avoided by the young person, due to insufficient attention to safety or lack of experience or training; or
– involves a risk to health from extreme heat or cold, noise or vibration.

However work in the above categories is **permitted** if it is necessary for the young person's training, there is supervision by a competent person and any risks are reduced to the lowest level reasonably practicable.

MEMO POINTS In addition there are further specific restrictions or prohibitions in relation to the following types of work:
– certain work with lead and ionising radiation; and
– supervising a vehicle carrying dangerous goods when it is parked.

4884 See also ¶3720 for the **working time restrictions** on young workers.

2. Worker's duties

4890 Workers have a corresponding obligation to **take reasonable care** for their own safety whilst at work and for the safety of others who may be affected by their acts or omissions (ss 3, 7 HSWA 1974). They also have a **duty to co-operate** with their employer to enable him to comply with his statutory obligations. Workers must not, therefore, work in a dangerous way, or refuse to wear or use necessary protective equipment, as this will amount to a breach of their statutory obligations even if it is only their own safety which is affected.

Further, workers have **particular duties** to use equipment and materials in accordance with the training that has been provided and to report any hazardous situations or shortcomings in the employer's arrangements to the employer.

4891 In order to benefit from the special protection afforded to **new and expectant mothers** and those who are breastfeeding, the worker must inform her employer in writing of her situation.

SECTION 2

Means of protection

A. Adequate management system

4900 Employers have a responsibility not only for the physical standards of health and safety at work, but also for the management system that ensures such standards are established and maintained. As a result, employers are required to have an adequate system of managing health and safety, in particular, **covering** the way in which health and safety matters are planned, organised, controlled, monitored and reviewed (reg 5 SI 1999/3242).

Further, the health and safety management system must provide **adequate emergency procedures** (reg 8 SI 1999/3242). Employers have an obligation to establish emergency procedures for the evacuation of the workplace in the event of serious and imminent danger and to ensure that employees do not return to the workplace until it is safe to do so. The procedures must include arrangements for informing employees of the nature of the hazard which has arisen and the appropriate steps to be taken. There must also be a sufficient number of competent persons to implement these procedures.

In **establishing** an adequate management system, the employer must:
- **consult** his safety advisers and other appropriate representatives (see section 3 below);
- **assess** where there are any risks and take appropriate action where necessary. In particular, risk assessments are required to be performed with regard to certain activities and groups; and
- **inform and train** employees and others who are working or visiting his premises.

Employers with **five or more employees** are required to make a written record of these arrangements and these can be incorporated into the overall health and safety policy. Further, employers are required to produce and, where necessary, update a written **statement of general policy** with respect to health and safety and the organisation and arrangements for implementing it (s 2(3) HSWA 1974). The health and safety policy, therefore, needs to detail, or make reference to, the responsibilities of key members of staff within the organisation and the health and safety procedures and standards that are implemented. **4901**

Risk assessment

Employers must make risk assessments as part of their health and safety management system and with regard to certain activities or groups of employees (SI 1999/3242). **4910**

The primary purpose of risk assessments is to identify the actions the employer needs to take to comply with legal requirements and, therefore, to ensure that risks are adequately controlled. Consequently, employers have a general duty to assess the risks present in their undertaking and identify the measures that are needed to adequately control these risks and meet the relevant statutory obligations. In addition, employers are required to undertake certain specific types of risk assessment, particularly in relation to work with hazardous materials, manual handling work, work with display screen equipment and fire safety. The employer is also required to take particular account of the risks to new or expectant mothers and young persons when undertaking risk assessments and considering control measures (see below).

Where the employer has **five or more employees**, the significant findings of the risk assessment must be recorded. **4911**

Specific risk assessments must be made regarding: **4912**
- manual handling which involves risk of injury (SI 1992/2793);
- noise (SI 1989/1790);
- personal protective equipment (SI 1992/2966);
- fire safety (SI 2005/1541);
- first aid (SI 1981/917); and
- workstations and display screen equipment (SI 1992/2792).

Women As well as the general duty to assess the risks to the health and safety of their workers, employers must make a risk assessment if there may be a possibility of any of the particular risks below. Consequently, it is advisable for employers to make a specific risk assessment if they have workers of childbearing age even before a worker becomes or is aware that she is pregnant. On completion, the employer must **provide** all workers of childbearing age with any comprehensible and relevant information on the risks to their health identified by the assessment (SI 1999/3242). The employer can also give the information to employee representatives. **4915**

Particular risks may occur to new or expectant mothers and their babies where: **4916**
- the workers in an undertaking include women of childbearing age, and
- the work could involve risk to the health and safety of a new or expectant mother due to her condition, or her baby, from any processes or working conditions, or physical, biological or chemical agents, including those specifically listed.

MEMO POINTS The specified list of agents, processes and working conditions is non-exhaustive and is summarised as follows:
1. **Physical agents** that may cause foetal lesions and/or are likely to disrupt placental attachment. These include shocks, vibrations or movement (for example, travelling in off-road vehicles may increase the risk of a miscarriage, and long-term exposure to vibration may increase risk of premature birth or low birth weight).
Manual handling of loads may present a risk of injury as hormonal changes can make the ligaments more susceptible to injury. Postural problems may increase as the pregnancy progresses.
Movements and postures, travelling, mental and physical fatigue, and other physical burdens (for example, fatigue from standing for long periods) may be associated with miscarriage, premature birth and low birth weight. Excessive physical or mental pressure may also cause stress and give rise to anxiety, fatigue and raised blood pressure, as may exposure to loud noise.
Ionising radiation and non-ionising electromagnetic radiation could cause harm by raising body temperature (for example, by over-exposure to radio-frequency radiation). However, such emissions from display screen equipment (VDUs) have been found (by the National Radiological Protection Board) not to present a risk.
Extremes of temperature, for example may cause pregnant women to faint or suffer heat stress.
Working in pressurised environments, for example pressurised enclosures and underwater diving may cause a risk to a pregnant woman.
2. **Biological agents** that may endanger the health of the worker or her unborn or breastfeeding child. For example, a child may be infected with hepatitis B, HIV, herpes, TB, syphilis, chickenpox and typhoid through the placenta, breastfeeding or close contact with the mother. A foetus may be aborted or physically and neurologically damaged by rubella, toxoplasma, cytomegalovirus and chlamydia. For most workers, the risk of infection is not higher at work than from living in the community but in certain occupations (for example, laboratory workers, healthcare staff, those looking after animals and dealing with animal products) exposure to infections is more likely. Pregnant workers should not be exposed to toxoplasma or rubella virus unless they have adequate immunisation.
3. **Chemical agents** including substances that may have irreversible effects, cause cancer and heritable genetic damage, harm to an unborn or breastfed baby. Carcinogenic agents, mercury and mercury derivatives and antimitotic (cytotoxic) drugs (which may be absorbed by inhalation or through the skin) may, in cases of long term exposure, cause damage to the genetic information in sperm and egg. Dangerous chemical agents (which are absorbed through the skin) including certain pesticides, carbon monoxide, and lead and lead derivatives (in so far as they are absorbable) also present a risk to health. Pregnant workers and workers who are breastfeeding may not be involved in absorbable lead and lead derivatives underground mining where there is a health or safety risk.

4917 If a worker **believes there is a risk** to her or her unborn baby's health or safety which the employer has not considered in the general risk assessment or a risk has been identified but the employer will not take preventive action, she should bring the risk to the attention of her employer or employee representative. If the employer discounts the risk and the worker remains concerned, she should discuss the matter with her doctor or get in touch with her local Health and Safety (HSE) office for advice.

4918 Where an employer **fails to carry out a risk assessment**, it may amount to a detriment entitling a pregnant or breastfeeding worker to claim discrimination. She may also have a negligence claim.
As well as breaching the relevant regulation, failure to carry out a risk assessment in respect of a pregnant woman who, as a result, suffers a detriment, will also amount to sex discrimination (*Hardman v Mallon t/a Orchard Lodge Nursing Home* [2002] IRLR 516, EAT).

4920 **Young persons and children** Employers who employ, or intend to employ, young persons must ensure that the risk assessment particularly takes account of the (SI 1999/3242):
- inexperience, lack of awareness of risks and immaturity of young persons;
- fitting-out and layout of the workplace and workstation;
- nature and degree of exposure to physical, biological and chemical agents;
- form, range and use of work equipment and the way in which it is handled;
- organisation of processes and activities;
- extent of the health and safety training provided; and
- risks from certain types of agents and processes.

Where the employer employs a child, the employer must ensure that the **parents** of the child are provided with comprehensible and relevant information on the risks identified in the risk assessment, any risks notified to the employer by another employer sharing the workplace and, in both cases, the required control measures. 4921

Information

As well as informing employees with regard to any **specific risks/issues**, employers must also provide their employees with certain **basic information** concerning their health, safety and welfare at work (Health and Safety Information for Employees Regulations SI 1989/682). This information is contained in both a poster and a leaflet approved by HSE. Employers can comply with their duty by either displaying the poster or providing employees with a copy of the leaflet. Employers can obtain copies of the poster and leaflet from HSE Books. The leaflet is also available on HSE's web site (www.hse.gov.uk). 4925

Training

An employer has considerable duties in relation to the provision of health and safety training for employees and the management system for health and safety should cover the need to provide adequate worker health and safety training (SI 1999/3242). Employers must, in particular, ensure that the selection of employees takes **account of their capability** in relation to health and safety matters and that employees receive **adequate** health and safety **training** in the following circumstances: 4930
- on being recruited into the employer's undertaking;
- on being exposed to new or increased risks because of a transfer or change of responsibilities, or due to the introduction of new technology; and
- with regard to work equipment or a new or changed system of work.

The requirements for health and safety training apply at all levels in an organisation, including senior managers and directors. The content of the health and safety training necessary will, of course, differ as while more junior staff may need specific training on particular work equipment or systems of work, senior staff will need training in health and safety responsibilities and the overall management of health and safety.

B. Reporting duties

Employers must report to the relevant health and safety enforcement authority (Reporting of Injuries, Diseases and Dangerous Occurrences Regulations SI 1995/3163): 4940
- **accidents resulting in a reportable injury** (i.e. death, or a specified major injury or injury resulting in absence from work for more than 3 days excluding the day of the accident but including any rest days when the employee would have been unfit for work) on the employer's premises or on other premises. These must be reported if they occur in connection with the work activity or due to work-related violence;
- **occupational diseases**; and
- **dangerous occurrences** relating to work that occur on premises under their control.

Road accidents involving work and **incidents involving gas** supplied through pipes or in containers and incidents involving gas fittings and equipment have additional reporting requirements.

As **good practice**, employers may find it appropriate to require all accidents be noted in an accident book so that it can be easily seen whether a particular incident requires/may require reporting. 4941

Procedure

4942 Employers must send the appropriate written report to the enforcement authority. The HSE has approved alternative systems of reporting (by telephone or email) with initiated pilot schemes in some areas. Where paperless reporting is approved, the HSE can require extra records be kept to demonstrate that reporting has taken place. Reports of death or specified major injury, injuries to members of the public and dangerous occurrences must be sent by the quickest practicable means (i.e. telephone or fax) with the written report on the requisite form (F2508) following no later than 10 days from the date of the accident.

Occupational diseases must be reported on form F2508A immediately following the receipt of notification from a medical practitioner. Gas incidents must be reported on a specified form F2508G within 14 days.

4943 **Records** of reports must be **kept for** 3 years and should contain the following information (reg 7 SI 1995/3163):
– date and time of the accident, dangerous occurrence or disease;
– brief description of the circumstances;
– full name, nature of the injury/disease and occupation of any relevant employee;
– full name, nature of the injury and status, e.g. school pupil, customer, passenger etc, of any injured member of public;
– date on which the event was first reported; and
– method by which the event was reported.

There is no legal requirement as to the **form** records should be in and records can be kept, for example by:
– keeping copies of report forms in a file;
– recording the details on a computer; or
– maintaining a written log.

SECTION 3

Specific issues

A. Stress

4945 Workplace stress is of growing concern as it can **affect the productivity and morale** of employees who are suffering from stress and may leave the employer **liable for damages** under a tortious or contractual claim due to their psychiatric illness.

Readers are recommended to read **ACAS' stress at work guide**, which aims to help organisations and individuals reduce stress at work as well as giving guidance as to how it can be prevented it from occurring in the first place; and/or the **booklet on work-related stress** for employers and employees from the **DTI and the Health and Safety Executive (HSE)**, together with the CBI, TUC, the Forum of Private Business and CEEP UK, which aims to provide guidance on, and increase general awareness of, work-related stress.

The HSE has also developed **stress management standards** to help employers measure their performance in managing the key causes of stress and identify areas for improvement. The key areas focus on:
– the demands made on employees;
– the level of control employees have over their work;
– the support employees receive from managers and colleagues;
– the clarity of an employee's role within the organisation;

– the nature of relationships at work; and
– the way that change is managed.

Scope for liability

Liability for psychiatric injury caused by stress at work is in general no different in principle from liability for physical injury i.e. liability arises where there is a **foreseeable injury** which has occurred as a result of the employer's **breach of duty of care** (*Hartman v South Essex Mental Health and Community Care NHS Trust and other linked appeals* [2005] IRLR 293, CA; *Sutherland (Chairman of the Governors of St Thomas Becket RC High School) v Hatton* [2002] IRLR 263, CA). The employer will breach his duty of care if he knows or should have known of the employee's problem or vulnerability and has failed to take reasonable steps to try and prevent the injury from occurring/re-occurring. **4946**

The employer's duty does **not extend** to protect employees from **feelings** such as anger and bitterness or **normal conditions** such as stress or anxiety which do not cause injury (and see ¶4950 below). The courts recognise that employers often have to take decisions (for example, in relation to disciplinary issues) which they know are likely to cause anger and anxiety and generally it is safe for an employer to assume that his workers **can deal with ordinary disciplinary matters** without worrying about how such disciplinary matters will affect their mental health (*Croft v Broadstairs and St Peter's Town Council* [2003] All ER (D) 273, CA). **4947**

However, where the employer has acted unreasonably in the **events leading up to his dismissal**, an employee will be able to claim for damages in respect of psychiatric injury that has been suffered because of the way the disciplinary procedure was conducted up to the actual dismissal (*McCabe v Cornwall County Council* heard jointly with *Eastwood and Williams v Magnox Electric plc* [2004] IRLR 733, HL). For such a claim to succeed the events which gave rise to the injury must be independent of, and prior to, the dismissal and must not immediately surround the dismissal. In *McCabe v Cornwall County Council* and *Eastwood and Williams v Magnox Electric plc*, the employees had a cause of action relating to the financial loss they had suffered as a result of psychiatric injury caused by their employers' treatment of them in the events leading up to dismissal, which was independent of the action they brought relating to the unfairness of the dismissal.

Compensation, however, is not recoverable for damages for on-going financial loss due to injury to feelings, psychiatric injury, loss of reputation and inability to find new employment arising from an employee's **dismissal or the manner of his dismissal** (*Johnson v Unisys Ltd* [2001] IRLR 279, HL; *Dunnachie v Kingston upon Hull City Council* [2004] IRLR 727, HL). Unfairness in the circumstances of dismissal does not give rise to a common law action, whether in contract or tort, but must be subject to employment tribunal proceedings.

The employer will only be liable for the **damages** that the breach of duty has **caused or materially contributed to** the harm suffered. The general rules of **apportionment** apply and an employer will only be liable for the proportion of damages which are attributable to his wrongdoing. Any assessment of damages will **take into account** any pre-existing condition or vulnerability and what chance the employee would have succumbed to a stress-related disorder in any event. **4948**

Susceptibility and foreseeability Although psychiatric damage may arise from the job that the employee is required to do, unless there is a **real risk of breakdown** with regard to that employee which the employer ought to reasonably have foreseen and which he should have properly averted, the employer will be not be liable for such damage. As it may sometimes be difficult to identify the difference between the risk of stress and the suffering of stress by an employee which may lead to a risk of psychiatric breakdown it is recommended that as a **practical approach**, where there are indications that an employee is showing signs that he is either under great pressure from work or is already suffering stress, the employer carries out an **assessment** of the causes of these signs and the exact state of the employee's health. If work-related stress is identified, appropriate action, support and monitoring may be required to ensure that the employer does not find himself in breach of his duty of care. **4949**

4950 The employer is **not expected to foresee** any greater susceptibility to injury from work pressures than that which would be expected from **other employees in the same or similar role** (*Sutherland (Chairman of the Governors of St Thomas Becket RC High School) v Hatton* [2002] IRLR 263, CA). An employer is also entitled to assume that the employee can **withstand the normal pressures** of the job and whilst an employer knew or ought to have known that a decision would cause an employee emotional upset in one form or another it does not necessarily follow that he knew or ought to have known that it would cause the employee to suffer a psychiatric illness such as depression (*Fraser v The State Hospitals Board for Scotland*, 11 July 2000, CS; *Morland v London Borough of Tower Hamlets*, 1 May 2003, High Court).

Likewise, no **job in itself** is intrinsically dangerous to mental health (*Sutherland (Chairman of the Governors of St Thomas Becket RC High School) v Hatton* [2002] IRLR 263, CA). However, the **nature and extent** of an employee's job will be a relevant factor when deciding what is reasonably foreseeable and whilst there are some occupations which appear intrinsically stressful such as traffic police officers who regularly deal with gruesome accidents, the courts have emphasised that it is not the job but the **interaction** between the individual and the job which causes the harm. Even where one employer has foreseen a **particular risk in a particular field of work**, it does not necessarily follow that all others in the same field should have done so as well (*Melville v The Home Office* [2005] IRLR 293, CA (one of the linked appeals to *Hartman v South Essex Mental Health and Community Care NHS Trust*)).

4951 It is generally reasonable for an employer to take what his employee tells him at **face value**, unless there are other indications to the contrary (for example, the employee has already had time off for stress). However, where an employer is aware of an employee's problem or vulnerability, there is a more positive requirement to **actively monitor** the situation and in such circumstances he should not solely rely on the employee informing him of his ongoing condition (*Barber v Somerset County Council* [2004] IRLR 475, HL) although employers will not be expected to require the employee to undergo intrusive medical assessments (for example a further visit to the employee's psychiatrist) and in such circumstances it is reasonable to rely on the employee's reassurances as to his health (*Vahidi v Fairstead House School Trust Ltd* [2005] EWCA Civ 765).

Usually, an employer knows or is aware about a specific employee's problem or vulnerability as they have been **informed** of the problem or vulnerability (for example, because the employee returns to work after a period of sick leave due to stress or a stress-related illness). However, an employer may also be liable if he **should have known** about a specific employee's problem or vulnerability, for example the employee behaviour should have highlighted to the employer that there was a problem. In assessing whether the employer should have been aware of a particular problem, the courts will take into account what a reasonable employer should have foreseen, such as **picking up signs** from the employee's absence and sickness records, and being aware that other employees have suffered injury to their health in the same job.

4952 Employers cannot be expected to have **knowledge of confidential information** to which they do not have access. For example, employers are not expected to know of an employee's vulnerability where the employee has declared it on a health screening questionnaire which was for the sole use by their occupational health service only (*Hartman v South Essex Mental Health and Community Care NHS Trust and other linked appeals* [2005] IRLR 293, CA). As a matter of note, the Court of Appeal in this case commented that in this situation, there may be circumstances in which an occupational health department's duty of care to an employee requires the department to seek the employee's consent for the disclosure of the information to the employer so that proper steps can be taken for the welfare of the employee.

4953 **Reasonable support** The employer is only in breach of duty where he knows or should have known of a specific employee's problem or vulnerability and he has failed to take whatever measures are possible and appropriate to try to support and help the employee. He is expected to **take reasonable steps** to protect the employee from an occurrence/re-occurrence of the psychiatric illness **taking into account** the magnitude of the risk, the cost of preventing it, and whether if taken, such steps would do any good (*Barber v Somerset County*

Council [2004] IRLR 475, HL; *Young v The Post Office* [2002] IRLR 660, CA). In other words, the employer must identify the steps that he both could and should take although he can only reasonably be expected to take steps which are **likely to do some good**.

Although it might be an appropriate course of action in certain circumstances, it is not reasonable to expect an employer to **dismiss** an employee to protect him from harm where the employee wants to go on working (*Sutherland (Chairman of the Governors of St Thomas Becket RC High School) v Hatton* [2002] IRLR 263, CA; *Vahidi v Fairstead House School Trust Ltd* [2005] EWCA Civ 765).

An employer who offers a **confidential advice service**, with referral to appropriate counselling or treatment service, is unlikely to be found in breach of duty. 4954

Guidelines

The above principles can all be found in the guidelines given by Lady Justice Hale in *Sutherland (Chairman of the Governors of St Thomas Becket RC High School) v Hatton*. The Court of Appeal has recently confirmed that these guidelines are **useful signposts** to help ascertain whether a worker has suffered psychiatric injury due to stress at work; and as a consequence are set out in the next paragraph. However, they are not intended to cover all the infinitely variable facts that are likely to arise in such cases and they need care in their **application to the particular facts** under consideration (as emphasised recently in the Court of Appeal decision of *Hartman v South Essex Mental Health and Community Care NHS Trust and other linked appeals*). 4955

MEMO POINTS The Court of Appeal, in confirming that the guidelines as set out in *Hatton* were useful signposts, commented that the preference given by Lord Walker (in his leading judgment of the majority view in *Barber v Somerset County Council*) for the statement of Swanwick J in *Stoke v Guest, Keen and Nettlefold (Bolts and Nuts) Ltd* [1968] 1 WLR 1776 was not an expression of disagreement with these guidelines but simply a word of caution that no two cases were the same and that each case had to be decided on its particular facts (*Hartman v South Essex Mental Health and Community Care NHS Trust and other linked appeals*). An even more recent Court of Appeal decision has also commented that the *Hatton* guidance "was for all practical purposes endorsed completely by the House of Lords in *Barber v Somerset County Council*" (*Mark Hone v Six Continents Retail Ltd* [2005] EWCA Civ 922).

The guidelines are **as follows**: 4956

1. There are no special control mechanisms applying to claims for psychiatric (or physical) illness or injury arising from the stress of doing the work the employee is required to do. The ordinary principles of employer's liability apply.
2. The threshold question is whether this kind of harm to this particular employee was reasonably foreseeable: this has two components: a. an injury to health (as distinct from occupational stress) which b. is attributable to stress at work (as distinct from other factors).
3. Foreseeability depends on what the employer knows or ought to know about the individual employee. Because of the nature of mental disorder, it is harder to foresee in a known individual than in the population at large. An employer is usually entitled to assume that the employee can withstand the normal pressures of the job unless he knows of some particular problem or vulnerability.
4. The test is the same whatever the employment: there are no occupations which should be regarded as intrinsically dangerous to mental health.
5. Factors likely to be relevant in answering the threshold question include:

a. The nature and extent of the work done by the employee. Is the workload much more than is normal for the particular job? Is the work particularly intellectually or emotionally demanding for this employee? Are demands being made of this employee? Are the demands being made of this employee unreasonable when compared with the demands made of others in the same or comparable jobs? Are there signs that others doing this job are suffering harmful levels of stress? Is there an abnormal level of sickness or absenteeism in the same job or the same department?

b. Signs from the employee of impending harm to health. Has he a particular problem or vulnerability? Has he already suffered from mental illness attributable to stress at work? Have there recently been frequent or prolonged absences which are uncharacteristic of him? Is there reason to think that these are attributable to stress at work, for example because of complaints or warnings from him or others?

6. The employer is generally entitled to take what he is told by his employee at face value, unless he has good reason to think to the contrary. He does not generally have to make searching enquiries of the employee or seek permission to make further inquiries of his medical advisers.
7. To trigger a duty to take steps, the indications of impending harm to health arising from stress at work must be plain enough for any reasonable employer to realise that he should do something about it.
8. The employer is only in breach of duty if he has failed to take the steps which are reasonable in the circumstances, bearing in mind the magnitude of the risk of harm occurring, the gravity of the harm which may occur, the costs and the practicability of preventing it, and the justifications for running the risk.
9. The size and the scope of the employer's operation, its resources and the demands it faces are relevant in deciding what is reasonable; these include the interests of other employees and the need to treat them fairly, for example, in any redistribution of duties.
10. An employer can only reasonably be expected to take steps which are likely to do some good: the court is likely to need expert evidence on this.
11. An employer who offers a confidential advice service, with referral to appropriate counselling or treatment service, is unlikely to be found in breach of duty. (The Court of Appeal in this case also applied this to an occupational health service).
12. If the only reasonable and effective step would have been to dismiss or demote the employee, the employer will not be in breach of duty in allowing a willing employee to continue in the job.
13. In all cases, therefore, it is necessary to identify the steps which the employer both could and should have taken before finding him in breach of his duty of care.
14. The claimant must show that that breach of duty has caused or materially contributed to the harm suffered. It is not enough to show that occupational stress has caused the harm.
15. Where the harm suffered has more than one cause, the employer should only pay for that proportion of the harm suffered which is attributable to his wrongdoing, unless the harm is truly indivisible. It is for the defendant to raise the question of apportionment.
16. The assessment of damages will take account of any pre-existing disorder or vulnerability and of the chance that the claimant would have succumbed to a stress-related disorder in any event.

Examples

4957

EXAMPLE **Not foreseeable/reasonable support**

1. In *Fraser v The State Hospitals Board for Scotland*, F brought a claim for a psychiatric illness that arose after he was **demoted**. The Court held that it was a considerable leap for an employer to go from a position where he might anticipate that the employee would be emotionally upset, to one where he knew or ought to anticipate that his decision would cause the employee to suffer a psychiatric illness. Consequently, it was not foreseeable that the demotion would cause the employee's illness.
2. *In Morland v London Borough of Tower Hamlets*, M, a local authority education officer, brought a claim for psychiatric illness due to stress which resulted from carrying out Ofsted inspections. The Court held that his workload was not unreasonable and that, as with every job, there were **periods of intense activity**, in this situation well balanced by periods of relative inactivity and long holidays. Consequently, it was not foreseeable that the work pressure would cause the employee's illness.
3. In *Bonsar v UK Coal Mining Ltd (named as RJB Mining UK Ltd)* [2004] IRLR 164, CA, B had started to show that she was under great pressure from her workload but this alone was not sufficient to result in her employer being in breach of its duty when, because she had a **particular vulnerability** that the **employer was unaware** of, she succumbed to a nervous breakdown.
4. In *Barlow v Borough of Broxbourne* [2003] EWHC 50, High Court, B brought a claim for psychiatric illness brought on by stress. Although the Court accepted that B held a **senior and demanding position**, he had held this for **many years without complaining** about his workload or indicating that he was suffering from stress and had always appeared laid back and in control. Consequently, it was not foreseeable that the work pressure would cause B's illness.
5. In *Harding v The Pub Estate Company Ltd* [2005] EWCA Civ 553, H, was an **experienced** pub manager employed to manage a pub on a temporary basis. He lived on site, worked long hours and suffered from violence in the pub and damage to the property. After managing the pub for nearly one and a half years, H suffered a heart attack and was dismissed. The Court of Appeal held that there was **no evi-**

dence in the employee's medical notes about stress or that the employee's doctor was alert to the **risk of either an impending heart attack or a psychiatric breakdown**. H's working hours were deemed to be in his own hands and even his own evidence suggested that it was the working environment which was the subject of his complaints, which his employer could not do anything about. Nothing was said which flagged up to the employers the risk of a breakdown in the employee's health and there was no clear sign to his doctor that such a warning should be passed onto his employer. The employer was therefore never given the kind of warning that required it to act.

6. In *Vahidi v Fairstead House School Trust Ltd*, V, a school teacher, had her **teaching methods re-organised** as a result of an inspection which had highlighted shortcomings in the school's procedures. She was unhappy about the new arrangements and became depressed resulting in 8 months off work. V **returned to work** when her psychiatrist informed the school that she was well enough to do so. The school, aware of the risk of a relapse, took her back initially on a **part-time** basis and organised **weekly support meetings**. Unfortunately, V still could not cope, suffered depression again and left the school. The Court held that although the relapse was clearly foreseeable, there was no breach as it considered that the school had taken all the reasonable steps it could in supporting V on her return.

Foreseeable/failure to give reasonable support

1. In *Young v The Post Office*, Y suffered a depressive condition as a result of an **increasing workload**. This was recognised by the employer and he had a period off work. On **return to work**, although the employer allowed him a flexible working environment, his workload was **not monitored** and he was sent on a training **course** which he found extremely stressful. The Court held it was plainly foreseeable that there might be a recurrence of his condition if appropriate steps were not taken to monitor his workload on his return to work and the employer owed him a duty to take such steps.

2. In *Barber v Somerset County Council*, B, a school teacher, took on **further responsibilities** following a restructure of the staffing at the school he worked in. This caused him to work long hours and he found the workload and the school life (in particular the manner of leadership of the senior management team after the restructure) stressful. Over the following year, B's condition worsened and he had to take sick leave for stress and depression. On his **return to work**, he initiated meetings with the senior management team but was dealt with unsympathetically and **no steps** were made by the school to investigate or remedy the situation other than urging B to prioritise his work. B continued to work under the same conditions or even possibly a slightly heavier workload until he suffered a nervous breakdown which caused him to leave the school. The House of Lords held that it was clear that the employer had been aware that B was suffering from stress after he returned to work and consequently the school should have taken appropriate measures which could have included making sympathetic enquiries about B's health and taking reasonable steps to reduce his workload. As they did not, the school was in breach of its duty of care.

3. In *Melville v The Home Office* [2005] IRLR 293, CA (one of the appeals linked to *Hartman v South Essex Mental Health and Community Care NHS Trust*), M, a prison healthcare officer, attended eight suicides of prisoners and subsequently suffered a stress-related illness. The Home Office recognised that those involved in dealing with such incidents might suffer psychiatric injury and had prison care teams to provide care and support. However, the **support procedure was not implemented** with regard to M and as a result the Home Office was held to be in breach of their duty of care. As M's employer had failed to implement their own scheme to provide support, they only had themselves to blame as they had set their own threshold.

4. In *Mark Hone v Six Continents Retail Ltd*, H, a pub manager, worked excessively long hours in the period before he left work after having collapsed from chest pains and giddiness. Prior to this, H had told SCR Ltd that he was working excessively long hours and, although he did not specifically refer to any adverse affects on his health, he did emphasise that he was tired and required help after other key workers, who could have deputised for H so as to allow him to take time off from work, had left, which had greatly exacerbated the situation. However, no additional help was forthcoming. The Court of Appeal held that SCR Ltd had breached its duty of care as it was aware of H's increased and excessive working hours and his need for assistance.

B. Drugs and alcohol

4960 It is advisable for an employer to have a drugs and alcohol policy in order to ensure compliance with his health and safety obligations. The policy will also serve to set the standards of behaviour required of employees, and failure to observe these standards will raise disciplinary and performance issues. However, the employer must distinguish between disciplinary issues arising out of drug/alcohol abuse and possession, and medical issues connected with addiction, which should be handled with sensitivity.

Health and safety issues

4962 Employers are under contractual and statutory duties to take reasonable care of the health and safety of their employees, which means that they must take reasonable steps to ensure that their workers are not under the influence of drugs or alcohol at work if this would harm the health and safety of other employees (¶4810) (HSWA 1974).

Employers may also be under a **duty to third parties** (e.g. customers) to take reasonable care of their health and safety.

An employer could be **prosecuted** for a breach of health and safety legislation, and could also be **liable in damages** if employees or third parties are injured as a result of the actions of an employee who is under the influence of drugs or alcohol.

MEMO POINTS It is a criminal offence for certain workers to be unfit through drugs or alcohol while working on railways, tramways and other guided transport systems, and the operators of those systems would also be guilty of an offence unless they had shown all due diligence in trying to prevent the offence being committed (Transport and Works Act 1992).

4963 It is a **criminal offence** for occupiers or managers knowingly to permit people to undertake certain activities on their premises, including producing or supplying controlled drugs, and smoking cannabis (Misuse of Drugs Act 1971).

MEMO POINTS If the employer or the employee is required to be registered with a **regulatory authority** (for example, in the financial services sector), drug or alcohol abuse may have an effect on these registrations, for example, because the employee must be a "fit and proper person". If an employee is dismissed for, or convicted of, drug taking, the employer may be required by applicable regulatory rules to notify the relevant regulatory body.

Setting up a policy

4965 If drug taking or alcohol abuse is a concern, it may be useful to have a specific policy dealing with those issues, in addition to the general disciplinary procedures. The drug/alcohol misuse policy could form part of the company's overall health and safety policy.

The HSE's "Drug Misuse at Work: Guide for Employers" recommends a **four step approach** to introducing a policy on drug misuse:
- find out if there is a problem;
- if there is, decide what to do;
- take action; and
- monitor the policy in practice.

The same approach could apply to alcohol abuse.

4966 In assessing **whether misuse is a problem**, the employer should:
- review sickness records for any periods of unexplained or frequently taken absence;
- check whether there have been any behavioural changes or unexplained drops in productivity;
- identify any performance or conduct problems; and
- review accident records for any increase in accidents or near misses or patterns involving particular employees.

If there is a problem, the employer will need to consult with employees (either directly or through elected representatives) and, where applicable, any union appointed safety representatives in order to consider **what action** to take. Such action may include: 4967
– implementing a programme (by group sessions, seminars etc.) to raise awareness among all staff of issues relating to drug/alcohol misuse;
– explaining the drugs/alcohol policy to all staff (this could be part of the induction process for new employees (see Chapter 3));
– training managers/supervisors to implement the policy and to recognise the signs of drug misuse;
– encouraging employees with a drugs/alcohol problem to seek help, giving assurances of confidentiality (unless this is not possible due to the commission of an offence); and
– identifying areas of operation which may be seriously affected by drugs/alcohol misuse problems, such as safety-critical work involving machinery, equipment or driving.

The HSE's guide identifies the **key elements** of a drugs/alcohol misuse policy as follows: 4968
– **aims**: i.e. why the policy exists and who it applies to (it must be seen to apply equally to all staff);
– **responsibility**: i.e. who is responsible for carrying out the policy. All managers/supervisors will have some responsibility but a senior employee should be named as having overall responsibility;
– **definition**: i.e. what constitutes drug/substance abuse;
– **rules**: i.e. behavioural guidelines to ensure work is not affected;
– **safeguards**: i.e. a statement that absence for treatment/rehabilitation will be treated as normal sick leave, a recognition that relapses may occur, and a commitment to monitoring and reviewing policy in consultation with employee representatives;
– **confidentiality**: i.e. an assurance of confidentiality, subject to legal requirements;
– **help**: i.e. a description of support available, which may include local advisory services, and encouragement to seek help voluntarily;
– **information**: i.e. a commitment to providing general information about the effects of drugs on health and safety; and
– **disciplinary action**: i.e. the circumstances in which action will be taken. This may include refusal to seek help/continued poor performance. The policy should include a warning that gross misconduct may lead to dismissal, and that possession/dealing will be reported to the police.

The policy should detail **unacceptable behaviour** and the procedures that will be applied in cases of alcohol or drug abuse. These procedures should be consistent with the **general disciplinary procedures**, which may be triggered by misbehaviour, misconduct or non-attendance due to excessive drinking. The disciplinary rules will often include a definition of **gross misconduct** entitling the employer summarily to dismiss the employee (¶6538). This may include being under the influence of drugs or alcohol at work.

For a **policy checklist** as to what such a policy may contain see the Appendix at ¶9940.

Employers should seek **medical advice** when dealing with an employee with an alcohol or drugs related problem. Addiction to or dependency on alcohol or any other substance is not a disability for the purposes of disability discrimination, so there is no duty to make reasonable adjustments (¶5515). However, alcoholics and drug addicts may benefit from **counselling or medical treatment**, possibly with sick leave covering any periods of absence. This may be advisable especially where it may be more costly to recruit and train a replacement than to permit an employee time off to get expert help. 4969

It may be appropriate to consider **suitable alternative employment**, especially if the employee's normal work is safety-critical.

An employee who performs unsatisfactorily at work or shows poor attendance levels having **declined help or treatment**, or who has discontinued treatment before satisfactory completion, will be subject to normal disciplinary procedures.

The employer should **monitor** implementation on a regular basis and consider whether any changes need to be made, and whether employees are aware of the policy and issues raised. 4970

Screening/testing

4972 Although not mentioned in the HSE guidelines as a key element for a policy, screening and drug testing is becoming more common, particularly in relation to safety-critical jobs. Screening may be used as part of the selection process, during the employment as a matter of routine (whether occasionally or on a random basis), or in specific circumstances, such as after an accident.

If a company is introducing screening for the first time, the workforce should be consulted (through trade union and/or employee representatives, as appropriate) and its agreement in principle obtained.

The use of screening and drug testing as a means of regulating an employee's private conduct could amount to an **infringement of an employee's right to privacy** under the Human Rights Act 1998 if the drug taking is unlikely to have any impact on public safety or the maintenance of the employer's reputation (*O'Flynn v Airlinks the Airport Coach Co Ltd*, EAT case 0269/01).

4973 Employers must make sure that they comply with the **data protection rules** in relation to information obtained from drug and alcohol testing, for example where the data are sensitive (¶5925), explicit consent should be obtained. For more details, see ¶5040 which sets out general core principles and good practice recommendations for employers to follow with regard to information about their workers' health and ¶5045 which set out specific **good practice recommendations** in relation to drug and alcohol testing.

Unfair dismissal

4974 The employer's **defence** to an unfair dismissal claim (¶8380) may be strengthened if he can show that he followed the company policy on drug/alcohol abuse. If the employer fails to follow company policy, any dismissal may well be unfair, even if the employer acted in accordance with his general disciplinary procedures. In particular, a dismissal may be unfair if no attempt has been made to help an employee with an alcohol or drug condition.

In order for a dismissal to be fair, the employee's conduct must in some way reflect on the employment relationship. An employee's **conduct outside the workplace** is therefore unlikely to amount to grounds for dismissal, unless the employee's day-to-day work was affected or the employer's reputation would be damaged by that employee's conduct.

EXAMPLE In *O'Flynn v Airlinks the Airport Coach Co Ltd*, above, the employer, whose disciplinary policy stated that being under the influence of drugs constituted misconduct, was justified in dismissing an employee who had taken drugs outside working hours since the employee could have been affected by her drug-taking whilst at work.

C. Smoking

4980 The employer has both common law and statutory **health and safety obligations**. As part of his **common law** duties, he must provide and maintain a working environment that is reasonably suitable, so far as is reasonably practicable, for the employee to do his work. Allowing smoking at work, such that employees must work in a smoke-filled environment, may breach this term and permit an employee to treat himself as constructively dismissed (*Waltons & Morse v Dorrington* [1997] IRLR 488, EAT).

The employer also has a **statutory** obligation to ensure, so far as is reasonably practicable, the health and safety and welfare of all his employees (Health and Safety at Work etc Act 1974). In particular, he must ensure that non-smokers using **rest areas** are protected from discomfort caused by tobacco smoke, and that **enclosed workplaces** are adequately ventilated (Workplace (Health, Safety and Welfare) Regulations SI 1992/3004).

MEMO POINTS The Government has indicated that, further to the response to its Public Health White Paper, it proposes to introduce legislation to restrict smoking in enclosed public places and workplaces in a staged approach so that, by the end of 2007, all workplaces will be **smoke-free**. This is, at the moment, in draft form as the Health Improvement and Protection Bill. The Scottish Executive has also announced its intention to ban smoking in workplaces in 2006 and draft regulations have been published (The Smoking, Health and Social Care (Scotland) Act 2005 (Prohibition of Smoking in Certain Premises) Regulations 2005).

Contractual terms

Employers may wish to include their no smoking policy or their smoking restrictions as contractual terms to emphasis that employees must strictly abide by these rules. Possible examples of **suggested wording** are as follows: 4981

EXAMPLE Total ban

The Company operates a no smoking policy. You are therefore not allowed to smoke on Company premises at any time. Failure to observe this policy may lead to disciplinary action.

Smoking restrictions

You are not allowed to smoke in [*location*] at any time. Smoking is only permitted in [*location*] at [*times*]. You should obtain your [manager/supervisor's] permission to take a smoking break. If this policy is abused, the Company reserves the right to refuse you permission to smoke other than [during your lunch break] [*other times*]. Failure to observe this policy may lead to disciplinary action.

No smoking policies

As with drugs/alcohol, having a policy on smoking can assist the employer to comply with his health and safety obligations. Indeed, the HSE recommends that all employers introduce a policy to control smoking in the workplace in order to eliminate the **risk of passive smoking**. 4983

MEMO POINTS The HSE has proposed an Approved **Code of Practice**, which would provide guidance for employers on their obligations under health, safety and welfare law in respect of passive smoking at work with a view to encouraging employers to introduce policies, in consultation with employees, to reduce employees' exposure to tobacco smoke. The code recommends a total or partial ban, but suggests alternatives where this is not possible, such as segregation of non-smokers. **Failure to comply** with the code will not be an offence, but the employer may be called on to justify non-compliance should the employee bring a complaint.

If smoking at work would constitute an obvious danger (for example, if flammable materials are present), the employer would clearly be justified in **imposing a ban**. Where there is no such obvious danger, the introduction of a no smoking policy may meet with some resistance if smokers have been allowed to smoke at work for some time. 4984

However, there is **no implied right** (by virtue of custom and practice) to smoke at work, and an employer is therefore entitled to introduce a no smoking policy imposing a total ban on smoking, although a period of **consultation** should be carried out before the policy is introduced (*Dryden v Greater Glasgow Health Board* [1992] IRLR 469, EAT).

If there is an **express right** to smoke at work, the employer will not be entitled to vary the term unilaterally (¶1645).

Setting up a policy

If the employer wishes to introduce a no smoking policy he should follow the **steps** outlined below: 4985

- consider whether to implement a **total ban** or simply to introduce **restrictions**, for example, having a designated area for smokers (but ensure that other areas remain smoke-free by ensuring good ventilation);
- carry out a **survey of opinion** in the workplace;
- provide **information** on smoking and health issues;
- **consult** with employees individually and via employee representatives, and take account of their wishes;
- consider providing **help** to smokers to reduce or give up smoking;

– help smokers to adapt, by introducing the policy over a **reasonable period** (the HSE recommends a minimum period of 3 months' notice); and
– make staff aware of the **details** of the policy and the consequences of **non-observance**.

4986 If an **employee breaches** a no smoking policy, the employer should implement his disciplinary procedures (¶6534). Dismissal for a first smoking offence will not normally be fair, and a disciplinary warning would generally be the appropriate response.

4987 For a **policy checklist** as to what such a policy may contain see the Appendix at ¶9940.

SECTION 4

Persons/bodies assisting and advising on health and safety

A. Safety advisers and first aiders

Assistance and advice

5000 Employers are required to appoint one or more **competent persons** for providing health and safety assistance and advice (SI 1999/3242). This can be the employer if he is an individual. The person(s) selected must be given sufficient training or have the requisite knowledge and experience to properly assist the employer. The actual level of training and competence required will depend on the risks in the employer's undertaking and the scope of advice required. The number of employees appointed must be adequate, having regard to the size and nature of the organisation and the type of risks involved.

The person(s) appointed can either be an employee or an external body or person, or a combination of both. However, where there is an appropriate employee with adequate competence, there is a legal preference to such an employee being appointed. Where there is insufficient or inadequate assistance within the organisation, then external competent assistance has to be sought.

In many cases, a range of different types of assistance may be needed, including professional health and safety practitioners and occupational health professionals, such as occupational health physicians, or occupational health nurses. In certain circumstances, other disciplines such as safety engineering staff and occupational hygienists may be needed.

5001 Where the employer is undertaking certain types of **specialist activity**, specific statutory appointments of trained and competent staff are needed. For example, work with ionising radiation will usually require the appointment of Radiation Protection Supervisors and a specialist Radiation Protection Adviser and work involving the transport or consigning for transport of hazardous goods will require the appointment of a Dangerous Goods Safety Adviser with particular qualifications and training.

Fire safety matters

5003 Employers must appoint one or more competent persons for providing assistance and advice on fire safety matters (SI 2005/1541). The requirements are identical to those for competent persons in relation to health and safety (see above) and the same considerations apply in relation to internal and external appointments. The same person can be used for both health and safety and fire safety, provided he is competent in both areas.

Emergencies and first aid

Employers must appoint a person to take charge of emergencies and first aid equipment 5005
and must also ensure that an adequate number of trained first aiders are provided except in small low risk organisations (SI 1981/917). Two or more employers can share arrangements for first aid provided the cover is adequate and the arrangements are agreed in writing.

Appointed persons are not required to have any formal training although they will need to 5006
know the procedures for calling the emergency services and the HSE strongly recommend that appointed persons attend a 4-hour emergency first aid course.

However, **first aiders** must be adequately trained and hold a valid certificate of training issued by a training organisation approved by the HSE. This type of training normally lasts 4 days and must be for a first aid at work qualification as opposed to another first aid qualification. Additional training will be needed where the employer has special risks, for example work in confined spaces or work with hydrofluoric acid. Certificates are valid for 3 years and before the expiry, refresher training and re-testing of competence must be undertaken to renew the certificate. If the certificate expires, the full training must be undertaken again to obtain a new certificate.

The HSE publish guidance on the **typical number of first aiders** required, as shown below. 5007
The minimum number of first aiders required must be maintained during **periods of holiday** and foreseeable **sickness** absence.

Category of Risk	Numbers Employed at any Location	Suggested number of First Aid Personnel
Lower risk e.g. shops, offices, libraries	Fewer than 50	At least one appointed person
	50-100	At least one first aider
	More than 100	One additional first aider for every 100 employed
Medium risk e.g. light engineering and assembly work, food processing, warehousing	Fewer than 20	At least one appointed person
	20-100	At least one first aider for every 50 employed
	More than 100	One additional first aider for every 100 employed
Higher risk e.g. most construction, slaughterhouse, chemical manufacture, extensive work with dangerous machinery or sharp instruments	Fewer than 5	At least one appointed person
	5-50	At least one first aider
	More than 50	One additional first aider for every 50 employed
	Where there are hazards for which additional first aid skills are necessary	In addition, at least one first aider trained in the specific emergency action

B. Employee representatives

Employers must consult with employees or their representatives on health and safety matters. 5010
The requirements differ depending on whether or not there is a recognised trade union representing the employers.

Establishments with recognised trade unions A recognised trade union has the right to 5011
appoint **safety representatives** who are employees of the employer (reg 3 Safety Representatives and Safety Committees Regulations SI 1977/500). An employee appointed as a safety representative shall, so far as is reasonably practicable, either have been employed by the employer for the previous 2 years, or have at least 2 years' experience in similar employment. Provided

the trade union notifies the employer in writing of the names of the safety representatives appointed and the group or groups of employees they represent, the safety representatives will have the rights and functions detailed below.

5012 **Employers** must **consult** appointed safety representatives with a view to ensuring the co-operation of employees in promoting and developing health and safety measures at the workplace and checking the effectiveness of those measures.

The employer must **specifically consult** safety representatives **on the following matters**:
– the introduction of any measure at the workplace which may substantially affect health and safety;
– the arrangements for appointing competent persons;
– any health and safety information the employer is required to provide to employees;
– the planning and introduction of health and safety training; and
– the health and safety consequences of the introduction of new technology to the workplace.

5013 In addition, **safety representatives** have the following **rights to** (regs 4-8 SI 1977/500):
– investigate potential hazards, dangerous occurrences and the causes of accidents at the workplace;
– investigate health and safety complaints from employees;
– make representations to the employer on general health and safety matters, or arising out of the above investigations;
– carry out an inspection of any part of the workplace not inspected in the preceding 3 months, after giving the employer reasonable notice in writing;
– carry out inspection where there has been a substantial change in the conditions of work, or if the HSE or HSC have published new information relevant to the hazards of the workplace;
– carry out an inspection following a notifiable accident, dangerous occurrence or disease provided it is safe for the inspection to be carried out, and the interests of employees represented might be involved;
– receive information from health and safety inspectors who are obliged to provide factual information relating to health and safety in the premises inspected and any action, or proposed action, the inspector intends to take;
– attend safety committees in the capacity of a safety representative;
– receive reasonable time off with pay for health and safety training which is normally provided by the trade union. The employer is entitled to a copy of the syllabus of the course requested; and
– inspect and take copies of any document which the employer is legally required to keep under health and safety legislation and which is relevant to the workplace, or the employees represented, except a document consisting of, or relating to, the health record of an identifiable individual.

5014 Employers are obliged to provide safety representatives with **information** necessary to enable them to fulfil their functions **including**:
– information regarding the plans and performance of the undertaking if they affect health and safety;
– technical information about hazards to health and safety and precautions necessary to minimise or eliminate them;
– information the employer keeps on accidents, dangerous occurrences and notifiable diseases;
– results of measurements taken to check the effectiveness of health and safety arrangements (for example noise, ventilation or exposure levels of toxic materials); and
– information on articles or substances issued to homeworkers.

It does **not include**:
– information, the disclosure of which would be against the interests of national security, or is prohibited from being disclosed by law;
– any information relating specifically to an individual, unless consent has been obtained for its disclosure;

– any information which if disclosed would cause substantial injury to the employer's undertaking, for reasons other than health, safety or welfare, or such damage to the undertaking of another person where the information was supplied by that other person; and
– any information obtained by the employer for the purposes of bringing, prosecuting or defending legal proceedings.

Employers must provide safety representatives with **facilities and assistance** that may be required to enable the representatives to fulfil their functions. This would normally include providing information as needed, giving access to relevant parts of the workplace, facilitating independent investigation of accidents and private discussions with employees. 5015

Where at least two safety representatives request, in writing, that a **safety committee** be established, the employer must consult with the safety representatives and representatives of recognised trade unions whose members work at the workplace to establish it (reg 9 SI 1977/500). This includes determining the exact composition of a safety committee, details of its membership and terms of reference. The employer must then post a notice, stating the composition of the committee and the workplace(s) covered by it, where it can be easily read by employees. The committee must be set up within 3 months of the written request. 5017

Safety committees should include elected representatives and representatives of management, together with other functions such as safety advisers, personnel/HR managers and works engineers. The management representatives should have adequate authority to give proper consideration to views and recommendations of the committee and the number of management representatives should not exceed the number of employee representatives.

Establishments/groups of employees without recognised trade unions Employers who do not have recognised trade unions, or who have groups of employees who are not represented by a trade union, must also **consult employees** on the same matters, on which safety representatives must be consulted (see above) (regs 3, 4 Health and Safety (Consultation with Employees) Regulations SI 1996/1513). 5020

The consultation must be either with employees directly (for example, in a small workplace), or with elected representatives of employee safety, who have been elected by the workforce, or a group of employees within the workforce. The elected representatives must be employed within the group that elects them and this group can cover multiple sites if appropriate. Employers can decide on the appropriate groups and numbers of representatives and the frequency of elections.

Representatives of employee safety have **similar functions** to those of a safety representative listed above, with the exception of those relating to investigations and inspections and receiving information from (as opposed to consulting with) health and safety inspectors. 5022

Employers must provide such **facilities and assistance** as the representatives may reasonably require for the purposes of carrying out their functions.

Employers must provide representatives of employee safety with such **training** in respect of the representatives' functions under the regulations as is reasonable in all the circumstances (reg 7 SI 1996/1513). Employers must meet the reasonable costs associated with the training, including travel and subsistence costs. 5023

Time off

Safety representatives and representatives of employee safety have the right to paid time off to attend training and fulfil their functions and must allow candidates for election reasonable time off with pay. The **amount** of time off must be that which is reasonable in all the circumstances rather than what is necessary (*Duthie v Bath and North East Somerset Council* [2003] ICR 1405, EAT). 5030

Such employees have the right to be remunerated for time off for the work that would have otherwise been done (¶3940).

SECTION 5

Data protection issues

5040 Collecting, handling and retaining information about workers' health is intrusive and, in certain circumstances, may be highly intrusive. Further, workers have a **legitimate expectation** that they can keep information about their personal health private. However, employers may **need or wish to process** health information, for example, the employer may want the worker to:
- fill out a health questionnaire;
- be assessed as to his fitness with regard to a particular job or in relation to certain benefits;
- inform the employer of any disabilities or special needs;
- take an eye-test if he is a VDU user;
- if appropriate to his job, have blood tests, etc to ensure he has not been exposed to hazardous substances;
- partake in random alcohol or drugs testing;
- undertake genetic testing; and/or
- inform the employer of his vaccination and immunisation status and history.

As well as the following specific recommendations in relation to information concerning their workers' health, employers are also advised to follow the DP Code's **general recommendations** with regard to data management (¶6000).

To process such information, employers must ensure that they comply with the **data protection rules** (¶5945), for example, where the data is sensitive (¶5925), **consent** must be **explicit and freely given** before any sensitive data is processed **unless** it can be shown that it was necessary:
- to enable the employer to meet his legal obligations, for example a health and safety requirement;
- for medical purposes, for example, for the provision of care or treatment, and undertaken by a health professional or someone who has an equivalent duty of confidentiality; or
- for actual or prospective legal proceedings.

Consent should be specific to the health information required and employers must make sure it covers not only any testing but also any subsequent handling, using and retaining of the results. Blanket consent obtained at the start of employment may not be sufficient.

5041 **To process** any such data, the employer must be clear about its purpose and benefits and that they are justified (part 4.1 DP Code).

Employers must **assess**, preferably by impact assessment (¶6165), whether the benefits from processing such data can justify the intrusion into their workers' privacy or any other adverse impact it may have, unless they are under a legal duty to process the data, for example, the duty to monitor for exposure to hazardous materials. The effectiveness of any collection of data must also be considered in ascertaining whether it is a proportionate response to a particular problem. The possible **adverse impact** that may occur which should be taken into consideration include its intrusiveness, who will see the data, how it may affect the duty of mutual trust and confidence and whether such collection of data is oppressive or demeaning. **Alternatives** should be considered, where possible, to ascertain whether it really is necessary for the data to be collected and, if so, whether a less intrusive method than the one proposed could be used. Employers should be careful not to collect more information than is necessary (part 4.1.5 DP Code). For example, an employer should not seek a worker's consent to the disclosure of all or substantial parts of his GP records unless it is genuinely necessary, but should limited himself to the relevant issues. Further, if commissioning a medical report on a sick worker, the information requested should focus on the worker's fitness for continued employment rather than medical details (part 4.1.5 DP Code).

The business purpose of all testing should be **recorded** along with which sensitive data condition has been satisfied.

Employers must **take into account their obligations** as to how medical information can be securely handled in accordance with the data principles. Employers should ensure that, where possible, only suitably qualified health professionals have **access to medical information** (part 4.1.4 DP Code). Where managers need to access information about a worker's health this should be limited, as far as possible, to information that is necessary to establish fitness to work. Safety representatives should be provided with anonymised information unless workers have given consent to the information being identifiable. Medical information should, unless the general standard of information security is sufficiently high, be kept separately from other personnel information. 5042

Employers must always realise that the **interpretation** of any piece of medical information should be left to suitably qualified health professionals.

Workers should be made **aware** of how any health information is held and the reasons for it.

Medical examination and testing

Where an employer requires medical examination or testing, as **good practice**, he should (part 4.3 DP Code): 5045

a. make sure the rules and standards are clearly set out in a policy where the information to be obtained is to be used to enforce the employer's rules and standards. Workers must be made aware of the policy;

b. obtain information through medical examination or testing of applicants only where there is a real likelihood of appointing them and the testing is a necessary and justified measure to determine fitness for the job in question, meet any legal requirements or determine the worker's eligibility to join a pension or insurance scheme. Applicants should be informed early on in the recruitment process that medical testing may be required. Where possible, less intrusive methods should be used, for example a health questionnaire instead of a medical examination; and

c. obtain information through medical examination or testing of existing workers only where it is part of an occupational health and safety programme which workers can choose whether or not to join and the procedures are a necessary and justified measure to:

- prevent significant risk to the health and safety of the worker/workers;
- determine a worker's fitness in relation to his specific job;
- determine whether a worker is fit to return to work after having been off sick and if so when;
- determine a worker's entitlement to health-related benefits;
- prevent discrimination on the grounds of disability and assess whether reasonable adjustments should be made; or
- comply with any other legal obligations.

The **parameters** as to who should be tested should be set and what precisely should be tested, the frequency of the testing and the consequences of the results. Samples obtained from testing should never be used for **any other purpose** than that for which it was originally obtained unless the worker is informed and his consent obtained. Further, bodily samples should not be covertly obtained as it is highly unlikely that this will ever be justifiable.

Only information that is required for the purpose of the medical examination/testing should be **retained** if it is necessary to do so. All extraneous and irrelevant information should be destroyed. 5046

SECTION 6

Enforcement and remedies

A. Enforcement

5050 Enforcement of health and safety legislation is undertaken by the Health and Safety Executive (HSE) for most industrial premises, or the Environmental Health Department of the local authority for offices not forming part of an industrial site, shops and a range of other premises (The Health and Safety (Enforcing Authority) Regulations SI 1998/494). The HSE is also the enforcement authority in relation to the safety of articles and substances supplied for use at work. Fire safety legislation is enforced by the local fire authority.

Enforcement authorities employ **inspectors** who have a wide range of powers, including the power of entry into premises without prior notice. Inspectors can issue enforcement notices, or bring prosecutions, depending on the seriousness of the offence in question.

5051 The HSE have adopted a **"name and shame" policy** in relation to health and safety prosecutions. Details of organisations prosecuted under health and safety legislation and the penalties imposed are now listed on their website (www.hse.gov.uk). This policy is aimed at enhancing the deterrent effect of prosecution.

1. Enforcement notices and prosecutions

Employers

5055 Health and safety, and fire, inspectors can issue enforcement notices to **employers** for breach(es) of the health and safety/fire precaution rules. **Failure to comply** with the requirements of any enforcement notice is a serious offence, which can result in an unlimited fine and imprisonment. Whilst the employer on which the notice has been served will be vulnerable to prosecution for the breach of the notice, any director or senior manager who allows or connives with such a breach will also be liable to personal prosecution.

5056 **Health and safety inspectors** can issue two types of enforcement notice. Where an inspector is of the opinion that legal requirements are not being met, an **improvement notice** can be served requiring the contravention to be rectified in a specified period of time. This period will be at least 21 days. An **appeal** against the notice can be made to an employment tribunal within 21 days of the issue of the notice and if an appeal is brought the notice is suspended until the appeal is heard.

Where, however, the inspector is of the opinion that the activities being, or likely to be, undertaken involve a risk of serious personal injury, a **prohibition notice** can be served directing that the activities in question are stopped. A prohibition notice can either take immediate effect, or come into force after a specified period of time. An **appeal** can be brought against the issue of the notice in the same way as described for an improvement notice above, but the notice will still remain in force until the appeal is heard.

MEMO POINTS In 2003, the HSE served its first **improvement notice on workplace stress** to a Hospital NHS Trust. This was served following an investigation by an HSE inspector regarding concerns about workplace stress at the Trust. The improvement notice set out the requirement for the Trust to make a suitable risk assessment of the risk of stress.

5057 **Fire safety inspectors** can serve enforcement notices where the fire authority is of the opinion that there has been a failure to comply with any aspect of workplace fire precautions legislation (reg 30 SI 2005/1541). An **appeal** against the notice can be made to the magistrate's court within 21 days, but the notice will remain in force until the appeal is heard. **Prohibition notices** can also be served where the fire authority is of the opinion that the risk to persons on the premises, in the event of fire, is so serious that the use of the premises should be prohibited or restricted (reg 31 SI 2005/1541). If the fire authority is of the opinion that the risk is imminent, the notice can take effect immediately. The same appeal procedures apply as for enforcement notices.

Workers

Enforcement action may also be taken against workers. When enforcement officers discover a breach of the worker's statutory duty of care (¶4890), it will be their duty to consider what action (if any) they should take in regard to the worker, by way of warning, improvement notice or prosecution. Consultation with workers' representatives is important at this stage. 5060

More often than not a warning will suffice or perhaps action through the workers' representative or a safety committee. Prosecution should be considered only if the worker had been warned before (either by an enforcement officer or by his employer) or if his employer can demonstrate that he has taken all reasonably practicable steps to see that safety devices were used and the offence by the worker was flagrant.

2. Offences

Offences under health and safety/fire precautions rules

Prosecutions under health and safety, and fire precautions, legislation can be brought by the relevant enforcement authority in either a magistrate's court or the Crown Court (s 33 HSWA 1974; s 9 Fire Precautions Act 1971). The maximum penalties are as follows: 5065

Offence	Maximum Penalty in Magistrates Court	Maximum Penalty in Crown Court
Breach of a general duty imposed by the HSWA 1974	£20,000 fine	Unlimited fine
Breach of regulations made under HSWA 1974 where no other penalty is specified	£5,000 fine	Unlimited fine
Failing to comply with the requirements of a prohibition or improvement notice	£20,000 fine and 6 months imprisonment	Unlimited fine and 2 years imprisonment
Undertaking an activity that requires a licence without having a licence	£5,000	Unlimited fine and 2 years imprisonment
Failing to comply with the terms of a licence	£5,000	Unlimited fine and 2 years imprisonment
Offences related to explosives	£5,000	Unlimited fine and 2 years imprisonment

MEMO POINTS The Health and Safety at Work (Offences) Bill, which will **increase the maximum fines/penalties** that can be imposed for offences under health and safety/failure to maintain insurance, is currently before Parliament.

The courts have held that it was impossible to lay down a tariff or formula, but stated that both mitigating and aggravating factors need to be considered when imposing fines (*R v F Howe & Son (Engineers) Ltd* [1999] 2 All ER 249, CA): 5066

Mitigating factors include:
- prompt admission of responsibility and a timely plea of guilty;
- steps taken to remedy deficiencies after they were drawn to the defendant's attention; and
- a good safety record.

Aggravating factors include a failure to respond to warnings and where safety has been compromised by profit motive.

5067 Each case has to be dealt with according to its own particular circumstances. When setting the level of the fine the court will balance the need for the fine to be large enough to show managers and shareholders that it was important to provide a safe environment in the workplace with the financial circumstances of the offending company.

5068 Prosecutions will usually only follow an improvement or prohibition notice. The inspectors can, however, choose to prosecute without notice.

Personal liability of directors

5070 Where an offence under health and safety or fire precautions legislation is committed by a company, or other body corporate, it is possible for senior individuals within the organisation to be personally prosecuted (s 37 HSWA 1974; s 23 Fire Precautions Act 1971). This occurs if the offence was committed with the consent or connivance of, or can be attributable to any neglect on the part of, a director, company secretary or senior manager. An example would be where a director of a company fails to ensure that corrective action was taken knowing that a particular safety problem existed, or if he refused to authorise expenditure on essential health and safety training. An example of connivance would be wilfully turning a blind eye such as allowing dangerous machinery to be operated whilst pretending not to know of the practice.

The courts have held that this type of offence is only applicable to senior staff who have the power to decide corporate policy and strategy (*R v Boal* [1992] IRLR 420, CA).

Corporate manslaughter

5072 A company may be prosecuted for **gross negligence manslaughter** where there is sufficient evidence to show that there has been gross negligence on its part (*R v DPP, ex parte Jones* [2000] IRLR 373, QBD). The test for gross negligence is an objective one, and the ordinary principles of the law of negligence apply to ascertain whether there has been a breach of duty to the person who has died i.e. the existence of the duty and the breach of it causing death. It is for the jury to decide whether the breach of the duty should be characterised as gross negligence and therefore a crime (*R v Adomako* [1995] 1 AC 171, HL). The prosecution may take place regardless as to whether the company is being prosecuted for breaches of HSWA 1974.

A company may only be found guilty of manslaughter if an identified individual's conduct, characterised as gross negligence, can be attributable to the company. Where the employer is clearly in breach of his obligations it is immaterial whether the employee who contributed to the breach was part of the employer's senior management team or not.

EXAMPLE In *R v British Steel plc* [1995] IRLR 310, CA, the employer was liable for a breach of s 3 HSWA 1974 even though the incident occurred under the supervision of an engineer who was not a member of senior management. Section 3(1) HSWA 1974 contained an absolute prohibition and it was not necessary to attribute corporate liability only for acts of the directing mind of the company.

5073 In the **absence of an individual's gross negligence** a company cannot be liable for manslaughter. Whilst absence of evidence as to state of mind will not prejudice a claim of gross negligence manslaughter, the absence of evidence establishing the guilt of an identified human individual will. A statutorily-created defendant (e.g. a company) cannot be convicted of gross negligence manslaughter (*Attorney-General's Reference (No 2 of 1999)* [2000] IRLR 417, CA).

MEMO POINTS 1. **Prosecutions** for manslaughter against corporate bodies have to date been restricted to relatively small companies where the senior management of the company is closely identified with its day-to-day actions.

2. The corporate killing bill presented to Parliament in March 2004 as a private member's bill has lapsed. However, the Government is now committed to addressing this issue and has published a draft bill for **reforming corporate manslaughter**. The draft bill would introduce a new offence for holding organisations to account for gross failings by their senior management that have

had fatal consequences. This would enable prosecutions against companies and other statutorily created organisations without the need to attribute the cause of death to an individual's gross negligence.

Whilst prosecutions under general health and safety law are initiated by the health and safety enforcement authorities, prosecutions for manslaughter are initiated by the Crown Prosecution Service following information provided by the police. The HSE, CPS and Police services now have a joint protocol for the investigation of such accidents. This involves a senior police officer attending the scene of any workplace death to establish if there is any evidence for manslaughter charges and HSE inspectors passing information to the CPS where such evidence is discovered in the course of an investigation. 5074

B. Remedies

Damages

Where there is a breach of the employer's duty to take care, a worker will be able to make a claim for damages if the damages suffered were as a result of the breach and were reasonably foreseeable (**tortious claim**) or are not too remote (**contractual claim**). It should be noted that the courts and tribunals often do not distinguish between claims for damages brought under tort or contract and, in practice, the result will be the same. A worker can also bring his claim for damages as a **civil claim** arising from his employer's breach of statutory obligations relating to health and safety. See section 1 for further details about the employer's liability and the extent of damages recoverable. 5080

Where an injury is due, in part, to the worker's own actions, any damages awarded against his employer may be reduced on the basis of such **contributory negligence**.

Damages awarded by the courts are generally covered by the compulsory employer's liability insurance that the employer is required to hold. 5081

Time off for safety representatives/representatives of employee safety

Such representatives or candidates have the right to complain to an employment tribunal if their employer has **failed to allow** them to take time off to attend training or fulfil their functions or has failed to pay them for such time taken off. The **tribunal can** make an order for compensation or an award for payment where appropriate (¶3960). 5090

Pay during suspension on medical grounds

An employee who is suspended on medical grounds has the right to complain to an employment tribunal if his employer **fails to pay him** during the period of suspension (¶4862). The **tribunal can** order the employer to pay the amount due (s 70 ERA 1996). 5092

Maternity-related rights

An employee who has been suspended by her employer on the grounds that she is pregnant, has given birth or is breastfeeding is entitled to be paid during the period of that suspension (s 68 ERA 1996). If her employer **fails to pay her** she may bring a claim before an employment tribunal and the tribunal can order the employer to pay her the amount that is due to her (s 70 ERA 1996). Furthermore, if her employer has **failed to offer** her alternative work, where it is appropriate to do so prior to her suspension, the tribunal can also award her compensation for the infringement of her rights and for any loss she has sustained as a result. 5093

Whistleblowing

5094 If an employee is concerned that his employer is failing in his responsibility to his employees' health and safety, or has a reasonable belief that there is a danger to the health and safety of any individual(s), he has **special protection** in certain circumstances if he discloses such facts (¶2700).

Constructive dismissal

5096 If the employer fails in his duty to take reasonable care, his breach may amount to a **fundamental breach of contract**, allowing the employee to bring a claim for constructive dismissal (¶8230).

Right not to be unfairly dismissed or suffer a detriment

5097 The following health and safety reasons are inadmissible reasons for the purpose of **automatic** (i.e. no qualifying period of service is required) unfair dismissal (s 100 ERA 1996):
- the employee was or proposed to be involved in activities relating to, preventing or reducing health and safety risks (having been designated by the employer to do so);
- the employee was acting or proposing to act as a health and safety representative or member of a safety committee, either in accordance with statutory arrangement or having been acknowledged by the employer as such;
- the employee took, or proposed to take, part in health and safety consultation or in an election of employee safety representatives (as a candidate or otherwise);
- the employee brought to the employer's attention by reasonable means circumstances relating to his work which he reasonably believed are or could be harmful to health and safety and where there is no health and safety representative or committee at the workplace or it was not reasonably practicable for him to raise the matter through those means. Reasonable means does not include unlawful industrial action (*Balfour Kilpatrick Ltd v Acheson and others* [2003] IRLR 683, EAT);
- the employee left, proposed to leave or refused to return to his workplace, believing there to be serious and imminent danger (from the workplace or other employees) which he would not reasonably be expected to avert; and
- the employee took, or was proposing to take, appropriate steps (determined by reference to all the circumstances, including his knowledge and the facilities and advice available to him at the time) to protect himself or others (not restricted to other employees) from what he reasonably believed to be serious and imminent danger.

EXAMPLE In *Harvent Press Ltd MaGaffee* [1999] IRLR 778, EAT, M was dismissed after he left his workplace in the middle of a shift because the abusive behaviour of a fellow worker made him fear for his safety. The EAT held that dangers caused by the behaviour of fellow employees are within the wide scope of the statutory protection.

5098 Further, employees have the right not to suffer detrimental actions on the same reason(s) or ground(s), as above (s 44 ERA 1996).

CHAPTER 16

Equality at work

OUTLINE ¶¶

5200 Discrimination on the grounds of **sex**, **race**, **disability**, **religion or belief**, **or sexual orientation** is prohibited. The most common **remedy** for a successful complaint is compensation and, unlike for general unfair dismissals, there is no cap on the amount which may be awarded where the worker has been dismissed due to discrimination.

As well as protection against **inequality of pay** with regard to workers of the opposite sex provided under the sex discrimination legislation, there is also a separate and additional form of action regarding equal pay and this is discussed separately in section 2 (¶5600).

MEMO POINTS It is expected that discrimination on the grounds of **age** will become unlawful from October 2006.

5201 Discrimination and/or inequality of pay may also give rise to:
- **non-discriminatory claims** under **other legislation**. For example, it is also automatically unfair to dismiss an employee or to subject a worker to any detrimental action short of dismissal in certain circumstances, say if the reason for such action is due to his taking part in protected industrial action or due to whistleblowing. Likewise, the employer, depending on the circumstances, may also find that he faces a complaint for redundancy and/or breach of other related legislation (for example, the Part-time Workers (Prevention of Less Favourable Treatment) Regulations SI 2000/1551);
- **common law claims**, for example, psychiatric injury; and/or
- **contractual claims**, for example, constructive dismissal and breach of the duty of mutual trust and confidence.

5203 Furthermore, a worker who experiences workplace **bullying** due to specific characteristics unrelated to grounds of sex, racial group, disability, religion or belief, or sexual orientation may suffer, and bring a claim for, psychiatric injury, including stress (¶4945). A claim may also be brought under the Protection from Harassment Act 1997. This legislation was originally introduced to provide protection from stalkers, but has been held to apply to harassment and bullying at work, and has also been used to restrain former aggressive employees (*First Global Locums Ltd and others v Cosias* [2005] EWHC 1147 (QB)). In addition, there could be other implications for employers since bullied members of staff may resign and, in certain circumstances, claim to have been constructively dismissed. Employers should therefore try to ensure workplace bullying is prevented by making workers aware of the issue in staff policies or, when it arises, dealing with it satisfactorily.

MEMO POINTS If a company procedure exists to address bullying in the workplace, it should be used. However, the procedure does not displace an employer's fundamental obligation to take reasonable steps to ensure that an employee is supported in times of difficulty (*Blackburn with Darwen Borough Council v Stanley*, EAT case 0429/04).

Illustrations of, and the effect of, discrimination and inequality regarding pay in the following **specific areas** of the employment relationship are also discussed outside this chapter: 5204

Illustrations of sex, racial and disability discrimination in relation to:	Para.
Pre-employment: advertisements, recruitment and selection procedures	Chapter 2 generally
Terms of employment including mobility clauses	¶¶1330, 1625
Training	¶¶6340, 6345
Appraisal and promotion	¶6468
Pensions	¶3435

Illustrations of sex discrimination in relation to:	Para.
Flexible working	Chapter 6
Pregnancy and maternity leave	Chapter 14

SECTION 1

Discrimination

To aid the reader in comprehending the five types of discrimination, we have brought together **key concepts** that recur throughout the anti-discrimination provisions. 5210

Further, we have brought together similar types of discrimination to give **three basic groups**:
- sex (including gender reassignment, marital and civil partnership status) and sexual orientation;
- racial and religion or belief; and
- disability.

For ease of reference, throughout this chapter the various strands of discrimination are **coded** as follows: S: Sex; SO: Sexual orientation; R: Race; RB: Religion or belief; D: Disability; and E: Equal pay. The three main acts are also abbreviated for ease of reference as follows: the Disability Discrimination Act 1995 (DDA 1995); the Sex Discrimination Act 1975 (SDA 1975) and the Race Relations Act 1976 (RRA 1976).

I. Key concepts

1. Scope

The scope of the legislation **covers** job applicants, workers (including those working under a contract of apprenticeship) and, in certain circumstances, ex-workers. 5215

Workers who work **wholly or partly in GB** are covered.

Generally, workers are excluded if they work, or it is contemplated that they will work, **wholly outside GB**. However, even if a worker works wholly outside GB, he will still be covered by the legislation if (S: s 10(1), (1A) SDA 1975, as amended by reg 11 Employment Equality (Sex Discrimination) Regulations SI 2005/2467; SO: reg 9 Employment Equality (Sexual Orientation) Regulations SI 2003/1661; R: s 8(1), (1A) RRA 1976; RB: reg 9 Employment Equality (Religion or Belief) Regulations SI 2003/1660; D: s 68(2), (2A) DDA 1995):

– his employer has a place of business at an establishment in GB;
– the work is for the purposes of the business carried on at that establishment; and
– the worker is ordinarily resident in GB at the time he applies for or is offered the employment or at any time during the course of that employment.

The **whole period of employment** should be taken into account to determine whether the employee works wholly outside Great Britain and tribunals should not focus only on the location of employment during the alleged discrimination (*Saggar v Ministry of Defence* [2005] IRLR 618, CA).

5216 Consequently, protection from discrimination is provided in respect of the following periods:

5218 **Before employment** Job applicants are specifically covered in respect of discrimination in the arrangements made by an employer in determining who should be offered a job, in the terms offered to applicants, and regarding an employer's refusal or deliberate omission to offer a worker a job (S: s 6(1) SDA 1975; SO: reg 6(1) Employment Equality (Sexual Orientation) Regulations SI 2003/1661; R: s 4(1) RRA 1976; RB: reg 6(1) Employment Equality (Religion or Belief) Regulations SI 2003/1660; D: s 4 DDA 1995).

5220 **During employment** Workers are covered in respect of discrimination which occurs during the employment relationship. Specifically, an employer must not discriminate in the way he affords access to opportunities for promotion, transfer or training, or any other benefits, facilities or services, or by refusing or deliberately omitting to afford such access, or by dismissing or subjecting a worker to any other detriment (S: s 6(2) SDA 1975; SO: reg 3(2) Employment Equality (Sexual Orientation) Regulations SI 2003/1661; R: s 4(2) RRA 1976; RB: reg 6(2) Employment Equality (Religion or Belief) Regulations SI 2003/1660; D: s 4 DDA 1995).

5222 **Post-employment** Ex-workers are covered in respect of discrimination and/or harassment after the employment relationship has ended (whether or not the act took place before the statutory provisions came into force), where it arises out of and is closely connected to that relationship (S: s 20A SDA 1975, as inserted by reg 3 SI 2003/1657 and reg 21 Employment Equality (Sex Discrimination) Regulations SI 2005/2467; SO: reg 21 SI 2003/1661; R: s 27A RRA 1976, as inserted by reg 29 SI 2003/1626, except in relation to colour and nationality: *Rhys Harper v Relaxion Group plc, and joined cases* [2003] IRLR 484, HL; RB: reg 21 SI 2003/1660; D: s 16A DDA 1995, as inserted by reg 15 SI 2003/1673).

2. Liability

Employer

5225 The scope of an employer's liability for a discriminatory act is wide and can cover:

5226 **Employer's acts** An employer can be **directly liable** for any unlawful discriminatory acts which he commits.

5227 **Workers' and agents' acts** An employer will be liable for his workers' acts which are carried out (S: s 41 SDA 1975; SO: reg 22(1) SI 2003/1661; R: s 32 RRA 1976; RB: reg 22(1) SI 2003/1660; D: s 58(1) DDA 1995):
– "in the course of their employment" whether or not it is done with the employer's knowledge or approval; or
– with the authority (express or implied) of the employer.

For example, implied or express authority of the employer for a discriminatory act may occur when an employment agency advertises a vacancy or selects job applicants.

5228 In the "**course of employment**" is to be interpreted in the sense in which the phrase is used in everyday layman's language and, accordingly, is said to include all acts committed **at work**, whether or not these acts are associated with the worker's duties (*Jones v Tower Boot Co Ltd* [1997] IRLR 168, CA). This is often described as establishing a sufficient "nexus" between the act and the job. For example, if a worker of a certain ethnic origin is repeatedly subjected to racist and physical abuse by colleagues at work, his employer is likely to be found liable for his other workers' behaviour when the worker resigns and complains of racial discrimination and constructive dismissal.

Even acts committed **outside working hours** and/or the **place of employment** can give rise to liability on the part of the employer if the acts were committed in circumstances connected to the employment. For example, if the acts occurred following a work conference or during or after a work drinks leaving party.

EXAMPLE In *Chief Constable of Lincolnshire Constabulary v Stubbs* [1999] IRLR 81, EAT, inappropriate sexual behaviour at an after-work drink and at a work-related leaving party was held to be sufficiently work-related to be in the course of the perpetrator's employment.

Lack of knowledge or approval by the employer of the discriminatory act is no defence. 5229
However, the employer will have a **defence** in such circumstances if he can establish that he took such **steps** as were reasonably practicable to prevent the worker or agent from committing the discriminatory act in question, or acts of that description/nature (S: s 41(3) SDA 1975; SO: reg 22(3) SI 2003/1661; R: s 32(3) RRA 1976; RB: reg 22(3) SI 2003/1660; D: s 58(5) DDA 1995). Only steps which the employer has taken **before the discriminatory act** took place are relevant and an employer cannot rely only on acts he has taken to remedy the discrimination (*Carter v Westcliff Hall Sidmouth Ltd*, ET case 31165/90).

EXAMPLE No defence

In *Chessington World of Adventures Ltd v Reed* [1997] IRLR 556, EAT, an employer was held vicariously liable for sex discrimination where he allowed the sexual harassment of a worker to take place by other employees in circumstances in which he could have prevented the harassment from occurring.

Defence

In *Balgobin & another v London Borough of Tower Hamlets* [1987] IRLR 401, EAT, where an employer had set up and made his workers aware of an appropriate equal opportunities policy and had provided adequate staff supervision, he was not held liable for discriminatory acts of which he was unaware.

Third parties' acts An employer may also be liable for the acts of third parties, for 5231
example clients and independent contractors, if the detrimental act was caused or permitted in circumstances in which the employer had sufficient control over whether or not the act happens and that the employer's failure to take reasonable steps to protect his employees from the discriminatory act was itself for a reason connected to the worker's sex or race (S & R: *Burton v De Vere Hotels* [1996] IRLR 596, EAT, as limited by *Pearce v Governing Body of Mayfield School* heard with *MacDonald (AP) v Advocate General for Scotland* [2003] IRLR 512, HL; D: *Ree v Redrow Homes (Yorkshire) Ltd*, EAT case 0035/03). It is expected that the same principles will apply to discrimination on the grounds of sexual orientation and religion or belief.

Consequently, employers must exercise good management to protect their staff whenever possible, for example, where appropriate, the employer could ask third parties to sign and adhere to his equal opportunities policy and/or instruct his staff to overview the conduct of a third party.

MEMO POINTS The decision in *Ree v Redrow Homes (Yorkshire) Ltd*, above, extended the principle laid down in *Burton v De Vere Hotels* (which had applied to sex and racial discrimination) to disability discrimination but it is expected that the limitation applied to *Burton v De Vere Hotels* in *Pearce v Governing Body of Mayfield School* is also extended to disability discrimination.

Worker

Where an unlawful discriminatory act is committed during the course of employment then, 5233
in addition to the employer's vicarious liability, **personal liability** can attach to the worker who performed the act (S: s 42 SDA 1975; SO: reg 23 SI 2003/1661; R: s 33 RRA 1976; RB: reg 27 SI 2003/1660; D: s 57 DDA 1995).

The worker will not escape liability even if the employer has a good defence (for example, 5234
that all reasonable steps to prevent the discrimination had been taken).

A worker has a **defence**, however, if he:
– acts in reliance on his employer's statement that he would not be acting unlawfully if he did the specific act; and
– it was reasonable for him to so rely on it.

EXAMPLE An organisation which has relied on word-of-mouth recruitment tells one of its supervisors to fill a vacancy "in the usual way." This is potentially (indirectly) discriminatory because it excludes persons from a different background for consideration. However, the supervisor may not be liable under this defence. By contrast, if he is instructed to eliminate Asian women from a recruitment exercise, he would be unable to claim that he reasonably believed this to be a lawful instruction and would not have a defence.

Other groups/bodies

5236 Further, the following groups can be also liable and are discussed in the relevant specific topics:

Liability of:	Para.
Trade unions, workers'/employers' organisations	¶7156
Authorities/bodies conferring an authorisation or qualification	¶6345
Providers/arrangers of vocational training	¶6348
Occupational pension scheme trustees/managers	¶3435

3. Forms of discrimination

Direct discrimination and victimisation

5240 **Direct discrimination** is arguably the most overt or easily-recognisable form of discrimination. This occurs when a person makes assumptions and judgements about another person based on inappropriate factors (for example, their race, religion, or sexual orientation) and, on such grounds, treats that person less favourably than others. Direct discrimination can also occur where an employee is treated less favourably because of someone else's religion, belief or race. The ambit of direct discrimination is therefore quite wide.

Victimisation is a specific form of direct discrimination. It occurs when a person is treated less favourably because he has previously made a complaint or assisted another in bringing a claim against the employer, provided his complaint was well-founded and made in good faith.

5241 Discrimination after the **employment relationship has ended** is a relatively uncommon form of direct discrimination or victimisation, but can have a significant impact on a former employee's future employment. The most common situation in which it is likely to occur is when an employee has left his employment and his employer has provided him with a discriminatory reference or has refused to provide him with a reference for discriminatory reasons.

5242 In certain circumstances, direct discrimination against job applicants and workers can be **justified** if there is a genuine occupational qualification or requirement for a particular position.

It may also be lawful, in certain circumstances, for an employer to give **preferential treatment** to an employee or group of employees. The rationale behind positive action is to recognise that some sections of the workforce may be under-represented and to rectify this under-representation or to compensate for certain disadvantages which particular employees or groups of employees might experience because of their particular characteristics. This does not mean that employers are permitted to positively discriminate, for example, they cannot use quotas or reserve jobs for particular individuals.

Indirect discrimination

Indirect discrimination occurs when an employer applies a **policy**, **provision**, **criterion or working practice** which, although on the face of it is neutral and applicable equally to all workers, in fact inadvertently puts a certain group of workers (for example, women or people of a certain religion) at a disadvantage in comparison to other workers. 5245

In certain circumstances, indirectly discriminatory provisions can be **justified** if the disadvantage suffered is proportionately balanced against the needs of the employer in the successful running of his business.

Harassment

Harassment occurs if, on grounds relating to sex, racial group, disability, sexual orientation, or religion or belief, a worker is subjected to **unwanted conduct** from his employer or another worker which has either the effect or purpose of violating his dignity or creating an intimidating, hostile, degrading, humiliating or offensive environment. 5246

Harassment after the employment relationship has ended, although relatively uncommon, can occur.

Bullying

Bullying is a more general term for unwanted conduct that has a detrimental effect on a worker's health or morale. More often than not, the **cause or underlying motive** for the bullying is connected to an individual's gender or membership of a particular group under one of the specific types of discrimination, and may well lead to a claim for indirect discrimination or harassment. However, if the bullying is a result of purely **specific characteristics** of that individual, which cannot be related to his/her gender or membership of a particular group, then there is no recourse under the discrimination or harassment provisions. 5247

Bullying in the workplace may also result in other, non-discriminatory implications and potential claims (¶5203).

II. Specific types of discrimination

Discrimination on the grounds of **sex**, **race**, **disability**, **religion or belief** and **sexual orientation** (save in certain circumstances outlined below) is prohibited (SDA 1975, as amended; RRA 1976, as amended; DDA 1995, as amended; Employment Equality (Religion or Belief) Regulations SI 2003/1660; Employment Equality (Sexual Orientation) Regulations SI 2003/1661). 5250

MEMO POINTS 1. There are various **Codes of Practice** which give practical guidance and provide examples of best practice to help employers ensure that they eliminate inequality. Whilst these Codes are not legally binding on employers, tribunals hearing an inequality claim must take into account any of the relevant Code's provisions which apply to that particular case. They are as follows:

– Code of Practice – Sex Discrimination (SD Code) published by the Equal Opportunities Commission (EOC).

– Code of Practice on racial equality in employment (RD Code) published by the Commission for Racial Equality (CRE). At the time of writing, a revised Code is awaited.

– Code of Practice on employment and occupation (DD Code) published by the Disability Rights Commission (DRC) (revised October 2004). In addition to the Code, the Secretary of State has issued Guidance notes to help employers understand the DDA 1995 (Guidance on matters to be taken into account in determining questions relating to the definition of disability (referred to as the Disability Guidance notes)). These are also not legally binding on employers yet they provide practical examples which must be taken into account by tribunals when dealing with disability discrimination complaints.

– Guidance on Sexual Orientation in the Workplace and Guidance on Religion or Belief in the Workplace published by ACAS.

2. Where **gender is of particular relevance**, 'he/she' will be used instead of 'he' in this section when referring to a worker/complainant.

5251 **Legal framework** Revisions to the race and sex discrimination legislation, together with the introduction of new provisions relating to discrimination on the grounds of religion or belief and sexual orientation, were made during 2003 resulting mostly from the implementation of two European Directives (EC Race Directive 2000/43; EC Employment Framework Directive 2000/78). Significant amendments to the disability legislation were introduced in October 2004. Further revisions have been made which update the Sex Discrimination Act 1975 and implement the Equal Treatment Amendment Directive (EC Directive 2002/73) provisions regarding harassment. These changes came into force in October 2005.

The Disability Discrimination Act 2005 (the relevant provisions of which are summarised where appropriate in this chapter) has also been passed and came into force in December 2005. Finally, at the time of writing, draft age discrimination regulations which are due to implement the remainder of the Employment Framework Directive (above) have been published and will be laid before Parliament in early 2006. The regulations, which are expected to come into force on 1 October 2006, are summarised below at ¶5254.

5252 As a result of the numerous changes that have taken place over the last couple of years, the existing discrimination framework is complex. However, with a few exceptions, it can be seen that greater **harmonisation** between the provisions governing the different strands of discrimination within the legislative framework has been achieved. This is principally because the majority of the new provisions and amendments originate from Europe. However, it should be noted that despite this increased uniformity, without specific clarification by the tribunals and courts, the **existing case law on sex and racial discrimination** cannot be taken as interpreting the relatively new law on sexual orientation and religion or belief. Consequently, at present, such cases can only be used for guidance as to how the tribunals and courts may or are likely to act (it is expected that more case law regarding religion or belief and sexual orientation will come through as the legislation beds down).

Further, on the whole, the **source** of the sexual orientation and religion or belief provisions is statutory whereas, because of the way the law has developed, the equivalent provisions with regard to sex and race are found in both statute and case law.

For these two reasons it is **necessary to distinguish** between **statutory and case references** for the various types of discrimination and they are therefore coded, as set out at ¶5210.

MEMO POINTS 1. The UK regulations on sexual orientation and religion or belief are, generally speaking, consistent in their treatment of the key concepts with the sex and racial discrimination rules. There are fewer common characteristics with the disability discrimination rules which, due to the nature of the protection provided, use different phraseology. However, the differences with the disability rules have diminished since the introduction of various amendments to the DDA 1995 on 1 October 2004 (Disability Discrimination Act 1995 (Amendment) Regulations SI 2003/1673). See ¶5452 for further details.

2. In certain circumstances, the UK implementing regulations offer greater protection than that provided for in the Race and Employment Framework Directives (for example, the definition in the regulations of 'harassment' is wider than the definition stipulated in the Directives) as a result of the principle of 'non-regression' (i.e. that new domestic legislation which implements EU laws cannot provide less generous protection than that previously enjoyed under the old domestic rules).

Age discrimination

5254 Discriminating on the grounds of age potentially prejudices both the young and old and can have a fundamental impact on the workplace.

At the time of writing, age discrimination is not specifically prohibited in the UK. However, as a result of the Employment Framework Directive, it is expected that direct and indirect age discrimination will become **unlawful from** 1 October 2006.

MEMO POINTS **Conduct** which effectively amounts to age discrimination has been held to be **unlawful on other grounds**.

For example, on the grounds of **sex**, it is unlawful for employers to stipulate different retirement ages for men and women or to provide male and female workers with different benefits under a pension scheme, as maximum age limits often prejudice women more than they do men (*Barber v Guardian Royal Exchange Assurance Group* [1990] IRLR 240, ECJ).

However, the challenge to the **upper age limit** to claim unfair dismissal on the ground that it is indirectly discriminatory against men failed before the Court of Appeal (*Rutherford and another v Secretary of State for Trade & Industry* [2004] IRLR 892, CA), although the House of Lords has agreed to hear an appeal.

The EAT has also heard a claim in which British Airways' **retirement age** of 55 for staff who joined the company after 1971 was challenged on the basis that it was indirectly discriminatory against women due to historical bargaining arrangements. The EAT agreed that whilst there was an adverse effect on women, such an effect could be justified due to the financial and organisational implications for the company (*Cross and ors v British Airways plc*, EAT case 0572/04). At the time of writing, this decision is also being appealed.

Age requirements have also been held to be indirectly discriminatory on the grounds of **race**, in relation to foreign applicants who have not been in the UK for very long or who have had to serve a period of time doing national service rather than completing their higher education (*Perera v Civil Service Commission and another (No 2)* [1983] ICR 428, CA).

The Government has published **draft** Employment Equality (Age) Regulations 2006, together with the final consultation document on age discrimination (Equality and Diversity: Coming of Age). The progress of, and any subsequent amendments to, the draft regulations will be outlined in future updates and newsletters and the next edition of this book will provide a detailed examination of age discrimination legislation. 5255

As the legislation will have potentially wide-ranging ramifications on many employment policies and practices ranging from pre-employment issues through to dismissal, it is recommended that employers **review their existing arrangements** to ensure that any potentially discriminatory policy or practice is removed **before October 2006**. To assist with this process, a summary of the key draft proposals is provided below. The draft regulations will also have a large impact on occupational pension schemes, retirement ages, redundancy and the law regarding unfair dismissal and these proposals will be noted in the relevant subject topics at ¶3444, ¶8207, ¶8990+ and ¶8390+ respectively.

Proposed direct and indirect The draft regulations propose that **direct** age discrimination will become unlawful where a person is treated less favourably on the grounds of his actual or apparent age, when compared with the treatment of another person in the same, or not materially different, circumstances. 5256

The draft regulations propose that **indirect** age discrimination will become unlawful when an employer applies to a worker:

- a provision, criterion or practice which is applied or would apply equally to a person of a different age group;
- which puts or would put members of the same age group as that worker at a particular disadvantage when compared with others; and
- puts the worker at that disadvantage.

5257

Both direct and indirect age discrimination may be **justified and lawful** if it is a proportionate means of achieving a legitimate aim. This is not the case under most of the other strands of discrimination legislation, under which direct discrimination can usually only be justified under narrow grounds (such as positive action or where there is a genuine occupational qualification or requirement (¶¶5280+, 5397+)). **Examples** are provided in the draft regulations of circumstances where direct age discrimination may pursue a legitimate aim, such as fixing a minimum age to qualify for certain advantages linked to employment or occupation in order to recruit or retain older people. Readers should note that these examples are not exemptions and an employer would still need to demonstrate that, in his circumstances, the discrimination pursues a legitimate aim and is a proportionate means of achieving that aim.

As noted above in relation to most other strands of discrimination legislation, age discrimination may also be **lawful** where positive action or genuine occupational requirements apply.

Positive action constitutes:

- providing individuals of a particular age or age group with access to facilities for vocational training; or

– encouraging individuals of a particular age or age group to take advantage of employment opportunities.

It is expected that both circumstances will be lawful if it reasonably appears that taking such steps will prevent, or compensate for, disadvantages linked to age suffered by people of that age or age group, doing that work or likely to take up that work. However, these provisions do not permit positive discrimination.

A **genuine occupational requirement** (GOR) may be relied on by an employer where, having regard to the nature of the employment or the context in which it is carried out, possessing an age-related characteristic is a genuine and determining occupational requirement and it is proportionate to apply that requirement in the particular case. Age can constitute a GOR in relation to recruitment, promotion, transfer, training and dismissal.

MEMO POINTS In addition to positive action and GORs, there are a **number of specific exemptions** where age-based requirements will be justified, including:
1. **statutory authority or provisions**. Where a statutory authority or provision operates to discriminate on the grounds of age, any act undertaken in order to comply with that authority or provision will be lawful. Age-based criteria are often applied in legislation: the consultation document provides the example of the Licensing Act 1964, which prohibits employing people under 18 in a bar when it is open for the sale or consumption of alcohol.
2. **national minimum wage**. The age bands contained in national minimum wage legislation (¶2865+) will also remain lawful. However, where employees in the lower age group and employees in the adult age group are paid at different levels, but both at or above the adult rate of the national minimum wage, there is no longer any reason to provide a special exemption based on the national minimum wage and the normal rules on objective justification will apply; and
3. **service-related pay and benefits**. These provisions comprise a general provision and two specific exemptions, all of which rely on length of service as a criterion to award or increase benefits. The provisions relate to pay and non-pay benefits, such as annual leave or company cars.
In respect of the **general provision**, any length of service requirement for employment benefits will be lawful if:
– awarding or increasing the benefit is meant to reflect the higher level of experience of the employee, reward loyalty or increase or maintain motivation;
– the employer has reasonably concluded that there will be a business benefit resulting from the higher level of experience of staff or from rewarding staff loyalty or increasing or maintaining staff motivation; and
– the employer applies the length of service criterion similarly to staff in similar situations.
The two **specific exemptions** are as follows:
– any length of service requirement of 5 years or less will be exempted and can continue if it is applied to all staff doing similar work; and
– any length of service requirement which mirrors a similar requirement in a statutory benefit will be exempted and can continue.

5258 **Proposed victimisation** The draft regulations propose that victimisation on the grounds of age will become **unlawful** if a worker is subjected to **less favourable treatment** than others by reason that he has:
– brought proceedings under the regulations against his employer or any other worker;
– given evidence or information in connection with such proceedings brought by another person against his employer or any other worker;
– taken any other action under or by reference to the regulations; or
– made any allegation against his employer or any other worker which would amount to a contravention of the regulations.

A worker will not be protected under these provisions if his allegation, evidence or information is false and not in good faith.

5259 **Proposed harassment** The draft regulations propose that harassment on the grounds of age will become **unlawful** if a worker has been subjected to **unwanted conduct**, which has the purpose or effect of:
– violating his dignity; or
– creating an intimidating, hostile, degrading, humiliating or offensive environment.

Conduct will only be regarded as having the above effect under the draft regulations if, having regard to all the circumstances, including the **worker's perception**, it should be reasonably considered as having that effect.

A. Sex and sexual orientation

Sex and sexual orientation discrimination is **divided** into direct discrimination (including victimisation), indirect discrimination and harassment. 5260

MEMO POINTS 1. The principal legislation governing sex and sexual orientation discrimination is the SDA 1975 and the Employment Equality (Sexual Orientation) Regulations SI 2003/1661 respectively.
2. Before 1 December 2003, discrimination on the grounds of sexual orientation was not unlawful in the UK (*Grant v South-West Trains Ltd* [1998] IRLR 206, ECJ) and no protection was provided by the SDA 1975 (*Pearce v Governing Body of Mayfield School* heard with *MacDonald (AP) v Advocate General for Scotland* [2003] IRLR 512, HL) except in very limited circumstances (*Smith v Gardner Merchant Ltd* [1998] IRLR 520, CA).

Sex discrimination

Sex discrimination is most commonly **defined** as discrimination based on a person's gender (i.e. the fact that a person is male or female). However, other instances of discrimination which are unique to sex discrimination include discrimination on grounds of: 5261
- marital or civil partnership status (i.e. the fact that a person is married or a civil partner (but not because he/she is single) (¶5325));
- the fact that a person has undergone, is undergoing or intends to undergo gender reassignment (¶5335);
- workplace dress code (¶5826);
- pregnancy, childbirth and maternity leave (¶5320); and
- flexible working (Chapter 6).

Both **female and male workers** are protected in equal terms, except obviously in relation to discrimination on grounds of pregnancy/maternity or childbirth and paternity.

MEMO POINTS The legislation refers to less favourable treatment on the ground of the **complainant's own sex** only (s 1(1)(a) SDA 1975). This is in contrast to the definitions of direct discrimination in the race, religion or belief or sexual orientation regulations.

Sexual orientation

Sexual orientation is **defined** as a sexual orientation towards persons of the (reg 2(1) SI 2003/1661): 5262
- same sex;
- opposite sex; or
- same sex and of the opposite sex.

Extended scope A worker is protected against discrimination even if the discrimination is on the grounds of **someone else's sexual orientation** (reg 3(1)(a) SI 2003/1661, as discrimination is "on grounds of sexual orientation" which is not limited to the complainant's sexual orientation). Consequently, a worker can bring proceedings if he/she objects to instructions given by an employer to discriminate on grounds of sexual orientation or the worker is discriminated against because his/her friends are gay. 5263

Moreover, less favourable treatment based on the **employer's or another employee's perception** of an individual's sexual orientation, whether that perception is rightly or wrongly held, is also covered. For example, there could be unlawful discrimination if an individual is treated less favourably because he/she is thought to look gay or is rumoured to be bisexual. It is not essential for a complainant to show **proof** of his/her orientation in order to bring a claim based on his/her perceived sexual orientation, but it is likely that the fact of a complainant's sexual orientation will emerge during tribunal proceedings.

1. Direct

5265 Direct discrimination is unlawful though there are certain exceptions and legal requirements which can result in lawful discrimination.

a. Unlawful

5270 Direct sex and sexual orientation discrimination occurs where there is "**less favourable treatment**" of an individual, **compared** with the treatment of another person of the opposite sex/of a different sexual orientation in the same, or not materially different, circumstances on the grounds of sex (of the individual concerned) or sexual orientation (S: ss 1(2)(a), 5(3) SDA 1975; SO: reg 3(1)(a), (2) SI 2003/1661).

Specifically, an employer is prohibited from discriminating against **job applicants and employees** (S: s 6 SDA 1975; SO: reg 6 SI 2003/1661):
– in the arrangements he makes for the purposes of determining who should be offered a position;
– in the employment terms and conditions on which he offers an individual a position;
– by refusing or deliberately omitting to offer an individual a position;
– in the way he affords access to opportunities for promotion, transfer or training, or to any other benefits, facilities or services, or by refusing or deliberately omitting to afford access to such opportunities and benefits; or
– by dismissing an individual, or subjecting him/her to any other detriment.

Moreover, it is unlawful for a person who has authority over another person or, in accordance with whose wishes that other person is accustomed to act, to give **instructions** to, or put **pressure** on, another person **to discriminate** against a worker on the grounds of sex (S: ss 39, 40 SDA 1975; SO: there is no express equivalent provisions in the Employment Equality (Sexual Orientation) Regulations SI 2003/1661, but see notes regarding extended scope of the regulations above). Only the EOC can bring proceedings in respect of unlawful instructions to discriminate on the grounds of sex, but currently there is no equivalent statutory body in respect of sexual orientation (¶5790).

MEMO POINTS Under amendments to the Employment Equality (Sexual Orientation) Regulations SI 2003/1661 which came into force at the same time (5 December 2005) as the Civil Partnership Act 2004 (an Act which gives same-sex couples the right to form a civil partnership and gain legal recognition of their relationship), the status of a **civil partner** will be comparable to a spouse. Therefore the fact that a person is married as compared to a being a civil partner will not be treated as a **material difference** for these purposes.

5271 It is irrelevant whether the alleged discrimination is **intentional** or not (S: *R v Birmingham City Council, ex parte Equal Opportunities Commission* [1989] IRLR 173, HL; *James v Eastleigh Borough Council* [1990] ICR 554, HL; SO: the regulations are silent as to whether any degree of intent is necessary for there to be a finding of unlawful discrimination or harassment, but it is expected that intention is not a relevant factor).

EXAMPLE Examples of direct sex discrimination:
1. In *Eke v Commission of Customs and Excise* [1981] IRLR 334, EAT, E, a worker, complained to her employer that she had been subjected to sexual harassment. Her employer refused to investigate the allegations and it was held that if the refusal to investigate the complaint was on grounds of her sex, it may amount to refusal of access to benefits and so be directly discriminatory.
2. In *Calder v James Finlay Corporation Ltd* [1989] ICR 157, EAT, the employer offered a non-contractual mortgage subsidy scheme for employees aged 25 and over. All male workers received the subsidy, but no female workers did. This was held to amount to unlawful sex discrimination.

Example of direct sexual orientation discrimination:
A worker, whose employer suspects he is gay, is passed over for promotion in favour of a less qualified straight worker because the employer is homophobic. This will amount to unlawful direct sexual orientation discrimination.

MEMO POINTS There have been a number of recent cases concerning unlawful discrimination on the grounds of sexual orientation. One case widely publicised as the first successful claim under the legislation prohibiting sexual orientation discrimination was reported to concern an office manager whose colleagues and managers constantly referred to, and used nicknames for him based on, his sexuality. He successfully claimed constructive dismissal on the grounds of sexual orientation (*Whitfield v Cleanaway*). It has also been reported that an employment tribunal has found an employer guilty of constructive unfair dismissal and discrimination on the grounds of sexual orientation after an employee was repeatedly referred to as "gay boy" and subjected to ongoing bullying and harassment by his manager (*Gismondi v (1) Council of the City of Durham (2) Tutty*, ET case 2502956/04).

Comparator In respect of **sex** discrimination, if there are **material differences** between the employee and his/her comparator, it may not be possible to establish less favourable treatment. However, it is not necessary that a minutely exact actual comparator must be found and where circumstances are **unidentical but not wholly dissimilar**, tribunals are free to consider whether the treatment is less favourable (*Chief Constable of West Yorkshire v Vento* [2001] IRLR 124, EAT, overturned on appeal on the issue of remedies only ([2003] IRLR 102, CA)). Only the **relevant circumstances** of the claimant and the comparator can be taken into account. The relevant circumstances are those which were taken into account by the employer when deciding how to treat the claimant and therefore all the characteristics of the claimant which were relevant to the way he/she was treated must also be found in the comparator (*Pearce v Governing Body of Mayfield School* heard with *Macdonald (AP) v Advocate General for Scotland* [2003] IRLR 512, HL). 5273

EXAMPLE A female worker fails to secure a promotion and complains of sex discrimination. She uses as a comparator a male worker who applied for the same post. The employer argues that the work experience of the two workers is so different as to make comparison of their treatment impossible. For the purpose of establishing an appropriate comparator, however, the relevant circumstances to be taken into account are limited to the fact that both workers applied for the same post. Their level of experience is not a relevant factor. It may, however, be relevant when the employer comes to explain why he offered the promotion to one worker and not the other (i.e. it will help to establish whether or not the complainant has, in fact, been subjected to less favourable treatment).

If a claimant cannot refer to the treatment of an actual comparator, it is appropriate that he/she refers to the treatment of a **hypothetical comparator** (*Balamoody v UK Central Council for Nursing, Midwifery and Health Visiting* [2002] IRLR 288, CA). When a hypothetical comparator is used, the comparison has to be made in the context of the same employment as the claimant's (*Grieg v (1) Community Industry (2) Ahern* [1979] IRLR 158, EAT; see also *Martin v Lancehawk Ltd t/a European Telecom Solutions*, EAT case 0525/03). 5274

Moreover, if a claimant tries to rely on a comparison with an **inappropriate comparator**, then the tribunal may compare him/her with a hypothetical comparator even if the claimant did not present his/her case on this basis (*Balamoody v UK Central Council for Nursing, Midwifery and Health Visiting*, above).

EXAMPLE 1. In *Grieg v (1) Community Industry (2) Ahern*, above, the claimant, a job applicant, was turned down on the basis that she would have been the only woman in an all-men team. Attempting to defend her sex discrimination claim, the employer argued that her treatment should be compared with that which would have been afforded to a hypothetical male applicant who would have joined a women-only team. This was rejected by the EAT which stated that for the purposes of making a comparison, it was appropriate to compare the treatment of Grieg with that of a male job applicant seeking to do the same job, with the same team.

2. In *Martin v Lancehawk Ltd t/a European Telecom Solutions*, above, a female employee was dismissed by her male manager following the termination of her affair with him and the breakdown of their personal relationship. In this case, the EAT held that the appropriate comparator was a hypothetical male employee with whom the manager had had a homosexual relationship and which had ended in similar circumstances. In applying such a comparator, the EAT held that in this case the reason for the dismissal was nothing to do with the claimant's sex.

Less favourable treatment In respect of **sex** discrimination, **mere unfavourable** or unfair **treatment** will not be discriminatory since it cannot be inferred from the fact that an employer has treated one employee unreasonably that he would have acted reasonably in respect of another employee in the same circumstances (*Zafar v Glasgow City Council* [1998] IRLR 36, HL). Therefore, an employer may act unreasonably, but provided he does not treat members of the opposite sex more favourably, he may escape a claim for direct discrimination. How- 5276 ever, the more unreasonable the treatment, the greater the possibility that the employer's **explanation for his conduct** will be challenged (*The Law Society v Bahl* [2003] IRLR 640, EAT, upheld on appeal ([2004] IRLR 799, CA)). The employer's conduct may, moreover, amount to indirect discrimination (¶5300).

5277 The **sex of the claimant** must also be at least a significant or important reason for his/her less favourable treatment, but it does not need to be the sole reason. In cases involving the application of gender-specific criteria, the question is whether "**but for**" the worker's sex, the employer would have acted differently (*James v Eastleigh Borough Council* [1990] IRLR 288, HL). However, recent case law has suggested that this test is limited to circumstances in which the less favourable treatment of the claimant by the employer stems from the application of gender-based criteria and where it arises from the selection of the claimant because of his/her gender (as confirmed by *Martin v Lancehawk Ltd (t/a European Telecom Solutions)*, EAT case 0525/03). In cases which do not involve the application of gender-specific criteria, a claimant must still demonstrate that the less favourable treatment was taken on the grounds of his/her sex and, to this end, the correct test is to ask the **reason why** the employer acted as he did, i.e. was this on the grounds of sex/race etc or was it for some other reason (*Nagarajan v London Regional Transport* [1999] IRLR 572, HL; *Chief Constable of West Yorkshire Police v Khan* [2001] IRLR 830, HL; *Shamoon v Chief Constable of the RUC* [2003] IRLR 285, HL; all considered by *Martin v Lancehawk Ltd (t/a European Telecom Solutions)*, above).

EXAMPLE An employer decides to defer training for a young female worker because it was site-based and all the other trainees would have been men. It was felt more appropriate for her to be given the training opportunity at a later date, provided some other female colleagues signed on for the same course. The decision is likely to be discriminatory.

5278 **Dismissing** a worker on grounds of his/her sex may constitute less favourable treatment amounting to unlawful sex discrimination. Moreover, where the principal reason for the dismissal is gender-neutral, there will be sex discrimination where the means by which the employer dismissed an employee are gender-specific, for example, in reliance on the statutory maternity leave provisions (*Lewis Woolf Griptight Ltd v Corfield* [1997] IRLR 432, EAT). In addition, where the employer's conduct is such that it entitles the worker to resign, the discrimination could also give rise to a complaint of constructive dismissal (¶8230).

5279 The test as to whether or not a worker has suffered a **detriment** is whether a reasonable worker would feel he/she had been disadvantaged at work by reason of his/her employer's acts, but it is not necessary to demonstrate that the employee has suffered any economic or physical consequence which is material or substantial (*Shamoon v Chief Constable of the RUC* [2001] IRLR 520, NICA, upheld on appeal ([2003] IRLR 285, HL)).

A **single incident** can amount to a detriment (*Bracebridge Engineering Ltd v Darby* [1990] IRLR 3, EAT; *Insitu Cleaning Co Ltd v Heads* [1995] IRLR 4, EAT). Where there are a **series of incidents**, each incident should not be considered in isolation but rather a tribunal will look at them in their entirety (*Driskel v Peninsula Business Services Ltd* [2000] IRLR 151, EAT).

---

b. Lawful

5280 Sex and sexual orientation discrimination may be **justified** if an employer can demonstrate that special provisions regarding preferential treatment or genuine occupational qualifications/requirements apply.

Moreover, an employer may be **required to take certain action** to comply with another law, even if this would otherwise amount to unlawful sex discrimination (s 51 SDA 1975), for example, health and safety legislation in relation to pregnant workers (¶4873).

MEMO POINTS Special rules also enable employers who provide **communal accommodation** (i.e. residential accommodation which includes dormitories or other shared sleeping accommodation which, for reasons of privacy or decency, or because of the nature of the sanitary facilities serving the accommodation, should be used by members of one of the sexes only, but which may include some shared or ordinary sleeping accommodation) to discriminate on the ground of sex against both male and female workers in the admission to communal accommodation and any benefit, facility or service which cannot properly and effectively be provided except for those using communal accommodation provided that the accommodation is managed in a way which, given the exigencies of the situation, comes as near as may be to fair and equitable treatment of men and women and the employer makes such arrangements as are reasonably practicable to compensate for the detriment caused by the discrimination (s 46 SDA 1975).

Preferential treatment

There are limited circumstances in which an employer is lawfully permitted to give preferential treatment to persons of a certain sex or sexual orientation, where such action would otherwise have constituted unlawful discrimination (S: s 48 SDA 1975; SO: reg 26 SI 2003/1661). This is otherwise known as **positive action**, but it should be noted that these provisions **do not permit positive discrimination** as such. 5282

Sex discrimination An employer may provide to individuals of a particular sex **access to facilities for training** (which would help to fit them for particular work) and encourage individuals of one sex to take advantage of **opportunities for doing particular work** where, in the preceding 12 months, there were no persons of that sex, or comparatively few persons of that sex in the organisation (s 48 SDA 1975). 5284

Broadly speaking, the provisions permit employers to provide targeted training to "level the playing field." They also permit employers to encourage applications for posts ("warming up the chill factor"). In more detail, an employer may: 5285
- provide a **special training programme** for members of one sex, either generally or because he thinks that members of that sex are likely to take up job opportunities or to facilitate a return to the employment market (for example, because they have been discharging family responsibilities). The targeted training may only be provided if the employer can identify clear under-representation of that sex in the specified job in the previous 12 months (unless in relation to return to work schemes); and
- encourage members of one sex to **apply for posts** where he can show that they were under-represented in the previous 12 months. Such encouragement could, for example, take the form of special advertisements and open days.

However, an employer is **not permitted** to make actual employment decisions, or to offer more favourable terms and conditions, on the basis of sex, even as a "tie-breaker". This is in contrast to some other European jurisdictions which permit this in specified cases and it has also been held permissible under EU equality laws (for example, *Marschall v Land Nordrhein-Westfalen* [1998] IRLR 39, ECJ). 5286

Consequently, in GB, these exceptions must be **construed narrowly** and an employer seeking to embark on a course of positive action should act cautiously. Positive action which falls outside these exceptions will amount to unlawful sex discrimination.

EXAMPLE **Lawful preferential treatment**

A financial services business wishes to promote clerical staff to junior management. It decides to recruit/promote on the basis of leadership and organisational skills. It permits examples of such skills to be demonstrated from a wide range of circumstances, including candidates' responsibilities in their home life, for example, voluntary work or play groups. This is not only permissible, but to exclude such consideration may, in fact, be unlawful.

Unlawful preferential treatment

In *ACAS v Taylor*, EAT case 788/97, an organisation carried out a complicated promotion procedure for higher management posts. Its sifting process required managers to decide which group of borderline employees should proceed to the second stage of the sifting process. All female borderline candidates were allowed to advance to the second stage, compared with only 37.5% male candidates. The EAT held that the policy amounted to unlawful positive discrimination even though it operated against a background of general under-representation of female workers in higher management as it fell outside the exceptions.

Sexual orientation discrimination An employer may provide to individuals of a particular sexual orientation **access to facilities for training** (which would help to fit them for particu- 5288 lar work) and encourage individuals of a particular sexual orientation to take advantage of **opportunities for doing particular work** where it reasonably appears to the employer that such treatment would prevent, or compensate for, disadvantages linked to sexual orientation suffered by persons of that sexual orientation doing that work or likely to take up that work (reg 26 SI 2003/1661).

Genuine occupational qualification/requirement

5290 In limited circumstances, an employer is permitted to lawfully discriminate if a genuine occupational qualification (GOQ) or requirement (GOR) applies. It should be noted that the concept of a GOQ (sex discrimination) and a GOR (sexual orientation discrimination) is the same, but different terminology is used under the two types of legislation. A GOQ/GOR though is no defence for a discriminatory dismissal.

In practice, only very few instances will qualify for the GOQ/GOR exception. Consequently, employers seeking to rely on a GOQ/GOR exception must act cautiously.

5291 **Sex discrimination** In respect of arrangements for recruitment (for example, advertisements, recruitment procedures, offers of employment, including a refusal to offer employment), in affording (or refusing) workers access to opportunities for promotion, transfer, and training, and in dismissing a worker, a **worker's gender is a GOQ** for a particular post only where some or all of the duties of the job fall within one of the following categories (s 7(2) SDA 1975):

a. the **essential nature of the job** calls for a member of one of the sexes for reasons of:
– physiology (excluding physical strength or stamina); or
– authenticity in dramatic performances or other entertainment;

because the essential nature would be materially different if carried out by a member of the opposite sex. For example, certain modelling and acting jobs;
b. the job needs to be held by a member of one of the sexes to **preserve decency or privacy** because:
– it is likely to involve physical contact with members of one of the sexes in circumstances where they might reasonably object to it being carried out by a member of the opposite sex; or
– the holder of the job is likely to do his/her work in circumstances where members of the opposite sex might reasonably object to the presence of a person of that gender because they are in a state of undress or are using sanitary facilities. For example, the post of lavatory attendant;
c. the job is likely to involve its holder **doing his/her work or living in a private home** and the job needs to be held by a member of one sex because there might reasonably be objections to allowing a member of the opposite sex to have the degree of physical or social contact with a person living in the home, or the knowledge of intimate details of such a person's life, which is likely to be allowed, or available, to the holder of the job. For example, a live-in home help;
d. the nature or location of the establishment makes it **impractical** for the holder of the job to **live elsewhere than in premises provided by the employer** and:
– the only available premises are lived in, or normally lived in, by members of one sex and are not equipped with separate sleeping accommodation and sanitary facilities for use by members of the opposite sex in privacy; and
– it is not reasonable to expect the employer either to equip those premises with such accommodation and facilities or to provide other premises for members of the opposite sex, for example posts in a live-in hostel;
e. the nature of the establishment, or of the part of it within which the work is done, **requires the job to be held by a member of one of the sexes** because:
– it is, or is part of, a hospital, prison or other establishment for persons requiring special care, supervision or attention;
– those persons are all members of the worker's sex (disregarding any woman or man whose presence is exceptional); and

– it is reasonable, having regard to the essential character of the establishment or that part, that the job should not be held by a member of the opposite sex;
f. the holder of the job provides individuals with **personal services** promoting their welfare or education, or similar personal services (for example, a family planning adviser), and those services can most effectively be provided by a member of one of the sexes;
g. the job needs to be held by a member of one of the sexes because it is likely to involve the **performance of duties outside the UK** in a country whose laws or customs are such that the duties could not, or could not effectively, be performed by a member of the opposite sex; and
h. the job is one of two to be held by a **married couple**.

MEMO POINTS There is a further exception in respect of **organised religions** which can lawfully discriminate in applying a requirement to a person to be of a particular sex if such a requirement has been genuinely imposed to comply with the doctrines of that religion or, because of the nature of the employment and context in which it is carried out, so as to avoid conflicting with the strongly-held religious convictions of a significant number of the religion's followers (s 19(1), (3) SDA 1975). For example, in some denominations, this might prevent a person from being employed as a minister, even if that person has obtained a gender recognition certificate in his/her acquired gender.

However, even if a job is covered by the instances of GOQ listed above, an employer **cannot rely** on the GOQ exception to justify discriminatory conduct against a worker of one of the sexes **where** (s 7(4) SDA 1975; *Etam Ltd v Rowan* [1989] IRLR 150, EAT): 5292
– the employer already employs workers of the opposite sex who are capable of carrying out the relevant duties of a vacant post;
– it would be reasonable to employ those workers to do the relevant duties of the vacant post; and
– there are sufficient workers capable of doing the relevant job without undue inconvenience.

EXAMPLE An employer turns down a male job applicant for the position of sales assistant in a women's clothing shop on the basis that the job involved contact with customers in a state of undress in fitting rooms and, thus, being a woman was a GOQ. However, this argument will fail if the employer has a sufficient number of female sales assistant workers who can perform the relevant duties (of assisting customers in the fitting rooms).

Sexual orientation discrimination In respect of arrangements for recruitment (including advertisements, recruitment procedures, and a refusal to offer employer procedures but not in respect of offers of employment), in affording (or refusing) workers access to opportunities for promotion, transfer, and training, and in dismissing a worker, a worker's sexual orientation is a GOR **for a particular post** where, having regard to the nature of the employment or the context in which it is carried out, regardless of whether or not the employment is for purpose of an organised religion, being of a particular sexual orientation is a **genuine and determining occupational requirement** and it is **proportionate** to apply that requirement in the particular case (reg 7(2) SI 2003/1661). 5294

It is expected that the exception for genuine and determining occupational requirements will be rarely invoked. However, in cases where the exception is invoked, it is likely that a complainant's sexual orientation would be at issue before the tribunal, for example, if he/she disputed the fact that he/she was gay, lesbian or bisexual.

In addition, where **employment is for the purposes of an organised religion**, an employer can lawfully impose a requirement that a position should be held by a worker of a particular sexual orientation where that requirement is applied so as to comply with the doctrines of that religion or, because of the nature of the employment and the context in which it is carried out, it is applied so as to avoid conflicting with the strongly held religious convictions of a significant number of the religion's followers (reg 7(3) SI 2003/1661). This GOR must be narrowly construed and applies specifically to ministers of religion, but is not likely to apply, for example, to a teaching position within a religious school (*R (on the application of AMICUS – MSF section and others) v Secretary of State for Trade and Industry* [2004] IRLR 430, QBD). 5295

MEMO POINTS 1. The exceptions set out in reg 7 SI 2003/1661 **do not apply** to the terms on which employment is offered, terms of employment, access to any other benefit (save for benefits for which marital status is a qualification) or subjection to any other detriment (apart from dismissal).
2. In respect of sexual orientation discrimination, there is also an exception regarding the **provision of benefits based on marital status** only in relation to any benefits accrued or payable in respect service prior to 5 December 2005 (the date on which the Civil Partnership Act 2004 came into force) (i.e. such discrimination is lawful) (reg 25 SI 2003/1661; see ¶5328). Under amendments to the regulations which bring them into line with the Civil Partnership Act 2004 (which gives same-sex couples the right to form a legally-recognised civil partnership), with effect from 5 December 2005, the exception regarding the provision of benefits based on marital status will be extended to civil partners. Employers can confer more favourable benefits on both spouses and civil partners based on their status to the exclusion of others.
3. The **validity of the GORs** set out in regs 7(2), 7(3) and 25 SI 2003/1661 have been **challenged** under an application for judicial review on the grounds that they were incompatible with the Employment Framework Directive and in breach of the European Convention on Human Rights. This challenge has failed (*R (on the application of AMICUS-MSF Section and others) v Secretary of State for Trade and Industry* [2004] IRLR 430, QBD), although the ruling is being appealed.

2. Indirect

a. Unlawful

5300 Indirect discrimination occurs where treatment which appears plausible and motivated by innocent considerations unconnected with sex, marital status, civil partnership status, gender reassignment or sexual orientation, nevertheless turns out to have a **disproportionately adverse impact** on members of a particular group.

It is irrelevant whether the alleged discrimination is **intentional** or not (S: *R v Birmingham City Council, ex parte Equal Opportunities Commission* [1989] IRLR 173, HL; *James v Eastleigh Borough Council* [1990] ICR 554, HL; SO: the regulations are silent as to whether any degree of intent is necessary for there to be a finding of unlawful discrimination but it is expected that intention will not be a relevant factor).

New regulations which update the SDA 1975 to bring its **definition of indirect sex discrimination** into line with the equivalent provisions in the RRA 1976 and sexual orientation and religion or belief discrimination regulations came into force on 1 October 2005. The amendments introduced by the new regulations reflect the recognition that it is not always possible, or indeed necessary, to use statistical calculations to demonstrate that a certain group of individuals have been particularly disadvantaged.

5301 Indirect discrimination is **defined** as when the employer applies to a worker (S: s 1(2)(b) SDA 1975, as amended by reg 3 Employment Equality (Sex Discrimination) Regulations SI 2005/2467; SO: reg 3(1)(b) SI 2003/1661):
– a provision, criterion or practice which he applies or would apply equally to a person of the opposite gender/different sexual orientation to that worker;
– which puts or would put members of the same gender/sexual orientation as that worker at a particular disadvantage when compared with the opposite gender/different sexual orientation;
– which puts that particular worker at that disadvantage; and
– which the employer cannot show to be a proportionate means of achieving a legitimate aim.

With regard to bringing a claim for sexual orientation discrimination, it should be noted that since a claimant must establish that persons of his/her sexual orientation have suffered or would suffer a disadvantage as a result of the provision, criterion or practice, **his/her own sexual orientation** may have to be established before the tribunal.

5302 Indirect discrimination by an employer may often be inadvertent. The phrase "provision, criterion or practice" is not defined, but is said to include not only formal conditions and requirements, but also **informal work practices**.

Examples of indirect sex discrimination where a policy or provision might inadvertently disadvantage more women than men include: 5303
- a change in working hours unilaterally imposed by an employer;
- a contractual provision requiring employees to be available to work their normal contractual hours without variation;
- a requirement on employees to work overtime;
- a contractual obligation or a practice or culture of employees being expected to undertake long working hours;
- an unreasonable refusal to allow an employee to work from home;
- a requirement to work without fixed hours but on an "as and when" basis;
- excluding a higher percentage of female than male workers from a category of worker; and
- excluding periods of part-time work, or even counting part-time work on a pro-rata basis, in order to calculate length of service.

EXAMPLE In *British Airways v Starmer*, EAT case 0306/05, an employee applied to her employer to halve her working hours. The employer refused her application and required that she work 75% of full time hours if she was to work part-time. The employer's actions were held to be indirectly discriminatory. The requirement that she work 75% of full time hours constituted a "provision, criterion or practice", even though it was claimed to be a one-off discretionary decision.

An **example of indirect sexual orientation discrimination** is in relation to an office function where spouses only are invited, or the provision of certain benefits (for example, concessionary travel) to employees' spouses only. Since same-sex partners are unable to marry (as UK law stands at the time of writing), they are put at a disadvantage and it is then for the employer to establish that such a provision or practice is a proportionate means of achieving a legitimate aim. In these examples, it is difficult to see how such a practice could be objectively justified. 5304

However, a provision, criterion, or practice will **not** be **unlawful** if an employer is able to demonstrate that there are sound reasons for the provision, criterion or practice and that it can be objectively justified by demonstrating that it achieves a legitimate aim and that it is a proportionate means of achieving that aim (¶5310). The definition of indirect sex and sexual orientation discrimination therefore recognises that it is not always possible, or necessary, to require detailed statistical analysis to demonstrate that a particular employee has suffered a disadvantage. Indeed, non-statistical evidence could be sought from experts or other witnesses. 5305

However, **statistical evidence** is likely to still play a role in providing evidence to tribunals as to whether a provision, criterion or practice causes disadvantage to a particular group of people. Therefore, it is considered that useful guidance is still provided by case law regarding the use of statistical evidence in indirect discrimination claims decided prior to the recent amendments to the SDA 1975. 5306

In appropriate cases, especially those which are reflective of social conditions generally, even a very small **marginal difference** can be enough to establish indirect discrimination (*London Underground Ltd v Edwards (No 2)* [1998] IRLR 364, CA). In this case, a female single parent was successful even though only 4.8% of women (compared with 0% men) could not comply with a requirement to work certain shifts. Tribunals are not restricted to looking at statistical evidence only, but may carry out a **general assessment of the impact** a provision, criterion or practice has on members of both sexes (*London Underground Ltd v Edwards (No 2)*, above; *Chief Constable of Avon & Somerset Constabulary v Chew*, EAT case 503/00).

EXAMPLE In *Chief Constable of Avon & Somerset Constabulary v Chew*, the difference between the number of female police officers unable to comply with a shift system compared with male police officers was only 2.26%. The EAT confirmed that, apart from statistical considerations, tribunals are entitled to take into account other factors to find that a disparate effect had been established, and that the female applicant had suffered indirect sex discrimination.

The **types of factors** which tribunals may consider are (*Chief Constable of Avon & Somerset Constabulary v Chew*, above): 5307
- the make up and overall numbers of the workforce under consideration;

– the point that no or very few members of the other sex were not disadvantaged;
– the effect of a change in numbers of men and women, for example, when the numbers of women were small, a reduction could have a dramatic effect on the proportion who were disadvantaged;
– the history in respect of or relevant to the workforce; and
– the inherent or inherently likely effect of the provision, criterion or practice.

It can reasonably be expected that tribunals will continue to conduct a general assessment of disparate impact, rather than one based purely on percentages and numbers.

Justification

5310 In certain circumstances, an employer may be able to justify an indirectly discriminatory provision, criterion or practice if he can demonstrate that the provision, criterion or practice is a **proportionate means** of **achieving a legitimate aim** (S: s 1(2)(b) SDA 1975, as amended by reg 3 Employment Equality (Sex Discrimination) Regulations SI 2005/2467; SO: reg 3(1)(b) SI 2003/1661).

In general, it would appear that a **legitimate aim** will include economic and administrative objectives which support the employer's business (*Rainey v Greater Glasgow Health Board* [1987] ICR 129, HL).

However, an employer cannot justify an apparently discriminatory practice by applying the "range of reasonable responses" test relied on in unfair dismissal claims (¶8435). Whilst the principle of proportionality requires the tribunal to factor in the reasonable needs of the business, the tribunal must make its own judgment as to whether the relevant practice is **reasonably necessary**, based on a fair and detailed analysis of the business considerations involved (*Hardys & Hansons plc v Lax* [2005] IRLR 726, CA).

MEMO POINTS Art 2(b) Employment Framework Directive EC Directive 2000/78 imposes a slightly **stricter test** on employers before they can justify an indirectly discriminatory provision, criterion or practice by requiring them to prove that the provision, criterion or practice was 'appropriate and necessary'. This means that employers have a less difficult test to satisfy under the implementing regulations. In addition, workers have a more difficult test to satisfy since they must show that there has been a disproportionately detrimental impact on themselves personally (thereby not allowing **hypothetical claims**), whereas the Directive does not require that a worker is in fact put at a particular disadvantage. Unless workers are employed by a **public authority** (for example, government departments, local authorities, health or education authorities), they cannot rely directly on the Employment Framework Directive if they believe that the UK has failed to implement it correctly, or that it gives them greater rights than the UK implementing regulations.

b. Lawful

5315 In limited circumstances, a provision, criterion or practice which is indirectly discriminatory on grounds of sex or sexual orientation may nevertheless be lawful (S: ss 7, 7A, 7B SDA 1975; SO: reg 7 SI 2003/1661). See ¶5280 for further details.

3. Application to specific situations

a. During pregnancy or maternity leave

5320 Following new regulations which came into force on **1 October 2005** and amend the SDA 1975, less favourable treatment on the grounds of pregnancy and maternity leave now expressly amounts to direct sex discrimination (s 3A SDA 1975, as inserted by reg 4 Employment Equality (Sex Discrimination) Regulations SI 2005/2467).

MEMO POINTS Prior to 1 October 2005, less favourable treatment on grounds of pregnancy or maternity leave already amounted to unlawful discrimination. However, this was on the basis of case law rather than, as is the position now, express provision in the SDA 1975 (*Webb v EMO Air Cargo (UK) Ltd* [1993] IRLR 27, HL).

Dismissing a woman because she is pregnant or **refusing to employ** a woman because she is of child-bearing age on the ground that she might become pregnant is unlawful direct sex discrimination since pregnancy and the capacity to become pregnant are exclusively female characteristics (*Webb v EMO Air Cargo (UK) Ltd*, above). 5321

Less favourable treatment will also be directly discriminatory if the pregnancy was the effective and predominant reason for it (even if it was not the only or main reason) (*O'Neill v Governors of St Thomas More RCNA Upper School and Bedfordshire County Council* [1996] IRLR 372, EAT; *Rees v Apollo Watch Repairs plc* [1996] ICR 466, EAT).

EXAMPLE The employer hires a temp to cover for an employee on maternity leave. The temp is found to do the job better than the absent employee. If the employer keeps the temp and dismisses the employee on maternity leave, the dismissal will be for a reason connected with pregnancy and, as such, will amount to unlawful sex discrimination. This is because the effective cause of the dismissal is the employee's absence on maternity leave and but for this absence, the temp would not have been hired and the employee dismissed.

Where discrimination is on pregnancy/maternity-related grounds and it occurs **during pregnancy or maternity leave**, no comparator (actual or hypothetical) is required. Consequently, the position of a pregnant worker (during pregnancy or maternity leave) must not be compared with that of a man suffering an illness (*Webb v EMO Air Cargo (UK) Ltd (No 2)* [1995] IRLR 645, HL). The EAT recently referred to the decision in *Webb v EMO Air Cargo (UK) Ltd (No 2)*, confirming that it is unnecessary for a pregnant woman to compare the treatment she receives with the treatment given to a sick man in order to succeed in a claim for sex discrimination and, equally, an employer dismissing a woman on the grounds of pregnancy cannot defend his action by arguing that he would have treated a sick man in the same way. However, as the purpose of the decision in *Webb v EMO Air Cargo (UK) Ltd (No 2)* is to protect women, the EAT noted that it should not rule out any comparison of more favourable treatment afforded to sick men, where appropriate, to demonstrate that a different rule is being applied in comparable circumstances and that discrimination has occurred (*Fletcher and others v Blackpool Fylde & Wyre Hospitals* [2005] IRLR 689, EAT). At the time of writing, this case is subject to an appeal. Further, under health and safety legislation, in respect of a failure to carry out a risk assessment of a pregnant woman, the woman does not need to demonstrate that she has been treated less favourably than a hypothetical male or non-pregnant woman (*Hardman v Mallon t/a Orchard Lodge Nursing Home* [2002] IRLR 516, EAT). 5322

However, where the discrimination on pregnancy/maternity grounds occurs **after maternity leave**, it may be appropriate to compare the woman's position with that of a man absent on sick leave (*Brown v Rentokil Ltd* [1998] IRLR 445, ECJ).

EXAMPLE In *Ministry of Defence v Williams*, EAT case 0833/02, a female employee was directly discriminated against when she was unable to attend a training course which clashed with her maternity leave and she was not selected for the course the following year on her return from maternity leave.

MEMO POINTS Pregnant women and those on maternity leave are also protected under the following specific **non-discriminatory claims**:
- the right not to be dismissed for a reason related to their pregnancy or maternity leave under the automatic unfair dismissal legislation (¶8394); and
- the right not to be subjected to any detriment (other than dismissal) for a reason due to their pregnancy, childbirth or maternity leave (¶¶4767, 4771).

b. Part-time work

Since most part-time work arrangements are **undertaken by women** who, statistically, often have the prime responsibility for childcare arrangements, a requirement that all workers work full-time is more likely to discriminate against workers with childcare responsibilities, a larger proportion of whom are likely to be women. Whether such a requirement can be justified, for example, on grounds of administrative efficiency of the organisation or business, will depend on all the facts. 5323

EXAMPLE **Full-time work objectively justified**

1. In *Greater Glasgow Health Board v Carey* [1987] IRLR 484, EAT, where the employer was providing health-visit services, the requirement to work full-time was found to be objectively justified on the particular facts of this case.
2. In *Nelson v Chesterfield Law Centre*, EAT case 1359/95, this same requirement was justified in circumstances where the vacancy in question required the successful applicant to collaborate closely with an existing worker so that further division of work by way of job sharing was undesirable.

Full-time work not objectively justified

In *The Home Office v Holmes* [1984] IRLR 299, EAT, this requirement applied to a civil servant was held to be unlawful as the employer could not justify the requirement on the basis that the bulk of industry was organised on a full-time work basis.

MEMO POINTS **Part-time workers** are further protected from less favourable treatment under the Part-time Workers (Prevention of Less Favourable Treatment) Regulations SI 2000/1551; and for a detailed discussion on part-time workers, see ¶1870.

c. Marital and civil partnership status

5325 It is unlawful to discriminate, directly or indirectly, against a worker who is **married or a civil partner** of either sex, on the ground that he/she is married or a civil partner (s 3 SDA 1975, as amended by reg 3(2) SI 2005/2467 and s 251 Civil Partnership Act 2004).

This does not, though, prohibit discrimination against **single persons** (including those who are getting married or become a civil partner), **cohabitees, divorced persons or parents** on the ground of their status. It is, therefore, important to note that the statutory provisions give more rights to married persons and civil partners than to others in stable, non-married or civil partnership, relationships.

MEMO POINTS 1. The Civil Partnership Act 2004 came into force on **5 December 2005** under which same-sex couples have the right to form a legally-recognised civil partnership. The Act amends the SDA 1975 to provide that discrimination in employment against both married persons and, equally, civil partners is unlawful. It is assumed that existing case law in relation to marital status discrimination will provide useful guidance as to how tribunals and courts would interpret cases involving discrimination relating to civil partners.
2. The protection afforded to workers from discrimination on grounds of marital status may become **less relevant** as greater numbers of children are being born outside marriage and/or as the divorce rate rises, resulting in a greater number of children having divorced parents. In such circumstances, unmarried workers complaining of discrimination arising from their childcare responsibilities must formulate their claim on the basis that they have been discriminated against on the grounds of their sex, as opposed to their marital status, or alternatively may opt to bring a claim **under other non-discriminatory protection**, for example the protection afforded to part-time workers (¶1870).
3. Actions which could amount to marital or civil partnership status discrimination may **also result in other types of discrimination**, for example if a worker can show that he/she was discriminated against on grounds of the employer's gender prejudices (for example, a belief that married female workers have children and cannot give as much to the job as male workers), he/she may have a complaint of sex discrimination (*McLean v Paris Travel Service Ltd* [1976] IRLR 202, IT).

Direct discrimination

5327 Direct discrimination against a worker who is married or a civil partner occurs if an employer treats him/her **less favourably** than he treats or would treat either a person of the same sex who is unmarried or not a civil partner or a person of the opposite sex who is married or a civil partner (s 3(1)(a) SDA 1975, as amended by s 251 Civil Partnership Act 2004; *Watkins v Jubilee Club & Institute*, ET case 5712/82). The married worker alleging discrimination must establish that the alleged discriminatory conduct came about **as a result of his/her status** as a married person (*Preece v Roadways International Hauliers*, ET case 73362/95), although this may not have to be the only reason.

EXAMPLE 1. In *Chief Constable of the Bedfordshire Police v Graham* [2001] IRLR 239, EAT, G was denied a promotion opportunity because had she been promoted she would have been managed by her husband. Her employer tried to justify the refusal on a number of grounds, including that to promote the

worker could have resulted in potential managerial and disciplinary problems (for example, persons working for the worker would be reluctant to complain as they would know that the complaint would be handled by her husband). The EAT held that the worker was directly discriminated against on grounds of marital status as the major reason to refuse promotion had been because of G's marriage, and thus she had been treated less favourably than a single woman would have been.
2. A council refuses to second a social worker to a two-year course in Maidstone because her husband has just been promoted to a post in London and the council thinks that the worker would stay with her husband rather than return to Wales when her course is finished. This will amount to unlawful sex and marital status discrimination.
3. An employer refuses to allow an employee to attend certain meetings (which she would, given her position in the company, be otherwise entitled to attend) because she has married someone working for a competitor.

An employer may in limited circumstances **lawfully discriminate** where there is a genuine occupational qualification (GOQ) on the grounds of marital or civil partnership status in relation to a particular job, for example, that the post is one of two to be held by a married couple or a couple who are civil partners of each other (s 7(2) SDA 1975, as amended by s 251 Civil Partnership Act 2004). For a detailed discussion on GOQs generally, see ¶5291. **5328**

MEMO POINTS There is a further exception in respect of **organised religions** which can lawfully discriminate in applying a requirement relating to not being married or to not having a civil partner (in addition to a requirement relating to whether a person has a living spouse/civil partner or to how that person has ceased to have a living spouse/civil partner) if such a requirement has been genuinely imposed to comply with the doctrines of that religion or, because of the nature of the employment and context in which it is carried out, so as to avoid conflicting with the strongly-held religious convictions of a significant number of the religion's followers (s 19(1), (3) SDA 1975).

Indirect discrimination

Indirect discrimination is **defined** as when the employer applies to a worker who is married or a civil partner (s 3(1)(b) SDA 1975, as amended by reg 3(2) SI 2005/2467 and s 251 Civil Partnership Act 2004): **5330**

- a provision, criterion or practice which applies or would apply equally to all workers who are not married or in a civil partnership;
- which puts or would put persons who are married or in a civil partnership at a particular disadvantage when compared with persons who are not married or in a civil partnership;
- which puts a married or civil partner worker at that disadvantage; and
- which the employer cannot show to be a proportionate means of achieving a legitimate aim.

EXAMPLE In *Chief Constable of the Bedfordshire Police v Graham*, above, the requirement to comply with a policy on conflict of interests involving partnerships and relationships was held to be also indirectly discriminatory as the proportion of married female workers who could comply with a policy of conflict of interests involving partnerships and relationships was considerably smaller than the proportion of unmarried female workers.

Justification An employer may be able to defend his allegedly discriminatory practices, criteria or provisions, if he can show that they are objectively justifiable on grounds other than marital or civil partnership status. Such grounds may relate to the nature of the job at hand, or to business, administrative or organisational reasons. Whether the defence of justification has been established is always a matter of fact and will depend on the particular circumstances of each case. **5332**

d. Gender reassignment

It is unlawful for an employer to treat a worker **less favourably** than he treats or would treat other persons on the ground that the worker has undergone, is undergoing, or intends to undergo gender reassignment (s 2A SDA 1975; Sex Discrimination Act (Gender Reassignment) Regulations SI 1999/1102). The appropriate comparator, in such circumstances, is an actual or hypotheti- **5335** cal person of the complainant's birth gender who is not intending to undergo, is not undergoing, or has not undergone, gender reassignment (*P v S* [1996] IRLR 347, ECJ).

In addition, **pay discrimination** on grounds of gender reassignment is specifically prohibited (s 8 SDA 1975).

MEMO POINTS 1. Gender reassignment is **defined** as a process which is undertaken under medical supervision for the purpose of reassigning a person's sex by changing physiological or other characteristics of sex, and includes any part of such a process (s 82 SDA 1975). Consequently, simple **transvestism** (the instance of a person wearing clothes of persons of the opposite sex) is not covered.
2. The Gender Recognition Act, which came into force on 4 April 2005, allows transsexuals who make an appropriate application to obtain **legal recognition** of their **acquired gender** (ss 1-4 Gender Recognition Act 2004). Such applications are determined by a Gender Recognition Panel which issues successful applicants who have demonstrated that they meet the evidential requirements with a gender recognition certificate which is effective from the date of recognition. In summary, the evidential requirements are that the person (s 2 Gender Recognition Act 2004):
- has or has had gender dysphoria;
- has lived in his/her acquired gender for 2 years prior to the application; and
- intends to live permanently in his/her acquired gender.
3. The Women and Equality Unit published new **guidance**, Gender Reassignment – A guide for employers (referred to as the Gender Reassignment Guidance), in January 2005, to assist employers in understanding the relevant law and to set out good workplace practice on how to deal with issues when an employee (or job applicant) is a transsexual person.

5336 **Protection starts** as soon as a worker has indicated an intention to commence gender reassignment and has taken a preliminary step to begin the process (for example, he/she has met with a specialist for a diagnosis of transsexualism or has begun the appropriate pre-treatment or hormone therapy).

5337 The Gender Resassignment Guidance recommends that employers discuss and write an **action plan** with their workers to agree the procedure and steps they wish to follow to handle the process and transition period, in particular if they are to avoid facing discrimination claims. For example, the action plan might include:
- whether the worker is to stay in his/her existing role or be redeployed;
- the expected timescale of the worker's medical and surgical procedures (if known) and any time off he/she requires for medical treatment;
- agreeing a procedure for adhering to a, or revising an existing, dress code;
- the expected point or phase of change of name, personal details and social gender;
- whether the employee wishes to inform his/her line manager, colleagues and clients him/herself, or would prefer this to be done for him/her, and whether training or briefing of colleagues and/or clients is necessary;
- what amendments will need to be made to records and systems;
- agreeing with the worker, if possible, the point at which the use of facilities such as changing rooms and toilets should change from one sex to the other; and
- discussing whether the worker is covered adequately by existing policies on insurance, confidentiality and harassment and, if not, how these may amended.

5338 The **use of single sex facilities** of the worker's "acquired" sex should be agreed between the employer and worker. This may be the stage at which the worker begins to present him/herself permanently in his/her acquired sex. It may be reasonable for an employer for a limited period to require the employee to use unisex facilities (for example, disabled toilets), but this is not an acceptable long-term solution. However, the employer must maintain a flexible approach and keep matters under review (*Croft v Royal Mail Group plc* [2003] IRLR 592, CA).

Further, since the process of gender reassignment is likely to lead to **absence from work**, there is specific protection for transgender workers from being discriminated against on such grounds (s 2A(2), (3) SDA 1975). Consequently, employers cannot treat a transgender worker less favourably than another worker who is absent due to sickness, injury or some other cause (if, in respect of other causes, having regard to the circumstances of the case, it is reasonable for the worker to be treated no less favourably). In such circumstances, the appropriate comparator is an actual or hypothetical colleague who is absent on account of illness or injury or, where there is some other comparable absence (for example, compassionate or study leave), a worker who can reasonably compare with the transgender worker.

Employers may have to take **additional steps** (over and above their existing equal opportunities policies and procedures) to ensure that the worker is not subjected to **harassment or other detriment by colleagues**, agents or other persons over whom the employer exercises the appropriate level of control. For example, it may be necessary to provide staff with general information about gender reassignment and specific information to enable them to understand the specific situation of the particular worker. 5339

Genuine occupational qualification (GOQ) **Corresponding provisions** to the GOQ rules in respect of sex discrimination generally (¶5291) exist in relation to workers who have undergone, are undergoing or intend to undergo gender reassignment (s 7A SDA 1975). However, these GOQs no longer apply in relation to discrimination against a person whose gender has become acquired under the Gender Recognition Act 2004 (s 14, Sch 6 Gender Recognition Act 2004). Therefore, once a person has obtained legal recognition of his/her "acquired" gender, these GOQs are no longer available to an employer. 5340

In addition, there are a number of **supplementary GOQs**, including cases where (s 7B SDA 1975):

a. the job involves intimate physical searches pursuant to statutory powers;
b. the job is done in a private home in certain specific circumstances;
c. the job involves the worker living in premises provided by the employer where accommodation and facilities have to be shared in certain circumstances and it is not reasonable to expect the employer to make alternative arrangements; and
d. the worker provides vulnerable individuals with personal services promoting their welfare or similar personal services and, in the employer's reasonable opinion, those services cannot be provided effectively by the transgender worker.

MEMO POINTS 1. These GOQs do **not apply** in relation to a person whose gender has become acquired under the Gender Recognition Act 2004 (s 7B(3) SDA 1975, as amended by Sch 6 Gender Recognition Act 2004).

2. The GOQ at **a**. above does not apply to the filling of a vacancy if an employer already employs employees who do not intend to undergo, are not undergoing gender reassignment and either they have not undergone gender reassignment or their gender has become acquired (see above) (s 7B(4), (5) SDA 1975, as inserted by reg 9 Employment Equality (Sex Discrimination) Regulations 2005/2467):
– who are capable of carrying out those duties listed at **a.**;
– whom it would be reasonable for the employer to employ on those duties; and
– whose numbers are sufficient to meet the employer's likely requirements in respect of those duties without undue inconvenience.

3. There is a further exception in respect of **organised religions** which can lawfully discriminate in applying a requirement to a person not to be undergoing or to have undergone gender reassignment if such a requirement has been genuinely imposed to comply with the doctrines of that religion or, because of the nature of the employment and context in which it is carried out, so as to avoid conflicting with the strongly-held religious convictions of a significant number of the religion's followers (s 19(1), (3) SDA 1975). For example, in some denominations, this might prevent a person from being employed as a minister, even if that person has obtained a gender recognition certificate in his/her acquired gender.

4. Victimisation

This occurs when a worker is subjected to **less favourable treatment** than others by reason that he/she has (in respect of the SDA 1975, the EPA 1970, ss 62-65 Pensions Act 1995 or the Employment Equality (Sexual Orientation) Regulations SI 2003/1661 (S: s 4(1) SDA 1975; SO: reg 4 SI 2003/1661)): 5350

– **brought proceedings** against his/her employer or any other worker;
– **given evidence or information** in connection with proceedings brought by another person against his/her employer or any other worker;
– taken any **other action** under or by reference to these provisions; or

– made any **allegation** against his/her employer or any other worker which would amount to a contravention of these provisions.

This extends to a **threat by the worker** to do any of these things or a suspicion by the employer that the worker intends to do any of them.

Further, a worker will not be protected if the allegation made by him/her, or evidence or information given by him/her was **false** and not made (or given) in good faith (S: s 4(2) SDA 1975; SO: reg 4(2) SI 2003/1661).

5351 Any claim must relate to an act which falls under one of the above grounds (*Waters v Commissioner of Police of the Metropolis* [1997] IRLR 589, CA).

EXAMPLE In *Waters v Commissioner of Police of the Metropolis*, above, W was harassed by another employee outside working hours. She complained to her employer who consequently treated her less favourably and she brought a claim for victimisation. However, since the harassment had taken place outside the course of employment, the employer was not vicariously liable and the harassment therefore did not fall within the SDA 1975. As a result, the subsequent less favourable treatment by her employer could not amount to victimisation.

5352 It is irrelevant whether the alleged victimisation is **intentional** or not (*Nagarajan v LRT* [1999] IRLR 572, HL).

5353 The **appropriate comparison** is between the treatment given to the worker bringing the complaint of victimisation and the treatment which was or would be given to other workers who had not done a protected act (i.e. brought discrimination proceedings, given evidence or information in connection with discrimination proceedings, taken any other action or made any allegation of discrimination etc) (*Chief Constable of West Yorkshire Police v Khan* [2001] IRLR 830, HL, which considered the RRA 1976). The "but for" test used to determine whether a worker has suffered less favourable treatment in a direct sex discrimination claim (¶5277) is not appropriate in determining whether a worker has been victimised "by reason" of a protected act he/she done (*Chief Constable of West Yorkshire Police v Khan*). Rather, there must be a **connection between** the worker's action (for example, in bringing or threatening to make a discrimination claim) and the alleged victimisation.

EXAMPLE In *Visa International Service Association v Paul* [2004] IRLR 42, EAT, in sex discrimination proceedings brought by P, VISA brought a counterclaim against P for repayment of P's enhanced maternity benefit. The EAT held that the counterclaim was a direct result of the proceedings and, consequently, amounted to victimisation since other employees (who had not returned to work and had not brought proceedings against VISA) had not been pursued by VISA for repayment by way of legal proceedings.

5354 However, where litigation is underway between an employer and employee, due to the adversarial nature of such proceedings, an **employer should have some latitude** in treating an employee in a manner which might otherwise amount to victimisation. This latitude includes honest and reasonable attempts to compromise the proceedings (*St Helens Metropolitan Borough Council v Derbyshire and others* [2005] IRLR 801, CA).

5. Harassment

5360 Harassment can form the basis of a distinct claim, separate to discrimination. With effect **from 5 October 2005**, the SDA 1975 has been revised to implement EC Directive 2002/73 (the Equal Treatment Amendment Directive) into UK law (s 4A SDA 1975, as inserted by reg 5 Employment Equality (Sex Discrimination) Regulations SI 2005/2467).This has resulted in two new definitions of 'harassment on the grounds of sex' and 'sexual harassment'. In addition, since discrimination on the grounds of sex includes discrimination on the grounds of gender reassignment (¶5335), there is also a definition to cover harassment on the grounds of gender reassignment.

MEMO POINTS 1. **Prior to October 2005**, sexual harassment (whether it be conduct on grounds of the recipient's sex or of a sexual nature in itself) was not explicitly defined in UK legislation, but it could constitute direct sex discrimination if the worker could demonstrate that he/she

had suffered a detriment (*Strathclyde Regional Council v Porcelli* [1986] IRLR 134, CS). This was often difficult, particularly where the nature of the conduct was not severe.
2. ACAS has produced revised guidance for employers and employees on bullying and harassment in light of the new definition of harassment on the grounds of sex and sexual harassment.
3. An additional reference code is used in this section only: GR (gender reassignment).

Harassment **on the grounds of a person's sex**, or the fact that a person intends to undergo, is undergoing or has undergone **gender reassignment** or **sexual orientation** occurs where an employer subjects a worker to unwanted conduct which has the purpose or effect of (S: s 4A(1)(a) SDA 1975; GR: s 4A(3)(a) SDA 1975; SO: reg 5 SI 2003/1661): 5361
- violating that worker's dignity; or
- creating an intimidating, hostile, degrading, humiliating or offensive environment for that worker.

Sexual harassment occurs when an employer (including any other person in respect of whose actions an employer will be vicariously liable – ¶5225) subjects a worker to any form of unwanted verbal, non-verbal or physical conduct of a sexual nature which has the purpose or effect of (s 4A(1)(b) SDA 1975):
- violating that worker's dignity; or
- creating an intimidating, hostile, degrading, humiliating or offensive environment for that worker.

In respect of harassment on the grounds of sex, gender reassignment and/or sexual harassment, harassment will also occur if an employer, on the grounds of a **worker's rejection of**, or **submission to**, any such **unwanted conduct**, treats that worker less favourably than he would treat him/her had the worker not rejected, or submitted to, the conduct (S: s 4A(1)(c) SDA 1975; GR: s 4A(3)(b) SDA 1975). There is no such equivalent provision in relation to sexual orientation.

It is irrelevant whether the alleged harassment is **intentional** or not. Even if the complainant cannot establish that the employer's conduct was intentional, the tribunal must consider whether, having regard to all the circumstances, including in particular the perception of the worker concerned, the conduct should reasonably be considered as having that effect (S: s 4A(2) SDA 1975; GR: s 4A(4) SDA 1975; SO: reg 5(2) SI 2003/1661). 5362

Consequently, the **test** is neither entirely objective nor subjective, since some account needs to be taken of the alleged victim's perception. However, it does mean that a complainant who **unreasonably takes offence** at an innocent comment would probably not be considered to have been harassed, although if the conduct was repeated after the complainant made his/her feelings known, then the repeat conduct could well constitute unlawful harassment.

An employer may also be **vicariously liable** for acts of harassment committed by his workers, agents or possibly third parties (¶5225). In this regard, the **use of email** and the **internet** at work is an increasingly common form of communication through which harassment of workers by other workers may take place. It is therefore vital for employers to prepare and implement an effective policy on the use of email and the internet to try to ensure that sexist, harassing and offensive communications are not sent and received in their workplaces (¶9958). 5363

EXAMPLE In *Moonsar v Fiveways Express Transport Ltd* [2005] IRLR 9, EAT, a case involving sexual harassment which was decided prior to the introduction of the new law, the use of pornography on a workplace computer by male employees in the presence of a female colleague gave rise to a claim for sexual harassment even though the female employee was not actually shown any of the pornographic images and she did not make a complaint at the time regarding the use of pornography. In this case, it was sufficient that the behaviour of the male employees had had an "obvious detrimental effect" that undermined the female employee's dignity at work for the burden of proof to shift to the employer to disprove that she had suffered any harassment.

If an employer **fails to investigate** a worker's grievance that he/she been harassed, then this failure might in itself constitute a further act of discrimination if it is due to the complainant's sex, gender reassignment or sexual orientation. However, if the failure to investigate is unrelated 5364 to the complainant's sex, then this will not amount to discrimination (*Coyne v Home Office* [2001] ICR 1443, CA).

5365 An employee is also able to bring a claim under the **Protection from Harassment Act 1997**, where the wrongdoer has engaged in a course of conduct (i.e. conduct or speech on at least two occasions) which is intentional and which the wrongdoer knew or ought to have known amounted to harassment (this is tested objectively) (*Majrowski v Guy's and St Thomas's NHS Trust* [2005] ICR 977, CA; *Banks v Ablex Ltd* [2005] ICR 819, CA).

This Act therefore gives employees who have been harassed or bullied at work another potential avenue. **Claims under this Act** do not need to be type specific (like harassment claims brought in relation to discrimination on the grounds of sex, sexual orientation, race, religion, belief and disability), nor do victims need to show that they have suffered a recognised psychiatric illness (general anxiety or distress will suffice) or that their injury was foreseeable as is required for personal injury claims.

Employers may also be **vicariously liable** for a breach of the statutory duty imposed on its employees under this Act if the relevant act or omission occurs during the course of employment (*Majrowski v Guy's and St Thomas's NHS Trust* [2005] ICR 977, CA).

MEMO POINTS At the time of writing, leave to appeal to the House of Lords has been granted in this case.

B. Racial and religion or belief

5375 Discrimination on the grounds of race or religion or belief is prohibited (RRA 1976; SI 2003/1660).

MEMO POINTS Prior to 2 December 2003, there was a prohibition against racial discrimination but no specific recourse for discrimination on the grounds of religion or belief (except in Northern Ireland). Consequently, individuals of a particular religion could only bring a claim for discrimination if they were also members of a certain race or ethnic origin. However, this is no longer necessary and such individuals can now bring distinct claims under the religion or belief regulations and no longer have to rely on the racial discrimination legislation.

5380 Discrimination on grounds of race, religion or belief is **divided** into direct discrimination (including victimisation), indirect discrimination and harassment.

5381 **Racial discrimination** "Racial grounds" are **defined** as including **colour**, **race**, **nationality or ethnic or national origins** (s 3(1) RRA 1976). Consequently, the legislation protects people from distinct racial groups who are defined by reference to any of these grounds.

Language, in itself, is not a racial ground, but it can be a factor in determining a person's racial group (*Gwynedd County Council v Jones* [1986] ICR 833, EAT).

As a racial group can be defined by **colour**, it can include more than one ethnic origin (for example, black people may be of more than one ethnic origin (*London Borough of Lambeth v Commission for Racial Equality* [1990] ICR 768, CA)). An individual may, therefore, fall into a number of different racial groups. For example, he may be a national of one country (for example, British), have his national origin in another country (for example, India) and be a member of a distinct ethnic group (for example, Sikh). Depending on the circumstances of the case, the individual may place himself in the appropriate racial group to proceed with his claim.

A person's "**national origin**" refers to his race, rather than his citizenship (*Ealing London Borough Council v Race Relations Board* [1972] 1 All ER 105, HL; *Tejani v Superintendent Registrar for the District of Peterborough* [1986] IRLR 502, CA). Persons of "**non-British**" origin could form a single racial group, even if they are of a number of different nationalities/national origins (s 3(2) RRA 1976). For example, therefore, where employment is conditional on residency in the UK for a period of time, all "non-British" job applicants who cannot meet the requirement may have a claim, whatever their individual nationality or national origin (*Orphanos v Queen Mary College* [1985] IRLR 349, HL).

"**Ethnic origin**" is wider than "race" and can include religious and cultural differences as well. It has been said to mean a segment of the population distinguished from others by a sufficient combination of shared customs, beliefs, traditions and characteristics derived from a common or presumed common past (*Mandla and anor v Lee and ors* [1983] IRLR 209, HL). This covers Sikhs, Jews and Romany gypsies (*Mandla and anor v Lee and ors*; *Seide v Gillette Industries Ltd* [1980] IRLR 427, EAT; *Commission for Racial Equality v Dutton* [1989] IRLR 8, CA).

However, Rastafarians are a religious, rather than an ethnic group, and so are not covered (*Dawkins v Department of the Environment* [1993] IRLR 284, CA) though they are covered by the prohibition against discrimination on the grounds of religion (see below).

MEMO POINTS Whilst discrimination on ground of nationality is unlawful under the RRA 1976, employers are nonetheless required to comply with UK immigration laws which, in effect, directly discriminate against non-UK citizens.

Religion or belief discrimination "Religion or belief" is **defined** as any religion, religious belief, or similar philosophical belief (reg 2(1) SI 2003/1660). This definition **excludes** any philosophical or political belief, unless such belief is similar to a religious belief. 5383

Relevant factors in determining what constitutes a religion or belief include whether there is collective worship, a clear belief system, or a profound belief affecting an individual's way of life or view of the world (para 5 Explanatory Memorandum).

Extended scope

Protection is **not limited to** the complainant's **own racial group**, **religion or belief**. Consequently, a worker can bring racial, religion or belief proceedings if he objects to instructions given by an employer to discriminate on racial, religion or belief grounds even if they do not relate to his own racial group or religion or belief (R: *Weathersfield Ltd (t/a Van & Truck Rentals) v Sargent* [1999] IRLR 94, CA; see also *Showboat Entertainment Centre Ltd v Owens* [1984] IRLR 7, EAT; RB: reg 3(1)(a) SI 2003/1660). 5384

MEMO POINTS "Racial grounds" should be interpreted widely and incorporates actions based on race, whether it is the race of the person affected by the action or of others. In *Redfearn v Serco Ltd t/a West Yorkshire Transport Service* [2005] IRLR 744, EAT, an employee who was summarily dismissed from a job working with Asian people following his employer's discovery that he was standing, and had been elected, as a Councillor representing the British National Party was held to be entitled to bring a claim under race discrimination legislation. It is understood that the employer in this case is seeking leave to appeal and further guidance is awaited.

Moreover, less favourable treatment based on the **employer's perception** of an individual's racial group, religion or belief, whether that perception is rightly or wrongly held, is also covered (R: *BBC Scotland v Souster* [2001] IRLR 150, CS; RB: reg 3(1)(a) SI 2003/1660). For example, there could be unlawful discrimination if an individual is treated less favourably because he is thought to look like he holds a particular religion or belief.

MEMO POINTS 1. Discrimination 'on racial grounds' or 'on grounds of religion or belief' (R: s 1(1)(a) RRA 1976; RB: reg 3(1)(a) SI 2003/1660) can refer to the racial group, religion or belief of a person other than the complainant (as noted above), but not the religion or belief of the alleged discriminator (RB: reg 3(2) SI 2003/1660).

2. A complainant does not need to show **proof of** his **religion or belief** in order to bring a claim since it is sufficient that he has suffered less favourable treatment due to the (incorrect) assumptions made about his religion or belief.

3. Workers in **private households** are protected from discrimination by employers only on grounds of their race, national or ethnic origins (as well as religion or belief) but discrimination on grounds of their colour and nationality is not covered (s 4(3) RRA 1976, as amended by reg 6 Race Relations Act 1976 (Amendment) Regulations SI 2003/1626).

Legal framework

The rules on **racial** discrimination originate from **three sources**: the Race Relations Act 1976 (RRA 1976), EC Race Directive 2000/43 and the Race Relations Act 1976 (Amendment) Regulations SI 2003/1626 which implemented the Race Directive on 19 July 2003. Although the scope of these sources overlap to a large extent, they are not identical. For example, the Race Directive and 5386 the Race Relations Act 1976 (Amendment) Regulations do not apply to discrimination on grounds of nationality, whereas colour and nationality is covered by the RRA 1976. In other respects, the Race Directive is wider in scope than the RRA 1976 and, where this is the case, it will be noted below.

In practice, the most significant effect of this is that the Race Relations Act 1976 (Amendment) Regulations apply to (and supersede the former provisions of the RRA 1976 in respect of) discrimination on grounds of race, ethnic and national origin, but do not apply to colour and nationality. However, with regard to discrimination on the grounds of colour and nationality, the provisions of the RRA 1976 existing prior to 19 July 2003 still apply. It is therefore necessary to take a **dual approach** to the racial discrimination legislation, although this is not ideal. Further legislative change and case law are awaited to clarify these inconsistencies.

MEMO POINTS Since EC Directive 2000/43 has been implemented by secondary (as opposed to primary) legislation (i.e. by implementing regulations), the regulations cannot cover colour and nationality. Had the Directive been implemented in the UK by primary legislation (i.e. by an Act), such a dual approach would not have been necessary. As a result, workers who feel that they have been discriminated against on the grounds of their colour or nationality do not benefit from the increased protection provided by the regulations and are therefore advised on their claim form to additionally specify the grounds of race, ethnic or national origin, if this is at all possible.

5387 A **summary** of the protection against discrimination on racial grounds and on the grounds of religion or belief is set out in the table below.

Ground of discrimination	RRA 1976	Race Relations Act 1976 (Amendment) Regulations	Race Directive	Religion or Belief Regulations
Race	✔	✔	✔	X
Ethnic origin	✔	✔	✔	X
National origin	✔	✔	X	X
Colour	✔	X	X	X
Nationality	✔	X	X	X
Religion or belief	X	X	X	✔

1. Direct

a. Unlawful

5390 Direct racial and religion or belief discrimination occurs where there is "**less favourable treatment**" of an individual, **compared** with the treatment of a person of a different racial group, religion or belief in the same, or not materially different, circumstances on grounds of race, religion or belief (R: ss 1(1)(b), 3(4) RRA 1976; RB: reg 3(1)(a), (2) SI 2003/1660).

The religion or belief referred to **excludes** the religion or belief of the alleged discriminator (reg 3(2) SI 2003/1660).

Specifically, an employer is prohibited from discriminating against **job applicants and employees** (R: s 4(1), (2) RRA 1976; RB: reg 6(1), (2) SI 2003/1660):
- in the arrangements he makes for the purposes of determining who should be offered a position;
- in the employment terms and conditions on which he offers an individual a position;
- by refusing or deliberately omitting to offer an individual a position;
- in the way he affords access to opportunities for promotion, transfer or training, or to any other benefits, facilities or services, or by refusing or deliberately omitting to afford access to such opportunities and benefits; or
- by dismissing an individual, or subjecting him/her to any other detriment.

Dismissal on the grounds of race, national or ethnic origin now includes a constructive dismissal on those grounds (s 4(4A) RRA 1976).

In addition, **segregating** a worker on racial grounds will amount to less favourable treatment (s 1(2) RRA 1976) and an employer cannot justify the segregation of workers of different racial groups on the basis that each racial group are provided with equally good (or bad) segregated facilities.

Moreover, it is unlawful for a person who has authority over another person or, in accordance with whose wishes that other person is accustomed to act, to give **instructions** to, or put **pressure** on, another person **to discriminate** against a worker on racial grounds (R: ss 30, 31 RRA 1976; RB: there is no express equivalent provisions in the Employment Equality (Religion or Belief) Regulations SI 2003/1660, but see notes regarding extended scope of the regulations above). Only the CRE can bring proceedings in respect of unlawful instructions to discriminate on racial grounds but currently there is no equivalent statutory body in respect of religion or belief (¶5790).

It is irrelevant whether the alleged discrimination was **intentional** or not (R: *Seide v Gillette Industries Ltd* [1980] IRLR 427, EAT; *R v Commission for Racial Equality, ex parte Westminster City Council* [1985] 426, CA; RB: the regulations are silent as to whether any degree of intent is necessary for there to be a finding of unlawful discrimination, but it is expected that intent is not a relevant factor). 5391

Comparator In respect of **racial** discrimination, the legal principles regarding the use of a comparator are the same as those under the SDA 1975 which are set out at ¶5273. The same rules are expected to apply to discrimination on grounds of religion or belief. 5393

It should be noted that a **hypothetical** comparator used in a racial discrimination claim does not need to be a clone of the claimant in every respect, including personality and personal characteristics, except that he is of a different racial origin to the claimant (*Madden v Preferred Technical Group Cha Ltd and anor* [2005] IRLR 46, CA).

Less favourable treatment In respect of **racial** discrimination, again, the legal principles relating to less favourable treatment are the same as those for sex discrimination (¶5276). The same rules are expected to apply to discrimination on grounds of religion or belief. 5395

In racial discrimination claims, tribunals must not simply focus on the worker's specific complaints but should also consider the **wider employment picture** beyond the matters complained of, in order to determine whether racial factors have influenced the employer in subjecting a worker to less favourable treatment (*Rihal v Ealing London Borough Council* [2004] IRLR 642, CA).

Moreover, in determining whether a worker has been treated less favourably, tribunals are not permitted to attribute **specific characteristics** to a particular national or ethnic group without evidence to support such assumptions (*Bradford Hospital NHS Trust v Al-Shabib* [2003] IRLR 4, EAT). The object of the RRA 1976 is to ensure that people are treated as individuals and are not assumed to belong to a **stereotype** of a particular racial group, whether or not in reality most members of that group do conform to such a stereotype.

EXAMPLE In *R (on the application of the European Roma Rights Centre and ors) v Immigration Officer at Prague Airport and anor* [2005] IRLR 115, HL, the system operated by immigration officials under which individuals of a particular racial and ethnic origin were treated with more suspicion and whose motives for travelling to the UK were questioned more sceptically than other individuals who did not look like they belonged to that particular racial or ethnic group, amounted to unlawful racial discrimination.

b. Lawful

An employer can **justify** racial and religion or belief discrimination **only if** special provisions regarding preferential treatment or genuine occupational qualifications/requirements apply. 5397

Moreover, an employer may be **required to take certain action** to comply with another law, even if this would otherwise amount to unlawful racial discrimination (s 41 RRA 1976), for example, where the employer refuses to engage, or dismisses, a worker because he does not have the legal right to work in the UK (¶750).

Preferential treatment

5399 There are limited circumstances in which an employer is permitted to **lawfully discriminate** in giving preferential treatment to persons of a certain racial group or religion or belief, where such action would otherwise have constituted unlawful discrimination (R: s 38 RRA 1976; RB: reg 29 SI 2003/1661). This is sometimes known as **positive action**, but it should be noted that the positive action provisions **do not permit positive discrimination** as such.

5400 **Racial discrimination** An employer is permitted to give preferential treatment to a particular racial group in connection with **access to training** (which would help fit them for particular work) and in encouraging them to take advantage of **opportunities for doing particular work** where, in the preceding 12 months, there were no persons of that racial group, or comparatively few persons of that racial group in the organisation (s 38 RRA 1976).

5401 **Religion or belief discrimination** An employer is permitted to give preferential treatment to individuals of a particular religion or belief in connection with **access to training** (which would help fit them for particular work) and in encouraging them to take advantage of **opportunities for doing particular work** where it reasonably appears to the employer that such treatment would prevent, or compensate for, disadvantages linked to religion or belief suffered by persons of that religion or belief doing that work or likely to take up that work (reg 29(1) SI 2003/1660).

Genuine occupational requirement/qualification

5402 In limited circumstances, an employer may be permitted to lawfully discriminate where a genuine occupational requirement/qualification (GOR/GOQ) applies.

5403 **Race, ethnic or national origin (GORs)** A genuine occupational requirement (GOR) allows employers, in limited circumstances, to discriminate in their arrangements for **recruitment** (for example, advertisements, recruitment procedures, offers of employment, including a refusal to offer employment), in affording (or refusing) workers **access to opportunities** for promotion, transfer, and training, and in **dismissing** a worker on the basis of the worker's race, ethnic or national origin (s 4A RRA 1976).

The circumstances in which an employer can lawfully discriminate on such grounds are limited to where, having regard to the nature of the employment, or the context in which it is being carried out, being of a particular race, ethnic or national origin is a **genuine and determining occupational requirement**, where such requirement is applied in a **proportionate manner**. The employer must be sincere in his view that a particular race, ethnic or national origin is an occupational requirement and that the requirement is decisive (para 24 Explanatory Memorandum). Until there is a body of reported case law on this issue, it is unclear how this criterion will be assessed in practice.

MEMO POINTS 1. The GOR provisions in s 4A RRA 1976 replace the former exception to direct racial discrimination in respect of the provisions set out in s 1(1B) RRA 1976, as inserted by reg 3 Race Relations Act 1976 (Amendment) Regulations SI 2003/1626, and are distinct from the genuine occupational qualification provisions (GOQ) in s 5 RRA 1976 (¶5404).

2. Art 4(1) EC Directive 2000/78 (Employment Framework Directive) sets down a **stricter test** under which employers must justify a genuine and determining occupational requirement by stipulating that the requirement must be for a legitimate objective. However, in the implementing regulations, there is no need for the requirement to be 'legitimate' and the DTI's Explanatory Memorandum states its belief that if an occupational requirement is a genuine one in order to carry out a particular job, then it also pursues a legitimate objective. Unless workers are employed by a **public authority** (for example, government departments, local authorities, health or education authorities), they will not be able to rely directly on the Employment Framework Directive if they believe that the UK has failed to implement it correctly or that it gives them greater rights than the UK implementing regulations.

Colour and nationality (GOQs) Where the GOR provisions above do not apply (i.e. in respect of discrimination on the grounds of colour and nationality), the following genuine occupational qualification (GOQ) provisions, which allow an employer to **lawfully discriminate** on the grounds of colour or nationality, apply (s5 RRA 1976). A worker's colour or nationality can be a GOQ where the position involves the following (s5(2) RRA 1976): 5404

- participation in a **dramatic performance** or other entertainment for which a person of a particular racial group is required for authenticity;
- participation as an **artist's or photographic model** in the production of a work of art, visual image or sequence of visual images for which a person of a particular racial group is required for authenticity;
- working in a place where **food or drink** is (whether for payment or not) **provided to and consumed by** members of the public or a section of the public in a particular setting for which, in that job, a person of that racial group is required for authenticity; or
- the holder of the job provides persons of that racial group with **personal services promoting their welfare** and those services can most effectively be provided by a person of that racial group.

These GOQs do **not apply** to job vacancies if an employer already has employees of the racial group in question who are capable of filling those vacancies, who the employer can reasonably employ on those duties and whose numbers are sufficient to meet the employer's likely requirements in respect of those duties without inconveniencing him unduly (s5(4) RRA 1976).

Religion or belief A genuine occupational requirement (GOR) allows employers, in limited circumstances, to discriminate in their arrangements for **recruitment** (for example, advertisements, recruitment procedures, including a refusal to offer employment), in affording (or refusing) workers **access to opportunities** for promotion, transfer, and training, and in **dismissing** a worker on the basis of the worker's religion or belief (reg 7(2) SI 2003/1660). It does not, though, apply to the terms on which employment is offered, terms of employment, access to any other benefit or subjection to any other detriment. 5405

The circumstances in which an employer can lawfully discriminate on such grounds are limited to where, having regard to the nature of the employment, or the context in which it is being carried out, being of a particular religion or belief is a **genuine and determining occupational requirement**, where such requirement is applied in a **proportionate manner**. The employer must be sincere in his view that a particular religion or belief is an occupational requirement and that the requirement is decisive (para 24 Explanatory Memorandum). Until there is a body of reported case law on this issue, it is unclear how this criterion will be assessed in practice.

MEMO POINTS Special protection is afforded to **Sikhs** from discrimination in connection with requirements as to the wearing of safety helmets on construction sites (reg 26 SI 2003/1660).

Employers who have an ethos based on religion or belief may also lawfully impose a requirement that a position should be held by a worker of a particular religion or belief where, having regard to that ethos and to the nature of the employment, and the context in which it is being carried out, being of a particular religion or belief is a GOR for the job and that it is proportionate to apply such a requirement (reg 7(3) SI 2003/1660). In these circumstances, the employer **need not demonstrate** that the requirement is determining (in contrast to provision relating to GORs based on religion or belief generally (reg 7(2) SI 2003/1660)). 5406

In addition, where employment is for the purposes of an **organised religion**, an employer can, in certain circumstances, also lawfully impose a requirement that a position should be held by a worker of a particular sexual orientation (¶5295) and/or refuse to employ a transsexual person (¶5340). 5407

2. Indirect

a. Unlawful

5410 Indirect discrimination occurs where treatment which appears plausible and motivated by innocent considerations unconnected with racial grounds or religion or belief, nevertheless turns out to have a **disproportionately adverse impact** on members of a particular racial group or religion or belief.

It is irrelevant whether the alleged discrimination was **intentional** or not (R: *Seide v Gillette Industries Ltd* [1980] IRLR 427, EAT; *R v Commission for Racial Equality, ex parte Westminster City Council* [1985] 426, CA; RB: the regulations are silent as to whether any degree of intent is necessary for there to be a finding of unlawful discrimination, but it is expected that intent is not a relevant factor).

It is possible for the **same set of facts** to give rise to a claim for both direct and indirect racial discrimination. However, this is not normally the case (*Jaffrey v Department of Environment Transport and Regions* [2002] IRLR 688, EAT).

5411 **Race, ethnic or national origin, religion or belief** Indirect discrimination (with the exception of colour and nationality) is **defined** as (R: s 1A RRA 1976; RB: reg 3(1)(b) SI 2003/1660):
– a provision, criterion or practice which an employer applies or would apply equally to all workers (or to all workers of a particular group), regardless of their race, ethnic or national origin, religion or belief;
– which puts or would put persons of the same race or ethnic or national origin, religion or belief as the complainant at a particular disadvantage when compared to other persons;
– which puts that particular worker at that disadvantage; and
– which the employer cannot show to be a proportionate means of achieving a legitimate aim.

The phrase "provision, criterion or practice" is not defined, but is said to include not only formal conditions and requirements, but also **informal work practices**, such as lax dress requirements or an expectation that alcohol will be consumed when entertaining clients.

EXAMPLE 1. A company which processes food requires its entire staff to be clean-shaven. This is apparently a neutral requirement, but one with which Sikh men will not be able to comply unless they are prepared to abandon one of the symbols of Sikhism.
2. An organisation requires applicants for a promotion to the post of manager to demonstrate "rapid career progression." This could discriminate against black candidates whose career may have progressed more slowly than their white counterparts.
3. A department has a pre-condition for access to training that all workers have good knowledge of the UK. This would be more difficult for non-British workers to meet.
4. A company requires all employees to work until 7pm on Friday. This could discriminate against Jewish employees who adhere to their religion's requirement not to perform any work during the Sabbath.
5. An employer who imposed a permanent change of rota hours that required an employee, a practising Christian who had made her religious commitments clear to her employer at the job interview, to work on a Sunday which would cause her to miss her local church's Sunday service, was found to have indirectly discriminated against the employee on the grounds of her religion or belief since, whilst the rota change applied to all staff, it placed the employee at a particular disadvantage. Since the employer had neither entered a defence nor attended the tribunal hearing, he had not demonstrated that the rota change was justified as being a proportionate means of achieving a legitimate aim (*Williams-Drabble v Pathway Care Solutions Ltd and anor*, ET case 260178/04).

MEMO POINTS Art 2(b) EC Directive 2000/78 (Employment Framework Directive) imposes a slightly **stricter test** on employers before they can justify an indirectly discriminatory provision, criterion or practice by requiring them to prove that the provision, criterion or practice was 'appropriate and necessary'. This means that an employer will have a less difficult test to satisfy under the implementing regulations. In addition, workers will have a more difficult test to satisfy since they must show that there has been a disproportionately detrimental impact on themselves personally (thereby not allowing hypothetical claims), whereas the Directive does not require that a worker is in fact put at a particular disadvantage. Unless workers are employed by a **public authority** (for example, government departments, local authorities, health or education authorities), they will not be able to rely directly on the Employment Framework Directive if they believe that the UK has failed to implement it correctly, or that it gives them greater rights than the UK implementing regulations.

Since there is little reported case law regarding the new indirect discrimination provisions relating to race, ethnic or national origin, religion or belief, some guidance might usefully be provided by cases which were decided under the unamended provisions of the RRA 1976, which are still applicable to racial discrimination on grounds of colour and nationality (see below). 5412

Colour and nationality In respect of colour and nationality, the unamended provisions of the RRA 1976 still apply and indirect discrimination is **defined** as (s 1(1)(b) RRA 1976): 5413
- a requirement or condition which an employer applies or would apply equally to all workers;
- which is such that the proportion of persons of a particular colour or nationality who can comply with it is considerably smaller than the proportion of persons not of that colour or nationality who can comply with it;
- which the employer cannot show to be justifiable irrespective of the colour or nationality of the worker to whom it is applied; and
- which is to the detriment of a worker of that particular colour or nationality.

MEMO POINTS Workers who feel that they have been discriminated against on the grounds of their colour or nationality do not benefit from the increased protection provided by the Race Relations Act 1976 (Amendment) Regulations SI 2003/1626 and are therefore advised on their claim form to additionally specify the grounds of race, ethnic or national origin, if this is at all possible.

In respect of the test for indirect discrimination, **how** a **condition or requirement** is **described** is less important than how it is applied in practice. Hence, a condition may be said to be "desirable" or a "preference", but in practice be applied as a strict condition (*Raval v Department of Health and Social Security and the Civil Service Commission* [1985] IRLR 370, EAT; *Falkirk Council v Whyte* [1997] IRLR 560, EAT). 5414

In order to assess whether a "considerably smaller" proportion of persons within a certain racial group can comply with a condition or requirement, compared to members of other racial groups, a tribunal must **identify a "pool"** for comparison. This will generally consist of all those to whom the condition or requirement is applied. The pool will then be divided into members of the complainant's racial group and members of other racial groups. To establish whether or not there has been racial discrimination, the "pool" is everyone to whom the requirement or condition could be applied, provided statistics are available. Proper identification of the relevant "pool" of workers is vital and can significantly affect the outcome of any dispute.

Tribunals will then determine the proportion of the complainant's group and the "**control group**" in order to see, in each case, what percentages can and cannot comply with the condition. This exercise can become quite complex especially as, in appropriate cases, tribunals are allowed to take their own knowledge into account, such as the cultural norms in the Indian Subcontinent. There is no hard and fast rule as to the required proportions, unlike some other jurisdictions.

EXAMPLE An employer requires good oral English. A job applicant complains that as a Moroccan he is less likely to be able to comply with the requirement than an English person, and produces statistics to prove his point about Moroccans. However, the requirement would not just be applied to Moroccans and he has therefore made his pool for comparison too small.

Justification

In respect of race, ethnic or national origin, colour or nationality and religion or belief, an employer may sometimes be able to justify an indirectly discriminatory provision, criterion, practice, condition or requirement. 5418

5419 **Race, ethnic or national origin and religion or belief** An employer can justify an indirectly discriminatory provision, criterion or practice if he can demonstrate that the provision, criterion or practice is a proportionate means of achieving a legitimate aim (R: s 1A RRA 1976, as inserted by reg 3 SI 2003/1626; RB: reg 3(1)(b)(iii) SI 2003/1660).

Cases decided under the unamended provisions (which are still applicable for discrimination on the grounds of colour and nationality) might usefully provide some guidance as to how the relatively recent statutory provisions will be applied in respect of race, national or ethnic origin, and religion or belief (see below).

5420 **Colour and nationality** There is little clear guidance from the tribunals and courts as to when an employer will be able to justify an indirectly discriminatory condition or requirement since each case will turn on its own particular facts. The Court of Appeal has, however, held that for a condition or requirement to be justifiable, this is an objective test and requires a balance between the discriminatory effect of the condition or requirement and the reasonable needs of the employer who is applying it (*Hampson v Department of Eduction and Science* [1989] IRLR 69, CA, which was overturned on different grounds in the HL ([1990] IRLR 302, HL)). Moreover, an employer must do more than establish that he himself considered his reasons adequate.

---

b. Lawful

5421 In limited circumstances, a provision, criterion, practice, condition or requirement which is indirectly discriminatory on racial, religion or belief grounds may nevertheless be lawful (R: s 4A, 5 RRA 1976; RB: reg 7(2), (3) SI 2003/1660). See ¶5397 for further details.

---

3. Victimisation

5425 This occurs when a worker is subjected to **less favourable treatment** than others because **he has** (in respect of the RRA 1976 or the Employment Equality (Religion or Belief) Regulations SI 2003/1660 (R: s 4(2) RRA 1976; RB: reg 4 SI 2003/1660)):
- **brought proceedings** against his employer or any other worker;
- given **evidence or information** in connection with proceedings brought by another person against his employer or any other worker;
- taken any **other action** under or by reference to these provisions; or
- made any **allegation** against his employer or any other worker which would amount to a contravention of these provisions.

This extends to a **threat** by the worker to do any of these things or a suspicion by the employer that the worker intends to do any of them.

However, a worker will not be protected if the allegation made by him, or evidence or information given by him was **false** and not made (or given) in good faith (R: s 2(2) RRA 1976; RB: reg 4(2) SI 2003/1660).

5427 It is not relevant whether the alleged victimisation was **intentional** or not (*Nagarajan v LRT* [1999] IRLR 572, HL).

5428 The **appropriate comparator** in a victimisation claim is a worker who has not brought discrimination proceedings on grounds of race, religion or belief (*Chief Constable of West Yorkshire Police v Khan* [2001] IRLR 830, HL).

There must be a **connection between** the worker's action (for example, in bringing or threatening to make a discrimination claim) and the alleged victimisation (see the example of *Visa International Service Association v Paul* [2004] IRLR 42, EAT at ¶5353).

4. Harassment

Different provisions govern harassment on grounds of race, ethnic or national origin, religion or belief from those in respect of harassment on grounds of colour and nationality. 5430

Race, ethnic or national origin and religion or belief Harassment on grounds of race, ethnic or national origin, religion or belief **occurs** where an employer subjects a worker to unwanted conduct which has the purpose or effect of (R: s 3A RRA 1976; RB: reg 5 SI 2003/1660): 5435

- violating that worker's dignity; or
- creating an intimidating, hostile, degrading, humiliating or offensive environment for that worker.

MEMO POINTS 1. In respect of race, ethnic or national origin, religion or belief, harassment is a distinct form of discrimination and, as such, it is not possible for a person to argue that his alleged harassment constitutes a detriment under the discrimination provisions (R: s 78(1) RRA 1976; RB: reg 6(2)(d) SI 2003/1660).
2. In respect of the definition of 'harassment', the regulations are slightly **less stringent** than the Directive, which requires that the unwanted conduct must both violate the worker's dignity and create an intimidating, hostile, degrading, humiliating or offensive environment for that worker (Art 2(3) EC Directive 2000/43).
3. The **criminal offence** of "religiously aggravated harassment" (s 39 Anti-Terrorism, Crime and Security Act 2001) outlaws hostility based on a victim's membership or non-membership of a religious group. A 'religious group' is defined as "a group of persons defined by reference to religious belief or lack of religious belief." This is likely to include individuals who are presumed to be members of a religious group (even if they are not), persons who say they are members of a religious group (even if no-one else is), and individuals who are not members of any or any certain religious group. The outlawed conduct is prohibited generally, including in the workplace. A successful prosecution under the Act (which may be brought by individuals, as well as the Crown Prosecution Service) could pave the way for a worker, subjected to harassment at work, to pursue a claim against the employer under SI 2003/1660 as well as the Protection from Harassment Act 1997, for example, for vicarious liability and/or for breach of the duty to protect the employee's health and safety.

It is irrelevant whether the alleged harassment is **intentional** or not. Even if the complainant cannot establish that the employer's conduct was intentional, the tribunal must consider whether, having regard to all the circumstances, including the perception of the worker concerned, the conduct should reasonably be considered as having that effect (R: s 3A(2) RRA 1976; RB: reg 5(2) SI 2003/1660). The **test** is neither entirely objective nor subjective, since some account needs to be taken of the alleged victim's perception. However, it does mean that a complainant who **unreasonably takes offence** at an innocent comment would probably not be considered to have been harassed, although if the conduct was repeated after the complainant made his feelings known, then the repeat conduct could well constitute unlawful harassment. 5436

Colour and nationality In respect of discrimination on the grounds of colour and nationality only, the unamended provisions of RRA 1976 apply, and therefore a worker who believes he has suffered racial harassment must **prove** that he has suffered a **detriment** under s 4(2)(c) RRA 1976. 5437

Being subjected to a detriment means suffering some sort of **disadvantage** (*Ministry of Defence v Jeremiah* [1980] ICR 13, CA). However, a victim of **racial abuse** cannot automatically be assumed to have suffered a detriment and a complainant must prove that the harassment was specifically targeted at him (*Thomas and anor v Robinson* [2003] IRLR 7, EAT).

See ¶5365 as to the further avenue open to complainants under the **Protection from Harassment Act 1997**. 5438

C. Disability

5450 It is unlawful for an employer to discriminate against a **disabled person** in relation to his employment (DDA 1995, as amended).

Specifically, an employer is prohibited from discriminating against disabled **job applicants and employees** (s 4 DDA 1995, as amended by reg 5 Disability Discrimination Act 1995 (Amendment) Regulations SI 2003/1673):
– in the arrangements he makes for the purpose of determining who should be offered a position;
– in the employment terms and conditions on which he offers an individual a position or affords him once he is employed;
– by refusing to offer or deliberately not offering an individual a position;
– in the way he affords opportunities for promotion, transfer or training or receiving any other benefit;
– by dismissing him or subjecting him to any other detriment; or
– by subjecting him to harassment.

This also covers those **with past disabilities** (even including those who recovered before the DDA 1995 came into force), providing the effects of the past disability had lasted at least 12 months or recurred within a period not exceeding 12 months following the first occurrence (s 2(1) DDA 1995).

However, it is not open to a **non-disabled employee** to complain that preferential treatment (for example, in the form of reasonable adjustments) is given to a disabled worker.

MEMO POINTS Since 1 October 2004, **small employers** (i.e. those with fewer than 15 workers in total) are no longer exempt from the ambit of the DDA 1995 and are now liable to fully comply with the provisions of the Act (reg 7 Disability Discrimination Act 1995 (Amendment) Regulations SI 2003/1673).

Legislative framework

5452 **Significant amendments** to the DDA 1995 were introduced on 1 October 2004, together with a raft of other changes to the disability legislative framework (Disability Discrimination Act 1995 (Amendment) Regulations SI 2003/1673, referred to in this chapter as the regulations); Disability Discrimination (Questions and Replies) Order SI 2004/1168 (as amended by Disability Discrimination (Questions and Replies) Order SI 2005/2703); Disability Discrimination Act 1995 (Pensions) Regulations SI 2003/2770; Disability Discrimination (Employment Field) (Leasehold Premises) Regulations SI 2004/153). In summary, the regulations:
– removed the small employer exemption (¶5450);
– extended the scope of the DDA 1995 to cover new occupations (¶5453);
– introduced a new definition of unlawful "direct" discrimination (¶¶5500, 5550);
– extended the scope of the duty to make reasonable adjustments and removed the defence of justification for a failure to make such adjustments (¶¶5515, 5548);
– introduced specific provisions relating to protection from harassment (¶5580);
– prohibited discrimination by qualifications bodies (¶6345);
– prohibited post-employment discrimination or harassment provided that such discrimination or harassment arises out of the employment which has come to an end and is closely connected to it (¶5222);
– clarified that instructions to discriminate and advertisements which demonstrate an intention to discriminate are unlawful (¶¶5590, 590); and
– made changes to the burden of proof in disability discrimination cases (¶5730).

In addition, a revised Code of Practice on Employment and Occupation (DD Code), as well as a separate Code on Trade Organisations and Qualifications Bodies, have been issued by the Disability Rights Commission (DRC). The Codes are not legally binding but they will be taken into consideration by tribunals and courts in assessing disability discrimination claims.

MEMO POINTS The majority of the Disability Discrimination Act 2005 (DDA 2005) came into force in **December 2005**. Where appropriate, the proposed provisions of the Act are summarised in this chapter.

Extended scope Since 1 October 2004, **previously excluded occupations** have been brought within the scope of protection given by the DDA 1995 (ss 4B, 4C-4F, 6A-6C, 7A-7D, 64(8), 64A DDA 1995, as amended by regs 5, 6, 8, 24, 25 SI 2003/1673). The occupations now covered are contract workers, certain statutory office-holders (subject to certain conditions), partners (and prospective partners) in firms, barristers (including Scottish advocates), police, prison officers and firefighters. 5453

1. Definition of disability

A person has a disability if he has a **physical or mental impairment** which has a **substantial and long-term adverse effect** on his ability to carry out **normal day-to-day activities** (s 1(1) DDA 1995). 5455

a. Impairment

An impairment is some damage, defect, disorder or disease compared with a person having a full set of physical and mental equipment in normal condition (*Rugamer v Sony Music Entertainment UK Ltd* [2001] IRLR 644, EAT). This can be either a cause or an effect (*College of Ripon and York St John v Hobbs* [2002] IRLR 185, EAT, approved by *McNicol v Balfour Beatty Rail Maintenance Ltd* [2002] IRLR 711, CA). 5457

Physical impairment **Identifying** a physical impairment will often be relatively straightforward compared with identifying a mental impairment. 5459

The term "impairment" bears its ordinary and natural meaning and may result from another illness (*McNicol v Balfour Beatty Rail Maintenance Ltd* [2002] IRLR 711, CA). This means that a physical impairment (for example, back pain) may result from a mental impairment, for example, clinical depression. (Note that until the DDA 2005 came into force (the majority of the DDA 2005 came into force in December 2005), a mental impairment, to qualify as a disability, must be a clinically well-recognised illness.) This has sometimes been referred to as "psychological or functional overlay" (*McNicol v Balfour Beatty Rail Maintenance Ltd*). 5460

The *McNicol v Balfour Beatty Rail Maintenance Ltd* case approves an earlier EAT decision (*College of Ripon and York St John v Hobbs*, above) in which there was no evidence that the cause of the worker's physical symptoms (progressive muscle wasting and weakness) was an organic disease, but the symptoms themselves were sufficient to fall within the term "physical impairment", even if it had been proved that the cause was a significant psychological disorder. Here, the EAT held that it was not necessary to identify the underlying disease or trauma in order to show that a person has a physical impairment.

The *College of Ripon and York St John v Hobbs* ruling is significant, since it demonstrates that physical symptoms which are caused by psychological disorders may nevertheless amount to physical impairments.

MEMO POINTS This ruling remains vital where a worker suffers from a psychological disorder which does not fall within the category of "clinically well-recognised" mental illness (¶5463).

Potential physical impairments include back, neck or other limb problems, internal organ problems (for example, liver disease) and sensory impairments such as deafness (para 12 Disability Guidance notes). A number of conditions have been recognised by tribunals as potential physical impairments, including ME, epilepsy, club-foot, cerebral palsy, diabetes and dyslexia. However, each case must be considered independently, and in each case the definition of disability must be fulfilled. 5461

Under the new DDA 2005, a person who has **HIV infection**, **multiple sclerosis** and **cancer** is now to be deemed to have a disability from the point of diagnosis (Sch 1 para 6A DDA 1995, as inserted by s 18 DDA 2005). Consequently workers will no longer have to prove that they suffer any substantial and adverse effects from these impairments in order to be deemed disabled.

Individuals who are **certified blind or partially sighted**, however, will automatically fulfil the criteria and will be deemed disabled for the purposes of the Act (Disability Discrimination (Blind and Partially Sighted Persons) Regulations SI 2003/712).

5463 **Mental impairment** By contrast to physical impairments, mental impairments can be difficult to identify. With effect from December 2005, a mental illness is no longer required to be "clinically well-recognised" to be capable of constituting a mental impairment (s 18 DDA 2005).

Where a claimant has a mental impairment which is not a mental illness (such as a learning disability), there is no further requirement for it to be clinically well-recognised nor is there any further burden of proof. Expert evidence of both an identified condition and the nature and degree of the condition should be produced (*Dunham v Ashford Windows* [2005] IRLR 608, EAT). As there is no longer a requirement for claimants to show a clinically well-recognised illness, this is useful guidance for all cases concerning mental impairment going forward.

5465 **Excluded conditions** Certain conditions are expressly excluded, for example a tendency to set fires, a tendency to steal, a tendency to physical or sexual abuse of others, exhibitionism, voyeurism and hay fever. **Addiction** to alcohol, nicotine or any other substance is also excluded unless the addiction is the result of taking medically prescribed drugs or because of other medical treatment.

However, an employee suffering from a mental impairment which results from an excluded condition such as alcoholism, can nonetheless satisfy the definition of disability (*Power v Panasonic UK Ltd* [2003] IRLR 151, EAT).

EXAMPLE In a recent case, the EAT confirmed that an employee may have both a legitimate impairment and an excluded condition and, where this is the case, the critical question is one of causation. If, for example, the reason for the less favourable treatment is the excluded condition and not the legitimate impairment, the employee's claim would fail. If, however, the legitimate impairment and the excluded condition together form the reason, and the legitimate impairment was an effective cause of the treatment, then prima facie discrimination is made out, despite the fact that the excluded condition also forms part of the employer's reason for the less favourable treatment (*Edmund Nutall Ltd v Butterfield* [2005] IRLR 751, EAT).

---

b. Effect

Substantial and adverse

5470 **Substantial** means more than "minor" or "trivial" rather than "very large" (*Goodwin v The Patent Office* [1999] IRLR 4, EAT; see also both the Disability Guidance notes and the DD Code). It is a limitation going beyond the normal differences in ability between people. Despite this seemingly low threshold, research carried out on behalf of the Department for Work and Pensions shows that in 54.1% of cases where a worker was found not to be disabled, the reason was that the adverse effects were not substantial (Monitoring the Disability Discrimination Act (phase 2), DWP In-house report 91).

The focus is on what the worker cannot do, or can only do with difficulty, rather than on what he can do. Just because a worker can carry out a number of normal day-to-day activities does not mean that the impairment does not adversely and substantially affect his ability to carry out other normal day-to-day activities (for example, *Vicary v British Telecommunications plc* [1999] IRLR 680, EAT).

EXAMPLE 1. In *Goodwin v The Patent Office* [1999] IRLR 4, EAT, G, a paranoid schizophrenic, was dismissed following complaints from colleagues about his odd behaviour. The EAT held that the symptoms of his illness which impaired his ability to concentrate and communicate did affect his ability to carry out normal day-to-day activities to a substantial degree.

2. In *Kapadia v London Borough of Lambeth* [2000] IRLR 14, EAT, K who suffered from reactive depression, had difficulty sleeping, suffered from mood swings, appetite loss, lack of motivation, increased difficulty in absorbing and organising information and in communicating. The EAT held that there was sufficient medical evidence to support a finding that K's symptoms had a substantial effect.

Whether an impairment has a substantial effect is a question of fact and there are a **number of factors** that will be taken into account including: 5471
- the **time** it takes the worker to **carry out an activity**, compared with the time in which the activity would be expected to be carried out if the worker was not disabled (para A3 Disability Guidance notes);
- the **cumulative effects of the impairment** on a person's ability to carry out normal day-to-day activities. A worker may suffer from one impairment that has several consequences, none of which alone amounts to a substantial adverse impact. But the cumulative effect of the condition may reach this threshold (para A5 Disability Guidance notes);
- the **cumulative effects of a number of impairments**. This is relevant where a worker suffers from a number of impairments, that when viewed separately do not substantially affect his ability to carry out normal day-to-day activities. When taken together the impact may be sufficient (para A6 Disability Guidance notes; *Vicary v British Telecommunications plc* [1999] IRLR 680, EAT);
- the effects of the **worker's behaviour**. It is permissible to take into account the extent to which modifications in the worker's behaviour will prevent or reduce the effects of the impairment. If the worker can behave in a manner which will lead to cessation of the adverse effects of the impairment, he may not meet the definition of disability (para A7 Disability Guidance notes). However, where it is possible that the worker's ability to manage the effects of his impairment will break down with the result that the effects recur, this possibility must be taken into account when considering whether the impairment has a substantial adverse effect on the worker (para A8 Disability Guidance notes). Where a worker is **medically advised** to modify his behaviour in order to reduce the impact of an impairment, this might have to be treated as medical treatment (see effect of medical treatment below) (para A9 Disability Guidance notes);
- the effect of **environmental factors** (for example, temperature, humidity, tiredness, stress etc.) (para A10 Disability Guidance notes). Where environmental factors arise from an employer's system of work, the employer may be under a duty to make reasonable adjustments to reduce the effect these have on the worker. For example, a worker's asthma is triggered by exposure to fumes at work, but improves when he is away from work. Before deciding to dismiss the worker, the employer should seek to make reasonable adjustments. The employer cannot rely on the fact that away from work the worker's condition would improve to such a degree that the impairment would no longer have a substantial adverse affect on their ability to carry out normal day-to-day activities (*Cruickshank v VAW Motorcast Ltd* [2002] IRLR 24, EAT); and
- the **effect of any medical treatment** (¶5473).

Controlled/corrected impairments Where an impairment is being controlled or corrected by **medical treatment**, the use of prostheses, or any other aid, it should be taken to have the effect it would have without the specific treatment/correction (the so-called "deduced effect") (Sch 1 para 6(1) DDA 1995). One exception, however, is impaired eyesight correctable by wearing **glasses or contact lenses** (Sch 1 para 6(3)(a) DDA 1995). If the worker's ability to carry out normal day-to-day activities is substantially and adversely affected even where spectacles or contact lenses are used, however, these effects ought to be considered (para A14 Disability Guidance notes). 5473

MEMO POINTS Individuals who are **certified blind or partially sighted**, however are automatically deemed disabled for the purposes of the Act (Disability Discrimination (Blind and Partially Sighted Persons) Regulations SI 2003/712).

Treatment that has ceased can be taken into account in assessing whether there is a current disability and **continuing medical treatment** may be taken into account if its consequence is to create a permanent improvement (*Abadeh v British Telecommunications plc* [2001] ICR 156, EAT). 5474

In cases where **successful medical treatment** has resulted in an alleged disability having to be deduced, the worker must provide clear and detailed medical **evidence** of the symptoms he would suffer had he not undergone treatment for his condition (*Woodrup v London Borough of Southwark* [2003] IRLR 111, CA). It should be noted, however, that this is a difficult and complex issue in respect of which further development is anticipated.

EXAMPLE In *Kapadia v London Borough of Lambeth* [2000] IRLR 14 EAT, the EAT ruled that the 20 or so **counselling sessions** which K had undergone over a 2 year period could be regarded as medical treatment and K's condition should have been assessed without reference to that counselling. Consequently, the tribunal had erred in failing to take into account the evidence which showed that, but for the counselling sessions, there was a very strong likelihood that K would suffer a mental breakdown.

In *Carden v Pickerings Europe Ltd* [2005] IRLR 720, EAT, it was considered that if plates and pins are surgically inserted to successfully correct an impairment and **continue to provide support** and assistance, the impairment is being controlled by an aid and it should be taken to have the effect it would have without the aid. However, if they **lose their functionality**, for example because the bones have successfully knitted together and have recovered their original function, then there is no continuing treatment and the employee's condition is taken as it is (i.e. successfully repaired) and he cannot be said to be suffering from a disability.

5476 **Progressive conditions** An impairment(s) suffered by a worker due to a progressive condition will be deemed to have a substantial adverse effect if it has **some adverse effect** on his ability to carry out normal day-to-day activities, and is **likely**, in the future, **to have a substantial effect** (Sch 1 para 8(1) DDA 1995; *Mowat-Brown v University of Surrey* [2002] IRLR 235, EAT). This can include an impairment which has resulted from **medical treatment** for the progressive condition (*Kirton v Tetrosyl Limited* [2003] IRLR 353, CA). In this case, the worker developed incontinence after medical treatment for prostate cancer and it was held that his incontinence was sufficiently linked to the cancer to result from it, notwithstanding the fact that the worker had undergone surgery in the intervening period.

Some impairments can have long periods of **remission** even though the condition is not extinguished (for example, epilepsy). Consequently, an **impairment** which is "**likely to recur**" will be treated as having a continuing adverse effect on a worker's ability to carry out normal day-to-day activities (Sch 1 para 2(2) DDA 1995). When considering the likelihood of recurrence, a tribunal will consider what is "more probable than not" in deciding whether a substantial adverse effect is likely to recur (*Swift v Chief Constable of Wiltshire Constabulary* [2004] IRLR 540, EAT). Note that it is not necessary for the physical or mental impairment itself to be likely to recur, but rather whether any substantial adverse effect which results from the impairment is likely to recur (*Swift v Chief Constable of Wiltshire Constabulary*). All the circumstances of the case should be taken into account, including what the worker could reasonably be expected to do to prevent recurrence, but bearing in mind that coping/controlling methods can break down in certain situations (para B5 Disability Guidance notes).

EXAMPLE In *HSBC Bank plc v Clarkson*, EAT case 205/01, the claimant, who had suffered from two episodes of depression separated by a period of nearly 10 years, was not deemed to be disabled unless it could be shown that each of the episodes of depression had a long-term adverse effect on the claimant's ability to carry out normal day-to-day activities.

MEMO POINTS Under the DDA 2005, persons with **HIV infection**, **multiple sclerosis** and **cancer** are now deemed disabled from the point of diagnosis. Such workers will no longer have to prove that they suffer any substantial and adverse effects from these progressive conditions.

5477 In some cases, the worker may be able to **prove the likelihood of future substantial effect** by producing medical evidence of his likely prognosis, but in others, he may be able to rely on statistical evidence (*Mowat-Brown v University of Surrey*, above).

5479 **Severe disfigurements** Most impairments which consist of a severe disfigurement are deemed to have a substantial adverse effect on the ability of the person affected to carry out normal day-to-day activities (Sch 1 para 3(1) DDA 1995). It appears to be a matter of degree as to whether a disfigurement will be considered sufficiently severe, but it may also be important to consider whether the feature in question is visible, for example, if there is facial disfigurement.

Certain disfigurements are expressly **excluded**, for example, tattoos and decorative body piercing (Sch 1 paras 3(2), (3) DDA 1995).

Long-term

An impairment has a long-term effect if, **at the date of the alleged discriminatory act** (*Cruickshank v VAW Motorcast Ltd* [2002] IRLR 24, EAT), it (Sch 1 para 2(1) DDA 1995): 5481
1. has lasted at least 12 months; or
2. is likely (i.e. it is more probable than not) to last:
– at least 12 months; or
– for the rest of the worker's life (even if this is less than 12 months).

Provided that one of these conditions is satisfied, it is irrelevant that the adverse effects of the **impairment may change or fluctuate** over the period (for example, certain activities may become more easy or difficult to perform or one adverse effect will be replaced by another) (para B2 Disability Guidance notes).

In **assessing** whether an impairment has a long-term effect, consideration will be given to the typical length of the particular effect on an individual and any relevant factors specific to this individual (for example, age and state of health) (para B8 Disability Guidance notes). The total period of impairment both before and after the alleged discriminatory act may also be relevant (*Greenwood v British Airways plc* [1999] ICR 969, EAT).

c. Normal day-to-day activities

An impairment is treated as affecting a worker's ability to carry out normal day-to-day activities only if it **affects** one (or more) of the following **listed activities** (Sch 1 para 4(1) DDA 1995): 5485

– **mobility**. This covers moving or changing position in a wide sense. Account needs to be taken of the extent to which a person is inhibited in getting around unaided or using normal means of transport, climbing stairs, walking a short distance, sitting, standing, bending, reaching, etc. Inability to use a basic form of public transport is likely to amount to a substantial effect on mobility. Difficulty walking unaided for about 1.5 kilometres without discomfort or having to stop (depending on the age of the person and the terrain) is unlikely to be so viewed (para C14 Disability Guidance notes). It has been said that social withdrawal does not amount to an impairment to mobility (*A v Chief Constable of West Mercia Constabulary* [2001] ICR 67, EAT);

– **manual dexterity**. This covers the ability to use hands and fingers with precision. Account should be taken of the ability to co-ordinate both hands and to manipulate the fingers of each hand; inability to press buttons, keyboards or keypads or an ability to do so only more slowly than is normal for most people (but not, for example, for a typist). Loss of function in a dominant hand is expected to have greater impact than loss of functions in a non-dominant hand (para C15 Disability Guidance notes; *Vicary v British Telecommunications plc* [1999] IRLR 680, EAT);

– **physical co-ordination**. This covers balanced and effective interaction of body movement, including hand and eye co-ordination. Account should be taken of a worker's ability to carry out "composite" activities such as walking and using hands at the same time, using a fork to place food in one's mouth without undue concentration/assistance; but not mere clumsiness (para C16 Disability Guidance notes).

– **continence**, i.e. the ability to control urination and/or defecation. Account should be taken of the frequency and extent of loss of control, as well as the worker's age (para C17 Disability Guidance notes).

– the **ability to lift**, **carry or otherwise move everyday objects**. Account should be taken of a person's ability to repeat actions or bear objects of moderate weights (for example, kettle, bags of shopping, a chair) over a reasonable period of time (para C18 Disability Guidance notes).

– **speech, hearing or eyesight**. This covers the ability to speak, hear or see and includes face-to-face, telephone and written or electronic communication. Account may have to be taken of ability to speak clearly, but inability to articulate fluently due to a strong accent or a minor stutter may not be regarded as having a substantial effect. The effect on a worker's hearing needs to be assessed without the use of a hearing aid and against a level of background noise which would not affect the hearing of most people. Inability to hear or understand a person who speaks clearly over the telephone would be regarded as a substantial adverse effect. As for sight, however, the effect on a worker should be considered while he is wearing glasses/contact lenses. Inability to pass an eyesight test for a driving licence or to read ordinary print (when wearing glasses/contact lenses) would be regarded as having a substantial effect (para C19 Disability Guidance notes). However, where a worker had poor vision in one eye only, he was held not to be disabled. He could rely on his good eye and, thus, it was held that there would be no adverse effect on day-to-day activities (*Hudson v The Post Office*, ET case 3100773/98). Individuals who are certified blind or partially sighted, however, will automatically fulfil the criteria and will be deemed disabled for the purposes of the Act without having to prove their normal day-to-day activities are substantially adversely affected (Disability Discrimination (Blind and Partially Sighted Persons) Regulations SI 2003/712).

– **memory or ability to concentrate**, **learn or understand**. Account should be taken of the worker's ability to remember, organise his thoughts, plan a course of action and carry it out, take in new knowledge, or understand spoken or written instructions. The meaning of 'ability to understand' has been extended to include an understanding of social interaction (*Hewett v Motorola Ltd* [2004] IRLR 545, EAT). Consideration should be given to whether the worker learns to do things significantly more slowly than is normal or with significantly more difficulty. It would be reasonable to regard the inability to adapt after a reasonable period of minor changes in work routine as a substantial adverse effect, but not inability to concentrate on a task requiring application over several hours (para C20 Disability Guidance notes); and/or

– **perception of the risk of physical danger**. This covers both underestimation and over-estimation of such danger. Relevant factors include neglecting basic functions such as eating, sleeping and keeping warm, as well as reckless behaviour which puts the worker or other persons at risk. The inability to operate safely properly-maintained equipment would be regarded as a substantial adverse effect, but underestimating risks which are not obvious in an unfamiliar work environment would not (para C21 Disability Guidance notes).

5486 These activities refer generally to **domestic activities** which are normal to and which are carried out fairly regularly by most people (Disability Guidance notes). It does not include activities which are normal only for a particular person or group of people. Thus, normal day-to-day activities will not include highly specialised activities such as playing a particular game, taking part in a particular hobby, playing a musical instrument or playing sport, or performing a highly skilled task. The EAT has held, however, that putting rollers in hair and applying make up could amount to normal day-to-day activities even though they are types of activities which are carried out almost exclusively by women (*Ekpe v Commissioner of Police of the Metropolis* [2001] IRLR 605, EAT).

However, the courts have held that evidence of a complainant's **activities at work**, including the manner in which he performs his duties, can be relevant (*Law Hospital NHS Trust v Rush* [2001] IRLR 611, CS). Although a worker's particular work duties cannot be equated with normal day-to-day activities, they can be relevant to the tribunal's assessment of the complainant's case, particularly if the work duties include some normal day-to-day activities.

Moreover, if a worker's ability to carry out normal day-to-day activities fluctuates and worsens at work due to the particular circumstances of his workplace (for example, if a worker's asthma is exacerbated by environmental conditions at work), then both his activities at work and outside work will be considered in determining whether his impairment has a substantial and long-term adverse effect on his ability to carry out normal day-to-day activities (*Cruickshank v VAW Motorcast Ltd* [2002] IRLR 24, EAT).

5487 In **assessing** whether a worker's activities are affected the focus is on what the worker cannot do or can only do with difficulty, as opposed to what he can do (*Goodwin v The Patent Office* [1999] IRLR 4, EAT).

2. Unlawful

An employer will be liable for unlawful disability discrimination if (ss 3A, 3B, 4A, 16C, 55 DDA 1995; *Clark v TDG Ltd t/a Novacold* [1999] IRLR 318, CA): 5500

a. for a reason which **relates to** a person's disability, the employer treats that person **less favourably** than he treats or would treat others to whom the reason does not or would not apply, and he **cannot justify** the less favourable treatment (i.e. if the reason for it is both material to the circumstances of the particular case and substantial);

b. the employer **fails** to comply with the **duty to make reasonable adjustments** in relation to the disabled person. It is no longer possible for an employer to justify such a failure;

c. on the **ground of** a disabled person's disability, the employer treats that disabled person **less favourably** than he treats or would treat a person not having that particular disability whose relevant circumstances, including his abilities, are the same as, or not materially different from, those of the disabled person (the recently introduced so-called strand of "direct discrimination"). It should be noted that it is **not possible** for an employer **to justify** such less favourable treatment;

d. he **victimises** a person (whether they have a disability or not) for a prohibited reason in respect of the DDA 1995;

e. he subjects a worker to unwanted conduct which amounts to **harassment**; or

f. he gives **instructions to discriminate** against a worker under any of the provisions of the DDA 1995 to a person under his authority.

MEMO POINTS 1. In order to fully implement EC Directive 2000/78 (the Employment Framework Directive), **two new 'strands' of disability discrimination** were introduced: direct discrimination on the ground of a disabled person's disability (**c**. above) and harassment (**e**.). These are broadly consistent with the definitions of discrimination on the grounds of sex, race, religion or belief, and sexual orientation and sit alongside the existing definitions of 'less favourable treatment for a reason related to a person's disability' (**a**.) and 'failure to comply with the duty to make reasonable adjustments' (**b**.).

2. **Less favourable treatment** can include dismissing the employee and, for the purposes of the DDA 1995, the term "dismissal" includes a reference to constructive dismissal and the non-renewal of a fixed term contract (s 4(5) DDA 1995, as amended by reg 5 SI 2003/1673; *Nottinghamshire County Council v Meikle* [2004] IRLR 703, CA; see also ¶8230).

As a result of the Disability Discrimination Act 1995 (Amendment) Regulations SI 2003/1673, **two significant changes** to the way in which the rules operate came into effect on 1 October 2004 (s 3A(3), (4) DDA 1995, as amended by reg 4 SI 2003/1673): 5501

- firstly, although the existing strand of discrimination involving less favourable treatment (**a**.) can still be justified by an employer in certain circumstances (¶5510), it cannot be justified if the treatment amount to "direct discrimination" which falls within the treatment described at **c**.; and
- secondly, it is no longer possible for an employer to justify his failure to comply with the duty to make reasonable adjustments.

It should be noted that where **other statutory obligations** of the employer conflict with the disability provisions, they will take precedence provided there are no reasonable adjustments which the employer can make (s 59 DDA 1995). For example, health and safety legislative obligations impose an absolute duty on the employer and, if it is clearly impossible for an employee to comply with a particular requirement (for example, to wear protective boots because of a skin condition) and there would be a risk to an employee's health and safety as a result, which could not be adequately controlled (for example, because suitable alternatives could not be found), then the employer's only viable option is not to employ the employee in that particular area. In such circumstances, the anti-discrimination legislation is subordinate to health and safety legislation and the employee cannot make a claim for discrimination if he is dismissed (*(1) Lane Group plc (2) North Somerset Council v Farmiloe*, EAT cases 0352 and 0357/03; see also ¶5510). 5503

a. Less favourable treatment for a disability-related reason

5505 The **existing definition** of less treatment of a disabled person for a reason which relates to the disabled person's disability remains the same, although it is to be found at a different section in the DDA 1995 (s 3A(1) DDA 1995, as amended by reg 4 SI 2003/1673).

EXAMPLE A job applicant has a disability which requires the use of a wheelchair. She has the skills and qualifications to perform the job, but the employer is concerned that the wheelchair will get in the way in the office. Consequently, the employer gives the job to a person who is no more suitable for the job but who does not use a wheelchair. The job applicant has been treated less favourably than the successful candidate (by not being offered the job); the reason for the less favourable treatment relates to the disability (the fact that she uses a wheelchair).

5506 Often, there will not be direct evidence that an employer has acted for a reason related to a worker's disability. Consequently, a tribunal may **infer** that discrimination has occurred in certain circumstances where the facts show a difference in treatment for which an employer cannot provide a satisfactory explanation (*Glasgow City Council v Zafar* [1998] ICR 120, HL; *Roberts v Warrington Borough Council*, EAT case 497/98; *Rowden v Dutton Gregory* [2002] ICR 971, EAT). For further discussion on the burden of proof in discrimination cases, see ¶5730.

5507 Difficulties can arise where a disability affects a person's performance in a job (for example, the person finds it hard to concentrate or is often absent on sick leave), but the **disability is not obvious** and/or the **employer has no knowledge** of it. The authorities are mixed on whether the employer could be liable in such cases but, on balance, the answer seems to be that he can, provided that the disability and the worker's treatment are related (*HJ Heinz Co Ltd v Kenrick* [2000] IRLR 144, EAT; *London Borough of Hammersmith & Fulham v Farnsworth* [2000] IRLR 691, EAT). It is arguable, however, that this will not apply where an employer has absolutely no reason to believe that a worker is disabled (i.e. there are absolutely no factors which alert or should alert the employer to the possibility that the worker might be disabled) and his lack of knowledge is reasonable (*Heggison v A & W Bernard*, EAT case 1276/99).

The employer's **motive and intent** may also not be relevant (*British Sugar plc v Kirker* [1998] IRLR 624 EAT, and see especially the ET decision).

EXAMPLE In *HJ Heinz Co Ltd v Kenrick*, K was off work on sick leave for a lengthy period. The cause, diagnosis and future prognosis of his condition was unclear. He attended an interview with the employer, whose medical adviser reported that he was not fit to return to work. K told the employer that he was due to see a specialist and asked him to wait for the result of this examination before deciding whether or not to dismiss him. The employer refused and dismissed K the following day. Shortly afterwards, K was diagnosed as suffering from Chronic Fatigue Syndrome. The EAT ruled that K had been directly discriminated against, even though the employer did not know he suffered from a disability.

5508 **Performance-related pay schemes** which discriminate against disabled workers (and, in respect of which, employers do not make any reasonable adjustments that could improve the performance of a disabled person – see ¶5515) are no longer justifiable since 1 October 2004 and constitute unlawful discrimination (reg 3 SI 2004/153 revoking reg 3(1) SI 1996/1456).

Moreover, discrimination against disabled persons in respect of **any other benefit under a scheme or arrangement** for the benefit of employees in respect of the termination of their employment, retirement, old age, death, accident, injury, sickness or invalidity is prohibited (s 18 DDA 1995).

See ¶3443 for details of disability discrimination in respect of occupational pension schemes.

5509 **Comparison** Workers to whom the disabled worker should be compared are those to whom the reason for the treatment (for example, long term absence, poor performance or persistent lateness caused by the disability) do not apply (*Clark v TDG Ltd t/a Novacold* [1999] IRLR 318, CA). Consequently, a claimant's position may be compared with that of:
- an able-bodied worker;
- a person who suffers from a different impairment; or
- a person who suffers from the same impairment but in different circumstances.

EXAMPLE In *Clark v TDG Ltd t/a Novacold*, a worker was dismissed after an injury to his back (which amounted to a disability) prevented him from doing his work. It was found that he was dismissed for a reason related to his disability, i.e. because following his injury he was unable to perform his work duties. The reason for his dismissal did not apply to other workers who were able to perform their job. This was sufficient to establish less favourable treatment and the question became whether the dismissal was objectively justified.

Justification

Once it has been established that a worker has been treated less favourably for a disability-related reason, the employer will only escape liability if he can show that this was justified. 5510

Treatment will only be justified if the **reason** for it is both material to the circumstances of the particular case and substantial (s 3A(3) DDA 1995, as amended by reg 4 SI 2003/1673). For a reason to be **material**, there must be a reasonably strong connection between that reason and the circumstances of the individual case (*Jones v Post Office* [2001] IRLR 384, CA). **Substantial** means more than minor or trivial (*Jones v Post Office*); the reason must carry real weight and be of substance (*HJ Heinz Co Ltd v Kenrick*, above). Consequently, a tribunal will not make its own analysis, for example where a properly conducted risk assessment provides a reason for the treatment of the worker which is on its face both material and substantial, and is not irrational (*Jones v Post Office*).

The Court of Appeal has recently reiterated the similarities between the test for justification and the "band of reasonable responses" test used by tribunals in unfair dismissal claims (¶8435). In determining whether an act of disability-related discrimination can be justified, a tribunal must decide whether the reason provided by the employer for the less favourable treatment of the claimant is within the range of what a reasonable employer would have relied on as a material and substantial reason for such treatment (J. Walter Thompson Group Ltd [2005] IRLR 376, CA). This test is less stringent than the test for justification laid down in respect of the other strands of discrimination.

However, less favourable treatment of a disabled person **cannot be justified** where it constitutes less favourable treatment on the ground of that person's disability which falls within the scope of the new definition of so-called 'direct discrimination' (s 3A(4) DDA 1995, as amended by reg 4 SI 2003/1673). See ¶5550.

EXAMPLE Not justified

1. A person with a learning disability has worked in a shop for many years, stocking shelves, without any problem. The employer appoints a new manager who decides that a risk assessment of the job should be carried out in respect of the worker with a learning disability but not for all the other staff who stack shelves. This is unlikely to be justified (and may even amount to 'direct' discrimination – see ¶5550) (para 6.10 DD Code).
2. A worker suffering from a mental illness which amounts to a disability is dismissed for persistent absenteeism caused by her illness. If the amount of time off the worker took is only slightly worse than the amount of time off the employer normally accepts as sick leave for other workers, the employer is unlikely to be able to establish that the reason for the dismissal was substantial.
3. A clerical worker with a learning disability cannot complete some of her tasks as quickly as her colleagues, however there is a little difference in productivity overall. She is dismissed for this reason. The dismissal is unlikely to be for a substantial reason.

Justified

1. A school dismissed a technician who was not taking medication for his schizophrenia. The reason for the dismissal was that the school was concerned that other staff and pupils would have been at risk if he had had an acute relapse. The EAT found that the discrimination was justified (*A v London Borough of Hounslow*, EAT case 1155/98).
2. A job applicant who suffers with severe back pain and cannot bend is rejected for a job as a carpet fitter since he is unable to carry out the essential function of the job, which is to fit carpets. It is likely that such treatment would be lawful since the reason for rejecting him is both substantial and clearly material to the particular circumstances of the case (para 6.3 DD Code).

Long-term absence and an employer's **health and safety obligations** are common reasons for less favourable treatment, for example, the dismissal of a disabled worker. If a worker is too ill to work and there is no likelihood of return to work in the foreseeable future, an 5511 employer may be justified in terminating the employment but only if he has considered whether there are any reasonable adjustments which could be made to enable the worker's return (for example, to another job, on reduced hours etc.) (para 6.16 DD Code).

An employer will only have a defence of justification for treating a disabled employee less favourably if he can show that the less favourable treatment which is the subject of the employee's claim would have been justified even if the required **reasonable adjustments** had been made (s 3A(6) DDA 1995, as amended by reg 4 SI 2003/1673).

EXAMPLE 1. In *Nottinghamshire County Council v Meikle* [2004] IRLR 703, CA, the employer could not justify paying Mrs Meikle half-pay after a prolonged period of absence (100 days) due to her disability (in accordance with its contractual sick pay scheme) since she would have been back at work and entitled to full pay had the employer complied with his duty to make the reasonable adjustments required.
2. An employer receives advice from an occupational health advisor in respect of an employee which states that the employee is 'unfit to work'. Despite this advice, the employer is under a duty to consider whether there are any reasonable adjustments which could be made to enable the employee to return to work (para 6.16 DD Code).

5512 One question is whether **lack of knowledge** of a worker's disability is material where an employer seeks to establish the defence of justification. The authorities on this point vary. On balance, however, it seems that lack of knowledge might make it harder for an employer to establish the defence of justification, but it will not preclude it (*Quinn v Schwarzkopf* [2002] IRLR 602, CA; *Callagan v Glasgow City Council* [2001] IRLR 724, EAT).

An employment tribunal will consider and make findings of fact on, in relation to establishing an employer's **credibility and rationality**, expert medical evidence obtained after an alleged discriminatory act, even if such evidence was not available to the employer at the time. However, it must not be used to judge whether or not an employer's decision was justified (*Surrey Police v Marshall* [2002] IRLR 843, EAT).

b. Failure to make reasonable adjustments

5515 The **existing duty** to make reasonable adjustments remains but significant changes were made to its scope on 1 October 2004 (s 4A DDA 1995, as amended by reg 5 SI 2003/1673).

The duty applies where a **provision**, **criterion or practice** is applied by or on behalf of an employer, or any **physical features** of premises occupied by the employer, place a disabled person at a **substantial disadvantage** compared with non-disabled people. In such circumstances, the employer, where it is reasonable to do so, will be under a duty to make adjustments or modifications to any provision, criterion or practice which causes more than a minor or trivial disadvantage to a disabled person in order to remove that particular disadvantage.

MEMO POINTS Prior to 1 October 2004, the duty applied to '**arrangements**' made by and on behalf of an employer, together with physical features of premises occupied by him. The new regulations state that 'arrangements' expressly fall within the scope of 'provision, criterion or practice' (s 18D(2) DDA 1995, as amended by reg 18 SI 2003/1673).

5516 The duty **applies** in relation to both job applicants and potential job applicants who have notified the employer that they may apply for employment with him.

The duty also applies during employment and is now **extended** to apply to all stages of the employment process, up to and including when an employer dismisses an employee or subjects him to a detriment. The duty also applies in relation to post-employment discrimination (¶5222). Consequently, arrangements for the continuation or termination of employment and redundancy selection criteria are covered, as are pre-dismissal breaches of duty which result in the worker's dismissal (*Clark v TDG Ltd t/a Novacold* [1999] IRLR 318, CA). Even if a worker is **subject to disciplinary proceedings** in which he faces serious allegations of misconduct, an employer will still be liable to comply with the duty to make reasonable adjustments in respect of that worker (*Beart v HM Prison Service* [2003] IRLR 238, CA).

EXAMPLE 1. A person suffering from dyslexia, which amounts to a disability, applies for a job where he would be required to write letters within fairly long deadlines. All applicants are required to sit a test on letter-writing abilities. The job applicant can generally write letters very well but finds it difficult to do so in the stressful situation of the test. The employer's criterion (the requirement that job applicants pass the particular test within a set period of time) could substantially disadvantage the applicant, compared to non-disabled people who would not find such arrangements stressful or, if they did, would not be so affected by them. The employer would be expected to allow the applicant more time to complete the test, as this would "remedy" the applicant's position, would not inconvenience the employer very much and would only briefly delay its decision on an appointment (para 5.3 DD Code).

2. In *Berry v GB Electronics Ltd*, EAT case 0882/00, an employer informed a deaf worker, together with 7 other workers, that he was dismissed for redundancy. Since the employer did not engage a person who could communicate properly with the deaf worker, he only understood that he was dismissed, but not that others had also lost their jobs or that the dismissal was for redundancy. The employer was found to have breached the duty to make reasonable adjustments (for example, the appointment of an interpreter versed in sign language). The discrimination was in the arrangements made for, and the manner of, dismissal.

Employers are now under a duty to make reasonable adjustments in respect of their **performance-related pay schemes** to improve the performance of their disabled workers who are subject to a substantial disadvantage under them (reg 3 SI 2004/153 revoking reg 3(1) SI 1996/1456). **5517**

Contractual sick pay which is paid by the employer directly to an employee is also included in the ambit of the duty to make reasonable adjustments (*Nottinghamshire County Council v Meikle* [2004] IRLR 703, CA). This might entail making an alteration to a scheme rule if such an adjustment is reasonable.

See ¶3443 for details of disability discrimination in respect of occupational pension schemes.

The duty is a strict one, with the result that **employers must consider** what reasonable adjustments they can make (*Cosgrove v Caesar & Howie* [2001] IRLR 653, EAT). This duty will be **assessed objectively**, consequently, if the employer has failed to make an adjustment which the tribunal has held to be reasonable, he will have discriminated against the disabled worker in question. **5518**

Where a **worker proposes certain adjustments**, the employer is required to consider them. Indeed, when assessing whether an employer met his duty of reasonable adjustments, tribunals will consider the extent to which all the adjustments requested by a worker might have alleviated his symptoms and assisted him at work (*Fu v London Borough of Camden* [2001] IRLR 186, EAT). If a particular adjustment is considered to be unreasonable an employer ought to consider whether he can make other, reasonable, adjustments. An employer cannot require a worker to contribute to the cost of a reasonable adjustment. **5519**

If the employer is not sure that the impairment actually exists (for example, because it is not visible or noticeable), he can ask the worker to produce evidence that the impairment is a disability. For example, where a worker claims to suffer from a mental illness which requires him to take time off work on a frequent but irregular basis, if his employer is not convinced that the worker has a disability, he can ask for evidence of the mental illness claimed.

The duty to make adjustments only arises if an employer **knows or could reasonably be expected to know** that a person (including a job applicant) is disabled and is likely to be placed at a substantial disadvantage by the employer's provisions, criteria, practices or premises (s 4A(3) DDA 1995, as amended by reg 5 SI 2003/1673). An employer cannot claim that he did not know about a job applicant/worker's disability if a worker or agent of the employer (for example, a supervisor, personnel officer or occupational health officer) knew that the job applicant/worker was disabled. This does not apply where such information is gained by a person who provides services to workers independently of the employer, for example, an independent counselling service. **5520**

Provisions, criteria, practices and physical features The **provisions**, **criteria**, **and practices** that are covered are those made by or on behalf of the employer in relation to determining to whom employment should be offered and any term, condition or arrange- **5521**

ment on which employment, promotion, a transfer, training or any other benefit is offered or provided (para 5.8 DD Code). Therefore the duty to make reasonable adjustments applies, for example, to selection procedures (including premises used for interviews), job offers, and any other contractual arrangements or working conditions. However, only job-related arrangements are covered (*Kenny v Hampshire Constabulary* [1999] ICR 27, EAT). Consequently, matters such as providing assistance to and from work are excluded. Moreover, requiring a disabled job applicant to undergo an **occupational health assessment** does not amount to an "arrangement", although the occupational health adviser's assessment of whether the job applicant is or is not fit for the job he has applied for and whether the job is stressful or not will amount to an "arrangement" and an employer will be under a duty to make reasonable adjustments in respect of the adviser's assessment to prevent the job applicant from being placed at a substantial disadvantage in comparison to non-disabled job applicants (*Paul v National Probation Service* [2004] IRLR 190, EAT). Such adjustments could include evaluating the occupational health report in more depth and consulting the job applicant's own medical adviser.

In a significant case, the House of Lords has held that "arrangements" can include an **implied condition** of an employee's employment that he will be **fit to work** at all times in the position for which he is employed and, consequently, results in a further condition that an employee will be liable to be dismissed if he is unfit to do the work for which he is employed (*Archibald v Fife Council* [2004] IRLR 651, HL). In this case, such implied terms placed the employee at a substantial disadvantage in comparison to others in the same employment who were not disabled from doing their work (and who were therefore not liable to be dismissed from their position) and, consequently, her incapability to work in her position as a result of her disability automatically triggered her employer's duty to make reasonable adjustments to prevent her from being placed at such a disadvantage (¶5527).

5522 **Physical features** are defined as any permanent or temporary (s 18D(2) DDA 1995, as amended by reg 18 SI 2003/1673):
- feature arising from the design or construction of a building on the premises;
- feature on the premises of any approach to, exit from or access to such a building;
- fixtures, fittings, furnishings, furniture, equipment or materials in or on the premises; or
- other physical element or quality of any land comprised on the premises.

There may be occasions where employers cannot, or are not required to make changes to physical features (for example, because the problem lies in premises which the employer does not occupy, such as clients' premises, or because it is not possible to change the premises). In such cases, employers still need to consider whether their work arrangements can be adapted (for example, whether the worker can be allocated other clients or be relocated to another office).

EXAMPLE An employer has an open plan office. As a result, a worker who has a hearing impairment has difficulty hearing colleagues. The disadvantage is caused by a physical feature of the premises. It might be that the employer cannot reasonably do anything in the circumstances to change this feature. However, it might be reasonable for the employer to transfer the worker to another workplace with better acoustics (or to a smaller office) or to provide appropriate supervision when instructions are given, and thus obviate any disadvantage which the worker would otherwise suffer (para 5.9 DD Code).

5523 Where an employer **occupies premises under a lease** which does not permit it to make alterations to the premises and he is under a duty to make reasonable adjustments, he must apply to the lessor in writing for consent to making the alteration. The lease will have effect as if it allows the occupier to make alterations with the written consent of the lessor and that the lessor will not withhold consent unreasonably. However, the lessor may attach reasonable conditions to the consent, for example that the occupier repays the lessor's costs in giving the consent and that on expiry of the lease the employer must reinstate the premises to their pre-altered state (s 18A DDA 1995, as amended by reg 14 SI 2003/1673). Further details as to the revised **procedure for granting consent** and the circumstances in which the lessor can **reasonably withhold consent** can be found in the Disability Discrimination (Employment Field) (Leasehold Premises) Regulations SI 2004/153 which revoked the Disability Discrimination (Employment) Regulations SI 1996/1456 and Disability Discrimination (Sub-leases and Sub-tenancies) Regulations SI 1996/1333. See also the DD Code.

Substantial disadvantage Substantial disadvantages are those which are not minor or trivial. For example, a worker who is confined to a wheelchair finds it impossible to get through a particular doorway or if there are clear glass doors at the end of a corridor which might present a workplace hazard for an employee with impaired vision. In the example of the worker who is confined to a wheelchair, if there is a reasonably easy alternative route to the same destination, the employer is unlikely to be required to widen the particular doorway to enable passage by the worker. 5525

Adjustments

The following are examples of the range of adjustments that might need to be considered depending on the particular disadvantages of the disabled worker in question: 5527

– **adjustments to premises**. For example, widening a doorway, providing a ramp or moving furniture for a wheelchair user, relocating light switches, door handles or shelves for someone who has difficulty in reaching, or providing appropriate contrast in décor to help the safe mobility of a visually impaired person;

– **reallocating duties** to another person. A situation in which this might arise is where a disabled worker suffers from vertigo and his job occasionally involves going onto an open roof of a building;

– **transferring to fill an existing vacancy**. When a worker becomes disabled or his disability worsens so that he cannot continue in his current job, and there is no reasonable adjustment that would enable him to do so, the worker should be considered for suitable vacancies. Reasonable re-training should also be provided. Furthermore, depending on all the facts of the case and, in particular, as to what is reasonable, a reasonable adjustment might be to transfer an employee to a job at a slightly higher grade (in addition to a position at the same or lower grade) and this would entail actually appointing the worker to the job as opposed to simply allowing him to apply for such a position (*Archibald v Fife Council* [2004] IRLR 651, HL). In reaching its decision in this case, the House of Lords held that such a reasonable adjustment could therefore entail treating a disabled worker more favourably than non-disabled workers. Employers are not, however, required to re-deploy workers if there are no vacancies or if a particular transfer will only have limited positive benefit for the worker;

– **altering working hours or training**. Flexibility in hours and the provision of additional breaks may be appropriate to accommodate the needs of a disabled person;

– **assigning to a different place of work or training**. It may be reasonable, for example, to transfer a person with a hearing impairment from an open plan office to a more acoustically suitable environment, or to move a wheelchair user from a third floor office to a ground floor office;

– **allowing time off for rehabilitation, assessment or treatment**. An employer should consider allowing a disabled person extra time off during work for the purposes of treatment.

– **appropriate training or mentoring** (whether for the disabled person or any other person). This may be training on equipment especially designed for the disabled person or training which is provided to all workers but which has to be adapted because of the disability. The EAT has allowed a decision of disability discrimination to stand even though the tribunal, which had held that the employer had failed to make reasonable adjustments by failing to retrain the worker, had failed to specify precisely what training the employer should have provided. The failure to retrain the worker at all meant that it was not necessary to be more specific (*Electronic Data Systems Ltd v Travis*, EAT case 0476/03).

– **acquiring or modifying equipment**. For example, an employer may need to provide special equipment such as an adapted keyboard to a worker affected by RSI or an adapted telephone for a worker with a hearing impairment. An employer is not required to provide or modify equipment for personal purposes unconnected with work;

– **modifying instructions/reference manuals**. An employer may be required to provide instructions and manuals in Braille, on audio tape or orally with individual demonstration;

– **modifying procedures for testing or assessment**. An example would be allowing a job applicant with restricted manual dexterity to give oral instead of written responses in a test;
– **providing a reader/interpreter**. An employer may be required to provide a person with a visual impairment with a reader at particular times during the working day, for example to read post; and/or
– **providing supervision or other support**. It could be appropriate for an employer to provide a worker whose disability leads to uncertainty or lack of confidence with help from a colleague.

5529 **Whether reasonable to make** Where the duty has arisen, the employer must make such adjustments that are reasonable in order to prevent the disadvantage (s 3A(2) DDA 1995, as amended by reg 4 SI 2003/1673).

5530 Whether a particular adjustment is reasonable will be **determined objectively**, i.e. on the basis of what a reasonable employer should have done. In making this evaluation tribunals will take account of a **number of factors**, in particular (s 18B DDA 1995, as amended by reg 17 SI 2003/1673):
– the **effectiveness** of the step in preventing a disadvantage. It is unlikely to be reasonable for an employer to have to make an adjustment involving little benefit to the disabled applicant/worker. The employer should consider consulting the worker on the proposed adjustment as he is most likely to know if it will be effective;
– the **practicability** of the step. It is more likely to be reasonable for an employer to take a step which is easy than one which is difficult. The amount of warning regarding the disability which the employer receives may be relevant. If, for example, a job applicant does not tell a prospective employer about his disability until the interview, this may cause adjustments that would otherwise be manageable to become impracticable;
– the **financial and other costs** of the adjustment and the **extent of any disruption**. An adjustment is likely to be regarded as reasonable if the cost of it is insignificant and the step entailed is not disruptive. However, the greater the **employer's financial or other resources**, the more likely it is that it will be reasonable for the employer to make a more costly adjustment. Further, if **financial assistance** is available, for example from a Government programme or voluntary body, it may be reasonable for an employer to make an adjustment where that adjustment would have been too costly without that assistance. In any event, as a matter of good practice, employers should first consider the effectiveness and practicability of a particular adjustment before assessing the financial aspect;
– the value of the worker's **experience and expertise** to the employer will also be relevant. Assessing this will involve consideration of: the amount invested in the worker, his length of service and his expected future service, his level of skill and knowledge, the quality of the worker's relationships with clients, and the level of the worker's pay; and
– the **nature of the employer's activities** and the **size of his undertaking**. The larger the number of staff employed by the employer, the more likely it is that it will be reasonable for the employer to make certain adjustments, for example, reallocating some of a disabled worker's duties or transferring him to an existing vacancy.

Other factors include the effect which any adjustment would have on other workers, adjustments made for other disabled workers, the extent to which the disabled worker co-operates with the employer's proposed adjustment and adjustments already made. In relation to the last factor, an employer who had already taken steps which satisfied the duty to make reasonable adjustments was not required to pursue the option of another adjustment (in this case a phased return), particularly as the employee did not have an expected return date (*Home Office v Collins* [2005] EWCA Civ 598).

In relation to **private households**, factors to be taken into account in determining the reasonableness of an adjustment include, in particular, the extent to which making the adjustment would disrupt that household or disturb any resident of the household (s 18B DDA 1995, as amended by reg 17 SI 2003/1673).

5531 A disabled person is **not required to contribute** to the cost of an adjustment. However, a disabled worker may offer to provide certain equipment to assist the performance of his work. If this is the case, it may be reasonable for the employer to accept the offer as well as to take additional steps to allow the disabled person to use the equipment.

EXAMPLE A disabled person applies for a job which involves the use of a company car for business travel. The worker has an adapted car of her own which she is willing to use on business. In these circumstances, it may be reasonable for the employer to allow this and to pay the worker a reasonable car allowance (even though it may not have been reasonable for the employer to provide an adapted company car or to pay an allowance to cover alternative travel arrangements).

In circumstances where a reasonable adjustment requires the **co-operation of other workers** (for example, where some duties are reallocated), the employer must ensure that such co-operation takes place. This might also lead to issues of **confidentiality** as other workers, supervisors, personnel officers etc. may have to be informed of the adjustment. In such cases the employer should keep the reason for making the adjustment confidential if he would not have made a similar revelation about a non-disabled worker for an equally legitimate management purpose. 5532

No justification It is no longer possible for an employer to try to defend a failure to comply with the duty to make reasonable adjustments since the justification defence has been removed (SI 2003/1673). Instead, employers are expected to focus on what adjustments are necessary and whether it is reasonable to make such adjustments. 5548

c. Less favourable treatment on the ground of a person's disability

A further strand of so-called "**direct**" disability discrimination was introduced on 1 October 2004. This occurs where an employer, **on the ground of** the disabled person's **disability**, treats the disabled person less favourably than he treats or would treat a person not having that particular disability whose relevant circumstances, including his abilities, are the same as, or not materially different from, those of the disabled person (s 3A(5) DDA 1995, as inserted by reg 4 SI 2003/1673). 5550

This strand of disability discrimination operates alongside the pre-existing definition of disability-related less favourable treatment but is perhaps distinguished from the disability-related definition since it occurs when the **disability itself** is the reason for the less favourable treatment taking place, rather than being for a reason related to the disability, although it is arguable that treatment on the ground of a person's disability is also disability-related treatment. It is, however, important that a distinction is made as to when which strand applies since whilst disability-related discrimination can, in certain circumstances, be justified by the employer, direct discrimination on the ground of disability cannot. However, until further guidance is received from the courts and tribunals, it is difficult to predict as to exactly when each of the two strands will apply. In the meantime, further guidance can be found in the DRC's revised Code of Practice (DD Code) and the Explanatory Memorandum published by the Government. 5551

The issue is whether a disabled person would have received the less favourable treatment from his employer **but for** his disability (para 4.7 DD Code). Consequently, if an employer who has generalised, **stereotypical views or assumptions** about a particular disability or its effects, treats a disabled person less favourably on these grounds, this is likely to be unlawful direct discrimination since the employer would not make such assumptions about a non-disabled person (para 4.8 DD Code). 5552

EXAMPLE 1. An employer who has advertised for a shop assistant rejects an applicant with a severe facial disfigurement solely on the ground that other employees would be uncomfortable working alongside her. The employer's conduct constitutes unlawful direct discrimination (para 4.9 DD Code).
2. An employer assumes (wrongly) that blind people cannot use computers and consequently rejects an application for a job involving computers from a blind person. Since the employer has not attempted to consider the individual job applicant's particular circumstances, and he has treated her less favourably because of his wrongly-held assumptions, by not short-listing her for the position, he is likely to have directly discriminated against her (para 4.8 DD Code).

5553 It is essential to **look behind the reason** provided for less favourable treatment by an employer since, although it may appear that an employer has acted for an apparently disability-neutral reason, upon further investigation, it may be discovered that this was merely a pretext for direct discrimination (para 4.19 DD Code).

However, direct discrimination may sometimes be **unconscious** as an employer may act on deeply-held prejudices without realising that he is doing so.

EXAMPLE An employer advertises an internal vacancy for a position within his workforce. The job description indicates that the job would not be suitable for persons with a history of mental illness. Such a 'blanket ban' on any employees who have suffered from mental illness will be unlawful since the employer has suggested that he would disregard anyone falling into this category without any consideration of their individual circumstances (para 4.11 DD Code).

5555 **Comparison** The **appropriate comparator** is a person without the particular disability whose circumstances (including his abilities) are the same as, or not materially different from, those of the disabled person concerned. In the first example at ¶5552, the appropriate comparator would have been someone without the severe facial disfigurement but who has the same ability as the disabled person to do the job of a shop assistant. It should be noted that it is not essential to find a comparator whose circumstances are the same in every respect provided the comparator's relevant circumstances (i.e. including his abilities) are the same as, or not materially different from, those of the disabled person.

In the second example of the blind woman who was rejected for a job involving computers (¶5552), the appropriate comparator would have been a person who is not blind but who has the same abilities as the blind woman to do the job (para 4.15 DD Code).

5556 **No justification** It should be noted that it is not open for an employer to try to justify direct discrimination on the ground of a person's disability (s 3A(4) DDA 1995).

d. Victimisation

5570 This occurs when a worker is subjected to **less favourable treatment** than others whose circumstances are the same as his because **he has** (in respect of the DDA 1995 (s 55 (1) DDA 1995, as amended by reg 19 SI 2003/1673)):
- **brought proceedings** against his employer or any other worker;
- given **evidence or information** in connection with proceedings brought by another person under the DDA 1995;
- taken any **other action** under or by reference to these provisions in relation to his employer or any other person; or
- made any **allegation** against his employer or any other worker which would amount to a contravention of the DDA 1995.

This extends to a **suspicion** by the employer that the worker intends to do any of these things.

MEMO POINTS It is **not necessary** for a person to have (or to have had) a disability to be able to claim victimisation under the DDA 1995, but where the person who suffers the less favourable treatment under these provisions has a disability, that **disability will be disregarded** for the purposes of comparing him/her to others whose circumstances are the same as his.

5571 However, there will be **no protection** for a worker if the allegation made by him, or evidence or information given by him was false and not made (or given) in good faith (s 55(4) DDA 1995).

5572 The **appropriate comparator** is a worker who has not brought discrimination proceedings on grounds other than disability (*Chief Constable of West Yorkshire Police v Khan* [2001] IRLR 830, HL, which considered the RRA 1976).

e. Harassment

Since 1 October 2004, harassment is now a distinct form of discrimination (s 3B DDA 1995, as amended by reg 4 SI 2003/1673). Harassment occurs where an employer, for a reason which relates to a disabled person's disability, subjects that person to unwanted conduct which has the purpose or effect of (s 3B(1) DDA 1995): 5580
- violating the disabled person's dignity; or
- creating an intimidating, hostile, degrading, humiliating or offensive environment for him.

MEMO POINTS Since it is possible to bring a **free-standing claim** of harassment, it is no longer possible (or indeed necessary) for a person to argue that his alleged harassment constitutes a detriment.

It is irrelevant whether the alleged harassment is **intentional** or not. Even if the complainant cannot establish that the employer's conduct was intentional, the tribunal must consider whether, having regard to all the circumstances, including in particular the perception of the disabled person, the conduct should reasonably be considered as having that effect (s 3B(2) DDA 1995). 5581

Consequently, the **test** is neither entirely objective nor subjective, since some account needs to be taken of the alleged victim's perception. However, it does mean that a complainant who **unreasonably takes offence** at an innocent comment would probably not be considered to have been harassed, although if the conduct was repeated after the complainant made his feelings known, then the repeat conduct could well constitute unlawful harassment.

See ¶5365 as to the further avenue open to complainants under the **Protection from Harassment Act 1997**. 5582

f. Instructions and pressure to discriminate

It is unlawful for a person who has **authority over another person** or, in accordance with whose wishes that other person is accustomed to act, to instruct that other person to discriminate against a worker under any provision of the DDA 1995 (s 16C DDA 1995, as inserted by reg 15 SI 2003/1673). It is also unlawful to induce (or attempt to induce) an unlawful act of disability discrimination by providing or offering to provide another person with a benefit or subjecting, or threatening to subject him, to a detriment. Such an attempted inducement will constitute unlawful conduct even if it is not made directly to the person in question, provided it is made in such a way that he is likely to hear of it. 5590

EXAMPLE The chairman of a holding company, Y Ltd, tries to exert pressure on the managing director of one of Y Ltd's subsidiaries, Z Ltd, to dismiss a disabled worker in contravention of the DDA 1995. Such pressure on the managing director will constitute unlawful conduct.

Only the DRC can bring proceedings in respect of unlawful instructions to discriminate (s 17B DDA 1995, as amended by reg 15 SI 2003/1673). 5591

SECTION 2

Equal pay

5600 Inequality regarding pay is a **separate and distinct form of action** (Equal Pay Act 1970, as amended (EPA 1970)). This is in addition to any claim regarding inequality of pay with regard to workers of the opposite sex under the **sex discrimination** legislation (SDA 1975; ¶5260). It should be noted that part-time workers and fixed-term employees may also be able to bring a **non-discriminatory claim** (Part-time Workers (Prevention of Less Favourable Treatment) Regulations SI 2000/1551, as amended; Fixed-term Employees (Prevention of Less Favourable Treatment) Regulations SI 2002/2034), if appropriate.

MEMO POINTS 1. The **sources** of this separate form of action stem from the implementation of EC Directive 1975/117 (Equal Pay Directive), EC Directive 1976/207 (Equal Treatment Directive), EC Directive 1986/378 and EC Directive 1996/96. These, together with Art 141 of the Treaty of Rome (which stipulates the principle of equal pay for equal work or work of equal value), underline the domestic rules and can assist interpretation of the EPA 1970.
Unless workers are employed by a **public authority** (for example, government departments, local authorities, health or education authorities) they cannot rely directly on these Directives and Art 141 if they believe that the UK has failed to implement them correctly, or that Art 141 and the Directives give them greater rights than the UK implementing regulations.
2. A **Code of Practice** on equal pay (EP Code), published by the EOC (revised December 2003) gives advice as to how employers can comply with the law as well as recommending good practice with respect to pay arrangements. The provisions of the code are admissible as evidence in any equal pay or sex discrimination proceedings.
3. The EOC has also published an **Equal Pay Review Kit** which gives clear advice to employers on good equal pay practice. It contains a 5-step equal pay review model with guidance on each step. These documents can be downloaded from the EOC website at www.eoc.org.uk. Employers should consider conducting an equal pay **audit** to ensure their reward structures are transparent and, if there is any inequality of pay between men and women, that such differences are objectively justifiable. The DTI has set up the Accounting for People Task Force to study the correlation between employers' human resource policies and their workers' pay. The Government has committed itself to reviewing the position on men and women's pay if the various measures currently in force are found to have failed to close the gender pay gap.

Scope

5603 Both **men and women** are equally covered by the EPA 1970 (s 1(13) EPA 1970).

The equal pay provisions **apply** to job applicants, workers (including those working under a contract of apprenticeship) and in certain circumstances ex-workers.

As with the other strands of discrimination (¶5215), workers who work **wholly or partly in GB** are covered. Generally, workers are excluded if they work, or it is contemplated that they will work, **wholly outside GB**. However, even if a worker works wholly outside GB, he will still be covered by the legislation if (s 10(1), (1A) SDA 1975, as amended by reg 11 SI 2005/2467):
– his employer has a place of business at an establishment in GB;
– the work is for the purposes of the business carried on at that establishment; and
– the worker is ordinarily resident in GB at the time he applies for or is offered the employment or at any time during the course of that employment.

5604 There are, however, **exclusions** from the EPA 1970. Most importantly, the compliance with laws regulating the employment of women and their special treatment in connection with pregnancy and childbirth are not covered (s 6(1) EPA 1970).

Equality clause

5605 The EPA 1970 does not only cover unequal pay as between men and women but is concerned with equalising **any term or condition** of employment that discriminates between men and women. However, instead of a prohibition on either direct or indirect inequality of pay, the

EPA 1970 implies into each contract of employment an equality clause if it does not already contain one (s 1(1) EPA 1970). Such a clause will operate to **modify a** woman's **employment contract** so that if any term of it is or becomes less favourable to the woman than a term of a similar kind in man's employment contract, so as to became as favourable as the term in the man's contract; or, if at any time the woman's contract does not include a beneficial term which is in a man's contract, so as to include such beneficial term, where she is undertaking (s 1(2), (3) EPA 1970):
- like work to the man;
- work rated as equivalent to work done by a man; or
- work of equal value to that done by a man.

MEMO POINTS These provisions apply equally in a converse case to a man.

"**Like work**" means that the work carried out by the complainant must be the same or of a broadly similar nature to that carried out by the worker of the opposite sex and that there are no important differences in the tasks actually performed. What is actually carried out in practice is significant, not what is simply in the employment contract (*E Coomes (Holdings) Ltd v Shields* [1978] IRLR 263, CA). Not only does this require an examination of what duties are carried out, but also the circumstances in which they are carried out, for example, the degree of responsibility in carrying out the job (*Eaton Ltd v Nuttall* [1977] IRLR 272, EAT). A difference in the times of day or night like work is carried out should be disregarded (*Dugdale v Kraft Foods Ltd* [1976] IRLR 368, EAT). Further, the fact that a promoted woman undertakes more duties than her male predecessor does not mean that they are not undertaking like work for the purposes of bringing an equal pay claim (*Sita (UK) Ltd v Hope*, EAT case 0787/04). 5606

"**Work rated as equivalent**" covers situations where a worker is not engaged on like work with a member of the opposite sex, but rather where a job evaluation has rated his/her job as equivalent to that of the member of the opposite sex under various headings, such as effort, skill and responsibility. This will also cover circumstances in which the jobs would have been rated as equivalent but for the fact that the evaluation was made using different values for men and women on the same demand under any heading. The evaluation must be carried out objectively and capable of being applied impartially (*Eaton Ltd v Nuttall* [1977] IRLR 71, EAT), and both parties must accept its validity in order for it to be relied on (*Arnold v Beecham Group Ltd* [1982] IRLR 307, EAT). 5607

"**Work of equal value**" applies where a worker is not engaged on like work with, or work rated as equivalent to, a member of the opposite sex, but his/her work is of equal value to the work done by a member of the opposite sex, in terms of the demands made on him/her with regard to effort, skill and decision etc. An evaluation must not take into consideration factors which discriminate on the grounds of sex (*Rummler v Dato-Druck GmbH* [1987] IRLR 249, CA). There is a special, complex, procedure for dealing with work of equal value claims which is beyond the scope of this book. 5608

Comparison

A comparator in an equal pay claim must be an **actual person** and it is for the complainant to select the person of the opposite sex with whom he/she wishes to be compared (*Ainsworth v Glass Tubes and Components Ltd* [1977] IRLR 74, EAT). The EPA 1970 is unusual in requiring the comparator to be an actual person, whereas it is possible under the SDA 1975, RRA 1976 and DDA 1995 to compare one's treatment to that of a hypothetical comparator (this issue is yet to be decided in respect of sexual orientation and religion or belief discrimination). However, in the case of *Allonby v Accrington and Rossendale College and others*, the ECJ held that the claimant did not have to rely on an actual comparator and could instead provide **statistical data** to prove a claim of indirect discrimination (the claimant's case concerned a pension scheme which was not open to agency workers and she had to prove that more women than men were affected by this limitation). This case is potentially of wider significance since it means that a claimant can challenge a discriminatory pay-related provision in a statutory scheme (this case involved the Teachers' Superannuation Scheme) or collective 5615 agreement without an actual comparator, despite the requirement in the EPA 1970 to the contrary.

The Court of Appeal has recently held that **no male comparator** was required for a claim involving pay increases which had not been taken into account in an employee's statutory maternity pay and that a claim for unpaid back-dated increases could be made under EPA 1970 despite the lack of male comparator (*Alabaster v (1) Barclays Bank plc and (2) The Secretary of State for Social Security* [2005] IRLR 576, CA).

5616 A comparator can include a worker of the opposite sex who is currently employed at the same time as the claimant, but also the claimant's **successor or predecessor** (*Kells v Pilkington* [2002] IRLR 693, EAT).

5617 Moreover, the chosen comparator can be a worker at **another establishment of the employer** in GB if he/she is employed under common terms and conditions of employment as the complainant (s 1(6) EPA 1970). It should be noted that, with regard to workers employed at the **same establishment**, there is no requirement for there to be common terms and conditions of employment.

5618 When pursuing a claim under Art 141 EC Treaty (which is directly enforceable by employees of a **public authority**) a worker can compare himself/herself to a comparator employed by another employer, provided he/she can demonstrate that any difference in pay is attributable to a '**single source**' (i.e. an entity or body which is responsible for the inequality of pay and which can restore equality of pay) (*Lawrence v Regent Office Care* [2002] IRLR 822, ECJ; see also *Allonby v Accrington and Rossendale College and ors* [2004] IRLR 224, ECJ).

EXAMPLE In *Robertson and ors v Department for Environment, Food and Rural Affairs* [2005] IRLR 363, CA, a case which involved a pay differential between civil servants working in two different governmental departments, each department had been delegated responsibility for setting its own employees' pay and conditions. The Court held that although the claimants and their comparators were all employed by the Crown, there was no single body which was responsible for the inequality and which could remedy any such inequality. The equal pay claim therefore failed. Leave to appeal to the House of Lords was refused.

It remains to be seen whether the approach taken in this case will be confined to claims relating to civil servants or whether it will have wider application outside the civil service.

5619 When making a **comparison of** a complainant's **terms** with those of his/her comparator, it has been held that the basic hourly rate, fixed bonuses and attendance allowances form part of the same contractual term, relating to the entire payment received for the performance of the contract by employees during normal working hours. On this basis, the basic hourly rate, fixed bonuses and attendance allowances should be aggregated when making the comparison, rather than looked at as separate and distinct terms of the contract (*Degnan and ors v Redcar and Cleveland Borough Council* [2005] IRLR 615, CA).

Establishing unequal pay

5620 Where inequality of pay exists in circumstances in which a comparator of the opposite sex benefits from more favourable terms than the complainant, the complainant must simply establish that the difference in contractual terms has resulted in him/her having been "less favourably treated" than the comparator of the opposite sex (although it should be noted this wording appears in the SDA 1975 and not the EPA 1970). Thus, in such straightforward cases of so-called "**direct**" inequality, the burden of proof will at that stage shift to the employer to establish that the difference in treatment of the complainant and his/her comparator is not on the grounds of sex (¶5630).

5622 It is more difficult to apply the equality clause to less straightforward cases where there is "**indirect**" inequality of pay, i.e. where, on the face of it, a complainant and his/her comparator will enjoy equally favourable contractual terms but in which a beneficial term of the contract is contingent on the fulfilment of a condition or requirement which, in reality, fewer members of one sex than the other can comply with. In the courts and tribunals, there has been uncertainty as to whether a complainant who alleges such "indirect" inequality must identify (as with the former provisions of the SDA 1975 relating to indirect sex discrimination, which have now been revised – ¶5301) (i) a condition or requirement; (ii) a pool for comparison; and (iii) disparate impact. The Court of Appeal has held that to prove disparate impact, it is necessary for the complainant to provide statistical data and that there should be harmony in the way in which tribunals approach the burden of proof whether such claims are brought under EPA 1970, SDA 1975 or Art 141 EC Treaty (*Nelson v Carillion Services Ltd* [2003] IRLR 428, CA).

However, the EAT has recently held that tribunals are not required, as a matter of law, to always adopt a formulaic approach, consistent with that of the SDA 1975, in considering whether there is sex-related pay discrimination and disparate impact for the purpose of the EPA 1970. A tribunal instead has to be satisfied on the evidence before it and the facts found, that the pay difference was caused by a factor related to the difference in sex between the claimant and his/her comparator. The fundamental question is whether there is a **causative link** between the claimant's sex and the fact that he/she is paid less and such a link can be established in a variety of different ways (*Ministry of Defence v Armstrong and ors* [2004] IRLR 672, EAT).

MEMO POINTS In *Ministry of Defence v Armstrong and ors*, above, the EAT confirmed that, as far as possible, the EPA 1970 should be construed harmoniously both with the SDA 1975 and Art 141 EC Treaty. However, it has to be borne in mind that the concepts underpinning discrimination under the equal pay legislation and the sex discrimination legislation are not identical (for example, the EPA 1970 does not contain a defined concept of indirect discrimination) and that, in reality, the concept of indirect discrimination under the EPA 1970, when read together with European equal pay legislation and case law, is broader than that which applies under the SDA 1975 (*Enderby v Frenchay Health Authority* (Case C-127/92) [1994] ICR 112, ECJ).

Defences

There are **two possible defences** to a claim under the EPA 1970. The first applies only in equal value claims, while the second is potentially available irrespective of the ground on which equality is sought. 5630

In respect of **work of equal value** claims, a claim will fail if a job-evaluation assessment has been undertaken and this has concluded that the worker and his/her comparator do work which is not of equal value (s 2A(2) EPA 1970). 5631

MEMO POINTS A revised **special procedure** for work of equal value claims which is designed to streamline cases and reduce time and costs came into effect on 1 October 2004 (s 2A EPA 1970, as amended by Equal Pay Act 1970 (Amendment) Regulations SI 2004/2352; Employment Tribunals (Constitution and Rules of Procedure) (Amendment) Regulations SI 2004/2351). The details of this special procedure are beyond the scope of this book.

In respect of claims regarding **like work** or **work rated as equivalent**, if the employer can prove that the difference in pay or benefits is genuinely due to a **material factor other than sex**, he will not be required to provide equal pay and benefits (s 1(3) EPA 1970). 5632

An employer will **not** be **required to objectively justify** material factors which he has raised in defence to an equal pay claim regarding differences in pay if there is no suggestion that those material factors are, on the face of it, either directly or indirectly discriminatory on the grounds of sex (*Parliamentary Commissioner for Administration and another v Fernandez* [2004] IRLR 22, EAT). However, an employer will be **required to objectively justify** material factors regarding a disparity in pay if a complainant has made out a case that, on the face of it, amounts to direct or indirect discrimination (i.e. a "prima facie" case).

MEMO POINTS At the time of writing, the EAT has declined to follow *Parliamentary Commissioner for Administration and another v Fernandez* (representing the domestic authorities in this area) and has instead taken the European approach, holding that the genuine material factor defence does require objective justification. The EAT has, however, granted permission to appeal to the Court of Appeal in view of the importance of this decision (*Sharp v Caledonia Group Services Ltd* [2005] EAT case, 0041/05).

For a prima facie case of discrimination to be made out, it is sufficient (in the case of "indirect" pay discrimination regarding inequality of pay between two groups of employees employed by the same employer) for the advantaged group to be predominantly composed 5633 of men as compared with the disadvantaged group which contained a significant number, if not a clear majority, of women (*Bailey and ors v Home Office* [2005] IRLR 369, CA). In this case, the Court held that tribunals are concerned to determine whether what, on the face of it, might seem like a gender-neutral practice, in reality disguises the fact that female employees are being disadvantaged as compared to male comparators to an extent that indicates that the inequality is, on the face of it, due to gender.

MEMO POINTS Some commentators consider the Court of Appeal's conclusion in *Bailey and ors v Home Office*, that the presence of a significant number of men (as well as women) in the disadvantaged group does not preclude a tribunal from requiring an employer to objectively justify the disparity in pay, surprising. The House of Lords has granted leave to appeal.

5635 **Examples** of 'material factor' defences which have been successful include:
1. responsibility and potential exercise of responsibility (*Edmonds v Computer Services (South West) Ltd* [1977] IRLR 359, EAT);
2. experience (*Tyldesley v TML Plastics Ltd* [1996] ICR 356, EAT);
3. the application of an objective non-discriminatory grading structure (*National Vulcan Engineering Insurance Co Ltd v Wade* [1978] IRLR 225, CA);
4. the amount of physical effort involved and whether a job is physically unpleasant (*Christie and others v John E Haith Ltd* [2003] IRLR 670, EAT);
5. where more favourable terms have been preserved at a particular level following a TUPE transfer and where the pay differential is genuinely due to a material factor other than sex (*King's College London v Clark*, EAT case 1049/02); and
6. where length of service has been taken into account in determining salary, even if this means that such pay differences have a disproportionately adverse effect on women (*Health and Safety Executive v Cadman*, EAT case 0947/02, following the decision of the ECJ in *Handels-og Kontorfunktionaerernes Forbund I Danmark v Dansk Arbejdsgiverforening (acting for Danfoss)* [1991] ICR 74, ECJ).

MEMO POINTS The decision in *Health and Safety Executive v Cadman*, above, has been appealed to the Court of Appeal which has, in turn, made a reference to the European Court of Justice regarding the question as to whether length of service as the principal differential in an "indirect" pay discrimination claim requires objective justification by the employer seeking to defend such a difference (*Cadman v Health and Safety Executive* [2004] IRLR 971, CA).

SECTION 3

Enforcement and remedies

5700 Workers have a range of remedies, the most common being compensation for which, in respect of discrimination claims, there is no limit. Further, various organisations also have enforcement powers.

For ease of reference, the various types of discrimination are **coded** as follows: S: Sex; SO: Sexual orientation; R: Race; RB: Religion or belief; D: Disability and E: Equal pay.

I. Tribunal claim

5710 Workers who suffer unlawful discrimination, harassment or unequal pay can make a complaint to a tribunal. To help them assess whether they have a claim or should bring a claim, they can serve their employers with a questionnaire.

Questionnaires

5711 To assist in deciding whether to bring proceedings and in formulating and presenting his/her case, workers can serve a discrimination or equal pay questionnaire, as appropriate, on his/her employer (S: s 74 SDA 1975; SO: reg 33 SI 2003/1661; R: s 65 RRA 1976; RB: reg 36 SI 2003/1660;

D: s 56 DDA 1995; E: s 7B(1) EPA 1970). With regard to discrimination questionnaires, the worker can also serve it on any other person against whom he/she may have a complaint.

The questionnaire and replies to the questionnaire must be in a **prescribed form** (S: Sex Discrimination (Questions and Replies) Order SI 1975/2048; SO: Sch 2-3 SI 2003/1661; R: Race Relations (Questions and Replies) Order SI 1977/842; RB: Sch 1-2 SI 2003/1660; D: Disability Discrimination (Questions and Replies) Order SI 2004/1168 (as amended by Disability Discrimination (Questions and Replies) Order SI 2005/2703); E: Equal Pay (Questions and Replies) Order SI 2003/722).

MEMO POINTS 1. A **revised disability discrimination questionnaire** came into force on 1 October 2004 (Disability Discrimination (Questions and Replies) Order SI 2004/1168 (as amended by Disability Discrimination (Questions and Replies) Order SI 2005/2703)). This provides that the questionnaire is consistent with the changes that have been introduced by the Disability Discrimination Act 1995 (Amendment) Regulations SI 2003/1673 and includes a new definition of 'direct' discrimination and provision for a person who has suffered harassment. There is now also a requirement for a response from the employer to the questionnaire within 8 weeks (¶5713).
2. The Equal Opportunities Commission (EOC) has published **guidance** on its website on how to use equal pay questionnaires. The guidance includes a brief explanation of the law, directions for completing the questionnaire and sample questions.
3. The prescribed form of the **sexual orientation** and **religion or belief** discrimination questionnaires is available on the DTI website.

In responding to questionnaires, an employer must ensure he does not breach his obligations regarding **data protection** towards the named comparator(s) (¶5940). It is advisable, therefore, particularly in relation to equal pay, that before disclosing details of salary, bonus and benefit packages, the employer obtains the consent of the comparator(s). If no consent is given, the employer should consider providing the requested information in terms of groups of relevant workers (for example, the range of bonuses in any given range of workers) as opposed to details of specific workers' packages. 5712

A questionnaire (and any replies) will be **admissible as evidence** in tribunal proceedings **if** it is **served**: 5713
- **before proceedings have been brought** though in the case of discrimination questionnaires this must be within 3 months of the act complained of being done; or
- **within** 21 days of the date **proceedings were lodged** (i.e. started), or later at the discretion of the tribunal.

Further, if admissible, the tribunal can also draw **inferences**, including an inference that a discriminatory act (including harassment) has taken place/worker has suffered unequal pay, if it appears that the employer deliberately and without reasonable excuse **failed to reply within** 8 weeks beginning on the day on which the questionnaire was served on him, or if his reply is evasive or equivocal (S: s 74(2A) SDA 1975, as inserted by reg 32 Employment Equality (Sex Discrimination) Regulations SI 2005/2467; SO: reg 33(2)(b) SI 2003/1661; R: s 65(2)(b) RRA 1976; RB: reg 36(2)(b) SI 2003/1660; D: s 56(3)(b) DDA 1995; E: s 7B(4)(a) EPA 1970).

MEMO POINTS In the case of racial discrimination on grounds of **colour and nationality**, the employer must reply **within a reasonable period** from the date of service of the questionnaire in order to avoid adverse inferences being drawn by the tribunal (s 65(2)(b) RRA 1976). This period may be shorter or longer than 8 weeks.

Bringing a claim

Workers may present a complaint to a tribunal if their employer has committed an unlawful act of **discrimination or harassment** against them or there is **inequality with regard to their pay** (S: s 63 SDA 1975; SO: reg 28 SI 2003/1661; R: s 54 RRA 1976; RB: reg 31 SI 2003/1660; D: s 8 DDA 1995; E: s 2 EPA 1970). 5720

For these purposes, a discriminatory act is deemed to have occurred if the complaint:
- concerns a contractual term: the "act" is treated as having been done throughout the contract;
- is about an "act" extending over a period of time: it is treated as having been done at the end of that period and can include acts which take place after the termination of employment if there is a sufficiently close connection between the employment relationship and the act in question; or

– is about a deliberate omission: it is treated as having been done when the person in question decided on the omission. As it can be difficult to determine when a person decided not to do something, the tribunal will look at inconsistencies and will consider periods of inactivity by the employer in order to determine that there has been an unlawful "deliberate omission".

MEMO POINTS To this end, in respect of **sex, racial and disability discrimination** respectively, the EOC, CRE and the DRC have a specific duty to consider and, where appropriate, **assist claimants**, for example by arranging legal advice or representation, by seeking to reach a settlement of any dispute, or by providing other suitable assistance. All three bodies have a number of on-line facilities for the assistance of claimants and employers. At present, there is no equivalent statutory body to assist in respect of claims regarding religion or belief or sexual orientation discrimination.

5722 **Time limit** The time limit for presentation of **discrimination and harassment complaints** is 3 months from the time that the act (or omission) complained of was done (S: s 6(1) SDA 1975; SO: reg 34 SI 2003/1661; R: s 68(1) RRA; RB: reg 37 SI 2003/1660; D: Sch 3 para 3(1) DDA 1995). However, the tribunal may consider a complaint which is made out of time, if in all the circumstances of the case, it considers that it would be just and equitable to do so (¶9475).

MEMO POINTS Note that **statutory dispute resolution procedures** came into force on 1 October 2004 under which it is normally necessary for an employee to raise a grievance with his employer first before his tribunal claim will be accepted (see ¶¶6500, 6773 for further details).

5723 The time limit for bringing an **equal pay claim** is ordinarily 6 months from the date the worker's employment ended, although a claim can be started at any time during a worker's employment and, in certain circumstances, the 6-month time limit can be **extended** where (s 2ZA EPA 1970, as amended by reg 3 SI 2003/1656):

– an employer has **deliberately concealed a fact** from the worker which is relevant to his/her equal pay claim and the worker did not or could not reasonably have discovered the concealment until after the employment relationship ended. In such cases, a claim must be brought within 6 months of the date on which the worker discovered the concealment (or could, with reasonable diligence, have discovered it); and

– a worker is either a **minor or of unsound mind** at any time during the 6 months which follows the end of his/her employment. In such cases, a claim must be brought within 6 months of the worker ceasing to be a minor or of unsound mind.

MEMO POINTS 1. In respect of workers who have been in a **stable employment relationship** with their employer, consisting of **two or more contracts of employment in succession** (whether or not there has been an interval between the contracts), a claim must be brought within 6 months of the date on which the stable employment relationship ended (s 2ZA(3), (4) EPA 1970, as amended by SI 2003/1656).

2. **Before 19 July 2003**, the time limit for presentation of a complaint was 6 months from the date the worker ceased to be employed and there was no provision for extension to this time limit. The position has been brought into line with the ECJ decisions of *Levez v T H Jennings (Harlow Pools) Ltd* [1999] ICR 521, ECJ and *Preston v Wolverhampton Healthcare NHS Trust* [2001] IRLR 237, HL, to ensure that the rules are no less favourable than those which apply to claims for breach of contract (¶9451).

Evidence

5725 Workers rarely have **direct evidence** of discrimination and employers will very rarely admit to such behaviour. Consequently, findings of discrimination are usually based on **inferences**, drawn by tribunals from any difference in treatment and circumstantial evidence as to the grounds for this. This can include any false or evasive answers by employers including any responses to questionnaires (*King v Great Britain-China Centre* [1991] IRLR 513, CA). See ¶5730 regarding the process by which tribunals should approach discrimination and harassment claims.

5726 When considering whether an adverse inference can be drawn, tribunals are under a duty to consider not only an employer's responses to a statutory discrimination questionnaire, but also **any other explanation for the alleged discrimination** provided by the employer in response to a claimant's question(s) in writing, for example, in his response to a tribunal claim (formerly referred to as a notice of appearance) or in reply to a request for additional information (formerly referred to as further and better particulars) (*Dattani v Chief Constable of West Mercia Police* [2005] IRLR 327, EAT). In this case, the EAT held that an inference could be drawn from the responses provided by the employer in his notice of appearance, further and better particulars and a written explanation sent to the claimant.

MEMO POINTS It should be noted that in *Dattani v Chief Constable of West Mercia Police* the EAT referred to an adverse inference being drawn from "incorrect information" provided by the employer but since this is not consistent with the wording of the legislation, which refers to an "evasive or equivocal" reply (see above), it is questionable as to whether this part of the judgment should be followed.

The **credibility of a witness** will be considered in the light of all the surrounding circumstances and previous history of the case, particularly where it is possible that he might have been subconsciously swayed by a prejudicial or discriminatory attitude (*Anya v University of Oxford* [2001] IRLR 377, CA; *Williams v YKK (UK) Ltd*, EAT case 0408/01). 5727

Burden of proof

Where, at a hearing, the **complainant proves facts** from which the tribunal could conclude in the **absence of an adequate explanation** that the employer (and any other respondent) has (or is to be treated as having) committed an unlawful act of discrimination, harassment or unequal pay, the tribunal must uphold the complaint unless the employer (and any other respondent) proves that he did not commit (or is not to be treated as having committed) the act complained of (S and E: ss 8, 63A SDA 1975; SO: reg 29(2) SI 2003/1661; R: s 54A(2) RRA 1976; RB: reg 29(2) SI 2003/1660; D: s 17A(1C) DDA 1995, as amended by reg 9 SI 2003/1673). Thus, there is a **two stage process**: 5730

1. The claimant must prove facts from which the tribunal could conclude, in the absence of an adequate explanation, that the respondent has committed, or is to be treated as having committed, an unlawful act against the claimant; and
2. To successfully defend a claim, the respondent must prove that he did not commit, or is not to be treated as having committed, the unlawful act.

In 2003 the EAT produced some guidance (referred to as the **Barton guidelines**) for tribunals regarding the shift in the burden of proof from employee to employer (*Barton v Investec Henderson Crosthwaite Securities Ltd* [2003] IRLR 332, EAT). These guidelines have recently been **revised** and upheld by the Court of Appeal and are summarised below (*Igen Ltd (formerly Leeds Careers Guidance) and ors v Wong; Chamberlin Solicitors and anor v Emokpae; Brunel University v Webster* [2005] IRLR 258, CA, with Equal Opportunities Commission, Commission for Racial Equality, Disability Rights Commission (interveners)). It should be noted that although the guidelines were originally stated to apply in respect of sex discrimination, they have also been applied to race and disability discrimination claims. 5731

1. A claimant must prove on the balance of probabilities facts from which the tribunal could conclude, in the absence of an adequate explanation, that the respondent has, or is to be treated as having, committed an act of unlawful discrimination against the claimant.
2. If the claimant does not prove such facts, his/her claim will fail.
3. In deciding whether the claimant has proved such facts, the tribunal must bear in mind that it is unusual to find direct evidence of discrimination and that, in some cases, the discrimination will not have been intentional but rather based on an assumption that the claimant "would not have fitted in".
4. Moreover, the tribunal must take into account the fact that the outcome of this first stage of the analysis will usually depend on what inferences can be properly drawn from the primary facts found by the tribunal.
5. The word "could" set out at 1. above is important since at this stage the tribunal is not required to reach a definitive determination that the facts proved by the claimant lead the tribunal to conclude that there was unlawful discrimination. Rather, the tribunal must consider the primary facts before it can determine what inferences can be drawn from them.
6. At this stage, in considering what inferences or conclusions can be drawn, the tribunal must assume that there is no adequate explanation for those facts.
7. An inference can include, if appropriate, any inference that it is just and equitable to conclude from an evasive or equivocal reply to a discrimination questionnaire etc.

8. The tribunal must consider whether any Code of Practice is relevant and, if so, take such Code of Practice into account. Consequently, inferences can be drawn from any failure by the respondent to follow a relevant Code of Practice.
9. If a claimant has proved facts from which the tribunal could conclude that the respondent has treated the claimant less favourably on the grounds of sex, race etc, then the burden of proof will shift to the respondent.
10. The respondent must then prove that he did not commit, or is not to be treated as having committed, the unlawful discriminatory act.
11. To discharge the burden of proof, the respondent must prove, on the balance of probabilities, that the treatment was in no sense whatsoever on the grounds of sex, race etc.
12. The tribunal must assess whether the explanation advanced by the respondent is adequate to discharge the burden.
13. To this end, the tribunal would normally expect cogent evidence from the respondent and must consider carefully any explanations provided regarding a failure to deal with a discrimination/equal pay questionnaire and/or relevant Code of Practice.

5732 An employee can make out a primary case where the **evidence is neutral** and equally points to a discriminatory or innocent explanation of the underlying reason for the conduct complained of and he is not required to prove facts which point towards discrimination more than towards an innocent explanation (*Cunningham v (1) Quedos Ltd (2) John Wyeth & Brother Ltd*, EAT case 0298/03).

Where there are sufficient facts to make a **primary case against a third party** accused of aiding an employer's discrimination, the burden of proof passes on to that third party, to disprove an inference of discrimination (*Cunningham v (1) Quedos Ltd (2) John Wyeth & Brother Ltd*, above).

5733 In equal pay claims, once a worker can prove that there is a **lack of transparency** in the **employer's pay structure** and/or he has failed to comply with the equal pay questionnaire, this will be sufficient for the claimant to satisfy the first stage of the two-stage process (*Barton v Investec Henderson Crosthwaite Securities Ltd* [2003] IRLR 332, EAT).

A. Remedies – discrimination (including harassment)

5735 Where a tribunal finds that a **complaint is well founded**, it may make such of the following orders as it considers just and equitable (S: s 65 SDA 1975; SO: reg 30(1)(a) SI 2003/1661; R: s 56 RRA 1976; RB: reg 33(1)(a) SI 2003/1660; D: s 8 DDA 1995):
a. declaration: this is an order declaring the rights of the complainant and the respondent in relation to the act complained of;
b. compensation: an order requiring the respondent to pay compensation to the complainant; and/or
c. recommendation: a recommendation that the respondent take, within a specified period, action appearing to the tribunal to be practicable (in cases of sex, sexual orientation, racial and religion or belief discrimination) or reasonable in all the circumstances of the case (disability discrimination cases) for the purpose of "obviating or reducing" the adverse effect on the complainant of any act of discrimination complained of.

1. Declaration

5738 If a tribunal finds that an applicant has been discriminated against or subjected to unlawful harassment, it can make a declaration as to the **rights of the parties** in relation to the matters which are the subject of the complaint. This may assist in ensuring, where there is a continuing relationship between the parties, that they each know what is required in order to avoid further discrimination in the future. It will also be the most appropriate remedy where there is no continuing relationship or financial loss but there has been an act of discrimination.

2. Compensation

The principal differences between compensation for discrimination and compensation for unfair dismissal (¶8570) are that in discrimination cases, compensation may be **awarded for injury to feelings** and there is **no upper limit** on the amount of compensation which may be awarded. 5740

Compensation for unlawful discrimination falls under **two heads**:
- **financial loss**: loss of earnings and benefits both past and future; and
- **non-financial loss**: an amount awarded for injury to feelings and, in certain circumstances, aggravated damages.

Where an employee has been unlawfully discriminated against and is **subsequently unfairly dismissed** by the employer, the fact of the subsequent dismissal does not operate to end the employer's liability for losses arising from the unlawful discrimination (which would have the effect of bringing all further losses from the date of the dismissal under the rules for unfair dismissal and would therefore be subject to the statutory cap) since the employer is not permitted to rely on a second unlawful act to terminate his liability for the first (*H M Prison Service v Beart (No. 2)* [2005] IRLR 171, EAT).

EXAMPLE In *H M Prison Service v Beart (No. 2)*, B's psychiatric injury arising from her employer's discrimination which impacted on her ability to work continued beyond the date of the unfair dismissal. Since B had been unfairly dismissed, there was no reason for her to not be compensated for losses flowing from the act of discrimination beyond the date of her dismissal.

The tribunal may also make an award of **aggravated damages** where the employer has behaved in a high-handed, malicious, insulting or oppressive manner in committing the act of discrimination or, where the employer's conduct of his defence of discrimination proceedings is designed to be intimidatory and cause maximum unease to the worker (*Zaiwalla & Co v Walia* [2002] IRLR 697, EAT). The employer's behaviour need not be deliberate or conscious (*Leeds Rhinos Rugby Club and others v Sterling*, EAT case 267/01). 5741

Aggravated damages are **distinct from compensation for injury to feelings** (*Scott v Commissioners of Inland Revenue* [2004] IRLR 713, CA) and, as such, in awarding aggravated damages, tribunals must not allow the amount to be dictated by the level of injury to feelings and must consider them as a compensatory, as opposed to punitive, award (*Singh v University Hospital NHS Trust*, EAT case 1409/01).

EXAMPLE In *British Telecommunications plc v Reid* [2004] IRLR 327, CA, the Court of Appeal upheld an award for aggravated damages where the employer took over a year to complete its investigation into the employee's grievance that he had been subjected to racially discriminatory language. This had been further exacerbated by the employer who, during the investigation, promoted the alleged perpetrators of the discrimination while relocating the employee.

Subject to three important exceptions, in cases of **indirect discrimination** tribunals may not make an award of financial compensation if the employer proves that the **discrimination was unintentional**. Instead, the tribunal can only make a declaration and/or a recommendation. 5742

The three exceptions are as follows:

a. tribunals can enquire into the **employer's state of knowledge** of the likely consequences of his policies and practices in order to determine whether the discrimination was or could be inferred to be intentional. Consequently, where a provision, criterion or practice (or requirement/condition) was applied with knowledge of its unfavourable impact, the intention to discriminate may be inferred, and in such cases it will be open to tribunals to award compensation (*London Underground Ltd v Edwards (No 2)* [1997] IRLR 157, EAT; see also *JH Walker Ltd v Hussain* [1996] ICR 291, EAT);

b. in cases of **indirect sex discrimination** only, tribunals can award compensation where they think that it would not be just and equitable not to make an award (Sex Discrimination and Equal Pay (Miscellaneous Amendments) Regulations SI 1996/438); and

c. in cases of **indirect sexual orientation and religion or belief discrimination**, a tribunal may however award compensation if it makes either a declaration or a recommendation, or both, and further considers that it is just and equitable to make a compensatory award as well (SO: reg 30(2) SI 2003/1661; RB: reg 33(2) SI 2003/1660).

5743 Where employers are **vicariously liable** for a worker's act of discrimination (¶5227), it will normally be the employer who is required to make a payment in compensation to the complainant. However, if an individual has been named by the complainant as a personal respondent to a claim, the fact that his employer is vicariously liable for his discriminatory act does not necessarily mean that he will escape the consequences of his liability. In such cases, the tribunal may make an order that the individual respondent should also make a payment of compensation to the complainant. If the employer successfully defends himself against a claim for vicarious liability by showing that he took such steps as were reasonably practicable to prevent his employee from unlawfully discriminating, the tribunal may order the individual worker alone to compensate the complainant.

5744 The **ordinary rules of mitigation apply**, so in discrimination cases a complainant is under a duty to try to mitigate his losses just as they would be in an unfair dismissal case (¶8620).

A woman **dismissed for a pregnancy-related reason** will not generally be able to recover compensation for a period of more than 6 months after the date of childbirth, unless she is actively looking for work after that date (*Ministry of Defence v Cannock* [1994] IRLR 509, EAT). However, a tribunal can take account of the **difficulties** faced by a woman with a young child when seeking work (*Ministry of Defence v Hunt* [1996] IRLR 139, EAT).

5745 The burden of having to **prove a failure to mitigate loss** is on the person who asserts it. If the employer wants to raise this point then he will have to produce comprehensive evidence of employment opportunities available to the complainant by such means as expert evidence, copy advertisements and the like. Moreover, it is not sufficient for an employer to show that such opportunities are reasonable – instead, he must prove that the worker acted unreasonably in failing to utilise such opportunities (*Wilding v British Telecommunications plc* [2002] IRLR 524, CA).

It is possible for an employee to fulfil the duty to mitigate his loss by deciding to **re-train in a new profession** for a job which would place his earnings on a par with the position he had lost in circumstances in which the employer is unable to demonstrate that there is any suitable alternative employment for which the employee should and could have applied (*Orthet Ltd v Vince-Cain* [2004] IRLR 857, EAT).

Financial loss

5746 The amount awarded must put the complaining worker, so far as is possible, in the position he would have been had the act of discrimination not occurred (*Ministry of Defence v Wheeler* [1998] IRLR 23, CA). It is the complaining worker's own personal loss (and/or estimated loss) which is to be taken into account by the tribunal, not any hypothetical loss which has been calculated on the basis of how a "reasonable employer" might have behaved. There is **no limit** on the amount of compensation which can be awarded under this head.

In cases where the complainant has shown that an unlawful act of **discrimination resulted in a lost chance** the tribunal will have to calculate the award of compensation in accordance with the percentage chance that has been lost.

EXAMPLE A woman applies for a job as a sales director at a salary of £60,000 per annum. The post involves extensive travel and as a mother of two small children she is asked searching questions at interview about her capacity to undertake travel. She does not get the job and she feels her performance at interview was badly affected by this line of questioning. The man who is appointed was not asked similar questions at interview about his ability to travel. Even if the employer proves that the man is the best person for the job on objective grounds, the tribunal will calculate an award of compensation in relation to the woman's lost chance of getting the job. So if the tribunal put the woman's chance of successfully obtaining the job at 10% (had the selection criteria for the job not been discriminatory) she would be awarded a sum equal to 10% of her potential losses for whatever period the tribunal considers just and equitable.

In cases of discrimination, tribunals are also entitled to make an award on a **joint and several basis**, as between the respondents (if there is more than one) (*Way and another v Crouch* [2005] IRLR 603, EAT). Regard should be had to the extent to which each party caused the damage and to their relative culpability. Tribunals should not, however, make a joint and several award on the basis of the parties' relative financial resources. 5747

Non-financial loss

Although an award for **injury to feelings** will not automatically be made since a sense of injury must be proved by the complainant, it will often be easy for a complainant to prove, in the sense that tribunals will not take much persuading, that an act of discrimination has injured the complainant's feelings (*Ministry of Defence v Cannock* [1994] IRLR 509, EAT). Thus, an award for injury to feelings will be made in almost every case. 5748

Compensation can be recovered for any losses which are a **direct consequence** of the discriminatory act, whether or not such losses were reasonably foreseeable (*Essa v Laing Ltd* [2003] IRLR 346, EAT, confirmed by the Court of Appeal ([2004] IRLR 313, CA)). However, compensation should not be awarded for losses which result from the actions of the complainant, for example, in unreasonably refusing medical treatment or failing to follow medical advice. 5749

The EAT has set out useful **guidance** for tribunals in **calculating an award** for injury to feelings (*(1) Armitage (2) Marsden and (3) HM Prison Service v Johnson* [1997] IRLR 162, EAT). The principles to be applied are as follows: 5750

a. awards for injury to feelings should be compensatory without being punitive. Feelings of indignation at the discriminatory conduct should not be allowed to inflate the award;

b. the amount awarded should not be so low as to diminish respect for the anti-discrimination legislation;

c. awards should be generally similar to the range of awards in personal injury cases;

d. tribunals should remind themselves of the value in everyday life of the sum they have in mind; and

e. tribunals should bear in mind the need for public respect for the level of awards made.

An award of damages in respect of injury to feelings in a discrimination claim is **not taxable** and, as such, tribunals do not need to take into account income tax when determining the amount to be awarded (*Orthet Ltd v Vince-Cain* [2004] IRLR 857, EAT).

In respect of injury to feelings in cases of **sex and race discrimination**, the Court of Appeal has set out three bands of compensation which should be applied in assessing such awards (*Vento v Chief Constable of West Yorkshire Police (No 2)* [2003] IRLR 102, CA): 5751

- Top band: £15,000 – £25,000 for awards in the most serious cases of discrimination, for example, where it has taken place over a long period of time;
- Middle band: £5,000 – £15,000 for cases which, although serious, do not merit an award in the top band; and
- Lowest band: £500 – £5,000 for less serious cases, for example, where the discrimination occurred in a single incident (see also *Essa v Laing Ltd*, above, in which it was held that an award of £5,000 was held to be in the appropriate band for a one-off incident of racial abuse).

Most cases will fall into the lowest band and it appears that an award of at least £500 is generally regarded as the **minimum** appropriate level, although an award of £750 for racial taunts has been held to be so inadequate by the EAT that it was wrong in law (*Doshoki v Draegar* [2002] IRLR 340, EAT). However, employers should note that there is **no cap** on the amount that can be awarded and awards reaching tens of thousands of pounds have been made on a number of occasions. Moreover, the EAT has demonstrated that it is willing to overturn tribunal awards which it considers inadequate (*Doshoki v Draegar*, above).

MEMO POINTS 1. It is expected that this guidance from the Court of Appeal will be followed in cases involving discrimination on **grounds other than sex and race** (*London Borough of Hackney v Adams* [2003] IRLR 402, CA, a case involving discrimination on trade union grounds).

2. The EAT has recently applied the Vento guidelines regarding compensation in respect of injury to feelings to a case of **sexual harassment** (*Carney v (1) Rouf (2) Islam*, EAT case 0353/04). In this case, in applying the guidelines, relevant factors included the fact that there was persistent harassment

over a matter of months, the employer's denial of any discriminatory behaviour (requiring the claimant to go through what had happened to her at the hearing) and the fact that the harassment had been conducted by one of the owners of the business and not a junior employee.

5752 Any injury to feelings suffered by the complainant which is not in fact **related to the act of unlawful discrimination** will be disregarded by the tribunal in assessing the level of award for injury to feelings.

EXAMPLE In *Coleman v Skyrail Oceanic Limited* [1981] IRLR 398, CA, a female travel booking clerk married a male employee in a competing agency. After it became evident that information was leaked from one agency to the other, the two employers met and decided that the female worker should be dismissed. Their assumption was that the husband was the main breadwinner. The dismissal was held to be unfair and discriminatory on the ground of sex. The tribunal's award of £1,000 for injury to feelings was based on the assumption that the dismissal would injure the claimant's reputation (i.e. it would be assumed that she leaked the confidential information). However, the Court of Appeal reduced the award to £100 as such injury did not relate to sex discrimination and, therefore, could not be the subject of an award for injury to feelings.

5753 When an act of discrimination has resulted in the onset of a **psychiatric illness**, the complainant may recover **compensation for personal injury** in addition to an award for **injury to feelings** (*Sheriff v Klyne Tugs (Lowestoft) Ltd* [1999] IRLR 481, CA). Note that in practice, it may be difficult to separate injury to feelings and psychiatric injury since it may be almost impossible to say with any precision when the distress inflicted on the complainant by the act of discrimination became a recognised psychiatric illness such as depression (*HM Prison Service v Salmon* [2001] IRLR 425 EAT). In such cases, where there is a risk of double compensation, a tribunal can make a single award for injury to feelings, which includes an element for psychiatric injury.

Because of developments in case law relating to psychiatric injury it is now extremely common for complainants to bring forward evidence of psychiatric injury and employers facing claims of discrimination should be aware that the state of health of the individual is likely to be an issue. In addition, tribunals often award damages for actual costs incurred, such as for counselling.

3. Recommendation

5760 The tribunal can make a recommendation that the **respondent take action** which the tribunal considers practicable (in cases of sex, sexual orientation, racial and religion or belief discrimination) or reasonable in all the circumstances of the case (disability discrimination cases) for the purpose of "obviating or reducing" the adverse effect on the complainant of any act of discrimination complained of. It must specify a period of time for compliance. It is not possible for a tribunal to make a recommendation which simply aims to rectify the effect of some other act(s), including those of a third party (*Leeds Rhinos Rugby Club and ors v Sterling*, EAT 267/01).

A recommendation might **relate to matters such as** the removal of a discriminatory requirement such a minimum height requirement. It should not be used where monetary compensation is more appropriate (i.e. a recommendation should not order an increase in pay) (*Irvine v Prestcold* [1981] IRLR 281, CA). Nor is it appropriate to recommend that an applicant who has been refused a job or promotion because of discrimination should be given the next job which becomes available as this would be unfair to other people who might be suitable (*Noone v N W Thames RHA (No 2)* [1988] IRLR 530, CA).

5761 The power to make a recommendation can be of limited practical effect. Tribunals are not able to recommend that an employer discontinues a discriminatory practice (*Ministry of Defence v Jeremiah* [1978] IRLR 402, EAT) nor are they able to recommend that an employer should promote a successful complainant to the next suitable vacancy since such a promotion without consideration of other applicants (who may have superior qualifications) could in itself amount to direct discrimination (*British Gas plc v Sharma* [1991] IRLR 101, EAT).

However, in *Chief Constable of Yorkshire Police v Vento (No.2)* [2002] IRLR 177, EAT, a tribunal recommended that the Chief Constable should send to the complainant a written apology in specific terms set out by the tribunal, marked for the attention of prospective employers. In addition, the tribunal directed (and the EAT upheld on appeal) that the Deputy Chief Constable should interview officers who were involved in the discrimination and discuss with them certain aspects of the judgment of the tribunals in the case. It was said that in cases of "institutional discrimination", it was good practice to discuss and address the tribunal's findings with those concerned. However, the EAT ruled that it was not appropriate to recommend that the officers concerned be invited to apologise in writing to the claimant nor that the Chief Constable report to the claimant the result of the interviews and whether or not individual officers agreed to apologise.

MEMO POINTS *Chief Constable of Yorkshire Police v Vento (No 2)* has been overturned on appeal to the Court of Appeal but this point remains unaffected ([2003] IRLR 102, CA).

If the employer, without reasonable justification, **fails to comply** with a recommendation, the tribunal can, if it thinks it just and equitable to do so, increase any compensation previously awarded (or may award compensation if it did not previously do so) (S: s 65(3) SDA 1975; SO: reg 30(3) SI 2003/1661; R: s 56(4) RRA 1976; RB: reg 33(3) SI 2003/1660; D: s 8(5) DDA 1995). **5762**

B. Remedies – equal pay

When an equal pay **claim is successful**, the complainant is entitled to an **order** declaring his rights. This is likely to have the practical effect that his **future pay** will be increased to the level of the comparator's pay or his contractual terms will be improved to match those of his comparator. Once the order has been made, the complainant has a contractual right to the increased pay/improved terms. **5770**

In addition, a tribunal may award **compensation** in respect of arrears of pay (in effect, damages for breach of the implied clause on equal pay) or in respect of breaches of other contractual terms. The amount recoverable by a worker is now up to 6 years' arrears, starting with the date of the claim (s 2AB EPA 1970, as amended by reg 4 SI 2003/1656).

MEMO POINTS 1. The 6-year limit on arrears is **extendable** in certain circumstances, namely in respect of a worker from whom an employer deliberately concealed facts relevant to his/her equal pay claim and a worker who is either a minor or of unsound mind (s 2AB(3)-(6) EPA 1970, as amended by reg 4 SI 2003/1656). These rules are outside the scope of this book.
2. **Prior to 19 July 2003**, the EPA 1970 originally limited the amount recoverable by a worker to 2 years' arrears of pay, starting with the date of commencement of proceedings (s 2(5) EPA 1970). However, this limitation was declared unlawful (*Preston v Wolverhampton Healthcare NHS Trust* [2001] IRLR 237, HL) and EPA 1970 has subsequently been amended to bring the position into line with damages claims in other contract claims.

Damages for **non-financial loss**, such as injury to feelings, together with aggravated or exemplary damages, cannot be recovered in equal pay claims (as recently confirmed in *Council of the City of Newcastle Upon Tyne v Allan and others; Degnan and others v Redcar and Cleveland Borough Council* [2005] IRLR 504, EAT). **5772**

In relation to claims regarding differential access rules to employers' **pension schemes**, claims can go back to 1976 but must be brought either during employment or within 6 years of its termination. See ¶3439. **5773**

II. Enforcement

5790 The **Equal Opportunities Commission** (EOC), the **Commission for Racial Equality** (CRE) and the **Disability Rights Commission** (DRC) have investigatory and enforcement powers in respect of sex, racial and disability discrimination respectively.

These statutory bodies can conduct **formal investigations** where they have a genuine belief that the person or organisation to be investigated has committed a discriminatory act or acts contrary to sex, racial or disability discrimination legislation (S: s 57(1) SDA 1975; R: s 48 RRA 1976; D: s 3 Disability Rights Commission Act 1999).

The EOC, CRE and DRC may also issue **non-discrimination notices** if, following a formal investigation, they discover that a person or an organisation has committed or is committing unlawful discrimination in breach of sex, racial or disability discrimination legislation (S: s 67 SDA 1975; R: s 58 RRA 1976; D: s 4 Disability Rights Commission Act 1999). A non-discrimination notice will require the relevant person/organisation to cease the discriminatory conduct and, thus, take certain action or make certain changes. The notice may also contain **recommendations** as to action which should be taken to avoid future repetition of the unlawful conduct.

Where the EOC, CRE or DRC believe that a person has committed persistent discrimination and is likely to do so again unless restrained then, provided certain conditions are met, it can apply to a county court for an **injunction** to prevent further commission of the unlawful acts.

MEMO POINTS At present, there is **no equivalent statutory body** which can provide guidance and advice or conduct formal investigations into and issue non-discrimination notices in respect of cases involving discrimination on the grounds of **sexual orientation and religion or belief**. However, a proposed **single statutory equality and human rights institution**, the Commission for Equality and Human Rights (CEHR), is expected to be established by 2007 under the new Equality Bill. The new institution will cover all types of discrimination and will also provide support for individual rights granted under the Human Rights Act 1998.

5791 The EOC, CRE and DRC can also bring proceedings in relation to unlawful instructions and pressure to discriminate against a person on the grounds of sex, race or disability respectively (S: ss 39, 40SDA 1975; R: ss 30, 31RRA 1976; D: s 17B DDA 1995, as amended by reg 15 SI 2003/1673).

SECTION 4

Best practice

5800 In brief, the term "best practice" encompasses the steps which an employer should take to comply with current UK equal opportunities legislation and future obligations that are on the horizon, recommendations by the Equal Opportunities Commission (EOC), Commission for Racial Equality (CRE) and Disability Rights Commission (DRC), and common practice within their sector.

This section contains **general guidance** on the steps employers can take to ensure best practice within their organisation. However, these guidelines must be used flexibly, since the action an employer should take will depend on and vary with its type, size, resources and needs.

As a **starting point**, however, it is safe to say that all employers should formulate, adopt and implement, on an on-going basis, written equal opportunities policies. Indeed, this is viewed by the EOC, CRE and DRC as the most effective starting point in the process of becoming an equal opportunities employer. A written policy focuses attention on the employer's commitment to develop and to use employment procedures and practices which do not discriminate and which provide genuine equality of opportunity for all workers. That commitment is expressed publicly in a manner that the employer can control and manage.

A **policy checklist** can be found at ¶9940.

Work practices and procedures

Before an employer adopts an equal opportunities policy for the first time, and thereafter at regular intervals, it is advisable to review the employment practices, procedures, systems etc., to ensure that they support equal opportunities in the workplace. It is not uncommon for employers to find that a practice or procedure which appears neutral in fact disadvantages workers of a particular age, sex, sexual orientation, race or religion or belief, married workers, civil partners or those with a disability, for reasons which are neither job-related nor required for the safe or efficient running of the organisation. Such procedures and practices are unlawful, even if the employer never intended to discriminate nor appreciated that they in fact had a discriminatory effect. 5805

There are eight specific areas for employers to consider when reviewing their practices and procedures. These are discussed briefly below: 5806

1. Recruitment practices and job advertisements Employers need to ensure that job advertisements comply with discrimination legislation. It is unlawful for an employer to publish or cause to be published an advert which indicates or might reasonably be understood as indicating an intention to discriminate on grounds of **sex or race** (S: s 38 SDA 1975; R: s 29 RRA 1976). With regard to sex discrimination, this includes the use of a job description with a sexual connotation, for example, 'waiter', 'salesgirl', 'postman' or 'stewardess'. 5807

With regard to adverts which are discriminatory on the grounds of **disability**, it is unlawful to publish or caused to be published an advert which invites applications for a relevant appointment or benefit and indicates, or might reasonably be understood to indicate, that an application will or may be determined to any extent by reference to the applicant not having (or not having had) any disability, or any particular disability; or any reluctance of the employer to comply with a duty to make reasonable adjustments (s 16B DDA 1995, as amended by reg 15 SI 2003/1673).

In addition to the specific words used in an advertisement, caution should be exercised with regard to graphics, photographs, illustrations and the overall impression given.

Further, an advert indicating that a job is open only to persons who are or who are not **union members** will lead to a conclusive presumption that work has been refused on union membership grounds and thus, in general, unlawfully (s 137(3) TULRCA 1992).

Therefore, as a matter of best practice, employers should: 5808
- avoid placing adverts in publications or areas which are generally restricted to, for example, members of one sex, since this may, effectively, preclude a wider range of applicants;
- word advertisements in a way that would encourage applications from all suitable candidates, regardless of age, sex, sexual orientation, race, religion or belief, or disability. Employers are allowed (and encouraged by the DRC) to include a statement on advertisements that they welcome applications from disabled persons. Employers who are committed to equal opportunities may state that they are equal opportunities employers;
- review all advertising material and accompanying literature, to ensure that it does not present workers in stereotyped roles. For example, it may not be appropriate to have a picture of a male skier when recruiting ski instructors; and
- avoid prescribing requirements which are not necessary for the performance of the job. For example, length of residence or experience in the UK is unlikely to be a justified requirement for most jobs. If a job is largely sedentary, there is no reason to specify that job applicants must be "energetic". Where a post requires limited load carrying, it may not be acceptable to say that only "strong, able-bodied" persons should apply.

EXAMPLE 1. An intention to discriminate on grounds of sex would be indicated by a job title/description that is not **gender neutral**, such as "waiter", "salesgirl", "fireman" or "postman".
2. An intention to discriminate on grounds of **racial group** would be indicated by specifying that applicants should be white.

5809 There are a number of recruitment practices which **should**, **generally**, **be avoided**. These include:

– recruitment solely or primarily on recommendation from existing workers, especially where the workforce is wholly or predominately of one race, religion or belief, sex or sexual orientation; and

– recruitment through trade unions, where this is likely to have the effect that a disproportionately high percentage of people from one race, religion or belief, sex or sexual orientation are put forward.

Likewise, when **recruiting through** employment agencies, job centres, career offices or schools, employers should not confine their recruitment efforts unjustifiably to agencies, job centres, career offices or schools which, because of their particular source of applicants, provide only or mainly applicants of a particular gender or from a particular racial or religious group.

5810 In a number of specific cases prescribed by law, employers are allowed to fill a post with a worker from a particular race, religion or belief, sex or sexual orientation (or who are married or in a civil partnership). These cases fall under the **genuine occupational qualification/requirement** (GOQ/GOR) exception. When a vacancy for such a post comes up, employers need to examine whether, in all the circumstances, they can still rely on the GOQ/GOR exception. If the answer is no, employers must open the vacancy to everyone.

Similarly, just because it might have been justifiable in the past not to offer a post to a person suffering from a disability, employers must not assume that the post should never be filled by a **disabled worker**. Every application must be considered individually in light of the applicant's situation and the relevant surrounding circumstances (including, for example, medical and scientific advances).

5811 **2. Selection criteria and methods** **Questions** asked at interview, **tests** given to candidates to complete and other **methods of assessing** a person's suitability for a particular post must not be unlawfully discriminatory. Thus, questions should not be put to job applicants of one sex or a sexual orientation only, or of a particular racial group, religion or belief, or to disabled workers (for example, asking female applicants only if they have effective childcare arrangements, asking black or Asian candidates only to provide evidence of the right to work in the UK, asking a disabled person only how many sick days he had in the previous year, or asking only gay applicants to undergo medical tests to prove they are HIV negative).

However, it is often assumed, incorrectly, that it is enough if an employer asks all candidates the same questions. Whilst this is a good starting point, employers must appreciate that how they use the information may also be discriminatory.

MEMO POINTS If an employer implements a test which measures levels of a **candidate's physical fitness**, he must ensure that such fitness tests are not discriminatory as between men and women.

5812 Questions on application forms **should not suggest** that the employer will take into account factors which can result in discrimination. For example, is it necessary to ask whether candidates are married, intend to marry, have children or practice any religion? This type of question can undermine applicants' confidence in the selection process; make it difficult for the employer to recruit the best person for the job; make it harder for selectors/interviewers to do their job in a non-discriminatory way; and make it almost impossible for the employer to defend himself if he later faces a discrimination claim. The EOC recommends that questions on marital status/civil partnership and number/age of children are removed from application forms.

On the other hand, some questions can improve selection by highlighting "hidden" skills and assets of workers. For example, questions on unpaid work may help female and disabled applicants to demonstrate that they have the necessary experience and/or skills relevant to the vacancy.

5813 It may be necessary for an employer to accept an application in a different form in order to accommodate **disabled job applicants** (for example, a voice-recorded application).

Where employers carry out a full monitoring process as part of their equal opportunities policy, details of workers' age, sex, marital status, sexual orientation, race, religion and state of health/disability will be needed. It is recommended that such **monitoring information** should be sought on a separate form or on a tear-off slip which should not be available to those making recruitment/selection decisions. Ideally, the employer should explain on the form its reasons for requesting the information. Employers should not use the information provided as part of the monitoring exercise to reach a decision about the suitability of a job applicant to a particular post. Employers must also be aware of their obligations under the Data Protection Act 1998 in relation to such information (¶¶5845, 5900). 5814

Employers should **examine their job selection criteria** (including any test or application form) to ensure that they are job-specific and are not (intentionally or otherwise) unlawfully discriminatory. In most cases, therefore, employers are advised to: 5815
- limit their required qualifications to those which are necessary for the proper and safe performance of the job. For example, employers should not ask for a higher level of education or a higher standard of English than is needed for the safe and effective performance of the job;
- allow job applicants to make an application in a different form/manner. For example, an employer should not disqualify a job applicant because he is unable to complete the application form unassisted, unless the ability to do this is a valid test of the standard of English and communication required for the safe and effective performance of the job;
- review requirements for a demonstrable career path. Unless such a career path can be objectively justified as a pre-requisite for the safe and effective performance of the job, there is a risk that the requirement will discriminate against female workers, non-English workers or disabled workers, whose career might not have followed the usual route;
- accept overseas qualifications which are comparable with UK qualifications; or
- review their selection tests and ensure that irrelevant questions or exercises are removed. For example, questions on matters which may be unfamiliar to racial minority applicants should be removed, unless knowledge of these matters is essential for the proper performance of the job.

3. Shortlisting, interviewing and selection Much of the guidance applicable to selection criteria and methods also applies in respect of shortlisting, interviewing and selection. In addition, however, **staff responsible** for shortlisting, interviewing and selecting candidates **should be**: 5816

a. informed of the job selection criteria;

b. instructed to apply the job selection criteria objectively and consistently; and

c. given guidance and training on equal opportunities. This should deal with, for example:
- the effects that generalised assumptions and prejudices can have on selection decisions;
- the possibility of misunderstandings occurring in the interview process between persons of different cultural backgrounds;
- the importance of thinking ahead when interviewing an applicant with a disability so that adequate preparations/reasonable adjustments are made. Staff should be aware that they may have to make an adjustment when an applicant with a disability arrives for an interview even if they did not know in advance of the disability;
- the need to consider a disabled applicant's ability to do the job effectively, on the assumption that a reasonable adjustment can be made, and what this adjustment needs to be;
- asking only about a disability if it is relevant for the performance of the job and it will be useful to discuss what could reasonably be done to adjust working arrangements to assist the applicant to perform the job safely and effectively. For example, it may be appropriate to ask whether the worker will require extra leave as a result of the disability, because this can be a substantial factor relevant to the person's suitability for the job; and
- how effectively to interview applicants who are returning to work after a period away (for example, because of childcare responsibilities), applicants with a disability, or applicants of a different race. For example staff should be instructed to ensure that the interviewer's eyes are at the same level as the applicant's when interviewing a wheelchair user.

5817 Wherever possible, shortlisting and interviewing should be done by more than one person or should, at least, be checked by a more senior manager.

5818 **4. Promotion, transfer and training practices** Where an employer considers the promotion of a worker, many of the factors which apply to the selection of an external applicant will apply. In addition, and more specifically, best practice suggests that employers should:
– publicise vacancies, training and transfer opportunities to all eligible workers in a way that will encourage a broad range of applicants;
– review selection, assessment and appraisal systems to ensure that they are not unlawfully discriminatory;
– review promotion and career development patterns to ensure that the required qualifications/career patterns are objectively justified for the job at hand. For example, is length of service a justified criterion? In some cases, it can lead to unlawful sex discrimination as it may adversely affect more women than men;
– objectively consider candidates with differing career patterns and general experience when general ability and personal qualities are the main requirements for promotion to a post;
– review rules which restrict or preclude transfer between certain jobs. It may be that employees of one sex, or particular racial group or religion, or who are disabled or are above or below a certain age are concentrated in sections from which transfers are traditionally restricted without real justification. If these rules are found to be unlawfully discriminatory, or potentially so, they should be changed;
– review policies and practices for selection for training and personal development. If considerably more workers of one group attend certain training/undertake certain forms of personal development the reasons for this need to be identified. It may be that the content of the course or the way workers are selected to attend is discriminatory. In such a case, assumptions, policies and practices may have to be changed; and
– consider removing age limits for access to training and promotion.

5819 **5. Terms of employment, benefits, facilities and services** To ensure that terms of employment, benefits, facilities and services are not unlawfully discriminatory, employers must, at the outset, **review** these, their potential and actual impact on all workers, **and consider** whether and how these terms, facilities etc. square with UK equal opportunities legislation. It is impossible to review the totality of terms of employment, benefits and facilities which employers need to consider. However, some matters come up more often than others, and these are reviewed briefly below.

The appropriate steps for an employer to take will depend on the particular circumstances, for example, the size of the organisation, the structure of the workforce (for example, male/female-dominant, multi-racial, small or large number of disabled workers), the resources of the organisation etc. Below are examples of a number of areas in which employers may need or want to take action.

Flexible work arrangements

5820 Jobsharing, part-time working, home-working and other atypical work patterns are often regarded as a concession to female workers with childcare responsibilities. However, as the EOC notes, workers of either sex increasingly seek to balance their work and personal lives. Accordingly, there is increased demand on employers to provide working patterns that allow workers to maintain a fulfilling career whilst having adequate time for life outside work. The EOC recommends that employers consider introducing or developing a standard flexible working policy which sets out the types of flexible working which they offer and the procedure for requesting such arrangements.

A flexible work arrangement policy should provide a consistent, universally accessible framework. Changes to working hours and patterns should not be made ad hoc on the basis of a "deal" between a worker and the employer (if only because this could lead to a claim of discrimination by a worker whose request is not accommodated). Any restrictions on eligibility under the policy must be based on real operational needs and must be objectively justifiable. Employers should review the restrictions regularly to ensure that they remain justifiable and, if not, they must be removed.

Ideally, a flexible working policy should: 5821
– offer flexible working to all workers irrespective of sex or other potentially discriminatory grounds;
– not impose obligatory restrictions on the type of post(s) open for jobsharing/flexible hours etc. Unless there are good operational reasons, flexible working should be offered regardless of seniority or grade. Any restriction ought to be based on real operational needs and not on any assumptions that certain jobs carry too much responsibility. Restrictions based on such assumptions may result in a "glass ceiling" preventing certain workers (for example, women or disabled workers) from reaching senior positions and thereby deprive the organisation of a valuable resource of managerial/senior expertise;
– ensure that training is available to all workers, regardless of their working hours or patterns;
– apply to workers regardless of their length of service (such a qualification can indirectly discriminate against women who tend to have shorter careers, or take more breaks in their careers because of domestic responsibilities);
– not set an arbitrary limit on the number of jobs that can be worked flexibly;
– include provision for real attempts to facilitate flexible working, for example, make efforts to find a jobshare partner where jobsharing is requested; and
– set out provisions for leave, pay and other benefits which are equal (but pro-rated) to those available to full-time workers.

MEMO POINTS Working parents have the **right to request flexible work arrangements** and there are specific procedures for employers and workers to follow when dealing with the request (¶4690).

Cultural/religious needs

Workers may have particular cultural/religious needs which conflict with their work requirements (for example, with regard to dress code and/or work patterns and working hours). In such cases, the CRE recommends that employers consider whether it is reasonably practicable to vary or adapt the work requirements to accommodate the workers' specific cultural and religious needs. For example, an employer should not generally refuse employment to a turbaned Sikh or an Asian woman wearing a sari merely because he/she cannot comply with the organisation's uniform requirements, unless the requirements can be justified objectively. Likewise, employers should consider allowing workers to observe prayer times and religious holidays if insistence on attendance at work during those times is not justifiable and working time could be made up by the workers at other times. 5822

MEMO POINTS Further guidance may be obtained from ACAS which has prepared a guide for employers designed to deal with the requirements of the various religions practised in the UK.

Leave policies

Generally speaking, annual leave, domestic leave and other special leave arrangements should be applied consistently. For example, if a worker requests extended leave to visit relatives in his country of origin and the employer has a policy which allows for the accumulation of annual leave, the policy should be applied consistently. 5823

Bereavement policies may have to be revised to reflect certain religions' requirements for burial within 24-48 hours of death.

Benefits and workers' partners

Where employers offer benefits to workers in respect of their spouses (for example, extending private medical insurance to a worker's spouse), they must offer the same benefit to workers who are in a civil partnership (¶5325). 5824

MEMO POINTS Regulations which prohibit pension-related discrimination to sexual orientation have come into force (Employment Equality (Sexual Orientation) (Amendment) Regulations SI 2003/2827). See also ¶5260.

Communication and language training

5825 Employers are not obliged by law to provide language training. But where an employer employs staff with limited English (for example, because they are foreign nationals), the CRE recommends that the employer considers providing language training as a means of improving efficiency, promotion prospects, health and safety, and understanding between the employer, staff and unions. By way of an example, an employer may consider providing:
– interpretation and translation facilities, for example, in the communication of terms of employment and employment policies and procedures;
– training in English language and communication skills;
– translated safety signs; and
– training for managers and supervisors about the background and culture of racial minority groups.

Dress and appearance

5826 Certain jobs may require employees to wear **uniforms** or **protective clothing** (for reasons of **safety** or **hygiene**) and some employers require employees to maintain a **high standard of dress** and appearance. If the employer has such expectations his requirements should be made a term of the contract, which should expressly state that a failure to adhere to the dress code may result in disciplinary action. A **policy checklist** as to what might go into such a policy can be found at ¶9940.

In **adopting a dress code**, the employer should be careful that, whilst it may be different for men and women, it should not be **discriminatory** on the grounds of **sex** or **race**. What will constitute sex discrimination in a dress code will, in some respects, **reflect social norms** that apply at the time. In 1977, for example, the EAT thought that it was entirely permissible to refuse female retail staff permission to attend work in trousers, even though they might have been required to go up and down book-stacks (*Schmidt v Austicks Bookshops Ltd* [1977] IRLR 360, EAT). However, by 1993, an employment tribunal concluded that dismissing a female employee for wearing trousers was unfair (*Stoke-on-Trent Community Transport v Cresswell*, IT case 23968/92).

Whilst the case law has moved on, it is fair to say that there is still room for employers to specify slightly different dress codes for male and female staff and to require conventional appearance. In this context, for example, it would not be unlawful to refuse workers permission to "cross-dress", although special care must be taken to accommodate those undergoing a gender reassignment process (¶5335). However, in general, employers should exercise caution in specifying different dress codes for men and women so to avoid claims of sex discrimination from both sexes.

The difficulty that still remains concerns the extent to which an employer may require his staff to maintain a **conventional appearance**. Workplaces that operate **dress-down policies** are likely to find it harder to benefit from a "conventional appearance" defence and dress-down codes should be formulated to be as unisex as possible. However, it has been held that requiring male staff to wear a collar and tie will not necessarily constitute less favourable treatment. The question is whether the level of smartness required by the employer can only be achieved by imposing such a requirement (*Department of Work and Pensions v Thompson* [2004] IRLR 348, EAT). **Uniforms** have now evolved so that they are nearly always unisex, however the employer may impose other standards of dress that may be discriminatory. In any event, the employer should have a **convincing reason** for requiring a particular dress code and should refrain from reasons based purely on subjective taste (*Catharell v Glyn Nuttall Ltd*, IT case 7935/81).

The dress code should also take into account the **racial and religious requirements** of employees. In general, the employer should be aware that certain members of his workforce may not be able to conform to a dress code that goes against their cultural or religious beliefs and should, wherever possible, allow for this. There are instances where the law specifically addresses religious requirements, for example, the requirement of wearing a helmet on a construction site does not extend to a Sikh who is wearing a turban (s 11 Employment Act 1989; see also reg 26 SI 2003/1660).

The Human Rights Act 1998 may also have an impact on the employer's ability to impose dress/appearance requirements as it enshrines the right to **freedom of expression** and the ability to exercise that right without discrimination. However, applications to the European Court of Human Rights to this effect have failed. UK courts are obliged to take account of such case law, but they are not compelled to follow it.

MEMO POINTS Note that there is now specific recourse for individuals who believe they have been discriminated against on the grounds of religion or belief (¶5375). Further developments in this area of the law are therefore likely.

EXAMPLE 1. In *McGonomy v Croft Inns Ltd* [1992] IRLR 561, HCNI, it was held that it was unlawful for the defendants, owners of a public house, to exclude a man wearing earrings, where female customers would not have been excluded.
2. In *Smith v Safeway* [1995] IRLR 1320, CA, the Court of Appeal upheld the employer's rule under which a male delicatessen assistant was dismissed for having such long hair that it would no longer keep under his cap. The argument that the rule that required him to keep his hair short went well beyond his appearance at work, and was discriminatory compared to the rules for female colleagues, was rejected. In that case the Court was prepared to permit the employer considerable leeway in establishing the image that he wanted to project.
3. In *Catharell v Glyn Nuttall Ltd*, above, C's dismissal for refusing to have his hair cut was unfair since provided the performance of his job (as an electrician) or the employer's business was not detrimentally affected, the length of his hair was a matter of his own personal taste.

6. Grievance and disciplinary procedures and victimisation It is unlawful to discriminate in the operation of any dispute resolution procedure, for example, by instigating a disciplinary procedure against a worker because he has complained of discrimination or harassment, or has assisted another to make such a complaint. 5829

It is vital that employers ensure that grievances which are based on or relate to a worker's sex, sexual orientation, race, religion or belief, disability, or age, are taken seriously, are investigated promptly and thoroughly and, as far as possible, are kept confidential. Employers ought not to treat complaints of such a nature lightly.

Employers should review and, where necessary, adjust their grievance and disciplinary procedures to avoid placing a disabled worker at a substantial disadvantage. For example, where a worker with a learning disability is required to attend a disciplinary hearing, he should be allowed to bring a colleague or a guardian or friend with him and may have to be given longer than normal to prepare for the hearing.

7. Dismissal, selection for redundancy and other detrimental treatment There is a risk of unlawful discrimination when an employer dismisses or selects a worker for redundancy. Employers must take appropriate precautions to ensure that their procedures and actions do not discriminate unlawfully on discriminatory grounds. What steps are needed will depend on all the circumstances, including the nature and size of the organisation, the employer's resources, the worker(s) in question etc. Generally speaking, employers are advised to ensure that: 5830

- staff responsible for selecting workers for dismissal or redundancy are given equal opportunities training and are instructed not to select workers on discriminatory grounds;
- their redundancy selection criteria are not directly or indirectly discriminatory (for example, selection on the basis of a sickness absence record can be unlawfully discriminatory against female and/or disabled workers);
- workers of one group are not dismissed for performance or behaviour which would be overlooked or condoned in a worker belonging to another group and any necessary reasonable adjustments are made before a disabled worker is dismissed for poor performance;
- eligibility conditions for voluntary redundancy apply equally to all workers in the same or not materially different circumstances, regardless of sex, race or disability, age, religion or belief, or sexual orientation;
- where there is a change in working conditions (for example, the employer has a new shift structure), the new arrangements do not contravene equal opportunities legislation (for example, a new shift system does not make it considerably harder for female workers than male workers to attend work); and

– employers take all reasonably practical steps to ensure that a standard of behaviour is observed which ensures dignity at work. Workers should not be subjected to unwanted conduct which has the purpose or effect of violating their dignity or creating an intimidating, hostile, degrading, humiliating or offensive working environment on discriminatory grounds. The careful formulation, dissemination and implementation of an equal opportunities policy should go a long way towards fulfilling an employer's obligations in this respect.

5831 **8. Preferential treatment** Where it is lawful for employers to give preferential treatment, the following are some of the steps that may be open to an employer:
– providing training to existing workers for work which is traditionally the preserve of workers of the opposite sex (for example, training female staff for technical or managerial jobs and training male staff to do administrative or secretarial work);
– providing training to staff of an under-represented racial group or religion or belief for promotion, for example, language training; and
– setting up recruitment and training schemes for school leavers which are designed to reach members of the under-represented group.

Monitoring equal opportunities

5835 An employer may benefit from monitoring the composition of his workforce. Although monitoring is **not a legal requirement**, the SD Code recommends that it be carried out. The fact that an employer has monitored the diversity of his workforce is also often **taken into account** by the tribunals when dealing with claims based on discrimination.

If the workforce is small the employer may not need to make a formal assessment of his workforce, as the diversity (or lack of it) will be readily apparent. The SD Code suggests that a workforce of more than 50 should be monitored although unnecessary collection of data should be avoided.

5836 Through monitoring, an employer will be able to identify areas where there may be existing problems, or potential problems, which may or may not indicate that there are equality issues. His findings may assist him in identifying:
– fairness in opportunities, which may be a result of unlawful discrimination;
– whether his workforce reflects the local community appropriately; and
– the effectiveness of his equal opportunities policy.

5837 Having identified areas of deficiencies the employer can decide how best to deal with them, if at all. If, for example, the findings show that there are differences in the pay rates of different groups of workers, he should ascertain whether there is a valid reason for this. Similarly, the results of the monitoring may show that workers are not being recruited from the local community. There may be valid reasons for this, but it may be indicative of racial discrimination in his recruitment methods. Unless the employer addresses such issues he will remain vulnerable and open to action under the discrimination legislation.

5839 The extent of the monitoring will depend on the employer's objectives. The following types of monitoring are likely to be acceptable:
– the constitution of the workforce based on ethnicity, sex, religion, sexual orientation, disability, age, part-time workers and their respective jobs (what section, what type of work, what grade);
– differences in pay between different groups, and the reasons for such differences;
– trends in training opportunities, transfers and promotions between the different groups, and if they are different, the reasons why;
– the effectiveness of company procedures on grievance/harassment;
– the disciplinary procedure and whether it has universal application across the workforce;
– accessibility of the workplace for those with disabilities; and
– whether one group of workers is more likely to resign than others.

Through monitoring the employer is more likely to have a secure basis to develop equality in the workplace and ensure that he reaches the widest pool of talent when recruiting. The employer will also benefit by retaining employees, thereby reducing recruitment and training costs. If it is evident that an employer is being pro-active and ensuring equality of opportunity the public perception of that employer may also be improved. There is also likely to be an improvement in the morale of the workforce if the employer is seen to be taking equality issues seriously.

Data protection issues

Monitoring the diversity of a workforce, and processing the related data, is clearly an accepted employment practice provided it is used to promote equality of opportunity (¶5951). However, employers must still ensure that they comply with the **data protection rules** (¶5945) (for example, where the **data is sensitive** (¶5925), explicit consent should be obtained). 5845

As **good practice**, employers should (part 2.5 DP Code):
- ensure that all equal opportunities monitoring satisfies a sensitive data condition;
- where possible ensure that the information is collected in anonymised form. Information that identifies individual workers should only be used where it is necessary to do so to enable a meaningful monitoring; and
- design questions to ensure data is accurate and not excessive. For example, employers should not limit the range of choices of ethnic origin to the extent that individuals are forced to make a choice they consider does not properly describe them.

Employers are also advised to follow the DP Code's general **recommendations** with regard to data management (¶6000).

CHAPTER 17

Data protection and privacy

OUTLINE ¶¶

5900 Employers are required by law to meet certain **obligations** when obtaining, handling or using workers' personal information or when monitoring their acts/communications (Data Protection Act 1998 (DPA 1998); Regulation of Investigatory Powers Act 2000; Human Rights Act 1998 and the implied duty of trust and confidence).

Email and internet policies are also discussed in this chapter. For a policy checklist as to what such a policy may contain see the Appendix at ¶9940.

SECTION 1

Data protection

When personal information is collected, used or stored by an employer he has an **obligation to protect** that information from being improperly used or distributed. The individual whose personal details are being held or used also has a **right to know** exactly what information is being held and the reasons why. 5910

Protection is provided under the Data Protection Act 1998 (DPA 1998) through the **data protection principles** which apply when personal information, relating to a living individual, is processed. Most of the principles amount to no more than good employment practice and the aim of the DPA 1998, and its related Employment Practice Data Protection Code (DP Code), is to ensure that employers develop a culture in which privacy, data protection security and maintaining the confidentiality of personal information are all taken seriously. 5911

The DP Code sets out **good practice recommendations** and key points and possible actions for employers to follow. There are four parts which deal respectively with recruitment and selection, employment records, monitoring at work and medical testing. The recommendations are designed to assist employers comply with the requirements of DPA 1998. In an enforcement action, the non-implementation of these recommendations may be cited by the Information Commissioner to show that the employer has not complied with his obligations under the data protection principles. Likewise, in a tribunal/court claim, failure to comply may be accepted by the tribunal/court as evidence of a breach of the DPA 1998 unless the employer can prove that the particular requirement was met in some equally, or more, effective way.

MEMO POINTS The **Information Commissioner** enforces and oversees the DPA 1998 and is an independent supervisory authority reporting directly to the UK Parliament. The Information Commissioner's duties include the promotion of good information handling and the encouragement of codes of practice for data controllers. The Information Commissioner produces the DP Code (see above) and a code of practice on CCTV monitoring. In addition, the Commissioner has also published **legal guidance** notes which serve as a reference document for employers and their advisers and **model contract clauses**.

There are **four parts** to the DP Code: 5912
- Part 1: Recruitment and selection, on job applications and pre-employment vetting. In particular it covers: advertising, dealing with applications, verifying applicants' details, short-listing, interviewing, vetting and the retention of recruitment records;
- Part 2: Employment Records, on the collecting, storing, disclosing and deleting of employment records. In particular it covers: managing data, collecting and keeping employment records, security, sickness and accident records, pension and insurance schemes, equal opportunities monitoring, marketing, fraud detection, workers' access to information about themselves and dealing with disclosure requests, references, publication and other disclosures, mergers and acquisitions, discipline, grievance and dismissal, outsourcing data processing and the retention of records;
- Part 3: Monitoring at work, on the monitoring of workers. In particular it covers: the monitoring of electronic communications, video and audio monitoring, covert monitoring, in-vehicle monitoring and monitoring through information from third parties. The Information Commissioner has also produced supplementary guidance which is designed to be read alongside the relevant good practice recommendations given in Part 3 and provides additional notes and examples; and
- Part 4: Medical information, on occupational health, medical testing, and drug and genetic screening.

A. Scope of protection

Data subjects

5920 **Workers** and other individuals who are working or who have worked (for example casual labour, agency workers or past workers), or might work for the employer (for example, job applicants), are **entitled to protection** by the data protection principles as data subjects.

Data controller

5922 As the **employer** determines the purpose for which personal data is to be kept, and the manner in which it is to be processed, he is a data controller and **must comply** with the data protection principles if he (s 5 DPA 1998):
– is established in the UK. This includes those who maintain an office, branch or agency or have a regular practice in the UK;
– processes personal or sensitive data in the context of his business; and
– determines (either alone or with other persons) the purposes for which and the manner in which the data is or is to be processed.

5923 Employers that are not established in the UK or any other EEA State but **use equipment in the UK** for processing data, otherwise than for transit purposes, will also be subject to the data protection principles.

EXAMPLE 1. A Ltd is a subsidiary company of B Ltd. The records of A Ltd's staff are kept on the computer of B Ltd. A Ltd use the records for general personnel management. B Ltd use them for staff allocation and progression planning within the group. Both A Ltd and B Ltd will be data controllers for the records of A Ltd's staff.
2. Personal data from country A is routed through the UK to country B. Unless some substantive processing operation is carried out on such data in the UK, it is deemed to be in transit and not subject to the data protection principles.

Personal and sensitive data

5925 The data protection principles apply whenever personal or sensitive data is **processed** (see Processing below). Information can be processed either by automated systems, such as computers, telephones, audio or video systems that process information automatically, or by the means of a **relevant filing system**, where information is contained within a system that is structured by reference to either individuals or to criteria relating to individuals and which is readily accessible. A relevant filing system can be either electronic (computer programmes) or manual (paper based) files from which specific information on the worker can be retrieved, for example files with the worker's name or individual reference number from which information such as his start date or last appraisal can be ascertained.

The Information Commissioner has given detailed **guidance** on when **manual files** will be deemed to be a relevant filing system and has indicated that such files will only be covered if they are sufficiently structured, indexed, divided or referenced to allow the retrieval of personal data without leafing through the files. To help identify whether a manual file is covered, the Commissioner has devised the "temp test":

"Would a temp be able to extract specific information from the manual files about an individual without any particular knowledge of the employer's type of work or documents?"

It should be noted that the Commissioner has commented that, as a result of this new guidance, very few manual files will be covered.

MEMO POINTS The Freedom of Information Act 2000 extends the definition of data with regard to information held by **public sector bodies** and as a result such authorities will have to ensure that from 2005 unstructured manual personal data (except for unstructured manual personnel records) are accurate, up-to-date and accessible.

Personal data is information that relates to a person who can be identified from that data or from other information that the employer has or is likely to have. It might include: 5926
- salary details;
- sickness and attendance records;
- notification forms naming next of kin/beneficiaries;
- annual assessments; or
- bank account details.

Also included are any opinions about a worker and any indication of the intentions of the employer or other person with respect to that person.

However, it does not necessarily follow that because a person is **mentioned by name** in a document held by a data controller that such a document amounts to personal data. A document will only constitute personal data if it is sufficiently **relevant or proximate** to the person concerned (*Durant v Financial Services Authority* [2003] EWCA Civ 1746). As a result of Durant, the Information Commissioner has issued a detailed commentary on what amounts to personal data and has confirmed that data will only be personal if it can be linked to an **identifiable individual** (for example, where his name appears together with his address, telephone number or information regarding hobbies, or where the data contains information about his medical history, salary, tax liabilities, bank statements or spending preferences).

However, **documents** that, when viewed on their own would not be regarded as "personal", could become construed as such when **viewed** all **together** (*Johnson v Medical Defence Union* [2004] EWHC 347, ChD).

Special protection is given when personal information, **considered as sensitive**, is processed such as (s 2 DPA 1998): 5927
- racial or ethnic origin;
- political opinions, religious beliefs or other beliefs of a similar nature;
- trade union membership;
- physical or mental health;
- sexual life; or
- the commission or alleged commission of any offence, or any proceedings for any offence committed or alleged to have been committed and/or the disposal of any such proceedings or sentence given.

Information is **not protected** if it does not identify an individual, such as: 5928
- general reports that do not name or use identifying information such as job titles;
- manual files that are not part of a filing system; or
- reports on individuals that are anonymised.

MEMO POINTS Information will be anonymised where it is stripped of all factors by which an individual may be identified. However, this does not apply where there is a cross reference to other information which identifies the individual.

Processing

Personal and sensitive data will be processed if the employer does any of the following with it (s 1 DPA 1998): 5930
- **obtaining, recording** or **holding** it; or
- carrying out **any operation** or set of operations on it including:
  - organisation, adaptation or alteration;
  - retrieval, consultation or use;
  - disclosure by transmission, dissemination or otherwise making available; or
  - alignment, combination, blocking, erasure or destruction.

These actions encompass most activities that are performed by an employer on personal information that he keeps on his workers. Even when an employer strips identifying factors from personal data in order to anonymise it he will be considered as processing that data.

EXAMPLE 1. Short listing job applicants on the basis of information provided on application forms (being a structured set of information) involves the processing of personal data as it requires consultation and use of the personal information. Interviewing and the obtaining and recording of informa-

tion from an interview will involve processing where information on the applicant is collated in a structured form.
2. The destruction of old personnel records, whether computerised or part of a "relevant filing system", will fall within the definition of processing.
3. The taking of a blood or urine sample and its subsequent analysis to test for drugs if the test results are to be kept on computer or recorded in a structured manner involves the processing of personal data. In any event, the analysis is likely to be processed if it is undertaken by automated equipment.

5931 Specific obligations apply to the data controller where **another entity**, known as a data processor, **processes data on his behalf**. A **data processor** can be any person, other than a worker of the data controller, who merely provides a processing service and operates under the data controller's instructions. Full responsibility remains with the data controller even where a data processor acts on his behalf. See ¶6005, for further details about using data processors.

EXAMPLE Examples of data processors:
1. From example 1 at ¶5923, B Ltd, if it makes no use of the information but merely provides the computer facility on which A Ltd maintains its staff records.
2. A self-employed consultant reorganising and updating A Ltd personnel records.
3. A payroll company used by A Ltd.
4. An organisation that provides a secure facility for storage of archived manual personnel records of A Ltd.

5933 **Right to prevent processing** Data subjects have the **right to prevent** processing if it may cause damage or distress (see Remedies below).

This right **does not exist** if the worker has given his **consent** to the processing or where it is necessary to comply with a legal obligation or to protect a workers' vital interests (s 10 DPA 1998). The worker has the **right to withdraw** his consent at any time.

B. Employer obligations

5940 When collecting, using or storing personal information the employer, as data controller, must observe **three fundamental obligations**:
- abiding by the data protection principles;
- observing the rights of data subjects to disclosure; and
- notification (where required).

1. Data protection principles

5945 The employer, as data controller must comply with the data protection principles when **personal or sensitive data is processed**. **Specific exceptions** apply in some employment situations, for example where it is necessary to safeguard national security or prevent or detect crime (ss 28-29 DPA 1998).

In summary, these principles state that data must be:
- fairly and lawfully processed;
- processed for limited purposes;
- adequate, relevant and not excessive;
- accurate;
- not kept longer than necessary;
- processed in accordance with the data subject's rights;
- secure; and
- not transferred to countries without adequate protection.

MEMO POINTS 1. The eight data protection principles are contained in Sch 1 of DPA 1998. Schs 2 and 3 set out the conditions required to meet the 1st principle requirements when processing personal and sensitive data. Sch 4 applies to cases where the 8th principle (transfer of data outside the EEA) does not apply. The processing of sensitive data is also subject to the provisions of the Data Protection (Processing of Sensitive Personal Data) Order SI 2000/417 which contains conditions additional to those of Sch 3.
2. Personal data held in a relevant filing system that **pre-dates 24 October 1998** is largely exempt from data protection principles 1-5 until 24 October 2007, as transitional arrangements provide an exemption until that date.

1st principle

Personal data must be **processed fairly and lawfully** and shall not be processed unless at least one of the conditions contained in Sch 2 is met. Where the **data is sensitive** at least one of the conditions of Sch 3 must also be met. 5948

Processed fairly Whether data is processed fairly will depend on the **manner** in which it was obtained and whether the worker was **aware** of the purposes for which it was being obtained, such as where the worker consents with full knowledge of the purpose for which the information is to be used, knows who the data controller is, and has all the information required to ensure that that the processing is fair (Sch 1 DPA 1998). Consent should be unambiguous and should be allowed to be withdrawn at any time. 5949

In addition, **personal data** may not be processed unless **at least one of the following conditions** is met (Sch 2 DPA 1998): 5950
1. the worker has given his **consent** to the processing; or
2. **processing is necessary**:
– for the performance of the worker's contract or the taking of steps at the request of a prospective worker with a view to entering into a contract;
– to comply with any legal obligations of the employer (other than obligations imposed by contract);
– to protect the vital interests of a worker (this possibly only applies to life threatening situations, for example, if the employer is badly injured and his employer has medical information that would be vital to his recovery);
– for the administration of justice or for the exercise of any function conferred by an Act of Parliament; or
– for purposes of a legitimate interest pursued by the employer or third party to whom data is disclosed except where this is prejudicial to rights and freedoms or legitimate interests of the worker.

Where **sensitive data** is processed the employer must **also meet one of the following conditions** (Sch 3 DPA 1998); 5951
1. the worker has given **explicit consent** to the processing;
2. **processing is necessary**:
– and imposed on the employer by law in connection with the employment;
– to protect the vital interests of the worker where his consent cannot be given or the data controller cannot be reasonably expected to obtain it;
– for the administration of justice or in the exercise of any function conferred by an Act of Parliament; or
– in connection with any legal proceedings or prospective proceedings, for obtaining legal advice, or otherwise necessary for the purpose of establishing, exercising or defending legal rights; or
3. the processing is required for the **purpose** of identifying or keeping under review the existence or absence **of equal opportunities**, on the basis of race or ethnicity, with a view to enabling such equality to be promoted or maintained.

MEMO POINTS 1. The Data Protection (Processing of Sensitive Personal Data) Order SI 2000/417 sets out more detailed provisions for the processing of sensitive data that is in the substantial public interest and necessary for the prevention or detection of an unlawful act, and where the consent of the individual need not be obtained. It also sets out the requirements for processing information in

establishing and administering an **occupational pension scheme** and information that is required to determine eligibility for, and benefits payable under, such a scheme.
2. Sch 3 DPA 1998 contains other conditions that do not apply to employment situations, including the right of **trade unions**, or other non profit organisations, to process personal data relating to its members subject to appropriate safeguards being in place, and requiring the data subject's consent prior to transferring personal data to others.

5952 Where an employer has received the personal data from a third party, for example where he has received information from a former employer, he **must inform the worker** as soon as is practicable that he holds such information as a data controller, the purpose for which that data is to be used and any further information necessary to ensure that the processing of that data will be fair. Failure to do this could amount to the processing of the data being deemed unfair (Sch 1 DPA 1998).

However, the employer **need not inform** the worker if to do so would involve a disproportionate effort, or if the processing is necessary for compliance of a legal (but not contractual) obligation of the employer. The Commissioner recognises that what is disproportionate will depend on the circumstances, taking into account the time and cost to the employer. Where an employer wants to rely on the **grounds of disproportionate effort** he should keep a record as to the circumstances he has taken into account. Neither of these exemptions removes the employer's obligation to process the information fairly and the worker is still entitled to ask to see the information.

5953 **Processed lawfully** Personal data will not be processed fairly if it has been **obtained through deception**, fraud or where there is a breach of the implied duty of trust and confidence.

2nd principle

5955 Personal data must be **obtained** only for **one or more specified and lawful** purposes and must not be processed further in any manner that is incompatible with that purpose.

3rd principle

5957 Personal data must be **adequate relevant and not excessive** in relation to the purpose or purposes for which they are processed i.e. the employer should only hold personal data that he actually needs.

4th principle

5959 Personal data must be **accurate** and where necessary kept **up-to-date**.

5th principle

5961 Personal data processed for any purpose or purposes must be **kept no longer than is necessary** for that purpose.

6th principle

5963 Personal data must be processed **in accordance** with the **rights of data subjects**.

7th principle

5965 Appropriate **technical and organisational measures** should be taken against unauthorised or unlawful processing of personal data and against accidental loss or destruction of or damage to personal data.

The employer should have **adequate security precautions** in place to prevent the loss, destruction or unauthorised disclosure of personal data. Where a data processor processes data on the employer's behalf, a written contract should be in place to ensure that the data processor has adequate security and will only process the data according to the employer's instructions.

8th principle

Personal data **must not be transferred** to a country or territory **outside the EU** unless that country or territory ensures an adequate level of protection of the rights and freedoms of data subjects in relation to the processing of personal data. However data may be transferred outside the EU with the data subject's consent. 5967

Where an employer wants to transfer personal data to a country outside the EU he should **consider using contractual terms** to protect that data. Standard contractual clauses which provide acceptable safeguards with respect to the protection of the privacy and fundamental rights and freedoms of individuals are attached as an Annex to the EC Decision of 15 June 2001 (Document No: EUA0500108) and can be obtained from the Commissioner.

MEMO POINTS 1. The EC decides which countries outside the EU provide an adequate level of protection to meet the requirements of the 8th principle and has powers to prohibit data flows to countries where there is inadequate protection. It has introduced a **voluntary model contract** which contains a declaration by both the data importer and the data exporter that they will process data according to basic data protection rules. The EC has accepted Switzerland, Canada and Hungary as the only countries outside the EU that provide adequate protection for personal data transferred from the EU.
2. Employers who are considering the transfer of personal data **to the USA** should be aware that the EC does not recognise any US system as being adequate to meet the 8th principle requirements. However, the self-regulatory framework of the Safe Harbor Agreement, entered into voluntarily by certain US firms has been accepted by the EC as providing adequate protection for the purposes of the transfer of personal information from the EU into the US. Consequently, when considering the transfer of personal data from an EU member state to the US the employer should consider 1) whether the importer of such data has signed the Safe Harbor Agreement; 2) whether it is appropriate to require the importer to execute the EC model contract; or 3) whether the importer's own policy on data protection will satisfy EC requirements.

2. Disclosure of information

When an employer decides to disclose information about workers he should balance the benefits against the reasonable expectations of his workers that their privacy will be respected and there is an implied duty of trust and confidence that personal information will not be disclosed where there is an expectation that it will remain confidential. 5970

Specific data protection issues regarding disclosure are covered as follows: 5971

Business mergers and acquisitions	¶5977
Fraud detection	¶5974
Marketing	¶5973
Occupational sick pay schemes (OSP)	¶4175
Pension/insurance schemes	¶3445 and ¶4206
Publication of personal and sensitive information	¶5975
References	¶8328
Sickness records	¶4223

Marketing The employer may wish to market his or third party products or services to workers. 5973
If so, as good practice, the employer should (part 2.6 DP Code):
– inform workers of any intention to use personal information to deliver advertising or marketing messages and should make sure that they can opt-out of any such campaigns; and
– obtain explicit and freely given consent.

Fraud detection The employer should not disclose any information gathered for fraud detection purposes to any third party unless (part 2.7 DP Code): 5974
– he is required to do so by law;
– he believes that failure to do so will prejudice the prevention or detection of a crime; or
– the disclosure is provided for in the worker's contract.

5975 **Publication of personal and sensitive information** There may be circumstances when the employer makes a discretionary disclosure, for example, where the employer publishes personal information in an annual report or in marketing material. Discretionary disclosure may also be expected by academic staff where information about their fields of expertise and research interests is to be widely disseminated, including on the internet. However, the majority of workers will not expect personal data to be so disclosed.

As good practice, the employer should only publish information where (part 2.11.1 DP Code):
- there is a **legal obligation** to do so;
- the information is clearly **not intrusive**;
- the worker has **consented** to the disclosure; or
- the information is in a form which does **not identify individual workers**.

Where the worker's consent has been obtained the employer should ensure that the worker is aware of the extent of the information and its use and publication, and the implications of this. The worker should be genuinely **free not to consent** to the publication of the information.

5976 Furthermore, personal/sensitive information should only be **supplied to trade unions** for its recruitment purposes if (part 2.11.3 DP Code):
- the trade union is recognised by the employer;
- the information is limited to that necessary for a recruitment approach; and
- each worker has been advised and has been given a clear opportunity to object.

Aggregated or statistical information about the workforce should be sufficient information for **collective bargaining purposes** and the employer should not assume that information about individual workers must be given to a trade union involved in collective bargaining negotiations.

5977 **Business mergers and acquisitions** Where the employer is involved in a business merger or acquisition he may be required to disclose personal information relating to his workers.

As good practice, the **employer should** (part 2.12 DP Code):
- wherever practicable, anonymise such data;
- apply conditions to its release, such as securing assurances that it will be only used in the evaluation of assets and liabilities, treated in confidence and that it will be destroyed or returned after use;
- advise workers of such disclosure wherever practicable and, if the merger or acquisition takes place, he should ensure that workers are aware of the extent to which their records are to be transferred to their new employer;
- ensure that a sensitive personal data condition (see data protection principles above) is satisfied if such data is to be transferred;
- if data is to be transferred abroad outside of the EEA ensure that there is a proper basis for making the transfer.

The **new employer** who acquires a workforce as a result of a merger or acquisition will take on the responsibility for the type and extent of personal data retained by him as well as the liability of data controller. He should, therefore, ensure that the records that he retains are accurate and relevant and should not retain excessive information.

3. Subject access requests

5980 A worker has a **right to know** what **information** is kept about him by his employer. This is known as "subject access". The information held by the employer may include records on health and sickness, disciplinary or training, performance reviews, emails and even interview notes. A worker may make a **request in writing** from a prospective, current or past employer for a copy of all his personal information that is processed by that person/organisation. The right to such information is not limited to information kept electronically but also extends to structured paper records (¶5925). The employer may **charge a fee** of up to £10 for responding to each request. The request does not have to state that it is made in connection with DPA 1998, although to do so will ensure that the employer recognises the request as such.

As good practice, the **employer should** (part 2.8 DP Code): 5981
- **establish a system** so that subject access requests are recognised and all information about a worker located so that the employer can **respond to the request within** 40 days of it being received;
- **check the identity** of anyone making a subject access request to ensure that information is only given to the person who is entitled to receive it. In smaller organisations, identity checks may not be necessary, but in larger organisations employers should not assume that all requests are genuine and appropriate checks will be necessary;
- **provide** the worker with a **hard copy** of information kept, making clear any codes and the sources for the information;
- **make a judgement** as to what information is reasonable to withhold which concerns the identities of third parties;
- **inform** managers and other relevant people in the organisation of the nature of the information that is to be released pursuant to subject access requests from workers;
- ensure that workers are promptly provided with, or in any event within 40 days, a **statement of** how any **automated decision-making process**, to which they are subject, is used and how it works; and
- ensure that any **computer system** that is purchased will enable the employer to retrieve all the information relating to any given individual without difficulty. The employer should ensure that if automated decisions about workers are to be used then the supplier of the system should provide him with information enabling him to respond fully to requests about that system.

In addition, the employer: 5982
- should ensure that the information given is intelligible, includes sources, and if possible is in **hard copy** form unless disproportionate effort is involved in copying it. Although disproportionate effort is not defined, factors to be taken into account would include the cost, the length of time involved, the difficulty and the size of the employer. Where there is a disproportionate effort some form of access still has to be given;
- should **remove all information** which identifies a third party (usually another worker(s)), for example, where a complaint has been made about the worker, the release of the document of complaint would identify the complainant. Whilst the employer could, in that case, remove the complainant's name, in other circumstances the third party may still be identifiable. The employer must strike a balance between the worker's right of access and the right of the third party to privacy. If the other person has consented to the information being released, or it is reasonable in all the circumstances to comply with the request without the other's consent, then the employer must make the disclosure. A recent High Court decision had confirmed that the names of third parties can be removed from data if they do not necessarily form part of the personal data. However, the Court held that in certain circumstances such data was disclosable without requiring the consent of those third parties (*Johnson v Medical Defence Union* [2004] EWHC 347, ChD); and
- is under no obligation to disclose documents which had been produced electronically but are **no longer in electronic form** and are only held in paper form. The form in which a document is stored at the time of the request is relevant to whether it is searchable and, to qualify as "data", the documentation has to be reasonably accessible by the data controller without needing to conduct a manual search (*Johnson v Medical Defence Union*, above).

4. Notification

Data controllers should notify the Commissioner before they process personal data. However, this will **not apply to most employers** as they will be exempt if they only process personal data **for the purposes of**: 5990
- staff administration (including payroll);
- advertising, marketing and public relations (of the employer's business); or
- accounts and records.

5991 In addition, notification is **not required** in any event where personal data is:
– recorded only in a manual filing system; or
– is a health or educational record;

unless the processing is likely to cause substantial damage or distress to the data subject or might significantly prejudice his rights or freedoms (s 17 DPA 1998).

Some **not for profit organisations** are also exempt from notification.

MEMO POINTS Detailed guidance about the notification exemptions can be found in the Commissioner's publication – *Notification Exemptions – A self-assessment guide*. Any data controller who believes he may be exempt must refer to this guidance.

5992 In all other circumstances, the employer will be **required** to notify the Commissioner and he must submit his notification prior to processing personal data. The notification details are then put on the register, which is a public document. The details show the employer's name and address and the name and address of his UK representative (if he has one); a description of the personal data being held by him and any recipient who might receive such data; any country outside the EEA where the data may be sent; and any exempt data.

If the personal data maintained by the employer falls partly within and partly outside the above exemptions, for example where personal data is recorded in both a manual filing system and on a computer, the employer should notify the Commissioner as to the non-exempt data and make a statement of fact confirming that he holds exempt data. Alternatively, he may choose to voluntarily notify the Commissioner of all the personal data he controls, regardless of whether it is held on computer or not.

5993 As part of the notification process a **registration fee** of £35 is payable. Notification is **valid for one year**, following which the employer is obliged to renew with any amendments that are necessary. The employer must also provide a general description of the security measures taken to protect the personal data, although this will not appear on the public register. Notification does **not equate to compliance** with the data protection principles.

Failure to notify the Commissioner is an offence (ss 17, 21 DPA 1998) and it remains open to the Commissioner to investigate and prosecute those who are required to notify but have not done so.

MEMO POINTS 1. Notification may now be completed on-line through www.dpr.gov.uk/notify. The site also provides an online self-assessment to determine if notification is required.
2. Employers who registered under the Data Protection Act 1984 were exempt from the prohibition on processing personal data without notification until the end of their three year registration period or their voluntary notification under the DPA 1998, whichever occurred earlier. If they did not voluntarily notify under DPA 1998 then on the expiry of their original registration period they should have notified the Commissioner in accordance with the DPA 1998.

C. Data management

6000 All employers hold personal data and probably some sensitive personal data on their workers. This will have been collected during the recruitment process, through appraisals, sick notes, the administering of certain benefits, for example permanent health insurance and through any monitoring of communications as discussed in the previous sections. Ideally, data protection compliance should be seen as an **integral part** of the employer's procedures and practices rather than as a standalone requirement. An employer's written procedures relating to the keeping of workers' records should incorporate the relevant good practice recommendations of DP Code, which should extend to all staff and the processing of all personal and sensitive data, not just to the more obvious departments such as human resources and payroll. Data protection compliance should be viewed as a multi-disciplinary matter so that all staff are aware that they each have a part to play in securing compliance. The procedures should be regularly reviewed and where necessary updated.

Consequently, employers should allocate responsibility, establish what personal data are processed and ensure that employment practices comply with the data protection principles. 6001
As good practice, **employers should** (managing data protection (part 0) DP Code):
- establish a person within the organisation **who is responsible** for ensuring employment practices and procedures comply with the data protection principles, for example, a senior manager in a human resources function or someone in a comparable position, or where the organisation is small, the employer himself. This is a continuing responsibility and a means of checking that procedures are followed in practice should be established;
- ensure that each departmental line manager and business area which may process workers' personal or sensitive information is **aware of their responsibilities** for data protection compliance, and if necessary, amend working practices to accommodate them;
- **assess** what personal information on workers is kept, and who is responsible for it;
- **eliminate** the collection of personal information that is irrelevant or unnecessary to the employment relationship. If sensitive data is collected then a sensitive data condition should be satisfied (¶5951);
- ensure that **workers are aware** of the extent to which they can be criminally liable if they knowingly or recklessly disclose personal data outside the employer's policies or procedures. Serious breaches of the data protection principles should be made a disciplinary offence;
- allocate responsibility for making a valid **notification** (if required, see above) to the Commissioner if required, and maintain it in accordance with the notification requirements; and
- **consult** with trade unions or other workers' representatives, if any, or workers themselves over the development and implementation of employment practices and procedures that involve the processing of personal information.

Specific data protection issues are covered as follows: 6002

Equal opportunities monitoring	¶5845
Discipline, grievance and dismissal	¶6504
Information about workers' health	¶5040
Occupational sick pay schemes	¶4175
Pension/insurance schemes	¶3445 and ¶4206
Recruitment and selection	¶676
Sickness records	¶4223

1. Collecting and handling records

It is not generally necessary to obtain workers' consent to keep general employment records and it will usually be sufficient to ensure that they are aware that records are being kept and for what purpose. However, consent may be necessary with regard to sensitive data. 6003
As good practice, the **employer should** (part 2.1 DP Code):
- ensure that newly appointed **workers** are made **aware** of the nature and source of any information stored about them, how it is used and to whom it may be disclosed;
- ensure that all **workers understand** their rights under the DPA 1998 and their right of access to information held about them;
- make sure that there is a **clear and foreseeable need for the information** and that the information collected meets that need. Any extraneous information should not be collected and/or removed;
- regularly **provide workers** with a copy of the **information about them that may be subject to change**, for example home addresses. Workers should be asked to check such information to ensure that their records are up-to-date and accurate; and
- **maintain and review** all systems for collecting and retaining information to enable accuracy, consistency and validity checks to be carried out.

Using data processors

6005 Often employers outsource the processing of information they hold to third parties, referred to here as data processors. When using a data processor the employer should ensure that appropriate security measures are adopted and complied with (part 2.14 DP Code). To this end, the employer should have a **written contract** with the data processor which ensures that security is maintained and that personal information is processed only on the employer's instructions. Where the use of a data processor would involve the transfer of information about a worker outside the EEA, the employer should ensure that there is a proper basis for making the transfer. The data processor should comply with the same standards for the collection, processing and retention of personal information as apply to the employer as data controller.

6006 Further, **contract/agency staff** will be data processors if they process personal data for the employer. The reliability of such staff that have access to workers' records and other personal data should be checked no less thoroughly than in the case of workers who have a similar level of access. Consequently, they should have written contracts that ensure they only process data in accordance with instructions and that they keep the data secure.

Prevention of unauthorised access

6010 The basic principle is that information about workers should **only be available** to those who need it to do their job. The employer should be aware that access rights should be based on genuine need and not seniority. Where workers need to access personal information as part of their job, the employer should check their reliability and they should be made aware of the security regime. Where appropriate, a confidentiality clause should be inserted into their contract of employment.

As good practice, the **employer should** (part 2.2 DP Code):
– apply proper **security standards** that take account of the risks of unauthorised access to or accidental loss or destruction of or damage to employment records;
– **institute a system** of secure cabinets, access controls and passwords that ensure staff access employment records only when they have a legitimate business need to do so;
– use the **audit trail** capabilities of automated systems to track who accesses and amends personal data;
– take steps to ensure the **reliability of staff** that have access to worker records. This will involve training and ensuring that workers understand their responsibilities. Confidentiality clauses should be included in contracts of employment;
– ensure that if **records are taken off-site**, for example on a laptop, that this is controlled and that only necessary information is taken. Staff should be made aware of appropriate security rules and procedures, for example, the laptop must be secure or in view at all times, to protect such information; and
– take account of the **risks of transmitting confidential information** by fax or email. Such information should only be transmitted between locations if a secure network or comparable arrangement is in place. In the case of email, employers should provide some technical means of ensuring security, such as effective password protection and encryption.

2. Retention of records

6015 As good practice, the **employer should** (part 2.15 DP Code):
– establish and adhere to **standard retention times** for categories of information held on the records of workers and former workers. The retention periods should be based on business needs, taking into account any professional guidelines;
– **anonymise** any data about workers and former workers where practicable;
– if the holding of records containing information on **criminal convictions** of workers is justified, ensure that the information is deleted once the conviction is 'spent' (¶616); and
– ensure that records which are to be **disposed of** are securely and effectively destroyed.

6016 No specific retention **period** is given in the DPA 1998, but the DP Code does provide that any period that the employer decides on must be based on **business need** and should take into account any **professional guidelines**. Employers should be aware that the DPA 1998 **does not override** any statutory requirement to retain records, for example in relation to certain aspects of health and safety or income tax. Therefore, the employer must strike a balance between ensuring that personnel information is not kept for longer than is necessary but not deleting it where there is a real business need to retain it. The retention of records for health and safety purposes, for example, is likely to be different in the case of those working with hazardous substances to those working in an office environment.

The employer should **not retain** personal information on the basis that it may be useful one day. Instead he should take into account any relevant professional guidelines or statutory requirement and should:
- adopt a risk analysis approach by considering what realistically would be the consequences for the business, the workers, former workers and others, if personal information that is only occasionally accessed is no longer available;
- treat items of information individually or in logical groupings. All of the information in a record should not be retained just because there is a need for some of it to be retained; and
- use the principle of proportionality to help decide which records should be retained i.e. records about a large number of workers should not be retained for a lengthy period on the off-chance that one of them at some point might question some aspect of his employment.

D. Remedies

6040 A worker may **ask his employer** in writing **not to process personal data**, or ask him to stop processing it, where it is causing, or is likely to cause, substantial unwarranted damage or substantial distress to the worker or anyone else. The employer who has received such a request must **respond within** 21 days stating whether he is going to comply with the request or not. If the employer believes that the request is unjustified then he must give the reasons.

A worker can also submit a **subject access request** to find out what personal or sensitive data is held about him (¶5980).

Applications to the Commissioner

6043 Workers can write to the Commissioner stating that their employer has failed to comply with his obligations. The Commissioner may:
- **make an assessment** as to whether it is likely or unlikely that the employer has complied with the data protection principles;
- **issue enforcement proceedings** if he is satisfied that the data controller has contravened one of the data protection principles; or
- **recommend** that the worker apply to court alleging a failure to comply with the subject access provisions.

6044 The Commissioner has a **wide discretion** as to how an assessment is carried out. Should he determine that there has been non-compliance then he may take the matter up directly with the data controller and is **empowered to enforce** the data protection principles against any data controller where he is satisfied that any of the principles have been, or are being, contravened.

6045 An employer who receives an enforcement notice from the Commissioner may **appeal** to the independent data protection tribunal. However, if the tribunal upholds the Commissioner's decision, failure to comply becomes a criminal offence. The tribunal may substitute its own decision for the Commissioner's if it sees fit.

Applications to civil courts

6047 The worker may also apply to the civil courts if (ss 7-12 DPA 1998):
- his employer fails to respond to his requests;
- personal data held by his employer is inaccurate; or
- the employer has based an opinion about the worker on inaccurate data.

The courts have the power to order the employer to comply with his obligations or, in the case of inaccurate data or an opinion based on such data, make an order to rectify, block, erase or destroy that data (s 14 DPA 1998).

In addition, the worker may be **entitled to compensation** if he can prove that he has suffered damage as a result of the employer not meeting his obligations (s 13 DPA 1998). The court may order compensation for any **associated distress** as well. A claim for distress alone is unlikely to succeed.

SECTION 2

Monitoring and surveillance

6150 Many employers make some **checks** on the **quantity and quality** of work produced by their workers, for example, counting the number of calls made on a daily or weekly basis by telesales workers. Such monitoring of work output is often termed **performance monitoring**. Employers may also check their workers' behaviour and their conformity with company policies, procedures and any legal requirements, for example compliance with health and safety rules or discrimination rules. This is commonly termed **surveillance**.

6151 Traditionally, performance monitoring and surveillance was conducted solely through human observation by way of managers and foremen. However, newer **methods of monitoring and surveillance** by automated and electronic means are now commonplace, such as telephone monitoring, CCTV cameras and email interception, and all have the potential of being extremely intrusive.

A. General standards

6160 Monitoring will usually be considered to be intrusive and workers have **legitimate expectations** to have a degree of privacy at work as well as to keeping their personal lives private. Any adverse impact on these expectations as a result from any monitoring must be **justified by** the benefits it gives to the employer (DPA 1998). Monitoring that cannot be justified and is excessive **may also be contrary** to the Human Rights Act 1998 and may breach the employer's implied duty of trust and confidence.

6163 **Policy on monitoring/surveillance** It is advisable that employers have or introduce a policy on monitoring if they plan to monitor their workers. The policy should be workable and user friendly.

If the reason for the monitoring is the **enforcement** of the employer's **rules or standards**, they should be clearly **set out** in a policy which refers to the associated monitoring and workers should be made aware of the policy. Where the rules and standards, for example, apply to the use of emails and internet access in the workplace, they should be set out in a policy that is made known and is readily accessible to the workers to which it applies. The employer should also specify the safeguards that he has in place to protect the worker's personal data and its confidentiality.

The most **widely applicable** monitoring policy is often on internet usage and emails which should set out what is acceptable use in the business culture in which employees work, and should emphasise the need for maintaining productivity, the problem of viruses and the legal consequences of sending emails as well as the fact that it is often no substitute for an actual conversation (¶6215). 6164

Impact assessments

Employers, in all but the most straightforward of cases, should carry out a formal or informal impact assessment to help them decide if and how to carry out any monitoring and this **will involve**: 6165

1. **identifying the purpose** for the monitoring and its proposed benefit;
2. **identifying any adverse impact**. This includes the intrusion the monitoring would have on the workers' private lives, whether workers will be able to limit any intrusion, whether confidential or sensitive information will be seen by others (for example, IT workers) and whether it will impact on the relationship with the employer or other bodies.
3. **considering any alternatives** to monitoring or different ways in which it could be carried out. For example, the employer should consider whether less intrusive methods would obtain the same desired benefit, such as effective training, supervision and clear communication from managers or limiting the proposed monitoring to a small group of workers which have either been suspected of wrong-doing or are in an area of high-risk to the business. Where the monitoring could be automated may also make the monitoring less intrusive as will spot-checking or auditing instead of continuous monitoring (although this may not be the case where the spot-checking or auditing requires human intervention).
4. **taking into account the obligations** that occur when monitoring. In particular, employers must ensure that they comply with the data protection principles which require that all personal information that is obtained through monitoring be processed legally and fairly and in accordance with the data protection principles (¶5945). They must also comply with the specific standards that apply to the processing of sensitive data and, when collecting sensitive data about a worker's health, racial origin or sex life must satisfy the sensitive data conditions (¶5951). Workers must also be informed of any monitoring and employers must consider the implications of the rights that workers have to obtain a copy of information about them that has ben gathered through monitoring; and
5. **deciding whether** the monitoring is **justified**. This must take due consideration of steps 1 to 4, balancing the benefits against any adverse impact while placing particular emphasis on the need to be fair to individual workers. Where electronic communications are involved, any intrusion must be no more than absolutely necessary. Any significant intrusion into the private lives of workers will not normally be justified unless there is a real risk to the employer's business. Account should also be taken of the results of any consultation with trade unions or other representatives.

Good practice recommendations

As good practice, the **employer should** (part 3.1 DP Code): 6167

- be clear about the **purpose** of the monitoring. This should be identified before the monitoring takes places. Employers should not monitor workers just because a customer for their products or services requires it unless it can be justified;
- be satisfied that the particular **method** chosen is justified by the benefits. This again should be identified before the monitoring is to start and it is best if this is done by an impact assessment (see above).
- make sure that **workers are aware** of the nature, extent and reasons for any monitoring, unless (exceptionally) covert monitoring is justified. This includes informing workers what monitoring is taking places and why and making sure that they are regularly reminded that monitoring is occurring;
- keep to a minimum those who have **access to the information**. Wherever possible, access should be confined to those with relevant responsibilities working in a specific function such as the human resources department. Access to personal information obtained through monitoring must be limited and those with such access should be subject to confidentiality and security requirements and should be properly trained as necessary.

– ensure that the information gathered should **not be used for any other purpose** unless it is clearly in an individual worker's interest to do so or it reveals an activity that the employer cannot reasonably be expected to ignore;
– ensure that where the information may have an **adverse impact on an individual worker**, he should be given the opportunity to see the information and make representations, for example to explain or challenge the information, before any action is taken against him; and
– make sure that the workers' **right of access** to information held about them is not compromised and that the monitoring system can meet this requirement.

B. Monitoring electronic communication

6190 Electronic communication **includes** the telephone, fax, email, voicemail and internet access. As well as the **requirement** to comply with the general standards in section A, there are also specific good practice recommendations in relation to the monitoring of electronic communication. Further, where employers intercept communications as part of their monitoring they must also ensure that they are acting lawfully (see below).

There are **risks and liabilities** (see ¶6260) associated with workers' use of electronic communications in particular email and internet access which may require monitoring. The **introduction of a policy** can serve to minimise the potential for these risks and abuses by setting out clear guidelines and restrictions and by stating what, if any, monitoring takes place.

1. Data protection compliance

6200 As good practice, if he is considering monitoring workers, the **employer should** (part 3.2 DP Code):
– ensure the monitoring is **legal** (see sub-section 2 below);
– consider whether the monitoring is **justified**, preferably by using an impact assessment. Alternatives should be considered, for example, if the issue is security, whether encrytion and passwords will be sufficient or whether the proposed monitoring can be automated as such systems are likely to be less intrusive. With regard to any monitoring, workers should be informed of its nature and extent and the purpose behind it. Information regarding private calls or email should not be used, unless they reveal an activity that no employer could reasonably be expected to ignore;
– with regard to **phone calls**: Particular care must be taken before phone calls or voicemails are, or are likely to be, monitored as it is more intrusive and therefore harder to justify. Where phone lines are provided at workers' homes or company mobile phones are provided for personal use, expectation of privacy will be even higher.

Where it is essential, alternatives should be considered such as whether itemised call records will suffice. If voice-mails need to be checked for business calls while workers are absent, they should be made aware of this and that in such circumstances it may be unavoidable that some personal messages may be heard. Where calls are monitored, ensure that external callers know that calls may be monitored and the purpose behind it, unless this is obvious.
– with regard to **emails and the internet**: Wherever possible, employers should avoid opening emails, especially those which are clearly shown to be private. To this end, workers should be encouraged to mark emails as personal where appropriate. Private emails should only be monitored in exceptional circumstances. If possible, email monitoring should be confined to the address/heading of the email, unless it is essential to examine the content.

If it is necessary to check emails while workers are absent, they should be made aware of this. A system of marking up emails to help identify private emails should be encouraged and where possible private emails should not be opened.

Workers should be informed of the extent to which information about their internet access and emails is retained in the system and for how long.

Policies

As good practice, employers should establish a policy if they wish to monitor electronic communication. Workers must be made aware of the policy and its contents. In particular, as good practice, the **policy should** (part 3.2 DP Code): 6205
- clearly state **when** phones (including mobile phones, where relevant), email systems and the internet can be used for **private access and communications**;
- clearly state the **extent of allowable private use**, for example whether overseas phone calls can be made and/or whether certain types of email attachments can be received or sent. This should also include what is allowable for private use with regard to the employer's equipment when it is used from home or off site.
- clearly state what, if any, restrictions apply to **internet access**, for example, whether there are prohibitions regarding downloading or copying information from the internet and/or whether certain material should not be viewed, for example offensive material (in such cases, what is considered to be offensive should also be defined, for example material which is racist or pornographic);
- advise workers of the general **need to exercise care** and what alternatives can be used to ensure confidentiality, for example medical reports should be sent by internal post rather than email;
- explain the **purposes and extent of any monitoring** and how it will be carried out; and
- explain how the policy is **enforced** and what penalties exist for a breach of policy.

2. Interception requirements

Interception of worker communication by employers is an **offence** (s 1 Regulation of Investigatory Powers Act 2000). The employer may, however, have the **lawful authority** to intercept such communications in certain circumstances, such as where there is specific consent. In addition, specific circumstances which give the employer lawful authority to intercept are contained in the Telecommunications (Lawful Business Practice) (Interception of Communications) Regulations 2000 (SI 2000/2699). 6220

Unlawful interception

It is unlawful for any person who controls a private telecommunications system or, with his consent, for another person to intercept communications made on that system unless they have lawful authority to do so (s 1(3) Regulation of Investigatory Powers Act 2000). Situations where a third party has hacked into an employer's private telecoms system and intercepted communications are not covered by the Regulation of Investigatory Powers Act. 6221

A **private telecommunications system** is defined as one attached to a public telecoms system by equipment located in the UK (s 2(1) Regulation of Investigatory Powers Act 2000).

> EXAMPLE Any company telephone or email system which is attached to a public system is included. Therefore, if an employer has a telephone system by which his workers can make internal telephone calls, it will be within the definition if these workers can also make external telephone calls using the same system. However, an internal system that is not connected in any way to a public system, will not be included.

Communication is **defined** as including speech, music, sounds, visual images or data of any description, for example, telephone conversations, emails and other written communication (s 81 Regulation of Investigatory Powers Act 2000). 6222

Communication is **intercepted** if the employer (or someone acting on his behalf) (s 2(2) Regulation of Investigatory Powers Act 2000): 6223
- **modifies or interferes** with the telecommunications system or its operation; or
- **monitors** transmissions made by:
  · means of the system; or
  · tapping to or from apparatus in the system;

to make some or all of the content available to the employer (or any other person other than the sender or the intended recipient).

Therefore, the monitoring of the **number of emails or telephone calls** is not interception unless the contents are opened or the calls are listened to.

Interception must occur **during transmission** of the communication (s 2(2), (7), (8) Regulation of Investigatory Powers Act 2000). This includes the period when the communication is being stored, for example an answerphone message or an email in an inbox. Interception must be **performed in the UK**. Either the sender or intended recipient of the communication must also be located in the UK.

Lawful interception

6225 Communication may be lawfully intercepted if the employer has reasonable grounds for believing that both the **sender and recipient have consented** (s 3(1) Regulation of Investigatory Powers Act 2000). This exception can be used where the communication is between workers of the same organisation and the employer has obtained consent from his workers (usually by incorporating written consent into their contracts of employment).

6226 In addition, an employer's interception of his worker's communications for **specific purposes** is recognised as being lawful. Even in these circumstances, however, the employer should make all reasonable efforts to **inform potential users** that the interception may be made. Examples of **making reasonable efforts** to inform potential non-worker users that interceptions may be made, could be putting an automatic message on all out-going emails etc warning that they may be monitored/read or having a recorded message for any customers telephoning which states that calls may be recorded for monitoring or training purposes.

The specific purposes include the **monitoring or keeping a record** of communications in order to (reg 3 SI 2000/2699):

– establish the existence of facts, or to ascertain compliance with procedures applicable to the employer's business;

– ascertain or demonstrate the standards followed by workers using the communications system, such as telephone operators or telesales teams; or

– prevent or detect crime, investigate or detect unauthorised use of telecommunications systems (for example, monitoring to ensure worker compliance with the employer's internet and email policy), or secure the effective operation of the system (for example, monitoring for viruses and other threats).

6227 Other instances of lawful interception are when the employer monitors communications between its workers and any confidential voice counselling or support service so long as it is free of charge and provides anonymity of the caller, or where he monitors incoming communications to determine whether they are business or personal communications.

C. Other specific forms of surveillance

6230 In some circumstances, employer may want to monitor his workers by other means for example, by CCTV cameras or audio devices. As well as the requirement to comply with the general standards in section A, there are also specific good practice recommendations in relation to the monitoring of video and audio, vehicle monitoring and monitoring through third party information.

Video and audio

6233 Video monitoring covers the use of CCTV within the workplace. Audio monitoring concerns the recording of face-to-face conversations (as opposed to telephone calls for which is electronic monitoring). Video and audio monitoring must be kept to an absolute minimum and, consequently, it is unlikely that **continuous use** of video or audio monitoring is justifiable save in circumstances where there are particular safety or security risks, for example, in a shop where there is a high likelihood of robbery. Covert monitoring (see below) by such equipment is only justifiable in specific circumstances where open monitoring would prejudice the detection of a crime or the apprehension of offenders.

MEMO POINTS The **separate** code of practice on CCTV monitoring which is of more general application than monitoring at work also provides useful guidance.

As good practice, the **employer should** (part 3.3 DP Code): 6234
- consider, preferably using an impact assessment, whether the benefits will **justify** the adverse impact. Where possible, any monitoring should be targeted to areas of particular risk and confined to areas where the expectations of privacy are low;
- give workers a **clear notification** that the monitoring is taking place and where, and the reasons for it, unless covert monitoring is justified (see below); and
- ensure that **non-workers**, such as visitors or customers, who may be inadvertently monitored by the system, are **aware** that the monitoring is taking place and the reasons for it.

In-vehicle monitoring

Monitoring of vehicle movements of company cars and vans etc, where the vehicle is **allocated to a specific driver**, for example by means of tachograph systems as well as tracking devices, must comply with the data protection standards. 6237

As good practice, the **employer should** (part 3.5 DP Code):
- consider, preferably using an impact assessment, whether the benefits will **justify** the adverse impact. In making an assessment the employer should consider whether the monitoring can be limited to exclude information on the private use of the vehicle. If the private use of the vehicle is allowed then monitoring of private usage will rarely be justified. Where vehicles are supplied both for business and private use, employers should provide workers with the ability to disable any monitoring device when the vehicle is being used privately. In the case where he is obliged by law to monitor the worker's use of the vehicle this will take precedence; and
- **make clear in a policy** the nature and extent of any monitoring and what extent of private use is allow. Workers affected must be made aware of the policy.

Non-employment information

Some employers may wish to monitor the behaviour of their workers through information **held by third parties** to which they have access, for example public record information such as the electoral roll and the Register of County Court Judgments. Information concerning criminal convictions must be obtained from the Criminal Records Bureau (¶619). 6240

Employers must not use credit reference agencies which check their customers to monitor or vet workers. Likewise, information which an employer has about a worker because they are also a customer/client/supplier must not be used.

As good practice, the **employer should** (part 3.6 DP Code):
- consider, preferably using an impact assessment, whether the benefits will **justify** the adverse impact. A worker's financial circumstances should not be monitored unless the employer has evidence that shows that a worker who is in financial difficulties poses a significant risk to the employer;
- **inform workers** what information sources are to be used to carry out the checks, and why they are to be carried out;
- ensure that those carrying out the monitoring are **properly trained** and that there are rules to prevent the disclosure of information obtained through the monitoring; and
- **avoid retaining** any information obtained by the monitoring. Only a record that the check took place and the result obtained should be kept. Any records should not normally be retained for more than 6 months.

D. Covert monitoring

6250 Covert monitoring, that is monitoring about which the subject of it is unaware, is only justifiable in **exceptional circumstances**, where informing the worker that surveillance is taking place may prejudice national security, the prevention or detection of crime, the apprehension or prosecution of offenders or the assessment of any tax or duty (Part IV DPA 1998). As well as the requirement to comply with the general standards in sections A and B, there are also specific good practice recommendations.

If a private investigator is used, the employer must make sure that the investigator is contractually required to act in accordance with the employer's obligations.

6251 As good practice, the **employer should** (part 3.4 DP Code):
– normally require that **senior management authorise** any covert monitoring. To be **justified** they must be satisfied that there are grounds for suspecting criminal activity or malpractice and that notifying the workers concerned would prejudice its prevention or detection;
– ensure that any covert monitoring is **strictly targeted** and performed within a specified limited timeframe. The number of people involved should be likewise limited;
– ensure that covert monitoring is **not used in** areas in which workers have a reasonable expectation of privacy, for example in private offices or toilets. Where exceptionally it is necessary to monitor such an area there should be an intention to involve the police; and
– ensure that there are clear rules limiting the **disclosure and access** to the information obtained. Any information obtained should **only be used** for the purpose of the covert monitoring and any other information gathered should be destroyed unless it reveals information that no employer could reasonably be expected to ignore.

6252 The **right to privacy** (¶6050) may also have an impact on any covert monitoring the employer undertakes. In a recent case, undercover surveillance cameras which were used to "spy" on an employee whom the employer suspected of falsifying his timesheets in relation to call-outs and periods in which he attended his workplace did raise a presumption that the right to respect for private life (Art 8 Human Rights Act 1998) was being breached but the determining factor was held to be whether the employer's actions in carrying out the surveillance was proportionate to the employee's alleged misconduct (*McGowan v Scottish Water* [2005] IRLR 167, EAT). In this case, the EAT held that the employee's alleged misconduct had forced the employer to investigate the matter and, since the objective of the surveillance was to establish how many times the employee left his house to attend the workplace which would then affect the accuracy or otherwise of his timesheet, the covert surveillance went to the **root of the investigation** that the employer was bound to carry out to protect its assets and was therefore not disproportionate. In effect, the employer (which was a public body) was allowed to investigate what had amounted to a criminal activity and was therefore justified and proportionate. Consequently, M's dismissal had not been unfair.

SECTION 3

Email and internet issues

6260 The use of internet and email at work is widespread and, whilst there are many commercial and organisational advantages, there are also risks and liabilities associated with employee use of these media, including viruses, legal claims, unauthorised access, and inadvertent formation of contractual obligations. The introduction of a policy on such use can serve to minimise the risk to the employer by setting out clear guidelines and restrictions. Breach of the email and internet policy should be made a disciplinary offence. The employer should monitor use to ensure compliance, although there may be restrictions on his right to do so.

Any monitoring of electronic communication requires compliance with the general standards (¶6160), specific good practice recommendations (¶6190) and, where appropriate, good practice recommendations on covert monitoring (¶6250). Further, where employers intercept communications as part of their monitoring they must also ensure that they are acting lawfully (¶6225). 6261

The key elements of an email and internet policy are: 6262
– notification that email and internet are provided for business-related purposes only, or guidelines as to what level of personal use is acceptable;
– guidelines on access to and use of computer systems and software, and details of computer security procedures;
– notification that emails may be read by the employer and use of computer facilities monitored;
– a ban on sending pornographic, discriminatory and other obscene material, and a warning that doing so may leave the employee open to criminal and civil liability;
– a ban on downloading and sending defamatory messages, informing employees that derogatory remarks, even when intended as a joke, can constitute libel or unlawful discrimination or harassment;
– a reminder that back-up systems and retrieval capabilities mean that deletion of a message or file may not remove it entirely from the system;
– a warning that legally binding contracts can (even inadvertently) be formed by email correspondence; and
– a warning that breach of the email and internet policy and any guidelines on access/use of computer systems and software may result in disciplinary action up to and including summary dismissal.

Some of these areas are expanded below. For a policy checklist as to what such a policy may contain see the Appendix at ¶9940.

Breach of confidentiality

The use of email increases the risk of accidental disclosure of the employer's confidential information, especially if the email goes to the wrong recipient. A company policy could protect against this by stating that no highly sensitive company information or confidential material should be sent by email. However, this approach should be weighed against the cost and environmental benefits of having a "paper-free" office. 6264

In order to minimise the effect of accidental disclosure, it is advisable to ensure that all emails carry a confidentiality statement.

Email also makes it easier for disgruntled employees to make unauthorised disclosures of sensitive information. Further, a departing employee can take confidential information with him by saving it on a disk or downloading it to his home computer or laptop. After the termination of employment, confidential information is only protected to the extent that it amounts to a trade secret (¶2301), or if there is an express restrictive covenant (¶2550).

Computer viruses

Computer viruses can be transmitted if software and other files are downloaded. The employer's policy should outline procedures to avoid the risk of his systems being corrupted, for example scanning all discs for viruses. 6266

Defamation

An email may constitute a defamatory statement (libel), as may a message posted on the internet. The employee may be liable for any damage caused to the reputation of the subject of the statement. The employer may also be liable by virtue of vicarious liability (¶1205) or as a publisher or disseminator of the offending statement. 6268

A defence may be available to the employer as disseminator of a defamatory statement if he can show that (s 1 Defamation Act 1996):
– he was not the author, editor or publisher of the statement;

– he took reasonable care in relation to its publication; and
– he did not know, and had no reason to believe, that what he did caused or contributed to the publication of a defamatory statement.

The courts will consider the extent to which the employer had responsibility for the statement and the nature or circumstances of its publication. The employer's defence will be strengthened if he has issued clear guidance to employees about acceptable usage of email and internet, and if he has monitored employee use in order to identify and deal with any abuse.

Formation of contracts

6270 Employees may inadvertently enter into contracts on the employer's behalf or vary terms which the employer will be obliged to honour. An email exchange (once printed out) is capable of amounting to an agreement in writing signed by the parties (*Hall v Cognos Ltd*, ET case 1803325/97).

Harassment

6272 The contents of email (for example, jokes or pornographic images or text) can give rise to complaints of harassment (i.e. unwanted, unsolicited and inappropriate words or conduct affecting the dignity of another person), and other claims on the grounds of racial or religious, sex, sexual orientation and disability discrimination. See ¶¶5360, 5430, 5580 and Chapter 16 generally.

> EXAMPLE In *Morse v Future Reality Ltd* [1996] ET case 54571/95, an employment tribunal awarded M compensation for sexual harassment based on the fact that her male colleagues often looked at pornography downloaded from the internet, which, together with their bad language and the general atmosphere of obscenity, caused her to feel uncomfortable at work.

6273 Employers are legally obliged to protect employees from harassment and may be liable for any discrimination perpetrated by their employees. In order to defend any claims, the employer must show that he took all reasonably practicable steps to prevent employees from committing acts of discrimination. This will include having and successfully implementing equal opportunities and harassment policies, supervising the use of emails, and dealing with any problems that arise.

The internet and email policy itself should draw employees' attention to the potential liability attached to email abuse, and set guidelines for acceptable usage.

6274 The employer's disciplinary and/or email and internet policy should also make it clear that downloading and/or circulating pornography constitutes gross misconduct (¶6537). If it is not clear, the mere use of the internet for these purposes may not be grounds for summary dismissal, unless the material is extreme enough to be classified as obscene (in which case publication would also be a criminal offence).

If the employee is not permitted to use the internet for personal use at all, downloading or circulating pornography will be a breach of contract in any case, and may result in disciplinary action. Whether summary dismissal is justified in those circumstances will depend on whether the employee's breach is repudiatory (¶1701). It will be easier for an employer to defend an unfair dismissal claim if the employee was made aware of the potential consequences of breach of the policy.

Intellectual property

6276 Copyright may be infringed where employees download articles and other materials from the internet. Software can also be downloaded and software licences may be infringed if unlicensed software is installed.

Personal use of the internet

6278 Employers may suffer a loss of productivity if employees are allowed unregulated access to the internet. The internet policy should establish the scope of permitted use. If the employee's work is suffering, the matter should be dealt with normally as a performance issue.

Unauthorised access/dissemination

Whilst outsiders can generally be kept out of an organisation's computer systems by means of security technology such as "firewalls", employees may be able to gain unauthorised access. It is therefore important for the employer to have rules governing proper use and access. This could be a separate computer and software usage policy, or could be combined with the internet and email policy. **6280**

The policy should state that computer misuse may result in disciplinary action, including summary dismissal for serious cases. If they do not, the employer may not be justified in summarily dismissing an employee who has gained unauthorised access, unless the case is sufficiently serious to warrant such action (for example, if the employee's activities constitute a criminal offence (Computer Misuse Act 1990; DPA 1998)).

If an employee deliberately gains unauthorised access to a computer containing information to which he is not entitled (for example, by using someone else's password), it is likely that a summary dismissal would be justified, especially where the employer has issued guidelines and warned of the consequences of breach (*Denco Ltd v Joinson* [1991] IRLR 63, EAT). Such action is comparable to dishonesty, which would breach the employee's implied duty of fidelity (¶1213).

Where, however, an employee is not authorised to use the computer system but nevertheless obtains access for legitimate work-related purposes to obtain information to which he is entitled, summary dismissal may not be justified (*British Telecommunications plc v Rodriguez*, EAT case 845/92).

Particular care should be taken when using email to **transmit confidential information**. **6281**
Failure to take appropriate security measures could result in a breach of the 7th data protection principle (¶5965). It should be noted that while encryption may protect email in transit the transmission may still be vulnerable at either end. Further, even when a confidential email is "deleted" a copy may nevertheless be retained on the system. There are also risks with the use of fax. A confidential fax message may be received on a machine to which many people have access. It can also easily be misdirected, for example, by mis-keying the fax number of the intended recipient.

To protect his workers from the unauthorised dissemination of personal data, the **employer should**:
- ensure that he has an information systems security policy which properly addresses the risk of transmitting worker information by email;
- only transmit information between locations if a secure network or comparable arrangements are in place or if, in the case of email, encryption is used;
- ensure that all copies of emails and fax messages received by managers which contain sensitive information are held securely and that access to them is restricted;
- provide a means whereby managers can permanently delete such emails from personal work-stations, and that they are held responsible for doing so. Checks should be made to ensure that "deleted" information is permanently deleted and not just stored on a server. The employer should be always aware that those providing IT support have access to the server; and
- draw to the attention of all workers the risks of sending confidential or sensitive personal information by email or fax.

SECTION 4

Right to privacy

6285 Many employers voluntarily act in a socially responsible manner with respect to personal information relating to their workers, but whilst a worker may expect that the employer will keep that information confidential and not distribute it to others under the **data protection principles** (see above), and public authority workers have the right to privacy under the **Human Rights Act** (see below), there is no distinct common law right to privacy.

Consequently, claims have been brought under **breach of confidence** to varying degrees of success (the most recent high profile successful claim was Naomi Campbell's claim against a well-known paper).

It should be noted that some recent judgments have suggested that a new tort of privacy is necessary and is developing (see in particular: *Douglas v Hello! Ltd* [2001] QB 967; *Venable & Thompson v News Group Newspapers* [2002] EWCA Civ 1143 and *H (A Healthcare Worker) v Associated Newspapers Ltd v N (A Health Authority)* [2002] EWCA Civ 195), other cases (including two House of Lords' decisions), have indicated that there is either no need to develop a new tort or that one cannot be developed (*Wainwright v Home Office* [2003] UKHL 53; *A v B & C* [2002] 3 WLR 542, CA; *Campbell v MGN Limited* [2004] UKHL 22, HL).

Human rights issues

6286 The Human Rights Act 1998 which directly incorporates the EC Convention on Human Rights, **offers protection** in relation to fundamental human rights, in particular in relation to employment matters, the right to privacy and family life, home and correspondence (¶6288), and the right to a fair trial (¶9435).

However, this only has direct application in the UK against public authorities. This means that an individual who believes his right to privacy has been infringed by a **public authority** may seek direct recourse in the UK courts. Consequently, workers can only directly rely on the Human Rights Act if the employer is a public authority employer. Hybrid (i.e. mixed bodies which are part authority/part public, such as the BBC) or a non-public body such as a private limited company or a PLC are not public authorities.

6287 There are, however, two ways in which the right may be **indirectly given** to workers in the **non-public sector**:

1. Firstly, UK courts and tribunals are public authorities and, as such, should act in conformity with the human rights principles (s 6 Human Rights Act 1998). They may be expected, therefore, to recognise the worker's right to a reasonable expectation of privacy in claims for unfair dismissal or breach of the implied terms of trust and confidence (*Halford v United Kingdom* [1997] IRLR 471, ECHR). A worker, for example, may possibly claim that his dismissal was unfair if the evidence behind the reason for dismissal was obtained from the secret use of CCTV surveillance which was in breach of privacy and not justifiable under the DP Code.

The same principles may also apply to intrusive body searching, drug and alcohol testing and similar activities. It must, however, be emphasised that this is an indication as to how courts and tribunals may act and there is no guarantee that they will do so in relation to private employers.

2. Secondly, UK courts and tribunals are bound to apply domestic legislation in a manner compatible with the EC Convention on Human Rights unless prevented from doing so by primary legislation i.e. Acts of Parliament (s 3 Human Rights Act 1998). Therefore, courts and tribunals are bound to interpret legislation to make it compatible unless it is impossible to do so i.e. unless it is clearly incompatible with the wording of an Act. This goes beyond interpretation and the courts **must take into account** the human rights principles in resolving any legislative ambiguity. They must also develop and apply the common law to make it compatible with the Convention.

The Human Rights Act gives the **right to privacy** and family life, home and correspondence. Private life can include activities of a professional or business nature (*Niemietz v Germany* [1992] 16 EHRR 97) and there is also an express reference to correspondence, which includes all types of communication, including email and telephones. **6288**

EXAMPLE In *Halford v United Kingdom* [1997] IRLR 471, which was a case taken to the European Court of Human Rights by a public employee (before the Act came into force, public employees had to take breaches of the Convention to the European Court), H was a senior police officer who alleged that the telephone line (which she had been given by her employer (a police authority) for her to make private calls) had been tapped by them. The Court held that unless H had been given prior warning that her calls were liable to interception, she had a reasonable expectation of privacy. Further, even if this was not so, the police authority would still need to justify the tapping under Article 8(2).

MEMO POINTS It was partly as a result of *Halford* that Parliament introduced the Regulation of Investigatory Powers Act 2000 to regulate interceptions on private telecommunications systems (¶6220).

However, there have been a couple of recent decisions which limit its application (*Pay v Lancashire Probation Service* [2004] ICR 187, EAT and *X v Y* [2003] ICR 1138, EAT). In both cases, activities out of work were not held to be private because they were done in public places and consequently, could be taken into account in deciding whether to dismiss the employee. For example, in the first case, the employer, in deciding whether to dismiss P, could take into account the fact that P, who was a probation officer working with sex offenders, was performing in fetish clubs and merchandising bondage, domination and sado-masochism goods. **6289**

CHAPTER 18

Training and performance

OUTLINE ¶¶

6300 **Training** ensures that employees have the **requisite skills** for their job. Further, developing employees' skills and abilities so that they can progress within the company should assist in their retention as well as ensuring a skilled and able workforce. Although there is no implied term requiring an employer to train an employee, failure to adequately train, properly instruct or support him may result in a variety of legal consequences.

As well as training employees, employers may also have **trainees and apprentices** who are required to undergo specific training and are subject to special rules. There are also a number of government backed **initiatives** that help young people and those who may find it more difficult to return to work.

Finally, **work-experience** can be a useful tool for those who like to find out more about a particular job/organisation and gain experience in that area. Employers also benefit in providing an opportunity to assess and encourage young graduates. Work experience can take a variety of forms: sandwich placements, participation in work-based projects, work placements, voluntary work, part-time work, work shadowing, internships and vacation work.

MEMO POINTS With regard to work-experience, readers are referred to the National Council for Work Experience at www.work-experience.org for more information.

6301 **Union learning representatives** (ULRs) are another potentially useful tool in the training of the workforce.

6302 The following groups are specifically **entitled to paid time off** to study or train:

Type of employee	Purpose of time off	Para.
Under notice of redundancy	to make arrangements for training for future employment	¶8885
Young person	study or training for a relevant qualification	¶6330

Type of employee	Purpose of time off	Para.
Trade union official	undergo training so that he can carry out his duties	¶7603
Union learning representative	to carry out training and learning functions	¶7607
Safety representative and representative of employee safety	undergo training so that he can carry out his duties	¶5030
Employee representative and candidate in election	undergo training so that he can carry out his duties	¶8931
Trustee of occupational pension scheme	undergo training so that he can carry out his duties	¶3432

There are various methods of **monitoring and assessing performance** of employees. On a larger organisational scale, benchmarking is often used to measure standards. 6304

SECTION 1

Training

The **induction stage** is usually the first time the employer will formally assess the employee's training requirements and formulate a personal training plan if necessary. Certain groups of employees may require special attention, such as school and college leavers and those who have been out of the workplace to care for children, change direction in their careers, or spend some time working abroad. For example, health and safety training is particularly important in the case of young new recruits who may have little or no experience of workplace environments, thus making them more vulnerable to accidents. Likewise, employees who have been out of the workplace may require additional training and experience to enable them to feel confident in their new jobs. 6310

After the induction stage, training and employee development is usually discussed and planned as a result of the employer's **appraisal/performance management system**.

Training may be **formal or informal** and is usually a combination of the two. 6311

Formal training and most qualifications are sought through specialist training providers such as universities, colleges of further and higher education and private training organisations. Some employers have obtained approval to run their own qualifications which as well as tailor-making the training to meet their needs, may also be cost effective where numbers are sufficiently large to justify the effort and costs involved in becoming a recognised centre. 6312

There are a large number of **qualifications** available. The Qualifications and Curriculum Authority (QCA) keeps an up-to-date database of qualifications and awarding bodies (for example, BTEC, City and Guilds, Edexcel and OCR) for each qualification, who in turn will usually be able to give details of the centres which are approved to run the qualifications they award.

As well as the main group of awarding bodies, there are sector oriented awarding bodies and others which focus on a particular group of employees, for example Hospitality Awarding Body (HAB) and Chartered Institute of Management.

An employer may also use NVQs (National vocational qualifications). Technical competence will usually include qualifications and working experience and assessment will be by a work based assessor with internal and external verification to ensure the requisite standards are met.

Informal techniques include, coaching, mentoring, job shadowing, buddy training and experiential learning. These are all work based and there is a measure of overlap between 6313 the various approaches. Due to their informality, this may result in a haphazard learning process and a training programme and/or checklist of the required learning points is often useful.

Where appropriate, secondment can also be a useful tool in developing the skills and experience of employees.

Requirement to train

6320 There is **no implied term** requiring the employer to train an employee (*White v London Transport Executive* [1981] IRLR 261, EAT).

However, **not providing** adequate training, proper instruction and support may result in:

1. A **breach of contract** if there is an express term relating to the training of the employee.
2. A **breach of** the common law **duty of care** if loss or injury is suffered by the employee or others to whom the employer owes a duty of care.
3. **Liability for sex**, **race**, **disability**, **sexual orientation**, **or religion or belief discrimination** (or age discrimination which is expected to come into force from 1 October 2006) if the employer has directly or indirectly discriminated against the employee. For example, management training that occurs at weekends or in the evenings may be difficult or impossible for women with family responsibilities to attain and is, therefore, indirectly discriminatory. Where there may be the potential for discrimination, reasonable alternative arrangements should be made available, for example by re-scheduling or providing alternatives to residential training. In the same context, employers must give equal access to training to part-time workers as they do to comparable full-time workers.

Liability for unlawful discrimination may also occur if managers and employees have not been trained how to correctly implement an equality at work policy as the mere fact of having a policy will not give the employer a defence against any such claim if it has not been implemented.

4. A contributing reason, and in exceptional circumstances the main reason, supporting a **claim for unfair dismissal** if the employee is dismissed for incompetence or poor performance (*J Davison v Kent Meters Ltd* [1975] IRLR 145, IT). This also covers providing inadequate training to a newly promoted employee (*F Burrows v Ace Caravan Co (Hull) Ltd* [1972] IRLR 4, IT) and unfairly dismissing an employee for poor performance where it was due to a lack of trained subordinates (*Woodward v Beeston Boiler Co Ltd* [1973] IRLR 7, IT).

Training is important as the issue of fair procedure is often crucial in determining whether a dismissal for incapability was fair. A tribunal will consider what steps a reasonable employer would have taken, and what steps the employer could have taken to minimise the risk of poor performance by providing adequate training and supervision to enable the employee to carry out his duties to a satisfactory standard.

5. In exceptional cases, a **claim for constructive dismissal**, where the failure to give adequate support is sufficiently serious (*Associated Tyre Specialists (Eastern) Ltd v Waterhouse* [1976] IRLR 386, EAT).
6. A **breach of** the employer's **health and safety obligations** and may have implications with regard to his insurance cover.

Refusal by employee to train

6325 Most **disciplinary procedures** will treat the failure to participate in training as an offence meriting disciplinary action, the severity of which would depend on the importance and type of the training refused. For example, if the employee has unreasonably refused to undertake training which is required by the health and safety rules, an employer may be entitled to dismiss him. Likewise, an employer may be able to insist that an employee undergoes training where he is seeking external accreditation for a quality standard, for example the ISO quality award where the holding of that quality standard may have implications for the type of work that the organisation can undertake.

Where an employee has refused to train, which may have a future negative impact on his employment conditions, this should be examined carefully to ensure that there are no **issues of discrimination**, for example because a female employee refused to attend weekend training session due to family responsibilities. In such cases, alternative arrangements should be made available where appropriate.

Employers may place a **contractual requirement** that employees will participate in appropriate training. In such cases, a refusal may also amount to a breach of contract. 6326

Where substantial costs have been incurred in training the employee, it may be possible to **recover** a genuine pre-estimate of the cost if he leaves the company within a set period after completing the course or fails to complete it successfully (¶2849). In such cases, there should be a separate written agreement to cover the potential recovery of training costs. 6327

Right of young persons to take time off

A young employed person has the right to take paid time off work for study and training (ss 63A-63C ERA 1996 (inserted by s 32 Teaching and Higher Education Act 1988)). A young person is **defined** as someone who is 16 or 17 years, who has not received full-time secondary or further education, and has not attained the prescribed standard of achievement. 6330

The employer must allow the employee a **reasonable amount** of time off taking into account all the circumstances and in particular: 6331
- the requirements of the study or training; and
- the circumstances of the business of the employer and the effect of the employee's time off on the running of that business.

This is **paid at** the appropriate hourly rate and see ¶3935. 6332

Discrimination by employers

An employer may not discriminate on the grounds of sex, race, disability, sexual orientation, or religion or belief in offering employees an **opportunity to undergo training**. Nor should an employer refuse to afford or deliberately not afford training to employees on such grounds (s 6(2) SDA 1975; s 4(2) RRA 1976; s 4(2) DDA 1995; reg 6(2) SI 2003/1661; reg 6(2) SI 2003/1660). 6340

EXAMPLE 1. Failure or refusal to offer a female employee a training course because she is pregnant will amount to direct sex discrimination.
2. Refusal to consider alternative training arrangements where access to a training room is impossible for an employee who is a wheelchair user is likely to constitute disability discrimination (failure to make reasonable adjustments).

In certain limited circumstances, an employer may take **positive action** which would otherwise give rise to a sex, race, sexual orientation, or religion or belief discrimination complaint (see Chapter 16). 6341

In addition, in certain circumstances, it is lawful to provide facilities or services **to meet the special needs** of persons of a particular group in relation to their education, training, welfare, or any ancillary benefits (see again Chapter 16 for further details).

EXAMPLE An employer may not be discriminating unlawfully if he provides language training to employees who were born overseas or who had disrupted education in their country of origin, with the result that they are unable to communicate effectively.

Special provisions requiring reasonable adjustments to be made for **disabled employees** in appropriate cases are discussed in detail at ¶5515. 6342

It is expected that discrimination by employers on the **grounds of age** will become unlawful from 1 October 2006 (see ¶5254 for a summary of the draft regulations). 6343

Discrimination and harassment by qualifying and training bodies

It is unlawful for authorities and bodies which can confer an **authorisation or qualification** which is needed for, or will facilitate, engagement in a particular profession or trade, to discriminate on the grounds of sex, race, disability, sexual orientation, or religion or belief 6345

(S: s 13(1) SDA 1975; R: s 12(1) RRA 1976; D: s 14A(1) DDA 1995; SO: reg 16 SI 2003/1661; RB: reg 16 SI 2003/1660):
- in the terms on which they are prepared to confer authorisation of qualification;
- by refusing or deliberately omitting to grant an authorisation or qualification; or
- by withdrawing or varying the terms on which an applicant holds a qualification or authorisation.

However, where an authority or body provides an **independent complaint and appeal process** (in this case, the Specialist Training Authority, by virtue of the Medical Act 1983), a claim for race discrimination may not be brought against that authority or body in an employment tribunal (*Chaudhary v Specialist Training Authority appeal panel and others (No. 2)* [2005] ICR 1086, CA). The Specialist Training Authority and its appeal panel provided the claimant with a fair and public hearing by an independent and impartial tribunal established by law and complied with his right to a fair trial under article 6 of the European Convention of Human Rights. The option of applying for judicial review of the appeal panel's decision remained available to the claimant.

MEMO POINTS Situations involving the grant of a qualification or authority often include granting authority to (and recognising the qualifications of) foreign-qualified workers (for example, in the medical profession) to practice in the UK.

6346 In addition, it is unlawful for a qualifications body to discriminate against a **disabled person** in the **arrangements** which it makes for the purpose of determining upon whom to confer a professional or trade qualification (s 14A(1) DDA 1995). Moreover, such bodies are under a duty to make **reasonable adjustments** to any provision, criterion or practice, other than a competence standard, applied by or on behalf of a qualifications body or any physical feature of premises occupied by such a body which places a disabled person concerned at a substantial disadvantage in comparison with persons who are not disabled in order to prevent the provision, criterion or practice, or physical feature, from having that effect (s 14B DDA 1995).

6347 Similarly, it is unlawful for such qualifying bodies to **subject to harassment** any person who holds or applies for such a qualification on the grounds of sex, race, disability, sexual orientation or religion or belief (S: s 13(1A) SDA 1975; R: s 12(1A) RRA 1976; D: s 14A(2) DDA 1995; SO: reg 16 SI 2003/1661; RB: reg 16 SI 2003/1660).

6348 Persons and bodies that provide, or make arrangements for the provision of, **vocational training** must not discriminate on the grounds of sex, race, disability, sexual orientation, or religion or belief (S: s 14(1) SDA 1975; R: s 13 RRA 1976; D: s 14C(1) DDA 1995; SO: reg 17 SI 2003/1661; RB: reg 17 SI 2003/1660):
- in the terms on which they are prepared to afford access to training;
- by refusing or deliberately omitting to grant access to training;
- by terminating the training; or
- by subjecting an applicant to any other detriment during the course of his training.

In respect of **sex discrimination**, it is also unlawful to discriminate in the arrangements made for the purpose of selecting people to receive vocational training (s 14(1) SDA 1975, as amended by reg 17 Employment Equality (Sex Discrimination) Regulations SI 2005/2467).

Again, it is unlawful for a provider of vocational training to discriminate against a **disabled person** in the arrangements which it makes for the purpose of determining who should be offered a **work placement** (s 14C DDA 1995). In addition, such providers are under the same duty to make reasonable adjustments in respect of a disabled person as qualifications bodies (s 14D DDA 1995).

In addition, it is unlawful for a provider of vocational training to **subject to harassment** any person seeking or undergoing vocational training (and in the case of disability discrimination, a work placement) on the grounds of sex, race, disability, sexual orientation, or religion or belief (S: s 14(1A) SDA 1975, as inserted by reg 17 Employment Equality (Sex Discrimination) Regulations SI 2005/2467; R: s 13(3) RRA 1976; D: s 14C(2) DDA 1995; SO: reg 17 SI 2003/1661; RB: reg 17 SI 2003/1660).

It is expected that discrimination by qualifying bodies and providers of vocational training on the **grounds of age** will become unlawful from 1 October 2006 (see ¶5254 for a summary of the draft regulations). 6349

A. Trainees and apprentices

Trainees under a **training contract** will often have an express term that makes the contract terminable if the trainee does not satisfactorily complete his training, or if there is no suitable position available for him with the company at the end of the traineeship. 6350

Trainees who are **not employees** under their contract, for example students on placements who are gaining experience in their chosen profession, are not entitled to the main body of employment rights though employers must ensure compliance with the health and safety regulations and the working time rules.

Apprenticeships, on the other hand, are governed by common law and are a **distinct entity**. 6351
The primary purpose is training and work done by the apprentice is considered secondary. As a consequence, the employer undertakes a much wider responsibility towards an apprentice than he does towards an employee (*Whitely v Marton* [2003] IRLR 197, EAT).

In return, the apprentice must serve his master. There is also greater degree of control than that normally given to an employer over an employee due to the training nature of the relationship. The amount of disciplinary power that a master may have over an apprentice will vary depending on the maturity and qualifications of the apprentice, and the extent to which he, like his master, is regulated by any professional code of conduct.

MEMO POINTS Pupil barristers have been held to have a binding contract (*Edmonds v Lawson QC* [2000] IRLR 391, CA).

An apprenticeship will be based on an **agreement** between the apprentice (or his parents 6352
or guardian if he is a minor) and the employer and must be for a fixed period or until specified qualifications are achieved. Consequently, an apprenticeship is not terminable on notice (*Whitely v Marton*, above). Apprenticeship contracts cannot be **terminated** for misconduct in the same way as an ordinary contract of employment nor can apprentices be made redundant unless there has been a fundamental change in the employer's business which has resulted in the redundancy situation (*Wallace v CA Roofing Services Ltd* [1996] IRLR 435, QBD).

A contract of apprenticeship, to be enforceable, must be made in writing. An oral contract of apprenticeship, although legally valid, is unenforceable unless and until it is acted upon (*Edmonds v Lawson QC* [2000] IRLR 391, CA).

Apprentices have the **right to equal treatment** (Part-time Employees (Prevention of Less Favourable 6353
Treatment) Regulations SI 2000/1551) and are protected by the **anti-discrimination** laws. Apprentices are also covered by the **national minimum wage** rules unless they are under 19 or under 26 and in the first 12 months of apprenticeship (reg 12(2) National Minimum Wage Regulations SI 1999/584).

See below for government backed apprenticeship programmes and national traineeship. 6354

B. Government backed training initiatives

6370 There are a number of initiatives that help young people and those who may find it more difficult to return to work, and that aid vocational training.

1. Apprenticeship programmes and national traineeships

6375 **Apprenticeship programmes** are grant-aided schemes which are aimed at enhancing the vocational skills of the workforce and are targeted mainly at those in the **16-24 age bracket** with employers receiving financial assistance towards the cost of training.

6376 There are two levels of apprenticeship: apprenticeships and advanced apprenticeships. The requirements of any apprenticeship programme will depend on the sector. There are also some regional variations in the frameworks. For more information, readers should contact their local Learning and Skills Councils in England, their local Education and Learning Wales (ELWA) in Wales, the Local Enterprise Company in Scotland and the Department for Employment and Learning in Northern Ireland as appropriate.

6377 **National Traineeships** are aimed primarily at 16 and 17 year old school leavers. It is a grant-aided scheme administered in a similar way to apprenticeships although it is not available in Scotland. It is possible for a trainee to transfer to an apprenticeship place on successful completion of the national traineeship.

Status

6378 Government-backed apprenticeships where there is a tripartite apprenticeship agreement in which the employer provides the opportunity for work experience, whilst the training is done under the auspices of and/or by a training agent or provider and/or a college or council, do not result in common law contracts of apprenticeship (*Flett v Matheson* [2005] IRLR 412, EAT). Instead, such arrangements result in contracts of employment. Where it is necessary to terminate such a contract before the end of the training period it is likely that there will be an implied term in the contract that would allow it to be terminated on reasonable notice; such reasonable notice being geared towards the time within which it would be reasonable to expect the training agent/provider/council/board in question to place the apprentice with another employer.

2. New Deal

6380 This initiative is aimed at **assisting** those, who would otherwise have difficulty entering paid employment. Employers will also get assistance, and in some cases funding, to help and encourage them to recruit such employees.

The New Deal strategy is based on **local partnerships** between employers, local authorities, training providers, Jobcentres, environmental groups, volunteer organisations and others. The partnerships are co-ordinated by the Jobcentre Plus or in some cases by the private sector. New Deal is developing at different rates in different parts of the United Kingdom, so it is worthwhile checking precise details of schemes offered in a particular area. Because different bodies have responsibility for promoting and developing the initiatives, the vocabulary and approach may also vary.

6381 There are **New Deal schemes** for the following:

– **young jobseekers (aged between 18-24)** (mandatory) who have been claiming jobseeker's allowance for 6 months or more;

– **jobseekers (aged 25 or over)** (mandatory) who have been claiming jobseeker's allowance for 18 months or more;

- **persons aged 50 and over** who are claiming benefits other than jobseeker's allowance and who want to work;
- **lone parents** (i.e. anyone who is looking after at least one school-aged child on their own, and claiming income support). Those who are a lone parent aged 18 to 24 and are currently claiming jobseeker's allowance, will fall under the New Deal for young jobseekers;
- **disabled persons** claiming disability or health-related benefits. Those claiming jobseeker's allowance but have a disability or health condition, will fall under the New Deal for young people or 25 +;
- **partners of people claiming jobseeker's allowance**;
- persons who want to be **self-employed**; and
- persons who want to make a career as a **musician**.

Employers who offer jobs to young jobseekers or jobseekers over 25 will receive a New Deal **subsidy** (consisting of a set contribution towards the wages for up to first 6 months of employment and contribution with regards to training). For more information and contact numbers, see the New Deal website: www.newdeal.gov.uk 6383

C. EU and UK Government assignment support

UK employers may be eligible for grants under a **European Community programme (Leonardo da Vinci programme)** when assigning or seconding an employee to another EU member state for vocational training. The programme is open to a wide range of public and private sector organisations and companies active in training or concerned by training issues. The vocational training, however, must be part of a structured vocational training programme leading to a recognised qualification in the UK. For more information, see www.leonardo.org.uk 6390

Periods of vocational training acquired in another EU member state can also be registered in a **Europass-Training document**. This provides the trainee with an individualised record of his training placements outside the Member State where the training is based. The document is issued by the European Commission and distributed in each Member State through the relevant National Agency. The Central Bureau for International Education and Training administers the system in the UK. For more information, see www.europass-uk.co.uk

The **Department of Trade and Industry's Global Watch secondments programme** also helps British businesses that want to second employees overseas to acquire skills, technology and connections and which enables employees to enhance their career prospects. The programme is aimed to help medium-sized companies send employees abroad (outgoing secondments) or receive key people from abroad (incoming secondments). It does not apply to intra-group assignments or those between joint ventures. For more information, see www.globalwatchonline.com 6392

SECTION 2

Evaluation, guidelines and benchmarking

6450 Performance can be judged, monitored, reviewed, assessed and encouraged by the following methods:

Job evaluation and banding

6451 Job evaluation provides a structured method of **comparing jobs** that are different in terms of duties and responsibilities with the aim of being able to position the jobs in terms of levels of authority and pay. Job evaluation is most often carried out when organisations are changing either in terms of growth or restructuring. However, in legal terms, its importance as a technique arises from its use in ensuring compliance with anti-discrimination legislation.

There are a number of job evaluation schemes available, usually through specialist providers. The essentials of the various schemes tend to be broadly similar although the detailed content may vary.

6452 Job evaluation is **based on** a set of defined factors which are further split into bands (commonly around five) though no single job evaluation system will be equally applicable to all organisations. Some adjustments will be needed to tailor a job evaluation system to an organisation. Further, while there are no essential differences to the approach in organisations of differing sizes or complexity, there is a tendency for smaller organisations or those with fewer "layers" to need fewer bands.

A rating system is often used to give a score for the different factors making up a job evaluation. Jobs can then be grouped to reflect their positioning within the selected factors by adding together the scores. A common approach is a score rating of up to ten points for each band level which allows for a degree of leeway between and within bands. The various factors can be given a weighting as well, for example one factor may be considered to be twice as important as another and this can be reflected in the rating system.

6453 The common **standard factors** are as follows:
- **skill, knowledge and expertise**, for example in terms of educational qualifications or in terms of the knowledge and understanding which are unique within the organisation;
- **management or supervisory responsibility**, for example in terms of the level and type of supervisory or management responsibility in terms of the activities that the employee is expected to undertake;
- **decision-making responsibility**, for example in terms of the degree of autonomy and the impact of the job on the organisation's core aims and objectives;
- **job difficulty**, for example in terms of the amount of disruption to plans that the employee has to tolerate, such as sudden changes in the workload that cannot be anticipated; and
- **adding value**, for example in terms of impact on the customer.

Behavioural guidelines

6455 There are a number of areas where behavioural guidelines remain key, mainly, discipline and standard operating procedures. These define the two extremes of behavioural guidelines:
- **disciplinary rules** define what is considered unacceptable behaviour and the associated procedures determine how breaches of those rules will be dealt with; and
- **standard operating procedures** define the desired or required "good" behaviour. Standard operating procedures are most often used in the context of quality control and assurance. Where the job, process or procedures add value to the final outcome, then the more closely defined they are the easier it is to ensure quality.

Competence statements

Competence statements are a definition of the **knowledge, skills and capabilities** underlying a job. There can be a degree of overlap between the competences required for a number of jobs. As a result, organisations that define jobs by their competences often do so in terms of groups of related jobs, usually called "Job Families." 6460

Job competence is commonly based on the working skills, knowledge and attitudes that underlie the ability to do a job effectively. The **key requirements** for the demonstration and assessment of competence are: 6461
- currency. This is usually a requirement for competence to be demonstrated recently;
- reliability. This must be demonstrated over a period of time and in different situations;
- validity, i.e. using procedures that are relevant to the skills or knowledge being assessed;
- authenticity, i.e. done in a way that ensures that the work or outcomes can be clearly assigned to the employee being assessed; and
- consistency. The same standard or level of performance must be demonstrated despite changing circumstances and conditions.

A **key method** of assessing competence is through training checklists.

Appraisals and performance management

Appraisals or performance management reviews are generally accepted as **good human resource practice**. The processes can have an indirect impact on discipline, promotion, redundancy and equal treatment situations and consequently must be performed fairly using best practice procedures. For example, in employment disputes and disciplinary cases, employees and employers may wish to refer to the content of appraisals or performance reviews as evidence of, for example, a history of problems or an exemplary working record. 6465

Both appraisal and performance management provide an opportunity for an employee to review his job and performance with his line manager as well as giving an opportunity to plan his development within the organisation and highlight any training needs.

Appraisal and performance management processes are, at first sight, very similar in the way they are conducted. The differences between them could be summarised as follows: 6466

Appraisal	Performance management
Regular interview procedure	Continual review of performance
Focus on working methods	Focus on job outcomes
Leading towards an Action Plan to be reviewed at a fixed period	Leading towards an Action Plan to be reviewed continuously
Information from manager to employee	Discussion of information to which both have prior access

There are a number of other reviews possible: 6467
- **group performance reviews** where output and performance are dependent entirely on group rather than individual effort;
- **360 degree feedback** resulting in assessment and feedback on performance from "all angles" essentially from the employee's peers, those that he manages, himself, and his line manager; and
- **self-assessment of performance**.

There should be an **internal appeal procedure** in place where an employee does not agree with the assessment of his performance and/or no agreement is possible on an action plan.

Discrimination in the appraisal and promotion process An employer must not discriminate, on the grounds of sex, race, disability, sexual orientation, or religion or belief against an employee in the appraisal process or in the way he affords an employee access to opportunities for promotion or by refusing or deliberately omitting to afford him access to such 6468 opportunities (s 6(2) SDA 1975; s 4(2) RRA 1976; s 4(2) DDA 1995; reg 6(2) SI 2003/1661; reg 6(2) SI 2003/1660).

MEMO POINTS Discrimination on the grounds of age is expected to become unlawful from 1 October 2006 (see ¶5254 for a summary of the draft regulations).

An appraisal can have a critical effect on an employee's career development, promotion prospects, pay rise, access to benefits and continuation of employment (for example, a poor appraisal may render an employee more susceptible to selection for redundancy). An employee who believes that his poor appraisal was **unjustified and biased** on the grounds of sex, race, sexual orientation, religion or belief, or disability, could complain of being subjected to a detriment. It is, therefore, vital to ensure that the staff who carry out appraisals are **adequately trained** and fully **understand** their **employer's equal opportunities obligations**. It is often advisable to train appraising staff and to carry out appraisal spot checks. In all cases, appraisals ought to be carried out objectively and consistently.

Special care and consideration should be taken when **appraising a disabled employee**. The appraisal process may have to be adapted to prevent substantial disadvantage to the employee. For example, if an employee is deaf, a person versed in sign language may have to be present at the appraisal meeting. In addition, appraisal criteria may need to be altered. Moreover, working arrangements may need to be reviewed as a result of the appraisal. For example, if a disabled employee's job performance has been affected by his disability, it will be necessary to consider making reasonable adjustments to facilitate his working arrangements (¶5515).

6469 Employers must also ensure that **selection procedures for internal promotion** are as carefully and objectively set as for external appointments. This means that selection criteria should be drawn up and a fair and objective process applied, which will generally include an internal advertisement. Any advertisement must not indicate, or be reasonably understood to indicate, an intention on the part of the employer to discriminate unlawfully. In most cases, they should be gender or race neutral and ought not to contain any indication that the employer will not accept applicants with a disability or will be reluctant to make reasonable adjustments (¶5515). Job advertisements are discussed generally at ¶590.

Quality assurance and benchmarking

6470 The term "benchmarking" in this context refers to identifying those **indicators of performance** by which an organisation measures its standards and quality. Benchmark indicators can relate to any area of performance. For example, in most working environments there is an expected relationship between the costs of materials and/or labour and the costs of the product or service.

Benchmarking enables an organisation to **measure the effectiveness** of what they do and to learn from how others organise and measure performance. Consequently, benchmarking should be against "industry best" by comparing performance against those who are acknowledged as the best at that activity. So, for example, if a manufacturing company wants to measure the performance of its distribution department, it should compare itself to a leading distribution company and not a competing manufacturing company.

6471 The **actual measures** that an organisation might benchmark itself against will vary considerably. The following table sets out examples of the activities that companies from different sectors might benchmark themselves against:

Distribution	Manufacturing	Export
Time between order and delivery	Changeover times	Time needed to recover investment
Number of late deliveries	Machine down time	Costs of changes to products
Condition of goods on arrival	Machine efficiency	Costs of marketing/advertising
Percentage of deliveries undertaken by own staff	Output per person hour worked	Training/skills needed for new market

Distribution	Manufacturing	Export
Percentage of deliveries undertaken by contractors	Management to work force ratios	Market size needed for profitable return on investment
Number of returns	Adherence to preventative maintenance schedules	
Training/qualifications of staff	Costs of quality measures	
Customer satisfaction information gathered and actual ratings	Workforce communications	

In any relationship it is better if both sides benefit equally. Identifying such partners, though, can be difficult. In recent years both employers' organisations and Government departments have taken steps to help organisations find suitable benchmarking partners. 6472

Where benchmarking exercises have applications across all organisations, it is common for them to be formulated into **recognised standards**, for example: 6473

a. ISO 9000 standards for manufacturing, service and other types of organisations. This is probably the most well known at an international level and is an externally assessed quality standard where the organisation is measured against its own internally generated quality procedures and systems. Also of growing importance and application is the ISO 14000 standards which relate to environmental management systems. For further details, see the ISO website: www.iso.org;

b. the Business Excellence Model of the European Foundation for Quality Management (EFQM) which is mainly an internally assessed quality standard, but external assessment is also possible and is gaining in use. For further details, see the EFQM website: www.efqm.org;

c. GoodCorporation standard which is a human resource focused quality and social responsibility standard covering the way in which the organisation behaves towards its employees, customers, suppliers, shareholders, the environment and the local community. For further details, see www.goodcorporation.com; and

d. Investors in People which is a human resource focused quality standard. It provides a best practice standard for the learning and development of the organisation's workforce and an external assessment process. The standard is based on four principles:

- commitment (the organisation is fully committed to developing its people in order to achieve its aims and objectives);
- planning (the organisation is clear about what the aims and objectives are and what the employees need to do to achieve them);
- action (the organisation develops its people effectively in order to improve its performance); and
- evaluation (the organisation understands the impact of its investment in people on its performance).

There are 12 indicators supporting these principles and 33 evidence requirements for an organisation to be recognised as an Investor in People. For further details, see the IIP website: www.iipuk.co.uk

CHAPTER 19

Discipline and grievance

OUTLINE ¶¶

6500 **Disciplinary issues** arise when problems of conduct or performance are identified by the employer, who consequently seeks to address them through his established procedures. **Grievances**, on the other hand, are raised by employees, who may have concerns or complaints about their terms and conditions of employment, their working environment or relationships with other staff.

Most employers will already have in place disciplinary rules and procedures and grievance procedures. On 1 October 2004, **statutory dispute resolution procedures** came into force, which contain minimum requirements that must be met in respect of any dismissal, disciplinary action or grievance (ss 29-34, Sch 2-4 EA 2002; Employment Act 2002 (Dispute Resolution) Regulations SI 2004/752, referred to as the regulations). See below for a discussion on their applicability, general requirements and the implications of failure to comply with the procedures (¶6510). The regulations are intended to encourage better co-operation between employers and employees, to resolve workplace disputes internally and to reduce the number of employment tribunal applications being made. **6501**

Existing dispute resolution procedures which employers have in place will remain in force insofar as they incorporate, and are consistent with, the statutory procedures. Employers are therefore able to keep their own existing disciplinary and grievance procedures provided that their procedures incorporate the basic minimum requirements which are stipulated by the regulations.

Throughout this chapter, the **statutory minimum requirements** specified by the regulations will be identified. However, it is important to emphasise that employers who follow these minimum requirements will not necessarily be rendered free from any liability for unfair dismissal even if they have followed the procedures to the letter. They are merely "building blocks" which provide a backdrop for the principles of best practice to be applied. For this reason, it is essential for employers to ensure that they are aware of, and implement, the **best practice principles** which are laid down in the ACAS Code of Practice on disciplinary and grievance procedures (DG Code) and other regulatory guidelines (¶6520).

At certain disciplinary or grievance hearings, there is a **statutory right to be accompanied** by a work colleague or trade union official (s 10 ERelA 1999). See ¶6780 for further details. **6503**

Employers must ensure that they comply with the data protection principles (¶5945) when **processing information** in relation to disciplinary or grievance proceedings. In particular, employers must make sure that those investigating such matters do not gather any information by deception and that unsubstantiated allegations are removed unless there is some exceptional reason not to do so. All records should be of a good enough quality to support any conclusion drawn from them. **6504**

As **good practice**, employers should (part 2.13 DP Code):
- not access or use information kept about a worker just because it might have some relevance, if such access or use is incompatible with the purpose for which the information was originally gathered or if it is disproportionate to the seriousness of the matter under investigation;
- have clear procedures about how spent disciplinary warnings are dealt with; and
- ensure that if a worker is dismissed, an accurate reason is recorded which ties in with what the worker has been told.

Employers are also advised to follow the DP Code's general **recommendations** with regard to data management (¶6000).

1. Scope

Most **employees** are subject to disciplinary rules and procedures, and grievance procedures. Whether an employer's disciplinary rules and procedures, and grievance procedures apply to **workers** (for discussion as to status see ¶13) will depend on the contractual arrangements between them. On the other hand, the **statutory dispute resolution procedures** apply only to employees. **6505**

However, as these rules and procedures have broader benefits in ensuring harmonious industrial relations at the workplace in general, it is recommended that, as a matter of **good employment practice**, the standards set out in the DG Code and the regulations are also applied to grievance and disciplinary proceedings involving workers (DG Code). Therefore, whilst the sections on discipline and grievance in this chapter refer to employees, the employer should consider the application of those sections to his workers in general.

However, some provisions mentioned in this chapter can only apply to employees, such as those referring to an employee's right to a statement of written particulars (¶1400), to bring a claim of unfair dismissal, and to request a written statement of reasons for dismissal.

The **right to be accompanied** at disciplinary and grievance hearings, on the other hand, specifically applies to all workers, including employees, regardless of the contractual arrangements as to discipline and grievance between them.

a. Statutory minimum requirements

6510 It is essential to first of all establish whether a statutory procedure applies to any particular circumstances. This is important since if a statutory procedure applies, there are various consequences for any party who fails to comply with them. This can impact the fairness or otherwise of a dismissal, the amount of compensation an employee can be awarded in respect of a tribunal claim, and whether any extension to the normal time limits for bringing an employment tribunal claim apply.

In general, the statutory procedures **apply to** (reg 18 SI 2004/752):
– any **dismissal** or **relevant disciplinary action** (¶6556) where the employer first contemplates dismissing or taking such action on or after 1 October 2004; and
– any **grievance** raised by an employee if the action complained of occurs or continues on or after 1 October 2004, but will not apply if the employee had raised a grievance about the action before that date.

MEMO POINTS The **DTI** has published **guidance** for employers on how the new regulations should be implemented in the workplace. Its principal guidance (Guidance on the Employment Act 2002 (Dispute Resolutions) Regulations 2004 and associated provisions in the Employment Act 2002) (referred to as the DTI guidance) explains in detail how the regulations are intended to work in practice. This guidance does not have legal force. It has also published a shorter version of its guidance which is intended primarily for managers in **small organisations** (DTI guidance for small firms). This guidance provides **sample letters** which can be used by employers when carrying out the statutory dismissal, disciplinary and grievance procedures. Again, this guidance does not have legal force.

6511 The statutory procedures will **not apply** if either party does not start a statutory procedure which would otherwise have been applicable on the basis that he (reg 11 SI 2004/752):
a. has reasonable grounds to believe that starting or completing a statutory procedure would result in a **significant threat** to himself, his property, or any other person or their property;
b. has been **subjected to harassment** and reasonably believes that starting or completing a statutory procedure will result in further harassment; or
c. considers it **not practicable** to start or complete a procedure **within a reasonable period**.
Notwithstanding the fact that where one or more of the above circumstances exists, a statutory procedure which would otherwise have been applicable will not apply, if either the circumstances in **a.** or **b.** above exists as a result of the behaviour of one party and this either prevents the other party from starting or completing an applicable procedure, then the party whose behaviour is in question will be deemed to have failed to comply with an applicable procedure (reg 12 SI 2004/752).

Where an applicable statutory **procedure has been started** but one of the reasons in **a.**, **b.** or **c.** above applies and, as a consequence, a party does not comply with a subsequent requirement of the procedure, the parties will be deemed to have complied with the procedure (reg 11 SI 2004/752). Nevertheless, if the reason for the failure to complete a subsequent requirement of an applicable procedure is that one of the circumstances in **a.** or **b.** exists, and it exists as a result of the behaviour of one of the parties, the fact that the subsequent requirement was not complied with will be deemed to have been a failure to comply with the procedure by the party whose behaviour is in question (reg 12 SI 2004/752).
See ¶¶6514-16 for further details as to the consequences of a failure (including a deemed failure described above) to comply with an applicable statutory procedure.
See ¶6636 for further details as to certain **types of dismissal** to which the statutory procedures do not apply.

Furthermore, if following the statutory procedures would require the disclosure of information which would threaten the **interests of national security**, then the statutory procedures will be deemed to not apply (reg 16 SI 2004/752).

MEMO POINTS **a.** This is intended to cover **violence** and threats of violence.
b. In this regard, **harassment** means conduct which has the purpose or effect of violating the person's dignity or creating an intimidating, hostile, degrading, humiliating or offensive environment for him (reg 11 SI 2004/752). For example, this might be on grounds such as gender, race, disability, religion or belief, or sexual orientation. Conduct will only be regarded as having that purpose or effect if, having regard to all the circumstances, including in particular the perception of the person who was the subject of the conduct, it should reasonably be considered as having that purpose or effect (reg 11 SI 2004/752).
c. This will include **long-term barriers** which effectively make it not practicable to start or complete a procedure within a reasonable period such as illness, incapacity or the cessation of the employer's business. It could also include a long period of absence abroad (s 1 para 31 DG Code). However, in these circumstances, an employer should consider appointing a different manager to deal with the procedure wherever possible.

It is important to establish whether there is a **complete exemption** from the procedures (¶6511) or whether the procedures apply but are to be **deemed to have been complied with** (¶¶6566, 6750). The principal significance is that if the procedures do not apply, there will be no time limit extensions available for bringing a tribunal claim, whereas if the procedures apply but are deemed to have been complied with, there are time limit extensions available for tribunal proceedings (¶9479). **6512**

In respect of each of the statutory procedures, there are a number of **general requirements** which the parties must also meet to ensure that the procedures are followed fairly and reasonably (Sch 2 Part 3 EA 2002): **6513**
- each step and action must be taken **without unreasonable delay**;
- the **timing** and **location** of meetings must be reasonable and they should be **conducted** in a manner that enables both the employer and the employee to explain their cases; and
- in the case of **appeal meetings** which are not the first meeting, as far as is reasonably practicable, the employer should be represented by a more senior manager than attended the first meeting (unless he attended that meeting).

Some of the concepts laid down in the general requirements are open to interpretation by the courts and tribunals and further guidance is awaited.

Failure to comply with an applicable statutory procedure, including any of the general requirements (¶6513), will be attributed to the party responsible for the failure and neither party will need to comply with any further requirements of the relevant procedure (reg 12 SI 2004/752). Note that in certain circumstances, the parties will be treated as complying with the applicable procedure by virtue of the regulations (¶6566 (disciplinary), ¶6750 (grievance)). This will not usually constitute a failure to comply with the regulations except where specified in the relevant section. **6514**

If an employer dismisses an employee without completing an applicable statutory dismissal and disciplinary procedure, and the failure is wholly or mainly attributable to him, then the dismissal will be **automatically unfair** (s 98A(1) ERA 1996 as amended by s 34 EA 2002) (although the employee will still have to satisfy the general qualifying conditions for unfair dismissal – ¶8410). In these circumstances (whether or not the dismissal is unfair or regarded as unfair for any other reason), the employee will receive a **minimum basic award** of at least 4 weeks' pay (ss 112(5), 120(1A) ERA 1996) (this will be subject to the statutory cap – ¶2920). Consequently, if a tribunal **awards compensation** and the basic award is less than 4 weeks' pay, it must increase the award to 4 weeks' pay (s 120(1A) ERA 1996). If the award is already greater than 4 weeks' pay, no additional payment will be made for the automatically unfair dismissal. See also ¶8577. If a tribunal does not award an employee compensation in an unfair dismissal claim but rather makes an **order for reinstatement or re-engagement** (¶8680), it must in addition make a minimum basic award to the employee of 4 weeks' pay (which, again, will be subject to the statutory cap on a week's pay – ¶2920). **6515**

MEMO POINTS The provisions regarding the minimum basic award apply in unfair dismissal claims only (and must be awarded whether or not the dismissal is unfair or regarded as unfair for any other reason). In contrast, it should be noted that the provisions regarding the adjustment of compensation at ¶6516 below apply not only to unfair dismissal claims, but also to any successful claim brought under one of the jurisdictions set out at ¶9985 where an award of compensation is made to an employee.

6516 If an employee brings a claim under one of the jurisdictions listed in the Appendix at ¶9985 and it appears to a tribunal that an applicable statutory procedure was not completed before proceedings were begun due to the employee's failure to comply with a requirement of the procedure or to exercise a right of appeal under it, the **tribunal must reduce any award of compensation** which it makes to the employee by 10% and may, if it considers it just and equitable in all the circumstances to do so, reduce it by up to 50% (s 31(2) EA 2002). It is worth noting that there is no obligation, under the statutory procedures, on an employee to actually exercise his right of appeal. Despite this, however, it appears that an employee will be penalised by a mandatory reduction to any compensation he may have been awarded in a successful claim should he fail to exercise his right of appeal, save in exceptional circumstances.

Similarly, in a claim under one of the jurisdictions set out at ¶9985, if the employer fails to start or complete an applicable statutory procedure before proceedings were begun, then the **tribunal must increase any award of compensation** which it makes to the employee by 10% and may, if it considers it just and equitable in all the circumstances to do so, increase it by up to 50% (s 31(3) EA 2002).

Only in **exceptional circumstances** where any reduction or increase would be unjust or inequitable, a tribunal can opt to make no reduction or increase or to make a reduction or increase of such lesser percentage as it considers just and equitable in all the circumstances (s 31(4) EA 2002).

MEMO POINTS As highlighted above (see memo point to ¶6515), the provisions regarding the adjustment of compensation for failure to comply with an applicable statutory procedure applies to any successful claim brought under one of the jurisdictions set out at ¶9985 where an award is made to an employee, and not just to unfair dismissal claims. Further details regarding the adjustment to the compensatory award in **unfair dismissal claims** and how the new provisions will impact on the operation of the pre-existing rules regarding procedural fairness are to be found at ¶¶8629-33.

b. Best practice principles

6520 The Advisory, Conciliation and Arbitration Service (ACAS) has revised its Code of Practice on disciplinary and grievance procedures (DG Code) (issued under statutory authority (s 199 TULRCA 1992)) to reflect the introduction of the new dispute resolution procedures. The DG Code contains **best practice guidance** on disciplinary practice and procedures, grievance procedures, and the statutory right of workers to be accompanied at disciplinary and grievance hearings.

The DG Code does not have legal force, so a failure on the part of an employer to observe any of its provisions does not of itself render him liable to any proceedings (s 207 TULRCA 1992). However, the DG Code is **admissible in evidence** in any proceedings before a tribunal, and any provision of the DG Code which appears to the tribunal to be relevant to any question arising in the proceedings (for example, whether a dismissal is unfair) is required to be **taken into account** in determining that question. It must also be taken into account by the arbitrators if the claim is being determined under the ACAS arbitration scheme (¶9360).

ACAS has also published an **advisory handbook**, which provides further practical guidance and expands on the DG Code's provisions relating to discipline (ACAS Advisory Handbook: Discipline and Grievances at Work) (referred to as the Handbook), together with a practical online **questions and answers** page on discipline, dismissal and grievances (found on the ACAS website at www.acas.org.uk).

6521 The guidance given in the DG Code and the Handbook is aimed at employers in all types and **size of organisation**. However, the procedures and practices best suited to a particular organisation will vary according to its size, complexity and resources. This will be taken into consideration by a tribunal in deciding whether a fair procedure was followed in any unfair dismissal claim. Nevertheless, all organisations, regardless of size must follow the minimum statutory dismissal and disciplinary procedures. However, the DG Code recognises that some smaller organisations may not find it practicable to adopt all of its detailed good practice guidance (s 1 para 7 DG Code).

2. Policies and procedures

Subject to a qualifying period of 1 month's continuous service, employers are obliged by statute to provide a **written statement of employment particulars** to all employees, containing specified information, **within** the first 2 months of an employee's employment (ss 1-7, 198 ERA 1996; ¶1405). 6525

The written statement must **specify** not only the disciplinary rules applicable to an employee but also any procedures (including any statutory procedures) relating to dismissing or taking disciplinary action in respect of an employee (or should refer the employee to a reasonably accessible document in which such procedures can be found) (s 3(1) ERA 1996, as amended by s 35 EA 2002). In addition, the statement must specify the grievance procedure applicable not only in respect of any disciplinary action taken in respect of an employee but also in respect of any decision to dismiss him (s 3(1)ERA 1996, as amended by s 35 EA 2002).

Small employers (with less than 20 employees) are no longer exempt from the requirement to provide information about disciplinary rules and procedures (s 36 EA 2002).

Failure to provide a written statement or if an employee's statement is found to be **incomplete** or **inaccurate** may give rise to the employer being additionally liable to pay compensation to an employee who has brought a claim before a tribunal in respect of a different matter under any of the jurisdictions set out at ¶9985 (s 38 Sch 5 EA 2002). 6526

A tribunal which finds in favour of an employee (whether or not it makes an award to him) in respect of his claim must make an **award** of 2 weeks' pay and can **increase** this award to 4 weeks' pay (if it considers it just and equitable to do so) if, at the time the proceedings began, the employer was in breach of his duty to provide a full and accurate written statement of particulars (s 38(2), (3) EA 2002). The amount of a week's pay is subject to a statutory cap, see ¶2920.

MEMO POINTS These provisions do not provide employees with a stand-alone remedy if an employer is in default of the requirement to provide written particulars.

SECTION 1

Discipline

Disciplinary arrangements should consist of two elements, namely disciplinary rules, and disciplinary procedures. 6530

There is **no direct obligation** on an employer to introduce disciplinary rules. However, employers should have disciplinary procedures in place if they are to ensure that any disciplinary dismissal or other action taken in respect of an employee is fair. In any event, employers are obliged to implement **statutory dismissal and disciplinary procedures** which set minimum standards required of employers when taking a decision to dismiss or discipline employees. Further, employers are obliged by statute to **provide written information** about their disciplinary rules and procedures (¶6525).

Disciplinary rules set standards to be observed by all staff to whom they apply, and make clear to employees what is expected of them, and the consequences of breaking the rules or failing to reach the required standards. 6531

It is advisable for disciplinary rules to be **contractual terms**, so that a breach by the employee will be a breach of contract.

6532 **Disciplinary procedures** are an aid to good management in that they can help the employer to deal fairly and consistently with any disciplinary problems.

It is advisable for the procedures to be **non-contractual**, so the employer can retain as much flexibility as possible when implementing them.

If they are **contractual**, an employee may be able to:
– argue that his contract has been breached if his employer deviates even slightly from the agreed procedures (*Gunton v London Borough of Richmond-upon-Thames* [1980] IRLR 321, CA);
– obtain an injunction, restraining the employer from dismissing in breach (¶1700);
– bring a claim of wrongful dismissal (¶8155) if the employer dismisses him in breach;
– resign and claim that he has been constructively dismissed if the employer commits a fundamental breach by imposing a disciplinary sanction (such as suspension or demotion) without following the contractual procedures (*Post Office v Strange* [1981] IRLR 515, EAT); and
– argue that, if the contractual procedure had been followed, he would still have been employed on the date that would give him sufficient qualifying service to bring a claim of unfair dismissal (¶8410).

MEMO POINTS For the time being, the Government has decided not to make the new statutory dispute resolution procedures **an implied contractual term** and has put on hold the coming into force date of the relevant statutory provision (s 30 EA 2002) in order to see how the new regulations work in practice.

A. Disciplinary rules

6534 The disciplinary rules should be fair and reflect the needs of the particular organisation, including the type of work, working conditions, size and location of the employer. One set of rules cannot cover every situation, and should, therefore, state that they are not exhaustive.

1. Formulation

6535 Policy on discipline should be formulated by the employer with the involvement of employees (and trade union or other employee representatives, where applicable) (s 1 para 52 DG Code).

6536 The disciplinary rules should be **reviewed** from time to time in order to reflect developments in employment legislation and/or good practice. If amendments or additions are made to the rules, these should only be implemented after reasonable notice has been given to employees and, where appropriate, their representatives consulted (s 1 para 62 DG Code). In general, changes to individual contracts will require employee consent (¶1600).

6537 When formulating disciplinary rules, the following **general principles** should be observed (s 1 paras 55, 56 DG Code):
– the rules should specify clearly and concisely those requirements that are necessary for the efficient and safe performance of work and the maintenance of satisfactory relations within the workforce and between employees and management;
– the rules should be set out clearly and concisely in writing and be readily available to all staff (for example, on a noticeboard or, in larger organisations, in the staff handbook or on the company intranet), and management is responsible for ensuring that employees know and understand them (for example, by giving each employee a copy, perhaps as part of the induction programme for new employees); and
– employees should be made aware of the likely consequences of breaking the rules, and the type of conduct which may warrant summary dismissal (¶8155).

The disciplinary rules should inform employees of the likely consequences of breaking the disciplinary rules. In particular, it is usual for disciplinary rules to **cover** issues of misconduct (including poor performance (¶6660), absence (¶6650), poor timekeeping, harassment or victimisation, and misuse of company facilities (for example, employee use of email and the internet)), and to specify that serious cases will be treated as gross misconduct. 6538

Misconduct and gross misconduct Misconduct is conduct which initially requires disciplinary action other than dismissal, such as persistent lateness, harassment or victimisation, bad behaviour (such as fighting or drunkenness), unauthorised absence and failure to meet known work standards. If further misconduct takes place, dismissal may ultimately be an appropriate sanction. 6540

Gross misconduct is generally considered to be misconduct serious enough to destroy the contract between employer and employee, and irretrievably break down the working relationship and trust between them. The rules should indicate that such conduct may warrant summary dismissal, i.e. dismissal without notice. Examples may include theft or fraud, physical violence, bullying or offensive behaviour, deliberate damage to company property, misuse of the employer's property or name, inappropriate internet or computer use, alcohol or drug use affecting work, causing loss, damage or injury through serious carelessness, a serious breach of the health and safety rules or a serious breach of confidence.

It is common for the employer to provide a **non-exhaustive list** of those acts which constitute misconduct, and those which amount to gross misconduct, including those determined by the nature of his business (see the checklist in the Appendix at ¶9955 for examples). Some types of conduct will obviously amount to misconduct (such as fighting) or gross misconduct (such as dishonestly claiming overtime), and it is, therefore, not always necessary to specify them as such in the rules (*C A Parsons & Co Limited v McLoughlin* [1978] IRLR 65, EAT; *Tesco Stores Ltd v Sams*, 27 January 1997, EAT). 6541

As it is not always obvious whether a particular offence amounts to gross misconduct, it is still useful to give examples of gross misconduct as the employer will more clearly be **justified in dismissing** an employee without warning if it is obvious that the employee should have known that such conduct would result in summary dismissal (*Meyer Dunmore International Ltd v Rogers* [1978] IRLR 167, EAT). Regardless of any stated examples, to avoid a claim of unfair dismissal, the employer must in any case be able to show that dismissal was a reasonable sanction to impose in the circumstances (*Ladbroke Racing Ltd v Arnott* [1983] IRLR 154, CS).

2. Application

Employers should ensure that their managers and supervisors are familiar with the disciplinary rules and are **trained** to apply them in a consistent and fair manner. 6545

The employer should ensure that every employee knows and understands the applicable disciplinary rules, including employees whose **first language is not English** or who have **reading difficulties** (s 1 para 55 DG Code).

Consistency The rules should be applied consistently but not inflexibly, and the employer must take into account any **mitigating or aggravating circumstances** in a particular case. He should deal with each case on its own merits, as employment tribunals hearing unfair dismissal claims will always consider whether the employer acted fairly in all the circumstances of the case (and consistency will merely be one factor). 6546

Inconsistency may arise as a result of:
– different treatment of employees in a sufficiently similar position (both in the past and subsequently) (*Post Office v Fennell* [1981] IRLR 221, CA; *Eagle Star Insurance Co Ltd v Hayward* [1981] ICR 860, EAT); or
– different treatment of a particular employee from one occasion to the next.

An employee may argue that the rules have been applied inconsistently if:
– he was led to believe that certain categories of conduct would be ignored or not punished by dismissal (*Bendall v Paine & Betteridge Eastbourne* [1973] IRLR 44, IT);
– decisions made in other cases support an inference that the reason stated by the employer for the dismissal is not the real reason; or
– decisions made by the employer in comparable cases support an argument that it was not reasonable to dismiss the employee in the circumstances.

If the employer wants to take a **different attitude towards a particular rule** (for example, where his established and well-known practice has been to ignore an express rule and he now wishes it to be observed), he must give employees sufficient advance warning of this change.

6548 **Discretion** The employer can retain some **flexibility** by stating in the rules that gross misconduct 'will normally' or 'may' result in summary dismissal. In unfair dismissal cases, a tribunal in deciding whether the employer acted reasonably in treating a particular case of gross misconduct as a sufficient reason for dismissal will take into account this element of discretion. The discretionary element will not, however, allow an employee to claim that dismissal was not the likely result of gross misconduct (*Proctor v British Gypsum Ltd* [1992] IRLR 7, EAT).

EXAMPLE In *Proctor v British Gypsum Ltd*, the rules stated that gross misconduct (including fighting) 'may result in dismissal.' P was dismissed for fighting. He argued that dismissal was inconsistent with the penalty imposed in similar circumstances in the past. The EAT held that the dismissal was fair, and that the discretionary wording could not be relied on to indicate that there was a general practice that dismissal would not be the likely result of the misconduct in question.

6550 **Dealing with several suspects** Where one of a number of employees could have committed a particular offence for which the sanction is dismissal, the employer should implement the minimum statutory disciplinary procedure in the usual way for each employee involved. The employer will be justified in **disciplining all members** of the group if:
– he has a reasonable belief that more than one person committed the act;
– the group of employees who could have committed the act has been reasonably identified;
– each member of the group was individually capable of committing the act; and
– the individual perpetrator cannot reasonably be identified.

The usual fairness requirement of having "a genuine belief on reasonable grounds after reasonable investigation" (¶8505) that a particular employee committed the offence does not apply.

The fact that one or more of those employees was not dismissed does not make the dismissal of any others unfair as long as the employer can show that he had "solid and sensible grounds", which do not have to be related to the relevant offence, for **differentiating** between the employees (*Frames Snooker Centre v Boyce* [1992] IRLR 472, EAT). Such differentiation should not, however, be made on discriminatory grounds.

B. Procedures

6555 If an employee breaches a disciplinary rule, the employer must consider whether to deal with the matter **informally**, or whether to invoke his **formal disciplinary procedures**. His decision is likely to depend on the seriousness of the breach, and whether it was a first offence.

The employer may have separate procedures for dealing with issues of **conduct and capability**.

In any case, any hearing which might result in a formal warning or some other disciplinary action will trigger the statutory **right to be accompanied** (¶6780).

6556 In certain circumstances, a **statutory minimum procedure** must be followed if an employer is contemplating dismissing an employee or imposing some other disciplinary penalty other than suspension on full pay or an oral or written warning (reg 2 SI 2004/752). For a discussion as to when the statutory dismissal and disciplinary procedure will apply, see ¶6510.

Depending on the circumstances, either a **standard** (i.e. three-step) or **modified** (two-step) procedure will apply.

1. Formulation

6557 A disciplinary procedure should be formulated to incorporate not only the statutory minimum requirements set out in the regulations but also the principles of best practice laid down by the DG Code and other government guidance.

Statutory dismissal and disciplinary procedures

6560 The statutory dismissal and disciplinary procedures are set out below (Sch 2 Pt 1 Ch 1 EA 2002). These three steps set out the minimum requirements that must be met in order for the statutory dismissal and disciplinary procedure to be completed.

However, following the relevant statutory procedure alone will not necessarily mean that an employer will not leave himself open to a claim of **unfair dismissal** in respect of the action he has taken. It is therefore important to consider and, as far as is practicable, implement the principles of best practice set out below (¶6570).

STEP 1: STATEMENT OF GROUND(S) FOR ACTION AND INVITATION TO MEETING	– Employer must **set out in writing** the employee's alleged conduct, characteristics, or other circumstances which lead him to contemplate dismissing or taking disciplinary action against the employee. – Employer must **send the statement** (or a copy of it) to the employee and **invite** the employee to attend a meeting to discuss the matter.
STEP 2: MEETING	– The meeting must **take place before** any action is taken, except in the case where the disciplinary action consists of suspension. – The meeting can **only take place** if: a. the employer has informed the employee what the basis was for including in the statement the ground(s) given in it; and b. the employee has a reasonable opportunity to consider his response to that information. – Employee must take **all reasonable steps** to attend the meeting. – After the meeting, employer must **inform** the employee of his decision and **notify him of the right to appeal** against the decision.
STEP 3: APPEAL	– If he wishes to appeal against the decision, **employee must inform** the employer. – If the employee informs the employer of his wish to appeal, the employer must **invite** him to attend a further meeting. – Employee must take **all reasonable steps** to attend the meeting. – The appeal meeting **need not take place before** the dismissal or disciplinary action takes effect. – After the appeal meeting, **employer must inform** employee of his final decision.

MEMO POINTS **Sample documents** are available in the DTI guidance for small firms.

6565 Where an employer is considering dismissing an employee for gross misconduct, a **modified statutory dismissal and disciplinary procedure** will normally apply (¶6640).

STEP 1: STATEMENT OF GROUND(S) FOR ACTION	– Employer must **set out in writing:** a. the employee's alleged misconduct which has led to the dismissal; b. what the basis was for thinking at the time of the dismissal that the employee was guilty of the alleged misconduct; and c. the employee's right to appeal against his dismissal. – Employer must **send the statement** (or a copy of it) to employee.
STEP 2: APPEAL	– If he wishes to appeal against the decision, the **employee must inform** the employer. – If the employee informs the employer of his wish to appeal, the employer must **invite** him to attend a meeting. – Employee must take **all reasonable steps** to attend the meeting. – After the appeal meeting, **employer must inform** employee of his final decision.

6566 **Deemed compliance** It should be noted that in certain circumstances, the statutory dismissal and disciplinary procedures will be deemed to have been complied with even if not all of the minimum requirements have been met. In these circumstances, since the statutory procedures are still applicable, the parties may be granted an **extension** of the time limits to complete the procedure to avoid the employee presenting a premature claim to the tribunal (¶9479). This **applies** where (reg 5 SI 2004/752):
– the employee presents an application for interim relief to an employment tribunal pending determination of his complaint (¶8700); or
– there is a right of appeal against dismissal or disciplinary action which has been incorporated into an employee's contract of employment by virtue of a collective agreement (¶1270).

An employee can, when claiming that he has been unfairly dismissed for certain reasons (¶8700), make a claim for **interim relief**, the purpose of which is to maintain the status quo pending the final determination of his case. If at the time the application for interim relief is presented, the parties have complied with Steps 1 and 2 of the standard procedure (i.e. the statement of ground(s) for action, invitation to meeting and the meeting), or Step 1 of the modified procedure (i.e. the statement of ground(s) for action), but not with Step 3 of the standard procedure or Step 2 of the modified procedure (i.e. the appeal stage), they will be deemed to have complied with the appeal stage of the appropriate statutory procedure.

Where there is a **collectively agreed appeal procedure** in place at the time of the dismissal or disciplinary action under which there is a right to appeal against such dismissal or disciplinary action, then the parties will be deemed to have complied with the appeal stage of the appropriate statutory procedure if the employee chooses to appeal under the collectively agreed appeal procedure.

MEMO POINTS The procedure must have been agreed by two or more employers or an employers' association and at least one independent trade union. This provision allows employers and employees to continue to use pre-existing appeal procedures which have been agreed at a national level. Employees are still free to choose to appeal under the employer's own statutory procedure however.

Best practice

6570 **Natural justice** demands that employees should be (s 1 para 59 DG Code):
– informed in advance of any disciplinary hearing of the allegations that are being made against them, together with the supporting evidence;
– subject to an unbiased and impartial tribunal;

– given the opportunity of challenging the allegations and evidence before decisions are reached; and
– given the right of appeal against any decisions taken against them.

A disciplinary procedure should therefore be designed to ensure compliance with these requirements, which should be observed in respect of all employees regardless of the size of the organisation. Breach of natural justice is not an independent ground of complaint if an employee is dismissed, but will be an important factor in **assessing fairness** for the purposes of an unfair dismissal claim (*Slater v Leicestershire Health Authority* [1989] IRLR 16, CA).

As a result of the broad concept of natural justice, the DG Code recommends that **good disciplinary procedures** should (s 1 para 60 DG Code): 6571
– be in writing, specify to whom they apply, and provide for matters to be dealt with without undue delay;
– be non-discriminatory;
– provide for proceedings, witness statements and records to be kept confidential;
– indicate the disciplinary actions which may be taken and specify the levels of management which have the authority to take the various forms of disciplinary action;
– provide for employees to be informed of the complaints against them and, where possible, all relevant supporting evidence, before any disciplinary hearing;
– provide employees with an opportunity to state their case before decisions are reached;
– provide employees with the right to be accompanied (¶6780);
– ensure that, except for gross misconduct, no employee is dismissed for a first breach of discipline;
– provide for careful investigation before disciplinary action is taken;
– ensure that employees are given an explanation for any penalty imposed; and
– provide a right of appeal (normally to a more senior manager) and specify the appeal procedure.

2. Operation

It is essential that all managers and, where appropriate, employee representatives understand the procedures. **Training** in their use and operation may be required (s 1 para 61 DG Code). 6574

The disciplinary procedure should be observed in all cases unless there are exceptional circumstances. Even if the procedure is non-contractual, a failure to follow it may give rise to a complaint of **unfair dismissal** if it indicates that the employer acted unfairly in the circumstances (*Polkey v A E Dayton Services Ltd* [1987] IRLR 503, HL). For example, an employer may be held to be acting unreasonably if he does not follow a collectively agreed procedure, unless it is inherently defective (*East Hertfordshire District Council v K Boyten* [1977] IRLR 347, EAT). However, a breach of agreed procedures will not automatically make the dismissal unfair (it will be a factor in assessing the overall fairness of the employer's actions) (*Westminster City Council v Cabaj* [1996] IRLR 399, CA). 6575

Moreover, **failure to comply with all the statutory minimum requirements** will have a number of implications for the party to whom the failure is wholly or mainly attributable. For example, this might result in any subsequent dismissal being held to be automatically unfair (¶¶6514-6516). 6577

MEMO POINTS Neither party will be expected to start or follow through the statutory procedure if they have reasonable grounds to suspect that by doing so they might be exposed to a **significant threat**, such as violent, abusive, or intimidating behaviour, or harassment or if it is **not practicable** to start or follow through a procedure **within a reasonable period** (¶6511).

To amount to a **fair dismissal**, the reason for the dismissal (i.e. the breach of the rules) must fall within one of the five statutory fair reasons, "conduct" being the most relevant (¶8422). The disciplinary procedures are especially important, as a tribunal hearing an unfair dismissal claim will take account of whether a fair procedure was followed, i.e. that the employer acted fairly in all the circumstances in dismissing the employee (¶8500). 6578

For details of the rules relating to **procedural defects** in disciplinary procedures in unfair dismissal claims, see ¶8629.

6579 When dealing with disciplinary cases, employers must also ensure that they do not **discriminate** against any employee in respect of their disciplinary rules and procedures on the grounds of sex, race (including colour, nationality, ethnic or national origin), disability, sexual orientation, religion or belief, or age (s 1 para 4 DG Code). For example, a pregnant woman may be disciplined for a reason that is unconnected with her pregnancy, such as theft, but not on the grounds of her pregnancy.

EXAMPLE In *Sidhu v Aerospace Composite Technology* [2000] IRLR 602, CA, the Court held that a disciplinary policy that ignored all types of provocation, including racial provocation, was not discriminatory because the application of the policy was not race-specific.

6580 **Grievance about the dismissal and disciplinary procedure** If the employee raises a grievance during the disciplinary procedure, for example, if he is **dissatisfied** with the **handling of the disciplinary matter** (for example, the behaviour of the investigating manager), the employer should consider suspending the disciplinary process for a short time in order to deal with the grievance (s 1 para 33 DG Code). It may be necessary for a different manager to deal with the remainder of the disciplinary process, although this may not be possible in smaller organisations.

6581 If the action taken, or contemplated, by the employer is **dismissal**, the statutory grievance procedure (¶6740) does not need to be followed and, instead, the employee's complaint will be the subject of the ongoing statutory dismissal and disciplinary procedure, if this is applicable (reg 6(5) SI 2004/752).

6582 If the employer takes, or is contemplating taking, **disciplinary action short of dismissal** (other than suspending the employee on full pay or giving him a warning) and he asserts that the reason for the action is related to the employee's conduct or capability, the dismissal and disciplinary procedure must be followed **except** if one of the reasons for the grievance is that (reg 6 SI 2004/752):
- the disciplinary action amounted to, or would amount to, unlawful discrimination; or
- the true reason for the action is not the reason given by the employer.

If one of these circumstances exists, either the standard or modified grievance procedure will apply (as the case may be – ¶¶6731, 6760) but the parties will be deemed to have complied with the applicable procedure if the employee has set out his grievance in writing to the employer (reg 7 SI 2004/752):
- where a statutory dismissal and disciplinary procedure is being followed, before any appeal meeting; or
- where neither statutory dismissal and disciplinary procedure applies, before presenting a claim arising out of his grievance to a tribunal.

MEMO POINTS **Unlawful discrimination** in this regard refers to any act or omission by the employer in respect of which the employee would have a right to bring a tribunal claim on the grounds of sex, race, disability, religion or belief, or sexual orientation discrimination or inequality of pay (reg 7 SI 2004/752).

6583 If the action taken, or contemplated being taken, by the employer is **suspending** the employee **on full pay** or giving him an **oral or written warning**, then the statutory grievance procedure will apply if the employee has any complaint regarding the disciplinary action (s 1 para 34 DG Code).

6584 In the above cases, the employee must raise a written grievance through the statutory procedure (¶6740) before bringing a tribunal claim (¶6773). However, if he raises his written grievance before any disciplinary appeal hearing (¶6690), the remainder of the grievance procedure does not need to be followed and, instead, the employer can use the disciplinary appeal meeting to discuss the grievance (s 1 para 34 DG Code). This will avoid unnecessary duplication of the disciplinary and grievance procedures. It should be noted, however, that if the employee raises his grievance only after the disciplinary procedure has been completed, he must complete the grievance procedure in full.

MEMO POINTS The DTI guidance provides that the letters and meetings under the disciplinary and grievance procedures can be **multi-purpose** if necessary.

Investigation

The first step when a disciplinary matter arises is for the relevant supervisor or manager to **establish the facts** as soon as possible before recollections fade (s 1 para 11 DG Code). He should, therefore, obtain statements from available witnesses where appropriate, and keep written records for later reference. 6585

Where an investigatory meeting is held **solely for the purpose of** establishing the relevant facts of the case, the supervisor or manager must inform the employee that it is not a disciplinary meeting (s 1 para 11 DG Code).

MEMO POINTS An investigation that continues longer than an ordinary investigation would do can amount to a detriment for **discrimination** purposes, even though the employee is unaware that the investigation is continuing (*Garry v London Borough of Ealing* [2001] IRLR 681, CA).

If any **informant** wishes to **remain anonymous**, his evidence should be treated with care. In such cases, the following **guidelines** should be observed (*Linfood Cash and Carry Ltd v Thomson* [1989] IRLR 235, EAT): 6586

1. A written statement should be compiled of the information given by the informant, taken initially without regard to the fact that anonymity is to be preserved. It may subsequently be necessary to omit or erase certain parts of the statement before it is disclosed to others in order to prevent identification. The statement should include information on:
- the date, time and place of any observation or incident;
- the informant's opportunity and ability to observe clearly and with accuracy;
- the circumstantial evidence, such as knowledge of a system or arrangement or the reason for the presence of the informer and why certain small details are memorable; and
- whether the informant suffered at the hands of the employee or has any other reason to fabricate, whether from a personal grudge or any other reason or principle.

2. Further investigation can then take place either to confirm or undermine the information given. Ideally that information should be corroborated, although in some cases it may not be possible.
3. It may be appropriate to make tactful inquiries into the character and background of the informant or any other information which may tend to add or detract from the value of the information.
4. If the employer is satisfied that the informant's fear of disclosing his identity is genuine, the employer will have to decide whether or not to continue with the disciplinary process. If it is to continue, the informant should be interviewed by the responsible manager at each stage of the process so that the manager can satisfy himself as to the weight to be given to the informant's evidence, and the informant's written statement (with omissions where necessary to prevent identification) should be made available to the employee and his representative.
5. It is particularly important where evidence has been taken from an informant that full and careful notes are taken during disciplinary procedures, and if evidence is to be taken from the investigating officer at the hearing, it should, where possible, be prepared in writing.

However, depending on the circumstances of the case, it may not always be necessary to strictly adhere to these guidelines. Where there are **real fears** that informants in a disciplinary investigation will suffer **retaliation and reprisals** for having cooperated with management, it is not unreasonable for an employer to protect the identities of such informants by restricting knowledge of their identities to only one member of management (*Ramsey and ors v Walkers Snack Foods Ltd* [2004] IRLR 754, EAT). In this case, the anonymity of the informants did not affect the fairness of the employees' dismissals, despite the informants' witness statements lacking in detail and the fact that the informants had not been questioned by the managers involved in the disciplinary investigation or subsequent dismissals. Even though the guidelines were not strictly adhered to in this case, there were two additional problems which had not arisen in *Linfood Cash and Carry v Thomson*: the informants refused to sign a witness statement unless it had been sufficiently edited to remove any chance of identifying them and they were unwilling to be questioned by any other members of management.

6587 The employer must also consider and investigate any **explanations** put forward by the employee, including whether there are any special circumstances to be taken into account, such as personal or other external factors affecting performance or conduct.

6588 To **defend a claim of unfair dismissal** on grounds of misconduct, the employer must have a genuine belief in the employee's guilt, held on reasonable grounds having carried out such investigation as was reasonable in all the circumstances (¶8505). An investigation is important for the following reasons:
a. to enable the employer to establish the facts on which his decision will be based; and
b. to provide the employee with an opportunity to:
– respond to the allegations against him; and
– reveal any mitigating circumstances (which may affect the disciplinary sanction imposed).

To **establish dishonesty**, for example, the employer must ask himself two questions (*R v Ghosh* [1982] QB 1053, CA):
1. Was what was done dishonest according to the standards of reasonable and honest people?
2. If so, did the employee realise that what he was doing was dishonest by those standards?
In many cases, there will be no doubt about the answer, but the circumstances may require investigation, for example, to ascertain the seriousness of the offence (*John Lewis plc v Coyne* [2001] IRLR 139, EAT).
There is no principle of law that dismissal will always be a **fair sanction** for dishonesty, and there may be mitigating factors in certain cases (*Tesco Stores Ltd v Othman-Khalid*, EAT case 385/00). However, case law indicates that even in trivial cases of dishonesty, dismissal will normally be within the range of reasonable responses open to an employer (*Murphy v Trust Houses Forte Hotels Ltd* [1977] IRLR 186, EAT; see ¶8508 regarding the 'range of reasonable responses').

If an employee has **admitted misconduct** (either at the investigation stage or during the disciplinary hearing (see below)), the employer can reasonably act on that admission (*RSPB v Croucher* [1984] IRLR 425, EAT). However, where the employee admits the physical elements of the offence but there is some **doubt as to his intention**, some investigation may still be required (*John Lewis plc v Coyne*). In any case, the employer will still be obliged to follow a fair procedure generally (*Whitbread plc (t/a Whitbread Medway Inns) v Hall* [2001] IRLR 275, CA). Similarly, if the employee **pleads guilty** to, or is convicted of, a criminal offence, the employer is entitled to assume the employee's guilt (*P v Nottingham County Council* [1992] IRLR 362, CA).

EXAMPLE In *John Lewis plc v Coyne*, the store had a rule against using work telephones for personal calls (which was considered to amount to dishonesty) and warned that misuse could lead to dismissal. C admitted making personal calls and the store dismissed her without further investigation as it considered her actions objectively dishonest. The EAT held that an investigation was required as the test for dishonesty is not simply an objective one but should be considered in the light of individual circumstances, including whether C considered her actions to be dishonest.

6589 The courts have not laid down rigid criteria of what an adequate investigation will involve (it will be a question of degree in each case) (*Bentley Engineering Co v Mistry* [1978] IRLR 436, EAT). An investigation may be **inadequate** for the following reasons, which may make a subsequent dismissal unfair:
– failure to allow the employee an opportunity to offer an explanation (*McLaren v National Coal Board* [1988] IRLR 215, CA);
– failure to take statements from available witnesses before recollections fade or delay in carrying out investigation (*RSPCA v Cruden* [1986] IRLR 83, EAT);
– employees' explanation rejected without proper enquiry (*Francis v Ford Motor Company* [1975] IRLR 25, IT);
– reliance on hearsay evidence alone (*Gordon v F Medhurst Ltd Bromley* [1972] IRLR 47, IT); and
– investigation after decision to dismiss had been taken was a charade and therefore insufficient (*Robert Whiting Designs Ltd v Lamb* [1978] ICR 89, EAT).

Suspension In most cases, it will not be necessary to suspend the employee during the investigation stage. However, suspension **with pay** should be considered in the following circumstances to allow unhindered investigations to be carried out (s 1 para 9 DG Code): 6595
- preliminary investigations indicate that there is a potentially serious case, i.e. one involving gross misconduct;
- the relationships at work have broken down; and
- it is considered that there are risks to the employer's property or he has responsibilities to other parties (e.g. other employees or customers).

If the employer is contemplating suspending an employee on **full pay**, the statutory minimum procedures will not apply to this action. They will, however, need to be followed if any other disciplinary action is being considered, including dismissal.

The employee should be informed that suspension on full pay is not itself considered as disciplinary action (s 1 para 9 DG Code).

A suspension **without pay** or with **reduced pay** is possible where the contract of employment so provides. However, this should be exceptional as it will, in itself, amount to a disciplinary penalty. Consequently, the statutory dismissal and disciplinary procedure must be followed.

Before suspending, the employer should consider whether there are alternatives to suspension, such as a transfer or a short period of leave. The suspension should be for **no longer than is reasonably necessary** to carry out the investigation, otherwise the employer may be in breach of contract. Even if there is a contractual right to suspend (¶6597), a failure to follow **correct procedures** before exercising the right may lead to a breach of contract claim. 6596

EXAMPLE In *Gogay v Hertfordshire County Council* [2000] IRLR 703, CA, G, a care worker was suspended pending the outcome of an investigation into allegations of sexual abuse of a child in her care. The Court of Appeal accepted that the Council was in breach of the implied term of trust and confidence because it had no reasonable and proper cause to suspend G, as it had not carried out preliminary investigations to determine the exact nature of the allegations. Consequently, there were no reasonable grounds for believing that the child would suffer harm unless G was suspended and the Council should have considered alternatives to suspension.

The employer should reserve an **express contractual right** to suspend the employee in order to defeat any argument that there is an implied obligation to provide work (¶1233). If there is no express right, the employer may be in breach of contract. 6597

Post-investigation Following the investigation, the **manager may decide** to (s 1 para 8 DG Code): 6600
- drop the matter (if the employee has a satisfactory explanation or the employer feels that there is insufficient evidence);
- deal with the matter on an informal basis (where the circumstances do not warrant implementation of the formal procedures because, for example, the matter is a minor one); or
- arrange for the matter to be dealt with under the formal procedures.

Minor cases of misconduct and most cases of poor performance may warrant **informal advice, coaching and counselling** (s 1 para 11 DG Code). If necessary, an **informal oral warning** could be issued, together with a discussion of how the employee needs to improve. This discussion should be held in private, where possible, and should be two-way, allowing the employee to put forward explanations of his conduct or performance. 6601

The employee should be informed how his performance or **conduct** will be **reviewed**, over what period, and any consequences of a failure to improve (for example, implementation of the formal disciplinary procedure). It should be made clear that informal warnings and/or counselling are not part of the formal procedures, although a note should be kept for reference purposes.

Letter to employee

If the employer decides that **formal action** is necessary, he must observe the statutory minimum requirements of the standard dismissal and disciplinary procedure set out above 6605

(¶6560). If the employer takes the action below (¶6606 +), he will have satisfied the minimum criteria required to meet **Step 1** of the standard dismissal and disciplinary procedure. In addition, by observing these principles of best practice, he will reduce the risk of tribunal proceedings being brought against him in respect of the dismissal or disciplinary action taken.

6606 As a matter of **good practice**, the first step in any formal process is to **inform** the employee in writing what it is that they are alleged to have done wrong and the reasons why his conduct or capability has not been acceptable (s 1 para 13 DG Code). This can be done in a letter or a note to the employee.

It is important at this stage for employers to take care that the disciplinary charge(s) is framed precisely and accurately, since an employee can only be found guilty of the charge which has been put to him (*Strouthos v London Underground Ltd* [2005] IRLR 636, CA).

The employer must **invite** the employee to attend a meeting at which the conduct or capability issue can be discussed. The meeting should be arranged at a mutually convenient time and location which is reasonable for both parties (Sch 2 Part 3 SI 2004/752; s 1 para 14 DG Code) and the employer should check that everyone who is required to attend the meeting is available. The employee should be given sufficient time to prepare his case, but there should not be an **unreasonable delay** so as to prevent the parties' memories from fading (Sch 2 Part 3 SI 2004/752; s 1 para 14 DG Code).

6607 **In advance** of making arrangements for the meeting, the employer should:

1. write to the employee confirming the **time, place, and purpose** of the meeting, giving details of the complaint, and advising him of his statutory right to be accompanied (¶6780), and of any rights he has under the disciplinary procedure;
2. consider whether any arrangements need to be made to cater for any **language difficulties** or **disability** of any person attending (bearing in mind the duty to make reasonable adjustments under disability discrimination legislation (¶5515; *Cave v Goodwin* [2004] EWCA Civ 391, CA; *Johnson & Johnson Medical Ltd v Filmer*, EAT case 1087/00) (for example, it may be necessary to provide wheelchair access));
3. plan how the meeting will be **structured**, making notes of points that need to be covered;
4. arrange for **witnesses** to attend (unless the employee accepts in advance that their statements are statements of fact), and arrange, where possible, for a second member of management to be present to take notes, and to act as a witness; and
5. establish what disciplinary action was taken in **similar circumstances** in the past.

6608 The employer must consider whether **documents** (e.g. witness statements) **or other evidence** (e.g. tapes of conversations) should be provided to the employee in advance of the hearing. In each case, he must consider whether any documents may be defamatory, sensitive or confidential. If so, rather than provide copies, the employer could allow the employee to arrive in advance of the hearing in order to read through any such documents in private beforehand (without taking copies), or alternatively could provide the employee with relevant extracts only. In either case, the employer must keep in mind the requirement to act reasonably in all the circumstances in order to defend an unfair dismissal claim. If the employee does bring a claim, the employment documents may be **disclosable** (¶9185).

Disciplinary hearing

6610 The employer must adhere to the statutory minimum requirements of the standard dismissal and disciplinary procedure with regard to the Step 2 (meeting) stage set out above (¶6560). If the employer takes the action recommended by the best practice principles regarding the disciplinary hearing and the employer's decision below (see ¶6625), he will have satisfied the minimum criteria required to meet **Step 2** of the standard dismissal and disciplinary procedure. Again, by observing the principles of good practice, he will reduce the risk of tribunal proceedings being brought against him in respect of the dismissal or disciplinary action taken.

As a matter of **good practice**, before any decision to dismiss or take disciplinary action (excluding suspension) is taken, a meeting (referred to as a disciplinary hearing) should be held to give the employee the opportunity to state his case and to answer the allegations made against him (s 1 para 14 DG Code). 6611

Attendance If an employee (or his companion – ¶6786) **cannot attend** a meeting, he must inform the employer in advance whenever possible (s 1 para 16 DG Code). 6612

If either party is unable to attend a meeting organised in accordance with the statutory procedure due to **unforeseen circumstances** which are beyond his control and which were not foreseeable when the meeting was arranged, such as illness, neither party will be treated as having failed to comply with the statutory procedure (reg 13(1) SI 2004/752). In this case, the employer must invite the employee to attend at another time. Where the employee is exercising his right to be accompanied, if he proposes an alternative time, this must be no more than 5 working days after the date originally agreed with the employer unless both parties agree to a longer period (reg 13(2) SI 2004/752; s 1 para 16 DG Code).

If the employee has been invited to attend **two meetings** under the statutory procedure and, on both occasions, it has not been reasonably practicable for the employee to attend due to unforeseen circumstances, the employer is not obliged to re-arrange a further meeting (reg 13(3) SI 2004/752). Instead, the statutory procedure will be deemed to have come to an end (i.e. they will be deemed to have been complied with), although this will not give rise to an adjustment of compensation in any tribunal claim being pursued by the employee (reg 13(4) SI 2004/752; ¶6516).

However, if the employee fails to attend a re-arranged meeting **without good reason**, the employer may decide the outcome of the procedure in his absence (s 1 para 16 DG Code). In these circumstances, any award of compensation made to the employee may be reduced if he brings a successful claim before a tribunal (¶6516).

MEMO POINTS The regulations make separate provision for when it becomes **not reasonably practicable** for one party to start or follow through an applicable statutory procedure within a reasonable period (reg 11(2), (3)(c) SI 2004/752). This is discussed at ¶6511.

Conduct Save for the statutory minimum requirements (¶6560) and the general requirements set out at ¶6513, there are no set legal rules to be followed for a disciplinary hearing, and much will depend on the particular circumstances, and if the employer has set out any procedural guidelines. To avoid any allegation of prejudice, the hearing should ideally be **conducted by** an independent person, i.e. someone other than the person who made the complaint against the employee or who carried out, or was involved in, the investigation stage, and further, that person should be impartial (i.e. have no personal interest, financial or otherwise, in the outcome). The person chosen should have the employer's **authority** to impose any relevant penalty, and must act in good faith. 6615

EXAMPLE In *R v Chief Constable of Merseyside Police ex parte Bennion* [2001] IRLR 442, CA, the Chief Constable was held to be impartial when hearing B's disciplinary case, despite the fact that her sex discrimination claim was pending against him as head of the force. He had no disqualifying personal interest arising from his involvement, in different capacities, in either set of proceedings and it was held that there was no real danger of bias.

MEMO POINTS The above case focuses on the statutory responsibility of a chief constable to hear disciplinary proceedings. It could, in practice, also apply to **chief executives in private organisations** (i.e. they should not regard themselves as disabled by tribunal proceedings from being involved in internal disciplinary matters, unless they have a personal interest in the outcome of the tribunal proceedings).

To avoid any **unnecessary interruptions**, the meeting should be held in a private location (s 1 para 14 DG Code). 6616

During the **introductory stage** of the hearing, the person conducting the hearing (normally a manager) should: 6617

a. introduce those present and explain the reason for their attendance;

b. confirm that the hearing is a disciplinary one to consider whether dismissal or any other disciplinary action should be taken; and

c. explain how the hearing will be conducted.

The employer should ensure that the employee's **personnel file** is available at the hearing to allow a review of his previous disciplinary record (including any current warnings) and employment history (including absence or sickness records, where relevant).

6618 The person conducting the hearing should then explain the nature of the complaint, reviewing the evidence, giving any witnesses an opportunity to comment and ensuring that the employee (and his representative) is allowed to see any witness statements or is told very clearly of the allegations and evidence raised (s 1 para 15 DG Code). As long as the employee is told of the accusations against him and given a full opportunity to respond, there will not necessarily be a breach of natural justice if witness statements are not disclosed. The fairness of the procedure will be a question of fact in each case (*Hussain v Elonex plc* [1999] IRLR 420, CA). The employee should have time to consider the evidence, so it may be appropriate to disclose any statements in advance of the hearing. If witnesses are called at the hearing, the employee should be given the opportunity to raise any issues with them, but it is not essential that he is given a chance to cross-examine them (*Santamera v Express Cargo Forwarding t/a IEC Ltd* [2003] IRLR 273, EAT).

The **employer** must strike a balance between the desirability of protecting informants who are genuinely in fear of reprisals, and the need to provide a fair hearing. If the employer is relying on the **statements of an informant** who wishes to remain anonymous, the informant's motives should be examined, and corroborative evidence sought at the investigation stage (¶6585). If the employee or his representative raises any issues which should be put to the informant, it may be desirable to adjourn the hearing so that the informant can be questioned on those matters.

6619 The **employee** should be invited to **state his case**, ask questions, present evidence, and call witnesses. If witnesses are unable to attend, the hearing should be adjourned unless it is clear that their evidence will not affect the substance of the complaint.

The employer should consider any explanations or other special circumstances put forward by the employee. If he has not offered an explanation, he should be invited to do so. The employer's approach should be formal but polite, using questions (both open-ended and closed, as appropriate) to clarify all the issues.

6620 If it becomes clear that the employee has provided an **adequate explanation** or that there is **no real evidence** to support the allegation, the proceedings should be stopped.

If **new facts** emerge during the hearing, the employer must decide whether further investigation is required, in which case the hearing should be adjourned to be reconvened when the investigation is completed.

6621 If the employee becomes **emotionally distressed** during the hearing, he should be given time to compose himself before continuing. If it is not possible to continue the hearing, it should be adjourned and resumed at a later date.

Whilst the employee (and perhaps some of the witnesses) may be highly charged, **abusive language**, threatened physical violence or other misconduct should not be tolerated. The interview should be adjourned and reconvened at a later date, where that misconduct can also be considered.

6622 At the end of the hearing, the employer should **summarise** the main points concerning the offence, the main points raised by the employee, and any matters that need to be checked.

6623 **Human rights impact** Disciplinary hearings may be affected by the **right to a fair and public hearing** by an independent tribunal (Human Rights Act 1998; Art 6 European Convention on Human Rights). However, previous attempts to apply that right to internal disciplinary hearings have been largely unsuccessful because the employer's decision to impose a disciplinary sanction (such as dismissal) cannot be described as the determination of a civil right, which is necessary for the human rights legislation to apply. Further, this right is satisfied if the individual has access to a court or tribunal which can deal with all aspects of the dispute, such as the availability of an application to a tribunal.

MEMO POINTS Disciplinary proceedings may be conducted by **professional bodies** (such as the General Medical Council and the Law Society), which can determine individuals' rights to practice a particular profession. In these cases, there is a determination of a civil right and the individual concerned may be protected by human rights legislation if the professional bodies can be said to be carrying out a public function in licensing professionals to practise. For example, the General Dental Council's disciplinary procedure was subject to human rights law and would have breached the right to a fair hearing due to a lack of impartiality and independence had there not been an ultimate right of appeal to the Privy Council, which conducted a complete rehearing of the case (*Preiss v General Dental Council* [2001] IRLR 696, PC). By extension, it may be possible to argue that employees accused of disciplinary offences which could affect their ability to carry out a particular kind of work (for example, those employees in financial services for whom regulatory approval is required) should also be covered.

Decision

Unless the case is particularly **straightforward**, the hearing should be adjourned before a decision is reached. This allows any further investigation to be completed, and a proper consideration of all the matters raised. The employee should be told about the result of any further investigations, and should be given the opportunity to respond if relevant. If the facts are disputed, the manager conducting the hearing should decide which version is the most probable. **6625**

If the employee is found to have committed an offence, before imposing a disciplinary sanction, the **employer should consider** (s 1 para 17 DG Code): **6626**
- the gravity of the offence, and whether the disciplinary procedure indicates what the likely penalty will be as a result of the offence in question;
- the penalty imposed in similar cases in the past (although each case must be considered on its merits and its own facts);
- any mitigating circumstances (e.g. health, domestic problems, provocation, ignorance of the rule or inconsistent treatment in the past);
- the employee's disciplinary record, employment history, age, position and length of service; and
- whether the proposed penalty is reasonable in all the circumstances.

The employer **should not consider** any further allegations which were not addressed at the investigation/disciplinary hearing stages, as this would be contrary to natural justice (and may be a breach of the employer's own procedures) (*Barros D'Sa v University Hospital Coventry and Warwickshire NHS Trust* [2001] IRLR 691, CA). Since it is not open to a disciplinary panel to find an employee guilty of matters which go beyond the charge originally put to him, it is important that the employer takes care, when formally framing the disciplinary charge, to ensure that it is framed precisely and accurately (*Strouthos v London Underground Ltd* [2005] IRLR 636, CA).

The employer can consider **previous warnings** given for other reasons in deciding whether to dismiss. The significance that can be given to **previous unrelated warnings** will depend on the particular case (*Auguste Noel Ltd v Curtis* [1990] IRLR 326, EAT). **6627**

EXAMPLE In *Auguste Noel Ltd v Curtis*, C was given a final warning in October 1987 concerning his relationship with other employees, and a final warning in February 1988 for unsatisfactory documentation and absenteeism. In March 1988, the employers dismissed him for mishandling company property. The EAT held that his employer was entitled to take into account the existence of the warnings, how many there had been, the substance of the complaint on each occasion, and the dates and periods between them, as long as to do so was fair and just in the circumstances.

Once a decision has been reached, the **meeting or hearing** should be **reconvened**. The employee should be given the **following information**: **6628**
- the decision, the reason for it, and the penalty;
- how long any warning given will last and the consequences of further misconduct;

– where improvement is required, what is expected, over what period, and how it will be assessed; and
– the procedure and timescale for lodging an appeal.

The above information should also be **notified in writing** to the employee in all cases other than oral warning, with a copy being kept on his personnel file. The letter should ideally be handed to the employee, who should be asked to sign a copy acknowledging receipt. If this cannot be achieved for any reason, a note should be placed on the personnel file, and a copy of the written notification sent to the employee's home address by recorded delivery.

3. Sanctions

6630 The factors the employer should consider when deciding on the appropriate sanction are discussed above. The following disciplinary sanctions are available (s 1 paras 19-25 DG Code):
a. formal oral warning;
b. first written warning;
c. final written warning;
d. penalties short of dismissal; and
e. dismissal (with or without notice).

Small organisations may be justified in foregoing one of the first two stages of the warning process. In any case, it is advisable for the procedures to state expressly that the employer **reserves the right** to implement the procedure at any stage if the employee's conduct warrants such action.

Warnings

6631 If the employer is contemplating disciplining the employee by issuing an oral or written warning, then the minimum statutory requirements will not apply and the employer will be free to follow a disciplinary procedure which does not meet the minimum requirements (reg 2(1) SI 2004/752). It is nevertheless advisable that the employer observes at least the principles of best practice to try to ensure that any disciplinary action taken is fair and reasonable.

Minor offences will usually merit a **formal oral warning**, in which case the employee should be informed that a note that it was given will be kept for reference purposes.

In more serious cases, or in the case of several minor offences, a **first written warning** should be given.

Where the matter is more serious still, or in the case of further misconduct (where the employee has received a previous warning), a **final written warning** may be given, together with a statement setting out what the consequences of recurrence of the offence would be. This should only be given once the employee has had an opportunity to present his case at a meeting with the employer (s 1 para 24 DG Code). The final written warning should provide the employee with details of, and the grounds for, the complaint and should warn the employee that if there is no improvement in his conduct, he may be subject to further disciplinary action, including dismissal. The employee should also be informed of the right to appeal against the warning (s 1 para 24 DG Code).

MEMO POINTS Employers should consider carefully whether a disciplinary offence justifies the imposition of a final written warning, since the **disproportionate use** of such a warning for a minor offence could constitute a fundamental breach of the employee's contract, entitling him to resign and claim constructive dismissal (*Stanley Cole (Wainfleet) Ltd v Sheridan* [2003] IRLR 52, EAT; see also ¶8230).

6632 **Spent warnings** Unless special agreed circumstances apply, a disciplinary warning should normally be disregarded for disciplinary purposes after a **specified period** of satisfactory conduct, which should be established when the disciplinary procedure is being drawn up. In general, warnings for **minor offences** should be disregarded after a maximum of 6 months, whilst final warnings may remain in force for 12 months or more.

In cases of **serious misconduct** (which verges on gross misconduct), it may be justifiable for disciplinary warnings to remain "live". In such circumstances, the employee should be told that the warning will remain active, and that any recurrence will/may lead to dismissal. If an employee's conduct or performance lapses soon after a warning expires, the employer should take this lapse into account when deciding how long any new warning should last.

Although a spent warning will be disregarded for disciplinary purposes, a record of it may be kept on file (¶6645).

Penalties short of dismissal

Provided these penalties are allowed for in the contract (for example, in disciplinary rules which have been incorporated), instead of, or following, a final written warning, the employer could consider imposing a penalty short of dismissal, such as **disciplinary transfer**, **disciplinary suspension without pay** (but only for such period as the contract permits, which must also be reasonable in the circumstances), **demotion**, **loss of seniority**, or **loss of salary increment**. If an employer is considering such penalties, the statutory disciplinary procedure will apply and he must follow Steps 1, 2 and 3 of this procedure (¶6560) and should consider adopting the best practice guidelines which complement the statutory minimum requirements. 6633

Note that if there is **no contractual right** to impose such penalties, then any demotion or other such penalties may amount to a fundamental **breach of contract**, allowing the employee to resign and claim that he has been constructively dismissed (*Hilton v Shiner Ltd – Builders Merchants* [2001] IRLR 727, EAT).

Dismissal

The **final disciplinary sanction** will be dismissal. 6634

If an employer is **contemplating dismissing** an employee which he asserts to be based wholly or mainly on the employee's conduct or capability, the statutory disciplinary procedure will apply and he must follow Steps 1, 2 and 3 of the procedure (¶6560) and should consider adopting the best practice guidelines which complement the statutory requirements. A modified procedure is available in certain circumstances (¶6640). 6635

Failure by the employer to comply with an applicable statutory procedure will result in the dismissal being automatically unfair (s 98A(1) ERA 1996) (although the employee will still have to satisfy the general qualifying conditions for unfair dismissal – ¶8410) and the employee being awarded a minimum basic award of 4 weeks' pay (this will be subject to the statutory cap – ¶2920) (¶6514).

The standard procedure must be followed in every case where an employer contemplates dismissing an employee and will cover all **types of dismissal**, including dismissals on the grounds of conduct or capability, redundancy, compulsory retirement and expiry of a fixed term contract which is not renewed (¶1996). 6636

In the case of **compulsory retirement** dismissals, the procedures need only be followed where an employee has been made redundant on the grounds of age in circumstances where he could claim unfair dismissal in respect of his retirement (i.e. before the normal retirement age for that job or before 65 (where there is no normal retirement age for that job)). However, if the retirement is by mutual consent, the procedures do not apply.

MEMO POINTS It is expected that direct and indirect age discrimination will become unlawful from 1 October 2006. The proposed legislation will have wide-ranging ramifications on a number of employment policies and practices, including dismissal and retirement (a summary of the proposed legislation is at ¶5254 +).

The following types of dismissal are **exempt from** the **statutory procedure** (reg 4 SI 2004/752):
– dismissals where **all the employees of a particular description** or in a category to which the employee belongs are dismissed, provided that the employer (or his successor or an associated employer) offers to **re-engage** all the dismissed employees either before or on the termination of their contracts;

– a dismissal which is one of a number of dismissals **in respect of which the duty to consult representatives** when proposing to make a certain number of collective redundancies applies (¶8916);
– if at the time of his dismissal, the employee is taking part in **strike or other industrial action** which is:
· unofficial; or
· neither unofficial nor protected, unless in the circumstances a tribunal would be entitled to determine whether the dismissal was fair or unfair (¶7521);
– if the reason (or, if more than one, the principal reason) for the dismissal is that the employee took **protected industrial action** and the dismissal would be regarded as unfair (¶7521);
– where the **employer's business suddenly ceases to function** because of unforeseen circumstances making it impractical for the employer to continue to employ any employees;
– if the reason (or, if more than one, the principal reason) for the dismissal is that the employee could not continue to work in his position without **acting in breach of legislation** (by either the employer or the employee) (for example, an employee who is employed to be a driver for a company and he loses his licence); or
– if a **dismissal procedures agreement** applies to the employee at the date of dismissal.

It should be noted that the **normal unfair dismissal rules** still apply in all these cases (¶8410).

6637 As a matter of **best practice**, the decision to dismiss an employee must only be taken by a manager who has authority to make such decisions (s 1 para 25 DG Code). This will commonly follow a formal oral warning, a first written warning, and a final written warning. In most cases, dismissal should be the sanction only if, despite warnings, conduct or performance does not improve. However, in some circumstances in may be appropriate to enter the procedure at the written warning or final written warning stage. Dismissals **for a first offence** may be justified in cases of gross misconduct, and also where the employee has made it clear that he is not prepared to alter his attitudes (such that a warning would be futile).

Other than cases of gross misconduct, the employee should receive the appropriate **period of notice** (statutory or contractual, whichever is greater) or payment in lieu of notice.

In exceptional cases, where the misconduct is not so serious as to destroy the relationship of trust and confidence between employer and employee, the employer should consider whether **suitable alternative employment** is available.

6638 If the employer is considering imposing the disciplinary sanction of dismissal, he should decide whether the breach of the particular rule constitutes a fair reason for dismissal, such as conduct (¶8490). If it does, the employer may have a defence to a claim of **unfair dismissal** if he has also followed a fair procedure (¶8500), which will also depend on whether the employee knew that his conduct would merit dismissal (¶6540).

However, simply following the minimum statutory requirements of the standard or modified dismissal and disciplinary procedure will not necessarily be sufficient to ensure that the employer will not be liable if the employee later brings a claim for unfair dismissal. It is recommended that the employer also observe the principles of best practice to reduce the risk of such a claim.

6639 It should be noted that employees with 1 year's service have a right to request a **written statement of reasons** for dismissal (¶8310).

6640 **Gross misconduct** If an employer is considering summarily dismissing an employee for gross misconduct, the **modified statutory procedure** must be followed (Sch 2 Pt 1 Ch 2 EA 2002; see also ¶6565 and ¶8155).

This will **apply** where an employee has been dismissed without notice by reason of his conduct and (reg 3(2) SI 2004/752):
– the dismissal occurred at or immediately after the time the employer became aware of the employee's conduct;
– the employer was entitled to dismiss the employee by reason of his conduct without notice or payment in lieu of notice; and

– it was reasonable for the employer to dismiss the employee before enquiring into the circumstances in which the conduct took place.

However, the modified procedure will **not apply** to a summary dismissal if the employee has presented a complaint relating to the dismissal to an employment tribunal at a time when the employer has not already complied with Step 1 of the modified procedure (reg 3(2) SI 2004/752). In these circumstances, the procedure is deemed not to apply and the employee will be able to bring a claim before a tribunal straight away (provided he has the requisite qualifying service for an unfair dismissal claim).

As a principle of **best practice**, the employer must give employees a clear indication of the type of misconduct that will warrant this sanction, which should only take place after the normal investigation process is completed (¶6540). The employee must still be told of the allegations against him, and given an opportunity to state his case before any decision to summarily dismiss him is taken. 6641

4. Records

In order to ensure consistency in the application of the disciplinary procedure, records of **decisions** should be kept. These should be confidential, and should be retained in accordance with the disciplinary procedure and data protection principles (Data Protection Act 1998; ¶5945). The records should give the following **details**: 6645
- the nature of any offence;
- the employee's defence or mitigation;
- the action taken and the reasons for it;
- whether an appeal was lodged and, if so, the outcome;
- any grievances raised during the disciplinary procedure; and
- any subsequent developments.

Copies of meeting records, including copies of any formal minutes that have been taken at meetings, should be provided to the employee, although in certain circumstances (for example, to protect the anonymity of a witness) an employer will be justified in withholding some information (s 1 para 51 DG Code).

C. Dealing with particular offences

1. Absence

The employer should ensure that employees know who to **notify** (and when) when they are absent from work. In cases of sickness, they should know when self-certification is acceptable, and when a doctor's medical certificate will be required. 6650

The employer should **monitor** absence levels by keeping records showing lateness, and the duration of and reasons for any absences. By examining such records, the employer will be able to identify those employees who are regularly absent, and a pattern may be identifiable, allowing problems to be addressed at an early stage.

Absence on medical grounds (such as injury, disability and illness (s 1 para 38 DG Code)) should be treated as a capability issue, whereas other types of absence may give rise to disciplinary issues. Medical absences should be treated sympathetically (¶4280). When considering how to handle such cases, the employer should consider (s 1 para 38 DG Code): 6651
- **how soon** the employee's health and attendance will improve;
- whether there is **suitable alternative work** available to give him;
- what the **effect** his absence will have on the organisation;

– whether there have been any **other similar cases** and, if so, how they were handled; and
– whether the illness is a result of a **disability**, in which case the employer should bear in mind his statutory obligations not to treat an employee less favourably for a reason relating to or on the ground of his disability, and his duty to make reasonable adjustments to accommodate disabled employees (¶¶5505, 5515, 5550).

6652 If the employee has a record of **frequent self-certified absences** without any medical advice in support, he should be asked to consult a doctor to establish whether any treatment is necessary, and it may be appropriate for the employer to carry out an assessment as to whether the underlying reason is work-related.

Employees suffering from **alcohol or drug addiction** should be encouraged to seek help and treatment. Alcohol or drug abuse and/or possession, on the other hand, will give rise to disciplinary issues. The employer may have a policy specifically aimed at dealing with such issues (¶¶4960, 9957).

6653 In some cases, an employee may suffer from a medical condition that makes him **unacceptable to fellow employees**, who may threaten or even take industrial action or otherwise bring pressure on the employer to dismiss. Such action/pressure will not be taken into account by an employment tribunal when assessing the fairness of a dismissal, so the employer must consider all relevant factors, as he will not be able to rely on disruption to production caused by industrial action to justify his decision (s 107 ERA 1996).

6654 Where the absence arises from the taking care of dependants, the employer should respect the employee's right to take reasonable time off (¶4740).

6655 All **unexpected absences** should be investigated promptly, and the employee asked to give an explanation. If there are no acceptable reasons for the absence, the matter should be treated as a conduct issue, and dealt with under the disciplinary procedure, in which case the employee should be told what improvement in attendance is expected, and warned of the likely consequences of failure to improve (s 1 para 37 DG Code). If there is no improvement, the employer should take into account the following factors when deciding the appropriate action:
– the employee's age, length of service, and performance;
– the likelihood of an improvement in attendance;
– the availability of suitable alternative work; and
– the effect of past and future absences on the business.

Persistent absence must be dealt with promptly, firmly, and consistently to show the employee (and staff in general) that absence is regarded as a serious matter and may result in dismissal.

6656 If an employee takes **holiday without authorisation**, or fails to return from holiday or a period of extended leave on the agreed date, the disciplinary procedure (including a full investigation) should be applied in the usual way.

Before deciding to dismiss an employee in these circumstances, the employer must take into account the employee's age, length of service, past attendance record, and any explanation put forward by him.

2. Poor performance

6660 Employees are contractually obliged to perform to a satisfactory level (¶1202). Employers should set **realistic and measurable standards** of performance for the job. Careful **recruitment and selection** will minimise the risk of poor performance, as the employer should carefully explain the required standards (and the consequences of failing to meet them) to employees at the outset of the employment (or promotion), and ensure that job descriptions convey the main purpose and scope of the job and the tasks involved.

Proper **training and supervision** are key to the achievement of satisfactory performance, and employers should give employees help and encouragement to reach the required standards.

Performance should be discussed on a regular basis, either informally or formally, by means of **appraisal or performance management** systems (¶6465).

Performance should be monitored closely during any **probation period** (¶940).

If an employee **fails to perform** to the required standard, the matter should be investigated to ascertain the reason for the poor performance (s 1 para 8 DG Code). 6661

Reason	Action
External factors, e.g. market forces affecting sales figures	not disciplinary issue
Change in nature of job	consider whether to treat as redundancy, rather than capability or conduct
Lack of required skills	where practicable, assistance through training/coaching, monitoring of performance, and reasonable time to reach required standard. If no improvement, consider disciplinary procedure
Sickness/disability	treat sympathetically as non-disciplinary, capability issue
Negligence or lack of application	disciplinary action through normal procedure or separate capability procedure

If the **matter is a disciplinary one**, the employer should normally issue a **warning**, and give the employee an opportunity to improve by setting a reasonable target and timescale (*Polkey v A E Dayton Services Ltd* [1987] IRLR 503, HL). 6662

An employee should only be dismissed for poor performance, **without previous warnings**, if the actual or potential consequences of his single, negligent error are, or could be, extremely serious (for example, pilot error endangering passengers) (*Taylor v Alidair Ltd* [1978] IRLR 82, CA). The disciplinary procedure should indicate that such cases may result in summary dismissal (s 1 para 56 DG Code).

Nevertheless, if an employer is considering dismissing or taking other disciplinary action against an employee which the employer asserts to be based wholly or mainly on the employee's capability, then depending on the circumstances, either the standard or modified **statutory procedures** must be followed.

There are no set rules as to the **period for improvement**, and the time will depend on the particular employee, his status, position, service, past performance, and the degree to which he is underperforming.

The **number of warnings** given in a particular case will depend on the levels of improvement required and on the seniority of the employee involved. **More senior employees** may be expected to have the necessary experience for their position, and so the employer may consider that only one warning is appropriate. Only in rare cases will an act of incapability justify immediate dismissal without warning.

The employer may need to put in place special arrangements for employees on **short-term contracts** and **probationary employees**, as the term of their contract or probation period may not accommodate the employer's usual warning procedures. 6663

Performance should be monitored and a review meeting scheduled (s 1 para 19 DG Code). 6664

If the employee **fails to improve** despite warnings and/or additional training, the employer should consider moving him to a suitable alternative job, if available and if provided for by the contract. Otherwise, this variation may require the employee's consent. A failure to consider alternative positions may render a dismissal unfair.

Demotion could be considered where provided for by the contract.

If there is no suitable alternative position, the employer may be justified in **dismissing** the employee. He should ensure that he acts fairly in all the circumstances and that he follows the minimum statutory requirements of the dismissal and disciplinary procedure (¶6560).

6665 The employer may be tempted to **penalise poor performance** by making a deduction from the employee's pay. However, employees are protected from **unlawful pay deductions** and compulsory payments (¶3050) and employers should ensure that any variation to an employee's contractual pay (for example, as a result of a demotion) is agreed to by the employee.

6666 **Records** A note of any discussions with the employee, and the decisions reached, should be kept.

D. Special cases

Trade union officials

6670 Normal disciplinary standards should apply to employees acting as trade union officials. However, if they are the subject of disciplinary proceedings, the circumstances of the case should be discussed with a senior trade union representative or full-time official before any disciplinary action beyond an oral warning is taken (s 1 para 42 DG Code). Otherwise, the action may be seen as an attack on the union's functions, which may lead to a serious dispute.

Criminal charges or convictions outside employment

6671 If an employee is charged with, or convicted of, an offence, the employer will need to consider the facts of the case and decide whether the employee's conduct should be treated as a formal disciplinary matter. The disciplinary procedure should only be implemented if the charge or offence **relates** (directly or indirectly) **to the employee's job** (i.e. it must affect the employer's business or undermine his confidence in the employee). The employer should take into account the nature of the offence, and the position and type of work carried out by the employee (including whether this involves contact with other employees or the public).

Off-duty conduct that has **no bearing on the employment** will not justify disciplinary action unless it is within the band of responses of a reasonable employer.

6672 An employee charged with a criminal offence is not necessarily guilty of it and he should not be dismissed solely because a **charge is pending**, even where he is employed in a sensitive post (*Securicor Guarding Ltd v R* [1994] IRLR 633, EAT). A **spent conviction** (¶616) will not provide proper grounds for dismissal (*Property Guards Ltd v Taylor and Kershaw* [1982] IRLR 175, EAT). On the other hand, **acquittal** of a criminal charge does not make any subsequent disciplinary action based on the same event illegal (*Saeed v Greater London Council (Inner London Education Authority)* [1986] IRLR 23, QBD).

6673 Any disciplinary decision should be made on a reasonable belief following a reasonable **investigation** into the circumstances of the case. The employer does not have to establish the employee's guilt by means of his own independent investigation but can rely on a **court decision** or the **verdict of a jury** (*P v Nottingham County Council* [1992] IRLR 362, CA; *The Post Office v Liddiard* [2001] EWCA Civ 940, CA), although he should still follow a fair procedure, including giving the employee an opportunity to explain his conduct. The **police** should not be asked to conduct any investigation on behalf of the employer, nor should they be present at any disciplinary hearing or interview (*Read v Phoenix Preservation Society* [1985] IRLR 93, EAT).

The employer should not postpone taking disciplinary action merely because the **outcome of the prosecution** is not known. Further, the disciplinary penalty should not depend on the outcome of any criminal trial.

The employee may be advised by his lawyer that taking part in a disciplinary investigation or hearing may prejudice the outcome of criminal proceedings. If the employee **refuses to co-operate** with the employer's disciplinary procedure, the employer should advise him in writing that unless he co-operates, a disciplinary decision will be taken on the basis of the information available, and could result in dismissal. The employer will then need to consider whether the evidence available to him is strong enough to justify a disciplinary warning or dismissal. Failure to comply with an applicable statutory procedure will result in a reduction in any compensation that the employee may be awarded if he subsequently brings a claim before a tribunal (¶6516).

If the employee will be absent from work while in **custody or on remand**, the employer must consider whether his job can be kept open during that time (this is not a disciplinary matter). If it is unlikely that the employee will be able to return to the job, it may be argued that the contract of employment has been frustrated, in which case there will be no dismissal (the contract terminates by operation of law). This argument may be accepted where the frustrating event (i.e. the imprisonment) makes performance of the contract clearly impossible (¶8285). **6674**

If the employee **loses a licence** (for example, his driving licence) as a result of a conviction such that continued employment in a particular job will be illegal, the employer should consider whether suitable alternative work is available.

The employer should not **automatically dismiss** the employee merely because of the charge or offence, or because of absence from work as a result of being remanded in custody. Dismissal will only be justified if this sanction is within the band of responses of a reasonable employer (¶8435), which will be the case where the offence is one that makes the employee unsuitable for his type of work (in which case the normal disciplinary rules and procedure should be followed). **6675**

As in the case of sickness-related absence discussed above (¶6650) the employer cannot rely on **pressure to dismiss** to justify the dismissal.

EXAMPLE 1. In *The Post Office v Liddiard* (¶6673), L was convicted of **football hooliganism**. Due to press coverage, the Post Office claimed that he had brought it into disrepute and therefore dismissed him. The Court held that misconduct unconnected to the workplace could justify dismissal if this sanction was within the band of responses of a reasonable employer.

2. In *Norfolk County Council v Bernard* [1979] IRLR 220, EAT, B, a drama teacher, was convicted of **possession of cannabis**. The EAT held that, in the circumstances, the dismissal was unfair.

3. In *Nottinghamshire County Council v Bowly* [1978] IRLR 252, EAT, B was convicted of a **sexual offence**. The dismissal was held to be fair.

4. In *Moore v C & A Modes* [1981] IRLR 71, EAT, M, a section leader in a retail store, was fairly dismissed after 20 years' service after being caught **shoplifting** in another store.

Isolated employees

The employer will need to give special consideration to the handling of disciplinary matters in the case of employees to whom the full procedure may not be immediately available, such as **nightshift** workers and employees in **isolated workplaces** (s 1 para 41 DG Code). For example, the employer could allow the employee paid time off so that he can attend a disciplinary hearing on the main site during normal working hours. Alternatively, if a number of the employee's colleagues need to attend as witnesses, it may be more practical to hold the hearing on the nightshift or at the employee's site. **6676**

E. Appeal procedure

Under both the standard and the modified **statutory dismissal and disciplinary procedure**, the employee is given the right to appeal against the decision to dismiss or take disciplinary action. The appeal stage is **Step 3** of the standard procedure and **Step 2** of the modified procedure. It is also a principle of **best practice** that employees who have had disciplinary action taken against them must be given an opportunity to appeal (s 1 para 44 DG Code). **6680**

Failure to appeal by an employee against the decision to dismiss him or take disciplinary action against him under the statutory procedure will normally reduce any compensation he might be awarded by the tribunal (¶6516).

An employee may wish to appeal a disciplinary decision on the **grounds** that he considers it to be unfair, the penalty too severe, or the disciplinary procedure defective, or he may wish to put forward new evidence.

6681 The appeal hearing may impact on the **date of dismissal** (¶8340).

1. Formulation

6685 As a matter of **best practice**, an opportunity to appeal against a disciplinary decision is essential to natural justice (s 1 para 59 DG Code). It is recommended that the appeal procedure should (s 1 paras 44-47 DG Code):
– provide for appeals to be dealt with as promptly as possible (a time limit for hearing the appeal should be set);
– specify any time limit within which the appeal must be lodged (this may vary between organisations but 5 working days is usually appropriate);
– provide for the appeal to be heard by a manager or managers who has/have not previously been involved in the disciplinary procedure (although this may not be possible in small organisations, in which case the person dealing with the appeal should act as impartially as possible); and
– specify the action which may be taken by the person dealing with the appeal.

2. Operation

Appeal hearing

6690 The employer must observe the statutory minimum requirements of the applicable dismissal and disciplinary procedure set out above (¶6560). If the employer takes the action below, he will have satisfied the minimum criteria required to meet **Step 3** of the standard and **Step 2** of the modified dismissal and disciplinary procedure. In addition, by observing these principles of best practice, he will reduce the risk of tribunal proceedings being brought against him in respect of the dismissal or disciplinary action he takes.

6691 As a matter of **best practice**, the employee should be informed of the **arrangements** for appeal hearings, including his statutory right to be accompanied (¶6780), and any other rights under the procedure (s 1 para 47 DG Code) These arrangements will be similar to those for the disciplinary hearing (¶6610). When preparing for the hearing, the employer should ensure that the relevant records are available. The person hearing the appeal should review these documents in advance of the hearing.

6692 It must be decided whether the appeal is a re-hearing or review. A **review** will be appropriate only where there is no new evidence and no question of there being any defects in the procedure to date, for example, where the employee does not dispute his guilt but feels that the penalty imposed is too harsh. A **re-hearing** will be appropriate in most other cases, in particular where there is new evidence or to remedy any defect in the earlier procedure. If there is any doubt, the appeal hearing should proceed as a re-hearing, as this may impact on the fairness of the dismissal (¶8500).

6693 The person/manager **conducting** the appeal should:
– introduce those present to the employee, explain the purpose of the hearing (i.e. whether it is a review or a re-hearing), how it will be conducted and what powers the appeal panel has;
– ask the employee to state the grounds of the appeal; and
– allow the employee, or his representative, the opportunity to comment on any new evidence.

As for the disciplinary hearing, the manager should deal with all the relevant issues, summarising them when concluding the hearing, and adjourn the hearing in order to consider the appropriate decision.

If an employee (or his companion – ¶6786) **cannot attend** a meeting, he must inform the employer in advance whenever possible (s 1 para 16 DG Code). See ¶6612 for a discussion on the consequences under the statutory procedure of one of the parties being unable to attend the appeal hearing. 6694

Decision

When deciding whether to uphold or revoke the disciplinary decision, the appeal panel should take into account the same **considerations** as applied to the earlier decision (¶6625), and also consider the reasons for that decision, if available, and any new evidence put forward by the employee. 6695

It is recommended that the appeal panel should not impose a penalty which is more severe than that being appealed. The appeal panel should not hesitate to **overturn a previous decision** where it is clear that it was incorrect, and impose a lesser penalty. If this action is taken, it will be useful for the matter to be subsequently discussed with the manager who took the disciplinary decision, and to consider whether further training of that manager is called for.

The appeal panel cannot find that the dismissal was **justified**, but for a **different reason** than that previously relied on, as the fairness of any dismissal is judged in the light of the reason relied on at the time of the dismissal (*Monie v Coral Racing Ltd* [1980] IRLR 464, CA). If the appeal panel finds that dismissal is justified but on **different grounds**, the original dismissal should not stand. To ensure that he acts fairly, the employer must look at the matter afresh in order to decide whether a subsequent dismissal on the new information is appropriate. 6696

New information which comes to light after the dismissal can be considered at the appeal stage to decide whether the decision to dismiss for the stated reason should stand (*The Board of Governors, The National Heart & Chest Hospitals v Nambiar* [1981] IRLR 196, EAT). 6697

EXAMPLE In *The Board of Governors, The National Heart & Chest Hospitals v Nambiar*, N twice refused to comply with a lawful order from his employer, and walked out of work. During the disciplinary investigation, N claimed that he had refused because of pressure or work. His employer rejected his claim and dismissed him with pay in lieu of notice. N appealed and presented new evidence (medical reports) to the internal appeal panel, which sought further expert medical opinion as to the cause of his conduct. The appeal panel upheld the decision to dismiss, but recommended that, in the light of the new evidence, the employer should seek to employ N in suitable alternative work, if available. N refused offers of other work and claimed unfair dismissal. The EAT held that N was not unfairly dismissed as, on the basis of all the evidence, the internal appeal tribunal had acted reasonably in recommending that he should not be reinstated to his original post.

The employee should be informed of the **outcome** of the appeal and the reasons for the decision as soon as possible (s 1 para 48 DG Code). The employee should also be informed if the decision constitutes the final stage in the appeal procedure. This information should be confirmed in writing, and the employee should be asked to acknowledge receipt. Where he refuses to do so, a note should be made on the personnel file, and the **written notification** sent to his home address by recorded delivery. 6698

Effect on tribunal claims

The employee may accept the outcome of the appeal decision or he may wish to make a tribunal claim, with or without instigating an internal appeal. When bringing a claim, he must comply with the relevant time limits. 6699

Time limits When bringing an employment tribunal claim, the employee should usually do so within the normal time limits (¶9450). This is usually 3 months from the date of the act or omission complained of. The tribunal has a continuing discretion to extend these time limits in certain circumstances (¶9465). 6700

With regard to cases where **no statutory procedure applies** (¶6511), if an **internal appeal** is **still in progress** as the time limit for bringing an employment claim approaches, it is advisable for the employee to consider preserving his position by presenting a claim with a request that the matter not be set down for hearing until the internal appeal has been completed.
However, if a **statutory procedure applies**, the regulations make provision for workplace discussions to continue without obliging employees to submit premature tribunal claims to avoid missing the relevant deadlines. See ¶9479 for further details.

6705 **Failure to appeal** A failure to appeal against dismissal does not amount to an acceptance that the dismissal was fair (the employee can still bring a claim of unfair dismissal (*Chrystie v Rolls-Royce (1971) Ltd* [1976] IRLR 336, EAT)) and will merely be of **evidential value** as to the employee's attitude at the time of dismissal.

EXAMPLE In *Chrystie v Rolls-Royce (1971) Ltd*, C was asked to attend a disciplinary hearing after he had assaulted a fellow employee. He failed to attend and the employers sent him a letter of dismissal. This letter crossed in the post with a letter from C, explaining that he had been ill and giving his account of the incident. The employers nevertheless allowed the dismissal to stand. The EAT rejected the argument that C had acquiesced in his dismissal by failing to appeal, and accepted that his dismissal had been unfair.

6706 If a **statutory procedure** applies but the **employee fails to appeal**, the amount of compensation which a tribunal can award him if he subsequently brings a successful claim under one of the jurisdictions set out at ¶9985 must be reduced by between 10 and 50% (s 31(2) EA 2002; see ¶6516). Similarly if the **employer fails to allow** the employee to complete the statutory procedure, the tribunal must likewise increase any award which it makes to the employee by between 10 and 50% (s 31(3) EA 2002; see ¶6516).

6707 If the **employer prevents the employee** from exercising a **contractual right of appeal**, the dismissal may be held to be unfair (*West Midlands Co-operative Society Ltd v Tipton* [1986] IRLR 112, HL). This will depend on whether the employee was thereby denied the opportunity of showing that the employer's real reason for the dismissal could not reasonably be treated as a sufficient one for the statutory test of fairness (*Westminster City Council v Cabaj* [1996] IRLR 399, CA).

MEMO POINTS See ¶8436 for a further discussion on the impact of procedural defects on the fairness of a dismissal in unfair dismissal claims.

SECTION 2

Grievance procedures

6730 Under the statutory dispute resolution procedures, a grievance is defined as a complaint by an employee about action (including any act or omission) which his employer has taken or is contemplating taking in relation to him (reg 2(1) SI 2004/752). A grievance procedure is a process whereby an employee's concerns, problems or complaints on a particular issue are raised and addressed. If grievances are not dealt with, or are badly handled, the situation may deteriorate, and may lead to poor performance, resignations, complaints to tribunals or courts (including constructive dismissal claims), and possibly a wider dispute with employees in general.

6731 Not only is it a matter of good employment practice for employers to have grievance procedures in place so that grievances can be dealt with fairly, consistently and efficiently (s 2 para 65 DG Code) but a **compulsory statutory grievance procedure** must also be implemented. Depending on the circumstances, either a standard (three-step) or modified (two-step) procedure applies in relation to any grievance about action by the employer that could form the basis of a complaint by an employee to a tribunal under one of the jurisdictions set out at ¶¶9985-6.

The statutory procedure contains **minimum requirements** that must be met in respect of any grievance raised by an employee where the grievance continues on or after 1 October 2004 (ss 29-34, Sch 2-4 EA 2002; SI 2004/752).

The statutory procedure will **not apply** to grievances where (reg 6(4), (5) SI 2004):
- the employee has already raised a grievance about such action before 1 October 2004; or
- neither the standard nor the modified procedure has been started and the employee is no longer employed and it is no longer reasonably practicable for him to comply with Step 1 of the statutory procedure;
- the grievance is that the employer has dismissed or is contemplating dismissing the employee (¶6581) or that the employer has taken or is contemplating taking disciplinary action against the employee except in certain circumstances (¶6582).

There is an **implied term** that an employee's grievances will be promptly and properly dealt with. It is also important to bear in mind the **general requirements** applicable to the statutory dispute resolution procedures which stipulate that each action and step under the procedure must be taken without unreasonable delay (Sch 2 Pt 3 EA 2002; ¶6513). 6732

An employee has a statutory **right to be accompanied** at grievance hearings (¶6780). 6733

Issues that may be the subject of employees' grievances include (s 2 para 92 DG Code): 6734
- terms and conditions of employment;
- health and safety;
- relationships at work;
- bullying and harassment;
- new working practices;
- organisational change; or
- equal opportunities.

An employee may also have a grievance in relation to the **operation of the disciplinary procedure**. Any action taken (or contemplated being taken) by an employer in relation to the employee will fall under either the dismissal and disciplinary procedure or the grievance procedure, but **not both** (see ¶6580 for circumstances in which each procedure will apply). However, the DTI guidance provides that the statements and meetings made under either one of the procedures can be multi-purpose and can be used for either the disciplinary or grievance procedure. 6735

It is advisable for the grievance procedure to be **non-contractual**. If the procedure is **contractual** and the employer fails to comply with even a minor part of it, the employee may have grounds to resign and claim constructive dismissal (¶8230). Note that there are other consequences of failing to comply with the statutory grievance procedure. For further details, see ¶6514. 6736

MEMO POINTS For the time being, the Government has decided not to make the new statutory dispute resolution procedures **an implied contractual term** and has put on hold the coming into force date of the relevant statutory provision (s 30 EA 2002) in order to see how the new regulations work in practice.

1. Formulation

A grievance procedure should be formulated to incorporate not only the statutory minimum requirements set out in the regulations but also the principles of best practice laid down by the DG Code and other government guidance. 6739

Statutory grievance procedure

The **standard** statutory grievance procedure is set out below (Sch 2 Pt 2 Ch 1 EA 2002). These three steps set out the minimum requirements that must be met in order for the statutory grievance procedure to be completed. 6740

STEP 1: STATEMENT OF GRIEVANCE	– Employee must **set out in writing** his grievance. – Employee must **send the statement** (or a copy of it) to the employer.
STEP 2: MEETING	– **Employer must invite** the employee to attend a meeting to discuss the grievance. – The meeting can **only take place** if: a. the employee has informed the employer what the basis for the grievance was when he made the statement; and b. the employer has had a reasonable opportunity to consider his response to that information. – Employee must take **all reasonable steps** to attend the meeting. – He has a right to be accompanied to the meeting by a companion (¶6780). – After the meeting, employer must **inform** the employee of his decision as to his response to the grievance and **notify him of the right to appeal** against the decision if he is not satisfied with it.
STEP 3: APPEAL	– If he wishes to appeal against the decision, **employee must inform** the employer. – If the employee informs the employer of his wish to appeal, the employer must **invite** him to attend a further meeting. – After the appeal meeting, **employer must inform** employee of his final decision.

MEMO POINTS The Step 1 requirement for the employee to send to the employer a statement of grievance will not be satisfied by the employee simply sending his employer a **discrimination or equal pay questionnaire** under the equal pay, sex, racial, disability, religion or belief or sexual orientation discrimination legislation (reg 14 SI 2004/752; see ¶5711 for information on discrimination and equal pay questionnaires generally).

6745 In certain circumstances, a **modified procedure** will apply (Sch 2 Pt 2 Ch 2 EA 2002). See ¶6760.

STEP 1: STATEMENT OF GRIEVANCE	– Employee to **set out in writing**: a. the grievance; and b. the basis for it. – Employee to **send the statement** (or a copy of it) to employer.
STEP 2: RESPONSE	– Employer must set out his **response in writing** and **send the statement** (or a copy of it) to the employee.

6750 **Deemed compliance** It should be noted that in certain circumstances, the statutory grievance procedures will be deemed to have been complied with even if not all of the minimum requirements have been met. In these circumstances, since the statutory procedures are still applicable, the parties may be granted an **extension of the time limits** to complete the procedure to avoid the employee presenting a premature claim to the tribunal (¶9479).

This **applies** where (regs 8-10 SI 2004/752):

– the employee has **ceased to be employed** and under the standard procedure the employee has complied with Step 1 (whether before or after the end of his employment) but since his employment ended, it has **ceased to be reasonably practicable** for the employee, or the employer, to comply with Steps 2 or 3 (reg 8(1) SI 2004/752). Note that in such circumstances where the requirements of Step 2 of the standard grievance procedure have been complied with, but the employer has not informed the employee of his decision in response to the grievance and notified him of the right to appeal, the employer shall be **treated as having failed to comply** with that requirement **unless** he informs the employee in writing of his decision as to his response to the grievance (reg 8(2) SI 2004/752);

– an appropriate representative has raised in writing a **collective grievance** and has specified in writing to the employer (whether in setting out the grievance or otherwise) the names of at least two employees, of whom one is the employee having the grievance, as being the employees on behalf of whom he is raising the collective grievance (reg 9(1) SI 2004/752); or
– at the time the employee raises his grievance, there is a **collectively agreed procedure** in operation made between two or more employers or an employers' association and one or more independent trade unions, that provides for employees of the employer to raise grievances about the behaviour of the employer and have them considered and the employee is entitled to raise his grievance under that procedure and does so (reg 10 SI 2004/752).

MEMO POINTS An **appropriate representative** can be (reg 9(2)(a), (b) SI 2004/752):
– an official of an independent trade union recognised by the employer for the purposes of collective bargaining in respect of a description of employees that includes the employee having the grievance (¶7200); or
– an employee representative elected or appointed by employees consisting of or including employees of the same description as the employee having the grievance and who, having regard to the purposes for which and method by which he was elected or appointed, has the authority to represent employees of that description under an established procedure for resolving grievances agreed between employee representatives and the employer.

Best practice

The **aim** of a good procedure is to deal with the employee's grievance quickly, fairly, and at the lowest possible level within the organisation. 6755

Senior management is **responsible** for developing the organisation's grievance procedure, but this cannot be done effectively without the input of employees and their representatives (including trade unions, where recognised), and of the levels of management responsible for the procedure's operation (s 2 para 90 DG Code).

Grievance procedures **should be** (s 2 para 91 DG Code):
– simple;
– in writing;
– enable an employee's line manager to deal informally with a grievance if possible; and
– allow the employee to be accompanied by a companion at meetings.

They should also be rapid in operation and confidential.

The employer should ensure that all employees are **aware of and understand** the procedure, with every employee being given his own copy or provided with access to it (for example, by including it in the staff handbook or by putting it on the company intranet) (s 2 para 94 DG Code). This may be covered as part of an induction programme, with explanations of the procedures being given as required (¶926). 6756

Special allowance should be made for individuals whose **first language is not English** or who have a **visual impairment** or some **other disability** (see also ¶5515).

2. Operation

If the employee's grievance is of a routine nature, it may best be resolved **informally** by discussion with his immediate line manager, who should keep a note of any such discussion (s 2 para 67 DG Code). Working out an informal solution to the grievance allows issues to be resolved quickly and may be beneficial where there is a close personal relationship between a manager and an employee (s 2 para 67 DG Code). 6757

If the grievance **cannot be resolved informally**, the formal grievance procedure should be implemented. Where an employee has a grievance which continues on or after 1 October 2004 (and the employee has not already raised it as a grievance before this date), a statutory grievance procedure must be followed unless certain exemptions apply (¶6511). 6758

If necessary, supervisors, managers, and employee representatives should be **trained** in the procedure's use.

6759 A failure to take an employee's grievance seriously may itself amount to **discrimination** (¶5829). For example, employers should not ignore or treat lightly grievances from **members of particular racial groups** on the assumption that they are over-sensitive about discrimination.

Further, any action taken against an employee because he has brought a complaint under a grievance procedure may amount to **unlawful victimisation** (¶5240).

6760 **Former employees** All grievances should ideally be dealt with while an employee is still employed (s 1 para 72 DG Code). However, if an employee has left employment, both parties can **agree** in writing that the **modified procedure will apply** provided the employer was (reg 6(3)(a)-(c) SI 2004/752):
– unaware of the grievance before the employee left employment; or
– aware of the grievance before the employee left employment but the employee had not instigated the standard procedure or the parties had not completed the standard procedure before the employee left employment.

6761 **Specific procedures** Some employers may have specific procedures to deal with particularly sensitive issues, such as **discrimination or bullying and harassment** (on grounds of sex, racial group, disability, sexual orientation, religion or belief etc) (¶5800). Where the employer has in place separate procedures for dealing with such issues, these should be used instead of the normal grievance procedure, provided they incorporate the statutory minimum requirements (s 2 paras 85, 93 DG Code). If there is no separate procedure, these issues should, at least, be addressed specifically in the general grievance procedure.

6762 Some employers may have a **whistleblowing** procedure to deal with concerns raised by employees about wrongdoing in their organisation (s 2 para 86 DG Code). This will encourage employees to raise such concerns internally, rather than going directly to a regulatory authority or, for example, the press (¶2700). The statutory procedures will not usually be used by an employee to make a **protected disclosure** under the whistleblowing legislation unless (Sch 2 Part 4 SI 2004/752):
– the information relates to a matter which the employee could raise as a grievance with his employer; and
– it is the intention of the employee that the disclosure should constitute the raising of the matter as a grievance.

6763 If the company has safety representatives and a safety committee, there may be no need for a separate **health and safety** procedure. In their absence, the employer may have such a procedure, so that employees can formally raise any grievances they may have.

Raising the grievance

6764 If the employee takes the following action, he will have satisfied the minimum criteria required to meet **Step 1** of the standard or modified grievance procedure.

6765 Employees should normally **raise** any grievance **with** their immediate line manager unless the employer's procedure indicates that another person in the organisation should be contacted (s 2 para 73 DG Code). The grievance, and the basis for it, should be set out **in writing** and sent to the employer.

If there are any reasons as to why the employee might find setting out his grievance in writing difficult, for example, if his **first language is not English** or if he has **reading difficulties**, he should be encouraged to seek assistance from colleagues, or a trade union or other employee representative (s 2 para 75 DG Code). Moreover, if the employee is **disabled**, the employer should consider whether any reasonable adjustments need to be made to assist him in formulating a written grievance if he is unable to do so by himself (s 2 para 75 DG Code).

If the grievance **concerns the person to whom the complaint would normally be addressed**, then the employee may approach that person's manager or another manager in the organisation. This may prove more difficult for smaller organisations where it may not be possible for a different person to hear the grievance. If this is the case, the person to whom the grievance is addressed should deal with it as impartially as possible.

Grievance meeting

In response to the statement of grievance, if the employer takes the following action, he will have satisfied the minimum criteria required to meet **Step 2** of the standard grievance procedure. 6766

On receipt of the written grievance, the manager concerned must invite the employee to attend a meeting to discuss the grievance as soon as possible and inform him that he has the right to be accompanied should he wish (¶6780). As a matter of good practice, the manager and employee should agree a **mutually convenient** time and location for the meeting where they will not, if possible, be interrupted (s 2 para 77 DG Code).

The meeting can only take place if the employee has informed the employer of the basis for the grievance when the statement was made and if the employer has had a reasonable opportunity to consider his response to the grievance. 6767

The employee must take all reasonable steps to attend the meeting. See ¶6612 for the consequences of either party **failing to attend** a meeting.

At the meeting, the employee should be given the opportunity to explain his complaint and how he would like to see it settled. If it becomes clear to the manager during the course of the meeting that he is not sure how to deal with the grievance or that further investigation is necessary, he should **adjourn** the meeting to seek further advice or make further enquiries (s 2 para 78 DG Code).

Before responding to the grievance, the manager must give the employee's explanation careful consideration.

He should respond in writing to the employee's grievance **within** a reasonable time and inform the employee of his right to appeal against the decision if he is not happy with it. It is usually reasonable for the employer to respond within 5 working days, but if this is not possible, the manager should explain the delay to the employee and inform him of when he can expect a response (s 2 para 81 DG Code).

Note that if the **modified procedure** applies, there will be no meeting and the employer must simply set out his response in writing and send it to the employee in order to fulfil Step 2 of the procedure.

Appeal

If the employee is not satisfied with the decision taken in respect of his grievance, he may wish to exercise his right of appeal. If he takes the following action, he will have satisfied the minimum criteria required to meet **Step 3** of the standard grievance procedure. 6768

The employee should **inform** his employer that he wishes to exercise his right of appeal. In response, the employer must invite the employee to attend a further meeting.

As with disciplinary appeal meetings (¶6680), if possible, the **appeal meeting** should be heard by a more senior manager than the one who heard the original grievance. Where this may prove difficult in smaller organisations, another manager should hear the appeal, if possible. However, if this is not an option, the person to whom the original grievance was raised should deal with the appeal as impartially as possible (s 2 para 82 DG Code).

After the appeal meeting, the employer should write to the employee to inform him of the **outcome** of the appeal meeting as soon as possible and should explain that this is the final stage of the grievance procedure. 6769

Although it is not a requirement of the statutory grievance procedure, in **large organisations**, it is good practice to allow a further (second) appeal to a higher level of management, for example, to a director (s 2 para 84 DG Code).

See ¶6705 for the consequences of **failing to appeal** against the employer's decision in respect of an employee's grievance. 6770

Records

6771 The employer should keep records giving the following details (s 2 para 87 DG Code):
– the nature of the grievance;
– a copy of the written grievance;
– the employer's response;
– any action taken;
– whether there was an appeal and, if so, the outcome; and
– any subsequent developments.

These records should be confidential, and should be retained in accordance with the data protection principles (¶5945). Copies of any meeting records should be given to the employee, although in certain circumstances some information may be withheld (for example, to protect a witness).

Impact of statutory procedures on tribunal claims

6772 For an overview of the impact of the statutory procedures on tribunal claims, see ¶6514. In particular, whether or not the employee has followed through the applicable statutory procedure will have an impact on the admissibility, and time limits for bringing, any subsequent claim in an employment tribunal which concerns the subject of his grievance.

6773 **Admissibility** In respect of complaints about grievances brought under one of the statutory jurisdictions set out at ¶9986, an employee **cannot start tribunal proceedings** in respect of the subject of his grievance **unless** (s 32(2)-(4) EA 2002):
– the employee has first raised a grievance in writing under Step 1 of the applicable statutory procedure and waited a further 28 days or more since he sent the Step 1 letter or note before presenting his tribunal claim; or
– the employee has sent the Step 1 letter to his employer no later than 1 month after the end of the original time limit in circumstances in which the employee has tried to submit a tribunal claim within the normal time limit (¶9480) but his claim has not been accepted by the tribunal on the grounds that he has not put his grievance in writing to his employer or he has not waited a further 28 days or more since sending the Step 1 letter to his employer.

A tribunal cannot consider a claim which breaches the above admissibility requirements if the tribunal is aware of the breach as a result of information supplied to it by the employee or the issue of compliance with the admissibility requirements having been raised by the employer (s 32(6) EA 2002).

MEMO POINTS An **exception** to these admissibility requirements is in respect of claims relating to a breach of contract.

6774 **Time limits** The normal time limits for bringing a tribunal claim will apply (¶9452), although in certain circumstances these time limits may be **automatically extended** to allow a statutory dispute resolution procedure to complete (¶9479).

6775 **Compensation** For an overview of the consequences of either party **failing to comply** with the minimum statutory requirements, see ¶¶6514-16.

SECTION 3

Right to be accompanied

Entitlement

Workers have a statutory right to be accompanied by a single fellow worker or trade union official where they are required or invited by the employer to attend disciplinary or grievance hearings, and reasonably request (orally or in writing) to exercise their right (ss 10-15 ERelA 1999; s 3 DG Code). **6780**

The employer should ensure that his dismissal, disciplinary and grievance procedures provide for the statutory right to be accompanied, and that it is applied at all disciplinary and grievance hearings. This will include the **Step 2 meetings** and **Step 3 appeal meetings** set out in the statutory dispute resolution procedures (¶¶6560, 6740).

This right is in addition to any contractual rights, and applies to all **workers** (¶13), regardless of length of service. For these purposes, the definition specifically includes agency and home workers (s 13 ERelA 1999). Casual, temporary, and part-time workers will also be covered if they meet the general definition of worker.

Type of hearing

A **disciplinary hearing** includes hearings that could result in (s 3 para 97 DG Code): **6781**
– the administration of a formal warning to a worker (i.e. a warning, whether about conduct or capability, that will be placed on the worker's record);
– the taking of some other action in respect of a worker by the employer (for example, suspension without pay, demotion or dismissal); or
– the confirmation of a warning issued or some other action taken (i.e. appeal hearings where a sanction might be endorsed or removed) (s 13(4) ERelA 1999).

The right to be accompanied will also apply to any disciplinary or grievance meetings held as part of the **statutory dismissal**, **disciplinary and grievance procedures**. This includes any meetings after an employee has ceased to be employed (s 3 paras 98, 102 DG Code).

Most formal disciplinary hearings will fall within the definition, although earlier **investigatory** stages in the process will not necessarily be covered.

EXAMPLE In *Skiggs v South West Trains Limited* IRLR 459, EAT, a meeting held to investigate a grievance about an employee who had previously been disciplined did not constitute a disciplinary hearing and the employee was therefore not entitled to be accompanied. It is a question of fact and degree in each case as to whether a preliminary factual inquiry has transformed into a disciplinary hearing.

Informal interviews or **counselling sessions** which do not result in a formal warning or other action will not be disciplinary hearings, and the right to be accompanied will not apply.

However, an **oral warning** which is **subsequently confirmed** in writing and becomes part of a worker's disciplinary record will constitute a formal warning and gives rise to the right to be accompanied (*London Underground Ltd v Ferenc-Batchelor* [2003] IRLR 252, EAT). Likewise, if it becomes clear during an investigative or informal interview that formal disciplinary action may be needed, the interview should be terminated and a formal hearing convened at which the worker will have the right to be accompanied (s 3 para 99 DG Code).

A **grievance hearing** is a hearing which concerns the performance of a duty by an employer in relation to a worker (s 13(5) ERelA 1999), which means a legal duty arising from statute or common law, such as contractual obligations (s 3 para 100 DG Code). It will be up to the courts to decide this question. However, the following examples may assist:

EXAMPLE 1. A worker's request for a pay rise will not amount to a grievance hearing unless it is specifically provided for in the contract, or it raises issues of equal pay.

2. A complaint following refusal of a request for new terms and conditions (for example, a request for car parking facilities) will not amount to a grievance where these are not already provided for in the contract. However, if the complaint is made by a disabled worker who needs such facilities in order to attend work, the employer may be under a statutory duty to the worker, in which case the right to be accompanied would apply.
3. A complaint about the application of a contractual grading or promotional exercise will amount to a grievance.
4. Grievances arising out of day-to-day friction between fellow workers are unlikely to involve breach of a legal duty unless the friction develops into incidents of bullying or harassment, which would give rise to a legal duty of care.

Choice of companion

6782 The worker's companion can be a **fellow worker** (again, a "worker" as defined above), or a **trade union official**, and it is for the worker and not the employer to decide (ss 1, 119 TULRCA 1992; s 10(3) ERelA 1999).

The employment **contract** may extend the category of person who may accompany the worker, for example to include a partner, spouse or legal representative (s 3 para 105 DG Code). For example, if a worker is **disabled**, the employer should consider whether it might be reasonable to allow him to be accompanied by his partner or spouse because of his disability.

MEMO POINTS A companion can only attend in a **union capacity** if he is either a full-time official, or certified by his union as having the necessary experience or training to perform such a role. Workers are free to choose a companion from any union, although where there is a recognised trade union, it is good practice for the union official to be from that union (s 3 para 106 DG Code).

6783 The **employer can refuse** the worker's request to be accompanied if it is not "reasonable". It would not be reasonable for a worker to insist on being accompanied by a colleague (s 3 para 103 DG Code):
– whose presence would prejudice the hearing;
– who might have a conflict of interest; or
– who is located at a geographically remote site when there is someone suitably qualified on site.

6784 The person who the worker chooses as his companion has the **right to refuse to accompany** him (s 3 para 107 DG Code). If he accepts, he has the right to a reasonable amount of **paid time off** during working hours to participate in and prepare for the hearing (¶3910) (s 3 para 109 DG Code; s 10(6) ERelA 1999).

Training

6785 Training will be important both for employers and trade unions (s 3 para 108 DG Code). Managers will need to know and be able to apply the rules and procedures. Unions should ensure their officials are both experienced in performing this role and are provided with periodic refresher training. Organisations may benefit from joint management/trade union training.

Arranging the hearing

6786 The employer is entitled to set the time and date of the hearing. However, it is **good practice** to agree a mutually convenient time and location and, where possible, the companion should have a say in the date and time of a hearing (s 3 para 110 DG Code). Where the **chosen companion cannot attend** on the date proposed, the worker can offer an alternative time and date so long as it is reasonable, and is within the following 5 working days (s 10(4)(5) ERelA 1999; s 3 para 110 DG Code). A "working day" does not include Saturdays, Sundays, Christmas Day, Good Friday, or statutory bank holidays (s 13(6) ERelA 1999).

It may be unreasonable for the worker to propose a new date where he knows that the relevant manager is going to be unavailable, unless another manager could conduct the hearing.

If the companion is **disabled**, the employer should cater for this by considering whether physical adjustments are necessary, in the same way as he would for a worker's disability. 6787

Companion's role

Before the hearing takes place, the worker should inform the employer who his companion will be. In certain circumstances, it may be useful for the companion and employer to make contact before the hearing (for example, where the companion is an official of a non-recognised trade union) (s 3 para 112 DG Code). 6788

The companion has the **right to address** the hearing in order to (s 10(2A)-(2C) ERelA 1999 as amended by s 37 ERelA 2004; s 3 paras 113, 114 DG Code):
- confer with the worker;
- put across the worker's case;
- sum up the worker's case; and
- respond on the worker's behalf to any view expressed at the hearing.

However, the companion has **no right** to (s 3 para 114 DG Code):
- answer questions on the worker's behalf;
- address the hearing if the worker does not want him to; or
- prevent the employer from explaining his case.

Beyond that, it is for the employer to decide the scope of the companion's involvement. Given the importance of his role, it is **good practice** to allow the worker's companion to ask questions and participate as fully as possible.

Enforcement and remedies

A worker can complain to an employment tribunal if his employer **fails to comply with a reasonable request** to be accompanied, or if the employer **refuses to rearrange** to a reasonably convenient date (s 3 para 115 DG Code; s 11(1) ERelA 1999). 6790

The tribunal can award **compensation** of up to 2 weeks' pay (this will be subject to the statutory cap – ¶2920). If the worker can show that his lack of opportunity to be accompanied rendered a dismissal unfair or was discriminatory, then compensation may also be awarded for those complaints.

A worker can also complain to the tribunal if his employer **subjects him to any detriment** as a result of his exercising, or seeking to exercise, his right to be accompanied or to have a hearing rescheduled (s 3 para 116 DG Code; s 12 ERelA 1999), or for acting or seeking to act as a companion (and, in the case of trade union officials, regardless of whether he has the same employer as the worker exercising the right to be accompanied). 6791

If a worker is **dismissed** on the ground that he exercised, or sought to exercise, the right to be accompanied or the right to have a hearing rescheduled, or for acting or seeking to **act as a companion** (and, in the case of trade union officials, regardless of whether he has the same employer as the worker exercising the right to be accompanied), that dismissal will be automatically unfair (¶8390). 6793

Further, **unfair dismissal protection** and compensation, including the right to interim relief (¶8700), is extended to apply to "workers", as well as "employees" (s 12(5), (6) ERelA 1999).

There is now a **right of appeal** to the EAT from the employment tribunal in respect of detriment and dismissal claims (s 21 Employment Tribunals Act 1996 as amended by s 38 ERelA 2004). 6794

CHAPTER 20

Payroll and NIC

OUTLINE ¶¶

6800 The Pay As You Earn (PAYE) system is a method of **collecting income tax at source** from employment income, pensions and taxable state benefits. Other topics which are closely related to PAYE earnings are benefits, expenses, and statutory payments, all of which are administered by the employer and interact closely with PAYE deductions.

Employed earners and their employers must also **pay National Insurance contributions** (NICs). The mechanics of the PAYE system are also used for collecting NIC.

SECTION 1

PAYE

A. General principles

The aim of the PAYE system is to ensure that the correct amount of tax is deducted from 6810 each individual's income, according to his personal circumstances, and paid to Revenue and Customs at regular intervals. The administrative burden is placed on the employer who has four main obligations:

a. to calculate and deduct the correct amount of income tax;
b. to pay the correct amount of income tax to Revenue and Customs by the correct day;
c. to keep detailed records for each employee, and make appropriate reports to Revenue and Customs; and
d. to provide each employee with the appropriate information to be able to complete his tax return correctly.

Persons liable

All **employers** are automatically obliged to operate PAYE for their employees, if they have 6812 a presence in the UK. For these purposes, the term employer is deemed to include the payer of taxable pension income (such as scheme administrators) and taxable state benefits (the Department for Work and Pensions (DWP)). The term **employee** includes: full and part-time employees, casual labour, pensioners, directors and office holders.

There are **special rules** in the following situations:

Situation	Details	Person liable	Reference
Agency workers [1]	– client pays worker direct; – agency is overseas; or – client pays someone else overseas (i.e. not the worker or agency)	Client	s 688 ITEPA 2003
	Otherwise	Agency	
Intermediaries	If an employee works for, and is paid by, a person who is not the contractual employer	Intermediary [2]	s 687 ITEPA 2003
	Individual caught by personal service company rules, so that deemed employment income arises		
Employees of a contractor	Employees work for a client whilst being employed by a contractor	Contractor, but can also be client [3]	s 691 ITEPA 2003
Tips distributed by person who is not employer [4]	Independent person, known as the troncmaster, distributes the tips. Employer has no involvement in the distribution	Troncmaster	s 692 ITEPA 2003 SI 2003/2682 reg 100
Employee of overseas employer	Working for an entity who has presence in the UK. Irrelevant who pays employee's earnings	UK entity [5]	s 689 ITEPA 2003
No UK employer or intermediary	Working for an entity who has no UK presence	Employee	SI 2003/2682 regs 141-147

1. This distinction is for PAYE purposes only.
2. Where intermediary fails to deduct tax under PAYE, employer becomes ultimately responsible.
3. Revenue and Customs can issue a direction to client to make deductions under PAYE.
4. Employer must notify Revenue and Customs where a tronc commences and must follow published guidance on the operation of PAYE in relation to tronc: Revenue and Customs' Booklet E24.
For NIC treatment, see ¶6946.
5. Where employee in UK for less than 60 days, income tax is not due, and PAYE is not required to be operated.

Income liable

6814 An immediate deduction under PAYE **applies to** all taxable cash payments (including cash vouchers) received from the employment relationship, including termination payments, pensions and statutory payments for sickness and parents (s 683 ITEPA 2003). In practice, with the exception of benefits in kind and reimbursed expenses, any items treated as employment income are earnings for this purpose.

In addition a PAYE deduction must be operated on any round sum allowances. The employee may then make a claim for tax relief in respect of any qualifying expenditure (¶3278).

6815 As a general rule, **payments in kind** are not subject to immediate deductions under the PAYE scheme (although they will be taken into account when the PAYE code for the next tax year is calculated).

MEMO POINTS However, in a bid to counter perceived avoidance, immediate PAYE deductions must be made in respect of payments in the form of **readily convertible assets**, basically assets where the employer has already arranged a sale for the employee or a market for the sale exists. The amount liable to PAYE is the cost to the employer of providing the employee with the asset. In addition **non-cash vouchers** will be liable where they are can be exchanged for cash, or a readily convertible asset.

Taxable period

6817 The **tax year runs** from 6 April to 5 April in the following year, for example the 2005-2006 tax year started on 6 April 2005 and ends on 5 April 2006. Most employees are paid weekly or monthly and therefore the tax year is **divided into** tax weeks and months, starting on 6 April. Tax months therefore end on the 5th day of each calendar month.

A tax year contains 52 weeks. However, as a calendar year has 52 weeks and an extra day (or two in a leap year), it is possible for employees to be paid during tax week 53, for which there are special rules (for further information see Revenue and Customs' Booklet CW62).

B. PAYE deductions

6820 The employer has many obligations concerning the calculation and deduction of PAYE, and the administrative requirements for earnings. Every employer must run a payroll, which identifies each employee, the gross amount paid, and the deductions withheld and paid over to Revenue and Customs.

For the administrative requirements applicable to benefits in kind, see ¶6895.

Setting up a new payroll

6821 When setting up a payroll system, the employer should **notify** Revenue and Customs who will then send a starter pack to the employer. The payroll will be given a unique PAYE reference which should be recorded on any correspondence and the employer will also be issued with a payment book and details of how to pay PAYE.

MEMO POINTS This pack includes a CD ROM which gives access to the main PAYE forms and booklets. In addition there is substantial guidance for employers on Revenue and Customs' website, and increasingly, the internet is being used as a forum for reporting and payment.

1. PAYE codes

6825 A PAYE code is issued by Revenue and Customs to tell the employer how much of an employee's salary can be paid without deduction of tax (SI 2003/2682).

The code generally consists of up to 3 digits and a suffix letter (although in some circumstances the letter will be a prefix, or there may be no numbers).

A **notice** (P2) showing the calculation will be issued to the **employee**, who can object to it, or subsequently alter it where his circumstances change. The **employer** will receive notification of the code to use (on P6), but not details of the calculation. He should continue to use the code until notified by Revenue and Customs of any amendments. Where an employer has not received a PAYE code in respect of an employee, he must notify Revenue and Customs where any payment he makes exceeds the PAYE threshold. 6826

If there is a **change to** the employee's **circumstances** during the tax year, a new P2 notice will be issued, and the employer will be informed via a new P6 notice.

When an individual first **starts work** for an employer the PAYE code is usually notified on form P45 (¶6850). 6827

Number

The number usually **indicates** the amount of tax-free salary for a tax year, with the exception of K codes (¶6833). The number is calculated by adding together all the allowances to which an individual is entitled, and then reducing this for anything on which tax needs to be recovered, taking into account the employee's personal circumstances. 6829

Once the total figure is arrived at, the last digit is dropped to give the PAYE code number.

Letters

The letter generally **indicates** the type of personal allowance to which the employee is entitled, and is used by Revenue and Customs to make re-coding easier. 6831

A **standard code** will include one of the following letters as the suffix, each corresponding to a different type of personal allowance and in some cases the expected highest rate of tax applicable. If allowances are changed, which usually happens in the Budget, Revenue and Customs can normally issue the employer with instructions on how to alter all codes with the same suffix, avoiding the need to issue revised codes. 6832

Letter	Meaning
L	Personal allowance
P	Maximum age related allowance for individuals under 75
V	Maximum married couple's allowance for under 75s and taxable at basic rate
Y	Maximum age related allowance for individuals aged at least 75

MEMO POINTS As an exception, where the suffix is the **letter T**, it means that the code must be reviewed annually by Revenue and Customs and the employer cannot automatically amend it. Revenue and Customs will issue a new code to take account of any changes.

The following **special codes** operate in a different way. 6833

Letter	Meaning	Situation where normally used
OT	Tax to be deducted at in the order of starting rate, basic rate and higher rate, with no allowances	Allowances already used against other income
NT	No tax to be deducted	Employee overseas
BR	Basic rate tax to be deducted with no relief for allowances	Employee has more than one employment and is using his allowances against the other employment income
D (followed by a number)	Whole of the employee's salary to be taxed at the higher rate	For some directors, or individual liable to higher rate tax who have more than one employment
K (followed by a number)	Creates additional taxable pay because code deductions (e.g. benefits in kind) exceed allowances	Employee with many benefits
E	Emergency code which gives personal allowance only, more commonly known as a suffix code of 489L	Employee starting work with no previous code

6834 Individuals with **more than one employment** require separate PAYE codes for each employment. The personal allowance will generally be given in full against the earnings from one of those employments.

2. Calculation

6840 Many payroll systems are **computerised and automatically calculate** the PAYE deductions.

Otherwise, there are **two alternative methods** which can be used:
– Revenue and Customs' PAYE tax tables; or
– the alternative method where the employer calculates the PAYE deductions using the actual tax rates and thresholds. Note that the taxable pay to date must still be calculated using the Revenue and Customs' pay adjustment tables.

For further details, see the Tax Memo or Revenue and Customs' Booklet E13.

Recording requirements

6842 Whichever method is used, a separate record should be maintained of the pay and tax deductions on a cumulative basis for each employee. The official form for recording the information is the **deductions working sheet**, **form P11**. There is no requirement to use the P11 (or an approved substitute) but, in all cases, the information required to complete the P11 must be maintained in some format. The P11 has a row for each tax week during the year, and entries should be made on the row for the tax week during which the payment is made.

MEMO POINTS If the employer has agreed that the **employee is to be paid free of tax**, or a fixed amount after deductions, the actual payment is deemed to be the net salary and must therefore be grossed up. Special tax tables are provided for this purpose, and a special deductions working sheet (**P11 (FOT)**) must be used.

Retention

6844 An employer is **obliged** to retain full details of the pay and benefits provided to his employees. This includes all the payroll records and other supporting documents, for example time sheets and petty cash vouchers. These records must be retained for a minimum of 3 years from the end of the tax year to which they relate.

Incorrect deductions

6846 It is the **responsibility** of the employer to ensure that the correct deductions are made from the employee's salary. The position for incorrect deductions depends on whether the mistake is discovered during the same tax year.

If the mistake is **discovered** after the **end of the tax year**, it is not possible for the employer to correct the error. Therefore, Revenue and Customs should be informed of the full circumstances of the case. If the mistake is discovered **during the tax year**, and the mistake is that **too much tax** has been deducted, the P11 should be annotated with the correct figures as appropriate (whilst leaving the original entries legible).

6847 An employee will be **obliged** to pay further tax where Revenue and Customs accept that:
– a genuine error occurred and that the employer took reasonable care; or
– the employee was complicit in the under-deduction, and had knowledge of it.

This will usually be achieved by amending the PAYE code. Under no circumstances may the employer simply make an increased deduction from the employee's next earnings.

An **employer may request** in writing that a Revenue and Customs direction is made to recover underpaid PAYE from an employee.

3. New and leaving employees

New employees

The **employee** is required to **supply form P45** to his new employer, in respect of his previous employment, and this automatically gives the employer sufficient information to process the payroll. 6850

The **employer** must complete part 3 of the form and forward it to Revenue and Customs.

If the employee **does not supply** form P45, it is usually necessary to complete **form P46**, unless the employee is going to work for the employer for less than a week. The employee and the employer should each complete the relevant sections of the form which is then sent to Revenue and Customs. 6851

The following codes should be used until another code is notified by Revenue and Customs.

Employee's situation	PAYE code
First job since leaving education and has not received unemployment benefits	E
Both first job since leaving education and only or main job	E
Only or main job, and not receiving a pension	E week 1/month 1 basis
Any other case	BR

Leaving employees

When an employee leaves the employment, the **employer must**: 6853
- complete **form P45**; and
- annotate the deductions working sheet (**form P11**) with the employee's leaving date.

If the **employee retires** and the employer is paying a future pension, this is not a cessation of the employment and form P45 is not required.

Where a **payment** is made to the employee **subsequent to the issue** of the P45, the employer must deduct basic rate income tax.

MEMO POINTS 1. **Agencies** must issue a P45 to an agency worker when the worker stops doing work for the agency, or when the agency has not paid him for 3 months.
2. When the employer is paying a pension **on retirement**, form P160 must be completed and submitted to Revenue and Customs within 14 days of the change of circumstances. A copy of the form should also be given to the employee within the same period.
3. **On the death** of:
a. an employee, the employer must provide a P45, deduct tax at the basic rate on any payments made subsequent to the issue of the form, and send it to Revenue and Customs;
b. a pensioner, pension payers should continue to deduct tax, except for payments where the P45 has been issued and the payment is made in the next tax year. In this case basic rate tax should be deducted.
In either case, no information needs to be provided on the P45 regarding the personal representatives or payments to be made.

Form P45 shows the pay and tax details to the date of leaving, the last tax week/month for which the employee was paid and the last recorded PAYE code. 6854

If **no further employment is taken up**, the form can be used to obtain a refund of tax if appropriate, for example in respect of the personal allowances for which relief has not yet been given. Alternatively a pension payer, or the unemployment office may require the P45.

4. Payment of tax

6860 The due date for the payment of deductions to Revenue and Customs is independent of when the employee receives his pay.

Amount

6862 The amount which must be paid to Revenue and Customs is calculated as follows (reg 68 SI 2003/2682):

	£
Income tax	X
Class 1 primary NIC	X
Class 1 secondary NIC	X
Student loan repayments	X
CIS deductions	X
	X
Less: Refunds of tax and NIC to employees [1]	(X)
Working tax credits paid to employee [2]	(X)
SMP, SAP, SPP [3]	(X)
Recoverable SAP [3]	(X)
PAYE due	X

1. Paid out of income tax deducted where possible.
2. Paid out of income tax deducted where possible. Excludes any amounts funded separately by Revenue and Customs. Note that payment of working tax credits (WTCs) through PAYE is being phased out between 7 November 2005 and 31 March 2006 (¶6909).
3. Paid out of NIC deducted where possible. Excludes any amounts funded separately by Revenue and Customs.

Electronic payments

6864 If the employer has **250 or more employees**, PAYE must be paid electronically, on time and in full, otherwise surcharges may apply (reg 199 SI 2003/2682). The due date for electronic payments is the 22nd of the month.

MEMO POINTS Where the 22nd falls on a **weekend or Bank Holiday**, the payment must reach Revenue and Customs' bank account no later than the last working day before the 22nd.

6865 A system of **surcharges** applies to electronic payment defaults: Revenue and Customs' Booklet MP2 part 4. The surcharge period begins on the day after the due date of the electronic PAYE payment and ends at 5 April of the tax year in which the employer has never been in default.

Non-electronic payments

6867 The **general rule** is that PAYE must be paid to the Collector of Taxes within 14 days of the end of the tax month to which it relates (reg 69 SI 2003/2682).

By **exception**, employers may make quarterly payments where the **average monthly PAYE is less than** £1,500. Payments must be made within 14 days of the end of each quarter which, for these purposes, ends on the following dates:
- 5 July;
- 5 October;
- 5 January; and
- 5 April.

Deductions made using the **direct collection method** are also made quarterly.

Interest

6869 Interest is automatically **charged** on any amounts outstanding on 19 April (22 April for electronic payments) following the end of the tax year. The amount outstanding is the net due after deducting any amounts recoverable from Revenue and Customs. Interest runs from the due date until the date payment is made.

Interest will also be due on any amounts **overpaid**, and will run from the due date (or date of payment if later) until the date a refund is made.

5. Year end routine

The tax year end is a busy time for employers, because compliance for the tax year just ended is required, and the new tax year must be started. 6875

Annual summaries

In addition to the forms completed on an ongoing basis, the employer must complete a number of **forms** at the end of the tax year. 6877

MEMO POINTS 1. Where a **termination payment** has been made in the tax year, the employer must report this by the following 6 July.
2. Where any event involving **shares or options** awarded to employees has occurred in the tax year, the employer must report this by the following 6 July.

Form	Function	Due date
P35	Annual summary of deductions employer has made	19 May
P38A	Annual summary of employees receiving pay gross	19 May
P14	Employee specific summary of pay and deductions made	19 May
P60	Employee's copy of P14	31 May
P11D	Employee specific summary of benefits and expenses (£8,500 + employees)	6 July
P9D	Employee's summary of benefits and expenses (lower paid employees)	6 July

Penalties Penalties are automatically imposed if the forms P35 and P14 are not **filed by** the due date, although by concession, no penalty will be charged if the forms are submitted within the following 7 days (s 98A TMA 1970). In addition, also by concession, any penalty will be **reduced** to the higher of £100 and the actual PAYE and NIC liability shown on the P35. 6879

The **calculation** of the penalty is initially determined by the number of employees who should be reflected on the P35. The penalty is £100 for each month (or part thereof) that the returns remain outstanding (up to a maximum of 12 months) for each batch of 50 employees (or part thereof). This penalty cannot be mitigated.

If the returns remain **outstanding for more than 12 months** after the deadline, a further penalty will arise equal to the amount of PAYE and NIC outstanding on 19 April following the end of the tax year, subject to any mitigation. 6880
If the employer, through fraud or negligence, **submits an understated return**, a further penalty equal to the amount of the understatement may be charged, subject to mitigation.

Online filing

Online filing **applies** where forms P14 and P35 are required to be submitted (regs 82-83 SI 2003/2682). There is no requirement to file forms P38A, P9D or P11D online. 6882

The forms must meet the Revenue and Customs' Quality Standard, which means that they must be fully and accurately completed.

Compulsory filing For 2005/06 and later years, **employers with 50 or more employees** are generally required to file online (regs 205-208 SI 2003/2682). An employer should receive an **e-filing notice** by 31 December relating to the next tax year, as notification of this requirement. An employer can appeal against such a notice on the basis that he has an insufficient number of employees. 6883

MEMO POINTS **Small employers** (those with fewer than 50 employees), do not have to start online filing until 2009/10, but can receive **tax free incentive payments** (£250 for 2005/06, £150 for 2006/07) from Revenue and Customs by filing online early (SI 2003/2495).
To qualify, the returns must be submitted electronically, and meet Revenue and Customs' Quality Standard.
The incentive payment will be credited to the employer's PAYE account, and set off against subsequent liabilities, unless the employer makes a request for the payment to be made directly to him.

6884 **Penalties** If the forms do not meet the Quality Standard, they will be treated as not having been submitted. Employers will face a penalty even if they try to put things right by filing return forms again online because the first item, or part of it, was not made in the right way. Failure to file correct returns on time will result in a **maximum** penalty of £3,000 (the exact amount will depend on the number of employees on the employer's payroll) (regs 209-210 SI 2003/2682). Interest will be charged on penalties paid late. There is a right of appeal against the imposition of penalties.

C. Other payments and deductions

6890 The employer often remunerates his employees in payments other than cash, namely benefits in kind. In addition, the employer is required to make certain payments in compliance with state imposed obligations.

1. Benefits and expense payments

6895 An employer providing an employee with benefits in kind or paying for expenses has reporting obligations to Revenue and Customs.

Reporting requirements

6897 An employer **must make** a return in respect of benefits provided to employees and expenses incurred, **unless covered** by a dispensation or PAYE settlement agreement. The return required is usually a **form P11D**, with the exception of an employee who earns less than £8,500 per annum (¶3146), when a **form P9D** is used instead. A form must be completed for each employee in receipt of taxable benefits in kind or expenses during the tax year, including employees who have left. In addition to the actual forms, the employer must submit a declaration (**form P11D(b)**) confirming that all required returns have been made and submitted. Where no returns are due the declaration should still be completed and submitted by the due date. The forms and the P11D(b) must be submitted to Revenue and Customs by 6 July following the end of the tax year.

The returns enable Revenue and Customs to adjust the employee's PAYE code to collect the additional tax due on any benefits, and also provide information for the employee to complete his self-assessment return where relevant.

In addition, a **form P46(car)** is required whenever there is a change in the details of a car provided to an employee. The P46(car) must be submitted within 28 days of the end of the quarter in which the circumstances change. Quarters end on 5 July, 5 October, 5 January and 5 April.

6898 **Penalties** Penalties may be charged if the **returns are filed late** (s 98 TMA 1970). The penalty is £300 per return, plus £60 for each additional day that the return remains outstanding.

If the employer, through fraud or negligence, **submits an incorrect return**, a further penalty of £3,000 per return may be imposed. In practice however, this penalty is rarely levied.

Dispensations

Where Revenue and Customs are satisfied that employees provided with a particular expense payment would be entitled to a tax deduction for that amount, a dispensation may be granted to the employer (s 65 ITEPA 2003 and Revenue and Customs' Leaflet IR 169). An employee will be **excluded** from a dispensation where it would result in his earnings being reduced below £8,500 per annum. 6900

Items covered by the dispensation are not subject to income tax or NIC, and commonly include business travel, subsistence and professional subscriptions.

A dispensation authorises the employer not to report the specific expense, and therefore the employee is not required to submit any related claim. This is simply a matter of administrative convenience and does not result in a reduction of tax, merely in a reduction of forms.

Once a dispensation has been agreed, the employer will be sent a notice setting out the exact terms of the agreement, which will specify the expenses which are covered. The dispensation **remains valid** for as long as the circumstances do not change. Revenue and Customs may withdraw the dispensation by giving notice to the employer.

PAYE settlement agreements

Where it would prove **difficult or impractical** to calculate the value of certain benefits and expenses provided to employees, the employer may decide to enter into a PAYE settlement agreement (PSA) (regs 105-107 SI 2003/683). Under the agreement, the **employer pays** tax and Class 1B NIC on the items covered by the PSA, and these items are excluded from any other PAYE return. As the settlement of an employee's liability is a benefit in itself, the tax due is calculated on a grossed up basis. Therefore, although the PSA may reduce the employer's administrative burden, there is a real tax cost which the employer suffers. 6902

The **types of items** which may be included in an agreement are (Revenue and Customs' SP 5/96):
- minor benefits, e.g. small gifts;
- benefits paid irregularly, such as relocation expenses in excess of £8,000;
- benefits shared between employees, e.g. an expensive staff party; or
- where it is difficult to compute the tax using the normal rules.

PSAs are **negotiated** annually with Revenue and Customs, at any time before 6 July following the tax year. Once a PSA is in force, it is renewable annually provided circumstances do not change. The scope of the PSA may be amended by negotiation with Revenue and Customs.

The tax due in respect of a PSA **must be paid by** 19 October (22 October if paying electronically) following the end of the tax year to which it relates. Interest may be charged on any amounts unpaid at that date. 6903

2. State imposed payments and credits

Increasingly, payroll systems are being used to administer certain state benefits. In addition to statutory sick pay, and statutory parental payments, employers are also required to pay working tax credit to certain employees and to make deductions in respect of student loan repayments. Revenue and Customs provides all employers with a manual providing guidance on the operation of each scheme and the tables used in calculating payments. 6905

SSP, SMP, SAP and SPP

Payments of SSP, SMP, SAP and SPP are subject to PAYE and NIC deductions and must be recorded on the deductions working sheet (P11) and on the annual returns. SMP, SAP and SPP also qualify as earnings for pension contributions purposes. 6907

For all other details regarding these payments, see Chapter 13 on Sickness, injury and absence and Chapter 14 on Family-friendly rights.

Working tax credits

6909 Payment of working tax credits (WTCs) **through PAYE is being phased out** between 7 November 2005 and 31 March 2006 (SI 2005/2200). Instead the money will be paid directly to working tax credit claimants by Revenue & Customs. From 7 November 2005, all **new claimants** will receive their WTC from Revenue and Customs. However, employers must continue to pay **existing claimants** until 31 March 2006. Employers should receive stop notices (**form TC702**), which include the date of last payment, well before 31 March 2006. Employers must notify employees about the change by sending a targeted letter before the changeover date, and displaying posters etc about the workplace. Revenue and Customs has also stated that it will be writing to all working tax credit claimants setting out the new procedure.

Payments of WTCs are not taxable, but where administered through PAYE must be recorded on the deductions working sheet (P11) and on the annual returns.

Student loan deductions

6911 Employers are also responsible for **collecting** student loan payments from employees, which are not deductible for tax or NIC purposes (reg 35 SI 2000/944). The loans are only repayable once the earnings from employment exceed a certain threshold (£15,000 from 6 April 2005). Revenue and Customs publishes a special table to show the amount of the deduction required.

Student loan deductions should be made where Revenue and Customs has sent a start notification, and should not be made after a stop notification. The P11 should be annotated to indicate that deductions are being made.

MEMO POINTS 1. **Earnings** is measured in the same way as for Class 1 NIC purposes.
2. If a **new employee** provides a P45 which indicates that student loan deductions are due, the new employer should make the deductions without notification from Revenue and Customs.
3. If an **employee leaves** whilst student loan deductions are being made, the P45 should be annotated accordingly.

SECTION 2

NIC in relation to employment

A. General concepts

6925 The UK maintains a National Insurance fund which aims to provide subsistence level benefits to those in need. All individuals covered by the scheme are given a National Insurance number. The collection of National Insurance is administered by the National Insurance Contributions Office (NICO), which is part of Revenue and Customs.

6926 Various contributions may be payable in **respect of the employment** of an employed earner as follows:

Class 1 contributions are payable in respect of earnings by both the employer and employee.

Class 1A contributions are paid in respect of benefits in kind by the employer.

Class 1B contributions are payable by the employer where he has entered into a PAYE settlement agreement with Revenue and Customs (¶6902).

An employer can deduct employer's Class 1, Class 1A and Class 1B NICs when computing taxable profits.

For National Insurance purposes, an individual is an **employed earner** if he is gainfully employed in the UK receiving employment income (s2 SSCBA 1992). Basically, the same rules apply to decide whether an individual is an employee for NIC purposes as for income tax, including the provisions relating to personal service companies.

Liability for contributions

Liability for contributions **starts** once an individual attains the age of 16. The specific rules for the starting date for each class of contribution are included in the appropriate section. 6928

Liability for most contributions **ceases** when an individual reaches pensionable age, except for contributions payable by the employer (Class 1 secondary, Class 1A and Class 1B) which remain payable after pensionable age is attained.

For men, **pensionable age** is 65. For women the pensionable age is also 65, except for those who were: 6929

a. born on or before 5 April 1950, for whom pensionable age is 60; and

b. born between 6 April 1950 and 5 April 1955, for whom the date of pensionable age is calculated as follows:

Step	Instruction
1	Calculate the number of tax months between 6 April 1950 and the woman's date of birth (including the final month)
2	Add the number of months to the date of the woman's 60th birthday
3	If the number of months in step 1 is: **a.** even, pensionable age is attained on the 6th day of the month immediately preceding the date in step 2; or **b.** odd, pensionable age is attained on the 6th day of the month immediately following the date in step 2.

Link between contributions and benefits

The entitlement to certain benefits is linked to an individual's contributions to the fund. In addition, some benefits, known as **contributory benefits**, are paid at a higher level based on contributions. **Non-contributory benefits** are generally paid from the general taxation revenues rather than from the National Insurance fund, and may be means tested. 6931

To be entitled to the maximum rate of **long term benefits** (i.e. earnings related state pension and widow's benefits) an individual is expected to have a full contributions record for approximately 90% of their adult life. Entitlement to **short term benefits** (for example sickness benefit) is based on contributions over a short period, and each benefit has specific rules.

Classes 1, 1A and 1B in relation to employment carry the following **entitlements to benefits**:

Class	Long-term benefits	Short-term benefits
1 (primary)	– earnings related state pension [1]; – bereavement allowance (previously widow's pension); – widowed parent's (previously mother's) allowance; and – bereavement (previously widow's) payment.	– incapacity benefit; – jobseeker's allowance (contribution based); and – maternity allowance.
1 (secondary)	None	None
1A	None	None
1B	None	None

1. Employees may decide to opt out of the earnings related element of the state pension scheme, and make independent arrangements. A reduced level of Class 1 primary contribution is payable in these circumstances.

National Insurance number

6933 All individuals within the National Insurance scheme are given an identifying number. The National Insurance (NI) number comprises a prefix of two letters, followed by six digits and a single letter suffix, for example AB123456C.

As a rule, an individual is **issued** with an NI number shortly before the school leaving date. If an individual has not been issued with a number, he should apply for a number at a social security office.

When an individual starts work for an employer, he will be asked for his NI number. If the number is not available, the employer may use a **temporary number**, which is comprised of the prefix TN followed by the employee's date of birth in 6 digit format and then a suffix of either M if male or F if female (for example TN010782M). If the employee does not provide his proper NI number within 8 weeks, the employer should apply to Revenue and Customs, either to trace an existing number or issue a new number as appropriate.

MEMO POINTS Any **year end returns** including the temporary number TN will be rejected, which may lead to penalties for late filing.

B. Contributions

1. Class 1 contributions

6940 Earnings of an employed earner, such as salary, are liable to Class 1 contributions. Contributions are only payable if earnings reach a minimum level, and the rate of contribution depends on who is paying the contribution. For the rules specific to directors, see ¶6967.

Persons liable

6942 Contributions may be payable by the primary contributor and the secondary contributor:
– the **primary contributor** is the employed earner, referred to throughout as the employee; and
– the **secondary contributor** will usually be the employer, or in the case of an office holder, the body responsible for paying the earnings (referred to throughout as the employer).

Contributions are only payable by employed earners over the **age** of 16 in respect of any earnings paid after the 16th birthday regardless of whether they were earned before that date. Primary contributions cease being payable once the employee reaches pensionable age and any earnings paid after that date are liable only to secondary contributions, for which there is no upper age limit.

Income liable

6944 Contributions are **payable in respect of** the gross earnings of the employment (Sch 3 SI 2001/1004 and Revenue and Customs' Leaflet CWG2). So dividend income, rent and interest on loan accounts are excluded.

In the main, taxable employment income is liable to Class 1 NICs as shown in the following table (s 3 SSCBA 1992):

Remuneration	Earnings for Class 1 NIC purposes	Taxable
Wages, salary, overtime and bonuses	✔	✔
Inducement payments	✔	✔
Restrictive covenant payments subject to income tax	✔	✔

Remuneration	Earnings for Class 1 NIC purposes	Taxable
Employment tribunal awards with regard to payments to an employee under: – a reinstatement order or a re-engagement order; – an order for the continuation of employment; or – a protective award	✔	✔
Payments in lieu of notice where contractual	✔	✔
Redundancy and termination payments	x	✔ (above £30,000)
Damages payment under contract when employee injured	✔	✔
Reimbursed expenses which are not all business related	✔	✔
Personal incidental expenses paid in excess of income tax limits	✔	✔
Tax paid on behalf of employee	✔	✔
Round sum allowance which does not cover specific business expenses	✔	✔
Council tax for living accommodation not job related	✔	✔
Clothing allowance other than for uniform	✔	✔
Meal allowances	✔	✔
Parking fines	✔	✔
Scholarship income	✔	x
Luncheon vouchers – excess over 15p per day	✔	✔
Non-cash vouchers (such as vouchers for transport and gift vouchers, but not vouchers for long service or social functions which fulfil the relevant income tax conditions)	✔	✔
Childcare vouchers in excess of £50 per week	✔	✔
Loans written off	✔	✔
Share remuneration outside an approved scheme	✔	✔
Statutory pay in respect of parenthood, adoption and sickness	✔	✔
Pension benefits	x	✔
Pension contributions into funded unapproved schemes (FURBS)	✔	✔

Class 1 NIC is also payable on the following **payments in kind** (Sch 3 SI 2001/1004): 6945
a. those which can be exchanged for cash (known as readily convertible assets); and
b. any pecuniary liability of the employee met by the employer, where the employee enters into a contract for any goods or services and the employer pays for it by reimbursing the employee's expenditure or settling the bill directly with the provider. Examples would include healthcare insurance or a mobile phone contract.

Tips and gratuities Tips and gratuities are not liable for NIC unless the **employer** has **control** over their distribution. Therefore, cash payments **given directly** to a waiter are not earnings, but tips included on the credit card slip, and therefore distributed by the employer, are earnings. 6946

If an **independent troncmaster** (even one appointed by the employer, but not a director or member of management) decides on the allocation of tips, the payments will be exempt from NICs. Where the employer retains some of the tip monies to cover his expenses, the remaining tips distributed by the troncmaster are still exempt from NIC. Tips and gratuities paid to an employee by a **person connected with the employer** are also not liable for NIC

provided the payment is made in recognition of some personal service which is not allocated by the employer, and either is:
– similar in amount to that which an unconnected person would make; or
– made by the person in his capacity as troncmaster (i.e. an organised arrangement for tips to be shared amongst employees by a person who is not the employer).

MEMO POINTS The following are still liable to NIC:
– any payment which is included for the purposes of the National Minimum Wage (NMW), although tips in excess of NMW can still be exempt; and
– any payment made as part of any employment contractual arrangements, even where a troncmaster is involved.

Time of recognition

6948 Contributions **become payable** at the earlier of:
– when earnings payment is actually made (e.g. when the payment is credited to the employee's bank account); or
– when the employee is absolutely entitled to be paid, even if the pay is not drawn until a later date.

Payments received by an employee after his contract had been terminated, in respect of restrictive covenants, are still subject to NIC (*RCI Europe Ltd v Woods* [2003] EWHC 3129, ChD).

6949 Where earnings are received in **advance** by an employee who is not a director, the NIC treatment of a payment depends on whether the:
– employee has an absolute entitlement to the income when the payment is received (when it will be liable to NIC); or
– payment is effectively a loan of money (which is not liable to NIC).

An inducement payment may be liable to NIC if it relates to the employment, even where that employment has not yet commenced.

a. Calculation

6950 Calculation of the NIC liability requires the application of specific rates to bands of income received in a measured period. The NIC must then be paid to Revenue and Customs.

Earnings periods

6952 An earnings period is simply the amount of time between payments of earnings, and is usually at least a week.

Earnings periods **must begin** on the first day of the tax year (i.e. 6 April) and run consecutively. This means that weekly or monthly earnings periods will correspond with the tax weeks and months used in the operation of the PAYE system (¶6817).

6953 Where an employee is paid at **regular intervals** (for example monthly), the earnings period is simply the interval at which the employee is usually paid (reg 3 SI 2001/1004). Where employees are paid at regular intervals but the actual **date of payment changes**, the earnings period is the regular interval.

Where payments are made **irregularly**, and there is **no overriding regular payment** interval, the earnings period for each payment will be the period for which the earnings are paid (or 1 week if longer) (reg 4 SI 2001/1004).

If an employee receives earnings on **two bases** (for example monthly salary with 6 monthly bonuses), the earnings period is the shortest interval between payments (reg 7 SI 2001/1004).

MEMO POINTS A **leaving** employee may receive payments bundled together, which would have been received separately if the employment had continued. In this case, the normal earnings periods will still apply to each payment, as follows:
– regular payments received after ceasing employment are subject to NIC in the usual manner, as if the ex-employee was still employed; and
– one-off payments after cessation are subject to a weekly earnings period.

Rates

The rates **depend on**: 6955
- who is liable for the contribution (employee or employer); and
- whether special circumstances apply (¶6965).

The standard rate is by far the most usual case and for the **employee's primary contributions** is 11% on earnings which fall between the employee's earnings and upper thresholds, and 1% on any excess earnings. The standard rate of the **employer's secondary contributions** is 12.8% and applies to all earnings in excess of the employer's earnings threshold.

MEMO POINTS Check the updates to this edition for any changes to these rates for 2006/07.

Calculation methods

To calculate contributions, the **following methods** can be used (reg 12 SI 2001/1004): 6957
- the tables provided by Revenue and Customs; or
- the exact percentage method. This is generally only used by **computerised payroll systems** (or for directors' earnings), and involves multiplying the exact amount of earnings subject to contributions for the earnings period by the appropriate rate. It must be used where the earnings period is more than a week, but not a multiple of a week or a month (for example, every 10 days), the exact percentage method must be used.

b. Payment

The person **liable** for the payment of both primary and secondary contributions, is the employer (secondary contributor), although the primary contributions are recoverable from the employee by deduction from salary (Sch 1 para 3 SSCBA 1992). 6960

Class 1 contributions are generally **collected** via the PAYE system, which determines the interest and penalties which apply to contributions paid late.

MEMO POINTS **Exceptionally**, contributions may be collected via a system known as **direct collection** which means that the primary contributor is liable for paying contributions to Revenue and Customs. The same payment requirements and penalty provisions apply as for contributions paid by the secondary contributor.

Where an **underpayment** of primary contributions has been made as result of a mistake, the employer can recover it by making deductions from the employee's subsequent earnings. The extra amount which can be deducted is however limited to the usual primary contributions due on his earnings. If recovery is not made by the end of the tax year following that in which the mistake arose, the employer must suffer any remaining cost. 6961

MEMO POINTS 1. Where an employee's earnings from more than one employment are **aggregated**, the primary contributions may be recovered from any part of his earnings.
2. Where an underpayment has occurred, the correct amounts actually due should be entered on the annual **payroll returns** (¶6877).

c. Special cases

For the following types of individuals, the rules outlined above are modified: 6965
- directors;
- employees with more than one job;
- employees who have chosen to contract out of part of the state pension; and
- married women who made an election before May 1977 to pay reduced rates.

Directors

Special rules apply when calculating contributions in respect of directors, because otherwise their remuneration packages could be subject to manipulation resulting in the deferral or avoidance of NIC: Revenue and Customs' Leaflet CA44. 6967

MEMO POINTS For these purposes a director is **defined** as:
– a member of the board of directors (or similar body) which manages the company;
– a single director (or similar person) who manages the company;
– a member of the company where the company is managed by its members; or
– a shadow director, being any person in accordance with whose directions (other than in a professional capacity) the company directors are accustomed to act.

6968 A director's earnings will **include** all the items treated as earnings for employees, as well as any fees paid to him.

If the director is also an employee of the company, both sets of earnings should be aggregated when calculating the contributions payable.

6969 A director's remuneration is usually approved by the members of the company, and so any amounts **received in advance** of such approval cannot strictly be earnings. However the rule for NIC is that income is recognised at the earliest of when:
– payment is made; and
– earnings are approved.

If any income is voted to a director but subsequently waived or refunded to the company, it is still included as earnings when voted upon.

6970 Where the director **maintains an account with the company** to which remuneration is usually credited, amounts are included as earnings (and therefore liable to NIC) when credited to the account. Provided the account remains in credit, no further contributions are due.

If the **account becomes overdrawn** (or the overdrawn amount increases), contributions will be due if the withdrawal is in anticipation of further earnings being credited to the account. If the withdrawal is in anticipation of the introduction of funds from another source (for example dividends), no contributions are payable.

6971 **Rates** The **general rule** is that each time a director is paid, contributions are calculated on the total earnings to date and any contributions already paid are deducted. Directors are deemed to have an annual earnings period regardless of the interval at which they are paid, so the rates are applied on an annual basis. Where a director resigns his position during the tax year, he will still have an annual earnings period for that tax year.

MEMO POINTS The only **exception** is where a director is appointed after the start of the tax year in question. In this case, the director has a pro rata annual earnings period. The pro rata period runs from the date the director was appointed to the end of the tax year and, for these purposes, the tax year is deemed to have 52 weeks (if the director is appointed in week 53, his earnings period will be 1 week).

6972 **Methods of calculation** Director's NIC may be calculated **using** either:
a. the alternative method, where:
– the director is paid at regular intervals (which is treated as the earnings period);
– the earnings exceed the lower earnings limit; and
– the director agrees to contributions being calculated in this way; or
b. the normal method, in any other case.

Either tables or the exact percentage calculation can be used in conjunction with either method.

MEMO POINTS The alternative method allows contributions to be calculated in accordance with the normal rules for employees throughout the tax year, with **an adjustment** when making the final earnings payment for the tax year (or the termination of the directorship if earlier). The adjustment recalculates the NIC liability using the annual thresholds. This should lead to a more even spread of NICs, although a large bonus soon after 6 April will result in a large amount of primary Class 1 NICs being due at the end of the year.

More than one employment

6974 Where an employee has more than one employment, each is normally considered separately when calculating NICs. In such cases it is **usual** to pay primary Class 1 NICs as normal in one employment, and apply for deferment in respect of any other (reg 13 SI 2001/1004). In certain circumstances, an employee may overpay contributions, and he may be entitled to a refund.

As an **exception**, earnings will be combined in the following situations (unless it is too impractical):
- employments with the same employer;
- the two employers are carrying out business in association, sharing profits or sharing resources such as accommodation or personnel; or
- where only one employer, or some other person, is treated as the secondary contributor.

Where **aggregation** applies, the secondary contributors must decide how to operate the primary Class 1 NIC deduction.

Contracted out employees

The contracted out rates **apply** to employees belonging to an occupational pension scheme which has received a contracting out certificate from Revenue and Customs: Revenue and Customs' Booklet CA39. Members of such schemes are not eligible for the earnings related element of the state pension scheme (known as S2P). 6976

Both primary and secondary contributions are payable at a discounted rate up to the upper earnings limit, with secondary contributions depending on whether the scheme is salary related or money purchase.

Married woman's election before 1977

Reduced rate contributions are **payable by** married women and widows who, before 12 May 1977, elected to pay reduced contributions, and their circumstances have not changed since (e.g. she has not divorced or remarried after becoming widowed): Revenue and Customs' Booklet CA13. Such an election can be withdrawn at any time. 6978

2. Class 1A contributions

Contributions are **payable** in respect of benefits in kind (see ¶3150) provided for relevant employees (broadly those employees earning at a rate of more than £8,500 per annum), by the secondary contributor (usually the employer) (s 10 SSCBA 1992 and Revenue and Customs' Leaflet CWG5). No contributions are payable in respect of benefits provided to lower paid employees. 6980

The following benefits are **excluded** from liability (Sch 3 SI 2001/1004):

Exemption
Earnings subject to Class 1 NIC
Exempt benefits for employment income purposes
Included within a PAYE settlement
Covered by a dispensation
Specifically exempted by legislation: – childcare [1]; – shares in the employer company [2]; – tips and gratuities; and – redundancy payments.
1. The provision of care for a child for whom the employee has parental responsibility. For this purpose, child care includes both full-time and part-time care, provided by a child minder, nanny or relative. 2. Only if not readily convertible assets. Exemption does not include deemed loans relating to shares which are taxable.

Calculation and payment

The employer's declaration form includes a calculation of Class 1A contributions. The method is simply to total all the relevant benefits on the P11D and multiply the total by the Class 1A contribution **rate**, which is set at the standard rate for secondary contributions. 6982

Contributions are **payable** in a single amount on 19 July following the tax year, unless payment is being made electronically, when the due date is 22 July. Interest may be charged on any amounts paid late.

Reporting requirements

6984 The employer's reporting requirements are satisfied by completion of form P11D(b) which includes a declaration by the employer that the details are fully and truly stated to the best of his knowledge.

The latest date that the form can be submitted is 6 July following the tax year.

3. Class 1B contributions

6990 Where an employer has entered into a **PAYE settlement agreement** (¶6902), known as a PSA, Class 1B NIC is due on the items covered by the agreement, payable in a single lump sum (s 10A SSCBA 1992).

The sum of the following **amounts are liable**:

– total value of the items covered by the PSA which would otherwise give rise to a Class 1 or Class 1A NIC liability; and

– the income tax payable by the employer.

Contributions are at the standard **rate** for secondary contributions and are **payable** on the same date as the related income tax, i.e. 19 October following the tax year to which it relates, extended to 22 October where payment is being made electronically.

C. Overseas issues

7000 NIC is generally payable by anyone working in the UK. Individuals working in the UK on a short term basis, and those leaving the UK who wish to maintain their entitlement to benefits, may be able to take advantage of special rules which exist between the members of the European Economic Area (EEA). The UK has also entered into a limited number of reciprocal agreements with certain other countries.

MEMO POINTS The term UK includes Great Britain and Northern Ireland, because even though Northern Ireland has its own system, the same principles apply.

1. General principles

7005 The liability for NIC is **linked to** an individual's residence status and whether he is present in the UK. Special rules apply to ensure that individuals do not pay contributions in more than one country during the period in which they arrive in, or leave, the UK.

On arrival in the UK, anyone planning to work should apply for a National Insurance number (¶6933).

Presence

7007 It is usually clear whether an individual is present in the UK, as presence is simply a matter of fact.

MEMO POINTS **Directors** of UK registered companies, if they are not resident in the EEA, or countries with which the UK has a reciprocal agreement, may ignore certain visits to the UK to attend board meetings, where:

– no more than ten board meetings each requiring a maximum presence of 2 days are attended in a year; or

– if there is only one board meeting, the meeting does not last more than 14 days.

Residence and ordinary residence

There is no statutory **definition** for either residence or ordinary residence for National Insurance purposes. Residence and ordinary residence are a question of fact, and although theses terms are generally given their meaning for income tax purposes, there are some differences as set out below. 7009

Residence has a greater permanence than presence, and may continue even while an individual is temporarily absent, if the individual intends to remain resident. Where an individual leaves the UK for an unknown period of time, this will usually bring his residence status to an end. 7010

Claiming contributory benefits is a strong indication that an individual is resident.

An individual will be **ordinarily resident** in a country where he normally lives, and has a settled mode of life. It can be generally concluded that it is difficult for an individual to make himself not ordinarily resident for NIC purposes, even when he is not present in the UK. 7011

Revenue and Customs have set out practical guidelines, which are summarised below.

Liability to UK NIC

An **employee** is liable for Class 1 primary contributions if he is either resident, present (subject to temporary absences), or ordinarily resident in the UK at the time of the employment. 7013

Whenever there is a primary contribution, there is usually is a secondary contribution. The **employer** is liable for Class 1 secondary contributions if the employer is either: 7014
- resident or present in the UK when the secondary contributions become payable; or
- has a place of business in the UK at that time.

MEMO POINTS 1. Revenue and Customs considers the following to be a **place of business**, where:
- the employer's premises is occupied lawfully; and
- employees undertake activity at the premises, in the course of the employer's business.

2. The following are used as **indicators of premises**:
- a registered office address;
- a lease or rental agreement;
- headed paper or business cards showing the address;
- an entry in the telephone or trade directory; and
- a name plate.

3. An **overseas company** with an UK branch will have a UK place of business, but a UK subsidiary, whilst itself having a UK presence, will not constitute a UK place of business for its overseas parent.

4. If expatriates are outside the scope of UK NIC, no **Class 1A** NIC is payable by the employer even where P11D forms are still completed.

2. Application of the rules

The operation of the above rules means individuals arriving in, or leaving, the UK may be liable to contributions in more than one country at the same time. Special provisions therefore apply to limit the **double charge** in some circumstances, by determining that an individual is subject to contributions in one country only. Unlike income tax, there is no set off of liabilities of one country against another. 7020

Summary of regimes

There are three different regimes which apply, depending on whether the individual is moving between the UK and: 7021

1. An EEA member state.
2. A country with which the UK has a reciprocal agreement, which may either be full, covering both NIC and benefits, or a Double Contributions Convention (DCC) which covers NIC liability only.
3. The rest of the world.

MEMO POINTS Further information can be found on the services and benefits area of the DWP's website, www.dwp.gov.uk.

Country	EEA [1]	Reciprocal agreements		Reference	Leaflet
		Full	DCC		
Austria	×			EC 1408/71	SA 29
Barbados		×		SI 1992/812	SA 43
Belgium	×			EC 1408/71	SA 29
Bermuda		×		SI 1969/1686	SA 23
Bosnia Herzegovina		×		SI 1958/1263	SA 17
Canada			×	SI 1995/2699	SA 20
Croatia		×		SI 1958/1263	SA 17
Cyprus	×			EC 1408/71	SA 29
Czech Republic	×			EC 1408/71	SA 29
Denmark	×			EC 1408/71	SA 29
Estonia	×			EC 1408/71	SA 29
Finland	×			EC 1408/71	SA 29
France	×			EC 1408/71	SA 29
Germany	×			EC 1408/71	SA 29
Gibraltar	×			EC 1408/71	SA 29
Greece	×			EC 1408/71	SA 29
Guernsey		×		SI 1994/2802	SA 4
Hungary	×			EC 1408/71	SA 29
Iceland	×			EC 1408/71	SA 29
Ireland	×			EC 1408/71	SA 29
Isle of Man		×		SI 1977/593	
Israel		×		SI 1957/1879	SA 14
Italy	×			EC 1408/71	SA 29
Jamaica		×		SI 1997/871	SA 27
Japan [2]			×	SI 2000/3063	
Jersey		×		SI 1994/2802	SA 4
Korea [3]			×	SI 2000/1823	
Latvia	×			EC 1408/71	SA 29
Liechtenstein	×			EC 1408/71	SA 29
Lithuania	×			EC 1408/71	SA 29
Luxembourg	×			EC 1408/71	SA 29
Macedonia		×		SI 1958/1263	SA 17
Malta	×			EC 1408/71	SA 29
Mauritius		×		SI 1981/1542	SA 38
Netherlands	×			EC 1408/71	SA 29
New Zealand		×		SI 1964/495	SA 8
Norway	×			EC 1408/71	SA 29
Phillipines		×		SI 1989/2002	SA 42
Poland	×			EC 1408/71	SA 29
Portugal	×			EC 1408/71	SA 29
Serbia and Montenegro		×		SI 1958/1263	SA 17
Slovak Republic	×			EC 1408/71	SA 29
Slovenia	×			EC 1408/71	SA 29

Country	EEA [1]	Reciprocal agreements		Reference	Leaflet
		Full	DCC		
Spain	×			EC 1408/71	SA 29
Sweden	×			EC 1408/71	SA 29
Switzerland [4]	×			EC 1408/71	SA 29
Turkey		×		SI 1961/584	SA 22
USA		×		SI 1984/1817	SA 33

1. The EEA rules are to be replaced sometime in 2006 with those in EC 883/2004. The terms of the existing bilateral treaties will continue to apply where this gives a more beneficial result (such as the agreements involving Malta, Cyprus and Slovenia).
2. Further information can be found at: www.hmrc.gov.uk/nic/japan
3. Further information can be found at: www.hmrc.gov.uk/nic/korea
4. Switzerland is treated as part of the EEA by the UK rules.

a. Moving within the EEA

The overriding principle is that nationals of any EEA member state should **only be subject** to the social security legislation of one state. 7025

MEMO POINTS From 1 January 2006, **access to healthcare** in other member states requires the production of a European Heath Insurance Card (EHIC).

As an employee is liable to social security contributions in the state in which he works, regardless of where he lives, or where the employer's place of business is, the NIC treatment of an employee **depends on** whether he is still working for his home employer whilst overseas, or taking on a new employment. 7026

So where an employee takes on **work overseas** under a contract with a **new employer**, he will be liable to contributions in the overseas state from day one. On the other hand, where an employee **remains employed by his home employer**, and he is posted overseas, the NIC treatment will depend on the length of the assignment.

MEMO POINTS Where an employee **works in multiple member states** at the same time (whether for the same or different employers), he will generally be liable to contributions in the state in which he habitually resides, if he undertakes any work in that state. Whilst the occasional business trip to another state will be ignored for these purposes, an employee working a couple of days a month on a regular basis would be working in more than one state.
If the employee **does not reside** in any of the states in which he works, he will be liable to contributions for the state in which his employer has its place of business or registered office.

Short temporary assignments

For these purposes, a short assignment is **not expected to last more than** 12 months. Where the employee is not replacing another employee whose posting has ended, he will remain liable to home contributions (i.e. contributions in the country in which he has his home), as long as a certificate of coverage (form E101) is obtained. 7028

It is possible to obtain an extension to the certificate, where the assignment's duration is longer because of **unforeseen circumstances**. The extension will only be for a maximum of another 12 months.

MEMO POINTS 1. To obtain a **certificate of coverage**, the employer should apply to the social security authority in the home state with the appropriate evidence (such as the employment contract) for a certificate of coverage. This document satisfies the authorities in the other member state that contributions are not required.
2. To obtain an **extension**, an application must be made on form E102 to the social security authority in the host state, before the original certificate period has expired.
3. An employee can go to a **third member state** without returning to the home state, as long as his total time away is less than 12 months.
4. A **new 12 month period** will become available once the employee has been back in his home state for more than 8 weeks.

Longer term temporary assignments

7029 The **default treatment** is that an employee will pay contributions in the overseas state from day one.

By **exception**, it may be possible to remain liable to home contributions for a period of up to 5 years, where any of the following criteria apply:
– the employee has special skills or knowledge which are not available in the local labour market;
– the employer has specific objectives with which the employee is familiar and for which his services are required; or
– unusually, it is shown to be in the employee's best interest (for example where the employee is nearing retirement).

MEMO POINTS 1. In this exceptional case, an **application** should be made to the social security authority in the home state setting out the circumstances of the case. If they agree with the application, they will seek the host state's approval to continuing home contributions. Often the host state will examine the employee's history to see that he has a sufficient contributions record in the home state, and has not just spent a minimal amount of time there in order to pay cheaper contributions.
2. Eventually, an employee may **develop stronger ties** with the state where he is working, which means that he would need to pay contributions in that state in any event.

b. Reciprocal agreement countries

7035 The UK has entered into reciprocal agreements with a number of countries. Each agreement is unique, although they have many common features and generally include provisions similar to those between EEA member states.

The **general aim** of a reciprocal agreement is to ensure that an individual is only liable to contributions in one of the countries concerned, usually the country in which the individual is working. Most of the reciprocal agreements cover both employees and self-employed individuals.

7036 An individual may continue to pay home contributions (i.e. contributions in the country in which he has his home) if he **works temporarily** in another country. The **definition** of temporary differs according to the country concerned, but is generally 12 months.

If the period of the assignment is extended due to **unforeseen circumstances**, the individual is generally permitted to continue to pay home contributions for a further period. These provisions only apply if the individual was paying contributions in the home country before the assignment.

Applications to pay home contributions should be made in the same way as for employees working in the EEA, using form E101 or form E102 as appropriate.

c. Other countries

7040 Where an individual moves between the UK and a country for which no special arrangements exist **liability for contributions** may arise in more than one country. The rules for determining whether contributions in the UK are required are set out below.

Broadly, an employee:
– arriving in the UK will not be required to pay NICs for the first 52 weeks of their stay; and
– leaving the UK is required to continue paying NICs for the first 52 weeks of their absence.

Coming to the UK

7042 Primary and secondary Class 1 NICs are generally **payable from** the date an individual takes up employment in the UK.

However, an exception will arise where the individual is **posted temporarily** to the UK and all of the following circumstances apply:
– the employee is not ordinarily resident or employed in the UK (apart from the temporary posting);
– the posting arises in the course of an employment carried on mainly outside the UK; and
– the employer has his main place of business outside the UK.

If these criteria are met, no primary or secondary Class 1 contributions are payable from the date of last entry into the UK until the employee has been resident in the UK for a continuous period of 52 contribution weeks.

MEMO POINTS **Students working in the UK** may be exempt from contributions in the following situations:
a. where a student pursuing a full time course of study outside the UK takes up temporary employment during a vacation (not at the end of the course) which is similar to, or related to, the course of study; or
b. where a student, who occupies a position comparable with that of an apprentice with someone outside the UK, commences employment in the UK before the age of 25 which is similar to, or related to, the apprenticeship.

Leaving the UK

In this case, the employer and employee will often have a **double charge** to NIC, in the UK and the host country. Primary and secondary Class 1 contributions continue to be payable for 52 weeks after the employee leaves the UK if all of the following apply: 7044
– the employee is ordinarily resident in the UK;
– the employee was resident immediately before taking up the employment overseas; and
– the employer has a place of business in the UK.

Otherwise all liability to NIC ceases on the leaving date.

MEMO POINTS If an individual employed abroad **changes employer**, the first employer's liability for contributions ceases with the last payment due from him. In this case, further liability for contributions will be dependent upon the three criteria above.

Return to the UK and further employment abroad

If the employee **temporarily returns** to the UK **before the end of the 52-week period**, in any of the following situations, contributions continue to be payable until the period has expired: 7046
– during paid leave (i.e. holiday);
– sick leave; or
– for a temporary period of employment.

If the temporary employment begins **after the 52-week period** has expired, contributions are not payable for the first 6 weeks of UK duties.

If the length of the temporary assignment lasts for more than 6 weeks, UK contributions may be payable in the normal way unless the duties are merely incidental to the overseas employment (for example training).

Full liability to UK NIC will recommence on an individual's **permanent return** to the UK and so contributions will be due on the first payment of UK earnings unless both of the following conditions are satisfied: 7047
– the employee is on paid leave from the employer pending termination of that employment; and
– the 52-week contribution period had ended before the return to the UK.

In this situation, contributions are not required for the period of paid leave unless the employee takes up employment with a different employer during that period. The new employer will, of course, be required to deduct contributions in the normal way.

If, **after returning to the UK** following employment abroad, the employee takes up **further employment abroad**, a further 52-week period of contributions will be due if the conditions 7048 in ¶7044 are satisfied. So if the employee was not resident in the UK before taking up the new post, no UK NICs will be due during the further employment abroad.

The question **depends on** whether the employee has resumed residence in the UK. Each case will be considered on its facts, and the following factors will be taken into consideration in relation to the employee:
- how long he was in the UK;
- whether he stayed at his own home or used temporary accommodation; and
- the reason for his return to the UK.

CHAPTER 21

Trade unions and industrial action

OUTLINE ¶¶

7100 Nearly one in three UK workers belongs to a trade union (referred to as a union throughout this chapter) and about four in ten have their employment contract regulated through collective bargaining between unions and employers. Union rights generally apply to workers (see general definition of worker at ¶13) and this term will be used throughout sections 1 – 4 of the chapter.

7101 **Unions** are subject to legislation that lays down the manner in which they must conduct their affairs. They are open to legal challenge, from members, employers and third parties, where they fail to comply with their duties as laid down by statute or as determined by the contractual relationship they have with their members.

Unions must be **independent**, that is, not under the domination or control of an employer, and have the **right to be recognised** by employers **for collective bargaining purposes** where they have recruited the majority of workers and/or have won a majority in a ballot. A non-independent union (for example, a staff association promoted or financed by the employer) is generally excluded from the statutory rights afforded to independent unions.

Recognised unions, which have obtained a certificate of independence from the Certification Officer, also have the right to information for collective bargaining purposes. In workplaces with recognised unions, employers must disclose this information, with certain limited exceptions. Union officials in recognised workplaces have the right to paid time off to take part in union activities.

7102 Unions also have **certain legal obligations**. They must maintain registers of names and addresses of members so that elections for senior officials of the union and ballots for industrial action can be carried out. They also have very substantive obligations in relation to the keeping of financial accounts. They are required to file annual returns and to make their financial accounts available for inspection to members, employers and third parties.

7103 **Union rights** may be categorised as collective or individual. **Collective rights** are those where the union itself, its officials or members gain protection or immunity in connection with the exercise of their collective functions. The protection of certain forms of industrial action is a clear example of a collective right. The right to recognition is another. Unions have immunity from legal action in certain specified situations. They can call industrial action, even though its impact will be to induce workers to break their contracts, and will be protected from legal challenge, provided that they have complied with legal rules regarding the nature and origins of the dispute and the process by which the action was called. Their legal funds are, at least in part, protected even where industrial action is called in breach of the legal rules.

Individual union rights, on the other hand, protect the individual worker in his relationship with the employer or the individual member in his relationship with the union. Members of independent unions are legally protected against victimisation or dismissal where it is on account of their membership or activities.

Most of the law which affects unions is to be found in the Trade Union and Labour Relations (Consolidation) Act 1992 (TULRCA 1992), as amended, which brought together all previous employment law dealing with unions or their members, together with the Employment Relations Act 1999 (ERelA 1999). **7105**

The Employment Relations Act 2004 (ERelA 2004), which amends the existing statutory framework, was enacted in stages, and the last provisions of the Act came into force in October 2005. The Act is the result of a wide-ranging review of Employment Relations Act 1999 (ERelA 1999), following which the Government published its proposals to improve, simplify and clarify aspects of trade union and industrial action law, principally in respect of the statutory recognition procedures (¶7200). The provisions of the Act are outlined where relevant below.

SECTION 1

The Certification Officer

The Certification Officer (referred to in this section as the CO) is a government-appointed official who is responsible for the registration and legal regulation of unions. The offices of the CO are housed within the ACAS head office at Brandon House, 180 Borough High Street, London SE1 1LW. In the exercise of his functions, the CO can appoint assistants and can delegate such functions, as are considered appropriate, to any such assistant. ACAS also provides administrative assistance to the CO. **7110**

The **main functions** of the CO are to (s 254 TULRCA 1992): **7111**
- maintain a list of unions;
- certify whether a union is independent;
- maintain a list of employers' organisations;
- produce an annual report; and
- ensure that the statutory requirements which relate to accounting records, annual returns, auditors, financial affairs, political funds, the procedures for amalgamations and transfers of engagements, and changes of union names are complied with.

The CO's records, in relation to the annual returns of unions and employers' organisations, accounts, copies of rules and other documents, are available for public inspection at the Certification Office and, where appropriate, the Office of the Assistant Certification Officer for Scotland, at all reasonable hours, either free or at a reasonable charge.

The CO must also deal with **complaints** by union members: **7112**
- that a union has failed to comply with the legal provisions relating to the holding of secret postal ballots for electing members of its executive committee, president and general secretary;
- that there has been a breach or threatened breach of the union's own rules;
- about alleged breaches of political fund rules; or
- about the conduct of merger ballots.

The CO must disclose to the union the identity of a member making a complaint unless, in the view of the CO, the circumstances are such that the identity should not be disclosed.

Union members making complaints to the CO must do so **within** 6 months of the alleged breach, threatened breach or conclusion of any internal enquiry. Before accepting a complaint, the CO has to be convinced that all reasonable steps were taken to resolve the claim internally. If a complaint is accepted, the CO will call a hearing and give the applicant and the union an opportunity to be heard.

At any stage of the proceedings, the CO may **strike out** an application or complaint on the grounds that (s 256ZA TULRCA 1992, as inserted by s 48 ERelA 2004):
– it, or anything in it, is scandalous, vexatious, has no reasonable prospect of success or is otherwise misconceived;
– proceedings have been conducted in a scandalous, vexatious or unreasonable manner; or
– there has been an excessive delay in proceedings.

If, however, the CO is satisfied that the complaint is successful, he can make a **declaration and an enforcement order** requiring the union to undertake the necessary steps to remedy the breach. He may also pay expenses to the complainant if these are incurred for the purpose of attending hearings.

Appeals from a decision on points of law of the CO go to the Employment Appeal Tribunal (EAT).

7114 More generally, the CO, or any authorised member of the CO's staff, has the right to **investigate the financial affairs** of a union where it appears to the CO that they have been conducted for a fraudulent or unlawful purpose or in breach of any statutory duty imposed upon it (s 37A TULRCA 1992).

A report on the outcome of any such investigation can be furnished, free of charge, to the union, its auditors and any member who has either initiated the complaint or requests a copy or where the CO believes that the report's findings are relevant to that member.

SECTION 2

Trade unions

7115 A trade union is defined as an organisation, whether temporary or permanent, which consists "wholly or mainly of workers" of one or more description. The definition includes an organisation consisting of constituent or affiliated trade unions (for example, the UK Trades Union Congress (TUC)).

7116 A union's **principal purposes** (which are usually to be found in its rulebook) must include "the regulation of relations" between workers and employers or employers' organisations. This is normally achieved through collective bargaining, which may be extensive or limited to cover specific areas of negotiation only. Regulation could also be solely through a consultation forum, for example where there is consultation over matters such as redundancies, the outcome of which is an agreement on the preferred course of action. An organisation consisting wholly or mainly of representatives of constituent or affiliated organisations, like the TUC, would also have, as a principal purpose, the regulation of relations between its constituent or affiliated organisations. The TUC, for example, exercises a role as an arbiter in disputes between its affiliated unions.

A union's **main aim** is to reach agreements with employers over the contractual terms under which their employees will work (s 1 TULRCA 1992).

MEMO POINTS The Union Modernisation Fund has been launched by the Government to provide financial assistance to trade unions. The Fund is aimed at supporting innovative projects which reflect modern working practices, involving, for example, the review of internal union structures and supporting greater efficiency in union management. Between £5 and £10 million is expected to be available over several years.

7117 A union has the right to **make contracts**, sue and be sued and can have criminal proceedings brought against it. It can be sued by its members in negligence save where the negligence arises in the course of a legal action which the union has employed solicitors to handle (*Friend v Institution of Professionals, Managers and Specialists* [1999] IRLR 173, QBD). However, unions cannot register as a company or friendly society and only have quasi-corporate status (s 10 TULRCA 1992).

A union cannot hold **property** in its own name, rather a union's property is held in the name of its trustees, and there are certain legal restrictions on the way that its funds can be utilised. Most notably it cannot use its property to indemnify unlawful conduct, for example by paying any penalties or compensation imposed for offences or contempt of court committed by one of its officials or members (s 12(1) TULRCA 1992).

Register of unions Unions register annually with the CO and the fact that an organisation is included in a list of unions, kept by the CO, is sufficient evidence that it is a union (s 2 TULRCA 1992). The most recent report of the CO lists approximately 200 unions as having registered, with approaching eight million members. Many of these unions are small, single employer organisations. Most of the larger unions affiliate to the TUC. Over 75 unions are affiliated, with a combined membership of nearly seven million. **7121**

Independent unions

The exercise of certain union rights are dependent on the union establishing that it is an independent body, not under the domination or control of, or subject to interference from an employer (s 5 TULRCA 1992; see further ¶7560). These are the rights: **7122**
- not to be victimised on union grounds;
- not to be dismissed or selected for redundancy on union grounds;
- not to be refused employment on union grounds;
- to prevent the employer from seeking, or preventing, or deterring a worker from becoming a union member;
- to information for collective bargaining; and
- to time off to take part in union activities.

Conclusive evidence of a union's independence comes in the form of a **certificate of independence** issued by the CO. Unions wishing to establish their independence must apply for this certificate. The CO can withdraw a certificate of independence, once issued, if he is of the opinion that a union is no longer independent (s 7 TULRCA 1992).

Recognised unions

Where a union has been recognised (¶7200), it can negotiate pay and other terms and conditions of employment on behalf of a group (or groups) of workers. This will result in a collective agreement being formed. **7123**

A **collective agreement** is an agreement or arrangement made by or on behalf of a union and an employer which **relates to** one or more of the following (s 178 TULRCA 1992):
- terms and conditions of work;
- physical conditions;
- engagement or non-engagement of workers;
- termination or suspension of employment;
- allocation of work between workers or groups of workers;
- disciplinary matters;
- union membership;
- facilities for union officials; and
- machinery for negotiation and consultation, and other procedures relating to these matters, including the recognition of a union by an employer to represent workers in the negotiation or consultation of such procedures.

In large sectors of industry, levels of pay and other principal terms and conditions for individual workers may be prescribed by terms negotiated between a union and one or more employers and agreed in a collective agreement.

MEMO POINTS The definitions of collective agreement and collective bargaining are different for unions recognised under the statutory recognition procedure.

The provisions of a collective agreement will be **legally enforceable** provided it is in writing and expressly states that the parties intend the agreement to constitute a legally binding contract as between the **union and the employer** (s 179(1), (2) TULRCA 1992). In addition, to be **7124** enforceable between **employer and worker** the collective agreement must be incorporated into the individual worker's terms and conditions of employment (¶1271). Such provisions will be enforceable between the employer and worker even if the collective agreement is not legally binding as between employer and union.

Some collective agreements might contain a **"no strike" provision**, which attempts to prohibit or restrict the right of workers to take industrial action. These clauses are dealt with at ¶7428 below.

A. Structure

7125 At the **head of the union** organisation there will commonly be a general secretary, president and principal executive committee, who are all elected by secret postal ballot.

A **member of the executive committee** is any person who "under the rules of the union" may attend and speak at all or some of the meetings of the executive, otherwise than for the purpose of providing the committee with factual information or with technical or professional advice.

The union may also employ **full-time officials**, who are not necessarily elected to their posts, unless required under the union's own rules or unless they have voting rights on the executive committee. To be a voting member of the executive committee, a person has to be entitled, in their own right, to attend at least some meetings of the executive committee and to vote.

In addition, the union will employ **administrative staff**, who service the organisation, its officers and its members. The union's trustees, usually elected by the membership as a whole, are responsible for checking that its finances and affairs are in order.

Beneath this structure are the union's **lay officials**, for example, branch secretaries, workplace representatives and members of regional bodies. The union rulebook will prescribe how they are selected. This layer most directly services the union's members by providing advice and representation at a local or workplace level.

7126 Employers are most likely to deal, on a day-to-day basis, with lay officials. However, **collective bargaining** may be conducted by a full-time official or by lay officials depending on the rules of the procedural agreement between the employer and union.

Membership

7128 The members of the union and the union itself are **governed by** its rules, which are its written rules or any other written provision forming part of the contract between a member and the other members (s 20(7) TULRCA 1992). The union rulebook sets out the terms of its contract with its members. It also usually includes the union's main principles and objectives. The union's rules may be amended through decisions taken by the union's policy-making bodies, for example, their annual conference.

All unions will have a general fund into which **members' contributions** are paid. The general fund is used to pay expenses incurred in carrying out the union's objectives as set out in the rulebook. If the union has political objectives that require funding, there must be a separate fund to support this (¶7181).

Amalgamations and transfers

7130 Amalgamations and transfers between unions are regulated by law (ss 97-106 TULRCA 1992, as amended by s 50 ERelA 2004). Notice of any such proposal has to be given in writing to members and approval of the instruments of amalgamation or transfer must be obtained from the CO. Union members have the right to vote upon a resolution to effect any amalgamation or transfer. Voting is conducted in a manner similar to that for union elections (¶7160). Members also have the right to complain to the CO if the voting did not take place in accordance with the legal rules.

B. Obligations to members

A union has a number of specified obligations imposed by law. These are additional to any obligations arising out of the union's own rules. They include the following duties: 7138

1. To keep accounts (s 28 TULRCA 1992) A union must keep proper accounting records of its transactions, assets and liabilities, which give a true and fair view of the state of the affairs of the union and explain its transactions. These records have to be kept for at least 6 years. 7139

2. To permit members to inspect records (s 30 TULRCA 1992) On payment of reasonable administrative expenses, if requested by the union, members have the right to see any accounting records going back 6 years. Where such a request is made, the union has to respond to it within 28 days. The member, who can be accompanied by an accountant, can inspect the records and take any copies required. The accompanying accountant can be required to agree to protect confidentiality, failing which, the union can refuse that person access. These rights of access are not limited to the right to see the accounts of the union at national level. A member can also inspect the accounting records relating to a branch or section of the union, whether or not a member of that branch or section. 7140

If a union **denies access** to accounting records, the member can apply to the CO or to the High Court (Court of Session in Scotland) for an order to allow inspection, accompaniment or the taking of copies, as required. Where the claim goes to the CO, the order will, as far as is reasonably practicable, be made within 6 months of the application.

3. To file annual returns (s 32 TULRCA 1992) Unions have to file annual returns with the CO. To carry out this duty properly, the union has to forward revenue accounts indicating income and expenditure, a year-end balance sheet and any other accounts which the CO might require. The returns must also give details of the salaries it pays to its executive, president and general secretary. It must also forward a copy of the auditor's report and a copy of the relevant accounting rules of the union, which will be found in the union's rulebook. The CO can require that the returns be in respect of a period other than a calendar year. 7141

4. To supply copies of the annual returns (s 32(5) TULRCA 1992) Any person, including the employer, has the right to ask the union for a copy of the union's most recent return, either free of charge or on payment of a reasonable sum. Annual returns are also available for public inspection from the CO. In addition, the union has to take steps to publish details of its financial returns to its members within 8 weeks of submitting its report to the CO. 7142

5. To appoint an auditor (ss 33, 35-37 TULRCA 1992, as amended by s 53 ERelA 2004) Unions must appoint a qualified auditor, unless the union is very small (i.e. has a membership of no more than 500 and assets and turnover of no more than £5,000 in a calendar year). Certain persons are specifically excluded from holding the office of auditor, namely officers or employees of the union or its branches or sections, their partners, their employers or employees. Corporate bodies can, however, be appointed as auditor. 7143

6. To maintain a register of members' names and addresses (s 24 TULRCA 1992) Unions must compile and maintain a register of the names and addresses of their members. This information will be used as the member's postal address when holding ballots for industrial action or where there is an internal election. Unions also have an obligation to ensure "as far as is reasonably practicable" that the entries in the register are accurate and are kept up-to-date. This does not mean that every record has to be correct at all times but that there must be systems in place designed to maintain accurate records. 7144

7. To permit members to see their entry Provided reasonable notice has been given, unions must allow their members, free of charge, to check the register to see if there is an entry for them and to supply a copy of the entry on request. A reasonable fee can be imposed for the copy. 7145

If a union **fails to comply** with any of the requirements relating to the register, a member can apply either to the CO or to the High Court (Court of Session in Scotland) for a declaration to that effect. The court or CO, as the case may be, will issue an enforcement order. This will set out the steps that have to be taken to remedy the declared failure or the action to be taken to ensure no future failure.

7146 **8. Not to unjustly discipline a member** (ss 64-67 TULRCA 1992, as amended by s 34 ERelA 2004). A union must not unjustifiably discipline a member. Disciplinary action includes expulsion, fines, refusal to accept contributions, depriving members of union benefits, encouraging another union to exclude the member or doing anything else which is detrimental to the member (*Nalgo v Killorn and Simm* [1990] IRLR 464, EAT). A suspension from membership also amounts to a disciplinary action, however, a mere recommendation for disciplinary action, without it having been carried out, would not give rise to a claim (*TGWU v Webber* [1990] IRLR 462, EAT).

The disciplinary action is unjust where it is imposed because the member has (s 65 TULRCA 1992):
– failed to support or participate in industrial action;
– continued to work to his contract despite the industrial action;
– asserted, otherwise than falsely and in bad faith, that the union, its officials or representatives have breached their legal obligations;
– encouraged others to continue working during industrial action;
– failed to comply with any unjustifiable disciplinary penalty already imposed;
– worked or is proposing to work with non-union members; or
– sought assistance from the CO.

7147 A member/former member can make a **claim** to an employment tribunal, which can declare that the discipline was unjustified (s 66 TULRCA 1992). The claim must be presented **within** 3 months of the action complained of, unless the tribunal believes that it was not reasonably practicable to have done so.

Once there is a **declaration** that a union has unjustifiably disciplined one of its members, it must take all necessary steps to ensure that the effects of the disciplinary action are revoked (*Beaumont v Amicus MSF*, EAT case 0122/03). This will involve positive and unequivocal action and not simply notifying the member's union branch that the disciplinary action has been reversed.

Further after such a declaration, the member/former member can also pursue a claim for **compensation** and/or **reimbursement** of any fine/penalty paid (s 67 TULRCA 1992). A claim can only be made after 4 weeks from the date of the declaration but must be made before the end of 6 months from this date.

The **maximum compensatory award** limit is £65,200 (i.e. 30 times the maximum amount of a week's pay for unfair dismissal (¶2920)) plus the maximum compensatory award for unfair dismissal (£56,800).

Compensation is awarded in accordance with what is just and equitable and this will not be limited to compensation for failure to revoke the unjustifiable disciplinary action and can include compensation for the manner of the disciplinary action and its effects on the member (*Beaumont v Amicus MSF*). Applications for compensation relating to the unjustifiable discipline of a member may no longer be made to the EAT.

MEMO POINTS These amounts are likely to increase in **February 2006**.

7148 **9. Not to unlawfully exclude or expel a member** (ss 174-177 TULRCA 1992, as amended by s 33 ERelA 2004) The closed shop (where union membership is a requirement of employment) is rarely found in the UK. Legislative changes have effectively limited or restrained union membership arrangements where these acted to require membership in return for work. However, if union membership is a **requirement of employment**, an individual seeking employment cannot be refused the right to join a union nor be unreasonably expelled by the union.

Whether it is **lawful** to exclude or expel a member on the grounds of his conduct **depends on** whether the conduct is **excluded** or **protected**. Excluded conduct includes conduct relating to being or ceasing to be a member of another trade union or being or ceasing to be employed at a particular place or by a particular employer. Protected conduct relates to a member being or ceasing to be a member of a political party. Undertaking political activities does not fall within protected conduct (s 174 TULRCA 1992, as amended by s 33 ERelA 2004).

A union is **able to exclude or expel** a member where the exclusion or expulsion is wholly attributable to conduct which is neither excluded nor protected. A union is also able to exclude or expel where the exclusion or expulsion is to some extent, but not wholly or mainly, attributable to protected conduct. However, a union **is not able to exclude or expel** where the exclusion or expulsion is to any extent attributable to excluded conduct. An exclusion or expulsion is therefore unlawful where excluded conduct is the sole, main or subsidiary reason for the union's decision and where protected conduct is the sole or main reason.

An individual who **claims** that membership has been denied or that the union has unreasonably excluded or expelled him can present a claim to a tribunal. An individual can claim compensation against the union and will be heard by an employment tribunal. 7149

The **maximum** employment tribunal **compensation** that can be awarded is £65,200.

An individual must make the claim **within** 6 months, which is calculated from the date of the refusal of membership or expulsion. The tribunal can extend this period where it believes that it was not reasonably practicable for the individual to present the claim in time (s 175 TULRCA 1992). The meaning of "not reasonably practicable" should be construed in the same way as the equivalent wording contained in the unfair dismissal legislation (s 111(2) ERA 1996) (*GMB v Hamm*, EAT case 246/00). Applications for compensation relating to the exclusion or expulsion of members may no longer be made to the EAT.

10. To abide by its own rules The union must abide by its own rules and non-compliance will amount to a breach of contract between the union and its member. For example, if a rule states that the union will provide members with professional assistance to pursue legal claims, a refusal to do so will amount to a breach of contract. 7150

A union member can make a **complaint** to the CO that the union has breached or threatened to breach its rules. This can occur where the alleged breach relates to (s 108A TULRCA 1992): 7151
- appointments or elections of officials, other than employees of the union;
- disciplinary proceedings;
- balloting, other than for industrial action; or
- the constitution or proceedings of any policy-making executive body of the union.

A union member making a complaint has to show that reasonable steps had been taken to resolve the matter internally. The complaint has to be made **within** 6 months.

Members of a union may also have a **contractual right to challenge**, in the civil courts, the validity of an executive council's or executive committee's decision where that decision is taken in breach of the union's own rulebook. A union member has an individual contractual right to do so (*Wise v Union of Shop Distributors and Allied Workers* [1996] IRLR 609, ChD). However, there are limits to how far the courts will go in investigating the internal affairs of a union. For example, the powers of investigation of the High Court do not extend to a situation where there had already been an internal process where alleged irregularities had been properly investigated (*Hamlet v GMB* [1986] IRLR 293, ChD). 7152

Where **funds** have been misused unlawfully, a member of the union can apply for a court order to make the union recover the property, to appoint a receiver or remove one or more trustees (s 16 TULRCA 1992). 7153

There may be cases where members have **conflicting claims** on the union. If this is the case then the union has the right to protect the collective interests of its members, even if this offends the individual interests of one or more members. For example, if a union agrees a new working arrangement to the advantage of a majority of its members, the fact that one 7154 or more individuals is inconvenienced or perhaps even has to leave work as a result, does not give that or those members a right to claim that the union has breached any general duty of care that it might have to its members (*Iwanuszekak v GMB* [1988] IRLR 219, CA).

7155 **11. To hold elections** Unions must hold elections for certain executive and official positions (¶7160).

7156 **12. Not to discriminate on grounds of sex, race, disability, religion or belief, or sexual orientation** Unions must not discriminate on grounds of sex, race, religion or belief, or sexual orientation against members or persons applying for membership of the union (s 12 SDA 1975; s 11 RRA 1976; reg 15 SI 2003/1660; reg 15 SI 2003/1661):
– in the terms on which they are willing to admit members;
– by depriving an existing member of his membership or varying his terms of membership; or
– by subjecting a member to any other detriment.

In addition, it is unlawful for a union to discriminate against a **disabled** person (s 13 DDA 1995 as amended by reg 13 SI 2003/1673):
– in the arrangements which it makes for the purpose of determining who should be offered membership;
– in the terms on which it is prepared to admit new members;
– by refusing to accept or deliberately not accepting his application for membership;
– in the way it affords him access to any benefits or by refusing or deliberately omitting to afford him access to them;
– by depriving him of membership, or varying his membership terms; or
– by subjecting him to any other detriment.

Moreover, trade unions are under a **duty to make reasonable adjustments** in respect of any provision, criterion or practice applied by or on behalf of the union or any physical feature of premises occupied by it which places a disabled person at a substantial disadvantage in comparison to persons who are not disabled in order to prevent the disabled person from suffering that disadvantage (s 14 DDA 1995 as amended by reg 13 SI 2003/1673).

C. Elections

7160 Unions must hold elections at least every 5 years for the **following positions** (s 46 TULRCA 1992):
– members of the executive;
– any position by which a person has the right to vote as a member of the executive;
– the president; and
– the general secretary.

These legal requirements override any conflicting union rules contained in a union rulebook.

7161 There are **exemptions** from the requirement to hold elections:
1. when an election is **uncontested**.
2. if the **president or general secretary** (s 46(4) TULRCA 1992):
– is neither a voting member of the executive nor an employee of the union;
– holds office for a period which ends within 13 months of taking it up; and
– there was a gap of at least 12 months during which he did not hold such office.

EXAMPLE In some unions, the president holds office for just a year and then must stand down. Provided that the office is held by a lay official with no voting rights there is no obligation that they stand for election, other than as determined by the union rulebook.

3. if the **president** (s 46(4A) TULRCA 1992, as inserted by s 52 ERelA 2004):
– has been elected or appointed in accordance with the rules of the union;

– at the time of the election or appointment as president, he was also an elected general secretary or member of the executive and it is less than 5 years since such election took place; and
– has at all times since his election or appointment as president been an elected general secretary or member of the executive.
4. if the union is **newly formed**.
5. in the **first year after amalgamation** for office-holders who had already been elected in one of the amalgamating unions (s 57 TULRCA 1992).
6. where elected post-holders have been employees of the union for at least 10 years, who will reach **retirement age** within 5 years and who, under the rules of the union, can continue to hold their position without re-election (s 58 TULRCA 1992).

Right to stand as a candidate

Unions may not unreasonably exclude members from standing as candidates in elections (s 47 TULRCA 1992). Therefore, all union members have the right to stand for office. 7163

EXAMPLE In *Ecclestone v National Union of Journalists* [1999] IRLR 166, ChD, the Court held that excluding a candidate, who did not have the confidence of the sitting executive, was unreasonable.

Further, a union cannot require that a candidate is "directly or indirectly" a **member of a political party** and, therefore, they cannot exclude a candidate on the basis that he is not directly or indirectly a member of a particular party. 7164

Unions can **exclude a whole class** of members (for example, retired members) from standing as candidates, but the exclusion has to be in accordance with the rules of the union. It is not unlawful for a union to limit the number of elected candidates from any one region (*R v Certification Officer, ex parte EPEA* [1990] IRLR 398, HL). 7165

Manifestos

All candidates have rights in relation to the **content and distribution** of the material produced in support of their candidature (s 47 TULRCA 1992). These rights are intended to ensure that members have equality of treatment from the union and that the resources of the union are not used to favour any one candidate over another. 7166

Election addresses

Candidates have to be given the opportunity of preparing an election address in their own words (s 48 TULRCA 1992). Copies of the address, as far as is reasonably practicable, should be distributed by post, along with the voting papers. Unions can require candidates to submit their election address to the union by a specified date. The union can also put a maximum length on the election address provided that at least 100 words are permitted. The union is not allowed to modify a candidate's address, other than at the candidate's own request. It also has to reproduce copies of the election addresses in such as way as to not advantage one candidate over another. The union must bear the cost of distribution of all the candidates' election addresses. 7167

Voting

All union members have the **right to vote** in elections (s 49 TULRCA 1992). However, where the election is for an executive member to represent a particular trade, occupation, geographical area or class of membership, voting can be restricted to those who are members of the appropriate grouping. This applies as long as it does not mean that some members lose the right to vote in every election. Additionally, unions can **exclude** unemployed members, members in arrears of subscription or members who are in training, apprentices or new members. 7169

The union has to appoint a qualified **independent scrutineer** to supervise the production, distribution and count of votes in any election ballot. Solicitors with a current practising 7170 certificate and accountants qualified as auditors are competent to act as qualified independent scrutineers. The scrutineer also has a duty to inspect the union's register of members and is bound by a duty of confidentiality (s 49 TULRCA 1992).

7171 **Voting papers** have to be numbered, show the name of the independent scrutineer and the address to which the paper has to be returned. Every person entitled to vote has to be sent a voting paper to their nominated address together with a list of the candidates. They must be able to vote by post and in secret, without interference from or constraint imposed by the union, any of its members, officials, or employees.

Completed voting papers are returned to the scrutineer, not the union, who retains custody of them for at least a year after the election result has been announced, or longer if a complaint has been made to the court or the CO (¶7177).

Outcome

7173 The outcome of the election is determined solely by counting the number of votes cast directly for each candidate, although there are circumstances where voting by single, transferable vote is permissible. Any **inaccuracies** in the counting of votes can only be disregarded if they are on a scale that would not affect the result of the election.

Where there is a **tie** between two candidates, and there is no express term in the union's rules to resolve such a situation, a tie-breaker term will be implied into the rules to resolve the tie (*AB v CD* [2001] IRLR, HC).

7174 The scrutineer has to prepare a **report** on the election. This must state (s 52 TULRCA 1992):
– the number of voting papers distributed, returned, votes cast and spoilt or otherwise invalid papers returned;
– whether he is satisfied that the ballot was held in accordance with the legal rules and that the arrangements for the handling of the ballot papers were such that they minimised the potential for unfairness or malpractice;
– whether he is satisfied that he was able to carry out his functions without interference; and
– whether he has inspected the register of members.

Publication of results

7176 The union cannot publish the election results until the scrutineer submits his report. Having received the report, it has to take steps to make its contents known to its members. Members have the right to a copy of the report on request, although the union may charge a reasonable fee.

Complaints over the conduct of elections

7177 A union member or a candidate at the election can make an application to the CO or to the High Court (Court of Session in Scotland) where he believes that the union has failed to comply with the election requirements (s 54 TULRCA 1992). The CO or the court, as the case may be, has the power to make a declaration and an enforcement order, which obliges the union to hold an election or to take appropriate steps to remedy any failure in the conduct of the election. It can also order that the terms of the enforcement order be carried out within a specified period.

The application has to be made **within** a year of the announcement of the election result.

D. Political objects

A union may have political objects, though its members cannot be required to belong to a political party nor to contribute to its political fund (¶7183) (ss 71-96 TULRCA 1992). 7180

The rules and objects of a union may require it to engage in political lobbying or indeed to support a particular political party or candidate for office (s 71 TULRCA 1992). The rules must provide for payments for political objects to be made out of a **separate fund**, the union's political fund. 7181

Unions must establish a separate fund if they wish to engage in any of the following activities:
- contribute directly or indirectly to a political party, whether by affiliation fee or any loan to the party;
- provide any service or property for use by or on behalf of a political party;
- support any candidate for election to a political office as a member of Parliament, member of the European Parliament or member of a local authority or any position within a political party;
- maintain any holder of a political office;
- hold conferences or meetings on behalf of a political party or any other meeting whose main purpose is the transaction of business in connection with a political party; or
- produce or support any material (regardless of the form that this takes) where it is intended to persuade people who to vote, or not vote, for.

No money can be put into the political fund other than contributions from members who have not opted out (¶7189). The law constrains unions from using their general funds for such political purposes or from discharging any liabilities arising from the political fund. 7182

Political resolution

To be able to make payments in any of the above situations a union **must adopt** a political resolution, passed by a simple majority of those voting in a ballot of union members (s 73 TULRCA 1992). Voting has to be in accordance with the political ballot rules of the union, which have to be approved by the CO each time there is a ballot. The CO can only approve rules where the requirements regarding the appointment of the independent scrutineer, entitlement to vote, voting and the scrutineer's report are in compliance with the law. The political fund election rules are the same as those in elections for members of the union's executive (¶7160). 7183

Once adopted, a political resolution operates as if it were a rule of the union and can be rescinded in the same way as other rules can (s 72A TULRCA 1992). 7184

If not rescinded, the resolution **ceases to have effect** at the end of 10 years after the date of the ballot that decided the establishment of the political fund. 7185

Unions can **re-ballot** before the end of the 10 years and if they do the new resolution takes effect from the date of the new ballot. If the union **fails to win** the re-ballot, the political fund resolution ceases to have effect 2 weeks after the date of the ballot. The union can continue to make payments out of the fund for another 6 months from the date of the ballot. It cannot, however, make any payments if the fund is, or would be, in deficit as a result, and can only add to the fund money paid before the political fund resolution ceased to have effect. The union has to take steps to end contributions into the political fund and as an interim measure must pay any further contributions received into another fund, for example, its general fund.

If a member asks for a **return of contributions** after the political fund resolution has been lost, the union has to make the refund. Members can go to court to get an order to ensure that the union repays and stops collecting political fund contributions.

7187 **Complaints** that a union has breached the political fund rules in the way that it has applied its funds can be made to the CO or to the High Court (Court of Session in Scotland). There is no time limit within which the complaint must be made, though it should be made without undue delay.

Member's right to opt out

7189 A union cannot compel its members to contribute to a political fund (s 82 TULRCA 1992). Unions' rules have to provide that a member of the union, who gives notice that he **objects to contributing** to the political fund, will not be excluded from any benefits of the union nor placed at any disadvantage. Further, **on adopting** a political fund, the **union must inform** its members that they can opt out of contributing to it and how they can obtain an exemption notice.

7190 **Opting out** is normally done by means of an exemption notice form, which should be provided by the union. It is also available from the CO who will approve the form, taking account of the existing practice and character of the union. The notice states that the member objects to contributing to the political fund and exercises the right not to do so. Once the exemption notice has been given it comes into effect the following 1 January. However, if the union has just voted to establish a fund, the notice is effective from the date that it is given. The union can either reduce the member's regular contribution accordingly or can periodically exempt the member from payment of contributions (s 84 TULRCA 1992).

7192 Where the **rules have been breached**, a member can complain to the CO, who, should the complaint be upheld, can make an order for the breach to be remedied.

7194 **Employer's administrative duties** Where **union contributions are deducted** at source by the employer, the employer must comply with any **notification** in writing from a worker that he is **exempt** from making payments to the political fund (s 86 TULRCA 1992). In such circumstances, the employer has to ensure that no amounts are deducted representing payments to a political fund. However, the employer is not allowed to refuse to deduct the rest of a member's union contribution, if contributions are deducted in respect of other members.

7195 A union member claiming that the employer has **not complied** with his duties can apply to the county court for a declaration. The complaint must be made **within** a period of 3 months. The court can order the employer to take steps to comply within a specified time.

SECTION 3

Recognition and derecognition

7200 A union is recognised by an employer (or two or more associated employers) if it is entitled to **negotiate pay and other terms and conditions of employment** on behalf of a group (or groups) of workers (s 178 TULRCA 1992). This process is called **collective bargaining** and its definition differs according to the method by which a union has been recognised, i.e. either by reference to the legislation ("**statutory recognition**") or by voluntary agreement between the parties where the employer has voluntarily agreed to recognise a union without reference to the legislation (see ¶7210). Many such voluntary arrangements existed prior to, and have continued to come into existence since, the introduction of the statutory procedures and a clear distinction must be drawn between such **non-statutory voluntary arrangements and statutory "voluntary"** arrangements (as set out at Part II Sch A1 TULRCA 1992). For the purposes of this chapter, the latter are referred to as "semi-voluntary" recognition arrangements (see ¶7320 below).

It is essential to establish how a union has been recognised since this will affect the union's powers for collective bargaining purposes.

Collective bargaining has a wide definition under TULRCA 1992 and means negotiations relating to one or more of the matters specified above (¶7123) (s 178 TULRCA 1992).

However, for the purposes of the statutory recognition procedure, the broad definition of collective bargaining is expressly superseded by a much narrower definition at various points in the procedure which provides that if a union is recognised for the purpose of conducting collective bargaining on behalf of a group (or groups) of workers, it will have authority to conduct negotiations with the employer relating only to **pay, hours and holidays** (para 3 Sch A1 TULRCA 1992). Pay is a broad concept and it has been held that, for statutory collective bargaining purposes, it should include bargaining about **defined pension matters** and all matters relating to the levels or amount of employer's pension contributions, although this is inconsistent with the new measures introduced in April 2005 by the Employment Relations Act 2004 which state that pay does not include terms relating to a person's membership of, rights under or employer's contributions to, an occupational pension scheme or a personal pension scheme (*UNIFI v Union Bank of Nigeria plc* [2001] IRLR 712, CAC). However, the parties can also agree other matters to be the subject of collective bargaining which may or may not include pay, hours and holidays (paras 3(4), 54(3) Sch A1 TULRCA 1992).

In spite of this, the broad definition of collective bargaining will ordinarily apply where reference is made to an existing collective bargaining agreement between an employer and a union, regardless of how the collective bargaining agreement was established, for example, when the CAC is determining whether a request for recognition passes the validity and admissibility tests set down under the statutory procedure (paras 33, 44 Sch A1 TULRCA 1992).

MEMO POINTS 1. The statutory recognition procedures came into force under Sch A1 TULRCA 1992 (as introduced by Sch 1 ERelA 1999). Sch A1 TULRCA 1992 provides for both statutory (i.e. compulsory) (Part I) and "semi-voluntary" (Part II) recognition.
2. References in this section to one union acting on its own also cover the situation where two or more unions are acting jointly together, unless specifically stated otherwise. Joint requests by unions are discussed below at ¶7254.

The **other rights on recognition** (voluntary or statutory) are: 7201
- the right for union members and officials to take time off work to carry out union duties (s 168 TULRCA 1992; ¶7600);
- the right to disclosure of information for the purposes of collective bargaining (ss 178, 181 TULRCA 1992);
- the right to be consulted on collective redundancies (s 188 TULRCA 1992; Collective Redundancies and Transfer of Undertakings (Protection of Employment) (Amendment) Regulations SI 1999/1925);
- the right to be informed and consulted about, and other rights in connection with, the transfer of an undertaking (Transfer of Undertakings (Protection of Employment) Regulations SI 1981/1794, as amended);
- the right to be informed and consulted about under the Health and Safety at Work etc. Act 1974 (Safety Representatives and Safety Committee Regulations SI 1977/500, as amended; Management of Health and Safety at Work Regulations SI 1999/3242, as amended);
- the right to be informed and consulted about occupational pensions (s 11(5) Pensions Schemes Act 1993; Occupational Pension Schemes (Contracting-out) Regulations SI 1996/1172, as amended; s 113 Pensions Schemes Act 1993, as amended; Occupational Pension Schemes (Disclosure of Information) Regulations SI 1996/1655, as amended); and
- the right to commence procedures for the establishment of a European Works Council (or equivalent consultative procedures at transnational level) (Transnational Information and Consultation of Employees Regulations SI 1999/3323).

However, unlike unions which are recognised by reference to the statute (save for semi-voluntarily recognised unions), voluntarily-recognised unions have no right to be informed and consulted about training (see ¶7295).

Employees are afforded some protection under the statutory recognition provisions if they 7205
are **dismissed** or **subjected to a detriment** for a reason in connection with union recognition or derecognition (paras 156-162 Sch A1 TULRCA 1992) (¶7598 and ¶7583). A dismissal on statutory

recognition or derecognition grounds will be for an inadmissible reason and therefore employees do not need to have any particular period of continuous employment in order to bring an unfair dismissal claim. In addition, employees over normal retiring age are not excluded. However, the employment protection in this respect only applies to unions which are recognised (or derecognised) under the statutory provisions set out in Schedule A1 TULRCA 1992 and, therefore, will not apply to purely voluntary recognition arrangements.

7208 A summary of the different **types** of recognition and the **main characteristics** of each is as follows:

	Statutory	Semi-voluntary	Voluntary
Recognition procedure	Prescribed by statute (see ¶7230)	Prescribed by statute (see ¶7320)	By agreement between employer and union(s) (see ¶7210)
Does the union need to be independent?	Yes	Yes	No
Enforceability/ derecognition	Recognition is legally binding on employer/ union and there are prescribed derecognition procedures (see ¶7340)	Recognition is legally binding on employer/ union and there are prescribed derecognition procedures (see ¶7340)	Not legally binding (so recognition can be withdrawn at any time) unless parties expressly agree otherwise
Subject of collective bargaining	Pay, hours and holidays, although parties can extend scope of collective bargaining by agreement	Pay, hours and holidays, although parties can extend scope of collective bargaining by agreement	Agreed by parties and not subject to any statutory restrictions
Consequences	Statutory duties to agree on method of collective bargaining (or have one imposed by CAC) and to consult on training (see ¶7285), in addition to principal consequences listed at ¶7201	Statutory duty to agree on method of collective bargaining (or have one imposed by CAC) (see ¶7325), in addition to principal consequences listed at ¶7201	Some or all of principal consequences set out at ¶7201, depending on whether union is independent or not
Right of union members and officials not to be dismissed/subjected to a detriment?	Yes	Yes	Only if union is independent
Right of union members and officials to time off for activities/duties?	Yes	Yes	Only if union is independent

I. Recognition

A. Voluntary recognition

Employers with **fewer than 21 workers** may or may not agree to recognise a union for the purposes of collective bargaining. However, it is an entirely voluntary matter for the employer as to whether he agrees to recognise a union for these purposes as he falls outside the scope of the statutory recognition procedure. Similarly, where a **union is not independent** (see ¶7122), the statutory recognition procedure will not apply and the only route open to the union is to seek voluntary recognition from the employer. There is **no obligation** on the employer to agree to voluntary recognition. 7210

However, provided that the 21-worker threshold has been passed and the union is independent, the union may choose whether to pursue statutory or voluntary recognition.

Since the introduction of the statutory recognition procedures in 2000, there has been a **marked increase** in the number of employers and unions **favouring the voluntary route** to recognition and, so far, the statutory route envisaged by Sch A1 TULRCA 1992 has been far less used than previously anticipated. One possible explanation is that an employer would prefer to voluntarily agree with a union the terms of a (purely) voluntary recognition arrangement rather than have a heavily-regulated statutory recognition arrangement imposed. There are also obvious advantages, in terms of saving management and union resources, to agree to a purely voluntary recognition arrangement. 7211

The **form** that a voluntary agreement should take is not set out by the legislation. However, a purely voluntary recognition agreement will not be a legally enforceable contract, unless the parties record in writing their express intention otherwise (s 179 TULRCA 1992). This means that, unless the parties expressly provide for the voluntary agreement to be legally enforceable, any deviation from the agreed terms of a collective bargaining method, or indeed a complete withdrawal of voluntary recognition, will not give rise to a legal challenge (although, the threat of industrial action should, of course, be borne in mind). 7212

It is also advisable that the agreement is **dated** and states that the employer recognises the union is entitled to carry out collective bargaining on behalf of a certain group of workers.

B. Statutory recognition

1. Procedure

a. Union request for recognition from employer

A union can only seek statutory recognition if the employer (together with any associated employer(s)) has **21 or more workers** on the day he receives the request, or an average of at least 21 workers in the 13 weeks ending with that day (para 4 Sch A1 TULRCA 1992). Moreover, a union must have a **certificate of independence** issued by the Certification Officer (¶7122). 7230

A union seeking recognition must first **request** it from the employer. This request must:
- be in writing;
- identify the union to be recognised and the proposed bargaining unit;
- state that it is being made under Sch A1 of TULRCA 1992; and
- be received by the employer (the onus is on the union to ensure that the employer physically receives the request).

MEMO POINTS 1. In order to establish the average number of workers in the 13 weeks ending with the day on which the employer receives the request, the aggregate of the number of workers (including part-timers) employed in each of the 13 weeks should be divided by 13 (para 7 Sch A1 TULRCA 1992).

2. Two employers are treated as being associated if one is a company of which the other has direct or indirect control, or both are companies of which a third company which has direct or indirect control (s 297 TULRCA 1992). Any workers employed by an associated employer incorporated outside GB should be ignored unless the day the recognition request was made fell within a period during which he ordinarily worked in GB (para 7 Sch A1 TULRCA 1992).

Agreement as to the bargaining unit and recognition

7232 After a valid request, the parties have 10 working days (starting with the day after the request is received by the employer) to agree which workers (known as the bargaining unit) will be covered by the recognition arrangement and, in addition, to agree that the union is to be recognised for the purpose of collective bargaining on behalf of that bargaining unit. If agreement is reached within 10 working days (known as the **first period**), the union will be deemed to be recognised and no further action will be required (para 10(1) Sch A1 TULRCA 1992).

MEMO POINTS For the purpose of the statutory recognition procedure, a working day is any day falling between Monday to Friday (inclusive), with the exception of Good Friday, Christmas Day or any other bank holiday.

7233 If, before the end of the first period, the **employer rejects the recognition** request but indicates he is **willing to negotiate** with the union, the parties have a further 20 working days (known as the **second period**) in which to agree a bargaining unit and that the union is to be recognised for the purposes of collective bargaining (para 10(2), (3) Sch A1 TULRCA 1992). The second period starts with the day after that on which the first period ends (or such longer period, starting on that day, as the parties may from time to time agree). If such an agreement is made before the end of the second period, the union will be deemed to be recognised and no further action will be required (para 10(4) Sch A1 TULRCA 1992).

7235 **Involvement of ACAS** Either party may request assistance from ACAS in negotiating an appropriate bargaining unit (para 10(5) Sch A1 TULRCA 1992).

If the employer requests that ACAS assists in the negotiation and, within 10 working days (starting with the day following that on which the employer makes the proposal), the **union rejects** the request to involve ACAS or **fails to accept** the proposal, the union will be precluded from making any subsequent application to the Central Arbitration Committee (below) to decide whether the union has the support of a majority of the workers constituting the bargaining unit.

---

b. References to the Central Arbitration Committee

7240 The Central Arbitration Committee (CAC) has a pivotal role in the statutory recognition procedure. The CAC is an independent public body which has several other industrial relations functions outside the scope of this book. **Applications** to the CAC are heard by a three-member panel, including the chairman or deputy chairman. The CAC has produced a publication (for guidance purposes only), Trade Union Recognition and Derecognition, which is available from its website, www.cac.gov.uk.

However, the union **cannot apply** to the CAC under this provision if it has previously rejected (or failed to accept) the employer's request that ACAS assists in the negotiations on a bargaining unit (para 12(5) Sch A1 TULRCA 1992).

If the **employer rejects** the request or **fails to respond** before the end of the first period or, if despite a willingness to negotiate, no agreement is reached by the end of the second period (see above), the union may apply to the CAC to decide whether (paras 11, 12 Sch A1 TULRCA 1992): 7241
- the proposed bargaining unit is appropriate; and
- the union has the support of a majority of the workers constituting the bargaining unit.

Further, where at the end of the second period, the parties have agreed on a bargaining unit but have **not agreed that the union is to be recognised** to conduct collective bargaining on behalf of that unit, the union may apply to the CAC to decide whether the proposed bargaining unit is appropriate and whether the union has the support of a majority of the workers constituting that unit (para 12 Sch A1 TULRCA 1992).

Acceptability and admissibility requirements

The CAC must decide whether a union's application is acceptable (paras 14, 15 Sch A1 TULRCA 1992) and admissible (paras 33-42 Sch A1 TULRCA 1992). 7245

MEMO POINTS The CAC is entitled to require a union, employer and worker to **supply** the CAC case manager with **specific information** within a specified period in relation to the workers in a specified bargaining unit or the likelihood of a majority of workers being in favour of a union conducting collective bargaining on their behalf (para 170A Sch A1 TULRCA 1992, as inserted by s 19 ERelA 2004). If they fail to comply, the report made by the CAC in accordance with such information must mention that failure and the CAC may draw an inference against the party concerned.

Acceptable If the CAC receives **two or more applications from different unions**, it must ascertain, in respect of each application in turn, whether 10% of the proposed bargaining unit are union members, within 10 working days of receipt of the last application (paras 14(4), (6) Sch A1 TULRCA 1992). If both or neither applications pass the 10% test, then the CAC will reject both applications (para 14(7) Sch A1 TULRCA 1992). If only one application passes the 10% test, the CAC will proceed to consider whether that application is valid and admissible (para 15(2) Sch A1 TULRCA 1992) and must not accept any other application (para 14(8) Sch A1 TULRCA 1992). If the CAC does not accept an application, no further steps will be taken in respect of that application (para 14(10) Sch A1 TULRCA 1992). 7246

Admissible The application should be made in a **form specified** and provided by the CAC and supported by documentation prescribed by the CAC (para 33 Sch A1 TULRCA 1992). The union should supply the employer with a **notice of the application**, together with a copy of the application and any supporting documentation (para 34 Sch A1 TULRCA 1992). It is sensible to send these by recorded delivery. 7248

The CAC will not accept an application unless it decides that the application passes the **10% test**, namely, that members of the union constitute at least 10% of the workers constituting the relevant (i.e. proposed) bargaining unit and that a majority of the workers constituting the relevant bargaining unit would be likely to favour recognition of the union (para 36 Sch A1 TULRCA 1992). In addressing the question of whether there is such a majority, the CAC does not take a purely mathematical approach and often relies on its own experience and the nature of unionisation in the industry concerned. 7249

An application will not be admissible if the CAC is satisfied that there is already in force an **existing collective agreement** under which one or more unions are recognised as entitled to conduct collective bargaining on behalf of any worker or workers within the relevant bargaining unit (para 35(1) Sch A1 TULRCA 1992). This restriction prevents a union from abusing the recognition procedure by trying to upset existing collective bargaining arrangements between the employer and another union. This will include any **pre-existing national agreement** if the employer is a party to, and uses, it for collective bargaining purposes (*TGWU and Riverstone Spinning Ltd*, TUR1/110/01, CAC). Likewise, this will include any **pre-existing voluntary recognition agreement** already in force which will prevent any further applications for recognition being admissible from the moment the pre-existing agreement is entered into. Moreover, it is not necessary for such an agreement to have been used to negotiate the terms and 7250 conditions of workers who make up the relevant bargaining unit and it is irrelevant that there is only one member of staff who belongs to the union voluntarily recognised by the employer (*R (on the application of the National Union of Journalists) v CAC and MGN Ltd* [2005] IRLR 28, QBD). Furthermore, the pre-existing collective agreement does not need to provide for collective bargaining on pay, hours, holidays or other terms and conditions of employment for it to prevent any further applications from being admissible (*Transport and General Workers' Union v Asda* [2004] IRLR 836, CAC).

Whether there is an existing collective agreement is a **question of fact** for the CAC, and the CAC is entitled to question whether the objectives of the alleged agreement do regulate relations between the employer and his workers (*BECTU v City Screen Ltd*, TUR1/309/03, CAC). In this case, a non-independent Forum, which the employer had set up in response to an application for recognition, was not held to be a union with collective agreement powers, as it did not, at the time of the hearing, include workers whose terms and conditions it was seeking to regulate. In *Amicus v 21st Century Logistics Ltd*, TUR1/445/05, CAC, one union (TGWU) was already recognised before an application for recognition from Amicus was heard by the CAC. The TGWU subsequently withdrew its recognition agreement prior to the hearing and as there was no collective agreement in force, the application from Amicus did not need to be rejected.

However, in certain circumstances a **union can make a second application** for recognition if (para 35(2) Sch A1 TULRCA 1992):
– the union is independent;
– it is the same union that is already recognised for the purposes of collective bargaining; and
– the existing collective bargaining agreement does not already cover negotiations relating to all of the "core topics": pay, hours and holidays.

Therefore, a union will not have to relinquish (purely) voluntary recognition in respect of collective bargaining covering matters other than pay, hours and holiday (for example, disciplinary issues) in its pursuit of statutory recognition.

7251 However, a **second union** can make an application for recognition where (para 35(4) Sch A1 TULRCA 1992):
– the existing recognised union is not independent;
– at some time there was a different agreement between the (non-independent) union and the employer (the old agreement) under which the (non-independent) union was recognised as being entitled to conduct collective bargaining on behalf of a group of workers which was the same, or substantially the same, as the group of workers covered by the current application; and
– that old agreement ceased to have effect within 3 years of the date of the current agreement.

7252 It is for the CAC to determine whether a group or groups of workers are the same, or substantially the same, as another. This provision aims to **prevent** an employer from re-recognising a non-independent union (including a staff association) following its derecognition arising from an application from workers, in an attempt to **bar any independent union** from seeking statutory recognition.

This issue was illustrated in a case in which the existence of a non-independent staff association, which had been continuously in operation for some time prior to the conclusion of a formal agreement (which took place shortly after the introduction of the new statutory procedures), effectively prevented an independent union from seeking statutory recognition (*Prison Officers' Association and Securicor Custodial Services Ltd*, TUR 1/5/00, CAC). In this case, the only alternative for the independent union would be to seek derecognition of the non-independent staff association before applying for recognition.

7253 Where the CAC has accepted an application from one union and a **second union applies**, and at least one worker is covered by both applications, the CAC will refuse to consider the second application until consideration of the first application has been concluded (para 38 Sch A1 TULRCA 1992).

7254 If **two (or more) unions submit a joint application**, the CAC will only accept it if the unions can demonstrate that they will co-operate with each other and that they agree (if the employer so requests) to enter into an agreement with the employer that the collective bargaining will be conducted by the unions acting together (para 37 Sch A1 TULRCA 1992). Therefore, the onus is on the unions to demonstrate that they operate with a united voice. In addition, joint applicant unions have the burden of convincing the CAC that they will maintain the stable and constructive collective bargaining arrangements.

An application from a union for recognition in respect of a **bargaining unit covering two or more employers** will not be admissible (*Graphical, Paper and Media Union v Derry Print Ltd* [2002] IRLR 380, CAC). In this case, the CAC determined that a single bargaining unit could not cover workers employed by more than one employer, even if the employers were associated. However, it indicated that it would be prepared to look behind the corporate veil if there was overwhelming evidence that two companies were, in reality, one entity. 7255

Three year rule

Nevertheless, once an application for recognition has been made by a union and the CAC has agreed to consider it, the union will have to wait a further 3 years before making a **second application** in respect of the same, or substantially the same, bargaining unit (para 39(2) Sch A1 TULRCA 1992). 7257

Similarly, if the CAC has issued a **declaration** that a union is **not entitled to be recognised**, a further application made by that union in respect of the same, or substantially the same, bargaining unit within 3 years starting with the day after the declaration was made will be inadmissible (para 40(2) Sch A1 TULRCA 1992).

Finally, if the CAC has issued a declaration that, in respect of a recognised union, the current union is to be **derecognised** (in accordance with para 121(3) Sched A1 TULRCA 1992, see below at ¶7352), an application by a union relating to the same, or substantially the same, bargaining unit within 3 years starting with the day after the declaration was issued will be inadmissible (para 41 Sch A1 TULRCA 1992).

Determination of the bargaining unit

Where the request is admissible and acceptable, the **CAC will** initially try to **assist** the parties to reach an agreement on the appropriate bargaining unit within 20 working days starting with the day after the CAC accepts the application. This period is known as the **appropriate period** (para 18 Sch A1 TULRCA 1992). 7259

It is possible to shorten the appropriate period. If the CAC decides that there is **no reasonable prospect** of the parties coming to an agreement on the bargaining unit before the end of the appropriate period, the CAC has the discretion to notify the parties that the period will end on an earlier date, thereby speeding up the process. The CAC must provide **reasons** in its notice.

The parties may also **apply** to the CAC to shorten the appropriate period and the CAC can provide a declaration to this effect. However, it remains open to the CAC to extend the period, even if previously reduced at the parties' request, to allow the parties more time to reach an agreement. Again, the CAC must provide reasons for any such extension.

Within 5 working days, starting with the day after the CAC notifies the employer of its acceptance of the application, **the employer must supply the following information** to the union and the CAC (para 18A Sch A1 TULRCA 1992, as inserted by s 3 ERelA 2004):
- a list of the categories of worker in the proposed bargaining unit;
- a list of the workplaces at which the workers in the proposed bargaining unit work; and
- the number of workers which the employer reasonably believes to be in each category at each workplace in the proposed bargaining unit.

The details provided to the union and the CAC must be the same and as accurate as is reasonably practicable in light of the information held by the employer at the time.

The union can **ask the CAC to decide upon the proposed bargaining unit** before the end of the appropriate period. If, either at the time the union's request is made or at a later time during the appropriate period, the CAC considers that **the employer has failed to provide** 7260

the requisite information (¶7259), it must decide whether the proposed bargaining unit is appropriate (and if not, it must decide a bargaining unit which is appropriate) **within** (para 19A Sch A1 TULRCA 1992, as inserted by s 4 ERelA 2004):
– 10 working days (starting with the day after the date the request is made); or
– such longer period as the CAC may specify by notice containing reasons.

If the **employer and the union fail to agree on the bargaining unit** by the end of the appropriate period and at the end of that period, the union has not asked the CAC to make a decision as to the bargaining unit or, if a request has been made, the CAC does not consider that the employer has failed to provide the requisite information, the CAC must decide whether the proposed bargaining unit is appropriate (and if not, it must decide a bargaining unit which is appropriate) **within** (para 19 Sch A1 TULRCA 1992, as inserted by s 4 ERelA 2004):
– 10 working days (starting with the day after that on which the appropriate period ends); or
– such longer period as the CAC may specify by notice containing reasons.

7261 In deciding the appropriate bargaining unit, the **CAC must take into account** the need for the bargaining unit to be compatible with effective management together with the following matters, in so far as they do not conflict with that need (para 19B Sch A1 TULRCA 1992, as inserted by s 4 ERelA 2004):
– the views of the parties;
– existing national and local bargaining arrangements;
– the desirability of avoiding small fragmented bargaining units within one business;
– the characteristics of workers falling within the bargaining unit under consideration and of any other employees whom the CAC considers relevant; and
– the location of the workers.

In taking the employer's views into account in order to decide whether the proposed bargaining unit is appropriate, the CAC must also take into account the employer's views about any other bargaining unit that he considers appropriate.

The CAC will pay **particular regard** to the requirement that the bargaining unit is compatible with effective management. The constitution of the bargaining unit is crucial to the statutory recognition procedure since evidence of union membership and support for recognition will vary according to whether the balance tips towards union or employer. For this reason, an employer may try to argue for a "whole company" approach so as to include as many middle management employees in the unit as possible, thereby attempting to shift the balance away from support for union recognition. In such cases, the union is likely to argue for smaller, distinct units. The CAC has held that a unit consisting of only shop-floor staff would be appropriate and was not incompatible with effective management (*Benteler Automotive UK and the ISTC*, TUR 1/4/00, CAC).

7263 **Modified bargaining unit** If the appropriate bargaining unit agreed by the parties (para 18 Sch A1 TULRCA 1992) or determined by the CAC (para 19 Sch A1 TULRCA 1992) differs from the bargaining unit originally proposed by the union, the CAC must ensure that the recognition request, in relation to the modified bargaining unit, is still valid (¶7320) and that the admissibility tests are satisfied (¶7245). The validity requirements must be determined by the CAC within 10 working days following the day on which the appropriate bargaining unit was agreed or decided (para 20 Sch A1 TULRCA 1992).

Appointment of independent person

7264 Once the CAC accepts an application to determine the proposed bargaining unit, the union may apply to the CAC for the appointment of a suitable independent person to enable it to **communicate with the relevant workers**. Before a bargaining unit is agreed or decided upon, relevant workers are those who fall within the proposed bargaining unit. After an appropriate bargaining unit is agreed or decided upon, relevant workers are those who fall within that unit (para 19C Sch A1 TULRCA 1992, as inserted by s 5 ERelA 2004). The union's right of communication starts on the day on which the CAC informs the parties of the name of the

person appointed and the date of his appointment and ends when the first of the following occurs:
- the union's application to the CAC is withdrawn;
- the CAC declares that the application is invalid;
- the CAC notifies the union that it is recognised as entitled to conduct collective bargaining on behalf of the workers in the bargaining unit; or
- the CAC informs the union of the name of the person appointed to conduct a ballot.

Once an employer is informed of the appointment of the suitable independent person, he must comply with certain **duties**, insofar as it is reasonable to expect him to do so (para 19D Sch A1 TULRCA 1992, as inserted by s 5 ERelA 2004). These are to **provide** the CAC with names and home addresses of all the relevant workers within 10 working days (starting with the day after that on which the employer is informed of the name of the person appointed and the date of the appointment) and to **update** this information if the relevant workers change as a result of an agreement or decision on the appropriate bargaining unit, or if they join or leave the bargaining unit. The appointed person must, if asked to do so by the union, **send** to any worker whose name and home address has been passed to him, and who remains a relevant worker, any information supplied to him by the union.

If the employer **fails** to fulfil any of its duties and the union's right of communication has not yet ended, the CAC may order the employer to remedy its failure within a specified period. If the employer fails to comply with the remedial order, the CAC must notify the employer and the union of that failure, drawing their attention to its **discretion to award recognition** if:
- the CAC is satisfied that the employer failed to comply with the remedial order;
- an appropriate bargaining unit has been agreed by the parties or decided upon by the CAC;
- the application to the CAC is not invalid; and
- the union's right of communication has not ended.

Declaration of recognition

If the **parties voluntarily agree a bargaining unit before** the CAC has made a declaration of automatic recognition or its duty to arrange a recognition ballot has arisen and they apply jointly to request that the CAC take no further action (para 17 Sch A1 TULRCA 1992), the union will be deemed to be **semi-voluntarily recognised** and entitled to conduct collective bargaining on behalf of a group or groups of workers under the terms of an agreement for recognition (see ¶7320). 7265

However, if the parties are **not in agreement**, the CAC will decide the question of recognition. In determining whether a union should be recognised following an application by a union, if more than half the workers in the bargaining unit are already members of the union, there will be a presumption of support for recognition and the CAC will issue a declaration of **automatic recognition** that the union is recognised to conduct collective bargaining on behalf of the bargaining unit (para 22(2) Sch A1 TULRCA 1992). However, the CAC will **not** issue a declaration of **automatic recognition** if (para 22(3), (4) Sch A1 TULRCA 1992, as amended by s 6 ERelA 2004): 7266
- it believes that a ballot should be held in the interests of good industrial relations;
- the CAC has credible evidence from a significant number of the union members within the bargaining unit that they do not want the union to conduct collective bargaining on their behalf; or
- membership evidence is produced which leads the CAC to doubt whether a significant number of members wish the union to conduct collective bargaining on their behalf.

If any one of these factors exist, the CAC must notify the parties that it intends to arrange for the workers within the bargaining unit to **vote in a recognition ballot** to indicate whether they want the union to conduct collective bargaining on their behalf (para 23(2) Sch A1 TULRCA 1992).

MEMO POINTS Membership evidence, for these purposes, is evidence about the (para 22(5) Sch A1 TULRCA 1992):
- circumstances in which the union members became members; and
- length of time for which union members have been members.

7267 **Membership evidence** should be assessed according to the union's normal rules so that only current and genuine members are counted in assessing evidence of membership and support. If there are discrepancies between membership information provided by the union and that provided by the employer, the CAC may arrange for the information to be checked by an independent third party.

7268 There is **no appeal** against the CAC decision whether or not to hold a recognition ballot. However, it is possible for a party to bring an application for judicial review of the decision in the High Court. Nevertheless, provided the reasons (if any) given by the CAC for its decision are not irrational and the manner in which the decision was reached does not breach the rules of natural justice, a party is unlikely to be able to successfully challenge the CAC's decision as to whether a recognition ballot is required (*Fullarton Computer Industries Ltd v CAC*, 28 June 2001 (CS)).

7270 **Recognition ballots** It is unlikely that the CAC will make a declaration of recognition on the basis of majority membership without holding a recognition ballot, particularly if it is aware that an employer objects to the recognition request. However, if the CAC is not satisfied that a majority of the workers within the bargaining unit are members of the union, then a ballot conducted by a qualified independent person will always be required.

7271 Once the duty to organise a ballot has arisen, the **CAC** should, as soon as is reasonably practicable, **notify the parties** of (para 25(9) Sch A1 TULRCA 1992):
– the name of the qualified independent person and the date of his appointment;
– the date by which the ballot must be held;
– the method of conducting the ballot; and
– where (if there is more than one workplace) the ballot will be held.

If the **union** within 10 working days (starting with the day on which the union receives the CAC's notification that it intends to arrange a recognition ballot (¶7266)), informs the CAC that it **does not want the ballot to take place**, the CAC must cancel the ballot and notify both parties of its actions and reasons for cancellation. If both the **union and employer** inform the CAC that they do not want the ballot to take place, the 10 working day period starts with the day on which the last of the parties receives the CAC's notification. The CAC may specify a longer period (para 24 Sch A1 TULRCA 1992, as amended by s 7 ERelA 2004).

7272 A **recognition ballot must** (para 25(2)-(4) Sch A1 TULRCA 1992):
– be **organised by** a qualified independent person appointed by the CAC;
– **take place within** 20 working days starting with the day after the qualified independent person was appointed (or such longer period as the CAC may decide); and
– be **conducted by** post or at a workplace or by a combination of the two.

A person is **qualified** to undertake this task if he is (Recognition and Derecognition Ballots (Qualified Persons) Order SI 2000/1306):
– a practising solicitor;
– a qualified accountant; or
– a member of one of six appointed bodies.

MEMO POINTS The six appointed bodies are The Association of Electoral Administrators; Election.Com Limited; Electoral Reform (Ballot Services) Limited; The Industrial Law Society; Involvement and Participation Association; and Twenty-first Century Press Limited.

7273 The **qualified independent person** must **ensure**:
– the names and home addresses of the workers to be balloted are accurate;
– the ballot is conducted properly and in secret;
– (if requested to do so by the union) that any information supplied by the union is sent to the balloted workers (this cost will be borne by the union) (para 26(6) Sch A1 TULRCA 1992); and
– that the CAC is promptly informed of the ballot result.

It is not the role of the independent person to listen to disputes on access to workers during the union recognition (or derecognition) process (¶7365).

The CAC will decide on the appropriate **method of conducting the ballot**. In doing so, it will take into consideration the risk of unfairness or malpractice if the ballot is conducted at one or more workplaces; costs and practicality; and any such other matters as it considers appropriate (para 25 Sch A1 TULRCA 1992, as amended by s 8 ERelA 2004). Unless factors such as the location of workers indicate that a **combination of methods** would be appropriate, the CAC will ordinarily decide on just one balloting method. 7274

During the balloting process, an **employer must**: 7275
- **co-operate** with the union and the qualified independent person (para 26(2) Sch A1 TULRCA 1992);
- provide the union with **access** to the workers as is reasonable to enable the union to inform the workers of the object of the ballot and to seek their support and opinions;
- **provide** the names and home addresses of the workers constituting the bargaining unit within 10 working days of being informed of the ballot, together with details of those who join and cease to be within the unit (para 26(4) Sch A1 TULRCA 1992);
- **refrain from making any offer** to workers in the bargaining unit which is likely to induce them not to attend meetings between the union and workers (which are organised to provide the union with access to workers and which the employer is required to permit) and is not reasonable in the circumstances (para 26(4A) Sch A1 TULRCA 1992, as inserted by s 9 ERelA 2004);
- **refrain from taking or threatening to take** any action against a worker solely or mainly on the grounds he took part in such meetings between the union and workers or indicated an intention to do so (para 26(4B) Sch A1 TULRCA 1992, as inserted by s 9 ERelA 2004); and
- **comply with** the Code of Practice on Access and Unfair Practices during Ballots for Trade Union Recogntion or Derecognition (¶7366).

An employer should give careful consideration to his duties during the ballot process, since any **failure to comply** on his part may lead to the imposition of penalties by the CAC. In deciding whether an employer has complied with the Code of Practice, the CAC may take into account the union's conduct (¶7384). 7276

If the **employer fails to fulfil** his duties during the balloting process, and the ballot has not yet been held, the CAC may order him to take specific reasonable steps to remedy the failure(s) as the CAC considers appropriate. The CAC will lay down a time limit within which the employer must comply with the steps specified (para 27 Sch A1 TULRCA 1992).

If the employer fails to comply with such an order from the CAC, and if the ballot has not been held, the CAC may (but is not required to) issue a declaration that the union is recognised to conduct collective bargaining on behalf of the bargaining unit without holding a ballot (para 27(2) Sch A1 TULRCA 1992). If so, the CAC will cancel the ballot and, if the ballot is nevertheless held, it will be null and void. The sanction for awarding recognition without a ballot due to an employer's failure to fulfil his duties means that, on a practical level, the employer should take steps to comply with his duties and/or any order issued by the CAC to remedy any failure to comply with his duties during the ballot process.

No corresponding duties or sanctions are imposed on the **union** in respect of its co-operation during the balloting process. However, the CAC may take into account the union's conduct in deciding whether the employer has complied with his duties in respect of the ballot process. 7277

Each party must, however, also refrain from using any **unfair practice**. A party uses unfair practice if it does any of the following to influence the outcome of the ballot (para 27A Sch A1 TULRCA 1992, as inserted by s 10 ERelA 2004): 7278
- offers to pay money or give money's worth to a worker in the bargaining unit in return for his agreement to vote in a particular way or to abstain from voting;
- makes an outcome-specific offer to a worker entitled to vote;
- coerces or attempts to coerce a worker in the bargaining unit to disclose whether he intends to vote or how he intends to, or did, vote;
- dismisses or threatens to dismiss a worker;
- takes or threatens to take disciplinary action against a worker;

– subjects or threatens to subject a worker to any other detriment; or
– uses or attempts to use undue influence on a worker entitled to vote.

Any **complaint** about such unfair practices must be made to the CAC on or before the first working day after either the ballot or, if votes can be cast in the ballot on more than one day, the last of those days. The CAC has 10 working days to decide whether the complaint is well-founded (starting with the day after which the complaint was received by CAC or such longer period as CAC specifies to the parties in writing, giving reasons for the extension).

If the complaint is well-founded, the CAC must issue a **declaration** to that effect as soon as is reasonably practicable. It may order the party concerned to take **specific action** as is reasonable to mitigate the effect of the party's failure. Where a party fails to comply with the order and/or uses unfair practice involving the use of **violence or the dismissal of a union official**, the CAC has the discretion to award recognition (if the party concerned was the employer) or to reject the union's application for recognition (if the party concerned was the union).

The CAC also has the discretion to arrange for a **further ballot** where unfair practice has occurred. If the CAC gives notice of its intention to hold a second ballot, the above provisions relating to the ballot apply with **modifications** (for example, the period within which the union or the employer can inform the CAC that it does not want the ballot to take place is reduced from 10 working days to 5 working days and the employer's duty to provide specific details to the CAC is limited) (para 27C, D, F Sch A1 TULRCA 1992, as inserted by s 10 ERelA 2004).

7279 There is also a difference regarding the **costs** of the ballot, depending on whether unfair practice has occurred. Where a complaint of **unfair practice** is well-founded, the gross costs of the ballot shall be borne by such of the parties and in such proportions as the CAC may determine. The CAC may therefore require the party who committed the unfair practice to pay all or the majority of the costs. Where unfair practice is **not applicable**, the union and employer must share the costs of the ballot equally (para 28(2) Sch A1 TULRCA 1992). If two unions are involved in the ballot, they will divide the unions' half of the costs into equal shares, unless they agree otherwise between themselves. Should two or more unions agree to share the costs in any other way, they must notify the qualified independent person of their agreed arrangement (para 28(3) Sch A1 TULRCA 1992).

The costs of the ballot will **include** (para 28(7) Sch A1 TULRCA 1992):
– costs incurred (wholly, necessarily and exclusively in connection with the ballot) by the qualified independent person (if relevant);
– a reasonable amount to be paid to the person who conducted the ballot for his services; and
– any other costs which the employer and union may agree together.

MEMO POINTS The **qualified independent person** will send the parties his **bill** (para 28(4) Sch A1 TULRCA 1992). They have 15 working days to pay the bill from receipt (para 28(5) Sch A1 TULRCA 1992) but if the bill is not paid, the qualified independent person may apply to the county court for an order enforcing payment. The parties may appeal against the demand within 4 weeks starting with the day after receipt of the demand. An appeal shall be dismissed unless it is shown that the gross costs of the ballot, or the costs to be borne by the recipient of the bill, are too great (para 165A Sch A1 TULRCA 1992, as inserted by s 14 ERelA 2004).

7281 The **CAC must inform** the parties of the **result of the ballot** as soon as is reasonably practicable once it receives notification from the qualified independent person (unless a further ballot is being held as a result of unfair practice (¶7278)) and it will **issue a declaration** that the union is either recognised or not recognised to conduct collective bargaining on behalf of the bargaining unit (para 29 Sch A1 TULRCA 1992).

However, if there are any **disputes over the ballot process**, the above requirement does not prevent the CAC from investigating and, if appropriate, annulling the ballot and ordering a further one (*R (on the application of Ultraframe (UK) Ltd) v CAC* [2005] IRLR 641, CA).

The union will be recognised as a result of a ballot if the union has the support of the majority of the workers voting and at least 40% of the workers within the bargaining unit (para 29 Sch A1 TULRCA 1992).

2. Obligations on recognition

a. Methods of collective bargaining

Agreed by parties

Once recognition has been granted, the parties have 30 working days (which can be extended by agreement), starting with the day after notification of the declaration of recognition, to agree on a method of collective bargaining (para 30 Sch A1 TULRCA 1992). 7285

Determined by CAC

If no agreement is reached within this time frame, either party may apply to the CAC for assistance. If agreement on the bargaining method is not reached **within** the further period of 20 working days, starting with the day after that on which assistance is sought, or such longer period as the CAC may decide with the consent of the parties, the **CAC will specify the method** to be used (para 31(3) Sch A1 TULRCA 1992). In doing so, it will have regard to the "**model method**". 7287

If at any time before the CAC imposes a specified method on the parties, the parties may jointly apply to the CAC requesting it to stop taking steps under these provisions. If such a request is received by the CAC, it will comply with it (para 31(7) Sch A1 TULRCA 1992).

MEMO POINTS 1. The "model method" is set out in the Trade Union Recognition (Method of Collective Bargaining) Order SI 2000/1300.
2. The parties may also apply to the CAC to determine a method of collective bargaining where, following a declaration of recognition, the parties have agreed on a method but one party has failed to carry out the agreement (para 32 Sch A1 TULRCA 1992).

Model method The model method **provides that a joint negotiating body** (JNB) (which comprises at least three representatives from the union and three from the employer) should be established to discuss and negotiate pay, hours and holidays of workers in the bargaining unit. Each union recognised by the employer is entitled to at least one seat on the JNB. The union representatives on the JNB may be workers employed by the employer or individuals employed by the union as union officials. 7288

Under the model method, the parties set aside half a working day for each **JNB meeting** unless agreed otherwise. Ordinarily JNB meetings should be held during normal working time but the JNB should schedule meetings at times which minimise disruption to the employer's business. The model method also lays down the minimum requirements for union members who are JNB representatives to **paid time off**. The employer and union are required to have regard to the ACAS Code of Practice on Time Off for Trade Union Duties and Activities (revised in 2003) and ensure that there is no unwarranted or unjustified failure to adhere to the Code (see also ¶3910).

MEMO POINTS The **Code** is not legally binding but its content is admissible in evidence and **will be taken into account** in any employment tribunal proceedings where the issue of time off is being considered.

A specific **bargaining procedure** is set out in the model method, including a suggested timetable, for the parties to deal with proposals to adjustments to pay, hours and holidays on an annual basis, although the parties can agree a different bargaining period. Any collective agreement affecting the pay, hours and holidays of workers in the bargaining unit, which the employer and union enter into as a result of JNB negotiations, must be recorded in writing. If one party considers that the other has failed to implement any part of the agreement, it can request a meeting of the JNB to discuss the failure. 7289

The method imposed by the CAC, including the model method, constitutes a **legally binding contract** between the parties. However, the parties may **agree to vary** its terms, including to remove its legally binding status. Once the CAC has imposed a method of collective bargain- 7290 ing, an employer cannot vary the contractual terms affecting pay, hours and holidays of any workers within the bargaining unit unless he has first negotiated his proposals with the union in accordance with the bargaining method. In addition, an employer cannot grant the right to negotiate pay, hours and holidays to any other union in respect of workers in the bargaining unit covered by the method of collective bargaining specified by the CAC. However, individual workers will not be prevented from discussing or negotiating with their employer terms of their contract of employment which differ from the terms of any collective agreement which has been entered into by the employer and union as a result of collective bargaining conducted by this method.

Disclosure of information

7292 The employer and the union must have regard to the ACAS Code of Practice on Disclosure of Information to Trade Unions for Collective Bargaining Purposes (2003) (available from the ACAS website, see www.acas.org.uk for details) and ensure that there is no unwarranted or unjustified failure to abide by it in relation to the bargaining arrangements specified by this method. The Code itself is not legally binding, but is admissible in evidence in any proceedings before the CAC.

Enforcement

7293 Either party may apply for an **order for specific performance** if the other party breaches any provision of the collective bargaining method (para 31(6) Sch A1 TULRCA 1992). A failure to comply with an order for specific performance would constitute a contempt of court.

---

b. Employer's duty to consult on training

7295 Once statutory recognition has been granted, a union will enjoy a number of rights under which the employer will be required to inform and consult the union on matters such as collective redundancies and health and safety. A list of the principal consequences of recognition is set out at ¶7201.

However, in addition, if a union has been **recognised by reference to the statutory procedure** described above (¶7230), in respect of which a specified method of collective bargaining is in force, the employer will also be under a duty to consult over training with the union (s 70B TULRCA 1992) (unless the agreement has been otherwise varied by the parties). This right **does not**, **it appears**, **extend** to unions which have been granted **semi-voluntary recognition**.

Six-monthly meetings

7296 From time to time, in respect of the workers in the bargaining unit, the employer must invite the union to send representatives to a meeting with the employer for the **purposes of** (s 70B(2) TULRCA 1992):

– consultation about the employer's training policy;

– consultation about the employer's training plans during the 6 months starting with the day of the meeting; and

– reporting about training since the previous 6-monthly meeting.

7297 The first meeting must be held within 6 months of the day on which the CAC specifies the bargaining method.

At least 2 weeks **before a meeting** the **employer must provide** the union with any information without which the union's representatives would be impeded, to a material extent, at the meeting (s 70B(4) TULRCA 1992). However, an employer is not required to provide information in this context which would not be required to be disclosed for the purposes of collective bargaining by virtue of the restrictions on the general duty of disclosure (s 182(1) TULRCA 1992).

An **employer must take account** of any **written representations from the union** about **matters raised at a meeting** within 4 weeks of receiving them (s 70B(6) TULRCA 1992). 7298

Enforcement

A union may bring a **complaint to an employment tribunal** if an employer fails to comply with his duties in respect of consultation over training (s 70C(1) TULRCA 1992). The **time limit** for bringing such a claim is 3 months beginning with the date of the failure to consult or within such further period as the tribunal considers reasonable in a case where it is satisfied that it was not reasonably practicable for the complaint to be brought before the end of that 3 month period (s 70C(2) TULRCA 1992). 7299

Where a complaint is successful, a tribunal may make a declaration to that effect and, in addition, may make an award of compensation to be paid by the employer to each person who was, at the time when the failure occurred, a member of the bargaining unit. The amount of the award shall not, in relation to each person, exceed 2 weeks' pay (¶2920). 7300

3. Changes to the bargaining unit

If a business experiences changes (for example, to its structure, organisation, workforce or activities), either the union or the employer may make an **application to the CAC** if it believes that the original bargaining unit is no longer appropriate or has ceased to exist. 7305

Bargaining unit is inappropriate

If either the employer or the union believes the current bargaining unit is no longer appropriate, they may apply to the CAC to make a decision as to what is an appropriate bargaining unit (para 66(2) Sch A1 TULRCA 1992). An application will be considered if the **CAC decides**, within 10 working days of the application, that it is likely that the original bargaining unit is no longer appropriate **due to a change** in the organisation, structure, or activities pursued by the employer, or due to a substantial change in the number of workers employed in the original unit (para 67(2) Sch A1 TULRCA 1992). If the CAC does **not consider** that there has been **any such change**, then the application is inadmissible and no further action will be taken (para 68(4) Sch A1 TULRCA 1992). 7306

Applications must be made in the **specified form** and accompanied by such **appropriate documentation** as set out by the CAC (para 92 Sch A1 TULRCA 1992). 7307

New unit agreed by parties If the CAC decides that an application is admissible, the **employer and the union have** 10 working days in which **to agree** a new unit (para 69(1) Sch A1 TULRCA 1992). 7308

If the **parties agree** the new bargaining unit, the CAC must ensure that the new unit does not contain any worker who also falls within an existing bargaining unit (in respect of which another union is recognised) (para 69(2) Sch A1 TULRCA 1992). If there is an **overlap**, no further action can be taken under this procedure. If there is **no overlap**, the CAC will issue a declaration that the union is recognised for the new unit and entitled to conduct collective bargaining on its behalf and the method of collective bargaining relating to the original unit will apply to the new unit, subject to any modifications deemed necessary by the CAC (para 69(3) Sch A1 TULRCA 1992).

If one or more workers originally fell within the original unit and do not now fall within the new unit, the CAC must issue a declaration that the bargaining arrangements will cease to have effect in relation to those workers on a date specified by the CAC (para 73 Sch A1 TULRCA 1992).

Determination by CAC If the **parties do not agree** on a new unit, then the CAC has 10 working days (or such longer period as the CAC may specify) in which to determine whether the original unit remains appropriate or, if not, to determine what would be an appropriate unit (para 70(2) Sch A1 TULRCA 1992). 7309

If the CAC decides that the **original unit is appropriate**, the existing bargaining arrangements will continue and no further steps will be taken under this procedure (para 71 Sch A1 TULRCA 1992). If the CAC decides that the original unit is **not appropriate** due to one or more of the changes described above, it will decide on an appropriate unit (or units) by taking into account (para 70(4), (5) Sch A1 TULRCA 1992):
– the need for the unit to be compatible with effective management;
– the views of the employer or union;
– existing local and national bargaining arrangements;
– the desirability of avoiding small fragmented bargaining units within an undertaking;
– the characteristics of workers falling into the original unit and of any other employees of the employer which the employer considers relevant; and
– the location of the workers.

If the CAC decides that **two or more bargaining units are appropriate**, it must ensure that no worker falls within more than one of them (para 70(6) Sch A1 TULRCA 1992).

Bargaining unit has ceased to exist

7310 An **employer who believes** that the original bargaining unit has **ceased to exist** and wishes the current bargaining arrangements to cease to have effect, must **notify** the union, providing a copy of its notice to the CAC, which (para 74(1), (2) Sch A1 TULRCA 1992):
– identifies the bargaining unit and the bargaining arrangements;
– states the date upon which the notice is given;
– states that the unit has ceased to exist; and
– states that the bargaining arrangements will cease to have effect on a date which is specified in the notice (which falls after the end of the period of 35 working days starting on the day after that on which the notice is given).

The CAC has 10 working days in which to decide whether the notice is valid (para 74(7) Sch A1 TULRCA 1992). If the notice does not comply with the above requirements, it will have no effect (para 74(4) Sch A1 TULRCA 1992).

7311 The **union may challenge** the notice, within 10 working days of receiving it, by applying to the CAC to determine whether the original bargaining unit has ceased to exist and, if not, to decide whether the original unit is no longer appropriate by reason of one of the prescribed changes (para 75 Sch A1 TULRCA 1992). If the union **does not challenge** the notice, recognition will automatically cease (para 74(6) Sch A1 TULRCA 1992).

7312 The **union's application** to the CAC must be made in the prescribed form and a copy sent to the employer (para 92 Sch A1 TULRCA 1992).

If the **CAC accepts an application** from the union, it will give both parties an opportunity to give evidence on the matter and must decide the questions within 10 working days (starting with the day after that on which it accepts the application) (para 77(1) Sch A1 TULRCA 1992).

If the **CAC decides** that the **bargaining unit has in fact ceased** to exist due to one of the prescribed changes, it must make a declaration to this effect and the bargaining arrangements will cease to have effect (para 77(2) Sch A1 TULRCA 1992). If the CAC decides that the **original unit still exists** and, moreover, is still appropriate, the employer's notice will have no effect (para 77(3) Sch A1 TULRCA 1992).

7313 **New unit agreed by parties** However, if the CAC decides that the **original unit is no longer appropriate** due to one of the changes referred to above, the CAC will give notice to that effect and the parties will have 10 working days in which to agree a bargaining unit (para 78 Sch A1 TULRCA 1992).

If the parties **agree a new unit** (or units) within this period, they should inform the CAC of what they have agreed (para 78(1) Sch A1 TULRCA 1992). Provided the CAC is satisfied that there is no worker falling within both the existing unit and proposed new unit(s), the collective bargaining arrangements will apply to the new unit(s) (para 78(3) Sch A1 TULRCA 1992) and the union will be derecognised in respect of any worker falling outside the new unit (para 81 Sch A1 TULRCA 1992).

If there is an **overlap** between the existing unit and the proposed new unit, namely, if the CAC decides that the new unit contains at least one worker falling within the original unit, no further action can be taken under this procedure (para 78(2) Sch A1 TULRCA 1992).

Determination by CAC If the **parties cannot agree** on the new bargaining unit, the CAC will determine the matter within 10 working days (para 79 Sch A1 TULRCA 1992). In deciding on an appropriate bargaining unit or units, the CAC must take into consideration the same criteria as specified above in respect of a bargaining unit which one party has claimed is no longer appropriate (¶7309) (para 79(3), (4) Sch A1 TULRCA 1992). 7314

If there is **no overlap** between the original and new bargaining units, then the CAC will decide whether the difference between the original unit and the new unit is such that **support for the union** within the new unit **needs to be assessed**. If so, it will inform the parties of its decision (para 85(1) Sch A1 TULRCA 1992). In assessing support for the union, the CAC will decide whether the union has at least 10% membership in the unit and whether recognition for the unit is likely to have majority support of the workers constituting the new unit (para 86(2) Sch A1 TULRCA 1992). 7315

If there is **no need for union support to be assessed**, the CAC will issue a declaration that the union is recognised for the new unit and the original method of collective bargaining will apply (together with any modifications the CAC may consider necessary) (para 85(2) Sch A1 TULRCA 1992).

If the CAC **cannot answer** these questions positively, then the union's recognition will cease and the bargaining arrangements will no longer have effect (para 86(3) Sch A1 TULRCA 1992). Otherwise, the CAC must issue a declaration of recognition to the union as entitled to conduct collective bargaining on behalf of the workers constituting the new unit (para 87(2) Sch A1 TULRCA 1992).

However, a more **likely scenario** is that a **ballot will be held** (para 87(4) Sch A1 TULRCA 1992, as amended by s 6 ERelA 2004) if the CAC considers any one of the following conditions applies: 7316

- a ballot should be held in the interests of good industrial relations;
- the CAC has credible evidence from a significant number of the union members within the bargaining unit that they do not want the union to conduct collective bargaining on their behalf; or
- membership evidence is produced which leads the CAC to doubt whether a significant number of union members within the new unit want the union to conduct collective bargaining on their behalf.

In any event, if the CAC is not satisfied that a majority of the workers in the new unit are members of the union, it must hold a ballot (para 88 Sch 1 TULRCA 1992).

The same requirements for conducting the ballot apply (¶7272).

If, as a result of the ballot, the CAC issues a declaration of recognition in respect of the new unit, the declaration shall supersede any declaration of recognition that the union is entitled to conduct collective bargaining on behalf of the original unit in so far as it affects workers in the new unit who fall within the original unit. In addition, the **method of collective bargaining** relating to the original unit shall have effect in relation to the **new unit** (subject to any modifications the CAC believes necessary) (para 89(6) Sch A1 TULRCA 1992). Finally, recognition will cease in respect of any workers who fell within the original unit but do not fall within the new unit (para 90 Sch A1 TULRCA 1992).

C. Semi-voluntary recognition

7320 Subject to the statutory recognition procedure described above at (¶7230) having been followed, a union will have a right to demand statutory recognition. However, at each stage of the procedure, the legislation tries to promote agreement between the parties instead of persisting with the formal procedure. If the parties are able to reach an agreement on recognition during the formal process, the agreement is commonly referred to as "semi-voluntary". Such an agreement is described in the legislation as an **agreement for recognition** (para 52 Sch A1 TULRCA 1992).

7322 In order to reach an agreement for recognition, the union's request must have fulfilled the validity requirements (¶7230) and agreement must have been reached within the permitted period (para 52(3), (4) Sch A1 TULRCA 1992). Moreover, the agreement must entitle the union to conduct collective bargaining for a group (or groups) of workers (para 54(3) Sch A1 TULRCA 1992). The broad definition of collective bargaining (¶7200) is disapplied (para 54(2) Sch A1 TULRCA 1992) but the **parties can agree** (in the agreement for recognition) the exact scope of the union's collective bargaining powers and are therefore not restricted to pay, hours and holidays.

7323 One or more of the parties may **apply to the CAC** for it to determine whether or not the agreement is an agreement for recognition (para 55 Sch A1 TULRCA 1992). The CAC will determine this question within 10 working days from receipt of the application (or such longer period as the CAC may specify) and, if it so decides, will issue a declaration to that effect.

Method of collective bargaining

7325 The method of collective bargaining can either be agreed by the parties (within a certain time frame) or it will be imposed on the parties by the CAC.

7327 **Agreed by parties** If the parties make an agreement for recognition, they **must** try to **negotiate** a bargaining method within 30 working days (para 58(2), (4) Sch A1 TULRCA 1992).

7328 **Determination by CAC** If **no agreement** is reached during the initial period, the parties may **apply to** the CAC for assistance (para 58(3) Sch A1 TULRCA 1992). References to the CAC must be in the prescribed form and satisfy the admissibility requirements (paras 60, 61 Sch A1 TULRCA 1992). This includes the requirement that the employer is over the 21-worker threshold (¶7230) and that the union has received a certificate of independence from the Certification Officer (¶7122).

7329 If the application is accepted and admissible, the **CAC will try to promote agreement** between the parties as to a collective bargaining method. If the **parties cannot agree** a collective bargaining method within the agreement period of 20 working days (starting with the date on which the CAC accepts the application), the **CAC will specify the method** by which the parties are to conduct collective bargaining (para 63(2) Sch A1 TULRCA 1992). As with the purely statutory recognition procedure set out above (¶7287), the CAC will **take into consideration** the model method when specifying the bargaining method to be implemented.

7330 The method specified can **only apply to** bargaining over **pay**, **hours and holidays** (para 54(4) Sch A1 TULRCA 1992). However, the **parties can widen the scope** of the matters to be dealt with by collective bargaining by agreement in the agreement for recognition.

MEMO POINTS If the parties have agreed a collective bargaining method but one or more of the parties fail to carry it out, either side may seek **assistance from the CAC** to specify the method of collective bargaining (para 59 Sch A1 TULRCA 1992).

7331 It will be **legally enforceable**, but the parties may **agree to vary its terms** in writing, including agreeing to remove its legally binding status (para 63(4) Sch A1 TULRCA 1992). A party to the agreement will be able to apply for **specific performance** in respect of any failure by the other party to carry out the bargaining method specified by the CAC (para 63(5) Sch A1 TULRCA 1992).

II. Derecognition

Derecognition is the process by which an employer **ceases to recognise** a union as being entitled to conduct collective bargaining on behalf of workers within the bargaining unit. The **statutory derecognition procedure** applies only to a union which has been recognised by a CAC declaration (para 96(1) Sch A1 TULRCA 1992) and may not be invoked until at least 3 years have passed from the date of the CAC declaration (para 97 Sch A1 TULRCA 1992). 7340

An independent union can be derecognised at any time under a **voluntary recognition arrangement**, usually without any legal recourse being available to the union. Moreover, there are **special procedures** to derecognise non-independent unions and unions which have had their certificate of independence withdrawn (¶7361).

A union which has been declared to be recognised by the CAC under a **semi-voluntary recognition agreement** (¶7320) cannot be derecognised **by the employer** for 3 years from the date on which the declaration was made (para 56(5) Sch A1 TULRCA 1992). Thereafter, the employer will be permitted to terminate the agreement through the normal derecognition procedures set out below, with or without the consent of the union. However, the **union may terminate** an agreement for recognition at any time, whether during or after the 3-year period (para 56(3) Sch A1 TULRCA 1992). If the agreement for recognition is terminated, the existing collective bargaining arrangements will cease to have effect (para 57(1) Sch A1 TULRCA 1992).

Derecognition due to number of employees

If the employer has **less than 21 workers**, it can notify the union that the collective bargaining arrangements will cease to have effect from a given date. This date must be at least 35 days after the union is notified but can be given during the 3-year minimum recognition period provided that the specified end date is after the end of the 3-year period (para 99(3) Sch A1 TULRCA 1992). 7342

The **notice** (which must also be sent to the CAC) **must**: 7343
- identify the collective bargaining arrangements which are the subject of the notice;
- specify the period of 13 weeks in which the employer had an average of less than 21 workers;
- state the date on which the notice is given;
- be given within 5 working days (starting with the day after the last day of the specified 13 week period);
- state that the employer had less than 21 workers within the 13 week period; and
- state the date on which the bargaining arrangements will cease to have effect.

If the notice **does not satisfy** the above conditions, recognition will continue and the CAC will inform the parties, within 10 working days of receipt of the notice, that the notice is to be treated as having no effect (para 100(2) Sch A1 TULRCA 1992).

MEMO POINTS The notice will be **invalidated** if:
- an earlier such notice was given or an application was made (either by the employer or worker, in order to end arrangements) within 3 years prior to the date of the current notice;
- this earlier notice or application related to the same bargaining unit; and
- the CAC decided this earlier notice complied with the above requirements or accepted the application (para 99A Sch A1 TULRCA 1992, as inserted by s 12 ERelA 2004).

If the notice does contain the requisite information, the notice will take effect (para 100(4) Sch A1 TULRCA 1992), **unless challenged by the union** within 10 working days (para 101 Sch A1 TULRCA 1992). If the union does not challenge the notice or if the union's challenge is not admissible, then the collective bargaining arrangements will cease on the day specified in the employer's notice (paras 100(4), 102(4) Sch A1 TULRCA 1992). 7344

7346 If the **union's notice is admissible**, the CAC will invite evidence from both parties on the matter and has 10 working days (starting with the date after that on which the CAC accepted the notice) in which to reach a decision (para 103 Sch A1 TULRCA 1992). If the CAC decides that the union's challenge has been successful, the employer's notice is deemed to have no effect.

Employer requests end of bargaining arrangements

7348 An employer may, at any time **after** 3 years have elapsed, request a union to end statutory recognition. The **request must** (para 104(2) Sch A1 TULRCA 1992):
- be in writing;
- be given to the union;
- identify the bargaining arrangements; and
- state that the request is being made under Schedule A1 TULRCA 1992.

7349 If an employer has requested an end to the bargaining arrangements and either the **union fails to respond** or **rejects the request** within 10 working days, then the employer may **apply to the CAC** to hold a (secret) **derecognition ballot** to decide whether a majority of workers support derecognition (para 106 Sch A1 TULRCA 1992). Again, the application for a ballot must be **admissible** (paras 108-111 Sch A1 TULRCA 1992). In addition, the CAC must be satisfied that at least 10% of the workers in the bargaining unit favour an end to the bargaining arrangements and that a majority of workers constituting the bargaining unit are likely to favour the end of recognition (para 110 Sch A1 TULRCA 1992).

The derecognition ballot requirements (paras 117-121 Sch A1 TULRCA 1992) almost mirror those of a recognition ballot (¶7270). Once a ballot has taken place, if derecognition is supported by a majority of the workers voting and at least 40% of the workers constituting the bargaining unit, then the CAC will issue a declaration that the bargaining arrangements are to cease on a specified date (para 121 Sch A1 TULRCA 1992).

7350 Alternatively, the **parties may reach agreement at an earlier stage**: if the union simply accepts the employer's request within 10 working days (the first period), no further steps will be taken under the procedure (para 105(1) Sch A1 TULRCA 1992); or, if the union does not accept the request but indicates it is willing to negotiate and the parties reach agreement within 20 working days (starting with the day after that on which the first period ends), then again, no further steps will be taken (para 105(4) Sch A1 TULRCA 1992).

Nevertheless, if **negotiations are not successful**, the employer may apply to the CAC to hold a secret derecognition ballot to decide whether the bargaining arrangements should end (para 107 Sch A1 TULRCA 1992), unless the employer had previously, during negotiations, refused the union's request to seek assistance from ACAS. The holding of a derecognition ballot is discussed above (¶7349).

Workers' application to end bargaining arrangements

7352 A worker (or group of workers) may **apply to the CAC** to end statutory bargaining arrangements provided, once again, 3 years have elapsed since the CAC's declaration of statutory recognition.

The application must be made in the **prescribed form** and the CAC must be satisfied that the application fulfils the **admissibility requirements** (paras 112-114 Sch A1 TULRCA 1992), including the requirement that at least 10% of the workers in the bargaining unit favour an end to the bargaining arrangements and a majority of workers constituting the bargaining unit are likely to favour the end of recognition.

7353 Provided the application is admissible, the **CAC will assist** the union, employer and worker(s) with **negotiations** with a view to ending bargaining arrangements or the worker(s) withdrawing the application (para 116 Sch A1 TULRCA 1992). The parties have 20 working days after the CAC's acceptance of the application, or any longer period that the parties (and the CAC) agree in which to reach agreement.

If an **agreement is reached** or an application is withdrawn, the CAC will take no further action.

If **no agreement** can be reached, a **ballot** must be held (paras 117-121 Sch A1 TULRCA 1992). There is a different sanction in the event that the employer fails to fulfil any of his duties imposed under this procedure and the ballot has not been held in respect of a worker's (or workers') application to an application made by an employer (para 119(3) Sch A1 TULRCA 1992). If the ballot results in a majority vote in favour of ending recognition and at least 40% of the workers in the bargaining unit have voted in support of derecognition, then the bargaining arrangements will cease to have effect (para 121 Sch A1 TULRCA 1992).

As with the obligation to refrain from using any **unfair practice** in relation to recognition ballots, similar provisions apply to derecognition ballots, which take into account that unfair practice in derecognition ballots could be committed by either the employer or union or a worker (¶7278) (para 119A-I Sch A1 TULRCA 1992, as inserted by s 13 ERelA 2004).

Derecognition in "majority membership" cases

There is a further procedure for dealing with derecognition of unions where the CAC had **7355**
declared the union entitled to recognition without holding a ballot on the ground that most of the workers in the bargaining unit were union members (namely, the union had received **automatic recognition** – see above ¶7266) (paras 122-133 Sch A1 TULRCA 1992). The procedure covers three possible eventualities:

– where the CAC declared recognition but the parties agreed their bargaining procedure: bargaining arrangements, for these purposes, mean the declaration and the parties' agreement (para 122(2) Sch A1 TULRCA 1992);

– where the CAC declared recognition and specified the bargaining method: bargaining arrangements, for these purposes, mean the declaration and anything effective as, or as if contained in, a legally enforceable contract between the parties (para 123(2) Sch A1 TULRCA 1992); and

– where the CAC imposed recognition in respect of a new bargaining unit (para 87(2) Sch A1 TULRCA 1992): bargaining arrangements, for these purposes, mean the declaration and the method of collective bargaining relating to the original unit which took effect in respect of the new unit (subject to any modifications the CAC considered necessary) (para 124(2) Sch A1 TULRCA 1992).

In each of these situations, the **employer may request derecognition** once 3 years have **7356**
elapsed since the CAC's declaration of recognition (paras 125, 127 Sch A1 TULRCA 1992). The employer's request must be made in the **prescribed form** and fulfil the **validity requirements**. The parties will have 10 working days in which to reach agreement (the **negotiation period**) (para 128 Sch A1 TULRCA 1992).

If agreement on derecognition is reached, no further steps will be taken under this procedure.

If not, the employer **may apply to the CAC** for the holding of a **ballot** to decide whether the bargaining arrangements should be ended. The application to the CAC must fulfil the **admissibility requirements**, including the condition that the CAC must be satisfied that fewer than half of the workers constituting the bargaining unit are members of the union (para 131 Sch A1 TULRCA 1992).

Provided the application to the CAC is valid and admissible, the CAC will organise a ballot **7357**
on the question of derecognition in accordance with statutory requirements (para 133 Sch A1 TULRCA 1992). If a majority of the votes support derecognition and at least 40% of the workers in the bargaining unit have voted in favour of derecognition, then the union will be derecognised and the bargaining arrangements (as defined in ¶7355) will cease to have effect.

Non-independent unions

Another procedure lays down the rules for the derecognition of a non-independent union **7359**
(paras 134-147 Sch A1 TULRCA 1992). This procedure is **commenced by a worker** (or workers) falling within the bargaining unit and may be commenced at any time (there is no 3 year

rule as in the case of derecognition of independent unions). The procedure in many ways mirrors that of the general derecognition procedure. However, the details of the procedure are beyond the scope of this book.

Union loses independence

7361 Finally, only a union holding a certificate of independence may be entitled to statutory recognition. If a union has its **certificate of independence withdrawn** by the Certification Officer (¶7122) any recognition of the union is **deemed voluntary** and, as a consequence, the bargaining arrangements which previously applied will cease to have effect (para 152 Sch A1 TULRCA 1992). On a successful challenge by the union to **restore its certificate of independence**, statutory recognition will be reinstated (para 153 Sch A1 TULRCA 1992).

III. Access to workers

7365 During recognition and derecognition ballots, employers must give the union such access to the workers within the bargaining unit as is **reasonable** to enable the union to inform the workers of the object of the ballot and to seek their support (para 26(3) Sch A1 TULRCA 1992).

7366 A **Code of Practice** on Access and Unfair Practices during Ballots for Trade Union Recognition or Derecognition (found on the DTI website at www.dti.gov.uk) combines guidance on requests by unions for access to workers during recognition or derecognition ballots with further practical advice arising from the provisions of the ERelA 2004, which require employers to refrain from making offers to induce workers to avoid meetings with unions, engaging in unfair practice and undertaking irresponsible campaigning (¶¶7275, 7278 and 7381). The Code is not legally binding but it will be admissible in evidence in any proceedings before any court, tribunal or the CAC where it considers the Code relevant.

MEMO POINTS This Code revises and supersedes the Code of Practice on Access to Workers during Recognition and Derecognition Ballots (2000).

Access arrangements

7367 Access will vary according to the type of workplace involved and the characteristics of the balloted workforce. The **overall aim** is to ensure that the union can reach the workers involved during the balloting process to inform them of their objectives and seek their support.

Once the CAC has given the parties notice of the fact that it intends to hold a ballot, preparations for establishing access arrangements should commence. The **parties should meet** at the earliest convenient time to discuss access arrangements. Where two or more unions are involved in either the recognition or derecognition process, they should act jointly in preparing and implementing access arrangements. At this meeting, the union should put forward its **proposals for accessing** the workers to the employer. If the **employer rejects the proposals** (because he considers the union's requirements to be unreasonable), he should **offer alternative arrangements** at the earliest opportunity, preferably within 3 working days.

7368 The parties should record an **access agreement in writing** before implementing the arrangements. An access agreement **should include**:
– the union's programme for when and how it will access the workers on site and/or during their working time (the parties will need to establish limits on the duration and frequency of the union's activities, although as a general rule, the employer should allow the union to hold at least one meeting of at least 30 minutes for every 10 working days of the access period);
– the union's programme for where it will access the workers (wherever practicable, this should be their workplace);
– details of whether the union will access the workers on-site or off-site; and

– details of any mechanisms which are in place for resolving disagreements about implementing access arrangements.

Where it is appropriate, the employer's existing methods of communicating with the workforce should be adopted.

The access agreement should also **specify** who should be given access to the workers who will be balloted. Employers should be prepared to give **access to**:
a. individual union members employed by the employer who are nominated by the union as the lead representative of their members at workplaces where the bargaining unit is located;
b. individual union members employed by the employer who are nominated by the union as the lead representative of their members at other workplaces in the employer's business, provided that it is practicable for them to attend events at workplaces where the bargaining unit is located; and
c. full-time union officials.

Sometimes an access arrangement may need to be **altered if circumstances change**. If this arises, the party whose situation has changed should notify the other party as soon as practicable and **offer alternative suggestions**. In general, the other party should accept the alternative suggestions if they are of an equivalent nature to the ones already agreed. 7369

The **period of access** will begin as soon as the parties have been informed by the CAC of the following arrangements for the ballot: 7370
– the fact that it is arranging the ballot;
– the name of the qualified independent person; and
– the period within which the ballot must be conducted.

The union should ensure that disruption to business is minimised, although access should usually take place **during normal working hours**. Consideration should be given to holding events **during rest periods. Off-site** events should usually take place **outside normal working hours**.

If there is a **postal ballot**, the period of access will cease on the closing date of the balloting period. If the ballot is to be conducted at the workplace, access will continue until the ballot has closed.

Employer's disclosure of information

In order for the union to formulate its access proposals, the union may require certain information from the employer. It is reasonable for the employer to be expected to disclose information **relating to the workplace(s)** such as: 7372
– typical methods of communicating with his workforce;
– workplace premises;
– patterns of work; and
– plans to put across his views, directly or indirectly, to the workers about the recognition or derecognition of the union.

The employer should **not disclose** information regarding workers' names, addresses (postal or email) of the workers in the bargaining unit, **unless** the individuals concerned have **authorised** the disclosure.

Role of ACAS

If an employer and union **fail to agree access arrangements** voluntarily, they may (separately or jointly) apply to ACAS to conciliate differences. ACAS should respond within one working day of receiving the request. The appointed ACAS officer will aim to assist the parties in resolving their differences on access arrangements in an impartial manner. However, if no agreement can be reached, the CAC may be asked to intervene. The CAC may consider delaying the ballot in order to provide extra time in which to reach an agreement on access arrangements or it may simply adjudicate and make an order. It is therefore sensible for the 7374 parties to try to reach agreement on access arrangements voluntarily in order to avoid having to be bound by an arrangement imposed by the CAC.

Union surgeries

7376 Where appropriate, union "surgeries" could be organised **at the workplace during working hours** in order to give each worker an opportunity to meet with a union official on an individual basis or in small groups. Workers who attend surgeries (or any other meetings with unions) should be **paid in full** unless the surgery or meeting takes place outside working hours when the worker would not have received payment from the employer in any event. Where a union wishes one of the employer's workers (as set out above at **a.** and **b.** at ¶7368) to hold a union surgery, the employer should normally grant the employee **paid time off**. However, in exceptional circumstances, it might be reasonable for the employer to **refuse time off** (for example, if there is no adequate cover for the worker's absence from the workplace and production process) (see also ¶¶3910, 7600). Moreover, an employer would be justified in refusing to allow surgeries to take place if this would lead to an unacceptable increase in tension in the workplace.

Communications with workers

7377 The **union should be able to**:
– display written material at the workplace (employers should, where practicable, provide a notice board for the union's use);
– use the employer's website; and
– use internal email.

If a union wants to make use of its website pages for campaigning purposes, an employer should allow his workers access to the union's material in the same way that he (whether expressly or tacitly) permits workers to download information in connection with non-work related matters. If the employer does not generally allow workers to download such material, then he should consider giving permission to one of his workers nominated by the union to download the material and disseminate it more widely among the workers.

7378 The employer should take into consideration the difficulties faced by unions in communicating with **workers who might not be present full-time** in the workplace, for example:
– shift workers;
– part-time workers;
– home-workers;
– off-site workers;
– those on parental, maternity, paternity or adoption leave; and
– those on sick leave.

The employer should be receptive to a union's suggestions for securing access to such workers.

7379 Employers should also **respect the privacy** of access meetings and an employer or any representative of his should not attend an access meeting unless invited to do so. Further, the employer should not use any unwillingness on the union's part to allow such attendance as a reason to refuse the access meeting, unless it is reasonable to do so. The union should therefore consider in advance whether it wishes to exclude supervisors or managers who fall within the bargaining unit from meetings to avoid any uncertainty and disruption.

Achieving privacy during access meetings may be difficult, particularly where employers have security cameras or other recording equipment permanently installed in the workplace. Where this is the case, employers should generally inform the unions so that both parties can discuss how to ensure the privacy of meetings.

7380 **Joint activities** between the employer and union should be encouraged. For example, the use of a joint notice board informing the workers of the union and the employer's activities or joint meetings where equal time is allocated to the union and the employer.

Whilst active **campaigning** by the parties is expected during recognition and derecognition ballots, it must be undertaken responsibly to avoid the use of unfair practices or distorting the balloting process. There is a fine line, for example, between fair comment about job prospects and intimidatory behaviour designed primarily to scare the workers to vote against recognition. Prior discussion is therefore encouraged between the parties to focus on the standards of conduct expected of campaigners to minimise the risk of any intimidation or duress which could give rise to undue influence. 7381

Non-compliance by the employer

The **union may ask the CAC** to decide whether the employer has failed to perform his statutory duties in relation to the ballot (¶7275). 7382

If the CAC is satisfied that the employer has failed to perform one or more of its duties the **CAC may order** the employer to take such steps to remedy the failure as the CAC considers reasonable within a reasonable time limit. If the **employer fails to comply** with the CAC's order within the time specified, and the ballot has not been held, the CAC may issue a declaration that the union is recognised, or that the union is not derecognised.

Non-compliance by the union

Complaints about an employer's failure to provide reasonable access can only be made by a union. However, in deciding whether the employer has complied with his duty to provide the union with access to workers in the bargaining unit, the **CAC may take into account** all relevant circumstances. This may include the behaviour of the union (¶7277). 7384

SECTION 4

Strikes and other forms of industrial action

There is **no general right to strike** or to take any other form of industrial action, including action short of a strike, and under the common law industrial action amounts to a breach of contract. **Strike action** is action that involves the total withdrawal of labour, although it does not have to be indefinite and includes one-day stoppages. **Action short of a strike** includes overtime bans or call-out bans, a work to rule or any other action that falls short of a total withdrawal of labour (s 220 TULRCA 1992). 7400

However, the law gives **legal immunities** in certain circumstances which protect unions and others taking industrial action, from the consequences of their potentially unlawful actions where the industrial action is conducted strictly in accordance with the statutory provisions guaranteeing immunity. These provisions include an obligation to ballot, a limit on the circumstances in which industrial action can be called and strict requirements regarding notice to employers.

While the union, its officers and individual strikers may all be legally liable where industrial action is not protected, a **court will not compel** an employee to work or attend his place of work by ordering specific performance or granting an injunction restraining the breach (s 236 TULRCA 1992). If the breach is sufficiently serious and amounts to a fundamental breach, the employer may be justified in **dismissing** the individual (¶1755). 7401

MEMO POINTS UK legislation on industrial action is very restrictive, when compared to that of other EU member states. Indeed, in a number of respects (for example, the total bar on secondary action (¶7435)) the UK has been held to be in breach of international standards.
Further, the issue of compliance assumes an added significance in light of the Human Rights Act 1998 which requires UK courts to interpret statutory and common law, where possible, in a way that is compatible with the standards laid down in the European Convention of Human Rights. Aspects of the UK law on industrial action are therefore subject to human rights challenges in the UK courts.

I. Industrial action

7410 For any industrial action to be **protected**, it has to be a trade dispute that has been **validly authorised and endorsed** by the union (¶7417) and supported by ballot. Further, a union will maintain its immunity, even where industrial action is unlawful or unsupported by ballot, where it has formally **repudiated** the action (¶7422). In such circumstances, any union member continuing to take unlawful industrial action will be risking dismissal, and will not have the right to submit an unfair dismissal claim to a tribunal.

7411 Industrial action **covers** any concerted action by workers to bring about changes to terms and conditions or to any other working arrangements. Industrial action is most commonly identified with strike action, but includes any action aimed at persuasion, for example, a work to rule, an overtime ban, a work without enthusiasm, a refusal to cover for others, or a refusal to do specific tasks. The fact that there is no contractual obligation to undertake certain duties (for example, overtime) does not mean that it cannot amount to industrial action, when taken with the aim of achieving changes at work. It is, therefore, irrelevant whether or not the action would involve a breach of contract.

7412 **Unions** have **specific protection** from certain tort (i.e. civil wrong) liabilities which arise "**in contemplation or furtherance**" of a trade dispute. This protection is **limited to the tort of**:
- inducing another person to break a contract; or
- interfering or inducing another person to interfere with its performance; or
- threatening to break or interfere with a contract, either by the union or by another person.

This gives unions protection where they **call on their members to take industrial action**, provided that it is in furtherance of a trade dispute. Certain forms of picketing can also come within the range of protected industrial action.

Certain forms of industrial action are **excluded** from protection, most notably secondary or solidarity action, or action taken with the aim of enforcing union membership (s 219 TULRCA 1992).

7413 A union will not be liable where the **breach was unintentional**.

EXAMPLE In *TimePlan Education Group v National Union of Teachers* [1997] IRLR 457, CA, the union was unaware that its call for a boycott would breach an existing contract. It, therefore, did not lose its immunity because it had no way of knowing that it could be inducing a breach.

7414 Where there is **no contract**, a union will not be liable for inducing a breach.

EXAMPLE In *Middlebrook Mushrooms v TGWU* [1993] IRLR 232,CA, the union was calling on potential customers of a retail outlet (by means of a leaflet campaign) to participate in a boycott of the produce of a particular employer, with whom the union was in dispute. The Court held that as there were no contracts between the potential customers and the retail outlet, the union's actions did not amount to the tort of lawful inducement.

7415 **Employers** may **challenge the lawfulness of industrial action** by applying the following four stage test (*Merker Island Shipping Corporation v Laughton* [1983] IRLR 218, HL):
- does the industrial action give the employer a cause of action in tort?
- if so, does the law provide immunity?
- has the cause of action been restored due to the immunity having been removed?
- what is the extent of the union liability?

Authorised and endorsed

7417 The union will not be liable only where it has authorised or endorsed the action complained of. An action is authorised or endorsed by a union where it was taken by:
- any person empowered under the rules of the union to do so;
- the executive committee or president or general secretary of the union; or
- any other committee of the union or any other official of the union.

A **committee of the union** is any group of persons constituted in accordance with the rules of the union. This is likely to include union branch committees, regional committees, trade groups and other bodies that are constituted according to the union's rulebook. However, it would not include ad-hoc groups of members who have no formal status under the union's rules. Groups, such as shop stewards' committees, that are referred to in the rules of the union are also likely to be included (s 20(2) TULRCA 1992). 7418

An **official of the union** is any official, whether full-time or lay. A lay official who induces or interferes with a contract will be assumed to have been authorised or endorsed by the union. If an official is a member of a group of persons organising or co-ordinating industrial action, he will be taken to have authorised or endorsed the action, if it was taken, authorised or endorsed by any member of the group. 7419

It is irrelevant that the action may have been taken in breach of the union's own rules. The actions of its executive committee, president, general secretary, committee, or of any official of the union are deemed to have been authorised, unless the action is repudiated (¶7422). The union is liable even in respect of action that would be a breach of its own rulebook or contrary to any contract or rule of law. The fact that the union itself may be deemed liable does not mean that its members or officials avoid liability, as individual union members can also be liable for inducing a breach of contract or interference or threats to contracts. 7420

Repudiated action

A union can avoid liability for unlawful industrial action if it repudiates the action "as soon as is reasonably practicable" after it comes to the knowledge of any member of its executive, its president or general secretary (s 21 TULRCA 1992). Repudiation must amount to "an open disavowal and disowning of the acts of the officials concerned" to be effective (*Express & Star Ltd v NGA (1982)* [1985] IRLR 455, QBD). 7422

If the union has repudiated the industrial action then the repudiation comes into force on the next working day after the repudiation took place.

Written notice To repudiate the action, the union has to give written notice of repudiation, without delay, to the **committee or official** who endorsed or authorised the action. The union also has to do its best to give **individual** written notice, of the fact and date of the repudiation, to every member who is, or might take part in the action. 7423

The notice to members must contain the **following prescribed words**:

"Your union has repudiated the call (or calls) for industrial action to which this notice relates and will give no support to unofficial industrial action taken in response to it (or them). If you are dismissed while taking unofficial industrial action, you will have no right to complain of unfair dismissal."

Finally, the union must also give the **employer** of every such member written notice of the repudiation.

Within 6 months after it has repudiated the unlawful industrial action, any person who is a **party to a commercial contract** whose performance has been or may be interfered with as a result of the industrial action, can demand from the union a written notice of repudiation. A commercial contract for this purpose is any contract other than one of employment or a contract to personally perform work or services. 7424

Failure to give notice as required or on request will invalidate the repudiation, leaving the union responsible for unprotected industrial action. 7425

Inconsistent union action A union cannot merely formally repudiate unlawful industrial action but continue to act in a manner that is inconsistent with its repudiation. Therefore, if a union issues a written notice of repudiation but its executive, president or general secretary continue to support industrial action (for example by providing financial or other assistance) the repudiation is invalid. 7427

"No strike" clauses

7428 Some collective agreements may contain a provision which attempts to prohibit or restrict the right of workers to strike or engage in other industrial action. Any such so-called "no strike" clauses will be precluded from being incorporated into the contract of employment of an individual worker unless the collective agreement (s 180 TULRCA 1992):
- is in writing;
- expressly states that the no strike provisions will or may be incorporated into an individual contract of employment;
- has been entered into by one or more unions, all of which are independent;
- is reasonably accessible at the place of work of a worker to whom the strike clauses apply and is available to be consulted upon during working hours; and
- (the terms relating to industrial action) are expressly or impliedly incorporated into the individual worker's contract of employment.

It is not possible for a collective agreement or individual contract of employment to **contract out** of the above conditions (s 180(3) TULRCA 1992).

A. Trade disputes

7430 For any industrial action to be protected, it must fall within the **statutory definition** of a trade dispute, namely a dispute, between workers and their employer, which relates wholly or mainly to one or more of the following (s 244 TULRCA 1992):
- terms and conditions of employment, or the physical conditions in which any workers are required to work. If a union has called for industrial action by its members regarding workers' terms and conditions of employment, it is irrelevant that a number of the union's members being balloted to strike are unaffected by the terms and conditions in contention (*British Telecommunications plc v Communication Workers Union* [2004] IRLR 58, QBD).
- engagement or non-engagement, or termination or suspension of employment or the duties of employment, of one or more workers;
- the allocation of work or the duties of employment between workers or groups of workers;
- matters of discipline;
- a worker's membership or non-membership of a union;
- facilities for officials of unions; and
- the machinery for negotiation or consultation and other procedures relating to any of the above matters, including the recognition by employers or employers' associations of the right of a union to represent workers in such negotiation or consultation or in the carrying out of such procedures.

A dispute that does not come within the strict terms of a trade dispute and, therefore, any industrial action taken in contemplation or furtherance of it, will not be protected.

The following disputes **fall outside** this definition:

7431 **1. To compel union membership** (ss 222,225 TULRCA 1992) Any action aimed at forcing the employer to employ union members is not a trade dispute. Therefore, industrial action which occurs due to the belief that an employer is employing, or might employ, a non-union member, or might fail to discriminate against a non-unionist is unprotected. Similarly, industrial action which amounts to an inducement or attempted inducement to introduce a requirement of union membership into a contract is unprotected.

Pressure to impose a union recognition requirement into a contract or a proposed contract or a refusal to deal with a person on the grounds of union exclusion is also unprotected.

7432 **2. Where the dispute is political** Any dispute that is in some way connected with government policies is likely to be defined as a political dispute.

Although the courts have provided some guidance as to what will or will not be included, the dividing line between protected and unprotected action sometimes seems fine.

EXAMPLE Protected actions

1. A dispute over the new national curriculum and its impact in schools on the working conditions of teachers (*London Borough of Wandsworth v National Union of Schoolmasters and Union of Women Teachers* [1993] IRLR 344, CA).
2. A dispute connected with the government's decision to end the National Dock Labour Scheme, a system that guaranteed job protection to dockworkers. This was held to amount to a genuine trade dispute over their future terms and conditions of employment (*Associated British Ports v TGWU* [1989] ICR 55, CA).
3. A union ban of the sale of performing rights to South Africa, as a protest against the then system of apartheid. Although it was argued that this action was "politically motivated", the High Court held that the boycott was carried out with the well-being of the union's actor members in mind and was within the powers conferred on the union by its rulebook.
4. A dispute about a change of employer following a proposal to "externalise" the functions of a local council to a private company, a proposal to which employees objected on the basis that they wished to remain employees of the local council (*Westminster City Council v Unison* [2001] IRLR 524, CA).

However, action by workers, which involves taking part in a public demonstration aimed at lobbying parliament for legislation to better their terms and conditions, is unlikely to come within the definition. 7433

3. In response to the dismissal of unofficial strikers (s 223 TULRCA 1992) Industrial action taken in response to the dismissal of unofficial strikers is not protected, regardless of whether the action is carried out in compliance with all of the legal rules and has been officially sanctioned by the union. 7434

4. Where workers are taking secondary action (s 224 TULRCA 1992) Industrial action is unprotected if it amounts to secondary action, other than lawful secondary picketing (¶7495). Secondary action, sometimes called **solidarity or sympathy action**, involves calling on those employed by another employer to take industrial action in support of the dispute where there is no actual dispute with the secondary employer. 7435

Industrial action taken by workers, employed by a third party employer, in support for those in dispute is outside the protection of the immunities. Secondary picketing, which aims to picket workers in another workplace, is similarly outside the protection.

5. Where reason for dispute differs If the reason that the union gives for calling industrial action is not the main cause of the dispute, the action will not be protected. However, where the union honestly believes that the dispute is over an issue, which it has identified, its immunity will not be lost (*London Borough of Newham v NALGO* [1993] IRLR 83, CA). 7436

6. Where there is no actual dispute Any industrial action will not be protected if there is no actual dispute in existence. 7437

EXAMPLE In *London Underground v NUR* [1989] IRLR 341, QBD, the Court ruled that industrial action would not be protected because matters were included in the ballot form which were not yet the subject of an industrial dispute.

7. A dispute between groups of workers or another party A demarcation dispute between one group of workers and another is not covered and would, therefore, never be protected. A dispute with a party other than the employer is also not covered. 7438

EXAMPLE In *Connex South Eastern v RMT* [1999] IRLR 249, CA, the Court ruled that the action, in protest at rail safety, was the responsibility of a separate company that was not their employer and, therefore, the dispute was not protected.

8. Disputes over future terms and conditions A dispute over future terms and conditions of employment cannot be the subject of a legitimate trade dispute (*UNISON v United Kingdom* [2002] IRLR 497, ECHR). Although the European Court of Human Rights held that the restriction in TULRCA 1992 on the right to strike in respect of such matters contravenes the right to freedom of association under Art 11 of the European Convention on Human Rights, in this case, such a restriction is both justified and proportionate in the circumstances. Further, the union would in 7439 any event be entitled to bring an action against any future (yet to be identified) employer in respect of future terms and conditions of employment.

7440 **9. Supply of goods** Industrial action is unprotected if it:
– interferes with the supply of goods or services or can reasonably be expected to do so; or
– there is an allegation that breaches of contracts have been induced or threatened; and
– the reason, or one of the reasons for this is that a supplier does not recognise unions or does not negotiate or consult with them.

A term in a contract for the supply of goods and services is void in so far as it purports to require a party to the contract to recognise a union or to negotiate or consult with it. A refusal to deal with a supplier of goods or services because the supplier does not recognise unions is also prohibited, as is the exclusion, for example from tender applications, of a supplier on similar grounds. Any party adversely affected by such action can bring a claim for a breach of statutory duty.

1. Supported by a ballot

7443 An act done by a union to induce someone to take part in or continue to take part in a trade dispute is not protected unless it has the support of a ballot (s 226 TULRCA 1992). Action is deemed to be supported by a ballot where the workers who are entitled to vote did so in favour of the action and it was reasonable to assume that the union's members would be called upon to take industrial action. It will only be taken to have the support of a ballot in the **following circumstances**:
– all of the rules about the procedure for holding the ballot, notification and declaration of the results are complied with;
– the majority voting in the ballot answered affirmatively to the question on industrial action; and
– the industrial action, authorised by the ballot, is called by the person specified in the ballot to do so.

A ballot would not be unlawful simply because the union had campaigned for its members to vote in a particular way. The fact that a union has called for a "yes" vote and is clearly partisan, does not nullify the ballot. A union is "perfectly entitled to be partisan" as long as it complied with the legislation (*London Borough of Newham v NALGO* [1993] IRLR 83, CA).

7445 **Ballots of over 50 members** Where the number of members who would be entitled to vote in an industrial action ballot exceeds 50, the union must appoint an **independent scrutineer** before the ballot takes place (s 226B TULRCA 1992). The role of the scrutineer is similar to that in union elections (¶7160).

The scrutineer has to take appropriate steps to enable **a report** to be made to the union on the conduct of the ballot, by no later than 4 weeks after the date of the ballot. The report must indicate whether the scrutineer is satisfied that the legal requirements on ballots were complied with. The report must also show whether the scrutineer was satisfied with the arrangements for producing, storing, distributing, handling and counting the voting papers. This has to include being satisfied that the ballot was carried out in such a way as to minimise unfairness or malpractice. His report must indicate whether he was able to carry out his functions without interference by the union, its officials, members or employees.

7446 An employer has the **right to see a copy** of this report, provided that a request is made to the union within 6 months of the ballot. Individual members of the union, who were entitled to vote in the ballot, also have this right. The union can specify a reasonable fee to provide the report.

7447 **Separate employers** Industrial action at one location, where all the relevant workers are covered by the **same terms and conditions**, can be by single ballot, even if the action would affect more than one employer. If the terms and conditions are different, separate ballots must be held.

EXAMPLE In *University of Central England v National and Local Government Officers' Association* [1993] IRLR 81, QBD, a single ballot which covered college staff employed by several different employers was still valid, since the subject matter of the dispute related to common terms and conditions.

Separate workplaces A union may be required to hold separate ballots, where members are working in different workplaces (ss 226(3), 228 TULRCA 1992). However, it can organise an aggregated ballot where there is at least one individual, who is affected by the dispute, in each of the workplaces aggregated into the single ballot. Ballots can also be aggregated where linked by occupation and employer(s). 7448

Where there are separate ballots for different workplaces, industrial action can only be taken to have the support of a ballot if the majority in the specific workplace has voted in favour of the industrial action.

Members to be balloted

The union has to give the right to vote in the ballot to all of its members who it is reasonably believed at the time of the ballot might be called on by the union to take part in industrial action (s 227 TULRCA 1992). Therefore, if the union ballots either too widely or too narrowly it could lose its protection in respect of the proposed action. However, where there is a failure to comply that is accidental and unlikely to affect the ballot result, the mere fact that some members were added in or left out will not jeopardise the lawfulness of the ballot. 7449

A member, whom the union could **reasonably have expected to be called** on to take industrial action and who has not been balloted, cannot subsequently be induced to take industrial action. If a union fails to send out ballot papers to a substantial number of members whom the union could reasonably have expected to be called on to take industrial action, the industrial action may be restrained on the basis that at least some of the members who were not balloted would have been induced to strike (*National Union of Rail, Maritime and Transport Workers v Midland Mainline Ltd* [2001] IRLR 813, CA). However, if members have joined the union after the date of the ballot it can still induce them to take industrial action (*London Underground Ltd v National Union of Rail, Maritime and Transport Workers* [1996] ICR 170, CA). 7450

Overseas members Where members of the union are working overseas during the period when votes are being cast are concerned, the union has the right to decide whether or not to give them entitlement to vote (ss 227-230 TULRCA 1992). If it does decide to do so it does not have to comply with the rules on entitlement to vote, separate workplace ballots, marking the ballot paper and the conduct of the ballot in relation to the votes of these members. However, it must, when providing information on the outcome of the ballot, be able to distinguish between the results of those who are overseas and those who are not. 7452

Member's right to a ballot

A member of a union who claims that members (including himself) are likely to be induced to take industrial action which does not have the support of a ballot, can apply for a court order (s 62 TULRCA 1992). If granted it will require the union to take steps to ensure that there is no further or continued inducement of members to take industrial action. It is irrelevant that the union's inducement may have been ineffective. 7453

2. Ballot requirements

To comply with **procedural** requirements, ballots must be: 7455
- commenced within a specified time-scale;
- notified in advance to the employer;
- in secret;
- by post;
- fairly and accurately counted;

– independently scrutinised (if ballot is of over 50 members only); and
– prepared so as to inform the employee of the extent of the legal protection against dismissal.

7456 A **Code of Practice** on Industrial Action Ballots and Notice to Employers (found at www.dti.gov.uk) gives guidance to employers and unions "to promote the improvement of industrial relations and good practice" in the conduct of industrial action ballots. It gives guidance on situations where a ballot would be appropriate and on the steps that unions must take to comply with the law on ballots. The Code also deals with how employers can challenge ballots that are not in compliance.

The Code is not legally binding but may be taken into account by a tribunal or court in deciding whether an industrial action is lawful.

MEMO POINTS This Code revises and supersedes the Code of Practice on Industrial Action Ballots and Notice to Employers (2000).

Ballot validity

7460 A ballot normally **ceases to have effect** at the end of 4 weeks from the last day on which voting could have taken place, **except** in the following circumstances (s 234 TULRCA 1992):
– if the date when the action should have begun has been delayed due to legal proceedings, the industrial action can be called within an overall 12 week period; or
– where the employer and union have agreed to extend the 4 weeks by up to another 4 weeks (8 weeks in total) to allow for further negotiation.

The **weeks are calculated** counting the last day for voting as day one.

7461 If industrial action commences and is suspended to allow for negotiations to take place a union may re-impose the action without having to re-ballot (*Monsanto plc v TGWU* [1986] IRLR 406, CA). However, the gap between the **suspension of industrial action** and its re-imposition should not be too long or the ballot will no longer provide immunity.

EXAMPLE In *Post Office v Union of Communication Workers* [1990] IRLR 143, CA, a break of several months during which changes in the composition of the workforce occurred, invalidated the ballot. Otherwise, workers who would be called upon to take strike action would not have been balloted and conversely workers who had been balloted would no longer be in the workplace and therefore not called upon to take industrial action.

Advance notice requirements

7463 There are **four key stages** when the union must communicate in writing with the employer and failure to comply with any of these stages will remove the immunity from the industrial action (s 226A TULRCA 1992, as amended by s 22 ErelA2004). The four notice requirements are:

7464 **1**. At least 7 days **before the opening day** of the ballot (i.e. the first day when a voting paper is sent to any member entitled to vote), the union must take reasonable steps to ensure that it gives the employer notice of its intention to hold a ballot. It must specify the date that it reasonably expects the ballot will begin and provide specific information (see below). Where the **validity** of a ballot notice is at **issue**, it is important to consider the notice objectively and in context, rather than the subjective intentions of the union or the subjective view of the company (*English, Welsh and Scottish Railway Ltd and anor v National Union of Rail, Maritime and Transport Workers* [2004] EWCA Civ 1539).

The union must provide certain information to the employer who the union believes will be the employer of those entitled to vote in the ballot. Unions must provide a **list** of the categories of employee to which the employees concerned belong and a list of the workplaces at which they work. Unions must also provide **figures** of the total number of employees concerned, in relation to each category and each workplace, together with an **explanation** of how those figures were arrived at. Where there are employees from whose wages the employer makes deductions representing payments to the union, either these lists, figures and explanation are required or further information is needed, enabling the employer to deduce the total number of employees concerned in relation to each category and workplace (s 234A TULRCA 1992, as amended by s 25 ERelA 2004).

2. At least 3 days **before the ballot commences** a sample copy of the voting paper, which will be sent to those employees who the union reasonably believes will be entitled to vote in the ballot, must be received by the employer. 7465

3. The union must notify the employer of the result as soon as is reasonably practicable **after the result** of the ballot has been declared. The union must take the necessary steps to ensure that the employer is informed of the number of votes cast. He must also be told of the number answering "yes" and the number answering "no" to the question or questions and the number of spoiled votes. 7466

4. At least 7 days **before the industrial action** is due to start, the employer must be given written notice of the date of commencement of industrial action. 7467

Voting paper

In order to comply with the rules as to its **content**, the voting paper must (s 229 TULRCA 1992): 7470
- state the name of the independent scrutineer where there is a ballot of over 50 members;
- clearly specify the address to which, and date by which, it must be returned;
- be differently numbered;
- contain a question (however framed) which requires the person answering it to say, by "yes" or "no", whether they are prepared to take part (or continue to take part) in a strike (where the action proposed is action short of a full strike, the question has to specify that form of action);
- specify who is authorised to call on members to take industrial action; and
- contain the following statement:

EXAMPLE *"If you take part in a strike or other industrial action, you may be in breach of your contract of employment. However, if you are dismissed for taking part in a strike or other industrial action, which is called officially and is otherwise lawful, the dismissal will be unfair if it takes place fewer than 12 weeks after you started taking part in the action, and depending on the circumstances may be unfair if it takes place later."*

This reference to industrial action being potentially in breach of contract must appear, even where it is the case that the action proposed would not amount to a breach of contract.

A union seeking a mandate both for a **strike and for action short of a strike** has to ask two separate questions. Asking the wrong question, or getting a yes vote for one form of action, but opting for the other, makes the ballot invalid and any resulting industrial action unlawful. 7471

However, the union does not have to aggregate the results of the answers to each question. If it obtains a simple majority for one question, it has the right to call industrial action that accords with that question. An employer cannot challenge the legitimacy of the industrial action because a higher proportion of workers had voted on the other question, even though they had, by a majority, rejected the call for that form of industrial action (*West Midlands Travel v TGWU* [1994] IRLR 578, CA).

The fact that the union has not defined or prescribed every single issue in dispute in the ballot paper will not make the ballot void (*Associated British Ports v TGWU* [1989] IRLR 291, HL).

Voting procedure

All members who are entitled to vote must be allowed to do so **without interference** from the union, its members, officials or employees (s 230 TULRCA 1992). There is, however, no prohibition on interference by the employer or any third party. 7473

The voting must be "as far as is reasonably practicable" **without cost to the individual**. This might mean that the union could be required to provide pre-paid envelopes for posting completed voting papers. 7474

Voting must be **in secret** and every voter has to have a voting paper sent **by post** to his home address or any other address that has been nominated by him to the union. The 7475 member must be given a convenient opportunity to vote by post. Failing to send out a few forms due to a minor error would not automatically invalidate the ballot.

At least 7 days have to be allowed for the **first class** return of the voting paper. If the ballot is being returned by **second class** post then at least 14 days should be allowed for return of the voting papers.

7476 The votes must be "**fairly and accurately**" counted.

Result of ballot

7478 The union must communicate the result of the ballot in writing to the employer and to the members who were entitled to vote "as soon as is reasonably practicable" after the result of the ballot has been declared (s 231 TULRCA 1992). In both cases, the union must take the necessary steps to ensure that they are informed of the number of votes cast, told of the number answering "yes" and the number answering "no" to the question(s), and the number of spoiled votes.

Right to challenge legality of a ballot

7480 **Employers and union members** can challenge the legality of a ballot. An employer may apply to the High Court where it is alleged that a union intending to authorise industrial action has not complied with all of the legal requirements concerning the ballot including:
– whether notice was properly served to the employer, before the ballot was held and before the industrial action began;
– whether the correct workers were balloted;
– whether the requirements regarding the conduct of the ballot were adhered to; and
– any other matters related to the ballot.

However, **minor unintentional errors** in conducting a strike ballot will not generally invalidate its results (*Re P, a minor* [2003] ICR 386, HL).

3. Calling an action

7485 Only the individual specified by the union as having the **authority to call** industrial action can do so (s 233 TULRCA 1992). In some unions, this power lies solely in the hands of the general secretary. In others, it may be the executive committee or a full-time official who can call on members to take industrial action.

The name of the person empowered to call industrial action must be included in any ballot form. Legality is preserved as long as this name is included.

EXAMPLE In *Tanks & Drums v TGWU* [1991] IRLR 373, CA, the Court rejected an employer's challenge to the legality of the strike on the grounds that, although the ballot paper specified that the union's general secretary was the specified person with the power to call the industrial action, the call was dependent on the judgement of local officials, as they were charged with concluding a satisfactory settlement.

7486 Additionally, there must have been no call for industrial action before the date of the ballot. The call for industrial action must be made while the ballot is still effective.

4. Notice of action

7490 Employers must be given **written notice** of the action at least 7 days **before the industrial action** is due to begin but no earlier than when the results of the ballot are announced (s 234A TULRCA 1992, as amended by s 25 ERelA 2004). The notice must include:
– specific information about the group of employees to be called upon to take industrial action, which almost mirrors the requirements for the written notice of the ballot (¶7464);

– the type of industrial action intended, including whether it is continuous (for example an all out strike) or discontinuous (where it is intended to take place only on some days, but not others); and
– the date or dates when it will begin.

If a union fails to take such steps as are reasonable to give proper notice, the industrial action will lose its immunity and will be open to challenge by the employer if it goes ahead. If the union ceases to authorise or endorse industrial action and then, at a later date, decides to re-authorise or endorse, the original notice to the employer no longer applies and the union will have to give new notice.

B. Picketing

Workers have the **right to picket** when they are involved in a trade dispute. However, their legal right is **limited** to where the picket is: 7495
- at their own workplace;
- peaceful; and
- held for the purpose of peacefully persuading others not to cross their picket.

A picket will be **unlawful** if it goes **further than peaceful persuasion** or communication. For example, picketing which tries to restrict or restrain individuals from entering or exiting a building would not be protected.
Therefore, a member "in contemplation or furtherance of a trade dispute" can attend "at or near his own place of work" but only if the purpose of doing this is peacefully to obtain or communicate information, or persuade a person to work or abstain from working.

EXAMPLE In *Rayware Ltd v TGWU* [1989] IRLR 134, CA, the Court held that **picketing at the entrance to a trading estate**, rather than the actual entrance of the company with which the pickets were in dispute, was lawful. This was because the company entrance was not publicly accessible. The entrance to the trading estate was the nearest point the pickets could reach without trespassing on private property. The employer had argued that the picket was not taking place "at or near" their place of work but the court disagreed, saying that the legislation had to be interpreted with an element of common sense.

Union officials (including lay union officials) have the right to attend at or near the place of work of their members who are in dispute and whom they represent. If a person is a union official elected or appointed to represent some members of the union only (for example the secretary of a union branch) then the right to attend applies only to a picket by members of that branch. Otherwise, a union official has the right to attend any picket. 7496

Difficulties are likely to arise where the workers have **no specified work location**, perhaps because they work from more than one location or actually travel in the course of their work. For such workers, the appropriate location for any picketing depends on how and where they normally work. If someone normally works at more than one place or somewhere where it would be impracticable to picket, their place of work, for the purpose of the right to picket peacefully, will be any premises of the employer from which they work or from which work is administered. 7497

EXAMPLE In *Union Traffic Ltd v TGWU* [1989] IRLR 127, CA, the Court held that drivers who normally worked from one depot, but occasionally from others, could not lawfully picket the other depots since these were not at or near their normal place of work.

If the **pickets are no longer employed** by the employer (i.e. because they have been dismissed) the appropriate location for the purpose of a lawful picketing is the location that would have been appropriate had the individual remained in employment. 7498

7499 While the legislation itself is silent as to the numbers who may picket at any one time, the guidance given by the Code is followed. Therefore, it is recommended that pickets and their organisers should ensure that in general the number of pickets does not exceed six at any entrance to a workplace; frequently a smaller number will be appropriate. Where issues relating to the number of pickets have come before the courts, they have generally viewed large-scale pickets as being in breach of the law.

EXAMPLE In *Thomas v National Union of Mineworkers (South Wales Area)* [1985] IRLR 136, ChD, the Court noted that a picket was in breach of the common law of nuisance, even though there were just six pickets that stood at the gate, because around 60 demonstrated across the road. Consequently, an injunction could be applied to restrain it.

II. Employer's rights

7510 Where there is an industrial action, employers may respond by withholding pay or by moving to dismiss those taking industrial action, provided that the dismissal is in compliance with the law (¶8101).

Further, an employer whose employees threaten or take industrial action which is not protected, has the right to commence legal proceedings. Proceedings can be brought against the union and/or the individuals taking the industrial action. The most commonly used remedy is the injunction, a court order which carries with it potential further penalties, including action for contempt of court, if not complied with.

A. Withhold pay

7515 An employer whose employees are taking any industrial action, regardless of whether it is protected of not, has the right to withhold pay. Where employees are taking partial industrial action, for example, by working to rule or refusing to handle specified pieces of work, the employer may withhold **part pay** in return for part performance of the contract (*Miles v Wakefield Metropolitan District Council* [1987] IRLR 193, HL). Indeed, an employer may even withhold **entire wages**, where employees refuse to undertake part of their contractual duties, no matter how small these duties are, provided that the employer makes it clear that part performance of the contract is not acceptable (*Wiluszynski v London Borough of Tower Hamlets* [1989] IRLR 259, CA). For an employee to sue for wages due under a contract, he must prove a readiness and willingness to discharge all contractual obligations, including implied obligations so that, provided the employer indicates that partial performance is not enough, he will defend any such claim.

7516 The employer's rights to withhold pay extend to employees who, though they are carrying out, or are willing to carry out, their full duties, are nevertheless still supporting an industrial dispute.

EXAMPLE In *British Telecommunications plc v Ticehurst and Thompson* [1992] IRLR 219, CA, an employee, on her return to work after a 2-day strike, was asked to sign a loyalty pledge specifying that she would not take part in any further industrial action for the duration of the dispute. She refused to sign and was excluded from work, on a daily basis, until the dispute was formally settled. She claimed that an unlawful deduction had been made to her wages, since she was at all times ready and willing to perform the full range of her duties. However, the Court held that, by withdrawing her "goodwill", she had breached an implied term in her employment contract to "serve her employer faithfully," even if the work she would have carried out would not have been disrupted.

Pay deductions, which are due to industrial action, do not come under the general protection which workers have against unlawful deductions (¶3050; *Sunderland Polytechnic v Evans* [1993] IRLR, EAT). In such cases, the worker can only challenge the contractual validity of the deduction. 7517

B. Dismiss workers

Where workers are taking industrial action an employer may **lawfully dismiss** them, **unless**: 7520

1) The industrial action is protected and the **date of dismissal** is (ss 237, 238, 238A TULRCA 1992, as amended by s 26 ERelA 2004): 7521
– within the protected period; or
– after the end of the protected period but:
· the employee had ceased to take part in the industrial action before the end of that period; or
· the employer has failed to take any procedural steps that might have been reasonable to attempt to resolve the dispute.

The **protected period** is the sum of the:
– basic period, which is the first 12 weeks of protected industrial action; and
– extension period, which is the number of days during which the employee is locked out by the employer during the period of protected industrial action.

To determine whether the **employer** has **taken any procedural steps** that might have been reasonable to attempt to resolve the dispute, it will be examined whether the union and the employer agreed to use a **conciliation or mediation services provider** and, if so, whether they co-operated in arranging meetings with that provider, fulfilled any commitments given during the process or answered any reasonable question put to them during the conciliation or mediation (s 238B TULRCA 1992, as inserted by s 28 ERelA 2004).

In such cases, any dismissal will be treated as being **automatically unfair**, regardless of the worker's age or length of continuous employment. Therefore, workers who have worked for less than a year (who are normally excluded from unfair dismissal rights (¶8410)) are covered, as are workers over retirement age (also normally excluded). 7522

2) At the date of dismissal (¶8340), during a protected industrial action or a lockout, other relevant employees involved in the action or lockout were not dismissed. 7523

Relevant employees are, in relation to a (s 238 TULRCA 1992):
– lock-out, employees who were directly interested in the dispute in contemplation or furtherance of which the lockout occurred; or
– strike or other industrial action, those employees at the establishment of the employer at or from which the complainant works, who at the date of his dismissal were taking part in the action.

This definition means that a wider group of workers is covered where a dismissal arises in a lockout, and therefore, it is more likely that an employee, dismissed in the course of a lockout, will have the right to pursue an unfair dismissal claim.

For **complaints** of unfair dismissal see ¶8380. 7524

C. Specific remedies

7525 The employer can pursue the following legal rights if the **industrial action is unprotected**:

Injunction

7526 An employer can apply to the High Court to obtain an injunction (or interdict, in Scotland) (ss 20(6), 221 TULRCA 1992; see ¶1771). If an injunction is made, the union will be required to take any steps that the court considers appropriate to ensure that there is no further inducement of persons to take part in industrial action. The injunction can require that any industrial action or picket does not take place or does not continue to take place. An employer can also apply for an injunction to stop a union from authorising or endorsing, or continuing to authorise or endorse industrial action that is not protected.

If a union fails to comply with the injunction, proceedings can be taken for contempt of court. Such proceedings can result in the imposition of a fine, sequestration or imprisonment (*Richard Read (Transport) Ltd and another v National Union of Mineworkers (South Wales Area)* [1985] IRLR 67, QBD).

Any application for an injunction should be brought to the attention of the party named in it (most commonly, the union), where that party is likely to claim that the action complained of was in contemplation or furtherance of a trade dispute and may wish to defend the application.

Damages

7527 Employers may also bring claims for damages against unions and individuals where unprotected industrial action has caused financial loss.

In general, claims for damages are relatively rarely sought for the following reasons:
– in claims against the union itself the amount of damages is limited, making it unlikely that the employer will successfully recover any financial loss; and
– claims against workers, although not subject to a statutory maximum, are rarely pursued because in most cases the employer's wish will be for the industrial action to end so that normal working can resume.

Further, taking workers to court, or even threatening that this should happen, is not likely to create an industrial relations climate that is conducive to an effective return to work.

7528 **Against individual members** If claims are pursued against individuals, the employer has to be able to allocate, to that individual, the amount of the loss directly attributable to that individual's actions. It is very difficult, in most cases, to do this and usually, where it has been attempted, the legal action has failed. For example, the court can order a claim for damages against individual pickets, though the employer must to be able, both to estimate the financial damages and also to allocate the damages, where a number of individuals collectively have been carrying out unlawful picketing.

7529 **Against unions** A union has legal protection against unlimited damages claims when an employer brings an action in tort for an unprotected industrial action that has been authorised or endorsed by the union (s 22 TULRCA 1992). Where the losses are reasonably foreseeable as a result of the union's actions, the courts can make an award of damages against the union. However, the amount of damages is subject to a maximum that is linked to the size of the union. Smaller unions are subject to a lower level of liability than are large unions as follows:

Size of union by membership	Maximum award
Less than 5,000	£10,000
Between 5,000 – 24,999	£50,000
Between 25,000 – 99,999	£125,000
100,000 or more	£250,000

An employer seeking to sue a union for damages as a result of unprotected industrial action needs to be aware of the size of the union as this, and not the loss sustained, could determine the amount awarded.

The maximum set under the legislation does not include any **award of interest** on the sum outstanding in respect of the loss sustained by the employer. The amount that can be awarded is at the discretion of the court (s 35A Supreme Court Act 1981). 7530

EXAMPLE In *Boxfoldia LTD v NGA (1982)* [1988] IRLR 383, QBD, the court exercised this discretion to award an additional amount of £50,000 in respect of interest, in addition to the maximum amount of £250,000 which it could award, based on the size of the union.

An award against a union, its trustees in whom property is vested, or against members or officials of a union can be made against any property of the union unless it is **protected property** (s 23 TULRCA 1992). Protected property includes: 7531
- the property of individual members of the union, officials and trustees;
- the contents of the political fund (but only where there is a rule which says that it cannot be used to fund industrial action); and
- any separate provident benefit funds.

Where there are such rules, they must already have been in operation at the time when the legal proceedings were begun. A union cannot retrospectively create protected property.

The **provident benefit funds** that remain protected are those from which payment is expressly made to members during sickness, injury, unemployment, retirement, in cases of accident, as funeral benefits or to compensate for the loss of a member's tools.

Exceptions These limits on damages do not apply in three situations where the proceedings in tort are: 7532
- for personal injury (including any disease or impairment of a person's physical or mental condition) as a result of negligence, nuisance or breach of duty;
- for breach of a duty, that is imposed by any rule of law or by or under any enactment, where this is in connection with the ownership, occupation, possession, control or use of property, whether real or personal; or
- by virtue of a claim related to product liability under the Consumer Protection Act 1987.

IV. Third party rights

Anyone who **claims that**: 7540
- a union or any other person has done, or is likely to do an unlawful act to induce industrial action; and
- the effect of the action will be to prevent, delay or reduce the quality of goods or services to him,

can apply to the High Court for an injunction or to the High or county court for damages. Therefore, parties who are not a party to the industrial dispute but who claim that it is, or could affect their rights to goods and services, can take steps to have the action stopped or prevented (s 235 TULRCA 1992).

EXAMPLE In *Falconer v ASLEF and NUR* [1986] IRLR 331, CC, F, a commuter who was unable to travel due to an industrial dispute successfully brought an action in the county court, but not against British Rail from whom he had bought a ticket and with whom he, therefore, had a contract. Instead, he brought a claim against the unions, which had authorised unprotected industrial action and interfered with F's contract with BR.

The person applying to the court does not have to have had a contract to be supplied with the goods or services in question. In effect, a **potential customer** can complain where a service, which he might have required, is affected in any way due to industrial action. 7541

V. Criminal penalties

7550 The police authorities have responsibility in relation to the **following circumstances** (s 241 TULRCA 1992):

7551 1. With regard to **unlawful picketing**, the police must ensure that there is no obstruction of the highway and no threats of violence to persons or property and have the power to arrest pickets who pose such threats or cause obstruction.

Individual pickets may also be criminally liable under the old offence of "watching and besetting". It is committed where, with a view to compelling another person to do or not to do something, which he has a legal right to do, a person "wrongfully and without legal authority":
- uses violence or intimidates;
- persistently follows that person;
- hides tools, clothes or property or otherwise deprives or hinders that person from using them;
- "watches or besets" his home or place of business; or
- together with two or more persons follows that person in a "disorderly" manner.

A police constable can **arrest, without warrant**, anyone who is reasonably suspected of committing any one of these offences. The **penalty** on conviction can be a fine and up to 6 months' imprisonment.

7552 2. Where the form of industrial action that workers take involves a "**work in**" or "**sit in**". This occurs when workers do not leave work premises but remain within whilst refusing to carry out their contractual duties.

EXAMPLE In *Galt v Philip and others* [1984] IRLR 156, HCJ, the Court ruled that a "work in" by laboratory staff was illegal. Denying access to the laboratory, with a view to compelling others not to do what they had a legal right to do, was held to amount to "besetting."

Payment of members' penalties

7554 A union may not use its funds for the payment of any member's penalty for an offence of contempt. Members of a union can apply for a court order where they believe that money has been unlawfully spent (s 15 TULRCA 1992).

SECTION 5

Individual trade union rights

7560 Potential employees have the right not to be refused employment because of their trade union involvement or lack of involvement. In addition, employees have the right not to suffer any detriment (short of dismissal) or be dismissed (or selected for redundancy) for not joining a trade union or for being members or prospective members (or taking part in activities) of an independent trade union. In addition, members, officials and union learning representatives (ULRs) of independent unions recognised by their employer have a statutory right to reasonable time off for union activities and duties, and, in the case of officials and ULRs, for training.

7561 **Employees and workers** The majority of the provisions in TULRCA 1992 refer to, and cover, 'workers' as opposed to 'employees'. However, the principal individual union rights described in this section 5 **apply to employees only**, with the exception of the newer worker rights in relation to the protections against detrimental treatment found in sections 145A-152 TULRCA 1992 (¶¶7572-81) and in relation to the statutory recognition and derecognition procedures (¶¶7583, 7598).

A. General right not to be refused employment

An employer cannot refuse to employ a person under a contract of employment (i.e. a potential employee) because he is (s 137(1) TULRCA 1992): 7563
– or is not a **member** of a union (whether independent or not); or
– unwilling to accept a **requirement to**:
· become or cease to be a member; or
· make payments or equivalent of union subscriptions if he is not a member.

The protection also covers action taken against an applicant on the ground of his prospective **union activities** as the EAT has held that it will not separate between union membership and union activities (*Harrison v Kent County Council* [1995] ICR 434, EAT).

The only **exception** is where the job is working for a union and there is a valid requirement that applicants are members (s 137(7) TULRCA 1992).

EXAMPLE In *Harrison v Kent County Council*, H, a known union activist, successfully brought a claim against his employer when he failed to obtain a new job even though he was told it was not because he was a union member but because he was unco-operative and "anti-management."

A **refusal of employment** occurs if the employer does any of the following: 7564
– refuses or deliberately **omits to consider** and process an application or enquiry, or causes the applicant to withdraw his application or enquiry;
– refuses or deliberately **omits to offer** the employment. For example, a person would be held to be refused employment if he was not selected for a vacancy after being asked at his interview whether there could be a conflict of interest between being a union representative and being a worker with a managerial role; or
– **makes an offer** of employment:
· conditional on the applicant becoming or ceasing to be a member or requiring him to make payments or suffer deductions if he is not a member and the applicant refuses because of the condition(s). For example, an individual is interviewed for a job and makes it clear that he has a strong objection to joining a union. The employer offers him the job but on the condition that he joins the union. As a result, the applicant is unable to accept the offer;
· on terms that no reasonable employer, wanting to fill the post, would offer and which is not accepted. For example, an individual applies for a job and is sent details of the main terms and conditions. In the course of his job interview, it is established that he is the best candidate but is also an active trade union member. The employer offers the job but on significantly worse pay and conditions than would be appropriate for the particular position on offer. As a result, the applicant is unable to accept the offer; or
· but **then withdraws it** or causes the applicant not to accept it. For example, an employer withdraws an offer made to the applicant on hearing that he is an active union member.

It is equally unlawful for an **employment agency** to refuse its services to someone on similar grounds (s 138(1) TULRCA 1992). 7565

A **refusal of service** occurs if the agency does any of the following:
– refuses or deliberately omits to make the service available;
– causes the applicant not to be available or cease to be available for the service; or
– does not provide the same service, on the same terms, as is provided to others.

Blacklists An employer must not have an arrangement or practice under which employment is offered only to persons **put forward** or **approved by a union**, and the union puts forward or approves only persons who are members of the union. If he does so, a **non-union** 7566

applicant who is unsuccessful because of this arrangement or practice, will be taken to have been refused employment because of his union status (s 137(4) TULRCA 1992).

7567 **Job advertisements** Advertisements cannot imply that there is a **requirement regarding union membership** (¶590). This applies to all forms of advertisements, whether public or not, and will include a notice on a company noticeboard, or even a letter which suggests that there is a requirement that relates to union membership.

If an employer or employment agency advertises a job so that it indicates, or might reasonably be understood as indicating, that there is such a requirement, any applicant who does not fulfil the requirement will be conclusively presumed to have been refused employment for that reason (s 137(3) TULRCA 1992). The test is a subjective one and an employer cannot argue that applicants would not have understood there to be such a requirement, if it was reasonable that the claimant might have understood there to be this requirement. Therefore, to avoid any doubt, it is recommended that even words such as "Trade Union members welcome" should be avoided.

7568 **Remedies** An applicant affected by a requirement regarding union membership has the right to complain to an employment tribunal (ss 139, 140 TULRCA 1999). A complaint can be **brought against** an employer and/or an employment agency as appropriate (s 141 TULRCA 1992). If the complaint is **brought against one only**, the applicant may request the tribunal to join the other. The request will be granted if it is made before the beginning of the hearing though may be refused once the hearing has begun. No request can be made after the tribunal has decided whether the complaint is well-founded.

If either the employer or the claimant claims that the refusal of employment was induced by a **third party**, usually the union, by calling or threatening industrial action, they can ask for them to be joined in the action if the refusal is on the grounds that the claimant was not a union member (s 142 TULRCA 1992). The tribunal will allow a third party to be joined prior to the beginning of the hearing though may refuse once the hearing has began. No request can be made after an award of compensation. Where a tribunal makes an award for compensation it shall be paid in full or partly by the third party if the claim against it is well-founded.

7569 The complaint has to be **presented before** the end of 3 months, beginning with the date when the conduct complained of occurred, except where the tribunal decides that it was not reasonably practicable to present the claim before the end of the period and extends the period as it considers reasonable (s 139 TULRCA 1992).

If a tribunal **upholds** the complaint it will make a declaration to that effect and order that the individual is paid compensation up to a maximum of £56,800 (s 140 TULRCA 1992). Where there is a **joined action**, the tribunal will choose if one of the parties should pay compensation in full or whether two or more should each pay part, if the action is successful (ss 141(3), 142(3) TULRCA 1992).

The tribunal can also recommend the employer/agency takes within a specified period, any action it thinks practicable to reduce the adverse effect suffered by the complaint (s 140 TULRCA 1992).

MEMO POINTS This amount is likely to increase in **February 2006**.

B. Right not to be victimised on union grounds

7570 Both non-members and members alike have the right not to be victimised, i.e. subjected to detrimental treatment short of dismissal, on the grounds of their union status.

There are a number of points to note regarding this section. The rights of **non-members** relate to non-membership of any union, or a particular union, or a branch or section of a particular union. These provisions therefore apply to independent unions (¶7122), but can also refer to unions which are not independent. However, the rights of **members** not to be victimised due to their membership or union activities etc. only applies to members of independent unions. However, the right of **workers** not to be vicitimised in relation to the grounds specified in the statutory recognition and derecognition procedures only apply to members of independent unions which are recognised by their employers.

1. Non-members

Right not to be a member or pay union subscriptions An employee has the right not to be subject to any detriment by any act, or deliberate failure to act, by his employer where the **employer's purpose** is to (s 146(1)(c), (3), (4) TULRCA 1992): 7572
- compel him to be or become a member of any union or of a particular union; or
- enforce a requirement that, in the event of the employee not being a member of any union or of a particular union, he must make one or more payments (or suffer deductions from his salary) for union subscriptions or equivalent.

2. Members

Right to be a member and participate in union activities A member of an **independent union** has the right not to be subject to any detriment by any act, or deliberate failure to act, by his employer where the **employer's purpose** is to prevent or deter him from (s 146(1)(a)-(b) TULRCA 1992): 7573
- being, or seeking to become, a member;
- taking part in union activities at an appropriate time or to penalise him for doing so; or
- making use of union services at an appropriate time or to penalise him for doing so.

An **appropriate time** is defined as a time outside the member's working hours (i.e. any time when, in accordance with his contract of employment, he is required to be at work) or within these hours in accordance with arrangements agreed with (or consented to by) his employer. This can be established by custom and practice but cannot be inferred by an employer's silence (*Marley Tile Co Ltd v Shaw* [1980] IRLR 25, CA). For example, an employer was held to impliedly consent if he allows members to talk while they work provided no disruption is caused (*Zucker v Astrid Jewels Ltd* [1978] IRLR 385, EAT).

The employer's consent or agreement is necessary for this right to be active during working hours and if the employer unreasonably withholds his consent, the member's remedy will be under the right to take time off for union activities (¶7601).

An employer who removes a worker, who is a union official, from a client's site because of pressure from that client to remove him due to his union activities does not have the purpose of preventing or deterring the worker from being a union member or from taking part in union activities, or of penalising him for doing so (*Smyth-Britt v Chubb Security Personnel*, EAT case 0620/03). In this case, the employer's purpose in removing the worker from the site to his detriment was not to prevent or deter the worker's union activities but to retain its contract with the client. Although it was the client's purpose to deter or prevent the worker from taking part in union activities, there is no statutory provision which makes such external pressure unlawful.

It has also recently been confirmed that any claim based on participation in union activities requires the claimant to establish that he is on the "trade union side" as opposed to the employer's side (*Yewdall v Secretary of State for Work and Pensions* [2005] EAT case, 0071/05). In this case, the claimant, whilst a trade union member and engaged in activities with the trade union, was acting in his capacity as a health and safety officer for the employer and was therefore held not to have been engaged in union activities.

Detriment includes denying a worker promotion, disciplinary action based on union activities, and altering a worker's shift patterns, if the reason for doing this is to thwart his union activities or victimise him. Further, if a worker makes a derogatory remark about another 7574 worker at a union meeting, which results in the employer taking disciplinary action, this may amount to victimisation.

Refusing to recognise or deal with a **union representative** will also amount to victimisation. Therefore, while it is lawful for an employer to de-recognise a union, where recognition was a result of a voluntary arrangement (¶7210), he cannot choose not to recognise particular representatives of a recognised union.

> EXAMPLE In *Cleveland Ambulance NHS Trust v Blane* [1997] IRLR 332, EAT, the EAT held that refusing to shortlist an employee for a promotion because of his trade union activities amounted to a detriment and entitled him to damages for injury to feelings in addition to any other compensatory damages.
>
> In *FW Farnsworth v McCoid* [1998] IRLR 362, EAT, the EAT held that an employer who had removed accreditation from a shop steward amounted to deterring him from taking part in union activities.

7575 In considering a complaint of detriment from a member, a tribunal will look to at the **employer's intentions** to decide whether such a detrimental act (or failure to act) has occurred. The employer will only be acting unlawfully if the action is taken with the purpose of deterring or preventing workers from being a union member or participating in union activities or, alternatively, compelling an individual to become a member.

> EXAMPLE No victimisation
>
> 1. If an employer decides to investigate the mileage claims of union local officers and the reason for the investigation is to correct any mis-information coming from the union, this would not amount to victimisation. The fact that the employer's investigation may deter some activists from their involvement in the campaign will not alone amount to victimisation. However, it will be for the employer to prove that he did not intend to victimise.
>
> Victimisation
>
> 2. If an employer offers an employee a promotion (together with a pay rise), but then informs the employee that his pay rise will be withheld until such time as he has given up his union duties, this will amount to victimisation if the employer's intention is to deter the employee from carrying out any further union duties (*London Borough of Southwark v Whillier* [2001] EWCA Civ 808).

7576 **Inducing workers to opt-out** Workers have the right not to have an offer by their employer made for the sole or main purpose of inducing the worker not to be or seek to become a member of an independent union; not to take part, at an appropriate time, in the activities of that independent union; not to make use, at an appropriate time, of the union's services, or to be or become a member of any union or of a particular union (s 145A TULRCA 1992, as inserted by s 29 ERelA 2004). Such inducements are also unlawful if the result of the worker's acceptance of the employer's offer would be that the worker's terms and conditions would not be determined by a collective agreement negotiated on behalf of a union which is recognised or seeking to be recognised by the employer (s 145B TULRCA 1992, as inserted by s 29 ERelA 2004).

These provisions came into force on 1 October 2004 with the aim of preventing employers from making "sweetener payments" to workers to give up their collective bargaining position and move to individual contracts and to ensure full compliance with the European Court of Human Rights' ruling in *Wilson and NUJ v United Kingdom* [2002] IRLR 568, ECHR. In this case, the employer's action in offering financial incentives to workers to discourage trade union representation in the light of derecognition of the union were held to be unlawful.

7577 **Remedies** A worker alleging that he has been victimised or that his employer has made an unlawful inducement relating to union membership, activities or collective bargaining, has the right to complain to an employment tribunal (ss 145A, 145B, 146 TULRCA 1992, as amended).

7578 The complaint has to be **presented before** the end of 3 months, beginning with the date when the act, failure or inducement occurred, except where the tribunal decides that it was not reasonably practicable to present the claim before the end of the period and extends the period as it considers reasonable (ss 145C, 147 TULRCA 1992, as amended).

7579 The employer must show that the purpose of the action was not victimisation to be able to successfully **defend** the action i.e. that the reason for the treatment was not due to the worker's union involvement or non-involvement. In respect of a claim relating to an unlawful inducement, it will be for the employer to demonstrate his sole or main purpose in making such an offer to the worker concerned.

If a tribunal **upholds** a complaint it will make a declaration to that effect and order that the employee is paid compensation (s 149 TULRCA 1992). In respect of victimisation claims, the **amount of compensation** will be the sum the tribunal regards as just and equitable in all the circumstances and having regard to the infringement and any loss sustained. Loss includes any: 7580
- expenses reasonably incurred; and
- loss of benefit which might have reasonably been anticipated were it not for the victimisation.

Non-financial loss, i.e. stress, injury to health or feeling, sustained because of the infringement can be compensated (*Brassington v Cauldon Wholesale Ltd* [1977] IRLR 479, EAT). The amount of any compensation for injury to feelings in such cases will not necessarily be lower than that awarded in claims involving any other types of discrimination and in each case, it is necessary to focus on the level of injury suffered (*London Borough of Hackney v Adams* [2003] IRLR 402, EAT; see also ¶5748).

In respect of a successful complaint of **unlawful inducement**, there is a fixed award of £2,500 (s 145E TULRCA 1992, as amended).

EXAMPLE 1. In *Cleveland Ambulance NHS Trust v Blane* [1997] IRLR 332, EAT, a worker who was not shortlisted for a promotional post because of his union activities won damages for injury to feelings.
2. In *London Borough of Hackney v Adams*, above, LBH withdrew an offer of promotion to A when it became aware of her trade union activities. A tribunal awarded her £5,000 compensation for the humiliation and distress suffered. The EAT held that although the award was on the "high side" (taking into account the fact that A had mitigated her losses by taking up a temporary role with LBH on a higher salary and grade than the position previously offered), it was not erroneous so as to be perverse.

A tribunal can **reduce** the compensation where it considers that the worker to any extent caused or contributed to the situation (s 149(6) TULRCA 1992). However, the tribunal must **not consider** the worker's conduct in assessing any contributory fault, where the conduct relates to (s 155 TULRCA 1992): 7581
- being or becoming a member of a union;
- ceasing or refraining from becoming a member of a union; or
- not taking part in the activities of a union.

3. Worker rights relating to recognition and derecognition

A worker has the right not to be subject to any detriment by any act, or deliberate failure to act, by his employer in connection with any of the specified grounds under the **statutory recognition and derecognition** procedures (paras 156-160 Sch A1 TULRCA 1992). These provisions apply regardless of the worker's length of continuous employment. 7583

In respect of workers (¶13), detrimental treatment may amount to a **dismissal**. However, if an employee suffers a detriment which amounts to dismissal, his recourse will be under the unfair dismissal legislation (¶7598).

Protection against detrimental treatment **only applies** in respect of statutory recognition and derecognition provisions and does not extend to purely voluntary recognition arrangements.

Remedy A worker who has been subjected to such a detriment can complain to an employment tribunal **within** 3 months of the date of the act or failure of the employer. 7584

Should a tribunal find that a complaint is well-founded, it may award **compensation** which it considers just and equitable in all the circumstances. If a worker's complaint is upheld and the detriment complained of is the termination of his contract (not a contract of employment), then compensation may be awarded, subject to the statutory limits for basic and compensatory awards under the unfair dismissal legislation (¶8570).

C. Right not to be dismissed/selected for redundancy on union grounds

7585 Both non-members and members alike have the right not to be unfairly dismissed or selected for redundancy on the grounds of their union status.

However, there are a number of points to note regarding this section. The rights of **non-members** relate to non-membership of any union, or a particular union, or a branch or section of a particular union. These provisions therefore apply to independent unions (¶7122), but can also refer to unions which are not independent. However, the rights of **members** not to be victimised due to their membership or union activities only applies to members of independent unions. However, the right of **workers** not to be victimised in relation to the grounds specified in the statutory recognition and derecognition procedures only apply to members of independent unions which are recognised by their employers.

1. Non-members

7586 **Right not to be a member or pay union subscriptions** An employee will be automatically unfairly dismissed if the **reason** or **principal reason** for his dismissal or selection for redundancy is that he (ss 152(1)(c), (3), 153 TULRCA 1992):
- was not a member of any union or of a particular union; or
- refused, or proposed to refuse, to become or remain a member of any union or of a particular union; or
- refused, or proposed to refuse, to pay the equivalent of union subscriptions or objected, or proposed to object, to make such payments (or suffer such deductions from his salary).

There is no requirement to have been employed for a **minimum qualifying period** or to be below the **upper age limit** before being able to bring a complaint of unfair dismissal in connection with one of these reasons (¶¶8393-4).

2. Members

7590 **Right to be a member and participate in union activities** An employee will be automatically unfairly dismissed if the **reason** or **principal reason** for his dismissal or selection for redundancy is that he (ss 152(1)(a), (b), (ba), (bb), 153 TULRCA 1992):
- was, or proposed to become, a member of an independent union;
- was not, or refused to become or remain, a member of an independent union;
- had taken part or was proposing to take part in union activities at an appropriate time;
- had made use of the services of his union at an appropriate time; or
- refused to accept an unlawful inducement (¶7576).

See ¶7573 for the definitions of 'appropriate time' and 'working hours' (s 152(2) TULRCA 1992). Again, there is **no minimum qualifying period** and **no upper age limit** for the right to bring a claim of automatic unfair dismissal in connection with one of these reasons (¶¶8393-4).

EXAMPLE 1. An employer dismisses an employee who, in the course of his union activities, **criticises the employer**. This will constitute unfair dismissal (*Bass Taverns v Burgess* [1995] IRLR 596, CA). An employer cannot argue the defence in such a case that the employee is a member of the management team and therefore has an obligation to advance harmonious relationships between the employer and staff.

2. An employer who dismisses an employee because he has become aware of the employee's **past union activities** in a previous job when the only rational basis for doing so is the fear that the employee will repeat those activities in his present employment will be guilty of unfair dismissal (*Fitzpatrick v British Railways Board* [1991] IRLR 376, CA).

The right not to be unfairly dismissed or selected for redundancy has been extended to employees **making use of** a **union official's essential services** in negotiating an employee's terms and conditions (*Discount Tobacco v Armitage* [1990] IRLR 15, EAT; affirmed by *Speciality Care plc v Pachela* [1996] IRLR 248, EAT). 7591

The **motive** of the employer in selecting an employee for redundancy is irrelevant. 7592

EXAMPLE Unfair selection

1. In *Dundon v GPT* [1995] IRLR 403, EAT, D, a senior shop steward, agreed with his employer that although he was employed and paid as a technical services operator, he could work as a packing operator, so that he could devote half of his time to his union activities. Following a reorganisation, the packing department closed down and D was made redundant after scoring badly on a work assessment. His selection was held to be unfair, even though the employer had not been malicious in selecting him for redundancy or deliberately dismissed him because of his union activities.

Fair selection

2. If an employee's work has been arranged to fit in with his union activities and he is chosen because the job that he is doing is clearly identified as being redundant, his selection for redundancy will not be unfair (*O'Dea v ISC Chemicals Ltd* [1995] IRLR 599, CA).

Remedies An employee can apply to a tribunal to have a dismissal (including a dismissal for redundancy) suspended pending a full hearing of his unfair dismissal claim (s 161 TULRCA 1992). The application has to be made to the tribunal within 7 days of the dismissal and has to be presented to the tribunal along with a certificate, in writing, signed by an authorised official of an independent union. The certificate must state that: 7593

- on the date of the dismissal the employee was a union member or was intending to join; and
- that there are reasonable grounds for considering that the dismissal was due to the employee's union membership or proposed membership.

A tribunal will not **postpone** the hearing of the application except where it is satisfied that special circumstances exist which justify it.

Once an application has been made, the tribunal has to give the employer a copy of the application and the union certificate, together with notice of the date, time and place of the hearing (s 162 TULRCA 1992).

At the **interim hearing**, the tribunal will state if it is likely to uphold the unfair dismissal claim. If so, it will ask the employer, if present, whether, pending the full hearing or settlement, he will reinstate the employee or re-engage him on no less favourable terms and conditions. If the employer agrees, the tribunal will make an **order** to that effect (s 163 TULRCA 1992). 7594

If the employer states that he is willing to re-engage the employee in another job, and specifies the terms and conditions on which he is willing to do so, the tribunal will ask the employee whether he is willing to accept the job on those terms and conditions. If the employee accepts the job, the tribunal will make an order to that effect. If not, the tribunal will make an **order for continuation** of the contract of employment if it considers the refusal is reasonable.

An order for continuation is an order that the contract of employment continues in force for the purposes of pay and all employment benefits purposes, including any benefits that are based on seniority (s 164 TULRCA 1992). The order will be in force from the date of the dismissal until the tribunal gives its decision on the substantive dismissal claim. The tribunal will state how much should be paid to the employee on each normal pay period and is based on what the employee would reasonably have been expected to earn. Any money paid under a continuation order will be taken into account on any assessment of compensation if the dismissal is found to be unfair.

If an employer **fails to attend** or states that he is unwilling to reinstate or re-engage, the tribunal will make an order for continuation (s 163 TULRCA 1992). If the employer **fails to comply** with a continuation order he will be ordered to pay compensation to take account of the fact that the employee's rights have been infringed together with any loss of earnings as a result of this failure (s 166 TULRCA 1992).

If there is a **change in circumstances**, the employer or employee can at any time after the continuation order has been made, apply to the tribunal to have the order revoked or varied (s 165 TULRCA 1992).

7595 If either the employer or the employee claims that a dismissal was induced by a **third party**, usually the union, by calling or threatening industrial action, they can ask for them to be joined in the action if the dismissal is on the grounds that the employee was not a union member (s 160 TULRCA 1992). The tribunal will allow a third party to be joined prior to the beginning of the hearing although it may refuse to do so once the hearing has begun. No request can be made after an award of compensation or an order for reinstatement or re-engagement.

7597 If the court **upholds** the claim at the **full hearing**, it may award compensation, reinstatement or re-engagement.

The **maximum compensatory award** limit is £65,200 (i.e. 30 times the maximum amount of a week's pay for unfair dismissal (30 x £280) plus the maximum compensatory award for unfair dismissal (£56,800)). The compensatory award is assessed under the standard rules for compensation (¶8585). Where a tribunal makes an award for compensation it may order that the compensation shall be paid in full or partly by the **third party** if the claim against it is well-founded. Further, if the tribunal orders reinstatement or re-engagement, but the employer refuses to comply, it will give an additional award of between 26 and 52 weeks' pay.

MEMO POINTS These amounts are likely to increase in **February 2006**.

3. Worker rights in relation to recognition and derecognition

7598 An employee who is dismissed (or selected for redundancy) for a reason connected with one of the specified reasons under the **statutory recognition and derecognition procedures** will be deemed to have been automatically unfairly dismissed for an inadmissible reason (paras 161, 162 Sch A1 TULRCA 1992; see also ¶¶8393-4).

MEMO POINTS A **worker** who is dismissed (or selected for redundancy) for a reason connected with the statutory recognition and derecognition procedures has the right to claim he has been subjected to a detriment (see ¶7590).

7599 **Remedy** An employee may bring a **complaint** of unfair dismissal under these provisions in accordance with the normal unfair dismissal rules (¶8380).

There is **no minimum qualifying period** and **no upper age limit** for the right to claim automatic unfair dismissal for the above reasons. (s 164 TULRCA 1992; see also ¶¶8393-4).

D. Time off on union grounds

7600 Members, officials and union learning representatives (ULRs) of independent recognised trade unions have a **statutory right to reasonable time off** for union activities and duties. Officials and ULRs are also entitled to be paid for any time taken off to perform their duties or for their training.

The **ACAS Code of Practice** on Time off for Trade Union Duties and Activities (revised in 2003 and referred to below as the Code) provides legal and practical **guidance** and is admissible in evidence and must be taken into account in any employment tribunal proceedings where the issue of time off is being considered. The Code emphasises co-operation between employers and unions in relation to time off and stresses the importance of reaching agreements on their own arrangements for handling time off.

MEMO POINTS 1. The Code was revised in April 2003, following the enactment of the Employment Act 2002, which set out specific legislation regarding paid time off during working hours for **union learning representatives** (ULRs) to undertake duties and undergo training (s 42 EA 2002).
2. Officials and ULRs are employees who have been elected or appointed as representatives of all or some of a union's members in a particular company or workplace.
3. The statutory right to time off only **applies to** members, officials and ULRs of **independent unions** which are **recognised** by their employers. For further information on statutory recognition, see ¶7200.

Members

An employee who is a member of an independent union recognised by his employer is entitled to take **reasonable time off** to (s 170(1) TULRCA 1992): 7601
- take part in union activities; or
- access the services of a ULR.

This will **include** time off for union meetings, attending union conferences and other union bodies like local councils and regional meetings of the union. It does **not include** taking time off for industrial action, whether or not in contemplation or furtherance of a trade dispute. The right to time off for the purpose of accessing the services of a ULR only applies if the ULR himself would be entitled to time off for the purpose of carrying out his duties in relation to the employee.

The union activity must be directly linked to the relationship between the employee, the employer and the trade union (*Luce v London Borough of Bexley* [1990] IRLR 422, EAT).

EXAMPLE In *Luce v London Borough of Bexley*, L, a teacher, who was a union member, attended a union-organised lobby of Parliament against the Education Reform Bill. This lobby presented political and ideological objections to the proposed legislation which would affect the teaching profession but did not directly concern the employer. As there was no direct link to the employer, L had no statutory right to time off to attend the lobby.

The **Code** recommends that members should get unpaid time off for attending workplace meetings to discuss and vote on the outcome of negotiations, meetings with full-time officials to discuss issues relevant to the workplace, voting in properly conducted ballots on industrial action and voting in union elections. It also recommends that where the member is acting as a representative he should be given time off to attend branch, area or regional meetings, meetings of official policy-making bodies, such as the union's principal executive or its annual conference, and meetings with full-time officials to discuss issues relevant to the workplace. 7602

Although there is **no right to be paid** for taking part in union activities, the Code recommends that consideration should be given to payment if this would ensure that meetings of union members are more representative.

Officials

An employee who is an official of an independent union recognised by his employer is entitled to take **reasonable time off** to carry out his official duties or undergo training (that has been approved by the Trades Union Congress or by the independent union of which he is an official), **concerned with** (s 168(1), (2) TULRCA 1992): 7603
- negotiations with the employer related to or connected with collective bargaining;
- the performance of functions which the employer has agreed may be performed by the union; or
- redundancies (¶8931) or TUPE (¶8071) following receipt of information by the employer and consultation by him.

The **Code** has given the following examples of matters that would be related to or connected with collective bargaining:
- terms and conditions of employment, or the physical conditions in which employees are required to work;
- engagement or non-engagement, or termination or suspension of employment or the duties of employment, of one or more employees;

– allocation of work or the duties of employment as between workers or groups of workers;
– matters of discipline;
– trade union membership or non-membership;
– facilities for officials of trade unions; and
– machinery for negotiation or consultation and other procedures.

There is **no right** to time off to carry out internal union duties or to be involved with another employer's employee disputes.

7604 The union must expressly or impliedly **require the attendance** of the official at its meetings in order for such attendance to amount to the carrying out of his duties as an official (*Ashley v Ministry of Defence* [1984] IRLR 57, EAT). It is the official duties that the union considers necessary for the official to attend and not the duties the official may subjectively think are desirable.

EXAMPLE In *Ashley v Ministry of Defence*, the unofficial meeting of shop stewards, which was not authorised by the union and which the union did not request its shop stewards to attend, was held not to be a meeting that the official had the right to time off to attend.

7605 A tribunal will consider all the circumstances in ascertaining whether a **meeting** is sufficiently close or proximate to industrial relations between the employer and his employees for an official to be entitled to have time off to carry out official duties (*British Bakeries (Northern) Ltd v Aldington* [1988] IRLR 177, EAT). This will be a question of fact.

Attending **preparatory, explanatory or advisory** meetings will be considered to be sufficiently proximate if such meetings have some direct relevance to the industrial relations between the employer and its employees (*Beal v Beecham Group Ltd* [1982] IRLR 192, CA). For example, attending a meeting to exchange information may not be directly relevant but determining policies nationally may be (depending what the policies are). A tribunal will consider all the circumstances in deciding whether a particular preparatory or advisory committee is sufficiently close to the carrying out of industrial relations negotiations.

7606 **Training** Training usually amounts to giving the official **reasonable time off** in the first year to take part in basic training provided either by the official's own union or by the TUC (which offers a one-day training course). After this initial training, the official may require **refresher training** as well as new training which takes account of developments, for example, where there are significant changes in the law which would affect how the representative should perform his duties. The Code notes that officials will perform their duties better if they have the right skills and knowledge and recommends that time off should be given as soon as possible after their appointment.

To determine whether attending a **training course** is carrying out trade union activities, the description of the people attending the course by those responsible for it will be a relevant factor that a tribunal will take into consideration (*Ashley v Ministry of Defence*, above). The **subject matter** of the course should be relevant to the functions that the official performs. The Code advises that there is no one recommended syllabus for training as duties may vary depending on the collective bargaining arrangement in the workplace, the structure of the union and the role of the official.

The **Code** also recommends that there are situations where an official should be given **additional time off** for training. These are where:
– the official has special responsibilities;
– there are proposals to change the structure or topics of negotiation or where organisational change is being contemplated; and
– legal changes could affect workplace industrial relations and existing agreements.

Union learning representatives (ULRs)

7607 An employee who is a member of an independent union recognised by his employer is entitled to take **reasonable time off** to carry out the duties of a ULR, provided that the union

concerned has given written notice to the employer and the ULR is sufficiently trained (¶7608). The **duties** for which ULRs are allowed time off are (s 168A(1), (2) TULRCA 1992):
- analysing learning or training needs;
- providing information and advice about learning or training matters;
- arranging learning or training;
- promoting the value of learning or training;
- consulting with the employer regarding learning and training;
- preparing to carry out any of the above activities; and
- undergoing the relevant training to carry out ULR duties.

MEMO POINTS Prior to April 2003 when the statutory provisions regarding ULRs came into force, many employers already had **established staff training and learning programmes**. The Code states that ULRs should liaise closely with employers to ensure their learning and training activities complement those established schemes and avoid duplication of duties.

Training In order for a ULR **to qualify** for paid time off to undertake his duties, he must be sufficiently trained by the date on which either his union gives written notice to the employer that he is a ULR, or within 6 months of the employer receiving such written notice (s 168A(3), (4) TULRCA 1992). In the latter case, the union will ordinarily confirm in writing that the ULR will be undertaking the necessary training and when this has been completed. It is also good practice for the union to give details of the training which has already been completed and any previous training which has been taken into account. In certain circumstances, a ULR may be able to **extend** the 6-month **training period**, by agreement with his employer, should he be absent from work for a prolonged period due to any significant unforeseen event (e.g. ill-health or pregnancy). 7608

A ULR can demonstrate to his union that he has received sufficient training to carry out ULR duties by completing a **training course** approved by the TUC or the independent union to which the ULR belongs, or by demonstrating that he has previously gained the necessary skills and experience to operate as a ULR. Such expertise could be gained from experience in other areas of work, including teaching, counselling, careers guidance or human resources etc.

Request for time off

The request for time off must be made and brought to the attention of the employer by the member, official or ULR concerned. Only then does the employee have a right to complain to a tribunal if the employer refuses, ignores it, or fails to respond (*Ryford Ltd v Drinkwater* [1996] IRLR 16, EAT). Employees should give employers as much notice as possible and provide details of the: 7610
- purpose of the time off;
- intended location; and
- timing and duration of time off required.

Time off is discussed further in Chapter 12.

Extent of time off

The extent of time off for members, officials and ULRs must be reasonable in all the circumstances having regard to the Code (ss 168(3), 168A(8), 170(3) TULRCA 1992). 7611

Factors such as the needs of the business, and the amount and duration of time off in relation to these needs are important considerations in deciding if the employer acted reasonably. The number and frequency of similar periods of time off, which have been permitted by the employer, will also be considered to determine if the employer acted reasonably (*Borders Regional Council v Maule* [1993] IRLR 199, EAT). 7612

EXAMPLE In *Thomas Scott & Sons (Bakers) Ltd v Allen* [1983] IRLR 329, CA, the employer was not unreasonable in refusing to give paid time off to all 11 shop stewards to attend a union meeting on the busiest day of the week.

7613 An employer can act reasonably even if he refuses a valid request for time off if he was not fully aware of the purposes for which time off was requested. There may be a range of reasonable conduct within which the employer may act (*Ministry of Defence v Crook and Irving* [1982] IRLR 488, EAT). Whether the employer acted reasonably is a question of fact.

EXAMPLE In *Ministry of Defence v Crook and Irving*, C, a shop steward, requested time off for a training course. The employer refused, as he was unaware that the course had been broadened and was now relevant to shop stewards. The EAT held that the employer had not acted unreasonably.

7615 The Code states that employers should consider each **application for time off** on its merits and consider the reasonableness of the request in relation to the amount of time already taken. The Code suggests that account should be taken of **factors such as** the:
- size of the organisation;
- production process;
- need to maintain a service to the public; and
- need for safety and security at all times.

7616 There may also be situations when **more time off** would be appropriate, for example:
- where the workforce is experiencing significant change;
- where there is substantial labour turnover;
- in the period leading up to pay negotiations;
- if there has been an increase in the number of disciplinary hearings; or
- if there have been changes in management personnel or in the ownership or control of the company.

As a result, the Code recommends that time off should **usually be permitted for**:
- regular union side meetings, involving either all the officials in the union, or indeed officials from more than one union, where the recognition agreement is multi-union;
- meetings prior to negotiations;
- national and district meetings to consider pay and other matters;
- preparing for negotiations;
- informing members of progress;
- explaining the outcomes to members; and
- preparing for meetings with employers.

7617 It is advisable for employers and unions to have an **agreement** that sets out those issues over which bargaining is to take place and makes clear the range of duties for which paid time off will be available. The Code recommends that formal time off agreements are reached, particularly in larger workplaces, that provide clear guidelines against which applications for time off can be determined to avoid misunderstandings, facilitate better planning and ensure fair and reasonable treatment. It suggests that the agreement should deal with the amount of permitted time off, when it can be taken, who gets paid time off and the procedures for requesting it.

Right to remuneration

7618 Officials and ULRs (but not members) have the right to be remunerated for time off for the work that would have been done (s 169 TULRCA 1992).

An employer only has to pay for the hours on the course when the worker would have worked.

EXAMPLE 1. In *Hairsine v Kingston upon Hull City Council* [1992] IRLR 211, EAT, H, a shift worker, worked an evening shift between 3pm and 11pm. He attended a union training course that took place between 9am and 4pm and then worked only part of his shift before going home. The EAT held that he was not entitled to be paid for the time spent on the training course prior to 3pm, or for that part of the shift which he had not worked because he had gone home.

7619 However, where this might amount to **unlawful discrimination** (for example, discrimination against part-time workers), officials and ULRs will be entitled to receive payment in respect of all the time spent on the training course and will not be subject to a cap at their normal weekly working hours (*Davies v Neath Port Talbot County Borough Council* [1999] IRLR 769, EAT).

EXAMPLE In *Davies v Neath Port Talbot County Borough Council*, above, a part-time employee who attended a full-time training course was entitled to be paid for the entirety of the time spent on the training course.

See ¶3930 for the calculation of remuneration payable for the time taken off. **7620**

Remedy

Union members, officials and ULRs can complain to an employment tribunal where an employer has failed to allow time off or, in the case of officials and ULRs, has failed to pay for time taken off, and can seek compensation or an award for payment where appropriate. (ss 168, 168A, 169, 172 TULRCA 1992; see ¶3960). **7621**

EXAMPLE In *Skiggs v South West Trains Limited* [2005] IRLR 459, EAT, the EAT confirmed that, where the employer failed to allow an employee time off to carry out union duties, the award of compensation was wide enough to include the concept of cash reparation for the employee for the wrong done to him, independent of any specific consequential loss the employee may have suffered.

CHAPTER 22

Information and consultation in the workplace

OUTLINE ¶¶

7650 Increasingly, employers are being required to inform and consult with their employees on matters affecting the workplace, for example, in respect of **collective redundancies** (¶8915) and **business transfers** to which TUPE applies (¶8060).

Under new domestic legislation, certain employers are now required to **inform and consult UK-based employees** on an ongoing basis about potential measures and decisions which will affect their employment prospects and which are likely to lead to substantial changes in the workplace. **Currently**, the regulations only apply to larger employers (i.e. those with at least 150 employees based in GB). However, **by 2008**, employers with 50 or more employees will be subject to the regulations. Domestic information and consultation requirements are discussed in section 1.

In addition, certain larger employers with **employees in more than one EU member state** have had to negotiate the establishment of a European Works Council (EWC) or an information and consultation procedure as a means of exchanging views and establishing dialogue between management and employees. EWCs are discussed in section 2.

SECTION 1

Domestic information and consultation

In April 2005 new legislation came into force under which certain employers are now required to establish information and consultation arrangements in their workplace (Information and Consultation of Employees Regulations SI 2004/3426, referred to in this chapter as the regulations). These regulations were introduced to give effect to the European Directive on Information and Consultation (EC Directive 2002/14). 7655

MEMO POINTS Employers cannot **exclude or limit** the **application of the regulations**, and any agreement (for example, an employment contract) which attempts to contract out of the regulations will be void (reg 39 SI 2004/3426).

I. Scope of the regulations

The regulations will come into force over a period of 3 years and currently apply only to larger employers with **150 or more employees** in the UK. From 6 April 2007, the regulations will cover employers with **100 or more employees** and, from 6 April 2008, employers with **50 or more employees**. 7658

Employers with **less than 50 employees** will not be subject to the regulations.

Number of employees	Date regulations apply
At least 150	6 April 2005
At least 100	6 April 2007
At least 50	6 April 2008

MEMO POINTS 1. With regard to employers who are **not yet covered by the regulations** but who will be subject to them in the future, the Government is encouraging employers and employees to consider the advantages of putting into place a valid **pre-existing information and consultation agreement** (¶7676) under which the parties can voluntarily agree the terms of their information and consultation arrangements. Under such an agreement, the parties could, for example, agree that the type of information to be provided and consulted on does not need to be as broad as the information stipulated by the "default" standard IC provisions (¶7745) and, in addition, the statutory enforcement provisions (¶7770) will not apply. Moreover, any valid pre-existing agreement is protected from being challenged by a 3-year moratorium (¶7667), during which any further employee requests to negotiate a negotiated agreement will be invalid.
2. Moreover, the Government has indicated that, as a matter of **good practice**, all businesses, regardless of their size or the nature of their activities and whether or not they will eventually fall within the scope of the regulations, are encouraged to inform and consult with their employees on an ongoing basis about matters which affect them in a way which is appropriate for their particular circumstances (para 2 DTI guidance).
3. ACAS has also revised its booklet on Employee Communications and Consultation, which aims to assist employers, employees and their representatives **develop effective arrangements for communications and consultation** (the booklet can be found at www.acas.org.uk).

Applicability

The regulations apply to **undertakings** whose registered or head office, or principal place of business is situated in GB (reg 3(1) SI 2004/3426). An undertaking is defined as a public or private undertaking carrying out an economic activity, whether or not operating for gain (reg 2 SI 2004/3426). Ultimately, whether an organisation falls within the definition of an undertaking carrying out an economic activity for the purposes of the regulations will be determined by the Central Arbitration Committee (CAC) and, on appeal, the EAT and higher courts. 7659

MEMO POINTS 1. **Further guidance** as to what may constitute an "**undertaking**" and an "**economic activity**" may be found in European Court of Justice and UK case law interpreting the application of the Acquired Rights Directive and the TUPE regulations respectively (¶¶7911, 7931). DTI guidance suggests that the regulations principally cover companies (as opposed to organisational entities such as establishments or business divisions within a company), partnerships, co-operatives, mutual, building and friendly societies, associations, trade unions, charities and individuals who are employers. It is possible that the regulations also cover educational establishments, NHS trusts and Government bodies.
2. Where an undertaking's registered office is situated in GB but its **head office or principal place of business** is located **in Northern Ireland** or vice versa, the regulations will only apply if the majority of its employees are employed in GB (reg 3(2) SI 2004/3426). Separate legislation implements the EC Directive on Information and Consultation in Northern Ireland. Once it is determined whether the regulations or the Northern Irish legislation applies, this legislation will apply to employees throughout the undertaking, whether they are employed in GB or Northern Ireland.
3. The Government intends to draft a Code of Practice in respect of information and consultation to operate alongside the regulations which will apply to **central government departments** which are not covered by the regulations.

Employee thresholds

7660 In order to determine whether the 150, 100 or 50 employee thresholds are met, it is necessary to calculate the number of employees working for that employer in the UK. This is done by taking the average number of employees employed (whether for whole or part of the month) in the previous 12 calendar months (reg 4(1) SI 2004/3426). This calculation refers to 12 completed calendar months prior to the event that triggers an obligation on the employer to negotiate an IC agreement (para 5 DTI guidance; ¶7665). If an organisation has **existed for less than twelve months**, the number of actual months that it has existed must be used (reg 4(4) SI 2004/3426).

EXAMPLE 1. If an employee request to negotiate an IC agreement is made on 30 Sept 2005, the relevant figure would be the total number of employees employed during each month starting on 1 Sept 2004 and ending with 31 Aug 2005, divided by 12.
2. If, using the above example, the employer has only existed since 1 April 2005, the relevant figure would be the total number of employees employed during each month starting on 1 April 2005 and ending with 31 Aug 2005, divided by 12.

7661 **Part-time employees** are normally to be counted as if they worked full-time. However, for the purpose of the number thresholds only, an employer can choose to treat any part-time employee who works **75 hours or less** in any whole month within the relevant 12 month period as representing half a full-time employee, but he is not obliged to do so (reg 4(3) SI 2004/3426). Any absence from work or overtime worked by the employee is disregarded when determining whether he is contracted to work 75 hours or less per month. In addition, the fact that a particular month may contain less than 21 working days is also ignored.

An employer can only choose to count a part-time employee as representing half a full-time employee for those months in which he was employed part-time throughout the whole month. If an employee is employed on a full-time basis during any whole or part month, he must be counted as a full-time employee for that month. Moreover, if an employee works under a contract for **more than 75 hours** per month, he is deemed to be a full-time employee even though his employer may regard him as "part-time" in comparison to other employees in the business (para 5 DTI guidance).

7662 For these purposes, only employees should be taken into account and certain categories of **workers who are not employees** (see ¶¶11, 13 for the respective definitions) must be disregarded, for example, temporary agency workers (¶2040) and sub-contractors (¶15).

MEMO POINTS 1. **Fixed-term** employees (¶1950) are included in the scope of "employee". Similarly, **executive company directors** who are employed under a service agreement (¶2101) are included.
2. If the company is part of a **group of companies**, any employees within the group (for example, working for a parent or subsidiary company) should be ignored (para 6 DTI guidance).

Access to employee data

Should employees wish to make an employee request to trigger the obligation to negotiate a negotiated agreement, they will need access to employee figures. An employee (or employee representative) is entitled to make a **data request** to his employer for information on the number of people employed by the undertaking in the UK to enable him to determine whether the employee threshold is met and to determine what number of employees constitutes 10% of employees employed by the undertaking for the purposes of the negotiations (¶7670) (reg 5 SI 2004/3426). The request must be **dated** and **in writing**. 7664

If the employer **fails to provide** the necessary employee data **within** 1 month of a valid data request or the data provided is considered false or incomplete in any material respect, the employee (or employee representative) can complain to the CAC which, if it considers the complaint to be well-founded, will order the employer to disclose the data within a given period, not being less than 1 week from the date of the order (reg 6 SI 2004/3426). Employees who believe their employer has failed to provide the required data are advised by the Government to consider trying to resolve the matter informally with their employer before making a formal complaint to the CAC (para 7 DTI guidance).

MEMO POINTS The term "**employee representative**" is not defined in the regulations and can be a trade union official or some other third party (para 7 DTI guidance). Note that employee representatives have the right not to be unfairly treated or dismissed (¶7782).

II. Negotiated agreement

The process of reaching a negotiated agreement will be **triggered by** either (regs 7, 11 SI 2004/3426): 7665
- a valid employee request to initiate negotiations (¶7670); or
- a valid employer notification of his decision to initiate negotiations (¶7695).

Whichever way the process of reaching a negotiated agreement is triggered, the rules governing the actual **process** of negotiations and the **requirements** for the negotiated agreement are the same (¶¶7700, 7718).

Three-year moratorium

There are **restrictions** as to when employee requests and employer notification can be made. A 3-year moratorium (i.e. suspension) on employee requests or employer notifications applies where the request or notification is made **within 3 years of** (reg 12 SI 2004/3426): 7667
- where a negotiated agreement (¶7665) is in place, the date the agreement was drawn up, unless it has been terminated during that period;
- where a standard agreement (¶7730) is in place, the date it started to apply; or
- where a pre-existing agreement (¶7675) is in place and an employee request to negotiate a new negotiated agreement has not been endorsed by ballot, the date of that request.

Once an agreement covering information and consultation is in place (whether it is under a negotiated, standard or pre-existing agreement), either party is prevented from unilaterally starting the process of putting new information and consultation arrangements in place, although they can mutually agree to terminate the current information and consultation arrangements (para 29 DTI guidance).

The moratorium will not apply where there have been **material changes in the undertaking** during the 3-year period which mean that either (reg 12(2) SI 2004/3426):
- there is no longer a valid pre-existing agreement(s) which covers all the employees in the undertaking(s) or can no longer be treated as being approved by employees; or
- where there has been a negotiated agreement, it no longer covers all the employees in the undertaking.

Such material changes could, for example, arise from a significant group restructuring.

1. Employee request

7670 The process of reaching a negotiated agreement will usually be triggered by an employee request to initiate negotiations. The request must be **in writing** and **specify** the names of the employees making it and the date on which it is sent. Employees are advised to sign and date their signatures to avoid disputes as to whether they do in fact support the request (para 14 DTI guidance).

To be **valid**, a request must consist either of (reg 7(2) SI 2004/3426):
– a single request made by at least 10% of the employees in the undertaking; or
– a number of separate requests made on the same or different days by employees which, when taken in aggregate, amount to at least 10% of the employees in the undertaking, provided the requests fall within a rolling 6-month period.

The figure of 10% of employees is **subject to a minimum** of 15 and a **maximum** of 2,500 so that if a company has less than 150 employees, a request will only be valid if at least 15 employees make the request. Similarly, in large companies with more than 25,000 employees, a request will be valid so long as 2,500 employees have made the request. Any part-time employee is to be counted as representing a full-time employee for the purposes of the request, even if the employer chooses to count him as representing half a full-time employee for the purposes of the number thresholds (¶7660).

EXAMPLE An undertaking employs a workforce of 30,000. A total of 2,900 employees make a request to initiate negotiations to reach a negotiated agreement. Although the normal 10% threshold has not been met, the request will nevertheless be valid since it is only necessary for 2,500 employees to make the request.

MEMO POINTS Employers are advised to **retain** records of **employee requests** for 6 months which, on their own, do not meet the 10% threshold, in case any further requests are made which would, in aggregate, amount to a valid request as set out above (para 14 DTI guidance).

7671 A request must be **sent to** the employer at its registered office, head office or principal place of business (reg 7(4) SI 2004/3426).

Should the employee(s) making the request **wish to remain anonymous**, he can send the request to the employer via the CAC (reg 7(4) SI 2004/3426). The CAC does not forward the names of the employees to the employer but will notify the employer that a request has been made and seek such information from the employer that is necessary to ascertain the number and names of the employees who have made the request (reg 7(5) SI 2004/3426). The employer must provide this information to the CAC as soon as reasonably practicable.

MEMO POINTS If an employer has already received other **employee requests during the previous 6 months** which, when taken alone, did not meet the 10% threshold, he is advised to provide the CAC with the names of the employees making the previous request(s) to avoid the problem of double-counting (para 14 DTI guidance).

7672 Each request must be **dated**. In the case of a single request, or a number of single requests made on the same day, this will normally be the date it is sent to the employer but in the case of anonymous requests, it is the date the CAC informs the employer and employees of how many employees have made the request (reg 7(7) SI 2004/3426). With regard to aggregated requests made on a different days, the relevant date is the day on which the 10% threshold (¶7670) is met, or the date the CAC informs the parties that the threshold has been met.

7673 Where an **employer believes** that an employee **request** is **not valid** on the grounds that (reg 13 SI 2004/3426):
– it does not meet one or more of the validity requirements (¶7670);
– a 3-year moratorium on further employee requests is in place (¶7667); and/or
– the regulations did not apply to the undertaking concerned on the date the request was made;

he may apply to the CAC, within 1 month of the date on which the request was made, for a **declaration** as to whether the request is valid.

If the CAC **upholds the complaint** that the employee request is not valid, the parties will be prevented from proceeding any further with the process of negotiating to reach an agreement covering information and consultation (reg 7(9) SI 2004/3426). If the CAC **rejects the complaint**, the employer must then initiate discussions for a negotiated agreement.

MEMO POINTS As a matter of **good practice**, employers are advised to acknowledge receipt of the request, inform the workforce as a whole of the request and explain how they intend to respond to it (para 14 DTI guidance), though these steps are not required by the regulations. This will assist in avoiding confusion as to whether or not an employer believes the request is valid.

a. Pre-existing agreement

If a valid **employee request** has been **made by fewer than 40% of employees** in the undertaking, an employer who already has in place one or more valid pre-existing agreements on the date the request is made will not necessarily be obliged to commence negotiations for a negotiated agreement. In these circumstances, an employer can choose either to ballot the workforce to establish whether it endorses the employee request (¶7685) or to not ballot the workforce but commence negotiations to reach a new agreement on information and consultation (reg 8(2) SI 2004/3426). 7675

If the employee request has been made by **40% or more of employees** in the undertaking, the employer has no choice but to initiate negotiations for a negotiated agreement (¶7700).

Criteria for pre-existing agreement(s)

For a pre-existing agreement to be **valid**, it must, on the date on which the employee request is made (reg 8(1) SI 2004/3426): 7676
- be in writing;
- cover all the employees of the undertaking, though it could include employees in other undertakings (for example, in group companies – ¶7678);
- set out how the employer is to inform and consult with employees or their representatives; and
- have been approved by the employees.

MEMO POINTS 1. The regulations do not stipulate what constitutes **employee approval** of a pre-existing agreement, but the DTI suggests that approval might be demonstrated by ballot endorsement, support through signatures, or agreement with employee representatives (including recognised union officials) who represent a majority of the workforce (para 20 DTI guidance).
2. Employers who wish to put in place a valid pre-existing agreement **prior to the regulations being applicable** to them should review their existing information and consultation agreements to ensure that they meet the criteria specified. This might include, for example, extending existing arrangements to cover all employees, putting in place new consultation arrangements covering the whole workforce, and/or seeking approval for existing agreements.

A **collective agreement** (¶7123) might be a valid pre-existing agreement even if it does not cover all the employees in the undertaking, provided one or more other valid pre-existing agreements cover the remainder of the employees who fall outside the scope of the collective agreement (para 20 DTI guidance). 7677

However, a **European Works Council (EWC) agreement** (¶7800) is not a valid pre-existing agreement since it focuses on transnational, rather than domestic, issues.

Pre-existing agreement covering more than one undertaking

Where a pre-existing agreement which meets all the validity criteria covers employees in more than one undertaking, the employers can choose to hold a **combined endorsement ballot** of the employee request rather than holding separate ballots in respect of each of the undertakings (reg 9 SI 2004/3426). 7678

A combined endorsement ballot can only be held if **fewer than 40% of employees** in all the undertakings covered by the agreement made one or more requests for the negotiated agreement. Requests from employees in different undertakings covered by one pre-existing agreement will be aggregated if they are made within a rolling period of 6 months. Note that, rather than holding a combined endorsement ballot, it is still open to the employer to simply hold an endorsement ballot in respect of the employees in the undertaking from which the request was made (reg 9(3) SI 2004/3426).

If **40% or more employees** in all the undertakings covered by the agreement made the request, then the obligation on the employer to negotiate a new IC agreement is triggered (¶7700).

EXAMPLE A valid employee request to negotiate an information and consultation agreement is made in respect of an undertaking, X. X already has in place a valid pre-existing agreement which covers employees in its two subsidiary companies, Y and Z. The employee request in relation to X, when aggregated with employee requests made by employees of Y and Z during the preceding 6 months, is made by 30% of the total number of employees employed by X, Y and Z. It is therefore possible for X, Y and Z to hold a combined endorsement ballot to endorse the request in respect of all the employees employed by X, Y and Z. However, X can alternatively choose to simply hold an endorsement ballot in respect of its own workforce.

7679 Similarly, it is possible for one pre-existing agreement to provide for different information and consultation arrangements to apply to different parts of one undertaking or for there to be several pre-existing agreements, each of which covers only part of an undertaking.

Complaints regarding pre-existing agreement(s)

7680 Where an employee (or employee representative) believes that there is no valid pre-existing agreement in place which entitles the employer(s) to hold an endorsement ballot (or, if applicable, a combined endorsement ballot), he can complain to the CAC provided he does so **within** 21 days of the employer's notification of his intention to hold an endorsement ballot (or combined endorsement ballot) (reg 10(1) SI 2004/3426). Where a complaint has been made, an employer is advised to wait for the CAC's decision before going ahead with the ballot (para 23 DTI guidance).

If the employee's complaint is **upheld by the CAC**, it must order the employer to start negotiations for a new negotiated agreement or, where an employer proposes to hold a combined endorsement ballot, it will either order the employer to initiate negotiations for a new negotiated agreement (if he has expressed a preference for this) or to conduct a single endorsement ballot in respect of the undertaking from which a valid employee request was made (provided there is a valid pre-existing agreement covering that undertaking).

If the complaint is **not upheld**, the employer is free to hold the endorsement ballot.

---

b. Endorsement ballot

7685 If a valid employee request has been made by **fewer than 40% of employees** in the undertaking, the employer can choose to hold an endorsement ballot rather than start negotiations for a negotiated agreement (reg 8(2) SI 2004/3426).

If he decides to hold a ballot, he must, **within** 1 month of the employee request, **inform in writing** all the employees in the undertaking (or, in the case of a combined endorsement ballot, all the employees in that group of undertakings) that he intends to do so (reg 8(3) SI 2004/3426).

An employee (or employee representative) who believes that his employer has **failed to inform employees** that he intends to hold an endorsement ballot within the time limit can apply for a declaration from the CAC which, if upheld, will oblige the employer to start discussions for a negotiated agreement (reg 8(7) SI 2004/3426).

7686 The employer must make arrangements for the ballot to be held as soon as is reasonably practicable but in any event **no earlier than** 21 days of having informed employees of the ballot. During this period, employees have an opportunity to complain about the validity of the pre-existing agreement(s) (¶7680).

If, having informed employees of his intention to hold an endorsement ballot, an employer **fails to hold a ballot**, an employee (or employee representative) can complaint to the CAC which, if the complaint is well-founded, must make an order requiring the employer to hold a ballot by a given date (reg 8(8), (9) SI 2004/3426).

Conduct of the ballot

The employer must ensure as far as is reasonably practicable that the arrangements for the ballot are fair and that every individual who is employed by the undertaking on the day of the ballot is entitled to vote in it (reg 8(4) SI 2004/3426). The ballot must be conducted so that voting takes place in secret and the votes are counted accurately. 7687

One way of ensuring the fairness of the endorsement ballot would be to appoint an **independent scrutineer** to supervise its conduct, such as an independent qualified person (¶7272), although this is not required by the regulations.

If an employee (or employee representative) believes that his employer has **failed to meet** any of the **ballot requirements**, he can complain to the CAC within 21 days of the ballot. If his complaint is upheld, the CAC will make an order that either the employer initiates negotiations for a new negotiated agreement (if, the employer has already indicated that he would prefer to do this) or that the ballot should be held again (reg 10(2), (3) SI 2004/3426). 7688

Result of the ballot

The **employer must inform** the employees of the result of the ballot as soon as is reasonably practicable. 7689

An **employee request** is **endorsed** if 40% or more of the employees in the undertaking, plus the majority of the employees who voted in the ballot, vote in favour of it (reg 8(6) SI 2004/3426). The employer will then be under an obligation to start the negotiation process to reach a negotiated agreement. Where a pre-existing agreement covers more than one undertaking, the employer's obligation to start negotiations applies in respect of all the undertakings in respect of which a ballot was held and not just in respect of the undertaking from which the employee request was made. Where there is more than one undertaking, an employer is free to negotiate a new negotiated agreement applying to all the undertakings covered by the pre-existing agreement or a separate agreement in respect of each of the undertakings (para 22 DTI guidance). 7690

This does not mean that pre-existing agreements already put in place by the employer no longer continue to have any force (for example, a collective agreement with a trade union which provides for collective bargaining over pay, hours and holiday). However, it means that the pre-existing agreement is not sufficient to fulfil the employer's obligations under the regulations and that a new negotiated agreement (or if the parties fail to reach an agreement, the standard IC provisions) must be put in place (para 25 DTI guidance).

However, if the **employee request** is **not endorsed**, the employer is not obliged to initiate negotiations for a negotiated agreement (reg 7(8) SI 2004/3426). Furthermore, **a 3-year moratorium** on any further employee requests from employees in any of the undertakings in which an endorsement ballot was held comes into effect from the date of the employee request (reg 12(1) SI 2004/3426) (¶7667). 7691

2. Employer notification

As an alternative to an employee request, the process of negotiations for a negotiated agreement can be initiated by an employer notification. 7695

A **valid** notification must (reg 11 SI 2004/3426):
– state that the employer intends to start negotiations for an IC agreement and that notification is given for the purpose of the regulations;
– state the date on which the notification is issued; and

– be published in order to bring it to the attention of, so far as is reasonably practicable, all the employees in the undertaking (or if the employer wishes to negotiate a single IC agreement covering more than one undertaking, the employees in each undertaking covered).

Once a valid notification has been given, the process of negotiating a negotiated IC agreement will begin (¶7700).

7696 Where an employee (or employee representative) considers that an employer notification is **not valid** on the grounds that it does not meet one of the above requirements above or that the employer is restricted from issuing a notification by a 3-year moratorium which is in place (¶7667), he may apply to the CAC, within 1 month of the date on which the notification was made, for a **declaration** as to whether the notification is valid (reg 13 SI 2004/3426).

Where appropriate, employees are advised to first inform the employer on an **informal basis** that they believe a notification is not valid, or that the regulations do not apply to the undertaking, before bringing a complaint to the CAC, in case there has been a misunderstanding between the parties regarding the application of the regulations to the undertaking concerned (para 30 DTI guidance).

If the CAC **upholds the complaint** that the employer notification is not valid, the employer will be prevented from continuing any further with the process of negotiating to reach an agreement (reg 7(9) SI 2004/3426). If the CAC **rejects the complaint** and declares the notification is valid, the employer will be required to initiate negotiations.

3. Negotiations to reach an agreement

7700 Before any negotiations can take place, the employer must first arrange for the election or appointment of negotiating representatives. The regulations lay down how such election or appointment must take place, as well as certain provisions regarding the conduct of the negotiations.

a. Negotiating representatives

Election or appointment

7702 Following a valid employee request (which, if necessary, has been endorsed by a workforce ballot – ¶7685) or employer notification, the employer must, as soon as is reasonably practicable, make arrangements for the election or appointment of negotiating representatives who will represent employees in the negotiations for an agreement with the employer (reg 14(1) SI 2004/3426). Whether negotiating representatives are elected or appointed is left to the discretion of the employer, although it is possible to use both methods, for example, with regard to different parts in an undertaking. The employer is not entitled, however, to take any part in the decision as to who is elected or appointed.

There are no requirements regarding the **number of representatives**, and the employer must simply ensure that a sufficient number are elected or appointed. If the undertaking is split into different parts, then it may be appropriate for employees to elect or appoint representatives from each part of the undertaking. Similarly, if it is proposed that a negotiated agreement will cover employees in more than one undertaking, for example, in a group of companies, then it may be appropriate to have one (or more) negotiating representative(s) from each undertaking to be represented.

The employer must ensure that all employees are entitled to take part in the election or appointment of the representatives and that, following their election or appointment, all employees will be represented by one or more representatives (reg 14(2) SI 2004/3426). If it is proposed that a negotiated agreement will cover more than one undertaking, employees in all the undertakings covered must be entitled to take part in the election or appointment (para 33 DTI guidance).

Once such representatives have been elected or appointed by employees, the employer must inform employees of the identity of the representatives and invite the representatives to enter into negotiations to reach an agreement (reg 14(1) SI 2004/3426).

MEMO POINTS 1. It will not always necessarily be the case that the individuals who are elected or appointed as negotiating representatives will be the same people as the **IC representatives** (¶7733) who will be informed and consulted by the employer under the arrangements set out in the negotiated agreement. In addition, it should not be assumed that **trade union representatives** should become negotiating representatives, although they are likely to be well placed to take on such a role (para 35 DTI guidance).
2. **Long haul crew members** in the merchant navy are precluded from acting as negotiating representatives (reg 43 SI 2004/3426).

Complaints regarding election or appointment

7704 If an employee (or employee representative) believes that one or both of the requirements for the election or appointment of negotiating representatives has not been met, he can, **within** 21 days of the election or appointment, bring a complaint to the CAC (reg 15(1) SI 2004/3246). Where the CAC upholds a complaint, it will order the employer to arrange for the process of election or appointment to take place again within a prescribed period.

Role

7705 The role of the negotiating representatives is significant in representing employees' interests when negotiating the information and consultation arrangements with the employer. Negotiating representatives will therefore need to ensure that they represent **employees' views** regarding what arrangements they wish to put in place, including, for example (para 35 DTI guidance):
- the method, subject matter, timing and frequency of information and consultation;
- how IC representatives will be chosen and replaced;
- who will represent the employer at information and consultation meetings;
- the method by which the employer will respond to the views put across at such meetings; and
- the circumstances in which the arrangements under the negotiated agreement can be amended or terminated.

Right to paid time off

7706 A negotiating representative has the right to take **reasonable** paid time off during his working hours to perform his functions (regs 27, 28 SI 2004/3426) and is entitled to be paid at the **appropriate hourly rate**, the amount of which will depend on whether his contractual hours vary or not (¶¶2935, 2937). It should be noted that any contractual remuneration paid to him in respect of a period of time off will go towards discharging any liability of the employer to pay remuneration in respect of the time off and vice versa (reg 28(7) SI 2004/3426).

7707 An employee who is **unreasonably refused** time off to perform his functions as a negotiating representative or is not paid (wholly or in part) in respect of such time off can bring a complaint to an employment tribunal (reg 29(1) SI 2004/3426). Complaints must be made within 3 months beginning with the day on which the time off was taken or on which it is alleged the time off should have been permitted (reg 29(2) SI 2004/3426). However, a tribunal can extend this period if it is satisfied that it was not reasonably practicable for the employee to make the complaint in time.

If the claim is successful, the **tribunal must** make a declaration to that effect and/or (reg 29 SI 2004/3426):
- order the employer to pay the employee the amount equal to the remuneration he would have been entitled to had the employer not refused to permit him to take time off; or
- order the employer to pay the amount due to the employee if he has taken time off but the employer has refused to pay him in whole or in part.

MEMO POINTS Before bringing any complaint before a tribunal, an employee must first raise his grievance under his employer's **statutory discipline and grievance procedures** (¶6772).

b. Conduct of negotiations

Time limit for starting negotiations

7710 The **employer must initiate** negotiations to reach a negotiated agreement with employee representatives as soon as reasonably practicable or, at the latest, **within** 3 months of the date of the request or notification (reg 14(3) SI 2004/3426).

The 3-month deadline for starting negotiations is effectively **suspended** in respect of any period during which (reg 14(3) SI 2004/3426):
– an endorsement ballot (including a combined endorsement ballot) is held (¶7685);
– any complaint regarding an endorsement or combined endorsement ballot is determined (¶7688);
– any dispute regarding the validity of the employee request or employer notification is determined (¶¶7673, 7696); or
– any complaint regarding the election or appointment of employee negotiating representatives is determined (¶7704).

If the employer **fails to initiate negotiations** within the time limit, the standard information and consultation provisions (¶7745) will apply from the earlier date of (reg 18(1) SI 2004/3426):
– 6 months from the date of the valid employee request or employer notification; or
– the election of information and consultation representatives under the standard information and consultation provisions.

7711 During the negotiations, the parties are under a duty to work in a **spirit of co-operation** and with due regard for their reciprocal rights and obligations, taking into account the interests of both the undertaking(s) and the employees (reg 21 SI 2004/3426).

Duration of negotiations

7712 Negotiations between the employer and employee representatives can **continue for up to** 6 months from the date beginning 3 months after the employee request or employer notification was made (reg 14(3) SI 2004/3426).

The 6-month negotiating period is effectively **suspended** in respect of any period during which any complaint regarding the employee approval ballot (¶7725) of a negotiated agreement is determined, including any further period during which the ballot is re-held if required by the CAC (reg 14(4) SI 2004/3426).

7713 If, before the end of the 6-month negotiating period, the parties have not yet reached agreement, the employer and a majority of the negotiating representatives can mutually agree to **extend** the negotiating period **without limit** (reg 14(5) SI 2004/3426). It is not possible for one party to unilaterally impose an extension.

Failure to reach agreement

7715 If the parties fail to reach an agreement within the 6-month period, or any extended period which has been agreed between the parties, the **standard information and consultation provisions** (¶7745) will **apply from** the earlier date of (reg 18(1) SI 2004/3426):
– 6 months from the date on which the time limit expires; or
– the election of the information and consultation representatives under the standard information and consultation provisions.

This provides the parties with an additional limited period in which the parties may be able to reach agreement before the standard information and consultation provisions begin to apply. Employers should note that if, at the end of this additional 6-month period they have failed to arrange for the election of information and consultation representatives (¶7733), they will be liable to a fine (¶7777).

4. Requirements for negotiated agreement

Form and content

Considerable flexibility is provided to the parties in agreeing the scope and provisions of the negotiated agreement so they can tailor the agreement towards the particular circumstances of the organisation. 7718

However, the regulations require that a negotiated agreement, which can be either a **single agreement** or consist of **separate parts** (e.g. sections, divisions, units or establishments) **covering different employees** which, when taken together, cover all the employees in the undertaking (or, if more than one, each of the undertakings), **must** (reg 16(1) SI 2004/3426):

a. set out the circumstances in which the employer must inform and consult the employees;

b. be:

- in writing;
- dated;
- approved by employees (¶7723); and
- signed by, or on behalf of, the employer (or, in the case of an agreement which covers more than one undertaking, each of the employers); and

c. either provide for the appointment or election of information and consultation representatives whom the employer must inform and consult or provide that the employer informs and consults directly with employees (or both) (¶7722).

Where a negotiated agreement consists of different parts, each part can make different provisions in respect of the requirements set out above (reg 16(2) SI 2004/3426).

MEMO POINTS The **date** of the negotiated agreement will determine the start of the 3-year moratorium on further employee requests or employer notifications.

Specific matters such as the method, subject matter, timing and frequency of information and consultation are not prescribed by the regulations, but must be determined by the negotiations between the employer and negotiating representatives. The "default" standard information and consultation provisions (¶7745) can be used as a guide as to content of the information and consultation arrangements should the parties wish. 7720

DTI guidance suggests the following framework of provisions could be used as a basis for deciding what arrangements need to be covered in any such negotiated agreement, including (Annex 1 DTI guidance):

- **coverage**. This might include a definition of "undertaking", which employees will be covered, whether separate arrangements will cover different parts of the undertaking and the scope of any agreements with trade unions;
- **methods** of informing and consulting. This might include the type of arrangements to be set up, including whether there should be representatives or direct consultation with employees (or both), how any representatives will be chosen, how long they will serve and how they will be replaced, any facilities and time off for employee representatives, and any obligations on the representatives to report back to employees and/or seek the views of the workforce;
- **frequency** and **timing** of information and consultation. This might include how often information and consultation will take place and when;
- **subject matter**. This might cover the types of topics which will be covered by the obligations to inform and consult and how those topics will be chosen, including how the agendas of meetings will be decided;
- **information and consultation**. This might include the type and nature of the information to be provided, how the views/opinions of the employees could be expressed, what the employer will do in response and who will represent management in any meeting with information and consultation representatives;
- **statutory consultation requirements**. This might include how other legal requirements on the employer to consult employees (for example, regarding collective redundancies, TUPE transfers, European Works Councils etc) will be handled and whether there will be any

overlap with the information and consultation arrangements set up under the negotiated agreement;
– **confidential information**. This might include how confidential or price-sensitive information will be dealt with, the obligations on any recipients of confidential information and any disciplinary measures for breaches of confidentiality;
– **disputes**. This might cover how disputes are resolved and the enforceability of any pre-existing agreement(s);
– **restructuring**. This might cover what the implications of any company restructuring would be for the information and consultation arrangements agreed; and
– **duration**. The parties might want to include provisions regarding the duration of the agreement and the circumstances in which it can be reviewed, revised or terminated.

MEMO POINTS Special provisions apply to **confidential information and documents** (¶7746).

Information and consultation representatives

7722 A negotiated agreement must provide for either the **election or appointment** of information and consultation representatives (referred to as IC representatives) or for the employer to inform and consult **directly** with the workforce. It is possible for an agreement to provide for both forms of arrangement and this is a matter for the parties to agree.

The employer and negotiating representatives must, if they agree that information and consultation should take place through IC representatives, also decide on how many IC representatives there will be, who they will represent, when and how they will be replaced, and whether anyone other than an employee can hold the position (para 38 DTI guidance).

Employee approval

7723 A negotiated agreement will be approved by the employees if it has been **signed by** (reg 16(3) SI 2004/3426):
a. all the negotiating representatives; or
b. a majority of the negotiating representatives and either approved:
– in writing by at least 50% of employees in the undertaking (or, where the agreement covers more than one undertaking, group of undertakings); or
– by at least 50% of employees voting in a ballot.

MEMO POINTS Where a negotiated agreement consists of **different parts**, each part must be approved in accordance with identical provisions (reg 16(4) SI 2004/3426).

Ballot

7725 An employer is not obliged to hold a ballot to seek employee approval of a negotiated agreement. However, if he chooses to do so, he must ensure, as far as reasonably practicable, that the arrangements he makes for the ballot are fair and that all employees (who are employed on the date of the ballot) in the undertaking (or, in the part of the undertaking to which the agreement relates, if appropriate) are entitled to vote in it (reg 16(5) SI 2004/3426).

The ballot must be **conducted** so that, as far as is reasonably practicable, the voting takes place in secret and that the votes are accurately counted. As soon as is reasonably practicable after the date of the ballot, the employer must inform the employees who were entitled to vote in it of the result (reg 16(6) SI 2004/3426).

MEMO POINTS One way of ensuring the fairness of the endorsement ballot would be to appoint an independent scrutineer to supervise its conduct, such as an independent qualified person (¶7272), although this is not required by the regulations.

7726 A negotiating representative who believes that the arrangements for the ballot do not satisfy all the requirements set out above can bring a **complaint regarding** the **conduct** of the ballot to the CAC **within** 21 days of the date of the ballot (reg 17 SI 2004/3426). Where the CAC upholds a complaint, it will order the employer to re-hold the ballot within a specified period.

III. Standard agreement

If, following a valid employee request or employer notification, the employer fails to initiate negotiations for a negotiated agreement or the parties enter into negotiations but fail to reach an agreement within the 6-month period (or any extended period which had been mutually agreed between the parties), the standard information and consultation provisions (referred to as the standard IC provisions) will apply (reg 18 SI 2004/3426). It should be noted that the standard IC provisions will apply to each individual undertaking separately and any information and consultation arrangements made under the standard IC provisions cannot cover more than one undertaking (para 44 DTI guidance). 7730

When implementing the standard IC provisions, the parties are under a duty to work in a **spirit of co-operation** and with due regard for their reciprocal rights and obligations, taking into account the interests of both the undertaking and the employees (reg 21 SI 2004/3426).

Negotiated agreement

It is important to note that where the standard IC provisions apply, the employer and the IC representatives who have been elected under the standard IC provisions can, at any time, reach a negotiated agreement under which provisions **other than the standard IC provisions** will apply (reg 18(2), (3) SI 2004/3426). Such an agreement can only take effect if it complies with the requirements for a negotiated agreement (¶7718) and is signed by a majority of IC representatives. 7731

Where such an agreement has been reached, the **3-year moratorium** will apply to any further employee requests or employer notification from the date of the agreement (¶7667).

1. Information and consultation representatives

Before the standard IC provisions start to apply, the employer must arrange a **ballot to elect** the relevant number of IC representatives (reg 19, Sch 2 SI 2004/3426). For each 50 employees (or part thereof), one representative must be elected, subject to a **minimum** of 2 and **maximum** of 25. Therefore, a company with 100 employees will need two IC representatives and a company with 180 employees will need 4. 7733

MEMO POINTS 1. It is not necessary for the same people who are elected **negotiating representatives** to also be elected as IC representatives.
2. **Long haul crew members** in the merchant navy are precluded from acting as negotiating representatives (reg 43 SI 2004/3426).

Arrangements for ballot

The requirements for the arrangements and conduct of the ballot are set out at Sch 2 SI 2004/3426. 7734

The employer can choose whether to hold a **single ballot** or **separate ballots** in respect of different constituencies if the employer considers that the IC representatives elected would better reflect the interests of the employees as a whole (para 1 Sch 2 SI 2004/3426). Once he has formulated his proposed arrangements for the ballot, he must, as far as reasonably practicable, **consult** with employee representatives (for example, trade union or negotiating representatives) or employees regarding the arrangements and make any necessary modifications following consultation. He must then **publish** the final arrangements for the ballot in such a way that they are, as far as reasonably practicable, brought to the attention of his employees (and employee representatives).

Any employee can stand as a candidate, provided he is employed at the latest time at which a person is allowed to stand. However, if, at any point, the **number of candidates** equals or is less than the relevant number of IC representatives (¶7733), those candidates will become the IC representatives and the employer will not have to conduct a ballot.

Every employee in the undertaking must be **entitled to vote**.

Conduct of ballot

7735 The employer must **appoint** an **independent ballot supervisor** to supervise the conduct of the ballot (para 2 Sch 2 SI 2004/3426). A person will be an independent ballot supervisor if the employer reasonably believes that he will carry out his functions competently and the employer has no reasonable grounds to believe that his independence might reasonably be called into question. The ballot supervisor must be able to carry out his functions without interference and the employer must comply with all reasonable requests made by the ballot supervisor in connection with the conduct of the ballot (para 8 Sch 2 SI 2004/3426).

The **role** of the ballot supervisor is to supervise the conduct of the ballot in accordance with the arrangements set out above (para 9 Sch 2 SI 2004/3426). The ballot cannot be held before the employer has published the final ballot arrangements and, where no complaint of defective ballot arrangements has been made, before the expiry of 21 days beginning with the date on which the arrangements were published. Alternatively, where a complaint regarding defective ballot arrangements has been made (¶7738), the ballot cannot be held before the complaint has been determined and the arrangements have been modified as required by the CAC.

The ballot must be conducted so as to secure that as far as reasonably practicable, all those entitled to vote can do so in secret, all those entitled to stand as candidates can do so, and that all the votes are fairly and accurately counted.

The ballot supervisor must publish the **results of the ballot** to the employer, candidates and voters as soon as reasonably practicable (para 10 Sch 2 SI 2004/3426).

7736 **Within** 1 month of the ballot results being published, the ballot supervisor can publish an **ineffective ballot report** if he considers (whether or not on the basis of representations made to him) that:

– any of the requirements regarding the conduct of the ballot were not met and the result of the ballot would have been different;

– there was interference with the carrying out of his functions; or

– the employer failed to comply with his reasonable requests so that he was unable to form a proper judgement as to whether each of the requirements for the ballot had been met.

This report should be published to the employer, candidates and voters.

Where such a report is published, the outcome of the ballot (or separate ballots, if appropriate) will be **void** and the employer(s) must re-hold the ballot(s).

7737 All **costs** relating to the conduct of the ballot, including payment of the ballot supervisor, must be paid by the employer, whether or not the supervisor has declared the ballot ineffective (para 15 Sch 2 SI 2004/3426).

Complaints regarding arrangements and conduct

7738 Any employee (or employee representative) who considers that the **ballot arrangements** are **defective** can **complain** to the CAC **within** 21 days of the final arrangements having been published (para 3 Sch 2 SI 2004/3426). The CAC will **uphold a complaint** if the arrangements for the ballot set out above are not met and may make an order specifying what modifications the employer must make to the arrangements or which requirements set out above should be satisfied.

If an employer has actually **failed to make arrangements** for such a ballot, an employee (or employee representative) can bring a complaint to the CAC (reg 19(4) SI 2004/3426). If the CAC **upholds the complaint**, it will order the employer to arrange, or re-arrange, and hold the ballot. Moreover, the employee (or employee representative) can, within 3 months of the CAC declaration, apply to the EAT for the employer to be issued with a fine (regs 19(6), 22(6) SI 2004/3426) (¶7772).

Right to paid time off

7740 An IC representative has the right to take **reasonable** paid time off during his working hours to perform his functions (regs 27, 28 SI 2004/3426) and is entitled to be paid at the **appropriate**

hourly rate, the amount of which will depend on whether his contractual hours vary or not (¶¶2935, 2937). It should be noted that any contractual remuneration paid to him in respect of a period of time off will go towards discharging any liability of the employer to pay remuneration in respect of the time off and vice versa (reg 28(7) SI 2004/3426).

An employee who is **unreasonably refused** time off to perform his functions as an IC representative or is not paid (wholly or in part) in respect of such time off can bring a complaint to an employment tribunal (reg 29(1) SI 2004/3426). Complaints must be made within 3 months beginning with the day on which the time off was taken or on which it is alleged the time off should have been permitted (reg 29(2) SI 2004/3426). However, a tribunal can extend this period if it is satisfied that it was not reasonably practicable for the employee to make the complaint in time. 7741

If the claim is successful, the **tribunal must** make a declaration to that effect and/or (reg 29 SI 2004/3426):
- order the employer to pay the employee the amount equal to the remuneration he would have been entitled to had the employer not refused to permit him to take time off; or
- order the employer to pay the amount due to the employee if he has taken time off but the employer has refused to pay him in whole or in part.

MEMO POINTS Before bringing any complaint before a tribunal, an employee must first raise his grievance under his employer's statutory discipline and grievance procedures (¶6772).

2. Standard information and consultation provisions

If the standard information and consultation provisions (referred to as the standard IC provisions) apply, the regulations require employers to comply with the standard IC provisions set out below in respect of the information to be provided and the way the consultation is to be conducted. The DTI has provided some guidance as to how these provisions will be interpreted, but ultimately it is a matter for the courts to decide how these provisions should be applied in practice. 7745

Confidential information

Under either a standard or negotiated agreement, an employer is permitted to **withhold or restrict** what information or documentation is released to IC representatives (and any persons to whom the IC representatives may wish to further disclose the information or documentation) where, when viewed objectively, such disclosure would seriously harm the functioning of, or would be prejudicial to, the undertaking (regs 25, 26 SI 2004/3426). This provision will apply when information is so confidential that if leaked, it would cause serious harm or prejudice to the functioning of the undertaking. 7746

MEMO POINTS Employers should bear in mind **their own confidentiality obligations** (if applicable) when deciding what information or documents can be provided to IC representatives, for example, under the UK Listing Rules or the City Code on Takeovers and Mergers.

Where there is a **dispute** between the employer and the IC representatives or, where no IC representatives have been elected or appointed, an employee or employee representative, **as to the confidentiality** of a piece of information or document which the employer has withheld, either party can apply to the CAC for a declaration as to whether or not the information or document is of such a confidential nature that, when viewed objectively, its disclosure would seriously harm the functioning of, or be prejudicial to, the undertaking (reg 26(2) SI 2004/3426). If the CAC makes a **declaration against the employer**, it will order the disclosure of the information or document, specifying the person(s) to whom the information or document should be disclosed, any terms on which it is to be disclosed and the date before which disclosure must take place (reg 26(3), (4) SI 2004/3426). Before applying to the CAC, however, the parties are advised to seek to resolve the dispute informally (para 77 DTI guidance). 7747

7748 Where an **employer releases** information or documentation to IC representatives on **terms that require them to keep it confidential** or restricts the categories of persons to whom the information or documentation can be further disclosed, the IC representatives must not disclose such information or documentation except, where the employer has expressly permitted them to do so (reg 25(1) SI 2005/3426). It is for an employer to ensure that he makes it clear what information and documentation is to be kept confidential and if any restrictions are to be placed on further disclosure by the recipients to other persons (para 77 DTI guidance). For example, an employer might allow IC representatives to disclose information to their professional advisers. Employers are advised, however, to make clear that any further recipients of the information are to be bound by an obligation of confidentiality as well.

If a recipient of information or documentation **breaches his duty of confidentiality**, the employer can bring an action against him for breach of a statutory duty (reg 25(3) SI 2004/3426). However, if the recipient reasonably believed that the disclosure was protected under the whistleblowing regulations (¶2700), there will be no breach of duty (reg 25(5) SI 2004/3426).

A recipient of information or documentation from the employer can apply to the CAC for a **declaration** as to **whether** it was **reasonable** for the employer **to impose a duty of confidentiality** in respect of the information or documentation (reg 25(6) SI 2004/3426). If the CAC considers that the disclosure of the information or document by the recipient would not or would not be likely to harm the legitimate interests of the undertaking, it will declare that it was not reasonable for the employer to require the recipient to hold the information or document in confidence (reg 25(7) SI 2004/3426). The recipient(s) of any such information or documentation will therefore no longer be under any duty of confidentiality.

---

a. Information to be provided

7750 The **specific matters** about which an employer must inform and consult with IC representatives are (reg 20(1) SI 2004/3426):

a. the recent and probable developments in respect of the undertaking's activities and economic situation;

b. the situation, structure and probable development of employment within the undertaking and any anticipatory measures envisaged, in particular, where there is a threat to employment within the undertaking; and

c. decisions likely to lead to substantial changes in work organisation or in contractual relations.

DTI guidance (below) suggests what type of information might be included within these categories, although it will depend largely on the particular circumstances of the undertaking concerned.

An employer is obliged to ensure that consultation on matters referred to in **b.** and **c.** above takes place. He must therefore ensure that the information is **provided at such time and in such a way with such content** as appropriate to enable the IC representatives to adequately study and, if necessary, prepare for consultation regarding such matters (reg 20(2) SI 2004/3426).

Category a: developments regarding activities and economic situation

7752 The standard IC provisions imply that the purpose of this category of information is to provide IC representatives with information which will enable them to understand the background against which subsequent decisions affecting employment, work organisation or contractual relations are made (para 53 DTI guidance). Information will include past and future probable developments, which implies that only matters which are more than just a mere possibility need to be disclosed (para 55 DTI guidance). It should be noted that an employer is not obliged to consult in respect of such information, but simply to provide it to IC representatives.

DTI guidance suggests that the following types of information might be included in respect of the undertaking's **activities** (para 55 DTI guidance):

– the launch of new products or services or the discontinuation of others;

- changes in senior management;
- takeovers, mergers, acquisitions, sales and other restructuring involving the undertaking;
- reorganisation of the workforce within the undertaking;
- developments in new methods of working; and
- changes to the aims, objectives, strategy or business plan of the undertaking.

DTI guidance regarding the undertaking's **economic situation** suggests that the following information might be included:
- trading conditions, the competitive market in which the undertaking operates, future forecasts for the sector and the level of demand; and
- the undertaking's financial situation based on its accounts.

Category b: situation, structure and development of employment

Unlike information to be provided in category a. above, the employer must consult with IC representatives regarding information provided under this category. 7754

DTI guidance suggests that the emphasis regarding this category of information is on the overall number of employees within the undertaking and that it therefore might include information regarding (para 55 DTI guidance):
- the recruitment of new staff and redundancies (both voluntary and redundancy);
- employee turnover;
- the possibility of moving to reduced hours working or the need for overtime;
- changes in retirement policy and early retirement schemes;
- the distribution of employees in the undertaking, both geographically and organisationally; and
- the reorganisation, redeployment or transfer of posts within an undertaking.

The DTI suggests that the term "threat to employment" refers to employee training and skill development so as to increase the "employability and adaptability" of affected employees.

Category c: changes in work organisation or contractual relations

This category of information includes information regarding collective redundancies (¶8730) and business transfers (¶7900). Again, employers are obliged to consult with IC representatives regarding any information provided under this category. 7756

DTI guidance suggests that information regarding changes in **work organisation** might include (para 55 DTI guidance):
- changes to the level or distribution of employment within the undertaking;
- changes to flexible working, part-time and overtime policies;
- the introduction of different work patterns, including shift work, reduced hours or overtime; or
- the introduction of new technology or equipment and any subsequent need for training.

DTI guidance also suggests that **contractual relations** refer to the contractual relationship between employer and employee and that such information would include:
- a change of employer resulting from a business transfer;
- variations to employees' terms and conditions, except for pay or benefits with a monetary value since these are specifically excluded;
- the introduction of, or a change to, compulsory retirement age;
- changes to an occupational pension scheme where there is a contractual right to become a member; and
- changes in disciplinary and grievance procedures.

---

b. Conduct of consultation

The employer must consult with IC representatives regarding **information provided under** categories b. and c. above. The employer must ensure that consultation is conducted in such a way so as to ensure that the timing, method and content of the consultation is appropriate (reg 20(4) SI 2004/3426), although there is no guidance as to the required **frequency** 7760 or **timing** of consultation, save that the regulations imply that consultation should be ongoing and regular (para 59 DTI guidance). The frequency and timing of consultation is likely to fluctuate depending on whether there is much change underway within an undertaking.

Consultation is designed to be a **two-way process based on** the information the employer provides as well as any opinion expressed by the IC representatives. Moreover, the IC representatives must be able to meet the appropriate level of management at the employer, depending on the subject matter, and to obtain a reasoned response from the employer to any opinion the representatives have given. These provisions are aimed at ensuring that there is a genuine consideration by the employer of any views expressed by the IC representatives during the course of the consultation process (para 57 DTI guidance). IC representatives may therefore disagree with decisions which have been made or may express suggestions for modifying employer's proposals. However, whilst an employer is not obliged to necessarily follow the opinions expressed by the IC representatives, the regulations do imply that meaningful consultation requires the employer to seek and consider views expressed prior to making such decisions (para 61 DTI guidance).

It is **good practice**, though not a requirement of the regulations, for the IC representatives to report back to the employees they represent and/or to obtain their views following consultation with the employer to ensure that the views of the workforce are reflected (para 57 DTI guidance).

7762 In addition, with regard to information in category **c**. regarding **collective redundancies** and **business transfers**, the consultation must take place with a view to reaching an agreement on decisions within the employer's power (reg 20(4) SI 2004/3426). This overlaps with the employer's separate consultation duties under TULRCA 1992 (¶8915) and the TUPE regulations (¶8060).

However, once an employer is under a statutory duty to consult representatives under the relevant legislative provisions, the **duty to inform and consult** under these regulations **will cease** provided he has notified the IC representatives in writing that he will be complying with his duty under either TULRCA or TUPE (as appropriate) (reg 20(5) SI 2004/3426). This notification needs to be made each time a collective redundancy situation or business transfer arises. However, an employer can choose to consult under both sets of legislation should he wish.

IV. Enforcement and remedies

7765 Where either a **negotiated agreement** or the **standard IC provisions** have come into effect, the following statutory enforcement provisions will apply. Employers who fail to implement their information and consultation obligations, whether under either type of agreement, risk being liable to a fine (¶7777).

Where, however, a valid **pre-existing agreement** is in place, the statutory enforcement provisions do not apply and such an agreement will only be enforceable if the methods of enforcement have been expressly agreed by the parties in the agreement itself or if the agreement has contractual force (¶1117).

7766 The regulations provide for a formal means of addressing an **employer's failure to comply** with his obligations under a negotiated agreement or, if applicable, the standard IC provisions, but employees (or their representatives) are advised to consider trying to resolve the matter informally before bringing a formal complaint to the CAC (para 66 DTI guidance). There is no provision allowing for an employer to bring a **complaint against IC representatives or individual employees** save in respect of a breach of confidentiality (¶7748).

7767 **Employee, IC and negotiating representatives** have a **statutory right to paid time off** to carry out their duties as representatives (¶¶7740, 7706). Moreover, both representatives and candidates have the **right not to be unfairly dismissed** or **suffer a detriment** in respect of their functions as a representative or candidate.

Furthermore, **general employees** within an undertaking are afforded the **right not to be unfairly dismissed** or **suffer a detriment** in respect of various matters connected to the negotiation of information and consultation arrangements within an undertaking.

a. Breach of negotiated or standard agreement

With regard to a **negotiated agreement**, a complaint might be brought if the employer fails to comply with one of the terms of the agreement. This could include, for example, that the employer has failed to: **7770**

- establish the information and consultation arrangements provided for by the agreement;
- arrange for the election or appointment of IC representatives;
- provide adequate or timely information; or
- consult in the way established by the agreement.

With regard to a **standard agreement**, a complaint can be brought regarding an employer's failure to arrange for the election of IC representatives (¶7738) or in respect of any failure by the employer to comply with one or more of the standard IC provisions (¶7745). This could include, for example, if the employer has failed to:

- arrange for the election of IC representatives;
- adequately provide the information in categories a., b. or c. (¶7750+) or to consult in a genuine and meaningful way;
- provide such information in a timely manner;
- meet the IC representatives or send the appropriate level of management to such a meeting; or
- listen to representatives' opinions being expressed and give a reasoned response to such opinions.

Complaint to CAC

Where an employer fails to comply with the terms of a negotiated or, if applicable, the standard IC provisions, a complaint can be made to the CAC in respect of such failure **within** 3 months of the alleged failure (reg 22(1), (2) SI 2004/3426). Where IC representatives have been elected or appointed, they can bring a complaint. If there are no IC representatives, an employee or employee representative can bring the complaint (reg 22(3) SI 2004/3426). **7772**

Any complaint or application to the CAC must be made **in writing** and in the **form** required by the CAC (reg 35(1) SI 2004/3426). The CAC will make any **appropriate enquiries** of the parties that it sees fit and, so far as is reasonably practicable, any party with a proper interest in the complaint or application will have an opportunity to be heard by the CAC (reg 35(2) SI 2004/3426). If, as part of its enquiries, the CAC makes a **reasonable request** for **information or documents** from one or both of the parties, it can draw adverse inferences from any failure to comply with such a request (reg 35(3) SI 2004/3426).

Where an employer fails to inform and consult as required by a standard agreement, he cannot rely on a **failure by** a **person who controls the employer** (either directly or indirectly) to provide information to the employer as a valid reason for the employer failing to inform and consult (reg 20(6) SI 2004/3426).

MEMO POINTS The **CAC** is expected to publish **further guidance** as to how to handle cases regarding the regulations.

If it considers that the matter is reasonably likely to be settled by conciliation, the CAC can **refer** the complaint or application **to ACAS** and will notify the parties accordingly (reg 38 SI 2004/3426). ACAS is not under a duty to assist the parties to conciliate and, if it decides that the matter is not appropriate for conciliation, or has unsuccessfully tried to resolve the dispute, ACAS will notify the CAC which must then hear and determine the complaint or application (reg 35(3)-(5) SI 2004/3426). See ¶9218 for a discussion as to ACAS' involvement in the conciliation process. **7774**

7775 Where the CAC **upholds a complaint**, it will make a declaration to that effect and may order the employer to take such steps as are necessary to comply with the terms of the negotiated agreement or, as the case may be, the standard IC provisions, specifying what steps the employer is required to take and the timeframe in which he must take them (reg 22(4), (5) SI 2004/3426). However, any order made by the CAC cannot have the effect of suspending, or altering the effect of, any act done or agreement made by the employer or preventing or delaying any such act or agreement he proposes to do or make (reg 22(9) SI 2004/3426).

The CAC must make any declaration or order under these regulations **in writing** and state its **reasons** for making it (reg 35(5) SI 2004/3426). If necessary, a CAC declaration or order can be **enforced** in the civil courts (¶9850).

Appeals

7776 Appeals from a CAC declaration or order on a point of law can be made to the EAT and will be subject to the usual rules regarding timing and form as appeals from the employment tribunal (¶9740).

Fines

7777 If the CAC makes a declaration and upholds a complaint regarding an employer's failure to (regs 19(6), 22(6) SI 2004/3426):
- inform and consult as required by a negotiated or (if applicable) standard agreement; or
- make arrangements for a ballot to elect IC representatives under the standard agreement;

the complainant can **apply to the EAT within** 3 months of the declaration for a penalty notice containing a fine to be imposed on the employer, which is payable to the Secretary of State for Trade and Industry (reg 22(6) SI 2004/3426).

Fines cannot be ordered in respect of any other complaints or applications to the CAC, for example, where an employer withholds information on employee numbers (¶7664).

The EAT can hear representations from the employer regarding his failure to comply with the terms of the negotiated agreement or, if applicable, the standard IC provisions. However, unless the EAT is satisfied that, on having heard the employer's representations, his failure resulted from a **reason beyond the employer's control** or that he has some other **reasonable excuse** for his failure, the EAT must impose a fine.

7778 The penalty notice will **specify** the (reg 23(1) SI 2004/3426):
- **amount** of the fine, which **cannot exceed** £75,000;
- **date** by which it must be paid, which cannot be earlier than the end of the period within which an appeal against a declaration or order by the CAC can be made (see ¶9756 regarding the timing of appeals to the EAT); and
- **nature** of the employer's failure and the period to which the fine relates.

In **determining the amount** of the fine, the EAT must take into account the (reg 23(3) SI 2004/3426):
- gravity of the failure;
- period of time over which the failure occurred;
- reason for the failure;
- number of employees affected by the failure; and
- number of employees in the undertaking(s).

The employer can **appeal** to the EAT against a CAC decision (¶7776) and, if he does, the penalty notice will be suspended while the appeal is ongoing.

7779 If an employer **fails to pay** the fine before the time limit specified in the penalty notice and the period during which an appeal may be made has expired without the employer having made an appeal or such an appeal has been made and determined (against the employer), the fine can be recovered by the Government from the employer as a civil debt (reg 23(5) SI 2004/3425).

b. Representatives' and candidates' remedies

Note the specific provisions relating to a representative's or candidate's **statutory right to reasonable paid time off** and any remedies for breaches of this right (¶¶7741, 7707). 7780

Right not to be unfairly dismissed or suffer a detriment

An employee representative, negotiating representative or IC representative (whether elected or appointed under a negotiated or standard agreement), or any candidate for such a position, will be **automatically** unfairly dismissed if the **reason** or **principal reason** is that (reg 30 SI 2004/3426): 7782
- he has performed or proposed to perform any of the functions or activities as a representative or candidate;
- he exercised or proposed to exercise his right to paid time off to carry out the functions of a representative or candidate; or
- he requested paid time off to carry out the functions of a representative or candidate.

A representative will not be unfairly dismissed if the reason or principal reason for his dismissal is that in his performance of his functions or activities, he **breached** his **confidentiality obligations** to the employer (¶7748), unless the employee reasonably believed that he had acted in accordance with the whistleblowing rules (¶2700). For the purposes of automatically unfair dismissal, no **qualifying period of service** is required and there is **no upper age limit** on the right to bring a claim of unfair dismissal (¶8390).

Further such representatives have the **right not to suffer a detriment** (which does not amount to a dismissal) on the same reason(s) or ground(s) as above (reg 32 SI 2004/3426).

Representatives and candidates who are **also employees** of the employer are further protected from the right not to be unfairly dismissed or suffer a detriment for the reasons and grounds listed below (¶7785).

MEMO POINTS Before bringing any complaint before a tribunal, an employee must first raise his grievance under his employer's **statutory discipline and grievance procedures** (¶6772).

c. General employees' remedies

Right not to be unfairly dismissed or suffer a detriment

An employee, whether or not he falls within one of the categories of representative mentioned above, is protected from being unfairly dismissed or suffering a detriment (which does not amount to a dismissal) if the **reason** or **principal reason** for his dismissal is that he (reg 30(6), (7) SI 2004/3426): 7785

a. brought, or proposed to bring, tribunal proceedings to enforce a right or secure an entitlement conferred on him by these regulations, whether or not the employee has the right or entitlement or whether or not it has been infringed, provided that the claim to the right (and, if applicable) the claim that it has been infringed has been made in good faith;

b. exercised, or proposed to exercise, any entitlement to apply or complain to the CAC or EAT, or to exercise the right to appeal, in connection with any rights conferred by these regulations;

c. requested, or proposed to request, data (¶7664);

d. acted with a view to securing that an agreement was or was not negotiated or that the standard IC provisions did or did not become applicable;

e. indicated that he supported or did not support the coming into existence of a negotiated agreement or the application of the standard IC provisions;

f. stood as a candidate in an election to become either a negotiating or IC representative;

g. influenced or sought to influence by lawful means the way in which votes were to be cast by other employees in a ballot arranged under these regulations;

h. voted in any ballot under these regulations;

i. expressed doubts, whether to a ballot supervisor or otherwise, as to whether the ballot had been properly conducted; or

j. proposed to do, failed to do, or proposed to decline to do, any of the things mentioned in **d.** to **i.** above.

MEMO POINTS Before bringing any complaint before a tribunal, an employee must first raise his grievance under his employer's **statutory discipline and grievance procedures** (¶6772).

SECTION 2

European works councils

7800 Most large employers, who have employees in more than one EU member state, must negotiate the establishment of a European Works Council (EWC) or an information and consultation procedure, as a means of **exchange of views** and the establishment of **dialogue between management and employees** (Transnational Information and Consultation of Employees Regulations SI 1999/3323, referred to in this section of the chapter as the regulations). The regulations do not apply if, on or before 22 September 1996, there was already in place a voluntary agreement for transnational information and consultation which fulfils the conditions laid down in the regulations (reg 45 SI 1999/3323).

The regulations apply if the company's central management responsible for conducting the negotiations is **situated in the UK** (regs 3, 4, 5 SI 1999/3323). Central management is usually in the country with the company head office or employing the largest number of employees. If it is not in the UK, the law of the EU country in which central management is based will apply. Where central management is based **outside the EU** (for example, because the company is a US or Japanese company), the employer can choose which local management based in the EU will take on the role of the central management. If that choice is not made, it automatically falls to the EU country which has the highest number of employees.

MEMO POINTS 1. Unlike the majority of legislation governing trade unions, EWC legislation refers specifically to 'employees' (¶11) as opposed to the wider category of 'workers' (¶13). See Chapter 1 for further details.

2. The regulations are a result of the implementation of the European Works Councils Directive (EC Directive 1994/45) extended to cover the UK with effect from 15 December 1999 by the Extension Directive (EC Directive 1997/74).

3. Whilst these regulations apply only to large multinational employers, the Information and Consultation Directive (EU Directive 2002/14) which governs **domestic information and consultation** is being implemented in the UK from 6 April 2005 (Information and Consultation of Employees Regulations SI 2004/3426). See Section 1 of this chapter for further details.

7801 Employees who are members or candidates of a Special Negotiating Body (SNB) (¶7814), EWC, or information or consultation body have the right not to **suffer a detriment** or be **unfairly dismissed** in relation to the exercise of their role. Any such dismissal would be automatically unfair and does therefore not require any qualifying period of employment before the entitlement to bring a claim arises (¶¶8393-4).

7802 Employees are afforded some **protection** under the regulations if they are **dismissed** or **subjected to a detriment** for a reason in connection with their membership, candidature or involvement as an information and consultation representative (s 105(7D) ERA 1996; reg 28 SI 1999/3323) (see below).

I. Scope of regulations

Only employers who are "**Community-scale undertakings**" are obliged to consider the setting up of an EWC. These are **defined** as undertakings which employ at least 1,000 employees within the EU and where at least 150 employees are employed in each of at least two EU states (reg 2 SI 1999/3323). The EU states are: Austria, Belgium, Cyprus, Czech Republic, Denmark, Estonia, Finland, France, Germany, Greece, Hungary, the Republic of Ireland, Italy, Latvia, Lithuania, Luxembourg, Malta, the Netherlands, Poland, Portugal, Slovakia, Slovenia, Spain, Sweden and the UK. **7804**

To calculate the **number of employees located in the UK**, the employer needs to (reg 6 SI 1999/3323): **7805**
- take the number of employees for each month in the previous 2 years;
- add those numbers together; and
- divide the total by 24.

All employees, without having had any absences or worked overtime, who work for **75 hours or less in any month** of 21 working days, are counted as the equivalent of half a person. For **employees located in other EU states**, the calculation will depend on the domestic law in force in each individual EU state.

II. Establishment of an EWC

The procedure for establishing an EWC can be **invoked** by the employer's management or by the employees (or their representatives). At various stages during the process, both employers and employees (and their representatives) have a number of rights and duties. The **principal rights and duties** are set out below. **7807**

A. Employer's duties

To provide information on employee numbers Employees or their representatives have the right to be given information on **employee numbers** for the purposes of enabling them to decide whether or not the undertaking comes within the definition of a "Community-scale undertaking". If this request is made, central management must state what the average number of employees has been in the UK and in each of the relevant EU states within the previous 2 years (reg 7 SI 1999/3323). The obligation to provide this information is triggered even where no controlling interest in a group of companies exists (and hence no obviously identifiable central management) (*Betriebsrat der Bofrost Josef H Boquoi Deutschland West GmbH & Co KG v Bofrost Josef H Boquoi Deutschland West GmbH & Co KG (Case C-62/99)* [2001] IRLR 403, ECJ). **7808**

Where a request for information regarding employees which is essential in order to begin negotiations for the establishment of an EWC is made to the central management (or deemed central management) of a Community-scale group of undertakings **by another undertaking within the same group** which is **based in another member state**, the central management (or deemed central management) is under an obligation to supply that undertaking with the information requested by its employee representatives where that information is not in the possession of that undertaking (*Betriebsrat der Firma ADS Anker GmbH v ADS Anker GmbH*, ECJ Case C-349/01).

Where **central management** of a group of Community-scale undertakings is **located outside the EU**, the responsibility to provide the information which is essential to commence negotiations to set up an EWC will fall to its representative agent within the EU, but if there is no such representative, the deemed central management will be the management of the undertaking within the EU which employs the greatest number of employees in any one EU member state (*Gesamtbetriebsrat der Kuhne und Nagel AG un Co KG v Kuhne und Nagel AG und Co KG* [2004] IRLR 332, ECJ). This deemed central management is under an obligation to obtain from other group undertakings within the EU the necessary information required to commence negotiations and those other undertakings are obliged to co-operate with any such request.

7809 If, once requested, an employer **fails to provide the information** on numbers or provides **false or incomplete information**, those making the request have the right to take a complaint to the Central Arbitration Committee (CAC). The CAC will not consider any complaint until 1 month has passed from the date when the request was made. The CAC, if it upholds the complaint, can make an **order** against the employer requiring him to provide the information and will specify a date (at least 1 week after the order is made) by which time the information has to have been provided (reg 8 SI 1999/3323).

The CAC can also make a **declaration** that employee numbers reach the required levels for the discussions on the establishment of an EWC (reg 8(3) SI 1999/3323).

7810 **To respond to a request to negotiate an EWC** An employer can decide to start the process of negotiations towards the establishment of an EWC. However, **central management must initiate negotiations** to establish an EWC **following a valid request** made by employees or their representatives where the undertaking is a Community-scale undertaking or group of undertakings (reg 9 SI 1999/3323).

A **valid request** will (reg 9(3) SI 1999/3323):
- be in writing;
- be sent to the central or local management;
- specify the date on which it was sent;
- (if there have been previous aborted negotiations) be no earlier than 2 years after previous negotiations had been concluded; and
- be a single request made by at least 100 employees or their representatives who represent at least that number in at least two member states; or
- be a number of requests which, when taken together, mean that the requisite number of employees is represented.

7811 If the employer's central management considers that the request is **not valid**, it can seek a declaration from the CAC. To do this, central management must apply within 3 months of the initial request for information and before any steps have been taken to start negotiations (reg 10 SI 1999/3323).

7812 **"Fall-back" position** If the employer's **central management refuses to begin negotiations** within a period of 6 months from the request to establish an EWC or fails to conclude an agreement within 3 years of the request, an EWC can be imposed (Sch 1 cl 18 SI 1999/3323).

7813 If, due to a failure of central management, an information and consultation procedure is not properly established, the SNB or any employee or employee representative (where there is no SNB) has the right to make a **complaint to the Employment Appeal Tribunal** (EAT). The EAT has the power to order central management to take the necessary steps to establish the EWC or information and consultation procedure. The order will specify the period within which it must be complied with (reg 20(1)-(4) SI 1999/3323).

The EAT can also issue a **written penalty notice**, under which central management has to pay a penalty to the Secretary of State unless it can show that its failure arose from matters outside its control (reg 20(7) SI 1999/3323). The penalty can be set up to a **maximum** of £75,000 and its size will reflect the gravity of the failure, the period of time over which the failure occurred and the number of employees affected by the failure.

To take steps to establish a Special Negotiating Body Following a valid request, steps should be taken to establish a SNB (reg 11 SI 1999/3323). Its **role** is to determine the scope, composition, functions and terms of office of the EWC or the arrangements for implementing an information and consultation procedure. 7814

European law leaves it to each member state to decide on the **size of the SNB**. The regulations state that the SNB should have **at least one member from each member state** where establishments are situated. For example, an undertaking with a base in Germany, France, Ireland and the UK would have to have at least four representatives from those states on the SNB. In addition, depending on its size, the SNB would also have the following additional members (reg 12(3) SI 1999/3323): 7815
- one additional member – if between 25% and 50% of employees are in that state;
- two additional members – if between 50% and 75% of employees are in that state; and
- three additional members – if 75% or more employees are from that member state.

EXAMPLE An undertaking with its HQ and central management in the UK employs in total 5000 employees. In the UK there are 2,500 employees. In France there are 600. In Germany there are 500 and in Ireland there are 1,400. Membership of the SNB is as follows:
UK (50% of employees) = 3 members
Ireland (28% of employees) = 2 members
Germany and France (10% and 12% of employees respectively) = 1 member each
Therefore the total size of the SNB will be 7 members.

UK employees must **elect** UK members of the SNB by ballot **unless** there is already an existing consultative committee (reg 13 SI 1999/3323). 7816

The **consultative committee** is one whose normal functions include or comprise the carrying out of an information and consultation function (reg 15(4) SI 1999/3323):
- without interference from the employer;
- representing all UK employees; and
- which consists wholly of persons who were elected by a ballot in which all UK employees had the opportunity to vote.

For these purposes, **information and consultation** includes information which may significantly affect the interests of UK employees and which is wider than just their specific interests, for example, relating to health and safety or redundancy. The committee must therefore be more than just a transitory committee, for example, dealing with a particular redundancy or business transfer consultation. It must be a **genuinely consultative body** that is consulted over a range of issues.

If such a consultative committee exists it can **nominate the SNB**. But it must nominate the right number of members. Too few or too many is treated as a failure to nominate. The committee has to **publish the names** of those whom it is nominating (reg 15(6) SI 1999/3323). 7817

If the employer, employees or their representatives believe that the consultative committee does not meet the standards required in the legislation, they can apply to the CAC for a declaration that the committee's **nominations are invalid** within 21 days of the date when the committee publishes its nominations (reg 15(7) SI 1999/3323). Where the committee fails to nominate members of the SNB or where the committee's procedure is declared invalid by the CAC, a ballot or ballots should be organised. 7818

To arrange for the holding of a ballot The **employer is responsible** for arranging the holding of the ballot (reg 14(1) SI 1999/3323). Where more than one representative is to be elected the employer can decide whether to divide employees into separate balloting constituencies if he believes that employees' interests would be better represented in this way. Employers also have to bear the full **costs** of the ballot, including the costs of any independent ballot supervisors appointed. 7819

Before going ahead with organising the ballot the employer, so far as is reasonably practicable, must **consult** with any existing employee representatives. When the final arrangements for the ballot have been formulated these have to be published so that they can be brought to the attention of employees and any existing representatives (reg 14(3) SI 1999/3323).

Any UK employees (or their representatives, including, in recognised workplaces, full-time union representatives who are not employed by the employer) are **eligible to stand for election** (reg 13(3) SI 1999/3323). **Voting** is open to all UK employees who are employed on the day of the balloting.

An **independent ballot supervisor** will supervise the ballot (reg 13(3) SI 1999/3323). Where **more than one ballot** is to be held the employer can decide to appoint additional supervisors.

7820 Employees (or their representatives) can complain to the CAC if they believe that the **arrangements for the ballot are defective** within 21 days of publication of the final arrangements (reg 13(4) SI 1999/3323). If the CAC upholds the complaint it will make a declaration to that effect and can order changes to the balloting arrangements (reg 13(5) SI 1999/3323).

7821 Provided that there have been no formal complaints over the procedure for the ballot, the employer must ensure that the **ballot supervisor** carries out his functions without interference. The employer is also obliged to comply with any reasonable requests made by the ballot supervisor in connection with his functions. Specifically, the ballot supervisor has to ensure, as far as reasonably practicable, that (reg 14 SI 1999/3323):
- employees entitled to vote have the opportunity to do so;
- those who have the right to stand as candidates have the opportunity to do so;
- voting is in secret; and
- votes are fairly and accurately counted.

He will also publish the results of the ballot. If there was anything wrong with the ballot he has to publish, within a month, an **ineffective ballot report** (reg 14(6) SI 1999/3323). If such a report is published, the ballot will be nullified.

7822 **To convene a meeting with the SNB** Once the SNB has been constituted, central management must convene a meeting with it and, at the same time, inform any local management of this (reg 16 SI 1999/3323). The SNB can decide to bring along **additional experts** if it so wishes. The employer has to pay any **reasonable expenses** incurred by the SNB in carrying out its functions (but only has to pay for a maximum of one expert). Subject to a two-thirds majority vote, it is for the SNB to decide whether to open negotiations with management and when it chooses to end them (reg 16(3) SI 1999/3323).

If the **SNB decides to end negotiations**, employees will be prevented from invoking the EWC establishment procedure for at least another 2 years, save with the employer's agreement.

All decisions of the SNB are by **majority vote**, with each member having one vote (reg 16(2) SI 1999/3323).

7823 **To negotiate with the SNB** Central management and the SNB are under a legal duty to negotiate in the **spirit of co-operation** with a view to reaching a **written agreement** on the detailed arrangements for the information and consultation of employees. If they decide that they want to set up an EWC they have to decide on the following (reg 17(4) SI 1999/3323):
- which undertakings will be covered;
- who will be on the EWC and what their term of office will be;
- what the functions and procedures for consultation will be;
- the venue, frequency and duration of its meetings;
- the financial and material resources to be allocated to it; and
- how long the agreement will last and the procedure for its renegotiation.

7824 **To provide information to assist negotiations** In the course of negotiations central management is expected to provide information to enable the negotiations to proceed. However, there is **no obligation to provide this information** where it would seriously harm the functioning of the undertaking or be prejudicial to it (reg 24 SI 1999/3323). Any **disputes** concerning the information to be provided may be referred to the CAC, which will make an order specifying whether or not it should be provided and if it should, the time limit for providing it.

To co-operate Central management has a **legal duty** to work in a spirit of co-operation and with due regard to their reciprocal rights and obligations (reg 19 SI 1999/3323). Therefore the employer should not operate in such a way as to frustrate the setting up of an SNB or the operation of an EWC. 7825

Not to victimise or dismiss An employer must not take action either to victimise or dismiss employees on the grounds of their actions as **candidates or members** of an **SNB or EWC** (reg 31 SI 1999/3323). Moreover, an employer must not take **detrimental action** against employees who are exercising their rights in relation to the establishment of an SNB or EWC. 7826

An employee who is a member of the SNB, an EWC, an information and consultation representative or a candidate for any of these positions has the **right not to be victimised** on the grounds that (reg 31(2), (3) SI 1999/3323): 7827
– the employee has performed any functions or activities as a member or candidate; or
– the employee, or someone acting on his behalf, requested time off to perform these functions.

This protection does not cover circumstances where the **employee** has **breached confidentiality** (¶1223) (reg 32(4) SI 1999/3323).

All employees, regardless of whether or not they are candidates or members of an SNB or EWC have the right to **protection from victimisation** where they had or proposed to (reg 31(5), (6) SI 1999/3323): 7828
– take proceedings to a tribunal, appeal court or CAC;
– exercise their rights to information;
– secure an SNB, EWC or information and consultation procedure;
– indicate support or otherwise for the EWC;
– influence voting or to vote; or
– question the conduct of the ballot.

This **protection applies** even if it transpires that the employee did not have the right he was attempting to exercise, provided that he was acting in good faith (reg 31(7) SI 1999/3323).

If an employee is **dismissed** for reasons connected with membership, candidature or activity in an SNB, EWC or information and consultation procedure he will be regarded as unfairly dismissed (s 105(7D) ERA 1996; regs 28-29 SI 1999/3323). 7829

Employees are similarly protected against unfair selection for **redundancy** if selection is due to their involvement in the SNB or EWC (¶8830).

To bring a claim of unfair dismissal or unfair selection for redundancy, there is **no minimum qualifying period** of employment and **no requirement** to be under the **normal retirement age** (reg 29 SI 1999/3323; see also ¶¶8393-4). The only circumstance in which an employee is not protected is where the dismissal occurs due to the employee having **breached his confidentiality** obligations (reg 28(4) SI 1999/3323).

Time off Employers must give candidates or members of an SNB, EWC or information and consultation body reasonable **paid time off during contractual working hours** to perform their functions (reg 25 SI 1999/3323). 7830

Employees are likely to seek time off:
– as candidates to meet with employees who will be voting for the SNB or EWC as appropriate;
– for meetings and pre-meetings of the SNB and EWC; and
– for report-back meetings to employees.

Employers may also be asked to grant time off for **preparation** prior to meetings. In general arrangements for time off will be agreed with the SNB and EWC at their initial meeting with the central management.

7831 **Employers must pay employees** during this time off (reg 26 SI 1999/3323). To **calculate** how much should be paid, the employee's weekly pay should be divided by the number of normal contractual working hours in the week. This gives the hourly rate. Where normal contractual hours differ from week to week, the hourly rate is calculated by averaging it over a 12-week period.

EXAMPLE An employee is paid £440 a week. However, he works different hours and different shifts in some weeks. In week one he works four 10 hour shifts. In week two he works five 8 hour shifts and in week three he works six 7 hour shifts. Over the 12 weeks he repeats this cycle four times. His total hours for the 12 weeks are:

$$\frac{(4 \times 10 \times 4) + (5 \times 8 \times 4) + (6 \times 7 \times 4)}{12} = 40.66$$

Therefore, his weekly pay of £440 is divided by 40.66 to calculate his hourly rate: £10.82 an hour.

7832 If an employee who works **varied hours** has not been employed for at least 12 weeks, employers should base payment on what would be fairly regarded as the number of normal hours in the week. This takes account of the average number of hours which he could be expected to work under his contract and the average number of hours worked (by comparable employees).

7833 If an **employer refuses paid time off**, in circumstances where it should have been granted to enable the employee reasonably to perform his functions as a candidate or representative, the employee will have the **right to bring a claim** in the tribunal **within** 3 months of the refusal. There may be circumstances where the tribunal will accept claims beyond the 3-month time limit, but only where it was not reasonably practicable for the complaint to be made in time.

If the tribunal upholds the employee's complaint it will make a declaration to that effect and will order the employee to pay any money due to the employee. If the complaint is that time off was unreasonably refused, the tribunal will **order the employer to pay the wages** the employee would have been entitled to had the time off not been refused, regardless of whether or not the employee in actual fact was paid because the refusal meant that he did not have any time off.

B. Employee representatives' duties

7835 Employee representatives also have certain legal duties in relation to the SNB and the EWC. These are:

7836 **To maintain confidentiality** Members and experts on the SNB are subject to a legal requirement to maintain confidentiality by not disclosing information given by central management where they have been **asked to keep it confidential** (reg 23 SI 1999/3323).

The CAC can hear disputes about whether or not information should be kept confidential and can rule on whether or not the request for confidentiality was reasonable (reg 24 SI 1999/3323). It will make this assessment **taking into account** whether the information would be likely to prejudice or cause serious harm to the undertaking.

Providing that there has been no ruling from the CAC which negates the requirement for confidentiality, employers can sue members or experts if they breach confidentiality.

7837 **To co-operate** Employees who are members of the EWC have a legal duty to work in a **spirit of co-operation** with employers and **with due regard to their reciprocal rights and obligations** (reg 19 SI 1999/3323). This means that the employer should not operate in such a way as to frustrate the setting up of an SNB or the operation of an EWC. Similar duties apply to information and consultation bodies where the parties have decided to set these up as an alternative to an EWC.

To inform Employees elected or appointed to the EWC under the statutory procedures have a legal obligation to inform employee representatives or, where they do not exist, employees directly of the **outcome of EWC meetings** with management, **subject only** to any obligations to maintain confidentiality (Sch 1 cl 9 SI 1999/3323). 7838

III. Functioning of the EWC

In general it is up to the **parties to agree** how the EWC should function. This means that arrangements can vary widely between one EWC and another. The only issues that **must be included** in any agreement are: 7840
- which companies and locations are covered;
- how seats on the EWC are distributed;
- what its tasks and procedures should be;
- arrangements over meetings;
- money and other resources; and
- how long the agreement should last.

"Fall-back" position to establish EWC

If, within the specified time limits, no agreement has been reached voluntarily through the SNB there is a **statutory default mechanism** for the formation of the EWC (Sch 1 SI 1999/3323). Under this procedure an EWC of **between 3 and 30 members** is established with at least one member representing each member state where there are establishments, with additional representatives based on the size of the workforce in the member state. The method of calculating this is the same as for the establishment of the SNB (¶7815). 7841

The procedure also requires that any UK members of the EWC be UK employees either **elected or appointed by employee representatives**. They are defined as union representatives of all the workforce or elected or appointed representatives, provided that the latter also represent all employees and are not appointed for one issue only (for example, to consult on redundancies). Where such representatives exist they have the right to choose which of their number will form the UK membership of the EWC.

Under the UK legislation, **full-time union officials**, who can sit as members of the SNB, cannot be members of the EWC although they may, of course, be called upon as experts.

Arranging a ballot Where there are **no valid employee representatives** the employer is under a legal duty to arrange for the holding of a ballot. The legal rules regarding these arrangements and the conduct of the ballot are identical to those for the election of SNB members (¶7819). 7842

Procedures The EWC so elected has a competence limited to information and consultation on matters concerning Community-scale undertakings. It adopts its **own rules of procedure** and can be **assisted by experts** of its choice, in so far as they are needed to help it carry out its tasks. These experts could, for example, be full-time trade union officials or independent experts, who are often academics (Sch 1 cls 6, 9 SI 1999/3323). In some cases, where its size would warrant it, the EWC can decide to establish a **select committee** that could take administrative responsibility for setting the agenda, organising meetings and general liaison. 7843

Unless otherwise agreed, the central management is liable for all of the **operating expenses** of the EWC and should provide any **financial and material resources** to enable the members of the EWC to perform their functions appropriately. This will include: 7844
- the expenses of up to one expert;
- the costs of organising meetings;
- interpreting costs; and
- accommodation and travel expenses.

7845 **Meetings** Meetings of the EWC must be held **at least once a year**. At this meeting members of the EWC should be **informed and consulted** on the progress of the business and its prospects. This consultation should revolve around a report drawn up by central management.

The meeting should **consider**:
– the structure, economic and financial situation;
– the probable development of the business and of production and sales;
– the situation and probable trend of employment;
– investments and substantial changes concerning organisation;
– introduction of new working methods or production processes;
– transfers of production, mergers, cut-backs or closures of undertakings or important parts of them; and
– collective redundancies.

Prior to the meeting the EWC members have the **right to meet separately** without the presence of central management (Sch 1 cl 9 SI 1999/3323).

7846 In addition to these annual meetings there may be times when it is necessary to have an **exceptional meeting** of the EWC, particularly where circumstances arise which are likely to affect considerably the employees' interests, for example, where closures, redundancies or transfers are anticipated. Members of the EWC, representing those plants or businesses which are most directly affected, must be given the opportunity to attend these meetings even if otherwise only members of the select committee would be attending (Sch 1 cl 8 SI 1999/3323).

The EWC can **request** an exceptional meeting with the central management or any other appropriate level of management. Management must then prepare a report, which the EWC will respond to at the end of the meeting, or within a reasonable period of time. Members of the EWC also have the right to meet without management prior to the exceptional meeting.

7847 **Disputes** If either the central management or the EWC believe that the EWC procedure is not being followed they can **complain** to the Employment Appeal Tribunal (EAT) which can order the defaulter to take such steps as are necessary to comply with the procedure. This order will set out what is to be done and the time limit for compliance. The EAT can also impose a **financial penalty** on central management where it is the party in default, unless it can show that the failure arose from a reason beyond its control (reg 21 SI 1999/3323). This penalty can be set up to a **maximum** of £75,000 and its size will reflect the gravity of the failure, the period of time over which it occurred and the number of employees affected by the failure.

7848 **Duration** This statutory EWC will **operate for** at least 4 years at the end of which it can decide whether it now wishes to negotiate a voluntary EWC or to continue with the statutory provisions. If it wants to negotiate a voluntary agreement it has to make a request in writing to the central management. This then would trigger the negotiation procedures (¶7810).

CHAPTER 23

Lay-off and short-time working

OUTLINE ¶¶

Where an employer cannot provide work, an employee may be entitled to a statutory guarantee payment. If the employee has been laid off or put on short-time working, he may be entitled to a statutory redundancy payment if he terminates his employment. These issues are discussed below. **7850**

SECTION 1

Guarantee payments

An employee has a statutory right to a minimum guarantee payment for every workless day where the employer cannot provide him with work. **7860**

Employers should pay full contractual pay in such circumstances unless there is an express term to reduce pay. Otherwise, he may be liable under his employee's implied right to be paid (¶2806).

To be entitled to a guarantee payment, **employees** must be **continuously employed** for 1 month ending with the day before the workless day (s 29 ERA 1996). **7861**

The right arises when **work** of the kind which the employee is employed to do **is not provided** to him during any part of his normal working hours in a workday **due to** (s 28 ERA 1996): **7862**

- a decrease in the employer's business requirements for that work; or
- any other event affecting the normal working of his business in relation to that work.

When this occurs, the day will be treated as a workless day.

Where a **shift or night worker**'s shift starts before midnight and ends the following day, the workless day will be taken to be the day he started the shift if it is, or would normally be, longer in duration before midnight. If not, it will be treated as falling wholly on the second day (s 28(4), (5) ERA 1996). **7863**

7864 **Exceptions** An employee is not entitled to a guarantee payment if (s 29(3), (5) ERA 1996):
– his employer fails to provide work as a result of a **strike**, lockout or other industrial action involving any employee of his employer or of an associated employer;
– his employer has offered **suitable alternative work** and he has unreasonably refused. Suitable alternative work need not be within his normal contractual duties but does have to take into account his skill, geographic location, pay and hours; or
– he does not comply with his employer's **reasonable requirements** which are made with a view to ensuring that his services are available, for example a requirement to telephone to find out about availability of other alternative work.

Amount payable

7865 The amount payable for a workless day is **calculated** by multiplying the number of normal working hours in that day by the guaranteed hourly rate (s 30 ERA 1996).

7866 The **guaranteed hourly rate** is 1 week's pay (¶2920) divided by the number of **normal working hours** for that week. If the employee works **variable hours** from week to week, the number of working hours for 1 week's pay is calculated by taking the average number of working hours over the 12 weeks ending with the last complete week before the workless day. If the employee has not been employed for 12 weeks, the working hours are calculated by the number which will fairly represent the number of normal working hours in a week taking into account the employee's reasonable expectations in accordance with his contractual terms and the experience of comparable employees (s 30(3) ERA 1996).

If the employee works on **short-time**, the calculation is based on the original contract (s 30(5) ERA 1996).

7867 This is subject to a **maximum amount payable** for a workless day of £18.40 (likely to be increased in February 2006) and is only payable **for a maximum of** 5 workless days in any 3 month period (Employment Rights (Increase of Limits) Order SI 2004/2989).

Any **contractual amounts** paid by the employer with regard to a workless day will go towards discharging this amount (s 32 ERA 1996). Therefore, if an employee is paid on a weekly or monthly basis, these payments will go towards discharging any statutory liability in that period. Off-setting the statutory entitlement does not discount the workless days in question and therefore will count towards the maximum of 5 workless days in any 3 month period (*Cartwright v G Claney Ltd* [1983] IRLR 355, EAT).

Remedies

7870 The employee can bring a claim to an employment tribunal if his employer has failed to pay the whole or part of a guarantee payment entitlement (s 34 ERA 1996).

The **time limit** for bringing a claim is 3 months beginning with the workless day. The tribunal can **extend** this period if it is satisfied that it was not reasonably practicable to have presented the claim in time. In such cases the tribunal will indicate what extension is reasonable.

7871 Where the tribunal finds that the complaint is well-founded it will **order** the employer to pay the worker as appropriate.

SECTION 2

Redundancy payments

If an employee has been laid off or put on short-time working, he may be entitled to a statutory redundancy payment under a specific statutory scheme if he terminates his contract by giving notice and satisfies the eligibility requirements (see below). 7875

Contractual redundancy schemes which give enhanced redundancy payments do not normally apply to lay-off or short-time working.

The **collective consultation obligation** does not apply as it arises only when the employer proposes to dismiss, and in the case of lay-off and short-time working, it is the employee who gives notice of termination. 7876

Scope

The **lay-off** provisions apply when an employee is not provided with the work he is employed to do and on which his contractual remuneration depends, such that he will not be entitled to any remuneration for the period of the lay-off (for example, pieceworkers) (s 147(1) ERA 1996). Receipt of a statutory guarantee payment (see above) will not prevent the lay-off provisions applying. 7877

The **short-time working** provisions apply when an employee is provided with less work by the employer, such that his remuneration for any week is less than half a week's pay (for example, pieceworkers and timeworkers) (s 147(2) ERA 1996) (¶2920). Again, guarantee payments do not affect the application of these provisions.

An employer needs a **contractual right** (express or implied) to lay off an employee or put him on short-time working. An implied right will only exist where there is a custom for that particular employment that is reasonable, certain and notorious such that the employee would have expected the term to be included as part of the agreement. 7878

If there is **no contractual right**, the employer will be in fundamental breach of contract if he imposes lay-off or short-time working, entitling the employee to accept the breach, resign, and claim constructive dismissal (including, possibly, a claim for a redundancy payment under the general rules). Alternatively, the employee can choose not to treat himself as dismissed, waive the breach, and claim redundancy under the specific lay-off/short-time working provisions by resigning with notice.

If the employee has **actually been dismissed** in connection with a period of lay-off or short-time working, he must bring a claim for a redundancy payment under the general rules (s 151 ERA 1996).

It has been held that there is an implied contractual term that any lay-off will only be **for a reasonable period**, and that breach of this term will entitle the employee to claim constructive dismissal for redundancy (*A Dakri & Co Ltd v Tiffen* [1981] IRLR 57, EAT), although it has also been held that the employee's remedy for a lengthy period of lay-off is to claim a redundancy payment under the specific statutory scheme (*Kenneth MacRae & Co Ltd v Dawson* [1984] IRLR 5, EAT). 7879

Eligibility

Firstly, the employee **must satisfy** the eligibility requirements under the general statutory redundancy payment scheme (including the completion of 2 years' continuous service) (¶8990). 7880

Secondly, the employee must: 7881
– work under a contract according to which his pay is dependent on the provision of work by the employer (for example, workers paid per piece of work done);
– have been laid off or put on short-time working for the requisite period (¶7882);
– have been available for work (i.e. an employee on sick leave will not be eligible);

– comply with the statutory notification procedure (¶7884);
– in contested cases, apply to the tribunal for a decision (¶7888); and
– resign his employment by giving notice (¶7886).

An employee may be entitled to a redundancy payment in these circumstances even if he also receives a statutory guarantee payment from the employer (see section 1).

7882 **Requisite period** The employee must have been laid off or put on short-time working (or a combination of the two) for either (s 148(2) ERA 1996):
– 4 or more consecutive weeks; or
– a total of 6 weeks (of which no more than 3 are consecutive) in any period of 13 weeks.

For these purposes, a week ends with a Saturday, unless the employee's pay is calculated by reference to a week ending with a different day, in which case it ends with that day (s 235(1) ERA 1996).

7883 A week of lay-off or short-time working caused wholly or mainly by a **strike or lock-out** will not count towards the requisite period (s 154(b) ERA 1996), whether or not:
– the employee participates in the strike or lock-out;
– the strike or lock-out is in the employee's trade or industry; or
– the strike or lock-out takes place in Great Britain.

MEMO POINTS For these purposes, a **strike** is defined as (s 235(5) ERA 1996):
– the cessation of work by a group of workers; or
– the refusal of workers to continue to work as a consequence of a dispute;
to compel the employer (or to aid other workers in compelling their employer) to accept/not to accept terms or conditions of or affecting employment.

A **lock-out** is defined as (s 235(4) ERA 1996):
– the closing of a place of employment;
– the suspension of work; or
– the refusal by an employer to continue to employ workers in consequence of a dispute;
with a view to compelling workers, or to aid another employer in compelling his workers, to accept terms or conditions of or affecting employment.

7884 **Notice of intention to claim** The employee must give the employer written notice of his intention to claim a redundancy payment on, or **within** 4 weeks of, the last day of the last of the weeks of lay-off or short-time working on which the claim is based (s 148 ERA 1996). This time limit cannot be extended.

The notice must be **served by** (s 179(2) ERA 1996):
– delivery to the employer or a person designated by him;
– post to the employer at the employee's workplace (or to the designated person at a designated address); or
– leaving it for the designated person at a designated place.

If the notice is **served before** the employee has completed the requisite period of lay-off or short-time working (¶7882), it will be invalid and the claim for a redundancy payment will fail (*Allinson v Drew Simmons Engineering Ltd* [1985] ICR 488, EAT), although the employee could cure the defect by sending another notice within the time limit.

7885 If the employee is dismissed for misconduct or taking part in a strike **after service** of the notice, he cannot claim a redundancy payment based on lay-off or short-time working, but will have to rely on the express dismissal and the general redundancy payment rules. However, in this case, the employer will not be able to rely on the fact that the dismissal was not for redundancy to thwart the employee's claim for a payment (¶8992), although the tribunal will have a discretion to reduce the amount of the payment (¶9006).

7886 **Notice of termination** The employee will not be entitled to a redundancy payment if his employment subsists, so he must terminate his employment by giving 1 week's (i.e. 7 days') notice (or contractual notice, if longer) either (s 150(1), (3) ERA 1996):
– within 3 weeks of the employer's failure to give, or his withdrawal of, a counter-notice (or his service of a late or invalid notice) (see below for service of counter-notice); or

– in contested cases, within 3 weeks of notification to the employee of the tribunal's decision (ignoring any appeal).

This notice does not have to be in writing.

Contested claims

If the employer opposes the claim, he must serve a **written counter-notice** within 7 days of service of the employee's notice (s 149 ERA 1996). It must clearly state that the employer intends to contest the employee's claim for a redundancy payment. 7887

The counter-notice must be **served by** (s 179(1) ERA 1996):
– delivery to the employee;
– leaving it for the employee at his usual or last-known place of residence; or
– post to the employee at that address.

The employer can **withdraw** his counter-notice at any time by giving a written notice of withdrawal.

If the employer has served (and not withdrawn) a counter-notice, the **employee must apply** to a tribunal for a decision (s 149 ERA 1996). 7888

If the employee does not satisfy the eligibility criteria (¶7880), the employer can **defend the claim** on that basis (whether or not he has served a counter-notice). 7889

Otherwise, the employer can only defend a claim if, when the employee served his notice, it was reasonably to be expected that a period of at least 13 weeks of normal working (i.e. no lay-off or short-time) (under the same contract of employment) would be resumed within the next 4 weeks (s 152 ERA 1996). To rely on this defence, the employer must have served a valid counter-notice. If the employee continues to be laid-off or on short-time working throughout the 4 weeks, the employer's defence will fail.

MEMO POINTS An employee who unreasonably refuses an offer of **suitable alternative employment** may lose his entitlement to a statutory redundancy payment (¶8996). It is not clear whether this applies to the specific statutory provisions relating to lay-off and short-time working, or whether it is confined to situations where there has been a dismissal for redundancy, although it is thought that the latter approach is more likely to be taken by the courts and tribunals.

Uncontested claims

If the employer does not serve a counter-notice (or withdraws his counter-notice), the employee who satisfies the eligibility criteria (¶7880) will be entitled to a redundancy payment as if he had been dismissed for redundancy. 7890

Calculation

The redundancy payment is calculated in the same way as the general scheme (¶8990). 7891

The **relevant date** for calculation purposes is the last day of the last week of lay-off or short-time working on which the employee is relying (s 153 ERA 1996).

Death of employer or employee

If an **individual employer** dies after the employee has been laid off or put on short-time working for 1 or more weeks but **before** he has served a **notice of intention to claim**, the week in which the employer dies and the week in which the employee is taken on by the employer's personal representatives are treated as consecutive weeks for the purposes of the requisite period (¶7882) if the personal representatives lay the employee off or put him on short-time working for 1 or more weeks (s 175(2) ERA 1996). 7892

If the employer dies within 4 weeks of receiving the employee's notice of intention to claim but before he has given **notice to terminate** (or before that notice expires), the position will depend on whether the employee is re-engaged by the personal representatives within 4 weeks of the date of service of the notice of intention to claim. If he is **not re-engaged**, the position is as if the employer had not died and the employee had terminated his employment by giving the required notice. However, the employer's defence is not available to the personal representatives, nor can they serve a counter-notice opposing his claim (s 175(3), (4) ERA 1996). If he is **re-engaged** and is laid off or kept on short-time working for at least 1 week, all the weeks of lay-off or short-time working are deemed to be consecutive and in the same employment (s 175(5) ERA 1996). The time limit for service of his notice of termination is extended by the number of weeks between the employer's death and the date of re-engagement.

7893 If an **employee dies after serving** his notice of intention to claim (but **before giving notice to terminate** the employment), and the time limit for serving a notice to terminate has not expired (see above), the requirement to serve such a notice disappears (s 176(6)(a) ERA 1996). The employee's estate can claim a redundancy payment although the employer is free to raise a defence.

If an employee dies **within 7 days of serving** his notice of intention to claim, the employer is treated as having served a counter-notice (even if he has not actually done so) and may contest any tribunal proceedings brought by the employee's estate (s 176(6)(b) ERA 1996).

CHAPTER 24

Transfer of the business

OUTLINE ¶¶

The sale of a business may be covered by **UK transfer regulations**. The **purpose** of these regulations is to protect employees in the event that the undertaking in which they are employed is transferred. Where a transfer of a business takes place, certain **rights and liabilities**, including the contracts of employment of the transferring employees, will transfer automatically to the transferee and the employees will preserve their statutory continuity of employment. **Changes to terms and conditions** for a reason connected to the transfer will automatically be unfair, although the employer may have a defence in certain circumstances. 7900

Information and consultation obligations may also apply, principally to the transferor but also to the transferee. These require the relevant party to inform and consult with appropriate representatives, not just of the transferring employees, but also any employees affected by the transfer.

The parties cannot contract out of UK transfer regulations if they apply, although the transferor and transferee are free to come to a **commercial agreement** as to who should bear the costs of such liabilities. The negotiation and detailed content of such agreements are outside the scope of this work, and specialist legal advice should be sought where appropriate.

At the time of writing, the **regulations governing** such transfers are the Transfer of Undertakings (Protection of Employment) Regulations SI 1981/1794, which were introduced to give effect to a European Directive known as the Acquired Rights Directive ("ARD") (EC Directive 1977/187). These regulations are usually abbreviated to "TUPE". UK courts and tribunals have **interpreted** TUPE in line with the ARD, by looking at the purpose of the ARD when making transfer-related decisions (*Litster v Forth Dry Dock & Engineering Co Ltd* [1989] IRLR 161, HL). 7901

MEMO POINTS 1. The European Commission can take legal action against the UK due to infringement of the ARD (*Commission of the EC v UK* [1994] IRLR 392, ECJ).
2. If the employer is an emanation of the state, i.e. a **public authority** (for example, government departments, local authorities, health or education authorities), its employees can rely directly

on the ARD if they believe that the UK has failed to implement it correctly, or that it gives them greater rights than the UK regulations.

7902 However, the ARD has been **amended by a new Directive** (EC Directive 1998/50, now consolidated in EC Directive 2001/23). The Government has published draft regulations which will implement this Directive into UK law and revise and supersede the existing regulations (Transfer of Undertakings (Protection of Employment) Regulations 2006). These will be referred to in this chapter as the **new TUPE regulations**. In addition to ensuring European Union compliance, the new regulations also aim to, where appropriate, reduce or eliminate confusion, address case law conflicts which have arisen over the interpretation of provisions and update provisions where well-established developments in case law have rendered the existing wording anachronistic or inadequate.

The principal **changes** introduced by the new TUPE regulations include:
- a broader definition of a "transfer of an undertaking" (see ¶¶7928, 7945);
- an extension of the definition to include "service provision changes" (see ¶¶7928, 7946);
- permitted contractual variations made in connection with the transfer (see ¶¶7929, 8015);
- an obligation on the transferor to notify the transferee of specific information regarding transferring employees (see ¶8082); and
- a limitation on the extent to which the liabilities of an insolvent transferor will transfer (see ¶7929).

7903 **At the time of writing**, the new TUPE regulations have been published in draft form and final regulations are **expected to become effective** on 6 April 2006, although further delay may occur. As the new TUPE regulations are expected to come into force during the life of this edition, the current draft regulations are summarised at the end of each section of this chapter, where appropriate, to indicate where they will either depart from the current regulations or introduce new provisions. Please refer to the online updates and newsletters for confirmation of any changes between the draft and final regulations and the date that the new TUPE regulations will come into force.

SECTION 1
Application

A. Types of transaction

7910 In order to decide whether TUPE applies to a particular transaction, it is necessary to identify whether an undertaking, or part of an undertaking, has transferred from the transferor to the transferee (reg 3(1) SI 1981/1794).

7911 "**Undertaking**" includes any trade or business (reg 2(1) SI 1981/1794). It must be **situated** in the United Kingdom immediately before the transfer. Undertaking has been held to include the carrying out of an activity pursuant to a contract, and the activities of a charitable foundation (*Dr Sophie Redmond Stichting v Bartol* [1992] IRLR 366, ECJ), but does not include administrative functions carried out by a public body pursuant to public law powers (*Henke v Gemeinde Schierke* [1996] IRLR 701, ECJ) (see ¶7928 and ¶7945 for the position under the new TUPE regulations).

7912 TUPE will apply to the transfer of **part of an undertaking** where this is capable of being regarded as a separate and self-contained part of the operations of the remainder of the business, for example by being geographically distinct, or carrying out a separate activity, with its own accounts, management structure and product line.

TUPE applies: 7913
– to the transfer of an undertaking (or part) if what is transferred is transferred **as a going concern** (reg 2(2) SI 1981/1794); and
– whenever there is a **change** in the natural or legal person (e.g. an individual or a company) responsible for the **operation** of the undertaking as a result of a legal transfer or merger (reg 3 SI 1981/1794).

It is, therefore, not limited to a change in **ownership**, but applies also where there is a change in the **employer**, whether or not ownership of assets used in the undertaking has been transferred (reg 3(4)(b) SI 1981/1794; *Landsorganisationen i Danmark v Ny Molle Kro* [1989] IRLR 37, ECJ).

EXAMPLE In *Landsorganisationen i Danmark v Ny Molle Kro*, TUPE applied when an owner of premises rescinded the lease of her premises for failure by the lessee to observe her obligations, such that the owner then took on the management of the undertaking directly, assuming responsibility for the employees.

The most **common transactions** giving rise to a TUPE transfer are mergers and acquisitions, the contracting out of an activity (¶7925), the transfer of a lease on a business (*Foreningen af Arbejdsledere i Danmark v Daddy's Dance Hall* [1988] IRLR 315, ECJ; *Landsorganisationen i Danmark v Ny Molle Kro*), and the transfer of business between two subsidiaries in the same group (*Allen v Amalgamated Construction Co Ltd* [2000] IRLR 119, ECJ). The following transactions may **also** amount to a transfer: 7914
– the termination and grant of franchises and licences;
– the grant of concessions, for example, by a public body (*Collino and Chiappero v Telecom Italia SpA* [2000] IRLR 788, ECJ);
– the transfer of an undertaking from a private body back to a public authority (i.e. where the activities carried out by a legal person governed by private law are taken over by a legal person governed by public law) (*Mayeur v Association Promotion de l'Information Messine (APIM)* [2000] IRLR 783, ECJ);
– the transfer of a state subsidy from one charity to another (*Dr Sophie Redmond Stichting v Bartol* [1992] IRLR 366, ECJ);
– operation of law (for example, the automatic transfer of a sole trader's estate on his death); and
– the carrying on of the business by the directors and sole shareholders with the same employees, after the company was struck off the register of companies (*Charlton and Charlton v (1) Charlton Thermosystems (Romsey) Ltd and (2) Ellis* [1995] IRLR 79, EAT).

TUPE will not apply to a mere transfer of an **asset** or assets (*Premier Motors (Medway) Ltd v Total Oil Great Britain Ltd* [1983] IRLR 471, EAT), nor to the transfer of **shares** in a company which carries on the undertaking, even where the transaction is structured in this way specifically to avoid TUPE (*Brookes v Borough Care Services* [1998] IRLR 636, EAT). 7915

EXAMPLE Company A runs a computer training business. Company B wants to acquire it. If B buys the business as a going concern from A, TUPE will apply and the employees of the business will transfer to B. If, however, B buys Company A's shares, it will own the business by virtue of its ownership of A, but TUPE will not apply and employees of the business will still be employees of A.

In most cases, the transfer is effected by one transaction. In some cases, however, the transfer may be effected by a **series of two or more transactions** (reg 3(4) SI 1981/1794). For TUPE to apply, the series of events must, as a matter of causation, implement the transfer. This is the case, even if there is an **interval of time** between the different transactions, provided the second (and any further) transaction was within the parties' contemplation as being part of a series of transactions at the time the first transaction took place (*Key Communications Ltd v Rose*, EAT case 1292/00). In this case there was a gap of several months between the sale of a business to a transferee which had bought it on behalf of a third party, and the subsequent sale of that business by the transferee to that third party. 7916

EXAMPLE In *Foreningen af Arbejdsledere i Danmark v Daddy's Dance Hall*, the lessee of restaurant premises dismissed his employees when the lease came to an end. The lessor granted a **new lease to a third party** who continued to run the business without any interruption, immediately re-employing the staff of the former lessee. TUPE applied even though the transfer took place in two phases: the transfer back to the owner, followed by the transfer to the new lessee.

7917 As long as the undertaking is located in the UK, TUPE will apply even if the transfer is **governed or effected by foreign law**.

7918 TUPE also applies to **liquidation proceedings**, although the ARD has been held not to apply to the transfer of an undertaking or business in the course of formal judicial liquidation proceedings (*Abels v Bedriifsveereniging voor de Metaalindustrie en de Electrotechnische Industrie* [1985] ECR 469, ECJ) (see ¶7929 for the position under the new TUPE regulations).

Where a receiver, administrator, or (in the case of a creditors' voluntary winding up) liquidator of a company transfers the business to a wholly-owned subsidiary in order to attract buyers for the viable part of the company's activities (known as a "**hive-down**"), TUPE will not apply unless the subsidiary ceases to be wholly owned by the company, or the business is transferred out of the subsidiary company to a third party. Although TUPE does not apply to the hive-down, it will transfer liabilities relating to the employees of the transferor to the ultimate purchaser when the sale of the subsidiary/its business eventually takes place, and there is deemed to be one transfer only at this stage (reg 4(1) SI 1981/1794; *In the matter of Maxwell Fleet and Facilities Management (Ltd) (in administration)* [2000] IRLR 368, ChD).

TUPE does, however, apply to the transfer of an undertaking which is being **wound up** by a court (if the undertaking continues to trade) (*Jules Dethier Equipment SA v Dassy* [1998] IRLR 266, ECJ) or voluntarily (*Europieces SA v Saunders*, ECJ (IDS 627)).

However, where a business has completely **ceased to operate** and a liquidator has been appointed to gather the business's assets and sell them for the maximum benefit of the creditors, TUPE will not apply (*Perth & Kinross Council v Donaldson and others* [2004] IRLR 121, EAT(S)).

7925 **Contracting out and in** A TUPE transfer may take place where an employer contracts out an **in-house service** (such as cleaning, catering, IT or payroll services) provided that the service forms an identifiable part of the employer's operation which retains its identity after the transfer (*Süzen v Zehnacker Gebäudereinigung GmbH Krankenhausservice und Lefarth GmbH* [1997] IRLR 255, ECJ; *Rask v ISS Kantineservice* [1993] IRLR 133, ECJ) (see ¶7928 and ¶7946 for the position under the new TUPE regulations). TUPE may apply in such cases even though the service transferred is only an **ancillary activity** of the transferor and the agreement relates to the provision of services provided exclusively for the benefit of the transferor in return for an agreed fixed fee. It may apply even where the services are performed by a **single employee**, and no tangible assets are transferred (*Schmidt v Spar-und Leihkasse der Früheren Ämter Bordesholm, Kiel und Cronshagen* [1994] IRLR 302, ECJ).

EXAMPLE In *Schmidt v Spar-und Leihkasse der Früheren Ämter Bordesholm, Kiel und Cronshagen*, the bank contracted out the cleaning of one of its branches. S was the only person engaged in that activity, but the ECJ held that her employment transferred nevertheless under TUPE to the contractor.

7926 Contracting in of a service (i.e. bringing it **back in-house**) is also likely to be covered by TUPE.

7927 TUPE can apply where a contract is transferred from one contractor to another on its expiry or termination (known as "**second generation contracting out**"). There is **no** need for a **contractual link** between the outgoing contractor and the new contractor. Therefore, it is possible for employees of one contractor to transfer under TUPE to a second contractor, even though the contractual link is between the contractors and the company contracting out the service (*Dines v Initial Health Care Services* [1994] IRLR 336, CA). TUPE will not, however, apply between an original contractor and a second contractor to whom the work has been moved if the reason for moving the contract was the client's genuine dissatisfaction with workers' performance and it was not done to avoid the application of TUPE (*Carlisle Facilities Group v Matrix Events & Security Services and ors*, EAT case 00380/04).

This principle also applies where a contractor **subcontracts** performance of the contract. In such cases, TUPE may apply to transfer employees from the sub-contractor to the new contractor, even though there is no direct contractual relationship between the subcontractors and the new contractor or between the subcontractor and the company awarding the contract (*Temco Service Industries SA v Imzilyen* [2002] IRLR 214, ECJ).

Expected changes under the new TUPE regulations

It is expected that the new TUPE regulations will apply to two broad types of transaction. The first such transaction is the transfer of an **undertaking or business** or part of an undertaking or business situated in the United Kingdom immediately before the transfer, where there is a transfer of an **economic entity** which retains its identity (¶7945). **7928**

The second type of transaction relates to the **contracting** of services. The Government has attempted to cover this key issue comprehensively, in order to introduce a "level playing field" and avoid uncertainty and unnecessary litigation. The scope of the new TUPE regulations has therefore been extended to **service provision changes**. These occur where a contract is:
- awarded by a client to a contractor (**"contracted out"** or **"outsourced"**);
- re-let to a new contractor (**"reassigned"**); or
- brought back "in-house" (**"contracted in"** or **"insourced"**).

For the new TUPE regulations to apply to such changes, further conditions must be met, which are outlined further at ¶7946. Once these conditions are met, the party responsible for carrying out the service before the change will be treated as the transferor and the party responsible after the change will be treated as the transferee.

As part of the Government's intention to promote "rescue culture" and the sale of insolvent businesses as going concerns, two changes have also been introduced in the new TUPE regulations to address their application to **insolvency proceedings**. **7929**

The first change relates to the transfer of pre-existing debts. Where the transferor is subject to certain insolvency proceedings, such as administration, company and individual voluntary arrangements and creditors' voluntary winding-up, certain **pre-existing debts** (i.e. statutory insolvency payments and statutory redundancy payments) owed by the transferor to relevant employees will not pass to the transferee. Relevant employees, for these purposes, are those employees who have passed to the transferee and those who would have done so but for the fact that they were unfairly dismissed by the transferor (either because of the transfer itself or a reason connected with the transfer that is not an economic, technical or organisational reason entailing changes in the workforce) (¶8030 +).

The second change introduced by the new TUPE regulations provides that where the transferor is subject to certain insolvency proceedings, the transferor or transferee (or insolvency practitioner) is not prevented from making **permitted variations** to contracts of employment which would normally be unlawful (that is, where the sole or principal reason for them is the transfer or a reason connected with the transfer that is not an economic, technical or organisational reason entailing changes in the workforce) (¶8010 +). However, the changes must be agreed with **appropriate representatives** and must be designed to **safeguard employment opportunities** by ensuring the survival of the undertaking or business.

In addition to the new insolvency provisions, the existing provision relating to hiving down (¶7918) has been removed from the new TUPE regulations, on the basis that, following consultation, it no longer serves any useful purpose.

Finally, in relation to the more general scope of the new TUPE regulations, it is also specified that the **administrative reorganisation of public administrative authorities** or the transfer of **administrative functions between public administrative authorities** will not fall within the regulations.

MEMO POINTS Public sector transfers are addressed by the Government in the Cabinet Office Statement of Practice (Staff Transfers within the Public Sector (2000)) and the Code of Practice on Workforce Matters in Public Sector Service Contracts (Cabinet Office Statement of Practice (March 2005)).

B. Identifying a transfer

7930 In many cases it will be obvious that there is a TUPE transfer. Where it is not clear, or where the matter is in dispute, the parties (or the tribunal determining the question) must examine the issue with great care and in some detail. The critical issue in establishing whether there has been a transfer to which TUPE applies is whether there is an economic entity which has retained its identity after the transfer (*Spijkers v Gebroeders Benedik Abbattoir CV* [1986] ECR 1119, ECJ) (see ¶7945 for the position under the new TUPE regulations). The correct approach is to consider the **two issues** (economic entity and transfer of that entity) separately, applying different factors to each issue (*Cheesman v R Brewer Contracts Ltd* [2001] IRLR 144, EAT).

7931 **Is there an economic entity?** An economic entity **means** an organised grouping of persons and assets facilitating the exercise of an economic activity which pursues a specific objective (for example, a contract cleaning business) (*Süzen v Zehnacker Gebäudereinigung GmbH Krankenhausservice und Lefarth GmbH* [1997] IRLR 255, ECJ). The question as to whether there is an economic entity often arises in cases where **part of an undertaking** is transferred, as where a company contracts out an ancillary in-house service.

An entity cannot be reduced to the **activity** entrusted to it, i.e. the activity does not, in itself, constitute an economic entity (*Süzen v Zehnacker Gebäudereinigung GmbH Krankenhausservice und Lefarth GmbH*). The identification of an economic entity will emerge from **other factors**, such as its workforce, the management of its staff, the way the work is organised, its operating methods or, if appropriate, the operational resources available to it (*Francisco Hernández Vidal SA v Gómez Pérez* [1999] IRLR 132, ECJ).

7932 The economic entity must also be "**structured and autonomous**" (*Sánchez Hidalgo v Asociación de Servicios Aser* [1999] IRLR 136, ECJ), which may, for example, mean that it has a distinct cost centre for accounting purposes, although it does not necessarily have to have significant **assets**. For example, even a 'package' of maintenance duties which were almost exclusively undertaken by one worker within a disciplined and technical framework has been held to constitute an economic entity which is capable of transferring under TUPE (*Dudley Bower Building Services Ltd v Lowe* [2003] IRLR 260, EAT). In certain sectors (such as cleaning and surveillance), the assets are often reduced to their most basic and the activity is essentially based on manpower. An organised grouping of wage-earners who are specifically and permanently assigned to a common task may, in the absence of other factors of production, amount to an economic entity (*Sánchez Hidalgo v Asociación de Servicios Aser*). It is the function of the employees and not merely their employment status that should be considered in identifying such an organised grouping (*Wynnwith Engineering Co Ltd v Bennett* [2002] IRLR 170, EAT). Often, where there are no significant assets, the starting point in establishing whether there is an economic entity is the wording of the transfer agreement which defines what constitutes the 'business' (whether this includes assets or not) being transferred (*McLeod and Welsh v Ingram (t/a Phoenix Taxis) and Rainbow Cars Ltd (t/a Rainbow Taxis)*, EAT case 1344/01).

7933 There is a need for **stability**. It is, therefore, unlikely that TUPE will apply where an operation is marked by extreme **fluctuations in the number of employees** and **changes in the tasks** carried out (*Initial Contract Services Ltd v Harrison*, EAT case 64/01), nor to an entity whose activity is limited to performing **one specific works contract** (*Rygaard v Stro Molle Akustik* [1996] IRLR, ECJ). Likewise, where the new contractor's **allocation of staff** to perform the contract is so significantly different to the allocation by the former contractor, this may cause the economic entity to not retain its identity following the transfer of the contract (*Computercenter (UK) Ltd v Swanton and ors*, EAT case 0256/04).

EXAMPLE 1. In *Rygaard v Stro Molle Akustik*, R was employed by Svend Pedersen A/S, a carpentry business, which was contracted to build a canteen for a company, SAS Service Partner. Svend Pedersen's contract was subsequently transferred to Stro Molle Akustik. The ECJ held that the ARD did not apply to the transfer as the subject matter of the transfer was merely the right to complete a **specific building project**. Although some employees and materials were made available

to Stro Molle, the ECJ held that there was no stable economic activity, there being no continuing and recurrent activity to which the ARD should apply.
2. In *Computercenter (UK) Ltd v Swanton and ors*, following a tender process, a computer maintenance service contract passed from one contractor to another. The original contractor, SCC, had employed a dedicated team of eight staff to perform the contract, some of which were based at the client's site. The new contractor, C, however, decided not to employ any of the eight SCC employees but instead to use its own employees to provide the maintenance service, although none of its employees spent more than 40% of their time on the contract and none were based at the client's site. There was no contractual link between SCC and C, no employees or assets were transferred and the tribunal had not found that C had deliberately not taken on any of SCC's employees to avoid the application of TUPE. In this case, the EAT held that, although the maintenance service contract was identical following the transfer, C's **allocation of staff** to perform the contract was so significantly different to the allocation by SCC that the economic entity could not be said to have retained its identity following the transfer of the contract.

However, there is no basis for automatically excluding all **single-contract undertakings** from the scope of the ARD and TUPE. In cases other than the completion of a specific building project which is discrete and limited in time, an activity limited to one specific contract may amount to an undertaking where the contract consists of **more than the mere activity** (*Argyll Training Ltd v (1) Sinclair and (2) Argyll & The Islands Enterprise Ltd* [2000] IRLR 630, EAT). 7934

EXAMPLE In *Argyll Training Ltd v (1) Sinclair and (2) Argyll & The Islands Enterprise Ltd*, S was employed by Business & Employment Skills Training Ltd (BEST) as a training adviser to provide in-house training and placement of trainees with local enterprise companies under a contract between BEST and ATL. BEST lost its contract, and ATL subsequently took over some of the placement trainees on BEST's books. The EAT held that, although the activity was limited to **one training contract**, it amounted to an undertaking (it was a stable economic entity) because the contract also included significant **intangible assets** (namely the contractual arrangements pertaining to the trainees).

Has it transferred? The decisive criterion is whether the economic entity **retains its identity**, as may be shown by the continuation of the undertaking's operation with the same or similar activities (*Schmidt v Spar-und Leihkasse der Früheren Ämter Bordesholm, Kiel und Cronshagen* [1994] IRLR 302, ECJ). All the factual circumstances of the transaction must be considered, and no single factor is overriding. The decisive criterion itself is not dependent on a single factor (*Cheesman v R Brewer Contracts Ltd*). 7937

Particular **factors** include (*Spijkers v Gebroeders Benedik Abbattoir CV*):
- the type of undertaking or business;
- whether tangible assets (such as buildings and moveable property) are transferred;
- the value of intangible assets (such as goodwill) at the date of the transfer;
- whether the majority of employees are taken over by the new employer;
- whether customers are transferred;
- the degree of similarity between the activities carried on before and after the alleged transfer; and
- whether there is a cessation of the activities and, if so, for how long.

MEMO POINTS The UK courts have had to decide the issue of whether an economic entity which is **fragmented** into two or more separate entities is capable of retaining its identity on transfer (*Fairhurst Ward Abbots Ltd v (1) Botes Building Ltd (2) Vaughan*, EAT case 1007/00, confirmed on appeal ([2004] IRLR 304, CA)). In this case, the EAT held that the fragmented part of the undertaking was still an economic entity capable of retaining its identity on transfer, but that each case will turn on its own facts. A matter of importance to the EAT was that future transferors might try to circumvent the application of TUPE by dividing up an undertaking into smaller fragmented parts.

It has been held by the ECJ that the ARD and TUPE will not apply on a **change of contractor** unless substantial tangible or intangible assets are transferred, or the new contractor takes over a major part (in terms of their numbers and skills) of the workforce assigned by its predecessor to the performance of the contract (*Süzen v Zehnacker Gebäudereinigung GmbH Krankenhausservice und Lefarth GmbH*; followed in *Whitewater Leisure Management Ltd v Barne* [2000] IRLR 456, EAT). The transfer of assets and staff will be very important factors, but not conclusive (*(1) RCO Support Services Ltd (2) Aintree Hospital Trust v Unison* [2002] IRLR 401, CA; *Pinnacle AIC Ltd v (1) Honeyman (2)* 7938

Cape Industrial Services Ltd, EAT case 411/01). There is, therefore, often a degree of uncertainty whether TUPE applies to a change of contractors in any given case (although see ¶7928 and ¶7946 for the position under the new TUPE regulations).

7939 Account must be taken of the type of undertaking or business in issue, and the degree of importance to be attached to the various factors will vary according to the activity carried on.

In **labour-intensive undertakings** with no significant assets (such as contract cleaning), a group of workers engaged in an entity on a permanent basis may constitute an economic activity. If the new contractor continues to pursue that activity and also **takes over a major part of the workforce** (in terms of their numbers and skills) previously assigned to that activity (which, in effect, is the key asset of such an undertaking), TUPE is likely to apply (*Süzen v Zehnacker Gebäudereinigung GmbH Krankenhausservice und Lefarth GmbH*; *Oy Liikenne Ab v Liskojarvi* [2001] IRLR 171, ECJ). The fact that physical assets and other items do not transfer may not have an impact in determining whether TUPE applies in such cases (*Allen v Amalgamated Construction Co Ltd* [2000] IRLR 119, ECJ).

The **ECJ case law** may lead to the conclusion that in such sectors, a new contractor may avoid the application of TUPE by **refusing to take on a major part** of the old contractor's workforce, even where that workforce (or a replacement workforce) is required by the new contractor to perform the contract (*Süzen v Zehnacker Gebäudereinigung GmbH Krankenhausservice und Lefarth GmbH*; *Oy Liikenne Ab v Liskojarvi*).

The **UK courts**, however, have indicated that the issue must be decided by reference to **all the facts of the case**, in particular, the factors identified in the *Spijkers v Gebroeders Benedik Abbattoir CV* case (¶¶7930, 7937), one of which is whether the majority of employees are taken over by the new contractor (*ECM (Vehicle Delivery Service) Limited v Cox* [1999] IRLR 559, CA; followed in *RCO Support Services Ltd (2) Aintree Hospital Trust v Unison*). A **failure to take on the majority of the workforce** (or to transfer significant assets) will not point conclusively against a TUPE transfer, but will be one of the factors, as will the **reason why** the transferor's employees were not taken on (*ECM (Vehicle Delivery Service) Limited v Cox*; *Fairhurst Ward Abbots Ltd v (1) Botes Building Ltd (2) Vaughan* [2004] IRLR 304, CA). If a tribunal finds that the reason, or principal reason, a transferee employer does not take on the transferor's workforce is the avoidance of the application of TUPE, then this is a relevant factor to take into account in applying the multi-factor approached stipulated in *Spijkers v Gebroeders Benedik Abbattoir CV* and could be determinative. If, however, the tribunal finds that, on the facts of the case, the avoidance of TUPE is not the reason, or principal reason, then the *Spijkers v Gebroeders Benedik Abbattoir CV* test should be considered without it (*Astle v Cheshire County Council* [2005] IRLR 12, EAT).

Whether the majority of the workforce is taken on may be a critical factor, and there may not be significant other factors pointing to a TUPE transfer. However, tribunals are likely to strive to avoid a rigid application of the *Süzen v Zehnacker Gebäudereinigung GmbH Krankenhausservice und Lefarth GmbH* case, as this may result in the protection of employees' acquired rights (i.e. the basic objective of the ARD and TUPE) being jeopardised. Indeed, it has been held that where new contractors took over the provision of cleaning and catering services without the transfer of any employees, TUPE was deemed to apply (*RCO Support Services Ltd (2) Aintree Hospital Trust v Unison*).

EXAMPLE **Valid reason**

1. An outsourcing company may be dissatisfied with the old contractor's performance of the contract and the competence of his workforce, which a new contractor will, therefore, not want to take on. If the new contractor employs a new workforce with new skills and training, and uses different working methods, a tribunal, taking into account all the relevant factors, may be inclined to find that there has not been a TUPE transfer in such circumstances (*Dickson v Compact Group (UK) Ltd*, EAT case 1037/99).

2. An overriding economic reason is a valid reason for a new contractor to refuse to take on the old contractor's workforce (*Ministry of Defence v (1) Carvey and (2) Rentokil Initial Security Ltd*, EAT case 202/00), although tribunals may not always find this to be the case.

Not valid reason
However, if the reason for not taking on the transferor's employees is a desire to avoid the application of TUPE, it has been held that the tribunal must assess the case as if the employees had been taken on, making it more likely that TUPE will apply (*ADI (UK) Ltd v Willer* [2001] IRLR 542, CA).

With regard to undertakings which are "**asset-orientated**" (i.e. not labour-intensive), the transfer (or not) of employees will not be a decisive factor in determining whether or not TUPE applies and it is therefore necessary to identify **other factors**, such as the transfer of physical assets (*Betts v Brintel Helicopters Ltd and KLM ERA Helicopters (UK) Ltd* [1997] IRLR 361, CA; *Carlito Abler v Sodexho MM Catering GmbH*, ECJ case C-340/01). The provision of catering services has been held to be an asset-reliant function (*Carlito Abler v Sodexho MM Catering GmbH*), where the ECJ held that the catering function was reliant on a significant amount of equipment, namely premises, together with water, energy and other essential equipment. 7940

It does not necessarily follow, however, that TUPE will not apply to a transfer involving an "asset-orientated" activity if there is not a significant transfer of those assets (*P & O Trans European Ltd v Initial Transport Services Ltd* [2003] IRLR 128, EAT). The transfer or otherwise of assets is only one factor to be taken into account and the circumstances of the entire transaction need to be considered.

EXAMPLE In *Carlito Abler v Sodexho MM Catering GmbH*, a contract to provide hospital catering services was awarded to a new contractor. The new contractor refused to take on the former contractor's employees, materials or other moveable assets. Instead, the incoming contractor had only taken over the use of water, energy and other essential equipment which the client (a third party) had provided for the former contractor. Nevertheless, the ARD was held to apply.

If the **activities are carried on** but **in a different way** (for example, by the introduction of new machinery and work methods) such that the economic entity can no longer be identified, TUPE will not apply (*Convy v Saltire Press Ltd*, EAT case 1269/99). Further, the mere fact that old and new contractors provide a **similar service** does not support the automatic conclusion that an economic entity has been transferred (*Süzen v Zehnacker Gebäudereinigung GmbH Krankenhausservice und Lefarth GmbH*). Also, the mere loss of a service contract to a competitor cannot by itself indicate the existence of a TUPE transfer. A contractor **losing one customer** in this way may, for example, continue to exist and carry out its business working on other contracts, albeit without the work brought in by the particular contract. 7941

The **absence of any contractual link** between the transferor and transferee may be evidence that there has been no TUPE transfer but it is not conclusive as there is no need for any such direct contractual relationship (*Sánchez Hidalgo v Asociación de Servicios Aser*).

The fact that work is performed continuously with **no interruption** or change in the manner or performance will be a factor that indicates that TUPE applies, but no particular importance should be attached to a gap between the end of the work by one sub-contractor and the start by the successor (*Allen v Amalgamated Construction Co Ltd*). 7942

The **parties' intentions** (indicated, for example, in the contractual documents or during a tendering process) may be a relevant factor in deciding that TUPE applies (*Lightways (Contractors) Ltd v Associated Holdings Ltd* [2000] IRLR 247, CS). However, if TUPE is found as a matter of law to apply, their intention that it should not will be irrelevant. 7943

MEMO POINTS The Cabinet Office's Statement of Practice states that it should be assumed that TUPE applies to the contracting out/contracting back in of services in respect of **public bodies** (January 2000). Tribunals may take this statement of intention into account when determining whether TUPE applies (*Lightways (Contractors) Ltd v Associated Holdings Ltd*).

Expected changes under the new TUPE regulations

When identifying a transfer under the new TUPE regulations, it is expected that **different provisions will apply** depending on whether there is a transfer of an undertaking or business, or a service provision change. 7944

7945 **Transfer of an undertaking or business** In relation to the transfer of an undertaking or business, there will need to be a transfer of an **economic entity which retains its identity** for the new regulations to apply. An economic entity is expressly defined under the new TUPE regulations as **an organised grouping of resources** which has the objective of pursuing an economic activity, whether or not that activity is central or ancillary. As is clear from the issues outlined above (¶7930 +), the new TUPE regulations have drawn on current case law in this area to develop the definition of an economic entity. The existing case law will therefore remain relevant and it is likely that the factors outlined in *Spijkers v Gebroeders Benedik Abbattoir CV* (¶7937) will still be relied upon to assess whether an economic entity has retained its identity.

7946 **Service provision change** In relation to a transfer involving contracting out, reassignment or contracting in (¶7928), **three further conditions** will need to be fulfilled for the new TUPE provisions to apply:

a. there must be an **organised grouping of employees** situated in the United Kingdom immediately before the change, whose principal purpose is to carry out the activities concerned on behalf of the client;

b. the client must intend that the **activities** will, after the service provision change, be carried out by the transferee **other than in connection** with a single specific event or task; and

c. the **activities** must **not consist** wholly or mainly of the procurement or supply of goods for the client's use.

There may also be an exemption from the provisions applicable to service provision changes for **professional business services**.

MEMO POINTS **a.** There must be an **identifiable and dedicated team of employees** carrying out the service activities. Where, for example, a courier service is provided by a contractor but the deliveries and collections are undertaken by different couriers on an ad hoc basis, rather than by an assigned team on a permanent basis, if the client subsequently engages a different contractor, this will not be covered by the new TUPE regulations. Equally, an organised grouping of employees whose principal purpose is to carry out service activities for clients in general, rather than one specific client, will be excluded from the new regulations.

b. The scope of the new TUPE regulations is not intended to apply to a client who **engages a contractor on a one-off basis** (for example, to organise a conference), who has no intention of having an on-going relationship with that contractor, and then does the same with a subsequent contractor. However, this exclusion means that tribunals will have to examine the client's intention at the relevant time, especially where there are a series of one-off events or tasks. It has been suggested that this exclusion may not survive the final new TUPE regulations.

c. Only **service-based activities** are intended to be caught by the new TUPE regulations.

At the time of writing, the Government has not confirmed whether the new TUPE regulations will also apply to **professional business services**. It was considered during the consultation exercise that whilst the existing scope of TUPE extends to "blue collar" services, such as office cleaning and workplace catering, it should not extend to "white collar" professional business services, such as consultants. It is difficult to define professional business services precisely and there is a risk that an exemption for such services would introduce uncertainty. It is also arguable that both blue and white collar workers should be entitled to the protection of transfer legislation. It has, however, been suggested that, as blue collar services have more often been the subject of dispute and case law in this area, professionally qualified employees who are key to providing such services are less in need of additional legal protection.

SECTION 2

Effect

A. Transfer of employees

TUPE applies to **transfer automatically** (by operation of law) to the transferee (as if their contracts of employment were originally made with the transferee), those employees: 7950
- employed by the transferor in the undertaking (or part) immediately before the transfer (reg 5(3) SI 1981/1794), i.e. "assigned" to the undertaking (or part); and
- whose employment would otherwise have been terminated by the transfer (reg 5(1) SI 1981/1794) (see ¶7963 for the position under the new TUPE regulations).

An **employee** includes an individual who works for another person under a contract of employment or apprenticeship or otherwise, but not someone who provides services under a contract for services (¶13) (reg 2(1) SI 1981/1794). There must be an employment relationship and a contract between the employee and the transferor. For example, a teacher employed by a local education authority will not transfer under TUPE if the governing body of a school reorganises it, as the teacher is not employed by that body (*Askew v Governing Body of Clifton Middle School* [1999] IRLR 708, CA). 7951

The employment contracts of employees who **ordinarily work outside the UK** (or whose employment is **governed by foreign law**) will transfer to the transferee, as will collective agreements and union recognition in appropriate circumstances (¶7990). However, such overseas employees will not (save for certain mariners) be protected against a dismissal in connection with the transfer (¶8030), nor will they be entitled to information or consultation (or a remedy for failure to inform or consult) (¶8060) (reg 13 SI 1981/1794) (although see ¶7966 for the position under new TUPE regulations). 7952

Assigned to the undertaking This usually means that the employee works wholly or mainly in that part of the business. Employees of the transferor not employed in the undertaking (or part) to be transferred will not transfer under TUPE. If an employee's contract allows the employer to require him to work in a part of the undertaking that is not being transferred, the employee could be transferred to that part prior to the transfer, and will therefore not be covered by TUPE. However, the existence of a **mobility clause** in the contracts of employees assigned to the undertaking will not of itself mean that they are not assigned for the purposes of a TUPE transfer (*Securicor Guarding Ltd v Fraser Security Services Ltd* [1996] IRLR 552, EAT). Further, if an employee has only been **temporarily** assigned to another undertaking (or part), then he is not assigned to that undertaking (or part) for the purposes of TUPE (*Securiplan v Bademosi*, EAT case 1128/02). Whether an employee is on a temporary assignment is a matter of fact in each case. In this case, the parties had expressly agreed that the assignment would be temporary. 7955

If an employee **works at two or more parts** of the undertaking and only one is being transferred, the courts will look to see where the employee predominantly worked (*Botzen v Rotterdamsche Droogdok Maatschappij BV* case 186/83 [1986] 2 CMLR 50, ECJ; applied in *Michael Peters Ltd v Farnfield* [1995] IRLR 190, EAT). UK tribunals have applied a percentage test, taking 80% of time spent in the undertaking as indicating assignment (*Anderson v Kluwer*, COIT 15068/85). This test is not applied by the ECJ, and the matter should be determined by undertaking a factual assessment of each case (*Duncan Webb Offset (Maidstone) Limited v Cooper* [1995] IRLR 633, EAT).

Relevant factors will include:
- the amount of time spent on one part of the business or the other;
- the amount of value given to each part by the employee;

– the terms of the employment contract; and
– how the cost to the employer of the employee's services is allocated between the different parts of the business.

MEMO POINTS In *CPL Distribution Ltd v Todd* [2003] IRLR 28, CA, T, a personal assistant, worked for a manager who was assigned to the part of an undertaking which did not transfer when CPL lost a contract after it was put to tender. The Court held that T had been **effectively assigned to her manager** and, accordingly, did not transfer to the transferee, even though most of her work related to the contract lost.

7956 The transferee is likely to seek a **warranty** in the transfer agreement as to the identity of the transferring employees. He may also seek an **indemnity** in respect of any employee who actually transfers to him under TUPE, but of whom he was unaware.

7958 **Immediately before the transfer** To transfer, the employees must be employed in the transferring undertaking immediately before the transfer (reg 5(3) SI 1981/1794). TUPE will also cover those employees who were **unfairly dismissed** by the transferor **shortly before the transfer**, if the transfer was the sole or principal reason for the dismissal (*Litster v Forth Dry Dock & Engineering Co Ltd* [1989] IRLR 161, HL). This means that such employees will be protected by TUPE from unfair dismissal even though they are not actually employed on the transfer date.

If the transfer is effected in stages, by means of **more than one transaction**, TUPE will apply to anyone employed in the undertaking immediately before any of the transactions in question (reg 5(3) SI 1981/1794).

7959 **Transfer date** Employees will transfer on the **transfer date**, i.e. the completion of the contract for the sale of the business, for example. The date of a transfer must be a **particular point in time** (which cannot be postponed to another date at the will of the transferor or transferee), i.e. when the responsibility as employer for carrying on the business of the unit transferred moves from the transferor to the transferee (*Celtec v Astley* (C-478/03) [2005] IRLR 647, ECJ).

7960 **Employee knowledge** If TUPE applies, such employees will be transferred **whether or not** they have been **informed** of the transfer (*Secretary of State for Trade and Industry v Cook* [1997] IRLR 150, EAT) (and regardless of any contrary intention of or agreement between the transferor and transferee (*Rotsart de Hertaing v J Benoidt SA* [1997] IRLR 127, ECJ)).

7962 **Employee objection** An employee can object to the transfer. An objection may be **evidenced** by a refusal to give consent to the transfer, which is communicated to the transferor or the transferee prior to the transfer (*Hay v George Hanson (Building Contractors) Ltd* [1996] IRLR 427, EAT). A mere expression of unhappiness or concern will not amount to an objection. "Opting out" of the transfer and accepting a severance payment from the transferor may not amount to an objection where the employee does in fact accept employment with the transferee (*Senior Heat Treatment Ltd v Bell* [1997] IRLR 614, EAT).

The **consequences** of an objection are that the employee's employment will be deemed to have terminated by operation of law, and he will not be entitled to compensation for unfair or wrongful dismissal (reg 5(4A), (4B) SI 1981/1794). There is no requirement that the employer inform an employee of the consequences of any objection. Note, however, that in certain circumstances the employee can bring a **constructive dismissal** claim against the transferor employer (¶8035).

If the employee objects to the transfer and is **retained by the transferor**, it may be possible to argue that a **subsequent dismissal** by the transferor is automatically unfair for being connected to the transfer (*Dunkinson v Meridian Technologies Ltd*, EAT case 0266/01).

Expected changes under the new TUPE regulations

7963 Both the transfer of an undertaking and a service provision change will have an effect on employees under the new TUPE regulations. Those employees employed by the transferor and **assigned to the organised grouping of resources or employees** which is the subject of the transfer will **transfer automatically** to the transferee (as if their contracts of employment were originally made with the transferee).

MEMO POINTS The new TUPE regulations refer to those employees who are "assigned to the organised grouping of resources or employees" in a number of places, often to clarify or replace the previous use of the term "undertaking".

Being **assigned means** being assigned other than on a temporary basis. It will be a question of fact in each case and, as the provisions in the new TUPE regulations reflect existing case law, it is likely that the factors assessed in *Botzen v Rotterdamsche Droogdok Maatschappij BV* case 186/83 [1986] 2 CMLR 50, ECJ, *Duncan Webb Offset (Maidstone) Limited v Cooper* [1995] IRLR 633, EAT and *Securiplan v Bademosi*, EAT case 1128/02 will continue to be considered (¶7955). 7964

The provisions apply to those employed immediately before the transfer or those who would have been employed had they not been unfairly dismissed where the sole or principal reason for the dismissal is the transfer or a reason connected with the transfer that is not an economic, technical or organisational reason. This reflects the judgment in *Litster v Forth Dry Dock & Engineering Co Ltd* [1989] IRLR 161, HL (¶7958).

However, **for the automatic transfer** to take place, there will no longer be a requirement that the employment contracts would have otherwise "been terminated by the transfer". The Government considers that this wording adds nothing of value and risks creating a loophole, allowing the transferor to retain employees who would otherwise automatically transfer, as such retention would mean that their employment would not be terminated by the transfer (¶7950). 7965

The existing provisions in TUPE which exclude its application to **overseas employees** (¶7952) do not feature in the new TUPE regulations, in order to make them consistent with all employment rights legislation. In future, it is expected that the normal principles of international law will be applied to ascertain whether an overseas employee can claim protection under the new TUPE regulations. 7966

B. Transfer of rights and liabilities

Effect on employment contracts TUPE operates to transfer the contracts of employment of transferring employees to the transferee (in legal terms, a "statutory novation of contract") (reg 5(1) SI 1981/1794; *Stirling District Council v Allan* [1995] IRLR 301, CS). Statutory **continuity of employment** will be preserved, i.e. the transferee must recognise the employee's period of service with the transferor. 7980

MEMO POINTS Note that a **continuation order** (¶7594) which has been imposed on an employer who has refused to reinstate or re-engage an employee will not transfer under TUPE to a new owner of the business since a continuation order does not constitute a continuing contract of employment but rather is a purely statutory relationship between the employer and the former employee which provides for the financial protection of the employee pending the full hearing of his claim (*Dowling v (1) ME Ilic Haulage (2) Berkeley Logistics Ltd*, EAT case 0836/03).

The transferee employer does not need to provide a new **statement of employment particulars** (¶1400), but must notify the transferring employees in writing of the change in the employer's identity, and give the date their period of continuous employment began. 7981

All the transferor's rights, powers, duties and liabilities under or in connection with the employment contracts (including his obligations in respect of the employees' contractual rights such as **pay, benefits, holiday entitlement**) transfer to the transferee, i.e. the employees' **existing terms and conditions** are preserved (reg 5(2)(a) SI 1981/1794). The transferor will no longer be liable to the employees after the transfer (*Stirling District Council v Allan*). For example, if the transferor owed the transferring employees wages prior to the transfer, the employees must claim any outstanding sums from the transferee after the trans- 7982 fer. Similarly, the transferee can sue an employee for a breach of contract that was committed against the transferor before the transfer.

Anything done before the transfer by or in relation to the transferor in respect of the employment contracts or the transferring employees is deemed to have been done by or in relation to the transferee (reg 5(2)(b) SI 1981/1794).

7983 **Restrictive covenants** will transfer under TUPE, but are construed so as to **protect the business** that was **transferred**, and not the whole of the transferee's business. As the subject-matter of the restriction will remain unchanged, a covenant against dealings with customers of the employer, for example, will be read as referring to **customers of the transferor** employer who fell within the definition of the covenant (*Morris Angel & Son Ltd v Hollande* [1993] IRLR 169, CA). This will clearly be problematic if the transferee wishes to enforce the covenant some time after the transfer, when the pool of customers may have changed. However, agreeing a new covenant with the transferring employees is also not without difficulty (¶8010).

7985 **Statutory and civil claims** Liability for statutory claims (or circumstances giving rise to them) existing prior to the transfer will transfer to the transferee. For example, the transferee will become liable for any act of **discrimination** done by the transferor in relation to a transferring employee prior to the transfer. This will be the case even if the liability related to a contract which preceded the one in place at the time of the transfer, as the ARD refers to rights and obligations arising from the "employment relationship", and TUPE is interpreted in line with this broad concept (*DJM International Ltd v Nicholas* [1996] IRLR 76, EAT). This broad interpretation means that liability to transferring employees for tortious acts of **negligence** (including personal injury claims) (whether direct or arising by virtue of the employer's vicarious liability for the acts of his employees), and for **breaches of statutory duty** will pass to the transferee as arising from the employment relationship (*Taylor v Serviceteam Limited & Waltham Forest Borough Council* [1998] 2CL 57, CC).

However, **liabilities owed to third parties** as a result of the employees' tortious acts will not transfer.

7986 **Personal injury claims** (whether based on the employer's tortious or contractual obligations) will be transferred. Further, the right of a transferor to an **indemnity** from his insurers in respect of his employees' personal injury claims (under the obligatory **employer's liability insurance**) will transfer along with liability for any such claims to the transferee, as it is a right arising from/in connection with the employment contract (*Bernadone v Pall Mall Services Group* [2000] IRLR 487, CA) (see ¶7998 for the position under the new TUPE regulations).

7987 Given that compulsory employers' liability insurance cover can transfer under TUPE, there is now a question as to whether **other types of insurance cover** that are provided for contractually (such as permanent health insurance) could also transfer, as arising from or in connection with the employment contract. It is essential for transferee employers to obtain details of any insurance claims by transferring employees, together with details of the relevant policies. Liability will then be a matter for negotiation between the parties (and possibly their insurers), as the transferee may seek an indemnity.

7989 **Criminal liabilities** These do not transfer (reg 5(4) SI 1981/1794).

7990 **Collective agreements** Collective agreements made between the transferor employer and a trade union recognised by him to any extent for the purposes of collective bargaining in respect of the transferring employees will have effect after the transfer as if made by the transferee employer and that trade union (reg 6 SI 1981/1794). In most cases, however, such agreements do **not** result in an **automatic incorporation** into individual employment contracts and are binding in honour only. Consequently, for example, where the transferor is **not legally bound to offer terms** contained in a collective agreement each time a fixed-term contract comes up for renewal, the transferee employer will similarly not be obliged to offer such collectively agreed terms (*Ralton v Havering College of Further and Higher Education* [2001] IRLR 738, EAT). Likewise, where at the date of the transfer of an undertaking from the public to the private sector, transferring employees' contracts of employment provided for their terms and conditions to be in accordance with a national collective agreement which made no provision for any successor agreement to be incorporated into the employees' contracts, it meant that no subsequent collective agreement could be deemed to apply to the employees' terms and conditions without any further reference or incorporation (*Ackinclose and ors v Gateshead Metropolitan Borough Council* [2005] IRLR 79, EAT).

If, however, **terms are incorporated** into the individual employment contracts, they will automatically transfer to the transferee under TUPE (reg 5 SI 1981/1794). A collectively agreed pay agreement, for example, (which has been incorporated into individual contracts) will be binding on the transferee employer even though he is not a party to it, and even where he derecognises the union (*Whent v T Carledge Ltd* [1997] IRLR 153, EAT).

If the transferred undertaking maintains an identity distinct from the rest of the transferee's **7991**
undertaking after the transfer, any **independent trade union recognised** by the transferor is deemed to be recognised by the transferee employer (reg 9 SI 1981/1794). Unlike the transfer of collective agreements, recognition is not restricted to employees who were employed at the date of the transfer, and so will apply to new joiners who are within the scope of the recognition agreement. However, it is open to the transferee to derecognise the union in the same way that the transferor was able to do so (reg 9(2) SI 1981/1794).

Share options and other incentives A transferring employee may hold share options in **7992**
the transferor company/group. If the business is transferred to the transferee, the employee will be leaving the company or group. Case law has indicated that TUPE will not affect any rights under share option schemes where these are separate contracts from the employment contract. Liability in respect of the options will, therefore, not transfer to the transferee (*Chapman & Elkin v CPS Computer Group plc* [1987] IRLR 463, CA).

Although they may technically transfer under TUPE, some **contractual terms** that are specific **7993**
to the transferor employer may be meaningless or difficult to implement after the transfer, such as **bonuses** or **profit-sharing schemes** calculated by reference to profits of the transferor employer's group of companies. A solution may be for the transferee to establish benefits of "substantial equivalence" to the transferor's scheme (*Mitie Managed Services Ltd v French* [2002] IRLR 512, EAT).

Pension rights Pension rights (i.e. rights and liabilities relating to provision of **occupa-** **7995**
tional pension schemes which relate to benefits for old age, invalidity or survivors) generally do not transfer under TUPE (reg 7 SI 1981/1794). The transferring employees are not legally entitled to equivalent pension benefits after the transfer, nor are future pension rights covered by the ARD or TUPE (*Adams v Lancashire County Council* [1997] IRLR 436, CA). There is, therefore, no legal obligation on a transferee to continue to pay premiums previously paid by the transferor to an occupational scheme as part of the employment relationship, nor is he obliged to provide an occupational pension scheme for transferring employees (*Eidesund v Stavanger Catering A/S* [1996] IRLR 684, EFTA).

However, new statutory provisions, under which a **minimum level of pension protection** is provided to employees who have transferred to another employer under TUPE, came into force on 6 April 2005 (ss 257, 258 Pensions Act 2004; Transfer of Employment (Pension Protection) Regulations SI 2005/649). Under the new provisions, a **transferee** employer **must offer, as a condition of employment**, any transferring employee who had an actual or contingent right (i.e. was an active member, eligible to be a member or was in a waiting period before becoming eligible to be a member) in relation to an occupational pension scheme with employer contributions immediately prior to the TUPE transfer, either:

a. membership of a defined benefit (i.e. final salary) occupational pension scheme in relation to which the transferee is the employer which provides for either:

– the value of the benefits to be provided to the member to equal at least 6% of his pensionable pay per year of employment, in addition to any member contributions, and where the member is required to make contributions, for him to contribute at a rate not exceeding 6% of his pensionable pay; or

– the transferee to match member contributions to the scheme up to a maximum of 6% of basic pay; or
b. membership of a money purchase occupational pension scheme in relation to which the transferee is the employer, to which the employer must match member contributions up to a maximum of 6% of basic pay (with either party being able to contribute more at their own discretion); or
c. to match member contributions up to 6% of basic pay to a stakeholder pension scheme of which the employee is, or is eligible to become, a member (with either party being able to contribute more at their own discretion).

MEMO POINTS 1. **Public sector employers** are obliged to protect any pension scheme rights which crystallise at the time of the transfer (i.e. **accrued rights**) (*Walden Engineering Co Ltd v Warrener* [1993] IRLR 420, EAT).
2. The public sector tends to contract out services on the condition that the contractor establishes a **comparable pension scheme** for transferring employees (HM Treasury Guidance Note, June 2004). This scheme often has to be approved by government actuaries as part of the tender process.

7996 Some pension schemes provide for age-related benefits (such as **enhanced redundancy entitlement** or **early retirement benefits** (*Beckmann v Dynamco Whicheloe Macfarlane Ltd* [2002] IRLR 578, ECJ, confirmed by *Martin and ors v South Bank University* [2004] IRLR 74, ECJ) which will fall outside the scope of the pension rights exclusion from TUPE. These entitlements may, therefore, transfer. Also, a transferor's obligation to make contributions to an employee's **personal pension** plan (whether this be an individual arrangement or a group plan) is likely to transfer under TUPE, as it is not within the definition of occupational pension scheme (s 1 Pension Schemes Act 1993).

7997 **TUPE consultation liabilities** Recent case law indicates that liability for failure to consult as required by TUPE (¶8060) will transfer. See ¶8079 for further details.

Expected changes under the new TUPE regulations

7998 The new TUPE regulations expressly refer to **employers' liability compulsory insurance**. The Government believes that the outcome in *Bernadone v Pall Mall Services Group* (¶7986), which applied to transfers between private sector employers, is satisfactory. However, in respect of transfers from public sector employers to private sector employers, there is generally no equivalent insurance cover to transfer (for example, because the public sector employer is not subject to, or is exempted from, the requirement to provide it). The new TUPE regulations therefore provide for the transferor and transferee to be jointly and severally liable to employees for injury or disease arising from pre-transfer employment where the transferor is a public sector employer.

In relation to **pensions**, although the provisions in the new TUPE regulations are broadly the same as those in the existing regulations, the Government has sought to clarify that an employee cannot bring claims against the transferor for breach of contract or constructive unfair dismissal where he has suffered a loss or reduction in relation to his occupational pension entitlement following the transfer.

C. Varying terms and conditions

8010 There may be good commercial/HR reasons for a transferee employer to want to **harmonise the terms** of transferee employees with his existing staff as soon as possible after a transfer. Employees who transfer under TUPE do so on their existing terms and conditions, and it is not possible to contract out of TUPE to avoid this (reg 12 SI 1981/1794).

If the **employment contract** gives the employer the **right to make** minor changes or certain specified variations without consent, the transferee employer can make such changes as fall within the scope of that right (¶1615).

If there is **no existing right** or the proposed change is outside the scope, any changes to contract terms that are made **for a reason connected with the transfer** will be legally ineffective, even if the parties have agreed the variation (*Wilson v St Helens Borough Council* [1998] IRLR 706, HL) and even if the variation is to the employee's advantage (*Foreningen af Arbejdsledere i Danmark v Daddy's Dance Hall A/S* [1988] IRLR 315, ECJ). However, this position will change under the new TUPE regulations (¶8015).

EXAMPLE In connection with transfer

In *Credit Suisse First Boston (Europe) Ltd v Lister* [1998] IRLR 700, CA, L transferred under TUPE to CSFB. As part of the transfer, L agreed to a **new restrictive covenant**, preventing him taking up competing employment in return for a substantial payment and other new terms that were beneficial to him. The Court refused to grant an injunction to enforce the covenant on the grounds that the variation had been agreed in connection with the transfer.

Not in connection with transfer

In *Solectron Scotland Ltd v Roper and others* [2004] IRLR 4, EAT, compromise agreements regarding the financial value of redundancy terms and conditions following a TUPE transfer were not rendered void since they did not purport to vary contractual terms and conditions but instead were being used to settle a financial claim (i.e. the value of a redundancy package).

MEMO POINTS The ECJ has ruled that the ARD does not preclude, in principle, the reduction of an employee's pay by the State where the employee's employment has transferred in accordance with the ARD from a private undertaking to the State in order to harmonise the employee's remuneration with the State's national pay rules, although the employee's length of service should be taken into consideration in determining the employee's new rate of pay (*Boor v Ministre de la Fonction Publique et de la Reforme administrative* [2005] IRLR 61, ECJ). The ECJ did, however, go on to hold that such a reduction in pay will constitute a substantial change in the employee's working conditions to his detriment and, consequently, any termination of the employment contract would be deemed to have resulted from the employer's actions and could give rise to a claim in respect of the dismissal. See also ¶8035.

If the changes are not disadvantageous to the employees, the **pragmatic approach** may be **8011**
to implement the changes with employee consent in the expectation that few, if any, employees will complain.

It is difficult to establish when the **link** between a variation of terms and the transfer will be **8012**
broken (*Taylor v Connex South Eastern Limited*, EAT case 1243/99). It may be on the particular facts that a variation is connected with the transfer even after a year or more has passed. Once the link is broken, a variation can be effected (*Wilson v St Helens Borough Council*), and the normal rules on variation apply (¶1600).

EXAMPLE In *Norris and others v Brown & Root Ealing Technical Services Ltd*, EAT case 386/00, variations to contractual terms (and dismissals) which took place two years after a TUPE transfer were held not to be connected to that TUPE transfer, but rather were the result of serious cash-flow problems facing the transferee during the intervening period.

As a result, in order to ensure that the new terms are legally binding, the employer could **8013**
consider **dismissing and re-engaging** the employees on new terms (*British Fuels Ltd v Baxendale and Meade* [1998] IRLR 706, HL). The **disadvantage** of this course of action is that the dismissals may be automatically unfair if they are for a transfer-connected reason, although the employer may have a defence if the dismissals are for an economic, technical or organisational reason entailing changes in the workforce (¶8041).

To **minimise his liability**, the employer could ask employees to waive any contractual claims and compromise their right to bring an unfair dismissal claim, in return for a payment calculated by reference to the unfair dismissal basic award (¶8575).

If the employee is made aware that, after the transfer, substantial detrimental changes will **8014**
be made to his contractual terms (which will amount to a fundamental breach of his employment contract), he can **object** to the transfer, and bring a **constructive dismissal** claim against the transferor (¶8035).

Expected changes under the new TUPE regulations

8015 It is expected that the new TUPE regulations will **expressly permit** contractual variations made in connection with the transfer to be agreed (see ¶7929 as to how this may be achieved in insolvency situations), where the **sole or principal reason** for the variation is not the transfer but an economic, technical or organisational reason entailing changes in the workforce (an **"ETO"** reason). However, where the sole or principal reason for the variation is the transfer itself or a reason connected with the transfer which is **not an ETO** reason any variation will be void.

Although the potential to vary contractual terms is a key development in light of the commercial difficulties faced by transferee employers (¶8010 +) and is consistent with the provisions regarding the defence for dismissals (¶8041), it **may be difficult for employers to demonstrate** that the reason for the transfer-related variation entails a change in the workforce. Wanting to harmonise the terms of transferring employees with existing employees, for example, may constitute an economic or organisational reason for a variation but it will not necessarily entail a change in the workforce. It is likely that employers will continue to take the commercial and pragmatic approach outlined above.

D. Dismissal

8030 **Protection under TUPE** Where the reason for the dismissal is **unconnected to the transfer**, it will not be automatically unfair, but may still be unfair under the normal rules (¶8380).

Where the transfer or a **reason connected** with it is the reason or principal reason for the dismissal, the dismissal will be effective (whether before, on or after the transfer) but will be automatically unfair (reg 8(1) SI 1981/1794). This protection applies to both transferring and non-transferring employees of the transferor, and existing employees of the transferee (reg 8(3) SI 1981/1794). In contrast to other automatically unfair dismissals, the employee must still satisfy the qualifying period (¶8411) in order to bring a claim. Whether the dismissal is by reason of the transfer is a question of fact for the tribunal to determine in all the circumstances.

If the employee is **dismissed prior to the transfer**, the transferee is not obliged to employ him (*Wilson v St Helens Borough Council* [1998] IRLR 706, HL).

8032 **Connection to transfer** To be connected to the transfer, it is not necessary for the transferor to have had in mind a specific transferee at the time of the dismissal, and it is enough that a **possible transfer** was the reason for the dismissal (*Morris v John Grose Group Ltd* [1998] IRLR 499, EAT), although it must be more than "a mere twinkle in the eye" (*Ibex Trading Co Ltd v Walton* [1994] IRLR 564, EAT).

8033 There is no hard and fast rule as to **when the link** between a dismissal and the transfer will be **broken**. A dismissal which took place nearly two years after the transfer has been held to be connected with it, partly because there had been ongoing negotiations throughout that period in relation to changes to the employee's terms and conditions (which he had resisted and which eventually led to his dismissal) (*Taylor v Connex South Eastern Limited*, EAT case 1243/99). Conversely, dismissals which took place two years after a TUPE transfer have been held to be unconnected with the transfer on the basis that they were caused by serious cash-flow problems facing the transferee in the intervening two-year period (*Norris and ors v Brown & Root Ealing Technical Services Ltd*, EAT case 386/00).

8035 **Constructive dismissal** The dismissal may be actual (by the transferee or the transferor), or constructive. The latter may arise where the transferee proposes to implement measures involving **substantial detrimental changes** to the employee's contractual terms which have resulted in a fundamental breach of the employee's contract (reg 5(5) SI 1981/1794; *University of*

Oxford v (1) Humphreys (2) Associated Examining Board [2000] IRLR 183, CA). However, it is essential that such a fundamental breach is established (*Rossiter v Pendragon plc*; *Air Foyle Ltd v Crosby-Clarke* [2002] IRLR 483, CA).

In some cases, if the **change in identity of the employer** is significant and detrimental to the employee, a constructive dismissal claim can be brought although no other terms and conditions are changed (reg 5(5) SI 1981/1794). For example, the transferee employer may have a bad record in relation to health and safety matters or industrial relations, or may have environmental or other policies that conflict with the interests or beliefs of a particular employee (see ¶8048 for the position under the new TUPE provisions).

The dismissal will be automatically unfair as connected with the transfer, although there may be a defence to any such claim if there are changes in the number or composition of the workforce (¶8042).

Liability The liability for dismissal of transferring employees will transfer to the **transferee** so that he becomes liable for both **pre- and post-transfer dismissals** (unless there is an ETO defence – ¶8041), as TUPE applies to employees employed in the undertaking immediately before the transfer and also extends to those employees who would have been so employed if they had not been unfairly dismissed for a reason connected with the transfer (¶7958). The transferee may, therefore, wish to seek appropriate indemnities from the transferor for pre-transfer dismissals. 8037

MEMO POINTS The transferee is not liable for the dismissals of employees who are not employed in the undertaking or part transferred, even though such dismissals may be automatically unfair under TUPE.

If the employee claims **constructive dismissal without first objecting** to the transfer, he will be treated as having been constructively dismissed for a reason connected with the transfer, and liability will pass to the transferee (reg 8(1) SI 1981/1794; *Euro-Die (UK) Ltd v (1) Skidmore (2) Genesis Diesinking Ltd*, EAT case 1158/98). 8038

However, if the employee also **objects to the transfer and is constructively dismissed** as a result of substantial changes proposed by the transferee, the **transferor** will be liable for the dismissal (despite the principle established in the *Litster v Forth Dry Dock & Engineering Co Ltd* case (¶7958), although this did not deal with objection to the transfer), and may wish to obtain an indemnity from the transferee (*University of Oxford v (1) Humphreys (2) Associated Examining Board*). In such cases, there will be no automatic unfair dismissal, but the employee may be able to bring a wrongful dismissal claim and a claim of unfair dismissal under the normal rules.

A **compromise agreement** between the employee and the transferor reached after the transfer date (perhaps because the parties had assumed that TUPE did not apply) cannot be relied on by the transferee to block an unfair dismissal claim against him (*Thompson v Walon Car Delivery* [1997] IRLR 343, EAT). 8039

Defence The employer may have a defence to an unfair dismissal claim if he can show that, although the **transfer was "a" reason** for the dismissal (in the sense that it was the occasion for it), the reason or **principal reason** was in fact an **ETO reason**, such as genuine redundancy or business reorganisation (reg 8(2) SI 1981/1794) (see ¶8049 for the position under the new TUPE regulations). Despite case law to the contrary (*Kerry Foods Ltd v Creber*, below), it seems that it is not open to an employee to argue that the employer is precluded from relying on an ETO defence where the dismissal is in connection with the transfer (*Collins v John Ansell & Partners Ltd*, EAT case 124/99). 8041

The reason must entail **changes in the workforce**, which means that the structure of the workforce must be changed, either by a reduction in the number of employees, or a change in job functions (*Crawford v Swinton Insurance Brokers Ltd* [1990] IRLR 42, EAT). The ETO reason will, therefore, not apply where employees are dismissed (or resign and claim constructive dismissal) for refusing to accept a variation to their existing terms and conditions (even where a change in numbers or composition may be a possible consequence of that variation) (*Berriman v Delabole Slate Ltd* [1985] IRLR 305, CA). 8042

8043 The ETO reason can be that of the transferor or the transferee (*Jules Dethier Equipment SA v Dassy* [1998] IRLR 266, ECJ).

If the **transferor dismisses** the employee and the main reason for the dismissal is an ETO reason, the employee will not be deemed to have been employed immediately before the transfer, and liability for his dismissal (for example, in relation to unfair dismissal procedure) will not transfer to the transferee (*Kerry Foods Ltd v Creber* [2000] IRLR 10, EAT). If the transferor cannot show an ETO defence, the dismissal will be automatically unfair and liability will transfer to the transferee (*Kerry Foods Ltd v Creber*).

It is unlikely that the transferor can rely on the ETO defence where he dismisses employees at the transferee's request to achieve a sale or in order to make the business more attractive, as the ETO reason must relate to the conduct of the business (with which the transferor will no longer be involved) (*Wheeler v (1) Patel (2) J Golding Group of Companies* [1987] IRLR 211, EAT; followed in *Ibex Trading Co Ltd v Walton*). The ETO defence may be available where **receivers of an insolvent transferor** dismiss at the request of the transferee in circumstances where all employees would have been dismissed had the transferee not agreed to take over the business (*Thompson v SCS Consulting Ltd* [2001] IRLR 801, EAT).

If the transferor can establish the ETO reason, he must also **act reasonably** in all the circumstances, which is likely to require him to consult and consider alternative employment, and possibly to satisfy himself that the transferee's reason for the dismissal is genuine. Given that the liability will rest with the transferor, he may be reluctant to implement dismissals at the transferee's request without obtaining appropriate **indemnities**.

If the transferor can dismiss in circumstances where an ETO defence is available, the transferee benefits from the fact that there are **separate pools for redundancy selection** purposes. If the transferee were to effect the dismissals, he may have to include his existing staff in the selection pool.

If the transferor gives notice of termination before the transfer which expires after the transfer, a tribunal would consider the transferor's reasons when determining the fairness of the dismissal (although liability for the dismissal will transfer to the transferee) (*BSG Property Services v Tuck* [1996] IRLR 134, EAT).

8044 If the **transferee dismisses** the employee, he will be liable for the dismissal, but may invoke the ETO defence. It is likely to be easier for him to rely on this defence, as he will be involved in the future conduct of the business. This defence may be available even where he dismisses as a condition of a contract for the provision of services being awarded to him by the transferor in order to reduce on-going staffing costs (*Whitehouse v Chas A Blatchford & Sons Ltd* [1999] IRLR 492, CA).

8045 If this defence is established, the employer will have made out one of the five statutory **fair reasons for dismissal**, namely "some other substantial reason" (¶8530) (although see ¶8049 for the position under the new TUPE regulations). To avoid liability, he will also have to show that he acted reasonably in all the circumstances in treating that reason as a fair reason for dismissal (¶8435). This may require the employer to consider alternatives to dismissal, and to consult with the employee.

8047 **Redundancy payment** The employee may be entitled to a redundancy payment if he is dismissed by the transferor prior to the transfer because he is about to go out of business in the place where the employee was employed or no longer requires work of the particular kind done by the employee, or if the transferee subsequently dismisses for these reasons (which may include in circumstances where the ETO defence applies (*Gorictree Ltd v Jenkinson* [1984] IRLR 391, EAT)).

Expected changes under the new TUPE regulations

8048 The Government has attempted to clarify the position where detrimental changes are made to an employee's terms and conditions (¶8035). Where a transfer involves a **substantial change in working conditions** which are to the detriment of a transferring employee, the employment contract will be treated as having been terminated and the employee treated as having been dismissed with notice. The new TUPE regulations separate this provision from the employee's right to resign and claim constructive dismissal where there is a repudiatory breach of contract by the employer, as a substantial change in working conditions may not be sufficient to amount to repudiatory breach. There is no equivalent provision under the new regulations referring to the effect of the change in identity of the employer (reg 5(5) SI 1981/1794; ¶8035).

In relation to the employer's **defence** for dismissal (¶8041), where the **sole or principal reason** for the dismissal is: 8049
– the transfer itself or a reason connected with the transfer that is **not an ETO reason**, the dismissal will be automatically unfair;
– not the transfer itself but a reason connected with it which **is an ETO reason**, the dismissal will be potentially fair and subject to the normal test of reasonableness. The dismissal will be regarded as having been for either **redundancy** (entitling the employee to claim a redundancy payment) if the appropriate test of redundancy is met (¶8730 +), or for **some other substantial reason** (¶8530).

SECTION 3

Information and consultation obligations

TUPE imposes a duty on employers to inform and consult with the appropriate representatives of employees who are affected by the transfer of an undertaking (reg 10 SI 1981/1794). Many of the requirements in relation to appropriate representatives, elections, protections and failure to comply are as for collective redundancy consultation, and reference will be made to those sections as appropriate. 8060

MEMO POINTS Consultation requirements are also imposed by the EU **Information and Consultation Directive**, which requires employers to consult employees before taking important business decisions, particularly where these affect employee rights. The Directive will be implemented in stages, depending on the size of the employer's organisation. The first stage, for employers with more than 150 employees, was implemented on 6 April 2005 (see Chapter 22).

Affected employees These are broadly defined as any employees of the transferor or the transferee who may be affected by the transfer or by measures taken in connection with it (reg 10(1) SI 1981/1794), and not just transferring employees. For example, an employee who remains with the transferor may be affected in that his job duties may change after the transfer, or he may be faced with redundancy. Similarly, the transferee's existing employees may be affected by measures after the transfer. 8061

Appropriate representatives The employer must inform and consult the affected employees' appropriate representatives (reg 11(A) SI 1981/1794). For further detail see ¶8925, where references to election/appointment for the purposes of redundancy consultation should be read as references to election/appointment for the purposes of TUPE information/consultation. 8062

Candidates and employee representatives have **rights** to paid time off, to access and facilities, and to receive relevant training. They also have the right not to suffer any detriment or be unfairly dismissed. Further detail is provided at ¶¶3910, 8380. 8063

Election requirements

The requirements for the election of representatives (and **replacement representatives**) for the purposes of TUPE information and consultation (reg 10A SI 1981/1794) are as for collective redundancies (¶8928), as are the consequences of **failure to elect** representatives within a reasonable time (reg 10(8A) SI 1981/1794) (¶8930). Where a transferor has no recognised union 8065 and there are **no elected employee representatives** (for example, as the result of a failure to elect them), the transferor is nevertheless obliged to invite "affected employees" to elect employee representatives for the purposes of TUPE and, should they fail to do so, the transferor is obliged to inform and consult all affected employees on an individual basis about the matters relating to the transfer prescribed by the regulations (*Howard v Millrise Ltd (t/a Colourflow) (in liquidation) and anor* [2005] IRLR 84, EAT).

Duty to inform

8067 The employer (i.e. the transferor in respect of his employees and the transferee in respect of his own staff) must inform the appropriate representatives of the **following** (reg 10(2) SI 1981/1794):
– the **fact** that a transfer is to take place (and **when**, approximately), and the **reason** for it (but he is not obliged to justify the transfer or discuss its merits);
– the legal, economic and social **implications** of the transfer for the affected employees, which may include an explanation of the legal effect in relation to employment contracts, collective agreements and statutory rights, the impact on pay and benefits, and any relocation plans; and
– the **measures** which he envisages he will take, in connection with the transfer, in relation to the affected employees (or, if no measures are envisaged, confirmation of that fact). If the employer is the transferor, any measures which the transferee envisages he will take in connection with the transfer, in relation to the transferring employees (or, if no measures are envisaged, confirmation of that fact). The transferee is obliged to provide the transferor with such information as will allow him to comply with this obligation (see ¶8074 for consequences of the transferee's failure to comply).

MEMO POINTS "**Measures**" are not defined, but are widely construed to include any action, step or arrangement amounting to a definite plan or proposal that the employer intends to implement, for example redundancies, relocation, changes to working practices, and effects on pensions and other benefits. Mere possibilities or hopes are excluded (*Institution of Professional Civil Servants v Secretary of State for Defence* [1987] IRLR 373, HC).

8068 A transferor is obliged to **take reasonable care** in providing information in a transfer situation (for example, in relation to pension rights following the transfer), or he may face a claim for breach of contract (¶1700) and/or negligent misstatement (*Hagen and ors v ICI Chemicals & Polymers Ltd* [2002] IRLR 31, QBD), as may a transferee in relation to information provided by him. However, liability for negligent misstatement will only arise where:
– a duty of care owed by the employer to the employees is breached (i.e. because the representations are false and could not have been made by someone exercising reasonable care);
– the employees reasonably relied on the representations and suffered loss as a result; and
– the loss is of a kind falling within the scope of the duty.

In most cases, it will be difficult to establish consequential loss, as most employees are not in a position to prevent a transfer going ahead or to secure more favourable terms (in the *Hagen and ors v ICI Chemicals & Polymers Ltd* case, it was accepted that had the transferring employees not been satisfied about the terms on offer, they would have sought, as a body, to resist the transfer and their resistance, in all likelihood, would have been successful and a more favourable arrangement negotiated between the transferor and transferee).

8069 **Procedure** The information to be provided must be given to the appropriate representatives directly, or sent to them **by post** to an address notified by them to the employer or, in the case of trade union representatives, to the union's head or main office (reg 10(4) SI 1981/1794). This requirement indicates that the information should be provided **in writing**. It is then up to the representatives to convey the information to the affected employees, which they may do by holding meetings in the workplace or by way of written information.

Duty to consult

8071 The duty to consult the appropriate representatives only arises where an employer envisages he will be taking measures (¶8067) in relation to the affected employees (reg 10(5) SI 1981/1794).

This means that the **transferor** is not obliged to consult if he is not envisaging taking any measures, nor is he obliged to consult in relation to measures envisaged by the transferee. The **transferee** is not obliged to consult with transferring employees prior to the transfer, as he is not yet their employer.

If consultation is required, it should take place "with a view to seeking their agreement to measures to be taken", and employers are expressly required to consider any representations made by the appropriate representatives, and to reply to those representations, giving reasons for any rejection of them (reg 10(6) SI 1981/1794). The employer must, therefore, give proper and genuine consideration to the views of the appropriate representatives, and allow them to canvass the opinions and suggestions of the affected employees.

Timing

Whether or not the employer is actually obliged to consult, the required information must be provided "long enough" before the transfer to enable consultation with the appropriate representatives to take place. The **duty is triggered** where there is a proposed or planned transfer, even if it does not eventually take place (*Banking Insurance and Finance Union v Barclays Bank plc* [1987] IRLR 495, EAT). The timing will, therefore, depend on the number of employees, their location, and the complexity of the transaction. If appropriate representatives already exist, a period of between 2 to 4 weeks may be appropriate. If representatives need to be elected, a longer period will be needed. **8073**

If the **employer is also obliged to consult**, this process should ideally start before the transfer agreement is signed, so that he can respond in a meaningful way to any representations raised. If it is not, the employer may have failed to comply with his consultation obligations. However, where the transfer is commercially sensitive, reasons of secrecy may outweigh potential liability for failure to fully inform and consult (although note that such reasons are unlikely to offer a defence).

Failure to comply/infringement of rights

Complaints may be brought to an employment tribunal for failure to **inform and consult** or to comply with **election requirements** as for collective redundancy consultation (reg 11(1) SI 1981/1794) (¶8946). **8074**

As for collective redundancy consultation, if a question arises as to whether or not a particular employee representative was an appropriate representative, it is for the employer to show that the **representative had the necessary authority** to represent the affected employees (reg 11(2A) SI 1981/1794). If necessary, he must also show that the requirements regarding elections have been satisfied (reg 11(2B) SI 1981/1794). **8075**

Defence As for collective redundancy consultation, **special circumstances** may be a defence for failure to consult in a TUPE case (¶8950) (reg 10(7) SI 1981/1794). Again, concerns about **confidentiality** or the **mere appointment of a receiver or administrator** will not provide a defence. **8076**

If the **transferee does not provide** the transferor with **information** on measures he envisages taking, the transferor may have a defence to any complaint that he has failed to fulfil his obligations on the basis that it was not reasonably practicable for him to do so (obviously he must have chased the transferee for that information). If the transferor wishes to rely on this defence, he must give the transferee notice of that intention, in which case the transferee becomes a party to the proceedings (reg 11(3) SI 1981/1794). **8077**

Remedies If the tribunal finds that the **employer** has failed to comply with **any of his obligations**, it can make a **declaration** to that effect and order him to pay appropriate **compensation** to the affected employees in respect of whom the complaint was brought (reg 11(4) SI 1981/1794). The **amount** will be such sum as the tribunal considers just and equitable having regard to the seriousness of the employer's failure to comply, subject to a maximum of 13 weeks' pay (uncapped) (reg 11(11) SI 1981/1794). **8078**

If the **transferee** has failed to provide information on measures to the transferor, the tribunal can order the transferee to pay appropriate compensation.

8079 It now seems that **liability to pay** compensation for **failure to inform and consult** will transfer to the transferee, even if the failure to consult is not his fault (*Alamo Group (Europe) Ltd v Tucker* [2003] IRLR 266, EAT, affirming *Kerry Foods Ltd v Creber* [2000] IRLR 10, EAT, cf. *Transport & General Workers' Union v James McKinnon, JR (Haulage) Ltd* [2001] IRLR 597, EAT). This is on the basis that the duty to consult arises from the individual contracts of employment which transfer automatically under TUPE.

MEMO POINTS In cases involving both collective redundancies and a TUPE transfer, a separate award for failure to consult may be made in relation to each, with no provision for one to be offset against the other.

8080 **Protection for voters, candidates and employee representatives** It is automatically unfair (¶8390) for an employer to **dismiss** any employee wholly or mainly because (s 103 ERA 1996):
– they have participated in the election either as a candidate or voters; or
– of their status or activities as union representatives or elected representatives.

It is also unlawful for an employer to victimise any such employee by subjecting him to a **detriment** short of dismissal by any act, or any deliberate failure to act, on those grounds (ss 47, 47(1A) ERA 1996).

Expected changes under the new TUPE regulations

8081 The provisions under the new TUPE regulations are broadly the same as those under the existing regulations, with a few key changes.

In respect of the failure to inform and consult, the transferor and transferee will be **jointly and severally liable** for any award of compensation made for the failure to comply with information and consultation requirements and therefore employees may bring proceedings against either the transferor or the transferee or, as is more likely, both. If liability passes wholly to the transferee, there is no incentive on the transferor to comply with the requirement so this provision is a commercial solution.

8082 Under the new regulations, the transferor will also be required to notify the transferee of **employee liability information**, namely all the information which is or ought to be known to the transferor as to his rights, powers, duties and liabilities under or in connection with any contract of employment of any employee who will be transferred. The transferor must also notify the transferee of any change in the employee liability information. The notification must be given **in good time** before the relevant transfer, no later than its completion and can be given indirectly through a third party.

A transferee may apply to the High Court (or Court of Session in Scotland) if the transferor has failed to comply with these obligations. If the High Court considers the claim well-founded, it may require the transferor to pay a **penalty** of up to £75,000 to the transferee.

CHAPTER 25

Ending employment

OUTLINE ¶¶

The **three main ways** an employment relationship can come to an end (termination by the employer, termination by the employee and termination by mutual agreement) are set out below. Termination may be with or without notice. 8100

In addition, the contract may automatically terminate in certain circumstances, such as where it is "frustrated" by the employee's long-term absence.

When **terminating** the employment of an employee, the employer must do so in accordance with the terms of the contract (for example, in relation to notice periods) or he will be liable for breach of contract (¶1700). 8101

In addition, all employees (and to a certain extent, some workers) also enjoy **statutory protection** on dismissal. If the dismissal is discriminatory, the employee may bring a claim of discrimination on the grounds of sex, racial group, disability, religion or belief, sexual orientation, or age (which is expected to come into force from 1 October 2006, see ¶5254+). If an employee is dismissed for an inadmissible reason, he can bring an unfair dismissal claim (with, generally, no requirement for qualifying service). In such cases, the dismissal will be automatically unfair. Dismissals to which the business transfer regulations apply are also automatically unfair and special rules apply (¶8030).

Employees with sufficient qualifying service can bring an unfair dismissal claim under the general scheme (¶8410).

Redundancy is a fair reason for dismissal unless: 8102
- there is no genuine redundancy situation;
- it is automatically unfair (for example, if the reason for dismissal is the employee's pregnancy); or
- the employer failed to act fairly in all the circumstances. This includes a requirement for individual consultation. In cases of collective redundancies, an employer is also required to consult with trade union or employee representatives and to notify the DTI.

An employee under notice of dismissal for redundancy has a statutory right to **time off work** to seek new employment or to make arrangements for retraining, and on dismissal may be entitled to a **statutory redundancy payment**. Employees may also benefit from contractual provisions relating to redundancy pay and procedures.

Employees have specific rights and protections if their **employer is insolvent**, including: 8103
- a right to apply to the DTI for certain state guaranteed payments;
- a right to be preferential creditors in respect of certain debts; and
- rights against an administrator in respect of amounts arising during the period of administration (or in rare cases administrative receivership).

SECTION 1

Termination of employment

There are three main ways an employment relationship can come to an end: termination by the employer (known as **dismissal**), termination by the employee (known as **resignation**), and termination by **mutual agreement**. Termination may be with or without notice. The contract may **automatically terminate** in certain circumstances, such as where it is "frustrated" by the employee's long-term absence. 8105

Extended meaning of dismissal To **bring a claim** of unfair dismissal or for a redundancy payment, the employee must show that he has been dismissed. The meaning of dismissal is extended by statute for these purposes to include: 8106
- the **expiry of a fixed-term contract** without its renewal (¶1996) or the termination of a contract for a **specific purpose**/terminable on the occurrence of a specified event;

– **constructive dismissal** (where the employee resigns in response to the employer's fundamental breach of contract) (ss 95(1)(c), 136(1)(c) ERA 1996) (except in redundancy cases, when the fundamental breach is a **lock-out** and the employee resigns without notice (s 136(2) ERA 1996)); and
– the resignation of the employee during the employer notice period under a special statutory procedure whereby he gives a **counter-notice** (for redundancy purposes only, this must be given during the "obligatory period") (ss 95(2), 142 ERA 1996) (¶9000).

For redundancy purposes, dismissal also includes the following:
– **voluntary redundancy** (in contrast to consensual termination/early retirement) (*Burton, Allton & Johnson Ltd v R R V Peck* [1975] IRLR 87, QBD; *Cole v London Borough of Hackney*, EAT case 973/99);
– termination by **operation of law** (¶8270) as a result of an act of the employer or an event affecting him (for example, death of an individual employer, frustration of the contract at common law, the dissolution of a partnership, the appointment of some receivers and some forms of winding up (s 136(5) ERA 1996; *British Airport Authority v Fenerty* [1976] ICR 361, EAT; *Pickwell v Lincolnshire County Council* [1993] ICR 87, EAT); and
– special cases where the employment is terminated **by statute** (for example, transfers from one statutory body to another) (s 172 ERA 1996).

A deemed dismissal may also occur in some cases of **variation**, where the changes are so significant that a court finds that the old employment has in fact been terminated and replaced by a new contract (¶1652).

When an employee reaches the applicable **retirement** age, the employment will terminate and this is also treated as a dismissal (technically it is the expiry without renewal of a fixed-term contract), but voluntary early retirement is not – see below.

8107 **No dismissal** There is no dismissal in the following cases:
– termination by **mutual agreement**. An employee who agrees to take **early retirement** will not, therefore, be dismissed (*Birch and Humber v The University of Liverpool* [1985] IRLR 165, CA; *Scott v Coalite Fuels and Chemicals Ltd* [1988] IRLR 131, EAT). If, however, an employee is given notice of redundancy and subsequently agrees to take early retirement, he will still be considered to have been dismissed for redundancy unless the employee agrees to the notice of redundancy being withdrawn (*Gateshead Metropolitan Borough Council v Mills*, EAT case 610/92);
– **resignation** (unless the circumstances give rise to a constructive dismissal or the employee has been forced to resign); and
– termination by **frustration** or **supervening events** (but note the extended meaning of dismissal for redundancy purposes in certain cases of termination by operation of law above).

In certain circumstances, an employee will be deemed not to have been dismissed where he is **subsequently re-engaged** (¶8850).

There is no dismissal when employees transfer automatically from one employer to another under the **business transfer** regulations (¶7950).

8108 How the employment ends affects whether an employee can bring a claim and the type of claim he may bring. To help him decide whether he may have a claim against the employer, certain employees are entitled to a **statement of the reasons** for dismissal. To avoid **liability for breach of contract**, the employer must comply with the terms of the contract (in relation to notice and any applicable termination procedures). To avoid statutory liability for **unfair dismissal**, he must have a fair reason for dismissal and follow a fair procedure. The employee may, depending on the circumstances, be entitled to a contractual and/or statutory **redundancy payment**. The dismissal may also be **discriminatory**, giving rise to a separate claim of sex, race, religion or belief, sexual orientation, disability or age discrimination (which is expected to come into force from 1 October 2006), which is discussed further in Chapter 16.

MEMO POINTS **Compulsory dispute resolution procedures**, including a statutory dismissal and disciplinary procedure, came into force on 1 October 2004. Such procedures have changed how dismissals can be carried out in the workplace. See ¶6500 for further details on the statutory procedures and ¶8435 regarding the new rules relating to procedurally unfair dismissals.

In some cases, the employer and employee may **negotiate the termination** of employment, which commonly involves the payment of a lump sum in return for a waiver of the employee's rights against the employer. This is discussed at ¶9259. The employee's **contract** of employment can deal with a number of issues arising on termination, such as notice requirements, post-termination restraints, return of company property and, in the case of directors, resignation of directorships. 8109

One particularly important issue on termination is the provision of **references**. For the employee, this may be crucial to his securing new employment. From the employer's point of view, he may incur liability, both to the employee and the recipient of any reference provided by him.

It is important to identify the **date of termination** for various reasons, including assessing continuous employment (in order to assess qualifying service periods and the amount of redundancy payments and unfair dismissal awards) and complying with time limits for tribunal claims. This date will depend on the form of termination and, for some purposes, it is postponed. These issues are discussed at ¶8340. 8110

Discrimination

It is unlawful for an employer to discriminate against a person on the grounds of sex, race, disability, religion or belief, sexual orientation or age (which is expected to come into force from 1 October 2006) by dismissing him (s 6(2) SDA 1975; s 4(2) RRA 1976; s 4(2) DDA 1995; reg 3 SI 2003/1660; reg 3 SI 2003/1661). See Chapter 16 for a detailed discussion of discrimination. 8111

Generally speaking, a dismissal which is unlawfully discriminatory is also likely to be unfair (¶8380). However, the statutory provisions are not the same and do not necessarily lead to the same result. It should be noted that there is **no qualifying service requirement** for bringing a claim in respect of a discriminatory dismissal. Further, for the claim to succeed, the individual only has to show that the prohibited ground was a significant reason for the dismissal – not that it was the only one. However, it is not enough merely to show that the employer was acting unreasonably in the unfair dismissal sense (*Glasgow City Council v Zafar* [1998] ICR, HL).

It should be noted that discrimination may also amount to constructive dismissal under discrimination laws (¶8249).

I. Forms of termination

The various forms of termination are discussed below. In some cases, it may not be clear whether the employment has in fact ended (for example, because of ambiguity as to words used or as to a party's true intentions, or where a party attempts to withdraw his words). 8115

Identifying a termination

There may be a dispute as to whether the employer (or employee) has in fact terminated the employment where the **actions or words used are ambiguous**. The tribunal or court will take an objective view and consider how those words or actions would have been understood by a reasonable employee (or employer) in the circumstances (including preceding and subsequent events and the nature of the workplace) (*B G Gale Ltd v Gilbert* [1978] IRLR 453, EAT). Further, the general principle of construction applies so that any ambiguity is construed against the party seeking to rely on it (*Graham Group plc v Garratt*, EAT case 161/97). 8116

If the **words are clear**, the employer (or employee) cannot later state that he did not intend them to have that meaning, unless special circumstances apply (such as words spoken in the heat of the moment, where the other party ought to know they are not meant to be taken seriously or where the employee is mentally impaired) (*Sothern v Franks Charlesly & Co* [1981] IRLR 278, CA; *Sovereign House Security Services Ltd v Savage* [1989] IRLR 115, CA; *Kwik-Fit (GB) Ltd v Lineham*

[1992] IRLR 156, EAT). Where such circumstances apply, the employer (or employee) would be advised to investigate the other party's **true intentions**.

8117 In general, words of dismissal or resignation cannot **unilaterally** be **withdrawn** once they have been communicated to the other party. However, it has been held that, as a matter of good employment relations, an employer should be able to withdraw words of dismissal if he does so almost immediately (*Martin v Yeoman Aggregates Ltd* [1983] IRLR 49, EAT). Notice of termination by either party can, of course, be withdrawn **by mutual consent**.

Once notice of termination has been given, it is still open to the employer (or employee as the case may be) to terminate immediately during the notice period if the employee (or employer) is in **fundamental breach** (*Ford v Milthorn Toleman Ltd* [1980] IRLR 30, CA).

A. Dismissal with notice

8120 **Statute** implies a minimum notice period into every contract terminable on notice. However, there may also be an **express or implied contractual term**. It is advisable (but not a legal requirement) that notice of termination is in writing. Even if the employer gives the requisite notice, the dismissal may still be **unfair**.

The employee is entitled to the longer of the contractual notice and the statutory minimum notice.

EXAMPLE 1. Employee A has been employed for 2 years and his contractual notice is 1 month. He is entitled to the contractual notice as it is longer than the statutory minimum (which is 2 weeks – see ¶8131 below).

2. Employee B has been employed for 8 years and his contractual notice is 1 month. He is entitled to the statutory minimum notice of 8 weeks (see ¶8131 below), as it is longer than the contractual period.

1. Notice periods

8123 To be valid, notice of termination must include the **date of termination** (or information from which it can be ascertained) (*Morton Sundour Fabrics Ltd v Shaw* [1967] ITR 84, DivCt) and be unequivocal. It is not sufficient for an employer to notify the employee that his employment will terminate if he does or does not perform a specified act since such notice could, in theory, be unilaterally withdrawn (*Rai v Somerfield Stores Ltd* [2004] IRLR 124, EAT). Similarly, a warning that the employment will end on or after a certain date does not constitute a valid notice of dismissal (*Doble v Firestone Tyre and Rubber Co Ltd* [1981] IRLR 300, EAT).

EXAMPLE In *Doble v Firestone Tyre and Rubber Co Ltd*, the employer's announcement that the plant at which D worked would close by a certain date did not amount to a notice of dismissal as the date of termination could not be ascertained with precision from that announcement (which further stated that notice of dismissal would be sent out to individual employees as appropriate).

8124 The date of termination may be **brought forward or postponed** by mutual agreement (*Mowlem Northern Ltd v Watson* [1990] IRLR 500, EAT). If the employee wants to leave before expiry of the employer's notice period, he may still be treated as having been dismissed if the employer so agrees or if he serves a statutory **counter-notice**. For unfair dismissal purposes, there are no formal requirements for such a notice (it need not be in writing or be equivalent to the statutory minimum or contractual notice). For redundancy purposes, specific requirements must be met (¶8340). The implications on the date of termination are discussed at ¶9000.

8125 Unless the contract states otherwise, notice can be given on any day and, where given **orally**, runs from the start of the next day (*West v Kneels Ltd* [1986] IRLR 430, EAT).

Where notice is given **in writing**, it appears that the notice period will not run until it is reasonable to expect the employee to have read it. It also appears that notice can run from the day the employee reads it (as opposed to the start of the next day (*West v Kneels Ltd*, above)).

Contractual notice

There is often an **express term** in the contract stating the period of notice required of the employer and the employee to terminate the employment. The following sample wording is taken from the model contract of employment for general staff (¶9910). 8126

EXAMPLE If you wish to terminate your employment, you must give [employer] [1 week's] prior written notice. Subject to [employer's] right to terminate without notice [or payment in lieu of notice] in cases of gross misconduct, if [employer] wishes to terminate your employment, you will be given 1 week's notice during your first 2 years of employment and then an additional week's notice for each additional complete year of service up to a maximum of 12 weeks' notice. [*cross refer to notice period during probation, if different*]

This term must be notified to the employee in writing as part of the obligation to give **written particulars** (¶1405). 8127
It is also advisable for the contract to require written notice of termination. If it does, oral notice may be ineffective.

The contract may specify a different period of notice in respect of any **probationary period** (see sample wording from the model contract of employment for general staff (¶9910)). 8128

EXAMPLE During the probationary period, your employment may be terminated by [employer] or by you giving [*notice period during probation, if different from general position*]. On successful completion of the probationary period, the provisions of clause [*general notice provisions*] will apply in respect of the termination of your employment.

If there is no express term, there is an **implied term** that the employment may be terminated on **reasonable notice**. Determining what is reasonable is a mixed question of law and fact, and will depend on all the circumstances of the case, including the level/grade and remuneration of the employee, his age, length of service, and the usual practice in that trade or industry. Broad guidelines are given in the following table: 8129

Employee	Reasonable notice
Manual workers	Between 2 and 4 weeks' notice
Skilled/managerial staff	3 months
Senior management/director level	Between 3 and 12 months

EXAMPLE In *Clarke v Fahrenheit 451 (Communications) Ltd*, EAT case 591/99, C, an equity director in a new company, was given 1 month's notice of dismissal after 3 months' service. The EAT held, taking into account the modest nature of the business, and C's length of service, status and seniority, that 3 months' notice would have been reasonable in the circumstances.

Statutory minimum notice

Unless he falls within one of the exceptions detailed below, after he has been continuously employed for 1 month, an **employee is entitled to receive** 1 week's notice (s 86(1) ERA 1996). Once he has been employed for 2 years or more, he is entitled to 1 week's notice for each complete year of continuous employment up to a maximum of 12 weeks' notice as set out in the following table. 8131

Length of continuous employment	Employee's notice entitlement
1 month up to 2 years	1 week
2 years	2 weeks
3 years	3 weeks
4 years	4 weeks
5 years	5 weeks
6 years	6 weeks
7 years	7 weeks

Length of continuous employment	Employee's notice entitlement
8 years	8 weeks
9 years	9 weeks
10 years	10 weeks
11 years	11 weeks
12 years and above	12 weeks

8132 An employee is also obliged to give statutory minimum notice (or the contractual notice, where greater) (¶8181).

8133 **Exclusions** Employees employed for a **specific purpose** not expected to last for more than 3 months who have actually worked for less than 3 months are excluded (s 86(5) ERA 1996), as are most employees on **fixed-term contracts** not terminable by notice. However, an employee on a fixed-term contract of 1 month or less who has been continuously employed for 3 months or more is entitled to statutory minimum notice as though he has a contract for an indefinite period (s 86(4) ERA 1996). Further, if a fixed-term contract is terminable by notice before its expiry, the statutory minimum notice provisions apply to any early termination. An **apprenticeship** normally terminates on its completion without any requirement for notice. If, however, it is terminated prior to its completion, the statutory minimum notice requirements will apply.

8134 **Waiver of rights** An employee **cannot contract out** in advance of his right to statutory minimum notice (s 203 ERA 1996). He can, however, waive his right to notice on a particular occasion (including the right to payment in respect of that notice), or accept pay in lieu of notice (see below) (s 86(3) ERA 1996; *Trotter v Forth Ports Authority* [1991] IRLR 419, CS).

8135 **Specific right to payment** Employees who work out their notice under normal working conditions will be paid according to their contract.

However, in certain circumstances an employee who **does not work** for all or part of the statutory minimum notice period is entitled to be paid a minimum wage where the employment is **terminated by notice** (given by the employer or employee), unless the contractual notice to be given by the employer exceeds the statutory minimum by 1 week or more (s 87(4) ERA 1996). This right does not arise if the employment is terminated without notice.

The right **applies** where the employee is:
– ready and willing to work but no work is provided for him;
– incapable of work because of sickness or injury (even where sick pay rights have been exhausted by date of dismissal);
– absent from work wholly or partly because of pregnancy, childbirth, or adoption, or on parental leave; or
– taking holiday in accordance with his contract.

EXAMPLE Employees C and D are contractually entitled to 4 weeks' notice. C's statutory minimum notice entitlement is 2 weeks and D's is 6 weeks. During the notice period C and D are both on unpaid parental leave. C's contractual notice is greater than his statutory notice by at least 1 week so he is not entitled to any payment while on parental leave. D, on the other hand, is entitled to be paid a minimum wage for the parental leave period which coincides with the statutory notice period.

8136 There is **no right** to be paid where the employee has given notice and subsequently goes on strike (s 91(2) ERA 1996) or where the employee is on leave at his own request (other than taking contractual holiday entitlement) (s 91(3) ERA 1996), although there may be a separate statutory right to be paid for this time off, for example to look for work in a redundancy situation. Further, if the employee otherwise breaches the contract during the notice period allowing the employer to terminate immediately, there is no right to payment for the rest of the notice period (s 91(4) ERA 1996).

The **amount payable** is determined by multiplying the number of hours covered by the above circumstances by the employee's hourly rate of pay (i.e. a week's pay (¶2920) divided by the number of normal working hours) (s 88 ERA 1996). Where there are no normal working hours, the amount payable is a week's pay for every week of the notice period in which the employee was ready and willing to do work of a reasonable nature and to earn a week's pay (s 89 ERA 1996). 8137

Any payment actually made (including holiday or sick pay) can be deducted from the amount payable.

If the employer terminates immediately in breach of contract during the notice period, any payment made is taken into account when assessing damages payable to the employee (s 91(3) ERA 1996).

The employee **cannot enforce** his right to a minimum wage during what would have been the statutory minimum notice period, but this loss will be taken into account when calculating damages for wrongful dismissal (¶8160) (s 91(5) ERA 1996).

State guaranteed payments The employee may be able to recover his statutory notice monies from the National Insurance Fund in certain circumstances, for example where the **employer is insolvent** (¶9045). 8138

Resignation during notice period An employee who is under notice of dismissal may wish to leave before the employer's notice expires. To preserve his right to a redundancy payment, he must either agree with the employer to vary the notice period or serve a **counter-notice** on the employer, following specific statutory provisions (¶9000). 8139

2. Pay in lieu of notice

In the employment contract, the employer can reserve the **right to terminate** the employment **immediately** by a payment in lieu of notice (PILON). This is useful when the employer wants the employee to leave work immediately rather than work out the notice period (an alternative would be to have a contractual right to put the employee on garden leave – see below). The employer may also wish to reserve the right to make a payment in lieu of **notice given by the employee**. 8145

Set out below is sample wording from the model contract of employment for general staff (similar wording is included in the model service agreement).

> EXAMPLE 16. Termination of employment
> [Employer] reserves the right, at his sole and absolute discretion, to pay salary (based on the basic salary set out above) in lieu of any required period of notice (whether given by you or [employer]), less any deductions [employer] is required to make by law.

If the employer exercises an **express PILON** and terminates immediately, there will be **no breach of contract** (the employee remains bound by his **post-termination contractual obligations**). Express PILONs are usually stated to be **based on** basic salary alone (i.e. not taking into account the value of any benefits that would have been provided to the employee during the notice period, had it been served), and are normally payable even if the employee finds another job immediately. 8146

If the express PILON is stated to be **discretionary** (i.e. "the employer may make a payment in lieu of notice to the employee…"), the employer has a choice whether to exercise that clause or give notice (for example, in order to preserve restrictive covenants) or to terminate in breach (so the employee has to mitigate his loss) (*Cerberus Software Ltd v Rowley* [2001] IRLR 160, CA).

The **letter of dismissal** should clearly state that the employment is being terminated immediately by payment in lieu of notice (i.e. that no notice is being given).

If there is **no express PILON**, the employer could terminate immediately (in breach of contract) and pay a sum representing damages for **wrongful dismissal** (see below), in which 8147 case the employee would have to **mitigate** his loss (for example, by finding another job), and damages could reflect the employee's net loss (i.e. salary after deduction of tax/national insurance). The employee would, in theory, have a right to bring an employment tribunal claim for damages, but the employer's payment may (depending on its calculation) in fact extinguish his loss. If the employer terminates in breach, the employee will not be bound by any **post-termination contractual obligations** (such as express confidentiality undertakings and restrictive covenants). Employers should be aware, however, that in such a case the payment of a PILON will not release them from any **express settlement agreement** obligations they have towards the employee (*CRS Computers Ltd v Mackenzie* [2002] All ER 173, EAT).

8148 If the contract contains a PILON (even where this is discretionary), the payment will be subject to the usual **income tax and national insurance deductions**. In contrast, damages for wrongful dismissal can be paid tax free up to £30,000 and are not subject to national insurance deductions. See ¶¶3123 +, 3134 + for detail on the taxation of termination payments.

3. Garden leave

8150 Garden leave describes the employer's ability to require the employee to stay at home during the notice period whilst continuing to pay him as if he was at work. In certain cases, an employer may be able to obtain a garden leave injunction to restrain the employee from competing during the notice period. Garden leave is discussed in detail at ¶2529.

B. Dismissal without notice

8155 An employer is entitled to dismiss the employee without notice (known as **summary dismissal**) if he is in fundamental breach (the contract can specify circumstances in which he may do so, such as for **gross misconduct** (¶6540)). The service agreements of directors and senior employees should also expressly set out the circumstances in which the employment may be terminated without notice.

If the employer is **not entitled** to dismiss summarily, he will be in breach of contract if he does not give the required period of notice (statutory or contractual) (known as **wrongful dismissal**), entitling the employee to a remedy (¶8160).

Even if notice is given (where required), the dismissal may be **unfair**. Conversely, a wrongful dismissal is not necessarily always an unfair dismissal (*BSC Sports and Social Club v Morgan* [1987] IRLR 391, EAT).

If the employer makes a **payment in lieu of notice**, a dismissal without notice will not be a wrongful dismissal. In those circumstances, the employee would have to sue for a sum due under the contract, rather than damages for breach (*Abrahams v Performing Rights Society* [1995] IRLR 486, CA).

The termination of a **fixed-term contract** not determinable on notice prior to its expiry, and the termination of a **contract for a specific purpose** prior to completion of that purpose will also amount to wrongful dismissal.

8156 The most common remedy for wrongful dismissal is damages, although in rare circumstances an injunction may be granted (¶1732). This section will focus on the **calculation of damages**. As for all breach of contract claims, the **basic aim** when calculating damages is to put the employee, so far as an award of money can do so, in the same situation as if the contract had been properly performed by the employer. If a claim for wrongful dismissal is made in a tribunal, any award is subject to a **statutory maximum** of £25,000. The civil courts are not subject to any such limit.

1. Calculation of damages

Period of loss

In making the calculation, the law assumes that if the employer had not wrongfully terminated the contract, he would have terminated lawfully at the first point when he could have done so (*Lavarack v Woods of Colchester Ltd* [1967] 1 QB 278, CA). The employee's losses are, therefore, limited by reference to that period. This approach contrasts with that taken in unfair dismissal cases where an employee may be awarded compensation for several years' loss of earnings, even where the contract could be terminated by, for example, 3 months' notice. 8160

EXAMPLE 1. Employee E is contractually entitled to **3 months' notice.** The employer dismisses him without any notice (in circumstances where he was not entitled to do so). E's losses will be limited to the 3 month period of notice which he should have been given. If E had been dismissed with only 1 month's notice, his losses would be calculated on the basis of the balance of the notice period, i.e. 2 months.
2. Employee F has a **fixed-term contract** for 2 years (not terminable by notice prior to expiry of the fixed term). The employer dismisses him (in breach of contract) after 6 months. F's losses will be calculated on the basis of the remaining 18 months of the contract.
3. The employer dismisses Employee G without notice (in circumstances where he was not entitled to do so). G's contract entitles him to 3 months' notice, but also incorporates a **contractual disciplinary procedure**, which would have taken 2 weeks to follow properly. The earliest the employment could lawfully have been terminated is therefore 3 months and 2 weeks after the date on which it was actually terminated and losses will be calculated accordingly (*Focsa Services (UK) Ltd v Birkett* [1996] IRLR 325, EAT).

Types of loss

General principles are discussed at ¶1700. The particular types of loss which may be included in the calculation of damages for wrongful dismissal are set out below. 8161

Loss of earnings and benefits Damages are calculated by reference to the employee's contractual pay and benefits, which may include pay, commission, bonus, tips, pensions, and share options. If an employee has a contractual right to a **bonus or a pay rise** during the notice period (or fixed term), this will be taken into account in calculating loss of earnings. Many employment contracts refer to discretionary bonuses or pay rises, where the employer may decide to make such payments but is not obliged to. The court or tribunal is entitled to form a view as to what the employer would have done, and is to assume that such discretion would have been exercised reasonably (*Clark v BET plc* [1997] IRLR 348, QBD). Even a bonus clause which appears to give the employer completely unrestricted discretion must be exercised in good faith and not irrationally or perversely (¶2833). 8162

Damages extend to **accrued pension rights** to which the employee would have become entitled had he been given the correct period of notice (*Silvey v Pendragon plc* [2001] IRLR 685, CA).

As the purpose of compensation is to put the employee in the position he would have been in had the employer not breached the contract, the calculation needs to **take account of the tax** he would have paid on his earnings and other benefits. The loss is, therefore, the **net salary and the net value** of any other benefits (such as a company car) after deducting the tax and national insurance contributions which would have been payable. 8163

Expenses Expenses that have been incurred as a result of the breach will be included if they would not have been incurred had there been a lawful termination of the contract. 8164

Loss of statutory rights An employee who has been summarily dismissed in breach of the employer's contractual **disciplinary procedures** cannot recover damages through a wrongful dismissal claim for the loss of the chance to claim unfair dismissal (*The Wise Group v Mitchell*, EAT case 0693/04, applying *Virgin Net Ltd v Harper* [2003] IRLR 831, EAT confirmed on appeal [2004] IRLR 390, CA and *Johnson v Unisys Ltd* [2001] IRLR 279, HL). 8165

MEMO POINTS 1. It is possible that the situation will be different where there has been a failure to apply the new statutory minimum requirements under **compulsory statutory dispute resolution procedures** and that failure has resulted in the loss of a chance to claim unfair dismissal. See Chapter 19 for a detailed discussion of the statutory dispute resolution procedures.
2. In coming to its decision in this case, the EAT considered that its earlier decision in *Raspin v United News Shops Ltd* [1999] IRLR 9, EAT was wrongly decided in light of *Virgin Net Ltd v Harper* and *Johnson v Unisys Ltd*.

8166 **Loss due to injury to feelings, etc.** Compensation is not recoverable for damages for on-going financial loss due to **injury to feelings**, **psychiatric injury**, **loss of reputation** and **inability to find new employment** arising from an employee's **dismissal or the manner of his dismissal** (*Johnson v Unisys Ltd* [2001] IRLR 279, HL; *Dunnachie v Kingston upon Hull City Council* [2004] IRLR 727, HL). Unfairness in the circumstances of dismissal does not give rise to a common law action, whether in contract or tort, but must be subject to employment tribunal proceedings.

However, a claim in respect of injury arising from events which are **independent** of, and **prior to** a dismissal can be brought, provided that the events do not immediately surround the dismissal itself (*McCabe v Cornwall County Council* heard jointly with *Eastwood and Williams v Magnox Electric plc* [2004] IRLR 733, HL). In these cases, the employees had a cause of action relating to the financial loss they had suffered as a result of psychiatric injury caused by their employers' treatment of them in the events leading up to dismissal, which was independent of the action they brought relating to the unfairness of the dismissal.

MEMO POINTS However, the implied term of trust and confidence in accordance with a provision in the contract of employment entitling the employer to terminate the **contract with notice for "good cause shown"** only ceases once a decision to dismiss has been made and consequently it subsists during the employer's investigation and evaluation of disciplinary charges (*King v University Court of the University of St Andrews* [2002] IRLR 252, CS).

8167 In rare cases, financial loss associated with **loss of reputation** resulting from a breach of the implied term of trust and confidence during the employment relationship ("**stigma damages**") may be awarded (*Malik v Bank of Credit and Commerce International SA* [1997] IRLR 462, HL), although actual (and not merely hypothetical) loss must be shown, and the stigma must be shown to be the cause of the former employee's failure to find work (*Bank of Credit and Commerce International SA v Ali (No 3)* [2002] IRLR 460, CA).

EXAMPLE In *Malik v Bank of Credit and Commerce International SA*, the bank went into liquidation after having operated for some time in a corrupt and dishonest manner in breach of the implied term of mutual trust and confidence. The employee was entitled to compensation for the financial loss associated with his damaged employment prospects, which had been tainted by the employer's reputation.

Adjustments to net loss

8169 Once the employee's net loss has been assessed, adjustments are made to increase or reduce the award as set out below. Note that an employee who becomes entitled to a **pension** on dismissal is not required to set off the amount which he receives from his pension against any damages for wrongful dismissal (*Hopkins v Norcross plc* [1992] IRLR 304, QBD).

8170 **Discount for accelerated receipt** If the award contains an element of future loss, which is most likely where there is a long notice period or a fixed-term contract with a long period to run when the award is made, the award will be adjusted to reflect the fact that the employee is receiving an accelerated payment (see ¶8600 for provision for decelerated receipt in relation to unfair dismissal). Instead of receiving his salary in monthly or weekly instalments over a period of time, he will receive his **damages in a lump sum** in advance of the due dates for payment. He will be able to invest this and so a lump sum of, for example, £24,000 paid on 1 January is in practice worth more than 12 monthly payments of £2,000 made over the course of the year. The lump sum is therefore discounted to reflect the amount of compensation awarded and the potential return on investment.

Mitigation The employee has a duty to mitigate his loss, and the most obvious way for him to do so is to **seek alternative employment**. If the employer has offered new employment on reasonable terms, the employee may have failed to mitigate his loss if he refuses (¶8620). 8171

The employer will be given credit for **sums earned** by the employee **from another employer** during the period for which compensation is being awarded (or which the employee could have earned had he taken reasonable steps to mitigate his loss). There is no obligation to mitigate if the employer exercises a contractual right to make a **payment in lieu of notice** (¶8145). Mitigation is discussed in more detail in the section on compensation for unfair dismissal (¶8620).

State benefits **Unemployment benefit** is set off (*Parsons v BNM Laboratories Ltd* [1964] 1 QB 95, 8172
CA). However, the court has to take into account any loss which is suffered by the employee as a result of the fact that, by not giving him notice, the employer has caused him to claim benefit earlier than would have been the case, so that he will also exhaust his entitlement earlier than he would have done (*Westwood v Secretary of State for Employment* [1984] IRLR 209, HL).

Taxation Damages for wrongful dismissal in excess of £30,000 will be taxable (tax being 8173
levied on the excess only) (¶3125; s 406 ITEPA 2003). Where the **damages exceed £30,000**, this tax liability also needs to be brought into the calculation to avoid the employee suffering double taxation. The approach taken is to calculate the total net damages and then gross that figure up to **take account of the tax** which will have to be paid on any excess over £30,000 (*Shove v Downs Surgical plc* [1984] IRLR 17, QBD).

2. Sample calculation

The following calculation illustrates the general principles described above. 8175

EXAMPLE A is employed under a contract which entitled him to 12 months' notice of termination. He is summarily dismissed in breach of that contract. His salary under the contract was £80,000 per annum and in addition he had other benefits with a taxable value of £10,000 per annum.
He has been able to find a lower paid job which, over the course of the 12 month period for which damages are being calculated, will enable him to earn £15,000 after tax.
Calculation based on tax rates and allowances for 2005/06.

a. *Calculation of award before grossing up for tax*

	£
Gross salary for 12 months:	80,000
Gross benefits for 12 months:	10,000
Total gross loss:	90,000
Tax on gross salary and benefits:	
Deduct personal allowance:	(4,895)
Taxable income:	85,105
Income tax @ 10% on £0 – £2,090	(209)
Income tax @ 22% on £2,091 – £32,400	(6,668)
Income tax @ 40% on taxable income over £32,400	(21,082)
Total tax payable	(27,959)
Total net loss after tax:	62,041
Less:	
Mitigation	(15,000)
	47,041
Deduction for accelerated receipt (e.g. 5%):	(2,352)
Total:	44,689

b. *Grossing up for tax*

	£
Award to be grossed up:	44,689
Less: tax free element	(30,000)
Amount to be grossed up:	14,689

To gross up for tax, the sum of £14,689 would be added to any other taxable income which A had (or could be expected to have) for the period in question to determine how much income tax would be payable on that sum. Assuming this results in a finding that it would be taxed at the basic rate of 22%, this would mean tax of £3,231.
The gross award made to A would therefore be:

	£
Pre-grossing up award:	44,689
Plus: grossing up sum	3,231
Total:	47,920

3. Overlap with unfair dismissal awards

8177 An employee might claim both unfair dismissal and wrongful dismissal. To some extent, the awards made may overlap. However, the employee is not entitled to be compensated for the same loss twice (*Babcock FATA Ltd v Addison* [1987] IRLR 173, CA).

Neither the **basic award** nor any **additional award** is set off against damages for wrongful dismissal as they are not based on any loss suffered by the employee and so there is no question of double compensation.

The **compensatory award** may well overlap with wrongful dismissal damages, in which case some **set off** will be required. It will be necessary to identify those elements of the compensatory award (assuming that award has already been made) which cover losses which would otherwise be included in the damages for wrongful dismissal. Obviously, if the wrongful dismissal case has been heard first then the reverse process will need to be carried out by the employment tribunal in calculating the compensatory award. If the cases are heard together, the tribunal will adopt a method of calculating damages to ensure that the employee is not compensated twice.

EXAMPLE Employee J is dismissed without notice when he should have been given 3 months' notice (at £2,500 per month). The tribunal (sitting 4 months after dismissal) finds that he was unfairly dismissed and makes the following award:

	£
Basic Award	540
Compensatory Award	
– Loss of earnings from dismissal to hearing (@ £2,500 per month)	10,000
– Future loss (6 months @ £2,500)	15,000
– Loss of statutory rights	200
Total	25,740

If J chose (and was able) to bring a subsequent case in the civil courts for wrongful dismissal, the court would have awarded him £7,500 (3 months @ £2,500) for his notice period but this has already been compensated by the loss of earnings awarded by the tribunal for the period from dismissal to the hearing, so J will get no further compensation.
If, for whatever reason, the tribunal had only awarded him loss of earnings for the first 2 months from dismissal (£5,000) and no loss of earnings after that, but had still awarded him a basic award of £540 and loss of statutory rights at £200, the £5,000 received for loss of earnings would be set off against losses during the notice period but not the basic award or loss of statutory rights as these are not items which are covered by the wrongful dismissal damages. J will, therefore, be awarded a further £2,500 compensation for wrongful dismissal.

C. Resignation

Termination by the employee is known as resignation and may be **with or without notice**. The employer can reserve the right to make a payment in lieu of notice given by the employee (¶8145). If the employee resigns, there will be no dismissal (i.e. the employee will not be entitled to bring a claim for redundancy, unfair or wrongful dismissal), unless he has resigned in response to the employer's fundamental breach (i.e. he has been constructively dismissed – ¶8230), has resigned during the employer's notice period by serving a statutory counter-notice (¶9000), or has been forced to resign. **8180**

Notice periods As for employer termination with notice (see above), the employee must give the longer of the **contractual** (express or implied) or statutory notice period. The **statutory minimum** period to be given by an employee who has been continuously employed for 1 month or more is 1 week (this does not increase with length of service) (s 86(2) ERA 1996). See ¶8135 for employee rights to payment during the statutory notice period. **8181**

The employee may ask to be **released before the expiry** of his notice period. If this is acceptable to the employer, he should ask the employee to confirm in writing the agreed termination date, and the fact that the employer is released from any further obligations under the contract. Without such confirmation, the employee could argue that the employer merely agreed to release him from his obligation to work out his notice.

Communication of resignation There are **no formal requirements** for a resignation but it must be communicated to the employer either orally, in writing or by conduct. It is not, therefore, strictly necessary for the employee clearly to state his intention to resign as this may be inferred from his conduct and the surrounding circumstances (*Johnson v Monty Smith Garages Ltd*, EAT case 657/79). It may be sufficient for the employee to walk out and fail to return to work. There is no need for the employer to **accept** the resignation. **8182**

Notice of an **intention to resign** (but without specifying a date) is unlikely to be a valid and effective termination of the employment (*Ely v YKK Fasteners (UK) Ltd* [1993] IRLR 500, CA).

EXAMPLE In *Ely v YKK Fasteners (UK) Ltd*, E told the employer that he planned to emigrate in order to take up a job offer. The employer recruited a replacement but E subsequently changed his mind. The employer claimed that E had resigned but this was not the case as no formal notice had been given and no termination date could be ascertained from the information he had provided.

Pressure to resign If the employer forces the employee to resign, there will be an express dismissal (rather than a constructive dismissal) (*Martin v MBS Fastenings (Glynwed) Distribution Ltd* [1983] IRLR 198, CA; *Bickerton v Inver House Distillers Ltd*, EAT case 656/91). If the parties agree that the employee should resign as an alternative to completing disciplinary proceedings (the end result of which could be dismissal), the agreed resignation will not amount to a dismissal (*Staffordshire County Council v Donovan* [1981] IRLR 108, EAT). If the employee is offered an inducement (for example, a financial incentive) to resign, there may be an agreed resignation or alternatively a termination by mutual agreement (¶8260). **8183**

MEMO POINTS Note that on 1 October 2004 **compulsory statutory dispute resolution procedures**, including a dismissal and disciplinary procedure, came into force. For further details, see Chapter 19.

Resignation without notice If the employee does not give the required period of notice, he will be in **breach of contract** unless he has resigned in response to a fundamental breach by the employer (¶8230). There is an argument that the employer can choose whether or not to accept this breach but in practice the employment terminates regardless of the employer's wishes. The employee cannot be compelled to work out his notice and although the employer could sue for damages, such actions are rare (¶1750). If the employer withholds the employee's wages, he may be liable for making an unlawful deduction (¶3050). **8184**

The employer could seek a **garden leave** injunction to ensure that the employee does not compete during the notice period (¶2645).

D. Retirement

8200 The employment will terminate when an employee reaches the applicable retiring age and this is considered a **dismissal** by the employer. If an employee chooses to take **early retirement**, this will be a **resignation** rather than a dismissal (in some cases it will be a termination by **mutual agreement** – ¶8260).

On retirement, the employee may be entitled to certain **benefits** (in particular, a **pension**).

1. Retiring age

Contractual retiring age (CRA)

8205 The employer may have a retirement policy giving a contractual retiring age for the employment (referred to here as the CRA), or one may have arisen by virtue of an established custom or practice (¶1180). Once an employee reaches the CRA, the employment will terminate without the need for an express dismissal or resignation. The policy can permit the employee to **remain in employment** at the employer's discretion (*Taylor v Secretary of State for Scotland* [2000] IRLR 502, HL) and/or give a maximum age but state that the employee may **retire before** reaching this age without losing his pension benefits. If there is **no applicable retiring age**, the employee can continue to work until he is dismissed or he resigns.

8206 If the employer wishes to **change the CRA**, the normal principles of variation of contract (as discussed at ¶1600) apply.

8207 **Equal opportunities** In order to avoid liability for sex discrimination, the CRA must be the same for **men and women** (s 6(4) SDA 1975; *Marshall v Southampton and South-West Hampshire Area Health Authority (Teaching)* [1986] IRLR 140, ECJ). The **state pension age** cannot be a CRA as it is differs according to sex (currently 60 for women, 65 for men). The CRA may, however, differ for **different occupations**.

If the employer has an **equal opportunities policy** that undertakes to exclude age discrimination, this will be construed not to override any CRA (i.e. the employer will not be in breach of contract if he dismisses an employee once he has reached the CRA).

The Department of Work and Pensions' (DWP) **code of practice** gives standards of good practice in employment, although it has no formal statutory authority (Code of Practice on Age Diversity at Work). The code **recommends** that employers:

– base any retirement policy on business needs while also giving individuals as much choice as possible;

– carefully evaluate the loss to their business in terms of skills and abilities in cases of early retirement and consider alternatives to early retirement;

– avoid using age as the sole criterion for early retirement schemes (subject to pension rules);

– use flexible retirement schemes, where possible;

– use phased retirement, where possible, to allow employees to alter the balance of their working and personal lives and prepare for full retirement (also preparing the business for the loss of the employee's skills); and

– make pre-retirement support available for employees.

MEMO POINTS Direct and indirect age discrimination is expected to become **unlawful from** October 2006. At the time of writing, the Government has published **draft** Employment Equality (Age) Regula-

tions 2006 (see ¶5254 for a summary of the draft regulations). The following key changes are proposed in relation to retirement:
a. **Compulsory retirement** will constitute age discrimination.
b. An employer will, however, be able to retire employees, or set retirement ages within his company, at or above the **default retirement age** of 65 without it constituting unlawful age discrimination or unfair dismissal (¶8422). The Government will review whether it is still appropriate to have a default retirement age in 2011.
c. An employer will only be able to retire an employee at a **lower age** if he can satisfy the test of **objective justification** (outlined at ¶5257);
d. An employee will have the **right to request** to work beyond the intended retirement age. This right to request will be modelled on the existing right to request flexible working (¶4690);
e. An employer will have a **duty to consider** an employee's request to work beyond the intended retirement age. The key rules of this procedure will include the following:
– an employer will have a duty to notify an employee of the intended retirement date and the employee's right to request working past this date, no more than 12 months and no less than 6 months before the intended retirement date. An employer who fails to comply with this duty may be liable to pay compensation of up to 8 weeks' pay;
– if an employer fails to notify an employee of the above information within the time limits, he will have an ongoing duty to do so until 2 weeks before the dismissal;
– if an employee asks to work beyond the intended retirement date, the employer will have to consider the request at the earliest 12 months and at the latest 6 weeks before the intended date of retirement (although this 6 week deadline does not apply if the employer has failed to inform the employee about the right to request);
– the employer should consider an employee's request in good faith and hold a meeting to discuss it. An employee will have the right to appeal against an employer's decision; and
– if a new retirement date is agreed, the duty to consider procedure will apply again as the new date approaches and, for each retirement occasion, an employee can make one formal request.

The **state pension age** is to be equalised at age 65, to be phased in over 10 years from 6 April 2010 (Pensions Act 1995).

Pensionable age under occupational pension schemes (which must also be the same for men and women as pension is "pay" for the purposes of EU equal pay provisions (*Barber v Guardian Royal Exchange Assurance Group* [1990] IRLR 240, ECJ)) is distinct from both the state pension age and any CRA, although it can be the same.

Statutory rights

Retirement at the CRA normally constitutes a **dismissal** for the purposes of **unfair dismissal** and **statutory redundancy payment** claims (voluntary early retirement does not). However, these claims are barred if the employee has reached the **normal retiring age** (referred to here as the NRA) (this being the same for men and women) for a person employed in that position in that undertaking (unfair dismissal)/in the business for which he was employed (redundancy), or, if there is no such age, the age of 65 (ss 109(1), 156 ERA 1996). Tapering provisions apply to payments to employees aged between 64 and 65 (¶9005). 8210

This upper age limit does not apply to automatically unfair dismissals (¶8390).

MEMO POINTS 1. It is proposed that the **upper age limit** applied to claims of unfair dismissal and redundancy will be **removed** under the draft Employment Equality (Age) Regulations 2006 (see ¶5254 for a summary of the draft regulations and ¶8390+ and ¶8990+ in relation to the specific changes proposed in relation to unfair dismissal and redundancy provisions respectively).
2. Meanwhile, the challenge to the upper age limit on the grounds that is **indirectly discriminatory** against men has recently failed before the Court of Appeal (*Rutherford and another v Secretary of State for Trade and Industry (No. 2)* [2004] IRLR 892, CA). At the time of writing, this case is awaiting an appeal hearing in the House of Lords.

Determining the normal retiring age (NRA) To determine the NRA, the reasonable expectations of the group of employees holding the employee's position at the date of dismissal must be examined. The relevant group is identified by reference to their status, nature of work and terms of employment, including any terms dealing in particular with retirement (*Barber v Thames Television plc* [1992] IRLR 410, CA). The expectations of the group are determined by reference to the group in general and not merely those employees approaching retirement (*Brooks v British Telecommunications plc* [1992] IRLR 66, CA). Normal is not to be equated with usual, which suggests a narrow, statistical approach. 8211

If there is a **CRA** (¶8205), which is well known and observed, this is the NRA. Where there is **no CRA**, the NRA is the normal retiring age for employees in that particular position or, if there is no such normal age, the age of 65.

If the employee occupies a **unique position**, in that there is no other employee employed by the undertaking with the same job, it does not mean that such an employee does not have an NRA (*Wall v British Compressed Air Society*, EAT case 169/02; confirmed on appeal ([2004] IRLR 147, CA)). In such cases, the NRA will ordinarily be the CRA.

If the **CRA is expressly abandoned** or **regularly departed from** in practice, it will be displaced as the NRA as the group's reasonable expectations will have changed (*Waite v Government Communications Headquarters* [1983] IRLR 341, HL; *Whittle v Manpower Services Commission* [1987] IRLR 441, EAT). However, **limited exceptions** to the CRA will not displace it as the NRA (*Barclays Bank plc v O'Brien* [1994] IRLR 580, CA).

If the employer lawfully **changes the CRA** and the relevant employees are made aware of this change, their expectations will also change and the NRA will be altered (*O'Brien*).

If, however, the employer attempts to **lower the CRA in breach of contract**, it seems that the NRA will not be affected (*Bratko v Beloit Walmsley Ltd* [1995] IRLR 629, EAT). If the employee refuses to agree to a lower CRA, the employer could terminate the current contract by notice and offer new employment on revised terms (¶1655).

8212 On the basis that an employee with a CRA has a reasonable expectation that he will not be compulsorily retired before this age, the **NRA cannot be lower than the CRA** (*Royal and Sun Alliance Insurance Group plc v Payne* [2005] IRLR 848, EAT). An employer who unilaterally makes the NRA lower than the CRA will therefore be acting in breach of contract. Where there is **no NRA**, the statutory alternative of 65 will apply.

2. Early retirement

8215 An employee can retire before reaching the CRA (¶8205) by giving the notice required under his contract.

The employer will be in breach of contract if he **forces the employee to retire** before the CRA is reached (or where there is no CRA). However, the employer will not be in breach if he gives the correct **notice of termination**, even if the reason for the dismissal is to enforce early retirement. However, a dismissal in these circumstances may be unfair (and the upper age limit applicable to unfair dismissal claims (the NRA) may not mirror any unlawful reduction in the CRA, such that the employee's claim could proceed (*Bratko v Beloit Walmsley Ltd*, above)).

Impact on pension entitlement

8216 Pension schemes are discussed at ¶3400. The relevant scheme rules may allow the employee to draw a pension before the employee reaches pensionable age, typically with the employer's consent. Early retirement may be offered as an alternative to redundancy and the scheme may provide for one or more of the following:
- immediate payment of the employee's full pension (with no reduction for early payment);
- payment of part of the pension as a lump sum;
- adding additional years service for the purpose of calculating pension entitlement; and
- allowing the employee to pay all or part of any termination payment into the scheme in order to increase entitlement.

MEMO POINTS Revenue and Customs approved occupational schemes cannot pay pensions before age 50, except in cases of ill health.

Retirement due to ill health

8217 If an employee is dismissed on the grounds of ill health, the employer may be liable for unfair dismissal and disability discrimination. When dealing with an employee who is on long-term sick leave, the employer may, therefore, wish to consider whether early retirement could be an option. Ill health retirement may entitle the employee to pension benefits.

The rules of an **occupational scheme** normally provide for early retirement due to ill health, commonly granting immediate payment of full pension, perhaps with additional pensionable service added on in order to calculate an enhanced ill health pension. Some schemes apply a tiered system, such that full prospective pensionable service is used for complete incapacity and actual pensionable service is used when the employee can do some work (but not his normal duties). 8218

Some schemes will also allow for commutation on the grounds of **serious ill health**. If so, and the employee's life expectancy is severely shortened, the scheme will commute the whole of his retirement benefit into a lump sum.

Medical evidence is normally required to prove that the employee's ill health prevents him from carrying out his normal employment. Often, the incapacity must be expected or likely to be permanent, with provisions for suspension of pension payments if the employee is able to resume work before reaching pensionable age. 8219

The employer is bound by his duty to act in **good faith** when deciding whether the employee meets any definition of incapacity (*Mihlenstedt v Barclays Bank International Ltd and Barclays Bank plc* [1989] IRLR 522, CA) and the scheme **rules must be construed** in a purposive and practical way (*Derby Daily Telegraph Ltd v The Pensions Ombudsman and Thompson* [1999] IRLR 476, ChD).

MEMO POINTS **Personal pensions** can also come into payment early, at a reduced rate, and the employee should check his policy, if necessary.

E. Constructive dismissal

If the employer commits a **fundamental breach** of contract (¶1715), the employee is entitled to treat himself as discharged (i.e. he can immediately terminate the employment without notice) (*Western Excavating (ECC) Ltd v Sharp* [1978] IRLR 27, CA). The contract will not automatically terminate; the employee must resign (he normally does so without notice but may give notice if he wishes) (see above) before bringing a claim based on the fact that he has been constructively dismissed. 8230

It is important to note that it is only the **employer's actions** that must be considered in determining whether there has been a fundamental breach justifying constructive dismissal and not those of the employee (*Tolson v Governing Body of Mixenden Community School* [2003] IRLR 842, EAT). Consequently, it is irrelevant that the employee failed to utilise the employer's grievance procedure as a response to his employer's actions.

MEMO POINTS Note that all employers and employees must also follow **compulsory statutory grievance procedures** (¶6740) although the principle in *Tolson v Governing Body of Mixenden Community School* regarding the establishment of a fundamental breach remains.

Fundamental breach often occurs in the context of a variation. If the employee **agrees to a variation**, there will be no breach of contract (and so no question of constructive dismissal). 8231

If the employer **unilaterally imposes radically different terms**, there may be a deemed express dismissal (¶1652).

Constructive dismissal in the context of a **business transfer** is discussed at ¶8035. 8232

An employer may also commit a fundamental breach if he unjustifiably imposes a **disproportionate disciplinary sanction** on an employee (¶6633).

A breach by the employer of the **implied term of trust and confidence** will always be a repudiatory breach for the purposes of a claim of constructive dismissal (¶1248).

Anticipatory breach The employee may be justified in resigning if the employer indicates that he **intends to commit** a fundamental breach (an "anticipatory breach"). There must be 8233 a clear and unequivocal statement of intention, and vague or conditional proposals of a variation to terms or working practices will not amount to an anticipatory breach. For example, in the absence of a unilateral variation of contract, the **lawful termination** of a contract, coupled with an offer of employment on new terms, will not of itself give rise to a breach of the implied term of trust and confidence nor will it constitute an anticipatory breach (*Kerry Foods v Lynch* [2005] IRLR 680, EAT). A **warning of redundancy** will not normally entitle the employee to claim he has been constructively dismissed (*Secretary of State for Employment v Greenfield*, EAT case 147/89), nor will a rumour that a particular employee is to be made redundant (*Quinn v Weir Systems Ltd*, EAT case 1317/00), although it has been suggested that a **threat to dismiss** with notice in the context of an anticipated unilateral variation of contract by the employer can be a fundamental anticipatory breach (*Greenaway Harrison Ltd v Wiles* [1994] IRLR 380, EAT).

The employee's choice to accept the breach and resign must be unequivocal as the employer can **withdraw** his anticipatory **breach** prior to the employee's acceptance of his repudiation (*Harrison v Norwest Holst Group Administration Ltd* [1985] IRLR 240, CA).

> EXAMPLE In *Harrison v Norwest Holst Group Administration Ltd*, the employer threatened to transfer H's workplace and remove H as a director. H indicated that he would resign if the matter could not be resolved amicably. The employer withdrew the threat before H resigned so he was unable to claim he had been constructively dismissed.

8234 **Cumulative breaches** A fundamental breach may be based on the cumulative effect of a **series of acts** (*Lewis v Motorworld Garages Ltd* [1985] IRLR 465, CA), such that the last act is the "**last straw**", justifying the employee's resignation. It is not necessary for each act in the series, or even for the last act, to be a fundamental breach in its own right. However, the last straw act must contribute in some way, when taken in conjunction with the cumulative breaches, to a breach of the implied term of trust and confidence, even though that contribution may be relatively insignificant (*London Borough of Waltham Forest v Folu Omilaju* [2005] IRLR 35, CA).

In addition, there is no requirement for the employee to demonstrate any particular degree of proximity between the acts relied upon (*Logan v Commissioners of Customs & Excise*, EAT case 686/00; confirmed by the Court of Appeal ([2004] ICR 63, CA)). Further, the series may comprise different incidents if they are united by a common thread (for example, the employer's failure to give the employee the necessary support (*Hamill v Strong & Co Ltd*, EAT case 1179/99)).

> EXAMPLE In *Abbey National plc v Robinson* (¶8245), R was on sick leave following a complaint that her manager had bullied her (which was upheld). The employer unreasonably failed to remove the manager from R's department so that she could return, thereby committing a fundamental breach. R remained on leave over the course of the next year whilst continuing to seek a way to return to work. During this time she suffered further insensitive, unsatisfactory and unreasonable treatment. Finally, she attended a meeting in which nothing was resolved. This was the "last straw" and R was entitled to resign and claim she had been constructively dismissed, 10 months after the initial fundamental breach.

8235 **Employer's intention** There is no need for the employer to intend to terminate the employment. A constructive dismissal may be identified even if the employer is keen for the employment to continue. There may be a constructive dismissal even where the **employer is unaware** that he is in breach (for example, he may be in fundamental breach of an implied term (*Bliss v South East Thames Regional Health Authority* [1985] IRLR 308, CA)). In cases of anticipatory breach, if the employer **genuinely but mistakenly believes** in a particular interpretation of the contract, there may be no repudiation if he puts forward his interpretation (but there probably will be if he insists on it) (*Financial Techniques (Planning Services) Ltd v Hughes* [1981] IRLR 32, CA). However, the employer's mistaken but genuine belief will not normally of itself prevent his conduct from amounting to a fundamental breach.

8236 An employer may be liable for constructive dismissal by virtue of his **vicarious liability** for acts done by employees in the course of their employment (*Hilton International Hotels (UK) Ltd v Protopapa* [1990] IRLR 316, EAT).

EXAMPLE In *Hilton International Hotels (UK) Ltd v Protopapa*, P was severely reprimanded by her immediate supervisor for making a dental appointment without first asking for permission to be absent from work. She resigned and claimed constructive dismissal. The EAT upheld her claim on the basis that the employer was liable for the acts of the supervisor as the latter was acting within the scope of her employment (the fact that she did not have authority to dismiss P was irrelevant).

Resignation

The employee's resignation must be **communicated** to the employer by words or conduct (*Edwards v Surrey Police* [1999] IRLR 456, EAT). This will be a question for the tribunal or court on the facts and evidence in each case. 8238

The tribunal or court must consider whether the fundamental breach **caused** the resignation (*TSB Bank plc v Harris* [2000] IRLR 157, EAT). It does not have to be the sole cause, and there can be a **combination of causes** provided the breach is the effective cause (*Jones plc v F Sirl & Son (Furnishers) Ltd* [1997] IRLR 493, EAT). It is not necessary for the employee to know that there has been a breach of contract – the essential element is the causal link between the employer's conduct and the resignation. 8239

EXAMPLE In *Jones v F Sirl & Son (Furnishers) Ltd*, J's hours of work, pay, petrol allowance and pension were cut and she lost significant areas of her job responsibilities following the appointment of another manager. She accepted a job offer from another company and claimed constructive dismissal. The EAT held that the first employer's fundamental breach, rather than the job offer, was the effective cause of her resignation.

It is not always necessary for the employee to make the **reason** for his resignation clear to the employer at the time in order to prove that he resigned as a result of the employer's breach (*Weathersfield Ltd (t/a Van & Truck Rentals) v Sargent* [1999] IRLR 94, CA). Whether he did so or not will be one of the factors to be considered by the tribunal when determining this question. 8240

EXAMPLE In *Weathersfield Ltd (t/a Van & Truck Rentals) v Sargent*, S commenced work as a receptionist at a car hire firm. She resigned after a few days in response to the employer's special policy for black and Asian customers (i.e. she was to tell them that no cars were available). She did not communicate the reason for her resignation until some days later. The Court held that she had been constructively dismissed.

The employee must choose **within a reasonable time** to treat the contract as at an end or he will normally be taken to have affirmed it (see below) (*Western Excavating (ECC) Ltd v Sharp* [1978] IRLR 27, CA). 8241

Affirmation of the contract

The employee can reject the employer's breach but choose not to treat himself as discharged, in which case the employment will continue and there can be no claim of constructive dismissal (the contract is "affirmed"). His remedies in this case are discussed at ¶1710. 8242

The contract may be affirmed by the **employee's behaviour** (i.e. if he acts in a way that is inconsistent with an intention to treat himself as discharged). The employee may avoid this if he tells the employer that he does not accept the breach but **continues to work** for a period **under protest**, perhaps to allow the employer to remedy the breach (*W E Cox Toner (International) Ltd v Crook* [1981] IRLR 443, EAT). However, this period cannot continue indefinitely and at some stage the contract will be deemed to have been affirmed. 8243
Working out the **notice period** does not affirm the contract.

Factors to be taken into account when deciding whether the contract has been affirmed include: 8244
a. the length of any **delay** in resigning (mere delay without more will be evidence of implied affirmation but will not be conclusive (*Allen v Robles* [1969] 3 All ER 154, CA; *W E Cox Toner (International) Ltd v Crook*)). There may be special circumstances to excuse a delay, such as:
– mental illness;

– stress-related illness during which the employee is not in a position to make a rational judgement (*The Governing Body of St Edmund of Canterbury Catholic High School v Hines*, EAT case 1138/02);
– time needed to investigate the true position (*The Post Office v Roberts* [1980] IRLR 347, EAT);
– the willingness of the employer to give the employee time to decide (*Bliss v South East Thames Regional Health Authority*);
– where new terms are imposed at short or no notice (a reasonable trial period is allowed (¶8876)); or
– absence from work for example, due to sickness (*Burton v Northern Business Systems Ltd*, EAT case 608/92; see also *El-Hoshi v Pizza Express Restaurants Ltd*, EAT case 0857/03);
b. continued acceptance of **wages or other benefits**, including sick pay (*Wood & Mott Ltd v Carr* EAT case 1025/95), although acceptance of sick pay will not necessarily indicate that the employee has affirmed the contract (*Forbes v Salamis (Marine & Industrial) Ltd*, EAT case 0085/03) and, moreover, it is reasonable for the employee to accept wages for a limited time while looking for another job (*Waltons & Morse v Dorrington* [1997] IRLR 488, EAT);
c. the **nature of the breach**; and
d. the employee's **length of service** (*Miceli v Signal House Ltd*, EAT case 180/95).

8245 In cases of **cumulative breach**, it does not matter if the employee has waived earlier acts in the series (even if they amount to a fundamental breach), as it is the end of the series that is relevant in order to identify if the contract has been affirmed (*Abbey National plc v Robinson*, EAT case 743/99). When deciding whether the final act is a sufficient "trigger" to revive the earlier ones, the tribunal will take into account (*Hamill v Strong & Co Ltd*):
a. the nature of the incidents;
b. the overall time span;
c. the length of time between the incidents;
d. any factors which may have amounted to a waiver of any earlier breaches; and
e. the nature of any waiver, namely:
– whether it was express or implied; and
– whether it was final or conditional on there being no further breach.

Further, if the individual acts are not fundamental breaches in themselves, there can be no affirmation until the "last straw" trigger.

8246 If the situation involves a **continuing breach** (for example, the failure to provide or operate a proper grievance procedure (*WA Goold (Pearmak) Ltd v McConnell* [1995] IRLR 516, EAT)), the contract is not affirmed by the employee delaying his resignation while the breach continues.

Remedies

8248 If an employee has been constructively dismissed, he may seek compensation for **wrongful dismissal** (¶8160) if he resigned without notice.

As constructive dismissal is a dismissal for the purposes of **unfair dismissal** and **redundancy payments**, the employee may also bring such claims, where appropriate (ss 95(1)(c), 136(1)(c) ERA 1996).

8249 A constructive dismissal will also be a dismissal for the purposes of **sex**, **racial**, **disability**, **religion or belief or sexual orientation discrimination** claims (the employer's conduct may also amount to "other detriment" for the purposes of such claims) (s 82(1A)(b) SDA 1975; *Derby Specialist Fabrication Ltd v Burton* [2001] IRLR 69, EAT; *Catherall v Michelin Tyre plc* [2003] IRLR 61, EAT; reg 6(5) SI 2003/1660; reg 6(5) SI 2003/1661). This should apply equally to claims made on the grounds of age discrimination which is expected to become unlawful from 1 October 2006 (see ¶5254).

A claim of discrimination (based on dismissal or some other detriment) must be **brought within** 3 months of the employer's fundamental breach (*Commissioner of Police of Metropolis v Harley* [2001] IRLR 263, EAT; *Cast v Croydon College* [1998] IRLR 318, CA). Note that this contrasts with the time limit for an unfair constructive dismissal claim, which runs from the effective date of termination (¶8340) (although this may be the same where the employee resigns without notice on the day the breach occurs). See ¶9460 for further detail on time limits for discrimination claims.

Unfair constructive dismissal A constructive dismissal may be fair or unfair. If an employee brings a claim of unfair constructive dismissal, he must comply with the general **qualifying conditions** and procedural rules applicable to all unfair dismissal claims (¶8410 and ¶8560). The tribunal will consider the **general questions**, namely whether the employee has been dismissed, whether the employer had a fair reason for dismissal, and whether he followed a fair procedure. 8251

In certain cases, a dismissal is **automatically unfair** (¶8390). For example, an employee can leave his workplace and claim automatic unfair constructive dismissal when he believes that his health and safety is in imminent and serious danger.

The **reason for the dismissal** is the employer's reason for committing the fundamental breach (*Berriman v Delabole Slate Ltd* [1985] IRLR 305, CA), and the tribunal will consider whether that reason was sufficient in the circumstances to justify the breach (the criteria applied are generally the same as those in cases of express dismissal – ¶8420). In defending a claim, the employer normally contests that a dismissal has in fact taken place at all, but he should also plead a reason for the dismissal in the alternative, as the tribunal will not investigate the reason of their own volition (*Derby City Council v Marshall* [1979] IRLR 261, EAT). 8252

In many cases the fundamental breach will make the dismissal unfair. However, the following situations may provide a **fair reason** for dismissal:
- conduct/capability dismissals (¶8450);
- redundancy (¶8510); and
- business reorganisations (capable of being a fair reason under the "some other substantial reason" limb – ¶8532).

EXAMPLE 1. In *Ross v What Every Woman Wants*, EAT case 474/87, R's **conduct** entitled his employer to dismiss him summarily but the employer chose to demote him (with a consequent pay cut). Although this was a fundamental breach, R's conduct constituted a fair reason for dismissal.
2. Employee K worked in London. The employer ceased to operate there and required K to move to his offices in Manchester (having no contractual right to do so). K resigned and claimed unfair constructive dismissal. **Redundancy**, however, could provide the employer with a fair reason for dismissal.
3. In *Genower v Ealing Hammersmith and Hounslow Area Health Authority* [1980] IRLR 297, EAT, the employer **reorganised his business** and the resulting **changes to G's job duties** amounted to a fundamental breach entitling him to claim constructive dismissal. However, the reorganisation amounted to a fair reason for dismissal.

Even if the employer establishes a fair reason, the dismissal may still be unfair if he failed to **act reasonably** in all the circumstances in treating that reason as a sufficient reason for dismissal (for example, he failed to consult when seeking to vary terms of employment). See ¶8420 for further detail on the criteria generally applied. 8253

F. Mutual agreement

Although relatively unusual, the employer and employee can agree (orally or in writing) to terminate the employment with effect at any time. This usually arises in cases of voluntary **early retirement**. There will be **no dismissal** (i.e. the employee will not be entitled to bring a claim for redundancy, unfair or wrongful dismissal) (*Birch and Humber v The University of Liverpool* [1985] IRLR 165, CA). 8260

In contrast, there will be a **dismissal** for redundancy purposes if the employee persuades the employer to dismiss him in a redundancy situation, or if he accepts **voluntary redundancy** or agrees to the employer's redundancy proposals (*Burton, Allton & Johnson Ltd v R R V Peck* [1975] IRLR 87, QBD).

If, however, the employee is under any **pressure to agree** (for example, a threat of dismissal in any case), the courts may find that he has actually been dismissed. However, if other factors also influenced the employee's decision (for example, he is offered a financial incentive), the courts may find that he has terminated by mutual agreement (*Sheffield v Oxford Controls Company Ltd* [1979] IRLR 133, EAT; *Hellyer Brothers Ltd v Atkinson and Dickinson* [1992] IRLR 540, EAT).

8261 There will be no termination by mutual agreement until **all the terms** of the agreement are agreed (*Asamoah-Boakye v Walter Rodney Housing Association Ltd* [2001] EWCA Civ 851).

EXAMPLE In *Asamoah-Boakye v Walter Rodney Housing Association Ltd*, A-B and his employer were negotiating terms in relation to the termination of his employment by mutual agreement. The employer required him to enter into a compromise agreement waiving his right to bring an unfair dismissal claim. A-B required the employer to provide an agreed form reference. A-B left his job before the agreement was signed. The Court held that there was no termination by mutual agreement as the agreement had not been signed and the form of reference had yet to be agreed.

8262 In contrast to a termination by mutual agreement, the employer and employee may negotiate the termination and agree that the employee resigns, or the employer dismisses the employee, on a certain date. **Negotiated terminations** are discussed at ¶9315.

8263 The employer and employee may have agreed that the employment should **automatically terminate** on the occurrence of a specified event (¶8270).

G. Automatic termination

8270 An agreement for automatic termination on the **occurrence of a specified event** may be ineffective to exclude statutory employment rights, unless it falls within one of the exceptions to the general prohibition on contracting out (¶9203). Therefore, an agreement that **overstaying holiday leave** would result in automatic termination was void as it purported to limit the employee's right not to be unfairly dismissed and to bring an unfair dismissal claim (*Igbo v Johnson Matthey Chemicals Ltd* [1986] IRLR 215, CA).

8271 The employment may also terminate automatically as a result of a **supervening event** or because it has been **frustrated**. In such cases, the employment terminates by operation of law and there is no actual dismissal or resignation. However, to preserve statutory rights, certain cases will be deemed to be a dismissal.

1. Supervening events

8275 Supervening events include death, certain cases of insolvency (¶8277), permanent closure of the employee's workplace, and automatic termination by statute (i.e. a change in the law makes performance impossible).

MEMO POINTS At common law, the transfer of an employer's business automatically terminates all existing contracts of employment. The employee's position is, however, normally protected by the **business transfer regulations**, which transfer the employment to the new employer (¶7950).

Death

8276 The death of the employer or the employee automatically terminates the employment unless there is a term (express or implied) to the contrary (*Farrow v Wilson* [1869] LR 4 CP 744, Court of Common Pleas). However, an employee whose contract is not renewed, or who is not re-engaged, by the person to whom the deceased employer's business passes is treated as dismissed for **redundancy** if the failure to renew or re-engage is wholly or mainly attributable to redundancy (¶9010). If the employee is **re-employed**, his statutory continuity of employment is preserved (s 218(4) ERA 1996).

Claims outstanding at the time of death (including claims of unfair dismissal and for a redundancy payment) can be brought against the deceased employer's personal representatives (s 206(1) ERA 1996) or by the deceased employee's personal representatives, as appropriate (ss 206(3), 207(1) ERA 1996; *Lewisham and Guys Mental Health NHS Trust v Andrews (deceased)* [2000] ICR 707, CA).

Insolvency

A detailed discussion of the law of insolvency is beyond the scope of this book and the following will deal only with its impact on the employment relationship. **8277**

The **bankruptcy** of an individual employer does not automatically terminate the employment. The **dissolution of a partnership** (as opposed to the addition or departure of individual partners) (*Briggs v Oates* [1990] IRLR 472, ChD), on the other hand, normally does. **Intervention by a regulatory body** may do so where it results in the regulated firm (for example, a partnership of solicitors) closing down (but does not where the partners are allowed to dispose of their practice as a going concern without dismissing the employees) (*Barnes t/a Barnes Thomas & Co v (1) Leavesley, (2) Taylors Solicitors*, EAT case 642/99).

If a company goes into **liquidation or winding up**, its assets are used to pay off its liabilities and the company is dissolved (i.e. it ceases to exist). There are three types of liquidation: compulsory, creditors' voluntary and members' voluntary. A company enters into **compulsory** liquidation by way of a court order, which automatically terminates the employment of all the company's employees. However, the liquidator can waive their dismissal if he needs to carry on the company's business during the winding up. A **voluntary** liquidation (creditors' or members') commences when the shareholders pass a resolution to wind the company up, and the employees' position depends on the circumstances. Their contracts of employment may provide that the company commits a fundamental breach if the business ceases or a resolution to wind the company up is passed. If not, the contracts will usually be terminated when the liquidator is appointed, unless the liquidator needs to carry on the company's business during the winding up. **8278**

Certain steps may be taken short of the company's liquidation. A company can be put into **administration** by the company, its directors, a qualifying floating charge holder or by court order (on application by the company, its directors or creditors) under which an administrator is appointed to manage the company's affairs. The appointment of an administrator does not of itself automatically terminate the employment of the company's employees as the administrator is said to be acting as agent of the company (para 69, Sch B1 Insolvency Act 1986). Employment contracts can either be adopted by the administrator or terminated by him within the law. If he causes an employment relationship to continue for more than 14 days after his appointment, he is taken to have adopted the contract (*Powdrill v Watson* [1995] 2 AC 394). **8279**

The company will go into **receivership** if the holder of a floating charge created before 15 September 2003 appoints an administrative receiver. The administrative receiver is also an agent of the company (s 44 Insolvency Act 1986) and so his appointment will not usually terminate the contracts of employment. If he causes an employment relationship to continue for more than 14 days after his appointment, he is taken to have adopted the contract (*Powdrill v Watson*, above). On the other hand, it will be terminated automatically where (*Griffiths v Secretary of State for Social Services* [1974] QB 468):
- the employee's employment is inconsistent with the receiver's activities;
- the receiver and employee enter into a new contract of employment contemporaneously or soon after the receiver's appointment, which is inconsistent with the old one; or
- the receiver's appointment is accompanied by a sale of the company's business.

MEMO POINTS The company also goes into receivership where a receiver (or receiver and manager) is appointed as a way of enforcing certain other security over the company's assets. The receiver can adopt a contract of employment, and will be taken to have done so if he allows an employment relationship to continue for more than 14 days after his appointment (*Powdrill v Watson*, above).

Where the **employment is not automatically terminated** by the insolvency, the employees may have to be dismissed. In such cases, the employer (or liquidator/receiver/administrator) should, before sending out dismissal notices, comply with the general rules on **collective redundancy consultation** (¶8915). **8280**

8281 If the employer's undertaking is **transferred** by a receiver, liquidator or administrator **to a wholly-owned subsidiary** in order to make it more attractive to a potential buyer, special provisions of the business transfer regulations will apply (¶7918, although see ¶7929 for the position under the new TUPE regulations).

8282 Employees of insolvent employers enjoy certain **specific rights and protections**, which are discussed at ¶9040.

2. Frustration

8285 A contract may be frustrated where an unforeseen event makes performance impossible or radically different from what the parties had originally contemplated (*Davis Contractors v Fareham UDC* [1956] AC 696, HL).

Although relatively rare in an employment context, frustration can occur in the following circumstances:
– prolonged or sudden serious illness or disability (discussed at ¶8458);
– imprisonment (see below);
– death (see above);
– total destruction of the workplace;
– conscription into the armed forces; and
– internment as an alien during wartime.

The party asserting that the contract has been frustrated has the **burden of proof**, and he cannot rely on a frustrating event if it has been caused by his **fault or default** (*F C Shepherd & Co Ltd v Jerrom* [1986] IRLR 358, CA).

In cases of frustration, the employment ends automatically by operation of law so that there is **no dismissal or resignation**, with the result that there can be no claim for wrongful or unfair dismissal, notice/payment in lieu of notice (*G F Sharp & Co Ltd v McMillan* [1998] IRLR 632, EAT), or for redundancy (unless the frustrating event affects the employer, in which case there is a **deemed dismissal** for statutory redundancy payment purposes (¶8106)), although the employee is entitled to payment for work done before the frustrating event.

The parties cannot choose to keep a frustrated contract alive (*G F Sharp & Co Ltd v McMillan*; *Collins v Secretary of State for Trade and Industry*, EAT case 1460/99), although continuity of employment may be preserved if the parties have a voluntary (as opposed to contractual) **continuing relationship** (¶1000).

Imprisonment

8286 If an employee is sentenced to imprisonment, the contract may, depending on the circumstances of the case, be **frustrated** (*F C Shepherd & Co Ltd v Jerrom*, above). Relevant factors include the following:
– the length of sentence/likely duration of the employee's absence;
– whether and at what stage it is necessary to replace the employee; and
– whether any replacement employee needs to be permanent rather than temporary.

An employer should not act too hastily, but should consider the likely duration of the employee's absence when making the decision whether to replace him (and not necessarily at the moment the sentence is passed) (*Chakki v United Yeast Co Ltd* [1982] ICR 140, EAT).

The contract may also be frustrated due to **restrictive bail conditions** (for example, that the employee lives in a certain place) or a **remand in custody** whilst awaiting trial (the factors discussed above will apply).

EXAMPLE In *Four Seasons Healthcare Limited (formerly Cotswold Spa Retirement Hotels Ltd) v Maughan* [2005] IRLR 324, EAT, the employee's employment contract was held not to be frustrated when the police launched an investigation into allegations of patient abuse at the care home at which the employee worked. Neither the act of abusing the patient nor the imposition of bail conditions which prevented the employee from entering the care home amounted to frustration of the contract. The contract was only frustrated when the decision was taken as to the employee's fitness to work (which, in this case, took place when the Crown Court convicted the employee and he was consequently rendered unfit to continue to work under the governing care home regulations).

If the contract is **not frustrated**, the employer may be able to dismiss fairly for some other substantial reason (¶8544). 8287

MEMO POINTS The employee will not be able to argue that by being imprisoned he has committed a fundamental breach of contract permitting the employer to treat himself as discharged in order to create a dismissal for the purposes of an unfair dismissal claim (*FC Shepherd & Co Ltd v Jerrom*).

II. Termination issues

In addition to **notice** provisions (including payment in lieu of notice and garden leave options) discussed above, the contract could include terms relating to **confidentiality** and **post-termination restraints**. These are discussed in Chapter 9. 8300

For directors, the agreement should also deal with resignation of **directorships** (¶2125). 8301

It is advisable for the contract to oblige the employee to **return company property** when the employment terminates. The following wording is from the model contract of employment for general staff (similar wording is included in the service agreement). 8302

EXAMPLE On the termination of your employment howsoever arising or at [employer's] specific request, you will immediately return to [employer] all property belonging or relating to [employer] that it is in your possession or under your control. [For the avoidance of doubt, this includes (but it is not limited to) [your company car, keys, security cards, *list other property*], and all documents, records, correspondence, papers and other materials (and any copies thereof), whether in hard copy or in electronic or machine readable form, made or kept by, or provided to, you during your employment.] You will not retain any copies or extracts of such material.

A. Statement of reasons for dismissal

If an employee is dismissed (with or without notice) or his fixed-term contract expires without being renewed, he is entitled to **request** (orally or in writing) a written statement of reasons for his dismissal, which must be provided within 14 days of the request (s 92(1) ERA 1996). 8310

The employee must normally have been **continuously employed** for 1 year ending with the effective date of termination (see below) (Unfair Dismissal and Reasons for Dismissal (Variation of Qualifying Period) Order SI 1999/1436). However, if an employee is dismissed whilst **pregnant or after childbirth** or on **adoption leave** where the dismissal ends her maternity or adoption leave period, no period of continuous employment is required (and no request for the statement need be made) (s 92(4), (4A) ERA 1996).

MEMO POINTS The **compulsory statutory dismissal and disciplinary procedure** requires the employer, prior to dismissal, to set out in writing the alleged circumstances which have led him to contemplate dismissing (or taking disciplinary action against) the employee. This will also provide evidence of his reasons for dismissal. See Chapter 19 for further details.

The employer may refer the employee to full reasons given in an **earlier written communication** (a copy must be sent with the employer's reply) (*Kent County Council v Gilham* [1985] IRLR 18, CA). 8311

The reasons given can be used as evidence in any **court or tribunal proceedings**.

8312 The employee can apply to an employment tribunal if the employer unreasonably **fails to provide** the statement of reasons or the employee believes that the reasons given are **inadequate or untrue** (s 93(1) ERA 1996).

It may be unreasonable for an employer to fail to comply even where the employee is fully aware of the reason for dismissal, as the provision enables him to show the reason for dismissal to third parties. The reason given must be sufficiently specific or it will be inadequate. It may be reasonable for the employer not to give a statement where he reasonably believes that there was in fact no dismissal (*Broomsgrove v Eagle Alexander Ltd* [1981] IRLR 127, EAT).

8313 The complaint must be **made within** 3 months from the effective date of termination (see below) (or within such further period as the tribunal considers reasonable where it was not reasonably practicable to comply with that limit) (s 93(3) ERA 1996).

If it upholds the employee's complaint, the **tribunal must order** the employer to pay him 2 weeks' pay (uncapped) (see ¶2920 for calculation of a week's pay) and may make a declaration in respect of the employer's reasons for dismissal (s 93(2) ERA 1996).

> EXAMPLE In *Marenghi v Western Baths Club*, EAT case 1508/00, M worked as a barmaid. The employer restructured the club so that the bar and kitchen were in the same place and asked M to serve food as well as drinks. She refused and her employment ended. The statement of reasons stated that she had been dismissed and had been made redundant. The EAT held that this statement was inadequate and untrue as the tribunal had found that the dismissal was for "some other substantial reason" (her refusal of a reasonable alternative to her duties). The employer had, therefore, given the wrong reason in the statement and the tribunal should have awarded M the mandatory 2 weeks' pay.

B. References

8320 There is **no implied term** entitling an employee to a reference. In some cases, the employer may be obliged to give a reference (for example, by a regulatory body or by the terms of a settlement agreement with the employee), or he may be willing to accede to the employee's request for one. As the employee may need a reference to obtain new employment (see ¶704 in relation to references as a pre-condition of employment), it is relatively unusual for the employer to refuse to supply one and a refusal may be discriminatory (see below).

A reference may be provided **orally** or, more commonly, **in writing**. All written references should be marked "private and confidential" to avoid their disclosure to third parties. References are often **requested by** prospective employers. Character references may also be sought from other organisations, for example in connection with legal proceedings. Financial references may also be requested by lenders or banks, for example in connection with a worker's application for a mortgage. Consequently, a reference may be **general**, or may be a response to a request for **specific details**. Regardless of the type of reference, the employer must take care not to breach the legal duties that he owes both to the recipient of the reference (the new employer) and to the subject (the employee/ex-employee).

8321 The **information provided** may depend on the status of the employee, with a fuller reference being provided for more senior employees. A reference for general staff will commonly include the following:
- length of service;
- positions held;
- competence;
- honesty/integrity;
- absence record;
- time-keeping; and
- reason for leaving.

When deciding whether to provide a reference (or the content of that reference), the employer must **avoid discriminating** against, or victimising, a particular employee (*Coote v Granada Hospitality (No 2)* [1999] IRLR 452, EAT). If the **reason for the refusal** to provide a reference is based on discriminatory grounds, the refusal in itself could amount to a discriminatory act (¶5222). The employer's reason is therefore a crucial factor in determining his liability. 8322

EXAMPLE **Victimisation**

In *Coote v Granada Hospitality (No 2)*, the employer victimised C by failing to provide her with a reference following her sex discrimination claim.

No victimisation

In *Chief Constable of West Yorkshire Police v Khan* [2001] IRLR 830, HL, K brought race discrimination proceedings against his employer. The employer refused to provide him with a reference for new employment while those proceedings were continuing. The Court held that K was not victimised because the reason for the refusal was not the fact that he had brought proceedings, but rather that providing a reference would have amounted to a reassertion of the alleged discriminatory views and would have compromised the employer's position in those proceedings.

The employee cannot bring a **libel** action based on the reference, unless the employer is motivated by malice and knows the information is incorrect. 8323

Duty of care If a **reference is provided**, the employer owes the employee (or ex-employee) a duty of care to ensure that it is **accurate**. In such circumstances, there is an implied term that the reference will be compiled (and the information on which it is based will be verified) with reasonable care. If it is not, the employee may have a remedy for **negligent misstatement** (*Spring v Guardian Assurance plc* [1994] IRLR 460, HL). For such a remedy to be available, the employer must **actually have provided** a reference (i.e. the employee cannot argue that any reference given would inevitably include a detrimental statement) (*Legal & General Assurance Ltd v Kirk* [2002] IRLR 124, CA). The **new employer** may also have a claim against the old employer if he suffers any loss as a result of inaccuracies in the reference (for example, if it gives a false picture of the employee's abilities). The employer must, therefore, ensure that a reference can be substantiated. 8324

Note that the duty of care does **not extend to** other statements made by the employer when generally disseminating the reasons for dismissing the employee (*Aspin v Metric Group Ltd* [2004] All ER (D) 221, QBD).

MEMO POINTS **While employed**, it has been held to be part of the implied contractual term of trust and confidence that the employer should exercise reasonable care and skill when providing a reference for existing employees (¶1245).

There is **no duty to provide a full and comprehensive reference** so employers may wish merely to provide an objective **standard form** reference, limited to basic facts and avoiding comments on more subjective issues. 8325

However, the reference must be in substance true, accurate and fair (*Bartholomew v London Borough of Hackney* [1999] IRLR 246, CA), and must **not be misleading** or create a false impression, or the employer will be negligent.

If the employee leaves while **disciplinary proceedings are pending**, the employer is not obliged to complete that investigation, but he should limit any **unfavourable statements** to matters that have been properly investigated and which he has reasonable grounds to believe are true (*Cox v Sun Alliance Life* [2001] IRLR 448, CA).

EXAMPLE **No breach of duty**

1. In *Kidd v Axa Equity & Law Life Assurance Society plc* [2000] IRLR 301, QBD, the employer gave a reference for K, a top salesman, which referred to the fact that he was in the process of **being investigated following seven complaints**. The employer omitted to answer a question about K's honesty and did not mention his excellent sales record, the particular nature of the products sold, or that he denied the allegations, was not in fact aware of all of the complaints and had had no reasonable opportunity to deal with them. Nevertheless, the Court held the employer was not in breach.

2. In *Bartholomew v London Borough of Hackney*, the reference referred to the fact that, at the time B left, he had been **suspended pending disciplinary action**. B alleged that the reference was negligent

as it failed to state that he strongly disputed the charges. Despite this omission, the reference was accurate and fair.

Breach of duty

3. In *Cox v Sun Alliance Life*, the employer led C's new employer to understand that C had left while disciplinary proceedings involving allegations of financial impropriety were pending. This was held to be an unfair reference because the unfavourable comments were not confined to matters which had been investigated and were, therefore, made without reasonable grounds.

MEMO POINTS 1. **While employed**, an employee has the right **not to suffer a detrimental act** or omission (s 44 ERA 1996) and an employer must ensure that any reference he provides is satisfactory, although this particular right only exists while the employee is still employed (*Fadipe v Reed Nursing Personnel* [2001] EWCA 1885).

2. In respect of employees who receive unsatisfactory references due to **whistleblowing**, see ¶2700.

8326 Where a settlement is agreed on termination, the wording of the **reference may be agreed** between the employer and the employee. The employer must, however, still be aware of his duty to new employers when supplying an agreed form reference.

8328 **Data protection** If the employer is asked to provide a reference, he should consider discussing the request with the employee. If **sensitive information** is requested, the employee's explicit consent to disclosure must be obtained to avoid a breach of data protection rules (¶5951).

As **good practice**, the employer should (part 2.9 DP Code):
- have a **clear company policy** which sets out who can give corporate references and in what circumstances. All referees should be made aware of the policy; and
- not give confidential references unless the referee is sure that this is the **worker's wish**. It may also be useful to include on file a record of whether the worker wants references to be provided after he has left.

Employers are also advised to follow the DP Code's general **recommendations** with regard to data management (¶6000).

8329 References given by the employer are excluded from the **right of access** to personal data held by him, although the employee may access the reference in the hands of the recipient (if the identity of the author can be protected or the author waives the right not to be identified (¶5980)).

8330 **Disclaimers** The employer may include a disclaimer of liability in the reference, but this is likely to be invalid as an unfair contract term prohibited by the law (¶1340) in relation to facts which are ordinarily within the knowledge of an employer (it may be reasonable (and therefore valid) in relation to statements of opinion not based on such facts).

C. Date of termination

8340 For the reasons set out below, it is necessary to ascertain the "**effective date of termination**" (EDT), known as the "**relevant date**" for redundancy payment purposes, but referred to here as EDT unless the two need to be distinguished.

The reasons are:
- to comply with **time limits** for tribunal or court claims (for example, unfair dismissal claims must be brought within 3 months from the EDT);
- to identify whether the employee has sufficient continuity of employment to **qualify for a particular statutory right**;
- to calculate the amount of any **statutory redundancy payment** or **unfair dismissal basic award** (which are based on length of continuous employment);

– to determine whether the employee has reached **normal retiring age**, which will preclude him from unfair dismissal and statutory redundancy payment claims (although see ¶¶5254, 8210, 8412 and 8992 as to the effect of the Employment Equality (Age) Regulations 2006, which are expected to come into force in October 2006);
– to identify the calculation date in order to ascertain a **"week's pay"** (for the purposes of various compensation awards, including unfair dismissal basic award, failure to consult under collective redundancy obligations, failure to provide written reasons for dismissal); and
– to determine whether a worker is a **protected shop or betting worker** throughout his period of continuous employment for the purposes of Sunday working.

The EDT depends on the **form of termination**, i.e. whether the termination is with or without notice or the expiry of a fixed-term contract. This is discussed in detail below. 8341

In summary, **it is the date** (Unfair dismissal: s 97(1) ERA 1996; Redundancy: s 145(2) ERA 1996):
– on which notice of termination expires; or
– (where no notice is served) the date on which termination takes effect; or
– the date of expiry of a fixed-term contract.

The **parties can agree** the EDT (even retrospectively) (*Lambert v Croydon College* [1999] IRLR 346, EAT). This will **not affect** the employee's statutory continuity of employment. If an employee who is under notice of dismissal (see ¶8343) agrees with his employer to bring forward the date of termination, the original notice period is withdrawn and replaced by a shorter notice period, with the result that the effective date of termination is brought forward. There does not need to be a positive withdrawal of the original notice of termination (*Palfrey v Transco plc* [2004] IRLR 916, EAT). For the purposes of other employee rights under ERA 1996, the **EDT** can **only be determined by** what happened between the parties over time and not on what they may have agreed to treat as having happened (*Fitzgerald v University of Kent at Canterbury* [2004] IRLR 300, CA). Consequently, when termination took effect is a matter of fact for the tribunal to decide and it will ignore any retrospective agreement setting out a different date. 8342

EXAMPLE In *Lambert v Croydon College*, L was on long-term sick leave from 11 September 1995. On 7 March 1996 he agreed with his employer that his employment terminated with effect from 31 December 1995. His unfair dismissal application to the tribunal on 6 June 1996 was, therefore, out of time.

Dismissal with notice

When an employee is dismissed with notice, the EDT is the date the notice expires (not the date on which notice was given, and whether or not the employee actually attends work during the notice period) (ss 97(1)(a), 145(2)(a) ERA 1996). The same applies to discrimination claims based on dismissal (*Lupetti v Wrens Old House Ltd* [1984] ICR 348, EAT). See ¶8120 in relation to notice periods. 8343

If the employer's **notice is ambiguous** as to the intended date for its expiry, it is interpreted to reflect what a reasonable employee would understand it to mean in the light of facts known to him at the time, and any ambiguity will be resolved in the employee's favour (*Chapman v Letheby & Christopher Ltd* [1981] IRLR 440, EAT). A written notice of dismissal will be interpreted without reference to any prior or subsequent oral or written communication, unless it is merely confirming an earlier oral notice of dismissal, in which case the letter can be used to clarify any ambiguity in the earlier notice (*Leech v Preston Borough Council* [1985] IRLR 337, EAT). 8344

If a **payment in lieu of notice** is made, the EDT is as for dismissal without notice (¶8349) unless the intention was actually to dismiss the employee with notice but release him from his obligation to work out the notice (i.e. paid or garden leave situations), in which case the EDT is as stated above. 8345

As noted above (¶8342), the parties can agree to **bring forward or postpone** the date of termination. If the employee gives a **counter-notice** to terminate which expires prior to the 8346 employer's notice (¶9000), he may still be treated as having been dismissed by the employer if he leaves before expiry of the employer's notice period, but the EDT will be the date the employee's notice expires (*Thompson v GEC Avionics Ltd* [1991] IRLR 488, EAT; s 145(3) ERA 1996 in relation to the relevant date).

8347 In **constructive dismissal** cases, where the employee resigns with notice, the date of termination is the date the notice expires (*Peterborough Regional College v Gidney*, EAT case 1270/97 and 1270A/97).

8348 Where the **employee or employer dies** during the employer's notice period, the contract is treated as having expired by notice terminating on the date of death (ss 133(1), 176(1) ERA 1996).

Dismissal without notice

8349 If the employee is dismissed without notice, the EDT is the date on which the termination takes effect (normally immediately, i.e. when the employer tells the employee that he is dismissed "with immediate effect" or when the employee ceases to work) (ss 97(1)(b), 145(2)(b) ERA 1996).

There is an argument that termination without notice, as a fundamental breach of contract, must be accepted by the innocent party in order to bring the contract to an end, rather than automatically terminating the contract. For statutory purposes, case law indicates that there is **no need for acceptance** (i.e. the employment is terminated automatically by the fundamental breach) (*Robert Cort & Son Ltd v Charman* [1981] ICR 816, EAT). Therefore, where the employer summarily dismisses the employee, the EDT is the date of dismissal.

If the **summary dismissal is oral**, it will take effect at the moment it is communicated to the employee (and not at the end of that day (or shift) (*Octavius Atkinson & Sons Ltd v Morris* [1989] ICR 431, CA)). If the communication is **in writing**, the EDT is the day on which the employee reads it. Tribunals will take into account when letters arrive in the ordinary course of post and the fact that people normally open their post promptly after it arrives. However, if there is a delay, the EDT will be when the employee has actual knowledge of the termination (unless he has deliberately avoided reading the letter) (*McMaster v Manchester Airport Plc* [1998] IRLR 112, EAT).

EXAMPLE In *McMaster v Manchester Airport Plc*, M's letter of dismissal (terminating the employment immediately) was posted to his home. He did not see it until the day after it arrived as he had been away in France on that day. The EDT was the date he read the letter.

8350 As for dismissal with notice, any **ambiguity** as to the effect of the dismissal is construed in favour of the employee. The date on which the employee is sent his **P45** is not relevant for the purposes of ascertaining the EDT (*London Borough of Newham v Ward* [1985] IRLR 509, CA).

8351 Where a **payment in lieu of notice** is made, the EDT is the date of dismissal (*Dedman v British Building & Engineering Appliances Ltd* [1973] IRLR 379, CA).

8352 In cases of **constructive dismissal** where the employee resigns without notice, the EDT is normally the date the employee accepts the breach as terminating the employment (as opposed to the date of the employer's breach). This acceptance must be communicated (by words or conduct) to the employer, so a letter of resignation which purports to terminate the employment immediately cannot do so until it is received by the employer (*Edwards v Surrey Police* [1999] IRLR 456, EAT; *Weathersfield Ltd (t/a Van & Truck Rentals) v Sargent* [1999] IRLR 94, CA). Nevertheless, a fax which sets out an employee's resignation without notice is deemed to have been received by the employer (and therefore communicated to him) at the time it is sent (*Potter and others v R J Temple plc (in liquidation)*, EAT case 478/03). It is irrelevant if the fax is sent out of office hours and that the employer will not actually see it until the next working day.

MEMO POINTS Only where the **breach itself inevitably terminates** the employer-employee relationship (for example, where the employee loses a directorship on which his employment depends) will the EDT be the date of the breach rather than the employee's resignation, where different (*BMK Ltd and BMK Holdings Ltd v Logue* [1993] IRLR 477, EAT).

Date of dismissal postponed Where the employer has given no notice or inadequate notice, the employee's **statutory notice** entitlement is **added on** (i.e. the EDT/relevant date is postponed) for the **following purposes** (ss 97(2), (3), 145(5), (6) ERA 1996): 8353
- assessing continuous employment for claiming:
· a written statement of reasons for dismissal (s 92(7) ERA 1996);
· unfair dismissal (s 108(1) ERA 1996); and
· a statutory redundancy payment (s 155 ERA 1996); and
- calculating the amount of an employee's continuous service in respect of:
· redundancy pay entitlement (s 162(1) ERA 1996); and
· unfair dismissal basic award (s 119(1) ERA 1996).

In relation to the EDT, this applies to both **express and constructive dismissal** cases (s 97(4) ERA 1996). The relevant date is not deemed postponed in cases of constructive dismissal.

Statutory notice is added on even where the employee has **waived** his right to notice or accepted a **payment in lieu** (*Secretary of State for Employment v Staffordshire County Council* [1989] IRLR 117, CA).

If the **employee dies** after the contract has been terminated but before the date on which proper notice (had it been given) would have expired, the relevant date will be the date of death (not the date on which statutory minimum notice would have expired) (ss 133(2), 176(2) ERA 1996).

EXAMPLE Employee L began work on 4 August 2003. He is dismissed without notice on 2 August 2004. On the face of it, he does not have the 1 year's continuous employment required to bring an unfair dismissal claim. However, his entitlement to statutory minimum notice (one week) is added on, which means that he qualifies to bring a claim.

No postponement Statutory notice is not added on where the employer is entitled to dismiss the employee summarily (for example, because of the employee's **gross misconduct**), or for the purpose of determining the **time limit** for tribunal claims. 8354

If the contract is terminated without notice just before the employee becomes entitled to a certain **contractual benefit** (for example, enhanced pension rights), no notice is added on but the loss will be recoverable as part of a wrongful dismissal claim (¶8161). Similarly, if the employee would have acquired a particular **statutory right** had the proper notice been given (for example, the right to claim unfair dismissal), the date of termination is not affected but the loss will be reflected in any award for wrongful dismissal. 8355

Fixed-term contracts

Where a fixed-term contract expires without being renewed, the EDT is the date of expiry (ss 97(1)(c), 145(2)(c) ERA 1996). 8356

Trial period in alternative employment

In redundancy cases, where the employee works for a trial period in alternative employment (¶8850) and leaves during that period, the relevant date for **qualifying service and payment calculation** purposes is the date of termination of the original contract (s 145(4)(b) ERA 1996). For **time limit** purposes, however, the relevant date is the date of termination of the trial period (or the last trial period, where more than one) (s 145(4)(a) ERA 1996). 8357

Appeals against dismissal

The employee may appeal the decision to dismiss him. If he is **reinstated** on appeal, there will be no dismissal (*Savage v J Sainsbury Ltd* [1980] IRLR 109, CA). If, however, the **decision to dismiss is confirmed**, the EDT will depend on the facts of the case and, in particular, the terms of the disciplinary procedure. Normally the employee is suspended pending the appeal decision and the contract does not subsist, such that the original date of dismissal stands (*Savage v J Sainsbury Ltd*). However, the contract may state that the employment subsists pending the appeal decision, with the dismissal not being implemented until that decision (*Drage* 8358 *v Governors of Greenford High School* [2000] IRLR 314, CA). Frequently, there is no express mention of the status of the employee pending the decision and the tribunal must ascertain the position from all the facts. Whether the employee continues to be paid while on suspension will be an important factor.

EXAMPLE In *Savage v J Sainsbury Ltd*, S's contract stated that, pending the appeal decision, S would be suspended without pay but if reinstated would receive full back pay. The Court held that the EDT was the original date of dismissal because the contract indicated that if the appeal failed, the employee would be deprived both of his pay and his right to work from the original dismissal date.

SECTION 2

Unfair dismissal

8380 All employees (and to a certain extent, some workers) also enjoy **statutory protection** on dismissal. If the dismissal is **discriminatory**, the employee may bring a discrimination claim on the grounds of sex, racial group, disability, religion or belief, sexual orientation or age (which is expected to come into force from 1 October 2006 – see ¶5254) discrimination. If he is dismissed for an inadmissible reason, he can bring an unfair dismissal claim (with no requirement for qualifying service). In such cases, the dismissal will be **automatically unfair** (¶8390).

Dismissals to which the **business transfer** regulations apply are also automatically unfair and special rules apply (¶8030).

Dismissals where an employer has failed to comply with an **applicable statutory dispute resolution procedure** (¶6511) will also be automatically unfair (s 98A(1) ERA 1996) but unlike the automatic unfair dismissal provisions set out below (¶8390), for a finding of automatically unfair dismissal in respect of the failure to comply with an applicable statutory dispute resolution procedure, an employee must satisfy the usual qualifying conditions for bringing an unfair dismissal claim under the general scheme (¶8410).

Employees with sufficient qualifying service can bring an unfair dismissal claim under the **general scheme** (s 94(1) ERA 1996; see ¶8410).

8381 In order to avoid a claim of unfair dismissal under the general scheme, an employer must be able to show a **statutory fair reason** for dismissal. If he cannot, the dismissal will be unfair.

If he does have a fair reason, the employer must also act fairly in all the circumstances in treating that reason as a fair reason for dismissal. This essentially means that he must follow a **fair procedure**.

8382 If an employee is unfairly dismissed, he can apply to an employment tribunal for a **remedy**.

I. Automatic unfair dismissal

8390 It is automatically unfair to dismiss an employee for **certain inadmissible reasons**.

If there are **several reasons** for dismissal, the dismissal will be automatically unfair if the inadmissible reason is the principal reason for dismissal.

MEMO POINTS It is expected that direct and indirect age discrimination will **become unlawful** from 1 October 2006 and, at the time of writing, the Government has published draft Employment Equality (Age) Regulations 2006. The draft regulations propose to make a **dismissal on the grounds of retirement automatically unfair** in certain circumstances (see memo points to ¶8422).
A summary of the draft regulations is provided at ¶5254. Other key proposals on age discrimination which apply to the law on unfair dismissal are outlined at ¶¶8411, 8412, 8422, 8575 and 8579).

A dismissal will also be automatically unfair if the employee was **selected for redundancy** for an inadmissible reason, where the circumstances constituting the redundancy applied equally to one or more other employees in the same undertaking who held positions similar to that held by the dismissed employee and who have not been dismissed (s 105 ERA 1996). 8391

In certain cases of automatically unfair dismissal, special provisions apply in relation to **remedies** (there may be no statutory cap on compensation, a minimum basic award may apply, and/or interim relief may be available). See the table at ¶8394 for further detail. 8392

Qualifying employees

Employees dismissed for the following inadmissible reasons **do not need** to have any particular period of **continuous employment** in order to bring an unfair dismissal claim. If the employee would not otherwise have sufficient continuity of employment to bring a claim under the general scheme (see below), he must prove that the reason for dismissal was an inadmissible one (such that no qualifying service is required) (*Smith v Hayle Town Council* [1978] IRLR 413, CA). 8393

For exclusions to the right to claim, see the table at ¶8412 below. However, employees over the **normal retiring age** are not excluded.

Some workers (for definition, see ¶13), who are not employees, whose contracts are terminated for one (or more) of the inadmissible reasons shown in the table below, can complain that they have suffered a detriment by the termination of their contracts. The position for workers contrasts with that of employees, who have to bring a claim under the unfair dismissal rules in such circumstances.

Inadmissible reasons

The following table lists the inadmissible reasons and shows who is protected against dismissal or detriment in those circumstances. Both employees and workers who are not employees are protected from being subjected to a **detriment** by any act or deliberate failure to act by their employer relating to one of the inadmissible reasons set out below. However, if the detriment in question amounts to a **dismissal**, then the only remedy available to an employee is a claim for unfair dismissal, whereas a worker, who is not an employee, whose contract is terminated, can complain that he has suffered a detriment. In such cases, compensation is awarded on the same basis as for unfair dismissal. 8394

Reason	Employee	Worker	Para.
Health and safety reasons	x		¶5097
Trade union reasons: – being, or proposing to be, a member of an independent trade union (or not being, or refusing to become/remain a member), or taking part, or proposing to take part in trade union activities, or making use of union services at an appropriate time; – taking protected industrial action; and – trade union recognition or derecognition – unlawful inducement	x x x x	x x x x	¶¶7560, 7521, 7573, 7583, 7598
Employee representation: – being an employee representative (or candidate) for collective redundancy consultation or business transfer consultation purposes, or taking part in an election of employee representatives for those purposes; and – membership of a special negotiating body or European Works Council, or being an information and consultation representative, or candidate for any of the above under transnational information and consultation legislation	x		¶¶8957, 8080, 7782, 7785
Pregnancy and maternity, paternity, adoption, parental, and dependant care leave reasons	x		¶¶4765, 4771
Assertion of a statutory right	x		¶8395

Reason	Employee	Worker	Para.
Seeking to enforce rights under part-time workers legislation	x	x	¶1920
Seeking to enforce rights under fixed term employees regulations	x		¶1997
Seeking to enforce rights under the working time regulations	x	x	¶4040
Making a protected disclosure for the purposes of the whistleblowing legislation	x	x	¶¶2763, 2769
Seeking to enforce rights under the national minimum wage regulations	x	x	¶2912
Exercising, or seeking to exercise, the right to be accompanied at a disciplinary or grievance hearing, or for accompanying a fellow worker to such a hearing	x	x	¶¶6791, 6793
Trusteeship of occupational pension scheme	x		¶3433
Protected shop/betting workers under Sunday trading legislation	x		¶¶3861-2
Spent convictions [1]	x		¶6672

1. Although it is not expressly stated in case law, it is generally accepted that a dismissal on the grounds of a spent conviction is automatically unfair without the need to have a particular period of continuous service.

8395 In relation to the **assertion of statutory rights**, the employee is protected if he brings proceedings to enforce the right or alleges that the employer has infringed the right (the allegation must be made prior to the dismissal) (s 104 ERA 1996). He need not have specified the right he sought to assert, as long as he made it reasonably clear to the employer what that right was (*Armstrong v Watler Scott Motors (London) Ltd*, EAT case 766/02). Further, provided the employee acts in good faith, he is protected regardless of whether he is actually entitled to the particular right and regardless of whether that right has in fact been infringed (*Mennell v Newell & Wright (Transport Contractors) Ltd* [1997] IRLR 519, CA). However, it appears that an employee will not be protected if he alleges that the employer has merely proposed or threatened to infringe such a right.

The **relevant statutory rights** include those relating to:
– employment documentation, including written statements of employment particulars, itemised pay statements, and written statement of reasons for dismissal;
– employee payments, including guarantee pay, medical/maternity suspension payments; protection against unlawful deductions from pay/unlawful receipt of payments by the employer, deductions of unauthorised or excessive union subscriptions, and requiring the employer to stop payment of a contribution to a union's political fund;
– time off (for public duties, antenatal care, trade union duties and activities, trade union learning representatives' duties or training, employee representatives and candidates' study or training, employee pension scheme trustee duties or training, or to look for work/arrange training prior to redundancy);
– maternity, paternity, parental, adoption and dependant care leave;
– working time, rest periods, breaks and annual leave;
– making a public interest disclosure;
– protection against detriment in health and safety cases, cases relating to Sunday shop or betting work, or on trade union grounds; and
– rights on dismissal, including statutory minimum notice, not to be unfairly dismissed, and to a statutory redundancy payment.

EXAMPLE In *Albion Hotel (Freshwater) Ltd v Maia e Silva* [2002] IRLR 200, EAT, Mr and Mrs S were hotel managers, entitled to an annual bonus dependent on occupancy levels. The hotel did not perform well under their management and at two review meetings when the couple **asserted their right to a bonus**, the employer indicated that no bonus was likely to be payable. They were subsequently dismissed. The EAT agreed that they had been dismissed for asserting a statutory right, namely the right not to suffer an unlawful deduction from wages (the refusal to pay the bonus).

II. General scheme

A. Qualifying employees

Employees who satisfy the requirements of continuous employment can bring an unfair dismissal claim, unless they are excluded (s 108(1) ERA 1996; Unfair Dismissal and Statement of Reasons for Dismissal (Variation of Qualifying Period) Order SI 1999/1436). 8410

Generally, an employee must have 1 year of **continuous employment** ending on the effective date of termination (¶8340). However, employees dismissed on medical grounds in consequence of certain health and safety requirements or recommendations only need 1 month's continuous employment (s 108(2) ERA 1996) (¶4862). 8411

MEMO POINTS Although potentially discriminatory, it is proposed that the above requirement of 1 year of continuous employment will be retained under the draft Employment Equality (Age) Regulations 2006. A summary of the draft regulations is provided at ¶5254.

For detail on **calculating** statutory continuity, see ¶1040.

Excluded employees

The following employees cannot bring an unfair dismissal claim: 8412

Employee	Para.
On **illegal contract**	¶1305
Reached **normal retiring age** for job or age of 65 if lower (although it is proposed that this age limit will be removed under the draft Employment Equality (Age) Regulations 2006: see ¶5254 for a summary of the draft regulations).	¶8210
Waived right to claim in valid **compromise agreement, ACAS-conciliated agreement**, or as part of ACAS **arbitration**	¶9259
On certain **fixed-term contracts**	1
Taking part in **certain industrial action**: – unofficial industrial action at time of dismissal (unless reason for dismissal is related to: family, time off for dependants, health and safety, working time, employee representative, or whistleblowing); or – lawful industrial action which is not protected industrial action, if dismissed whilst such action is taking place and all other employees who are taking part are also dismissed	¶7520
Covered by **dismissal procedures agreement** exempted by Order made by Secretary of State for Employment	2

1. This includes employees on **fixed-term contracts** for 1 year or more who agreed in writing before 25 October 1999 to waive the right to claim on expiry without renewal of that contract (or any extension to which the waiver applies agreed before that date). Waivers agreed after that date are not effective to exclude unfair dismissal rights.
2. The parties to the **dismissal procedures agreement** apply jointly to the Secretary of State to substitute the agreement for the statutory unfair dismissal provisions. The Secretary of State will make an exemption order if he is satisfied that:
– every trade union who is party to the agreement is independent;
– the agreement provides for procedures to be followed where an employee claims that he has been/is being unfairly dismissed;
– these procedures are available to all employees to which the agreement applies;
– the remedies provided are on the whole as beneficial as (but not necessarily identical with) the statutory scheme;
– the procedures provide for arbitration in every case, or at least in cases where a decision cannot be reached and the right to submit any question of law arising out of a decision to arbitration; and
– the provisions are such that it can be determined with reasonable certainty whether a particular employee is covered by the agreement.

B. Reason for dismissal

Dismissal

8420 If it is disputed, the first step in any unfair dismissal claim is for the **employee to show** that he has been dismissed. The definition of dismissal for these purposes is discussed at ¶8106.

8421 Certain employees can ask their employer to provide a written **statement of reasons** for dismissal (¶8310), which can be used as evidence in tribunal proceedings.

8422 Once the employee has shown that he was dismissed, the **employer must show** that the dismissal was for one of the statutory fair reasons (s 98(1) ERA 1996). If he cannot, the dismissal will be substantively unfair (*Timex Corporation v Thomson* [1981] IRLR 522, EAT).

The five fair reasons are:
- incapability;
- misconduct;
- redundancy;
- contravention of a duty or restriction; and
- some other substantial reason.

MEMO POINTS It is proposed under the draft Employment Equality (Age) Regulations 2006 that a dismissal on the **grounds of retirement** will be a fair dismissal if it is conducted in accordance with the draft regulations (see ¶5254 and ¶8207 +).

It is proposed that there will be a distinction between planned retirement dismissals and other retirement dismissals. A **planned retirement** will take effect on the date on which the employee reaches the default age of 65 or the employers normal retirement age (if this is below 65, it would need to be objectively justified (see ¶5254)) or where the employer has informed the employee of the retirement date at least 6 months in advance. In the case of a planned retirement, it will be assumed that the employer is correct in saying that the reason for the dismissal is retirement. The employee will have a heavy burden of proof if he wants to show the dismissal was for a different reason.

In **other retirement** situations, the burden of proof will be on the employer to show that the reason for the dismissal was retirement.

It is also proposed that employers will need to follow the **duty-to-consider** procedure to avoid the retirement being an unfair dismissal. The normal statutory dismissal procedures (¶6510) will not apply to genuine retirement dismissals.

A dismissal on the grounds of retirement will also be **automatically unfair** if, prior to the intended retirement date, an employer has not informed an employee at all of the intended retirement date and the employee's right to request working past this date, or has done so less than 2 weeks before the retirement date. It will also be automatically unfair if a dismissal takes effect while the duty-to-consider procedure is underway and an employer has not yet held a meeting with the employee or informed him of the decision.

8423 The tribunal will investigate the **real reason** for the employee's dismissal and may find that the employer has incorrectly labelled the dismissal, in which case it may substitute the correct reason provided the necessary facts have been established (*Abernethy v Mott, Hay and Anderson* [1974] IRLR 213, CA; *Marenghi v Western Baths Club*, EAT case 1508/00). It will not do so, however, if the employee would be prejudiced where the difference in grounds goes to facts and substance such that he might have conducted his case in a substantially different way (*Hannan v TNT-IPEC (UK) Ltd* [1986] IRLR 165, EAT). The employer should, therefore, take care when deciding which reason for dismissal to plead when defending a claim (he may plead a different reason in the alternative). This is particularly important as different factors may need to be taken into account when judging the reasonableness of the dismissal for a given reason (*Wilson v Post Office* [2000] IRLR 834, CA). If the tribunal **wrongly categorises** the reason for dismissal, this amounts to an error of law (which can, therefore, be appealed) (*Amor v Galliard Homes Ltd*, EAT case 47/01; *Wilson v Post Office*, above).

If the **employee disputes** the reason given for dismissal, it is for the employer to prove which reason was the principal reason for dismissal (*Maund v Penwith District Council* [1984] IRLR 24, CA).

EXAMPLE **Categorisation of reason for dismissal**
In *Wilson v Post Office*, the employer's tribunal defence stated that W was dismissed for "incapability by reason of unsatisfactory attendance record". The Court held that the tribunal incorrectly treated the case as one of incapability by reason of health rather than a case involving dismissal for another substantial reason (namely W's failure to meet the requirements of an agreed attendance procedure). The case was remitted for consideration on the correct basis.

The reason for dismissal in **constructive dismissal** cases is the employer's reason for committing the fundamental breach. Unfair constructive dismissal is discussed in detail at ¶8251. 8424

If the employer **dismisses by giving notice**, the reason for dismissal is determined by reference to the reason when the employment terminates and also by reference to the reason for giving the notice (*Parkinson v March Consulting Ltd* [1997] IRLR 308, CA). The employer may only rely on **facts known to him at the time** of the dismissal when putting forward a potentially fair reason for dismissal. If the facts change between the date of giving notice and the date of termination, the tribunal can have regard to the latter date and the changed facts (*Parkinson v March Consulting Ltd*). 8425

However, the employer cannot rely on **facts** which **emerge after the dismissal** to justify his decision to dismiss, although such facts may affect the amount of compensation awarded (*Devis & Sons Ltd v Atkins* [1977] IRLR 314, HL). Evidence of post-termination events are not, therefore, admissible in tribunal proceedings to establish the fairness or otherwise of a dismissal. It may be admissible in exceptional circumstances if it is relevant to the credibility of a witness or otherwise shows that other evidence given in relation to pre-termination events is inaccurate (*Overton v Healthcall Services Ltd*, EAT case 282/01). If there is an **internal appeal**, the employer can rely on new information which comes to light to confirm the dismissal for the original reason (but not for a different reason) (*Monie v Coral Racing Ltd* [1979] IRLR 54, EAT; *West Midlands Co-operative Society Ltd v Tipton* [1986] IRLR 112, HL).

If the employer is **pressured to dismiss** by reason of the calling, organising, procuring or financing a strike or other industrial action (or the threat of such), that pressure is ignored when determining whether the employer had a fair reason for dismissal (and also whether it was fair in the circumstances to dismiss) (s 107 ERA 1996). However, the trade union/individual who induced the employer to dismiss may be joined in the proceedings and ordered to pay all or part of any compensation awarded (s 160 TULRCA 1992). 8426

C. Procedure

Where the employer has established one of the five fair reasons for dismissal, the **tribunal will then consider** whether he acted reasonably in all the circumstances (taking into consideration the size and administrative resources of his undertaking) in treating that reason as a sufficient reason for dismissal (s 98(4) ERA 1996). 8435

This is essentially a question of fact and so the **tribunal's decision** cannot normally be **appealed** (the EAT hears appeals on points of law only and will only otherwise interfere if the tribunal has misdirected itself as to the law, reached a decision contrary to the facts, or if the decision is perverse).

Dismissal must be within the band or **range of reasonable responses** which a reasonable employer might make, and the tribunal must not substitute its own view for that of the employer (*Iceland Frozen Foods Limited v Jones* [1982] IRLR 439, EAT; *Post Office v Foley and HSBC Bank (formerly Midland Bank) v Madden* [2000] IRLR 827, CA; *Aitkin v Weatherford UK Limited (Court of Session)* [2005] CSIH 26; *Anglia Home Improvements v Kelly* [2005] ICR 242, CA). Whether or not the employer's decision to dismiss falls within that range depends on the employer's state of knowledge at the time the decision was taken (*Asda Stores Ltd v Malyn*, EAT case 0066/00).

The question is determined in accordance with equity and the substantial merits of the case (i.e. the tribunal should adopt a **broad approach of common sense and fairness**, avoiding legal and other technicalities (*Earl v Slater & Wheeler (Airlyne) Ltd* [1972] IRLR 115, NIRC)). The **tribunal should**, therefore, not only **consider** the way in which the dismissal was carried out, but also whether the employer acted reasonably in relation to the situation leading up to the decision to dismiss. As noted above, pressure on the employer to dismiss by reason of industrial action is ignored when determining the question of reasonableness.

Relevant factors

8436 **Procedural defects** It is essential that if an employer is contemplating dismissing an employee, he must establish whether or not a **statutory dismissal and disciplinary procedure** applies (¶6511). If a statutory procedure is applicable, it is essential that an employer implements it fully. Full details of the procedures are found in Chapter 19.

If a statutory procedure applies and an employer fails to comply with it before dismissing an employee, the dismissal will be **automatically unfair** (s 98A(1) ERA 1996) (although the employee will still have to satisfy the usual qualifying conditions for unfair dismissal under the general scheme to be able to bring a claim – ¶8410). In addition, whether or not an applicable statutory procedure is complied with (by either party) will have implications as to the amount (if any) of any adjustment to a **compensatory award** which may be made to the employee in a successful claim for unfair dismissal (¶8629 +).

However, for the purpose of determining whether a dismissal was fair under the test set out above (¶8435), a **failure** by the employer **to follow a procedure** (other than a statutory dismissal and disciplinary procedure) will not, by itself, be regarded as making the employer's action unreasonable if the employer can demonstrate that he would have decided to dismiss the employee in any event had he followed the procedure (s 98A(2) ERA 1996). This new provision came into force on 1 October 2004 and effectively statutorily reverses the common law concept formerly known as the "Polkey principle".

8437 However, even if an employer meets the statutory minimum requirements of the dismissal and disciplinary procedure in taking action against an employee, it will not necessarily follow that the subsequent dismissal of the employee will be fair. An employer must also take into account the **best practice** principles set out in any relevant **code of practice** (for example, the ACAS code on disciplinary and grievance procedures), and a tribunal will consider whether best practice guidance has been followed, even where the parties themselves do not refer to it (*Lock v Cardiff Railway Co Ltd* [1998] IRLR 358, EAT).

Examples of defects (notwithstanding that the statutory minimum requirements have been met – ¶6560) might include:
- a failure to warn an employee of sub-standard performance;
- a failure to give an employee sufficient detail of the allegations he must face at a disciplinary hearing;
- a failure to warn an employee that the disciplinary sanction of dismissal could be imposed; and
- an appeal being heard by someone with previous involvement in the disciplinary matter.

8438 **Size and administrative resources** Tribunals will also take into account the size and administrative resources of the employer's undertaking. For example, it may not be possible for a small employer to offer alternative employment (see below) (*Bevan Harris Ltd v Gair* [1981] IRLR 520, EAT), or to have an elaborate disciplinary or appeals procedure (*MacKellar v Bolton* [1979] IRLR 59, EAT) (provided the dismissal and disciplinary procedure meets the statutory minimum requirements set out at ¶6560). However, the size of the undertaking will not justify a failure to properly investigate complaints made against the employee (and which lead to his dismissal) (*Henderson v Granville Tours Ltd* [1982] IRLR 494, EAT), nor will it excuse a complete failure to consult with a potentially redundant employee (although it may affect the nature or formality of the consultation process) (*De Grasse v Stockwell Tools Ltd* [1992] IRLR 269, EAT).

8439 **Investigation** The employer must make his decision having **ascertained all the relevant facts**, and the fairness of that decision is determined by reference to the circumstances known to him **at the time of the dismissal** (or confirmation of the dismissal following an internal appeal (*West Midlands Co-operative Society Ltd v Tipton* [1986] IRLR 112, HL)). Any investigation conducted by an employer into an employee's alleged misconduct should fall within the same **range of reasonable responses** as in relation to the dismissal itself (*Sainsbury's Supermarkets Ltd v Hitt* [2003] IRLR 23, CA, see ¶8508).

Consultation and alternative to dismissal As a matter of best practice, a fair procedure will commonly oblige the employer to consult with the employee and consider alternatives to dismissal. 8440

Internal appeal against dismissal As both a requirement of the statutory dismissal and disciplinary procedure and of best practice, there should be a **right of appeal** against the decision to dismiss. **Procedural defects** in the conduct of the appeal could also make an otherwise fair dismissal unfair. An appeal hearing that amounts to a complete rehearing can **cure any defects** (for example, in the consultation process), making a potentially unfair dismissal fair. 8441

Other factors Other factors commonly taken into account by tribunals include: 8442
- **length of service**; and
- **consistency** (in the treatment of employees in a sufficiently similar position and in the treatment of a particular employee from one occasion to the next) (¶6546).

D. Application to specific cases

1. Incapability

a. Fair reason

The employer will have a fair reason if the reason (or principal reason) for dismissal relates to "the **capability or qualifications** of the employee for performing work of the kind which he was employed by the employer to do." 8450

The incapability must relate to the kind of **work the employee was employed to do**, which is determined by reference to his current contractual obligations. For the dismissal to be fair, it is not necessary that the employee is unable to perform all of his contractual duties (*Shook v London Borough of Ealing* [1986] IRLR 46, EAT).

Capability

Capability is assessed "by reference to skill, aptitude, health or any other physical or mental quality" (s 98(3)(a) ERA 1996). Incapability, therefore, covers the employee's **incompetence** and also his inability to do the job as a result of **illness**. The approach taken by the employer should vary depending on the type of incapability. 8451

Incompetence Incapability will **include** employees who fail to meet the employer's standards, who work too slowly, or who are physically incapable of doing their job. It also includes those whose mental qualities prevent them from fulfilling their duties. 8452

EXAMPLE 1. In *A J Dunning & Sons (Shopfitters) Ltd v S Jacomb* [1973] IRLR 206, NIRC, J was fairly dismissed for incapability because he lacked the necessary aptitude and mental qualities to be co-operative with, and helpful to, important clients.

2. In *Abernethy v Mott, Hay and Anderson* [1974] IRLR 213, CA, A was dismissed for unreasonably refusing to work at a site other than the head office. The Court held that his inflexibility and lack of adaptability supported a fair dismissal for incapability.

8453 The **test** for a fair capability dismissal is whether the employer **honestly believes** that the employee is incompetent, and that he has **reasonable grounds** for his belief (*Taylor v Alidair Ltd* [1978] IRLR 82, CA). The tribunal cannot substitute its own view of the employee's competence. The employer does not need to prove that his belief was correct. He must show that there was **evidence** available to him that satisfied him of the employee's incompetence and that, relying on that evidence, it was reasonable to dismiss. His belief may, for example, be founded on performance figures or exam results which directly relate to the employee's abilities, customer complaints, complaints from other employees, or evidence from the employee's supervisor or manager (*Cook v Thomas Linnell & Sons Ltd* [1977] IRLR 132, EAT).

The employer's position will be weakened if he has made **other statements** that are **inconsistent** with his assertion of the employee's incapability (for example, in a reference to a prospective employer).

8454 **One act** of incompetence is not normally sufficient to support a fair dismissal, unless the consequences are so serious that it would be too risky and dangerous to continue the employment (*Taylor v Alidair Ltd*). On the other hand, a **number of minor incidents** over a relatively short period of time resulting in a loss of confidence in the employee's abilities could be a sufficient reason for dismissal, even though individually the incidents would not justify such action (*Miller v Executors of John C Graham* [1978] IRLR 309, EAT).

EXAMPLE In *Taylor v Alidair Ltd*, T, a **pilot**, was dismissed after landing a plane carrying fare-paying passengers so hard that there was serious damage to the plane. The Court held that this **one-off error of judgement** justified a dismissal for incapability.

8456 Incapability can be difficult to establish in the case of **managers** and other **senior employees**, as the quality of management may be difficult to assess precisely. Case law indicates that it is sufficient for a fair dismissal if the employer comes to the view over a period of time that the employee is incompetent, as long as he has supporting evidence for his view (for example, a fall-off in trade or feedback from colleagues or clients) (*Cook v Thomas Linnell & Sons Ltd*, above).

8457 In some cases, the employee's incompetence may really be **misconduct** (for example, where the employee fails to meet the required standard through his own carelessness, negligence or idleness (*Sutton & Gates (Luton) Ltd v Boxall* [1978] IRLR 486, EAT)). This will affect the way in which the employer should deal with the matter (¶8490).

8458 **Ill health** Incapability due to ill health may relate to **persistent short-term illness** or to **long-term illness**. The employee's ill health may reduce his performance levels or prevent him from carrying out his duties at all if he is absent. In exceptional circumstances, the employee's ill health may **frustrate the contract**, in which case there will be no dismissal (and therefore no possibility of an unfair dismissal claim (¶8285)).

More commonly, the employee's ill health may be a fair reason for dismissal and the question will depend on all the facts of the particular case. The following **factors** will be relevant:
- the nature of the illness;
- the length and frequency of absences;
- the likely length of continuing or future absences;
- the employer's need to have work done by that employee; and
- the effect of the absence on his colleagues.

EXAMPLE An employee who refused to provide unequivocal consent to her occupational health report being passed to her employer was fairly dismissed on the grounds of capability after 3.5 months on sickness absence. Without access to the occupational health report, the employer was entitled to conclude that she was incapable on the basis of the limited material available to it. (*Elmbridge Housing Trust v O'Donoghue* [2004] EWCA Civ 939).

Ill health is likely to be a fair reason for dismissal. The question of fairness normally focuses on the second limb, i.e. whether the employer has acted reasonably in dismissing the employee for that reason.

If the ill health has been **caused by the employer's treatment** of the employee, the employee may be able to bring a personal injury claim against him. The fact that the employer caused the illness will not always of itself make a dismissal unfair, although the tribunal can take this into consideration (*London Fire and Civil Defence Authority v Betty* [1994] IRLR 384, EAT; approved on this point only by *Frewin v Consignia*, EAT 0981/02) (although where the employer's actions are wilful or malicious, it could make the dismissal unfair (*Edwards v Governors of Hanson School* [2001] IRLR 733, EAT)). The employer may be expected to show greater sympathy towards the employee where he has caused the illness, and his actions are likely to be relevant to an assessment of compensation (*Edwards v Governors of Hanson School*). 8459

It may be fair for the employer to dismiss where the employee's ill health makes it **unsafe for him to continue** in his position because of the danger presented to himself or to other employees (*Harper v National Coal Board* [1980] IRLR 260, EAT). 8460

EXAMPLE Fair dismissal

In *Harper v National Coal Board*, H, an epileptic, had on three occasions had a fit during which he (unknowingly) **attacked other employees**. His dismissal was fair despite the fact that his epilepsy did not interfere with his actual job performance.

Unfair dismissal

In *Converform (Darwen) Ltd v Bell* [1981] IRLR 195, EAT, B was a works director at the employer's factory. His dismissal after a heart attack was unfair because the **risk of another heart attack** did not make it unsafe for him to continue in his position, given the nature of his work.

Qualifications

"Qualifications" means "any degree, diploma or other academic, technical or professional qualification relevant to the position" (s 98(3)(b) ERA 1996). It is not always necessary for the employment contract **expressly** to refer to, or require, specific qualifications, as these may be **inferred** from a job advertisement (*Tayside Regional Council v McIntosh* [1982] IRLR 272, EAT), or **implied** from the nature of the position. 8461

In some cases, an employee is engaged on the understanding that he **will obtain a certain qualification**. If he subsequently fails to do so, the dismissal is likely to be fair, even if his performance has otherwise been satisfactory (*Blackman v The Post Office* [1974] IRLR 46, NIRC). 8462

The employer's **requirements** for particular qualifications **may change** over time. A dismissal may be fair where an employee does not meet the new requirements, but the employer must take special care to follow a fair procedure (see below). 8463

A dismissal is likely to be fair where the employee **loses his qualifications** (or if they lapse), although the employer should offer any available suitable alternative employment. 8464

EXAMPLE In *Tayside Regional Council v McIntosh* (see above), M, a car mechanic, was fairly dismissed when he **lost his driving licence** as the job advertisement for the position had specified this as an essential requirement.

b. Fair procedure

In cases of incompetence and ill health alike, the issue of fair procedure is often crucial in determining whether a dismissal for incapability was fair. A **tribunal will consider** what steps a reasonable employer would have taken, and what steps the employer could have taken at the outset to minimise the risk of poor performance and to enable the employee to carry out his duties to a satisfactory standard. These may include the provision of adequate training and supervision, and a satisfactory physical working environment. 8470

It should be noted that a **statutory dismissal and disciplinary procedure** will apply where an employer is contemplating dismissing (or imposing a disciplinary sanction other than a warning or suspension on full pay against) an employee and, consequently, certain minimum requirements must be met. For further details, see ¶6560. However, simply following the statutory minimum requirements will not automatically mean that the dismissal is fair and, therefore, employers should consider the principles of best practice set out below to ensure as far as possible that every employee is dealt with fairly.

8471 **Incompetence** Where the employee's incapability is not due to his own negligence or idleness, the matter should be dealt with more sympathetically than cases of misconduct, with plenty of opportunity for improvement. It may still be appropriate, however, to treat incompetence as a disciplinary matter, in which case the employer should follow his **disciplinary procedure**. Handling poor performance is discussed at ¶6660.

This will normally require him to take the **following steps**:
– carry out an appraisal of the employee to identify the areas of concern;
– give guidance, supervision and, where necessary, additional training (particularly where an employee is promoted to a new job);
– give the employee a specific period of time for improvement;
– warn the employee of the consequences of failure to improve; and
– review the employee's performance after the specified period.

It may not always be necessary to follow each step, for example in cases of **gross incompetence** ("irredeemable incapability"), a failure to give a warning/opportunity to improve may not make a dismissal unfair (*James v Waltham Holy Cross U.D.C.* [1973] IRLR 202, NIRC; *Taylor v Alidair Ltd*). Similarly, in the case of **senior employees** (who, it is argued, should be aware of the standards to be met and whether they are meeting them), a warning may not always be necessary (*James v Waltham Holy Cross U.D.C.*).

8472 An employee who has been **promoted** to a job that requires new skills that he proves incapable of acquiring is not automatically entitled to return to his old job (unless the contract provides such a right).

8473 Where, after the above steps have been taken, the employee still fails to meet the required standard (and in particular, where a promoted employee fails to meet the new requirements), the employer should normally consider the availability of **suitable alternative employment**, although this is not always required in cases of incompetence (*Bevan Harris Ltd v Gair* [1981] IRLR 520, EAT).

8474 Under both the statutory procedure and the best practice guidance in the ACAS Code of Practice, there should be a **right of appeal** against the decision to dismiss.

8475 **Ill health** The management of ill health differs according to whether the illness is short-term or long-term. These issues are discussed in detail at ¶4245. Handling absence generally is discussed at ¶6650. Persistent short-term illness is commonly treated as a disciplinary matter, whilst in **long-term** cases the employer will normally take the **following steps**:
– consult with the employee;
– obtain medical evidence (to ascertain whether the employee's health will improve and, if so, whether it will do so within a timescale that the employer's business requirements can accommodate);
– give a warning if there are a large number of short absences and where dismissal is being considered; and
– consider alternatives to dismissal (for example, changing work hours or offering suitable alternative employment).

8476 Again, as both a minimum statutory requirement and as a matter of best practice, there should be a **right of appeal** against the decision to dismiss.

8477 The employer should also consider the impact of **disability discrimination** legislation (¶5450). A dismissal could be unfair but not amount to disability discrimination (for example, because the employee's illness does not amount to a disability, as defined). However, it is likely that a discriminatory dismissal will almost always also be unfair.

2. Misconduct

a. Fair reason

The employer will have a fair reason if the reason (or principal reason) for dismissal relates to the conduct of the employee. **8490**

To constitute a fair reason, the misconduct must in some way reflect on the employer-employee relationship (*Thomson v Alloa Motor Co Ltd* [1983] IRLR 403, EAT). Misconduct **includes**:
– a breach of the employer's workplace or disciplinary rules (or of the standards of behaviour commonly required by employers) (*McPhie and McDermott v Wimpey Waste Management Ltd* [1981] IRLR 316, EAT);
– a refusal to obey a lawful order (*R Farnborough v The Governors of Edinburgh College of Art* [1974] IRLR 245, NIRC); and
– in limited circumstances (principally relating to criminal charges or convictions), misconduct committed outside the employment (¶6671), although there may be possible human rights implications in such cases (¶6052).
It is the employee's own conduct which is relevant and not the conduct of those around him (*Wadley v Eager Electrical Ltd* [1986] IRLR 93, EAT).

EXAMPLE In *Wadley v Eager Electrical Ltd*, W's summary dismissal following his **wife's dismissal for theft** was unfair.

Dismissal for misconduct may be appropriate after a **series of incidents** (provided the employer follows a fair procedure – see below) or, in serious cases of misconduct (known as **gross misconduct** (¶6640)), after a **single incident**. **8491**

Misconduct may still be a fair reason for dismissal where an employee is dismissed where there is **more than one suspect** (¶6550). **8492**

Breach of disciplinary rules or acceptable standards of behaviour Disciplinary rules are discussed in detail at ¶6534. In summary, to support a fair dismissal: **8493**
a. the rules must be:
– relevant to the employment;
– clear and unambiguous; and
– consistently applied;
b. the matter must be dealt with promptly;
c. other factors, such as length of service should be taken into account; and
d. the sanction of dismissal must be appropriate in the circumstances.

Refusal to obey The dismissal may be fair if the employee has refused to obey a **lawful order**, which is one which the employer is entitled to give according to the employee's contract (for example, refusing to relocate where the contract contains a wide mobility clause). However, not all cases of refusing to obey a lawful order will justify dismissal. **8494**

If the employee refuses to obey an order which is outside the scope of the contract (an **unlawful order**), a dismissal may be unfair, but this will depend on the circumstances (*Farrant v The Woodroffe School* [1998] IRLR 176, EAT). The tribunal may find that the employee has caused or contributed to the dismissal (which will affect the amount of compensation awarded). **8495**

EXAMPLE Unlawful orders
1. In *C W Graham v Anthony Todd (Haulage) Limited* [1975] IRLR 45, IT, G, an apprentice mechanic, was dismissed when he refused to **work overtime**. As the employer could not lawfully require him to work overtime, the dismissal for refusal to obey the unlawful order was unfair.
2. In *Brandon and Goold v Murphy Bros* [1983] IRLR 54, EAT, B and G were dismissed for refusing to **work over New Year** so that their employer could meet the demands of its main customer. Despite the fact that they were contractually entitled not to work, the dismissal was fair in all the circumstances.

3. In *Ferrie v Western No 3 District Council* [1973] IRLR 162, IT, F was an assistant gardener. He was unfairly dismissed for **refusing** to clear out a pond unaccompanied, as his refusal was reasonable given the **danger** presented by the task.
4. In *R F Deegan v T T Norman & Sons Ltd* [1976] IRLR 139, IT, D was the only tacker in the employer's footwear business. He refused the employer's unlawful instruction to **work overtime** so as to process an important order in time. The dismissal was unfair but D's refusal to co-operate had contributed to his dismissal and his compensation was reduced by 50%.

b. Fair procedure

8500 The employer's liability for unfair dismissal will be minimised if he implements and follows an applicable **statutory dismissal and disciplinary procedure**. Since 1 October 2004, it has been compulsory for an employer to meet the minimum statutory requirements of the statutory dismissal and disciplinary procedure (if applicable) when contemplating dismissing or taking disciplinary action (other than a suspension on full pay or an oral or written warning) (reg 3 SI 2004/752). In addition, the ACAS Code of Practice on disciplinary and grievance procedures provides guidance on best practice to employers. This and other issues relating to fair procedure in misconduct cases is discussed in Chapter 19. Details on procedure in relation to **specific topics** are found as follows:

Absence	¶6650
Poor performance	¶6660
Trade union officials	¶6670
Employees facing criminal charges/conviction	¶6671
Isolated employees	¶6676

8501 In summary, **best practice** requires that a fair procedure will normally **include**:
– having clear rules as to required standards of conduct (and sanctions for breach) and making employees aware what actions amount to gross misconduct (¶6540);
– applying the disciplinary rules consistently but not inflexibly (¶6546);
– carrying out an investigation to establish the facts (¶6585);
– giving the employee the opportunity to put his side of the case (¶6619), although it is not essential that an employee accused of alleged misconduct be allowed to cross-examine his accusers (¶6618; see also *Santamera v Express Cargo Forwarding t/a IEC Ltd* [2003] IRLR 273, EAT);
– taking account of the employee's representations before making any disciplinary decision (including any mitigating circumstances);
– deciding on the appropriate sanction (¶6630);
– if the employer decides to dismiss, clearly explaining the reason for the dismissal; and
– giving the employee the opportunity to appeal (¶6680).

Note that there is a statutory **right to be accompanied** at certain disciplinary and grievance hearings (¶6780).

8505 The tribunal needs to be satisfied that the employer, at the time of dismissal (*British Home Stores v Burchell* [1978] IRLR 379, EAT, approved in *Post Office v Foley and HSBC Bank (formerly Midland Bank) v Madden* [2000] IRLR 827, CA):
– had a **genuine belief** in the employee's guilt of that misconduct;
– had **reasonable grounds** to hold this belief; and
– carried out such **investigation** as was reasonable in all the circumstances.

This does not apply where there is **more than one suspect** (¶6550).

The first limb relates to fair reason, whilst the second and third are concerned with the reasonableness of the decision to dismiss (*HSBC Bank v Madden*). Each of the three limbs must be satisfied for a fair dismissal. For example, if the employer had a genuine belief in the employee's guilt, having carried out a reasonable investigation, but based his decision on inadequate and unreliable evidence (such that his belief was not held on reasonable grounds), the dismissal will be unfair (*Granges Building Systems Ltd t/a Glostal Monarch v Hill*, EAT case 666/99).

It is irrelevant to the fairness of the dismissal **whether the employee actually committed** the misconduct (*Ferodo Ltd v Barnes* [1976] IRLR 302, EAT). However, where the employee is facing **very serious allegations** of misconduct, including **criminal conduct**, then the seriousness of the criminal charges and their potential implications are relevant circumstances to consider and, as such, a very thorough and careful investigation must be carried out by the employer (*A v B* [2003] IRLR 405, EAT).

EXAMPLE In *McGowan v Scottish Water* [2005] IRLR 167, EAT, undercover surveillance cameras used to "spy" on an employee who was suspected of falsifying timesheets were deemed to be proportionate to his alleged misconduct. Covert surveillance went to the root of the investigation, enabling the employer to protect its assets, and the dismissal of the employee was therefore deemed to be fair.

In determining whether the test has been satisfied where an employee has been dismissed **before** he attended a **disciplinary hearing**, the tribunal will consider not only what would have happened at that disciplinary hearing had it taken place, but also whether the dismissal would have been fair or unfair, i.e. had the dismissal been made after a disciplinary hearing (*Panama v London Borough of Hackney* [2003] IRLR 278, CA). Note, however, that if an employer fails to complete an applicable statutory dismissal and disciplinary procedure (which will include holding a disciplinary meeting as Step 2 of the procedure), then this will render the dismissal automatically unfair (¶8436).

To satisfy the fair procedure test, the **employer should have concluded** that it was more likely than not that the employee committed the alleged misconduct. He **cannot take into account** matters which were not known to him at the time of the dismissal in order to defend an unfair dismissal claim (*Devis & Sons Ltd v Atkins* [1977] IRLR 314, HL) (¶8425).

Dismissal must be within the **range of reasonable responses** which a reasonable employer might make. The tribunal should not substitute its own view for that of the employer (i.e. it should not ask itself whether a lesser penalty would have been reasonable but rather whether or not dismissal was reasonable). In addition, any **investigation** conducted by the employer into an employee's alleged misconduct should fall within the same range of reasonable responses as in relation to the dismissal itself (*Sainsbury's Supermarkets Ltd v Hitt* [2003] IRLR 23, CA). 8508

In cases where the **employee admits to the offence** but fails to offer any explanation for his actions at every opportunity he is given to do so, the employer is not under a duty to enquire further into the employee's reason for committing the offence (*Weatherford UK Ltd v Aitken*, EAT case 0049/03).

3. Redundancy

The employer will have a **fair reason** if the reason (or principal reason) for dismissal is redundancy (as defined – see ¶8740). A **business reorganisation** may not always fall within the statutory definition of redundancy. In such cases, the dismissal may still be fair for some other substantial reason (¶8530). 8510

Although redundancy is a fair reason for dismissal, it is **automatically unfair** to select an employee for redundancy for certain reasons, including pregnancy and health and safety (¶8390). 8511

In order to show that he has acted reasonably, the employer must follow a **fair procedure**. This is discussed at ¶8800. He must also ensure he follows an applicable statutory dismissal and disciplinary procedure (¶¶6511, 6636) otherwise this will impact on how the fairness of his actions are judged (¶8436). 8512

4. Contravention of a duty or restriction

a. Fair reason

8520 The employer will have a fair reason for dismissal if he can show that he would be acting in breach of legislation by continuing to employ the employee, for example where an employee employed as a driver loses his driving licence (*Fearn v Tayford Motor Co Ltd* [1975] IRLR 336, IT), or where an employee is refused a work permit and so cannot legally work in the UK. The continued employment must **actually contravene** legislation (a genuine but mistaken belief does not suffice, although it may amount to some other substantial reason – ¶8545).

b. Fair procedure

8525 The employer's obligation to act reasonably may require him to consult with the employee, informing him of the situation and inviting his views. He should consider whether he could make any reasonable adjustments to the employee's duties to allow him to continue in employment (for example, where an employee's driving duties could be reallocated and other tasks given to him) and/or whether any suitable alternative employment is available.

The statutory dismissal and disciplinary procedures will not apply in these circumstances (reg 4(1)(f) SI 2004/752).

5. Some other substantial reason

a. Fair reason

8530 This is the "**catch-all**" category which covers fair reasons not covered by the preceding four categories. To fall within it, the employer must show that the reason (or principal reason) for dismissal is a "substantial reason of a kind such as to justify the dismissal of an employee holding the position which the employee held" (s 98(1)(b) ERA 1996). This is known as the "SOSR" defence. Tribunals must not substitute their own views in such cases but, instead, consider whether the reason advanced by the employer could constitute a SOSR and, if so, whether the employer's decision to dismiss was a reasonable response (*Scott & Co v Richardson*, EAT case 0074/04). SOSR applies to many varied situations which cannot be fully listed here. In all cases, the general principles set out below should be taken as guidance, and careful attention paid to following a fair procedure.

SOSR **most commonly applies** to action taken by the employer to protect his business, including:
- business reorganisations/changes requiring variations to employment terms to which the employee refuses to agree; and
- dismissal of employees who refuse to enter restrictive covenants necessary for the protection of the employer's legitimate business interests.

Other SOSR situations are described further below.

8531 The SOSR defence is available in the case of an employee who is dismissed for an economic, technical or organisational reason entailing changes in the workforce in the context of a **transfer of an undertaking** (¶8041).

Business reorganisations

8532 A dismissal of an employee who refuses to accept a change in terms and conditions as part of a business reorganisation may be fair if the employer has a "**sound, good business reason**" for the reorganisation (*Hollister v National Farmers' Union* [1979] IRLR 238, CA). There may be an overlap with dismissal for redundancy and it is open to the employer to plead both redundancy and SOSR in the alternative.

The employer must have evidence of the advantages of the changes (*Banerjee v City and East London Area Health Authority* [1979] IRLR 147, EAT), but he need not show that the variation was essential. However, making the business more profitable is unlikely to be seen as a good business reason in itself – the employer should be under some kind of pressure to make the reorganisation.

> EXAMPLE In *Genower v Ealing, Hammersmith and Hounslow Area Health Authority* [1980] IRLR 297, EAT, a prosecution in the supplies department in which G worked had led to a reorganisation of the department and a decision that control of the department should not rest with one person for too long. As a result, G's duties and place of work were changed, and he resigned. The EAT held that the dismissal was fair. Referring to *Hollister v National Farmers' Union*, it found that a reorganisation may be a fair reason for dismissal even if the alternative is not that the business would come to a standstill but is merely that there would be a **serious effect on the business**.

Changing working hours The changes to terms and conditions often involve a requirement to **work overtime** or to agree to **flexible working patterns**. 8533

> EXAMPLE 1. In *L Moreton v Selby Protective Clothing Co Ltd* [1974] IRLR 269, IT, the employer sought to vary M's contract to require her to work during the school holidays. This was essential to maintain production and M was given 12 months' notice of the change. M's dismissal for refusing to agree was fair.
> 2. In *B E Robinson v Flitwick Frames Ltd* [1975] IRLR 261, IT, R was the only employee who refused to work overtime to meet peaks in demand. As the employer's request was reasonable (and also because R would have remained in the bonus pool, making calculation of his entitlement compared to those who worked overtime difficult), he was fairly dismissed.
> 3. In *Kerry Foods Limited v Lynch* [2005] IRLR 674, EAT, the employer sought to persuade L to work a 6 day week to avoid a two tier system of working, increase the perception that Saturday was a working day and improve the quality of supervisory cover. The employer was able to show an improvement in Saturday trading performance and this was deemed to be sufficient to pass the "low hurdle" of establishing the SOSR defence. There was no need for the employer to demonstrate the quantum of improvement which would be achieved if the changes were made.
> 4. In *Copsey v WWB Devon Clays Ltd* [2005] IRLR 811, CA, it was held to be fair to dismiss a Christian employee who refused to work on Sundays. The employee argued that the dismissal infringed his freedom to manifest his religion under Art 9 of the European Convention on Human Rights. Whilst there was diverging views as to whether Art 9 was relevant in this context, it was agreed that any infringement (under the law of unfair dismissal with or without reference to Art 9) had been justified as the employer had compelling economic reasons requiring the introduction of a 7-day shift. This case was brought prior to employees having the right not to be discriminated against due to their religion or belief (¶5375). However, the outcome is unlikely to have been different as the change of practice could be justified as a proportionate means of achieving a legitimate aim (in this case, a business necessity which required a change to a 7-day shift pattern).

Relocation A refusal to relocate in order to be within a reasonable distance of the place of work may be a fair reason for dismissal (*Farr v Hoveringham Gravels Ltd* [1972] IRLR 104, IT). 8534

Opposing interests The tribunal will also take into account the **interests of the employees** when determining whether the employer had a good business reason for dismissal. The reasonableness (or otherwise) of the employee's refusal will also be relevant (*Evans v Elemeta Holdings Ltd* [1982] IRLR 143, EAT). 8535

> EXAMPLE In *Evans v Elemeta Holdings Ltd*, the employer sought to introduce a new contract which included an obligation to work mandatory and unlimited overtime. The EAT found that there was no evidence of an immediate need to introduce that requirement and that it was **reasonable for E to refuse** to agree (his dismissal was, therefore, unfair).

In some cases, however, the **interests** of the employees and those of the employer may be **irreconcilable** and the fairness of the dismissal will be determined by considering whether the employer's decision to dismiss was within the band of responses of a reasonable employer (see below). 8536

Confidentiality and competition issues

8537 The employer may wish to **introduce a new term** to protect his business interests, i.e. to prevent the disclosure of confidential information to a competitor, or to restrict the ability of employees to resign and set up a competing business. A dismissal for refusal to agree to the new term may be fair. The EAT has recently confirmed this (refusing to follow its previous approach in *Forshaw v Archcraft* [2005] IRLR 600, EAT) and held that a **dismissal for a failure to agree** to restrictive covenants is capable of constituting a SOSR situation, unless the contract that the employer was seeking to make was so manifestly unreasonable that the purported reason was in fact a cover or a ruse to get rid of the employee (*Willow Oak Developments Ltd t/a Windsor Recruitment v Silverwood and others*, EAT case 0339/05). Consequently, the consideration of the reasonableness of the new contract, including the **reasonableness of the covenants** sought to be imposed, arises at the stage of deciding fairness (¶¶8435, 8550) and the EAT outlined the approach that should be taken:

a. if the proposed covenant appears plainly unreasonable and not severable, it may be easier for a tribunal to conclude that there was unfairness;

b. if the proposed covenant is arguably unenforceable (and/or severable), greater consideration should be given to the approach of the employer (in particular, the amount of time given to consider proposals and the opportunity given for legal advice); and

c. if the covenant is plainly reasonable, then there will still need to be consideration of the fairness of the procedure but the tribunal may well be satisfied that the dismissal was fair.

EXAMPLE In *R S Components Ltd v Irwin* [1973] IRLR 239, NIRC, the employers' business was being damaged by departing sales employees, who were setting up in competition. In reaction to this, the employers sought to **introduce a new restrictive covenant** in the contracts of the remaining employees, which aimed to prevent competition for 12 months after the termination of their employment. I refused to accept the new covenant and he was dismissed. The NIRC held that the dismissal was fair on the grounds of SOSR, as the employers were entitled to protect their business interests.

8538 It may be fair to dismiss an employee where there is a real **risk of a leak of trade secrets** which could substantially damage the employer's interests, for example, where an employee has close **connections with a competing business**.

EXAMPLE 1. In *D C Foot v Eastern Counties Timber Co Ltd East Harling* [1972] IRLR 83, IT, F was a wages and accounts clerk. She was dismissed when her husband set up a competing business and her dismissal was fair.

2. In *Coleman v Skyrail Oceanic Ltd (t/a Goodmos Tours)* [1981] IRLR 398, CA, C was a booking clerk with the employer's travel agency. She was dismissed on her marriage to an employee of a rival firm. Her dismissal was unfair (partly because, despite the fact there had been leaks, C was never accused of being the source, and partly because she was given no warning).

3. In *Chandlers (Farm Equipment) Ltd v Rainthorpe*, EAT case 0753/04, C was dismissed on the grounds that her husband had left the company to work for a competitor. However, there was nothing in C's past conduct to lead her employer to reasonably think that any disclosure to her husband, even unintentionally, would occur. Both she and her husband were long-standing employees with good records and reputations. C's employer had therefore acted unreasonably and her dismissal was unfair.

Temporary contracts

8539 The SOSR defence may apply to the dismissal of an employee who was taken on as a temporary worker, provided it was explained at the outset that the job was only temporary (*Terry v East Sussex County Council* [1976] IRLR 332, EAT; approved in *North Yorkshire County Council v Fay* [1985] IRLR 247, CA).

This applies specifically to employees who are engaged as **replacements** for permanent workers who are absent due to pregnancy or childbirth, or on medical or maternity suspension, provided the return of such workers is the actual reason for dismissal and as long as the employee was informed in writing of the temporary nature of the post (s 106 ERA 1996).

8540 A fair procedure must still be followed, in particular, the employer should offer any available suitable alternative employment (see below).

Breakdown of mutual trust and confidence

Where, as a result of an act of the employee (for example, a conviction for dishonesty), the employer (or his customers) has lost trust and confidence in him, the SOSR defence may apply (*Wadley v Eager Electrical Ltd* [1986] IRLR 93, EAT). 8541

Breakdown of working relationship

The SOSR defence may apply where the working relationship has broken down (for example, because of a clash of personalities between employees (*Treganowan v Robert Knee & Co Ltd* [1975] IRLR 247, QBD; *Perkin v St George's Healthcare NHS Trust* [2005] EWCA Civ 1174). However, the breakdown must be irreparable, and the employer should seek to improve relationships and investigate alternatives to dismissal (*Turner v Vestric Ltd* [1981] IRLR 23, EAT). 8542

Dismissal at request of third parties

The SOSR defence may apply in exceptional circumstances where the employer is requested to dismiss an employee by a third party, for example a major customer (*Scott Packing & Warehousing Co Ltd v Paterson* [1978] IRLR 166, EAT). The employer must be able to show that he had tried to reason with the third party (if he disagreed with them) and that he gave due consideration to the potential injustice suffered by the employee. The SOSR defence will not, however, be available where the reason given by the third party is unfair in itself. 8543

Imprisonment

Imprisonment may bring the employment to an end by **frustration**, in which case there will be no dismissal (¶8286). 8544

If, on the facts, the contract cannot be said to be frustrated, the SOSR defence may apply, depending on the nature of the offence, the position held by the employee, and the length of the sentence (*Kingston v British Railways Board* [1984] IRLR 146, CA). Misconduct may also apply (¶8490).

Genuine belief that dismissal fair

The SOSR defence may be available where the employer had a genuine belief that the **reason for dismissal** was fair, even where modern sophisticated opinion can show that his belief has no scientific foundation (*Harper v National Coal Board* [1980] IRLR 260, EAT). 8545

Similarly, SOSR may apply to a genuine but mistaken belief that continued **employment would be unlawful** (for example, a breach of the immigration rules) (*Bouchaala v Trust House Forte Hotels Ltd* [1980] IRLR 382, EAT).

A mistaken belief that the **employee had resigned** (and an insistence on the employment ending when the employee belatedly changed his mind) has been held to be a fair dismissal for SOSR (*Ely v YKK Fasteners (UK) Ltd* [1993] IRLR 500, CA).

Takeover of the business

An employer may be able to argue the SOSR defence in respect of the dismissal of an employee following a successful takeover of the undertaking in which the employee is employed, provided that due regard is given to the position held by the dismissed employee and the dismissal fell within the range of reasonable responses which could be taken by the employer (*Cobley v Forward Technology Industries Ltd* [2003] IRLR 706, CA). In this case, C, the Chief Executive of FTI Ltd, led a failed management buy-out and was dismissed by the eventual successful bidder. The Court of Appeal placed importance on the fact that C was the most senior employee in the undertaking and that the company which took over FTI Ltd was entitled to treat him differently to, say, a manual worker or administrative employee employed by the same company. 8546

b. Fair procedure

8550 Since 1 October 2004, an employer must meet the **minimum requirements** of the statutory dismissal and disciplinary procedure when contemplating dismissing an employee in certain circumstances (reg 3 SI 2004/752; see ¶6560). To ensure that any such dismissal is fair, as a matter of best practice the employer must normally:
– consult with employees (even if there is an urgent financial need to introduce changes);
– discuss proposed changes with them in advance;
– explain the impact of proposed changes;
– consider and respond to representations and objections raised; and
– consider alternatives to dismissal, such as finding alternative jobs or moving staff to other locations.

The employer's decision to dismiss must be within the **range of responses of a reasonable employer** and the **following factors** will be relevant:
– the terms of the offer, and the number of employees who accepted it (*St John of God (Care Services) Ltd v Brooks* [1992] IRLR 546, EAT);
– the employer's motives (for example, if less favourable terms are offered because the employer was suffering financial difficulties and was trying to increase profits or avoid bankruptcy) (*Catamaran Cruisers Ltd v Williams* [1994] IRLR 386, EAT);
– the trade union's recommendation of the changes (*Catamaran Cruisers Ltd v Williams*);
– whether the employees are adversely affected financially (if so, it will be more difficult to persuade a tribunal of the employer's reasonableness); and
– whether the employer is acting reasonably in deciding that the advantage to him of implementing the changes outweighs any disadvantage which the employee might suffer (*Richmond Precision Engineering Ltd v Pearce* [1985] IRLR 179, EAT; *Chubb Fire Security Ltd v Harper* [1983] IRLR 311, EAT).

III. Enforcement and remedies

8560 An employee who wishes to bring an unfair dismissal claim must **apply to** an employment tribunal **within** 3 months of the effective date of termination (¶8340). Where the dismissal is connected with industrial action, the time limit is 6 months. The tribunal has a discretion to **extend the time limit** where it was not reasonably practicable for the claim to be presented on time (it must then be submitted within a reasonable time). For further information on time limits, see ¶9450.

It should be noted that where there is a **dismissal with notice**, it is possible to bring a claim after the notice of dismissal has been given (¶8343) but before the EDT (s 111(3) ERA 1996).

An **ACAS conciliation officer** will contact the parties if a fixed period of conciliation applies (¶9219) or, if no fixed conciliation period applies, where a claim is brought with a view to reaching an agreed settlement of the claim (¶9223).

As an alternative to tribunal proceedings, unfair dismissal claims may also be dealt with by way of **arbitration** (¶9360).

8561 If the **employee dies**, his personal representative can apply to the tribunal or continue existing unfair dismissal proceedings.

8562 If the employee becomes **bankrupt**, he can still pursue a claim of unfair dismissal since the complaint constitutes a claim for **personal relief** as opposed to a propriety remedy (for example, such as a declaration and/or compensation for injured feelings) and does not therefore vest in his trustee in bankruptcy (*Khan v Trident Safeguards Ltd* [2004] IRLR 961, CA).

8663 It should be noted that an employee **cannot commence tribunal proceedings** (except in relation to a breach of contract claim – ¶1710) in respect of the subject of any grievance he may have **unless** he has first raised a grievance in writing under the appropriate statutory grievance procedure and has waited a further 28 days or more since raising the grievance with his employer before presenting the tribunal claim (s 32(2), (3) EA 2002). For further details as to the statutory grievance procedure and its impact on time limits for tribunal claims, see ¶¶6772, 9479).

Three remedies are available for unfair dismissal: reinstatement or re-engagement and/or compensation (ss 113, 118 ERA 1996). The employee can indicate which of these remedies he is seeking when submitting his unfair dismissal claim (he is not bound by this indication), and again, if his claim is upheld, when the tribunal explains the remedies available to him. The tribunal can only order reinstatement or re-engagement if the employee so requests (s 112(3) ERA 1996). If he does not, the tribunal can only consider compensation. 8565

In certain circumstances, the employee can apply for **interim relief** (including reinstatement, re-engagement, and continuation of the employment contract) pending the final determination of his claim.

The **table** at the end of this section shows the circumstances in which particular remedies may be available (¶8710).

A. Compensation

Compensation is by far the most commonly made order. An award is in two parts: the basic award and the compensatory award. In some cases, an additional award (¶8680) may also be ordered. 8570

Unlike wrongful dismissal awards, a tribunal award for unfair dismissal is not itself taxable as earnings, but instead will be treated in the same way as payments which are taxed under sections 401 and 403 ITEPA 2003 (¶3125).

Where the employee is **paid less than the national minimum wage**, neither the calculation of a week's pay (¶2920) for a basic award nor the assessment of any compensatory award should be based on what the employee was being paid but should be based on the national minimum wage he should have received (*Paggetti v Cobb* [2002] IRLR 861, EAT). 8571

1. Basic award

If the tribunal finds that an employee has been unfairly dismissed and makes a compensation order, it must make a basic award (s 119(1) ERA 1996). This is calculated by reference to age, length of service to the effective date of termination (¶8340), and salary as follows (s 119(2) ERA 1996): 8575
- for each complete year of employment in which the employee was aged 41 to 64: 1.5 week's pay;
- for each complete year in which he was aged 22 to 40: 1 week's pay; and
- for each complete year in which he was aged under 21: 0.5 week's pay.

The table at ¶9007 for redundancy payments can also be used to calculate the employee's entitlement to a basic award, unless years when the employee was aged under 18 need to be taken into account for the basic award.

A **week's pay** is subject to a statutory cap. For details on this cap and on calculating a week's pay see ¶2920. **Length of service** is subject to a maximum of 20 years, and is calculated according to statutory continuity of service (contractual agreements relating to continuity are ignored) (¶1040).

The **current maximum** basic award is, therefore, £8,400 (£280 × 20 × 1.5).

EXAMPLE An employee, who commenced employment in 1979, was dismissed in 2004. He has 25 years service but only the last 20 of these will be included in the calculation. Assuming he is aged 63 and earns more than £280 per week, his basic award will be £8,400 (20 x 1.5 x £280).

MEMO POINTS Under the draft Employment Equality (Age) Regulations 2006, it is proposed that the length of service requirement and statutory cap should remain. However, it is also proposed that the level of multiplier based on age bands (ranging from 0.5 week's pay for younger employees to 1.5 week's pay for older employees, as outlined above) will be removed (although the level of the new multiplier has not yet been determined). Further, the tapering down rule (¶8578) will also be removed.

8576 In the situations discussed below, the amount of the basic award may be subject to a minimum level, a specific reduction or limit, or a general reduction (¶8578).

Minimum basic award

8577 If the employee is dismissed (or selected for redundancy) for **certain inadmissible reasons**, there is a specified minimum basic award (before any general reductions (¶8578) are made), currently £3,800 (s 120 ERA 1996, s 156 TULRCA 1992).

The inadmissible reasons are:
- trade union membership or activities;
- being an employee representative, candidate, or voter in relation to collective redundancy or business transfer consultation;
- being a workers' representative for health and safety purposes or a member of a safety committee;
- carrying out (or proposing to carry out) health and safety activities (having been designated by the employer to do so);
- being a workforce representative for working time purposes (or a candidate to become one); and
- being a trustee of an occupational pension scheme.

If an employer has dismissed an employee without completing an applicable **statutory dismissal and disciplinary procedure** and such failure is wholly or mainly attributable to the employer, then the dismissal will be automatically unfair and the employee will be awarded a minimum of 4 weeks' pay as a basic award unless the tribunal considers that this would cause injustice to the employer (s 120(1A), (1B) ERA 1996). This will be subject to the statutory cap on a week's pay (¶2920). If a tribunal makes no award for compensation but instead orders reinstatement or re-engagement (¶8680), then it must, in addition, make a basic award of 4 weeks' pay (subject to the statutory cap – ¶2920) (s 112(5), (6) ERA 1996). See ¶6515 for further details.

Note that the basic award will not be affected by any adjustment to compensation under the statutory dispute resolution procedures in respect of the failure by either party to follow an applicable procedure. However, the compensatory award may itself be adjusted (¶8629).

MEMO POINTS The minimum basic award figure of £3,800 is likely to increase in **February 2006** and will be covered in updates to this edition.

Reductions

8578 In the following circumstances, the basic award is subject to a reduction or limit.

8579 **Employee aged 64** If the employee has **passed his 64th birthday** at the EDT, the basic award is reduced by a fraction, which is formed by dividing the number of complete months which have elapsed between the employee's 64th birthday and the EDT by 12.

EXAMPLE An employee is 64 on 23 February. He is dismissed on 28 June. Four complete months have elapsed. His basic award would be reduced by 4/12 (i.e. 1/3).

MEMO POINTS It is proposed that this reduction will be removed under the draft Employment Equality (Age) Regulations 2006.

8580 **Redundancy dismissals** The basic award payable to an employee who has been dismissed because of redundancy is limited to 2 weeks' pay if (s 121 ERA 1996):
- he has unreasonably refused (or left) suitable alternative employment;
- his contract has been renewed; or
- he has been re-engaged.

8581 **Unreasonable refusal of offer** If the employee has unreasonably refused an offer from the employer which would have effectively **reinstated** him as though he had not been dismissed, the tribunal can reduce the basic award to the extent it considers just and equitable (s 122(1) ERA 1996). The tribunal will consider whether the employee acted unreasonably in refusing the offer, but it is not sufficient for the employer to show that such an offer was reasonable (*Wilding v British Telecommunications plc* [2002] IRLR 524, CA).

However, if the **employment** offered **differs** in any way **from his previous terms**, this reduction will not apply even if the employee's refusal could be considered unreasonable.

Employee conduct The tribunal may also reduce the basic award if it feels that it would be just and equitable to do so as a result of the employee's conduct **before the dismissal** (or if the dismissal was with notice, before notice of dismissal was given) (s 122(2) ERA 1996). 8582

The tribunal can take into account **any conduct** on the part of the employee, and not just conduct which caused or contributed to the dismissal. This applies even if the conduct is **discovered after the dismissal** (or giving of notice).

The basic award will not be reduced for employee conduct where the reason (or principal reason) for the dismissal was **redundancy**, unless the reason for selection was an inadmissible one attracting a specified minimum basic award (see above), in which case the reduction only applies to that part (s 122(3) ERA 1996). In most redundancy cases, the basic award and the statutory redundancy payment will be the same amount. This provision enables the tribunal to reduce the part of the basic award over and above the normal basic award which the employee is only entitled to because he was selected for an inadmissible reason.

EXAMPLE An employee is dismissed for capability (because the employer does not feel he is doing his job well enough) but for procedural reasons, the dismissal is unfair. The employer subsequently discovers that the employee has been defrauding him. The tribunal is likely to decide that it would not be just and equitable to order the employer to pay a basic award.

Receipt of other employer payments If the employee has received a **redundancy payment**, this will be set off against the basic award provided that the dismissal was genuinely because of redundancy (s 122(4) ERA 1996; *Boorman v Allmakes Ltd* [1995] IRLR 553, CA). 8583

If the employee has received an award under a designated **dismissal procedures agreement**, the tribunal can reduce the basic award to the extent it considers just and equitable (s 122(3A) ERA 1996).

An **ex gratia payment** made by the employer will only reduce or extinguish the basic award if it can be shown that it was intended to cover this liability. If the ex gratia payment is made in settlement of liability for unfair dismissal in general, there appears to be a presumption that this is intended to cover both the compensatory award and the basic award (*Chelsea Football Club and Athletic Co Ltd v Heath* [1981] IRLR 73, CA). The tribunal must determine as a question of fact whether any part of the payment which was made was intended to cover the basic award.

2. Compensatory award

The **purpose** of compensation is to put the employee, as far as possible, in the position which he would otherwise have been in had he not been unfairly dismissed. It is **not intended to punish** the employer (i.e. the compensation awarded does not increase according to the degree of unfairness). There is, therefore, no award of punitive or exemplary damages. 8585

The compensatory award will be such amount as the tribunal considers just and equitable in all the circumstances having regard to the loss suffered by the employee as a result of the dismissal, subject to the statutory cap (see below) (s 123(1) ERA 1996). Essentially, the tribunal should ask itself two questions: first, is the claimant's dismissal one of the causes of his loss of earnings (this will be a question of fact) and secondly, what compensatory award is just and equitable in all the circumstances (this is a matter of discretion) (*Dignity Funerals Limited v Bruce* [2005] IRLR 189, CS). A tribunal should only consider the second question if there is factual proof that the claimant's loss of earnings was caused to a material extent by his dismissal.

The starting point is, therefore, the employee's losses, but the tribunal has a **wide discretion** and it can refuse to award any compensation at all, even if the employee's loss is significant.

It may do so, for example, if the **employee committed serious misconduct** during his employment which did not come to light until after the dismissal, as it may consider that had the employer been aware of the misconduct at the time of the dismissal, he would have been justified in dismissing and could have done so fairly. If an employee is dismissed for incapability, the tribunal may take into account allegations that the **employer caused his illness** when deciding whether it is just and equitable to make a compensatory award (*Edwards v Governors of Hanson School* [2001] IRLR 733, EAT). It should also be noted that tribunals must consider the specific facts of each case and should not be constrained by compensation given in earlier tribunal decisions (*Elkouil v Coney Island Ltd* [2002] IRLR 174, EAT).

8586 The amount of the compensatory award may be **reduced or adjusted** to reflect:
– sums paid by the employer;
– the employee's failure to mitigate his loss;
– the possibility that the employee could have been fairly dismissed;
– any contributory fault; and
– whether either party has failed to comply with an applicable statutory dispute resolution procedure.

If the employee has received **social security benefits**, part of the award may be recouped by the Government. These are discussed further below. The order in which any such reductions are made is set out at ¶8665 below.

8587 The compensatory award is subject to a **statutory cap** of £56,800 which is applied once all other deductions and reductions have been made.

There is **no cap** for certain types of automatically unfair dismissal, namely "whistleblowing" or health and safety reasons (or selection for redundancy for those reasons). Further, if an award of compensation is made with a reinstatement or re-engagement order (see below), the tribunal can disregard the cap and award compensation equal to the employee's actual loss between termination of employment and the date of reinstatement/re-engagement (s 124(3), (4) ERA 1996).

MEMO POINTS The statutory cap is likely to increase in **February 2006** and will be covered in updates to this edition.

a. Losses for which compensation can be awarded

8590 The loss for which the tribunal can award compensation **includes** (s 123(2), (3) ERA 1996):
– expenses reasonably incurred by the employee as a result of the dismissal; and
– loss of any benefits which he might reasonably be expected to have had but for the dismissal (though any loss of the right to a redundancy payment (statutory or otherwise) will only be taken into account to the extent that it exceeds the basic award).

In making an award of compensation, the tribunal should **set out** the types of loss which it has included and explain how it has carried out the calculation (*Blackwell v GEC Elliott Process Automation Ltd* [1976] IRLR 144, EAT).

Causation

8591 The tribunal can only award compensation in respect of losses which flow from the **employer's actions** (*Leonard v Strathclyde Buses Ltd* [1998] IRLR 693, CS). Therefore, if something happens after the dismissal which breaks the chain of events, the tribunal will not award any further compensation. For example, if an employee suffers a stroke between being dismissed and the tribunal hearing such that he is permanently unable to work, any loss of earnings after that date is attributable to his medical condition and not to the actions of the employer.

8592 Complications can arise if the employee, after being dismissed **obtains another job which he subsequently loses**.

If the employee takes a **short-term temporary job** which comes to an end, or a job on a short **trial basis** in which he is not kept on, the tribunal may be persuaded that he was only in the position of having to take such a job because the first employer's actions had left him out of work. The earnings from the second employment will be taken into account in calculating compensation, but he should be able to claim further compensation from the original employer for the period after the second job ends.

If, however, the employee takes a **new job** which **lasts for a reasonable period** of time and then is, for example, made redundant or dismissed for misconduct, it will be more difficult to persuade the tribunal that the original employer should be held responsible for subsequent losses as this will be an intervening event which breaks the chain of causation.

If the employee **enrols on a course** after being unfairly dismissed, he may be entitled to compensation for future losses beyond the date of enrolment (*Khanum v IBC Vehicles Ltd*, EAT case 685/98).

EXAMPLE In *Khanum v IBC Vehicles Ltd*, K enrolled on a degree course after being unfairly dismissed. She was entitled to compensation for future losses beyond the date of enrolment as she decided to follow the course because she was unable to obtain a suitable job in her chosen career and needed to retrain. As such, losses incurred while studying were a direct result of her dismissal.

Earnings and other benefits

When calculating compensation for loss of earnings and other benefits, it is the **net equivalent** of such payments which is taken into account (as the employee would have had to pay tax and national insurance on his earnings and other benefits and, therefore, using the gross figures would result in over-compensation). 8593

Loss of earnings is generally separated into **two parts**:
– loss from dismissal to the date of the hearing; and
– future loss.

Loss prior to hearing The tribunal calculates the **earnings** which the employee would have earned from the employer between the date of the dismissal and the date of the hearing, taking into account any **pay increases or bonuses** which the employee might have been expected to receive during that period. It is not necessary to show a definite contractual entitlement to such bonuses or increases as long as the tribunal is satisfied on the evidence that in practice they would have been received (*York Trailer Co Ltd v Sparkes* [1973] IRLR 348, NIRC). 8594

The tribunal also takes into account **other benefits** such as company car, private health insurance, mobile telephone, and share schemes. The tribunal places a **value** on each benefit, usually on the basis of what it would cost the employee to obtain similar benefits privately. Often the taxable value of the benefit shown on a P11D or the value ascribed by the AA (for company cars) is used as a guide. For items such as company cars and mobile telephones, the tribunal only awards compensation if (and to the extent that) the employee was also allowed to use them for **private use**. 8595

Future loss This is more difficult to assess. The tribunal takes into account not only **salary** but also the value of **other benefits** (¶8593). 8596

MEMO POINTS Where the tribunal is quantifying loss, such as the loss of share options, which is dependent on a number of **uncertain future events** (for example, the likely flotation of a company and resulting share values), it must assess the chance of that event materialising in percentage terms and not on the balance of probabilities (*Selective Beauty UK Ltd v Hayes*, EAT case 0582/04).

If the **employee is still suffering a loss** at the date of the hearing, either because he remains out of work or has only been able to obtain work at a lower rate of pay, the tribunal will consider how long such loss might be expected to continue, which naturally requires a degree of speculation. The tribunal may also take into account the fact that the old employment would have ended fairly in any case, or that the employer had a good reason for dismissal but failed to follow a fair procedure. It can make a reduction to reflect its findings which is discussed further below. 8598

Where an employee has **not found a new job** at the date of the tribunal hearing, the tribunal has to decide when or if he is likely to find a job, and if so, the likely salary. The tribunal takes into account its own knowledge of the local employment situation, the age of the employee, his range of skills and his previous experience. It is essentially a matter of judgement for the tribunal and since it has a wide discretion, it is rarely possible to challenge its decision on appeal.

MEMO POINTS It should be noted that "Ogden tables" (which provide for an actuarial adjustment of future loss of earnings and benefits) may only be used when the future loss to be assessed is expected to last for the rest of the employee's working life (*Dunnachie v Kingston upon Hull City Council*, EAT case 726/02; *HSBC Bank plc v Drage*, EAT case 1036/02).

8599 If the employee has **obtained a new job** which is likely to continue indefinitely, the loss is the difference between the old pay and the new pay. The tribunal will decide for how long the employee should be compensated in this way. Its task in making this determination is similar to the task it faces in assessing how long an unemployed applicant will remain out of work (see below).

If the employee's new job **pays more** than the old job (taking into account the value of any benefits), and is likely to continue, then he has no continuing loss.

If, at the date of the hearing, the employee is working but it appears likely that his new job **will come to an end** for some reason, then in deciding if any further loss after the end of that employment should be attributed to the original employer, the tribunal will apply the same principles as are described at ¶8591.

8600 As compensation for future loss will be **awarded in a lump sum**, rather than earned over a period of months or years, the tribunal may (particularly if the period in question is a long one) make a reduction to reflect **accelerated receipt**. This is normally around 5%, although the Court of Appeal has expressed the opinion that this figure is out of line with, and somewhat higher than, the percentage applied in other civil cases (for example, the discount for accelerated receipt applied in personal injury cases is 2.5%) (*Bentwood Brothers (Manchester) Ltd v Shepherd* [2003] IRLR 364, CA). A tribunal is also entitled to make allowances for delayed payment when considering compensation and apply a premium to **delayed or decelerated** payments in the same way as deductions are made for accelerated receipt (*Melia v Magna Kansei Limited* [2005] IRLR 449, EAT).

EXAMPLE An employee, aged 60, was earning £25,000 per year and now earns £20,000 per year in his new employment. The tribunal believes that had he not been dismissed, he would have remained in his previous employment until retiring at 65. It also believes that having found this new job, it is likely that he will remain in it until the same age. The loss is, therefore, £5,000 per year for 5 years: £25,000 (which will probably be subject to a deduction for accelerated receipt).

Pension rights

8601 One of the most difficult aspects of calculating a compensatory award can be the assessment of pension loss, as the calculations required are often complex and based on actuarial values. The summary below provides an overview of the approach taken by tribunals but is no more than a general outline of the principles involved as a more detailed discussion is outside the scope of this book.

Tribunals have been given **guidance** on the assessment of pension loss by a booklet prepared by a committee of Chairmen of Employment Tribunals, the Government Actuary and a member of his department entitled "Compensation for Loss of Pension Rights – Employment Tribunals" (third edition (2003)). Whilst the guidance outlines the position regarding potential loss in relation to state pension provision (for example, the basic state pension, the State Earnings-Related Pension Scheme ("SERPS") and the State Second Pension ("S2P")), the difficulties surrounding the calculation of pension loss arise more frequently in relation to occupational pension schemes.

8602 **Occupational pension schemes** fall into **two main categories**:
– final salary (also known as defined benefit); and
– money purchase (also known as defined contribution).

In **final salary** schemes, the pension is based on a fraction (often around 1/60) of the employee's final salary for each complete year of service. An employee's **loss on dismissal** in relation to a final salary scheme is clearly based on him losing the right to a pension based on his final salary. The employee may, however, be entitled to a deferred pension (see further below) and his loss is therefore broadly based on the difference between the deferred pension and the pension and other benefits he would have received had he not been unfairly dismissed.

In **money purchase** schemes, the pension is based on the level of contributions made by employer and employee. An employee's **loss on dismissal** is therefore equal to the value of the further contributions the employer would have made. This is normally a fixed percentage of salary and can be worked out fairly easily. The tribunal must then decide how many years worth of contribution ought to be awarded, which it does by considering what is likely to happen in the future, including the likelihood of the employee finding another job, when, and whether that job will have a pension attached to it. The tribunal also has to consider the other factors considered above in relation to future loss generally. There is no loss in respect of the **employee's own future contributions** as the compensation awarded for loss of earnings or any earnings from a new job can be paid into a new pension scheme. However, a dismissed employee may be required to pay a penalty for leaving a money purchase scheme early, which will be a loss directly associated with the dismissal.

The guidelines suggest that tribunals should select one of **two different approaches to calculate** future pension loss:
- the simplified approach; or
- the substantial loss approach.

The tribunal's choice of approach will be significant and may make a substantial difference to the amount of compensation awarded for pension loss. Whilst the simplified approach entails a three-stage assessment of loss, the substantial loss approach relies on actuarial tables to calculate the value of the pension rights which would have accrued up to retirement. The difference in the approaches is outlined below.

MEMO POINTS Calculating loss, particularly in relation to final salary schemes, can be complex and **expert actuarial advice** may be required to produce an accurate assessment.

Simplified approach The simplified approach is likely to be appropriate in most cases of assessing pension loss. It **involves calculating three stages** of loss: 8603

1. in the case of a final salary scheme, the loss of enhancement of the pension rights which had already accrued at the date of dismissal (because the pension is calculated on the basis of the salary at dismissal, rather than the higher salary which the employee would have had if he had remained in employment until retirement);
2. in all cases, the loss of rights from the date of dismissal to the date of the hearing; and
3. the loss of future pension rights.

In relation to **stage 1**, an employee who leaves a final salary pension scheme early (either because he is dismissed or for any other reason), is entitled to a pension payable at what would have been his retirement date as an annuity for the rest of his life. This is a **deferred** pension. The early leaver therefore receives a deferred pension representing, usually, 1/60th of his salary at the time he leaves, for each year of service with the employer. However, even though this deferred pension will be recalculated to incorporate increases in the cost of living, the deferred pension is likely to be much less as it is based on the salary at the time of dismissal, rather than the final salary the employee would have had if he had remained with the company until retirement. 8604

The guidance recommends that there should be **no compensation** for loss of enhancement of pension rights where the employee is **near to his anticipated retirement date** i.e. within 5 years of retirement.

Similarly, the guidance suggests that it is not appropriate to award compensation for the loss of accrued pension rights where the tribunal makes a finding of fact that the **employment would have terminated in any event** within 1 year.

However, **compensation may be awarded** where the employee had **5 years or more to retirement** and the calculation can be undertaken using an actuarial method, based on a number of assumptions, provided in the guidance.

MEMO POINTS Different methods are provided for the private and public sector based on their different approaches to final salary schemes, for example, the former will usually provide a pension of 1/60th final salary, whereas the latter usually provides 1/80th final salary.

8605 **Stage 2** of the simplified approach covers the loss of pension rights from the date of dismissal to the date of the hearing. In relation to a **money purchase** scheme, the calculation will be based on the money value of the additional benefits the employee would have received during this period in relation to the employer's contributions. In relation to a **final salary** scheme, the calculation is not as easy. It is suggested that the employee's loss of earnings during this period should incorporate a sum representing what the employer would have contributed to the pension fund during this period, had the employee still been in employment. If the percentage contributed to the pension fund by the employer is unclear, a figure of 15% (or 20% for non-contributory schemes) of pensionable pay is suggested.

Stage 3 of the simplified approach addresses the loss of future pensions rights from the date of the hearing, and should be used where the period of future earnings is not likely to be more than 2 years. Where the pension is a **money purchase** scheme, the value of the loss during the relevant period is the amount of the contributions which the employer would have made to the scheme. In relation to a **final salary** scheme, the value of the loss is generally the amount of contributions which the employer would have made to the pension fund. Allowances for accelerated payment must be made in both cases.

8606 **Substantial loss approach** The guidance suggests that the substantial loss approach may be most **appropriate** where the employee dismissed has been in employment for a lengthy period, the employment is stable and unlikely to be affected by the economic cycle and the employee dismissed has reached an age where he is less likely to be looking for a new position.

This approach may also be appropriate where the employee:
– has found permanent new employment by the time of the hearing and is not likely to move on to a new position in due course;
– has not found new employment and the tribunal is satisfied that, on the balance of probabilities, he will not find new employment before state pension age (this may be the case if an employee is significantly disabled and will find it difficult to obtain new employment); or
– has not found new employment but the tribunal is satisfied that he will find new employment requiring the tribunal to value all losses to retirement and beyond before reducing the total loss by the percentage chance that the employee would not have continued to retirement in the lost employment.

The simplified approach is **not appropriate** in these circumstances as there is a quantifiable loss which can be assessed using pensions data and the actuarial tables set out in the guidance.

8607 Note that the application of either approach will involve the use of the appendices to the guidance, which are useful for parties and tribunals alike. For example, appendix 1 sets out a checklist for assessing pension loss and appendices 4 to 7 contain the tables of multipliers and factors necessary to calculate pension loss under both the simplified and substantial headings.

Expenses

8608 The tribunal can include a sum for expenses incurred by the employee as a result of the dismissal, including **travelling expenses** incurred looking for a new job, and, in some cases, **removal costs** if the employee can show that the only way he could find a new job was to move house and that it was reasonable for him to do so (*Co-operative Wholesale Society Ltd v Squirrell* (1974) 9 ITR 191, NIRC). If the employee, instead of taking up new employment, **sets up his own business** he may be able to recover the costs of doing so (*Gardiner-Hill v Roland Berger Technics Ltd* [1982] IRLR 498, EAT). The employee **cannot recover** the cost of bringing any legal proceedings under this heading.

Expenses incurred in attending tribunal hearings are dealt with separately and do not form part of the compensatory award (¶9712).

Statutory rights

As many statutory rights are only available to those with certain periods of qualifying service, the dismissed employee is disadvantaged, as he will lose the **built up period of qualifying service** with the old employer, and will have to start again with a new employer. This will mean that he will have a period of time during which he does not have, for example, the protection of the right not to be unfairly dismissed or the right to a redundancy payment, and will also have to build up his rights to minimum statutory notice again. The tribunal will award a sum, usually around £200, to compensate for this (*S H Muffett Ltd v Head* [1986] IRLR 488, EAT). 8609

Manner of dismissal

The manner of the dismissal will not of itself attract compensation (i.e. there is **no award for injury to feelings** for unfair dismissal) (*Vaughan v Weighpack Ltd* [1974] IRLR 105, NIRC). This has recently been confirmed by the House of Lords (*Dunnachie v Kingston upon Hull City Council* [2004] IRLR 727, HL). 8610

On rare occasions, the manner of dismissal will be relevant to the issue of compensation where it has **financial implications**, chiefly in relation to mitigation, i.e. if the manner of the dismissal makes it more difficult for the employee to find a new job (for example, because it causes him to become ill), such that the period for which compensation may be ordered is extended.

---

b. Adjustments to compensation

As discussed above, the compensatory award will be such amount as the tribunal considers just and equitable in all the circumstances, thus giving it **broad discretion** to reduce or adjust compensation as it sees fit. In addition, the compensatory award may be reduced or adjusted in the circumstances set out below, and in the order given at ¶8665. 8615

Sums paid by the employer

Once the tribunal has calculated the total amount of the loss, the employer is entitled to credit for any sums which he has paid to the employee, such as pay in lieu of notice (*MBS v Calo* [1983] IRLR 189, EAT). This will also include any sums paid to the employee from the **transferee** of the employer's business (*Steele v Boston Borough Council*, EAT case 1083/01). 8616

The order in which this reduction is made in the calculation of compensation is discussed below.

> EXAMPLE In *MBS v Calo*, MBS made an ex gratia payment of 3 months' gross salary to C on dismissal. It was assessed that C would be unemployed for 7 months. The EAT held that the correct approach was to work out 7 months' net pay and then deduct the 3 months' gross salary already paid.

In cases where the tribunal decides that the employee would have been dismissed in any event, perhaps at some later date, the tribunal will have to consider whether any **payment** made by the employer **would have been made anyway** (*Babcock FATA Ltd v Addison* [1987] IRLR 173, CA). If the payment would have been made anyway, it is not deductible from the compensatory award. If the payment would not have been made anyway, it is deductible. 8617

> EXAMPLE No set off
> An employee is dismissed and is given an ex gratia payment of £500. The tribunal decides that if a proper procedure had been followed, he would still have been dismissed but that dismissal would have taken place 6 weeks later. However, as the employer had a practice of making an ex gratia payment of £500 to any employee who was dismissed, whatever the circumstances, the employee would have received the payment whenever he was dismissed. In those circumstances, the tribunal would not set off the £500 payment against the loss which it finds the employee to be entitled to for the 6 week period when he should have remained in employment.
>
> Set off
> In *DCM Optical Clinic plc v Stark*, EAT case 0124/04, a payment made to an employee (who was subsequently found to be unfairly dismissed) pursuant to an agreement by the employee to continue to work his contractual notice period, was deemed to be deductible from the compensatory award.

8618 If the employer makes a payment by way of **redundancy compensation**, any surplus after an amount equivalent to the statutory redundancy payment has been set off against the basic award (¶8575) is set off against the compensatory award. The order in which these reductions are made in the calculation of compensation is discussed below. If the employee's loss exceeds the statutory maximum (¶8587), the employer's payment may in fact have no impact on the amount awarded to the employee by the tribunal.

EXAMPLE The tribunal assesses total net loss at £80,000. The employer has made an ex gratia payment of £20,000 which is deducted from the total loss, leaving a net loss of £60,000. There are no other deductions so the statutory maximum is then applied and the tribunal awards the employee £56,800. The tribunal would have awarded exactly the same sum to the employee if the employer had made no payment at all, as it would have assessed total loss at £80,000 and then applied the statutory maximum to make an award of £56,800.

8619 Any **sums for breach of contract** (including wrongful dismissal) which an employee has been awarded (or received by way of settlement) in other proceedings are also set off to the extent that they cover the same losses, as the employee is not entitled to be compensated for the same loss twice over (¶8177).

Mitigation of loss

8620 The compensatory award may be reduced if the employee has **not taken reasonable steps** to reduce his loss (for example by seeking alternative employment), i.e. if he has "failed to mitigate" his loss (s 123 ERA 1996). If he has taken steps to mitigate, earnings from his new employment will be offset against the compensatory award. This issue is discussed below.

8621 If the employee has **not found alternative employment** by the date of the hearing, or has taken up **employment at a lower rate of pay**, the employer may allege that he has failed to mitigate his loss, in which case the tribunal can reduce his compensation accordingly.

Strictly speaking, it is for the **employer to prove** such a failure, and he should give evidence of jobs which have been advertised locally during the relevant period for which he believes the employee would have been suitable. He does not have to prove that the employee would have obtained a particular job, only that it is likely that some employment would have been obtained if reasonable efforts had been made. It is sensible for an **employee** to have **evidence** of the steps which he has taken to find work, including copies of any applications which he has sent off (and any replies), details of his contacts with the employment service or recruitment agencies, and evidence of any other efforts which he has made.

Reasonable steps

8622 The tribunal must look at the individual employee and decide whether on the basis of his particular skills, age and background, he has taken reasonable steps to find alternative employment. The employee is expected to do what is reasonable, which means that he is expected to do what a reasonable person would have done if they had no prospect of recovering compensation (*Archbold Freightage Limited v Wilson* [1974] IRLR 10, NIRC). He is not necessarily expected to take the first job that comes along but he will be expected to be able to show that he has been looking for work.

8623 Rather than seek alternative employment, a dismissed employee may decide to **set himself up in business**. Depending on the circumstances of the employee, the tribunal may well find he has acted reasonably by doing so. This is particularly the case where the employee is older, has been with the same employer for a long period of time, and is in a relatively specialist area where alternative employment might be difficult to find (*Gardiner-Hill v Roland Berger Technics Limited* [1982] IRLR 498, EAT). The tribunal will need to be satisfied that the business has a reasonable prospect of producing an income for the employee.

8624 **Failure to mitigate** An employee is likely to have failed to mitigate his loss if he **turns down a job** on a rate of pay which, while lower than that which he received from the employer, would have gone some considerable way to reducing his loss. What it is reasonable for an employee to do will depend on the particular employee and the evidence of the alternative jobs which were available. On the other hand, if an employee is dismissed from a £40,000 per year job and accepts a £10,000 per year job and then makes no further effort to find employment at a higher rate of pay in order to replace the remainder of the lost earnings, he is also likely to be found to have acted unreasonably.

A **refusal to accept employment with the same employer** who has dismissed the employee is less likely to be unreasonable. Further, at the tribunal stage, the employee may indicate that he does not want an order for reinstatement or re-engagement (see below), and this will not be considered as a failure to mitigate his loss.

When the **tribunal has found a failure to mitigate**, it has to reduce the compensatory award accordingly. In doing so, it considers when it believes the employee ought to have found alternative employment, and what rate of pay the employee would have received. This is not done on a percentage basis, but is approached by treating the employee as though he has earned the amount the tribunal believes he could have earned from the date when the tribunal believes he could have started earning it. **8625**

EXAMPLE 1. Employee A is dismissed on 31 March. The tribunal finds that, had he made a reasonable effort, A would have found alternative employment on the same rate of pay not later than 30 June. The tribunal will award compensation for the period between 1 April and 30 June and no compensation thereafter.

2. Employee B is dismissed on 30 April. Prior to his dismissal, he was earning £100 per week. The tribunal sitting on 1 November decides that he could have obtained a job on £80 per week not later than 30 September. It will award him £100 per week for the period up to 30 September, £20 per week for the period from then until the tribunal hearing, and will calculate future loss on the basis of £20 per week.

Earnings from new employment Where the employee has been **able to find alternative employment** by the date of the tribunal hearing, the tribunal **off sets** the amount of any earnings from such employment from the amount which it awards for loss to date and also projects this forward in order to set it off against future loss. **8626**

However, it seems that if an employee **obtains higher paid employment** during the period between dismissal and the tribunal hearing, he is entitled to his full loss up to the date on which he obtains that higher paid employment and is not required to give credit for the excess of his earnings thereafter (*Whelan v Richardson* [1998] IRLR 114, EAT).

EXAMPLE In *Whelan v Richardson*, W was dismissed in August 1995 from a job in which she earned £72 per week. She was unemployed for 2 weeks and then obtained a new job which paid £51.60 per week. She remained in that job for 18 weeks before starting a new job in December 1995 which paid £95.82 per week. The tribunal hearing took place in November 1996, by which time she had been in the higher paid job for nearly a year. The total earnings since dismissal were actually higher than those she would have earned had she remained in the job from which she was dismissed. However, the EAT upheld the tribunal's decision to award loss of earnings up to the point at which she obtained the higher paid employment in December 1995 (i.e. 2 weeks at £72 and 18 weeks at £20.40 (£72 – £51.60)).

At the time of writing, the position is unclear as to whether account will be taken of **money earned in new employment during the notice period** of the old employment, for the purposes of assessing compensation. **8627**

Where an employee has been dismissed summarily, without any payment in lieu of notice, he will be under a duty to mitigate his loss and, consequently, if he obtains new, higher-paid employment during what would otherwise have been his **statutory notice period**, his earnings from his new employment will be taken into consideration in determining the compensatory award to be made (*Hardy v Polk (Leeds) Ltd* [2004] IRLR 420, EAT).

However, it has also been held that an employee who has been unfairly dismissed and has taken up new employment during what would have been his notice period is not required to give credit for any earnings from his new employment (i.e. have an amount equivalent to his new earnings deducted from his compensatory award), despite having received a payment in lieu of notice from his former employer (*Voith Turbo Ltd v Stowe* [2005] IRLR 228, EAT).

MEMO POINTS In reaching its decision in *Hardy v Polk (Leeds) Ltd*, the EAT refused to follow two well-established decisions (*Norton Tool Company Ltd v Tewson* [1972] IRLR 86, NICR; followed in *Babcock FATA Ltd v Addison* [1987] IRLR 173, CA) on the basis that neither case had specifically addressed the statutory mitigation of loss provisions (¶8620).

However, in reaching its decision in *Voith Turbo Ltd v Stowe*, the EAT upheld the decision in *Norton Tool Company Ltd v Tewson* but did not follow its own earlier decision in *Hardy v Polk (Leeds) Ltd*. This point of law is further complicated by the EAT's decision in *Morgans v Alpha Plus Security Ltd* [2005] IRLR 234, EAT, outlined further at ¶8647.

Employment would have terminated in any event

8628 In assessing compensation, the tribunal aims to put the employee in the position that he would have been in had he not been dismissed. If, therefore, the tribunal believes that his old employment would have come to an end anyway in circumstances where the termination of his employment would have been fair, it will take this into account (considering also when the dismissal would have taken place) (*James W Cook & Co (Wivenhoe) Ltd v Tipper* [1990] IRLR 386, CA).

EXAMPLE In *James W Cook & Co (Wivenhoe) Ltd v Tipper*, T claimed he had been unfairly dismissed from the employer's shipyard in May 1986. The Court held that he could not claim loss beyond September 1986 when the whole shipyard closed and all staff were made redundant. Even if he had not been dismissed in May, his employment would have ended anyway in September and so he did not suffer any loss beyond that point.

Procedural defects

8629 Save in exceptional circumstances, there will be a **mandatory adjustment** of any compensatory award made to an employee in a successful tribunal claim brought under any of the jurisdictions set out at ¶9985 in respect of a matter to which a statutory dispute resolution procedure applies and where the relevant procedure was not completed before proceedings were commenced (s 31 EA 2002; s 124A ERA 1996).

Where non-completion of the procedure is wholly or mainly attributable to a **failure by the employer** to comply with a requirement of the procedure, the tribunal must make an increase of 10% to the compensatory award, and may, if it is just and equitable in all the circumstances to do so, increase it by up to 50% (s 31(3) EA 2002). If the non-completion of the procedure is wholly or mainly attributable to a **failure by the employee** to comply with a requirement of the procedure or to exercise a right of appeal under it, then the tribunal must make a reduction of 10% to the compensatory award, and may, if it is just and equitable in all the circumstances to do so, reduce it by up to 50% (s 31(2) EA 2002). In exceptional circumstances, where an adjustment of 10% would be unjust or inequitable, the tribunal may, at its discretion, make no adjustment or make such lower adjustment as it considers just and equitable (s 31(4) EA 2002).

Note that under the statutory dispute resolution procedures there is no actual obligation on an employee to exercise his right to appeal against his employer's decision. However, it appears that if an employee fails to appeal, he will nonetheless suffer a mandatory reduction to his compensatory award (if any) if he subsequently brings a successful tribunal claim.

8630 It is possible for a dismissal to be unfair (both procedurally and/or substantively), even if an employer complies with an applicable statutory dismissal and disciplinary procedure.

There are some cases where the employer had a **good reason for dismissing** the employee but the dismissal is unfair because of a procedural defect. In such cases, the tribunal considers what would have happened had a fair procedure been followed. If the employer would have dismissed in any event, the tribunal may reduce any compensatory award to reflect the likelihood that the employee would have been dismissed in any event (*Polkey v A E Dayton Services Ltd* [1987] IRLR 503, HL; see also ¶8436 for details of the rules regarding procedural fairness) (known as a "**Polkey reduction**"). For example, an employee dismissed for misconduct without first being given the opportunity to give his version of events is likely to have been procedurally unfairly dismissed. The evidence, however, might show that even if the employee had been given that opportunity, there would still be sufficient evidence of misconduct to have justified the dismissal.

If the tribunal is unable to say with certainty what the outcome of a fair procedure would have been, it has to assess the chances that the **employee would have stayed in employment**. If it believes that there is a 25% chance that a fair procedure would have resulted in the employee remaining in employment, it should award 25% of the compensation which it would otherwise have given to the employee. It will be up to the **employer to show** that the employee would (or might) have been dismissed in any event (*Britool Ltd v Roberts* [1993] IRLR 481, EAT). It may not be appropriate to assess chance in percentage terms where the tribunal is considering the likelihood of the employee being **fairly dismissed at some point in the future** (as a sliding scale would have to be used). Instead, the tribunal may identify a date by which it concludes the employment would have terminated in any event, and calculate compensation by reference to that period (*O'Donaghue v Redcar and Cleveland Borough Council* [2001] IRLR 615, CA). The correct approach will depend on the facts and circumstances of each particular case. It is clear, however, that if the tribunal is considering making a Polkey reduction to an employee's compensation, then both parties must have an **opportunity to make submissions** on any such reduction (*Market Force (UK) Ltd v Hunt* [2002] IRLR 863, EAT).

Since 1 October 2004, the principle behind the Polkey reduction continues to operate in conjunction with the new statutory dismissal and disciplinary procedures, albeit with some differences. Prior to October 2004, a Polkey reduction of up to 100% might have been made to an employee's compensatory award. This is still the case in circumstances where an employer has failed to comply with an applicable statutory procedure and any subsequent dismissal will be automatically unfair (s 98A(1) ERA 1996) but the employee's compensatory award may nevertheless be reduced by up to 100% by way of a Polkey reduction since the new procedural fairness rules (¶8436) will not apply. However, if an employer has complied with an applicable statutory procedure but the dismissal is otherwise procedurally unfair in other respects, it is probable that a Polkey reduction of only up to 50% can now be made since an employer will have a "defence" to a procedurally unfair dismissal if he can demonstrate on the balance of probabilities that he would have taken the decision to dismiss the employee in any event even if he had followed a procedure (other than a statutory procedure) (i.e. that there is a greater than 50% likelihood that he would have taken such a decision). 8631

A similar principle applies in a case of **unfair selection for redundancy**. The tribunal may be able to say that a fair selection procedure would have meant that the employee was not the one selected for redundancy and so would have stayed in employment. Alternatively, it may only be able to say that had a fair procedure been carried out there was, for example, a 30% chance that the employee would have remained in employment or would have been offered alternative employment. In such a case, it will reduce the compensation accordingly. It should be noted that statutory dismissal and disciplinary procedures apply to redundancy dismissals too (¶6636). 8632

Compensation for **failure to consult** prior to a redundancy dismissal is conventionally calculated by reference to the length of time that a proper consultation process would have taken (for example, if it is decided that consultation would have taken 2 weeks, compensation may be calculated on the basis that the employee would have been employed for those further 2 weeks) (*Mining Supplies (Longwall) Ltd v Baker* [1988] IRLR 417, EAT). However, tribunals should not be constrained by this convention but should assess compensation by reference to what would have happened if the employer had acted properly in all the circumstances (*Elkouil v Coney Island Ltd* [2002] IRLR 174, EAT).

EXAMPLE In *Elkouil v Coney Island Ltd*, E was notified on 27 July 1999 that he was being made redundant with immediate effect. The tribunal found that, had the employer followed established procedure and consulted with him, E would have been employed for a further 2 weeks. However, as it had been clear to the employer by May 1999 that E would be made redundant, the EAT held that he should have been warned earlier and his compensation should, therefore, be calculated by reference to a 10 week period.

Procedural defects (other than in relation to a statutory dismissal and disciplinary procedure) may be **so fundamental** that it is not possible for the tribunal to come to any sensible conclusion about what would have happened if a fair procedure had been followed. In such cases, it is appropriate for the tribunal to award full compensation without making 8633 any Polkey reduction, and the tribunal should not indulge in an exercise of pure speculation (*King v Eaton Ltd (No 2)* [1998] IRLR 686, CS; *Valueunion Ltd v White*, EAT case 875/99).

EXAMPLE In *Valueunion Ltd v White*, W only found out that he had been dismissed when he read the employer's notice of appearance in respect of his application for unlawful deductions from wages. In the circumstances, the tribunal was not able to form any view as to what might have happened if a fair procedure had been followed and the EAT upheld its decision to make no reduction.

Contributory fault

8635 If the tribunal finds that the employee has, by his actions, caused or contributed to his dismissal, it **must reduce** compensation by such amount as it considers just and equitable (s 123 ERA 1996; *Optikinetics Ltd v Whooley* [1999] ICR 984, EAT). It is open to a tribunal to make a reduction of 100% on the basis of contributory conduct (*Devis & Sons Ltd v Atkins* [1977] IRLR 314, HL; *Perkin v St George's Healthcare NHS Trust* [2005] EWCA Civ 1174).

This reduction can only be made on the basis of the **employee's own conduct** – not the conduct of any other person (unless that person is acting as the employee's agent or under his instructions).

The employee must be allowed to give **evidence** in respect of any question of contributory fault. If the tribunal does make a reduction, it must specify the conduct which has caused it to do so (*Parkers Bakeries Ltd v Palmer* [1977] IRLR 215, EAT).

8636 Unlike reductions to the basic award which apply to any conduct, reductions to the compensatory award are limited to conduct which **caused or contributed** to the dismissal. This means that it is open to the tribunal to reduce the basic and compensatory awards by different proportions, although it is common to apply the same percentage deduction to both (*Charles Robertson (Developments) Ltd v White* [1995] ICR 349, EAT).

The conduct must have contributed to the dismissal, but **not necessarily to the unfairness** of the dismissal. Further, where the employee's conduct gave rise to a situation in which he was dismissed, the tribunal can find that he contributed to his dismissal even where the contributory conduct did not relate to the real reason for dismissal, provided it played a part in the process which led to dismissal (*Robert Whiting Designs Ltd v Lamb* [1978] ICR 89, EAT).

EXAMPLE 1. Employee C commits an act of gross misconduct. For procedural reasons, the employer's disciplinary process is found to be inadequate and the dismissal is held to be unfair. C's conduct has not contributed to the **procedural unfairness**, but has, however, contributed to the dismissal (it is because of his conduct that he was dismissed). The conduct can, therefore, be taken into account to make a finding of contributory fault.

2. According to the employer, Employee D is dismissed for persistent (unjustified) absenteeism. After examining all the matters discussed during the disciplinary process, the tribunal finds that the real reason for dismissal was, in fact, a general lack of competence. The tribunal can still regard the absenteeism as having **contributed to the dismissal**, as it was because the employee was persistently absent that the disciplinary process was initiated and it was one of the matters which ultimately led to his dismissal.

3. In *Lindsay v General Contracting Ltd t/a Pik a Pak Home Electrical*, EAT case 1096/00 & 1126/00, L's letter of dismissal stated that she was dismissed for bad work ethics, bad attitude and disruptive behaviour. The tribunal found that the real reason for dismissal was her joining a trade union. There should have been no reduction for contributory fault as her behaviour **did not contribute** to the dismissal.

8637 The tribunal has a broad discretion in relation to the **types of conduct** which it can take into account. The conduct has to be "**blameworthy**", i.e. action which is "perverse, foolish… or bloody-minded… [or] unreasonable in all the circumstances" (*Nelson v BBC (No 2)* [1979] IRLR 346, CA). The conduct need not amount to a breach of contract or a tort such as negligence. Conduct is not blameworthy if, for example, it consists of refusing to obey an order which would have involved breaking the law. Participating in industrial action (even where this is in breach of contract) is not, in itself, blameworthy (*Courtaulds Northern Spinning Limited v Moosa* [1984] IRLR 43, EAT). Further, circumstances which are beyond the control of the employee, such as ill health or incompetence (where the employee has made appropriate effort to do his job properly), will not normally be regarded as blameworthy.

Unlike reductions to the basic award, conduct by an employee can **only** be taken into account if it occurred, and was discovered by the employer, **before the dismissal**. This is because conduct that the employer did not know about when he dismissed cannot be said to have contributed to the dismissal. However, in such cases it is still open to the tribunal to find, on the basis of **conduct discovered after the dismissal**, that it would not be just and equitable to award compensation at all (*Devis & Sons Ltd v Atkins* [1977] IRLR 314, HL). 8638

Social security benefits

The treatment of social security benefits is discussed below. 8643

Income support and job seeker's allowance Where the employee has received one of these benefits, the Government can recoup payments made from any award (Employment Protection (Recoupment of Jobseeker's Allowance and Income Support) Regulations SI 1996/2349). The tribunal will ask the employee when it is assessing compensation whether or not either of these benefits has been received and if so, it will structure its order so as to comply with the requirements set out below. 8644

The regulations do not apply where the parties **settle the case privately** (whether or not a conciliation officer has been involved). This can act as an incentive to settling rather than having the award made by the tribunal.

These benefits are treated differently from other types of income when assessing compensation. The tribunal calculates the employee's loss without making any deduction to reflect receipt of these benefits. However, when it makes its award, it must specify how much relates to **loss of earnings** for the period **between dismissal and the date of the award**. This is called the "**prescribed element**", and is arrived at after all appropriate deductions and reductions have been made, and the statutory maximum has been applied. In working out how the prescribed element is affected by the application of the statutory maximum, it is deemed to have been reduced in the same proportion as the compensatory award as a whole. For example, if the loss for the period from dismissal to the date of the award is £40,000 and the compensatory award is £113,600, the latter will be reduced to £56,800 when the statutory maximum is applied. This means that of the £56,800, £20,000 is deemed to be the prescribed element. 8645

The Government is entitled to recoup from the employer an amount in respect of benefits paid to the employee by serving a **recoupment notice** on the employer. The notice must be served within 21 days of the conclusion of the hearing or within 9 days after the decision is sent to the parties (21 days if judgment has been reserved), whichever is later. Recoupment is limited to the amount of the prescribed element. This means that the employer may only pay to the employee the balance of the total award over and above the prescribed element until the period for service of a recoupment notice has expired. For example, if the award is £56,800, of which the prescribed element is £20,000, the employer may only pay the employee £36,800 initially. The tribunal will inform the employer of this and will tell him that he should not pay the employee any part of the prescribed element until either he has received a recoupment notice or has been informed that no notice is to be issued. If a notice is issued, the employer pays the Government the amount which it wishes to recoup from the prescribed element, and any surplus is then paid to the employee. 8646

Incapacity benefit In assessing the compensatory award of an employee who has been unfairly dismissed, a tribunal is permitted to **deduct in full** an amount equivalent to the amount of any incapacity benefits which the employee has received between the date of his dismissal and the date of the tribunal remedies hearing (*Morgans v Alpha Plus Security Ltd* [2005] IRLR 234, EAT). It was concluded by the EAT in this case that there is no authority to allow a tribunal to disregard any monies received by the employee and that to not take such receipts into account would be to reward an unfairly dismissed employee a "bonus" which would place him in a better position than he would have been in had he not been dismissed. 8647

MEMO POINTS It is difficult to reconcile this decision of the EAT with the decision arrived at in *Voith Turbo Ltd v Stowe* (see ¶8627) and further clarification on this point of law is required.

8648 **Contributory benefits** In relation to benefits such as **invalidity benefit** which are contributory in nature, the EAT has given guidance which suggests that credit should been given to the employer for 50% of the amount of the benefits. This is on the basis that it is not just and equitable for either party to benefit fully from the amount of benefits which have been received by the employee but which he has contributed to through the national insurance system (*Rubenstein v McGloughlin* [1996] IRLR 557, EAT).

8649 **Housing benefit** No credit is given to the employer in respect of housing benefit received by the employee. This is on the basis that housing benefit relates to the needs of the family/household as a whole and not directly to the position of the employee as an individual. It also reflects the fact that the local authority may be able to recover the amount of any housing benefit which it has paid out from any award of compensation which the employee receives, and so a deduction by the tribunal might leave the employee in a position of having effectively to pay it back twice.

c. Order for calculating compensatory award

8665 The order for calculating the compensatory award is as follows (*Digital Equipment Co Ltd v Clements (No2)* [1998] IRLR 134, CA, *Heggie v Uniroyal Englebert Tyres* [1999] IRLR 802, CS):

a. calculate the total loss attributable to the employer's actions;

b. give full credit for sums paid by the employer (other than contractual severance payments to the extent that they exceed the basic award) and money earned in mitigation (i.e. earnings since dismissal);

c. reduce this amount, if appropriate, to reflect that the employment may well have terminated anyway had a fair procedure been followed (the "Polkey reduction");

d. if appropriate, adjust the amount if either party has failed to complete a requirement of an applicable statutory dispute resolution procedure;

e. increase the amount in respect of any failure by the employer to provide a full or accurate statement of written particulars (¶6525);

f. reduce this amount further, if appropriate, to reflect any contributory fault on the part of the employee;

g. deduct the excess of any contractual severance payment over the basic award;

h. apply the statutory maximum if the amount arrived at exceeds £56,800; and finally

i. indicate, if appropriate, what part, if any, is a prescribed element for recoupment purposes due to benefits received.

The following example shows the difference which can occur by using a different order of calculation.

EXAMPLE An employee is out of work for 6 months after dismissal with total loss of earnings of £95,000. The employer has made an ex gratia payment of £20,000. The tribunal finds that compensation should be reduced by 20% to reflect contributory fault.
Using the correct order set out above, £20,000 would first be deducted from £95,000 to give a net loss of £75,000. This would then be reduced by 20% to give £60,000. As this exceeds £56,800 (the statutory maximum), the cap would then be applied so that the compensatory award would be £56,800.
If instead, the total loss of 95,000 was reduced by 20% to give 76,000, before deducting the ex gratia payment of £20,000, the compensatory award would be only £56,000.
Another alternative, with even more drastic implications for the employee, would be to apply the statutory cap before making the reduction for ex gratia payment and contributory fault. This would mean that the total loss of £95,000 would be capped at £56,800. £20,000 would then be deducted to leave £36,800, which would then be reduced by 20% to give a compensatory award of only £29,440.

B. Reinstatement and re-engagement

Reinstatement and re-engagement orders require the employer to take the employee back in either the same or a similar role and to pay compensation for earnings lost in the meantime (¶8593). 8680

In deciding whether or not to make one of these orders, the tribunal considers reinstatement first (s 116(1) ERA 1996). If it decides not to order reinstatement, it then goes on to consider re-engagement and, if so, on what terms (s 116(2), (3) ERA 1996).

MEMO POINTS If, in a claim brought under one of the jurisdictions set out at ¶9985, the tribunal makes an order for reinstatement or re-engagement instead of a compensatory award, it must also make a minimum basic award of 4 weeks' pay if it appears that the employer failed to comply with an applicable statutory dispute resolution procedure (¶¶6514, 8577).

Effect of reinstatement

If an employee is reinstated, he is treated as if he had not been dismissed (his employment is treated as having continued uninterrupted and **statutory continuity** of employment is preserved) (s 114(1) ERA 1996). 8681

The employee will be entitled to an amount in respect of **loss of benefits** (including **arrears of pay**) between the date of dismissal and the date of reinstatement (s 114(2) ERA 1996). In calculating the sum payable, the tribunal will take into account pay in lieu of notice, ex gratia payments by the employer, and any pay received from any other employer during the relevant period (s 114(4) ERA 1996). If the employee would have benefited from any **improvement** in his terms and conditions (for example, a pay rise or promotion) had he not been dismissed, the employer will be required to give him the benefit of such an improvement with effect from the date on which it would have taken effect had the dismissal not occurred (s 114(3) ERA 1996).

The order will also specify any **other rights and privileges**, such as seniority or pension rights that must be restored to him and will set a time limit for compliance by the employer.

Effect of re-engagement

An order for re-engagement requires the employee to be re-employed (and his **statutory continuity** of employment is preserved), but not necessarily in the same job or on the same terms. It need not even be by the same employer, but can require the employee to be engaged by a **successor** to that employer (i.e. someone who has taken over the business) or an **associated** employer (s 115(1) ERA 1996). 8682

MEMO POINTS Employers are treated as being "associated" if one is a company of which the other (directly or indirectly) has control, or both are companies of which a third party (directly or indirectly) has control (s 231 ERA 1996).

In such cases the employee must be engaged in employment **comparable** to that from which he was dismissed, or other suitable employment. The tribunal must specify the **terms** on which re-engagement is to take place. These must, as far as is reasonably practicable, be as favourable as an order for reinstatement, unless the employee has partly contributed to his own dismissal (s 116(4) ERA 1996). The tribunal cannot order re-engagement on substantially more favourable terms (*Rank Xerox (UK) Ltd v Stryczek* [1995] IRLR 568, EAT). The terms of the order will include (s 115(2) ERA 1996): 8683
- the identity of the employer;
- the nature of the employment;
- the remuneration for the employment (i.e. pay and other benefits);
- any amount payable for loss of benefits (including arrears of pay) between the date of dismissal and the date of re-engagement;
- any rights and privileges such as seniority and pension rights which must be restored; and
- the date for compliance.

As in the case of reinstatement orders, any pay in lieu, ex gratia payments or pay from other employers during the relevant period is taken into account in calculating how much the employer must pay for **loss of benefits** (s 115(3) ERA 1996).

Relevant factors

8684 In addition to the **applicant's wishes**, the following factors are taken into account by the tribunal when deciding whether to make an order for reinstatement or re-engagement.

8685 **Practicability** The tribunal has to consider whether it is practicable for the employer to comply with such an order. However, practicability is a relevant but not conclusive factor, so a tribunal may still make an order where it considers that compliance may not be reasonably practicable if it believes that there is still a chance it may succeed (*Timex Corporation v Thomson* [1981] IRLR 522, EAT). In such cases, doubts about the practicability of the order are relevant if the tribunal is subsequently asked to award compensation for non-compliance by the employer (¶8688).

In **assessing** practicability, the tribunal will look at all the circumstances, including the likely atmosphere in the workplace if the employee returns, the degree of trust and confidence which remains, whether there will be any (or enough) work for the employee to do, and the likely attitude of customers or the public (if the job involves contact with these groups). Each case has to be looked at individually. The tribunal will be reluctant to make an order which seems likely to lead only to further trouble.

EXAMPLE 1. In *Wood Group Heavy Industrial Turbines Ltd v Crossan* [1998] IRLR 680, EAT, C was dismissed following allegations of drug dealing in the workplace. The dismissal was held to be unfair (there had not been an adequate investigation). However, as the employer genuinely believed the allegations to be true, the EAT agreed that the relationship of trust and confidence between employer and employee had broken down such that an order for re-engagement was inappropriate.
2. In *Coleman and Stephenson v Magnet Joinery Ltd* [1974] IRLR 343, CA, C and S were dismissed after the rest of the workforce threatened to go on strike if the employer continued to employ them after they ceased to be union members. The dismissal was unfair (because the main reason for it was their exercising the right not to be trade union members), but re-engagement was inappropriate as such an order would lead to industrial unrest in the workplace.

8686 The tribunal will not take into account the fact that an employer has taken on a **permanent replacement** for the employee (s 116(5) ERA 1996). The tribunal can make an order for reinstatement or re-engagement even if a permanent replacement has been taken on, unless the employer can show that:
- it was not practicable for him to arrange for the employee's work to be done without engaging a permanent replacement (i.e. it could not be done by a temporary replacement or absorbed by other members of staff); or
- the employer waited for a reasonable period after the dismissal (and did not during that time hear from the employee that he wanted to be reinstated or re-engaged) before engaging the permanent replacement, and by that time it was no longer reasonably practicable for him to arrange for the employee's work to be done without engaging a permanent replacement.

8687 **Contributory fault** Where the applicant caused or contributed to his dismissal, the tribunal must consider whether it would be just to order his reinstatement. If, for example, a tribunal has found that an employee was guilty of serious misconduct but his dismissal was unfair for purely procedural reasons, it might be reluctant to order the employer to take him back.

A tribunal may consider that it would not be appropriate to order an employee to be taken back into the same workplace if there is **ill feeling** between him and other employees or management. It might, however, be appropriate in such cases for him to be taken back in a different job elsewhere in the employer's business.

Failure to comply

8688 If an order for reinstatement or re-engagement is made, further remedies are available to the employee if the employer fails to comply. Non-compliance may consist of a total failure or refusal to reinstate or re-engage the employee. Alternatively, it may be that the employee is reinstated or re-engaged but the terms of the order are not fully complied with (perhaps because the employer fails to pay all that it is ordered to pay, or because the employee is taken back on different terms from those ordered). In either case, the tribunal can award **compensation** (s 117 ERA 1996).

If there is **partial compliance** (i.e. reinstatement or re-engagement but failure to comply fully with the terms of the order), the compensation is calculated on the basis of the loss sustained by the employee as a result (which may exceed the statutory cap to the extent necessary to compensate for any amount which should have been paid under the original order) (ss 117(2), 124(3) ERA 1996).

If the non-compliance means that the employee has **not been reinstated or re-engaged at all** (or supposed reinstatement but on much inferior terms (*Artisan Press v Srawley and Parker* [1986] IRLR 126, EAT)), the compensation is calculated in the same way as for unfair dismissal.

The tribunal will (unless an exception applies) also make an **additional award** (s 117(3) ERA 1996). A tribunal is entitled to reconsider the amount of loss incurred by an employee between dismissal and the date originally set for reinstatement, even though this exercise will have already been carried out when making the original reinstatement order (¶8681) (*Awotona v South Tyneside Healthcare NHS Trust* [2005] ICR 985, CA). The statutory cap can be exceeded to the extent necessary to enable the aggregate of the compensatory and additional awards fully to reflect the amount which should have been paid under the original order (s 124(4) ERA 1996; *Selfridges Ltd v Malik* [1997] IRLR 577, EAT). The tribunal has a wide discretion in setting the amount of an additional award, which will be between 26 and 52 weeks' pay (subject to the statutory cap on a week's pay – ¶2920) (s 117(3) ERA 1996). The employer's conduct will be an important factor in deciding the amount payable. 8689

An additional award is **not payable** if the employer can satisfy the tribunal that it was not reasonably practicable for him to comply (s 117(4) ERA 1996). This means that the tribunal has to consider practicability again at this stage. The same considerations will apply as when considering practicability before making the order in the first place (see above). If the employer shows that it was not practicable to comply, the tribunal will award compensation in the normal way.

If the **employee** changes his mind and does not return, he can still ask for compensation but the tribunal must take his **failure to take up reinstatement or re-engagement** into account when considering whether or not he has mitigated his loss unless he had good reasons for not returning (s 117(8) ERA 1996). 8690

Where an **employer fails to comply** with a reinstatement or re-engagement order, an award for loss of benefits (including arrears of pay) forms part of the compensation award and is therefore subject to the statutory cap. The employer is not obliged to pay the compensatory award plus a further sum relating to lost pay and benefits (*Parry v National Westminster Bank plc* [2005] IRLR 193, CA).

C. Interim relief

The **purpose** of an interim relief order is to maintain the status quo pending the final determination of the case. It is only **available** where the applicant claims to have been **unfairly dismissed** for one of the reasons for which a minimum basic award is payable (¶8577) and also in respect of the following reasons (s 161 TULRCA 1992; para 161(2) Sch A1 TULRCA 1992; s 128 ERA 1996): 8700
- the right to accompany/be accompanied at disciplinary/grievance hearing;
- certain activities relating to trade union recognition/derecognition; and
- making a protected disclosure (i.e. whistleblowing).

Procedure An **application** for interim relief must be made within 7 days of the EDT (¶8340), and can only be made if an originating application claiming unfair dismissal on one 8701 of the grounds set out above has also been presented (the two applications will normally be presented together).

If made on grounds of **trade union membership or activity**, the application must be accompanied by a certificate signed by an authorised trade union official. The certificate must state that the applicant was (or proposed to become) a member of the trade union at the date of dismissal and that there are reasonable grounds for believing that the dismissal was on trade union grounds.

8702 The tribunal will hear the application as soon as possible after it is submitted. The tribunal will give the employer a copy of the application and (where applicable) the certificate at least 7 days before the **hearing**, along with details of the time, date and place of the hearing.

At the hearing (which may only be **postponed** if the tribunal is satisfied that special circumstances exist), the **applicant must satisfy** the tribunal that it is likely that at the full hearing of his originating application it will be found that he was unfairly dismissed for one of the specified reasons.

If the **tribunal is satisfied** that such a finding is likely, it will explain to the parties the powers available to it. It will then ask the employer (if present) whether or not he is willing to reinstate or re-engage the applicant (on terms not less favourable than would have been applicable had he not been dismissed), pending the final determination of the case.

8703 **Possible orders** If the employer is **willing to reinstate**, the tribunal will make an order accordingly. If the employer is **willing to re-engage on specific terms**, the tribunal will ask the employee if he is willing to accept those terms. If he is, the tribunal will order re-engagement accordingly. If he is not willing, the tribunal will only make an order for the **continuation of the employee's contract** of employment if it considers that the employee's refusal of those terms is reasonable (otherwise it will make no order).

If the employer is **not present** or states that he is **not willing to reinstate or re-engage**, the tribunal will (if satisfied that the unfair dismissal claim is likely to succeed) make an order for the continuation of the employee's contract of employment.

MEMO POINTS A continuation order will not transfer from a transferor employer to the transferee employer in respect of a business transfer under the TUPE regulations (¶7980).

8704 The **effect of a continuation order** is that from the EDT or settlement of the case, the contract remains in force:

– for the purposes of pay or any other benefit derived from the employment, seniority, pension rights and other similar matters; and

– to determine for any purpose (for example, the amount of a basic award or statutory redundancy payment) the employee's period of continuous employment (¶1040).

In the order, the tribunal will specify how much the employer is to pay the employee in respect of each pay period between the date of dismissal and the final determination of the case (based on the amount which the employee could reasonably have been expected to earn during that period). If the employer has made any payment in respect of a particular pay period (either under the contract, e.g. by way of notice pay, or as compensation for breach of contract), that payment will be set off. The recoupment provisions (see above) will be applicable to any sum which the tribunal orders the employer to pay in respect of arrears of pay between dismissal and final determination of the proceedings.

8705 If there is a **change of circumstances** after the making of the order, either party may make a further application to have it revoked or varied.

8706 **Failure to comply** If the tribunal orders reinstatement or re-engagement and the employer fails to comply, the employee can return to the tribunal to ask for:

– an order for continuation of the contract of employment; and/or

– damages.

D. Table of specific remedies

The following table shows the circumstances in which particular remedies may be available. 8710

Reason	Minimum basic award (general) (¶8577)	Minimum basic award (statutory procedure) (¶8577)	No cap on compensation (¶8587)	Interim relief (¶8700)	Additional award (¶8689)	Increase to compensatory award (¶8629)
Trade union membership/ non-membership or activities	x			x		
Certain activities relating to trade union recognition/ derecognition				x		
Being an employee representative, candidate, or voter in relation to collective redundancy or business transfer consultation	x			x		
Being a workers' representative for health and safety purposes, or a member of a safety committee, or carrying out (or proposing to carry out) health and safety activities (having been designated by the employer to do so)			x	x		
Other health and safety reasons			x			
Being a workforce representative for working time purposes (or a candidate to become one)	x					
Making a protected disclosure (i.e. whistleblowing)			x	x		
Right to accompany/ be accompanied at disciplinary/grievance hearing				x		
Trusteeship of occupational pension scheme	x			x		
Refusal to comply with order for reinstatement/ re-engagement			x		x	
Employee automatically dismissed where employer fails to follow a statutory dismissal and disciplinary procedure		x				
Employer fails to follow applicable statutory dispute resolution procedure						x

SECTION 3

Redundancy

8730 In broad terms, an employee is redundant if he becomes surplus to his employer's requirements. Redundancy can be a distressing experience for employees, and employers are advised to develop strategies for managing human resources in order to avoid or reduce job losses, minimise disruption to company performance and ease the process of change (ACAS: Redundancy handling).

8731 An employee under notice of dismissal for redundancy has a statutory right to time off work to seek new employment or to make arrangements for retraining. If he is dismissed by reason of redundancy, or laid off or put on short-time working (see Chapter 23), an employee may also be entitled to a statutory redundancy payment, although he may lose this entitlement if he unreasonably refuses an offer of suitable alternative employment. Employees may also benefit from contractual provisions relating to redundancy pay and procedures.

8732 Although redundancy is a fair reason for dismissal, an employer may incur liability for unfair dismissal if there is no genuine redundancy situation or the dismissal is automatically unfair (for example, if the reason for dismissal is the employee's pregnancy), or if he fails to act fairly in all the circumstances. This last requirement obliges the employer to implement fair selection, to consult, and to consider alternatives to dismissal.

8733 In addition to individual consultation in order to ensure a fair dismissal process, in cases of collective redundancies, an employer is also required to consult with trade union or employee representatives and to notify the DTI.

I. Identifying a redundancy dismissal

8740 **Definition** An employee is dismissed by reason of redundancy if the dismissal is wholly or mainly attributable to (s 139(1) ERA 1996):
– the fact that his employer has ceased or intends to cease (i) to carry on the business for the purposes of which the employee was employed by him, or (ii) to carry on that business in the place where the employee was so employed; or
– the fact that the requirements of that business (i) for employees to carry out work of a particular kind, or (ii) for employees to carry out work of a particular kind in the place where the employee was so employed, have ceased or diminished or are expected to cease or diminish.

8741 The **business** of the employer is treated as one business with the business of any **associated employer** (s 139(2) ERA 1996). Employers are "associated" if one is a company controlled by the other (who may be a company or an individual), or if both are companies controlled by another employer (either a company or an individual) (s 231 ERA 1996). "Company" means a limited company, and "control" means control of more than 50% of the votes attaching to shares. For example, Company A has a 75% stake in both Company B and Company C. The businesses of all three companies are treated as one and the redundancy selection procedure can be applied across the whole group such that, when faced with a redundancy situation, Company C could select employees for redundancy from Company A and B as well as from itself, even if there is no redundancy situation in Company A or B. See "Bumping" at ¶8784 below for further detail.

1. Redundancy situations

According to the statutory definition, **three redundancy situations** can be identified: 8745
- closure of the entire business;
- closure of the employee's workplace; and
- a diminishing need for employees to carry out work of a particular kind.

For the purposes of the definition, **cease** and **diminish** mean either a temporary or permanent cessation or diminution respectively, and it is a question of fact for the tribunal whether a temporary closure amounts to a cessation. For example, a 13-week closure of the business for repairs was held to be a temporary cessation for redundancy purposes (*Gemmell v Darngavil Brickworks Ltd* [1967] ITR 20, ET), whilst a 4-week closure for refurbishment was not (*Whitbread plc t/a Whitbread Berni Inns v Flattery*, EAT case 287/94).

In cases of temporary cessation, employees may be laid off or put on short-time working (¶7850).

If the employer transfers the business (or the part in which the employee is working) to a new owner, the **business transfer regulations** may apply automatically to continue the employee's employment with the new owner (¶7910). Specific considerations apply to dismissals in transfer situations (¶8030). 8746

Closure of business

The closure of the business may be **permanent or temporary**. A tribunal will not question the justification for the closure (*James W Cook & Co (Wivenhoe) Ltd v Tipper* [1990] IRLR 386, CA). 8747

A **change in the type of business** may amount to a closure of the old business if the new business is sufficiently different in nature and not merely a new way of operating the old business (*Whitbread plc t/a Whitbread Berni Inns v Flattery*, EAT case 287/94). 8748

Closure of employee's workplace

This redundancy situation will arise if the employer ceases to carry on business at his workplace, even if the **business is transferred** to another site. 8749

The tribunals currently apply a "geographical" or factual (as opposed to "contractual") test in order to determine **where the employee was employed** for redundancy purposes (*Bass Leisure Ltd v Thomas* [1994] IRLR 104, EAT; approved in *High Table Ltd v Horst* [1997] IRLR 513, CA). This means that they will take into account where the employee has actually worked under his contract. In most cases, there is one identifiable place of work or, in the case of "travelling jobs" (such as a travelling salesperson), one identifiable area. A temporary change in location is ignored. 8750

Mobility clause The mere existence of a contractual **right to transfer the employee** (a mobility clause) will not, therefore, deprive the employee of a redundancy payment. However, if the employer seeks to exercise that right and the employee refuses, a dismissal may be by reason of misconduct (rather than redundancy), in which case the employee will not be entitled to a redundancy payment. 8751

If there is **no such right**, the employee may be entitled to resign and claim constructive dismissal (¶8230) (and a redundancy payment) if the employer requires him to transfer. However, if the transfer to another workplace amounts to an offer of **suitable alternative employment**, the employee will not be entitled to a redundancy payment if he unreasonably refuses (¶8865).

Diminishing need for employees

This redundancy situation may arise in the following circumstances: 8752
- where work of a particular kind has diminished (i.e. there is **less work**) resulting in a diminished need for employees to carry it out; and

– where work has not diminished, but **fewer employees are needed** to do it, either because they have been replaced (e.g. by outside contractors or new technology) (i.e. the employees are no longer needed for the work), or because of a reorganisation resulting in a more efficient use of labour (i.e. fewer employees are needed for the work).

A redundancy situation may be triggered by the **employer's expectation** that there will be a diminishing need for employees (for example, in a merger situation where job losses commonly occur as a result of the streamlining of the merged companies, or where the employer plans to introduce new technology), even where temporary staff are brought in the interim period.

8753 The **test applied** to determine whether an employee is redundant in this situation is as follows (*Safeway Stores plc v Burrell* [1997] IRLR 200, EAT; approved in *Murray v Foyle Meats Ltd* [1999] IRLR 562, HL):

1. Was the employee dismissed (¶8765)?
2. If so, had the requirements of the employer's business for employees to carry out work of a particular kind ceased or diminished, or were they expected to cease or diminish?
3. If so, was the dismissal of the employee caused wholly or mainly by (i.e. "attributable to") the cessation or diminution (¶8767)?

8754 **Less work of a particular kind** If there is **less work** resulting in **fewer employees** being needed in the business, there will be a redundancy situation. There is no need for a diminishing need for employees to do the kind of work for which the dismissed employee was employed, and his **contractual terms** are only relevant when determining whether the redundancy situation was the operative reason for his dismissal (*Stankovic v City of Westminster*, EAT case 0696/00).

8755 There may also be a redundancy situation where the requirements of the business for a particular kind of employee to carry out work of a particular kind change (*Murphy v Epsom College* [1984] IRLR 271, CA), causing the employer to redistribute the **same amount of work** among the **same number of employees** (i.e. replacing one employee with another). The **skills and attributes** of the employees will be relevant (*British Broadcasting Corporation v Farnworth* [1998] ICR 1116, EAT). Whether a reorganisation amounts to redundancy is a question of fact to be decided by the tribunal, and the mere fact of reorganisation (in particular, that an employee is replaced by someone doing a slightly different job) is not conclusive of redundancy (*Shawkat v Nottingham City Hospital NHS Trust* [2001] IRLR 555, CA).

In contrast, there will be no redundancy situation where the work and number of employees required remains the same, but an employee of the same kind but of lower grade or status is required to do it, as **status or qualifications** will not make the work "of a particular kind" (unless they imply special skills, attributes or knowledge) (*Pillinger v Manchester Area Health Authority* [1979] IRLR 430, EAT). Further, the employee's **personal attributes** are not relevant unless they affect his ability to perform the work.

EXAMPLE Redundancy situation

1. In *Murphy v Epsom College*, M was one of two plumbers but he also did some engineering work. When he refused to continue with the engineering work, he was dismissed and replaced by an engineer who also did some plumbing. The Court agreed that the requirements for work of a particular kind had changed, in that the business first required a plumber who could do some engineering, and subsequently required an engineer who could do some plumbing. M was therefore redundant despite the fact that overall requirements for work and employees remained the same (i.e. there was no diminution in the work to be done).

2. In *British Broadcasting Corporation v Farnworth*, F was a radio producer graded "Mark 1". The BBC decided it needed a more senior producer and replaced her with a "Mark 2" producer. The EAT held that F was redundant because the BBC required an employee with a different specialism (in terms of experience and ability), even though the overall requirements of the business for employees had not diminished.

No redundancy situation

3. In *Shawkat v Nottingham City Hospital NHS Trust*, S was appointed as a thoracic surgeon. Following a merger, S was required to do cardiac work as well, thereby cutting down on his thoracic work. S refused, was dismissed and claimed redundancy. The Court held there was no redundancy because, despite the change in work, the employer's requirements for employees to carry out thoracic surgery had not ceased or diminished.

4. In *Pillinger v Manchester Area Health Authority*, P was a grade II research officer working on a particular project. When he was promoted to grade IIS, he was dismissed because it was felt that the project warranted only a grade II researcher. The EAT held that there was no redundancy as the work involved was exactly the same, regardless of the grade of researcher who undertook it.

If a redistribution of duties results in the **work done** being **fundamentally different**, such that the new job is "in a different league", there may be a redundancy situation (*D N Robinson v British Island Airways Ltd* [1977] IRLR 477, EAT). If the work changes such that it is of a **different particular kind**, there will be a redundancy situation (*R Denton v Neepsend Ltd* [1976] IRLR 164, ET). Work of a particular kind means work which is distinguished from other work of the same general kind by requiring special aptitudes, skills or knowledge (*J C Amos v Max-Arc Ltd* [1973] IRLR 285, NIRC). If the work changes but nevertheless is of the same kind as the old work, there will be no redundancy. 8756

EXAMPLE Work of a different particular kind

In *R Denton v Neepsend Ltd*, D was employed as a cold saw operator. The cold saw was replaced by an abrasive cutting machine, which D refused to operate. Although the purpose of the work was the same, the operational technique now needed was more sophisticated and onerous as the machine worked at higher speed. The working environment was also different as the machine gave out vapours, fumes and dust not present with the cold saw.

A **change in employment terms** (for example, the introduction of new working hours or arrangements) will not give rise to redundancy unless the kind of work (in terms of the tasks to be performed) changes or employee numbers are reduced (*N Johnson v Nottinghamshire Combined Police Authority* [1974] IRLR 20, CA; *Aylward v Glamorgan Holiday Home Limited* [2003] All ER(D) 249, EAT). 8757

EXAMPLE Night-shift to day-shift

1. In *Macfisheries Ltd v Findlay* [1985] ICR 160, EAT, a change from the night-shift to the day-shift gave rise to **redundancy** as the night-shift was "work of a particular kind", as identified from the nature of the work done on the two shifts, the impact of the shifts on the employee's personal life, and a contractual term protecting F's right not to transfer to the day-shift.

2. In *Maher v Photo Trade Processing Ltd*, EAT case 451/83, there was **no redundancy** situation following a change from the night-shift to the day-shift as the work on each shift was substantially the same, and was merely carried out at different hours.

Part-time to full-time

3. In *Ellis v GA Property Services Ltd*, ET case 13453/89, E, a part-time audio typist, was replaced by a full-time secretary who had other duties in addition to audio typing. The tribunal held that the work was of a different kind and gave rise to **redundancy**.

4. In *Barnes v Gilmartin Associates*, EAT case 825/99, B, a part-time secretary, was replaced by a full-time secretary. There was **no redundancy** as the requirement for employees to carry out secretarial work had not diminished.

Fewer employees needed There will be a redundancy situation where fewer employees are needed as a result of **technological change**, for example the introduction of new machinery or computers (*Scarth v Economic Forestry Ltd* [1973] ICR 322, NIRC). There will, however, be no redundancy situation where the new technology is simply a **new way of performing the same job** (i.e. the work remains of the same particular kind, albeit that the method of doing that work has changed) with no resulting decrease in the need for employees (*Cresswell v Board of Inland Revenue* [1984] IRLR 190, ChD). 8758

A redundancy situation may also arise where the employer replaces employees with **independent contractors**, because he will require fewer "employees" to do the work (although the number of "workers" may be the same as before) (*Baxter v Limb Group of Companies* [1994] IRLR 572, CA). However, if the business need for employees does not diminish and contractors are used as a fallback measure, there will be no redundancy situation (*Bromby & Hoare Ltd v Evans* [1972] ICR 113, NIRC). 8759

MEMO POINTS If the employer contracts out the operation of a service, the business transfer regulations may apply (¶7925).

8760 A redundancy situation may arise where there has been a **reorganisation** (for example, because of over-staffing) resulting in a reallocation of duties even though the amount of available work is the same or even greater (*Carry All Motors Ltd v Pennington* [1980] IRLR 455, EAT). The focus of this situation is on the requirements of the business for employees to carry out the work. However, not every reorganisation dismissal will be a dismissal for redundancy, and the reason for the dismissal must be examined in each case (*Frame It v Brown*, EAT case 177/93).

8761 If the employee is dismissed simply because the employer cannot afford to keep him on, the dismissal will not be for redundancy unless the employer has decided to reorganise in order to reduce staff numbers. If the employee is **not cost-effective** (for example, because he works too slowly) the dismissal may be by reason of capability (¶8451).

8762 **Flexibility clause** If an employee appears to be redundant, the employer may seek to avoid a redundancy situation by **redeploying** him to other duties within the scope of his contract (under a "flexibility clause" (¶1618)). The courts used to accept this "contract" test when deciding whether an employee was redundant, but the correct test to be applied is currently as set out above. The employee's contractual terms will now only be relevant to the question of whether the dismissal is wholly or mainly attributable to the redundancy situation (¶8767).

2. Dismissal

8765 To satisfy the definition of redundancy, an employee must prove that he has been dismissed. The concept of dismissal includes termination by the employer (with or without notice) and is further extended in certain circumstances, whilst certain forms of termination will not amount to a dismissal. These issues are discussed in detail at ¶8116.

3. Reason for dismissal

a. "Causation" issues

General principles

8767 There will only be a redundancy dismissal if the dismissal is **attributable wholly or mainly** to redundancy (s 139(1) ERA 1996). If there appears to be **more than one reason** for the dismissal, the tribunal will decide on the balance of probabilities which was the real, or main, reason for the dismissal.

Although tribunals will not concern themselves with the **economic or commercial reason** for the redundancy itself (*James W Cook & Co (Wivenhoe) Ltd v Tipper* [1990] IRLR 386, CA), they will review evidence to determine the **real reason** for dismissal (*Maund v Penwith District Council* [1982] IRLR 399, EAT; *West Kent College v Richardson* [1999] ICR 511, EAT). The test is an objective one, namely (*Baxter v Limb Group of Companies* [1994] IRLR 572, CA):
– was there a redundancy situation at the time of the dismissal?
– if so, was that the reason for the dismissal?

In claims for a redundancy payment (but not in unfair dismissal cases) there is a **presumption** that a dismissal was for redundancy (s 163(2) ERA 1996), so to avoid payment the employer must prove that there was no redundancy situation, or that the redundancy situation was not the sole or main reason for the dismissal.

8768 The **timing** of the dismissal may be an important factor. If the dismissal occurs at the same time as the closure of the business or workplace, the presumption of redundancy will be strengthened (*R A Marshall v Harland & Wolff Ltd* [1972] IRLR 90, NIRC).

The employee's **contractual terms** may also be relevant. If the employer exercises a flexibility clause (i.e. a contractual right to transfer the employee to other work), the dismissal may be for misconduct rather than redundancy if the employee refuses to obey. If the dismissal is attributable to the redundancy situation, it will be irrelevant that the employer could have transferred the employee to other work. It may, however, be more difficult to identify a redundancy situation in the case of an employee who could have been moved to other work, or who was not carrying out the work in respect of which there was a diminished requirement. 8769

Once a redundancy situation has arisen, the employer will select employees for redundancy by applying **selection criteria**. These criteria (for example, experience, attendance, disciplinary record) will normally be subsidiary reasons for dismissal, but in rare cases the tribunal may conclude that the criterion itself (for example, incapability) was the real reason for dismissal (*Timex Corporation v Thomson* [1981] IRLR 522, EAT). 8770

It is possible for the **reason** for dismissal **to change**. For example, an employee who has been given notice of dismissal for redundancy may actually be dismissed for misconduct if, during the notice period, he commits a serious disciplinary breach. 8771

Once an employer has decided to dismiss an employee for redundancy, he is prevented from dismissing the employee for some other reason in order to avoid a contractual obligation to make a contractual redundancy payment to the employee, unless the dismissal is for good cause. A summary dismissal for gross misconduct would, for example, constitute good cause (*Jenvey v Australian Broadcasting Corporation* [2002] IRLR 520, QBD) (¶8820). 8772

Specific cases

Causation issues in relation to specific cases where there may be some doubt are discussed below. 8775

Voluntary redundancy If there is a genuine redundancy situation, an employee who agrees to, or volunteers for, redundancy will still be considered to have been dismissed for redundancy (as will an employee who agrees to **early retirement** following a notice of redundancy which has not been withdrawn – see ¶8106). 8776

Fixed-term contracts An employee whose fixed-term contract expires and is not renewed because of a redundancy situation is considered to be dismissed by reason of redundancy. This may occur in the case of lecturers who are employed for single academic terms on a series of fixed-term contracts. The employee may be dismissed for redundancy when each contract expires (*(1) Pfaffinger v City of Liverpool Community College; (2) Muller v Amersham & Wycombe College* [1996] IRLR 508, EAT). They will only be entitled to a redundancy payment if they have sufficient continuity of service (¶8990). 8778

If, however, an employee has been working under a **temporary fixed-term contract** in order to cover for an absent employee, the non-renewal of the contract on the latter's return will not be by reason of redundancy.

Non-renewal of certain fixed-term contracts which cannot be renewed, such as **contracts of apprenticeship or training**, will not give rise to a redundancy dismissal (*North East Coast Ship Repairers Ltd v Secretary of State for Employment* [1978] IRLR 149, EAT).

Misconduct If an employee is dismissed for misconduct at a time when a redundancy situation exists, the misconduct rather than the redundancy may be considered to be the main reason for the dismissal, in which case he will not have been dismissed for redundancy. An employee dismissed for misconduct may lose his entitlement to a redundancy payment (¶9001). 8780

Industrial action Closure of the business and/or job losses often provokes industrial action. In such cases, it may be difficult to identify whether employees who take part in the action are dismissed for doing so, or for redundancy, and the tribunal will have to decide the matter on the evidence of each case (*K R Sanders v Ernest A Neale Ltd* [1974] IRLR 236, NIRC). If the industrial action itself forced the employer to cut back his workforce or close down the 8782 business, the employees will, depending on the evidence, still be dismissed by reason of redundancy (*K R Sanders v Ernest A Neale Ltd*, above). If there may be more than one reason for the dismissal, the tribunal must decide on the facts of the case which was the main reason (*Baxter v Limb Group of Companies* [1994] IRLR 572, CA).

EXAMPLE In *Baxter v Limb Group of Companies*, B refused to give up an overtime ban in which he was participating in connection with a dispute over bonuses, and was dismissed. He was subsequently replaced by an independent contractor. The Court reversed the tribunal's ruling that the decision to contract out work meant that there was a redundancy situation when B was dismissed, and found that industrial action was the real reason for the dismissal.

8784 **Bumping** An employee may be dismissed for redundancy where he is **replaced** by another employee who is surplus to requirements within the employer's business, even though there is **no diminution** in the **particular kind of work** carried out by the dismissed employee (known as "bumping" or "transferred redundancy") (*W Gimber & Sons Ltd v Spurrett* [1967] 2 ITR 308, DivCt; applied in *Elliott Turbomachinery Ltd v Bates* [1981] ICR 218, EAT).

EXAMPLE In *W Gimber & Sons Ltd v Spurrett*, S, a warehouse manager, was dismissed and replaced by a sales representative whose job had become redundant. The Court held that the dismissal of S was by reason of redundancy.

Indeed, the EAT has held that it may be unfair for an employer, when proposing to dismiss an employee on the grounds of redundancy, not to give consideration to alternative, including subordinate, positions for that employee, even where this may entail bumping another employee. Whether or not a **failure to consider bumping** another employee amounts to unfairness depends on the particular circumstances of each case, including factors such as (*Lionel Leventhal Ltd v North*, EAT case 0265/04):
- whether or not there is a vacancy;
- how different the two positions are;
- the difference in pay between the two positions;
- the relative length of service of the two employees;
- the qualifications of the employee in danger of redundancy; and
- any other factors which may be relevant to the particular case.

MEMO POINTS The EAT in *Lionel Leventhal v North* did not consider the decision in *Byrne v Arvin Meritor LVS (UK) Ltd*, EAT case 239/02, which held that there is **no duty** on an employer **to consider** bumping one employee in order to avoid making another employee redundant.

8785 A bumping redundancy may occur where an employee is displaced because of a redundancy situation elsewhere within his employer's group of **associated companies** (¶8741). However, bumping can only occur within the **same business** (*Babar Indian Restaurant v Rawat* [1985] IRLR 57, EAT). The test to be applied is whether the two businesses could be viewed as a "single enterprise".

EXAMPLE In *Babar Indian Restaurant v Rawat*, R was employed at a restaurant operated by two partners who also operated a frozen food concern, which they closed down. R was sacked to make way for employees from the frozen food concern. The EAT held that he was not redundant because the businesses were separate businesses, and there was no redundancy situation at the restaurant.

b. Unfair dismissal

8790 Redundancy is one of the five statutory **fair reasons** for dismissal (¶8422). Note that where the employee claims that his dismissal was not, in fact, by reason of redundancy, there is no statutory presumption of redundancy. However, the employer may dismiss for redundancy and still be **liable** for unfair dismissal if:
- the dismissal, or selection for dismissal is for an **inadmissible reason** which makes the dismissal **automatically unfair** (¶8390); or
- the employer has **not acted reasonably** in treating redundancy as a sufficient reason for dismissal (for example, because the employer failed to follow a fair procedure – ¶8800).

II. Managing redundancy

If the employer faces a redundancy situation, he must identify the employees at risk of redundancy (i.e. the appropriate selection pool – see ¶8831 below) and then address a number of **issues**, which are summarised in the following table: 8800

Number of employees in redundancy pool	Fair selection (¶8830)	Individual consultation (¶8910)	Alternatives to dismissal (¶8850)	Collective consultation (¶8915)	Notice of dismissal (¶8802)	Time off (¶8885)
One	n/a	x	x	n/a	x	x
Between 2 and 19	x	x	x	n/a	x	x
20 or more	x	x	x	x	x	x

If he is proposing to dismiss 20 or more employees within 90 days, the employer may have to put in place arrangements for **collective consultation** (including the election of representatives). Where 100 or more employees are to be dismissed, consultation must begin at least 90 days before the expiry of the first notice of dismissal, so the employer should make the necessary arrangements as early as possible. The detailed requirements of collective consultation are discussed at ¶8915. 8801

Individual consultation will be relevant in all cases and should also begin as early as possible. As part of this process, the employer should consider alternatives to dismissal, including any suitable alternative employment. These issues are discussed at ¶8910 and ¶8850.

To avoid liability for breach of contract, the employer must give **notice of dismissal** to terminate the employment of an employee who has been selected for redundancy. 8802

Certain employees under notice of dismissal for redundancy have a **right to time off** during working hours to look for new employment or to make arrangements for training for future employment (¶8885). 8803

Although redundancy is a fair reason for dismissal (see above), to avoid **liability for unfair dismissal** the employer must also **act reasonably** in treating redundancy as a sufficient reason for dismissal, so the careful management of a redundancy situation will be crucial. The general obligation on an employer to act reasonably when dismissing for a fair reason is discussed at ¶8435. In a redundancy context, in order to show that he has acted reasonably, the employer should (*Williams v Compair Maxam Ltd* [1982] IRLR 83, EAT; *Polkey v A E Dayton Services Ltd* [1987] IRLR 503, HL): 8804
- adopt and apply an objective and fair selection procedure;
- warn and consult the relevant employees;
- consult any recognised trade union; and
- consider any alternatives to dismissal.

Moreover, since the statutory dismissal and disciplinary procedure (¶6560) ordinarily applies to redundancy dismissals, the employer will also have to follow the statutory minimum requirements of the applicable procedure to minimise his liability for unfair dismissal. See Chapter 19 for further details.

If the employee **appeals against his dismissal**, an appeal hearing that amounts to a complete rehearing (as opposed to a mere review of the original decision to dismiss) can cure any **defects** (for example, in the consultation process), making a potentially unfair dismissal fair (*Lloyd v Taylor Woodrow Construction* [1999] IRLR 782, EAT).

If the redundancy is unfair, the **employee's remedies** may include, in addition to a statutory redundancy payment, compensation for unfair dismissal (¶8560). The redundancy payment will extinguish the entitlement to the basic award, but a compensatory award may be made.

A. Redundancy policies

8810 If a redundancy situation arises, the employer may deal with it according to the circumstances of the particular case on each occasion, or he may have a **formal redundancy policy** setting out the general approach to be adopted. This policy may be contractual or may serve as mere guidelines, and could be included in the staff handbook. In some cases, the procedure is agreed with union or employee representatives, resulting in a **formal redundancy agreement**. A redundancy selection procedure contained in a **collective agreement** is unlikely to be contractual, as it is not apt for incorporation given its lack of day-to-day significance in the employer-employee relationship (*LTI Ltd v Radford*, EAT case 16/00). If an employer wishes to establish a formal policy, it is good practice to involve his employees and/or their representatives. Further, adoption and implementation of a reasonable procedure may help the employer avoid liability for unfair dismissal.

8811 The **contents** of a formal procedure will vary according to the size and nature of the employer's organisation, but will normally include:
– a commitment to maintaining job security, wherever practicable;
– details of consultation arrangements with trade union or employee representatives (¶8915);
– measures for minimising or avoiding compulsory redundancies;
– guidance on selection criteria (¶8830); and
– details of
· severance terms;
· relocation expenses;
· appeals/hardship procedures; and
· training and assistance in finding other work.

8812 If the employer wishes to **depart from an agreed procedure**, he should seek the agreement of the trade union or employee representatives, as appropriate. It is useful for the procedure to specify the circumstances in which departures may be necessary. The procedure itself could allow for a degree of **flexibility** so that it can be applied to different redundancy situations and take account of changing economic circumstances. If the procedure is contractual, a failure to follow it will entitle the employee to a remedy for breach of contract (¶1710). In any case, failure to follow agreed procedures may result in industrial action, and may render a dismissal unfair.

8813 Any procedure should be reviewed periodically to ensure that it operates fairly.

B. Contractual terms

8820 In a redundancy situation, in order to avoid liability for breach of contract, the employer must terminate the employment in accordance with the terms of the employee's contract, including any contractual redundancy procedure (see above).

8821 **Notice** The employer must give the employee the **specified period** of notice of termination (or payment in lieu, if applicable). The contractual notice period is subject to statutory minimum requirements (¶8131).

8823 **Redundancy payments** The employer may be obliged by an **express or implied term** to enhance the employee's statutory entitlement. An express right may be set out in the contract of employment or an ancillary document, such as a redundancy policy document or a collective agreement, whilst an implied term may arise by virtue of custom and practice

(¶1180). It should be made clear **whether** the contractual payment is **in addition to or inclusive of** the employee's **statutory redundancy entitlement**.

A contractual redundancy payment may be **based on** a wider variety of factors than the statutory scheme, and different employers may attach different weight to different factors (taking care not to unlawfully discriminate) (*Barry v Midland Bank plc* [1999] IRLR 581, HL).

If an employee can establish a contractual right to an enhanced redundancy payment, the employer will not be able to deny the employee this entitlement by **dismissing** the employee for **another reason without good cause**. A summary dismissal for gross misconduct, for example, would constitute good cause (*Jenvey v Australian Broadcasting Corporation* [2002] IRLR 520, QBD).

MEMO POINTS An employee might be able to argue that a redundancy policy offering enhanced severance terms has become an implied contractual term of his contract by virtue of custom and practice. If an employer wishes to avoid this, he should ensure that he makes clear that the enhanced terms are discretionary and for the purposes of the current redundancy exercise only. If further exercises are envisaged for the future, the employer should consider varying the terms and structure of the enhanced packaged on offer, in order to avoid elevating the terms into implied contractual provisions by virtue of custom and practice.

Redundancy procedure The employment contract (or an ancillary document) may set out an agreed redundancy procedure (¶8810). 8825

C. Selection

The employer may have an **agreed selection procedure**, in which case this should be followed (unless the employer considers that, in all the circumstances, a departure from it can be justified) (¶8810). 8830

Selection pool Unless all employees are to be dismissed, employers must take care to ensure that the pool of employees from which employees may be selected for redundancy is fairly defined, as the application of otherwise fair selection criteria (see below) to the wrong group will probably amount to unfair dismissal. An agreed or customary procedure may specify a particular selection pool, otherwise the employer must consider the matter and act from genuine motives. In the light of the broad test of redundancy (¶8740), employers may be justified in using a wide pool for selection. When considering whether the employer acted reasonably, a tribunal may consider the following factors: 8831

- the extent to which other groups of employees are doing the same or similar work;
- the extent to which employees' jobs are interchangeable;
- the employees' contractual job descriptions;
- any agreement with unions as to the selection pool; and
- any background facts which may show that a pool was defined solely for the purposes of weeding out a particular employee.

Selection criteria An agreed procedure may specify the selection criteria to be applied to the pool. If there is no agreed procedure, the employer must adopt fair and objective selection criteria that are most suitable for his business. He must ensure that the balance of skills and experience within the remaining workforce is appropriate to his future operating requirements. The employer should be able to substantiate the criteria adopted (for example, by verifying them by reference to data such as attendance records). Where there is a recognised union, it should be consulted. 8833

Tribunals will rarely set aside an employer's selection criteria unless the criteria fall outside the band of responses open to a reasonable employer (*Drake International Systems Ltd v O'Hare*, EAT case 0384/03). In *Drake International Systems Ltd v O'Hare*, the tribunal refused to interfere with the employer's decision not to exclude industrial injuries from the absence records which were taken into consideration in applying the redundancy selection criteria.

8834 An acceptable method of selection is **voluntary redundancy**, whereby employees volunteer to be considered for redundancy dismissal. This may be an expensive method as longer serving employees tend to apply, thus attracting higher statutory redundancy payments. Further, it is common for employers to offer enhanced payments as an incentive to attract staff to volunteer. A further disadvantage is that voluntary redundancy may create an imbalance in the skills and experience of the remaining workforce. To avoid this, the employer could retain the right to confine applications to selected categories of employees, and/or to decide whether a particular employee is actually dismissed. On the positive side, voluntary redundancy is an effective way of reducing staff numbers where necessary without damaging staff morale.

8835 **Early retirement** may be considered as an alternative to redundancies. This usually involves the payment of a pension, and thus has its own financial implications. Where specialised staff are involved, early retirement may also result in deficiencies in skills and experience in the remaining workforce.

8836 Where the situation is not resolved by voluntary redundancy or early retirement, **compulsory selection criteria** must be considered. Such criteria are likely to include:

Criterion	Comment
Attendance record	Reasons for poor attendance may be a relevant factor, and period of assessment should be reasonable, not arbitrary. Extent of absences will also be relevant. To avoid disability discrimination, absences due to disability must not be taken into account. Absence due to pregnancy/maternity/paternity/adoption/parental leave should also be ignored. Employer should verify employee's state of health and offer suitable alternative work, where available
Age	Employees above normal retirement age cannot claim unfair dismissal (unless automatically unfair – see above), and can therefore be fairly retired (but note that it is expected that age discrimination will become unlawful from 1 October 2006 (¶5254))
Length of service	Last In First Out may be fair (even where used as sole criterion – each case depends on its own facts (*Blatchfords Solicitors v Berger*, EAT case 207/00)), but may lead to imbalance in skills of workforce. Part-time service should be taken into account as for full-time. Possible liability for indirect sex discrimination may arise if women are found to change jobs more frequently than men
Disciplinary record	Records must be compared over reasonable period of time to ensure that they are representative
Skills/qualifications	Assists retention of workforce balanced in terms of skills
Performance/capability	Fair criteria, provided that assessment of performance itself was objective, and performance criteria clearly defined from outset

It will not be fair to select an employee for redundancy because of his **attitude to his work** as this criterion is too subjective.

8837 In order to avoid unfair dismissal liability, the selection criteria adopted must also be fairly **applied** (*Boulton & Paul Ltd v Arnold* [1994] IRLR 532, EAT).

EXAMPLE In *Boulton & Paul Ltd v Arnold*, the selection criteria were performance, length of service, discipline and attendance. The employers took into account every day of absence, which in A's case included an authorised doctor's appointment lasting half an hour. She had no unapproved absence or lateness on her record. She was made redundant on the basis of her low attendance rating, which was held to be unfair.

8838 The employer should also take care to ensure that the selection criteria adopted are consistently applied and **do not discriminate** on the grounds of sex, racial group, disability, religion or belief, or sexual orientation, or he may face both an unfair dismissal and a discrimination claim (s 6(2) SDA 1975; s 4(1) RRA 1976; s 4 DDA 1995; reg 6 SI 2003/1660; reg 6 SI 2003/1661). Selection on the basis of working part-time or on a fixed-term contract may be discriminatory, and need to be objectively justified in order to be lawful (*Whiffen v Milham Ford Girls' School* [2001] IRLR 468, CA; see also *Hendrickson Europe Ltd v Pipe*, EAT case 0272/02).

The employer should also exercise caution before applying selection criteria such as Last In First Out (LIFO), or those based on length of employment or hours of work, since these could have a greater detrimental effect on women (*Brook v London Borough of Haringey* [1992] IRLR 478, EAT). It will be up to employers to establish a defence of justification in these cases. It should be noted that **fixed-term** employees who have been discriminated against in their selection for redundancy do not have to argue that their selection constitutes indirect sex discrimination and have a remedy under the Fixed-term Employees (Prevention of Less Favourable Treatment) Regulations SI 2002/2034 (¶1951).

Employees in the pool for selection are commonly **assessed** by being marked against selec- **8839**
tion criteria adopted by the employer. In some cases the different criteria may be given a particular weighting. The fact that the manager selecting employees for redundancy relied on assessments of employees made by others who had direct knowledge of their work does not render the dismissal unfair (*Eaton Ltd v King* [1995] IRLR 75, EAT).

Employees are not entitled to **disclosure of assessment forms** of all staff considered for **8840**
redundancy (note that an employee has the right to make a subject access request to his employer for information kept about him although the employer has the right to withhold information to protect the identity of others: ¶5980). The employer need only show that the method of selection was fair in general terms, and that it was reasonably applied to the employee concerned (*Buchanan v Tilcon Ltd* [1983] IRLR 417, CS; approved in *British Aerospace plc v Green* [1995] IRLR 433, CA). However, the employer may be found to have failed in his duty to consult with the employee (¶8900) if he fails to disclose details of the **employee's own assessment**, and allow him the opportunity to contest his selection (*John Brown Engineering Ltd v Brown* [1997] IRLR 90, EAT; see also *Alstrom Traction Ltd v Birkenhead*, EAT 1131/00).

The employer should consider establishing an **appeals procedure** to deal with complaints **8842**
that an employee has been unfairly selected (¶8810).

D. Alternative employment

The employer should offer any available suitable alternative employment to redundant **8850**
employees. There are two **implications**, the first relates to unfair dismissal, and the second to entitlement to a redundancy payment. Further, there is a specific obligation to offer alternative employment to employees who become redundant while on ordinary or additional **maternity or adoption leave** (¶4564).

The employer will be obliged to give the employee a statement of change of his **written** **8851**
particulars (¶1400) if he accepts and starts a new job.

Offers of suitable alternative employment from a deceased employer's **personal representa-** **8852**
tives are discussed below (¶9014).

Unfair dismissal As part of a fair redundancy procedure, employers should take reason- **8853**
able steps to find suitable alternative employment **within the company** and, where appropriate, within any **associated employer** (¶8682) (s 146(1) ERA 1996) (this will not be required where the associated employer carries out work completely independent of and distinct from the employing company). The suitability of alternative employment is relevant to a consideration of unfair dismissal. In particular, if the **terms** of the alternative employment **are unreasonable**, the dismissal of an employee who refuses the offer is likely to be unfair. The employer should not, however, discount alternative employment which involves a **decrease in salary or status**, but should raise any such possibilities as part of the consultation process, although it would normally be appropriate for a senior employee who is prepared

to accept an inferior position to make this clear to the employer at an early stage (*Barratt Construction Ltd v Dalrymple* [1984] IRLR 385, EAT).

Where there is more than one possibility of suitable alternative employment available, the employer should normally inform the employee of the **financial prospects** of those positions (*Fisher v Hoopoe Finance Limited*, EAT case 0043/05).

MEMO POINTS The EAT also noted in this case that if an employee fails to indicate an interest in a particular position and/or fails to request further information (including financial information), the tribunal can take this into account by reducing the basic and compensatory awards on the grounds of **contributory fault** (¶¶8578, 8635).

8854 The reasonableness of the dismissal depends on the circumstances of which the employer was aware at the time of the dismissal. If an alternative job comes up **after the dismissal**, a failure to offer it to the employee will not make the dismissal unfair (unless the employer already knew that work would become available within a short time) (*Octavius Atkinson & Sons Ltd v Morris* [1989] IRLR 158, CA). Similarly, if, after the dismissal, the employer discovers that the employee would not have accepted any alternative employment, this will not rule out a finding of unfair dismissal (although it may affect compensation).

8856 **Entitlement to a statutory redundancy payment** If a redundant employee accepts an offer of suitable alternative employment (subject to his right to a 4-week statutory trial period) or if he unreasonably refuses such an offer, he may lose his entitlement to a statutory redundancy payment.

Offer

8858 If the situation has improved since the employer served notice of dismissal, he may be able to offer to re-employ the employee in his old job (i.e. to **renew** his contract). More commonly, the employer (or an associated employer) makes an offer of alternative employment on different terms (i.e. to **re-engage** him). Where terms of employment are different, the employee has a right to a statutory trial period (see below).

8859 There are no statutory requirements as to the form of the offer of re-engagement (it can be **oral or in writing**) (ss 138(1), 141(1) ERA 1996), although it must be sufficiently clear for the employee to understand what is being offered. A written offer is obviously better evidence that an offer has been made. The employer can offer the employee **several different jobs** at once as long as what is offered is specific enough to be capable of acceptance (*Curling v Securicor Ltd* [1992] IRLR 549, EAT).

The offer does not need to be detailed (for example, it does not need to contain all the statutory written particulars (*McKindley v William Hill (Scotland) Ltd* [1985] IRLR 492, EAT)), but it is advisable that it specifies any **difference in terms** between the new and old employment (*Havenhand v Thomas Black Ltd* [1968] 2 All ER 1037, DivCt). It is also advisable that the offer states the **date** on which the new employment is to begin (unless it is obvious that it is to continue straight on from the old employment). If the employer cannot give a definite date, the employee may be justified in looking for work elsewhere, and his refusal of the employer's offer may, therefore, be reasonable.

8860 The offer may be **made collectively** (for example by placing it on a staff notice board), as long as it is brought to the employee's notice, is capable of being understood by him, and is in fact read by him (*McCreadie v Thomson and MacIntyre (Patternmakers) Limited* [1971] 2 All ER 1135, HL). If an employee is on sick leave and therefore does not read an offer posted on a staff notice board, no offer will have been made to him (*F Maxwell v Walter Howard Designs Ltd* [1975] IRLR 77, IT).

8861 An offer of renewal or re-engagement should be made even if the **employee indicates that he will refuse** any such offers, as the employer cannot rely on the employee's unreasonable refusal to justify not making a redundancy payment unless an offer is actually made (*Simpson v Dickinson* [1972] ICR 474, NIRC).

8862 If an offer of alternative employment is accepted **before notice of dismissal** is served, this will be an agreed variation to the existing employment contract and there will be no redundancy dismissal. It is also possible for an employee to agree to the variation subject to a trial period, which does not need to be the same as the statutory trial period (see below).

If the offer is made **after notice of dismissal** has been served, the statutory rules apply, in which case the offer should be communicated to the employee by the employer (or the associated employer) before the existing contract terminates (ss 138(1)(a), 141(1) ERA 1996). 8863

In either case, the **new employment must commence** immediately after the termination of the old employment or after an interval of not more than 4 weeks (ss 138(1)(b), 141(1) ERA 1996), in which case the employee is treated as not having been dismissed (for the purposes of redundancy payments but not for unfair dismissal purposes) and statutory continuity will be preserved (s 213(2) ERA 1996). The new employment will be treated as commencing immediately after the old where the latter ends on a Friday, Saturday or Sunday, and the new commences on or before the following Monday (s 146(2) ERA 1996). If the new employment does not commence immediately, the 4-week interval is calculated as if the old employment ended on that following Monday.

MEMO POINTS There is some uncertainty as to whether an **offer of renewal** needs to be made in order for the employee to lose his entitlement to a redundancy payment if the renewal takes place within 4 weeks of the ending of the old contract. However, if the employer wants to rely on an employee's unreasonable refusal of an offer of **suitable alternative employment** (or termination during the trial period) (see below), an offer must be made, so the safest course is to make an offer (whether of renewal or re-engagement) in every case.

Refusal

The employee will lose his right to a redundancy payment if he **unreasonably refuses** (either immediately or during a trial period) an offer to **renew** his contract or an offer of **suitable alternative employment** (s 141(2)-(4) ERA 1996). If the employer offers to renew (i.e. on the same terms), the only issue is whether the employee's refusal is reasonable. If he offers to re-engage, the employer must show that the job was suitable and, if so, that the employee's refusal was unreasonable. The employer should, therefore, seek an explanation for any refusal (*Jones v Aston Cabinet Co Ltd* [1973] ICR 292, NIRC). 8865

If the alternative employment is **not suitable**, or if the employee's refusal of renewal or suitable alternative employment is **reasonable**, he will still be entitled to a redundancy payment.

Suitability and reasonableness

The suitability of alternative employment is judged objectively, while the reasonableness of an employee's refusal of such employment is considered subjectively from his point of view at the time of the refusal (*Cambridge & District Co-operative Society Ltd v Ruse* [1993] IRLR 156, EAT). When considering these separate questions, there may be factors common to both (*Spencer and Griffin v Gloucestershire County Council* [1985] IRLR 393, CA). For example, the employee may refuse to accept a job of a lower standard than he considered reasonable. Whilst the alternative employment may be objectively suitable, it may be reasonable for the employee to refuse it on the ground of his personal perception of it. 8867

EXAMPLE In *Cambridge & District Co-operative Society Ltd v Ruse*, R was the manager of a butcher's shop. He was offered alternative employment as manager of a supermarket butchery department. The EAT held that although the job was suitable alternative employment, R's perceived loss of status made it reasonable from him to refuse it.

Suitability covers **factors** relating to the nature of the new employment as they affect the particular employee, such as job content, responsibility, status, terms and conditions (including pay and other benefits, location, working hours), and job prospects. If the job is suitable, a tribunal will go on to consider the question of **reasonableness**, which will involve a consideration of **factors** relating to the employee's personal circumstances, such as domestic arrangements (including childcare responsibilities), housing, schooling, medical grounds, and more general factors, such as the timing of the offer, whether the employee has found other employment, and the employer's financial stability. 8868

8869 If the employer makes a **collective offer** of alternative employment, suitability must be assessed in relation to each individual employee. If the employer states that his offer must be accepted by all or none, the offer will only be considered suitable if it is suitable for all of the employees concerned (*E & J Davis Transport Ltd v Chattaway* [1972] ICR 267, NIRC). Similarly, the reasonableness of refusal must be judged in relation to each employee (*John Fowler (Don Foundry) Ltd v H Parkin* [1975] IRLR 89, QBD).

Statutory trial period

8872 Where there is a **difference in the terms** of the new employment, the employee benefits from a mandatory trial period in order to decide whether the new employment is suitable for him (s 138(2)(a) ERA 1996). There is no right to a trial period where an employee is re-employed on the **same terms**.

The period **begins** when the employee starts work under the new contract (which must start not more than 4 (calendar) weeks after the old contract ends), and lasts for 4 (calendar) weeks (s 138(3) ERA 1996; *Benton v Sanderson Kayser Ltd* [1989] IRLR 19, CA).

The employer and employee can agree to **extend** the trial period in order to retrain the employee for the new job (s 138(3)(b)(ii) ERA 1996). The agreement must be (s 138(6) ERA 1996):
– made before the new job starts; and
– in writing and specify:
· the date on which the period of retraining will end; and
· the terms and conditions of employment that will apply after the period of retraining.

The employer should warn the employee that he will lose his redundancy entitlement if he **works beyond** the end of the trial period (without agreeing an extension), or the end of the agreed extended period.

8873 If the employee is **dismissed during the trial period** for a reason connected with or arising out of the new employment (such as the employee's incapability or unsuitability), the employee will be treated as having been dismissed for redundancy when the old job came to an end (s 138(2)(b)(ii), (4) ERA 1996), and will be entitled to a redundancy payment. If the employee is dismissed for a reason unconnected with the new employment (for example, for misconduct), he will lose his entitlement to a redundancy payment.

If the employee **leaves during the trial period**, he will be treated as having been dismissed for redundancy when the old job came to an end (s 138(2)(b)(i), (4) ERA 1996). He will be treated as having refused the offer of alternative employment and will therefore not be entitled to a redundancy payment if the new job was suitable and he acted unreasonably in leaving it (s 141(4) ERA 1996).

If the employee leaves or is dismissed within the trial period, he will be treated, for **qualifying service and redundancy payment calculation purposes** (¶8990), as having been dismissed when the old job came to an end. For the purposes of an application to the tribunal, however, the **time limit** runs from the date of termination of the trial period (¶8876).

8874 There can be **more than one trial period** if the employee is offered different alternative positions. If none of the alternatives works out and the employee is ultimately dismissed, he is deemed to have been dismissed for redundancy when the original contract ended.

Common law trial period

8876 Where the employer, faced with a redundancy situation, **imposes new terms and conditions** in fundamental breach of contract, the employee can resign and claim constructive dismissal, accept the new terms (resulting in an agreed variation), or continue working for a reasonable trial period in order to decide whether to accept the changes or to resign (*Air Canada v Lee* [1978] IRLR 392, EAT). This period may be longer than the statutory trial period, but should not be much longer or the employee may be deemed to have accepted the new terms.

However, if the **employer expressly terminates** the old employment and offers alternative employment under a new contract, the employee will be entitled to the statutory trial period only, as no question of constructive dismissal will arise.

E. Time off

Certain employees under notice of dismissal for redundancy (see ¶8120 for further details on notice of dismissal) have a **statutory right** to reasonable time off with pay during working hours to look for new employment or to make arrangements for training for future employment (s 52 ERA 1996). The entitlement to **paid time off** is limited to 40% of a week's pay for the whole notice period (s 53(5) ERA 1996). For detail on the rate of pay see ¶3930. The employee's **contract** may enhance the statutory right, for example by providing for further time off with pay. 8885

The **right applies to** employees (workers are excluded) who have been continuously employed for 2 years on the later of the following dates: 8886
– the date on which the notice is due to expire; and
– the date on which notice would have expired, had the statutory minimum notice been given.

The right to time off does not depend on **entitlement to a redundancy payment** (which may have been lost, for example due to an unreasonable refusal of suitable alternative employment (*Dutton v Hawker Siddeley Aviation Ltd* [1978] IRLR 390, EAT)).

Reasonable time off The employee is entitled to take time off **during working hours**, which is defined as any time when his contract requires him to be at work (s 52(3) ERA 1996). The **amount** of time off is whatever is reasonable in the circumstances, which will depend on the following factors: 8888
– the employee's length of service and attendance record;
– when the dismissal will take effect;
– how easy/difficult it will be for the employee to find another job;
– the timing of the request for time off and the proposed arrangements (i.e. how much time and when); and
– how the time off will affect the employer's work schedules.

It may, therefore, be reasonable for an employer to refuse time off in certain circumstances, such as where the employee refuses to provide details of any appointments or interviews for which he seeks time off (*Dutton v Hawker Siddeley Aviation Ltd*, above).

Remedies If the employer **unreasonably refuses time off** or **fails to pay** the amount due, the employee can apply to an employment tribunal for a remedy (¶3960). 8889

III. Consultation and notification requirements

Unfair dismissal A redundancy dismissal will normally be unfair where the **employee** has not been given prior warning or been consulted (*Polkey v A E Dayton Services Ltd* [1987] IRLR 503, HL). Warning and consultation do not need to be separate steps, rather warning (i.e. giving notice of the risk of redundancy) is an essential prerequisite of the consultation process (*Elkouil v Coney Island Ltd* [2002] IRLR 174, EAT). Only in exceptional circumstances, such as where the employer, at the time of the dismissal, may reasonably take the view that warnings or consultation would be utterly useless or futile, will such dismissals be fair. The test of fairness in such cases is whether an employer acting reasonably could have failed to consult in the given circumstances, and does not require the employer to make a deliberate decision not to consult the employee (*Duffy v Yeomans & Partners Ltd* [1994] IRLR 642, CA). 8900

To ensure a fair procedure, it is advisable also to consult with **any recognised union** as to the selection criteria and their application. In cases of **collective redundancies**, there is a statutory duty to consult with union or employee representatives (see below), and compli- 8901 ance with this duty is a further factor to be taken into account when assessing the reasonableness of a dismissal (*Williams v Compair Maxam Ltd* [1982] IRLR 83, EAT). However, compliance with collective consultation obligations does not make individual consultation unnecessary and the collective consultation obligation is independent of, and in addition to, the individual consultation obligation.

8902 It will be a question of fact and degree in each case whether the consultation that has taken place is so inadequate as to render a dismissal unfair (*Mugford v Midland Bank plc* [1997] IRLR 208, EAT). **Fair consultation** (both collective and individual) will require consultation when proposals are still being formulated, providing adequate information, giving adequate time for a response, and giving proper consideration to any points raised (*R v British Coal Corporation and Secretary of State for Trade and Industry ex parte Price* [1994] IRLR 72, DivCt; applied in *King v Eaton Ltd* [1996] IRLR 199, CS). Merely informing staff of potential redundancies will not constitute fair consultation (*Mofunanya v Richmond Fellowship*, EAT case 449/03). The extent and length of consultation necessary will depend on the facts of each individual case.

A. Individual consultation

8910 Consultation with individual employees selected for redundancy (including those redundant due to expiry and non-renewal of a fixed-term contract (*University of Glasgow v Donaldson and McNally*, EAT(S) case 951/94)) should **begin** as far in advance as possible (and before notice of dismissal is given).

The **employer should**:
- explain the reason for the redundancies;
- explain the selection process, seek the employee's views on the selection criteria and give him an opportunity to explain any factors which may have resulted in his selection for redundancy, such as domestic problems temporarily affecting his performance;
- explain any requirements during the notice period, including the right to time off to look for alternative work (¶8885), and any assistance (such as outplacement counselling) to be provided by him;
- explore with the employee ways of avoiding redundancy, such as retraining for other work, making it clear that he will look for suitable alternative employment within the organisation (¶8850); and
- ask for volunteers for redundancy.

B. Collective consultation

8915 If the redundancies arise in the context of a **business transfer**, separate TUPE consultation obligations may apply (¶8060).

MEMO POINTS Consultation requirements are also imposed by the EU Information and Consultation Directive, which requires employers to consult with employees before taking important business decisions, particularly where these affect employee rights. The Directive will be implemented in stages, depending on the size of the employer's organisation. The first stage, for employers with more than 150 employees, was implemented on 6 April 2005. See ¶7655 for further details.

Scope

8916 For the consultation obligations to arise, the dismissals must be on the grounds of redundancy, which is presumed to be the case (s 195(2) TULRCA 1992). The duty arises in the **redundancy situations** identified above and may also apply where the employer seeks to impose a **variation to employment terms** by dismissal and re-engagement (¶1677).

Where 20 or more redundancies are proposed at one establishment within 90 days, the employer must consult with "appropriate representatives" of the employees who may be affected by the proposed dismissals or by measures taken in connection with them ("**affected employees**") (s 188 TULRCA 1992, as amended). The employer is also required to notify the DTI (¶8970). If there is any dispute about who are the affected employees, it is for an employment tribunal to decide.

EXAMPLE The employer is proposing 30 redundancies from among the sales force team. The effect of the redundancies will be to increase the workload of the remaining members of the team and to transfer some of the team's clerical responsibilities to the clerical staff. The employer must consult with elected representatives of both the sales force team and the clerical workers whose working conditions may change as a result of the dismissals.

MEMO POINTS 1. The relevant legislation was amended by the Trade Union Reform and Employment Rights Act 1993 and the Collective Redundancies and Transfer of Undertakings (Protection of Employment) (Amendment) Regulations SI 1995/2587 and SI 1999/1925, implementing an EC Directive now consolidated in the EC Collective Redundancies Directive 1998/59.
2. The **definition** for consultation purposes is broader than that used for redundancy payment purposes, in that it applies to employees dismissed for a reason or reasons which is/are not related to the individual concerned (s 195(1) TULRCA 1992). If there are **mixed reasons** for dismissal, there will arguably be no redundancy dismissal for consultation purposes if one of the reasons relates to the individual.

Number of redundancies When calculating the number of employees an employer proposes to dismiss as redundant for the purposes of collective redundancy obligations, an employer must **include** any employees he is proposing to **redeploy**, if his proposals objectively amount to withdrawing an employee's existing contract or the proposed changes to the existing contract are so substantial so as to constitute a withdrawal of the entire contract (*Hardy v Tourism South East* [2005] IRLR 242, EAT). 8917

Employees who accept **voluntary redundancy** count as being dismissed for the purposes of the collective consultation provisions, and are entitled to protective awards in the event of a failure to consult (see below) (*Scotch Premier Meat Ltd v Burns* [2000] IRLR 639, EAT).

Where an employer has started consultation in relation to proposed redundancies, the number of those redundancies is ignored when considering his obligation to consult should **further redundancies** be proposed, unless bad faith can be identified (i.e. the employer intended from the outset to dismiss the combined group as redundant) (s 188(3) TULRCA 1992; *Transport and General Workers' Union v Nationwide Haulage Ltd* [1978] IRLR 143, IT). 8918

EXAMPLE An employer proposes 25 redundancies and starts consulting. He subsequently proposes 15 further redundancies. There is no duty to consult in relation to the additional redundancies as they are less than the threshold of 20 and the original 25 are not counted. If he had originally proposed 15 redundancies and subsequently (within 90 days) proposed a further 25, there would have been no obligation to consult initially, but there would have been an obligation to consult in respect of all the redundancies when the further 25 redundancies were proposed, as the threshold of 20 redundancies within 90 days would have been exceeded.

The consultation provisions **do not apply** to workers who are not employees (for example, independent contractors), nor to short-term employees (i.e. those employed for a fixed term of 3 months or less, or for a specific purpose not expected to last for more than 3 months, who have actually worked for less than 3 months) (s 282 TULRCA 1992). 8919

MEMO POINTS **Overseas employment** is not excluded from the duty to consult (although it is excluded from the duty to notify the DTI – ¶8970).

Collective agreements dealing with redundancy procedures or the provision of alternative employment which are covered by an exemption order issued by the DTI following application by all the parties to the agreement can **disapply** the statutory obligation to consult. 8920

Meaning of establishment The total number of redundancies proposed by the employer may be unimportant – the obligation to consult depends on the number of redundancies at one establishment. There is no statutory definition of establishment and so tribunals have 8921

taken a practical approach when deciding whether to add together the number of employees to be made redundant in a business which has **several sites**. The ECJ has held that "establishment" means the unit to which the redundant employees were assigned to carry out their duties, regardless of whether the power to effect redundancies lies with that unit (*Rockfon A/S v Specialarbejderforbundet i Danmark, acting for Nielsen* [1996] IRLR 168, ECJ), and it is a matter of judgment, depending on the circumstances of the particular case, as to whether a business operation constitutes an independent unit or merely forms part of a larger unit. **Relevant factors** may include (*Lord Advocate v Babcock and Wilcox Ltd* [1972] 1 All ER 1130, HL):
- the exclusive occupation of the premises;
- a degree of permanence;
- some organisation of employees working there;
- administrative functions; and
- the site being a contractual workplace.

EXAMPLE One establishment

1. In *Barratt Developments (Bradford) Ltd v UCATT* [1977] IRLR 403, EAT, the EAT held that 14 building sites linked to headquarters by telephone was one establishment.
2. In *Mills & Allen Ltd v Bulwich*, EAT case 154/99, the EAT held that a nationwide direct sales team was one establishment, as the team was capable of being a unit of the employer's organisation to which employees at different offices had been assigned.

Distinct establishments

3. In *National Union of Footwear, Leather & Allied Trades v K Shoemakers Ltd*, COIT 1300/65, unreported, it was held that five factories were distinct establishments as each had a degree of managerial independence, was geographically separate from the others, and was a permanent not a temporary site.

8922 The number of redundancies is calculated by reference to one employer only, and redundancies made in **associated companies** (¶8682) at the same establishment are treated separately.

8923 **Proposal to dismiss** The collective obligation applies to **actual and constructive dismissals**, and expiry of fixed-term contracts. There is no duty to consult where there is no dismissal, for example, where the redundancy situation arises as a result of a frustrating event, such as the death of an individual employer.

The obligation may arise in the case of **involuntary redundancies**, such as the making of a **winding-up order**, given that the underlying EC law now requires consultation where an establishment's activities are terminated as a result of a judicial decision (it was previously argued that the order, rather than the employer, caused the dismissal, such that there was no proposal to dismiss (*Re Hartlebury Printers Ltd (in liquidation) and others* [1992] IRLR 516, ChD; *GMB v Rankin and Harrison* [1992] IRLR 514, EAT)). Where a **liquidator, receiver or insolvency administrator** dismisses, he does so as the company's agent such that the duty to consult should apply (although the insolvency may give rise to a defence to claims of failure to consult – ¶8950). It could be argued that an employer in financial difficulties could anticipate his business collapsing and therefore "contemplates" redundancies, which may be sufficient to trigger the duty to consult (see below).

8924 The duty to consult is triggered when the employer "proposes" to dismiss and **arises** when the employer has decided the redundancies are necessary (and even only when he can identify the employees likely to be affected and is in a position to supply the required information) (*R v British Coal Corporation, ex parte Vardy* [1993] IRLR 104, QBD; *Griffin v South West Water Services Ltd* [1995] IRLR 15, ChD). A proposal to dismiss may arise where an employer has decided on a plan of action which has two alternative scenarios, only one of which necessarily includes redundancies (even if the other is still being considered) (*Scotch Premier Meat Ltd v Burns*). The word "propose" in this context connotes an intention on the part of the employer (*Scotch Premier Meat Ltd v Burns*). It does not matter that the proposal is yet to be approved by the company's shareholders (*Dewhirst Group v GMB Trade Union*, EAT case 0486/03) or that the proposal is made by a Council officer but not yet ratified by a formal political Council decision (*Leicestershire County Council v Unison* [2005] EAT case, 0066/05). The EAT's construction of "proposing to dismiss" in this case followed the judgment in *Junk v Wolfgang Kuhnel* [2005] IRLR 310, ECJ (which requires consultation to begin before notice of dismissal for redundancy is given (see ¶8939 below)) and therefore indicated that this phrase could be read as "proposing to give notice of dismissal". A proposal to dismissal may also arise where there is a proposal to redeploy employees, particularly when the proposal amounts to, or constitutes, a withdrawal of an employee's contract (¶8917; *Hardy v Tourism South East*). The EAT referred in this case to *GMB v Man Truck and Bus UK Ltd* [2000] IRLR 636, where it was held that an employer who seeks to harmonise his employees' terms and conditions by giving them notice to terminate and re-engage them on new terms is also proposing to dismiss them as redundant.

For consultation to be seen to be meaningful, it is essential for an employer to consult before making any definite redundancy plans and it is not open to an employer to argue that consultation would be futile or utterly useless as a defence for failing to do so (*Middlesbrough Borough Council v TGWU* [2002] IRLR 332, EAT). In any case, the employer must comply with the requirement to consult "in good time" (¶8939).

MEMO POINTS According to the EC Directive, the duty to consult is triggered when the employer is "**contemplating**" redundancies, which is believed to require consultation at an earlier stage, when the employer's ideas are still forming. It appears that this broader obligation is not compatible with the UK obligation and is not imposed by the UK tribunals (*MSF v Refuge Assurance Plc* [2002] IRLR 324, EAT).

Consultation requirements

The employer must consult the affected employees' **appropriate representatives**. These are either (ss 188(1B), 196(1) TULRCA 1992): 8925

- **representatives of the union** if the employees are of a description in respect of which an independent trade union (¶7122) is recognised for collective bargaining purposes (¶7200); or
- in any other case, employee representatives, employed by the employer at the time of their election or appointment, and who may be either:

· **existing representatives** elected or appointed by the affected employees for purposes other than redundancy consultation but who, having regard to those other purposes and the method of election/appointment, have authority from those employees to receive information and to be consulted about the proposed dismissals on their behalf (for example, members of an existing works council, but not, in the case of redundancies amongst sales staff for example, a committee specifically established to consider the operation of a staff canteen (DTI guidance: Redundancy Consultation and Notification)); or

· employee representatives who have been **specially elected** for the purposes of redundancy consultation (see below).

If there are **trade union representatives**, they must be consulted and, further, the employer can consult with them in respect of affected employees who fit the description of employees within the scope of the recognition agreement, whether or not they are actually union members. If any affected employees do not fit that description, they will be entitled to information and consultation via employee representatives.

The employer is **not required to consult about** the reasons for redundancies, including, for example, whether or not a plant should close (*R v British Coal Corporation, ex parte Vardy*, above). He is **required to consult** in good faith "with a view to reaching agreement" with the appropriate representatives on the proposed redundancies, in particular in **relation to** ways of (s 188(2) TULRCA 1992): 8926

- avoiding the dismissals;
- reducing the number of dismissals; and
- mitigating the consequences of the dismissals (which may include assistance in redeployment or retraining).

Employers are therefore under an absolute obligation to consult and to do so meaningfully (*Susie Radin Ltd v GMB* [2004] IRLR 400, CA). 8927

Further, employers are **obliged to negotiate** with employee representatives to find ways to avoid and/or reduce the number of redundancies which may need to be made (*Junk v Wolfgang Kuhnel* [2005] IRLR 310, ECJ). Employee representatives should therefore be given the opportunity to understand the proposals, and should give proper consideration to any counter proposals before reaching a final decision on the redundancies, although the employer will not be in breach of his duty if agreement is not actually reached.

8928 **Election requirements** The election of employee representatives must satisfy the requirements set out in the table below (under "First election") (s 188A TULRCA 1992). If, following an election, an elected representative ceases to act leaving any of the affected employees unrepresented, the employees must elect a replacement representative, satisfying the requirements as indicated in the table (s 188A(2) TULRCA 1992).

Requirement	First election	Replacement representative
Employer must: – make such arrangements as reasonably practicable to ensure election is **fair**	x	x
– determine **number of representatives** to be elected so all affected employees' interests are sufficiently represented (in terms of their number and classes)	x	n/a
– determine whether affected employees should be represented by representatives **of all the affected employees** or by representatives **of particular classes** of those employees	x	n/a
– decide their **term of office** (must be long enough to enable relevant information to be given and consultations to be completed)	x	n/a
Candidates for election must be affected employees as at election date	x	x
No affected employee should be **unreasonably excluded** from standing	x	x
All affected employees on election date are **entitled to vote** (they may vote for as many candidates as there are representatives to be elected to represent them or their particular class of employee, as the case may be)	x	n/a
Election must be conducted to ensure, as far as is reasonably practicable, that voting is **in secret** and votes are **accurately counted**	x	x

8929 If the **affected employees delay in electing representatives** where the employer invited them to do so long enough before the time when consultation was required to begin (or information was required to be given), the employer will be taken to have complied with his obligations if he consults or informs as soon as is reasonably practicable after the election (s 188(7A) TULRCA 1992).

8930 If affected employees **fail** to respond to the employer's invitation **to elect representatives** within a "reasonable" time, the employer has to give (in writing) to each affected employee the information which otherwise he would have been required to give to the elected employee representatives (see below) (s 188(7B) TULRCA 1992). "Reasonable" time is not defined, but it is likely to be no later than when the consultation with employee representatives would have begun had any been elected. In these circumstances, the employer may be excused his duty to consult, as the "special circumstances" defence may be available to him (¶8950).

8931 **Rights of employee representatives and candidates** Employee representatives (including union representatives) and, where relevant, candidates have the following rights:
a. reasonable time off with pay to carry out their functions or undergo appropriate training (ss 168, 169 TULRCA 1992; s 61 ERA 1996); and
b. access to (s 188(5A) TULRCA 1992):
– affected employees; and
– appropriate accommodation and facilities.

8932 There is no definition as to how much **time off** is "reasonable" (it may, therefore, be useful for employers to indicate in advance what would be considered reasonable as this is likely to avoid disputes later on). **Candidates** may require time off to lobby affected employees on an individual basis, and to prepare for and hold a general meeting to allow them to present their candidature. **Representatives** should be allowed paid time off to prepare for and attend consultation meetings with the employer, and to report back to affected employees. Time off should also be permitted for appropriate **training** to enable them to perform their functions, although there is no obligation on the employer to investigate or provide such training.

Details on the **payment** for time off and **remedies** for refusal of time off (or failure to make the appropriate payment) are discussed at ¶3960.

Legislation does not prescribe the range of **facilities** that should be provided, but employers may find it useful to establish early, before the election is called, what facilities will be provided. This could include the use of a telephone and facilities relevant to the production of the candidates' election material and its distribution to affected employees. To avoid claims of discrimination, facilities should be provided equally to all candidates (for example, it would be inappropriate to distribute the election material of one candidate and not of another). **8933**

Information to be provided

Employers must provide the representatives with relevant information that gives them "enough information about the employer's proposals to be able to take a useful and constructive part in the process of consultation" (DTI guidance). **8935**

Each representative should be given, in writing, information which complies with the above description. It **should include** (s 188(4) TULRCA 1992):
- the reasons for the proposed redundancies;
- the numbers and descriptions of employees he proposes to dismiss as redundant;
- the total number of employees of any such description employed by the employer at the establishment;
- the proposed method of selecting for redundancy;
- the proposed method and time-scale for carrying out the dismissals (with due regard for any agreed procedures); and
- the proposed method of calculating the amount of any non-statutory redundancy payments.

However, it is not essential that the employer provides information regarding the **economic background** or **context** in which the proposal to make redundancies has arisen (*Securicor Omega Express Ltd v GMB* [2004] IRLR 9, EAT).

The information should be disclosed before the consultation begins, and although the employer is not required to give every last detail of his proposals at the initial stage, he must give **provisional details** in respect of the required information as a basis for discussion with the representatives (*E Green & Son (Castings) Ltd v ASTMS* [1984] IRLR 135, EAT).

The employer must also give the representatives a **copy of the notification** made to the DTI (¶8970). **8936**

The information should be **given** to each of the appropriate representatives **or sent** to an address notified by them to the employer or, in the case of union representatives, posted to the union's main or head office (s 188(5) TULRCA 1992). **8937**

Employee representatives may be asked to accept **confidentiality constraints** for a specified period, so long as this does not inhibit their rights to be sufficiently informed so as to be able to take part in meaningful consultation. Further, Stock Exchange rules do not preclude employee representatives being informed and consulted in advance where collective redundancies are planned in connection with a take-over. **8938**

Timing

Following a significant ECJ ruling, consultation must now **be completed before the notice of dismissal** is given (*Junk v Wolfgang Kuhnel* [2005] IRLR 310, ECJ). **8939**

Readers should note, however, that the UK legislation rules on when consultation **must commence** still apply and employers must also ensure that where the number of redundancies proposed at one establishment:
- are between 20 and 99, consultation must commence at least 30 days before the first of the dismissals takes effect, i.e. before the expiry of the first notice of dismissal; or
- are 100 or more, consultation must commence at least 90 days before the first of the dismissals takes effect, i.e. before the expiry of the first notice of dismissal.

As consultation must now be completed before the notice of dismissal is given the UK rules will usually be complied with in any event. This is because it is expected that this additional requirement will mean employers will have to ensure that they start their consultation period earlier than before. However, where the consultation period is concluded quickly and the notice period is relatively short, it is possible that employers may find that they have to allow for the 30/90 day requirement.

Employers must ensure, as emphasised by the DTI in its revised guidance note (Redundancy Consultation and Notification), that the process of consultation begins in **good time**. Indeed, there should be a period of **meaningful consultation** before the notices of termination are sent out (*TGWU v Ledbury Preserves (1928) Ltd*), especially given the requirement to consult "with a view to reaching agreement" (¶8926). Consultation should also **precede any public announcement** of the redundancy programme.

MEMO POINTS Following the ECJ ruling in *Junk v Wolfgang Kuhnel*, it may appear artificial that the DTI has maintained the 30/90 day rule in its guidance, especially given the ECJ's comments that the effectiveness of the information and consultation provisions in the EC Directive on Collective Redundancies would be jeopardised if employers were allowed to inform and consult subsequent to their decision to terminate employees' contracts of employment. This very clearly imposes an obligation on employers to undertake meaningful consultation to achieve the Directive's objectives of finding ways to avoid and/or reduce the number of redundancies which need to be made.

8940 If they are to comply with these requirements, employers need to have the **structure for consultation** already in place before the relevant period of consultation is due to commence. This may make it more convenient to have a standing representative body with which to consult. Otherwise, if elections need to be held, there is a risk that plans over redundancies are indirectly revealed at too early a stage.

8941 In order to calculate the applicable consultation period, where the employer subsequently proposes **further redundancies**, each batch in respect of which the employer has already started consultation is, in the absence of bad faith, considered separately (s 188(3) TULRCA 1992).

8942 The employer will not be in breach of the consultation period if he consults or informs as soon as is reasonably practicable after the election of employee representatives where this has been **delayed by the affected employees** (¶8929).

8943 If the employer dismisses before the consultation period has expired, he will be in breach of his statutory obligations and could face a compensation claim. To avoid claims, the employer should **delay the date** of the dismissals.

Failure to comply/infringement of rights

8946 If an employer fails to **consult** as required, or fails to comply with **election requirements**, a complaint may be brought to an employment tribunal as follows (s 189 TULRCA 1992):

Failure:	Complaint by:
Election of employee representative(s)	Any affected employees/employees dismissed as redundant
Any other failure relating to employee representative(s)	Any employee representative(s) to whom failure related
Relating to trade union representative(s)	The trade union
Any other case	Any affected employees/employees dismissed as redundant

It appears, therefore, that where there are employee or trade union representatives, the affected employees have no direct right to complain of a failure to inform and consult.

If the employer fails to **organise the election** of employee representatives (or fails to carry out the election according to the requirements), any affected employee can bring a complaint.

If the employer fails to **give sufficient information** to the trade union representatives (or, if none, to the employee representatives), the trade union (or the employee representatives, as the case may be) can bring proceedings. If there are no union representatives and the employees fail to elect representatives (such that the employer provides information directly to all affected employees), any affected employee can bring a complaint if this information is insufficient.

Affected employees have no remedy if their **representative does not perform** his duties properly, as the right to complain is confined to complaints against the employer. 8947

If a question arises as to whether or not a particular employee representative was an appropriate representative, it is for the employer to show that the **representative had the necessary authority** to represent the affected employees (s 189(1A) TULRCA 1992). If necessary, he must also show that the **requirements regarding elections** have been satisfied (s 189(1)(a), (1B) TULRCA 1992). 8948

Complaints must be brought either before the date on which the last of the dismissals takes effect or within 3 months beginning with that date unless, in the view of the tribunal, it was not reasonably practicable for the complaint to be made in time, in which case it must be brought within such further period as the tribunal considers reasonable (s 189(5) TULRCA 1992) (¶9466). 8949

Defence There is a defence for an employer who finds it not reasonably practicable to perform his information and consultation obligations due to **special circumstances**. In such cases, the employer must take all such steps towards performing his duties as are reasonably practicable in those circumstances (s 188(7) TULRCA 1992). It is for the employer to establish the defence (s 189(6) TULRCA 1992). "Special circumstances" is not defined, but case law indicates that the circumstances must be special to the particular case, and "out of the ordinary" or "uncommon" (*Clarks of Hove Ltd v Baker's Union* [1978] IRLR 366, CA). If the circumstances are not sufficient to support the defence, they may nevertheless be taken into account by the tribunal when awarding compensation for failure to comply (see below). 8950

The employer cannot rely on the defence where he **has not received necessary information** from the person controlling him (directly or indirectly) (for example, a head office or parent company), where the latter has made the decision leading to the proposed dismissals.

Moreover, any **delay** between taking decision which leads to the proposed dismissals and the date on which the employer is informed of it should be disregarded when considering whether the employer can rely on the special circumstances defence (*GMB v Amicus (AEEU and MSF)*; *Amicus (AEEU and MSF) v Beloit Walmsley Ltd (in administration)*, EAT cases 1094/02 and 1095/02).

It is clear that concerns about **confidentiality** will not provide a defence, and the Stock Exchange rules do not preclude consultation in advance of a transaction involving a listed company. It may be possible to consult with appropriate representatives on a confidential basis, although this will obviously be more difficult if employee representatives need to be elected.

There are no special circumstances attaching to the **appointment of a receiver or administrator** (*Re Hartlebury Printers Ltd (in liquidation) and others* [1992] IRLR 516, ChD), unless the financial deterioration into insolvency or receivership is sufficiently sudden, such as the collapse of take-over negotiations and the immediate denial of further credit by the bank (*USDAW v Leancut Bacon Ltd* [1981] IRLR 295, EAT), or the insolvency is combined with, for example, the destruction of the employer's plant, a general trading boycott or a sudden withdrawal of supplies from the main supplier (*Re Hartlebury Printers Ltd (in liquidation) and others*).

Remedies for failure to consult/comply with election requirements If a tribunal upholds a complaint, it must make a **declaration** to that effect and may make a **protective award**, which the employer will be obliged to pay (s 189(2) TULRCA 1992). It appears that only those employees who have been dismissed as redundant, or whom it is proposed to dismiss as redundant, will be covered by the award (s 189(3) TULRCA 1992). Those employees who are otherwise affected by the redundancy situation (¶8916) do not appear to have a right to receive a protective award. 8951

The award is **calculated** by reference to a week's pay (¶2920) (uncapped) for each week of the "**protected period**" (s 189(2), (3) TULRCA 1992), which begins with the date on which the 8952 first of the dismissals to which the complaint relates takes effect, or the date of the award if earlier, and is as long as the tribunal decides is just and equitable bearing in mind the seriousness of the employer's failure to comply, subject to a maximum of 90 days (s 189(4) TULRCA 1992). Tribunals, in deciding the appropriate period, should make the maximum award of 90 days and should only make reductions to it if there are mitigating circumstances which the tribunal, in its discretion, considers just and equitable (*Susie Radin Ltd v GMB* [2004] IRLR 400, CA; *Transport and General Workers Union v Morgan Platts Ltd (in administration)*, EAT 0646/02). In *Susie Radin Ltd v GMB*, the Court of Appeal emphasised that the purpose of the protective award is punitive but should not serve to compensate the employee and, consequently, it is the **seriousness of the default** that should be the primary consideration in calculating the amount to be awarded. The EAT has recently applied the decision in *Susie Radin Ltd v GMB* and examined **mitigating factors** alongside the seriousness of the employer's default (*Amicus v GBS Tooling Ltd (in administration)* [2005] IRLR 683, EAT).

EXAMPLE In *Amicus v GBS Tooling Ltd (in administration)*, the employer failed to carry out any consultation with the union after formulating a proposal to dismiss all employees as redundant because of the company's insolvency. However, the employer had, in **prior consultation**, kept the union informed of the situation and that redundancies were likely. Although this consultation had taken place prior to formulating the proposal to dismiss, it was deemed to constitute a mitigating factor going to the seriousness of the employer's breach, justifying a reduction in the award.

The tribunal should not focus on the employer's **ability to pay** the protective award and it will be irrelevant that a payment may have to be made by the Government instead of the employer if the latter is insolvent (*Smith and anor v Cherry Lewis Limited* [2005] IRLR 86, EAT).

Therefore, if any reduction to the 90 day period is to be made, the tribunal is likely to **take into account**:
a. the number of consultation days actually lost;
b. the employee's loss of notice/remuneration;
c. whether the breach was merely technical or minor (for example, providing the information orally rather than in writing) and whether the employer complied in part;
d. the employer's attitude to the consultation process;
e. whether the employer made a genuine mistake in relation to, or was ignorant of, his legal obligations;
f. whether the breach was deliberate;
g. the employer's efforts to find alternative employment;
h. any previous practice of non-consultation; and
i. the extent to which employee representatives were also responsible for the failure.

Therefore, if there is no consultation, or the consultation is meaningless (for example, where there is no exploration of alternatives to redundancy), the maximum award is likely to be made. On the other hand, if, despite the employer's failure fully to comply with his consultation obligation, the employee has not suffered any adverse effects, the tribunal may reduce the award, or make no award at all, although in most cases, an award will be made.

8953 If the employee is paid a **Jobseeker's Allowance or income support** during the protected period, the employer must deduct the amount paid from the award and repay it to the Department of Work and Pensions. Note that a **contractual payment** or a payment by way of **damages for breach of contract** in respect of any part of the protected period will not go towards discharging the employer's liability to pay a protective award (and similarly, the protective award will not go towards discharging the employer's liability to make those payments) (*Commission of the European Communities v United Kingdom* [1994] IRLR 392, ECJ).

8954 The **protective award will be lost** to the extent that an employee would otherwise have remained employed where he is employed during the protected period but is fairly dismissed for a non-redundancy reason (see ¶8916 for definition of redundancy), or unreasonably terminates his employment (s 191(1) TULRCA 1992).

Further, if an employee **unreasonably refuses** an offer of **suitable alternative employment**, he loses the protective award for the period during which he would have been employed, had he not refused (s 191(2), (3) TULRCA 1992). If the employee accepts the alternative employment but reasonably leaves during the trial period (see above), he will still be entitled to the protective award.

If an **employee dies** during the protected period, that period will, for the purposes of calculating his award, end on his death (s 190(6) TULRCA 1992).

If the employer **fails to comply with the award**, the employee can bring a complaint to the tribunal within 3 months of the last day on which the employer failed to make the payment, unless it was not reasonably practicable to bring it within that period (s 192(2) TULRCA 1992). 8955

If the **employer is insolvent**, the employee can apply to the DTI for payment of the protective award (¶9053). 8956

Protection for voters, candidates and employee representatives It is **automatically unfair** (¶8390) for an employer to dismiss any worker wholly or mainly because (s 152 TULRCA 1992; s 103 ERA 1996): 8957
- they have participated in the election either as a candidate or voters; or
- of their status or activities as union representatives or elected representatives.

It is also unlawful for an employer to victimise any such worker by subjecting him to a **detriment short of dismissal** by any act, or any deliberate failure to act, on those grounds (s 146 TULRCA 1992; ss 47, 47(1A) ERA 1996). 8958

EXAMPLE The employer transfers Employee A, removing him from the group of affected employees. The reason, or one of the reasons for this, is to do with the fact that A is a representative. This amounts to detrimental action and gives A the right to a remedy.

C. Notification to DTI

An employer must notify the DTI of his proposal to dismiss employees as redundant. The timing for this notification is as for the commencement of consultation (¶8939) (s 193(1), (2) TULRCA 1992). 8970

MEMO POINTS In light of the effect of the ECJ's decision in *Junk v Kuhnel* (see ¶8939), the Government is proposing to make a small legislative change to clarify that an employer must notify the DTI before any redundancy notices are sent to affected employees.

The notification provisions **are excluded** in the same circumstances as the consultation provisions (see above). In addition, however, overseas employment is excluded from the duty to notify the DTI (s 285 TULRCA 1992). 8971

It is irrelevant whether the redundancies are compulsory or voluntary. Where the employer has already notified the DTI of one batch of redundancies, any **further redundancies** are counted separately (s 193(3) TULRCA 1992). 8972

Employers may notify by letter or use form HR1. The **information required** is similar to that to be provided to employee representatives (¶8935), and must, if consultation is required, identify the trade union or employee representatives concerned and give the date when consultation began. The DTI should also be informed if the employer's **proposals change significantly** after the notification has been given – for example, if the dismissal dates change or the numbers to be dismissed increase by twenty or more.

A **copy of the notification** must be provided to the employee representatives, although there does not appear to be any sanction for failure to comply with this requirement (s 193(6) TULRCA 1992).

Failure to notify may lead to criminal proceedings, which could result in a fine, although the special circumstances defence (see above) may apply. Ignorance of the obligation to 8973 notify does not amount to special circumstances for the purposes of the defence (*Secretary of State for Employment v Helitron Ltd* [1980] ICR 523, EAT).

IV. Statutory redundancy payments

Entitlement

8990 An employee who has been dismissed by reason of redundancy (¶8740) will be entitled to a statutory redundancy payment if he has completed at least 2 years' continuous employment, unless he is an excluded/disqualified employee.

MEMO POINTS It is expected that direct and indirect **age discrimination** will become **unlawful** from 1 October 2006. At the time of writing, the Government has published draft Employment Equality (Age) Regulations 2006. However, although potentially indirectly discriminatory, the Government proposes to retain the 2-year qualifying length of service.
See ¶5254 for a summary of the draft regulations and ¶¶8836, 8991, 8992, 8997, 9005 and 9007 in relation to other key proposals on age discrimination which apply to the law on redundancy).

If the **employer is insolvent or refuses to pay**, the state will guarantee the statutory redundancy payment from the National Insurance Fund. This is discussed at ¶9049.

Taxation of redundancy payments is discussed at ¶3132.

8991 **Continuous employment** is calculated as at the "relevant date", which is discussed at ¶8340. Periods before the employee's 18th birthday are not counted, and overseas employment and receipt of a genuine statutory redundancy payment will break continuity (see ¶1025).

MEMO POINTS It is proposed that periods of service before the age of 18 will no longer be discounted under the draft regulations on age discrimination.

Excluded/disqualified employees

8992 The following employees are not entitled to statutory redundancy payments:
- employees who have reached the normal retirement age for the job (if this is the same for men and women) (or the age of 65 if lower than the normal retirement age) (s 156 ERA 1996) (see ¶8211 for further details on "normal retirement age");
- employees who have contracted out of their entitlement (¶¶8993, 8995); and
- employees who have lost their entitlement in certain circumstances (¶¶8996 – 9001).

Domestic servants who are close relatives of their employers are also excluded (s 161 ERA 1996).

MEMO POINTS The challenge to the upper age limit on the grounds that it is indirectly discriminatory against men has recently failed before the Court of Appeal (*Rutherford and another v Secretary of State for Trade and Industry (No. 2)* [2004] IRLR 892, CA). At the time of writing, this case is awaiting an appeal to the House of Lords.
However, the draft regulations on age discrimination propose to remove the upper age limit for entitlement to statutory redundancy payments (¶5254).

8993 **Contracting out in advance** **Collective agreements** covered by an exemption order issued by the Secretary of State can disapply the statutory redundancy scheme in respect of employees within the scope of the agreement, and set out agreed severance payments and procedures (s 157 ERA 1996). The agreement must indicate that, in the event of disagreement, certain issues (the right to a payment and/or its amount) may be referred to an employment tribunal for decision.

8994 Employees on **fixed-term contracts** of 2 years or more can no longer contract out in advance on an individual basis (¶2003).

Contracting out once right has arisen It is only possible to contract out of the employee's right to redundancy pay (or to a statutory trial period in alternative employment – ¶8872) if the agreement between employer and employee meets the statutory requirements of a valid compromise agreement (¶9333) or reached through an ACAS appointed conciliation officer (¶9305). 8995

Re-employment or refusal of suitable alternative employment An employee will lose his entitlement if he is re-employed (such that continuity is preserved), or unreasonably refuses an offer of reinstatement or suitable alternative employment (or unreasonably leaves during the statutory trial period) (s 141(2)-(4) ERA 1996) (¶8873). 8996

Entitlement to occupational pension An employer may choose to **reduce or exclude** the employee's entitlement to a statutory redundancy payment if the employee is entitled to receive an occupational pension (whether by way of **lump sum or periodical payment**) on the termination of his employment (unless the pension payments have already started when the employee is made redundant (*Royal Ordnance plc v Pilkington* [1989] IRLR 489, CA)) if the following **conditions** are satisfied (Redundancy Payments Pensions Regulations SI 1965/1932; s 158 ERA 1996): 8997
a. the pension scheme is satisfactory to the Secretary of State; and
b. the pension is payable:
– by reference to the employee's last period of continuous employment with the employer;
– on or within 90 weeks of the termination (even where the employee defers payment until after this period); and
– for life or commutable into a lump sum.

MEMO POINTS The draft Employment Equality (Age) Regulations 2006 **propose to revoke** the Redundancy Payments Pensions Regulations 1965/1932.

If the employer can, and wishes to, reduce or exclude the redundancy payment, he must give **written notice** to the employee of his intention, and must set out how the redundancy payment has been reduced or excluded, and what payment will be made. The employer must give the notice within a reasonable **time** of becoming aware of the employee's claim to a redundancy payment, which is a question of fact for the tribunal to decide (*Stowe-Woodward BTR Ltd v Beynon* [1978] ICR 609, EAT; *British Telecommunications plc v Mahoney*, EAT case 101/86; *British Telecommunications plc v Burwell* [1986] ICR 35, EAT). Three months has been held to be unreasonable (*Stowe-Woodward BTR Ltd v Beynon*), whilst 42 days was considered reasonable in light of the 6-month time limit for redundancy claims (¶9010) (*BT v Mahoney*). If the employer **fails to provide** such a notice, he is liable to pay the employee's redundancy entitlement in full (*Thomas v Consolidated Pneumatic Tool Co Ltd*, ET case 18936/78). 8998

Redundancy payments can be reduced or excluded as follows: 8999

Annual value of pension [1]	Reduction/exclusion
1/3 or more of annual pay [2]	Where **pension payable immediately** on termination [3], redundancy payment can be excluded entirely
	Where **pension not payable immediately** on termination, employer pays weekly value of pension for each week between termination and beginning of pension payment (up to 90 weeks) up to value of full redundancy payment
Less than 1/3 of annual pay [2]	Where **pension payable immediately** on termination [3], redundancy payment can be reduced by proportion which annual value of pension bears to one-third of annual pay i.e. reduction will be (redundancy payment x annual value of pension) (1/3 of annual pay)
Less than 1/3 of annual pay [2]	Where **pension not payable immediately** on termination, employer pays amount that would have been payable if pension payable immediately (see above) plus the weekly value of pension for each week between termination and beginning of pension payment (up to 90 weeks) up to value of full redundancy payment

1. Annual value of pension is the gross amount payable during the first year of the pension plus 10% of any gross sum payable or, in the case of a lump sum pension, 10% of the lump sum.
2. Annual pay is the employee's week's pay (subject to the statutory cap (¶2920)) multiplied by 52.
3. "Immediately" means within one week of the termination.

9000 **Resignation during notice period** An employee who is under notice of dismissal may wish to leave before the employer's notice expires. To preserve his right to a redundancy payment, he must serve a **counter-notice** on the employer (s 136(3) ERA 1996). Although it appears that he can give short, even minimal notice (*Ready Case Ltd v Jackson* [1981] IRLR 312, EAT), he must give written notice within the obligatory period of the employer's notice (i.e. the minimum notice required by statute or contract, or the actual notice period if less), which is counted backwards from the date of dismissal specified in the employer's notice. For example, if the employee is entitled to 2 weeks' notice, but the employer actually gives 3 weeks' notice, the employee must serve his counter-notice within the last 2 weeks of the 3-week notice period (and not before).

The **employer may contest** the employee's counter-notice by serving a further written notice on the employee, requiring him to withdraw his counter-notice and serve out the original notice period, and warning him that the employer will contest his right to a redundancy payment if he fails to comply (s 142 ERA 1996). If the **employee refuses**, he is not entitled to any redundancy payment unless he applies to the tribunal, and the tribunal can award all, part or none of the redundancy payment, as it considers just and equitable. If the **employee dies** during the period of his counter-notice, the employer is deemed to have contested that notice (if he has not actually done so), and the employee's estate must apply to an employment tribunal for a redundancy payment (s 176(5) ERA 1996).

9001 **Gross misconduct** If an employee is **potentially redundant**, he will lose his entitlement if it is subsequently discovered that summary dismissal for gross misconduct is justified (¶6640), and the employer either dismisses without notice, with shorter notice than required by the contract or the statutory minimum, or with full notice but accompanied by a written statement that he would have been entitled to dismiss without notice (s 140(1) ERA 1996).

If the employer has **already given notice of redundancy** when the employee commits the act of gross misconduct, the employer may be able to avoid making a redundancy payment by giving **further notice** that he would have been entitled to summarily dismiss the employee. However, a tribunal may award the whole or part of any redundancy payment in such circumstances (s 140(3), (4) ERA 1996).

If an employee is **on strike** during the redundancy notice period, the employer cannot exclude the right to a redundancy payment by dismissing for gross misconduct (s 140(2) ERA 1996). However, he may make **payment conditional** on the employee working an extended notice period (to make up for days lost during the strike) by serving a written **notice of extension**, warning that he will dispute the employee's right to a redundancy payment if he does not comply (s 143 ERA 1996). If, on each day of the extension, the employee turned up for work, was unable to comply or reasonably refused to comply, a tribunal can award all or part of the redundancy payment. If not, the tribunal may not make any award.

Calculation

9005 The statutory redundancy payment is calculated by reference to age, length of service (subject to a cap – see below) to the relevant date (¶8340), and salary (subject to a cap – see below) as follows (s 162(2) ERA 1996):
– for each complete year of employment in which the employee was aged 41 to 64: 1.5 week's pay;
– for each complete year in which he was aged 22 to 40: 1 week's pay; and
– for each complete year in which he was aged 18 to 21: 0.5 week's pay.

The table on the next page can be used to calculate the employee's entitlement.

A **week's pay** is subject to a statutory cap (see ¶2920). **Length of service** is subject to a maximum of 20 years (s 162(3) ERA 1996), and is calculated according to statutory continuity of service (contractual agreements relating to continuity are ignored) (¶1020).

The **current maximum** statutory redundancy payment is, therefore, £8,400 (£280 (the current statutory maximum; this is likely to increase in February 2006 (see ¶2920)) x 20 x 1.5).

The entitlement of an employee who is made redundant **after his 64th birthday** is reduced by one-twelfth for each month of service past that age (s 162(4), (5) ERA 1996).

MEMO POINTS – The draft regulations on age discrimination propose the following in relation to the calculation of statutory redundancy pay:
– the reference to **length of service** and the cap of 20 years will be retained.
– the **reduction** for those employees who are within 1 year of the upper age limit will be removed.
– the level of the **multiplier** based on age bands (ranging at present (see above) from 0.5 week's pay for younger employees to 1.5 week's pay for older employees) will be removed. The level of the new multiplier has not yet been determined.

A tribunal has a **discretion to reduce** the amount of a redundancy payment in the following circumstances: **9006**
– where the employee served a counter-notice on the employer, seeking to bring forward the date of dismissal given in the employer's notice, but the employer serves further notice requiring him to work out the notice period in full (¶9000);
– where the employee is dismissed for misconduct after notice of dismissal for redundancy was served (¶9001) or after he served a notice of intention to claim a redundancy payment in a lay-off or short-time working case (¶7884); and
– where an employee fails to comply with a notice of extension after being on strike (¶9001).

Read off the employee's age and number of complete years' service (discounting any week which began before the employee attained the age of 18). The table will then show how many weeks' pay the employee is entitled to. **9007**

(See next page)

MEMO POINTS Note that figures in this table **will change** from 1 October 2006, when it is expected that the draft regulations on age discrimination will come into force.

Claims for payment

In order to **secure his entitlement** to a statutory redundancy payment, the employee must, **before** the end of 6 months beginning with the relevant date (¶8340) (s 164 ERA 1996): **9010**
– agree and receive the payment from the employer;
– make a written claim for payment from the employer;
– bring a claim for payment in an employment tribunal; or
– bring a complaint of unfair dismissal in an employment tribunal.

If the employee secures his entitlement (for example, by making a written claim from the employer), there is no time limit for a **subsequent application** to a tribunal if his entitlement is not paid in full. **9011**

EXAMPLE In *The Bentley Engineering Co Ltd v Miller* [1976] IRLR 146, QBD, M was paid a redundancy payment based on 8 years' service within 6 months of the relevant date, thus satisfying the initial time limit. Two years later, an employment tribunal accepted his claim for a redundancy payment based on 23 years' service.

The time limit for tribunal claims can be **extended** up to within 12 months of the relevant date (but no further) if the tribunal considers it just and equitable to do so, having regard to all the circumstances of the case (¶9475), including whether the employee should receive a redundancy payment (s 164(2) ERA 1996). **9012**

The statutory time limit only applies to claims under the statutory redundancy scheme. The time limits for **contractual schemes** (for example, exempt schemes set out in a collective agreement – ¶8993) may set out their own time limits. If they do not, the general limitation period for contractual claims will apply (¶9450). **9013**

Service (years)	2	3	4	5	6	7	8	9	10	11	12	13	14	15	16	17	18	19	20
Age (years)																			
20	1	1	1	1	-														
21	1	1 1/2	1 1/2	1 1/2	1 1/2	-													
22	1	1 1/2	2	2	2	2	-												
23	1 1/2	2	2 1/2	3	3	3	3	-											
24	2	2 1/2	3	3 1/2	4	4	4	4	-										
25	2	3	3 1/2	4	4 1/2	5	5	5	5	-									
26	2	3	4	4 1/2	5	5 1/2	6	6	6	6	-								
27	2	3	4	5	5 1/2	6	6 1/2	7	7	7	7	-							
28	2	3	4	5	6	6 1/2	7	7 1/2	8	8	8	8	-						
29	2	3	4	5	6	7	7 1/2	8	8 1/2	9	9	9	9	-					
30	2	3	4	5	6	7	8	8 1/2	9	9 1/2	10	10	10	10	-				
31	2	3	4	5	6	7	8	9	9 1/2	10	10 1/2	11	11	11	11	-			
32	2	3	4	5	6	7	8	9	10	10 1/2	11	11 1/2	12	12	12	12	-		
33	2	3	4	5	6	7	8	9	10	11	11 1/2	12	12 1/2	13	13	13	13	-	
34	2	3	4	5	6	7	8	9	10	11	12	12 1/2	13	13 1/2	14	14	14	14	-
35	2	3	4	5	6	7	8	9	10	11	12	13	13 1/2	14	14 1/2	15	15	15	15
36	2	3	4	5	6	7	8	9	10	11	12	13	14	14 1/2	15	15 1/2	16	16	16
37	2	3	4	5	6	7	8	9	10	11	12	13	14	15	15 1/2	16	16 1/2	17	17
38	2	3	4	5	6	7	8	9	10	11	12	13	14	15	16	16 1/2	17	17 1/2	18
39	2	3	4	5	6	7	8	9	10	11	12	13	14	15	16	17	17 1/2	18	18 1/2
40	2	3	4	5	6	7	8	9	10	11	12	13	14	15	16	17	18	18 1/2	19
41	2	3	4	5	6	7	8	9	10	11	12	13	14	15	16	17	18	19	19 1/2

Service (years)	2	3	4	5	6	7	8	9	10	11	12	13	14	15	16	17	18	19	20
Age (years)																			
42	2 1/2	3 1/2	4 1/2	5 1/2	6 1/2	7 1/2	8 1/2	9 1/2	10 1/2	11 1/2	12 1/2	13 1/2	14 1/2	15 1/2	16 1/2	17 1/2	18 1/2	19 1/2	20 1/2
43	3	4	5	6	7	8	9	10	11	12	13	14	15	16	17	18	19	20	21
44	3	4 1/2	5 1/2	6 1/2	7 1/2	8 1/2	9 1/2	10 1/2	11 1/2	12 1/2	13 1/2	14 1/2	15 1/2	16 1/2	17 1/2	18 1/2	19 1/2	20 1/2	21 1/2
45	3	4 1/2	6	7	8	9	10	11	12	13	14	15	16	17	18	19	20	21	22
46	3	4 1/2	6	7 1/2	8 1/2	9 1/2	10 1/2	11 1/2	12 1/2	13 1/2	14 1/2	15 1/2	16 1/2	17 1/2	18 1/2	19 1/2	20 1/2	21 1/2	22 1/2
47	3	4 1/2	6	7 1/2	9	10	11	12	13	14	15	16	17	18	19	20	21	22	23
48	3	4 1/2	6	7 1/2	9	10 1/2	11 1/2	12 1/2	13 1/2	14 1/2	15 1/2	16 1/2	17 1/2	18 1/2	19 1/2	20 1/2	21 1/2	22 1/2	23 1/2
49	3	4 1/2	6	7 1/2	9	10 1/2	12	13	14	15	16	17	18	19	20	21	22	23	24
50	3	4 1/2	6	7 1/2	9	10 1/2	12	13 1/2	14 1/2	15 1/2	16 1/2	17 1/2	18 1/2	19 1/2	20 1/2	21 1/2	22 1/2	23 1/2	24 1/2
51	3	4 1/2	6	7 1/2	9	10 1/2	12	13 1/2	15	16	17	18	19	20	21	22	23	24	25
52	3	4 1/2	6	7 1/2	9	10 1/2	12	13 1/2	15	16 1/2	17 1/2	18 1/2	19 1/2	20 1/2	21 1/2	22 1/2	23 1/2	24 1/2	25 1/2
53	3	4 1/2	6	7 1/2	9	10 1/2	12	13 1/2	15	16 1/2	18	19	20	21	22	23	24	25	26
54	3	4 1/2	6	7 1/2	9	10 1/2	12	13 1/2	15	16 1/2	18	19 1/2	20 1/2	21 1/2	22 1/2	23 1/2	24 1/2	25 1/2	26 1/2
55	3	4 1/2	6	7 1/2	9	10 1/2	12	13 1/2	15	16 1/2	18	19 1/2	21	22	23	24	25	26	27
56	3	4 1/2	6	7 1/2	9	10 1/2	12	13 1/2	15	16 1/2	18	19 1/2	21	22 1/2	23 1/2	24 1/2	25 1/2	26 1/2	27 1/2
57	3	4 1/2	6	7 1/2	9	10 1/2	12	13 1/2	15	16 1/2	18	19 1/2	21	22 1/2	24	25	26	27	28
58	3	4 1/2	6	7 1/2	9	10 1/2	12	13 1/2	15	16 1/2	18	19 1/2	21	22 1/2	24	25 1/2	26 1/2	27 1/2	28 1/2
59	3	4 1/2	6	7 1/2	9	10 1/2	12	13 1/2	15	16 1/2	18	19 1/2	21	22 1/2	24	25 1/2	27	28	29
60	3	4 1/2	6	7 1/2	9	10 1/2	12	13 1/2	15	16 1/2	18	19 1/2	21	22 1/2	24	25 1/2	27	28 1/2	29 1/2
61	3	4 1/2	6	7 1/2	9	10 1/2	12	13 1/2	15	16 1/2	18	19 1/2	21	22 1/2	24	25 1/2	27	28 1/2	30
62	3	4 1/2	6	7 1/2	9	10 1/2	12	13 1/2	15	16 1/2	18	19 1/2	21	22 1/2	24	25 1/2	27	28 1/2	30
63	3	4 1/2	6	7 1/2	9	10 1/2	12	13 1/2	15	16 1/2	18	19 1/2	21	22 1/2	24	25 1/2	27	28 1/2	30
64	3	4 1/2	6	7 1/2	9	10 1/2	12	13 1/2	15	16 1/2	18	19 1/2	21	22 1/2	24	25 1/2	27	28 1/2	30

9014 **Death of employer or employee** If the **employee dies**, his entitlement to a redundancy payment passes to his estate, and his personal representatives can pursue his claim. If the employee dies within 6 months of the relevant date, the basic **time limit** is 1 year beginning with the relevant date (s 176(7) ERA 1996). If the employee dies during the 6 months following expiry of the normal 6-month time limit, the tribunal may extend this second 6-month time limit to twelve months.

The deceased employee's estate will not be entitled to a redundancy payment if he had been offered **suitable alternative employment**, it would have been unreasonable for him to refuse, and he died (ss 176(3), (4)(a), (b) ERA 1996):
- after the offer was made but before deciding whether to accept or reject it;
- during the trial period; or
- having given notice to terminate the trial period.

9015 The death of an **individual employer** amounts to a dismissal of the employee for statutory redundancy purposes, and the employee may be entitled to a redundancy payment from the employer's estate (ss 136(5), 139(4) ERA 1996). If, however, the employee accepts an offer of **suitable alternative employment** (¶8867) from the employer's personal representatives, continuity will be preserved and there will be no liability to pay statutory redundancy. The statutory trial period will apply (¶8872), although in this case the new employment must begin within 8 weeks of the termination of the old job, and the offer of new employment does not have to be made before the old job came to an end (s 174 ERA 1996).

9016 It is possible that the transfer of the business from the deceased employer to his personal representatives may amount to the transfer of an undertaking for the purposes of the **business transfer regulations** (¶7910) (although arguably the employees' contracts would not otherwise have been terminated by the transfer, as required by the regulations, but by the employer's death). See Chapter 24 for further discussion about the transfer regulations.

Statement of entitlement

9017 When making a redundancy payment, the employer must provide the employee with a statement showing how it was calculated (see above), unless that amount is determined by an employment tribunal following a claim for payment (s 165(1) ERA 1996). It is advisable for the statement to make it clear that the calculation represents the employee's statutory redundancy payment.

Failure to provide the statement is a criminal offence. Further, the employee can give written notice to the employer **demanding a statement** by a specified date (allowing the employer at least 1 week), and failure to comply without reasonable excuse is a further offence (s 165(4) ERA 1996).

SECTION 4

Employee rights on insolvency

9040 A detailed discussion of the law of insolvency is beyond the scope of this book. The **impact** of employer insolvency **on the employment relationship** is discussed at ¶8277. This section will focus on specific employee rights and protections, including the employee's right to apply to the DTI for certain state guaranteed payments, his treatment as a preferential creditor in respect of certain debts, and his rights against an administrator (or, in rare cases, an administrative receiver) in respect of amounts arising during the period of administration (or receivership).

1. State guaranteed payments

a. Types of payment

Employees of an insolvent employer can apply to the DTI for the following state guaranteed payments (payable from the National Insurance Fund): 9045
- **statutory redundancy payments**;
- certain **debts**; and
- unpaid **pension contributions** to an occupational pension scheme or a personal pension scheme.

An employee of an insolvent employer can recover her **statutory maternity pay** from the Commissioners of Revenue and Customs (reg 7 Statutory Maternity Pay (General) Regulations 1986, as amended; s 1(2) Social Security Contributions (Transfer of Functions, etc) Act 1999). Likewise, **statutory paternity pay** and **statutory adoption pay** may be recovered (reg 43 SI 2002/2822).

MEMO POINTS Where an employer has his registered office in one EU state but also employs workers in **another EU state**, the guarantee institution of the state in which the employee is employed is responsible for making the guaranteed payment (*Everson and Barrass v Secretary of State for Trade and Industry and Bell Lines Ltd* [2000] IRLR 202, ECJ).

The **definition of insolvency** depends on whether the employer is an individual or a company (s 166 ERA 1996 (redundancy payments); s 183(2) ERA 1996 (debts)). 9046

An **individual employer** is insolvent if:
- he has been declared bankrupt or has entered a composition or arrangement with his creditors; or
- he has died and the court has ordered that his estate be administered as an insolvent estate (s 421 Insolvency Act 1986).

MEMO POINTS In **Scotland**, an individual employer is insolvent under the first limb if sequestration of his estate has been awarded, or he has executed a trust deed for his creditors or has entered into a composition contract. For detail on an insolvent estate, see s 11A Judicial Factors (Scotland) Act 1889.

A **corporate employer** is insolvent if: 9047
- a winding-up order or administration order has been made, or a resolution for voluntary winding-up has been passed;
- an administrator, a receiver or a manager of the company's undertaking is appointed, or possession has been taken of any company property by or on behalf of debenture holders; or
- a voluntary arrangement under certain insolvency provisions has been approved (Part I Insolvency Act 1986).

MEMO POINTS 1. If the employee is employed by a **partnership**, each and every partner must meet the definition of individual insolvency (*Secretary of State for Trade & Industry v Forde* [1997] IRLR 387, EAT).
2. Appointment of a manager/possession by or on behalf of debenture holders does not apply in **Scotland**.

An employer is not insolvent merely because he is unable to pay debts as they fall due or simply stops trading. When making a claim, the **employee must prove**, by direct evidence, that the employer is insolvent (*Secretary of State for Trade and Industry v Walden* [2000] IRLR 168, EAT). 9048

Statutory redundancy payments

The employee can recover a so-called employer's payment from the DTI if he can show that the employer was liable to make such a payment, he has not been paid (or has been paid only in part) and either: 9049
- he has taken all reasonable steps short of legal proceedings to obtain payment from the employer; or
- the employer is insolvent, as defined (see above).

For these purposes, **legal proceedings** does not include tribunal proceedings, but does include enforcement proceedings, so an employee is normally expected to bring a tribunal claim for a redundancy payment before applying to the DTI, but is not required to take enforcement proceedings in respect of a tribunal decision before doing so.

The Secretary of State will make the payment if he is satisfied that the above conditions are met, and in making his decision he must make reasonable enquiries to ascertain the facts and to apply them to the law current at that time (*Secretary of State for Trade and Industry v Lassman* [2000] IRLR 411, CA).

The employee must have completed the necessary period of **qualifying service** to claim a redundancy payment (¶8990).

MEMO POINTS An employee claiming under a contractual scheme covered by an exemption order (see below) must also have completed the statutory period of qualifying service to claim from the National Insurance Fund, regardless of the scheme rules, although the period of continuous employment is computed in accordance with these rules rather than the statutory provisions (s 167(2) ERA 1996).

9050 The **type of payment** recoverable includes a statutory redundancy payment and also (s 166 ERA 1996):
– an amount payable under an ACAS-conciliated settlement or a compromise agreement (including an agreement to submit a dispute to arbitration under the ACAS scheme) in respect of a statutory redundancy payment; or
– a termination payment payable in accordance with a collective agreement covered by an exemption order (¶8993).

9051 The **amount of payment** recoverable is as follows:

Claim	Amount
Statutory redundancy payment	Calculated in normal way, with credit given for any amount actually paid by the employer (s 168(1)(a) ERA 1996)
Sum owing under ACAS-conciliated settlement or compromise agreement	Lesser of amount owing under agreement or amount of redundancy payment employer would otherwise have been liable to pay (s 168(1)(aa) ERA 1996)
Sum payable under exempt scheme	Lesser of amount due under scheme and "relevant redundancy payment" (see memo points) (s 168(2) ERA 1996)

MEMO POINTS Relevant redundancy payment is the statutory redundancy payment to which the employee would otherwise have been entitled, calculated according to the exempted scheme's computation of continuous employment and determination of the relevant date, where different from the statutory provisions.

9052 Where a tribunal has specified the amount of a redundancy payment owing to an employee (or made appropriate findings permitting the amount to be calculated), the employer may be liable to pay **interest** on that amount from 42 days after the tribunal's decision. The interest owing can also be claimed from the DTI (*Secretary of State for Employment v Reeves* [1993] ICR 508, EAT).

Debts

9053 The debts listed below may be recovered from the DTI if the employer is insolvent (see above), the employment has been terminated, and the employee was entitled to all or part of the debt on the appropriate date (s 182 ERA 1996).

Relevant debt (s 184(1), (2) ERA 1996)	Limit	Appropriate date
Arrears of pay [1]	8 weeks [2]	Date employer becomes insolvent (except protective awards – see below)
Accrued holiday pay [3]	6 weeks	
Protective award	8 weeks [2]	The latest of: – date employer becomes insolvent; – date employment terminates; and – date on which award made
Unfair dismissal basic award		
Statutory minimum notice	[4]	The later of: – date employer becomes insolvent; and – date employment terminates
Reimbursement of whole or part of any fee/premium paid by apprentice/articled clerk		

1. Pay includes commission, overtime, guarantee and time-off payments, protective awards (for failure to consult in collective redundancy situations), and medical and maternity suspension pay. These are assessed on the basis of salary net of tax and national insurance contributions (which are deducted after the statutory cap (see below) is applied) (*Morris v Secretary of State for Employment* [1985] IRLR 297, EAT; confirmed in *Titchener v Secretary of State for Trade & Industry* [2002] IRLR 195, EAT).
2. The employee can choose the 8 weeks for which he is owed most, where relevant (*Mann v Secretary of State for Employment* [1999] IRLR 566, HL).
3. This relates to the employee's entitlement in the 12 months ending with the appropriate date and is assessed by reference to net pay – see memo point 1.
4. If the employee was wrongfully dismissed, the amount recoverable in respect of statutory notice will reflect his duty to mitigate his loss (*Westwood v Secretary of State for Employment* [1984] IRLR 209, HL) and any state benefits received (which would not have been paid had he not been dismissed) (¶8160).

EXAMPLE **Appropriate date**
Employee A's employer becomes insolvent on 14 October 2002 when a receiver is appointed out of court as agent for the company. The receiver dismisses A with immediate effect on 18 October. A can apply to the DTI for **arrears of pay** and **accrued holiday pay** up to 14 October (not up to 18 October).

The total amount recoverable for any debt (except for fees/premiums paid by apprentices or articled clerks) is subject to a **statutory cap** of £280 per week or such amount as the Secretary of State may order (or pro rata for a period less than 1 week) (s 186 ERA 1996). If the **employee is owed more** than the statutory maximum, the rest of the debt will be considered as part of the employer's insolvency proceedings. 9054

The Secretary of State can deduct any amount which the employer would have been able to **off set** (for example, a debt owed by the employee to the employer) (*Secretary of State for Employment v Wilson and BCCI* [1996] IRLR 330, EAT). If the statutory cap is applicable, the Secretary of State is entitled to apply this to the sum and then deduct NICs and other appropriate amounts which the employer would have been able to off-set (*Titchener v Secretary of State for Trade & Industry* [2002] ICR 225, EAT). However, if the employee has a claim for arrears of pay in respect of periods before the reference period (in addition to arrears in the reference period), payments made by the employer during the reference period are set against the earlier claims rather than the arrears during the reference period (*Regeling v Bestuur van de Bedrijfsvereniging voor de Metaalnijverheid* [1999] IRLR 379, ECJ). 9055

Pension contributions

Contributions recoverable are those to be paid by the employer on his own behalf or on behalf of an employee from whose pay a deduction has been made for that purpose, where these remain due from the employer at the date of his insolvency (s 124(2) Pension Schemes Act 1993). 9056

The **maximum amount payable** depends on whether the contribution is an employer or employee contribution as follows: 9057

Type of contribution	Amount payable
Employer	The least of: – arrears of employer contributions accrued within the 12 months immediately preceding date of insolvency; – an amount equal to 10% of the total amount of remuneration [1] paid or payable to employees covered by the scheme in respect of the 12 months immediately preceding date of insolvency; and – (in relation to defined benefit schemes) the amount certified by an actuary as required to pay employees' benefits on dissolution of the scheme
Employee	The amount deducted from the employee's pay in respect of his contributions during the 12 months immediately preceding the date of insolvency [2]

1. Remuneration includes statutory sick and maternity pay, guarantee and time off payments, medical or maternity suspension payments, protective awards, and holiday pay.
2. If an employee recovers a payment in respect of arrears of pay from which his employee contribution would normally have been deducted, he should consider paying his contribution into the scheme in order to preserve his benefits.

9058 The Pensions Act 2004 has introduced **new provisions** to address pension rights on insolvency. In summary, where, in the case of an occupational pension scheme, an insolvency event has occurred (which includes, in relation to a company, the appointment of an administrative receiver or entering into administration (see ¶8277+)), the insolvency practitioner is obliged to give notice of this, and the status of the scheme, to the Board of the Pension Protection Fund, the Pensions Regulator and the trustees or managers of the scheme. Schemes eligible for pension protection are certain defined benefit pension occupational pension schemes and defined benefit elements of other schemes.

If the Board of the Pension Protection Fund assumes responsibility for eligible schemes, which it may do under a number of complex provisions in the Pensions Act 2004, compensation may then be payable to affected members of the scheme. The compensation may be payable on a periodic or lump sum basis and the amount will vary depending on the age of the member.

b. Application procedure

9065 The **employee** applies for payment by filling in an **application form** (RP1) (available from the administrator, receiver, liquidator or trustee) (RP2 for payments in respect of statutory minimum notice) and returning it to the Redundancy Payments Office of the DTI. An application for payment of pension contributions is made by the **administrator** of the pension scheme (in respect of the total amount due to the scheme).

9066 There are no express **time limits**. However, as the state guaranteed redundancy payment depends on the employer's liability to pay, the time limits for claiming a redundancy payment must normally be observed (¶9010). The employee may then apply to the DTI if the employer refuses to pay or is **insolvent**. The employee may make an **application to a tribunal** for a redundancy payment from the employer before applying to the DTI (if the employer is **not insolvent**, he may be required to do so as part of the obligation to take all reasonable steps to recover payment).

9067 In order to determine the claim for payment, the DTI can require the employer or other persons to provide the necessary **information and documents** (s 169 ERA 1996 (redundancy payments); s 190 ERA 1996 (debts); s 157 Pension Schemes Act 1993), and failure to comply without reasonable excuse is a summary offence punishable by a fine. A more serious offence is committed if the employer deliberately or recklessly provides false information.

9068 The Secretary of State can apply to a tribunal **contesting the employee's redundancy entitlement** or the amount claimed (or both) (s 170(1) ERA 1996), even if an earlier tribunal application resulted in an award being made to the employee (*Secretary of State for Employment v Banks* [1983] ICR 48, EAT). There is no time limit.

If an administrator, receiver, liquidator or trustee in bankruptcy is required by law to be appointed, the Secretary of State must delay making any payment in respect of relevant **debts** until he has obtained a **statement** from such person as to the **amount owing** to the employee (unless he is satisfied that he can determine the amount without a statement) (s 187 ERA 1996). Similar provisions apply in relation to **pension contributions** but note that the Secretary of State cannot dispense with the requirement of an actuary's certificate, where applicable (s 125 Pension Schemes Act 1993). 9069

Transfer of rights If the Secretary of State makes a payment to the employee, the employee's rights and remedies against his employer are transferred to the Secretary of State, who is therefore entitled to any **money subsequently recovered** from the employer (ss 167(3), (4), 189 ERA 1996). This also applies in relation to the rights of the administrator of the pension scheme in the insolvency proceedings (s 127(1) Pension Schemes Act 1993). 9070

Remedies

Complaints are made to an employment tribunal and the procedure will depend on the type of payment claimed. 9071

Redundancy payments The employee can apply to a tribunal if the Secretary of State **refuses his application** for a redundancy payment or **pays less** than the correct amount (the application can be made against the Secretary of State alone, or the employee can join the employer as a party (*Jones v Secretary of State for Employment* [1982] ICR 389, EAT)). There is no time limit. 9072

MEMO POINTS In (1) *Scanfuture UK Ltd (2) Link v Secretary of State for Trade and Industry* [2001] IRLR 416, EAT, the EAT found that employment tribunals, when hearing cases against the DTI, were **not independent and impartial** as required by the European Convention on Human Rights (incorporated by the Human Rights Act 1998), as they are paid for, largely appointed by, and administered by the Secretary of State. Subsequent amendments to procedures for appointment, payment and termination of lay members' contracts mean that the right to a fair trial is no longer breached.

Debts and pension contributions The applicant for payment can complain to an employment tribunal that the Secretary of State has **failed to make the payment** or has **paid less** than the correct amount (s 188 ERA 1996; s 126 Pension Schemes Act 1993). 9073

He must bring the claim **within** 3 months beginning with the date on which the Secretary of State's decision was communicated to him (or where not reasonably practicable, within such further period as the tribunal considers is reasonable).

If the **tribunal upholds the complaint**, it will make a declaration to that effect and state the amount due (it does not actually order payment).

2. Preferential creditor

An **employee**'s claim to remuneration is treated as a preferential debt and given precedence over other creditors' claims (s 386, Sch 6 Insolvency Act 1986). **Workers'** claims for payment do not rank as preferential debts. 9080

Remuneration is **limited to** the 4-month period immediately preceding the employer's insolvency and **includes** wages or salary (including commission), guarantee and time-off payments (to look for work or arrange training on redundancy, for antenatal care, for trade union duties etc.), protective awards for failure to consult on collective redundancy, medical and maternity suspension pay, sick pay and accrued holiday pay (Sch 6 paras 9-15 Insolvency Act 1986).

The employee's claim is subject to a **statutory cap** of £800, although this does not apply to accrued holiday pay (Sch 6 Insolvency Act 1986; Insolvency Proceedings (Monetary Limits) Order SI 1986/1966). Claims over the cap and claims other than for remuneration (contractual or statutory) will not rank as a preferential debt.

9081 If the employer's **assets cannot meet all claims** for remuneration, each claim ranks equally and is paid in equal proportions to the other claims.

3. Administrators

9085 An administrator can be **appointed by** the company, its directors, a qualifying floating charge holder or by court order (on application by the company, its directors or creditors) (paras 10, 14, 22 Sch B1 Insolvency Act 1986 as amended by Enterprise Act 2002). The administrator does not incur personal liability to pay sums due to employees. Instead, if the employment contract was adopted by the administrator, certain sums due to employees may have to be paid out as an expense of the administration at the cessation of an administrator's appointment. In such cases, liability for the payments falls on the company's property in the custody or control of the administrator and has priority to most other charges and securities, including the administrator's own remuneration and expenses (para 99 Sch B1 Insolvency Act 1986 as amended by Enterprise Act 2002).

The **sums due to employees** under the above provisions are:
- wages and salary (including holiday pay and sick pay); and
- contributions to an occupational pension scheme.

MEMO POINTS The Court of Appeal has confirmed that the expenses of an administration rank ahead of paying protective awards (¶8951 +) and payments in lieu of notice (¶8145 +) and that therefore protective awards and payments in lieu of notice (subject to a minor exception in relation to the latter) do not attract "super-priority" (*Krasner v McMath* [2005] EWCA Civ 1072).

Under old insolvency rules, holders of a floating charge pre-dating 15 September 2003 may be able to appoint an **administrative receiver**. A receiver (or, a receiver and manager) may also be appointed by the court as a way of enforcing certain other security over the company's assets. The provisions relating to payments by administrative receivers and receivers are similar to those of administrators, except that administrative receivers are personally liable for certain payments under the contracts (broadly, wages, salary and occupational pension contributions for the period after adoption of the contract during his appointment) and receivers are personally liable for payments during their appointment without any statutory limitation (s 44, 37 Insolvency Act 1986 respectively). The exact details are outside the scope of this book.

CHAPTER 26

Handling disputes and alternative resolution

OUTLINE ¶¶

9100 Where an employment dispute arises, it is usually in the interests of both employer and employee to resolve it without resorting to litigation if possible, although in some cases the aggrieved party (usually the employee) may want his day in court. Section 1 examines the identification of disputes, sources of advice, and the gathering of information and evidence. Section 2 discusses alternative methods of resolving disputes, including negotiation/conciliation and arbitration, and examines the documenting of agreed settlements. Litigation is discussed in the following chapter.

Although reference will be made throughout this section to litigation in employment tribunals, the same principles generally apply to litigation in the courts.

SECTION 1

Handling potential litigious disputes

9110 If litigation cannot be avoided, the parties should prepare themselves as thoroughly as possible in order effectively to bring or defend the case.

In any event, the following steps should be considered:
- identifying possible disputes at an early stage;
- taking appropriate advice;
- identifying the strengths and weaknesses of each side;
- gathering and preserving all relevant evidence (which will include physical evidence, documentary evidence and the evidence of witnesses);
- identifying and using opportunities to resolve the dispute by means other than litigation; and
- knowing the potential costs and other consequences involved in pursuing (and possibly losing) litigation.

A. Identifying potential disputes

9115 Complaints can more easily be resolved if they are identified before a tribunal claim is actually brought. The employer should, therefore, be alert to the possibility of a dispute situation arising and be aware of, and have a means of addressing, employee grievances.

Dispute situations

9116 A dispute may arise where the employer's actions will or may **change the employment relationship**, for example, where he is contemplating a dismissal, the introduction of a new shift system, alterations to commission schemes, adjustments to lunch hours, or the introduction of a dress code.

Changes to the law may give employees new rights which make current practices unlawful. For example, the introduction of the national minimum wage created potential disputes where employees continued to be paid below the minimum rate.

Disputes may also arise between the employer and non-employees, such as a discrimination claim from an unsuccessful candidate in relation to the **recruitment process**.

An employer may be liable for the actions of his employees (or even third parties), for example in connection with racial or sexual harassment (¶¶5227-31), and should therefore be alert to **disputes or friction between staff**.

Recognising and avoiding potential disputes

The factors set out below will be relevant. 9118

Knowledge of the law An **employer** needs to have at least a basic understanding of employment law, and the rights and obligations imposed by it, in order to identify potential disputes and to avoid or deal with them satisfactorily. Ignorance of the law is no defence to a claim. 9119

Although the ability to avoid a dispute is normally in the hands of the employer, an **employee** needs to know whether there is any legal basis for his complaint.

Policies and procedures The following written procedures will assist the proper handling of a potential dispute (both employer and any aggrieved employee should consult the relevant procedure): 9120
- a dismissal and/or disciplinary procedure;
- a grievance procedure;
- an equal opportunities procedure;
- a redundancy procedure; and
- staff rules of conduct.

MEMO POINTS **Statutory dispute resolution procedures** set out minimum standards which must be followed (¶6500).

The employer must ensure that any written procedures are effectively **implemented** and, indeed, it is compulsory for employers to implement the statutory dispute resolution procedures, if they are applicable (¶6510). To achieve this, **those who make decisions** affecting employees (e.g. line managers) must be made aware of the applicable procedures, and know and understand their responsibilities. 9122

Following a fair procedure is crucial to defending a claim of **unfair dismissal**, as the employer must have a fair reason for dismissal and follow a fair procedure. Proper implementation of any written procedures will make it easier to satisfy a tribunal that a fair procedure has been followed, and a **departure from the normal procedure** may result in an unfair dismissal unless it can be justified and was carefully considered. These issues are discussed further at ¶8435.

It may also be useful for both employer and employee to consult any **code of practice or guidance** which covers the particular situation issued by ACAS or another body (for example, ACAS' publication on discipline at work). 9123

B. Taking advice

Availability

Both employers and employees should consider taking legal advice in order to understand their rights and obligations. Advice becomes particularly important if the matter proceeds to litigation, and is available from a number of sources, including: 9130
- solicitors, citizens advice bureaux, and law centres;
- employers' associations;
- trade unions;
- ACAS; and
- employment consultants.

Some solicitors offer a **free initial interview** at which they will discuss the case, give an outline of what needs to be done and estimate the likely costs.

Tribunal staff will give assistance in respect of the procedural aspects of claims but cannot give legal advice in relation to the merits of the case.

ACAS advisers give objective and impartial advice to employers, employers' associations, workers and trade unions (s 213 TULRCA 1992), which may be given at the parties' request or at its own instigation.

9131 **Legal aid** is not available for pursuing employment tribunal claims in England and Wales (although publicly-funded representation may be available for representation at the EAT). It is, however, available in limited circumstances for claims to employment tribunals in Scotland.

Employees in England and Wales may be entitled to a limited form of aid known as **legal help**, which is subject to a means test and enables a solicitor to give advice and assistance (e.g. advising on the merits of a claim, writing letters and preparing the tribunal application). It may also cover the cost of mediation. These costs will be paid by the Legal Services Commission but if the employee subsequently recovers any damages, the costs payable under the legal help scheme will be deducted from the amount recovered.

MEMO POINTS Despite arguments that this may conflict with the right to a fair trial under the Human Rights Act 1998 (which succeeded in Scotland), there are currently no plans to extend legal aid to such claims in England and Wales. Legal aid is available in Scotland where the case is both arguable and too complex for the applicant to present the case himself to a minimum level of effectiveness, and the award of legal aid is reasonable in the circumstances of the case (Advice and Assistance (Advice By Way of Representation) (Scotland) Regulations SI 1997/3070).

Timing

9133 Once a potential dispute has been identified, appropriate advice should be taken at the earliest possible opportunity. If a **dismissal for misconduct**, for example, is being considered, advice should be taken before the disciplinary process begins or as soon as possible thereafter. If **redundancies** are thought necessary, advice should be taken immediately so that a proper consultation procedure can be devised and implemented. Further, it is likely to be more cost effective to take advice before taking action rather than seek legal advice once a dispute has arisen.

9134 Most employment claims must be presented within relatively short **time limits** (¶9452). If, therefore, an employee is seeking advice about a potential claim after the dismissal (or other act complained of) has taken place, or if an employer is seeking advice after a claim has been started by an employee, swift action is needed.

First appointment

9136 The adviser will need to see all **relevant documents** (it may be helpful to send them in advance). He will require all the relevant information so that he can identify both the **strengths and weaknesses** in order to give a proper assessment of the case and the likely consequences. If a weakness is identified at the outset, an appropriate strategy can be adopted to minimise its impact. If it only comes to light during the tribunal hearing it will be more difficult to deal with, and the tribunal may question the veracity of a party's evidence if it suspects that the party has withheld information from his own adviser.

C. Gathering information and evidence

9140 Relevant information should be gathered and retained, including:
- documentary evidence (e.g. correspondence, notes of meetings, contractual documents);
- physical evidence (e.g. property which has allegedly been damaged); and
- witness evidence.

All relevant documents (or at least copies of them) and other items should be **preserved** so that they can, if necessary, be produced to the tribunal. If the company automatically disposes of or shreds documents, or automatically deletes electronic data, this should be stopped until all relevant information has been retrieved.

Employees will also need to gather any relevant evidence in the same way. They may be able to use their rights under the Data Protection Act 1998 to gain **access to records** held by the employer in their personnel file.

The ability to produce relevant documents which support a party's case is also often crucial in conducting successful **negotiations**, as the outcome is inevitably influenced by the parties' views of the relative strengths and weaknesses of each side's case.

Any **letters written in relation to a dispute** should not be unduly emotional, abusive or aggressive, but should be clear, precise and businesslike. If some response or action is required, this should be clearly stated and, if appropriate, should include the time scale for compliance. Correspondence within the employer's organisation (for example, between line managers and the human resources department) may have to be disclosed at the tribunal stage, unless they are covered by "privilege" (discussed below). 9141

It may be appropriate to mark letters relating to a genuine attempt at settlement of a dispute "without prejudice" (¶9230).

1. Documents

A **separate file** should be opened to keep all documents relevant to the dispute in chronological order so that they can be easily produced either to an adviser or as part of the disclosure process during litigation (¶9545). **Indexing** these documents will make it less likely that a document is subsequently overlooked, and will save time and expense if it later becomes necessary to compile a full list of documents for disclosure. 9143

If the **original** of a document cannot be retained (for example, where a letter is sent out), then a **photocopy** (or a second print of a document produced by computer) should be retained. 9144

All documents (or copies) must be complete and legible. It may be necessary for a **typed transcript** of any **hand-written notes** to be prepared (retaining the original in case it is important to show the content of contemporaneous notes if, for example, there is a dispute about what was said at the time). 9145

Where it is important to show that a particular document has been seen or received, an **acknowledgement of receipt**, or other proof (for example, recorded delivery post) should, where possible, be obtained and retained with the document. 9146

The **date of receipt** of a document may be important. If the document arrived by post, the envelope showing the postmark should be retained. Alternatively, a date stamp or handwritten note on the document itself may be helpful. 9147

The documents set out below are normally **relevant** in employment disputes. 9148

Contract of employment This may be contained in a single document or encompass a number of documents, such as an offer letter and staff handbook. 9149

There may be a number of different contractual documents over a long period of employment with the same employer. The contract governing the employment at the time of the matter in dispute will be most relevant, but **previous contracts** may be helpful for comparison purposes. Where there has been a transfer of the business, the contract may be a document produced by a previous employer.

Any **amendments** to the contract (whether by way of individual letters to the employee or general notices to staff) should also be made available.

Evidence of receipt and/or acceptance of these documents will often also be important.

Personnel file This will contain most, if not all, of the relevant employment documentation. **Background information** which, although not directly relevant to the particular dispute, may be useful. For example, information about the employee's **past conduct** could form the 9150 basis of an argument that it is not just and equitable to award him any compensation, even though it played no part in the decision to dismiss him.

9151 **Dismissal and/or disciplinary procedure** This may be contained in the employment contract, the staff handbook, or a separate document, and will be most relevant in unfair dismissal cases. Any evidence that the employee is aware of the disciplinary procedure will be important (for example, an acknowledgement of receipt of the staff handbook containing the procedure).

MEMO POINTS For details as to what information regarding disciplinary rules and procedures should be included in an employee's **written statement of particulars**, see ¶6525.

9152 **Documents arising from disciplinary action** Any previous **written warnings** should be made available, together with evidence of receipt.

Written notes of any **oral warning** should also be retained in accordance with the disciplinary procedure, as well as copies of all **other documents** used in the disciplinary process, including any letter to the employee setting out the complaints against him, requiring him to attend a disciplinary meeting and advising him of his right to be accompanied, any statements or other documents considered at the disciplinary hearing, notes of the meeting, and a copy of the written confirmation of the outcome (including written notice of any rights of appeal).

9153 **Notes of meetings** It may be crucial to prove what was, or was not, said in particular meetings, so comprehensive and accurate notes of any relevant meeting should be kept. Ideally, meeting notes should:

a. be **made**:

– **contemporaneously**, preferably by someone whose sole purpose in attending is to take notes, otherwise by the person conducting the meeting (even if these are only rough notes to form the basis of a more detailed minute to be prepared afterwards). If the employee is accompanied at a disciplinary or grievance hearing, he may wish his companion to take notes on his behalf; or

– **immediately after** the meeting, recalling what was said in as much detail as possible;

b. **identify** who is present at the meeting, the date and the location. The start and finish times (and the timing of any breaks) should also be recorded, as the length of the meeting can give a better impression of the nature of that meeting. For example, a meeting appearing to have lasted only 5 minutes is unlikely to have included detailed discussion of an allegation of misconduct followed by serious consideration of the appropriate sanction;

c. **contain**:

– as far as possible, a **verbatim account** of what is said, identifying who said what; or

– a **detailed summary** of what was said by each party; and

d. **refer to** any documents or other items which were considered in the course of the meeting.

All participants in the meeting should be **provided with a copy** of the note and asked to acknowledge that they agree that it accurately reflects what was said in the meeting or to specify any points which they believe are inaccurate. A party who has been given this opportunity and not raised an objection will find it harder later to convince a tribunal that the note is inaccurate. Evidence that copies of the notes have been sent to the participants (for example, a copy of a covering letter) should be retained. Where there is to be an appeal from the decision of that meeting, the relevant meeting note should be made available prior to the appeal hearing.

If a **typed transcript** is prepared of any hand-written notes, each participant should be provided with a copy of the original notes and the transcript and should be asked to agree both.

9154 **Correspondence** The file relating to the dispute should contain:

– copies of all letters sent out;

– copies or originals of all letters received; and

– evidence of the date of despatch or receipt.

Evidence relating to remuneration This may be important with regard to: 9155
– liability (for example, where it is alleged that an employee has been **underpaid** in a breach of contract or unlawful deductions claim); or
– compensation in any type of claim.

The file should, therefore, contain copies of payslips, P45, P60 and P11D (particularly important if the employee's pay is variable because of, for example, overtime or shift allowances), and any documents relating to bonus schemes or commission arrangements (if not included in the contract itself).

Medical evidence In a case involving ill-health or disability, copies of sick notes, correspondence with the employee's GP and any medical reports should be included in the file of documents. The employer may also have attendance records or self-certification forms, which may also be necessary to prove absence. 9156

The employee would also be advised to keep copies of any such documents and may also wish to obtain a letter from his GP confirming his condition.

Evidence relating to mitigation If an **employer** wishes to claim that an employee has not fully mitigated his loss (i.e. taken steps to minimise it) in order to reduce any compensation payable (¶8620), he should compile a dossier containing copies of any job advertisements which the employee might reasonably be expected to pursue. There is no need to prove that the employee could have obtained any particular job. 9158

Conversely, an **employee** should retain copies of all applications, letters of rejection, and a note of any interviews or other efforts made to find alternative employment (for example, a diary noting his contacts with the local job centre or recruitment agencies). He should also be able to produce evidence of pay and other remuneration received from any employment which he has obtained since his dismissal.

Diaries Those involved in a potential dispute should make a note in a diary as and when any incident or discussion occurs. This will be helpful in later demonstrating to a tribunal that a party's version of events is correct. 9159

Handling documents

The tribunal or court normally prefers to see the document in its original form. If, therefore, the parties wish to make **annotations** on a document, this should be done on a copy. Similarly, if certain sections of a document need to be **blacked out** for reasons of confidentiality, a clean copy should be retained. 9162

2. Physical evidence

Physical evidence will be important where, for example, an employee is accused of damaging employer property. Items of physical evidence may include damaged equipment, computer records, tachograph records, stolen property, alcohol or drugs found in the employee's possession, or examples of deficient workmanship. Care should be taken to ensure that any such items (assuming they belong to the employer) are taken out of the employee's custody. 9165

If the damaged item can be **retained**, it should be placed somewhere secure. Steps should be taken to ensure that it is not interfered with prior to any tribunal hearing. 9166

If the item is too large, or if it needs to be repaired or cleaned, **photographs** should be taken as soon as possible after the incident/damage occurs or is discovered. The date and time at which the photographs are taken should be recorded. Where possible, the actual damage should be **inspected** by the person who is conducting the disciplinary process before any repairs or cleaning take place. A note should be made identifying who was present at the inspection, what was seen and the date and time it took place. If an employee is suspected of having caused the damage, a **joint inspection** may be appropriate.

If the dispute relates to **computer records** then a screen print, paper print-out or back-up copy of the relevant records should be made in order to record and demonstrate the problem.

3. Witness evidence

9170 **Statements taken when dealing with the dispute** As part of a proper disciplinary procedure, the employer should obtain written statements from all relevant witnesses. He should certainly do so once a potential litigious dispute is identified. There are **three types** of statement:
– statements taken for use as evidence in the disciplinary process;
– statements taken after the relevant event(s) in order to provide information in relation to it; and
– formal statements prepared for use at a tribunal hearing.

The statements prepared during a disciplinary process or as part of an information-gathering exercise may not necessarily be those which are used at the tribunal. The latter are likely to be prepared by the parties' legal advisers in a more formal format, taking into account any additional matters which come to light in the course of preparing for the hearing.

The **more informal statements** taken for the purposes of a disciplinary procedure or in the early stages of preparing for litigation (discussed below) may form the basis of any formal statements subsequently prepared. They will also be important as they will have been prepared during or shortly after the events in question before memories fade. They may also serve as a basis for challenging any different version of events put forward by any witness at a later stage.

Preparation

9172 Statements are **generally** prepared in **one of two ways**:
– the witness is asked to write down in as much detail as possible his recollection of the relevant events; or
– the party seeking the statement interviews the witness and writes out a statement on the basis of that interview.

Whichever method is adopted, the statement must, as far as possible, be in the witness' own words. An attempt to influence what is said or put a more helpful gloss on the evidence may result in harmful discrepancies if the witness is subsequently (during tribunal proceedings) cross-examined on his statement.

If the statement is not prepared by the witness himself, he should be encouraged to make any **corrections, additions, or deletions** so that the statement accurately reflects his own recollection.

To obtain a balanced assessment of the case, statements should ideally be taken from **everyone who has been involved** in, or has witnessed, the relevant events (and not only from those who are thought likely to be most helpful to that party's case).

Each witness should **prepare** his own statement **independently** where possible, rather than after having read the statements of other witnesses. Once all the statements have been gathered, **supplementary statements** can be sought from witnesses if points made in one statement cast doubt or cause confusion in relation to points made in another.

Evidence of a party's spouse or other closely connected person who is **not independent** is not worthless and should still be obtained. A tribunal will take into account the lack of independence when assessing their credibility.

If a professional adviser is engaged, the task of interviewing witnesses and preparing statements is likely to be taken on by him.

Content

Witnesses should give a full and frank account of their recollection of events, including anything which is detrimental to a party's case, as it is better to identify any weaknesses at the outset (rather than in the course of the hearing). Statements should be confined to **relevant facts** so far as possible, and should not contain legal argument. 9174

Witnesses should make clear in their statements what they actually saw or are aware of from their own **direct knowledge**, and what they are recounting on the basis of having been told by someone else, and whether something they say is merely their **opinion or speculation**, as opposed to a statement of fact.

If a witness' evidence relies on a document, it is sufficient to **refer to the document** and, if necessary, to a particular paragraph or section (rather than recite its entire contents).

Nicknames and abbreviations should not normally be used. Where a person is referred to, that person's position in the business should be identified where appropriate. If a term is used which is **technical** or has a **specific meaning** within a particular business, an explanation should be given. If **locations** are being described, a photograph or a plan showing the layout could be attached.

If a witness cannot recall exact dates or times, an **approximation** should be given (but it should be made clear that it is an approximation). Similarly, if there is anything that the witness cannot remember with certainty, he should make this clear.

Format

It is desirable for witness statements to: 9176
- be **typed** (where relevant, the original hand-written version should be retained);
- be divided into **numbered paragraphs**;
- start with a brief **introduction** explaining who the witness is and what his involvement is;
- deal with events in **chronological** order; and
- be **signed and dated** by the witness (after having read through it) to show that he agrees with its contents.

Use at tribunal

The witness should be advised that his statement may later form the **basis of his evidence** at a tribunal hearing under oath. If this is likely, each witness should be asked to confirm in writing whether he is prepared to attend a tribunal hearing to give evidence if required. This will indicate whether or not **witness orders** will be needed (¶9553). 9178

4. Disclosure and privilege

The parties may be ordered by the tribunal to disclose **relevant documents** (irrelevant documents do not need to be disclosed) (¶9545). Those involved in a potential dispute should be made aware that documents they create may have to be disclosed in this way, unless they are protected from disclosure by a legal rule called "privilege". This applies to correspondence between a party and his legal advisers and other documents (e.g. early drafts of witness statements) prepared for the purpose of litigation. Privilege is discussed further at ¶9551. 9185

When a party is preparing his file of documents in readiness for litigation, it is important to distinguish between evidential documents (including final drafts of witness statements) and any earlier draft statements or other documents which are not intended for disclosure (including statements of any witnesses whom the party does not intend to call). Preferably these should be kept in a separate file or otherwise marked in order to prevent inadvertent disclosure.

SECTION 2

Resolving employment disputes

9200 If the parties have not already attempted to resolve their dispute, they should consider the prospect of settlement once proceedings are commenced or threatened and before the matter comes to a hearing. The likelihood of settlement will depend on the relative strengths and weaknesses of the opposing cases, the reasonableness of the parties involved, the demands and expectations of the claimant and the ability (and willingness) of the other party to meet those demands.

Statutory dispute resolution procedures set out the minimum steps which must be followed before a dismissal or other disciplinary action can be taken and how the parties should deal with any grievance an employee may have against the employer (including in relation to any dismissal or disciplinary action which has been taken against him). Failure to follow the minimum steps will impact on the admissibility of any subsequent claim and any compensation which may potentially be awarded. See ¶6500 for further details.

9201 The Advisory Conciliation and Arbitration Service (**ACAS**) often plays a significant role in the resolution of employment disputes. It is a statutory body set up to provide advisory, conciliation and arbitration services, with a general duty to promote the improvement of industrial relations. It intervenes both in individual employment disputes (discussed below) and in wider trade disputes.

Certain claims which are accepted by the tribunal are subject to a statutory **fixed period of conciliation** during which period ACAS is under a duty to conciliate between the parties. Certain types of claim are exempt from the fixed period of conciliation. The **standard period** for conciliation is 13 weeks, although a **short period** for conciliation of 7 weeks applies in certain cases. After the **expiry** of the fixed conciliation period, ACAS will only intervene to conciliate at its own discretion. For a detailed discussion on fixed conciliation periods, see ¶9219.

9202 Whether or not the services of ACAS are available, the parties should consider conducting their own negotiations, either directly or through professional advisers such as solicitors, with a view to arriving at an **agreed settlement**, which should be **documented** in a compromise or settlement agreement as appropriate.

9203 In order to avoid pressure being put on employees to sign away their rights, there is a **general prohibition on contracting out of statutory rights** such that any provision in an agreement is void in so far as it purports to exclude or limit the operation of those rights or prevents an employee from bringing or continuing a claim under them (s 203(3) ERA 1996). For example, any attempt to exclude the right to bring a claim of unfair dismissal will be, on the face of it, void.

There are three main **exceptions**:
– where an agreement is made with the involvement of an ACAS conciliation officer under the statutory conciliation procedures (¶9305);
– where a valid compromise agreement has been reached (¶9333); and
– where ACAS has referred the dispute to arbitration (¶9360).

9204 If the parties cannot agree a settlement, the matter may be referred to **arbitration** (in cases of unfair dismissal claims), or may come before an employment tribunal or court. Litigation is discussed in Chapter 27.

I. Settlement through negotiation/conciliation

A. Assessing the merits of settlement

Before entering into negotiations, each party should **assess**: 9210
- his chances of winning the case if it were to go before a tribunal or court;
- the level of compensation (or other remedies) available to the successful party;
- the amount of time and effort that will need to be devoted to bringing or defending the case (particularly for the employer);
- the legal and other costs involved, including the likelihood of the successful party recovering his costs from the unsuccessful party;
- what sort of adverse publicity the case may generate; and
- what the other party actually wants from the proceedings.

Initially, each party will only be able to form a provisional view on the above matters, with each factor being **reassessed** in the light of further information obtained during a negotiation process. For example, the employee may have evidence of which the employer was unaware, legal arguments which he had not considered, or may be more interested in obtaining an apology or a reference than compensation. If relevant, the employer should also find out whether the employee has found another job, which will affect any estimate of compensation.

Even if the **employer** believes, or is advised, that he has a **strong case**, it may still be commercially sensible for him to make a **token offer** in order to avoid incurring significant **legal costs** (not usually recoverable from the employee (¶9705)), and wasting **management time and resources** in preparing for and possibly attending a tribunal hearing. Dealing with tribunal claims can also be **stressful** for those involved and result in **adverse publicity**, even if the case is ultimately won. 9211

Where the **employer** has a **weak case** (or it is not clear who is likely to succeed), a more **substantial offer** may be required to settle the matter without the need for a hearing. 9212

Similar factors are relevant when an **employee** is deciding whether or not to accept an offer of settlement, although he may, as a **matter of principle**, have a greater interest in proceeding to a tribunal hearing to have his day in court. The employer may also, however, be unwilling to settle where the case against him has no merit, and may prefer to continue to defend it regardless of the cost. 9213

B. The negotiation/conciliation process

The settlement process should be **started** at the earliest possible opportunity in order to maximise the potential costs savings. The process **may continue** until all matters (i.e. both liability and remedy) are decided by the tribunal. If properly handled, the negotiation process should not prejudice either party's case in the event that it is not possible to reach a settlement. 9215

The parties are often unwilling to make the **first move** in commencing negotiations because they fear that it will prejudice their case and/or that it will be seen as a sign of weakness. Where **ACAS** is involved, this fear is often reduced as ACAS takes the initiative by contacting each party.

The **format** for the conciliation procedure will depend largely on the particular conciliation officer involved and the attitudes of the parties. In most cases, the conciliation officer consults with both parties by telephone and passes their respective views back and forth in the hope of achieving some common ground. This often assists in identifying those facts which are agreed and those which are in dispute, highlighting the perceived strengths and weaknesses of each case and identifying each party's estimate of any possible compensation. In some cases, meetings may be arranged with the parties either jointly or separately.

When discussing a case with the conciliation officer, a party may give certain information to him so that he has a complete picture of the case but may prefer not to have that information communicated to the other party. Parties should take care to ensure that the conciliation officer is aware of which information he can pass on and which he cannot.

1. Involvement of ACAS conciliation officers

9218 ACAS appoints officers to intervene in the conciliation of disputes, with the **aim** of assisting their resolution without the need for a tribunal hearing (s 211 TULRCA 1992). A conciliation officer may be an ACAS employee or an independent external appointee (the latter might be more appropriate if, for example, specialist knowledge of a particular industry is required) (s 210(2) TULRCA 1992).

The conciliation officer's **role** is to impartially and objectively promote a settlement of the dispute without the need for a tribunal hearing. He will not put forward a particular settlement or attempt to decide the merits of a case. He has no duty to advise either party on the effect of relevant legislation. Further, where a financial settlement is reached, he is not obliged to ensure that such an agreement is fair to both parties (*Moore v Duport Furniture Products Limited* [1982] IRLR 31, HL).

If he acts partially or adopts unfair methods, any agreement reached may be set aside (*Slack v Greenham* [1983] IRLR 271, EAT).

The conciliation officer is required, where appropriate, to encourage the **use of other procedures** available for the settlement of grievances (for example, the employer's internal grievance or appeal procedures, if these have not already been used (s 18(6) Employment Tribunals Act 1996)).

In **unfair dismissal** cases, the conciliation officer's priority is to try to promote the reinstatement or re-engagement of the complainant. If this is not possible, he will seek to promote settlement by way of compensation (s 18(4), (5) Employment Tribunals Act 1996).

MEMO POINTS Note that an employee is obliged to raise his grievance in writing under the **statutory grievance procedure** before his claim can be accepted by the tribunal (¶9513).

9219 Save for certain types of claim which have **no fixed conciliation period** (¶9223), all proceedings which are brought before a tribunal under any legislation which provides for conciliation will be subject to a statutory **fixed period of conciliation** during which ACAS has a duty to assist the parties to reach a settlement if possible. During this time, a full hearing cannot take place (although a case management discussion and/or pre-hearing review can be held (rule 22(3) Sch 1 SI 2004/1861)).

The conciliation period **starts** on the date on which the Secretary of the Employment Tribunal Office sends a copy of the claim to the respondent (if there is more than one respondent, there will be a conciliation period in relation to each respondent).

If, during proceedings, an order is made to stay (or in Scotland, sist) proceedings, any fixed period of conciliation will be **suspended**. If proceedings are subsequently re-started, the conciliation period will resume for the greater of the unexpired portion of that period or 2 weeks (rule 24 Sch 1 SI 2004/1861).

The conciliation period **ends** at the expiry of the 13 or 7 week period (depending on whether a standard or short conciliation period applies) unless it has been extended in limited circumstances. After the expiry of the fixed period, ACAS will only remain involved in a conciliation exercise in exceptional circumstances.

Either the short or the standard conciliation period will **end early** in relation to a particular respondent if (rule 23(1) Sch 1 SI 2004/1861):
– the claimant withdraws the claim;
– the claim is struck out or a default judgment is given in an uncontested case;

– the claimant and/or the respondent has notified ACAS in writing that he is unwilling to cooperate with the conciliation process and there is therefore no realistic prospect of a successful conciliation; or
– the parties have reached a settlement either through ACAS or through a separately negotiated compromise agreement, provided the agreement satisfied the conditions for a valid compromise agreement (¶9333).

Where a respondent's right to respond to a claim has been re-established (for example, following revocation of a default judgment), a **further fixed conciliation period** may be ordered by the tribunal and any previous conciliation period will be deemed not to count towards the further period of conciliation (rule 23(2), (3) Sch 1 SI 2004/1861).

Short conciliation period For more straightforward claims, there will be a short conciliation period of 7 weeks, although this period can be **extended** to the standard conciliation period (¶9221) if the Chairman considers that the complexity of the claim requires a longer period of conciliation. The **following claims** are subject to a short conciliation period (rule 22(5) Sch 1 SI 2004/1861 as amended by SI 2005/1865): 9220
– breach of contract claims which are the subject of tribunal proceedings (¶9425);
– claims in respect of failure to pay wages or unauthorised deduction of wages;
– guarantee payment claims;
– statutory annual leave claims;
– time off for public duties claims;
– time off and remuneration to look for work or arrange training claims;
– time off and remuneration for antenatal care claims;
– claims in respect of failure to pay remuneration during suspension for medical reasons;
– claims regarding remuneration whilst suspended on maternity grounds;
– redundancy payment claims;
– claims regarding the right not to suffer deduction of unauthorised union subscriptions;
– time off and remuneration for carrying out trade union duties claims;
– time off for trade union activities claims;
– protective award payment claims; and
– claims regarding failure to pay compensation following failure to inform and consult under the TUPE regulations.

MEMO POINTS If the claimant's claim involves an element of **discrimination** or **equal pay**, or a claim under the **whistleblowing** legislation, there will be no fixed conciliation period (¶9223).

Standard conciliation period In all other statutory claims, where there is a provision for conciliation in the legislation, there will be a standard conciliation period of 13 weeks (rule 22(6) Sch 1 SI 2004/1861). This can be **extended** by a further 2 weeks if, before the expiry of 13 weeks, ACAS notifies the Secretary in writing that all the parties agree to the extension, a proposal for settlement has been made by a party and is under consideration by the other party and if ACAS considers it probable that a settlement will be reached during the extended conciliation period (rule 22(7) Sch 1 SI 2004/1861). 9221

Currently, the conciliation officer can act in respect of the **following claims** which are the subject of tribunal proceedings (s 18 Employment Tribunals Act 1996):
– unfair dismissal claims;
– protection from suffering detriment claims (except whistleblowing legislation ¶9223);
– claims under the national minimum wage legislation;
– claims for contravention of the Part-time Workers (Prevention of Less Favourable Treatment) Regulations 2000;
– claims under the Fixed-term (Prevention of Less Favourable Treatment) Regulations 2002;
– redundancy claims;
– itemised pay statement claims;
– claims relating to written reasons for dismissal;
– parental leave claims;
– claims under the right to request flexible working;
– claims under the working time regulations (except for statutory annual leave claims);

– time off to care for dependants claims;
– time off for pension scheme trustees claims;
– time off for employee representative claims;
– time off for young persons for study or training claims;
– various other claims under the TULRCA 1992;
– claims under the Transnational Information and Consultation of Employees Regulations 1999; and
– claims under the Information and Consultation of Employees Regulations 2004.

MEMO POINTS If the claimant's claim involves an element of **discrimination** or **equal pay**, or a claim under the **whistleblowing** legislation, there will be no fixed conciliation period (¶9223).

9223 **No fixed conciliation period** There will be no fixed conciliation period in respect of claims for equal pay or discrimination on the grounds of sex, race, disability, sexual orientation, or religion or belief, or claims that a worker has suffered a detriment for having made a protected disclosure under the whistleblowing legislation or that an employee has been dismissed or selected for redundancy for having made such a disclosure (rule 22(1) Sch 1 SI 2004/1861).

In respect of these claims, the conciliation officer has an ongoing duty to conciliate until the case is disposed of and **will become involved** if he is requested to do so by one of the parties, which can be before tribunal proceedings are actually issued if he is informed of a complaint which could form the basis of such proceedings. Otherwise, he can volunteer to intervene if he considers that he could do so with a reasonable prospect of success (s 18(2) Employment Tribunals Act 1996). Whenever proceedings are commenced in a case to which conciliation applies, the Secretary of the Employment Tribunal sends copies of all relevant documents to a conciliation officer, who then contacts the parties to advise them of the availability of conciliation. If the parties wish to try to resolve the matter by means of an ACAS agreement, they will need to involve a conciliation officer at a relatively early stage, as ACAS will not simply rubberstamp agreements where it has not been involved in the negotiation process.

MEMO POINTS If the Secretary fails to send copies of relevant documents to a conciliation officer, this does not affect the validity of any subsequent proceedings.

2. Admissions of liability

9227 In some cases, where the employer's liability is obvious, he may **admit liability** so that the parties can move on to **discuss compensation**. In most cases, however, liability is **contested**, but the negotiations may, nonetheless, be successfully concluded without any admission by the employer. This may be acceptable to the employee if he is satisfied with the terms of the settlement, although sometimes it is important to him to prove that the employer was in the wrong (or get the employer to acknowledge that).

3. Without prejudice negotiations

9230 "Without prejudice" means that if discussions take place with a view to **trying to agree a settlement** but this is not achieved, the contents of those **discussions** (and even the fact that they have taken place) **cannot be disclosed to the tribunal** and a party will not be prejudiced by any offer made in the process. Although the tribunal is aware that, in most cases, some discussion takes place, it will not be influenced by that fact when deciding whether or not a party is liable.

EXAMPLE In the course of negotiations, an employer offers £10,000 in settlement. The employee seeks £14,000 and it is not possible to reach agreement. A tribunal finds the employer liable and awards the employee £8,000. The employee cannot argue that the employer should be ordered to pay at least £10,000 because he had previously offered that sum. The offer cannot be disclosed to the tribunal and if for any reason it is disclosed, the tribunal must disregard it.

If a tribunal is satisfied that the **purpose of the discussions** was to explore settlement, it will generally be prepared to regard them as without prejudice even if they have **not** been **expressly described** as such. However, it is sensible to specify that discussions or offers are "without prejudice" to avoid unnecessary arguments. On the other hand, the **mere use of the words** will not automatically result in protection from disclosure if the discussions do not relate to a genuine attempt to settle a dispute and if the parties are not on an equal footing (*BNP Paribas v Mezzotero* [2004] IRLR 508, EAT). Further, the EAT held that **discriminatory remarks** will never be protected. Consequently, it is recommended that employers ensure that they: 9231

– are attempting to resolve an existing dispute before embarking on any "without prejudice" discussions;
– give advance notice that the meeting is proposed to be "without prejudice" where possible and before starting any such discussion that they explain what it means and find out if the employee wishes to accept or decline the chance to have such a discussion;
– clearly state what dispute the discussions are aimed at settling and that the discussions are an alternative to dealing with this issue in the usual way, again emphasising that the employee is not forced to take part. In particular, it should be highlighted that whatever is proposed is an option to be considered rather than a stark choice between acceptance or dismissal;
– adjourn the meeting after any proposal has been made to allow the employee to consider the contents of the proposal before making a decision;
– put the proposal in writing where appropriate; and
– take extra care that nothing is said which will either undermine the duty of trust and confidence (¶1245) or is discriminatory.

EXAMPLE In *BNP Paribas v Mezzotero* [2004] IRLR 508, EAT, M, after raising a grievance with her employer about her treatment on return from maternity leave, was called to a meeting at which she was told after it had begun that it was on a "without prejudice" basis and that her job was no longer viable and a "redundancy" package was proposed. M was told that this was independent of her grievance which was still being investigated. The EAT held that M could use the contents of this meeting as evidence of further discrimination in her claim of sex discrimination because it was not a genuine attempt to settle M's complaint (although M had wanted changes to her job, she had wanted for her employment to continue). It further held that M had been in a vulnerable and unequal position, having only been informed that the meeting was "without prejudice" once it had started. Finally, the EAT held that discriminatory remarks will never be protected by the "without prejudice" rule.

An offer should clearly indicate whether it includes an **admission of liability**, as if a party appears to admit liability without any qualification, he may be held to that admission and only the remainder of the discussion (relating to remedies) will be regarded as without prejudice. If a party does not intend to be held to an admission of liability, he should state that such admission is made only for the purposes of negotiation and that he reserves the right to **dispute liability** if negotiations fail and the matter proceeds to a hearing. 9232

The protection afforded to "without prejudice" negotiations is largely removed **once agreement is reached**. If one party, having accepted a settlement offer without qualification then tries to get out of that agreement (whether ACAS has been involved or not), evidence can be put before the court or tribunal to prove the **existence of a settlement agreement** settling the proceedings. 9233

All **negotiations conducted through ACAS** are without prejudice and confidential. Therefore, any information communicated to a conciliation officer by a party to a case, is not admissible in evidence before a tribunal except with the consent of that party, even if it is the only evidence in relation to a certain matter (s 18(7) Employment Tribunals Act 1996). Evidence which exists separately from any communication to a conciliation officer can be put before the tribunal if it would otherwise be admissible (for example, a document provided to a conciliation officer which was already available to both parties). 9234

C. Settlement proposals and terms

Scope

9240 It is recommended that settlement proposals are set out in writing to avoid confusion and misunderstanding as to the scope of any proposed settlement. For example, when discussing compensation for unfair dismissal, the parties should **clarify** whether **any figures** mentioned include the basic award or are in addition to it. If **more than one claim** is being made, it should be made clear whether any offer is intended to settle both claims or just one of them.

9241 **A dismissal in connection with the transfer of an undertaking** to which the business transfer regulations apply (¶8030) gives rise to a potential litigious dispute. It is, therefore, advisable for the employer to obtain a waiver of the employee's right to bring a claim for unfair dismissal. In these cases it is not always clear **who should be a party** to the agreement. If the dismissal takes effect prior to the transfer date, the **transferor employer** should be a party to the agreement. In this case, his rights under the agreement would, in theory, pass to the **transferee employer**, if the employee were successful in claiming that his employment had transferred to the transferee under those regulations. However, to ensure that he can rely on it, a transferee employer would also be advised to be a party to the agreement. If the agreement is held to be void for not meeting the prescribed requirements (¶9333), the employee may be able to bring an unfair dismissal claim against the transferee (*Thompson v (1) Walon Car Delivery and (2) BRS Automotive Ltd* [1997] IRLR 343, EAT).

EXAMPLE In *Thompson v (1) Walon Car Delivery and (2) BRS Automotive Ltd*, BRS' business was to transfer to Walon under the transfer regulations. Walon did not want to take on T and other BRS staff, and so BRS intended to dismiss them, asking them to enter into compromise agreements. The agreements were not signed prior to the transfer date, and liability for the employees' dismissals transferred to Walon. The agreements were signed after the transfer date but as Walon was not a party, T could bring an unfair dismissal claim against it.

9242 A party should ensure that all the **terms** which he requires are included in the package **before agreement is reached**. For example, the employer might want the employee to agree to keep the terms of the settlement and the circumstances leading to his dismissal confidential. If the employee has already agreed to withdraw his claim in return for payment of a sum of money, he may be unwilling to accept a new confidentiality provision. Similarly, if the employee subsequently requests a reference as part of the settlement, the employer may refuse.

9243 While the terms of the settlement are still subject to negotiation, it is advisable to head any draft agreements "**subject to contract**" to indicate that final agreement has not yet been reached. Once it has (and prior to the execution of the agreement), the heading (and any "without prejudice" label (¶9233)) should be removed.

9244 Unless a party has been deliberately misled by the other party, he will not usually be able to **withdraw from an agreement** simply because he has become aware of some matter which would have caused him not to make the agreement had he known about it at the time.

9245 Reference should be made to the **model compromise and settlement agreement** provided at Appendix ¶9930. Whilst sample clauses are included below, it is advisable to review the model agreement in its entirety before adopting any of its provisions. It is intended to be **used as a starting point** and **should be tailored** according to the employer's requirements, proposed negotiation tactics and the circumstances of the compromise.

In addition to meeting the statutorily prescribed conditions for compromise agreements (¶9333), a settlement agreement may contain the terms discussed below, depending on the circumstances.

Agreed termination

A settlement commonly involves an agreed termination of the employment. It is advisable for this not to be described as a **resignation**, as the employer may not be able to make a bona fide damages payment for breach of contract in these circumstances, which could particularly be a problem with regard to the dismissal of a director. 9247

This may also have **adverse tax implications**, in that the payment may not fall within the favourable treatment applied to genuine compensation payments for loss of office/position (¶3125). Note that case law indicates that any payment made in connection with a consensual termination will not benefit from favourable tax treatment but will be taxed in full as an emolument from employment (*Richardson (HM Inspector of Taxes) v Delaney* [2001] IRLR 663, ChD). To fall within the favourable tax treatment, the employer would have to terminate before terms are agreed or offer settlement on a non-negotiable basis. If the parties attempt to agree terms informally prior to termination and subsequently document those terms in an agreement, Revenue and Customs may nevertheless argue that the termination was in fact by mutual agreement.

If the settlement is agreed before the termination actually takes effect, Revenue and Customs may attempt to argue that the settlement is a variation of the employment contract, with the result that payments made under the varied contract are fully taxable as earnings (¶3125). 9248

Consideration

As for any legally binding agreement, a settlement or compromise agreement must be supported by consideration. This is usually the payment of money to the employee in return for his waiver of rights (see Appendix ¶9930). 9250

Settlement payment The starting point for any settlement proposal is normally a **calculation of the likely award** which would be made to the employee if he succeeded at the tribunal. This notional figure could be reduced if it is thought likely that the tribunal would make **reductions** for factors such as mitigation, contributory fault or the likelihood of dismissal having occurred in any event. The employer would then argue that this figure should be further reduced to reflect what is known as "**litigation risk**". In other words, if, for example, the likely award to an employee if he is successful is £10,000 (after appropriate reductions), but the employer's view is that the employee has only a 60% chance of winning the case, then he may consider an offer of £6,000 to be appropriate. 9251

When considering an offer, an **employee** should take into account: 9252
- his chances of success and the likely award;
- the possibility of reductions (for example, for contributory fault);
- his chances of finding alternative employment; and
- the costs which he will save by accepting an offer.

An employee who is confident of obtaining £9,000 at the tribunal may think it prudent to accept an offer of £8,000 if it is likely to cost him £1,500 to get to the tribunal.

The employer could propose that the **payments are staggered**, for example, to take account of the fact that the employee may quickly find new employment (thus reducing his potential loss). In such cases, the agreement could provide that payments will cease if the employee starts a new job. The employee could be asked to give an undertaking, when entering the settlement agreement, that he has not yet started or obtained new employment (see clause 20 of the Appendix at ¶9930). 9253

If there is **no formal compromise of statutory claims**, an employer may consider staggering payment of the settlement monies, with the final payment being made, for example, 4 months after the termination date, on condition that no tribunal claim has been brought. The period reflects the time within which the majority of tribunal claims must be brought (although the tribunal does have discretion to extend these time limits). This wording may provide the employee with a financial incentive, but without a valid compromise agreement, it would not prevent him from bringing statutory claims against the employer. It is therefore a risky approach and not advisable.

9254 If the employee participates in an **approved retirement benefit scheme**, it may be possible for all or part of the termination payment to be made into the scheme, with advantageous tax treatment (¶3127). A further option would be for the employer to purchase an approved annuity for the employee.

9255 The **timing** of the termination payment (i.e. whether it is made before or after the termination of employment and delivery of the P45) will be relevant to its tax treatment.

9257 **Other forms of employer consideration** See sample wording set out below. These include allowing the employee to **keep his company car**. In this case, the employer should check the terms of the leasing and insurance arrangements to ensure that this would be permitted. The employer could offer to continue the employee's **health insurance** cover, again checking that the policy allows this.

> EXAMPLE The Company will [transfer ownership in the Employee's company car to him] [allow the Employee to continue to use his company car until [*date*]] [continue to provide the Employee with [permanent health insurance, life assurance and accident insurance] until [*date*] or until he obtains alternative employment, whichever is the earlier, subject to the terms of those schemes from time to time in force].

9258 An employee may be prepared to accept a lower sum in compensation in return for the employer agreeing to a settlement which also includes items which the tribunal could not include in any order, such as a **reference**, which is discussed below.

Some employees attach great importance simply to obtaining an **acknowledgement from the employer** that his actions were wrong.

9259 **Employee's waiver of rights** It is important to ensure that the agreement specifies **all possible claims** which the parties wish to settle. Although it is common to use words such as "in full and final settlement of all claims arising from the employee's employment or its termination", such words will be construed as being limited to matters within the presumed contemplation of the parties at the time, and will not extend to any possible claims outside of this (*Livingstone v Hepworth Refractories plc* [1992] IRLR 63, EAT; *Bank of Credit and Commerce International SA v Ali* [2001] IRLR 292, HL). The waiver should, therefore, be **carefully drafted** to specify all actual claims to be waived, together with any potential claims (however remote), so that it is clear that such claims are contemplated at the time of the agreement.

> EXAMPLE In *Bank of Credit and Commerce International SA v Ali*, the employee had signed a compromise agreement which was stated to be "in full and final settlement of all or any claims whether under statute, common law or in equity of whatsoever nature that exist or may exist". Some time later, the employees sought to claim "stigma" damages arising out of the fact that the way in which BCCI had been conducting its business had made it more difficult for them to find employment because of their previous association with it. Such a claim was not recognised at the time the compromise agreement was signed (it only became subsequently recognised as a claim by the House of Lords some 8 years later). Consequently, despite the very wide wording of the compromise agreement, the House of Lords in this case held that it could not be construed as covering claims which neither the employer or employee could have had in mind when signing the agreement. The House of Lords did suggest however that it would be possible, by using suitably specific wording, to exclude such claims if that was what was intended.

9260 Waivers of any **future rights** may be unenforceable as a matter of public policy and/or because the parties were unaware of such rights at the time of the agreement. If a waiver of future rights is included, it is advisable for further wording to state that the waiver does not extend to any claim or other right of action which would render it void or unenforceable.

> EXAMPLE Employee A, enters into a settlement agreement with his employer, a car manufacturer, waiving his future rights against the employer. Some years later, A buys a car made by the former employer which, due to defect, causes A to have an accident in which he suffers severe injuries. A court deciding A's claim against his former employer is likely to refuse to uphold the waiver on grounds of public policy.

It is common specifically to exclude any claims for **personal injury** or **accrued pension rights** from any general words of settlement. 9261

If the employer is part of a **group of companies**, it may be appropriate to extend the employee's waiver (and other undertakings) to cover other group companies (see sample clauses below). 9262

EXAMPLE 25. Any Group Company or any officer or employee of the Company may enforce the terms of [this Agreement] subject to and in accordance with the provisions of the Contracts (Rights of Third Parties) Act 1999.
26. In this Agreement "Group Company" includes the Company and all of its holding, subsidiary, or associated companies (as defined in section 736 of the Companies Act 1985).

Tax issues

These are often important in the context of agreed settlements. The tax treatment of termination payments is discussed at ¶3125. It is possible to **allocate separate consideration** to the various elements of the settlement. In addition to showing that there has been valid consideration for the employee's waiver of statutory or contractual claims (as the case may be), the tax treatment may differ (¶3132). 9265

If there is any doubt as to whether tax should be deducted from the settlement payment, advance clearance could be sought from Revenue and Customs. If there is insufficient time to seek clearance, the employer could consider seeking a tax indemnity (see sample clause below) from the employee so that he can recover from the employee any tax found to be payable if all or part of the payment is paid gross. However, the indemnity is only of benefit to the employer if the employee has the financial means to meet it. 9266

EXAMPLE 7. The Company gives no warranty as to whether income tax or employee National Insurance Contributions are payable in respect of any payments made to the Employee under this Agreement and the Employee is responsible for the payment of any tax and any liability to employee national insurance arising in respect of any payment set out in this Agreement. The Employee will indemnify the Company and each and every Group Company and keep it and them indemnified on a continuing basis against any liability to such taxation or national insurance.

Benefits

The termination may have an impact on benefits provided to the employee and his contract or relevant scheme rules, such as pension, share scheme, bonus, should be checked for this. The settlement agreement should cover what will happen to any such benefits on termination. Share scheme rules, for example, may provide for the employee's **share options** to be exercisable within a certain period of the termination date, or to lapse on termination, subject to the directors' discretion. In the latter case, the employer is in a strong negotiating position. As part of the settlement, the employee may agree not to exercise his options, and to waive any rights which he may have in respect of the scheme. This **waiver** may not be covered by the employee's general waiver and should be dealt with **separately**. 9268

References

The provision of a reference is likely to be of some value to the employee as he may encounter great difficulty in securing alternative employment without one. The settlement terms may, therefore, include an **agreed form of reference**, which will either be given to the employee to submit to future prospective employers or which the former employer agrees will be supplied in response to any requests for a reference. The wording should be consistent with any reason for the termination given in the settlement agreement and any reports to regulatory bodies. For further information on the provision of references generally, see ¶8320. 9270

Return of company property

9272 As part of the settlement, the employer may have agreed that the employee can retain certain property until the termination date, or may have given such property to him as part of the settlement package. If the employment has not yet terminated, the employee may acquire further company property after the date of the agreement. The wording of the agreement (see sample wording below) should reflect the arrangements made.

> EXAMPLE 12. The Employee agrees to return to the Company on [the Termination Date] [*specify other date*] all property belonging or relating to the Company or any Group Company that is in his possession or under his control. For the avoidance of doubt, this includes (but is not limited to) [the Employee's company car, keys, security cards, credit or charge cards, *list other property*], and all documents, records, correspondence, papers, discs and other materials (and any copies thereof) whether in hard copy or in electronic or machine readable form, made or kept by, or provided to, the Employee during his employment [except for [*property to be retained by Employee*]]. The Employee warrants that he has not retained any copies or extracts of such material.

Resignations

9274 The employer should ensure that the employee resigns all directorships and other offices (for example, company secretary, pension scheme trustee) as part of the settlement (see sample wording below).

> EXAMPLE 3. The Employee will resign any directorship or other office held in the Company or any Group Company [on the signing of this Agreement], such resignations to take effect [immediately] [on [*date*]].

Confidentiality and restrictive covenants

9276 There may be provisions in the employee's existing service agreement/contract of employment which are stated to apply after the termination, such as confidentiality undertakings and restrictive covenants. The employee should be reminded of these **existing obligations** in the settlement documentation (see sample wording below).

> EXAMPLE 13. [In consideration of the sum of [£ *such sum to be taxable*], the Employee acknowledges and reaffirms his obligations to the Company under clauses [*clause number – e.g. restrictive covenants*] of the Employee's [Service Agreement] [Contract of Employment] dated [*date*]].
>
> 14. [[In consideration of the sum of [£ *such sum to be taxable*],] the Employee acknowledges and reaffirms his obligations under clause [*clause number*] of his [Service Agreement] [Contract of Employment] dated [*date*] relating to confidential information.] OR
>
> [The Employee agrees not to use or disclose to any person any trade secrets or other confidential information ("Confidential Information") of the Company or any Group Company which he may have received or obtained during his employment with the Company.
>
> This restriction will not apply to information which becomes public (other than through unauthorised disclosure by the Employee), and is not intended to exclude or restrict the Employee's right to make a protected disclosure under the Public Interest Disclosure Act 1998.
>
> For the purpose of this clause, Confidential Information includes [client or trade secrets and confidential or commercial information relating to the organisation, business, finances, clients, customers, dealings and affairs of the Company and any Group Company]. [*define confidential information further, if possible*]]
>
> 15. The Employee agrees to keep confidential the terms of this Agreement, the circumstances giving rise to it, and the payment the Company has agreed to make, save as may be required by law or by any regulatory authority, or in order to instruct professional advisers.

9277 If the employer has terminated the employment in breach of contract, he will not be able to enforce these existing post-termination obligations and, if agreed within the settlement, the employer must **repeat the obligations** (as opposed to merely referring to them) in the settlement agreement (they could be annexed as a schedule).

If there are no existing provisions, or if existing obligations are insufficient, the employer could seek to include completely **new obligations** in the settlement agreement. For further detail on drafting confidentiality clauses and on restrictive covenants, see ¶2450 and ¶2520 respectively.

If the settlement agreement repeats or imposes restrictive covenants, the consideration for those covenants is subject to **special tax treatment**, normally resulting in their being fully taxable as an emolument (¶3140). To mitigate the amount that may be taxable as a result, a separate amount (reflecting the value of the covenants to the employer) should be allocated to the covenants to avoid the risk that the whole settlement payment may become taxable under this special tax regime. As confidentiality undertakings are arguably also restrictions on the employee's activities, there is a risk that they would also be subject to this special tax treatment. 9278

Reporting requirements

The employer may be legally obliged to report the **employee's dismissal** to the stock exchange, and/or regulatory bodies. In some cases, reasons for the dismissal must be given. Care should be taken to ensure that the reasons given for the dismissal are consistent in the settlement documentation and the report (and any reference – see above). 9280

Any **confidentiality undertaking** in relation to the termination and the terms of the agreement must allow for any required disclosures (see sample wording above).

Employee's legal fees

It is not uncommon for the employer to pay a **contribution** towards an employee's legal costs in entering into a compromise or settlement agreement (see sample wording below). There is a **tax concession** (i.e. no tax will be payable) if the payment is made direct to the employee's adviser in full or partial discharge of fees incurred in connection with the termination of the employment, and the payment is provided for in the settlement documentation. 9282

EXAMPLE 24. The Company will, within [*insert period*] of receipt of a copy of the Adviser's bill, pay up to [£*amount*] ([inclusive/exclusive of VAT]) to the Adviser as a contribution to the Employee's reasonable legal expenses in connection with this Agreement.

Governing law and jurisdiction

If the employment has an international element, the employer should consider including an express jurisdiction and governing law provision (see sample wording below) (¶2255). 9284

EXAMPLE 28. This Agreement will be governed by and interpreted in accordance with English law. The Company and the Employee submit to the exclusive jurisdiction of the English Courts and Tribunals in relation to any claim or matter arising in connection with this Agreement.

D. Settlement documentation

All agreements should be recorded **in writing**. If the agreement is reached through ACAS, the conciliation officer will prepare the written agreement. Otherwise, the agreement may be in the form of: 9300

- a formal compromise agreement which satisfies the various statutory requirements (¶9333);
- a less formal settlement agreement (which may be satisfactory if the time limit for any further statutory claims by the employee has passed);
- a combination compromise and settlement agreement; or
- an order made by the court or tribunal recording the terms of the parties' settlement.

MEMO POINTS If the terms of the settlement agreement are **not** recorded **in writing**, there is a danger that they will be difficult to prove and enforce later, and it is also possible that there could be a dispute as to whether the terms were agreed in full and final settlement (*Whiley v Christopher Clark Workshops Ltd*, EAT case 1403/01).

1. Agreements reached through conciliation officers

9305 In order for the exception to the prohibition on contracting out of statutory rights to apply (¶9203), the conciliation officer must be involved in the process which leads to the agreement. He must have "taken action" which means that ACAS will not simply approve agreements which have already been reached without its involvement (s 203(2)(e) ERA 1996). In such cases, the parties will have to draw up a compromise agreement instead.

Form

9306 ACAS will normally draw up the agreement using a standard form known as a "**COT3**", though any form of agreement will be sufficient. Although it is advisable (and standard practice) for the agreement to be in writing, an **oral agreement** may be sufficient (*Gilbert v Kembridge Fibres Limited* [1984] IRLR 52, EAT). Therefore, if a party reaches an agreement through the conciliation officer but subsequently refuses to sign the written record of that agreement, the other party can put forward evidence to demonstrate that agreement was reached. If this is accepted, the agreement will be valid. The normal contractual principles of offer and acceptance are applied, and a binding agreement will only exist where both parties intend it (*Duru v Granada Retail Catering Ltd*, EAT case 281/00).

Content

9308 Settlement terms are discussed above. See the model settlement and compromise agreement in ¶9930 for sample wording, which can also be included in COT3 agreements.

2. Compromise and settlement agreements

9315 If a conciliation officer is not involved, the parties should document their agreement in a compromise or settlement agreement (or a combined compromise and settlement agreement).

9316 Where a claim is compromised for an agreed amount and the employee remains in employment, that compromise does not affect his **continuity of employment** and he can rely on the period of service dating back to the commencement of his employment to satisfy any necessary qualifying period with regard to any subsequent claim.

a. Types of claim

9318 The method of settlement will depend on whether the matter deals only with contractual entitlements or involves statutory rights.

Contractual claims

9320 An agreement between the parties to settle a contract claim will prevent the parties from bringing or continuing a claim before a court or tribunal (which has jurisdiction to hear certain contractual claims (¶9425)) (Employment Tribunals Extension of Jurisdiction (England and Wales) Order SI 1994/1623 and s 3(2) Employment Tribunals Act 1996). There is **no prohibition against contracting out** of the right to bring such claims, and there is no requirement for a settlement agreement to be drawn up by a conciliation officer, or to be in a prescribed form.

Statutory rights

9322 There is an **exception to the general prohibition** on contracting out of statutory rights if the agreement meets the statutorily prescribed conditions for compromise agreements (see below). If the conditions are not met, the relevant provision will be void, and the employee will be free to bring a claim even if he has already received a payment in respect of that agreement (*Council of Engineering Institutions v R E Maddison* [1976] IRLR 389, EAT). However, if such a payment is made, the tribunal may take it into account in making any award of compensation.

EXAMPLE In *Council of Engineering Institutions v R E Maddison*, the employer made M redundant and gave him a letter enclosing a cheque for £1600 for severance (including his redundancy entitlement), acceptance of which was stated to be in final settlement of all claims. The letter did not meet the requirements for a compromise agreement, and the EAT confirmed that M could pursue his unfair dismissal claim.

The same statutory requirements apply to any **agreement as to the level of compensation** made between the parties after the tribunal has determined liability, but before it has awarded compensation. If such a payment is made but the agreement does not meet the statutory requirements, the tribunal may decide that it would not be "just and equitable" to award any further compensation if the agreement was reached without undue persuasion or pressure (*Courage Take Home Trade Ltd v Keys* [1986] IRLR 427, EAT), or may take any such payment into account in making any compensation award. 9323

The **complaints** that may be compromised are: 9324

Complaint	Reference
Sex discrimination	SDA 1975
Equal pay/equal treatment	EPA 1970/SDA 1975
Racial discrimination	RRA 1976
Religion or belief discrimination	SI 2003/1660
Sexual orientation discrimination	SI 2003/1661
Disability discrimination	DDA 1995
Infringement of certain trade union rights, including: • not to be unjustifiably disciplined • not to suffer deduction of unauthorised/excessive subscriptions • exemption/objection to contributing to political fund • not to be refused employment or service of employment agency on grounds related to union membership • not to suffer action short of dismissal on grounds related to union membership or activities • to paid time off for carrying out trade union duties and time off for union activities and training • to paid time off for carrying out trade union learning representative activities and training • not to be excluded/expelled from union • to consultation in cases of collective redundancies • to protective award for failure to consult	TULRCA 1992, as specified in Employment Tribunals Act 1996
Infringement of general employment rights, including: • to an itemised pay statement • not to suffer unauthorised deductions from wages or to have to make payments to employer • to a guarantee payment • to a written statement of reasons for dismissal • to a redundancy payment • not to suffer detriment on grounds of: – health and safety issues – Sunday working for shop and betting workers – being a trustee of an occupational pension scheme – being an employee representative – taking time off for study or training • to time off: – for public duties – to look for work/make arrangements for training in redundancy situations	ERA 1996, as specified in Employment Tribunals Act 1996

Complaint	Reference
– for antenatal care – for pension scheme trustee duties – for employee representative duties – for young persons for study or training – to care for dependants • to remuneration on suspension on medical grounds • not to be unfairly dismissed	
Infringement of rights under working time regulations, including: • to minimum rest periods • to weekly rest periods • to rest breaks • to annual leave/holiday pay • to compensatory rest	SI 1998/1833
Infringement of rights under national minimum wage legislation, including: • to access to records • to minimum wage • not to suffer detriment for enforcing minimum wage rights	NMWA 1998, as specified in Employment Tribunals Act 1996
Infringement of rights of part-time workers not to be treated less favourably	SI 2000/1551
Infringement of rights of fixed-term employees not to be treated less favourably	SI 2002/2034
Infringement of right not to be subjected to a detriment or unfairly dismissed on grounds connected with pregnancy, childbirth, taking maternity, adoption or paternity or parental leave regulations	ERA 1996; SI 1999/3312; SI 2002/2788
Infringement of right to request flexible working	ERA 1996
Infringement of rights under the transnational information and consultation regulations	SI 1999/3323
Infringement of rights under the information and consultation of employees regulations	SI 2004/3426

9325 It is not possible for an employee to contract out of his right to **statutory minimum notice** (i.e. he will be entitled to the statutory minimum despite any term in his contract providing for less notice), although he can waive his right to notice on a particular occasion or accept a payment in lieu of notice, which, depending on the amount, may extinguish his right to damages, as he may effectively have already been compensated for his loss (s 203(1)(a) ERA 1996; s 86(3) ERA 1996).

b. Types of agreement

9330 A **compromise agreement** is used to compromise statutory claims. It is an agreement between employer and employee to settle a dispute and to refrain from commencing or continuing with certain tribunal proceedings. A compromise agreement is not, therefore, limited to complaints that have already been presented to an employment tribunal (*Lunt v Merseyside Tec Ltd* [1999] IRLR 458, EAT).

A **settlement agreement** is used to settle contractual claims.

It is possible for a **single combined agreement** to be used to settle both statutory and contractual claims, although this document must comply with the strict requirements applicable to statutory claims. A combined compromise and settlement agreement is provided at ¶9930.

If both contractual and statutory claims are waived in the same agreement, it is possible for the waiver (i.e. the term stating that the parties will refrain from commencing or continuing with certain proceedings) to be upheld in respect of the contractual claims, even if the agreement is void in respect of statutory claims (for failure to meet the statutorily prescribed requirements) (*Sutherland v Network Appliance Ltd* [2001] IRLR 12, EAT).

EXAMPLE In *Sutherland v Network Appliance Ltd*, S's employer agreed in a letter to pay him a sum of money in respect of the termination of his employment with a waiver "in full and final settlement of any claims". The letter did not comply with the conditions for valid compromise agreements. The EAT held that the agreement was void only in so far as it purported to exclude statutory rights, and that S's contractual claims had been validly compromised. S could, therefore, only pursue his statutory claims.

c. Conditions for a valid compromise agreement

Reference should be made to the **model compromise and settlement agreement** provided at ¶9930, in which clauses marked with an asterisk indicate that the material must be included for a valid compromise of statutory claims. 9333

In order to be valid, the compromise agreement must meet a number of conditions, which are set out below.

Form

The agreement must be **in writing**. 9335

Particular complaint or proceedings

The agreement must relate to the particular complaint or proceedings and should not attempt to include potential tribunal claims other than the ones that have actually been raised. A "**blanket**" **agreement** (e.g. "in full and final settlement of all claims which the applicant has or may have against the respondent arising from his employment or the termination thereof") is not permitted in respect of statutory claims. This has been recently reinforced by the Court of Appeal in *University of East London v Hinton* where it held that a general clause in a compromise agreement purporting to be in full and final settlement of all claims was not sufficient to prevent a subsequent claim (*University of East London v Hinton* [2005] ICR 1260, CA). The Court emphasised that compromise agreements must "**relate to the particular proceedings**" to be compromised and set out **good practice standards** as follows: 9337

- if actual proceedings are to be compromised: the particulars of the proceedings and of the particular allegations made in them should be inserted in the compromise agreement in the form of a brief factual and legal description; and
- if the compromise is of a particular claim raised which is not yet the subject of proceedings: the particulars of the nature of the allegations and of the statute under which they are made or the common law basis of the alleged claim should be inserted in the compromise agreement in the form of a brief factual and legal description.

It is also not good practice use a standard form of compromise agreement which simply contains a list of examples of statutory claims, further to a general clause that the agreement is in full and final settlement of all claims. Compromise agreements must be **tailored to the individual circumstances** of each particular case otherwise it will not be effective.

MEMO POINTS It should be noted that given this decision, doubt must be cast as to the correctness of an earlier EAT decision (*Byrnell v British Telecommunications plc*, EAT case 0383/04). In this case, a clause which purported to be "in full and final settlement of all claims, both contemplated and not contemplated at the date hereof" was held to cover a claim that had been contemplated by the parties prior to the agreement having been signed.

Where tribunal **proceedings have already been brought**, the case number can be used to identify the claim. Otherwise, the compromise agreement should refer to the circumstances that could give rise to such a claim. 9338

If there are **several claims** to be compromised, they should be listed separately. A single compromise agreement can cover claims under more than one statute (*Lunt v Merseyside Tec Ltd*, see above).

Although there is no requirement to do so, it may be convenient to include any **contractual claim** in the compromise agreement where the facts relied on support both a statutory and a contractual claim (thus making a single combined agreement). If it is included, the particular breach of contract should also be clearly described.

Relevant independent adviser

9339 The employee must receive advice from a "relevant independent adviser" as to the terms and effect of the agreement and, in particular, its effect on his ability to pursue his rights before a tribunal. The agreement must identify the adviser (see sample clauses below). A relevant independent adviser **can be**:

– a qualified lawyer (i.e. a barrister who is practising or employed to give legal advice, a solicitor who holds a practising certificate, or a person other than a barrister or solicitor who is an authorised advocate or authorised litigator, for example, certain legal executives (Courts and Legal Services Act 1990));
– an officer, official, employee or member of an independent trade union who has been certified in writing by the trade union as competent to give advice and as authorised to do so on its behalf;
– a person who works at an advice centre (whether as an employee or a volunteer) who has been certified in writing by the centre as competent to give advice and authorised to do so on its behalf; and
– a qualified legal executive who is employed by a solicitors' practice and who is supervised by a solicitor who holds a practising certificate in providing such advice in relation to compromise agreements.

The adviser is **not independent** if:
– he is employed by or acting for the employer or an associated employer;
– in relation to trade union or advice centre advisers, the trade union or advice centre is the employer or an associated employer; or
– in relation to advice centre advisers, the employee pays for the advice.

EXAMPLE 21. The Employee warrants and undertakes that, before signing this Agreement, he received independent legal advice from [*name of adviser*] (the "Adviser"), [a qualified lawyer] OR [a certified union official] OR [a certified advice centre worker] OR [a qualified legal executive supervised by a solicitor who holds a practising certificate], as to the terms and effect of this Agreement and in particular its effect on his ability to pursue his rights or bring any statutory claim before an employment tribunal or any court of law.
22. By signing this Agreement, the Adviser confirms that:
22.1. he has advised the Employee as to the terms of this Agreement and in particular its effect on his ability to pursue his rights before an employment tribunal; and
22.2 he is not acting (and has not acted) in relation to this matter for the Company or any Group Company (as defined in this Agreement); and
22.3. he is covered by a current contract of insurance or an indemnity provided for members of a profession or professional body covering the risk of a claim by the Employee in respect of any loss arising in consequence of the advice; and
22.4. when giving the advice he was a "relevant independent adviser".

9340 The adviser must be covered by a contract of **insurance or an indemnity** provided for members of a profession or professional body covering the risk of a claim by the employee in respect of any loss arising as a result of his advice (see sample wording above).

9341 It is advisable for the employer to get **written confirmation** from the employee's adviser (either in the compromise agreement or in a separate letter) that he qualifies as a relevant independent adviser, has the necessary insurance cover, and has advised the employee as to the terms and effect of the agreement. There is no statutory requirement for the adviser to sign the compromise agreement, but this is often done in practice, and avoids the need for separate confirmation. However, some advisers prefer to sign a Schedule to the agreement, rather than the agreement itself.

Reference to statutory conditions

The agreement must state that the statutory conditions are satisfied. Statutory claims that can be legally compromised can only be excluded if the compromise agreement or contract refers to the relevant provisions of each statute. 9344

EXAMPLE In *Lunt v Merseyside Tec Ltd*, see above, although L's letter to her employers did contemplate a sex discrimination claim, the compromise agreement did not state that the conditions regulating compromise contracts in the SDA 1975 had been satisfied. L was therefore allowed to proceed with her sex discrimination claim.

3. Signing

The agreements are often signed by the **parties' representatives** rather than the parties themselves, and each side should take care to check that the representative with whom they are negotiating has **authority** to do so (for example, by being named in the appropriate box on the claim or response form). 9350

Where a representative signs the agreement, the party will be bound by the agreement provided his representative has actual or apparent (or "ostensible") authority to act on his behalf. **Ostensible authority** is taken to exist in the case of legal advisers and has also been held to exist in relation to an adviser from a Citizens Advice Bureau who was named as representative by a party and held himself out as having authority to negotiate and reach settlement on behalf of that party (*Freeman v Sovereign Chickens Limited* [1991] IRLR 408, EAT). Ostensible authority arises not from what the apparent agent says to the third party but from what the person for whom he claims to act says or does (*Gloystarne & Co Ltd v Martin* [2001] IRLR 15, EAT).

EXAMPLE In *Gloystarne & Co Ltd v Martin*, the trade union official who had conducted negotiations with the employers was not named as representative on M's originating application, and M had not indicated to the employers in any way that the official had authority to act on his behalf. The EAT accepted that the official had **no ostensible authority**, so M was able to proceed with his claim for unfair dismissal even though his "representative" had concluded an agreement with the employers.

If the adviser has **no actual authority to act**, the party for whom he signs may have a case against him, but the other party to the dispute will be able to rely on the agreement if the adviser had ostensible authority. 9351

4. Enforcement

Compromise and settlement agreements (including COT3 agreements) made **before termination** can be enforced as a contract claim in a tribunal, or by way of an action in the civil courts. 9353

However, a tribunal does not have jurisdiction to enforce agreements entered into **after termination** and any claims would have to be brought in the civil courts.

II. Arbitration

Scope

9360 As an alternative to bringing tribunal claims for unfair dismissal (¶8380) or in relation to the statutory right to request flexible working (¶4690), such claims can be referred to the ACAS Arbitration Scheme. Arbitration is different from conciliation (where a conciliation officer attempts to promote agreement between the parties), as the arbitrator (after hearing from both parties), decides how the dispute should be resolved. The scheme is intended to be confidential, relatively fast, cost-efficient, non-legalistic and informal.

Once the parties have agreed to refer the unfair dismissal or request for flexible working claim to arbitration, they cannot then return to the tribunal in respect of that claim. If the applicant also has **other claims** (even where these are linked to the unfair dismissal or request for flexible working claim), those claims will still have to be pursued in the tribunal (and the relevant time limits must still be observed).

MEMO POINTS The scheme has been extended to **Scotland** and the revised scheme is now contained in the Schedule to the ACAS Arbitration Scheme (England and Wales) Order SI 2004/753. Further guidance is available from ACAS which has published a guide to the scheme (The ACAS arbitration scheme for resolution of unfair dismissal disputes: a guide to the scheme) (referred to in this section as the "ACAS Guide") and an introductory leaflet (How ACAS can help: choosing our arbitration scheme).

9361 Once the parties consent to arbitration, this will be an **exception to the general prohibition on contracting out** of statutory rights (¶9203).

9362 The scheme is not designed to deal with complex legal issues (for example, **jurisdictional issues** such as qualifying service and compliance with time limits are not considered). The ACAS Guide indicates that arbitration is not suitable for cases which raise questions of **EC law** (for example, where the reason for the dismissal is sex discrimination or relates to the transfer of an undertaking or the exercise of rights under the working time regulations). However, the arbitrator must apply EC law and the Human Rights Act 1998 and can appoint a legal adviser to provide guidance if any such issues arise. Alternatively or additionally, a party to the arbitration can (with the permission of the arbitrator or the agreement of the other party) apply to the High Court or the Central London County Court for it to determine any such point of law.

9363 The **arbitrator's role** is twofold: he decides whether the dismissal was **fair or unfair**, and he determines remedies. He will take account of general principles of fairness and good practice (including principles set out in the ACAS Code of Practice "Disciplinary and grievance procedures" and the ACAS Handbook "Discipline at work" current at the time of dismissal), rather than applying strict law or legal precedent (i.e. he need not follow the statutory concept of reasonableness or the test for a fair dismissal laid down by case law). Although he should not substitute what he would have done for the actions taken by the employer, the arbitrator can make use of his own experience of accepted standards in the workplace.

In respect of unfair dismissal claims, the scheme operates on the assumption that there has been an actual dismissal and will, therefore, not be suitable in cases of **constructive dismissal** (unless the employer concedes that there has been a dismissal or a tribunal has made such a finding). Further, there is no explicit requirement for arbitrators to consider whether the reason for dismissal is one of the statutory fair reasons, which suggests that the potentially fair reasons for dismissal will not be confined to those reasons. Arbitrators only need to "have regard to" statutory provisions on **automatically unfair dismissal**, which means that the particular reason for dismissal will merely be a factor to be taken into account when deciding the fairness of a dismissal (rather than being determinative), so these claims will not normally be suitable for arbitration.

Access to the scheme

The employee must have either an **existing tribunal application** pending or grounds to bring such a claim. To use the scheme, both parties to the dispute must enter an **arbitration agreement** (reached with the assistance of an ACAS conciliator or in the format of a compromise agreement drawn up by their advisers), and must also sign a **waiver form** (one for each party), confirming they understand and accept the arbitration process and waiving certain rights (including, for example, the right to a public hearing and the cross-examination of witnesses). The agreement cannot seek to vary the provisions of the scheme. 9365

The agreement (and waivers) must be received by ACAS **within** 6 weeks of its conclusion by the parties (although an arbitrator can extend this time if it was not reasonably practicable to comply with it). Where such consent is given, ACAS will refer the dispute to the arbitration of an arbitrator (who is a person (other than an ACAS officer or employee) appointed by ACAS for the purpose). The arbitrator is obliged to disclose any circumstances which may affect his impartiality in the matter.

Withdrawal and settlement

The employee may withdraw from the arbitration by giving written notice, and the claim will be dismissed. There is no right to re-open the original claim to the tribunal. Once an arbitration agreement has been concluded and accepted by ACAS, the employer cannot withdraw from the scheme. 9367

The parties are free to reach a settlement of their dispute at any stage, in which case the arbitrator can terminate the arbitration on receipt of a joint written request of the parties, and (if so requested by the parties) can record the settlement (in so far as it is relates to the unfair dismissal claim and the remedies he can award) as an "agreed award". 9368

Pre-hearing procedure

Where a tribunal application had been made, the parties are invited to submit details of their claim or defence (as the case may be). In any case, they should submit a **written statement of their case** at least 14 days before the arbitration hearing, together with any supporting documentation (for example, the contract of employment, warning and dismissal letters) or evidence (for example, witness statements), and (where appropriate) a list (including title/role) of the people who will attend the hearing or be called as witnesses. 9370

The arbitrator may issue **directions**, for example, in relation to the production of relevant documents and the attendance of witnesses, although he has no power to compel a party to comply (but may draw an adverse inference from such a failure). He can also call the parties to a **preliminary hearing**, for example to address differences between the parties over the availability or exchange of documents. 9371

Hearing

An arbitration hearing must be held which, unlike a tribunal hearing, will be in private, and held at a location convenient and accessible to the parties. The arbitrator can set the date and location of the hearing if the parties do not agree. 9373

The hearing will normally last for not more than half a day. If a **party does not attend** the hearing without good cause, the arbitrator can hear the matter in his absence or adjourn it. Where the absent party is the employee, the arbitrator can dismiss the claim if the employee does not subsequently give a satisfactory explanation for non-attendance.

The hearing will be **inquisitorial** rather than adversarial (i.e. the arbitrator will ask the parties questions in order to find out the facts, as opposed to each party giving evidence and being cross-examined by the other, as in tribunal cases). The arbitrator will not apply strict rules as to the admissibility, relevance or weight of evidence.

The parties may be **represented**, although no special status is given to representatives (the parties will be liable for any fees or expenses incurred as a result). **Legal aid** may be available under the Legal Help scheme for limited initial advice and preparation for the hearing (¶9131).

9374 The ACAS Guide suggests a hearing procedure, although it emphasises that the procedures are flexible and can be adapted by the arbitrator to suit the circumstances. According to the suggested procedure, the hearing will be in **four sections** as follows:
– introduction (of those present and points of procedure);
– oral presentations (opening statements (the employer usually goes first) summarising the parties' main arguments and commenting on the other party's written submissions);
– discussion of the issues (the arbitrator questions the parties, seeks views on remedies, and requests information relevant to the calculation of compensation); and
– closing statements.

Decision

9376 The arbitrator will not announce his decision at the hearing but will send the parties (through ACAS) a written decision, called an **award** within 3 weeks of it being signed and dated by him. In it, the arbitrator will summarise each party's case, set out his main considerations, his decision and any remedy. The award is confidential.

9377 The **remedies** that an arbitrator can grant include compensation and orders of reinstatement or re-engagement. Awards are enforceable in the High Court or county courts. Where the employer fails to comply with an order of reinstatement or re-engagement, the employee can apply to a tribunal for appropriate compensation.

9378 **Costs** are not recoverable from the other party, although the arbitrator may include an element for costs incurred by the employee personally attending the hearing in any award of compensation.

Appeals

9380 The award of an arbitrator sitting in England and Wales is final (except on certain narrow grounds relating to EC law and the Human Rights Act), although a right of appeal to the Court of Session is given in respect of arbitrations held in Scotland. In England and Wales, the arbitrator's award can be **challenged** (as opposed to appealed) on the following grounds:
– **substantive jurisdiction**, i.e. that the dispute was not in fact one which should have been referred to arbitration or that the award dealt with matters outside the scope of the arbitration agreement; or
– **serious irregularity**, i.e. on the basis of the way in which the arbitration was conducted.
Such challenges must be made in the High Court or Central London County Court within 28 days of the date of the award.

CHAPTER 27

Employment claims

OUTLINE ¶¶

9400 If a **dispute cannot be resolved**, the aggrieved party (normally the employee) will have to bring legal proceedings in order to seek a remedy. However, some statutory employment rights are only available after a qualifying period of continuous employment (¶1080). Before commencing any litigation, an employee will, therefore, have to find out whether such a period is required, and if so, whether he fulfils that requirement. No such qualifying period is required in relation to breach of contract claims.

As the majority of employment claims are heard by employment tribunals, this chapter will focus on tribunal procedure, with a summary only of civil court procedure at ¶9850.

SECTION 1

Jurisdiction and time limits

9410 The aggrieved party must identify in **which forum** his claim should be commenced. In most employment disputes, claims must be brought in the employment tribunals. Some claims (for example, personal injury claims) must be brought in the ordinary civil courts (i.e. the High Court or the county court). In some cases the choice will be influenced by factors such as cost, time limits, speed, convenience and funding. In certain circumstances, a claimant may be estopped (i.e. prevented) from bringing a claim in one court when he has already issued proceedings in another forum (¶9629).

9411 A claim must be presented within the **time limit** specified for that type of claim. Most employment disputes are heard by employment tribunals, a forum which is intended to provide a quick and informal means of resolving disputes, and the time limit within which the action must be brought is generally short.

I. Where to bring a claim

9415

Forum	Claim	Para.
Tribunal	Statutory claims	¶9424
Civil courts	Personal injury claims Breach of contract: – during employment – over tribunal cap – where tribunal time limit expired – particular types of breach	¶9442 ¶9425 ¶9425 ¶9428 ¶9442 ¶9442
Choice	Breach of contract: – arising or outstanding on termination – within tribunal cap – within tribunal time limit	¶9425 ¶9425 ¶9428 ¶9452

A. Employment tribunals

Employment tribunals (referred to in this chapter as "a/the tribunal") **can hear** statutory claims and certain claims for breach of contract. 9420

The constitution and **rules of procedure** (referred to in this section as "the Rules") for the tribunals are set out in legislation (Employment Tribunals (Constitution and Rules of Procedure) Regulations SI 2004/1861 ("the Regulations")). A **revised** set of Rules and Regulations came into force on 1 October 2004 and **apply to** any proceedings commenced on or after that date, including proceedings which were commenced prior to that date provided that a copy of the former originating application was not sent to the respondent prior to that date.

MEMO POINTS 1. Tribunals were formerly known as industrial tribunals.

2. Tribunals are subject to the **overriding objective** to deal with cases justly, which includes ensuring the parties are on an equal footing, saving expense, dealing with the case in ways which are proportionate to the complexity or importance of the issues, and ensuring that it is dealt with fairly and expeditiously (reg 3(1) Sch 1 SI 2004/1861). They must give effect to this objective when exercising any power or interpreting any provision under the Rules and Regulations.

3. It is proposed that the Employment Tribunals and the Employment Appeal Tribunal (EAT) will be merged, along with a number of other major tribunals, to form part of a **single tribunal service** in order to improve service standards. The unified service would not include ACAS, the Central Arbitration Committee or the Certification Office.

Geographical jurisdiction The Rules and Regulations cover England, Wales and Scotland. 9423

Tribunals in **England and Wales** can deal with cases where (reg 19(1) Sch 1 SI 2004/1861):

– the respondent (i.e. the party defending the claim) (or one of the respondents) resides or carries on business in England or Wales; or

– if the matter had given rise to a county court action, the cause of action would have arisen (wholly or partly) in England or Wales (for example, if the breach of contract occurred in England and Wales); or

– the proceedings are to determine a question which has been referred to the tribunal by a court in England or Wales.

Similar, but different, provisions apply to tribunals in **Scotland** which can only deal with proceedings where (reg 19(2) Sch 1 SI 2004/1861):

– the respondent (or one of the respondents) resides or carries on business in Scotland; or

– the proceedings relate to a contract of employment which is or was executed or performed in Scotland; or

– the proceedings are to determine a question which has been referred to the tribunal by a sheriff in Scotland.

Cases can be **transferred** between Scotland and England and Wales where appropriate (for example, if a number of claims against a company with employees around the UK are brought in both Scotland and England, it may be convenient for them all to be heard by the same tribunal if they all involve the same issue) (rule 57 Sch 1 SI 2004/1861).

Statutory claims

9424 Tribunals do not have any inherent or common law jurisdiction. Nevertheless they have a wide and growing statutory jurisdiction – the **main complaints** which may be brought by **employees** (and in appropriate cases, by **workers**) are set out below:

Complaint	Statute
Written statement of employment particulars Deductions from wages Detriment for exercising various statutory rights Time off for various circumstances, such as for antenatal care, performance of public duties, and to care for dependants Maternity, adoption, paternity and parental leave Right to request flexible working Written reasons for dismissal Unfair dismissal Redundancy payments	ERA 1996
Equal pay	EPA 1970; SDA 1975
Sex discrimination	SDA 1975
Race discrimination	RRA 1976
Disability discrimination	DDA 1995
Sexual orientation discrimination	SI 2003/1661
Religion or belief discrimination	SI 2003/1660
Working time	SI 1998/1833
Minimum wage	NMWA 1998
Equality for fixed-term employees	SI 2002/2034
Equality for part-time workers	SI 2000/1551
Continuity of employment on transfer of undertaking	SI 1981/1794
Trade union rights	TULRCA 1992
Health and safety rights	HSWA 1974

Breach of contract

9425 Tribunals can hear **claims** brought by **employees** for damages for breach of, or any sum due under:

– a contract of employment; or

– any other contract connected with employment including compromise agreements concluded before termination of employment (*Rock-It Cargo Ltd v Green* [1997] IRLR 581, EAT).

The tribunal's **jurisdiction is limited**, however, to claims which either arise on **termination** of the contract of employment or which are outstanding on its termination.

Consequently, tribunals have **no jurisdiction** to hear a breach of contract claim in respect of compromise agreements not finalised until **after termination** even if the claim arose because of the termination (*Miller Bros and F P Bulter Ltd v Johnston* [2002] IRLR 386, EAT followed in *Byrnell v British Telecommunications plc*, EAT case 0383/04). Likewise, tribunals have no jurisdiction to hear a breach of contract claim that was commenced **before the termination** (*Capek v Lincolnshire County Council* [2000] IRLR 590, CA). Any such claims must be brought in the High Court or county court as appropriate.

EXAMPLE 1. An employer fails to pay his employee holiday pay due to him under his contract. The **employment continues**, so his breach of contract claim cannot be brought in the tribunal and must be brought in the civil courts. Note, however, that he may be able to make a tribunal claim based on a statutory breach under the working time regulations.
2. If, however, the **employment ends** for whatever reason, he may bring his breach of contract claim in the tribunal.
3. If both parties agree in a valid **compromise agreement** on a lump sum to be paid on termination, and the employer fails to pay the employee, he could bring a claim to enforce the agreement in the tribunal. If, however, the compromise agreement is agreed after termination, it will not be enforceable in the tribunal and a claim would have to be brought in the civil courts.

MEMO POINTS The tribunal's jurisdiction comes from an extension order (Art 3 Employment Tribunals Extension of Jurisdiction (England & Wales) Order SI 1994/1623).

An **employer** cannot bring a breach of contract claim against an employee in the tribunal unless he is first claimed against by the employee, in which case he can **counterclaim** against the employee for any damages or other sum which he claims to be owed under the contract (Art 3 SI 1994/1623). If the employer does counterclaim, he will be allowed to proceed with that claim even if the employee's own claim is dismissed, withdrawn or settled. If the employee has not made a claim, the employer would have to bring his claim in the civil courts. 9426

Tribunals have **no jurisdiction** to hear breach of contract claims based on any of the following (Art 5 SI 1994/1623): 9427
- confidentiality obligations;
- covenants in restraint of trade (e.g. non-competition or non-solicitation clauses);
- terms relating to the provision of living accommodation for the employee; and
- terms relating to intellectual property.

Compensation The amount of compensation which a tribunal can award in a breach of contract claim is limited to £25,000 (Art 10 SI 1994/1623). The full range of remedies available in breach of contract cases is considered at ¶1700. 9428

European Union Law

Tribunals cannot hear claims brought directly under the law of the European Union if the complaint is a free-standing one and not linked to a complaint under domestic UK legislation (*Barber v Staffordshire County Council* [1996] IRLR 209, CA). 9432

EXAMPLE In *Barber v Staffordshire County Council*, it was held that Article 119 of the Treaty of Rome, which deals with equal pay, did not create any separate right to claim unfair dismissal or a redundancy payment. The claimant could only claim those rights on the basis of the UK statutes.

However, tribunals must, of course, have regard to and apply EU law when hearing any case under domestic legislation (*Biggs v Somerset County Council* [1996] IRLR 203, CA). 9433

EXAMPLE In *Biggs v Somerset County Council*, it was pointed out that the tribunal could have used Article 119 to override the requirement which then existed for employees to work a minimum number of hours per week before they could claim unfair dismissal (as this made it more difficult for women to claim).

Human Rights Act 1998

As tribunals are public authorities, they must not act in a way which is incompatible with any of the rights set out in the Human Rights Act (such as the right to a fair trial, the right to respect for private and family life and freedom of expression). 9435

In practice, the **right to a fair trial** (Art 6(1) European Convention on Human Rights) has the most immediate impact on tribunals, although many of the principles inherent in this right are already imposed by the tribunal's rules of procedure and the rules of natural justice. Tribu-

nals will have to ensure that their decisions do not infringe this right. This may affect the following decisions:
– whether evidence should be excluded (for example, if evidence has been obtained by means of covert surveillance or monitoring of communications in breach of the right to privacy);
– whether parties should be allowed to call witnesses of whom the other party has not been given notice;
– whether parties presented with a large amount of documentation just before the hearing should be allowed an adjournment to consider it;
– whether hearings should be postponed if a witness is not available; and
– whether the tribunal or court is independent and impartial (¶9612). In deciding this, the test has been held to be whether a fair-minded and informed observer would conclude that there was a real possibility of bias (*In Re Medicaments and Related Classes of Goods* [2001] ICR 564, CA).

The right to a fair trial will also involve an effort by tribunals to avoid unnecessary delay in resolving a claimant's claim (*Somjee v UK* [2002] IRLR 886, ECHR).

An argument has been put forward, so far without success, that the non-availability of **legal aid** for tribunal proceedings in England and Wales breaches the right to a fair trial (this argument succeeded in Scotland). The availability of legal advice is discussed at ¶9131.

9436 Tribunals also have to **interpret domestic legislation** in a way which is compatible with the rights in the Human Rights Act 1998 (¶6053).

EXAMPLE In *MacDonald v Ministry of Defence* [2000] IRLR 748, EAT, the Scottish EAT interpreted the word 'sex' in the Sex Discrimination Act 1975 to include sexual orientation as this was the definition used in the European Convention on Human Rights. Although the decision was subsequently overruled, and relied on the Convention rather than the 1998 Act (which was not in force at the relevant time), it demonstrates the type of argument which is likely to be put forward. Note that separate sexual orientation discrimination provisions are now in force (¶5260).

B. Civil courts

The High Court

9440 The High Court of Justice is the principal court of civil jurisdiction for England and Wales. It is **divided into** three Divisions – the Family Division (FD), the Chancery Division (ChD) and the Queen's Bench Division (QBD). Employment cases are heard in either the Queen's Bench Division or the Chancery Division.

MEMO POINTS The **rules of procedure** of the High Court are set out in the Civil Procedure Rules SI 1998/3121, as amended.

9441 The High Court has **no jurisdiction** to hear claims regarding the various statutory claims which are reserved for the tribunal (see above).

EXAMPLE In *Barber v RJB Mining (UK) Limited* [1999] IRLR 308, QBD, the Court decided that it did not have jurisdiction to deal with any complaint that the limit on a worker's average weekly working time had been exceeded as this was specifically reserved for enforcement by the Health and Safety Executive, nor could it hear any complaint of detriment, which was a matter for the tribunal.

9442 The High Court has **jurisdiction** to hear any dispute not specifically reserved to another tribunal, including:
– breach of contract claims (of any amount and especially where the tribunal time limit has expired, see below), including claims to enforce restrictive covenants by way of injunctions or damages;
– disputes as to the interpretation of employment contracts, where a declaration is sought; and
– personal injury claims arising out of employment.

The county courts

The county courts deal largely with the same type of claims as the High Court (the more complex a claim is or the higher its value is, the more likely it is that it will be heard by the High Court rather than the county court), are governed by the same rules of procedure (see above), and may award the same remedies. 9443

II. Time limits

In deciding whether or not the time limit has been complied with, it is important to be able to ascertain (a) when the period of time commenced and ended, and (b) when the application was presented. These are discussed below. 9450

Courts

In the High Court or county court, breach of contract claims must be **brought within** 6 years of the breach, whilst personal injury claims must be made within 3 years. 9451

Tribunals

In the tribunals, most applications must be **made within** 3 months of the matter complained of occurring, and some time limits are even shorter. 9452

A **table** showing the time limits for the main types of tribunal claim is at ¶9480.

Time limits are strictly enforced, which means that a party who fails to present his claim within the specified time is likely to lose any chance of doing so. The parties **cannot agree to extend or waive** the time limit, although a tribunal has power to do so in certain circumstances, set out below. Unless the time limit has been extended, a tribunal cannot hear a case which is presented out of time (*Rogers v Bodfari (Transport) Ltd* [1973] IRLR 172, NIRC), and if it does, its decision will be a nullity (even if the employer did not raise the issue) and can be set aside.

1. Calculating the relevant period

The periods for presenting claims are expressed in different ways in respect of different types of claim. If an application has to be presented within a specified period "**beginning with**" a certain date, then in calculating the period, that date should be included (*Trow v Ind Coope (West Midlands) Ltd* [1967] 2 All ER 900, CA). This is the most commonly used formula. If, however, the application must be presented within a specified period "**after**" or "**from**" a particular date, that date is not included. 9455

In either formulation, time runs from the beginning of the relevant day, and runs until midnight on the last day of the period.

Where reference is made to a "**month**", this is interpreted as meaning a calendar month.

EXAMPLE 1. A complaint of race discrimination must be presented before the end of the period of 3 months **beginning when** the act complained of was done as follows (s 68(1) RRA 1976):

Date of act complained of	Last day for presentation
31 March	30 June
1 April	30 June
26 June	25 September
1 December	28 February (or 29 February if a leap year)

2. If, however, something is to be done within 14 days **after** 1 January, then it would have to be done by midnight on 15 January.

9456 The time limit may expire on a Saturday, Sunday or public holiday when the **tribunal office is closed**. In general, this does not affect the time limit, as presentation of an application does not involve any action on the part of the tribunal and it is sufficient for it to be posted through the office's letterbox (for example, by hand delivery on that day) (*Swainston v Hetton Victory Club Ltd* [1983] IRLR 164, CA). If the tribunal has no letterbox or other means to allow applications to be delivered when it is closed, presentation on the next day on which it is open may be regarded as having taken place on time (*Ford v Stakis Hotels & Inns Ltd* [1988] IRLR 46, EAT). However, as this is not entirely certain, the safest course is to ensure that applications are presented well within the appropriate time limit.

Identifying the relevant start date

9457 The relevant start date for calculating the relevant period depends on the type of claim, as set out below.

9458 **Unfair dismissal/redundancy** With regard to unfair dismissal claims, the relevant start date is the effective date of termination ("EDT"). The relevant start date for redundancy payment claims is referred to as the "relevant date". Both are discussed at ¶8340. For time limit purposes, the EDT/relevant date is not extended by the addition of statutory minimum notice.

An employee who has been given **notice of dismissal** can present his unfair dismissal claim before the EDT, even though the limit does not start to run until then (s 111(3) ERA 1996). This will also apply in cases of **constructive dismissal** where an employee has given notice to terminate his employment (*Presley v Llanelli Borough Council* [1979] IRLR 381, EAT).

> EXAMPLE On 1 February, an employee is told by his employer that he is being dismissed with effect from 28 February. He can present his application to the tribunal at any time after receiving notice on 1 February, but the final date on which he may do so is still calculated by reference to 28 February (so he must present his application by 27 May).

9459 However, if an employee presents an application before he has been given notice of dismissal or if no question of notice arises (for example, where he is told that his fixed-term contract will not be renewed and he issues his application before the date of expiry of that contract), the **application is premature** and will be rejected.

9460 **Discrimination** The relevant date is normally the date on which the act (or omission) complained of was done. It is, therefore, necessary to identify that act (or omission) and then determine when the time limit expires. If the act of discrimination is a **dismissal**, time will normally run from the date on which the dismissal takes effect (¶8341) and will not be affected by any internal appeal procedure (unless the employment contract states that employment continues pending the outcome of the appeal) (¶8358).

However, if it can be shown that the **rejection of an appeal against dismissal** was itself tainted by discrimination, this can constitute a separate act of discrimination so that the time limit can be calculated from the date of rejection.

A discriminatory act that **extends over the period** of an individual's employment is treated as having been done at the end of the employment (*Cast v Croydon College* [1998] IRLR 318, CA). A tribunal will consider whether there was an act of discrimination extending over a period of time as opposed to a series of unconnected acts (*Hendricks v Commissioner of Police of the Metropolis* [2003] IRLR 96, CA, overturning the EAT ruling). Where there is a **continuing act or a series of linked acts**, time is calculated from the last date of either the continuing act or the series of acts. Note that a continuing act of discrimination can include acts which take place after the termination of employment if there is a sufficiently close connection between the employment relationship and the acts in question (*(1) BHS Ltd (2) Hough v (1) Walker (2) Premier Model Management Ltd*, EAT case 0001/05). However, discrimination which takes place after a tribunal claim has been lodged cannot be taken into account in determining whether or not there has been a continuing act of discrimination (*Robertson v Bexley Community Centre t/a Leisure Link* [2003] IRLR 434, CA).

A **job claimant** cannot complain of a policy of continuing discrimination based on a general discriminatory recruitment policy. Time runs in relation to the specific post for which the claimant applied (*Tyagi v BBC World Service* [2001] IRLR 465, CA).

EXAMPLE In *Cast v Croydon College*, the employer refused to allow C to work part-time. This was a continuing act because there was evidence that the employer had a policy which required the holder of C's post to work full-time. C was allowed to proceed with her claim even though it was submitted more than 3 months after the initial rejection of her request to work part-time.

There is a distinction between a continuing act and the **continuing consequences** of an act (*Barclays Bank plc v Kapur* [1991] IRLR 136, HL). A rule or policy which remains in place and continues to have a discriminatory effect for as long as it remains in place, is treated as continuing (*Cast v Croydon College*). On the other hand, a decision not to promote an employee which means that he remains on a lower level of pay is treated as a one-off act and is not regarded as a continuing act simply because he continues to suffer from the consequences of that lower rate of pay from this date. 9461

Unlawful deductions from wages Where there is a **series of deductions**, time runs from the last of such deductions. Therefore, if an employee should be paid £30 per week but by reason of an unlawful deduction is only paid £25 per week for 6 months, he can present his claim within 3 months from the last date on which a deduction was made. 9462

Breach of contract Claims made to the tribunal cannot be presented before the termination of employment and must be submitted within 3 months after the employment ends (*Capek v Lincolnshire County Council* [2000] IRLR 590, CA). 9463

2. Extension of time limits

Although time limits are strictly enforced, the tribunal can extend on **two principal grounds**: 9465
- where it was not reasonably practicable for the complaint to be presented in time and the delay is reasonable (the "not reasonably practicable" test, applicable to the vast majority of claims, including unfair dismissal); and
- where the tribunal considers it just and equitable to extend time in all the circumstances (the "just and equitable" test, applicable principally to discrimination cases).

The **table** of time limits given at ¶9480 identifies which test is applied in considering requests for extensions.

In addition, following the introduction of the **statutory dispute resolution procedures**, under these procedures there are certain grounds on which the normal time limit for submitting a tribunal claim may be extended (¶9479).

Not reasonably practicable test

This is the stricter test of the two, and the tribunal must be satisfied that: 9466
- the claimant has shown that it was not reasonably practicable to present his application in time; and
- the application has been presented within a reasonable time.

The tribunal will consider the above steps in order and will only go on to consider the second limb if it is satisfied in relation to the first.

What constitutes "not reasonably practicable"? To satisfy the first limb of the test, the employee does not have to prove that it was not physically possible, although he must go further than showing that he had a good excuse for failure and that it was not reasonable to have expected him to comply. The test lies somewhere between the two and has been described as a requirement to show that it was not "reasonably feasible" (*Palmer & Saunders v Southend-on-Sea Borough Council* [1984] IRLR 119, CA). 9467

Each case has to be decided on its own facts and the tribunal has to decide if the excuse given by the employee effectively prevented him from submitting his application in time. In considering this, the tribunal will weigh up all relevant factors, including the prejudice to each party of allowing or not allowing an extension of time (*Elizabeth Duff Travel Ltd v Bray*, EAT case 0517/01).

9468 A **serious illness** which prevents a claimant taking professional advice during the period where an application could be presented might be sufficient. In such circumstances, the tribunal will consider when and for how much of the period the claimant was afflicted by this condition. A claimant who hopes to resolve the case through the use of internal appeal procedures during the first few weeks of the time limit and then is struck down by illness for the remainder of the period may be able successfully to argue that it was not reasonably practicable for him to submit the application in time (*Schultz v Esso Petroleum Ltd* [1999] IRLR 488, CA). However, a claimant who is ill during the first few weeks of the time limit but in good health for the remainder of the period is likely to be unsuccessful.

A **serious drug addiction** may also prevent a claimant from presenting his claim within the required time limit (*Imperial Tobacco Ltd v Wright*, EAT case, 0919/04). In this case, the employee (who was an existing heroin addict) had been summarily dismissed by his employer and returned to heroin abuse following his dismissal. In holding that it was not reasonably practicable for him to present his claim for unfair dismissal within the time limit, the EAT emphasised that tribunals must make a finding on the facts of each case as to whether it was reasonably practicable for an employee to present his claim in time. It was unreal, in the circumstances of this case, to regard the impracticability of presenting the claim in time as being the result of the claimant's voluntary choice.

9469 A claimant who is aware of his right to bring a claim but chooses not to for **commercial or other reasons** is unlikely to persuade a tribunal that it was not reasonably practicable to act earlier (*Birmingham Optical Group plc v Johnson* [1995] ICR 459, EAT).

9470 It used to be the case that a claimant's failure to present his claim in time arising from his own **ignorance of his rights** (or even from **incorrect advice** given to him by his legal advisers) will not generally justify an extension of time (*Walls Meat Co Ltd v Khan* [1978] IRLR 499, CA) (unlike the approach taken under the "just and equitable" test (see below)). However, the EAT has recently begun to take a less stringent view allowing an employee's claim to proceed even though it was out of time because she had been given incorrect advice (*Marks and Spencer plc v Williams Ryan* [2005] ICR 1293, CA). In this case, the employee was unaware that, in order to protect her position, she needed to present her unfair dismissal complaint to the tribunal within the 3-month time limit as she had received **advice from** the **Citizens Advice Bureau** that she needed to exhaust her employer's internal dispute resolution procedures before submitting a claim. Erroneous advice by a member of the **tribunal's own staff** has also been held to give grounds for an extension (*Jean Sorelle Limited v Rybak* [1991] IRLR 153, EAT).

9471 A claimant who becomes **aware of new facts** which change his understanding of his situation may be able to persuade a tribunal to extend time. For example, an employee may be made redundant and subsequently become aware of facts (such as the engagement of other employees) which suggest that there was not a genuine redundancy situation after all (*Machine Tool Industry Research Association v Simpson* [1988] IRLR 212, CA).

9472 An extension will not be granted on the grounds that the employee delays in order to await the **outcome of other civil or criminal proceedings**. In such a case, an appropriate course of action is to present the tribunal application but ask for it to be **adjourned** pending the outcome of those other proceedings. For extensions relating to the completion of a statutory dispute resolution procedure, see ¶9479.

9473 If a posted application **fails to arrive in time**, the tribunal will consider whether it was reasonable for the claimant to have expected that it would arrive in time. For these purposes, a claimant can rely on the **ordinary course of the post** and, if an application would, in the normal course of post, have been presented before the expiry of the time limit (although not immediately after), then the claimant should not be penalised for posting the application at the last possible moment (*Consignia v Sealy* [2002] IRLR 624, CA). Further guidance on the presentation of claims was laid down by the Court of Appeal in *Consignia v Sealy*, which, amongst other things, states that a first class letter will, in the ordinary course of the post, be **delivered on** the second day after it was posted, excluding Sundays, public and bank holidays. A tribunal might be prepared to grant an extension where the failure is due to a **postal strike or other postal delay**.

An EAT decision has also held that an **email communication** will be deemed to arrive within a very short time after being sent: 30 or 60 minutes would be the normal maximum (unless there is any indication that it has not been received) (*Initial Electronic Security Systems Limited v Advic* [2005] IRLR 671, EAT).

Where applications are submitted towards the end of the time limit period, the tribunal is also likely to consider what **efforts** have been made to **check receipt** (for example, by telephoning the tribunal to confirm that it has been received). However, in the case of a claimant who is **not legally represented**, the EAT has indicated that there is no duty to check whether their application has been received (*Grossman v Barnet Healthcare*, EAT case 0134/01; see also *Peters v Sat Katar Co Ltd* [2003] IRLR 574, CA, in relation to appeals to the EAT).

Reasonable time Once the reason for not being able to present an application is removed, 9474
the second limb of the test is that a claimant should present his application as quickly as possible. How long will be allowed for this will depend on all the circumstances of the particular case and not just the length of the delay (*Marley (UK) Limited v Anderson* [1994] IRLR 152, EAT).

Just and equitable test

In cases to which this test applies, the tribunal has a wide discretion to extend the time limit 9475
if it believes that it is just and equitable in the circumstances of the case. The tribunal is entitled to take into consideration any factors which it considers to be relevant, including whether the claimant can show a good reason for not presenting the claim in time and whether he acted reasonably promptly once it became apparent to him that a claim was appropriate.

In relation to the **delay**, the tribunal will also take into account:
- the length;
- whether it will affect the ability of witnesses to give their evidence;
- whether it has been contributed to in any way by the other party (for example, by refusing to provide relevant information); and
- what steps have been taken by the claimant to obtain appropriate professional advice.

A **good reason** for the delay may be:
- defective professional advice, including incorrect legal advice as to the time limit in which the claimant needed to submit her claim (*Chohan v Derby Law Centre*, EAT case 0851/03);
- where a claimant becomes aware of old documentation which changes his understanding of his position (*Southwark London Borough Council v Afolabi* [2003] IRLR 220, CA); and
- (with regard to circumstances to which the statutory dispute resolution procedures do not apply – ¶6510) pursuing an internal appeal or grievance procedure (although this will merely be one of the factors to be taken into account (*Robinson v Post Office* [2000] IRLR 804, EAT; confirmed in *Apelogun-Gabriels v London Borough of Lambeth* [2002] IRLR 116, CA)). See ¶9479 regarding completion of an applicable statutory dispute resolution procedure.

EXAMPLE 1. In *Robinson v Post Office*, it was held that it would not be just and equitable to allow R to proceed with a late application under the Disability Discrimination Act (he had waited until after his internal appeal) as he was aware of the time limit, was able to conduct his own affairs, and chose not to submit his application in time.

2. In *Southwark London Borough Council v Afolabi*, there was a delay of 9 years before the claimant discovered old documents which changed his understanding of his position. In this case, the Court of Appeal emphasised that such a delay was exceptional and that its decision was also based on the fact that the respondent had failed to provide any evidence supporting its submission that such a delay would not allow there to be a fair trial.

9476 The tribunal will consider the **prejudice to the parties**, i.e. that which the claimant would suffer as a result of not being allowed to proceed, compared to that which will be suffered by the respondent if the case is allowed to go ahead.

9477 An extension is more likely to be granted if the **claim is connected** to another claim which has already been submitted within the appropriate time but not yet heard (for example, where an attempt is being made to add a sex discrimination claim to an unfair dismissal claim which has already been submitted).

9478 It may be that a higher authority, such as the EAT or the Court of Appeal, makes a decision which **changes the interpretation of the law**. This could provide grounds for granting an extension if it was reasonable for the claimant to have concluded, on the previous interpretation of the law, that he had no case and only to realise after the expiry of the time limit and the change in the law that he did have a potential claim.

Completion of statutory dispute resolution procedures

9479 In certain circumstances, the normal time limits for presenting a tribunal claim under one or more of the jurisdictions set out at ¶¶9985-6 may be **extended automatically by** 3 months to allow the parties to complete an applicable statutory dispute resolution procedure (¶6500). The normal time limits will be extended beginning with the day after the date on which the time limit would otherwise have expired (reg 15(1) SI 2004/752). It should be noted that where a **statutory procedure does not apply**, no extension of the normal time limits will be available. However, where the parties are deemed to have complied with an applicable statutory procedure, an extension will be available if these circumstances apply (¶6512).

See ¶9480 below for a table of the normal time limits. It should be noted that any discretion which a tribunal may have to extend a normal time limit under the 'not reasonably practicable' or 'just and equitable' tests (¶¶9466, 9475) must be ignored for these purposes. However, the tribunal is still able to exercise any discretion to extend the normal time limits under these two common law tests.

Where a **statutory dismissal and disciplinary procedure applies**, the normal time limit for presenting a claim will be extended where an employee (reg 15(2) SI 2004/752):
- presents a claim after the normal time limit; but
- had reasonable grounds for believing, when that time limit expired, that a dismissal or disciplinary procedure (whether statutory or otherwise) was being followed in respect of matters that consisted of, or included, the substance of the tribunal claim.

Where a **statutory grievance procedure applies**, the normal time limit for presenting a claim will be extended by 3 months where an employee presents a tribunal claim within the normal time limit but in circumstances in which he is not permitted to do so, i.e. he has (reg 15(3) SI 2004/752; s 32(2), (3) EA 2002):
- not complied with the requirement to write a Step 1 letter to start the statutory grievance procedure; or
- complied with the Step 1 letter but has not waited a further 28 days before presenting his tribunal claim.

In these circumstances, the employee can submit his tribunal claim once he has complied with Step 1 and waited a further 28 days after having done so. However, the employee must start the statutory grievance procedure within 1 month of the expiry of the original time limit otherwise the tribunal will not be permitted to consider his claim (s 32(6) EA 2002; ¶6773). Note that the DTI guidance (para 128) regarding the operation of this bar provides that a tribunal may, in these circumstances, use its discretion to extend the normal time limit under the two common law tests referred to above. However, this interpretation is inconsistent with the provisions of the regulations and it is recommended that the regulations are followed in this regard.

Finally, the normal time limit will be extended where an employee presents a tribunal claim out of time (i.e. outside the normal time limit) having, within the time limit, sent a Step 1 letter to his employer to start the statutory grievance procedure (reg 15(3) SI 2004/752). In these circumstances, the time limit will be extended automatically on submission of the employee's claim.

3. Time limits for main tribunal claims

The following table sets out the main time limits and the test which will be applied in deciding whether or not extensions should be granted. "J & E" refers to the "just and equitable" test (see above), while "NRP" refers to the "not reasonably practicable" test (see above). See ¶8340 for detail on the EDT (effective date of termination) and relevant date. 9480

Complaint	Time Limit	Test for extension	Reference
Sex or racial discrimination – general claim	3 months beginning with date of act complained of	J & E	SDA 1975; RRA 1976
Appeal against a non-discrimination notice	6 weeks from date of service of notice	J & E	
Application by EOC/CRE as appropriate to enforce provisions relating to discriminatory advertisements, instructions and pressure to discriminate	6 months beginning with date of act	J & E	
Disability discrimination	3 months beginning with date of act complained of	J & E	DDA 1995
Application by DRC to enforce provisions relating to discriminatory advertisements, instructions and pressure to discriminate	6 months beginning with date of act	J & E	
Sexual orientation discrimination	3 months beginning with date of act complained of	J & E	SI 2003/1661
Religion or belief discrimination	3 months beginning with date of act complained of	J & E	SI 2003/1660
Equal pay/equal value	6 months beginning with termination of employment	None	EPA 1970
Unfair dismissal (*)	3 months beginning with EDT	NRP	ERA 1996
Unfair dismissal for taking part in official industrial action	6 months from date of dismissal (which is date notice given (if employer gave notice) or else EDT)	NRP	
Interim relief pending determination of certain complaints of unfair dismissal (¶8700)	7 days immediately following the EDT	None	
Written statement of reasons for dismissal (*)	3 months beginning with EDT	NRP	
Redundancy payment (*)	6 months beginning with relevant date	J & E (and see ¶9010)	
Written statement of employment particulars (*)	3 months beginning with date on which employment ceased	NRP	ERA 1996
Itemised pay statement	3 months beginning with date on which employment ceased	NRP	
Guarantee pay (*)	3 months beginning with day for which payment claimed	NRP	
Time off for: – public duties – dependants – pension scheme trustees – redundant employee to look for work (*)	3 months from date of failure to allow time off/day taken off or date when time off should have been allowed	NRP	ERA 1996; Health and Safety (Consultation with Employees) Regulations SI 1996/1513;

Complaint	Time Limit	Test for extension	Reference
– employee representatives – study or training – health and safety representatives and candidates – trade union duties and activities			Safety Representatives and Safety Committees Regulations SI 1977/500; TULRCA 1992
Refusal to permit exercise of rights or failure to make payments in respect of annual leave	3 months beginning with date when exercise of right should have been permitted or date when payment was payable	NRP	Working Time Regulations SI 1998/1833
Time off for ante-natal care	3 months beginning with date of appointment	NRP	ERA 1996
Parental leave (*)	3 months beginning with date of matters complained of	NRP	
Maternity, paternity and adoption leave and pay (*)	3 months beginning with date of matters complained of	NRP	
Infringement of right to request flexible working	3 months beginning with date of last act or failure	NRP	
Suspension from work on medical, or maternity, grounds (*)	3 months beginning with first day of suspension	NRP	
Less favourable treatment and detriment relating to part-time workers	3 months beginning with date (or last date) of less favourable treatment or detriment	J & E	Part-time Workers (Prevention of Less Favourable Treatment) Regulations SI 2000/1551
Less favourable treatment and detriment relating to fixed-term employees	3 months beginning with date (or last date) of less favourable treatment or detriment	J & E	Fixed-term Employees (Prevention of Less Favourable Treatment) Regulations SI 2002/2034
Right to be accompanied at a disciplinary or grievance hearing: – failure (or threat to fail) to comply – detriment relating to right	3 months beginning with date of failure or threat	NRP	ERelA 1999
Detriment relating to: – health and safety, – Sunday working – working time – protected disclosure – duties of occupational pension trustee – functions of employee representative – leave for study/training, family or domestic reasons – enforcement of rights to national minimum wage	3 months beginning with date of last act or failure	NRP	ERA 1996; NMWA 1998

Complaint	Time Limit	Test for extension	Reference
Transfer of undertaking: – failure to inform or consult – failure to comply with compensation order for failure to inform or consult	3 months beginning with date of completion of transfer 3 months beginning with date of tribunal's order	NRP	TUPE Regulations SI 1981/1784
Redundancy consultation: – failure to consult – failure to pay protective award	Before dismissal or 3 months beginning with date on which dismissal takes effect 3 months beginning with last day in respect of which complaint made	NRP	TULRCA 1992
Unauthorised deduction of union subscriptions	3 months beginning with date of deduction	NRP	
Trade union membership: refusal of employment	3 months beginning with date of conduct complained of	NRP	
Trade union membership or activities or making use of union services: dismissal and victimisation	3 months beginning with date of last act or failure	NRP	
Unlawful inducement relating to trade union membership, activities or collective bargaining: dismissal and victimisation	3 months beginning with date of last act or failure	NRP	
Breach of contract claim by employee	3 months beginning with EDT or (if no EDT) last working day (6 years from breach in civil courts)	NRP	SI 1994/1623
Breach of contract counter-claim by employer	6 weeks beginning with date of receipt of employee's claim (6 years from breach in civil courts)	NRP	

* A qualifying period of service applies (¶1080)

SECTION 2

Tribunal claims

The **litigation process is commenced** by lodging a claim. If the other party wishes to defend the proceedings, he will need to file a response. 9500

In order to bring cases to a hearing as quickly and efficiently as possible, and to ensure that the issues to be determined at the main hearing are clear both to the parties and the tribunal, the tribunal may deal with the following matters **before the main hearing** (and can be the subject of an **interim order** granted by the tribunal): 9501
- the contents of the claim and the response;
- disclosure and exchange of documents;
- witness statements and witness orders;
- the issue of a default judgment in an uncontested case;
- striking out of hopeless cases.

Pre-hearing procedure is covered at ¶9530.

9502 Tribunal procedure **at the main hearing** (discussed at ¶9600) aims to ensure the fair and efficient handling of the case, with rules governing the composition of the tribunal, representation, publicity and evidence.

9503 Tribunal decisions may be **appealed** on points of law to the Employment Appeal Tribunal (EAT), and from there, to higher courts. Appeals are discussed further at ¶9740, together with details on relevant European issues.

I. Commencement of proceedings

Commencement of a claim

9510 A claim is commenced by presenting details of the claim in writing to an Employment Tribunal Office (rule 1(1) Sch 1 SI 2004/1861).

The claim should be **addressed to** the Secretary of the Employment Tribunal Office (the "Secretary"). The Secretary will submit it to the appropriate regional Employment Tribunal Office. These offices are set up to cover specific geographic areas and each has a Regional Secretary who deals with the administration of the employment tribunal within his region. Any function of the Secretary may be performed by the Regional Secretary or by a person acting with the authority of the Secretary (rule 60(3) Sch 1 SI 2004/1861). The term Secretary will be used throughout this section even though a Regional Secretary may be acting with his authority. The **appropriate Regional Office** might be the one that covers the postcode area specified in the ET1 form, i.e. where the claimant worked or where the subject matter of the complaint occurred, although it could also be presented either at the Central Office or at any other regional Employment Tribunal Office (rule 61 Sch 1 SI 2004/1861).

9511 **Form** From 1 October 2005, the **revised** standard form (**form ET1**) is mandatory (SI 2005/435). This form which can be obtained from tribunals and from Jobcentres requires the **following information** to be given:
– the name and address of the employee ("the claimant");
– a UK address for correspondence if different;
– the name and address of those against whom the case is brought ("the respondent(s)");
– the grounds on which relief is sought (i.e. sufficient information to show what sort of complaint is being made);
– whether or not the claimant is or was an employee of the respondent;
– whether or not the claim includes a complaint that the respondent has dismissed the claimant or has contemplated doing so; and
– whether or not the claimant has raised the subject matter of the claim with the respondent in writing at least 28 days prior to presenting the claim to an employment tribunal and, if the claimant has not done so, why (¶6773); and
– if whether, since leaving the employment of the respondent, the claimant has obtained new employment and, if so, to give details of his new salary.

Where a claimant is required to provide minimum information in his claim form, his failure to do so should not immediately render it inadmissible (*Richardson v U Mole Limited* [2005] IRLR 668, EAT). In this case, the EAT suggested that the Rules are unsatisfactory and should be revisited and confirmed that the **claimant's failure to state expressly** in his claim form that he was an employee (as is required under the Rules) did not prevent the claim form being admitted. As the claimant responded to other questions relating to the job he did for the employer and his dates of employment, it could be implied that the claimant was asserting that he was an employee.

In another recent case on the admissibility of claim forms, the EAT again criticised the the Rules and has emphasised that they must **not be interpreted** so as to **deny a claimant access** to the tribunal system (*Grimmer v KLM Cityhopper UK* [2005] IRLR 596, EAT). Consequently, a claimant will have given sufficient details of a **complaint** if it **can be discerned** from the details provided on the claim form that the claimant is complaining of an alleged breach of an employment right which falls within the jurisdiction of the tribunal. The EAT in giving its judgment emphasised that this threshold for access should, in the interests of justice, be kept low. If it becomes necessary, as a case proceeds, for additional information to be obtained (for example, to clarify the issues) this can be done, either by application from either party or by the chairman of the tribunal on his own initiative (¶9539).

MEMO POINTS 1. If a claimant fails to use the form after this date, his claim will be returned to him together with an explanation of why the claim has been rejected and a copy of the prescribed form (rule 3(1) Sch 1 SI 2004/1861).
2. References to **dismissal** in this regard do not include references to a constructive dismissal.

Presentation The claim may be **presented by** hand, post, fax or other means of electronic communication (rule 61(1) Sch 1 SI 2004/1861). It is also possible to submit a claim online on the Employment Tribunals' website. 9512

It is presented upon **receipt** in the tribunal office (*Hammond v Haigh Castle & Co Ltd* [1973] 2 All ER 289, NIRC). A claim is **deemed** to have been **received** (unless proved otherwise) either when delivered in the ordinary course of the **post** or (in the case of **fax**) on the day of transmission or (in the case of **personal delivery**) on the date of delivery (rule 61(2) Sch 1 SI 2004/1861), or (in the ordinary course of **email**) within a very short time of being sent (30 or 60 minutes would be the normal maximum unless there is any indication that it has not been received) (*Initial Electronic Security Systems Limited v Advic* [2005] IRLR 671, EAT).

It is advisable that **confirmation of receipt** should always be obtained.

For discussion of the **timing** of presentation see ¶9450.

Pre-acceptance procedure When the claim is received, the Secretary will **review** it to establish whether or not the claim (or part of it) can be accepted by the tribunal (rule 2(1) Sch 1 SI 2004/1861). 9513

A claim will **not** be **accepted** if one or more of the following circumstances applies (rule 3(1), (2) Sch 1 SI 2004/1861):
– (after 1 October 2005) the mandatory claim form has not been used;
– the claim form does not include all the relevant information required;
– the tribunal does not have power to consider the claim (for example, if it seeks a relief which the tribunal does not have power to give); or
– the admissibility requirements of the statutory grievance procedure have not been met (¶6773).

The Secretary will refer the claim, together with his statement of reasons for not accepting it, to the Chairman who will decide whether the claim (or part of it) should be allowed to proceed. The Secretary will inform the claimant in writing of the Chairman's decision as soon as reasonably practicable, together with information on how that decision may be reviewed or appealed (rule 3 Sch 1 SI 2004/1861).

Where the **admissibility requirements** under the statutory grievance procedure have not been met, the Secretary will notify the claimant as to the time limit which applies to the claim and of the consequences of not complying with the requirements (rule 3(6) Sch 1 SI 2004/1861).

MEMO POINTS The claimant can apply to the tribunal to **review its decision** not to accept his claim on the grounds that the decision was wrongly made as a result of an administrative error or that it is in the interests of justice to do so (see ¶9720 for further details).

Tribunal action on acceptance of claim If the claim (or part of it) is accepted, the **Secretary sends a copy** of it to each respondent and records in writing the date on which it was sent (rule 2(2)(a) Sch 1 SI 2004/1861). He will give **notice to every party** (in writing) of the case number which has been assigned to it and the address to which notices and other communications to the Secretary must be sent (rule 2(2)(b) Sch 1 SI 2004/1861). The Secretary sends a **further notice to the respondent** which includes information about the means and time limit for entering a response to the claim, the consequences of the failure to do so and the right to receive a copy of the decision. 9514

MEMO POINTS If only **part of a claim** is **accepted**, the Secretary will inform the parties which part(s) of the claim has/have not been accepted and that the tribunal will not deal with those part(s) unless they are accepted at a later date.

9515 The Secretary must notify the parties (in every case where legislation provides for conciliation) that the **services of a conciliation officer** are available to them (rule 2(2)(d) Sch 1 SI 2004/1861) (¶9218). Where the requirement for a **fixed period** of conciliation applies (¶9219), the Secretary will notify the parties of the date on which the conciliation officer's duty to conciliate ends and, that after that date, the services of the conciliation officer will be available only in limited circumstances (rule 2(2)(e) Sch 1 SI 2004/1861).

9516 **Copies of all documents** and notices in the case are sent by the Secretary to:
- an appropriate conciliation officer, if relevant;
- the Secretary of State for Trade and Industry if the proceedings may involve payment out of the National Insurance Fund (for example where a redundancy payment or notice pay is being claimed from an insolvent employer); and
- the Equal Opportunities Commission, the Commission for Racial Equality or the Disability Rights Commission, as appropriate, in equal pay, sex, race and disability discrimination cases.

9517 The Secretary is responsible for maintaining a **public register** of applications, appeals and decisions (reg 17 Sch 1 SI 2004/1861). The Secretary must enter a copy of the following documents in the register (rule 32 Sch 1 SI 2004/1861):
a. any judgment (including any costs, expenses, preparation time or wasted costs order); and
b. any written reasons provided in relation to any judgment (unless the evidence has been heard in private and the tribunal or Chairman orders otherwise).

MEMO POINTS In cases which involve allegations of the commission of a **sexual offence**, the Secretary can omit or delete from the register or any judgment, document or record of proceedings any identifying matter which is likely to lead members of the public to identify any person affected by or making such an allegation (rule 49 Sch 1 SI 2004/1861) (¶9583).

9518 **Multiple claimants** Often a number of claimants will have identical or very similar cases, for example, where a large number of claimants have been made redundant by the same employer. In such cases the tribunal can order one claimant to represent the interests of all the claimants, order all the applications to be heard and dealt with together, or permit two or more applications to be submitted in a single document by claimants claiming the same relief in respect of the same set of facts (rules 10(2)(j), 1(7) Sch 1 SI 2004/1861).

Submission of a defence

9519 If he wishes to contest the proceedings, the respondent must enter a defence to the proceedings called a **response** (rule 4(1) Sch 1 SI 2004/1861).

9520 **Form** A **revised** standard form (**form ET3**) is sent out to the respondent by the Secretary along with the copy of the ET1, and from 1 October 2005 must be used (SI 2005/435). The following **information** will be required:
- the respondent's full name and address;
- a correspondence address in the UK if different;
- a statement of whether or not he intends to defend the claim (in whole or in part); and
- if he does intend to defend it, on what grounds.

MEMO POINTS If a respondent fails to use the form after this date, his response will be returned to him together with an explanation of why the response has been rejected and a copy of the prescribed form (rule 6(1) Sch 1 SI 2004/1861).

9521 **Entering a defence** The response must be **addressed to** the Secretary and be **presented** by the respondent (using the same **methods** of presentation as are allowed for the claim (¶9512)) **within** 28 days of the date on which a copy of the claim was sent to him (not including the date of receipt). For discussion of the timing of presentation, see ¶9450.

Where a respondent wishes to present a **late response**, an application for an **extension of time** must be made (rule 4(4) Sch 1 SI 2004/1861). The application must be presented to the tribunal **within** 28 days of the date on which the respondent was sent a copy of the claim (excluding the date on which the claim was received) and must explain why the respondent cannot comply with the time limit. 9522

A respondent may apply for more than one extension of time to enter his response (*Skinners Hastings Ltd v Wilkin*, EAT case 1023/00).

In considering the application, the tribunal (which may consist of a Chairman sitting alone) will have regard to the following **factors**:
- the reasons given for the failure or anticipated failure to present the response in time;
- the relative prejudice to the parties of granting or not granting the extension; and
- the merits of the respondent's proposed defence.

This will often be done without the tribunal requiring the parties to attend a hearing, but it is open to the tribunal to invite the views of the claimant in writing, and/or convene a hearing before making its decision.
The Chairman will only extend the time limit in which a response can be presented if he considers that it is just and equitable to do so.

Pre-acceptance procedure On receipt of the response, the Secretary will consider whether the response should be accepted (rule 5(1) Sch 1 SI 2004/1861). 9523

The response will **not** be **accepted** if one or more of the following circumstances applies (rule 6(1), (2) Sch 1 SI 2004/1861):
- (from 1 October 2005) the mandatory response form has not been used;
- the response does not include all the required relevant information; or
- the response has not been presented within the relevant time limit.

If the Secretary considers that the response should not be accepted for either of the two latter reasons, he must refer the response, together with an explanation as to why he does not accept it, to the Chairman who will decide whether or not the response should be accepted in respect of these grounds.

If the Chairman decides that the response **should be accepted**, he will inform the Secretary in writing and the Secretary will accept the response and deal with it accordingly (¶9524).

If the Chairman decides that the response **should not be accepted**, he will record his decision, together with the reasons for it, in writing in a document signed by him and the parties will be informed of his decision by the Secretary. The Secretary will also notify the respondent of the consequences for the respondent of that decision and that the respondent may apply for the decision to be reviewed or appeal against it. The response will be returned to the respondent and the claim will be dealt with as if no response had been presented (rule 6(5), (6) Sch 1 SI 2004/1861).

MEMO POINTS The respondent can apply to the tribunal to **review its decision** not to accept his response on the grounds that the decision was wrongly made as a result of an administrative error or that it is in the interests of justice to do so (see ¶9718 for further details).

Tribunal action on acceptance of response If the response is accepted, on receipt, the **Secretary sends a copy** of it to each other party and records in writing the date on which he does so (rule 5(2) Sch 1 SI 2004/1861). 9524

Multiple claimants Where there are multiple claimants (¶9518), the response form can include the response to more than one claim where the relief sought arises out of the same set of facts provided that the respondent (rule 4(5) Sch 1 SI 2004/1861): 9525
- intends to resist all the claims and the grounds for doing so are the same in relation to each claim; or
- does not intend to resist any of the claims.

Moreover, a single response form can be used by more than one respondent to a single claim provided that (rule 4(6) Sch 1 SI 2004/1861):

– each respondent intends to resist the claim and the grounds for doing so are the same for each respondent; or
– none of the respondents intends to resist the claim.

9526 **Default judgments** A default judgment can be ordered by the Chairman in circumstances in which the claimant's claim is effectively uncontested. If, at any time after the relevant time limit for presenting a response has passed (and the respondent has not been granted an extension of time in which to submit a response), the Chairman may issue a default judgment to determine the claim without a hearing if he considers it appropriate to do so and either (rule 8(2) Sch 1 SI 2004/1861):
– the respondent has **failed to enter a response**; or
– the **response** has **not been accepted**;

and the claimant has not informed the tribunal office in writing either that he does not wish a default judgment to be issued or that the claim has been settled.

A default judgment can determine liability only or both liability and a remedy. The remedy must be determined by the Chairman as appropriate on the basis of the information before him (rule 8(3) Sch 1 SI 2004/1861).

The default judgment must be in writing and signed by the Chairman. The Secretary will then send a copy of it to the parties, ACAS, and, if the proceedings were referred to the tribunal by a court, to the relevant court.

A respondent may, however, apply to have the default judgment reviewed in certain circumstances (¶9726; rules 8(5), 33(1) Sch 1 SI 2004/1861).

9527 **Taking no further part in proceedings** If a respondent **fails to enter a response**, or his response is **not accepted**, he is not entitled to take any further part in the proceedings except to (rule 9 Sch 1 SI 2004/1861):
– apply for a review of a default judgment (¶9726);
– apply for a review of the tribunal's decision not to accept his response under its pre-acceptance procedure (¶9718);
– take part as a witness if called by another person; or
– receive a copy of a decision.

A party who has been precluded from taking any further part in employment tribunal proceedings for having failed to enter a response will **nevertheless be able to** appeal a decision of the employment tribunal since appeals to the EAT are governed by different rules of procedure (*Atos Origin IT Services UK Ltd v Haddock* [2005] IRLR 20, EA) (¶9745).

II. Pre-hearing

1. Amendments to the claim or defence

9530 It is obviously advisable when submitting a claim or response to ensure that it accurately states the case which the party wishes to put forward. It is often the case, however, that a party will subsequently wish to amend his claim or response because of a **mistake** in the original document or as a result of **new facts** which have since come to light. The tribunal has a general discretion to allow amendments (rule 10 Sch 1 SI 2004/1861).

9531 **Timing** An application to amend may be made at any time – before, at, or even after the hearing of the case (*Selkent Bus Co. Ltd v Moore* [1986] ICR 836, EAT). The application should ideally be made as soon as it becomes apparent that it is necessary, as a tribunal will not look favourably on a party changing the basis of his case at a late stage due to the additional time and costs incurred as a result.

Procedure Most applications for amendment are made in advance of the hearing. Amendment applications are one of the interlocutory matters which can be dealt with by a Chairman sitting alone (¶9607). 9532

The application can be made either in the form of a letter setting out the amendment required or by submitting a copy of the ET1/ET3 marked up with the proposed amendments.

The tribunal may be able to determine the application to amend without the need for a hearing and, if the application relates to a **simple minor or clerical error** or is **not particularly controversial**, without seeking the views of the other party. If the other party is not consulted, he will have the **opportunity to object** after being notified of the amendment and his objections should then be considered and, if necessary, a further order made.

If the proposed amendment is **more serious or controversial**, the tribunal will write seeking the views of the other party. If he has no objection, the tribunal can go ahead and make the order approving the amendment. If the **other party does object**, a hearing is normally held so that both parties can put forward their arguments.

Decision In making its decision, the tribunal will attempt to strike a balance between the interests of the parties, and will take account of all the circumstances, including the **following considerations** (*Selkent Bus Co. Ltd v Moore* [1986] ICR 836, EAT): 9533

- the nature of the amendment (i.e. whether it is minor or substantial);
- if it would effectively introduce a new claim, whether the relevant time limit for such a claim has expired and if so, whether time should be extended under the appropriate statutory provision; and
- whether there has been a delay in making the application and if so, the reason for the delay.

Given the possibility that time limits for new claims may have expired, amendments to the claim often raise more difficult questions than amendments to the response. Further, the Court of Appeal has recently held that a **new claim** can **only be introduced** as an amendment to the original claim form **if** the grounds on which this new claim is to be based was particularised in the original claim form (*Ali v Office of National Statistics* [2005] IRLR 201, CA).

EXAMPLE In *Ali v Office of National Statistics*, the Court of Appeal held that as there was nothing in the applicant's original claim of race discrimination which supported his later request for an amendment to include a claim of indirect race discrimination his amendment could not be granted.

Claim

In addition to considering the general factors mentioned above, the tribunal will consider whether the effect of the application would, in fact, be to introduce a **new claim**, or merely to apply a **new label** to facts already presented. Tribunals are more willing to allow amendments which fall into the second category. 9534

EXAMPLE New claim

1. A claimant has submitted an unfair dismissal claim. He then tries to amend his claim to include a race discrimination claim based on **different facts** from those on which the unfair dismissal claim is based. The tribunal is likely to consider it to be a whole new claim, and will have to consider the relevant time limit for the new claim and the rules for extending that limit if necessary (¶9450).

New label

2. If the claimant has set out various facts which he claims amount to unfair dismissal, and then later seeks to amend his claim form to say that the **same facts** also amount to race discrimination, the tribunal is likely to consider the amendment and whether the relevant time limit should be extended if he is out of time.

New respondents The application may be to add a new respondent who was not previously involved in the proceedings, for example, if there is confusion as to which member of a group of companies is the correct employer, or if it transpires that there has been a transfer of an undertaking covered by the business transfer regulations. 9535

The only person who may be joined to the proceedings is a person against whom the claimant is seeking relief (not a person whom the respondent considers ought to share/take liability) (*Eemtrans v McMahon*, EAT case 797/00).

The tribunal can order the addition or substitution of respondents, either of its own motion or on the application of any person (which could be someone other than a party to the proceedings, such as the Secretary of State, who could apply to be joined in proceedings in which he has an interest, for example where the DTI could be liable to meet redundancy payments) (rule 10 Sch 1 SI 2004/1861). It can also (of its own motion or upon application) dismiss from the proceedings any party which appears to it not to have had, or to have ceased to have, any direct interest in the claim.

A tribunal can order the addition or substitution of the respondent regardless of the **time limits**, provided the original claim was itself submitted within the appropriate time limit. The tribunal **approaches** the question in the following way (*Cocking v Sandhurst (Stationers) Limited* [1974] ICR 650, NIRC):

1. It will consider whether the original unamended **claim** is **valid** (¶9511). If it is not, then it cannot be amended and a new claim will be required.
2. If it is valid, the tribunal will consider whether it was presented within the relevant **time limit** for the amended claim. If it was not, the tribunal will not allow the proposed amendment.
3. If it was, the tribunal has a **discretion** whether or not to allow the addition or substitution.

In deciding whether or not to exercise this discretion the tribunal should:
- be satisfied that the mistake as to the correct respondent was genuine, and was not misleading or such as to cause reasonable doubt as to the identity of the person intending to claim (or, as the case may be, to be claimed against); and
- have regard to all the circumstances of the case, in particular any injustice or hardship which may be caused to any of the parties, including those proposed to be added, if the proposed amendment was allowed or refused.

9536 It is even possible for the correct respondent to be substituted for another **after the final decision** has been made by the tribunal, although the new respondent may be able to apply for a review of the original decision if he was not aware of the proceedings (*Watts v Seven Kings Motor Company* [1983] ICR 135, EAT).

> EXAMPLE In *Watts v Seven Kings Motor Company*, the tribunal had made an order awarding compensation against a particular respondent (Seven Kings Motor Company Limited), but it was subsequently discovered that the true employer was in fact an individual trading as Seven Kings Motor Company (i.e. not a limited company). The EAT made an order substituting the true employer for the named respondent as it was satisfied that the true proprietor had been aware of the proceedings.

Response

9537 The tribunal is only entitled to find for the respondent on the grounds that have been specifically pleaded. If, therefore, the respondent has put forward a defence on the basis of one ground when, in fact, the evidence suggests that another would be more appropriate, his defence will fail. It may be essential, therefore, for a respondent to seek an amendment to his response.

If applications are made **during the hearing**, the tribunal will **consider** whether or not the amendment would substantially alter the basis on which the case has been proceeding and in particular, whether it would require the presentation of substantial additional evidence or the recalling of witnesses.

If the respondent is simply seeking to apply a **new label** to the same set of facts, an application will generally be allowed, even at a late stage.

If the proposed amendment introduces a whole **new line of defence**, a tribunal will be less willing to grant a late amendment.

> EXAMPLE New label
> 1. In an unfair dismissal claim, the employer's defence referred to the employee's failure to meet the required standards of work. This could amount to either a capability reason for dismissal or a reason related to conduct. As it is often difficult to determine whether someone is unwilling (misconduct) or unable (capability) to do their job properly, the tribunal will look favourably on a request to amend.

New defence
2. The claimant has claimed that he has been constructively dismissed. The respondent's defence has been that there was no dismissal but, at a late stage, he attempts to introduce a new line of argument suggesting that, if there was a dismissal, then there was a good reason for it. Such an amendment is likely to be rejected.

2. Additional information

A copy of the claim is sent to the respondent, and a copy of the response is sent to the claimant. These documents give the parties formal notice of either the claim which they face or the defence which will be put up against it. It may be that either the claimant or the respondent feels that the document sent to him does **not** contain **enough information** to enable him properly to understand the other party's case, in which case, he can apply to the tribunal for an order for additional information. The tribunal can order a party to provide in writing additional information as to the grounds on which that party relies and of any facts and contentions relevant to those grounds (rule 10(1), (2)(b) Sch 1 SI 2004/1861). 9539

The **purpose** of seeking additional information is not to produce evidence but to clarify the main points of the case put forward by a party. If, for example, a respondent simply stated that the reason for dismissal was that the claimant was not capable of doing his job, it is likely that the respondent would be ordered to provide additional information which establishes the reason for the incapability. If a claimant states that he has been victimised, it would be reasonable to require him to state by whom and in what way.

Written answers The tribunal may require a party to provide written answers to any question where it considers that the answer may help to **clarify any issue** likely to arise for determination in the proceedings, and that it would be likely to assist the progress of the proceedings for that answer to be available to the tribunal (rule 10(1), (2)(f) Sch 1 SI 2004/1861). Its **purpose** is to narrow the issues before the hearing begins. 9541

Timing and procedure The tribunal may make an order for additional information or written answers of its own motion or on the application of either party (who is normally expected to have first requested the other party to provide them **voluntarily**). No particular form of request is required. 9542

An order can be made at any time and can be issued by the Chairman in considering the papers before him in the absence of the parties or at a hearing. The tribunal may lay down a **time limit** for provision of the additional information or written answers (rule 10(3) Sch 1 SI 2004/1861), and will send copies both of the questions and the answers to all the relevant parties.

Failure to comply If a party fails to comply with an order for additional information or written answers, the sanctions are the same as for failure to comply with other orders and practice directions, namely striking out and/or costs or preparation time (¶9562). 9543

3. Disclosure and inspection of documents

Unlike the High Court, in the tribunal there is no automatic process of disclosure (also known as "discovery") or inspection (including the taking of copies) of documents. A party **does not need voluntarily to disclose** any documents to the other party (but if he does disclose some documents, he must not be selective in order to give an unfair or misleading impression of the case) (*Birds Eye Walls Ltd v Harrison* [1985] IRLR 47, EAT). Documents will, of course, form a very important part of many cases. The tribunal, therefore, can order disclosure of **relevant** documents. 9545

The **purpose** of disclosure and inspection is to bring to light the documents which are relevant, and to ensure that the whole picture is presented. A party must, however, have a case to begin with, and must be able to show that the document of which he is seeking 9546 disclosure is relevant to it. He cannot simply go on a "fishing expedition" and demand the production of all types of documents in order to try and deduce whether or not there is a case to be made. The claimant will also have to show that disclosure is necessary for the fair disposal of the claim or to save expense (rule 10(5) Sch 1 SI 2004/1861). For example, in cases arising out of selection for redundancy, the tribunal will only order disclosure of documents relating to the selection process if the claimant can show some basis for saying that the process was unfair. It will not simply order production of the documents to enable the claimant to find out if the process was fair or not (*British Aerospace plc v Green* [1995] IRLR 433, CA).

9547 **Timing and procedure** Either of its own motion, or on the application of either party, the tribunal can order such disclosure and/or inspection of documents and information as might be granted by a county court (or, in Scotland, a sheriff) (rule 10(2)(d) Sch 1 SI 2004/1861). It is normal, before applying to the tribunal for an order, to request the other party to give disclosure or inspection **voluntarily**.

Such requests or applications for orders should always be made as early as possible. The application may be made at any time and no particular form is required. The tribunal can set a **time limit** for complying with any order it makes and can specify the place at which disclosure or inspection of material should take place. The order can be made by a Chairman sitting alone.

9548 **Failure to comply** If a party fails to comply with such an order without reasonable excuse, he will be liable to be punished on summary conviction (i.e. conviction by the Magistrates' Court) by a **fine** (currently up to £1,000) (s 7(4) Employment Tribunals Act 1996). The order must contain a statement warning of the consequences of failure to comply and the amount of the current maximum fine (rule 10(6) Sch 1 SI 2004/1861).

In addition, the tribunal can impose the same sanctions as for failure to comply with other orders and directions, namely striking out and/or costs or preparation time.

Confidentiality issues

9549 Such issues often arise in relation to documents which a party wishes to have disclosed to him. This happens particularly in discrimination cases where the claimant is seeking disclosure of documents which he hopes will show that another employee had been treated more favourably. A party might have in his possession:
- documents which are relevant to the case but which contain additional information which either is not relevant or is confidential; or
- documents which are relevant but disclosure of which might breach a duty of confidentiality to other people not involved in the case.

9550 **Procedure** Tribunals may review the documents in order to consider whether there is any way in which the confidential elements of the documents could be deleted or concealed so that the general substance of the document can be disclosed. For example, an objection to disclosing names of certain people referred to in the documents could be overcome by replacing the names with letters of the alphabet. This review may be carried out either by the tribunal hearing the case or, in advance, by another tribunal depending on the circumstances (such as the availability of tribunal members). Another option is for a fresh document to be prepared which recites the relevant parts of the original documents whilst omitting the confidential details. The fresh document would then be checked against the originals by, for example, the tribunal Chairman. In this way, the relevant parts could be disclosed to the parties without disclosing those parts which it was felt should not be disclosed.

EXAMPLE In *Asda Stores Ltd v Thompson* [2002] IRLR 245, EAT, in which T and others were dismissed for allegedly supplying and using drugs at an office party, witness statements were given by other employees who wished to remain anonymous. The EAT held that it had not been necessary for the tribunal to order full disclosure of the statements in order for the proceedings to have been conducted fairly, but instead the tribunal should have considered ordering the statements to be disclosed subject to the identities of the witnesses not being revealed.

Legal professional privilege

A party cannot require another party to disclose documents and other communications which are **privileged from disclosure** on the grounds of legal professional privilege. This **covers** communications between: 9551
– a party and his legal advisers, provided the communications were confidential and made for the purpose of obtaining or giving legal advice; and
– a party or his legal advisers and a third party if those communications have been made for the purpose of existing or contemplated litigation.

The term "**legal adviser**" is limited to professionally qualified advisers, such as solicitors and barristers and does not extend to non-legally qualified advisers such as employment consultants (*New Victoria Hospital v Ryan* [1993] IRLR 202, EAT; confirmed in *Knight v King Edward Grammar School*, EAT case 936/98).

4. Witness orders

Most witnesses **attend** tribunal hearings **voluntarily** at the request of a party, and they should be invited to do so before any application is made for a witness order (*Dada v Metal Box Company Limited* [1974] IRLR 251, NIRC). However, tribunals can order the attendance of any witness and can also order him to produce any document or information which relates to the claim (rule 10(2)(c) Sch 1 SI 2004/1861). 9553

Where a witness attends voluntarily, it will usually be possible for the party calling that witness (or his representative) to prepare a **written statement** of the witness' evidence in advance of the hearing (¶9635). This enables the party to approach the hearing with some confidence as to what the witness is going to say. This is unlikely to be possible where a witness has to be compelled to attend and so the risks involved in calling such a witness are much greater.

Timing and procedure If a witness order is required, it may be made by a tribunal of its own motion or on the application of a party at any time. No particular form is required. The order may be made by a Chairman sitting alone (rule 12 Sch 1 SI 2004/1861). A tribunal will be unlikely to grant a witness order at the main hearing unless there is good reason as to why the order has not been applied for earlier (for example, that the witness' relevance to the proceedings only became known in the course of the hearing, or that prior to the hearing it was reasonable to believe that the witness would attend voluntarily). Where a witness order is made at the hearing, the hearing may have to be **adjourned** until the witness attends, unless there are other witnesses who can be conveniently dealt with in the meantime (which is only likely to be possible if the hearing is listed for more than 1 day). 9554

The tribunal has **discretion** as to whether or not to grant a witness order. In exercising its discretion, the tribunal will **consider**: 9555
– whether the witness is able to give **evidence which is relevant** to the issues in dispute; and
– whether the party applying for the order can satisfy it that it is **necessary** to issue a witness order.

The party applying for the order will need to give the tribunal some indication of the substance of the evidence which the witness would be able to give (it is not necessary to produce a full proof (i.e. statement) of that evidence), and demonstrate the extent to which it is relevant. The tribunal does not have to be satisfied in every case that the proposed witness would be **unwilling to attend voluntarily**. An order may also be appropriate if the proposed witness is **equivocal** in his response to a request to attend, if he **fails to respond** to such a request, or where it would be easier for a willing witness to attend if a witness order were to be obtained (perhaps because his **employer** is **unwilling** to release him).

If a witness is ordered to attend, he can apply to the tribunal to have the order varied (for example, as to the date or time) or set aside (rule 11 Sch 1 SI 2004/1861).

9556 **Failure to comply** Failure to comply with a witness order is an offence punishable on summary conviction (i.e. conviction by the Magistrates' Court) by a **fine** (currently up to £1,000) (s 7(4) Employment Tribunals Act 1996). The order must contain a statement warning of the consequences of failure to comply and the amount of the current maximum fine (rule 10(6) Sch 1 SI 2004/1861).

The tribunal can also make an award in respect of costs or preparation time or strike out the claim or response where there is non-compliance with a witness order (presumably only where one of the parties is in default in failing to comply with the witness order).

5. Directions

9560 Although tribunal procedure is intended to be relatively informal, tribunals can give directions at any time on any matter arising in connection with the proceedings to ensure that cases proceed as swiftly and efficiently as possible (rule 10(1) Sch 1 SI 2004/1861). Effective case management can narrow the issues, define them more clearly and reduce the time which has to be devoted to the final hearing.

Tribunals can conduct **case management discussions** (i.e. interim hearings) at any time during the tribunal process in order to address matters of procedure and case management. These discussions shall be held in private and, consequently, matters such as a person's civil rights or obligations cannot be dealt with at such a discussion (rule 17 Sch 1 SI 2004/1861 as amended by SI 2005/1865). Directions as to how the claim should proceed can be decided at such case management discussions.

9561 **Timing and procedure** Directions may be given by the tribunal of its own motion or on the application of a party made by notice in writing to the Secretary (no particular form is required).

The **nature and extent** of the directions given depend on the complexity of the case. In **most cases**, tribunals will, as a matter of course, issue standard directions dealing with:
– exchange of witness statements;
– exchange of relevant documents; and
– preparation of an agreed bundle of documents for use at the hearing.

In **more complicated cases**, directions may be required to cover matters such as:
– agreed chronology of events;
– submission of skeleton arguments;
– exchange of medical evidence;
– matters to be dealt with as preliminary issues;
– statements of agreed facts; and
– time estimate for the hearing (as in most cases the standard directions or listing order issued by the tribunal will allow for 1 day only).

Directions can be given by a Chairman sitting alone (this has been encouraged by the EAT), and may be made with or without a hearing (*Halford v Sharples* [1992] ICR 146, EAT). The need for a hearing will generally be determined by the complexity of the case. Parties will often try to **agree directions** to avoid the need for a hearing. The agreed directions are then submitted to the tribunal for approval.

9562 **Failure to comply** If a party fails to comply with a direction, the tribunal can strike out the whole or part of his claim/response and, where appropriate, may make an award of costs or preparation time against him (rules 40(4), 44(4) Sch 1 SI 2004/1861). Such orders are not made, however, until the party who has not complied has been given an opportunity to put forward reasons as to why the tribunal should not do so.

6. Expert evidence

The EAT has issued the following **guidelines** as to how expert evidence should be obtained (*De Keyser Ltd v Wilson* [2001] IRLR 324, EAT): 9565
- before instructing an expert, a party should seek guidance from the tribunal (by correspondence or at a directions hearing) as to whether such evidence will be acceptable;
- joint instruction of experts is preferred (in which case the parties should agree how the expert's fees and expenses will be shared);
- the tribunal may set a time limit for the parties to agree the identity of the expert and the terms of a joint letter of instruction (if the parties do not agree within that time, the tribunal can intervene to assist them to reach agreement), and set a date for his report to be made available;
- if one party instructs his own expert, the weight of his evidence may be increased if the terms of his instruction were submitted to the other party for agreement (or at least for comment) before being finalised;
- any letter of instruction should specify in detail any particular questions that the expert is to answer and any general subjects he is to address (in all cases, the tribunal can give formal directions as to these issues);
- instructions are to avoid partisanship and the letter should emphasise the expert's overriding duty to the tribunal;
- where each party instructs his own expert, the tribunal should, in the absence of agreement between the parties, give a timetable for disclosure/exchange of their reports and for meetings between them (see below), and possibly for the raising of supplementary questions and disclosure/exchange of answers; and
- where separate experts are instructed, they should meet on a "without prejudice" basis to try to resolve points of dispute. Where possible, a schedule of agreed issues/points of dispute should then be produced and disclosed.

The guidelines suggest that tribunals should consider awarding costs against a party who **fails to follow** the above steps.

7. Hopeless or vexatious cases

In order to try to eliminate hopeless or vexatious cases at an early stage (and thus alleviate the burden on tribunal resources and save the parties time and expense), the tribunal has the power to order a pre-hearing review at which the tribunal may make various orders including the payment of a deposit in order to continue the proceedings or the **striking out** of a claim and/or response in whole or in part. 9566

A party who has acted vexatiously, abusively, disruptively or otherwise unreasonably, or whose bringing or conducting of the proceedings has been misconceived, may have a **costs or preparation time order** awarded against him (¶9702). 'Misconceived' includes having no reasonable prospect of success. Tribunals can issue a '**costs warning**' to try to deter misconceived applications, but before doing so, must consider the effect of such a warning on the claimant's decision to proceed with his claim, taking into account whether such a warning is proportionate to the actual risk of substantial costs being awarded against the claimant (*Gee v Shell UK Ltd* [2002] IRLR 82, CA).

A party who repeatedly brings vexatious claims may have his **right to submit new claims** restricted (¶9576).

Pre-hearing reviews

The **purpose** of a pre-hearing review is to carry out a preliminary consideration of the proceedings at which the tribunal may (rule 18(2) Sch 1 SI 2004/1861): 9567
- determine any interim or preliminary matter relating to the proceedings;
- issue any order within its powers;
- order that a deposit be paid without hearing evidence (¶9570);

– consider any oral or written representations or evidence; and
– deal with any application for interim relief (¶8700).

In addition, despite the preliminary nature of a pre-hearing review, it is possible for the tribunal to make a judgment or order at the pre-hearing review which results in the proceedings being **struck out** (¶9573) or **dismissed** or otherwise determined with the result that a full hearing is no longer necessary (rule 18(5) Sch 1 SI 2004/1861).

9568 **Timing and procedure** The pre-hearing review may be ordered either by the tribunal of its own motion or on the application of either party, at any time **prior to the main hearing**, by notice in writing to the Secretary (no particular form is required) (rule 11(1) Sch 1 SI 2004/1861). If one of the parties has requested that such a judgment or order be made, then the judgment or order must be made at the pre-hearing review (or the full hearing) but if no request has been made, then the tribunal can make such judgment or order in the absence of the parties. The party against whom an order or judgment is proposed to be made must be given **advance notice** of the pre-hearing review so that he has an opportunity to submit written representations or put forward oral arguments as to why the judgment or order should not be made (rule 19(1) Sch 1 SI 2004/1861).

A pre-hearing review can be **conducted by** a Chairman sitting alone, although it can be conducted by a tribunal if a party so requests in writing at least 10 days before the date on which the pre-hearing review is due to take place and the Chairman considers that one or more substantive issues of fact are likely to be determined and that this would be desirable (rule 18(3) Sch 1 SI 2004/1861). The members of the tribunal which sit to determine the pre-hearing review (or the Chairman if sitting alone) are not allowed to play any part in the tribunal which ultimately sits to hear the case if, at the pre-hearing review, a requirement to pay a deposit has been considered (rule 18(9) Sch 1 SI 2004/1861).

9569 The tribunal **will consider** the contents of the claim and response, any representations made in writing and any oral argument advanced by or on behalf of a party. It is not a hearing of the evidence of the case.

Deposit to continue proceedings

9570 If, at the pre-hearing review, the tribunal believes that the contentions put forward by a party in relation to any matter to be determined by it have **little reasonable prospect of success**, that party may be **ordered to pay** a deposit of up to £500 as a condition of being allowed to continue to take part in the proceedings relating to that matter (rule 20(4) Sch 1 SI 2004/1861). A tribunal can only make this order if it has taken reasonable steps to ascertain that party's **ability to pay** and has taken such information into account in determining the amount (rule 20(2) Sch 1 SI 2004/1861).

The tribunal can reconsider its decision if there is a **material change** in the factual circumstances or a relevant change in the law (it will therefore need to consider the basis of its previous decision in order to assess whether such a change has occurred) (*Maurice v Betterware (UK) Ltd* [2001] ICR 14, EAT).

The tribunal's decision and its reasons must be **recorded** in writing, and a copy must be sent to the parties, accompanied by a **note explaining** that if the party against whom the order is made persists in participating in the proceedings, he may have an award of costs or preparation time made against him and could lose his deposit (rule 20(3) Sch 1 SI 2004/1861).

9571 An order to pay a deposit as a condition of being allowed to take part in proceedings does not constitute a judgment and **cannot be reviewed** (*Sodexho Ltd v Gibbons*, EAT case 0318-0320/05). However, a **strike out** of such an order does constitute a judgment and can be reviewed (¶9720).

9572 **Payment of the deposit** The deposit must be paid within 21 days from the day on which the written order is sent to the party who is required to pay it. That party can ask the tribunal to extend the 21-day period by up to 14 days, but to do so he must make his application in writing within the 21-day period (rule 20(4) Sch 1 SI 2004/1861). If the deposit is **not paid** within the required period (including any extension), the claim/response (or the relevant parts of such documents) is automatically struck out and the tribunal has no discretion to overlook the failure.

If the party pays the deposit and proceeds with the case but ultimately has a costs or preparation time order made against him, the deposit is **used** in satisfaction or part satisfaction of the award of costs, with any balance of the deposit which exceeds the costs award being returned to him (rule 147(2) Sch 1 SI 2004/1861). If a deposit is paid and the party continues and wins (or loses but does not have an award of costs made against him) his deposit will be **refunded** to him. It will also be refunded if he withdraws from the proceedings before they reach the final hearing.

MEMO POINTS It is likely that the power to order a deposit will be used less frequently now that there is an express power to strike out hopeless cases at the pre-hearing review stage.

Striking out

At the pre-hearing review, the tribunal can strike out or amend all or part of any claim or response on the grounds that it is **scandalous, vexatious, or has no reasonable prospect of success** or if the claimant or respondent (or their representatives) has **conducted the proceedings** in a scandalous, unreasonable or vexatious manner (rule 18(7)(b), (c) Sch 1 SI 2004/1861). 9573

The misconduct does not have to **take place** in the tribunal hearing room as long as it can be said to take place in the conduct of the proceedings (*Harmony Healthcare plc v Drewery*, EAT case 866/00; *Bolch v Chipman* [2004] IRLR 140, EAT).

A tribunal can also exercise its discretion to strike out a claim on the basis that the claimant has acted unreasonably in his **preparation for an appeal** (*Neckles v Yorkshire Rider Ltd*, EAT case 1267/01). In this case, the claimant had produced a transcript made from an unauthorised tape recording of the tribunal hearing but had refused to explain to even the employment tribunal how he had obtained the transcript. The unauthorised recording had been a deliberate breach of rules and constituted scandalous conduct.

A striking-out order must be **proportionate** to the offensive conduct (*De Keyser Ltd v Wilson* [2001] IRLR 324, EAT). In discrimination cases, there is a higher threshold and therefore only in the most exceptional cases should a claimant's claim be struck out (*Jiad v Byford* [2003] IRLR 232, CA).

EXAMPLE 1. In *Harmony Healthcare plc v Drewery*, the employer's representative assaulted D's representative in the **tribunal waiting room** when demanding the return of witness statements. The tribunal was entitled to strike out the response.
2. In *De Keyser Ltd v Wilson*, the employer was granted an order to appoint a medical expert to examine W's allegation that her illness was attributable entirely to her work. The employer's representatives attempted to prejudice the doctor to her disadvantage. The EAT held that striking out was **disproportionate** and that the correct response would have been to ensure the correct instruction of another doctor.
3. In *Edmondson v BMI Healthcare*, EAT case 0654/01, the claimant's lay representative repeatedly interrupted proceedings during the hearing, interfered with evidence being given by E and acted in an agitated manner. The tribunal's decision to strike out E's claim on the basis that not only was her representative's conduct unreasonable, but also on the ground that it was impossible for a fair trial to continue, was upheld by the EAT.

The tribunal can also strike out a claim for **want of prosecution** by the claimant (i.e. where the claimant does not take appropriate steps to bring the proceedings to a hearing or does not do so quickly enough) (rule 18(7)(d) Sch 1 SI 2004/1861). 9574

Moreover, the tribunal can strike out a claim where it considers that it is **no longer possible to have a fair hearing** in those proceedings (rule 18(7)(f) Sch 1 SI 2004/1861).

Timing and procedure An order to strike out may be made at any stage of the proceedings either by the tribunal of its own motion or on the application of either party. An order to strike out for want of prosecution may be made either of the tribunal's own motion or on the application of the respondent. In all cases, the order must not be made until the party 9575 to be struck out has been given an **opportunity to show cause** why (i.e. persuade the tribunal that) the order should not be made (*En'Wezoh v London Forum Hotel Ltd*, EAT case 1153/98). The tribunal normally writes to the relevant party inviting him to respond.

Restriction of proceedings orders

9576 A party who **repeatedly issues** "vexatious" (i.e. **hopeless or malicious**) applications can have a restriction of proceedings order made against them by the EAT (s 33 Employment Tribunals Act 1996). Such an order is not a denial of the right to a fair hearing protected by the Human Rights Act 1998 (*Attorney General v Wheen* [2001] IRLR 91, CA). The order has the **effect** of requiring the party in the future to obtain permission from the EAT before they can commence or continue any proceedings.

9577 **Timing and procedure** The order can only be made on the application of the Attorney General, and can be for a specified period or indefinite. The procedure is rarely used. It is no defence for the allegedly vexatious claimant to say that he has always withdrawn his applications once a tribunal has ordered him to pay a deposit.

> EXAMPLE In *Attorney General v Wheen* [2000] IRLR 461, EAT (approved by Court of Appeal [2001] IRLR 91, CA), W had over a period of time launched 13 sets of tribunal proceedings, all of which had failed. The EAT held that he had issued vexatious proceedings 'habitually, persistently and without any reasonable ground', thus justifying the order.

8. Entitlement to bring or contest proceedings

9580 There may be a question as to the entitlement of a party to bring or contest the proceedings, which may be dealt with at the **pre-hearing review** (rule 18(7)(a) Sch 1 SI 2004/1861). Situations where this could occur include:
- where it appears that the claimant may not have sufficient **qualifying service** to bring the claim which he has presented (¶1080);
- where the claim may have been presented **out of time** (¶9450); or
- where there may be a question as to the **true status of the claimant** (i.e. whether he is employed or self employed).

> EXAMPLE An employee commenced employment on 25 April 2005 and presented an unfair dismissal claim after he was dismissed on 20 April 2006. As it appeared that he had not completed the requisite 1 year of continuous employment, it will be appropriate to decide the question of continuous employment first as a separate issue. If the tribunal then finds that he does not have sufficient continuous employment, the claim will be dismissed and the parties will not be put to the effort and expense of preparing and presenting evidence in relation to the fairness of the dismissal. If, on the other hand, the tribunal finds that there was sufficient continuous employment (for example, because it appears he was dismissed for a reason which does not require any qualifying period (¶1080) or because his effective date of termination is extended by the addition of his statutory minimum period of notice (¶8131)), the case can proceed to a full hearing.

9581 **Timing and procedure** For a discussion as to the timing and procedure for an application by a party for a judgment or order to be made at a pre-hearing review in respect of the entitlement of the other party to bring or contest proceedings, see ¶9568.

The hearing of such an issue will generally also involve the hearing of **evidence**. It is, however, possible to deal with such an application at the beginning of the main hearing. However, if the evidence required to determine the issue of entitlement to bring or contest proceedings and the evidence required to determine the claim **overlap** to a large extent, the tribunal may prefer to consider the whole picture and deal with all the issues at once at the main hearing.

> EXAMPLE An employee is dismissed without notice a few days short of completing 1 year's service. If he is not guilty of gross misconduct, he is entitled to 1 week's statutory notice which he can add on to take him over 1 year's continuous service. If he is guilty of gross misconduct, he is not

entitled to such notice. Since the question of whether or not there was gross misconduct is also likely to be highly relevant to the fairness of the dismissal, the tribunal will probably want to deal with all the issues at the main hearing after having heard all the evidence.

9. Restricted reporting orders

The tribunal can make a restricted reporting order (either temporary or full) in any case which involves allegations of sexual misconduct or in a disability discrimination claim in which evidence of a personal nature is likely to be heard by the tribunal (rule 50(1) Sch 1 SI 2004/1861), as can the EAT (rule 23 Employment Appeal Tribunal Rules SI 1993/2854, as amended). 9583

Sexual misconduct is defined as the commission of a sexual offence, sexual harassment or other adverse conduct of whatever nature related to sex (whether such conduct is of a sexual character itself or is sexual by reference to the sex or sexual orientation of the person at whom the conduct is directed). **Evidence of a personal nature** means any evidence of a medical or intimate nature which might reasonably be assumed to be likely to cause significant embarrassment if reported.

MEMO POINTS There is no power under the Rules to make such an order in cases of sexual discrimination not involving allegations of sexual misconduct (for example, to protect the **anonymity of a transsexual** (*Chief Constable of the West Yorkshire Police v A* [2000] IRLR 465, EAT)), although European law may provide such a power where the claimant would be deprived of an effective remedy if the order were not made.

Timing and procedure The order may be made at any time **before** the **tribunal's decision** in respect of the claim, and may be made either on the application of a party by notice in writing to the Secretary (no particular form is required) or of its own motion (rule 50(2) Sch 1 SI 2004/1861). If a party thinks that a restricted reporting order is appropriate, it is obviously sensible to make the application in advance of the main hearing and certainly not later than the start of the main hearing (otherwise the damage may have been done before the order is made). If the application is made in advance of the hearing, the order can be made by a Chairman sitting alone. 9584

Before making such an order, the tribunal must give each party the opportunity to advance oral arguments at a **hearing** (either the main hearing or at a pre-hearing review) if they wish to do so.

Decision In deciding whether or not to make a restricted reporting order, the tribunal will balance the interests of all concerned, including the interest of the public and the press. Such orders are not granted automatically and are a matter for the tribunal's discretion. 9585

The **order must specify** the persons who are not to be identified. It will remain in force (unless revoked earlier, which might happen if it was no longer intended to call the evidence which had led to the order being made) until the final decision of the claim (which means the decision at a remedies hearing if the matter is adjourned following a "liability only" decision (*Chief Constable of the West Yorkshire Police v A* – see memo point above)).

The Secretary must ensure that a notice of the fact that a restricted reporting order has been made is **displayed** on the tribunal notice board along with any list of the proceedings taking place before the tribunal and on the door of the room in which the proceedings are taking place.

It is an **offence** to publish identifying matter in contravention of a restricted reporting order, and on summary conviction (i.e. conviction by a Magistrates' Court) a fine (not exceeding £5,000) can be imposed. Those who may be convicted of the offence include editors and publishers of newspapers, corporate bodies responsible for the publication and directors or managers of such corporate bodies (s 11(2)(3) Employment Tribunals Act 1996). 9586

10. Freezing injunctions

9590 In a recent significant ruling which may strengthen the tactics of applicants with potentially large claims, the High Court has confirmed that it has jurisdiction to grant a freezing injunction in respect of a pre-existing action which is in the employment tribunal. To succeed **there must be** a pre-existing cause of action at the time of the application which presents a very strong case for compensation. Further, it must be shown that there is a **real risk** that the respondent's assets will be dissipated unless he is prevented from doing so (*Amicus v Dynamex Friction Ltd and another* [2005] IRLR 724, HC).

MEMO POINTS A freezing injunction **freezes the assets** of a party pending an action to ensure that those assets will still be available to satisfy any award which may be made in the future. Freezing injunctions can be made at any time after a cause of action has been brought although such injunctions are **usually brought** as soon as the claim is made as, where there is a real risk of dissipation of assets, time is very often of the essence.

III. Main hearing

9600 After all the preliminary issues have been dealt with, the case will be heard by the tribunal to determine the outstanding procedural or substantive issues or to dispose of the proceedings.

1. Composition of tribunal

9605 When an employment tribunal sits to hear a case, it will usually be made up of a **Chairman** (drawn from a panel of legally qualified chairmen (e.g. solicitors or barristers)), and **two lay members**: one drawn from a panel of lay members from the **employee side** of industry (e.g. with a trade union background) and one from a panel of lay members from the **employer side** of industry (reg 8 SI 2004/1861). When hearing cases, lay members are impartial and independent, and must not show bias based on their own particular background (see below). Some chairmen are appointed on a full-time basis, while others sit only part-time. The lay members are all part-time.

By convention, in **sex or race discrimination cases** at least one member of the tribunal will be a woman or, as the case may be, have special experience of race relations. There is, however, no statutory requirement that this should be the case and the hearing will still be valid if this convention is not followed.

9606 If the parties consent, the hearing can be conducted by a **Chairman and one lay member**, in which case the Chairman has a casting vote if necessary (reg 9(3) SI 2004/1861; s 4(1)(b) Employment Tribunals Act 1996). If, for example, a member of the tribunal is taken ill on the day of the hearing and no replacement is available, the parties may prefer to proceed rather than have the hearing postponed to another day.

Such **consent must be informed** (*Rabahallah v BT Group plc* [2005] IRLR 185, EAT). In this case where a lay member of the panel became unavailable during the proceedings, the unrepresented applicant should have been told the identity of the remaining lay member (i.e. whether they represented the employer's or the employee's side of the industry) before her consent to continue the case was requested.

MEMO POINTS This applies the Court of Appeal's ruling in *de Haney v Brent Mind* (that informed consent must be given before the EAT can hear an appeal by just the judge and one lay member)(¶9789) to proceedings at tribunal level.

9607 **Chairman sitting on his own** The Chairman can hear a matter on his own where the parties have **consented** (perhaps in order to obtain an earlier hearing date), in which case he may do so even if consent is subsequently withdrawn, and where the **respondent is not**

contesting the case. Additionally, the **following complaints** can be heard by a Chairman sitting on his own (s 4(3) Employment Tribunals Act 1996):
– certain deductions of trade union subscriptions from wages;
– failure to supply a written statement of particulars of employment;
– unlawful deductions from wages;
– failure to consult under the regulations relating to business transfers;
– failure to keep records under the national minimum wage legislation;
– breach of contract;
– redundancy payments;
– guarantee payments and certain claims relating to insolvent employers; and
– complaints relating to medical and maternity suspensions.

A Chairman can also sit alone to determine the **entitlement** of a party **to bring or contest** proceedings (¶9580). However, this power should not be used as a matter of course as many of these issues (particularly where the facts are in dispute) would benefit from the **input of the lay members**, with their experience of industrial practice (*Sutcliffe v Big C's Marine* [1998] IRLR 428, EAT).

A case must be heard by a **full tribunal** if the Chairman decides that this is appropriate (s 4(5) Employment Tribunals Act 1996). When reaching his decision, he will have regard to the **following factors**: 9608
– any views of any of the parties as to whether or not the proceedings ought to be heard in either of those ways;
– whether there is a likelihood of a dispute arising on the facts which makes it desirable for the proceedings to be heard by a full tribunal;
– whether there is a likelihood of an issue of law arising which would make it desirable for the proceedings to be heard by a Chairman sitting alone; and
– whether there are other proceedings which might be heard concurrently but which are not proceedings specified as being capable of being heard by a Chairman sitting alone.

The Chairman **must consider** these factors before proceeding to sit on his own. If he fails to do so, his decision can be **challenged**. It does not, however, affect his jurisdiction and so the decision is not a nullity. If, for example, the parties had expressly agreed to the Chairman sitting alone, then his decision is likely to be upheld even if he had not explicitly considered the various factors (*Post Office v Howell* [2000] IRLR 224, EAT).

2. Fairness and natural justice

The tribunal, like any court, has a duty to follow the principles of natural justice at all stages in the proceedings but particularly at the final hearing. The two most important principles involved are that each side should be given a proper **opportunity to be heard** and present his case, and that the tribunal should be **impartial** and not be biased or give the appearance of bias. 9610

Opportunity to be heard

Each party (or his representative) must be allowed to **put his case** or **make submissions** on any issue upon which the tribunal is asked to decide. The tribunal should, therefore, not prevent a party from commenting on points raised by the other side. Further, the tribunal should not decide on an issue which it has identified as being of importance to the decision which it has to make without hearing from both parties. For example, if the parties have not addressed the question of contributory fault during a hearing, the tribunal cannot make a decision in relation to contribution without first asking the parties to express their views (or call evidence) in relation to the matter, nor can it rely on previous legal decisions without giving the parties the opportunity to make submissions on those decisions (*Albion Hotel (Freshwater) Ltd v Maia e Silva* [2002] IRLR 200, EAT). However, once the tribunal has raised a particular issue, the parties must ensure that all relevant evidence is brought to support their contentions (¶9660). 9611

Bias

9612 The right to a fair trial by an **independent and impartial tribunal** is a statutory right (Human Rights Act 1998) and a basic principle of natural justice. The principle is so important that the appearance of bias ("apparent bias") is as unacceptable as "actual bias" (*Locabail (UK) Ltd v Bayfield Properties Ltd* [2000] IRLR 96, CA). These are discussed below.

9613 **Actual bias** This arises where a judge (or tribunal member) is actually affected in his decision by **partiality or prejudice** towards or against one party. Such cases are rare and, for obvious reasons, difficult to prove.

9614 **Apparent bias** This usually arises where a **judge** (**or tribunal member**) has an **interest in the outcome**. If such an interest exists (even if he has put it entirely from his mind), it is not acceptable for him to be involved in the case. The issue is not whether the judge is linked to one of the parties, but whether the outcome of the case could realistically affect the judge's own interests and, therefore, his decision (for example, where he has a substantial shareholding in a company which is involved in a case, or he plays an active part in a charity which promotes a cause which is also supported by one of the parties (*R v Bow Street Metropolitan Magistrate, ex parte Pinochet Ugarte (No2)* [1999] 2 WLR 272, HL)). The test is whether a fair-minded and informed observer would conclude that there was a real possibility or danger that the tribunal was biased (*In Re Medicaments and Related Classes of Goods* [2001] ICR 564, CA).

There is no apparent bias if his **personal interest is so small** that it would be incapable of affecting his decision. If there is any doubt, the judge or tribunal member will be disqualified. **Indirect interests**, such as those of a spouse or other relative of the judge, are considered in the same light.

The issue of apparent bias can also arise in the context of a **tribunal's preliminary views** regarding the outcome of a case before it. It is acceptable for a tribunal to indicate to the parties its current thinking before the case has been concluded, provided only if it stresses that such views are provisional (*Jiminez v London Borough of Southwark* [2003] IRLR 477, CA). In this case, no apparent bias arose when a tribunal expressed a preliminary view on the treatment of the employee by the employer, having heard almost all the evidence save for evidence to be given by an insignificant witness, but before the parties had made their closing submissions.

Apparent bias can also occur if a **tribunal member cannot give his full attention** to the proceedings, for example, if he has consumed alcohol or has fallen asleep (*Stansbury v Datapulse plc and another* [2004] IRLR 466, CA).

9615 A further situation of possible apparent bias is where **counsel who has previously sat as a part-time judge** at the EAT appears as an advocate before one or more of the EAT lay members. With regard to this, the House of Lords has stated that this practice should cease since confidence in the judicial system would be reduced (*Lawal v Northern Spirit Ltd* [2003] IRLR 538, HL).

On the other hand, the EAT has held that there was no bias where the **Chairman** of the tribunal hearing the case had made, in an **earlier unconnected case**, a **costs order** (because of the way the proceedings had been conducted) against a party the claimant had represented in his capacity as a union representative (*Lodwick v London Borough of Southwark*, EAT case 116/05). This decision was given after the Court of Appeal had ruled that the EAT did have jurisdiction to hear the issue and the EAT in coming to its decision drew upon the Court of Appeal's ruling that in these circumstances "**something more**" is required to establish bias. The EAT also confirmed that, had it been in any doubt as to the issue of bias, the matter would have been put firmly beyond doubt due to the way in which the claimant was assisted by the tribunal during the hearing and in the formulation of his case.

9616 **Impact of bias** The judge (or tribunal member) himself must be alert to the possibilities of bias, and should stand down from the case at the earliest possible moment (preferably before any objection is raised). If a party is aware of a judge's interest, he should draw it to the attention of the tribunal before the start of the hearing. If he fails to raise the matter at the hearing, a party may waive his right to complain of bias (*Anthony v Governing Body of Hillcrest School*, EAT case 1193/00).

The Court of Appeal has provided **guidance** as to the procedure tribunals should adopt in cases in which there is a real possibility that the test for apparent bias would be met (*Jones v DAS Legal Expenses Insurance Co Ltd* [2004] IRLR 218, CA). In such cases, the Court of Appeal stated that if another Chairman or tribunal member is available to hear the case they should do so, otherwise:
– the Chairman should take time to fully explain to the parties what the facts are, why the issue of bias has arisen at such a late stage in the proceedings, and why (if appropriate) there is no other Chairman or tribunal who is available to hear the case on that day;
– the Chairman's explanation should be mechanically recorded, if possible;
– the Chairman should explain the parties' options to them, including asking the Chairman or tribunal to stand down. They should be told that if they do not object at this stage of the proceedings, they will lose the right to object on this issue later on;
– if the parties decide not to proceed with the case that day, they should be informed of the likely re-listing dates; and
– the parties should be informed that they have time to reflect on the issue before deciding whether to object to the Chairman or tribunal continuing to hear the case. If a person is not legally represented, he might be referred to the Citizens' Advice Bureau, chief clerk or listing officer.

Bias will normally mean the judge's disqualification from further involvement in the case. If the **case has already been determined**, such bias will normally give a party grounds for having the decision set aside (¶9795).

3. Public hearings

Unless an exception applies (see below), tribunal hearings must be held in public and **failure to have a public hearing** will make any decision which the tribunal has made unlawful and liable to be set aside (rule 26(3) Sch 1 SI 2004/1861). **9617**

The **test** for deciding whether a hearing is in public is whether the public has unimpeded access to it (and not whether a member of the public is actually prevented from attending it) (*Storer v British Gas plc* [2000] IRLR 495, CA).

EXAMPLE In *Storer v British Gas plc*, there was no tribunal room available to deal with S's case. Instead, it was heard in the Chairman's office which was in an area of the building marked "private no admittance to public beyond this point" and secured by a door with a push button coded lock. The Court decided that this did not constitute a hearing in public and so set aside the tribunal's decision, and remitted the case to be reheard by another tribunal.

In *Storer v British Gas plc*, the Court of Appeal appeared, in passing, to suggest that **all hearings** (including pre-hearing reviews) should be held in public. **9618**

The tribunal will exercise its discretion to **hear evidence in private** in the following circumstances: **9619**
– if disclosure of information contained in the evidence would **contravene any statute**, (for example, the Official Secrets Act) (rule 16(1)(a) Sch 1 SI 2004/1861);
– if the evidence consists of information which has been communicated to a witness in confidence or which he has obtained under a **duty of confidence** (rule 16(1)(b) Sch 1 SI 2004/1861); or
– if the evidence consists of information which if disclosed would cause substantial **injury to any undertaking** of the witness (or any undertaking in which he works) for reasons other than its effect on negotiations in respect of a trade dispute (for example, the disclosure of trade secrets) (rule16(1)(c) Sch 1 SI 2004/1861).

MEMO POINTS A hearing may be held in private if a Minister of the Crown has directed a tribunal to sit in private on grounds of **national security** (rule 54(1)(a) Sch 1 SI 2004/1861) or if the evidence relates to matters which would be against the interest of national security to be heard in public (where no order has been made by a Minister) (rule 54(2)(a) Sch 1 SI 2004/1861).

9620 An **application** for a hearing to be held in private will normally be made at the commencement of the hearing or during the hearing if the need arises in respect of a particular witness.

If a tribunal does sit in private, it has to decide **who should be allowed to attend** the hearing. Obviously, the members of the tribunal, the tribunal staff, the parties and their representatives, and the witness giving evidence at the time will have to be present, but more difficult questions arise in relation to, for example, a party's spouse whom that party wishes to be in attendance. The tribunal will decide whether there is any need for that person to be there (for example, if their assistance is required in presenting a case) and whether any prejudice would be caused by their presence.

9621 Where the specific rules discussed above do not apply, a tribunal cannot use its **general power to regulate its own procedure** (rule 10(1) Sch 1 SI 2004/1861) to sit in private (*R v Southampton Industrial Tribunal, ex parte INS Newsgroup Ltd and Express Newspapers plc* [1995] IRLR 247, EAT), and the parties' and witnesses' only recourse is an application for a restricted reporting order, where such orders are available (¶9583).

EXAMPLE In *R v Southampton Industrial Tribunal, ex parte INS Newsgroup Ltd and Express Newspapers plc*, allegations of indecent assault were raised. The tribunal had made a restricting reporting order which had allegedly been breached by a newspaper. The tribunal then made an order excluding the public and the press at certain stages in the proceedings when "salacious or sensitive" evidence was to be read. It did so under its general power to regulate its own procedure. The EAT held that this was not a legitimate use of that power.

4. Listing the case for hearing

9623 The President of the Employment Tribunals, Vice-President, or a regional Chairman will decide when and where the hearing of the claim should take place (rule 27(1) Sch 1 SI 2004/1861). Unless they consent to shorter notice, the parties must normally be given at least 14 days' notice of the hearing date (rule 14(4) Sch 1 SI 2004/1861). The **notice of hearing** will also set out information about:

a. attending the hearing;
b. where the case will be heard, the date and the time of the hearing;
c. the calling of witnesses and the bringing of documents; and
d. the opportunity to be represented by another person or to make written representations.

The tribunal normally lists more cases on each day than could actually be heard in the expectation that many will settle prior to the hearing. If too few settle, some cases may have to be removed from the list shortly before the hearing date, start later than the allocated time, or even be postponed on the day itself.

9624 **Time estimate** Cases are normally listed for hearing on 1 day only. If a party believes that the case will take **more than 1 day** because of the number of witnesses or the amount of legal argument involved, he must notify the tribunal beforehand, preferably having agreed a time estimate with the other party. Often this is dealt with at the pre-hearing review, if there is one.

If no estimate is given (or if the case takes longer than expected) and the case is **not completed** in the time allotted, it is not normally possible to continue the case on the following day, as the lay members (and sometimes the Chairman) are part-time. The case will be **adjourned** to a later date that is convenient to all those involved, resulting in a potential **delay** of several weeks or months, which may make it more difficult to deal with the evidence in a coherent way.

9625 **Requests for postponements** In most cases, the tribunal initially sends out a notice of hearing without consulting the parties as to convenient dates. In cases where finding a date convenient to all concerned is likely to be difficult, the tribunal often gives an indication of the period during which it intends to hold the hearing and asks the parties to submit a list of dates within that period which would not be suitable.

If a party requests a postponement of the hearing date **due to illness**, the onus is on him to prove that his inability to attend is genuine and that a postponement is necessary (*Teinaz v London Borough of Wandsworth* [2002] IRLR 721, CA; *Andreou v Lord Chancellor's Department* [2002] IRLR 728, CA). If a claimant receives **medical advice** informing him **not to attend a tribunal hearing**, then he cannot be expected to attend to prove he is unable to attend (*Teinaz v London Borough of Wandsworth*, above). However, if a claimant simply receives **medical advice** informing him **not to attend work**, then it does not automatically follow that he is unable to attend a tribunal hearing (*Andreou v Lord Chancellor's Department*, above).

Unless there are exceptional circumstances, requests for postponements **must be made** in writing within 14 days of the date of the notice of hearing. It is important, therefore, as soon as the notice of hearing is received, that the party or his representative confirms the availability of all potential witnesses on the date allocated. 9626

A Chairman has a wide **discretion** to postpone the day or time fixed for a hearing (rule 10(2)(m) Sch 1 SI 2004/1861), especially where this will allow the parties to pursue efforts towards conciliation. In any event, if the parties are subject to a statutory fixed period of conciliation, the hearing must be postponed until after the conciliation period has ended (¶9219). The Chairman's duty is to do as he thinks best in the interest of justice in each individual case (*Carter v Credit Change Ltd* [1979] IRLR 361, CA). He also has to take into account the Human Rights Act (in particular, the right to a fair trial).

Before deciding on a request for a postponement, the tribunal normally gives each party the opportunity to make **representations** (orally or in writing) as to why the hearing should or should not be postponed.

If the tribunal grants a postponement on the application of a party, it can make an order in respect of **costs or preparation time** in favour of or against (depending on the circumstances) the party requesting the postponement (rules 40(1), 44(1) Sch 1 SI 2004/1861).

> EXAMPLE In *London Fire and Civil Defence Authority v Samuels*, EAT case 450/00, a directions hearing was held at which the main hearing was listed for 14-18 August. The employer's barrister was unaware that a key witness was unavailable on those dates (he therefore raised no objection). The employer's subsequent request for a postponement was refused as the barrister should have had available dates at the directions hearing and the key witness would not be greatly inconvenienced by having to attend. The interests of justice/administrative efficiency in bringing the matter to a hearing were also taken into account.

Requests for postponement pending decisions by other courts Employment disputes can give rise to cases not only in the tribunal but also in the High Court and county court, and there will often be a significant degree of **overlap** between such cases. For example, a dismissal could give rise to an unfair dismissal case in the tribunal but also to a wrongful dismissal (breach of contract) case in the High Court or county court (where, for example, the employee's loss exceeds the £25,000 limit on contractual claims in the tribunals). Although the legal remedies sought are different, many of the facts to be considered will be the same. Tribunals will, therefore, often be asked to postpone the main tribunal hearing until after the High Court (or county court) has made its decision in any related case. 9628

When faced with such an application, the tribunal will consider **factors** such as:
- the delay which will inevitably result;
- the degree of overlap between the issues in the two sets of proceedings;
- the complexity of the issues;
- the nature of the evidence;
- the sums being claimed in each case; and
- the legal principle of "res judicata".

In basic terms, **res judicata** (sometimes referred to as "issue estoppel") means that once an issue has been decided in one court it should not be reopened in another court. Therefore, if a tribunal makes a decision on the facts of a case after hearing the evidence, such a finding could bind a High Court judge who had to determine similar issues in an overlapping case. Further, if a claimant **withdraws** his claim before it is decided such that it is dismissed, 9629 he may be prevented from bringing a fresh claim based on the same facts ("cause of action estoppel"), depending on the reason for his withdrawal, which the tribunal should ascertain (*Ako v Rothschild Asset Management Ltd* [2002] IRLR 348, CA). Consequently, the **reasons** for the withdrawal must also be made clear (*London Borough of Enfield v Sivanandan* [2005] EWCA Civ 10).

However, if he has **reserved** the right to bring proceedings in a different court, he may be allowed to do so (*Sajid v Sussex Muslim Society* [2002] IRLR 113, CA).

> EXAMPLE In *London Borough of Enfield v Sivanandan*, the Court of Appeal was satisfied that the claimant's breach of contract claim in the tribunal had been struck out with her other claims (of race and sex discrimination, victimisation, and unfair dismissal) on the grounds that they were scandalous, vexatious and with no reasonable prospect of success. As a result, her attempt to re-litigate it in the High Court on the basis that her breach of contract claim had been withdrawn from the tribunal to allow her to pursue the civil proceedings (where the amount that could be rewarded was not limited to £25,000) failed.

9630 It may be **undesirable** for the tribunal **to deal** with the case before the High Court (or county court) for the following reasons:

– the rules of evidence in the High Court are much stricter and the procedures are more formal (a High Court judge could, therefore, find himself forced to accept a finding of fact by a tribunal which it would not have been appropriate for him to have made applying the stricter rules of evidence);

– the High Court claim will often involve much larger sums than could be awarded by the employment tribunal;

– the High Court claim may also involve counterclaims by the employer which could not be made in the employment tribunal; and

– the successful party in the High Court would be able to recover his costs from his opponent, which is less likely to be the case in the tribunal.

The tribunal may, therefore, be inclined to postpone the main hearing (or any preliminary hearing dealing with overlapping factual issues) until after concurrent High Court or county court proceedings, particularly if the claimant indicates that he has only issued his tribunal proceedings in order to comply with the applicable time limit for tribunal claims.

Similar consideration will apply where there are concurrent proceedings in **foreign jurisdictions** or **criminal proceedings**.

9631 **Dismissals in connection with industrial action** Where a claimant alleges that he has been dismissed for participation in official industrial action and court proceedings are taking place to determine whether or not that industrial action is covered by the protections given by trade union legislation, the tribunal may adjourn the application until those court proceedings have been concluded (rule 10(2) Sch 1 SI 2004/1861).

5. Preparation for the hearing

9633 The tribunal will usually give directions on matters such as the exchange of witness statements and preparation of bundles of documents (¶9560). Even if it has not done so, it is clearly in the interests of both the parties and the tribunal that such matters should be addressed.

9634 **Bundle of documents** Cases often involve a lot of documents and to be dealt with efficiently, these need to be presented in a way which makes them easy to find and identify during the hearing. The parties should agree a bundle of documents **containing** all correspondence and other documents on which they intend to rely at the hearing. The bundle should be in chronological order and have numbered pages.

If there is any dispute as to the **admissibility or authenticity** of any document, then (unless it can be dealt with at a case management discussion or pre-hearing review) such documents should still be included in the bundle but the issue should be raised at the beginning of the hearing.

Where a full tribunal is hearing the claim, **at least six copies** of the bundle should be prepared – three for the tribunal, one for each party and one for use by witnesses as they give evidence. The party preparing the bundle (which will usually be the claimant or his representative) should ensure that all the photocopies in the bundle are legible. It is helpful to include an **index** at the beginning of the bundle identifying the page numbers of each document.

Witness statements Unless the tribunal has specifically ordered this, there is no requirement for parties to exchange (or indeed prepare) written witness statements. Most tribunals will, however, **order** that there should be **simultaneous exchange**, a certain number of days prior to the hearing, of statements of **all witnesses which each party intends to rely on**, and that no further witnesses may be called at the hearing without the tribunal's permission. The statements prepared for the tribunal hearing may be based on statements produced at an earlier stage in the dispute, or as part of a disciplinary process (see ¶9170 for information as to their preparation, content and format). 9635

If written witness statements are used then, as with bundles of documents, **at least six copies** should be prepared for use at the hearing. Where statements have been exchanged, they will often be included either in the main bundle of documents or in a separate bundle which contains the statements of all witnesses for both parties.

Even if the tribunal has not ordered exchange of witness statements, a party will usually find it helpful to prepare witness statements for each witness. This saves time **at the hearing** because the tribunal will normally allow each witness simply to read out his statement. It also ensures that all the salient points which the witness wishes to make are there in writing and less likely to be forgotten or omitted in the course of giving evidence.

Tribunals should exercise their discretion in relation to **confidential witness statements** and order disclosure in an anonymised and redacted form if necessary (*Asda Stores Ltd v Thompson* [2002] IRLR 245, EAT). In exercising its discretion, a tribunal will consider the risk of reprisals, any promise of confidentiality and whether the disclosure of the statements and their origin are necessary for the fair disposal of the case. 9636

Written representations Parties can submit written representations to be considered at the hearing. If they wish to do so they should send them to the Secretary at least 7 days before the hearing and copy them to the other parties at the same time (rule 14(5) Sch 1 SI 2004/1861). This will generally happen if a party does **not intend to appear** at the hearing. The tribunal will have to decide **how much weight** to attach to such representations. They will not normally be given as much weight as evidence which has been given orally and tested by cross-examination. 9637

Occasionally, a tribunal will direct that the parties supply written submissions before the hearing. However, if it does so, the tribunal must wait to receive written submissions from both parties before making its decision, particularly if there was no delay in the lodging of the submissions by either party (*Mayor and Burgesses of London Borough of Haringey v Akpan*, EAT case 0974/00).

6. Representation

A party can present his case in person or be represented by a barrister or solicitor, a trade union representative or employers' association representative, or by any other person of his choice (s 6(1) Employment Tribunals Act 1996). Most parties are represented at hearings (statistics suggest that respondents are more likely to be legally represented than claimants). See ¶9130 for details on the availability of legal advice. 9640

A tribunal has no power to interfere with a party's **choice of representative** and **cannot exclude** a representative, although it does have power to control the way in which a representative conducts a case before it (*Bache v Essex County Council* [2000] IRLR 251, CA, confirmed in *Dispatch Management Services (UK) Ltd v Douglas* [2002] IRLR 389, CA; rules 10(1), 27(1) Sch 1 SI 2004/1861). 9641

MEMO POINTS It should be noted that a tribunal can make a **wasted costs order** against a party's representative in certain circumstances (¶9711).

9642 If a party is **unrepresented** (and particularly if his opponent is represented), the tribunal will attempt to ensure that he is not prejudiced as a result. The Chairman cannot present his case for him or tell him what evidence to call, but he will try to explain the procedure and the relevant law, and to assist him in presenting his case properly. For example, if an unrepresented party is giving evidence, a Chairman may adopt a more interventionist approach by asking questions to elicit the evidence which the party wishes to put before the tribunal.

7. The hearing itself

Form

9645 Tribunal procedure is designed to be relatively **informal**. A tribunal has a **wide discretion** as to how the proceedings should be conducted, and can conduct the hearing in such way as it considers most appropriate for the clarification of the issues before it and for the just handling of the proceedings, making such enquiries of the people appearing before it and the witnesses as it considers appropriate (rule 10(1) Sch 1 SI 2004/1861). Tribunals are specifically required to avoid formality as far as is appropriate, and are not bound by the strict rules of evidence which are applied in court (so that for example, a more relaxed approach is taken to hearsay evidence (¶9667)). Parties, their representatives and witnesses remain seated while addressing the tribunal or giving evidence.

Some degree of **structure** is, of course, necessary to ensure that the proceedings are dealt with efficiently and to this extent the procedure is similar to that in court. The more complicated a case, the more likely it is that a greater degree of formality will be introduced to ensure that all the issues are properly explored and that the case is properly understood.

9646 Each party may give evidence, call and question witnesses, and address the tribunal (rule 27(2) Sch 1 SI 2004/1861). The Chairman is obliged to make notes of the evidence and representations put forward during the hearing. There is no right to make any **opening statement**, but the party going first will often, particularly in more complicated cases, give the tribunal a brief outline of his case before calling the first witness. Whether or not this is allowed is within the discretion of the Chairman.

9647 In England and Wales (though not in Scotland), **witnesses** are allowed to be present in the tribunal room before they have given their evidence. A party may, however, ask the tribunal to exclude any witness prior to giving his evidence.

The tribunal may require witnesses to give evidence on oath or by affirming (rule 27(3) Sch 1 SI 2004/1861). When witnesses are giving their evidence, they should address the tribunal even though the questions are being put by a party or his representative. The tribunal Chairman should be addressed as Sir or Madam.

Failure to attend

9648 Where a party fails to attend the hearing and is not represented, the tribunal has to decide whether to dismiss the application, dispose of it in the absence of either the claimant or the respondent or adjourn the hearing to a later date (rule 27(5) Sch 1 SI 2004/1861). Before making its decision, however, the **tribunal must consider**:
– the claim/response submitted by the absent party, and any written representations or answers (rule 27(6) Sch 1 SI 2004/1861); and
– any information available to it as to the reason for non-attendance and whether the absent party had intended to appear.

In doing so, the tribunal must be **pro-active in making enquiries** to try to ascertain why the absent party has not attended and if they had intended to appear (*Cooke v Glenrose Fish Co.* [2004] IRLR 866, EAT). In most cases this means that the tribunal should telephone the absent party or at the very least consider whether it is appropriate to do so. Further, enquiries should be made of the other party as to any news they may have and whether they knew if the absent party had intended to come and, consequently, whether it was possible that the absence was due to the absent party being delayed or having forgotten the matter.

In making its decision, the **tribunal must explain its reasons** as to why it has taken the decision to dismiss, dispose of, or adjourn the application (*Robinson v Home Office*, EAT case 0553/01). Failure to do so will result in a breach of the right to a fair trial under the Human Rights Act. However, the tribunal is not under a duty to be satisfied that the respondent has established a good defence to the claim being brought by a non-attending claimant before dismissing such a claim (*Roberts v Skelmersdale College* [2004] IRLR 69, CA).

A party who is unable to attend for whatever reason, or who is going to be late, should, therefore, make every effort to contact the tribunal before the time appointed for the hearing in order to explain their absence.

Normally, the tribunal clerk will try and contact the absent party to find out whether or not **9649** he **intends to appear**. If he does and he is able to get to the tribunal within a reasonable time, the tribunal may be prepared to **give him time** to get there (particularly if it has other cases which it may deal with in the meantime). Alternatively, if he does intend to appear but is unable to get there on that day and has a **good reason**, the appropriate decision for the tribunal is to **adjourn** to a later date.

In either case, if the delay results in the case not being finished on that day, it is likely that the tribunal will make an order for **costs or preparation time** against the absent or late party, unless he can put forward a good reason (rules 40(4), 44(4) Sch 1 SI 2004/1861).

If the clerk finds that the absent party **does not intend to appear**, the tribunal will normally **9650** dismiss the case (if the party in question is the claimant) or deal with the case in the absence of that party (either the claimant or the respondent). In either case, it is likely that a **costs or preparation time order** will be awarded against the absent party, although in the case of an absent respondent, a costs or preparation time award is only likely if the claimant is successful in the case.

If **no contact** can be made or if the tribunal nonetheless continues with the hearing and **9651** dismisses the case or proceeds with it in the absence of a party, the absent party is entitled to apply to the tribunal for a **review** of the tribunal's decision, which may be successful if he had a good reason for not attending the hearing (rule 34 Sch 1 SI 2004/1861).

Initial matters

There are often a number of "**house-keeping**" points to be dealt with at the start of a hearing, **9655** including any of the following applications:
- for a restricted reporting order;
- for the hearing to be held in private;
- to amend the claim/response;
- with regard to disputed documents; or
- for permission to call witnesses whose evidence has not been exchanged in accordance with directions.

The Chairman may also give, or be requested to give, **guidance** as to how he intends to deal with different issues. For example, it is common practice in **unfair dismissal** cases for liability to be dealt with first and only if the claimant is found to have been unfairly dismissed, for the tribunal then to hear evidence in relation to compensation and other remedies. There may also be questions as to whether any allegation that a claimant has contributed to his dismissal should be dealt with as part of the main evidence on the dismissal or as part of the subsequent determination of remedy. It is useful for all concerned to know exactly how the tribunal wishes to deal with these matters at the outset so that evidence can be led and representations made at the appropriate time.

Who goes first?

The **general rule** is that the party who has the burden of proving his case should present his **9656** case first (*Gill v Harold Andrews Sheepbridge Ltd* [1974] IRLR 109, NIRC). This is, however, subject to the tribunal's discretion, and it may decide that it is more convenient to take the evidence in a different order.

In **unfair dismissal cases**, this will depend on whether or not the dismissal is admitted. If the respondent does **not admit dismissing** the employee (which most often arises in constructive dismissal cases), the claimant will have to present his case first as he must prove the dismissal. If the respondent **does admit** that the claimant was dismissed then, since the respondent must prove the reason for the dismissal, the respondent will go first. In most unfair dismissal cases, therefore, the employer's case is presented first.

In **discrimination cases**, once the claimant has established a prima facie case (i.e. a case to be answered), the burden of proving that the actions taken were not discriminatory shifts to the respondent (Sex Discrimination (Indirect Discrimination and Burden of Proof) Regulations SI 2001/2660; Employment Equality (Sexual Orientation) Regulations SI 2003/1661; RRA 1976; Employment Equality (Religion or Belief) Regulations SI 2003/1660; DDA 1995). The question of who goes first is, therefore, likely to depend on whether the tribunal feels from the claim and the response that a prima facie case exists before any evidence is heard.

Evidence

9660 The presentation of evidence at the main hearing and the rules relating to admissibility of evidence are discussed below.

9661 **Presentation** Each party will call the witnesses that he believes can produce the evidence to support his case. Although a contrary view has been expressed in some cases, the general view is that it is up to a party or his representative to decide the **order** in which he puts forward his witnesses (*Barnes v BPC (Business Forms) Ltd* [1975] IRLR 313, QBD).

It is up to the parties to ensure that **all relevant evidence** is put before the tribunal. The tribunal does not have any obligation to point out any gaps in the evidence or make any further investigation to try and fill them (*Mensah v East Herts NHS Trust* [1998] IRLR 531, CA), although it may try to be helpful, particularly where a party is unrepresented.

9662 Each witness (including the parties themselves if giving evidence) will give their evidence in turn. If there is a **written witness statement**, they may be allowed by the tribunal to give their evidence by reading it out. Sometimes the tribunal may simply ask the witness to confirm that it is his written statement and that he has signed it and accepts it as his evidence, in which case the tribunal members will read the statements themselves. Where the witness has difficulty in reading, the tribunal may ask his representative to read the statement on his behalf.

Where a written statement is read, the tribunal normally allows the party presenting the case (or his representative) to ask **further questions** of the witness either as he proceeds with the statement or after it has been read. It is sensible, however, to check with the tribunal at the beginning of the hearing as to how it wishes to handle this. The tribunal members will often ask questions of their own during or after the reading.

A party (or his representative) must not ask leading questions of his witnesses. A **leading question** is one which suggests its own answer (and usually can be answered simply yes or no). For example, "when you went into the room, did you see Fred taking money from the till?" is a leading question, whereas "when you went into the room, did you see anyone there and, if so, what were they doing?" is not. Leading questions asked in relation to non-controversial matters, such as "are you Fred Smith?", "did you work for the respondent?" will not normally be objected to.

9663 Once a witness has completed his evidence (and been asked any additional questions by the party who has called him or his representative), that witness is **cross-examined** by the other party or his representative. Cross-examination involves questioning the witness about any parts of his evidence which are disputed. It will also involve putting to the witness the contrary version of events which the other party wishes to prove. It is important in cross-examination that any aspect of a witness's evidence which is disputed is put to him and tested. If it is not, the tribunal may find that that evidence is not disputed. **Leading questions** are allowed in cross-examination.

Once the first party's witnesses have given evidence and been cross-examined, the same process is repeated with all the witnesses for the other party.

Sometimes, as a matter of convenience, it may be necessary to depart from this sequence. 9664
For example, if a witness is, for good reason, only able to attend the hearing at a certain time then it may be necessary for that witness's evidence to be heard **out of sequence**.

Parties should take care to ensure that they bring out from each witness all the relevant 9665
information which that witness has whilst they are giving evidence as the tribunal will be reluctant to allow a party to **recall a witness** later without good reason.

Rules Tribunals are **not bound** by the strict rules of evidence applied in the civil courts, 9666
although those rules are not to be completely disregarded. These rules have developed in order to ensure fairness and consistency in the way in which evidence is dealt with and so tribunals do follow the basic principles.

A tribunal may admit "hearsay evidence" (which would not normally be admitted in civil 9667
courts), unless it considers that doing so could adversely affect its ability to reach a proper decision in the case (*Coral Squash Club Ltd v Matthews* [1979] IRLR 390, EAT). **Hearsay evidence** is evidence given by someone who does not have direct knowledge of the facts which he is putting forward but was told of them by someone else. For example, "I saw Fred hit Jim" is not hearsay evidence but "Jim told me that Fred hit him" is.

Tribunals are also able to take a less restrictive approach to what is known as "**similar fact** 9668
evidence". In a criminal court, it will not normally be admissible to try and prove that someone did something on a particular occasion by leading evidence to show that he has done the same thing on a previous occasion. A tribunal is entitled to admit such evidence, although it will consider what weight should be attached to it (*Docherty v Reddy* [1977] ICR 365, EAT).

The tribunal is also entitled to consider **confessions or admissions** made in circumstances 9669
which would make them inadmissible in criminal proceedings (*Dhaliwal v British Airways Board* [1985] ICR 513, EAT), but will, of course, have to have regard to the right to a fair trial under the Human Rights Act.

Communications which are "**without prejudice**" (¶9230) are privileged from disclosure and 9670
so inadmissible in tribunal proceedings in the same way as in any other court.

Submissions of no case to answer

As the party bearing the formal burden of proving his case normally presents his evidence 9675
first, it sometimes becomes clear **at the end of the first party's case**, that it has no prospect of success. The other party may make a submission that there is no case to answer, i.e. that the first party has not put forward any evidence which would enable the tribunal to find in his favour. If the tribunal agrees, it will dismiss the case without the need for the other party to present his case. Alternatively, where a case is clearly misconceived (i.e. has no reasonable prospects of success), the tribunal may exercise its power to **strike out** (¶9573).

However, the use of submissions of no case to answer is not encouraged and should only be made in 'exceptional or frivolous' cases (*Logan v Commissioners of Customs and Excise* [2004] IRLR 63, CA). Instead, the **preferred approach** is to hear from both sides before making a decision (*Ridley v GEC Machines Ltd* [1977] 13 ITR 195, EAT; *Clark v Watford Borough Council*, EAT case 43/99, confirmed by *Logan v Commissioners of Customs and Excise*, above).

In **unfair dismissal** cases where the **dismissal is admitted** and the respondent goes first, the 9676
preferred view is that it is not appropriate for the case to be determined at the end of the respondent's case without hearing from the claimant (*Hackney London Borough Council v Usher* [1997] ICR 705, EAT). This is partly because there is not strictly any burden of proof on any party

in unfair dismissal cases, and also because there may be questions of contributory fault which have to be determined (which can only be done after hearing evidence from the claimant).

However, where the dismissal is **not admitted**, the claimant goes first, and if at the end of his case it is clear that there is no evidence to support the contention that he was dismissed, a submission of no case to answer may be appropriate and successful.

Final submissions

9680 After both parties have presented their evidence, each party (or his representative) may put forward submissions to the tribunal, **summarising** the evidence in support of his case, **highlighting** the perceived weaknesses in the other side's case, referring the tribunal to the appropriate law and explaining how (in his view) it should be applied to the facts of the case.

Such submissions are usually put forward **orally at the hearing**. The tribunal may ask the parties to put forward **written submissions** for consideration subsequently if they consent (*London Borough of Barking & Dagenham v Oguoko* [2000] IRLR 179, EAT). Written submissions are submitted to the tribunal, which must serve a copy on the other party. If the receiving party has any comments to make on the other party's submissions, he should send those comments to the tribunal within a stated period. **Comments in reply** (to oral or written submissions) are limited to correcting factual errors in the submissions or replying to new points of law raised in the other side's submissions. It is not an opportunity to make good any deficiencies in that party's own original submissions. If a party **fails to comment**, the tribunal will assume that he has no further comment to make and will make its decision on the basis of the submissions which it has received. A party who had **no opportunity to comment** is entitled to apply for a review of the decision and to state what further comments he would have made had he been given that opportunity.

IV. Decision

1. Points of procedure

9690 Decisions are **taken by** majority with each of the three tribunal members having one vote (rule 28(4) Sch 1 SI 2004/1861). It is, therefore, quite legitimate for the lay members to outvote the legally qualified Chairman. Although this does sometimes happen, **most decisions are unanimous**. If only a Chairman and one lay member are sitting, the Chairman has a **casting vote**.

The Court of Appeal has given **guidance** on tribunals **giving majority judgments** (*Anglia Home Improvements v Kelly* [2005] ICR 242, CA). The Court commented that it is undesirable, on the whole, for tribunals to reach split decisions although it accepted that in some cases it is inevitable. Tribunals should, if it is possible to do so, make all efforts to reach an unanimous decision and to this end should allow themselves more time to make the decision by reserving the decision rather than giving it extempore (i.e. at the time). Extempore decisions of majority judgments were also criticised in that they may not provide an adequate set of extended reasons (as happened in this case). Further, practically speaking, where a tribunal cannot agree, it was preferable, in general, for the Chairman to reserve the decision so that it could be written up and circulated to the lay members giving them not just the opportunity to see that their views were correctly expressed but also the opportunity to reflect on the grounds of disagreement, especially where they are in disagreement with the Chairman as to the outcome of the case.

Form The decision must be recorded in writing and signed by the Chairman (rule 29(1) Sch 1 SI 2004/1861). As well as giving its decision (for example, whether or not the claimant has been unfairly dismissed), the tribunal will also give **written reasons** for its decision provided (rule 30(3) Sch 1 SI 2004/1861): 9691

- a party makes a written request for extended reasons within 14 days of the date on which the judgment is sent to the parties (although this time limit can be extended where the tribunal considers it just and equitable to do so); or
- they have been requested by the EAT.

Written reasons must be signed by the Chairman, and the Secretary will send a copy of them to all the parties in the proceedings (rule 30(2), (4) Sch 1 SI 2004/1861). In practice, the decision and the reasons will generally be given in the same document but this need not be the case.

Written reasons provided must also include a **statement of any compensation** or payment awarded, and a breakdown or description of its **calculation**. Where a decision on compensation has been deferred to a later hearing, the written reasons for the decision on the merits and the statement setting out the tribunal's reasoning in relation to compensation may be in different documents. As well as the statement of compensation, written reasons will go into detail regarding the evidence, the tribunal's analysis of it and the application of the law. It is essential that written reasons should be requested in any case where an **appeal** is being considered. A notice of appeal can only be lodged after written reasons have been given.

Timing In many cases, the Chairman announces the tribunal's decision **at the end of the hearing**, together with the tribunal's reasons. The practice is for these to be tape recorded as the Chairman is delivering them. They are later typed up and sent out to the parties if a request is made for written reasons. 9692

Alternatively, perhaps because of a shortage of time, the Chairman only announces the tribunal's decision (i.e. which side has won) at the end of the hearing. The reasons are then prepared separately and sent out to the parties **at a later date**.

In some cases, the tribunal may **reserve its decision**. This means that the parties will not be notified of the outcome of the case on the day of the hearing. The decision and the reasons will be prepared, perhaps after further deliberation by the tribunal at a later date, and sent out **in due course** to the parties. This is likely to happen in more complicated cases or where there is insufficient time at the end of the hearing for the tribunal to complete its deliberations and deliver its decision.

The right to appeal a decision of an employment tribunal as set out by statute is confined to questions of law and consequently the **unsafeness of a decision due to the delay** cannot be an independent ground of appeal and it is not possible to equate unsafeness of the decision with the loss of the right to a fair trial as a matter of fact (*Bangs v Connex South Eastern Ltd* [2005] IRLR 389, CA, followed in *Wandsworth Borough Council v Warner* EAT case 0671/04). The ground of appeal must be whether the delay made the decision unsafe **on the grounds of perversity** (i.e. as a result of the delay the decision was one which no reasonable tribunal properly directing itself under law would have reached). This is often extremely difficult to establish (see ¶9749). 9693

However in exceptional cases, unreasonable delay may be treated as a serious procedural error or material irregularity giving rise to a **question of law "in the proceedings before the tribunal"**, for example if this resulted in the appellant being deprived of the substance of his right to a fair trial (under Art 6 of the European Convention on Human Rights (incorporated into domestic law by the Human Rights Act 1998)) and as a result it would be unfair or unjust to allow the delayed decision to stand. The Court commented that this test was, on the one hand, less stringent than the perversity ground of appeal, but it was, on the other hand, more stringent than the previous "unsafe" decision test formulated and applied by the EAT (*Kwamin v Abbey National plc*; *Birmingham City Council v Mitze*; *Martin v London Borough of Southwark*; *Connex South Eastern Ltd v Bangs* [2004] IRLR 516, EAT (overturned by CA decision)) as it required the existence of a question of law.

MEMO POINTS The House of Lords have given the parties leave to appeal the Court of Appeal's decision in *Bangs v Connex South Eastern Ltd* so this guidance may change.

9695 **Content** A tribunal decision consists principally of two parts. It first sets out the tribunal's **findings of fact**, followed by the tribunal's **application of the law** to those facts. It may also summarise the arguments put by each side.

9696 **Written reasons** must set out the issues identified as being relevant to the claim, which issues (if any) were not determined and why, findings of fact relevant to the issues which have been determined, a concise statement of the applicable law, and how the relevant findings of fact and applicable law have been analysed by the tribunal in order to determine the issues (rule 30(6) Sch 1 SI 2004/1861). In particular, they must provide **sufficient information** to enable the parties to understand why they have won or lost (*Meek v City of Birmingham District Council* [1987] IRLR 250, CA), and to enable the EAT or the Court of Appeal in any subsequent appeal to understand the basis on which the tribunal has reached its decision in order to determine if any question of law arises. This will involve **identifying the evidential documents** upon which it has made its finding and explaining how it reached its decision (*Tran v Greenwich Vietnam Community* [2002] IRLR 735, CA). At the same time, however, tribunals are discouraged from being overly formal or legalistic. In **unfair dismissal cases**, the tribunal must specify what it has found to be the principal reason for the dismissal (and the facts which have lead to that conclusion), and show that it has applied the correct test in deciding whether or not the employer has acted reasonably in all the circumstances. If it reduces compensation because of the employee's contributory fault, it must also specify the behaviour which it is relying on in order to make this reduction.

Where the decision has been **reached by majority**, the views of the majority and minority should be set out separately and distinctly in separate paragraphs (*Parkers Bakeries Ltd v Palmer* [1977] IRLR 215, EAT).

9698 **Registration** Once a tribunal decision and the reasons for it have been recorded in writing, they are entered by the Secretary in the register (rule 32(1) Sch 1 SI 2004/1861). This means that the decision and reasons are open to **public inspection**. If the hearing has been held in private, only the decision (and not the reasons) is registered (rule 32(2) Sch 1 SI 2004/1861).

MEMO POINTS Where the case involves the alleged commission of a **sexual offence**, the identity of the alleged victim or offender is deleted from the reasons before it is registered (rule 49 Sch 1 SI 2004/1861).

2. Remedies

9700 The remedies which the tribunal can order differ according to the type of claim, and are, therefore, discussed in the relevant chapters. A summary for the main claims is given in the table below.

Claim	Remedy	Para.
Unfair dismissal	Reinstatement	¶8680
	Re-engagement	¶8680
	Compensation	¶8570
	Interim relief	¶8700
Discrimination	Declarations	¶5738
	Recommendations	¶5760
	Compensation	¶5740
	Non-discrimination notices	¶5790
Breach of contract (memo point)	Declaration	¶1740
	Compensation (subject to financial limit ¶9428)	¶1725

MEMO POINTS Injunctions are only available as a remedy for breach of contract in the civil courts.

9701 The most common remedy is **compensation**, which is an option for the tribunal in most types of case. The purpose of a compensation award is not to punish the employer but to attempt as far as possible to put the employee in the position he would have been in but for the employer's default. In the vast majority of cases, the principal element of any compensation award will be **loss of earnings**. This is likely to include (a) loss of earnings between the date of the act complained of and the tribunal hearing and (b) a sum to represent the tribunal's estimate of future loss of earnings.

An employee seeking compensation has a duty to **mitigate** his loss, i.e. he must take reasonable steps to minimise the loss which he suffers. The most obvious example is that an employee who is claiming compensation as a result of being dismissed must make reasonable efforts to find another job.

3. Recovering costs or preparation time

Costs or preparation time

Tribunals are permitted to make orders in respect of either a party's costs in relation to a set of proceedings or the time a party (the receiving party) who is not legally represented at the main hearing has spent in preparing for the proceedings (rules 38-47 Sch 1 SI 2004/1861). Preparation time **covers** time spent up to, but not including any time spent at, a main hearing (rule 42(3) Sch 1 SI 2004/1861): 9702

- by the receiving party or his employees in carrying out preparatory work directly relating to the proceedings; and
- by the receiving party's legal or other advisers relating to the conduct of the proceedings.

Unlike the civil courts where the loser normally pays the winner's costs, the tribunal can only award orders for costs or preparation time in certain circumstances. Whether an order is made for costs or for preparation time will depend on whether the receiving party is legally represented or not. If the receiving party is **legally represented**, only a costs order can be made. Whilst, if the receiving party is **not legally represented**, only a preparation order can be made. A tribunal cannot, therefore, make both a preparation time order and a costs order in favour of the same party in the same proceedings. However, where a preparation time order has been made in favour of one party, the tribunal can make a costs order in favour of another party in the same proceedings (rule 46(1) Sch 1 SI 2004/1861).

MEMO POINTS 1. In **Scotland**, the term 'costs' and 'costs orders' are references to 'expenses' and 'orders for expenses' respectively.
2. A party who is **represented by in-house lawyers** is entitled to recover his costs in the same way as a party represented by independent solicitors (*Wiggin Alloys Ltd v Jenkins* [1981] IRLR 275, EAT).

Circumstances in which order can be made A costs or preparation time order (as appropriate) can be made **against** either a claimant or a respondent where (rules 40, 44 Sch 1 SI 2004/1861): 9703

- costs have been incurred, allowances paid or preparation time spent as a result of a **postponement or adjournment** of a hearing or pre-hearing review on the application of a party; and/or
- a party has **not complied with** an order or practice direction made by the tribunal.

Moreover, if a party, in bringing the claim, or he or his representative in conducting the claim, has **acted vexatiously, abusively, disruptively or otherwise unreasonably**, or the bringing of conducting of the claim has been **misconceived**, the tribunal must consider making a costs or preparation time order against him (rules 40(2), 44(2) Sch 1 SI 2004/1861).

A claim is **misconceived** (i.e. it has no reasonable prospect of success) when it is so poor that the other side does not even have to respond to the points raised for the claim to fail. If this is the case, however late the claimant comes to this conclusion, the claimant must abandon his case and should not regard the tribunal hearing as "a free opportunity to come to court simply because the case is listed" (*Thorpe v Eaton Electrical Limited*, EAT case 0497/04). In other words, a claimant cannot have his day in court if he knows he has no chance of success without the danger of a costs order being made against him of wasted time and expense. A claimant acts **vexatiously** if he brings a hopeless claim out of spite to harass his employers or for some other improper motive, rather than in order to recover compensation.

This is an abuse of the procedure. **Demonstrating** that a claimant has acted vexatiously or that his claim was misconceived is not an easy task. It is not enough that the case has been lost, or that by the end of the case it becomes clear that the case was hopeless. The tribunal has to consider whether the parties should have realised prior to the hearing that the case was hopeless.

Unreasonable conduct covers a wider range of circumstances, such as behaviour by a party or his representative which unnecessarily extends the length of the hearing or the cost to the other party. Such conduct may occur either before or during the hearing. It may also take place in the context of settlement negotiations and EAT has recently held that a tribunal did not err in making a costs order against a claimant on the grounds that part of her complaint was seriously misconceived and that her failure to accept a substantial settlement sum offered by her employer during proceedings was unreasonable (*Kopel v Safeway Stores plc* [2003] IRLR 753, EAT).

9704 The same rules apply to a **respondent**. Pursuing a defence which has no merit carries the same risks as pursuing a hopeless application. A respondent has the same responsibility not to conduct his case unreasonably before and during the hearing. Note, however, that it is the respondent's conduct in relation to the proceedings which is considered, not his conduct in relation to the actual dismissal or other cause for complaint.

9705 Furthermore, where a party has been ordered to pay a **deposit** as a condition to being permitted to continue to take part in the proceedings (¶9570) and the tribunal has found against that party but no award of costs or preparation time has been made against him, the tribunal must consider whether or not to make a costs or preparation order against that party on the ground that he conducted the proceedings unreasonably in persisting in having the matter determined (rule 47(1) Sch 1 SI 2004/1861). However, the tribunal must have considered the document recording the order to pay a deposit and believe that the grounds for judgment against the party are the same grounds as those for considering that his contentions had little reasonable prospect of success.

9707 **Circumstances in which order must be made** A costs or preparation time order (as appropriate) must be made against a respondent where, in an **unfair dismissal claim**, the main hearing has been **postponed or adjourned** and (rules 39, 43 Sch 1 SI 2004/1861):
- the claimant has expressed a wish for reinstatement or re-engagement which has been communicated to the respondent not less than 7 days before the hearing; and
- the postponement or adjournment of the hearing has been caused by the respondent's failure, without special reason, to provide reasonable evidence as to the availability of the job from which the claimant was dismissed or of comparable or suitable employment.

Such an order will relate to any costs incurred or preparation time spent as a result of the postponement or adjournment of the hearing.

9708 **Timing and procedure** A costs or preparation time order may be made by the tribunal acting on its own motion or at any time during the proceedings on the **application of a party** (rules 38(7), 42(5) Sch 1 SI 2004/1861). An application by a party can be made at the end of a hearing or in writing to the Employment Tribunal Office **within** 28 days from the date of the judgment (this will be the date of the hearing if the judgment was issued orally or the date on which the written judgment was sent to the parties). An application made after this date will not be accepted or considered by the tribunal unless it considers it in the interests of justice to do so.

No order can be made unless the party against whom the order may be made has been given the opportunity to give **reasons why the order should not be made** (this will include the opportunity to give reasons orally to the tribunal at the hearing) (rules 38(9), 42(7) Sch 1 SI 2004/1861).

The **tribunal's written reasons** as to why the order has been made will be provided if a request has been made for reasons within 14 days of the date of the order. Any such written reasons will be sent to all parties to the proceedings (rules 38(10), 42(8) Sch 1 SI 2004/1861).

Amount of the order The tribunal can order **costs** in three ways (rule 41(1) Sch 1 SI 2004/1861): 9709
- an order for a specified sum not exceeding £10,000;
- an order for a specified sum agreed by the parties (whether more or less than £10,000); or
- an order for the whole or part of the costs to be assessed if not otherwise agreed (this can exceed £10,000).

This means that the tribunal's own power to decide a figure for costs is **capped** at £10,000. If it believes that the costs payable should exceed this, then it will make an **order for assessment** of those costs and the party who is to have his costs paid must submit a detailed bill to the county court where it will be assessed, usually by a District Judge. The process of assessment involves the judge determining whether or not it was reasonable for the party to incur costs in respect of each aspect of the case, and whether the amounts claimed are themselves reasonable. The parties are entitled to make submissions to the judge as to why they believe the costs claimed are or are not reasonable and the judge can strike out or reduce particular elements of the costs in order to arrive at a final figure, which can be more or less than £10,000.

In **assessing** the **amount of preparation time** spent, the tribunal must assess the number of preparatory hours on the basis of (rule 45(1) Sch 1 SI 2004/1861):
- information provided by the receiving party; and
- the tribunal's own assessment of what it considers to be a reasonable and proportionate amount of time to spend on such preparatory work. In doing so, the tribunal can consider matters such as the complexity of the proceedings, the number of witnesses and documentation required.

Having assessed the amount of preparation time, the tribunal must apply an **hourly rate** of £25 to that figure in order to calculate the amount payable to the receiving party. The preparation time order is, however, subject to a **maximum** amount of £10,000.

MEMO POINTS From **6 April 2006**, the hourly rate will be increased by £1 annually.

In deciding on the level of costs or preparation time, the tribunal may take into account the paying party's **ability to pay** (rules 41(2), 45(3) Sch 1 SI 2004/1861). The tribunal can also take into account the **means of a trade union** which is supporting the claimants in deciding whether or not to make an award of costs. This is only likely to happen, however, if some fault on the part of the union has led to the costs order (*Beynon and others v Scadden and others* [1999] 700, EAT). 9710

Wasted costs

Tribunals (and the EAT) now have the power to make 'wasted costs' orders directly against a **party's representative** who is then personally liable to make the payment under the order (rule 48 Sch 1 SI 2004/1861). Before the order is made, the representative will be given the opportunity to make oral or written representations as to why an order should not be made. 9711

Wasted costs are **defined as** any costs incurred by a party as a result of any improper, unreasonable, or negligent act or omission by a party's representative, or, if the costs were incurred after the representative's act or omission but the tribunal considers that, in the light of such act or omission, it is unreasonable to expect that party who incurred the costs to pay them (rule 48(3) Sch 1 SI 2004/1861). A party's wasted costs may be disallowed or a representative may be ordered to meet the whole or part of any wasted costs of any party, including his own client, or to reimburse the Secretary of State the amount paid in any allowances in connection with a person's attendance at the hearing (rule 48(2) Sch 1 SI 2004/1861). The party in whose favour the wasted costs order is made does not have to be legally represented.

There is no limit as to the amount of a wasted costs order. However, before making a wasted costs order, the tribunal can take into account the representative's **ability to pay**. On request within 14 days of the date of the wasted costs order, the tribunal will provide written reasons as to why such an order was made.

MEMO POINTS 1. A **legal representative** will not include a representative who is not acting in pursuit of profit with regard to the tribunal proceedings.
2. A representative who is an **employee of a party** cannot have a wasted costs order made against him.

Expenses

9712 Both **parties and witnesses** who attend at tribunal hearings are entitled to claim allowances from the Secretary of State in respect of loss of earnings, travelling and other expenses. This does not, however, cover the costs of legal representation (s 5 Employment Tribunals Act 1996). Such allowances are paid on a **fixed scale** and there is a limit to the amount which can be claimed for loss of earnings. The allowances are claimed by filling in a form which should be requested from the tribunal clerk at the end of the hearing. A party and his witnesses can claim these allowances regardless of whether or not that party was successful in the case.

4. Enforcement of awards

9715 The tribunals do not have their own enforcement procedure. If a party fails to pay any money which is due under a tribunal order, the other party has to seek enforcement **via the county court** by filing an affidavit (i.e. a statement sworn before a solicitor or commissioner for oaths) verifying the amount which has not been paid under the order and producing a copy of the order. The outstanding balance can then be recovered using the same enforcement **procedures** as are available where there is non-compliance with a county court order, including:
- attachment of earnings (an order whereby the employer of the defaulting party is ordered to make a deduction from that party's wages and pay it direct to the court);
- execution against goods (where the bailiffs are sent to seize property owned by the defaulting party which can then be sold to raise money to satisfy the debt);
- garnishee proceedings (where the contents of bank accounts can be seized);
- bankruptcy proceedings; and
- charging orders against land (where the debt is secured against land owned by the defaulting party so that the debt can be satisfied out of the proceeds of sale).

Interest

9716 Where a tribunal orders a sum of money to be paid (other than costs and expenses), interest will eventually accrue if it remains unpaid (Employment Tribunals (Interest) Order SI 1990/479). If the full sum is paid within 42 days of the date on which the tribunal's written decision containing the order to pay is sent to the parties (the "**relevant decision day**"), no interest will be payable. If, however, it remains unpaid at that time, interest will be calculated from the end of that period (the "**calculation day**") until payment at a **rate** specified by statute (currently 8% per annum). Effectively, therefore, interest only starts to accrue after the period for lodging an appeal ends (¶9756).

The Secretary of the tribunal is obliged to send with the decision containing the award a **notice** specifying the relevant decision day, the calculation day and the rate of interest. If he omits to do so, this does not affect the liability to pay interest.

The relevant decision day remains the same even if the **amount** is subsequently **varied on appeal** (although interest will be calculated on the basis of the revised amount). If the amount awarded on appeal is subsequently varied again in a further appeal, then again this does not affect the relevant decision day. If the original tribunal decision did not award any money but a subsequent appeal decision does, then the relevant decision day is the date on which that appeal decision is sent to the parties.

EXAMPLE 1. The tribunal's written decision is sent to the parties on 3 January, containing an order to pay £1,000. The relevant decision day is 3 January. The calculation day is 15 February. If payment is made before 15 February, no interest will be payable. If payment is made after 15 February, interest will be calculated at 8% (from 15 February until the date of payment) on £1,000.

2. An appeal is lodged against the above decision and no payment is made while the appeal is pending. The EAT decides in December that the award should be £750 instead of £1,000. The relevant decision day remains 3 January, which means that the calculation day remains 15 February. Interest will be calculated from 15 February until the date of payment, but on £750 rather than £1000.

A further appeal goes to the Court of Appeal, which decides that the correct award is in fact £2000. Interest will still be calculated from 15 February but on £2,000.
3. The tribunal finds that the employee has been unfairly dismissed but orders no compensation because it finds that he contributed to his dismissal to the extent of 100%. The decision is sent out in December. On appeal to the EAT, the tribunal's finding on contribution is overturned and the EAT orders the employer to pay him the sum of £1,000. The EAT's decision is sent to the parties on 4 June. The relevant decision day will be 4 June and the calculation date will be 42 days after that.

Interest is not payable on any part of the award which is **recouped** by the government in respect of benefit payments (¶8586). 9717

EXAMPLE The tribunal awards £1000 for loss of earnings, of which £250 is subject to recoupment. Interest will only be payable on £750.

5. Review

In a review, the tribunal reviews its own judgment or decision. In contrast, in the case of an appeal, a superior court or tribunal is asked to decide whether or not the tribunal's judgment or decision was correct. The following **judgments or decisions** can be reviewed (rules 33(1), 34(1) Sch 1 SI 2004/1861): 9718
- a default judgment;
- a decision not to accept a claim, response or counter-claim; and
- a judgment other than a default judgment, but including an order for costs, preparation time or wasted costs.

MEMO POINTS 1. **Default judgments** are dealt with separately and are discussed at ¶9726.
2. The EAT recently reiterated that a tribunal has the power to review a decision by a chairman **not to accept a claim form** (*Richardson v U Mole Limited* [2005] IRLR 668, EAT, the judge referring in particular to his earlier judgment in *Moroak t/a Blake Envelopes v Cromie*).

Grounds for review A judgment or decision can only be reviewed on the **following grounds** (rule 34(3) Sch 1 SI 2004/1861): 9719
- the decision was wrongly made as a result of an administrative error by the tribunal staff;
- a party did not receive notice of the proceedings leading to the decision;
- the decision was made in the absence of a party; or
- new evidence has become available since the conclusion of the hearing (but only if its existence could not have been reasonably known of or foreseen at the time of the hearing).

MEMO POINTS 1. An application for review will be properly constituted if the grounds for review **can be discerned** from the application (*Sodexho Ltd v Gibbons* [2005] ICR 1647, EAT). In the event of any doubt, the Chairman, either on his own initiative or on an application of the opposing party, may seek additional information.
2. **Administrative error**, covers errors by the parties as well as tribunal staff (*Sodexho Ltd v Gibbons*). For example, where a mistake or procedural shortcoming has been made by both parties and the Chairman, there may be grounds to review the decision in the interests of justice (*Williams v Ferrosan Ltd* [2004] IRLR 607, EAT).

A decision may also be reviewed if the **interests of justice** require it and this should not be construed restrictively (*Sodexho Ltd v Gibbons*). Where a tribunal reviews a decision not to accept a claim, response or counter-claim on these grounds, the EAT has held that the power to review applies not just to the **content** of the claim/response/counter-claim in question, but also to its **timing** (despite the strict time limits which normally apply) (*Moroak t/a Blake Envelopes v Cromie* [2005] IRLR 535, EAT). In this case, the response was 44 minutes late and the EAT held that, in the interests of justice, the decision to reject the response on this ground could be reviewed. 9720

Further, where a **mistake or procedural shortcoming** has been made by both parties and the Chairman, there may also be grounds to review the decision in the interests of justice (*Williams v Ferrosan Ltd* [2004] IRLR 607, EAT). For example, a tribunal may review a decision in the interests of justice where there has been a procedural shortcoming which was a consequence of the parties having been denied a fair opportunity to present their case (*Trimble v Supertravel Ltd* [1982] IRLR 451, EAT). If this happens, even significant errors of law which have resulted from the procedural shortcoming can be reviewed. However, where both parties have a fair opportunity to present their case and where the tribunal decision was reached in the light of all relevant arguments, errors of law should be dealt with by way of appeal.

9722 **Procedure** A review can take place either following an application by a party or if the tribunal itself decides that it is appropriate.

A **party can apply** for a review either orally at the hearing or in writing to the Secretary (setting out the reasons for requesting a review), not later than 14 days after the written decision has been sent to the parties (rule 35(1) Sch 1 SI 2004/1861), although this can be extended by the tribunal.

If the **tribunal itself decides** that a review should be carried out, it must send a notice to each of the parties explaining why it proposes to do so and giving them the opportunity to make representations as to why there should be no review. A tribunal may decide to hold a review if, for example, it had decided the case on the basis of the law as it understood it but subsequently discovered that the EAT or a higher court had made a decision altering the law. The **tribunal's notice** must be sent out not later than 14 days after the date on which the decision was sent to the parties (rule 36(2) Sch 1 SI 2004/1861).

9723 Given the relatively short period in which an **appeal** may be lodged (¶9756), a party wishing to appeal may often have to lodge his appeal whilst a review is still pending. In such cases, the tribunal will decide whether to **adjourn the review** pending the outcome of the appeal or proceed as normal. The decision is likely to depend on whether the appeal is on the same or different grounds as the request for a review.

9724 **Conduct** **Applications** for review are **heard by** the original tribunal which decided the case unless this is not practicable (for example, because one of the members has died or is not available within a reasonable period of time for other reasons), in which case a freshly constituted tribunal will deal with the review. If the review is taking place at the instigation of the tribunal itself rather than on the application of a party, then only the original tribunal (or Chairman) can conduct such a review. If that is not practicable, a different tribunal or Chairman will be appointed.

9725 **Outcome** After hearing the review, the tribunal can confirm its decision, vary it, or revoke it (rule 36(3) Sch 1 SI 2004/1861).

If the decision is **revoked**, the tribunal has to order the decision to be taken again which may be either before the same tribunal or a differently constituted tribunal. The power to **vary** a decision is, however, a wide one and may enable the tribunal to substitute an entirely different decision without having to revoke the original decision and then hold a rehearing. If it is clear after the review not only that the original decision cannot stand but also what the decision ought to have been, then variation is the most appropriate course. If, however, it is only clear that the original decision cannot stand but further consideration of the evidence or further argument is required, revocation and rehearing will be the most likely outcome.

Default judgments

9726 A party can apply to have a default judgment against or in favour of him reviewed (rule 33(1) Sch 1 SI 2004/1861). His application must be made in writing to the Employment Tribunal Office **within** 14 days of the date on which the default judgment was sent to the parties. This time limit can be **extended** by a Chairman if he considers it just and equitable to do so. In his application, the party must state why the default judgment should be varied or revoked. If the **respondent** is the party **applying** for the review, he must also include his proposed response to the claim, an application for an extension of the time limit for presenting the response and an explanation as to why he did not comply with the rules for submitting a response (rule 33(2) Sch 1 SI 2004/1861).

A review of a default judgment must be **conducted by** a Chairman in public and notice of the hearing and a copy of the application must be sent to all other parties to the proceedings.

The jurisdiction to review a default judgment is a just and equitable one and the Chairman must have regard to whether there is a "**good reason**" for the response not having been presented in time, although this is not determinative, and does not rule out the consideration of other discretionary factors (*Pendragon plc t/a CD Bramall Bradford v Copus*, EAT case 0317/05). **9727**

If the respondent has a **reasonable prospect of successfully responding** to the claim or part of it, the Chairman may **revoke or vary** all or part of the default judgment. If the Chairman decides that the default judgment should be varied or revoked and that the respondent should be allowed to respond to the claim, the Secretary will accept the response and the tribunal will take the usual steps that apply on acceptance of a valid response (¶9514).

The Chairman may **refuse** the application for a review, or vary, revoke or confirm the default judgment. The judgment must be revoked if the whole of the claim has been **settled** by ACAS conciliation or a valid compromise agreement (¶9333).

V. Appeals

Appeals from decisions of tribunals on points of law are heard by the Employment Appeal Tribunal (EAT), and from there, by the higher courts. **9740**

A. Employment Appeal Tribunal

Appeals from employment tribunals on questions of law are dealt with by the Employment Appeal Tribunal (EAT), which (although it may sit at any time and in any place throughout GB) in practice sits permanently in Glasgow and London, and only occasionally sits elsewhere. **9745**

The EAT is a statutory body whose constitution is set out in Part II of the Employment Tribunals Act 1996, and whose **rules of procedure** are set out in the Employment Appeal Tribunal Rules 1993 (SI 1993/2854), as amended the Employment Appeal Tribunal (Amendment) Rules 2001 (SI 2001/1128 and SI 2001/1476) and the Employment Appeal Tribunal (Amendment) Rules 2004 (SI 2004/2526) (referred to in this section as the 'EAT Rules'). The EAT Rules were **amended** on 1 October 2004 to coincide with the introduction of new employment tribunal rules of procedure (Employment Appeal Tribunal (Amendment) Rules SI 2004/2526; see ¶9420). The EAT issued a **Practice Direction (PD)** in December 2004, which applies to all appeals from tribunals, unless specifically excluded by the EAT Rules. The full text of the PD is set out at [2005] IRLR 94.

MEMO POINTS 1. The EAT is subject to the **overriding objective** of dealing with cases justly (rule 2A SI 1993/2854; as inserted by reg 3 SI 2004/2526). As with employment tribunals, this includes ensuring that the parties are on an equal footing, saving expense, dealing with the case in ways which are proportionate to the importance and complexity of the issues and ensuring that it is dealt with expeditiously and fairly.

A recent EAT decision (judgment delivered on 16 February 2005) also emphasised that it has a **broad and generous discretion** in applying its Rules and Practices so as to achieve the overriding objective of dealing with cases justly (¶9759).

2. A refusal by the EAT to **sit in Wales** where the appeal is against a decision of an employment tribunal sitting in Wales, and a refusal to conduct a hearing in Welsh, does not contravene the Welsh Language Act 1993 or the European Convention on Human Rights (*Williams v Cowell* [2000] ICR 85, CA).

3. The **rules of procedure** are slightly different in **Scotland**, for example the system of case management does not apply to appeals in Scotland.
4. The Lord Chancellor's Department has announced that Employment Tribunals and the EAT will be merged (along with a number of other tribunals) to form a **single Tribunal Service** with the aim of providing a better service to users. The structure and governance of the proposed unified system is, at the time of writing, under consideration.

9746 The EAT also hears appeals on a question of law arising in any proceedings of the **Central Arbitration Committee** in connection with European Works Councils, domestic information or consultation requirements or from any declaration or order made by it. It also has jurisdiction to hear appeals from decisions of the **Certification Officer** for Trade Unions and Employers' Associations.

9747 Any documents sent to the EAT should be addressed to the **Registrar** (rule 35 SI 1993/2854), who has both administrative and quasi-judicial functions.

1. Grounds

Final orders

9748 A tribunal decision can only be appealed on a **question of law**. To succeed in an appeal, therefore, a **party must show** that (*British Telecommunications plc v Sheridan* [1990] IRLR 27, CA):
– there is no evidence to support a particular conclusion or finding of fact;
– the decision was either perverse (i.e. one which no reasonable tribunal properly directing itself under law would have reached) or obviously wrong; or
– the tribunal misdirected itself in law, or misunderstood or misapplied the law.

Unless one of these categories applies, the EAT cannot interfere with the tribunal's **finding of fact**.

EXAMPLE 1. Witness A says in his evidence to the tribunal that he personally handed a letter to witness B. Witness B in his evidence denies ever having received such a letter. The tribunal, having heard both witnesses and assessed their credibility, decides that it believes witness A rather than witness B. This is a **question of fact** for the tribunal to decide and the EAT will not interfere with this decision.
2. The facts are as in the previous example, but there is also a question as to the effect of the letter. The letter, which is dated 14 March, states that B's employment is 'terminated forthwith'. The tribunal finds that the letter was handed to B by A on 17 March. The tribunal has to decide whether the effect of the letter is to terminate B's employment on 14 March (the date of the letter) or 17 March (the date on which it was received). This is a **question of law**, which could be the subject of an appeal.

9749 The Court of Appeal has set out guidance as to when an **appeal** on the **grounds of perversity** can be brought (*Yeboah v Crofton* [2002] IRLR 634, CA).

9751 **New points of law** Exceptionally, the EAT may allow a point of law to be raised on appeal where it was not raised in the tribunal. It **may do so** if, for example, the legal point is so fundamental and well established that the tribunal should have considered it, even if it was not argued by the parties (such as the test for a fair dismissal for misconduct, i.e. whether the employer had a reasonable belief in the employee's guilt, held on reasonable grounds, following a reasonable investigation).

The respondent has an **opportunity to object** to a new point of law being raised by stating his objection in writing **within** 14 days of the receiving the notice of appeal (if a preliminary hearing has been ordered) or, if the appeal is listed for a full hearing without a preliminary hearing, in a respondent's answer.

9752 **New evidence** The EAT will exercise its discretion as to whether to admit evidence not put before the tribunal, having regard to its overriding objective (¶9745). This will only be permitted in limited circumstances. A party seeking to put new evidence forward must be

able to show the EAT that it (*Ladd v Marshall* [1954] 1 WLR 1489; *Wileman v Minilec Engineering Limited* [1988] IRLR 144, EAT):
– could not have been obtained with reasonable diligence for use at the tribunal;
– is relevant and would probably have an important influence on the result of the case (though it need not necessarily be decisive); and
– is apparently credible (though it need not be incontrovertible).
A party who decides to withhold evidence at the tribunal hearing stage will not, therefore, be able to introduce it at the EAT.

Bias Bias by the Chairman or a tribunal member in reaching their decision will normally give a party grounds for appealing to have the decision set aside (¶9612). In **considering allegations of bias** against tribunal members (including Chairmen) where the allegations involve conduct during a hearing, the EAT has recommended that the following steps be taken (*Facey v Midas Retail Security* [2000] IRLR 812, EAT): 9753
– unsworn statements will be taken from witnesses to the alleged conduct, including the tribunal members;
– sworn statements may then be required from witnesses other than the tribunal members;
– sworn statements may be invited from tribunal members but they cannot be required to give them;
– witnesses other than tribunal members may be cross-examined before the EAT but tribunal members may not; and
– the EAT may not draw adverse inferences from a tribunal member's refusal to be cross-examined, but may draw adverse inferences from a refusal to give a sworn statement.
The Court of Appeal has also recently provided guidelines on how appellate tribunals and courts should handle such complaints and has stated that the appellate tribunal may have to make judgments of fact to be able to resolve any factual disputes relating to such a complaint (*Stansbury v Datapulse plc and another* [2004] IRLR 466, CA).

Interim orders and decisions

A party can also appeal to the EAT against an interim order or decision made by the tribunal (for example, an order for disclosure of certain documents or a striking out order). As with final orders, the EAT can only intervene if the tribunal has made an **error of law**, i.e. if (*Adams and Raynor v West Sussex County Council* [1990] IRLR 215, EAT): 9754
– the order is not one which the tribunal has power to make;
– the tribunal has not followed the relevant "guiding legal principles" (which will depend on the order made) in relation to the exercise of its discretion; or
– the tribunal has exercised its discretion in an unreasonable or irrational manner (i.e. can be challenged on what are known as "Wednesbury principles").

2. Commencement

Form The **notice of appeal** must be, or be substantially, in accordance with **Form 1** (in the amended form annexed to the Practice Direction (most recently substituted by Employment Appeal Tribunal (Amendment) Rules SI 2005/1871)) or **Forms 1A or 2** of the Schedule to the Rules and must **identify** the date of the judgment, decision or order being appealed (para 2.1 PD). It must also clearly identify the grounds of appeal and state the order the appellant seeks (para 2.4 PD). With regard to **perversity appeals**, it will not be sufficient to merely state words to the effect that "the judgment or order was contrary to the evidence" or that "there was no evidence to support the judgment or order" or that "the judgment or order was one which no reasonable tribunal could have reached and was perverse" unless the notice of appeal also sets out full particulars of the matters relied on in support of these general grounds (para 2.6PD). 9755

Copies of the judgment, decision or order appealed against and of the employment tribunal's written reasons, together with a copy of the claim (ET1) and the response (ET3) must be attached, or if not, a written explanation must be given. A notice of appeal without such documentation will not be validly lodged (para 2.1 PD).

Notices of appeal can be **sent** to the EAT **by** post, hand delivery, fax or other electronic communication.

9756 **Timing** The notice of appeal must be **submitted within** 42 days (rule 3(3) SI 1993/2854; as amended by reg 4 SI 2004/2526):

1. in the case of an appeal against a **judgment of the employment tribunal**:
– from the date on which written reasons were sent to the parties, where those written reasons were requested orally at the hearing or within 14 days of the date on which the written record of the judgment was sent to the parties, or were reserved and given in writing by the employment tribunal;
– from the date on which a document containing edited reasons for the tribunal judgment given in relation to national security proceedings were sent to the parties; or
– from the date on which a written record of the tribunal judgment was sent to the parties where the written reasons for the judgment were not requested orally at the hearing before the employment tribunal or in writing within 14 days of the date on which the written record of the judgment was sent to the parties and were not reserved and given in writing by the employment tribunal; or
2. in the case of an appeal against an **order of the employment tribunal**, from the date of that order.

MEMO POINTS The Practice Direction gives **additional guidance** as follows (para 1.8 PD):
– the day that the employment tribunal decision is sent to parties does not count and the notice of appeal must arrive at the EAT on or before that day 6 weeks (i.e. 42 days) later;
– when a date is given for serving a document or for doing some other act, the complete document must be received by the EAT or the relevant party by 4 pm on that date. Any document received after 4 pm will be deemed to be lodged on the next working day; and
– all days count, but if a time limit expires on a day when the central office of the EAT, or the EAT office in Edinburgh (as appropriate), is closed, it is extended to the next working day except where the time limit is 5 days (e.g. an appeal against a registrar's order or direction) in which case Saturdays, Sundays, Christmas Day, Good Friday and bank holidays do not count.

9757 If it appears that compliance with the **time limit** may be **difficult**, it was previously recommended that the party serves a notice of appeal containing as much information as possible, accompanied by a covering letter indicating the difficulty in which he finds himself, and that it may be necessary to apply to amend the notice at a later date (¶9759). However, where the appellant is not able to provide a copy of the tribunal's written reasons with his notice of appeal, the EAT has indicated that it will take a strict approach in such cases (*Kanapathiar v London Borough of Harrow* [2003] IRLR 571, EAT).

9758 If the **time limit is missed**, an extension of time can be applied for, but it must be accompanied by a notice of appeal in proper form, together with a written application for an extension of time, explaining clearly and concisely the reasons for the delay in lodging the notice of appeal (para 3 PD). An **extension** will usually only be **granted** if there is a full, honest and acceptable explanation of the reasons for the delay (*Aziz v Bethnal Green City Challenge Co Ltd* [2000] IRLR 111, CA). The EAT in a Practice Statement issued on 3 February 2005 (to be found at [2005] IRLR 189) emphasised the importance of strict compliance with the time limit, and that it will not accept ignorance of the limit as an excuse. However it is worth noting that the EAT has even more recently (June 2005) taken a less stringent view with regard to time limits for commencing a claim (¶9473) and in another decision (16 February 2005) emphasised that it does have a broad and generous discretion in applying its Rules and Practices so as to achieve the overriding objective of dealing with cases justly (¶9759). If the reason for the missed time limit is due to a **postal delay**, the EAT has indicated that **represented** appellants will be expected to have enquired in good time to ensure that their appeal has been received by the EAT. However in respect of **unrepresented** appellants, there is no duty to check with the EAT as to whether the appeal has been received (*Peters v Sat Katar Co Ltd* [2003] IRLR 574, CA; see also ¶9473 in respect of employment tribunal claims).

It is not usually a good reason to miss the time limit on the grounds that an application for litigation support from public **funds** has been made, but not yet determined; or that support is being sought from, but has not yet been provided by, some other body, such as a trade union, employers' association or one of the equality Commissions (para 3.8 PD).

The **Registrar will** usually **determine** whether or not such a request should be granted, but it is possible to **appeal from his decision** to a judge. The judge can either hear the appeal on his own or refer it to a full decision of the EAT. Any appeal against the registrar's decision must be made within 5 days of the date when the registrar's decision was sent to the parties.

MEMO POINTS In any case of doubt or difficulty, a notice of appeal should be lodged in time and an application made to the registrar for direction (para 3.9 PD).

Amendment of the notice of appeal The notice of appeal may only be amended by an order of the EAT on a separate **interim application** and that application should be made as soon as need for the amendment is known (rule 19 SI 1993/2854; para 2.7 PD). The application must be accompanied by a draft of the amended notice of appeal which makes clear the precise amendments sought. Parties are encouraged to make such applications at the preliminary hearing (PH) (see below) or (if one is ordered) at the directions hearing (para 4.1 PD). **9759**

Permission may be granted if the proposed amendment is produced at the hearing. However, if the other party has not been notified of the proposed amendment and the appeal cannot proceed but for the amendment, then the opposing party can apply on notice to vary or discharge the permission to proceed.

If the proposed amendment is **not produced at the PH**, then the appellant can apply in writing for permission to amend the notice of appeal within 14 days of the PH, provided he gives notice to the other party. If the proposed amendment is critical to the appeal being allowed to proceed, then the EAT can at the PH order for the appeal to be dismissed if the appellant does not apply for permission to amend.

If the appellant is **permitted** to amend his appeal, then he must make any amendments within a period of time specified by the EAT. The respondent will be sent a copy and will have 14 days in which to object. **Objections** are only likely to be sustained if the amendment would cause prejudice to the other party. If permission to amend the notice of appeal is given, and the respondent has already filed an answer, he is allowed to make consequential amendments to his answer without permission within the same 14-day period. If the amendment is **not permitted**, then either party can apply to the EAT as to the hearing or disposal of the appeal.

The EAT has given **guidance** as to the principles which should be applied when considering applications to amend notices of appeal (*Khudados v Leggate* [2005] ICR 1013, CA). It emphasised that it has a **broad and generous discretion** in applying its Rules and Practices so as to achieve the overriding objective of **dealing with cases justly**. In doing so, the following are among the **matters to be taken into account** in determining whether an amendment should be allowed:

– whether the applicant has complied with the requirement that an application for permission to amend a notice of appeal should be made as soon as the need for the amendment is know (as set out above). This is of considerable importance and it is not simply aspirational or an expression of hope;

– whether the applicant has given a full, honest and acceptable explanation for any delay or failure to comply;

– the extent to which, if any, the proposed amendment if allowed would cause any delay. For example, proposed amendments that raise a crisp point of law closely related to existing grounds of appeal, or offer limited particulars that flesh out existing grounds, are much more likely to be allowed than wholly new grounds of perversity raising issues of complex fact and requiring consideration of a volume of documents, including witness statements and notes of evidence, which would, if allowed cause delay and extra expense;

– whether the amendment would cause prejudice to the other party, and whether refusing the amendment would cause prejudice to the applicant by depriving him of fairly arguable

grounds of appeal. It should be noted though that any prejudice caused by refusing permission to amend to an applicant who seeks permission to amend by adding fairly arguable grounds, but who has failed in a significant way to comply with the Rules and Practice Direction, or who has delayed excessively, is likely to carry less weight than where an applicant has not delayed and has acted in accordance with the Rules and Practice Direction;
– in some cases it may be necessary to consider the merits of the proposed amendments as, as a general rule, they must raise a point of law which gives the appeal a reasonable prospect of success at a full hearing; and
– regard must be had to the public interest in ensuring that business in the EAT is conducted expeditiously and that its resources are used efficiently.

3. Case listing

9760 On receiving a notice of appeal, instead of listing every appeal for a preliminary hearing (PH), a judge or the Registrar will decide which one of **four case tracks** the appeal should occupy and will give directions to the parties (para 9 PD):
1. where it appears to a judge or the Registrar that a notice of appeal discloses no reasonable grounds for bringing an appeal or is an abuse of the EAT's process or is otherwise likely to obstruct the just disposal of the proceedings, the appeal will be dealt with in accordance with rule 3(7) (¶9761);
2. the appeal will be listed for a preliminary hearing (PH) to determine whether the appeal has merit and a reasonable prospect of success (if so, it will go to a full hearing);
3. the appeal will be listed for a full hearing (FH), without the need for a PH; or
4. the appeal will be listed for a fast track full hearing (FTFH) due to its importance or if it deals with an interim order of the tribunal requiring compliance within a specified time limit.

Rule 3(7) cases

9761 If, having received a notice of appeal, the judge or Registrar decides that the notice of appeal discloses no reasonable grounds for bringing the appeal or is an abuse of the EAT's process or is otherwise likely to obstruct the just disposal of the proceedings, the judge or Registrar will notify the appellant of his reasons and no further action will be taken on the notice of appeal (rule 3(7) SI 1993/2854; as amended by reg 4 SI 2004/2526).

If the claimant **accepts** this, no further action will be taken on that appeal but he can lodge a fresh appeal either within the original time limit (if still applicable) or within 28 days from the date the notification was given to him. On the other hand, if the appellant **contests** this, the appellant must activate the prescribed procedure (rule 3(8)-(10) SI 1993/2854, as amended) within 28 days of the date the notification was given to him. The claimant can request an oral hearing before a judge to challenge the decision and if it appears to the judge or registrar that the notice of appeal gave insufficient grounds of, or lacked clarity in identifying, a point of law, he can postpone any decision under rule 3(7), pending further explanation or clarification (para 2.5 PD).

Preliminary hearing (PH) and directions

9762 Where the EAT's jurisdiction is not at issue, the judge or Registrar may nevertheless decide to list the appeal for a PH, the **purpose** of which is to determine whether the notice of appeal raises a valid point of law which gives rise to a reasonable prospect of success (para 9.7–9.18 PD). Alternatively, the EAT may consider that there is some other compelling reason that the appeal should go to a FH.

The aim of the PH is to eliminate at an early stage those appeals which have **no prospect of success**.

9763 **Hearing and decision** Only the appellant (or his representative) need **attend**, unless the respondent has indicated that he intends to cross appeal. The appellant will be invited to make submissions on whether the notice of appeal raises a reasonably arguable point of law. The respondent will not be allowed to present any arguments relating to the merits of the appeal, although he may make submissions in relation to directions, and will be allowed to make submissions in relation to any cross appeal (see below).

The hearing will be short (usually not more than an hour), and if a reasonably arguable point of law is established, the EAT will allow the **appeal to go forward** to a full hearing on all or only some of the grounds of appeal. If the appeal is **allowed to proceed**, it will be assigned to a listing category (as set out in para 9.18 PD) and the EAT may also give **directions** covering matters such as exchange of documents, time estimates, applications for fresh evidence, production of the Chairman's notes of evidence (¶9782), and amendments to the notice of appeal.

If a reasonably arguable point of law has not been established, the EAT will give a judgment explaining why the **appeal** is to be **dismissed**, whether in whole or in part.

Further directions In order to ensure that appeals are dealt with as swiftly and efficiently as possible, parties are encouraged to ensure that all necessary directions are obtained at the PH. Later applications for directions are only considered if the EAT is satisfied that there was a **good reason** for failing to apply for them at the PH (rule 19 SI 1993/2854). Such applications are also likely to result in the party applying being ordered to pay the costs (even if he is successful in obtaining the directions). 9764

The EAT also has power to give directions of its own motion at any stage in the proceedings (rule 25 SI 1993/2854). At this stage, it will give further directions relating to, for example, a time estimate, any application for fresh evidence, the exchange of skeleton arguments and the appellant's chronology, and bundles of documents and authorities for use at the FH.

Full hearing (FH) and fast track cases (FTFH)

If a judge or the Registrar decides to list the case for a FH without the need for a PH, then he will consider what directions should be given to the parties (see below). 9765

Although FH cases are generally heard in the order in which they are received by the EAT, in certain circumstances an appeal may be listed for the fast track, in which case it will be heard as soon as it can be fitted into the list.

Fast track appeals are normally one of the following appeals where (para 9.20 PD): 9766
- the parties have applied, and there are merits, for an expedited hearing;
- the parties are appealing against an interim order, directions, or decisions of the tribunal which require action within a specified period;
- other applications to the tribunal or EAT depend on the outcome of the appeal;
- one or both parties have sought a reference to the European Court of Justice or a declaration of incompatibility under the Human Rights Act 1998; or
- one of the parties has sought an order for reinstatement, re-engagement, interim relief or (in discrimination cases) recommendation for action.

4. Procedure

Contesting the appeal and cross appeals

After the appeal has been allocated to a particular track listing, or after a PH at which an appeal has been permitted to proceed to FH, the **EAT will send** to the respondent the **notice of appeal**, together with any permitted amendments, written submissions and/or skeleton argument lodged by the appellant. 9770

If the respondent wishes to contest the appeal, he must deliver a **written answer** within 14 days of the date of the notice of appeal (para 10.1 PD). If he fails to meet this time limit, the respondent may be prevented from taking part in the appeal unless he obtains permission to serve his answer out of time. 9771

At the same time as lodging and serving the written answer, the respondent may also wish to **appeal against the tribunal decision** (or a certain aspect of it) (known as a **cross appeal**). If his answer contains a cross-appeal, the appellant must lodge and serve his reply within 14 days of service. In his written submissions he must state whether his cross appeal is **conditional**, i.e. he intends to cross appeal only if the other party's appeal is allowed to proceed to a FH or whether it is **unconditional**, i.e. he wishes to cross appeal regardless of whether or not the other party's appeal is allowed to proceed.

In such cases, the cross appeal is also **considered at the PH**. The party putting forward the cross appeal is entitled to appear and must satisfy the EAT that there is a reasonably arguable point of law in the cross appeal. The EAT treats the cross appeal in the same way as it does the original appeal and will decide whether or not it should be allowed to go forward to a FH.

> EXAMPLE A tribunal finds that an employee has been unfairly dismissed but reduces compensation by 80% to reflect contributory fault. The employee may wish to appeal against the finding of contributory fault, while the employer may wish to cross appeal against the finding of unfair dismissal itself.

9772 **Directions** After the respondent has lodged and served his written answer (and any cross appeal), the Registrar may invite the parties to apply for directions. At this stage, he may give any appropriate directions that he sees fit of his own motion or, alternatively, may fix a date for the parties to attend a directions hearing (para 10.2 PD).

9773 **Failure to deliver answer** A respondent who fails to lodge his written answer may be prevented from taking any further part in the proceedings, but the EAT has discretion to make such order as it thinks just in the circumstances. As for notices of appeal, it is possible to apply for an **extension of time** (see above).

9774 **Amendment of answer** The procedure for amending a respondent's answer is as for the notice of appeal (see above).

Interim applications

9775 While parties are encouraged to ensure that all directions are given at the PH, it is possible to make interim applications (for example, amendments to notice of appeal or answer, joinder of additional parties, consolidation with other appeals, directions dealing with evidence and arrangements for the hearing).

9776 **Form and procedure** Such applications should be made in writing and must specify the direction or order sought. An interim application will in the first instance be dealt with by the Registrar who will serve a copy of the application on the other party and notify both parties of how he intends to deal with it. In general, applications will be dealt with at an **oral hearing** unless the application is not opposed (in which case an order may be made without the parties having to attend) or where the Registrar decides that it can be dealt with by way of **written submissions** from the parties. If the application is to strike out pleadings or to prevent a party in default from taking any further part in the proceedings, the application will usually be heard before the start of the main appeal hearing.

9777 **Conduct and appeal** The Registrar will normally deal with interim applications himself, having regard to the EAT's overriding objective. However, the Registrar may refer the matter either to the President or a judge (who may themselves refer it on to a full division of the EAT if they think it appropriate or refer it back to the Registrar with such directions as they think fit). Interim applications for a **restricted reporting order** or for permission to **start or continue** to make **a claim** in any proceedings before an employment tribunal must be disposed of by the President or a judge (rule 20 SI 1993/2854; as amended by reg 13 SI 2004/2526).

Decisions made by the Registrar can be appealed to a judge, who again can refer it to a full division of the EAT or determine the appeal himself. Notice of any such appeal should be given to the EAT within 5 days of the Registrar's decision.

Preparation for the hearing

Preparation will include the collation of relevant documents, (possibly) the production of the tribunal Chairman's notes, and the service of a skeleton argument. 9779

Documents Any documents **relevant** to the point of law on which the appeal is based (i.e. not necessarily all documents produced at the tribunal stage) should be sent to the EAT as soon as possible, and subject to the time limits set out below. 9780

Responsibility for the preparation of the **core bundle** of papers for use at the hearing lies with both parties and their advisers, although ultimately, the appellant is responsible, following consultation with the other parties (para 6.1 PD). **Guidance** as to which documents should appear in the core bundle is found in the Practice Direction (para 6 PD).

If the **parties disagree** over the content of the bundles, they can apply to the Registrar for directions, or he may give such directions of his own motion.

The **time limits** for lodging a core bundle vary depending on where the appeal has been allocated (i.e. which track). For **PH cases**, lodge four copies (two copies if judge is sitting alone) of the bundle as soon as possible after service of the notice of appeal and no later than 21 days from the date of the relevant order (para 6.5 PD). In **FH cases**, the parties must agree on a core bundle and the appellant is responsible for lodging four copies (two if the judge is sitting alone) of the bundle with the EAT no later than 35 days from the date of the relevant order (para 6.6 PD). In respect of **warned list** and **fast track** cases, the bundles should be lodged as soon as possible and (unless the hearing date is earlier than 7 days later) not later than 7 days after the parties have been notified that the case is expedited or in the warned list (para 6.7 PD). 9781

Evidence before employment tribunal and Chairman's notes Parties who consider that it is necessary to **refer to evidence** heard before the employment tribunal which does not sufficiently appear from the tribunal's decision or reasons, can apply for such evidence to be produced before the EAT (para 7 PD). 9782

Ordinarily, an **appellant should make his application** when he submits his notice of appeal. However, in exceptional circumstances, he can apply later (para 7.1 PD). A **respondent** must make such an application with his answer, or before if possible.

The party seeking production **must state** the issues in the appeal in respect of which the evidence is required, the names of those witnesses in respect of whose evidence the notes are required, the parts of the witness' evidence alleged to be necessary.

The application will be **considered on** the papers, **or by** the Registrar or a judge at PH stage. The Registrar or judge may: 9783

- determine the application; or
- give directions for written representations (if they have not already been lodged).

However, he will **ordinarily make** an order requiring the party to give notice to the other party(ies) to the appeal/cross-appeal. The notice will require the other party(ies) to co-operate in agreeing, within 21 days (unless a shorter period is ordered), a statement or note of the relevant evidence. All parties are required to use their best endeavours to agree such a statement or note (para 7.3 PD).

If the parties **fail to agree**, either party may apply for directions from the EAT within 7 days. The directions may include (para 7.4 PD):

- resolution of the disagreement on the written submissions or at a hearing;
- the administration by one party to the other(s) of, or a request to the Chairman to respond to, a questionnaire; or
- if the EAT is satisfied that it is necessary, a request that the Chairman produce his notes of evidence either in whole or in part.

9784 The **EAT must be satisfied** that production of the notes is necessary to enable the appeal to be dealt with fairly, for example if it is alleged that there is no evidence to support a particular finding of fact, or that the tribunal failed to make a relevant finding of fact which it ought to have made on the basis of the evidence as put forward, or that a finding of fact is perverse in the sense that no tribunal properly directed could have reached that conclusion. If the EAT considers that the notes should be produced, the Chairman is then obliged to provide them.

If a party believes that the Chairman's **notes of evidence are inaccurate**, the EAT has suggested that the proper procedure should be as follows (*Dexine Rubber Company Limited v Alker* [1977] ICR 434, EAT):
– the party should submit his criticism to the advocate for the opposite party;
– the criticism should then be submitted to the Chairman; and
– if the Chairman, having considered the criticisms, confirms that in his view his note is accurate, then unless there is a joint confirmation from both opposing advocates that they believe otherwise, the EAT will accept the Chairman's notes as being accurate.

A note of evidence is not to be produced and supplied to the parties to enable the parties to embark on a "**fishing expedition**" to establish grounds or additional grounds of appeal or because they have not kept their own notes of the evidence. If an application for such a note is found by the EAT to have been unreasonably made or if there is unreasonable lack of co-operation in agreeing a relevant note or statement, the party behaving unreasonably is at risk of being ordered to **pay costs** (para 7.7 PD).

9785 **New Evidence** Any application to include new evidence should be **lodged at** the EAT with the notice of appeal or the respondent's answer, as appropriate (para 8 PD). The application and copy should be served on the other parties. Details of the nature and substance of such evidence together with the date when the party first became aware of its existence document should be included and copies of any relevant documents should be lodged and served. The evidence and representations in support of the application must address the principles set out at ¶9752.

The application will be **considered by** the Registrar or a judge on the papers (or, if appropriate, at a PH) who may determine the issue or give directions for a hearing or may seek comments from the Chairman (para 8.4 PD).

A party wishing to **resist the application** must, within 14 days of it being sent, submit any representations in response to the EAT and other parties.

9786 **Skeleton arguments** Parties in all appeals are required to serve a skeleton argument on the EAT **in advance of** the hearing date for the appeal.

The skeleton argument should briefly **identify and summarise** the points in the legal argument to be put forward by that party, specifying statutory provisions and authorities to be relied on. The skeleton argument should also set out the **form of order** which the party seeks from the EAT. As well as the skeleton argument, the appellant should also submit a **written chronology** of relevant events. Where possible, the chronology should be agreed by both parties.

9787 The **time limits** for submitting skeleton arguments varies depending on where (i.e. which track) the appeal has been allocated (para 13.9 PD).

In respect of **FH appeals**, parties must lodge with the EAT and exchange their skeleton arguments no later than 21 days before the hearing. For **PH appeals**, the skeleton arguments must be lodged with the EAT no later than 10 days before the date fixed for the PH or, if the PH is listed for less than 7 days' notice, the skeleton arguments should be lodged as soon as possible after notification of the hearing date. If both parties are to be present at the PH, then they must also exchange them within these time limits. In respect of **warned list** (see ¶9792) and **fast track** cases, the skeleton arguments must be lodged as soon as possible and, unless the hearing date is at less than 7 days' notice, in any event within 7 days of notification of the hearing date.

Appeal hearing

The appeal will be heard by an appeal panel, as described below. 9788

Composition of appeal panel When an appeal is heard, the EAT panel will in **most cases consist of** a judge and either two or four (usually two) lay members (s 28 Employment Tribunals Act 1996). The parties can consent to an appeal being heard by a judge and either one or three lay members. Where there is an even number of lay members, there must be an equal number representing employers and employees. 9789

If the parties are asked to consent to an appeal being heard by just the judge and one appointed lay member, then the consent must be informed (*De Haney v Brent Mind* [2004] ICR 348, CA). In this case, the unrepresented appellant had given her consent for the appeal to be heard by the judge and one lay member, but she had not realised until the hearing itself that the lay member had represented the employer's side of industry (see memo point below).

MEMO POINTS EAT **judges** are selected from judges of the High Court and Court of Appeal (and at least one judge of the Court of Session in Scotland) (s 22(1) Employment Tribunals Act 1996). Additional judges can be appointed either to fill vacancies temporarily or to assist in the disposal of business. The **lay members** are appointed on the basis of their experience of industrial relations, some of whom represent the employee's side of industry and others the employer's side (s 22 Employment Tribunals Act 1996).

If the tribunal decision appealed against was taken by a Chairman sitting alone, then the appeal would be heard by a **judge sitting alone** unless the judge directs otherwise (s 28 Employment Tribunals Act 1996). 9790

MEMO POINTS There are special provisions regarding cases involving **national security**. If a Minister of the Crown so directs, then such an appeal is heard by the President of the EAT sitting alone.

Representation and legal aid As in the tribunal, a party may appear in person or be **represented** by a barrister or a solicitor, a trade union representative, an employer's association representative, or by any other person whom he desires to represent him (s 9(1) Employment Tribunals Act 1996). 9791

Legal aid is available for bringing or defending cases in the EAT.

EXAMPLE The Legal Aid Board which used to administer legal aid has now been replaced by the Legal Services Commission (LSC). Eligibility for funding is made to the LSC through a solicitor or advice agency.

Date of hearing The EAT will normally try to agree a date for the main appeal hearing with the parties. Cases will either be given a **fixed date** or placed in a **warned list**, which is prepared at the beginning of each month. The parties (or their representatives) are informed if their case is included in this list. If fixed date cases settle or are withdrawn, cases from the warned list will be called on in their place and the parties will be notified as soon as possible of the hearing date. 9792

Procedure EAT hearings are **held in public** but the same exceptions apply as in the case of employment tribunals (¶9617). 9793

As appeals are on a point of law, most appeals will only involve **legal argument**. However, if **witness evidence** is required, the EAT can hear evidence on oath and can order witnesses to attend.

The appellant will normally **go first**.

Decision

Decisions can be **made by** majority (most are unanimous). 9794

If **judgment is reserved**, the parties are notified of the date on which it will be handed down in writing and a copy of the transcript will be provided to all parties (para 18 PD). Where a

judgment is delivered at the FH, no transcript of it will be provided unless either party applies for it within 14 days or if the EAT so directs that the judgment should be transcribed (para 18.4 PD). It should be noted that all judgments which are transcribed or handed down will be posted onto the EAT website and are accessible by the public.

9795 **EAT orders** After hearing an appeal, the EAT can make an order:
– **dismissing** the appeal; or
– **allowing** the appeal and:
· substituting its own decision for that of the tribunal; or
· remitting the case (i.e. sending it back) to either the same or a different tribunal for a complete re-hearing or further consideration of a particular point.

The EAT's order is **sealed** by the Registrar before being sent to the parties.

9796 Where an **appeal is allowed**, the nature of the error of law identified will determine whether the EAT **substitutes its own decision or remits** the case. If the tribunal has misdirected itself as to the law, its decision can only stand if the EAT considers that the conclusion is plainly and unarguably right notwithstanding the misdirection (*Moore v University of Greenwich*, EAT case 0924/01). However, if the EAT believes that **further consideration of the facts** is required, then it will remit the case. If however, no further consideration of the facts is necessary but the **decision is plainly wrong** because of the way in which the tribunal has applied the law, the EAT will be more willing to substitute its own decision. It can only do so if a proper application of the law would inevitably have lead the tribunal to a certain conclusion. If, however, in applying the law properly, the tribunal could have come to one of a number of different conclusions, the case will be remitted. The EAT can also remit the case for **fuller reasons** from the tribunal prior to a further hearing on appeal (*English v Emery Reimbold and Strick Ltd* [2003] IRLR 710, CA; *Burns v Consignia plc (No. 2)* [2004] IRLR 425, 710, EAT followed and confirmed in *Barke v Seetec Business Technology Centre Ltd* [2005] IRLR 633, EAT).

If a case is to be remitted, the EAT will also decide whether it should be remitted **back to the same tribunal** that heard the case originally or when it should be remitted **to a fresh tribunal** (which would require a full rehearing of the case). The **relevant factors** which will be considered are as follows (*Sinclair Roche and Temperley and ors v Heard and anor* [2004] IRLR 763, EAT):
– **proportionality**. Where there is sufficient money at stake the question of costs does not offend on the grounds of proportionality although this may not be a decisive, or even an important, factor. Likewise, the distress and inconvenience of the parties in reliving a hearing must be weighed up although this will not be greatly less by virtue of the extra time taken by a fully, rather than partially remitted, hearing;
– **passage of time**. A matter should not be sent back to the same tribunal if there is a real risk that it will have forgotten about the case. However, tribunals should normally be able to refresh their minds from notes of evidence and submissions if the case occurred relatively recently. Further, the longer the case the more likely a tribunal is to remember it. In this case, the hearing which was over a year ago was held to be in the minds of the original tribunal as the hearing was relatively lengthy and the tribunal had come back to the case over that year in giving its reserved decision followed later by its promulgated decision, as well as having a remedies hearing and various chambers' meetings;
– **bias or partiality**. A matter will not be sent to the same tribunal where there is a question of bias or the risk of pre-judgment or partiality;
– **totally flawed decision**. It is not ordinarily appropriate to send a matter back to a tribunal where the first hearing was wholly flawed or there was a complete mishandling of it. The appellate tribunal must have confidence that, with guidance, the tribunal can get it right second time;
– **second bite at the cherry**. A matter must not be sent back to the same tribunal if, on the face of it, the tribunal has already made up its mind in relation to all the matters before it; and
– **tribunal professionalism**. On the balance of all the above facts, an appellate tribunal should ordinarily consider that, in the absence of clear indications to the contrary, it should be assumed that the tribunal below is capable of a professional approach to dealing with a matter on remission. It follows that where a tribunal is corrected on an honest misunder-

standing or misapplication of the legally required approach (not amounting to a "totally flawed" decision), then, unless it appears that the tribunal has so thoroughly committed itself that a rethink appears impracticable, there is the presumption that it will go about the tasks set out on remission in a professional way, paying careful attention to the guidance given to it by the appellate tribunal.

Consent orders The EAT should be informed immediately if: 9797
- an appellant decides to **abandon or withdraw an appeal**;
- the parties agree a **compromise**; or
- the parties agree that the **appeal should be allowed** and that the tribunal order should be reversed or varied or the matter remitted on the ground that the decision contains an error of law.

The EAT's permission is required in order to **withdraw an appeal**. If the parties have agreed an order for withdrawal, it should be submitted to the EAT for approval. If the parties are agreed that the appeal should be withdrawn but do not agree to the terms of a proposed order (which might arise if the respondent wishes to apply for costs against the appellant), the EAT will arrange a hearing to determine the outstanding matters. If the application to withdraw is made close to the main appeal hearing, the EAT may require the attendance of the appellant (or his representative) to explain the reasons for the delay in making a decision not to pursue the appeal, and in such circumstances may be minded to award costs and/or wasted costs (¶9800).

If the agreement is that the **appeal should be allowed**, the EAT normally has a hearing to decide whether or not the order should be made (although it can decide on the papers alone). To save costs it may only require one party to attend to put forward the reasons why the order should be made.

Previous decisions and precedent The EAT is bound by decisions of the **Court of Appeal** and **House of Lords** on English Law, and decisions of the Court of Session (Inner House) and House of Lords on Scottish Law (i.e. it must follow these decisions in later cases). 9798

Decisions of the **High Court** in England and Wales, and of the Outer House of the Court of Session in Scotland are regarded as being highly persuasive (i.e. the EAT will normally follow them unless it is persuaded that there is a good reason why it should not do so).

The EAT is not bound by its **own previous decisions**. It will, however, depart from them only in exceptional circumstances or where there are previous inconsistencies. When faced with **inconsistent decisions** the EAT attempts to resolve any conflicts and, if necessary, will direct employment tribunals as to which decision should be followed and which should be disregarded.

Decisions of the EAT (whether sitting in England and Wales or Scotland) are binding on all employment tribunals in England, Wales or Scotland. 9799

Costs The position on costs is similar to that in the tribunal (¶9702). An order for costs may be made where the EAT considers that **proceedings were unnecessary**, **improper or vexatious**, or that there has been **unreasonable delay** or **other unreasonable conduct** in bringing or conducting the proceedings (rule 34A SI 1993/2854; as inserted by reg 21 SI 2004/2526). This might include a party who pursued an obviously hopeless appeal, or if a party abandoned an appeal at the last minute or failed to attend the appeal hearing without good excuse. For discussion of vexatious proceedings, unreasonable conduct etc., see ¶9566. 9800

The fact that an appeal has gone through the sifting stage (¶9761) does not prevent it from having a costs order made against the appeal (*Iron and Steel Trades Confederation v ASW Ltd (in liquidation)* [2004] IRLR 926, EAT). However, it will be a factor in deciding whether such an order should be made.

A party may be ordered to pay all or part of the costs or expenses **occurred by another party**. The EAT may either **assess the costs** itself or refer the matter to the taxing officer authorised by the President of the EAT to assess costs or expenses. Where the taxing officer assesses costs, his decision may be appealed to a judge. Alternatively, the parties may agree on a sum to be paid between themselves. 9801

There is **no cap** on the costs which may be awarded by the EAT. However, the EAT will take into account the paying party's **ability to pay** when considering the amount of a costs order (rule 34B SI 1993/2854; as inserted by reg 21 SI 2004/2526).

Where the EAT makes a costs order **in favour of** a **party who is not legally represented**, the costs (excluding disbursements) cannot exceed two-thirds of the amount which would have been allowed if the party had been legally represented (rule 34D SI 1993/2854; as inserted by reg 21 SI 2004/2526). The **costs allowed** include costs for work and disbursements which would have been allowed if the work had been done or the disbursements made by a legal representative on the party's behalf, payments reasonably made by him for legal services relating to the conduct of the proceedings, costs in obtaining expert assistance in assessing the costs claim and other expenses incurred by him in relation to the proceedings (including expenditure on his employees, but not including any allowance paid to a witness to attend the appeal hearing). If the unrepresented party can prove his financial loss for the time reasonably spent on doing the work in relation to the proceedings, the costs will cover this amount. Where he cannot prove his financial loss, his costs will be calculated by the EAT for an amount of time which the EAT considers reasonably spent on doing the work at the rate of £25 per hour.

9802 **Wasted costs** The EAT is now also able to make a wasted costs order against a party's representative if he considers that the representative has acted improperly, unreasonably, or negligently in relation to the proceedings (rule 34C SI 1993/2854; as inserted by reg 21 SI 2004/2526). The rules relating to wasted costs are the same as in respect of the employment tribunal (see ¶9711 for further details).

Review and appeals

9805 The EAT has a similar power to **review** its own orders (and, if appropriate, to revoke or vary them) as the tribunal (¶9718). It **can do so if** (rule 33 SI 1993/2854):
- the order was wrongly made as a result of an error on the part of the EAT or its staff;
- a party did not receive proper notice of the proceedings leading to the order; or
- the interests of justice require a review.

The EAT can decide of its own motion to have a review (though it rarely does so), or a party can apply for a review within 14 days of the date of the order (rule 33 SI 1993/2854). A clerical mistake in any order may be corrected at any time by order of a judge or a member of the appeal panel.

9806 Where an application for review is made, it may be considered on paper by the judge who heard the original appeal or made the original order (para 20 PD). In such circumstances, where the judge in question had sat alone without lay members, he will deal with the application as he thinks fit. If, on the other hand, the judge had sat with lay members and, on consideration of the application on paper, thinks that an order may need to be varied or revoked, he will give notice to the other party and consult with the original lay members either on paper or in open court.

9807 Decisions of the EAT can be **appealed** to the Court of Appeal on a point of law. The appeal procedure is discussed below.

B. Court of Appeal

9820 Appeals from the EAT and the High Court are dealt with by the Court of Appeal (Civil Division), which has appellate jurisdiction only (i.e. it only hears appeals against the decisions of lower courts in England and Wales, cases do not start there). The Court of Appeal sits in London at the Royal Courts of Justice. In Scotland, the appeal is to the Inner House of the Court of Session, which sits in Edinburgh.

Like the EAT, the Court of Appeal can only consider appeals on a **point of law** and cannot interfere with findings of fact.

The appeal must be **lodged** with the Court of Appeal not later than 4 weeks after the date on which the EAT's order is sealed by the Registrar of the EAT. 9821

Before lodging an appeal, an application for **permission to appeal** must be made at the EAT hearing or when a reserved judgment is handed down (para 21 PD). If not made at this stage, or if the EAT refuses permission, then permission must be sought from the Court of Appeal within 14 days of the sealed order, or where a transcript has been ordered, within 14 days of receiving the transcript. If a transcript is requested after the hearing with a view to making an application for permission to appeal, then the potential appellant must apply for an extension of time for permission to appeal if necessary. The application **must state** the point of law and the grounds on which the appeal is based.

Appeals are **heard by** a panel of three senior judges (known as Lord or Lady Justice X), who decide whether or not to allow the appeal by majority if they are unable to reach a unanimous decision. 9822

Further, where the Court of Appeal disagrees with the decision of the court or tribunal below, it will normally substitute its own **decision** (unlike the EAT which often remits cases to be heard again by the same or another tribunal). 9823

Decisions of the Court of Appeal may be **appealed** to the House of Lords (see below). 9824

C. House of Lords

The House of Lords is the highest appellate court in the United Kingdom. It hears appeals on a **point of law** from the Court of Appeal (and from the Inner House of the Court of Session in Scotland). **Permission to appeal** is required either from the Court of Appeal (or Court of Session) or the House of Lords. Permission is normally only granted in cases where the point at issue is of general public importance. 9830

Appeals to the House of Lords must generally be **lodged within** 3 months of the date of the decision appealed against as set out in the HL Practice Direction, November 2000. The appeal is commenced (after leave has been granted) by lodging a petition in the Judicial Office of the House of Lords. 9831

The **appellate committees** of the House consist of members of the House of Lords known as Lords of Appeal in Ordinary ('Law Lords'). The Lord Chancellor is the head of the judiciary and sometimes sits with other Law Lords to hear appeals, in which case he will preside. When the Lord Chancellor does not sit, the appellate committee is presided over by the most senior Law Lord present. 9832

Appeals are normally **heard by** five judges. In cases of particular importance, seven judges may sit. Appeals are decided by majority if a unanimous decision cannot be reached.

The **judgment** is delivered in the chamber of the House of Lords, but the speeches of individual Law Lords are printed and given to the parties rather than being given orally. 9833

The House of Lords is not bound by its own **previous decisions**.

The decision of the House of Lords is final, i.e. there is **no further right of appeal**. 9834

D. Referral to the European Court of Justice

9840 The courts of Member States (including the EAT but not employment tribunals) can refer questions relating to the **interpretation of EU law** to the European Court of Justice (ECJ) for a **preliminary ruling**. EU law does not usually have direct effect – it needs to be implemented by the introduction of domestic laws in each member state (for example, the Working Time Regulations 1998 implement the EU Working Time Directive). Questions may, therefore, arise as to whether a Member State has fully complied with its obligation or as to the interpretation which should be given to domestic legislation in order to give effect to the EU law. Such questions may be referred to the ECJ so that it can give guidance and ensure uniform application across the Member States.

The ECJ comprises 15 judges and eight advocates general, appointed by the Member States. The judges select one of their number to serve as President. An **advocate general** delivers an impartial opinion on a case (in open court) before the **judges** make their decision. The judges do not have to follow the advocate general's opinion but his opinion can nearly always be taken as a guide to the way in which the ECJ will ultimately decide the case.

9841 **Procedure** The national court **submits the questions** which it wishes to have determined (usually in the form of a judgment). This is then translated into all the official EU languages and distributed to all Member States, the Commission and the Council of Ministers. A **notice** is published in the Official Journal of the European Communities.

The parties and those to whom the request is distributed have 2 months in which to **submit written observations** to the ECJ. Unlike domestic claims, **legal aid** may be applied for, the decision being made by a chamber of the ECJ.

The case is summarised in a **report** which is made public. A **public hearing** is then held at which the parties argue the case and are questioned by the judges and the advocate general. The ECJ sits either in **plenary session** (all 15 judges) or in **chambers** of three or five judges. A plenary session is held if a Member State or EU institution which is a party to the case requests it to do so, or if the case is particularly complex or important.

A few weeks later the advocate general delivers his **opinion** in open court. The judges will subsequently deliberate on the basis of a draft judgment which one of them has prepared.

When they have all agreed on the final text of the **judgment**, it will be delivered in open court. Decisions of the ECJ are by majority. No dissenting opinions are given.

MEMO POINTS The EU Commission or another member state may bring proceedings against a **member state** alleging that it has **not fulfilled its obligations** under EU law. For example, the ECJ ruled that the UK Government was obliged to implement the Working Time Directive, rejecting the UK Government's argument that the UK was not bound by the Directive.

SECTION 3

Claims in the civil courts

9850 The county courts are governed by the same rules of procedure as the High Court, and may award the same remedies.

Commencing proceedings

9851 Claims are commenced by service of a **claim form** setting out the basis for the claim and the remedies sought. This form may include the particulars of the claim, or these may be sent separately. The person making the claim is called the Claimant, and the other party, the Defendant.

The Defendant must serve an **acknowledgement of service** within 14 days service of the claim form stating whether or not he intends to defend the claim. Within 28 days from service of the particulars of claim, he must serve a defence in which he sets out his grounds for defending the claim. 9852

Directions

The Court plays an active part in the management of the case and will give directions to bring it to trial as efficiently as possible. The procedural rules require the parties to proceedings to disclose the existence of relevant documents to each other and/or to allow inspection of such documents. The directions set out a timetable for discovery and inspection, and also deal with matters such as exchange of witness statements, exchange of expert evidence, and preparation of trial bundles. 9853

Hearing

The trial will be held in public before a judge, sitting without a jury. The procedure at the trial is similar to, but more formal than, that at a tribunal hearing. Each party (normally represented by a barrister) will make an **opening statement**. They will then call their **witnesses** who will each give their evidence and be cross-examined by the other party's representative. The judge may also ask questions. Each party will then make his **closing submissions**. As in the tribunal, the party with the burden of proof will generally go first. 9854

Decision

The judge may either give his decision at the end of the trial or reserve it to be handed down later. When the judge gives his decision, he normally also gives a **judgment** setting out his reasoning. If the judgment is not handed down in writing, a transcript may be obtained later through the Court Service. 9855

Remedies

The High Court may award damages, and also has the power to grant injunctions and declarations. 9856

Costs

In the High Court, the party who loses the case normally has to pay the costs of the party who wins. If the parties cannot agree the figure for costs, costs are assessed as described above for tribunal claims. Costs are also awarded at interlocutory stages so that if, for example, a party has to make an application to the Court in relation to inspection of documents, the party who "wins" that application is normally entitled to have his costs (in respect of that application) paid by the other party regardless of the final outcome of the case. 9857

Appeals

A decision of the High Court may be appealed initially to the Court of Appeal on a point of law (see ¶9820). 9858

APPENDIX

OUTLINE ¶¶

The following model documents comprise:
- a written statement of particulars;
- a contract of employment for general staff; and
- a service agreement for directors or senior executives.

Each of the model documents contains a number of example clauses and is intended to be **used as a starting point** when drafting key employment terms. In order to maximise certainty for both parties, each model document **should be tailored** according to the circumstances of each employer and should also be consistent with other documents, such as company policies (¶9940).

Specialist legal advice should be sought before finalising employment documentation.

Model statement of particulars

9900

Name and address of Employer:

Name of Employee:

Date:

This statement sets out the particulars of your employment with [employer] which are required to be given to you under the Employment Rights Act 1996. The particulars are correct as at [*date*].

1. **Start date and period of continuous employment**

Your employment commenced on [*date*]. [Your period of continuous employment began on [*date*]] OR [No employment with a previous employer counts as continuous employment with [employer]].

2. **Job title**

Your job title is [*insert job title*]. [The main duties of your position are [set out in the attached job description] OR [*describe main characteristics of job duties*]]. [From time to time and at its absolute discretion, [employer] may require you to perform other duties to meet its business needs].

3. **Duration of employment**

[If you wish to terminate your employment, you must give [employer] [1 week's] prior written notice. Subject to [employer's] right to terminate without notice [or payment in lieu of notice] in cases of gross misconduct, if [employer] wishes to terminate your employment, you will be given 1 week's notice during your first 2 years of employment and then an additional week's notice for each additional complete year of service up to a maximum of 12 weeks' notice].

OR

[Your employment is for a fixed-term and will terminate on [*date*].] [It may be terminated at any time before expiry of the fixed-term by either party giving to the other [*insert applicable notice period*] prior written notice.]

OR

[Your employment is not intended to be permanent and is expected to continue until [*date*]. Either party may terminate your employment by giving to the other [*insert applicable notice period*] prior written notice.]

See clause 16 of ¶9910 for suggested wording for a payment in lieu of notice clause and provisions relating to gross misconduct.

4. **Place of work**

Your usual place of work is [*address*] [although from time to time and at the absolute discretion of [employer] you may be required to work at [*specify other locations*] on a temporary or permanent basis].

[You may also be required at the absolute discretion of [employer] to [live and] work in [*location outside UK*]. Further details are provided [in clause [12] below]].

5. **Hours of work**

Your normal hours of work are from [*time*] to [*time*] [Monday to Friday inclusive], with a [1 hour] [paid/unpaid] lunch break per day. [You will not be required to work overtime.] OR [You may from time to time be required to work overtime. If overtime is worked, you must complete the overtime sheets and return them to [the HR Department] to enable [employer] to comply with its obligations under the Working Time Regulations 1998.]

6. **Remuneration**

Your remuneration is £[*amount*] per [*time period*] subject to deductions for tax and NICs, payable by [*method of payment*] [*interval of payment*] on or about [*time of payment*].

[You are not entitled to any payment for overtime [unless agreed in advance with [your manager]]]. OR [Any overtime worked will be paid at the rate of £[*amount*] per hour].

You authorise [employer] at any time during your employment or in any event on the termination of your employment, howsoever arising, to deduct from your salary payment and any sums reimbursable to you by [employer] any amount from time to time which you owe to [employer] including but not limited to any outstanding loans, advances, payments for excess holiday and overpayment of wages and you expressly consent to any such deductions pursuant to Part II of the Employment Rights Act 1996.

7. **Holidays**

The holiday year runs from [*date*] to [*date*]. You are entitled[, in addition to English and Welsh [or Scottish] bank and public holidays,] to [*number*] days' paid holiday in each holiday year, accruing on a [daily] basis. [1] You will be paid [your normal basic remuneration] during such holidays. Your entitlement will be pro-rated in the year of joining and leaving [employer].

[You are required to use part of your annual entitlement during [employer's] shutdown period in [*time/dates*]. [Employer] will notify you by [*method and timing of notification*] of the exact number of days' holiday affected by this provision and the dates on which they must be taken].

You must take your holiday at times convenient to [employer] and you must obtain the prior written approval of [your manager] before taking a holiday. You are required to give at least [2 weeks] notice of a proposed holiday. [No more than [*number*] days' holiday can be taken together unless [your manager] gives permission]. [You must take at least [*number*] consecutive days' holiday in each holiday year]. [You cannot carry over holiday entitlement from one holiday year to the next and any holiday entitlement not used in a holiday year will be forfeited.]

You will be entitled to a payment in lieu of any accrued but untaken holiday on the termination of your employment. [You will not accrue any contractual holiday entitlement during any period of notice (whether given by [employer] or you), save that your entitlement to annual leave pursuant to the Regulations shall continue to accrue during such period]. If, on the termination of your employment, you have taken holidays in excess of your entitlement, [employer] may deduct from your final salary an amount that is equal to the gross salary paid to you in respect of such holidays and you expressly consent to any such deductions pursuant to Part II of the Employment Rights Act 1996.

8. **Sickness absence**

[Employer's] sick pay arrangements are explained in [*reasonably accessible document*].

OR

If you are absent from work due to sickness or injury, you (or someone on your behalf) must inform [your manager] of the reason for and likely duration of your absence no later than [*time*] on the first day of absence [*note: for SSP purposes, the employer cannot specify notification before a specific time on the first qualifying day*]. If your sickness absence lasts 7 calendar days or less, you must complete a self-certification form on your return to work [*note: for SSP purposes, the employer cannot insist on evidence of incapacity in the first 7 days of sickness*]. For absences lasting more than 7 calendar days, you must produce a medical certificate from your doctor stating the reason for your absence. You must keep [your manager] regularly informed of your absence and likely duration of your absence. Further medical certificates are required for each further [week] of sickness absence. [Failure to notify [employer] of your absence may render you subject to disciplinary action and may also bar you from receiving sick pay.]

[Employer] may require you to undergo a medical examination at its expense and the results of any such examination may be disclosed to [employer [and its advisers]].

[Subject to any right [employer] may have to terminate your employment, you will be paid your normal basic remuneration (inclusive of any Statutory Sick Pay (SSP)) [and provided all contractual benefits] for [*number*] working days of absence due to sickness or injury in any calendar year. Any payments to which you are entitled under any social security scheme (whether or not claimed by you) may be deducted from any sick pay paid to you by [employer]]. OR [[Employer] does not operate a sick pay scheme. Your entitlement is to Statutory Sick Pay (SSP) only].

9. **Pension arrangements**

[Employer's] pension arrangements are explained in [*reasonably accessible document*].

OR

[Employer] does not operate a pension scheme in relation to your employment [*Use only if employer falls outside scope of stakeholder pension legislation.*]

OR

[Employer] has set up a Stakeholder Pension Scheme which you are eligible to join [on commencement of employment/after completing [*number*] weeks'/months' employment], subject to the rules of the scheme from time to time in force. [[Employer] does not contribute to the scheme]. Further details of the scheme are set out in a separate pensions booklet available from [*insert details*].

OR

[Employer] operates a [non-contributory] pension scheme, which you will be eligible to join [on commencement of employment after completing [*number*] weeks'/months' employment], subject to the rules of the scheme from time to time in force. Further details of the scheme are set out in a separate pensions booklet available from [*insert details*].

AND

A contracting-out certificate in relation to the [State Earnings Related Pension Scheme (SERPS)]/[State Second Pension] [is]/[is not] in force in respect of your employment.

10. **Discipline and grievances**

The disciplinary rules applicable to you are [attached to this statement] OR [set out in [*reasonably accessible document*]. These rules form part of the terms and conditions of your employment. [2]

[The disciplinary procedure is [attached to this statement] OR [If you are dissatisfied with any disciplinary decision taken in relation to you (including dismissal), you should apply [in writing] within [*number*] days of the decision to [*specify person/job title*]. If you are still dissatisfied with the disciplinary decision (including dismissal) following [*person's/job title's*] review of that decision, you should apply [in writing] within [*number*] days of receiving their decision to [*specify further person/job title*]].

[Further details of [employer's] disciplinary procedure are set out in [*reasonably accessible document*]]. [3]

[The grievance procedure is [attached to this statement] OR [If you have a grievance regarding your employment you should apply [in writing] to [*specify person/job title*]. If you are dissatisfied with the decision taken by [*person/job title*] you should apply [in writing] within [*number*] days of receiving their decision to [*specify further person/job title*]].

[Further details of [employer's] grievance procedure are set out in [*reasonably accessible document*]].[3]

11. **Collective agreements**

[There are no collective agreements which affect the terms and conditions of your employment].

OR

[The collective agreement(s) between [*specify parties*] directly affect your terms and conditions of employment. [*give details of terms and conditions affected*]].

12. **[Work outside the UK]**

[It is anticipated that your posting to [*location*] will be for [*period*][, subject to the absolute discretion of [employer] to change the period of your posting.] During that time your salary will be paid in [*specify currency*] and you will additionally be entitled to [*additional remuneration or benefits, if any*]. At the end of your posting, [*terms and conditions relating to return to UK*]]. OR [There are no terms and conditions relating to the requirement to work outside the United Kingdom.]

I acknowledge receipt of this statement.

Signed .... (employee)

Dated ....

MEMO POINTS 1. Paid leave on bank or public holidays will **count towards** annual statutory entitlement (see ¶4009).

2. If **disciplinary rules** are set out in either an appendix to the statement or a reasonably accessible document, such as a Staff Handbook (rather than in the body of the statement), it should be clearly and expressly stated in that document that the rules form part of the contract of employment, so that any breach by the employee will constitute a breach of contract (see ¶6530).

3. Disciplinary and grievance procedures, like other company policies and procedures, can also be contained in a **reasonably accessible document**, such as a Staff Handbook.

Model short form contract of employment for general staff

* Clauses marked with an asterisk indicate that the information is required to be provided as part of the employer's obligation to give written particulars (¶1400). 9910

This Contract of Employment is made on [*date*] between:

(1) * [Employer] of [*address*] ("[employer]") and

(2) * [Employee] of [*address*] ("you").

This Contract sets out the terms of your employment with [employer].

1. * **Start date and period of continuous employment**

[Your employment commenced on [*date*]] OR [Subject to the conditions set out in your offer letter/set out below [*list any conditions, e.g. satisfactory medical, references satisfactory to [employer], work permit etc*] being fulfilled, your employment will commence on [*date*]].

[Your period of continuous employment began on [*date*]] OR [No employment with a previous employer counts as continuous employment with [employer]].

2. * **Job title and duties**

Your job title is [*insert job title*]. [The main duties of your position are [set out in the attached job description] OR [*describe main characteristics of job duties*]]. [From time to time and at its absolute discretion, [employer] may require you to perform any other duties within your capabilities and/or to move you to [another department] in order to meet its business needs]. [You will report to [*name of manager/supervisor*] or such person(s) as may be notified to you from time to time].

[[Employer] reserves the right to transfer your employment to [another group company] and/or to second you to [such a company, *other company/organisation*]].

3. **[Probation]**

Your employment is subject to a probationary period of [*number*] months, during which your performance and conduct will be appraised and monitored. [Employer] reserves the right to extend your probationary period should this be considered necessary by [your manager].

During the probationary period, your employment may be terminated by [employer] or by you giving [*notice period during probation, if different from general position*]. On successful completion of the probationary period, the provisions of clause [16] will apply in respect of the termination of your employment.

4. * **Place of work**

Your usual place of work is [*address*] [although from time to time and at the absolute discretion of [employer] you may be required on reasonable prior notice to work at [*specify other locations*] on a temporary or permanent basis]. [*specify any relocation provisions or refer to any policy*]

[You may be required at the absolute discretion of [employer] to undertake travel within the United Kingdom and internationally from time to time for the proper performance of your duties].

[You may also be required at the absolute discretion of [employer] to [live and] work in [*location outside UK*]. Further details are provided [in clause [11] below]].

5. * **Hours of work**

Your normal hours of work are from [*time*] to [*time*] [Monday to Friday inclusive], with a [1 hour] lunch break per day.

[You will not be required to work overtime.] OR [You may from time to time be required to work overtime. You are not entitled to any payment for overtime [unless agreed in advance with [*your manager*]]] OR [Any overtime worked will be paid at the rate of £[*amount*] per hour].

[Compliance with regulations on working time]

[If overtime is worked, you must complete the overtime sheets and return them to [the HR Department] to enable [employer] to comply with its obligations under the Working Time Regulations 1998, as amended (the "Regulations")].

The Regulations prohibit employees from exceeding the average weekly limit on working time (48 hours per week) unless they have agreed that the limit will not apply to them.

[You agree that the 48-hour limit on average weekly working time specified in the Regulations will not apply to your working time (including any overtime worked). This agreement will apply indefinitely, subject to your giving [employer] [*period of notice – up to 3 months*] written notice if you wish to withdraw your agreement].[1]

[You will record your working hours [*describe applicable recording method*] or as notified by [employer] from time to time. Failure to do so will be a disciplinary offence and [employer's] disciplinary procedures may be invoked].

[You may, with [employer's] prior written permission, take up employment with another employer. If you do so, you must notify [employer] of any hours worked for the other employer. If your total working time (including those additional hours) may result in your exceeding the limit on average weekly working time, you agree to opt-out of that limit].

In this contract, "working time" means any time during which you are working at [employer's] disposal and carrying out your duties, and will include [*examples*]. "Working time" does not include [*examples*].

6. * **Remuneration**

Your remuneration is £[*amount*] per [*time period*] subject to deductions for tax and NICs, payable by [*method of payment*] [*interval of payment*] on or about [*time of payment*].

Salary will be reviewed annually on or around [*date*] in each year. [There is no obligation on [employer] to increase the level of your basic salary at a review. [Employer] reserves the right to decrease salary at a review if deemed appropriate.] Any increase awarded in one year will not create any right or entitlement or set any precedent in relation to subsequent years. Any revision to your salary will take effect from [*date/period after review*].

[You may be eligible to participate in [employer's] [discretionary] bonus scheme, subject to the rules of that scheme from time to time in force. [The decision to award a bonus in any given year and the amount of any such bonus is at [employer's] absolute discretion. Payment of a bonus in a particular bonus year will not create any right or entitlement to a bonus in any subsequent bonus years]].

You authorise [employer] at any time during your employment or in any event on the termination of your employment, howsoever arising, to deduct from your salary payment and any sums reimbursable to you by [employer] any amount from time to time which you owe to [employer] including but not limited to any outstanding loans, advances, payments for excess holiday and overpayment of wages and you expressly consent to any such deductions pursuant to Part II of the Employment Rights Act 1996.

7. **Other benefits**

7.1. * **Pension**

[[Employer's] pension arrangements are explained in [*reasonably accessible document*]]. OR [[Employer] operates a [non-contributory/contributory] pension [and life insurance] scheme, which you will be eligible to join [on commencement of employment/after completing [*number*] weeks'/months' employment], subject to the rules of the scheme from time to time in force. Further details of the scheme are set out in a separate pensions booklet available from [*insert details*]]. OR [[Employer] does not operate a pension scheme in relation to your employment.] [*Use only if employer falls outside scope of stakeholder pension legislation*] OR [[Employer] has set up a Stakeholder Pension Scheme which you are eligible to join [on commencement of employment/after completing [*number*] weeks'/months' employment], subject to the rules of the scheme from time to time in force. [[Employer] does not contribute to the scheme]. Further details of the scheme are set out in a separate pensions booklet available from [*insert details*]].

* A contracting-out certificate in relation to the [State Earnings Related Pension Scheme (SERPS)]/[State Second Pension] [is]/[is not] in force in respect of your employment.

7.2. **[Private medical cover]**

You will, subject to meeting any conditions or eligibility criteria imposed by the insurance provider and subject to the rules of any such scheme from time to time in force, be eligible for such free private medical insurance as [employer] may from time to time arrange. Further details [are set out in the Staff Handbook/will be provided to you separately].

[Employer] reserves the right to cease to offer private medical insurance or to substitute another provider, or to alter the benefits available to you under, or the terms and conditions of, any scheme or schemes at any time and no compensation will be paid to you. [Employer] will not be liable in the event of any failure by or refusal from any provider or providers to provide cover or any application of any conditions or limitations to the benefit or benefits by any provider or providers.

7.3. **[Permanent health insurance]**

Subject to [employer's] right to terminate your employment, if you comply with any eligibility or other conditions imposed by [employer] or by the relevant insurance provider, you may be eligible to receive payments under [employer's] permanent health insurance arrangements. The terms and level of such cover will be in accordance with the [employer's] policy from time to time in force. Further details [are set out in the Staff Handbook/-will be provided to you separately].

[Employer] reserves the right to cease to offer permanent health insurance or to substitute another provider, or to alter the benefits available to you under, or the terms and conditions of, any scheme or schemes at any time and no compensation will be paid to you. [Employer] will not be liable in the event of any failure by or refusal from any provider or providers to provide cover or any application of any conditions or limitations to the benefit or benefits by any provider or providers.

7.4. **[Company car]**

You will be eligible to participate in [employer's] company car scheme, subject to the rules of the scheme from time to time in force. Participation is conditional on you having and retaining a valid full UK driving licence. Further details [are set out in the Staff Handbook/will be provided to you separately].

7.5. **Other (share schemes, professional subscriptions, lunch vouchers)**

[*insert details*]

8. * **Annual leave**

The leave year runs from [*date*] to [*date*]. You are entitled[, in addition to English and Welsh [or Scottish] bank and public holidays,] to [*number*] days' paid holiday in each holiday year, accruing on a [daily] basis. [[2]] You will be paid [your normal basic remuneration] during such holidays. Your entitlement will be pro-rated in the year of joining and leaving [employer].

[You are required to use part of your annual entitlement during [employer's] shutdown period in [*time/dates*]. [Employer] will notify you by [*method and timing of notification*] of the exact number of days' holiday affected by this provision and the dates on which they must be taken].

You must take your holiday at times convenient to [employer] and you must obtain the prior written approval of [your manager] before taking a holiday. You are required to give at least [2 weeks] notice of a proposed holiday.

[No more than [*number*] days' holiday can be taken together unless [your manager] gives permission]. [You must take at least [*number*] consecutive days' holiday in each holiday year]. [You cannot carry over holiday entitlement from one holiday year to the next and any holiday entitlement not used in a holiday year will be forfeited].

You will be entitled to a payment in lieu of any accrued but untaken holiday on the termination of your employment. [You will not accrue any contractual holiday entitlement during any period of notice (whether given by [employer] or you), save that your entitlement to annual leave pursuant to the Regulations shall continue to accrue during such period]. If, on the termination of your employment, you have taken holidays in excess of your entitlement, [employer] may deduct from your final salary an amount equal to the gross salary paid to you in respect of such holidays and you expressly consent to any such deductions pursuant to Part II of the Employment Rights Act 1996.

9. **[Expenses]**

9.1. [Employer] will reimburse (against production of satisfactory receipts) all your reasonable travelling, hotel and other expenses properly incurred by you in the performance of your duties.

9.2. [Any credit or charge card provided to you by [employer] must only be used for expenses properly incurred by you in the performance of the duties of your employment].

10. * **Sickness absence**

10.1.[[Employer's] sick pay arrangements are explained in [*reasonably accessible document*]].

OR

[If you are absent from work due to sickness or injury, you (or someone on your behalf) must inform [your manager] of the reason for and likely duration of your absence no later than [*time*] on the first day of absence [*note: for SSP purposes, the employer cannot specify notification before a specific time on the first qualifying day*]. If your sickness absence lasts 7 calendar days or less, you must complete a self-certification form on your return to work [*note: for SSP purposes, the employer cannot insist on evidence of incapacity in the first 7 days of sickness*]. For absences lasting more than 7 calendar days, you must produce a medical certificate from your doctor stating the reason for your absence. You must keep [your manager] regularly informed of your absence and likely duration of your absence. Further medical certificates are required for each further [week] of sickness absence.] [Failure to notify [employer] of your absence may render you subject to disciplinary action and may also bar you from receiving sick pay.]

10.2. [Employer] may require you to undergo a medical examination at its expense by a medical practitioner appointed or approved by [employer] and you authorise that medical practitioner to disclose to [employer [and its advisors]] the result of the examination and discuss with it [or them] any matters arising from the examination which might impair the proper performance of your duties.

10.3 [[Employer] does not operate a sick pay scheme. Your entitlement is to Statutory Sick Pay (SSP) only]. OR [Subject to any right [employer] may have to terminate your employment, you will be paid your normal basic remuneration (inclusive of any Statutory Sick Pay (SSP)) [and provided all contractual benefits] for [*number*] working days of absence due to sickness or injury in any calendar year. Thereafter, you will be paid half your normal basic remuneration (inclusive of any Statutory Sick Pay (SSP)) [and provided all contractual benefits] for a further [*number*] working days of absence due to sickness or injury in that calendar year. Any payments to which you are entitled under any social security scheme (whether or not claimed by you) may be deducted from any sick pay paid to you by [employer]. Entitlement to payment is subject to your compliance with this clause [10].]

[10.4. [Employer] at all times reserves the right to withhold, discontinue or request repayment of any contractual sick pay if:

10.4.1. you fail to follow [employer's] absence procedure;

10.4.2.[employer] is satisfied that there has been an abuse of the sick pay arrangements or misrepresentation of your health; or

10.4.3. you behave in a way likely to delay, hinder or impede recovery.]

11. * **[Work outside the UK]**

[It is anticipated that your posting to [*location*] will be for [*period*] [, subject to the absolute discretion of [employer] to change the period of your posting.] During that time your salary will be paid in [*specify currency*] and you will additionally be entitled to [*additional remuneration or benefits, if any*]. At the end of your posting, [*terms and conditions relating to return to UK*]]. OR [There are no terms and conditions relating to the requirement to work outside the United Kingdom.]

12. **Outside interests**

For the duration of this contract (including without limitation any period of garden leave), you will not undertake any other employment without the prior written permission of [*job title*], or engage in any outside activity, paid or unpaid, which might interfere with the effective discharge of your duties or adversely affect [employer] in any way. If such permission is given, you must advise [employer] of your additional working hours and [employer] reserves the right to withdraw its consent at its absolute discretion.

13. **Confidentiality and return of company property**

You will not, except as authorised by [employer] or as required by law or your duties, use, divulge or disclose to any person, firm or organisation, any client or trade secrets or other confidential information relating to the organisation, business, finances, clients, customers, dealings or affairs of [employer] which may come to your knowledge during your employment.

For the purposes of this contract, trade secrets and confidential information include [*insert examples, such as information relating to the employer's trading position (e.g. client/customer lists, details of suppliers), product and sales information, and documents marked as confidential*]. This list is by way of illustration only and is not exhaustive.

[A breach of this clause may render you subject to disciplinary action.]

This restriction will continue to apply after the termination of your employment but will not apply to information which becomes public (other than through unauthorised disclosure by you).

This clause is not intended to exclude or restrict your right to make a protected disclosure under the Public Interest Disclosure Act 1998 if you reasonably believe a harmful or illegal activity is being undertaken. In such a case, you [are encouraged to discuss your concerns with [*job title*]/should refer to [employer's] whistleblowing policy].

On the termination of your employment howsoever arising or at [employer's] specific request, you will immediately return to [employer] all property belonging or relating to [employer] that is in your possession or under your control. [For the avoidance of doubt, this includes (but is not limited to) [your company car, keys, security cards, *list other property*], and all documents, records, correspondence, papers and other materials (and any copies thereof), whether in hard copy or in electronic or machine readable form, made or kept by, or provided to, you during your employment]. You will not retain any copies or extracts of such material.

14. **[Intellectual property]**

See clause 18 of ¶9920 for suggested wording. Note that this clause contains defined terms which would need to be incorporated or adapted as appropriate.

15. * **Discipline and grievances** [3]

The disciplinary rules applicable to you are [set out in Appendix X below] OR [set out in [*reasonably accessible document*]. These rules form part of the terms and conditions of your employment [4].

[The disciplinary procedure is set out in Appendix X below] OR [If you are dissatisfied with any disciplinary decision taken in relation to you (including dismissal), you should apply [in writing] within [*number*] days of the decision to [*specify person/job title*]. If you are still dissatisfied with the disciplinary decision (including dismissal) following [*person's/job title's*] review of that decision, you should apply [in writing] within [*number*] days of receiving their decision to [*specify further person/job title*]. Further details of [employer's] disciplinary procedure are set out in [*reasonably accessible document*]].

[The grievance procedure is set out in Appendix X below] OR [If you have a grievance regarding your employment you should apply [in writing] to [*specify person/job title*]. [If you are dissatisfied with the decision taken by [*person/job title*] you should apply [in writing] within [*number*] days of receiving their decision to [*specify further person/job title*]. Further details of [employer's] grievance procedure are set out in [*reasonably accessible document*]].

16. * **Termination of employment**

16.1. [If you wish to terminate your employment, you must give [employer] [1 week's] prior written notice. Subject to [employer's] right to terminate without notice [or payment in lieu of notice] in cases of gross misconduct, if [employer] wishes to terminate your employment, you will be given 1 week's notice during your first 2 years of employment and then an additional week's notice for each additional complete year of service up to a maximum of 12 weeks' notice]. [*cross refer to notice period during probation, if different*]

OR

[Your employment is for a fixed-term and will terminate on [*date*] without any further notice.] [It may be terminated at any time before expiry of the fixed-term by either party giving to the other [*insert applicable notice period*] prior written notice.]

OR

[Your employment is not intended to be permanent and is expected to continue until [*date*]. Either party may terminate your employment by giving to the other [*insert applicable notice period*] prior written notice.]

16.2. [[Employer] reserves the right, at his sole and absolute discretion, to pay salary (based on the basic salary set out above) in lieu of any required period of notice (whether given by you or [employer]), less any deductions [employer] is required to make by law].

16.3. Notwithstanding the other provisions of this clause [16], your employment may be terminated immediately by [employer] without notice [or payment in lieu of notice] if you are guilty of gross misconduct or in any way fundamentally breach your employment contract with [employer]. The following are examples of conduct which would entitle [employer] to terminate your employment summarily:
- theft, fraud or any act of dishonesty;
- any act or attempted act of violence or abusive behaviour towards people or property;
- any serious act of insubordination or refusal to carry out reasonable requests;
- [*this list should be consistent with policies on disciplinary matters*].

This list is intended as a guide and is not exhaustive.

16.4. If you are absent for a total period of [*period*] (including Saturdays, Sundays and public holidays) in any period of 12 months due to sickness or injury, [employer] may terminate your employment [immediately by written notice] OR [by giving you [*shorter period of notice than clause [16]*]. [5]

16.5. [Employer] reserves the right at any time to suspend you on full pay [and contractual benefits] from the performance of some or all of your duties under this contract in connection with any investigation or matter with which you are involved for such period as [employer] in its absolute discretion shall decide.

16.6. During any such period referred to in clause [16.5]:

16.6.1. you shall, if requested by [employer], refrain from contacting [employees, customers, clients and professional contacts] of [employer];

16.6.2. [employer] shall be entitled to make such announcements or statements to its [employees, customers, clients and professional contacts] concerning you as [employer] in its absolute discretion shall decide; and

16.6.3. [employer] shall be under no obligation to provide any work for you and you shall continue to be bound by the express and implied duties of your employment.

16.7. [In any event and without prior notice, this contract will determine on the last day of the month in which you attain the age of [*age*]]. [6]

17. **[Garden leave]**

See clause 21 of ¶9920 for suggested wording. Note that this clause contains defined terms which would need to be incorporated or adapted as appropriate.

18. **[Post-termination restrictive covenants]**

See clause 24 of ¶9920 for suggested wording. Note that this clause contains defined terms which would need to be incorporated or adapted as appropriate.

19. **Data protection**

In relation to Personal Data and Sensitive Personal Data (as defined by the Data Protection Act 1998) provided by you to [employer], you give your consent to the holding and processing of that data for all purposes relating to your employment. In particular, you agree that [employer] can hold and process Personal and Sensitive Personal Data in order to pay and review your remuneration and other benefits, provide and administer any such benefits, provide information to professional advisers and to legal and regulatory authorities such as Revenue and Customs and the Contributions Agency, administer and maintain personnel records (including sickness and other absence records), carry out reviews of your performance, provide information to potential purchasers of [employer] or the business area in which you work, give references to future employers, and transfer Personal and Sensitive Personal Data concerning you to a country outside the EEA.

20. **Statutory particulars**

This contract [and the attached Appendix] contain the written particulars of employment which [employer] is obliged to provide you under the Employment Rights Act 1996.

21. *** Collective agreements**

[There are no collective agreements which affect the terms and conditions of your employment.] OR [The collective agreement(s) between [*specify parties*] directly affect your terms and conditions of employment. [*give details of terms and conditions affected*]].

22. **Policies and procedures**

You agree to comply with the rules, policies and procedures of the [employer] from time to time in force, although these do not form part of your contract of employment (unless stated otherwise).

23. **Whole agreement**

This contract supersedes any previous oral or written agreement between [employer] and you in relation to the matters dealt within it. It contains the whole agreement between [employer] and you relating to your employment as at the date of the contract, except for any terms implied by law that cannot be excluded by the agreement of the parties.

24. **Governing law and jurisdiction**

This contract will be governed by and interpreted in accordance with English law. [Employer] and you submit to the exclusive jurisdiction of the English Courts and Tribunals in relation to any claim or matter arising in connection with this contract.

Please sign and return the duplicate copy of this Contract of Employment to indicate your acceptance of its terms.

Signed .... Date.................................

For and on behalf of [employer]

I agree to the above terms and conditions.

Signed .... Date.................................

[Employee]

APPENDIX [7]

Unless expressly stated otherwise, the following particulars do not form part of your Contract of Employment [4]

[Disciplinary procedure]

[*insert full disciplinary procedure here*]

[Grievance procedure]

[*insert full grievance procedure here*]

MEMO POINTS 1. The ECJ recently emphasised that a worker's **consent to opt out** of the average weekly time limit should be **given expressly and freely** (see ¶3688).

2. Paid leave on bank or public holidays will **count towards** annual statutory entitlement (see ¶4009).

3. Note that the exemption for **small employers** who employ less than 20 employees to provide information relating to their disciplinary rules and procedures has been removed (see Chapter 19 for further details).

4. If **disciplinary rules** are set out in either an appendix to the contract or a reasonably accessible document, such as a Staff Handbook (rather than in the body of the contract), it should be clearly and expressly stated in that document that the rules form part of the contract of employment, so that any breach by the employee will constitute a breach of contract (see ¶6530).

5. Although this clause is useful, employers should ensure that they also comply, where relevant, with **disability discrimination legislation**, including the duty to make reasonable adjustments in relation to a disabled person (see ¶5450 +).

6. It is expected that direct and indirect **age discrimination** will become unlawful from 1 October 2006. Draft regulations on age discrimination make a number of proposals in relation to retirement and it is likely that this will need to be addressed both in employment contracts and company policies (see ¶5254 for a summary of the draft regulations).

7. Disciplinary and grievance procedures, like other company policies and procedures, can also be contained in a **reasonably accessible document**, such as a Staff Handbook.

Model service agreement

In line with the above model documents (¶¶9900, ¶9910), the following model service agreement is intended to be **used as a starting point**. Whilst it provides example clauses and guidance for drafting key terms for either a director or senior executive, it **should be tailored** to reflect the requirements of the employer and the articles of association of the company. The service agreement should also be consistent with other documents, such as company policies (¶9940). 9920

As service agreements are **often subject to detailed negotiation**, specialist legal advice should also be sought.

* Clauses marked with an asterisk indicate that the information is required to be provided as part of the employer's obligation to give written particulars (¶1400).

[SUBJECT TO CONTRACT] [1]

This Agreement is made on [*date*] between:

(1) * [the Company] whose registered office is at [*address*] (the "Company") and

(2) * [Employee] of [*address*] (the "Executive").

This Agreement sets out the terms on which the Executive will serve the Company.

1. **Definition and Interpretation**

In this Agreement:

1.1. "the Board" means the board of directors for the time being of the Company;

1.2. "Company Clients" means any person, firm or company who was at the Termination Date and/or at any time during the [*number*] months prior to the Termination Date a customer or client of, or in the habit of doing business with, the Company or any other Group Company and in respect of which the Executive had dealings, whether directly or indirectly;

1.3. "Confidential Information" includes but is not limited to client or trade secrets and confidential or commercial information relating to the organisation, business, finances, clients, customers, dealings and affairs of the Company and other Group Companies [*define confidential information further, if possible*];

1.4. "the Employment" means the employment governed by this Agreement;

1.5. "the Group" means the Company and all of its holding or subsidiary companies (as defined in section 736 of the Companies Act 1985) [2];

1.6. "Group Company" means a member of the Group [2];

1.7. "Incapacity" means any illness, injury, accident or other similar cause which prevents the Executive from carrying out his duties under this Agreement;

1.8. "Intellectual Property Rights" means all rights in and to intellectual property in the UK and internationally including without limitation patents, trade marks, copyright, design rights and rights in databases whether or not any of the above are registered and including applications for registration of any of them;

1.9. "Inventions" means all inventions, works and information including, without limitation, discoveries, designs, databases, ideas, methods, programs, diagrams and reports (and any drafts thereof) made or discovered by the Executive (alone or with others) in connection with the Employment or relating to or capable of being used in those parts of the businesses of the Company or any Group Company in which the Executive is involved;

1.10. "Termination Date" means the date of termination of the Employment;

1.11. words importing one gender include all other genders and words importing the singular include the plural and vice versa;

1.12. references to any statutory provisions include any modifications or re-enactments of those provisions;

1.13. the clause headings do not form part of this Agreement and shall not be taken into account in its construction or interpretation.

2. * **Term of employment**

2.1. Subject to the satisfaction of the conditions set out in clause [2.2] below, the Employment will commence on [*date*]. [The Executive's period of continuous employment began on [*date*]] OR [No employment with a previous employer counts as continuous employment with the Company].

2.2. The conditions to which clause [2.1] refers are as follows:

[*list any conditions, e.g. medical satisfactory to the Company, references, work permit, etc*].

2.3. Subject to the Company's right to terminate in accordance with clause [19], the Employment will continue until terminated by either party giving not less than [*number*] months' notice in writing to the other.

OR

Subject to the Company's right to terminate in accordance with clause [19], the Employment will continue for an initial fixed-term of [*initial term*], after which it may be terminated by either party giving not less than [*number*] months' notice in writing to the other.

OR

Subject to the Company's right to terminate in accordance with clause [19], the Employment will be for a fixed-term of [*period*], expiring on [*date*], but may be terminated prior to that date by either party giving not less than [*number*] months' notice in writing to the other [, to expire at any time on or after [*date*]].

2.4. [The Company reserves the right, at its sole and absolute discretion, to pay salary (at the rate set out in clause [6.1]) in lieu of any required period of notice (whether given by the Executive or the Company), less any deductions the Company is required to make by law.

2.5. [In any event and without prior notice, the Employment will determine on the last day of the month in which the Executive attains the age of [*age*]]. [3]

2.6. [If the Executive shall cease by reason of his own act or default to be a director of the Company he shall be deemed to be in breach of this Agreement and the Employment shall immediately terminate.]

3. * **Duties**

3.1. The Executive will serve the Company in the capacity of [*insert job title*] and will carry out such duties as the Board may from time to time direct. The Executive accepts that the Company may in its discretion require him to perform other duties or tasks outside the scope of his normal duties or to perform his duties for the Company or any Group Company in conjunction with another member of the Board and the Executive agrees to perform those duties or undertake those tasks as if they were specifically required under this Agreement.

3.2. The Executive agrees that he will:

3.2.1. devote all of his time, attention and skill to the Employment;

3.2.2. properly perform his duties and exercise his powers;

3.2.3. accept such offices or directorships as may reasonably be required by the Board;

3.2.4. comply with the proper and reasonable directions of the Board and all rules and regulations issued by the Company;

3.2.5. use his best endeavours to promote, develop and extend the business, interests and reputation of the Group; and

3.2.6. promptly disclose to the Board any information that comes into his possession which adversely affects the Company or the Group.

3.3. The Executive will keep the Board promptly and fully informed (in writing if so requested) of his conduct of the [business, finances or affairs] of the Company or any Group Company.

3.4. The Company may appoint another person to act jointly with the Executive.

3.5. The Company may, with the Executive's consent (which will not be unreasonably withheld), require him to perform duties for any Group Company [, and may transfer the Employment to any such company].

4. * **Place of employment**

4.1. The Executive's usual place of employment is [*address*] [but from time to time and at the absolute discretion of the Board the Executive may be required on reasonable prior notice to work at other places [within the United Kingdom], on a temporary or permanent basis].

4.2. The Executive may be required at the absolute discretion of the Board to undertake travel within the United Kingdom and internationally from time to time for the proper performance of his duties.

4.3. [The Executive may also be required at the absolute discretion of the Board to live and work in [*location outside UK*]. Further details are provided [in clause [12] below]] [*details of any relocation policy*] OR [Unless otherwise agreed with the Board, the Executive will not be required to live and work outside the United Kingdom.]

5. * **Hours of work**

5.1. The Company's normal hours of work are from [*time*] to [*time*] [Monday to Friday]. The Executive will comply with such hours and will also work any further hours as may from time to time become necessary in order to perform his duties to the satisfaction of the Board. He will not be entitled to receive any additional remuneration for work done outside his normal hours of work.

5.2. [The Working Time Regulations 1998 (the "Regulations") prohibit employees from exceeding the average weekly limit on working time (48 hours per week) unless they have agreed that the limit will not apply to them. The Executive therefore agrees that this limit will not apply to him. This agreement will apply indefinitely, subject to the Executive giving the Company [*period of notice – up to 3 months*] written notice if he wishes to withdraw his agreement] [4]

OR

[The parties acknowledge that the Executive has autonomous decision-taking powers and that he is able to determine the duration of his own working time, and that, as a result, the exemptions available in Regulation 20 of the Regulations will apply].

6. * **Salary [and Bonus]**

6.1. The Executive will be paid a salary of £[*amount*] per annum subject to deductions for tax and NICs, payable by [*method of payment*] [*interval of payment*] on or about [*time of payment*]. Salary will accrue from day to day and will be inclusive of any directors' fees payable to the Executive by the Company or any Group Company.

6.2. Salary will be reviewed annually by the Board on or around [*date*] in each year. [There is no obligation on the Board to increase the level of the Executive's salary at a review. The Board reserves the right to decrease salary at a review if deemed appropriate.] Any increase awarded in one year will not create any right or entitlement or set any precedent in relation to subsequent years. Any revision to the Executive's salary will take effect from [*date/period after review*].

6.3. [The Executive may be eligible to participate in the Company's [discretionary] bonus scheme, subject to the rules of that scheme from time to time in force. [*insert any conditions to eligibility*] [The decision to award a bonus in any given year and the amount of any such bonus is at the Company's absolute discretion. Payment of a bonus in a particular bonus year will not create any right or entitlement to a bonus in any subsequent bonus years]].

6.4. The Executive authorises the Company at any time during the Employment or in any event on the termination of the Employment, howsoever arising, to deduct from the Executive's salary payment and any sums reimbursable to the Executive by the Company any amount from time to time which the Executive owes to the Company (or any Group

Company) including but not limited to any outstanding loans, advances, payments for excess holiday and overpayment of wages and the Executive expressly consents to any such deductions pursuant to Part II of the Employment Rights Act 1996.

7. * **Holidays**

7.1. The holiday year runs from [*date*] to [*date*]. The Executive is entitled, in addition to English and Welsh [or Scottish] bank and public holidays, to [*number*] days' paid holiday in each holiday year, accruing on a [daily] basis.

7.2. The Executive's entitlement will be pro-rated in the year of joining and leaving the Company. On the termination of the Employment, the Executive will be entitled to a payment in lieu of any accrued but untaken holiday. [The Executive will not accrue any contractual holiday entitlement during any period of notice (whether given by [the Company] or the Executive), save that the Executive's entitlement to annual leave pursuant to the Regulations shall continue to accrue during such period]. If, on the termination of the Employment, the Executive has taken holidays in excess of his entitlement, the Company may deduct from his final salary payment an amount equal to the gross salary paid to him in respect of such holidays and the Executive expressly consents to any such deductions.

7.3. The Executive must obtain the Board's prior approval to the dates on which he proposes to take his holiday.

8. **Other benefits**

8.1. * **Pension**

8.1.1. [The Executive will be eligible to join the Company's [contributory] pension scheme [on commencement of the Employment/after completing [*number*] weeks'/months' service], subject to the rules of the scheme from time to time in force].

OR

[The Company does not operate a pension scheme in relation to the Employment. The Company will pay contributions to the Executive's personal pension arrangements at the rate of [*amount of contributions*], subject to any applicable Revenue and Customs requirements].

8.1.2. * A contracting-out certificate in relation to the [State Earnings Related Pension Scheme (SERPS)]/[State Second Pension] [is]/[is not] in force in respect of the Employment.

8.2. **Permanent health insurance**

Subject to the Company's right to terminate the Employment, if the Executive complies with any eligibility or other conditions imposed by the Company or by the relevant insurance provider, the Executive may be eligible to receive payments under the Company's permanent health insurance arrangements. The terms and level of such cover will be in accordance with the Company's policy from time to time in force.

The Company reserves the right to cease to offer permanent health insurance or to substitute another provider, or to alter the benefits available to the Executive under, or the terms and conditions of, any scheme or schemes at any time and no compensation will be paid to the Executive. The Company will not be liable in the event of any failure by or refusal from any provider or providers to provide cover or any application of any conditions or limitations to the benefit or benefits by any provider or providers.

8.3. **Private medical cover**

The Executive [and his wife and minor children] will, subject to meeting any conditions or eligibility criteria imposed by the insurance provider and subject to the rules of any such scheme from time to time in force, be eligible for such free private medical insurance as the Company may from time to time arrange.

The Company reserves the right to cease to offer private medical insurance or to substitute another provider, or to alter the benefits available to the Executive under, or the terms and conditions of, any scheme or schemes at any time and no compensation will be paid to the Executive. The Company will not be liable in the event of any failure by or refusal from any provider or providers to provide cover or any application of any conditions or limitations to the benefit or benefits by any provider or providers.

8.4. **Company car**

The Executive will be eligible to participate in the Company's company car scheme, subject to the rules of the scheme from time to time in force. Participation is conditional on the Executive having and retaining a valid full UK driving licence.

8.5. **Share schemes**

The Executive may be eligible to participate in the Company's share scheme arrangements from time to time in force. Details of such arrangements will be provided separately.

8.6. **Other (e.g. professional subscriptions)**

[*insert details*]

9. **Expenses**

9.1. The Company shall reimburse the Executive (against production of satisfactory receipts) all reasonable travelling, hotel and other expenses properly incurred by him in the performance of his duties.

9.2. [Any credit or charge card provided to the Executive by the Company must only be used for expenses properly incurred by him in the performance of the duties of the Employment.]

10. * **Sickness absence**

10.1. If the Executive is absent from work due to Incapacity, he (or someone on his behalf) must notify the Company on the first day of absence. If the sickness absence lasts 7 calendar days or less, the Executive must complete a self-certification form on his return to work. For absences lasting more than 7 calendar days, the Executive must produce a medical certificate from his doctor stating the reason for his absence. The Executive must keep the Company regularly informed of his absence and likely duration of his absence. Further medical certificates are required for each further [week] of sickness absence. [Failure to notify the Company of his absence may render the Executive subject to disciplinary action and may also bar him from receiving sick pay.]

10.2. Subject to the Company's right to terminate the Employment under clauses [2] and [19] of this Agreement and the Executive's compliance with this clause [10], the Executive will be paid salary (inclusive of any Statutory Sick Pay (SSP)) [and provided all contractual benefits] during absence due to his Incapacity for a total of [*period*] in any period of 12 months. [Thereafter any further payment in respect of absence due to the Executive's Incapacity will be at the sole discretion of the Company].

10.3. Any payments to which the Executive is entitled under any social security scheme (whether or not claimed by the Executive) may be deducted from any sick pay paid to the Executive by the Company.

10.4. If the Incapacity is caused by the fault of a third party in respect of which compensation for loss of [salary] under this Agreement is or may be recovered, the Executive will, if required by the Board, repay to the Company any money it has paid to him as [salary] for the same period of absence.

[10.5. The Company all times reserves the right to withhold, discontinue or request repayment of any contractual sick pay if:

10.5.1 the Executive fails to follow the Company's absence procedure;

10.5.2. the Company is satisfied that there has been an abuse of the sick pay arrangements or misrepresentation of the Executive's health; or

10.5.3. the Executive behaves in a way likely to delay, hinder or impede recovery.]

11. **Medical examination**

The Company may require the Executive to undergo a medical examination by a medical practitioner appointed or approved by the Company and the Executive authorises that medical practitioner to disclose to the Company [and its advisors] the results of the examination and discuss with it [or them] any matters arising from the examination which might impair the proper performance of the Executive's duties.

12. * **[Work outside the UK]**

[It is anticipated that the Executive's posting to [*location*] will be for [*period*] [, subject to the absolute discretion of the Company to change the period of his posting.]] During that time the Executive's salary will be paid in [*specify currency*] and the Executive will additionally be entitled to [*additional remuneration or benefits, if any*]. At the end of the posting, [*specify terms and conditions relating to return to UK*]].

13. * **Collective agreements**

[There are no collective agreements which affect the terms and conditions of the Executive's employment].

14. **Directorships**

14.1. Any office or directorship held by the Executive is subject to the Articles of Association of that company. In the case of any conflict between the Articles and this Agreement, the Articles will prevail.

14.2. The Executive will not, without the consent of the Company, resign any office or directorship held by him, and will not do or omit to do anything that would provide grounds for his disqualification as a director of any Group Company.

14.3. The Executive will resign from any office or directorship held in the Company and any Group Company and all other companies of which he shall have been appointed as a director by any member of the Group, if so requested by the Board.

14.4. If the Executive fails to comply with clause [14.3] above, the Company is hereby appointed to act as the Executive's attorney to execute any document or do anything in his name necessary to effect his resignation. If there is any doubt as to whether such a document or action has been executed or carried out within the authority conferred by this clause, a certificate in writing signed by any director or the secretary of the Company will be conclusive evidence that such is the case. [5]

15. **Outside interests**

15.1. The Executive will disclose in writing to the Board all his interests in any business (apart for any interest in a Group Company) throughout the Employment.

15.2. Subject to clause [15.3] below, during the Employment (including without limitation any period of garden leave), the Executive will not, without the prior written consent of the Board or except as a representative of the Company, be engaged, concerned, or interested, directly or indirectly, in the conduct of any other business of a similar nature to or which competes with that of the Company (or any Group Company) [or which is a supplier or customer of the Company (or any Group Company)].

15.3. The Executive may hold or be interested in shares or other securities of any company [which are listed or quoted on any recognised stock exchange or dealt on the Alternative Investments Market] provided that the interest of the Executive in such shares or other securities does not extend to more than [5%] of the total amount of such shares or securities.

16. **Dealings in securities**

The Executive will comply (and will procure that his wife and minor children comply) with all applicable rules of law (including, in particular, Part V of the Criminal Justice Act 1993), Stock Exchange codes, rules and regulations, and all rules, policies and codes of conduct of the Company as issued from time to time in relation to the holding of and dealing in shares, debentures or other securities.

17. **Confidentiality**

17.1. The Executive acknowledges that during the course of the Employment, he will have access to and is likely to obtain Confidential Information.

17.2. Without prejudice to any common law duties owed to the Company, the Executive agrees that he will not, during or after the Employment, except as authorised by the Company or as required by law or his duties, use, divulge or disclose to any person, firm or organisation, any Confidential Information which may come to his knowledge during the Employment. The Executive further agrees to use his best endeavours to prevent the unauthorised use or disclosure of such information.

17.3. This restriction will not apply to information which becomes public (other than through unauthorised disclosure by the Executive), and is not intended to exclude or restrict his right to make a protected disclosure under the Public Interest Disclosure Act 1998.

17.4. The Executive is likely to obtain Confidential Information belonging to or relating to other Group Companies. The Executive will treat such information as falling within the terms of clauses [17.2 and 17.3] above, and those clauses will apply with any necessary amendment to such information. The Executive will, at the Company's request, enter into an agreement or undertaking with other Group Companies in the same terms as clauses [17.2 and 17.3] above.

17.5. Unless it is [a formal/an agreed] part of the Executive's duties, the Executive will not, without the prior written consent of the Board, communicate with any press, radio or television representative on any issue relating to the business or affairs of the Company or any Group Company or to any officers, employees, customers or clients of any such company.

18. **Intellectual Property**

18.1. The Executive will promptly communicate full details of any Inventions to the Company. All Intellectual Property Rights in the Inventions will belong to the Company or the appropriate Group Company, as the case may be.

18.2. The Executive will not disclose or exploit any Invention unless authorised by the Company or in the proper performance of his duties.

18.3. The Executive hereby assigns to the Company or any other Group Company as appropriate to the extent allowed by law all his existing and future rights (including Intellectual Property Rights), title and interests in all Inventions.

18.4. To the extent that any right in such Inventions may not be assigned to the Company or other Group Company, the Executive will hold all such rights on trust for the Company.

18.5. In any event, at the request and expense of the Company, the Executive will give it all information and assistance as may be necessary to enable the Company effectively to exploit the Intellectual Property Rights, and will execute all documents and do all things which may be necessary to vest all such rights in the Company (or as it may direct) as legal and beneficial owner and to secure appropriate protection for all such rights anywhere in the world.

18.6. The Executive hereby irrevocably appoints the Company to take any action in his name and execute any document on his behalf for the purpose of giving to the Company (or its nominee) the full benefit of the provisions of this clause. If there is any doubt as to whether such a document or action has been executed or carried out within the authority conferred by this clause, a certificate in writing signed by any director or the secretary of the Company will be conclusive evidence that such is the case. [[5]]

18.7. The Executive waives all of his moral rights (as defined in the Copyright, Designs and Patents Act 1988) and any corresponding foreign rights in respect of all Inventions where the Intellectual Property Rights belong to the Company or appropriate Group Company by virtue of this clause, to the extent that such waiver is permitted by law.

18.8. The Executive will promptly notify the Company in writing if he becomes aware of any infringement or suspected infringement of any Intellectual Property Rights in any Invention.

18.9. Rights and obligations under this clause will survive the termination of the Employment in respect of Inventions made during the Employment and will be binding on the Executive's personal representatives.

19. **Termination and suspension of employment**

19.1. **Termination for long-term incapacity**

If the Executive is absent for a total period of [*period*] (including Saturdays, Sundays and public holidays) in any period of 12 months due to Incapacity, the Company may terminate the Employment [immediately by written notice] OR [by giving the Executive [*shorter period of notice than clause [2.3]*]. [6]

19.2. **Summary termination**

The Employment may be terminated immediately without notice [or payment in lieu of notice] if the Executive:

19.2.1. is guilty of any gross misconduct or conducts himself (in connection with the Employment or otherwise) in a way which is detrimental to the Company or any Group Company; or

19.2.2. commits a serious or persistent breach or non-observance of his obligations under this Agreement or has failed to perform his duties to the standard required by the Board; or

19.2.3. does not comply with any lawful order or direction given to him by the Board; or

19.2.4. becomes bankrupt or makes any arrangement or composition with his creditors or has a receiving order made against him; or

19.2.5. is guilty of insider dealing or of dishonesty or is convicted of an offence (other than a motoring offence not resulting in imprisonment); or

19.2.6. is disqualified from being a director of a company; or

19.2.7. ceases to be a director of the Company or a Group Company without the consent of the [Board/Company/Group Company]; or

19.2.8. by his actions or omissions brings the name or reputation of the Company or any Group Company into disrepute or prejudices the interests of the business of the Company or any Group Company; or

19.2.9. fails to comply in any material respect with any policy of the Company or any Group Company; or

19.2.10. becomes of unsound mind.

This list is intended as a guide and is non-exhaustive.

If the Employment is terminated in accordance with this clause [19], the Executive will have no claim for damages or any other remedy against the Company by reason of such termination.

19.3. On the termination of the Employment for any reason or if the Executive shall cease for any reason to be a director of the Company, the Executive shall if so requested by the Company resign immediately without compensation from his office as director of the Company, all other companies of which he is a director within the Group, and all other companies of which he shall have been appointed as a director by any member of the Group.

19.4. The Company reserves the right at any time to suspend the Executive on full pay [and contractual benefits] from the performance of some or all of his duties under this Agreement in connection with any investigation or matter with which he is involved for such period as the Company in its absolute discretion shall decide.

19.5. During any such period referred to in clause [19.4]:

19.5.1. the Executive shall, if requested by the Company, refrain from contacting [employees, customers, clients and professional contacts] of the Company or any Group Company;

19.5.2. the Company shall be entitled to make such announcements or statements to [employees, customers, clients and professional contacts] of the Company or any Group Company concerning the Executive as the Company in its absolute discretion shall decide; and

19.5.3. the Company shall be under no obligation to provide any work for the Executive and the Executive shall continue to be bound by the express and implied duties of the Employment.

20.* **Discipline and grievances**

The Company's disciplinary rules and disciplinary and grievance procedures as set out in the Staff Handbook from time to time apply to the Executive. [7]

21. **Garden leave**

[Once notice to terminate the Employment has been given by either party in accordance with clause [2.3] of this Agreement,] OR [During the last [*number*] months of the [initial fixed-term/fixed-term,] or if the Executive resigns without giving the required period of notice and the Company does not accept that resignation, the following provisions will apply for [such period as the Company in its absolute discretion may decide/a maximum period of [*period*]]:

21.1. the Company will not be obliged to provide the Executive with any work or require him to perform any duties or may require him to perform such specific duties as are expressly assigned to him by the Company for such period as the Company in its absolute discretion may decide;

21.2. the Company may exclude the Executive from its premises or the premises of any other Group Company and may require him not to be involved in the business of such companies;

21.3. the Executive's salary and all contractual benefits [excluding any bonus] will continue to be paid or provided;

21.4. the Executive will remain bound by his obligations under this Agreement and, in particular, by clause [15] [*outside interests*];

21.5. the Executive will return all of the Company's property including without limitation all Confidential Information;

21.6. the Company may require the Executive not to have any contact or communication with any of its [employees, customers, clients, or professional contacts] in relation to the business of the Company or any Group Company;

21.7. the Company may make such announcements or statements to any of the [employees, customers, clients, or professional contacts] of the Company or any Group Company or any other third parties concerning the Executive as it in its sole and absolute discretion may decide;

21.8. the Company may require the Executive immediately to resign without claim for compensation from any office which he holds in the Company or any Group Company. If he fails to do so, the Executive hereby irrevocably appoints the Company to be his attorney to execute any document or do anything in his name necessary to effect his resignation.

[The Company reserves the right to require the Executive to take holiday which is accrued up to the commencement of garden leave and which will accrue to the date the Employment terminates during the period of garden leave on such day or days as the Company may specify. No contractual holiday entitlement shall accrue during such period, save that the Executive's entitlement to annual leave pursuant to the Regulations shall continue to accrue during such period.]

[At the end of any period of garden leave imposed, the Company may make a payment in lieu of the balance of [any required period of notice (whether given by the Executive or the Company)] OR [the initial fixed-term/fixed-term], less any deductions the Company is required to make by law.]

22. **Return of company property**

On the termination of the Employment howsoever arising or at the Company's specific request, the Executive will immediately return to the Company all property belonging or relating to any Group Company that is in his possession or under his control. For the avoidance of doubt, this includes (but is not limited to) [the Executive's company car, keys, security cards, *list other property*], and all documents, records, correspondence, papers and other materials (and any copies thereof), whether in hard copy or in electronic or machine readable form, made or kept by, or provided to, the Executive during the Employment. The Executive will not retain any copies or extracts of such material.

23. **Reconstruction or amalgamation**

If the Employment is terminated by reason of the liquidation of the Company in order to effect its reconstruction or amalgamation, the Executive will have no claim against the Company provided that he is offered employment with the company or undertaking resulting from the reconstruction or amalgamation on terms and conditions that are no less favourable to him than the terms of this Agreement.

24. **Post-termination restrictive covenants**

24.1 During the Employment, the Executive is likely to obtain trade secrets and confidential information and personal knowledge of and influence over the Group's clients, customers and employees. As a result, the Executive agrees to observe the following restrictive covenants after the Termination Date. [8]

24.1.1. The Executive covenants that he will not, for a period of [*period*] from the Termination Date [(less any period of garden leave imposed by the Company)] and within [*insert geographical area of restriction*], on his own account or for or with any other person, directly or indirectly carry on or be engaged in any activity or business which is or is intended to be in competition with the business of the Company or any Group Company which was carried on by such company at the Termination Date and with which the Executive was concerned or connected at any time during the [*number*] months prior to the Termination Date.

24.1.2. The Executive covenants that he will not, for a period of [*period*] from the Termination Date [(less any period of garden leave imposed by the Company)], in competition with the Company or any other Group Company, on his own behalf or for or with any other person, directly or indirectly seek orders from or solicit the custom of Company Clients.

24.1.3. The Executive covenants that he will not, for a period of [*period*] from the Termination Date [(less any period of garden leave imposed by the Company)], in competition with the Company or any other Group Company, on his own behalf or for or with any other person, directly or indirectly deal or otherwise do business with Company Clients.

24.1.4. The Executive covenants that he will not, for a period of [*period*] from the Termination Date [(less any period of garden leave imposed by the Company)], in competition with the Company or any other Group Company, on his own behalf or for or with any other person, directly or indirectly entice or try to entice away from the Company or any other Group Company any person who was at the Termination Date and/or any time during the [*number*] months prior to the Termination Date [a senior or key employee, director, *list class of employee*] of such a company and with whom the Executive had worked closely at any time during that period.

24.1.5. The Executive shall at the request of the Company enter into a direct agreement or undertaking with any other Group Company by which he will accept restrictive covenants corresponding to the restrictive covenants contained in this clause [24]. The Executive acknowledges that the provisions of this clause [24] constitute severable undertakings given for the benefit of the Company and all other Group Companies and may be enforced by the Company on its own behalf or on behalf of any other Group Company.

24.1.6. Before accepting any employment, appointment or engagement with any third party either during the Employment or at any time during the period of [*period*] after the Termination Date, the Executive shall draw the provisions of this clause [24] to the attention of such third party.

24.1.7. [Each of the covenants set out above and is entirely separate and independent of the others and is considered and accepted by the parties [each of whom has taken legal advice] to be reasonable and necessary for the protection of the legitimate interests of the Company and the Group Companies. If any covenant or part thereof shall be found void, invalid or unenforceable by any court of competent jurisdiction, but would be valid if some words were deleted, or the period reduced, such covenants shall apply with such modification as may be necessary to make it valid and effective.]

24.1.8. [In the event of any covenant or part thereof being declared void, invalid or unenforceable by any court of competent jurisdiction, all other covenants or parts thereof shall remain in full force and effect and shall not be affected.]

24.1.9. After the Termination Date, the Executive will not without the consent of the Company represent himself still to be connected in any way with the Company or any Group Company.

25. **Data protection**

In relation to Personal Data and Sensitive Personal Data (as defined by the Data Protection Act 1998) provided by the Executive to the Company, the Executive gives his consent to the holding and processing of that data for all purposes relating to the Employment. In particular, the Executive agrees that the Company can hold and process Personal and Sensitive Personal Data in order to pay and review his remuneration and other benefits, provide and administer any such benefits, provide information to professional advisers and to legal and regulatory authorities such as Revenue and Customs and the Contributions Agency, administer and maintain personnel records (including sickness and other absence records), carry out performance reviews, provide information to potential purchasers of the Company or the business area in which the Executive works, give references to future employers, and transfer Personal and Sensitive Personal Data concerning the Executive to a country outside the EEA.

26. **Notices**

Notices may be given by letter or fax. Notices to the Company must be addressed to [its registered office] for the time being. Notices to the Executive must be given to him personally or sent to his last known address. Any notice sent by letter or fax will be deemed to have been given at the time at which the letter or fax would be delivered in the ordinary course of post or transmission. A notice delivered by hand is given on delivery.

27. **Statutory particulars**

This Agreement contains the written particulars of employment which the Company is obliged to provide the Executive under the Employment Rights Act 1996.

28. **Miscellaneous**

28.1. This Agreement will be governed by and interpreted in accordance with English law. The Company and the Executive submit to the exclusive jurisdiction of the English Courts and Tribunals in relation to any claim or matter arising in connection with this Agreement.

28.2. This Agreement supersedes any previous oral or written agreement between the Company and the Executive in relation to the matters dealt within it. It contains the whole agreement between the Company and the Executive relating to the Employment as at the date of the Agreement, except for any terms implied by law that cannot be excluded by the agreement of the parties.

28.3. The Executive cannot assign this Agreement to anyone else.

28.4. [This Agreement may only be modified by the written agreement of the parties] OR [The Company reserves the right to vary or amend these terms and conditions on giving not less than [*number*] weeks' prior written notice to the Executive].

EXECUTED as a DEED [5] [9] by
[*the Company*] acting by
Director
Director/Secretary

EXECUTED as a DEED [5] [9] by
[*the Executive*]
in the presence of:
[*signature of witness*]
Name
Address
Occupation

MEMO POINTS 1. If the service agreement is the **subject of negotiation**, it is advisable to head the drafts "subject to contract" to indicate that final agreement has not yet been reached. Once it has (and prior to the execution of the agreement), the heading should be removed.
2. The employer may be part of a **group of companies**. If this is the case, consideration should be given to the Executive's involvement with other group companies and the implications for the drafting of the agreement. The definitions used must be tailored as appropriate. Should "Group" include the employer's holding company? Associated company has a broader meaning than subsidiary: should "Group" include both?
3. It is expected that direct and indirect **age discrimination** will become unlawful from 1 October 2006. Draft regulations on age discrimination make a number of proposals in relation to retirement and it is likely that this will need to be addressed both in employment contracts and company policies (see ¶5254 for a summary of the draft regulations).
4. The ECJ recently emphasised that a worker's **consent to opt out** of the average weekly time limit should be **given expressly and freely** (see ¶3688).
5. As drafted, the service agreement contains powers of attorney in favour of the Company to allow it to effect the resignation of the Executive's directorships and to execute any documents or take any necessary action to vest intellectual property rights in the Company. **In order to be valid**, a power of attorney must be executed as a deed.
6. Although this clause is useful, employers should ensure that they also comply, where relevant, with **disability discrimination legislation**, including the duty to make reasonable adjustments in relation to a disabled person (see ¶5450 +).
7. See ¶9910 (clause 15) for **suggested wording** and ¶6500 for a discussion of the relevant issues.
8. Post-termination restrictive covenants are, in principle, void and unenforceable because they seek to restrict an individual's freedom to earn a living and use his skill and knowledge. However, such covenants may be enforceable if the employer has legitimate business interests to protect and the restraint is no wider than necessary to protect those interests (see ¶2550 +). Restrictive covenants must therefore be **carefully drafted**. They should correspond with the circumstances of the individual employer and employee (for example, terms such as "customers", "clients" and "key employees" should not be generalised but instead be defined and tailored to the business) and should be reviewed on a regular basis to meet the ongoing needs of the employer.
9. Agreements which are executed as a deed **need to be signed either by** two directors or one director and the company secretary.

Model compromise and settlement agreement

The format and content of compromise and settlement agreements can vary widely, depending on a number of factors, such as the nature of the compromise (i.e. whether or not proceedings have commenced), the complexity of the terms, the seniority of the employee concerned and the progress of negotiations between the parties. 9930

The following model document provides examples of key clauses which can be **used as a starting point** when putting together settlement terms. However, in order to maximise protection for the employer, the model document **should be tailored** according to the employer's requirements, proposed negotiation tactics and the circumstances of the compromise.

Specialist legal advice should be sought before drafting any compromise agreement.

* Clauses marked with an asterisk must be included for a valid compromise of statutory claims.

[WITHOUT PREJUDICE]

[SUBJECT TO CONTRACT]

This Agreement is made on [*date*] [1] between:

(1) [Employer] of [*address*] (the "Company" [or "Respondent"]) and

(2) [Employee] of [*address*] (the "Employee" [or "Claimant"]).

Background

[*If the compromise relates to actual proceedings, insert a brief factual and legal description of the particulars of the proceedings (including the relevant case number) and the allegations made in them*]

[*If the compromise instead relates to a particular claim which has been raised but which is not yet the subject of proceedings, insert a brief factual and legal description of the particulars of the nature of the allegations and of the statute under which they are made, or the common law basis of the alleged claim*] [2]

The parties have agreed as follows:

1. The Employee's employment terminates/terminated on [*date*] (the "Termination Date"). The Employee will receive/has received his salary [, payment in lieu of accrued but untaken holiday] and benefits due to him up to and including the Termination Date, subject to deductions for tax and National Insurance Contributions in the usual way. Except as otherwise expressly provided for in this Agreement, all salary payments and benefits extended to the Employee will cease/ceased with effect from the Termination Date.

2. An appropriate sum will be deducted from the Employee's [final salary payment] in the event that he has taken any holiday in excess of his entitlement or there are any outstanding monies due from him to the Company or any Group Company as at the Termination Date.

3. [The Employee will resign any directorship or other office held in the Company or any Group Company [on the signing of this Agreement], such resignations to take effect [immediately] [on [*date*]]].

4. The Employee's Form P45 will be made up to the Termination Date and issued to the Employee as soon as possible and in any event before the payment of the sums outline in clause [5].

5. Subject to the Employee complying in full with this Agreement and the Adviser signing this Agreement in accordance with clause [22] below, the Company will pay to the Employee the total sum of [£*amount*] within [*insert period*] of [the Termination Date], made up as follows:

   5.1. [[£*amount*] as compensation for the termination of his employment [inclusive of the Employee's entitlement to statutory redundancy pay, if any]; and

   5.2. [£*amount*] in lieu of notice.]

6. [The sums under clause [5] above will be paid subject to the deduction of income tax and employee National Insurance Contributions [except as to the first £30,000 of the sum

under clause [5.1] above, which the Company understands may be paid free of tax but gives no guarantee or warranty to that effect]].

7. The Company gives no warranty as to whether income tax or employee National Insurance Contributions are payable in respect of any payments made to the Employee under this Agreement and the Employee is responsible for the payment of any tax and any liability to employee national insurance arising in respect of any payment set out in this Agreement. The Employee will indemnify the Company and each and every Group Company and keep it and them indemnified on a continuing basis against any liability to such taxation or national insurance.

8. The Employee warrants that there are no sums owed to him or any sum which could become due to him from the Company or any Group Company including any payments under any bonus [*insert other relevant schemes*], except as set out in this Agreement.

9. The Company will [transfer ownership in the Employee's company car to him] [allow the Employee to continue to use his company car until [*date*]] [continue to provide the Employee with [permanent health insurance, life assurance and accident insurance] until [*date*] or until he obtains alternative employment, whichever is the earlier, subject to the terms of those schemes from time to time in force].

10. [*document share scheme/other relevant scheme arrangements on termination*]

11. [The Company agrees to provide a written reference to prospective employers of the Employee, [in the terms set out in the Schedule] [in terms to be agreed between the Employee and the Company] subject to the Company's overriding legal duties and obligations to prospective employers].

12. The Employee agrees to return to the Company on [the Termination Date] [*specify other date*] all property belonging or relating to the Company or any Group Company that is in his possession or under his control. For the avoidance of doubt, this includes (but is not limited to) [the Employee's company car, keys, security cards, credit or charge cards, *list other property*], and all documents, records, correspondence, papers, discs and other materials (and any copies thereof) whether in hard copy or in electronic or machine readable form, made or kept by, or provided to, the Employee during his employment [except for [*property to be retained by Employee*]]. The Employee warrants that he has not retained any copies or extracts of such material.

13. [In consideration of the sum of [£ *such sum to be taxable*], the Employee acknowledges and reaffirms his obligations to the Company under clauses [*clause number – e.g. restrictive covenants*] of the Employee's [Service Agreement] [Contract of Employment] dated [*date*]]. [3]

14. [[In consideration of the sum of [£ *such sum to be taxable*],] the Employee acknowledges and reaffirms his obligations under clause [*clause number*] of his [Service Agreement] [Contract of Employment] dated [*date*] relating to confidential information.] [3] OR

[The Employee agrees not to use or disclose to any person any trade secrets or other confidential information ("Confidential Information") of the Company or any Group Company which he may have received or obtained during his employment with the Company.

This restriction will not apply to information which becomes public (other than through unauthorised disclosure by the Employee), and is not intended to exclude or restrict the Employee's right to make a protected disclosure under the Public Interest Disclosure Act 1998.

For the purpose of this clause, Confidential Information includes [client or trade secrets and confidential or commercial information relating to the organisation, business, finances, clients, customers, dealings and affairs of the Company and any Group Company]. [*define confidential information further, if possible*]]

15. The Employee agrees to keep confidential the terms of this Agreement, the circumstances giving rise to it, and the payment the Company has agreed to make, save as may be required by law or by any regulatory authority, or in order to instruct professional advisers.

16. The Employee agrees that he will not disparage the Company or any Group Company or their businesses or any of its or their respective officers, directors or employees, or take part in any conduct likely to bring such companies or persons into disrepute.

17. The Employee accepts the terms of this Agreement and the sum(s) under clause [5] above in full and final settlement of all and any claims or other rights of action which the Employee has now or may have against the Company or Group Company or any of its or their officers or employees (whether arising under common law, statute, tort, European law or otherwise) arising directly or indirectly out of his employment by the Company or any Group Company or the termination of such employment or any other matter. The Employee hereby waives any such claims or other rights of action and will refrain from instituting or continuing and will withdraw any legal proceedings before an employment tribunal. [This clause [17] also waives and releases any and all claims and rights which are not contemplated at the date of this Agreement by the parties.] For the avoidance of doubt, nothing in this Agreement prevents the Employee from bringing any proceedings for personal injury or in connection with accrued pension rights. The Employee warrants that he is not aware of any circumstances which may give rise to such claims for personal injury or accrued pension rights. [*This clause should be tailored, where possible, to the circumstances of the individual employee*]

18. * For the avoidance of doubt, this Agreement and the waiver and release in clause [17] expressly relates to each and every one of the following statutory claims or complaints for: [*list all particular claims/complaints and corresponding legislation (for example, "unfair dismissal under the Employment Rights Act 1996") which are relevant to the circumstances of the individual employee. This should be consistent with the "background" of the Agreement and* [2]].

19. [For the avoidance of doubt, the waiver and release in clause [17] expressly includes the Employee's agreement to refrain from continuing and to forthwith withdraw within [*period*] of his signature of this Agreement his complaint[s] before an employment tribunal for [*insert the particulars of the claim[s], the relevant case number and the allegations made, which should be consistent with the "background" of the Agreement and* [2]]].

20. The Employee also warrants that:

20.1. the statutory claims referred to in clause [18] above are the only statutory claims that he has or may have against the Company or any Group Company or its or their officers or employees; and

20.2. he has not received or accepted any offer of, or commenced any employment.

The Employee acknowledges that the Company is entering into this Agreement in reliance on the Employee's warranties in this clause [20].

21. * The Employee warrants and undertakes that, before signing this Agreement, he received independent legal advice from [*name of adviser*] (the "Adviser"), [a qualified lawyer] OR [a certified union official] OR [a certified advice centre worker] OR [a qualified legal executive supervised by a solicitor who holds a practising certificate], as to the terms and effect of this Agreement and in particular its effect on his ability to pursue his rights or bring any statutory claim before an employment tribunal or any court of law.

22. * By signing this Agreement, the Adviser confirms that:

22.1. he has advised the Employee as to the terms of this Agreement and in particular its effect on his ability to pursue his rights before an employment tribunal; and

22.2. he is not acting (and has not acted) in relation to this matter for the Company or any Group Company (as defined in this Agreement); and

22.3. he is covered by a current contract of insurance or an indemnity provided for members of a profession or professional body covering the risk of a claim by the Employee in respect of any loss arising in consequence of the advice; and

22.4. when giving the advice he was a "relevant independent adviser".

23. * The parties agree that the conditions regulating compromise agreements under [*list relevant legislation and ensure list is consistent with clause [18]*] have been satisfied in relation to this Agreement.

24. [The Company will, within [*insert period*] of receipt of a copy of the Adviser's bill, pay up to [£*amount*] ([inclusive/exclusive of VAT]) to the Adviser as a contribution to the Employee's reasonable legal expenses in connection with this Agreement.]

25. Any Group Company or any officer or employee of the Company may enforce the terms of [this Agreement] subject to and in accordance with the provisions of the Contracts (Rights of Third Parties) Act 1999.

26. In this Agreement "Group Company" includes the Company and all of its holding, subsidiary, or associated companies (as defined in section 736 of the Companies Act 1985).

27. The terms of this Agreement contain the entire understanding between the Employee and the Company and any Group Company with respect to the termination of the Employee's employment and supersede and abrogate all (if any) other agreements, arrangements or understandings in such respect which shall be deemed terminated by mutual consent.

28. This Agreement will be governed by and interpreted in accordance with English law. The Company and the Employee submit to the exclusive jurisdiction of the English Courts and Tribunals in relation to any claim or matter arising in connection with this Agreement.

Upon signature by both parties and the Adviser of the Agreement, this Agreement shall cease to be without prejudice and subject to contract and shall become binding upon the parties.

SIGNED by
on behalf of: }

[*the Company*]

SIGNED by
[*the Employee*] }

SIGNED by
[*the Adviser*] [4] }

MEMO POINTS 1. See ¶9353 for details as to how the date of the compromise and settlement agreement may affect **where the agreement can be enforced** (i.e. in the employment tribunal or the civil courts).

2. A "blanket" agreement (i.e. purporting to be in full and final settlement of all claims without further particulars) is **not effective** to compromise statutory claims. Compromise agreements should therefore relate to the particular complaint to be compromised and be tailored to the individual circumstances of each case (see ¶9337).

3. If the employer has, for any reason, breached the employee's contract of employment (for example, by seeking to make a payment in lieu of notice when such a PILON clause does not exist in the contract), it is suggested that such breach by the employer could entitle the employee to treat himself as discharged from any ongoing obligations or post-termination restrictive covenants under his contract. In these circumstances, the employer might want to **consider allocating some additional consideration** (which will be taxable) to these clauses in order to ensure that they are enforceable against the employee despite the breach of contract.

4. An adviser may be reluctant to sign the body of the agreement itself, in which case the **clause relating to the adviser** (clause 22 in this agreement) can be inserted into a Schedule to the agreement.

Policy checklists

The aim of the following section is to give guidance on the setting up and running of policies and procedures. Policy checklists are given on common policies which can be **used as a starting point**. Note that employers may require specific terms or adaptations depending on their specific requirements and specialist legal advice should be sought before adopting any policy. 9940
To aid the reader in understanding the requirements for an effective and productive policy, this section sets out the **general contents** common to all good policies followed by more **specific contents** in the form of checklists for the most common policies.

Adoption

It is important that sufficient consideration is given not just to the contents but also to how a policy is adopted and maintained. Consequently, **before** adopting any policy employers should make sure that they: 9941
– consult with recognised trade unions or worker representatives in advance about the contents of the policy; and
– give clear guidance, and appropriate training where required, on the relevant law and the purpose, contents and requirements of the policy to HR personnel, managers and other personnel responsible for administering and overviewing the policy.

Further, employers should consider whether the policy will be **contractual or non-contractual** (see ¶1480 for more information). If any policy is to be contractual, this may be a **variation** of existing employees' terms and conditions and for details on how to vary employees' contracts, see ¶1600.

After adopting the policy, employers should make sure that they:
– communicate the policy to all those covered by it, e.g. via the intranet and obtain an appropriate acknowledgement of receipt;
– apply the policy regularly and consistently;
– keep records of all complaints of wrongdoing/infringements and action taken by the employer to deal with any such complaints; and
– review the relevant law regularly and update the policy as necessary to ensure on-going compliance.

A. General contents checklist

1. Where appropriate, employers should decide whether they intend to provide employees with the **minimum statutory rights** or **enhanced rights**. 9945

If the employer plans to give employees enhanced rights (over and above the minimum statutory rights), then he must go on to decide:
– whether or not these are to be contractual; and
– if they are to be reserved for certain categories of employees only (e.g. those with a certain minimum period of employment). However, any such limitations must not be discriminatory.

2. Every **policy should**: 9946
1. start with an introductory paragraph setting out the **aims** of the policy. This will be useful in clarifying the purpose of the policy;
2. **identify** the persons to whom the policy applies. In particular, consider whether the policy should apply to employees only or to anyone who works for the employer: employees, workers, freelance staff, agency staff etc.;

3. give the **nature and scope** of the rights, obligations and requirements, setting out any **procedures** that should be followed;
4. **cross-refer to other policies** (or the contract of employment) where appropriate, for example it may useful in a maternity/adoption/paternity leave policy to refer to the employer's policies on flexible work arrangements, parental leave and dependants' leave;
5. give the **sanctions for breach/abuse** of the policy. Make it clear that abuse will be considered a disciplinary matter which is likely to trigger disciplinary proceedings and may, in appropriate circumstances, result in dismissal;
6. give the job title or name of a person whom employees may **contact** if they have any questions regarding the policy and/or the rights and obligations it covers, for example the employee's manager/head of department and/or HR officer;
7. state whether the policy and procedures **form part of** employees' contract of employment and whether the employer reserves the power to amend it at any time; and
8. state the **date** from which the policy takes effect.

B. Specific policy checklists

9950 Each policy checklist below details the **specific scope, issues and procedures** that such a policy would usually contain. The eight general contents points as set out above are not repeated each time unless there is a specific point that needs to be made.

9951 The policies checklists covered are **as follows**:
1. data protection and privacy;
2. discipline and grievance;
3. dress code and appearance;
4. drugs, alcohol and smoking;
5. email and internet;
6. equal opportunities;
7. maternity/adoption/paternity/parental leave;
8. remuneration and benefits;
9. right to flexible working;
10. sickness and accident/unauthorised absence;
11. time off to care for dependants; and
12. whistleblowing.

It should be noted that given that internal **discipline and grievance procedures** are now legally required, all employers should have in place a policy on how to deal with discipline and grievances. Employers with existing policies are also advised to check that their policies comply with the legal minimum requirements.

1. Data protection and privacy policy

9954 For the law in relation to data protection and monitoring especially with regard to the principles and best practice guidance, see Chapter 17.

1. A data protection and privacy policy is likely to have many **aims**, including:
– facilitating the necessary use and retention of information about individuals working for the employer, whilst ensuring compliance with UK data protection laws;
– enabling clear communication of the employer's requirements, standards and policy regarding data protection and privacy issues;
– informing individuals who work for the employer of their rights and obligations under the Data Protection Act 1998;
– setting out a framework for compliance with UK data protection and privacy laws; and
– helping to maintain a good working relationship.

2. Because of the complexity of UK data protection laws, it is advisable to include in the policy the **definition** of a number of important terms, including: "data", "personal data", "sensitive personal data", "processing" and "data controller".

Confirm whether the employer is the data controller (or data processor). State the name or specific job title of the person within the employer who is the **data protection officer** (i.e. the person responsible for the administration of the data protection and privacy policy) and how he may be contacted.

Treatment of personal data

3. Outline the **type of data** which is **processed** by the employer for employment, administrative and business purposes etc. The list need not be comprehensive, but should include the major categories of information, for example:
- recruitment, promotion, training and/or career development;
- payroll administration;
- determination and calculation of benefits;
- compliance with legal requirements (e.g. the supply of certain information to Revenue and Customs, Benefits Agency and other public bodies or agencies);
- monitoring employees' performance and conduct and, where appropriate, taking disciplinary action; and
- providing references or reports.

Include any other data, the processing of which may be unique to the employer.

4. Make it clear that **employees** are responsible for ensuring that any **data they provide** to the employer in connection with their employment is accurate and kept up-to-date. Consider requiring employees to inform a designated individual or the HR Department of any changes to data which they have provided (e.g. change of address) or of any errors they have detected.

5. Confirm that in processing data, the **employer** intends to **comply** with the data protection principles set out in the Data Protection Act 1998. It is advisable to set out these eight principles (obtain and process data for specified purposes only, by lawful and fair means and, where appropriate, with the knowledge or consent of the employee concerned; ensure that data is adequate, relevant and not excessive in relation to the purposes for which it is processed, etc.).

Make it clear that the employer is required to process **sensitive personal data** relating to employees for various reasons and set these out. Confirm that the employer will only process sensitive personal data where one or more of the statutory conditions are met (e.g. where processing is necessary in the exercise of, or to comply with, any legal right or obligation of the employer in connection with the employment, where the processing is necessary for medical purposes and is done by health professionals or by another person who is subject to an equivalent duty of confidentiality, or where processing is carried out with the employee's explicit and freely given consent (note that according to the Information Commissioner, in the context of employment, consent is rarely likely to be given freely)).

Confirm that the employer will **retain** data for varying periods of time, in line with his business, financial and legal obligations. Either set out the relevant periods of time in relation to categories of data or state a number of general principles (e.g. in general, employees' names, addresses, position held and leaving salary will be held indefinitely, though other information relating to the employment will be kept for 6 years following the termination of the employment). Information relating to income tax, NICs, statutory pay and other similar payments will be retained for the period of time required by statute (3 and 6 years, as appropriate).

If the employer **publishes** certain personal data to the public (e.g. employees' work email address and telephone numbers appear on the employer's website or on marketing material) it may be advisable to give employees the option to object to the publication and limit access to it. If this option is made available, state whom employees should contact to ensure that data concerning them is not published and how their request may be dealt with.

6. Make it clear that data should only be **accessible** to those who need, and are authorised to, use it.

Require employees to ensure that any data concerning others which they process is **kept securely** and is not disclosed, whether accidentally or intentionally, to any unauthorised person, nor lost, damaged or destroyed without prior written authorisation from a named senior employee. Make it clear that employees must observe all internal security procedures regarding the processing of manual data (e.g. data should be kept in locked cabinets) and electronic communication systems (e.g. using a password and not disclosing it etc). Consider whether it is necessary to require employees to de-personalise or key-code certain data (in which case employees must be required to keep the information necessary to interpret the code securely and separately from the information). If it is likely that data may be taken away from the employer's premises (e.g. if employees work from home or use laptops), consider setting restrictions on such use. For example, employees may have to obtain prior written authorisation before removing data from the premises. Make it clear that employees must take due care to prevent the risk of loss, theft, damage or unauthorised access to data.

Set out the employer's security measures regarding the **deletion and disposal** of data. Separate guidelines may apply to sensitive personal data or data which is considered confidential (e.g. such data may have to be shredded or disposed of as "confidential waste").

Consider making line managers/heads of departments **responsible for ensuring compliance** with the above requirements within their individual lines/departments. Consider whether line managers/heads of departments should be responsible for keeping the data protection officer informed of any changes in relation to data collected, used or processed within their department and any security measure taken in connection with such data.

Make it clear that employees who knowingly or recklessly use, disclose or otherwise process data in **breach** of this policy will be subject to disciplinary proceedings including, where appropriate, dismissal for gross misconduct, and may face criminal charges.

Employees' rights

7. Set out the **range of rights** that employees have under the Data Protection Act 1998 (e.g. subject access request, the right to have incorrect information amended or deleted etc). In respect of employees' **right to access data** concerning them that is kept by the employer, it is advisable to set out in detail the procedure which employees are required to follow when seeking such access (e.g. whether requests should be made in writing, who to, and whether an administration fee will be charged), steps which the employer may take in response to such a request (e.g. the employer may require confirmation of the employee's identity), and any power the employer may wish to reserve to withhold information in the case of unreasonably repeated access requests or where the data is excluded through legislation. It is also advisable to state the circumstances in which the employer may refuse to reveal information.

CCTV

8. If the employer operates CCTVs, employees must be **informed** of this fact and of the employer's reasons for doing so (e.g. to enhance the security of employees, visitors and property). Confirm that the location of CCTV cameras may not be obvious, but may be disclosed to employees following a written request to a named individual. State the period of time within which information obtained by CCTV will be processed, the persons who will have access to such information, that as far as practicable such information will be viewed in a private area and that it will be kept confidential and securely.

Make it clear, however, that if CCTV footage discloses activity which the employer cannot reasonably ignore, the information may be disclosed to an outside authority, e.g. the police.

In-vehicle monitoring

9. If the employer monitors the use of his vehicles by employees, this should be made clear in the policy. State the reasons for carrying out such monitoring and the means by which monitoring will be performed. Confirm that monitoring will be carried out in accordance with the principles set out in this policy.

Disclosure outside the EEA

10. If it is possible that the employer may transfer data to countries or territories outside the European Economic Area (EEA), confirm that this will be limited to countries or territories which ensure an adequate level of protection for the rights and freedoms of employees in relation to the processing of data; otherwise with employees' consent or where it is permitted by law (e.g. where the transfer is necessary for the performance of a contract of employment or for the purposes of legal proceedings).

Notification

11. Confirm that the employer, if required to do so, has notified the Information Commissioner of the data he processes and his reasons for doing so. Make it clear that it is the employer's policy to process data in accordance with his terms of notification. State how and where employees may obtain information summarising the type of data processed by the employer. Confirm that the employer will update his notification to reflect any material changes in the type of data he processes or his reasons for doing so.

Miscellaneous

12. As with other policies, the sanctions on breach should be stated. Specifically with regard to this policy, it is useful to specify that a breach is likely to result in disciplinary action including, where appropriate, dismissal for gross misconduct. It is also advisable to state that employees who knowingly or recklessly disclose data in breach of this policy may also be guilty of a criminal offence.

13. As with other policies, state who can be contacted with regard to any question about the policy. Specifically with regard to this policy, consider stating that employees who have any concerns in relation to the application of this policy may raise the matter with their line managers/heads of departments or, if the matter is not resolved, with the data protection officer. Confirm that employees may also raise a grievance in accordance with the employer's grievance policy and procedures.

2. Disciplinary and grievance policy

For the law in relation to disciplinary and grievance issues, especially the requirements of the statutory dispute resolution procedures, which came into effect on 1 October 2004, see Chapter 19; and for the law on unfair dismissal, see Chapter 25. 9955

Note that new regulations establish:

– two **statutory disciplinary and dismissal procedures**: a standard procedure and a modified procedure. As these are minimum procedures only, compliance with them does not guarantee that the disciplinary action and/or employee's dismissal will be considered "fair" should the employee bring an unfair dismissal complaint or another complaint based on detrimental treatment. Consequently, this policy checklist contains detailed disciplinary procedures which **incorporate, and exceed**, the minimum statutory procedures. Employers may adopt some or all of the procedural stages proposed below, depending on the size of their organisation and their administrative resources; and

– two **statutory grievance procedures**: a standard procedure and a modified procedure which are both set out in the policy checklist. The standard procedure applies to the majority of grievances and should be used in the majority of cases.

1. A disciplinary and grievance policy is likely to have many **aims**, including:

– clearly communicating the standards of performance and conduct required by the employer and the sanctions for failing to achieve these standards;

– establishing a framework for dealing speedily, effectively, fairly and consistently with personnel management issues, including performance and conduct;

– facilitating internal dispute resolution, without the need to resort to tribunals and courts;

– setting out a framework for compliance with the law on unfair dismissal and statutory dispute resolution procedures; and
– helping to maintain a good working relationship.

The introductory paragraph on the aims of the disciplinary policy and procedures could include enabling the employer to maintain satisfactory standards of work and conduct and to facilitate improvement where required, and those of the grievance policy and procedure could include enabling employees to raise issues concerning their work with management.

2. A disciplinary and grievance policy would **normally be divided** into two sections: disciplinary policy and procedures, and, grievance policy and procedures.

Like with all policies, the identity of the persons to whom it applies should be stated. Specifically with regard to this policy, employers should consider whether the policy **applies to** all employees or is limited, for example, to employees who completed a minimum probation period and/or who are not above a certain level of seniority/executive directors. Where the policy does not apply to all employees, employers must bear in mind that the statutory dispute resolution procedures may nonetheless apply to the excluded employees and have to be complied with. Employers should also consider whether to extend the policy to workers other than employees, e.g. contract workers, temps, agency workers etc.

Disciplinary procedures

3. Set out the **various stages** of the procedures:

a. Consider whether the first stage of the procedure would consist of an **oral warning**. It is often appropriate to deal with minor breaches of discipline and/or poor performance by giving an employee a formal oral warning. This warning, like all other formal warnings, will be recorded in the employee's personnel file. It is important to state the period for which the warning will remain "live" (this will depend on the facts of the case and will usually not exceed 6 months).

Set out what will be included in a warning, for example:
– the reasons for the warning;
– the fact that it is the first stage of the disciplinary procedure;
– the person who will give the warning (e.g. the employee's direct manager);
– the improvements required of the employee and the timescale for achieving them;
– the period for which the warning will remain live;
– the employee's right to appeal against the warning; and
– the appeal procedure (e.g. whether the employee is required to submit a written notice of appeal within a certain period of time, the person to whom the notice should be sent, how the appeal will be dealt with and how and when the employee will be notified of the outcome of the appeal).

b. Written warnings are often issued where an employee's misconduct, poor performance etc is serious; there is a recurrence of an earlier minor "offence"; or there is no improvement following the issue of an oral warning. This warning, like all other formal warnings, will be recorded in the employee's personnel file. It is important to state the period for which the warning will remain "live" (this will depend on the facts of the case and may, depending on the seriousness of the offence, last up to 12 months).

Set out what will be included in a warning, for example:
– the reasons for the warning;
– the person who will be issuing it (e.g. the employee's departmental manager);
– the improvements required of the employee and the timescale for achieving them;
– the consequences of any failure to improve (e.g. the employee may be given a final written warning);
– the period for which the warning will remain live;
– the employee's right to appeal against the warning; and
– the appeal procedure.

c. Final written warnings should only be issued where:
– an employee's first offence is sufficiently serious;
– there is a recurrence of an earlier offence in respect of which the employee received a written warning; or

– the employee failed to improve his performance in accordance with the requirements of a written warning.

A final written warning, like all other formal warnings, will be recorded in the employee's personnel file. It is important to state the period for which the warning will remain "live" (this will depend on the facts of the case and may, depending on the seriousness of the offence, exceed 12 months).

Set out what will be included in a warning, for example:
– the reasons for the warning;
– the person who will be issuing it (e.g. the employee's departmental manager or head of HR);
– the improvements required of the employee and the timescale for achieving them;
– the consequences of any failure to improve (e.g. the employee may be demoted, transferred to another department or dismissed);
– the period for which the warning will remain live;
– the employee's right to appeal against the warning; and
– the appeal procedure.

d. It may be appropriate to **dismiss** an employee or apply other sanctions in respect of him where an offence is very serious; there is a recurrence of a previous serious offence; or there is no improvement following a final written warning. **Sanctions other than dismissal** may include demotion (with or without pay reduction), suspension without pay, transfer to another role or department, etc.

State the circumstances in which the standard disciplinary and dismissal procedure will apply. For example, it could be where the employer contemplates the dismissal of an employee for reasons connected to him personally, including dismissal for redundancy or another sanction (other than suspension on full pay or the issuing of a warning) in respect of an employee's conduct (other than gross misconduct) or capability. Set out the **procedure** (which should incorporate the minimum statutory standards and best practice principles).

4. It is advisable to reserve power for the employer to terminate an employee's employment immediately, without notice or pay in lieu of notice, should the employee be found guilty of **gross misconduct**. It is advisable to list in the policy **examples of conduct** which constitute gross misconduct (whilst making it clear that this list is non-exhaustive). Such conduct may include: threatening or committing verbal or physical abuse on colleagues, customers, suppliers, agents etc; any act of discrimination or harassment; any act of dishonesty or fraud in respect of the employer; serious or repeated subordination etc.

Explain that the **modified** disciplinary and dismissal **procedure** will apply to certain cases of gross misconduct (the regulations limit the application of the modified procedure to cases where the employee was dismissed for gross misconduct as soon as or immediately after the employer became aware of the conduct in question, and the facts were such that the employer was entitled to terminate the employment summarily and it was reasonable for him to do so). Clarify that the modified procedure consists of the first and third stages of the standard procedure only, i.e. that a written notice of the dismissal will be served by the employer and that the employee has a right to appeal against his dismissal. However, there is no requirement to hold a meeting.

5. Consider and make clear whether, and if so the circumstances in which, the disciplinary procedures may be used in respect of **conduct outside working hours** and/or **away from the employer's premises**. This may be appropriate where, for example, an employee's conduct brings or has the potential of bringing the employer into disrepute or the employee is imprisoned for an extended period of time.

6. Set out **general principles** which apply to **disciplinary matters**. It is advisable to confirm the following matters within the policy (and to ensure that they are followed in practice):
– as far as reasonably practicable, the employer will deal with disciplinary matters quickly and consistently, and only after carrying out a reasonable investigation of the relevant facts;
– employees will be informed of the allegations made against them and be given the opportunity to state their case;
– any stage of the procedure may be implemented, and decisions may be taken, by a more senior employee than any referred to in the policy;

– the employer reserves the power to suspend an employee on full pay during the investigation of a disciplinary complaint; and
– the employer may, in his absolute discretion, begin the procedure at any stage he considers appropriate in the circumstances.

Grievance policy and procedures

7. State whether the grievance procedures contained in the policy should be used for all complaints or whether, for example, employees are encouraged in the **first place** to resolve routine complaints and grievances **informally** and directly with their line managers.

Consider stating that use of the policy and procedure will not prejudice employees' position within the employer.

8. Set out the steps which employees are required to take if a routine grievance cannot be resolved informally with a line manager, if an employee feels uncomfortable raising the matter with his line manager for any reason or if the grievance is not a routine matter. Set out the **procedure** (which should incorporate the minimum statutory standards and best practice principles), making it clear that this will apply in all situations except in the limited circumstances mentioned at point 9.
Confirm that the employer will **endeavour to complete** each of the steps of the procedure without unreasonable delay.

Consider confirming that, as far as reasonably practicable, the employee's grievance will be kept and dealt with in **confidence**.

9. Set out the circumstances in which the **modified** statutory grievance **procedure** will apply. These are when the **employment has terminated**, the employer was unaware of the grievance at the time of the termination (or was aware of it but the procedure had not started or completed by the time the employment terminated), and the employer and employee agree in writing to use the modified procedure. Confirm that in these circumstances, only the first and third stages of the procedure outlined above will be held (i.e. a hearing will not take place).

Make it clear that an employee may not raise a grievance because the employer has taken, or is contemplating taking, disciplinary action (except the issuing of a warning or suspension on full pay and except in circumstances where the disciplinary action amounts to unlawful discrimination) or dismissing the employee.

10. Confirm that employees who wish to **inform** their employer of a **wrongdoing** (or suspected wrongdoing) in accordance with the legislative whistleblowing protection can choose whether to do so via this grievance policy or the employer's whistleblowing policy.

Right to be accompanied

11. Confirm employees' right to be accompanied at all hearings (disciplinary and grievance) by a fellow worker or a trade union official of their choice. Make it clear that if an employee or his companion cannot attend the meeting on the appointed date, they can offer an alternative date for the meeting. The employer will rearrange the meeting accordingly. However, an employee who twice fails to attend a meeting may forfeit his right to a meeting.

3. Dress code and appearance policy

9956 For more information and the legal implications behind a dress code and appearance policy, see ¶5826. Before formulating a policy, employers should consider whether they have real business needs for adopting such a policy.

1. The **aims** of a dress code and appearance policy are **likely to vary** from employer to employer, and may include:
– complying with relevant health and safety requirements;
– promoting a company image;
– conforming to a brand image;

- facilitating a professional working environment; and
- boosting morale among the workforce, e.g. dress down days.

A dress code and appearance policy can require a **fine balancing act** and employers may wish to bear in mind that overly restrictive policies may alienate the workforce, whereas a highly permissive environment may make some employees uncomfortable and/or present an inappropriate image to clients. Further, it is very important that employers make sure that they are not **discriminating** against one group of workers with regard to their policy requirements.

2. Set out clearly the dress code and appearance **requirements** which apply to each category of employee. It is not unusual to have different dress requirements for **different categories of employee**. For example, sales staff may have to present a professional attitude, whereas the dress code of maintenance and canteen staff will focus on prevention of health and safety risks.

Where a requirement is designed to meet the employer's **health and safety** duties, it is vital that the policy is very clear as to what is required of employees (e.g. employees must at all times wear a protective hat, protective gloves and safety boots). Employers should bear in mind certain exceptions under UK equal opportunities legislation (e.g. regarding Sikhs and head protection equipment).

Where the employer has or introduces a **uniform**, this should be described in detail, including any variation between male and female uniform (providing this is not discriminatory on grounds of sex). In the **absence of a uniform**, a general description of the appropriate code should be given, e.g. "professional appearance suitable for a business environment". Ideally, this would be followed by some specific examples, e.g. suits for all employees, ties for men etc. Consider setting out any unacceptable dress, e.g. denim, jeans, shorts, trainers, leggings etc.

Consider dealing with **other matters of appearance** such as hairstyles, jewellery, facial hair etc, bearing in mind, for example the various requirements of different religions (e.g. Orthodox Jews may be required not to shave).

If the employer has a "**dress down**" day, the policy should stipulate what day of the week it is and what is acceptable and unacceptable.

Assess whether the rules on dress and appearance need to be revised in relation to employees who **work away** from the office or travel on business (e.g. to countries where strict dress codes are the norm) and ensure that this is dealt with in the policy as required.

3. Like with other policies the sanctions on breach should be stated. Specifically with regard to this policy, state clearly the sanctions for **breach** of the policy, e.g. whether an employee will be sent home to change his clothing, or requested on put on an item/change on site (for example, a protective hat), whether persistent breaches will result in disciplinary proceedings, etc. It may be appropriate to note that breaches with regard to health and safety requirements, will be treated very seriously.

4. Drugs, alcohol and smoking policy

For more information and the legal implications behind a drugs, alcohol and smoking policy, see ¶¶4960 – 4987. Employers should consider the business needs and reasons for adopting a drugs, alcohol and smoking policy and should set out their reasons in the policy. As well as setting out the standards of behaviour that will be required by employees and the sanctions for breach of the policy, it should also detail any testing procedures and the employer's procedure for dealing with employees who suffer from alcohol or drug addiction. 9957

1. A drugs, alcohol and smoking policy may have one or more of the following **aims**:
- promoting a healthy and safe work environment;
- enabling the employer to comply with their health and safety obligations;
- setting out clear standards of conduct in relation to drugs, alcohol and smoking;
- making it clear to employees their duties in relation to alcohol and drug use and smoking, both at work and outside it;

– enabling the employer to deal consistently and fairly with employees who use or abuse drugs or alcohol and/or suffer from a medical condition as a result of such abuse;
– ensuring that the employer treats fairly employees who are required to take prescribed medication for health reasons;
– ensuring that the employer deals fairly and consistently with problems which arise as a result of use of drugs, alcohol or smoking;
– ensuring that use or possession of drugs and alcohol is properly reported and recorded; and
– helping to maintain a good employment relationship.

2. Set out the **reasons** for adopting the policy. Most employers are likely to adopt a drugs, alcohol and smoking policy for one or more of the following reasons:
– to ensure that the workplace is safe;
– to maintain the highest level of work performance, productivity and attendance;
– to protect the health and safety of employees and visitors;
– to maintain a positive public image; and
– to ensure compliance with a wide range of health and safety legislation and criminal law.

3. The policy should set out in **precise terms** the conduct it prohibits. Consider defining the term "drugs" (e.g. all substances covered by the Misuse of Drugs Act 1971 (so-called "controlled drugs"), prescribed and over-the-counter medication, and solvents and other substances). The policy should include a commitment to provide **general information** about the effects of drugs on health and safety.

Stipulate the **nature** of the prohibition, e.g. whether all alcohol and drugs consumption and all smoking is prohibited. All **exceptions** should be outlined, e.g. moderate consumption of alcohol during work functions, consumption of drugs which are medically prescribed to an individual by a qualified medical practitioner to deal with a recognised medical condition (providing the employee notifies his line manager of this), smoking outside work premises outside working hours or during specific work breaks. In many cases, **different principles** may apply to the consumption of alcohol, drugs and smoking.

Set out the **extent** of the prohibition, e.g. whether the prohibition is limited to working hours and/or consumption on work premises or whether it also extends to consumption outside working hours and/or away from work.

Make it clear that the dispensation, distribution, possession, use, sale or offer to buy any controlled drugs at work is strictly prohibited, will be reported to the police and is likely to result in disciplinary action.

4. Consider reserving power to carry out **alcohol and/or drugs testing**, where justified and make the position clear in the policy. Stipulate whether testing will cover controlled drugs only or all drugs and solvents. Make it clear that testing will be at the employer's expense.

State **when** the testing will be carried out, for example whether testing will be carried out on recruitment, randomly or regularly during the employment, following the occurrence of a specific event (e.g. road or work-related accident) or otherwise. Testing may be more appropriate at different times and circumstances, depending on the nature of a specific job.

Set out the **method** of testing likely to be used (bearing in mind the various statutory requirements and limitations, e.g. under the Data Protection Code of Practice). Identify the persons who are likely to carry out testing (e.g. a designated external agency). Set out the testing procedure, including the likely timescale and publication of results.

Consider reserving **power to search** employees and their property (including private property on work premises) for alcohol and drugs on the basis of a reasonable suspicion of a breach of this policy. State the procedure for a search and the persons who are expected to carry it out.

Set out the consequences of an employee's **refusal** to submit to a test and/or search.

5. Employers should treat **addiction to alcohol and drugs** differently to other forms of use/abuse of these substances. Employers should define what they consider by alcohol or drug addiction (e.g. the employer may require a diagnosis from a medical practitioner).

Employers should set out the **conduct** expected of employees who suffer from such an addiction. Employees are likely to be asked to inform a member of the employer of their problem, e.g. discuss their condition in confidence with a member of HR or the occupational health department (if there is one). Employers can give an assurance of confidentiality, subject to legal requirements. Employers should set out the help that will be available, which may include local advisory services, and encouragement to seek help voluntarily. Employees are likely to be required to receive help, for example counselling via the employer's Employee Assistance Programme, undergo inpatient or outpatient treatment if appropriate, attending of meeting of Alcoholics or Narcotics Anonymous etc. as appropriate.

Employers should consider treating **time off** for treatment/rehabilitation as sick leave.

State whether **disciplinary proceedings**, based on poor performance due to an employee's addiction will be postponed and, if so, for how long. Set out the period for which an employee's job will normally be kept open during treatment. Employers should also consider including a statement that recognises that relapses may occur.

Make clear the consequences of an employee's **refusal to undergo** recommended **treatment**, failure to follow and complete the required treatment or repeat use of alcohol or drugs following treatment.

6. Consider whether to impose a **duty** on members of staff **to report** to a designated individual suspected infringement of the policy by other members of staff (this is more likely to be accepted where breach of the policy is likely to endanger life).

5. Email and internet policy

For the law in relation to email and internet policy, data protection and monitoring issues and especially with regard to the principles and best practice guidance of the requirements of the Data Protection Code, see Chapter 17. 9958

1. An email and internet policy is likely to have many **aims**, including:
- ensuring that employees' use of emails and the internet does not expose the employer to legal risks and liabilities nor affect business productivity;
- maintaining a safe and efficient operation of the employer's email and internet facilities;
- safeguarding the rights of employees in the workplace and protecting them from harassment and bullying through the use of emails and the internet;
- setting out a framework for compliance with UK laws regarding use and monitoring of the use of email and the internet; and
- helping to maintain a good working relationship.

2. In particular, an email and internet policy is **likely to include**:
- rules on use of emails and the internet;
- procedure for monitoring use of the email and internet systems;
- security and confidentiality requirements; and
- restrictions on internet access, downloading etc.

The use of emails and the internet is **governed by** various strands of UK law, one of which is the Data Protection Act 1998. As this Act applies to virtually all individuals, in the context of employment it protects not only employees but also job applicants, workers, contractors, consultants, agency workers etc. In addition, employers may be exposed to legal liabilities due to improper use of emails or the internet not only by employees but also by other workers. It is, therefore, advisable to apply the policy to all individuals who work for or provide work to the employer (as well as to job applicants). Consider making it clear that the policy only applies to individuals who work in the UK.

Monitoring

3. Decide in advance and state clearly in the policy the **purposes** for which the employer's email and internet systems may be used. Some employers may limit use to **business purposes** only. Employers which allow personal use should make clear any limitations and/or conditions which apply to such use (e.g. personal use may be limited to employees' breaks, may have to be reasonable, may require access to a personal email account etc). Where **personal use** is permitted in limited circumstances, make clear what sanctions will apply to use in breach of these limitations (e.g. excessive personal use of the employer's email and internet systems will be regarded as a disciplinary matter and may trigger disciplinary proceedings). Consider making it clear that the email and internet systems must not be used for purposes which are **detrimental** to the employer, in breach of any of his policies, and/or for personal gain.

It may be advisable to remind employees that the same standards of communication apply to emails as to **written correspondence**.

Set out the employer's policy on the use of **group messages**.

4. Make clear that the employer reserves the **right to monitor** employees' use of the email and internet systems from time to time, without advance notice, in accordance with the terms of the policy. Explain why such monitoring may be carried out (e.g. indicate that whilst employees are entitled to expect a level of privacy at work, the employer needs to ensure that this policy and his other rules and procedures are followed). In addition, consider making it clear that the employer has a legitimate interest in protecting his business, reputation and communication systems, limiting his exposure to legal liability and ensuring that employees conduct themselves and perform their work to the level expected of them.

Ideally, the employer should be able to confirm that he aims to conduct **monitoring** on an automated and/or anonymised basis, where this is practicable and allows him to achieve the purposes of the monitoring. Provide examples of automated/anonymised processing (e.g. internet access monitoring may be confined to duration of access and/or web addresses). However, it is advisable to retain the power to monitor the contents of email and/or internet sites accessed where, in the opinion of the employer, this is necessary (e.g. to detect misuse of the systems, breach of employment duties or because the employer suspects that unlawful activity is taking place).

Consider confirming that the employer will only monitor emails marked as **personal** and emails sent from employees' personal email accounts using the employer's email systems in exceptional circumstances (e.g. where there are suspicions of unlawful conduct such as harassment).

Make it clear that emails addressed to an employee which are received during that **employee's absence from work** (e.g. due to sickness or holiday), may be accessed by the employer and acted upon. This may require the employer to access personal communications to employees (in which case, consider confirming that the employer will aim to treat as private such communication, subject to any law requiring disclosure and the employer's right to enforce his rules and procedures and to protect himself from legal liability).

Consider advising employees that personal information of a **confidential nature**, such as letters to the employer's doctor (if there is one), should not be transmitted using the email system, but should be sent via the internal post, marked 'confidential'.

5. Confirm that, as far as reasonably practicable, the employer will endeavour to ensure that email and internet **monitoring** is **carried out by** employees with relevant functions (e.g. HR employees) who are suitably trained to carry out the task and who are required to keep secure, and to treat with confidence, any data obtained as a result of monitoring.

6. Stipulate that the employer aims **not to use information obtained** as a result of email and internet monitoring for a purpose **other than** that for which the monitoring was carried out, unless the monitoring reveals information that the employer cannot reasonably be expected to ignore (e.g. evidence of activities of criminal activities).

7. State that information obtained as a result of email and internet monitoring will be **retained** by the employer for such periods as are deemed necessary, in accordance with legal requirements.

Security and confidentiality

8. Set out detailed and specific guidance regarding the use of and transmission, receipt, access or other forms of processing of information relating to the employer, his business, clients, customers or employees, via email.

Relevant security measures **may include** a requirement that employees:

– use correct email addresses;

– not use email to send internal or external transmission of data judged confidential or sensitive where another secure medium is available (or if no other medium is available,

ensure that the transmitted data is encrypted or secured by other means and, following transmission, is permanently deleted from the system); and
– before sending any confidential or sensitive data externally by email make sure that the intended recipient is aware of the potential for interception and agrees to receive the information by email.

In addition, consider requiring employees to include a **suitable warning** whenever transmitting by email confidential or sensitive data, making it clear that the transmission is confidential and is for the exclusive use of the addressee.

Make clear that employees have a **duty to take due care** of their PCs and all other electronic communication equipment, and access to such equipment (e.g. by keeping passwords confidential and locking their PCs if they are away from their desks for a certain period of time). On termination of the employment or at any time upon request by a named individual (e.g. the IT Director), employees must deliver up or allow access to their PC or other relevant equipment to designated individuals, and disclose their PC password(s).

Prohibitions and restrictions

9. Consider including a statement that employees who use the employer's email and internet systems must ensure that no material accessed, transmitted or received contravenes any UK law. Stipulate that employees **must not** knowingly access, transmit, download, view, retrieve, receive or otherwise process the **following information** using the employer's email and internet systems:
– defamatory material: any material or information held on any medium (e.g. video, picture or sound files), which has the potential to injure the reputation of a person or class of persons;
– obscene material: any material which may deprave or corrupt persons who are likely to see it or which may be regarded as offensive;
– copyrighted material: most documents and other medium e.g. photographs, videos, music etc. are subject to copyright and as such permission may be required before transmitting, receiving or downloading copies of documents or extracts from documents; and
– discriminatory material: any material which is or may be discriminatory on grounds of race, colour, nationality, national or ethnic origin, religion or belief, sex, sexual orientation, marital status, disability or otherwise, and any material which may cause harassment, violate an individual's dignity, or create an intimidating, hostile, degrading, humiliating or offensive environment to any person or class of persons on these grounds.

10. Confirm that **unauthorised access** to another employee's emails at work, without due cause or prior authority, is strictly prohibited. The same is true regarding tampering with, amending or deleting email or other information held on the employer's communication systems without prior authorisation or due cause. Further, prohibit employees from sending emails and other communications in another employee's name without that employee's advance express consent and without informing the recipient that the communication is made on behalf of that other employee.

Make it clear that **breach** of either of these prohibitions is a disciplinary offence.

11. Make it clear that it is strictly forbidden to **download any software** from, or to load software onto, the employer's systems, whether from the internet or otherwise (but consider whether downloading may be permissible with the prior written authorisation of a named individual). Stipulate that the deliberate or reckless importation of a computer **virus** into the employer's systems is strictly prohibited. Make it clear that such conduct may also amount to a criminal offence by an employee under the Computer Misuse Act 1990. Clarify that viruses can be imported unintentionally when opening attachments (often cartoon or graphic joke files) to emails and require employees not to open email attachments unless the employer's virus checking procedures have been complied with.

Confirm that **breach** of any of these prohibitions is likely to constitute gross misconduct and may result in summary dismissal.

6. Equal opportunities policy

9959 For the law in relation to equal opportunities and the legal implications of discrimination, victimisation, harassment and bullying, see Chapter 16.

1. An equal opportunities policy is likely to have a number of **aims**, including:
- promoting equal opportunities within the workplace;
- emphasising the employer's commitment to equal opportunities;
- safeguarding the rights of workers to work in an environment free from discrimination and protecting them from harassment and bullying on discriminatory grounds;
- setting out a framework for compliance with UK laws regarding discrimination; and
- helping to maintain a good working relationship.

2. In particular, an equal opportunities policy is **likely to include**:
- a definition of direct and indirect discrimination in respect of the various strands of discrimination;
- a statement of the employer's commitment to equal opportunities;
- the name(s) of the worker(s) responsible for the policy;
- details of the structure for implementing the policy;
- an obligation on workers to respect and act in accordance with the policy;
- the procedure for dealing with complaints of discrimination;
- examples of unlawful practices; and
- details of monitoring and review procedures.

3. It is important to **set out clearly**, often at the beginning of the policy, the **employer's commitment** to equal opportunities. This commitment should be stated to apply throughout the employment relationship on an ongoing basis, encompassing recruitment, promotion, transfers, training, salary, benefits and all other terms of employment. Emphasis should also be placed on the employer's aim to maintain a workplace free from discrimination, victimisation, harassment and bullying.

4.The policy should **clarify who it applies to**, for example, all the employer's workers, consultants and employees, irrespective of seniority.

5. The **different strands of discrimination legislation** should be summarised accurately within the policy. All the different grounds of discrimination (such as sex, race and disability etc.) can be set out in the policy, together with an outline of what constitutes direct and indirect discrimination, victimisation, harassment and bullying (see further below in relation to harassment and bullying).

Separate reference may be made to those workers who are disabled within the meaning of the disability discrimination legislation, to emphasise that the employer will discuss with such workers whether there are any adjustments which could reasonably be made to the job or working environment to assist with the effective discharge of duties. The policy can also refer to the possible appointment of a doctor to advise on such matters.

Examples of discrimination should be provided in the policy, indicating what would and would not constitute acceptable behaviour in the workplace (the examples should be stated to be non-exhaustive).

6. The policy should also outline the **procedure** that workers should follow if they believe that some form of discrimination has occurred either to them or other workers. This procedure can involve formal and informal stages. The policy should, in any event, cross refer to, and be consistent with, the grievance procedure which can be used for these purposes. The procedure should also emphasise that a breach of the policy may lead to disciplinary proceedings under the employer's disciplinary policy and that the individual may also be personally liable for unlawful discriminatory treatment.

7. **Harassment and bullying** can be dealt with separately within the policy, so that is clear to workers what this constitutes and how it will be addressed by the employer.

Examples of harassment and bullying will also be useful, indicating what would and would not constitute acceptable behaviour in the workplace (the examples should be stated to be non-exhaustive).

The policy may also contain a **procedure** for workers who believe that they, or other workers, are being harassed or bullied. This may comprise informal and formal stages. It should, in any event, cross refer to, and be consistent with, the grievance procedure which may also be used for these purposes. Again, it should be emphasised that a breach of this part of the policy may lead to disciplinary proceedings.

8. Whilst an equal opportunities policy is vital for all employers, it is not, however, enough to adopt the written policy without ensuring that it is also **effective in practice**. Employers may therefore wish to take the following steps in order to operate an equal opportunities policy effectively:

– **allocate overall responsibility** for the policy, ideally with a member of senior management;

– depending on the size and resources of the employer, **form a committee of workers** who are responsible for the content and implementation of the policy. If the employer is too small for this, one member of management can be given responsibility for the policy and for reporting to a member of senior management;

– **ensure all workers are aware** of the policy and any updates to it (for example, it is expected that age discrimination will become unlawful from 1 October 2006 and this will need to be reflected in all equal opportunities policies); and

– provide ongoing equal opportunities **training and guidance** (both written and practical) to all workers, including supervisory staff and those involved in recruitment, selection for promotion, transfers, training and/or dismissal.

7. Maternity/adoption/paternity/parental leave policies

For the law in relation to maternity/adoption/paternity/parental leave and pay, see Chapter 14. 9960

These policies outline the **statutory minimum rights** and requirements. The procedural requirements in the parental leave policy are the statutory fallback position.

1. A maternity/adoption/paternity/parental leave and pay policy may have one or more of the **following aims**:

– enabling the employer to establish and implement a systematic approach to such leave;

– keeping workplace disruptions to a minimum by effective planning;

– informing employees of their rights and obligations during their leave;

– minimising the disadvantages that may be suffered by employees during such leave;

– enabling employees to combine their career and family responsibilities; and

– enabling the employer to apply good employment practices and avoid discriminating against employees as a result of their pregnancy or for a maternity/adoption/paternity/parental-related or care responsibility reason.

a. Maternity leave

Ordinary maternity leave

2. Set out the conditions, in particular the **notification and any evidential requirements**, which employees must meet in order to qualify for ordinary maternity leave (OML). Clarify that failure to comply with the requested notification requirements would jeopardise certain rights in relation to OML. State the steps which the employer will take in response to the employee's notification – the employer must respond in writing within 28 days of receipt of an employee's notification setting out the leave end date (i.e. the end date of OML, or AML if entitled, going from the employee's proposed start date). Some employers also send a detailed letter, others hold an informal meeting, in which employees are advised generally of their maternity-related rights and duties. 9961

3. Confirm the **period of OML** and state the earliest **date** on which employees may commence maternity leave. Confirm that employees may continue working right up until the birth, providing there are no medical conditions which prevent them from carrying out their duties. Confirm that OML must begin at the latest on the date after the child's birth and must last for at least two weeks following the birth. Set out employees' position in the event of stillbirth after the 24th week of pregnancy.

Set out the notification requirements for employees who wish to **change** their OML start date; the person to whom notification should be sent; and the contents of the notice (e.g. the new OML start date).

Stipulate employees' rights in relation to sickness, being careful to distinguish between absence for **maternity-related illness** and absence for other sickness. Clarify that employees who are absent from work for a pregnancy-related reason after the beginning of the 4th week before the expected week of childbirth (EWC) will commence their OML automatically from the day after the first day of absence following the beginning of the 4th week before EWC. Employers may wish to indicate that short periods including odd days of absence may be disregarded at their discretion if the employee wishes to defer the start of her OML to her chosen date.

It is important to set out the sanctions for employees' failure to notify the employer of the true reason for their absence (e.g. employees may adversely affect their entitlement to statutory maternity pay, statutory sick pay or maternity allowance and may be subject to disciplinary action).

Inform employees that they have a duty to notify the employer (HR department/their line manager etc.) of the **date of the child's birth**, as soon as reasonably practicable after the birth.

4. Decide and inform employees whether the employer will hold an **appraisal meeting/** performance review/transfer of duties meeting before employees commence OML.

Additional maternity leave

5. Set out the **conditions** which employees must meet in order to qualify for additional maternity leave (AML). Set out the **date** on which AML will commence, the AML period and employees' **expected date of return** (at the end of AML unless the employer is notified otherwise by employees). Clarify that the employee may return from AML **earlier** if they give the employer at least 28 days' advance written notice. Warn of the consequences of an employee's failure to return to work at the end of AML (be careful to distinguish between failure to return due to sickness and failure to return due to other reasons).

Rights and obligations during maternity leave

6. Clarify that the contract of employment continues to exist during both OML and AML and that **continuity of employment** is preserved for the purpose of statutory employment rights. Set out the employee's surviving **contractual rights and obligations** during OML and AML (making sure that the differences between OML and AML are clear).

Inform employees of their rights and obligations regarding any **occupational pension scheme** (for example, whether continuity of employment accrues for the purpose of pensionable service, whether employees are expected to continue making pension contributions and whether the employer will make pension contributions during OML and AML, and if so, on what basis). Make sure that any difference in the employee's rights and obligations during OML and AML is made clear in the policy. Provide the job title or name of a person to whom employees may turn if they have queries concerning their pension rights during maternity leave.

7. Set out any arrangements for **keeping in touch** with employees during maternity leave (e.g. sending employees minutes of departmental meetings or internal reports, inviting employees to the employer's social functions). State whether expenses related to such arrangements will be borne by the employer.

8. Consider how the employer will deal with employees' **untaken holiday** entitlement during the period of OML. It will often be necessary to require employees to take their statutory holiday entitlement before they begin OML. A right to carry forward untaken holiday into the next leave year, or to receive a pay in lieu of it, only applies if enhanced contractual holiday terms allow for this. State whether any enhanced contractual holiday terms apply during AML.

9. Set out employees' notification obligations regarding their **return to work** (e.g. no notice is required if the employee intends to return immediately after the end of AML, but advance notice will be appreciated for operational reasons; 28 days' written advance notice required if the employee intends to return earlier than she originally indicated or before the end of AML). State the consequences of an employee attempting to return to work without due notice.

10. State the job to which employees are entitled to return, as provided for by legislation. Outline the various factors which may affect the job to which employees have a right to return, including whether the employee returns to work immediately after OML or AML or following a period of OML and AML which has been combined with another other leave period (e.g. unpaid parental leave).

Set out employees' position on return to work regarding their seniority, pension rights, salary and any other rights which may be affected by their absence. This depends on whether the employee returns to work following OML or AML.

Consider advising employees of the steps they ought to take if they would like to return to work on different terms, e.g. set out their request in writing to the HR department/line manager. Clarify when requests should be made, whether a particular form should be used, and how they would be processed (e.g. under the employer's flexible work policy).

Consider informing employees of their statutory rights in the event that they are selected for redundancy during maternity leave.

Decide and state whether the employer will hold a meeting with employees before they return from leave, e.g. to update employees of developments in their job, consider any retraining needs, consider any requests for flexible work arrangements, discuss any changes in job duties, etc.

11. Decide whether the employer will **pay** statutory maternity pay (SMP) only or **enhanced** maternity pay and, if the latter, whether to all employees or to certain categories only and for how long (e.g. part/whole of OML, part/whole of AML). For example, all employees who meet the statutory conditions may be entitled to SMP and employees with a certain minimum period of employment (e.g. one year) may be entitled to enhanced maternity pay.

Set out the **qualifying conditions** for SMP and enhanced maternity pay (if relevant). Set out any additional notification and evidential requirements.

Set out the **periods** for which SMP and enhanced maternity pay will be paid and the rates of payments. Confirm whether payments will be made gross or net of tax and NICs. If no payments are made during AML (i.e. under an enhanced scheme), it is best to set this out clearly in the policy. If the employer pays the employee enhanced maternity pay, it is advisable to make it clear that these payments will be taken to include any statutory payments to which employees may be entitled (e.g. SMP). Where employees are entitled to maternity allowance only, consider whether the enhanced payment will be reduced by the amount of maternity allowance.

State the **dates and interval of payments** (usually these follow employees' normal pay days and intervals). Set out all the deductions which may be made from the payments (e.g. tax and NICs, private medical insurance contributions, employees' pensions contributions etc).

Where the employer pays enhanced maternity pay, state whether he will seek to **recoup** all or part of the payments (to the extent that they exceed SMP) in the event that employees fail to return to work from maternity leave (or to return and remain at work for a minimum period of time).

State that employees who do **not qualify for SMP** may be able to claim statutory maternity allowance and will be given a form SMP1 on which to submit their claim to the benefits agency. Pregnant employees may also be eligible for a Sure Start Maternity Grant. Other possible benefits include income support, housing and council tax benefits, and tax credits.

Miscellaneous

12. Inform employees of their right to take a reasonable amount of paid time off work for **antenatal care**, setting out the relevant conditions.

Consider whether to include in the policy a statement to the effect that the employer will carry out **pregnancy-related risk assessments** in respect of employees who have informed the employer that they are pregnant, breastfeeding and/or have given birth in the preceding 6 months; the person/department responsible for carrying out the assessment; the employees' responsibilities (e.g. to complete and return a risk assessment form); and the range of steps which may be taken if a significant occupational risk is identified which may affect the employees or their unborn children (e.g. reallocation of certain duties, offer of alternative employment and the possibility of paid maternity-related suspension if no suitable steps can be taken).

13. State whether, and if so what, facilities the employer provides for **breastfeeding** employees (e.g. a room to express milk and cold storage facilities).

---

b. Adoption leave

Ordinary adoption leave

9962 **2**. Set out the **qualifying, notification and any evidential requirements**, which employees must meet in order to qualify for ordinary adoption leave (OAL). State the person within the organisation whom the employee should contact and whether the employee is required to complete any forms. Clarify that failure to comply with the notification requirements would jeopardise certain rights in relation to OAL. State the steps which the employer will take in response to the employee's notification. At the very least, the employer should respond in writing to the employee's notification within 28 days of receipt of his notification. Some employers send a detailed letter, others hold an informal meeting, in which employees are advised of their adoption leave and pay rights and duties.

3. Confirm the **period of OAL** and state the earliest **date** on which employees may commence adoption leave. Confirm that OAL must begin by the date of the child's placement.

Set out the notification requirements for employees who wish to **change** their OAL start date; the person to whom notification should be sent; and the contents of the notice (e.g. the new OAL start date).

State that employees have a duty to inform the employer in the event that the **placement is cancelled** (even if the employee is already on leave); the child dies during placement, or the child is returned to the adoption agency after the placement started. Set out the consequences of a **premature termination** of the placement (the employee's leave period is reduced to the lesser of 8 weeks or the remainder of the AAL period); and of failure to inform the employer of this (e.g. the employee may be subjected to disciplinary proceedings and the possibility of dismissal).

4. Decide and inform employees whether the employer will hold an appraisal **meeting**/performance review/transfer of duties meeting before employees commence OAL.

Additional adoption leave

5. State that, generally speaking, employees who qualify for OAL **also qualify** for additional adoption leave (AAL). Set out the exceptions to this rule (e.g. if the placement did not take place after all).

Set out the **date** on which AAL will commence, the AAL period and employees' **expected date of return** (at the end of AAL unless the employer is notified otherwise by employees). Clarify that the employee may return from AAL **earlier**, but only if they give the employer at least 28 days' advance written notice. Warn of the consequences of an employee's failure to return to work at the end of AAL (be careful to distinguish between failure to return due to sickness and failure to return due to other reasons).

Rights and obligations during adoption leave

6. Follow the same checklist as set out for OML, AML and SMP in the Maternity leave policy, though ignore any references to maternity allowance.

---

c. Paternity leave

2. Set out the **qualifying, notification and any evidential conditions**, which employees must meet in order to qualify for paternity leave (PAL). Make sure that the differences in these conditions, between cases where leave is taken in respect of a newly born child and where leave is taken in respect of a newly adopted child, are clear. State the person (e.g. line manager/HR officer) whom the employee should contact and whether the employee is required to complete any specific forms. Clarify that failure to comply with the notification requirements would jeopardise certain rights to PAL. 9963

Consider whether it will be necessary to inform the employer of any steps which the employer will take in response to the employee's notification. Some employers send a detailed letter, others hold an informal meeting, in which employees are advised of their PAL and pay rights and duties.

3. Confirm the **period** of PAL; state that it cannot **start** before the date of the child's birth or adoption; confirm that PAL must be taken in blocks of one or two weeks and, in any event, within 56 days (8 weeks) of the child's birth/adoption (unless the employer chooses to have more lenient rules). Reiterate that PAL may only be taken for the purpose of caring for the child or supporting his mother or adopter. Set out the notification requirements for employees who wish to **change** their leave start date; the person to whom notification should be sent; and the contents of the notice (e.g. the new PAL start date). Inform employees that they have a duty to notify the person of the **date of the child's birth**, as soon as reasonably practicable after the birth (there is no similar requirement in respect of a child placed for adoption).

4. Decide and inform employees whether the employer will hold an **informal meeting** to discuss the employee's rights and obligations during PAL and any cover arrangements for the leave period.

Rights and obligations during PAL

5. Follow the same checklist as set out for OML and SMP in the Maternity leave policy, though ignore any references to maternity allowance and point 8 regarding untaken holiday leave is unlikely to be relevant.

---

d. Parental leave

2. Set out the **statutory (or enhanced) qualification and entitlement requirements** for parental leave. 9964

Set out the **nature** of parental leave, e.g. unpaid leave, limited to 13 weeks in total in respect of each child under the age of 5 (18 weeks in respect of a disabled child under the age of 18), whether or not leave must be taken in blocks of one week, how a week will be calculated etc. (unless the employer chooses to have more lenient rules).

Set out the employer's **application requirements** with which employees must comply, e.g. whether employees are required to complete a prescribed form and submit it to a prescribed person (e.g. line manager/HR officer) within a set number of days before they wish to take parental leave.

3. Outline how the employer intends to deal with the **employee's request**, e.g. the employer will normally respond within 14 days, a meeting will be arranged to discuss the employee's request etc.

Consider reserving the power to require the employee to submit **evidence** of his entitlement to take parental leave (e.g. the child's birth certificate).

State the employer's **attitude to requests** for parental leave (e.g. in so far as reasonably practicable the employer would seek to approve employees' request). It is advisable to inform employees that, in certain circumstances, the employer may turn down/postpone a request (unless it relates to an employee taking leave from the date of birth or date of placement) and outline those circumstances (e.g. where the operations of the employer would be unduly disrupted by the employee's parental leave, this may be postponed by up to six months). Set out the steps which employees may take if they are unhappy with a decision to postpone their leave (e.g. discuss the matter informally first, then raise a grievance using the employer's grievance policy).

Rights and obligations during parental leave

4. Follow the same checklist as set out for OAL (except for the right to return to work which should outline the various factors which may affect the job to which employees have a right to return, including whether the employee returns to work immediately after parental leave which lasted up to 4 weeks, after a longer-period leave or after combining parental leave with another leave period, e.g. ordinary or additional maternity or adoption leave). Note that parental leave is unpaid (unless the employer gives enhanced terms in which case, set out what pay will be given and for how long etc).

Miscellaneous

5. It is advisable to reserve the power to **ask new employees** to confirm the **amount of parental leave taken** with previous employer(s) and to seek a confirmation of this from previous employers. In addition, the employer should state that he would provide information about parental leave taken by employees, if requested by future employers.

8. Remuneration and benefits policy

9965 For the law in relation to remuneration and benefits, see Chapter 10, which deals with remuneration and pension issues. Employers who operate or intend to operate share option and/or long-term investment schemes should obtain specialist advice.

1. The **aims** of a remuneration and benefits policy **may vary** from employer to employer, but are likely to include:
– recruitment and retention of high calibre individuals who are most suitable to do the job in question;
– encouragement and recognition of individual, departmental and corporate performance;
– compliance with internal and external regulatory requirements, e.g. the revised Combined Code on corporate governance; and
– linking shareholders' interests with the interests of senior management.

Employers should consider whether the policy **applies to** all employees or is limited, for example, to senior executives, members or the board of directors and non-executive directors etc.

2. In large, publicly listed organisations, it is **customary** to have a remuneration committee which is manned and chaired by non-executive directors. Such a committee is usually independent of the board, but may report to it and/or to the chief executive on certain matters. In smaller employers, remuneration and benefits decisions may be made by a senior management, on recommendations of the HR department. It is also often customary and necessary for employers to receive outside advice on various elements of the remuneration package (e.g. pensions and share option schemes) and in order to assess competitive pressures and market forces.

Consequently, state the body or persons that will **make decisions** on remuneration. Consider setting out the names of the remuneration committee members (if there is one); the scope of that body's/person's responsibilities (e.g. remuneration only, executive directors' notice periods and other contractual terms etc); the intervals at which the body/persons meet; whether the body/persons report to the board of directors/chief executive etc; and whether the body/persons receive advice from outside advisers and, if so, the advisers' identities.

Where relevant and appropriate, an employer may choose to confirm that the policy takes into account the revised Combined Code on Corporate Governance.

Elements of remuneration and benefits

3. Consider and select the elements of remuneration and benefits which are relevant to the employer from the following examples and any advice received from outside advisers: basic annual salary, benefits in kind (e.g. company car, private health insurance, long-term disability insurance, life assurance etc), performance bonus payments, long-term and share option incentive plans, pension arrangements etc.

Consider whether this policy should also deal with directors' notice periods and compensation on termination of employment, and the employer's position in respect of loans to employees.

The policy is unlikely to set out individuals' basic annual **salaries** (this is usually reserved for contracts of employment and reports on directors' remuneration). It is customary, however, to state in the policy the **bands or levels** at which basic salaries are set, e.g. by reference to the industry or market within which the employer is operating (e.g. "around mid-market", "between mid-market and the upper quartile ranges in comparable employers" or "around mid-market but upper quartile will apply to sustained excellent performance").

If the basic annual salary element is small in **comparison** to the performance bonus and/or share incentives, consider explaining the employer's thinking behind these arrangements (e.g. that it is important that a significant element of the remuneration should be linked to individual, departmental and/or corporate performance, to ensure that the employer maintains his growth and profit record, competitiveness and/or market position).

If the policy applies to **non-executive directors**, set out their annual basic fee and indicate whether additional fees are payable, e.g. for membership or chairmanship of certain committees within the employer (and, if so, the level of such fees).

State how often salaries and non-executive directors' fees are reviewed (e.g. annually) and how the assessment is conducted (e.g. by making a comparison with named or unnamed competing employers in the same industry which are of similar size and/or business diversity and growth and/or on the basis of the advice of external advisors etc). It is usually advisable for all pay reviews and revisions to be discretionary.

Performance bonus payments

4. State who **qualifies** for performance bonus payments (this may be limited to some, but not all, employees covered by the policy).

State **when**, and on **what basis** bonus payments will be made out, e.g. are they discretionary, are they based on group, business unit and/or individual pre-determined performance targets based on turnover, revenue, profit or working capital (or any combination of these), will they be paid to employees who are under notice of termination? Set out the **intervals** at which performance bonuses are paid (e.g. annually or quarterly).

It is customary to establish minimum and maximum payment **benchmarks**, which may relate to employees' salaries, e.g. the bonus payment may not be less than 80% nor more than 120% of an employee's basic annual salary. State how target-achievement **assessment** will be carried out, e.g. on the basis of approved audited accounts following the end of the relevant financial year and/or individuals' appraisal and scoring procedures.

Consider whether the bonus scheme should have a **deferral element** (whereby a proportion of the annual bonus is withheld and invested in shares, which become available to employees after a period of time) and, if so, make this clear in the policy. Set out the relevant deferral elements and their implications (e.g. tax), if any.

Long-term and share option incentive plans

5. State whether the employer operates any long-term incentive plans and/or share option incentive schemes. If so, state the categories of employees who qualify to join either scheme (it is customary to limit eligibility and, as a result, not all employees who are covered by this policy may qualify). Consider setting out the **aim** of the scheme(s), e.g. to align the interests of shareholders with those of the scheme members and to enable the employer to attract, motivate and retain key staff.

Set out the **main provisions** of the employer's scheme(s). This will depend on the nature of the scheme (LTIP or share option) and may include: stating whether the scheme is Revenue and Customs approved or unapproved; identifying the body that decides how many shares may be awarded each year and on what basis; the period in which shares may be awarded; the circumstances in which options may be exercised and/or shares will vest and any attached conditions, the basis on which shares exercise price will be determined; the periods of time within which employees may exercise their options under the scheme, the circumstances in which options may not be exercised (e.g. if an employee is dismissed for gross misconduct) etc. State where full details of the relevant scheme can be found.

State whether the employer operates **other incentive schemes**, e.g. saving related schemes and, if so, set out their main provisions and where detailed information may be found.

Benefits in kind

6. Consider whether the policy should set out the **range** of benefits in kind which may be offered to employees (e.g. company car, private health insurance etc) and any eligibility conditions (e.g. minimum period of employment).

Pension arrangements

7. State the **name** of the pensions scheme(s) operated by the employer and the **categories of employees** who are eligible to join. Set out the **main provisions** of each scheme and indicate where detailed information may be found. Relevant information includes: eligibility requirements, the nature of the scheme (e.g. final salary or defined contributions); the employer's and individual's levels of contributions; the scheme's retirement age etc.

Directors' notice periods/compensation on termination of employment

8. Consider setting out the employer's policy on directors' notice periods and pre-determined termination payments (bearing in mind, if appropriate, the revised Combined Code on Corporate Governance).

Other benefits

9. Consider and stipulate whether it is the employer's policy to grant or guarantee personal **loans** to employees and, if so, the terms on which such loans may be made/guaranteed.

State whether executive directors may hold **external non-executive appointments**, e.g. where these are likely to be valuable in personal and professional terms. Consider limiting the number of such appointments. Indicate whether executive directors may retain the fees or other benefits derived from such appointments.

Consider introducing a **minimum shareholding obligation** for certain employees (e.g. members of the Board of directors) and set out the nature and duration of this obligation and how it may be met.

9. Right to flexible working policy

9966 For the law in relation to a right to flexible working policy see ¶4690, and for:
- examples of different types of flexible working arrangements, see ¶1810;
- legal and practical considerations regarding part-time workers, see ¶1870; and
- the contractual and practical considerations regarding working at home, see ¶1820.

This policy outlines the statutory minimum requirements.

1. A flexible work policy is likely to have many **aims**, including:
- communication of the employer's policy on flexible work arrangements;
- enabling employees to combine their career and family responsibilities;

– establishing a framework for dealing with requests for flexible work effectively, fairly, consistently and in accordance with the law;
– setting out the various forms of flexible work open to employees of the employer; and
– helping to maintain a good working relationship.

Employers should consider whether the policy is limited to employees who have a statutory right to request flexible working or will extend to other employees (e.g. all employees with child-care responsibilities/all employees who have caring responsibilities/all employees).

Set out the **types of flexible work arrangements** which may be requested. These may include part-time work, job-share, home working, term-time working etc. It is advisable to make it clear that the employer will consider requests for flexible work arrangements in line with this policy, but that there is no guarantee that all requests will be accommodated.

Procedure

2. Set out the procedure for dealing with requests for flexible work arrangements. Require employees to make a written, signed and dated request (e.g. on a prescribed form of the employer). Stipulate that the request must make it clear whether the employee has made another request to work flexibly in the previous 12 months, and if so, when. Specify that the request must be made at least 14 days before the 6th birthday of the employee's child (18th birthday if the child is disabled). Stipulate to whom the request should be made (e.g. an HR manager or the employee's own line manager).

It is advisable to confirm that the employer will consider every request on its own merits, taking into account the employee's personal circumstances and the employer's needs.

If the **request is accepted**, the employee will be notified in writing within 28 days. The notification ought to specify the new arrangements, the date from which they will take effect and the impact these will have on the employee (e.g. the employee's salary and holiday entitlement will be pro-rated if he/she begins to work part-time). If the request cannot be agreed to automatically, the employer will convene a meeting to take place within 28 days of receipt of the application. State who would normally conduct the meeting (e.g. a member of the HR department). Confirm that the employee will be informed of the outcome of the meeting within 14 days of it being held. If the **request is agreed** following the meeting, state that the employee will be notified of the new arrangements, the date from which they will take effect and the impact they will have on him (e.g. the employee's salary and holiday entitlement will be pro-rated if he begins to job-share). Confirm that if the employee's request is **rejected** following the meeting, the employee will be informed of this in writing within 14 days, together with the grounds for the refusal, his right to appeal and the appeal procedure.

3. Stipulate that employees who wish to **appeal** against a decision have a right to do so within 14 days of receipt of the employer's decision. Appeals must be made in writing (signed, dated and setting out the grounds of appeal). Stipulate to whom appeals should be made.

Explain how the employer will deal with appeals. If, after considering the appeal notice, the employer agrees to the employee's request, the employee will be notified in writing of the new arrangements, the date from which they will take effect and the impact they will have on him. If a decision cannot be made on the basis of the appeal notice, a meeting will be arranged to take place within 14 days of receipt of the notice of appeal. The employer will notify the employee of his decision in writing, within 14 days of the date of the appeal meeting, either setting out the new arrangements, the date from which they will take effect and their impact on the employee, or the fact that the appeal was dismissed and the grounds for refusing the employee's request.

Grounds for refusal

4. Confirm that the employer will only refuse a request for flexible work arrangements on one of the eight permitted statutory reasons. It is advisable to set out these grounds in the policy as they appear in the legislation.

Conditions for agreeing flexible work arrangements

5. Consider whether the employer's agreement to flexible work arrangements would be **conditional** in any way. For example, the employer may require a trial period before the new arrangements are confirmed, employees may be required to adapt their new work arrangements in certain circumstances, e.g. where a job sharer is ill or on holiday, or the employer may reserve the right to terminate the flexible work arrangements if an employee's performance or conduct is unsatisfactory or if the arrangements are otherwise detrimental to the employer's operations.

State whether the new arrangements are **intended to be permanent** (i.e. to continue in operation even after the employee's child reaches the age of 6).

Some employers impose **specific conditions** to certain types of flexible work arrangements, e.g. home working and job-share. For example, job-sharing employees may be required to follow certain hand-over arrangements and/or to be at the workplace together at least one day during the week. A home-working employee may be required to be available at home and to log onto his PC during certain hours, to attend the workplace regularly or on an ad-hoc basis for meetings and training, to have a policy of insurance which covers home working, to ensure that family members do not have access to personal data in breach of the Data Protection Act 1998 etc.

Right to be accompanied

6. Confirm that employees have a right to be accompanied by a work colleague in both the initial and appeal meetings. The companion may address the meeting and confer with the employee, but may not reply to questions on the employee's behalf. Confirm that if the date of a hearing is not convenient to the employee or his representative, it may be postponed to an alternative date within 7 days of the original meeting date.

10. Sickness and accident/unauthorised absence policy

9967 For the law in relation to absence from work, see Chapter 13 which outlines the law on sickness absence, sick pay and managing sickness, and Chapter 17 which deals with data protection and employee monitoring.

1. A sickness and accident/unauthorised absence policy may have one or more of the following **aims**:
- enabling employers to adequately monitor sickness/accident/unauthorised absence;
- helping the employer to deal consistently and fairly with sickness/accident/unauthorised absence;
- ensuring that sickness/accident/unauthorised absence is properly reported and recorded; and
- helping to maintain a good employment relationship.

Employers may want to state how the employer **intends to treat employees** on sick leave (e.g. sympathetically/as far as possible secure their employment etc), and highlight the fact that absences have a detrimental effect on the employer, his employees and legal obligations.

A sickness/accident/unauthorised absence policy **would normally**:
- outline the relevant notification procedure;
- set out the employer's procedures for handling absence in general, and short-term intermittent and long-term sickness absence in particular;
- state what payments will be made during an employee's absence (if any); and
- stipulate any sanctions for breach or abuse of the policy.

Note that it is not unusual to apply **different rules and procedures** for agency staff (who may need to report absences to the agency through which they have been hired) or free lancers (who may not receive any sick pay) and senior management (who may receive more favourable sick pay).

Procedure

2. Set out the general **reporting requirements** where an employee is absent due to sickness/ absence or another unauthorised reason (the term 'unauthorised reason' should be defined, e.g. absence which has not been approved in advance and which does not fall within the employer's dependants' leave policy). State:

– how the employee should notify his absence (e.g. by telephoning in person wherever possible? Would an email or a phone call from a close relative be acceptable?);

– who the employee should contact (his line manager, the HR department etc? Can a colleague/the switchboard be informed? It is generally advisable to refer to individual's post in the organisation, rather than by name);

– the time by which employees should notify their absence (e.g. within one hour of the start of the working day or as soon as practicable thereafter. Where employees work shifts or have irregular working hours, whether they are required to contact the employer as early in the day as possible, rather than at the commencement of their shift); and

– what information employees are required to provide (e.g. the reason for their absence, the nature of any illness, the anticipated length of absence and date or time of return to work, details of any outstanding urgent work that needs to be dealt with during their absence etc).

It is customary to include specific notification requirements for cases where an employee is **absent from work for more than 1 day** but less than [7] consecutive days (including weekends and public holidays). For example, whether the employee is required to confirm his absence daily or on another mutually agreed regular basis. Stipulate whether, on return to work from absence which lasts up to [7] calendar days, the employee is required to complete and sign a self-certification form; the person from whom the form can be obtained; and the person to whom a completed form should be submitted. In addition, it is advisable to set out the specific notification procedure for absences which **last more than [7] consecutive days** (including weekends and public holidays). It is customary to require employees to send in a doctor's certificate which covers the whole of the absence period as soon as possible. Indicate to whom the employee should send the certificate (his line manager/the HR department etc).

Consider what procedure should apply where employees fall **sick whilst at work** (e.g. should they see a company doctor or a first-aider where relevant? Should employees receive a manager's approval before absenting themselves? etc). State whether a day in which the employee has attended work and then became sick will count as a sick day (note that for SSP purposes such a day does not count as a day of absence).

It is imperative to set out the **consequences of failure** to comply with the notification procedures set out in the policy, e.g. the employee may not be entitled to sick pay or any other remuneration, absence may be treated as unauthorised, the disciplinary procedure may be initiated and sanctions may be imposed, including dismissal where appropriate.

3. Consider whether to include a statement that employees should not **return to work** before they are recovered and able to carry out their duties. Consider whether, in certain circumstances and as a precautionary measures, employees may be asked to undergo a medical examination before they return to work to ensure that they are fit to carry out their duties. If so, state this clearly in the policy.

It is customary to require employees, on return to work from sickness/accident and unauthorised absence, to report to their line manager, complete and sign a sickness self-certification form and/or provide a doctor certificate (as relevant).

Consider holding an informal "return to work" interview, where an employee was absent for a prolonged period of time for reasons which could give rise to employer's liability (e.g. stress, disability, harassment etc) or for an unauthorised reason. Depending on the reason for the employee's absence, the interview may be formal or informal. The interview can provide the employer with an opportunity to find out more about the employee's reasons for absence, identify potential underlying issues and consider any steps which the employer needs to take to meet his legal obligations.

4. With regard to **monitoring sickness**, consider whether:
– managers/heads of departments etc would be required to monitor sickness etc absences and report any patterns that give rise for concern to the HR department; or
– whether the HR department would regularly monitor absence and report any causes of concern to managers/heads of departments.

Monitoring will need to be carried out in compliance with the Data Protection Act 1998. Some employers include a statement to this effect in the policy.

5. It is often customary, and conducive to good employment relations, to treat **repeated/intermittent short-term absence** differently from long-term absence.

Where this is the case, it may be advisable to explain what is considered by the employer to be "repeated short-term absence", e.g. 5/7 periods of absence within one year or at least 10 days' intermittent absence within any 6/9/12 months period).

Set out the employer's procedure for dealing with short-term absence. It is customary to investigate the reasons for the absence, allowing the employee to state his case and, if improvement is required, set out what steps the employee should take, within what period of time, and what might happen if improvement is not achieved. It is customary to raise the matters initially in a sickness absence interview, rather than in a disciplinary meeting. Where appropriate, a medical report should be sought. State what steps the employer will take if no improvement is made, or if improvement is unsatisfactory. For example, a further, disciplinary, meeting may be appropriate. State how many days' notice the employee will be given before each meeting and that the employee has a right to be accompanied by a colleague or a trade union representative. Ensure that employees have a right to appeal against any decision and that the procedure complies with the statutory dispute resolution procedures.

6. Define the period considered by the employer to be **prolonged absence** (e.g. in excess of 4, 6 or 8 consecutive weeks).

Set out the employer's procedure for dealing with long-term illness. Is the employee required to keep the employer up to date on his condition, future prognosis and likely return to work? Will the employer take the initiative to maintain contact with the employee?

It is customary to investigate long-term sickness absence and hold a meeting to discuss the employee's condition, future prognosis, date of likely return to work and any adjustments which the employer may need to make to facilitate the employee's return. Consider whether the meeting would be arranged by the employee's line manager/HR department/occupational health professional; who would be present in the meeting and where it would be held (e.g. at the employer's premises, at the employee's home, by written submissions?).

Set out whether the employee may be accompanied in the meeting and, if so, by whom (a colleague, a trade union representative and/or a family member).

Consider how the employer will obtain information in advance of the meeting, e.g. by requesting information from the employee's GP or hospital consultant (in which case the employer will need to comply with the Access to Medical Reports Act 1988), by requiring the employee to undergo examination by a doctor appointed by the employer (in which case, the employer would usually pay for the examination), by undergoing an examination by an independent doctor etc. State the possible consequences if the employee refuses to supply the necessary information/attend the medical examination (including, where justified, dismissal).

Outline the range of steps which the employer may take after receiving medical advice and holding a meeting with the employee, e.g. seek to adjust the employee's job duties to facilitate his return to work, look for an alternative position for the employee. State clearly that the employment may be terminated if neither option is open to the employer. Set out the employee's options on termination, e.g. retirement on ill-health, mutually agreed termination, dismissal. Ensure that employees have a right to appeal against any decision and that the procedure complies with the statutory dispute resolution procedures.

7. State whether the procedure will be modified in any way where absence is due to **alcohol/drug or other substance abuse**. If so, outline the relevant procedure including, for example, whether the employee will be offered paid time off to attend a rehabilitation centre/receive counselling etc. State the employer's expectations of the employee (e.g. that he stays sober/ clean) and the sanctions for failing to meet those expectations, including the possibility of dismissal.

8. Stipulate the employer's policy in respect of **sickness during annual leave**. For example, whether sickness during annual leave will qualify as sickness absence or holiday absence (this may depend on whether the sickness absence lasts more than a certain number of days and/or is medically certified). State whether sickness during public holidays (medically certified or not) entitles the employee to a holiday day in lieu.

Pay

9. State whether the employer intends to offer statutory sick **pay** (SSP) or enhanced sick pay.

Set out the employee's "**qualifying days**". These are, normally, the employee's usual working days, e.g. Monday to Friday.

Where the employer offers SSP, it is advisable to set out employee's **entitlement** under the statutory procedure. For example: employees' qualification conditions, when SSP becomes payable, the period for which SSP is payable, the forms which must be completed for SSP to become payable; employees' rights and benefits once their SSP entitlement expires.

Where the employer offers **enhanced** sick pay: state whether this is discretionary or contractual (and, if discretionary, consider stating what factors may be relevant), what is covered by the entitlement (e.g. basic pay only), and whether entitlement is subject to certain conditions (which must not be discriminatory), e.g. length of employment, employees' grades, length of absence etc. Make it clear that payments under the enhanced scheme will be offset against any SSP or other state payments/benefits to which the employee may be entitled. State the periods for which payments will be made and the amount (e.g. a percentage of the employee's salary and benefits or salary only).

Make it clear that **tax and NICs** will be deducted from all sickness payments in the usual way.

Consider reserving power not to make payments if the employer considers that an employee **abuses** the sick pay scheme.

Make it clear that the employee will not receive his normal salary and benefits for periods of **unauthorised absence**.

Where an employee's absence is due to an **accident** which gives rise to a negligence or similar claim by the employee against a third party, consider whether the payments made by the employer to the employee are to be treated as a loan to the employee which is repayable on recovery of damages for loss of earnings from the third party (in which case it is advisable to take advice on the employer's tax liabilities).

Permanent health insurance

10. If the employer provides employees with long-term sickness cover/permanent health insurance, set out in brief the circumstances in which employees may become eligible to participate in the scheme (subject always to the rules of the scheme from time to time in force) and/or refer them to an appropriate source of information (e.g. the HR Department). It is advisable to reserve the power to change the scheme provider and entitlement under the scheme and to end the scheme membership.

Records

11. Keep records of all sickness absence, return to work interviews, sickness absence meetings and related disciplinary meetings, sick payments made to employees, for at least 6 years.

11. Time off to care for dependants

9968 For the law in relation to leave to care for dependants (referred to as dependants leave, below) see ¶4740+.

Consider whether to give discretionary periods of **compassionate leave** (paid or unpaid) where appropriate.

1. Set out the **nature of the leave**, i.e. unpaid time off work to deal with specific unexpected or sudden emergencies concerning a "dependant" and state **who is entitled** to take dependants leave.

2. Define the term "dependant" as set out in the legislation and state the **types of emergencies** which are **covered** by the statutory right to dependants leave (or any enhanced rights offered by the employer). For example, to deal with an unexpected breakdown in the care arrangements of a dependant. Consider setting out examples of the type of situations **not covered**, e.g. a domestic emergency such as a broken down boiler or a flooded kitchen. State the type of leave which may be taken to deal with such emergencies (e.g. annual leave). Clarify that employees who know in advance that they will need to take time off to care for a dependant, who require a prolonged period of absence or repeated short periods of leave, are not entitled to dependants leave. Outline the other leave rights which such employees have, e.g. parental leave, annual leave etc.

Clarify that only a limited, reasonable, **amount of time-off** may be taken under this policy. State that dependants leave should only be taken to deal with the immediate problem and arrange long-term cover. Consider making it clear that, generally, the right to time off is limited to a matter of hours, or one or two days.

Make it clear that time off under this policy is **unpaid** (**unless** the employer gives employees enhanced rights, in which case a separate section on pay should be inserted, setting out the periods for which and rate at which pay will be available).

3. Set out the **notification requirements** with which employees are required to comply in order to take dependants leave. Some flexibility will be necessary, e.g. during working hours employees may be required to inform a member of management or the HR department that an emergency has occurred and they need to leave work. But, where an emergency occurs outside working hours or the employee cannot easily locate a member of management, it may be reasonable to delay notification until the first suitable opportunity. Ideally, the policy should state the job title of the person whom employees should contact if they wish to take dependants leave (e.g. direct line manager/HR manager).

State the **means by** which requests/notification should be made, e.g. by phone or email, by the employee himself or close family member. Detail the information which employees are required to supply, e.g. the reason for absence and expected period of absence. Confirm whether employees are required to continue to inform the employer of their absence on a regular basis, e.g. where absence extends over more than one day or over a longer period than originally anticipated. State that where an employee is unable to inform the employer in advance of the need to take dependants leave, he should provide the necessary notification as soon as possible, e.g. during their absence or at the latest on return to work.

State whether employees are required **to confirm** the reasons for their absence in writing (if so, a prescribed form may be provided) within a set period of time following their return to work. Consider reserving the power to require employees to produce evidence confirming the emergency.

12. Whistleblowing

9969 1. A whistleblowing policy may have one or more of the **following aims**:
- encouraging openness within the employer;
- providing an adequate internal mechanism for probity and accountability; and/or
- ensuring that matters of serious concern are dealt with within the employer rather than in public.

A whistleblowing policy **should set out** the procedure for raising wrongdoings at work or matters of serious concerns about practices, conduct, and operations etc of the employer internally. It should offer protection from reprisal and outline how the employer will deal with complaints which workers raise.

For the law in relation to whistleblowing, see ¶2700.

2. Set out **workers' rights and duties** in connection with the making of a disclosure. Explain that workers have legal protection when making protected disclosures. Outline workers' duties to the employer, e.g. to serve the employer faithfully, not to disclose confidential information etc. Explain the potential interaction between workers' duties and rights, namely an expectation that a worker who reasonably believes that a qualifying wrongdoing or malpractice has taken place, is taking place, or is likely to take place in the employer should use the procedure set out in the policy to bring the matter to his employer's attention. Confirm that workers who make a disclosure in accordance with the terms of the policy have a right not to be dismissed, disciplined, victimised, harassed or otherwise penalised because they made the disclosure. State what workers should do if they believe that they are being penalised because they made a disclosure in accordance with this policy.

3. State whether (and if so in what circumstances) **disclosures would be treated as confidential** within the employer and the **confidentiality of the whistleblower** would be maintained. State whether, and if so when and how, the employer may deal with anonymous disclosures. Consider whether, as an alternative, workers are allowed to raise a grievance in relation to wrongdoings which fall under this policy.

State what **action** will be taken **following a disclosure**, e.g. an internal investigation (the progress of which should be communicated to the worker) followed by a decision, followed by action. Set out what the worker may do if he is not satisfied with the action taken by the employer (e.g. contact a more senior member of management, contact an external appropriate public authority).

The policy should include a clear statement to the effect that workers who make disclosures outside the scope of the policy (e.g. in bad faith or of a non-qualifying disclosure), or in breach of the policy's procedure, will not be protected under it and could be subject to disciplinary action (including, where appropriate, summary dismissal).

4. Outline the **types of disclosures** covered by the policy and provide examples.

Employers need to decide whether they follow the legislative framework or extend protection to other types of disclosure. Employers following the legislative framework need to make it clear that a disclosure only **qualifies for protection** if, in the reasonable belief of the person making it, it shows that one of the "relevant failures" has happened, is happening or is likely to happen. Employers may wish to emphasise that the policy applies to disclosure of matters which are of public concern.

5. Outline the **procedure for making disclosures**. The policy should make it clear that protection only applies if:

– a qualifying disclosure is made in the manner outlined in it (this usually means to a specified person or body);
– the disclosure is made in good faith; and
– that, in the first instance, workers should be required to raise concerns internally.

The job title of the person to whom the workers should refer should be supplied, with an alternative in the event that the concern relates to that person or the worker does not feel comfortable approaching that person.

Consider whether all workers should be required to make **disclosure to** the same person (e.g. should agency workers make disclosure to the same person as other workers? Should senior staff be required to make a disclosure to members of the board of directors or to a non-executive director?). Consider whether all matters of concern should be raised with the same person. For example, should health and safety concerns be raised with a health and safety officer, concerns for breach of legal obligations with the director of legal affairs, and other concerns with the HR department?

In all cases, determine whether workers should **first be required** to contact their direct manager, with an option to contact another person (e.g. a member of the HR department or a line manager) if they do not feel comfortable contacting their direct supervisor or if their concern relates to this individual. Alternatively, workers may be required to contact an HR person or a senior member of management in the first place. In general, it is better to refer to a person's post rather than name, so that the policy will not have to be amended when there is a change in personnel.

Explain the **limited circumstances** when disclosures **may be made externally** (including to the media) and the conditions which attach to such disclosures.

6. Outline cases **when the policy may not be used**. For example, in relation to matters which have already been raised under the employer's grievance or anti-harassment policies.

7. Designate a person (and state their position) whom workers may **contact** if they are not clear about the operation of the policy or whether their concerns falls within its scope.

8. Set out the **sanctions for breach** of the policy. Make it clear that summary dismissal for gross misconduct is an option, in appropriate circumstances.

Whistleblowing – appropriate authorities

9980

Appropriate public authority:	Disclosures must relate to:
Accounts Commission for Scotland and auditors appointed by the Commission to audit the accounts of local government bodies	Proper conduct of public business, value for money, fraud and corruption in local government bodies.
Audit Commission for England and Wales and auditors appointed by the Commission to audit the accounts of local government, and health service, bodies	Proper conduct of public business, value for money, fraud and corruption in local government, and health service, bodies.
Certification Officer	Fraud, and other irregularities, relating to the financial affairs of trade unions and employers' associations.
Charity Commissioners for England and Wales	Proper administration of charities and of funds given or held for charitable purposes.
The Scottish Ministers	Proper administration of charities and of funds given or held for charitable purposes.
Chief Executive of the Criminal Cases Review Commission	Actual or potential miscarriages of justice.
Chief Executive of the Scottish Criminal Cases Review Commission	Actual or potential miscarriages of justice.
Independent Police Complaints Commission	The conduct of a person serving with the police (as defined in s 12(7) of the Police Reform Act 2002) or of any other person in relation to whose conduct the Independent Police Complaints Commission exercises functions in or under any legislation.
Civil Aviation Authority	Compliance with the requirements of civil aviation legislation, including aviation safety.
Office of Communications	Matters relating to the provision of electronic communications networks and services, broadcasting and the provision of television and radio services, media ownership and control and competition in communications markets.
The competent authority under Part IV of the Financial Services and Markets Act 2000	Listing of securities on a stock exchange; prospectuses on offers of transferable securities to the public.
Commission for Healthcare Audit and Inspection	Matters connected with the provision of healthcare for the purposes of the NHS, independent health services or any other activities in relation to which the Commission for Healthcare Audit and Inspection exercises its functions.
Commission for Social Care Inspection	Matters relating to the provision of regulated social care services as defined in the Care Standards Act 2000 and the inspection and performance assessment of local authority social services.
Commissioners for Her Majesty's Revenue and Customs	Value added tax, insurance premium tax, excise duties and landfill tax. Import and export of prohibited or restricted goods. Income tax, corporation tax, capital gains tax, petroleum revenue tax, inheritance tax, stamp duties, national insurance contributions, statutory pay, tax credits, child benefits, collection of student loans and the enforcement of the national minimum wage.

Appropriate public authority:	Disclosures must relate to:
Comptroller and Auditor General of the National Audit Office	Proper conduct of public business, value for money, fraud and corruption in relation to the provision of centrally-funded public services.
Auditor General for Wales	Proper conduct of public business, value for money, fraud and corruption in relation to the provision of public services.
Auditor General for Scotland and persons appointed by or on his behalf under the Public Finance and Accountability (Scotland) Act 2000 to act as auditors or examiners for the purposes of sections 21 to 24 of that Act	Proper conduct of public business, value for money, fraud and corruption in relation to the provision of public services.
Audit Scotland	Proper conduct of public business, value for money, fraud and corruption in public bodies.
Gas and Electricity Markets Authority	Generation, transmission, distribution and supply of electricity, participation in the operation of an electricity interconnector and activities ancillary to these matters. Transportation, shipping and supply of gas through pipes, participation in the operation of a gas interconnector and activities ancillary to these matters.
Director General of Water Services	Supply of water and the provision of sewerage services.
Water Industry Commissioner for Scotland	Supply of water and the provision of sewerage services.
Director of the Serious Fraud Office	Serious or complex fraud.
Lord Advocate, Scotland	Serious or complex fraud.
Environment Agency	Acts or omissions which have an actual or potential effect on the environment or the management or regulation of the environment, including those relating to pollution, abstraction of water, flooding, the flow in rivers, inland fisheries and migratory salmon or trout.
Scottish Environment Protection Agency	Acts or omissions which have an actual or potential effect on the environment or the management or regulation of the environment, including those relating to flood warning systems and pollution.
Food Standards Agency	Matters which may affect the health of any member of the public in relation to the consumption of food and other matters concerning the protection of the interests of consumers in relation to the food.
Financial Services Authority	Carrying on of investment business or of insurance business; operation of banks and building societies, deposit-taking businesses and wholesale money market regimes; operation of friendly societies, benevolent societies, working men's clubs, especially authorised societies, and industrial and provident societies; the functioning of financial markets, investment exchanges and clearing houses; functioning of other financial regulators; money laundering, financial crime, and other serious financial misconduct, in connection with activities regulated by Financial Services Authority.
General Social Care Council	Matters relating to the registration of social care workers under the Care Standards Act 2000.
Care Council for Wales	Matters relating to the registration of social care workers under the Care Standards Act 2000.
Scottish Social Services Council	Matters relating to the registration of social services workforce by the Scottish Social Services Council.
Children's Commissioner for Wales	Matters relating to the rights and welfare of children.

Appropriate public authority:	Disclosures must relate to:
Health and Safety Executive	Matters which may affect health or safety of any individual at work; matters, which may affect health or safety of any member of public, arising out of or in connection with activities of persons at work.
Housing Corporation	Registration and operation of registered social landlords, including their administration of public and private funds and management of their housing stock.
Local authorities which are responsible for the enforcement of health and safety legislation	Matters which may affect the health or safety of any individual at work; matters, which may affect the health and safety of any member of the public, arising out of or in connection with the activities of persons at work.
Information Commissioner	Compliance with the requirements of legislation relating to data protection and to freedom of information.
Scottish Information Commissioner	Compliance with the requirements of legislation relating to freedom of information.
National Care Standards Commission	Matters relating to the provision of regulated care services, as defined in the Care Standards Act 2000.
National Assembly for Wales	Matters relating to the provision of social care services under the Care Standards Act 2000 and the Children Act 1989, the inspection and performance assessment of Welsh local authority social services, the review of and investigation into the provision of health care by and for Welsh NHS bodies and the registration and operation of registered social landlords, including their administration of public and private funds and management of their housing stock.
Scottish Commission for the Regulation of Care	Matters relating to the provision of care services, as defined in the Regulation of Care (Scotland) Act 2001.
Pensions Regulator	Matters relating to occupational pension schemes and other private pension arrangements.
Office of Fair Trading	Matters concerning the sale of goods or the supply of services, which adversely affect the interests of consumers. Competition affecting markets in the UK.
Rail Regulator	Provision and supply of railway services.
Standards Board for England	Breaches by a member or co-opted member of a relevant authority (as defined in s 49(6) of the Local Government Act 2000) of that authority's code of conduct.
Local Commissioner for Wales	Breaches by a member or co-opted member of a relevant authority (as defined in s 49(6) of the Local Government Act 2000) of that authority's code of conduct.
Standards Commission for Scotland and the Chief Investigating Officer	Breaches by a councillor or a member of a devolved public body (as defined in s 28 of the Ethnical Standards in Public Life etc, (Scotland) Act 2000) of the code of conduct applicable to that councillor or member under that Act.
Treasury	Carrying on of insurance business.
Secretary of State for Trade and Industry	Fraud, and other misconduct, in relation to companies, investment businesses, insurance businesses, or multi-level marketing schemes (and similar trading schemes); insider dealing. Consumer safety.
Secretary of State for Transport	Compliance with merchant shipping law, including maritime safety.
Local authorities which are responsible for the enforcement of consumer protection legislation	Compliance with the requirements of consumer protection legislation.
Local authorities which are responsible for enforcement of food standards	Compliance with the requirements of food safety legislation.

Statutory dispute resolution procedures – relevant jurisdictions

9985 The statutory jurisdictions referred to at ¶6516 in respect of which a **statutory dispute resolution procedure** has **not been completed** are as follows (Sch 3 EA 2002):

Equality clauses (s 2 EPA 1970).

Discrimination in employment in relation to:
- sex (s 63 SDA 1975)
- race (s 54 RRA 1976)
- disability (s 4 DDA 1995)
- religion or belief (reg 28 Employment Equality (Religion or Belief) Regulations SI 2003/1660)
- sexual orientation (reg 28 Employment Equality (Sexual Orientation) Regulations SI 2003/1661)

Detriment in relation to trade union membership and activities and union recognition rights (s 146, Sch A1 para 156 TULRCA 1992)

Unauthorised deductions and payments (s 23 ERA 1996)

Detriment in employment (s 48 ERA 1996)

Unfair dismissal (s 111 ERA 1996)

Redundancy payments (s 163 ERA 1996)

Detriment in relation to national minimum wage (s 24 NMWA 1998)

Breach of employment contract and termination (Employment Tribunal Extension of Jurisdiction (England and Wales) Order SI 1994/1623; Employment Tribunal Extension (Scotland) Order SI 1994/1624)

Breach of Working Time Regulations (reg 30 SI 1998/1833)

Detriment relating to European Works Councils (reg 32 Transnational Information and Consultation of Employees SI 1999/3323)

Detriment relating to domestic information and consultation in the workplace (reg 30 Information and Consultation of Employees Regulations SI 2004/3426).

9986 The statutory jurisdictions referred to at ¶6773 in respect of which an **employee wishes to commence tribunal proceedings** are as follows (Sch 4 EA 2002):

Equality clauses (s 2 EPA 1970)

Discrimination in employment in relation to:
- sex (s 63 SDA 1975)
- race (s 54 RRA 1976)
- disability (s 4 DDA 1995)
- religion or belief (reg 28 Employment Equality (Religion or Belief) Regulations SI 2003/1660)
- sexual orientation (reg 28 Employment Equality (Sexual Orientation) Regulations SI 2003/1661)

Detriment in relation to trade union membership and activities and union recognition rights (s 146, Sch A1 para 156 TULRCA 1992)

Unauthorised deductions and payments (s 23 ERA 1996)

Detriment in employment (s 48 ERA 1996)

Unfair dismissal (s 111 ERA 1996)

Redundancy payments (s 163 ERA 1996)

Detriment in relation to national minimum wage (s 24 NMWA 1998)

Breach of Working Time Regulations (reg 30 SI 1998/1833)

Detriment relating to European Works Councils (reg 32 Transnational Information and Consultation of Employees SI 1999/3323)

Detriment relating to domestic information and consultation in the workplace (reg 30 Information and Consultation of Employees Regulations SI 2004/3426).

Main social benefits

Below are details of the main social benefits. Claims should always been made straight away or as soon as possible otherwise the benefit may be lost. 9990

Contact details for a person's:

- **local social security office** and **local jobcentre** can be found at http://www.dwp.gov.uk/localoffice/search/index.asp; and
- **nearest Revenue and Customs enquiry centre** can be found at http://www.hmrc.gov.uk/enq/index.htm

Alternatively, the relevant telephone numbers can be found in the phone book.

Main social benefits	What is it?	How to claim
Income Support	Income support for people on a low income and generally with savings of £8,000 or under. If have to sign on at the Jobcentre, cannot get Income Support.	Claim forms available from local social security office.
Jobseeker's Allowance	Paid if capable of working and available and actively seeking work.	Contact local jobcentre.
Council Tax Benefit	Help towards council tax. Paid by local councils. Do not have to get any other benefits to be eligible. Does not matter if already get discount on council tax, for example if living alone.	Claims can be made up to 13 weeks before entitlement. Claim forms available from local social security office. If Income Support or Jobseeker's Allowance is being claimed, a person will get relevant forms with claim pack. In such cases, he should return them as appropriate with his Income Support or Jobseeker's Allowance claim form.
Housing Benefit	Help towards rent. Paid by local councils. Does not have to get any other benefits to be eligible. If claiming Income Support or Jobseeker's Allowance, may be able to get help with other housing costs as part of benefit.	Claims can be made up to 13 weeks before entitlement. Claim forms available from local social security office. If Income Support or Jobseeker's Allowance is being claimed, a person will get relevant forms with claim pack. In such cases, he should return them as appropriate with his Income Support or Jobseeker's Allowance claim form.
Incapacity Benefit	Paid if SSP has ended or you cannot get SSP.	Claim forms available from local social security office.
Disability Living Allowance	Paid if need help looking after, have severe difficulty walking or need help getting around. Different rates depending on how disability affects person.	Claim forms available from local social security office.
Child Benefit	A benefit for people bringing up children. Paid for each child. Not affected by income or savings.	Claim packs available from local social security office or by ringing Child Benefit Centre on 0845 302 1444. If child has just been born, claim pack may be included in Bounty Pack from hospital.
State Pension	Retirement pension when obtained state pension age. Made up of Basic pension and SERPS/Second State Pension.	Claim form available if less than 4 months away from state pension age. Contact pension centre or local social security office.

Main social benefits	What is it?	How to claim
New Deal for Lone Parents	Help and support to improve job prospects if lone parent, thinking of starting work and getting Income Support. It can offer help with looking for a job, childcare and training.	Ask job centre or call the helpline on 0800 868 868.
New Deal for Partners	Help if been getting Jobseeker's Allowance, Income Support, Incapacity Benefit, Severe Disablement Allowance or Invalid Care Allowance and have been claiming for a partner or are the partner of someone so claiming.	Ask local jobcentre or call the helpline on 0845 606 2626.
New Deal for Young people	Help and support to improve job prospects if aged 18 to 24, claiming Jobseeker's Allowance and have been unemployed for 6 months or more.	Ask local jobcentre or call the helpline on 0845 606 2626.
New Deal for people aged 25 plus	Help and support to improve job prospects if aged 25 or over, claiming Jobseeker's Allowance and have been unemployed for 18 months or more.	Ask local jobcentre or call the helpline on 0845 606 2626.
New Deal for people aged 50 plus	Help and support to improve job prospects if aged 50 or over and have been getting one or more of the following for 6 months or more: Jobseeker's Allowance, Income Support, Incapacity Benefit, Severe Disablement Allowance, National Insurance credits, Invalid Care Allowance or Bereavement Allowance. Or if partner has been getting an increase in benefit for person for 6 months or more.	Ask local job centre or call the helpline on 0845 606 2626.
New Deal for Disabled People	A voluntary programme which offers help and support to improve job prospects if have been getting disability- or health-related benefits but wish to work.	Contact Job Brokers at http://www.jobbrokersearch.gov.uk or call helpline on 0800 137 177 (textphone 0800 435 550).
New Deal for Self-employment	Help and support in setting up own business if currently unemployed.	Ask local jobcentre or call the helpline on 0845 606 2626.
New Deal for Musicians	Help and support to improve job prospects for instrumentalists, vocalists, composers, songwriters and performing DJs of any age who are serious about wanting a career in music industry and are already on the New Deal for Young People or New Deal for 25 plus.	Ask local job centre or call the helpline on 0845 606 2626.
Job Grant	£100 tax-free payment on going into full-time work.	Must tell local social security office or jobcentre that have started job. If aged 25 years or over, starting full-time work expected to last for 5 weeks or more and been getting Income Support, Jobseeker's Allowance, Incapacity Benefit or Severe Disablement or a combination of these benefits for at least 26 weeks, claim will be automatically made.

Main social benefits	What is it?	How to claim
Statutory Maternity Pay	Paid by employers to pregnant women for up to 26 weeks.	Usually by informing employer at least 28 days before intention to stop work. Maternity certificate (form MAT B1) should be given to employer.
Statutory Adoption Pay	Paid by employers to adopters for up to 26 weeks.	Usually by informing employer at least 28 days before intention to stop work. Matching certificate should be given to employer.
Statutory Paternity Pay	Paid by employers to new fathers for one or two weeks.	Usually by informing employer at least 28 days before intention to stop work. Self-certificate should be given to employer.
Maternity Allowance	For pregnant women who cannot get Statutory Maternity Pay. Paid for up to 26 weeks.	Claim after pregnant for 26 weeks by contacting local social security office.
Working Tax Credit	Tax credit for working households on low incomes. Administered by employers.	Application packs are available from local Revenue and Customs enquiry centre, social security office and jobcentre.
Child Tax Credit	Tax credit for those (whether or not they work) who are responsible for child/children or qualifying young person(s).	Application packs are available from local Revenue and Customs enquiry centre, social security office and jobcentre.

Index

The numbers refer to paragraphs and the plus sign (+) indicates that the entry covers a number of paragraphs.

A

D

F

G

H

M

O

P

Q

R

S

T

W

Y

Composition réalisée par NORD COMPO

PRINTED IN FRANCE BY HÉRISSEY (CPI GROUP)
27092 EVREUX CEDEX 9

Dépôt légal : décembre 2005
N° d'impression : 100713